The Concept Connector Solution

The Concept Connector Solution is an engaging way for you to connect with World History. As you study different civilizations, you will again and again encounter enduring Essential Questions and issues that people have wrestled with throughout history and that still challenge us today. The Concept Connector Solution will help you:

· **Connect to experience the past**
· **Connect to succeed today**
· **Connect to understand today and tomorrow**

Connect to Experience the Past

Experience the excitement of history for yourself. Video, audio, and digital interactivities make history come alive as you experience and interact with people and events of the past.

 WITNESS HISTORY VIDEO

With a Discovery Channel video program for every chapter, the sights and sounds of each era come to life through historical reenactments and expert analysis.

WITNESS HISTORY 🔊 AUDIO

Audio symbols throughout your text let you know when you can listen to primary sources, music, and sounds from the past on your Witness History Audio CD or Interactive Textbook.

History *Interactive*   **Geography** *Interactive*

Use the Web Codes to go online for interactive animations, maps, timelines, and more. Listen to the people who were there and see dramatic images of the past.

Go Online at PHSchool.com

History *Interactive*

For: Interactive map, audio, and more
Visit: PHSchool.com
Web Code: nap-2941

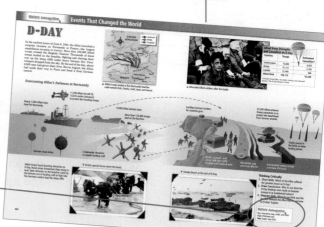

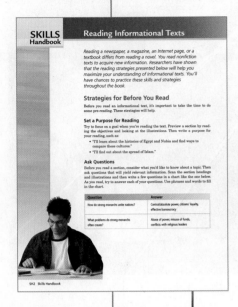

Connect to Succeed Today

Prentice Hall World History's Concept Connector Solution provides you with a variety of strategies and tools to help you truly understand the past, demonstrate your knowledge of world history, and succeed on quizzes, projects, and high-stakes tests.

21st Century Skills Handbook

The 21st Century Skills Handbook at the front of your textbook lets you brush up on important skills that you will use throughout your World History course and throughout your life. With 21st century knowledge and skills, you will succeed in school and succeed in life. Skills instruction to help you read, learn, and demonstrate your knowledge of world history includes:

- Reading Informational Texts
- Writing Handbook
- Geography Skills Handbook
- Critical Thinking About Texts, Visuals, and Media Sources
- Speaking and Listening

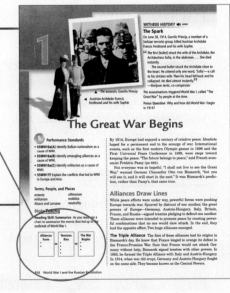

Note Taking

At the start of every section, you'll find suggestions on how to take notes using graphic organizers, timelines, and outlines. Use these to take notes in your own notebook, in your Reading and Note Taking Study Guide, or on the Note Taking Worksheets which you can download.

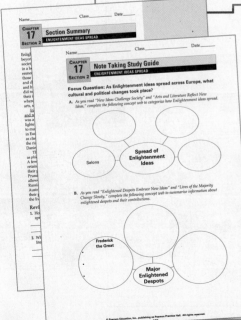

Reading and Note Taking Study Guide

Use your print or online study guide to develop vocabulary, practice reading and note taking skills, and record main ideas in different graphic formats. Use the easy-to-read summaries to help you learn the main ideas.

Progress Monitoring Online

Web codes at the end of every section take you to online quizzes with multiple choice questions on section content and vocabulary. At the end of each chapter, you'll find an online self-test on chapter content and a crossword puzzle to test your vocabulary mastery.

Go Online at PHSchool.com

Progress Monitoring *Online*
For: Self-test with vocabulary practice
Web Code: naa-2961

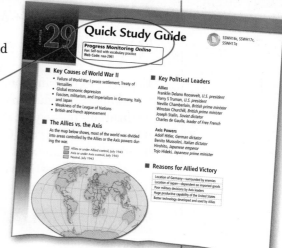

Quick Study Guides

At the end of each chapter, use the Quick Study Guide to make sure you have mastered the chapter contents and are ready for tests. Each Quick Study Guide organizes and reviews main ideas in a variety of formats, including:

- charts, graphs, and tables
- maps and illustrations
- graphic organizers and concept webs
- outlines and summaries
- timelines (Interactive timelines available online at PHSchool.com)

Prepare for the GHSGT

At the end of each chapter, the Prepare for the GHSGT contains several documents followed by multiple-choice questions that help you analyze documents and practice your map, graph, visual learning, and critical reading skills. A writing task helps you compare, contrast, and draw conclusions about the various documents.

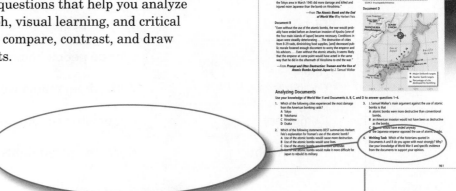

Connect to Understand Today and Tomorrow

Explore 18 enduring concepts and Essential Questions that people are still wrestling with today. In each chapter, you can explore how people and civilizations of the past dealt with these tough questions. You can record what you learn in your Concept Connector Journal, as you gradually build your own answers to these Essential Questions. By learning about the Essential Questions of world history, you will develop the knowledge needed to understand your world today and tomorrow.

Concept	Essential Question
Belief Systems	How do religions and belief systems affect society?
Geography's Impact	How do geography and people affect one another?
Conflict	When, if ever, should people go to war?
Cultural Diffusion	Why does cultural diffusion occur?
Trade	What are the intended and unintended effects of trade?
Science and Technology	What are the benefits and costs of science and technology?
Political Systems	How do political systems rise, develop and decline?
Impact of the Individual	How can an individual change the world?
Economic Systems	How should resources and wealth be distributed?
Revolution	Why do political revolutions occur?
Nationalism	How can nationalism be a unifying and a divisive force?
Migration	Under what circumstances do people migrate?
Empire	How does a state gain or lose power over others?
Dictatorship	Why do people sometimes support dictators?
Genocide	Why do people sometimes commit the crime of genocide?
Cooperation	With whom should we cooperate and why?
Democracy	Under what conditions is democracy most likely to succeed?
Human Rights	How are human rights won or lost?

View or make an Essential Questions Video

Go on a Web Quest

Access your Journal

View Concept Connector Online

It's all here! As you start or finish a chapter, you can go online to find out which Essential Questions are most pertinent to the chapter. For each Essential Question, you can explore a full-page feature, engage in various interactivities, pursue a Web Quest, or make and submit your own video or digital presentation. You will record what you learn in your Concept Connector Journal. Finally, you will transfer your knowledge of the past into a better understanding of your world today and tomorrow.

Go Online at PHSchool.com
Web Code: nah-3008

Concept Connector Feature Pages

Each of the 18 Essential Questions is highlighted in a full-page feature. Suppose the question is "When, if ever, should people go to war?" The full-page feature in the chapter you are studying will show you how people of that time dealt with conflict. A timeline will give you ideas on why people of other times and places went to war or avoided war. Most importantly, you will transfer your knowledge and explore how people today are still dealing with conflict and war.

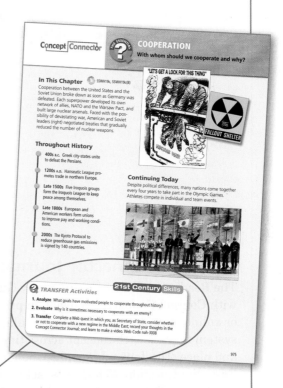

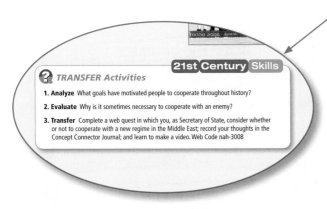

Transfer Activities and Student-Made Projects Online

After working with the full-page feature, you can go online to transfer what you have learned about the past into a clearer understanding of what's happening in your world today. You might go on a Web Quest, play a role-playing game, interact with digital primary resources, or make and submit your own video or digital presentation.

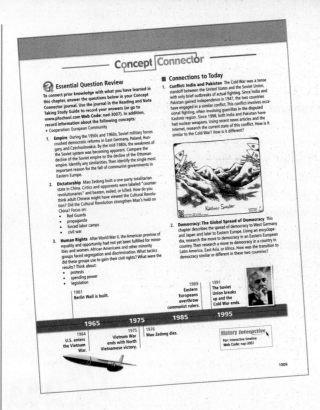

Cumulative Review and Connections to Today

At the end of every chapter, you can review what you have learned about the Essential Questions and big ideas and concepts that are most significant in the chapter. The Connections to Today questions help you transfer what you have learned into a better understanding of your world today. You can record responses in your Concept Connector Journal.

Concept Connector Journal

The Reading and Note Taking Study Guide with Concept Connector Journal, in print or online, provides you with a note taking system to track each concept across time and place. The Journal prepares you for Essential Question Web Quests, activities, and essays. The essays are just like thematic essays on high-stakes tests. In your essays, you will respond to enduring Essential Questions on big ideas and concepts by drawing on your knowledge of different historical eras and civilizations.

A message for you from Grant Wiggins

The Concept Connector Solution will help you gain understanding of big ideas—not just for "the test," but for life. Essential Questions are the foundation of the system. Each Essential Question is designed to guide your inquiry into important ideas of World History. How is an essential question different from any other question?

There are three basic kinds of questions that you face as a student.

1. **The factual question:** *When did World War II begin?* The answer is in the textbook.

2. **The opinion question:** *Should the United States have dropped the atomic bomb on Japan?* The answer is your personal response, based on your values and the facts that you know.

3. **The Essential Question:** *When, if ever, should people go to war?* This is clearly an important and timeless question that is not linked to only one chapter or era. You will build an answer to this question as you study history, do research, and complete a Web Quest. But, in some ways, you will never be finished answering the question because it is a question that every generation must face, from your great grandparents who lived through major wars in the twentieth century to you who will face the conflicts of the twenty-first century.

Essential Questions are challenging, but need not be overwhelming. Take a step-by-step approach.

Step 1. Don't become buried by a blizzard of facts. Look for the key ideas, themes, and trends implied by the question, around which facts are presented. What is the key issue or dispute? What matters to us in the present about this past event? Use the Concept Connector Journal to take notes not only on the facts, but also on ideas about the question that are sparked by those facts in the text. Think about the question throughout the course and note details related to it regularly in your journal.

Step 2. You often need to question the question itself. Consider the question above: *When, if ever, should people go to war?* Does *when* refer to events outside the country? For example, someone might say that we should go to war when our allies are invaded. Or does *when* refer to the politics inside our own country in terms of the decision-making process? Then, the answer to *when* might be that we should only go to war when all citizens strongly support the cause. The question refers to both meanings, and both should be carefully considered.

Step 3. Consider the alternatives, weigh the evidence and arguments, and reach a thoughtful conclusion—like a jury member. All important historical and political questions can be looked at from different points of view. The best historians carefully explore alternative narratives, theories, and arguments. They know all sides of an argument, and they can offer good reasons why their argument is a better explanation than the alternatives. By exploring Essential Questions in this way, you will build understandings that will have lasting value beyond the classroom—and be more thoughtful about issues that you will face in the future.

"I want you to really see the value of history! That's our aim here: to help you achieve useful and interesting insight. We want you to understand . . . the goal is understanding, not superficial knowledge." —Grant Wiggins, World History Program Consultant

▲ Phoenician vase

◄ Spartan woman athlete

▼ Ruins of Machu Picchu, Peru

▲ Mehmet II

▼ Bayeux Tapestry,
c. 1000s

UNIT 3 EARLY MODERN TIMES

(1300–1800)

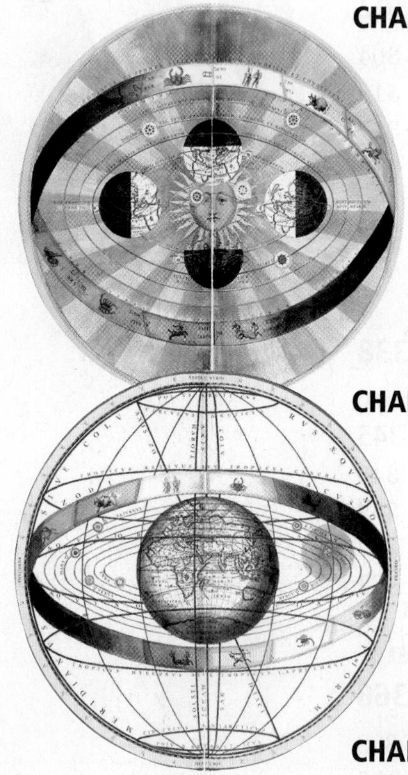

▲ Copernican (top) and Ptolemaic (bottom) solar systems

▲ Catherine the Great

◀ Shuttles for the fly shuttle loom, introduced in 1733

▲ Sepoy fighter in India

▶ Nazi dictator Adolph Hitler with member of Nazi Youth, 1930s

(1945–Present)

▼ Mother Teresa

▼ Mongolian yurt with satellite dish

SPECIAL FEATURES AND MULTIMEDIA

Witness History: Janina's War Story

"It was 10:30 in the morning and I was helping my mother and a servant girl with bags and baskets as they set out for the market. . . . Suddenly the high-pitch scream of diving planes caused everyone to freeze. . . . Countless explosions shook our house followed by the *rat-tat-tat* of strafing machine guns. We could only stare at each other in horror. Later reports would confirm that several German Stukas had screamed out of a blue sky and . . . dropped several bombs along the main street—and then returned to strafe the market. The carnage was terrible." 🔊 AUDIO

—Janina Sulkowska,
Krzemieniec, Poland,
September 12, 1939

WITNESS HISTORY 🔊 AUDIO

Primary source audio accounts throughout the text bring the voices and sounds of history to life.*

*Available on Witness History Audio CD and online at PHSchool.com

WITNESS HISTORY VIDEO

Witness History Discovery School™ videos for each chapter bring the events you read about in the text to life.

Ruins of Great Zimbabwe

History *Interactive* — Events That Changed the World

Audio, video, and animation-filled features help you explore major turning points in history.

Concept Connector

Explore World History's essential questions and go beyond the facts to connect with the issues that people are still wrestling with today.

Primary Sources

Full page excerpts allow you to relive history through eyewitness accounts and documents.

In-text Primary Sources

Gain insights as you read by reading the words of people who were there.

Matthew Perry arrives in Japan.

Traveler's Tales

View historic places through the eyes of those who traveled there.

COMPARING VIEWPOINTS

Explore issues by analyzing two opposing viewpoints.

HUMANITIES

Experience great literature and arts from around the world.

BIOGRAPHIES

Meet fascinating history makers.

Marie and
Pierre Curie

● INFOGRAPHICS

Photographs, maps, charts, illustrations, audio, and text help you understand the significance of important historical events and developments.

● INFOGRAPHIC

Taiping Rebellion

Taiping Rebellion leader Hong Xiuquan (at right), was a village schoolteacher. Inspired by religious visions and Christian missionaries, he wanted to establish a "Heavenly Kingdom of Peace"—the Taiping. Hong endorsed ideas that Chinese leaders considered radical, including community ownership of property and the equality of women and men.

◀ Chinese coins c.1850

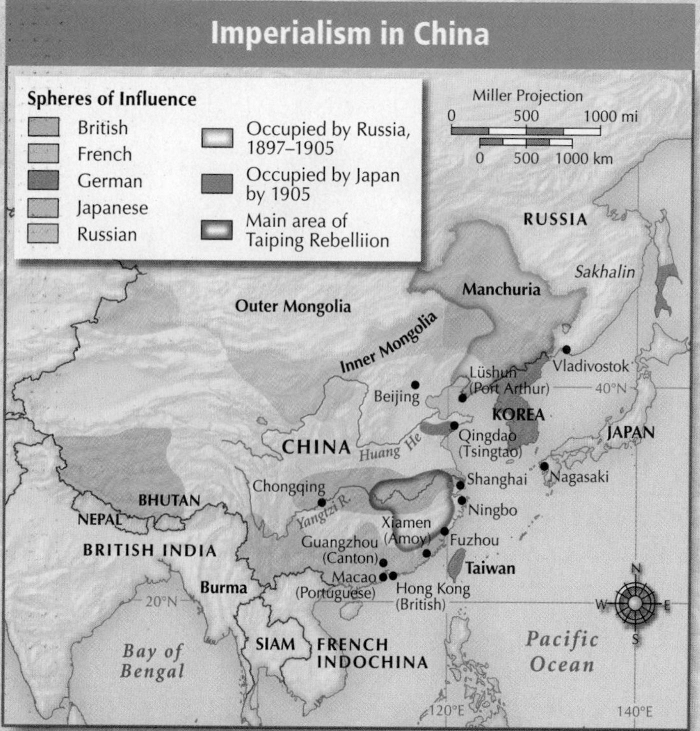

Imperialism in China

Spheres of Influence
- British
- French
- German
- Japanese
- Russian

- Occupied by Russia, 1897–1905
- Occupied by Japan by 1905
- Main area of Taiping Rebelliion

Miller Projection
0   500   1000 mi
0   500   1000 km

RUSSIA

Sakhalin

Manchuria

Outer Mongolia

Inner Mongolia

Lüshun (Port Arthur)   Vladivostok   40°N

Beijing

KOREA   JAPAN

CHINA   Huang He   Qingdao (Tsingtao)

Chongqing   Shanghai   Nagasaki

BHUTAN   Yangtze R.   Ningbo

NEPAL   Xiamen (Amoy)   Fuzhou

Guangzhou (Canton)

BRITISH INDIA   Macao (Portuguese)   Taiwan

Burma   Hong Kong (British)

20°N

Bay of Bengal   SIAM   FRENCH INDOCHINA   Pacific Ocean

120°E   140°E

● INFOGRAPHICS

▼ Battle scene of the
Taiping Rebellion

Julius Caesar

Prepare for the GHSGT

Practice the art and science of a historian by analyzing an event by examining multiple historical documents, data, and images.

Cause and Effect

Diagrams help you see the short- and long-term causes and effects of history's most important events.

Charts and Graphs

Diagrams and data help you understand history through visuals.

Charts and Graphs

Charts and Graphs

Daily Life in the United States, 1920s		
	1922	**1929**
Households with radios	60,000	10.25 million
Local telephone calls	36,831	61,034
Motion picture attendance per week	40 million	80 million
Dwellings with electricity	40%	68%

SOURCE: *Historical Statistics of the United States, Colonial Times to 1970*

Maps Geography *Interactive*

Interactive maps and Audio Guided Tours for each map with a Web code help you understand where history happened.

Maps Geography *Interactive*

(GA) Especially for Georgia

Reading Georgia's Performance Standards

Throughout this textbook, you will see a special coding system used to identify the **Georgia Performance Standards for World History**. The example below will help you understand the codes.

SSWH9g

SS: Social Studies

WH: World History

Standard 9: The student will analyze change and continuity in the Renaissance and Reformation.

Topic g: Explain the importance of Guttenberg and the invention of the printing press.

SSWH9g Explain the importance of Guttenberg and the invention of the printing press.

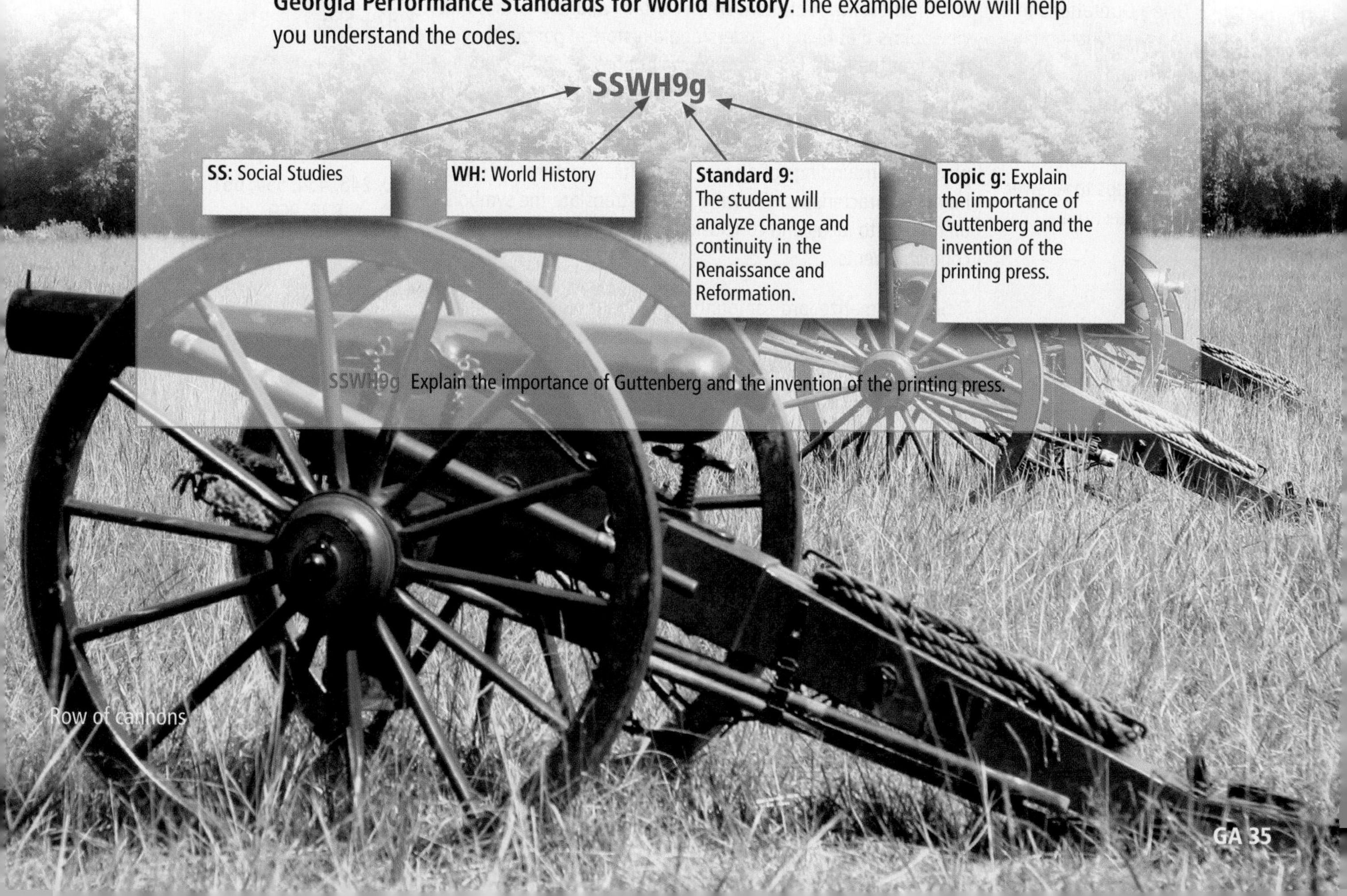

Row of cannons

GA

Social Studies Skills Practice

This guide allows you to practice the skills you need to succeed on social studies tests and the World History section of the **Georgia High School Graduation Test (GHSGT)**. Using a variety of practice materials, it shows you how to approach different kinds of multiple-choice questions. These are the kinds of questions you will probably encounter on any social studies test.

Remember that although the Georgia Performance Standards for World History covers content that starts with prehistory, the World History portion of the GHSGT only tests material that begins with the Renaissance/Reformation era.

On the following pages, review the sample questions and step-by-step instructions to help you answer each question. Then, practice your skills on pages GA44-GA50.

Social Studies Skills Practice		
Social Studies Skill	**What it Means to You**	**Review Pages**
Answering Multiple Choice Questions	Multiple-choice questions are a common format used in tests and quizzes. While the key to performing well on any test is understanding the content, there are techniques and strategies for approaching multiple-choice questions that can increase your chances of success.	27, 301, 443, 719, 849, 961, 1129
Using Quotations to Answer Questions	Quotations are a type of primary source—information that comes directly from a participant in or witness to a key historical event. Quotations often contain valuable details and viewpoints that help us understand a historical period. They represent the most important voices or phrases connected with a time period or incident in history.	9, 379, 559, 758, 819, 961
Using Maps to Answer Questions	Maps contain large amounts of information about the physical surroundings of a place, its political features, or its human characteristics. Knowing how to translate the symbols on maps into ideas and conclusions can help you understand complex events.	10, 248, 454, 554, 661, 837, 969
Using Tables to Answer Questions	Tables summarize large amounts of information and organize it into columns and rows. Being able to read and understand data presented in tables can help you compare different subjects and also identify broad generalizations or historical trends.	5, 216, 426, 569, 673, 820, 968
Using Graphs to Answer Questions	Graphs present numerical information in an easy-to-read format. Being able to read graphs can enable you to identify specific pieces of data, to recognize far-reaching trends, and to make quick comparisons.	83, 609, 788, 835, 1035, 1041, 1057
Using Timelines to Answer Questions	Timelines present events from a particular time period in chronological order. They can help you identify cause-and-effect relationships between seemingly unrelated events. They can also help you trace the progress of trends as they develop over time.	108–109, 298–299, 430–431, 536–537, 652–653, 878–879, 1126–1127

Answering Multiple-Choice Questions

Multiple-choice questions are a common format used in tests and quizzes. Multiple choice questions usually consist of a stem and four answer options. Only one answer option will be correct. The incorrect options are known as *distracters*.

This skill will help you answer questions like the one below. Follow the steps to apply the skill. Then answer the multiple-choice item below.

1 Which answer BEST explains why the first human civilization grew up in the region known as Mesopotamia?

A The Syrian Desert provided ample water supplies and rich natural resources.

B The arrival of traders from Europe brought new ideas for organizing government.

C The need to cooperate in the control of floodwaters and irrigation projects helped spur organization and, eventually, civilization.

D Flooding from the Tigris and Euphrates Rivers wiped out rival communities in the region.

Step 1 Read the directions. Be sure you understand what rules govern the test.

Step 2 Read the question, or stem, to determine the topic.

Step 3 Look for key words that tell you exactly what the question is asking. For example, are you looking for the single correct answer or the best answer? Or, are you looking for the one answer that is incorrect?

Step 5 If possible, eliminate any obviously wrong answers. Select the best answer from the remaining options.

Step 4 Read all of the answer choices—even if you think you know the correct answer.

Using Quotations to Answer Questions

Quotations are a type of primary source—information that comes directly from a participant in or witness to a key historical event. Quotations contain details and viewpoints that help our understanding. Quotations need to be read critically, with an eye towards the author's point of view and purpose for writing. You also need to use your knowledge of history to place the quotation in its proper context.

This skill will help you answer questions like the one below the following primary source. Follow the steps to apply the skill. Then answer the multiple-choice item below.

> Here the question arises: is it better to be loved than feared, or vice versa? I don't doubt that every prince would like to be both; but since it is hard to accommodate these qualities, if you have to make a choice, to be feared is much safer than to be loved. For it is a good general rule about men, that they are ungrateful, fickle, liars and deceivers, fearful of danger and greedy for gain. While you serve their welfare, they are all yours, offering their blood, their belongings, their lives, and their children's lives, as we noted above—so long as the danger is remote. But when the danger is close at hand, they turn against you. Then, any prince who has relied on their words and has made no other preparations will come to grief; because friendships that are bought at a price, and not with greatness and nobility of soul, may be paid for but they are not acquired, and they cannot be used in time of need.
>
> —Niccoló Machiavelli, from *The Prince*, 1513

Step 1 Read the quotation to gain understanding of the topic. Then summarize its main message. What information does it provide?

Step 2 Identify the author or creator of the document and, if possible, when and why it was created.

Step 3 Identify the purpose of the document. Ask: "Why was this document created?"

Step 4 Consider the reliability of the source. Does the author give an opinion or just the facts?

1 **Which answer represents an accurate summary of the message in this passage?**

A For the safety of the ruler, government must be based upon the highest and noblest ideals.

B It is impossible to rule people by fear because eventually people will turn against you.

C Above all, a good ruler must ensure that he or she is feared, for being feared is the best protection against angry people.

D A ruler must strive to avoid upsetting the people he or she rules because that will lead to danger.

Step 5 Read the question and determine how it relates to the subject matter of the quotation.

Step 6 Using your understanding of the quotation and any prior knowledge you may have, test each answer to the question. Select the best answer to the question.

Using Maps to Answer Questions

Maps contain geographic information about a place, its political features, or its human characteristics. Knowing how to translate the symbols used on maps into ideas and conclusions can help you understand complex events and developments.

This skill will help you answer questions like the one below the following map. Follow the steps to apply the skill. Then answer the multiple-choice item below.

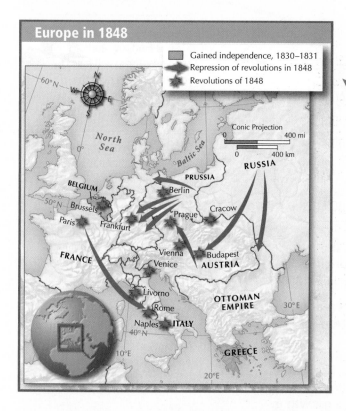

Step 1 Read the title to get an idea of the map's topic.

Step 2 Read all the map's labels.

Step 3 Locate the legend. Understand the meaning of the colors and symbols. Use the legend to interpret the map.

Step 4 Draw conclusions about what the map is trying to convey.

Step 5 Read the question and test each answer choice against your conclusions about the contents of the map.

Step 6 Select the best answer to the question.

1 **Which answer is supported by the contents of the map?**

A Independence movements in Greece and Belgium led immediately to revolution across Europe.

B The year 1848 was a time of widespread revolution and turmoil all across Europe.

C The revolutions of 1848 were well organized and executed.

D Russia was at the heart of the revolutions and turmoil of 1848.

Using Tables to Answer Questions

Tables summarize large amounts of information and organize it into columns and rows. Being able to read and understand data presented in tables can help you compare different subjects and identify historical trends.

This skill will help you answer questions like the one below the following table. Follow the steps to apply the skill. Then answer the multiple-choice item below.

Step 1 Read the title of the table to determine its topic.

Step 2 Find row and column headings. These will help you understand how the information is related.

Population of Major Cities		
City	1850	1900
Berlin, Germany	419,000	1,889,000
London, England	2,685,000	6,586,000
Moscow, Russia	365,000	989,000
New York, United States	696,000	3,437,000
Paris, France	1,053,000	2,714,000

Step 3 Read the data in the table. Look for trends or patterns in the data.

Step 4 Formulate a statement or conclusion that summarizes the information in the table.

1 Which conclusion BEST summarizes the information in the table about major cities in Europe and the United States in the late 1800s?

A The population of Europe was decreasing as that of the United States was increasing.

B The urban population of the United States and Europe was decreasing.

C Rural populations were decreasing.

D The major cities experienced rapid growth in the final years of the 1800s.

Step 5 Read the question, and use your conclusions about the contents of the table to test each answer choice.

Step 6 Select the best answer to the question.

Using Graphs to Answer Questions

Graphs present numerical information in an easy-to-read format. Line and bar graphs show how quantities and trends change over time. Circle graphs show how parts relate to a whole. Being able to read graphs can enable you to identify specific pieces of data, to recognize far-reaching trends, and to make quick comparisons between different items.

This skill will help you answer questions like the one below the following graph. Follow the steps to apply the skill. Then answer the multiple-choice item below.

Step 1 Read the graph's title to learn its subject.

Unemployment, 1928–1938

SOURCES: *European Historical Statistics* and *Historical Statistics of the United States*

Step 2 Read the graph's labels. They will tell you the type of data being presented and how it is being measured. On line and bar graphs, read the *x*-axis (horizontal) and *y*-axis (vertical).

Step 3 Look at the key to find out what the lines represent.

Step 4 Look at the lines on the graph. After examining all the lines, formulate a general conclusion about the graph and what it is saying about the subject.

Step 5 Read the question, and test each answer choice using your conclusions about the graph.

1 The graph shows unemployment trends in Germany, Great Britain and the United States during the Great Depression. Based on the graph, unemployment

A was lower in Germany in 1938 than in 1928.

B remained steady between 1928 and 1938.

C was higher in United States in 1938 than it was in 1935.

D was highest for each nation in 1932.

Step 6 Choose the best answer.

GA 41

Using Timelines to Answer Questions

Timelines present events in chronological order. They can help you identify cause-and-effect relationships between seemingly unrelated events. They can also help you trace the progress of trends as they develop over time.

This skill will help you answer questions like the one below the following timeline. Follow the steps to apply the skill. Then answer the multiple-choice item below.

Step 1 Read the title to determine the subject.

World Events, 1985–1995

1986	1990	1995
Nuclear accident occurs in Chernobyl.	Germany is reunited.	The WTO forms.

1985   **1990**   **1995**

1988	1991	1994
Osama bin Laden forms al Qaeda.	Soviet Union collapses.	NAFTA is created.

Step 2 Locate the starting and ending points on either end of the timeline. What period of time does the timeline cover?

Step 3 Read the individual entries on the timeline in chronological order.

1 The timeline shows recent world events from 1985 to 1995. Which of these statements can be supported by information on the timeline?

A Anti-Americanism grew around the world.

B Nations cooperated more in addressing economic issues.

C The accident at the Chernobyl nuclear power plant led directly to the collapse of the Soviet Union.

D The collapse of the Soviet Union allowed Germany to reunify.

Step 4 Determine if there is any connection between events on the timeline or a common theme linking different entries.

Step 5 Read the question, and test each answer against the information in the timeline.

Step 6 Choose the best answer.

Prepare for the GHSGT

The practice questions on the following pages are similar to those you will see on the **GHSGT** and social studies tests. The questions in each exercise are based on the seven units covered by your textbook and address the **Georgia Performance Standards for World History**. This skills practice section is organized as follows:

Fast Track to the GHSGT			
GHSGT Practice	**Georgia World History**	**Georgia Performance Standards**	**Review Pages**
1	Unit 1: Early Civilizations (Prehistory–A.D. 1570)	SSWH1a, SSWH2b, SSWH3b, SSWH3c, SSWH8a	38, 65, 80, 138–140, 165, 187
2	Unit 2: Regional Civilizations (730 B.C.–A.D. 1650)	SSWH3d, SSWH5e, SSWH4a, SSWH5f, SSWH6c	226, 258–259, 283, 306, 346–350
3	Unit 3: Early Modern Times (1300–1800)	SSWH9d, SSWH9b, SSWH10a, SSWH10c, SSWH10b	526, 414, 448, 449. 491
4	Unit 4: Enlightenment and Revolution (1700–1850)	SSWH13b, SSWH14b, SSWH14c, SSWH15a, SSEWH14b	569, 558–560, 597, 622–623, 648–651
5	Unit 5: Industrialism and a New Global Age (1800–1914)	SSWH15a, SSWH15b, SSWH15a, SSWH15c, SSWH15d	788, 692–695, 726–729, 776–777, 792–793
6	Unit 6: World Wars and Revolutions (1910–1955)	SSWH17b, SSWH16a, SSWH17d, SSWH17c, SSWH18a	904–905, 816–818, 865–867, 915, 938
7	Unit 7: The World Since 1945 (1945–PRESENT)	SSWH20a, SSWH19c, SSWH20b, SSWH19b, SSWH21b	1038, 967–968, 1002–1003, 1033, 1103

Downtown Atlanta

Skills Practice 1

After completing chapters 1–6, complete the exercise below.

Use this quotation to answer question 1.

"In the eighteenth year of my rule I crossed the Euphrates for the sixteenth time. [King] Hazael of Damascus put his trust upon his numerous army and called up his troops in great number…. I fought with him and inflicted a defeat upon him, killing with the sword 16,000 of his experienced soldiers. I took away from him 1,121 chariots, 470 riding horses as well as his camp…. I followed him and besieged him in Damascus, his royal residence. I cut down his gardens…. I marched as far as the mountains of Hauran, destroying, tearing down and burning innumerable towns, carrying booty away from them which was beyond counting. I marched as far as the mountains of Ba'li-ra'si…and erected there a stela [stone pillar] with my image as king."
—From King Shalmaneser III of Assyria

1 This quotation helps illustrate what feature of Assyrian civilization?

A their well-planned cities and social organization

B their reputation as fearsome warriors

C their devotion to knowledge

D their use of iron weapons

2 Buddhism differed from Hinduism in what key respect?

A Buddhism focused on individual enlightenment through meditation, while Hinduism focused on formal rituals.

B Buddhism embraced the caste system while Hinduism did not.

C Buddhism did not spread beyond India while Hinduism did.

D Buddhism rejected the Hindu principle of nonviolence.

3 Which figure is MOST responsible for the spread of Ancient Greek culture throughout the Mediterranian world and the Middle East?

A Pericles

B Plato

C Alexander the Great

D Socrates

4 Which of the following BEST represents Rome's legacy?

A the commitment to democratic principles

B the policy of bread and circuses

C the development of dictatorship

D the commitment to the rule of law

5 Which of the following was NOT a characteristic of the Inca Empire?

A an efficient government

B an extensive network of roads

C a lack of personal property

D an intricate system of writing

Skills Practice 2

GHSGT Skills Practice

Regional Civilizations (730 B.C.–A.D. 1650)

After completing chapters 7–12, complete the exercise below.

Use this map to answer question 1.

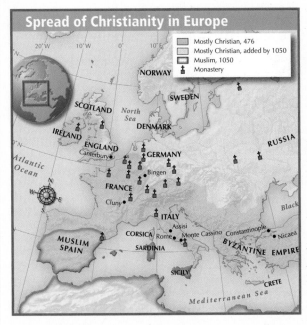

Spread of Christianity in Europe

Mostly Christian, 476
Mostly Christian, added by 1050
Muslim, 1050
Monastery

1 **Based on this map, which statement about Christianity is correct?**

A Christianity was threatened by the growth of the Muslim World.

B Christianity failed to find acceptance in much of Europe following Rome's fall.

C Christianity continued to spread across Europe and into Russia following Rome's fall.

D Christianity was unable to grow because of a lack of monasteries.

2 **The Crusades led to**

A the collapse of European economies

B the destruction of Muslim power

C the strengthening of European monarchs and the Pope

D the spread of the Black Death

3 **Justinian's Code was**

A a secret message painted into the walls of the Hagia Sophia

B the compilation of Roman law created by the Byzantine emperor

C the religious text used by the Byzantine Christians

D a tale about life in Medieval Europe

4 **According to Muslim belief, Jews, Christians, and Muslims represent**

A the Three Pillars of Islam

B the People of the Path

C the People of the Prophet

D the People of the Book

5 **Which development spurred the growth of the great kingdoms of West Africa—Ghana, Mali, and Songhai?**

A the start of the trans-Saharan trade in salt, gold, and other goods

B the spread of Christianity in West Africa

C the conquests of Mansa Musa

D the Bantu migrations

GA GHSGT Skills Practice
Early Modern Times (1300–1800)

After completing chapters 13–16, complete the exercise below.

Use this political map to answer question 1.

Europe in 1648

NORWAY

SCOTLAND   SWEDEN

North Sea   DENMARK   Baltic Sea   PRUSSIA

IRELAND   ENGLAND   Dutch Neth.   BRANDENBURG   Berlin

Atlantic Ocean   London   Spanish Neth.   WESTPHALIA   SAXONY   Silesia   Prague   Bohemia   Vienna   TRANSYLVANIA

Paris   Alsace   Lorraine   BAVARIA   SWISS FED.   AUSTRIA   HUNGARY   OTTOMAN EMPIRE

FRANCE   Milan

Papal States

Corsica   Rome   Naples

PORTUGAL   Madrid   SPAIN

Sardinia

Mediterranean Sea   Sicily   Crete

Controlled by Spanish Hapsburgs
Controlled by Austrian Hapsburgs
Italian city-states
Controlled by Prussian Hohenzollerns
Boundary of Holy Roman Empire

1 What does this map suggest about the results of the Thirty Years' War?

A Catholicism spread throughout the Holy Roman Empire.

B Protestantism spread throughout the Holy Roman Empire.

C The Holy Roman Empire remained fragmented.

D The effort succeeded in unifying the Holy Roman Empire.

2 Why is Leonardo da Vinci regarded as the ideal "Renaissance man"?

A He was born at the start of the Renaissance.

B He coined the term Renaissance.

C He excelled as an artist.

D He embodied many of the skills and interests that defined the era.

3 Vasco da Gama is remembered for

A being the first to sail from Europe around the Cape of Good Hope to India

B assembling expert cartographers and scientists at Sagres, Portugal, to plan voyages of discovery

C circumnavigating the globe

D reaching the Americas by sailing west

4 The Columbian Exchange refers to which of the following?

A what Christopher Columbus paid native peoples in return for his safety

B the shift of power that occurred in Europe as a result of Columbus's voyages

C the global exchange of goods that occurred when Columbus first linked Europe with the Americas

D the European markets that were built in the Americas

Skills Practice 4

GA **GHSGT Skills Practice**
Enlightenment and Revolution (1700–1850)

After completing chapters 17–20, complete the exercise below.

Use this table to answer question 1.

Selected Enlightenment Thinkers		
Thinker	Lifespan	Nationality
Jean D'Alembert	1717–1783	French
Jeremy Bentham	1748–1832	English
Cesare Beccaria	1738–1794	Italian
Denis Diderot	1713–1784	French
David Hume	1711–1776	Scottish
Immanuel Kant	1724–1804	E. Prussian
John Locke	1632–1704	English
Charles Montesquieu	1689–1755	French
Jean-Jacques Rousseau	1712–1778	French
Adam Smith	1723–1790	English
Voltaire	1694–1778	French

1 According to this table, which country produced the greatest number of great Enlightenment thinkers?

A Italy

B England

C France

D Scotland

2 Simón Bolívar is associated with which of the following independence movements?

A Spanish South America

B Mexico

C Haiti

D Brazil

3 Which of the following was MOST responsible for Napoleon's defeat in Russia in 1812?

A superior Russian weapons

B the enormous size of the Russian army

C the arrival of reinforcements from Spain and Austria

D the effects of the harsh Russian winter on Napoleon's troops

4 The English thinker Adam Smith is associated with which of the following?

A labor unions

B the spread of child labor

C laissez-faire economics

D utilitarianism

5 Which of the following best describes the reason for the American Revolution?

A The colonies did not like the British system of government.

B The American colonists felt that the British were not respecting their rights as English citizens.

C The French encouraged the colonists to rebel.

D The colonists were angry at British actions during the French and Indian War.

GHSGT Skills Practice
Industrialism and a New Global Age (1800–1914)

After completing chapters 21–25, complete the exercise below.

Use this bar graph to answer question 1.

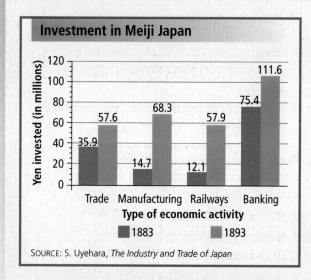

Investment in Meiji Japan

SOURCE: S. Uyehara, *The Industry and Trade of Japan*

1 What does this graph suggest about the changes taking place in Meiji Japan in the late 1800s?

  A Meiji Japan was trying hard to slow the pace of change sweeping its society.

  B Meiji Japan was making large investments in its economy in order to modernize.

  C By far the biggest priority in Meiji Japan was improving trade.

  D Meiji Japan's investment in railways would prove disastrous to the economy.

2 The French exploited Indochina for which of the following raw materials?

  A gold

  B rubber

  C salt

  D tin

3 Germany's Chancellor Otto Von Bismarck

  A failed to recognize the importance of industrialization

  B provoked a disastrous war against France that ended in crushing defeat

  C united Germany and established the German empire

  D promoted the spread of socialism in Germany and Europe

4 During the late 1800s and early 1900s, the British government responded to growing demands of the working class by

  A outlawing labor unions

  B establishing penal colonies for unruly workers

  C outlawing slavery

  D passing a series of social welfare laws, such as health insurance and old-age pensions

5 Which of the following best describes the cause of the Boxer Uprising in China?

  A anger over the growing foreign influence in China

  B anger at corruption by Empress Ci Xi

  C popular rejection of Confucian values

  D strong popular support for westernization

Skills Practice 6

GA GHSGT Skills Practice
World Wars and Revolutions (1910–1955)

After completing chapters 26–29, complete the exercise below.

Use this line graph to answer question 1.

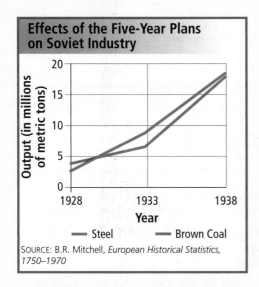

Effects of the Five-Year Plans on Soviet Industry

Output (in millions of metric tons)

— Steel   — Brown Coal

SOURCE: B.R. Mitchell, *European Historical Statistics, 1750–1970*

1 Which of the following answers is supported by the information in this graph?

A Industry lagged behind agriculture during the first two five-year plans.

B Industrial output fell during the first five-year plan.

C Industrial output rose during the first five-year plan.

D The Soviet Union's workers suffered greatly during the first five-year plans.

2 Mohandas Gandhi is associated with the nationalist movement in which country?

A China

B India

C Turkey

D Egypt

3 Which BEST describes the cause of World War I?

A religious conflict between Christians and Muslims

B the breakdown of traditional alliances and friendships among European nations

C class conflict resulting from industrialization in Europe

D entangling alliances and growing nationalism in Europe

4 Adolf Hitler and Benito Mussolini were similar in what way?

A Both believed in socialism.

B Both fought against totalitarianism.

C Both gained power through a violent civil war.

D Both based their appeal on intense nationalism and the promise of restoring past glory.

5 The United States entered World War II following which event?

A the D-Day invasion

B Germany's invasion of Poland

C the Japanese attack on Pearl Harbor

D the German siege of Leningrad

Skills Practice 7

GA

GHSGT Skills Practice
The World Since 1945 (1945–Present)

After completing chapters 30–34, complete the exercise below.

Use this timeline to answer question 1.

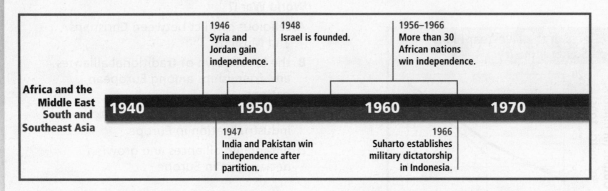

1 Which of the following would be the most appropriate title for this timeline?

A Key Events of the Cold War

B New Nations Emerge in the Post-War World

C New Empires After World War II

D The United States Promotes Freedom

2 The establishment of Israel in 1948 was followed by which of the following?

A the British withdrawal from Palestine

B an Arab-Jewish peace accord

C the attack of Israel by several Arab states

D the United Nations decision to divide Palestine into a Jewish and Arab state

3 The World Trade Organization is MOST associated with which development?

A higher tariffs on trade

B increasing economic globalization

C the fall of the Soviet Union

D the growth in multinational corporations

4 Which represents the correct order in which these events from the Cold War occurred?

A the Korean War, the Soviet invasion of Hungary, the Cuban Missile Crisis, the fall of the Berlin Wall

B the Cuban Missile Crisis, the Korean War, the fall of the Berlin Wall, the Soviet invasion of Hungary

C the Soviet invasion of Hungary, the Cuban Missile Crisis, the Korean War, the fall of the Berlin Wall

D the Cuban Missile Crisis, the fall of the Berlin Wall, the Korean War, the Soviet invasion of Hungary

5 Mikhail Gorbechev's attempts to introduce *glasnost* and *perestroika* resulted in

A increased tensions with the United States and its NATO allies

B the Soviet Union invasion of Afghanistan

C a burst of economic growth by the Soviet economy

D the breakdown of central authority in the Soviet empire

SKILLS Handbook

Contents

A series of handbooks provide skills instruction to help you read, learn, and demonstrate your knowledge of world history.

Reading Informational Texts

Writing Handbook

Geography Skills Handbook

Critical Thinking About Texts, Visuals, and Media Sources

Speaking and Listening

21st Century Skills

SKILLS HANDBOOK

SKILLS Handbook

Reading Informational Texts

GA SSWHRC1c, SSWHRC1d, SSWHRC1d(A), SSWHRC1d(B), SSWHRC1c(C)

Reading a newspaper, a magazine, an Internet page, or a textbook differs from reading a novel. You read nonfiction texts to acquire new information. Researchers have shown that the reading strategies presented below will help you maximize your understanding of informational texts. You'll have chances to practice these skills and strategies throughout the book.

Strategies for Before You Read

Before you read an informational text, it's important to take the time to do some pre-reading. These strategies will help.

Set a Purpose for Reading

Try to focus on a goal when you're reading the text. Preview a section by reading the objectives and looking at the illustrations. Then write a purpose for your reading, such as:

- "I'll learn about the histories of Egypt and Nubia and find ways to compare these cultures."
- "I'll find out about the spread of Islam."

Ask Questions

Before you read a section, consider what you'd like to know about a topic. Then ask questions that will yield relevant information. Scan the section headings and illustrations and then write a few questions in a chart like the one below. As you read, try to answer each of your questions. Use phrases and words to fill in the chart.

Question	Answer
How do strong monarchs unite nations?	Central/absolute power, citizens' loyalty, effective bureaucracy
What problems do strong monarchs often create?	Abuse of power, misuse of funds, conflicts with religious leaders

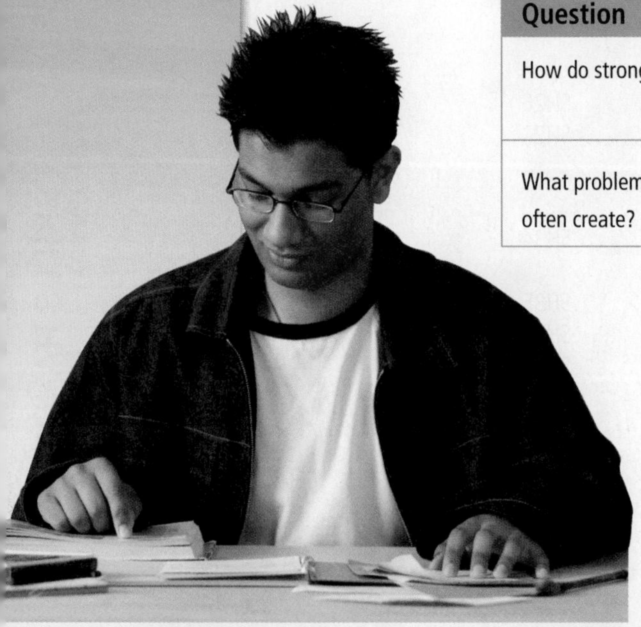

Predict

Engage in the reading process by making predictions about what you are preparing to learn. Scan the section headings and the visuals. Then write a prediction, such as:

- "I will find out what caused feudalism in Europe to develop and later to disappear."

Keep your predictions in mind as you read—do they turn out to be accurate or do you need to revise them?

Use Prior Knowledge

Research shows that if you connect the new information in your reading to your prior knowledge, you'll be more likely to remember the new information. You'll also see the value of studying history if you see how it connects to the present. After previewing a section, create a chart like this one. Complete the chart as you read the section.

What I Know	What I Want to Know	What I Learned
Many people today are Calvinists or Lutherans.	How and when did these religions begin?	John Calvin and Martin Luther led people to start new Protestant churches during the sixteenth-century Reformation.

Strategies for During Reading

It's important to be an active reader. Use these strategies as you read an informational text.

Reread or Read Ahead

If you don't understand a certain passage, reread it to look for connections among the words and sentences. For example, look for cause-and-effect words that link ideas, or sequence words that show when events took place. Or, try reading ahead to see if the ideas are clarified later on. Once you find new clarifying information, return to the confusing text and read it again with the new information in mind.

Paraphrase

To paraphrase is to restate information in your own words, as in the example below. Paraphrasing is a good way to check your understanding of the reading. Think of it this way—if you can explain it to someone else, you understand it.

Original Paragraph	Paraphrase
When Ireland won independence in 1922, Britain retained control of six northern counties where there was a Protestant majority. Faced with widespread discrimination, Catholics demanded civil rights and the reunification of Ireland. Protestants wanted to remain part of Britain.	After Irish independence in 1922, Britain controlled six Protestant-dominated counties in the north. People in these counties divided along religious lines: Catholics called for both civil rights and reunification of the Irish nation; Protestants supported British control.

Summarize

Summarizing—a version of paraphrasing—can also help you confirm your understanding of the text. Summarizing focuses on restating the main ideas of a passage, as you can see in the example below. Include a few important details, such as the time period, to orient yourself or other readers to the text.

Original Paragraph	Summary
Ottoman expansion threatened the crumbling Byzantine empire. After several failed attempts to capture Constantinople, Muhammad II finally succeeded in 1453. Over the next 200 years, the Ottoman empire continued to expand.	The Byzantine empire gave way to the Ottoman empire around 1453, resulting in 200 years of Ottoman rule.

Identify Main Ideas and Details

A main idea is the most important point in a paragraph or section of text. Some main ideas are stated directly, but others are implied. You must determine these yourself by reading carefully. Pause occasionally to make sure you can identify the main idea.

Main idea

<u>Europeans continued to seek new routes around or through the Americas.</u> In 1513, the Spanish adventurer Vasco Núñez de Balboa, with the help of Native Americans, hacked a passage through the tropical forests of Panama to reach what he called the South Sea. In November 1529, Spanish nobleman Ferdinand Magellan sailed through a passage at the tip of South America. After a difficult journey filled with brutal storms, rushing tides, and unpredictable winds, Magellan's ships emerged into Balboa's South Sea, which Magellan renamed the Pacific—that is, peaceful—Ocean.

Main ideas are supported by details. Record main ideas and details in an outline format like the one shown here.

Main idea

Details

European Exploration in the Americas
I. Continued as Europeans sought new routes around or through the Americas
    A. Balboa and Native Americans found a passage across Panama.
    B. Balboa named the South Sea.
    C. Magellan found passage around tip of South America.
    D. Magellan reached the South Sea and renamed it the Pacific Ocean.

Vocabulary

Here are several strategies to help you understand the meaning of a word you do not recognize.

Use Context Clues You can often define an unfamiliar word with clues from the surrounding text. For example, in the sentence "Crusaders fought on and off for more than 200 years, and many died for their cause," the words *fought* and *died* are clues indicating that a Crusader was someone who fought wars. Context clues can be in the same sentence as the unfamiliar word or in nearby sentences or paragraphs.

Analyze Word Parts Use your knowledge of word parts to help you define unfamiliar words. Break the word into its parts—root, prefix, suffix. What do you know about these parts? For example, the suffixes *–ify* and *–ation* mean "make into" and "action or process." The word *desertify* means "turn into a desert." *Desertification* means "the process of turning into a desert."

Recognize Word Origins Another way to figure out the meaning of an unfamiliar word is to understand the word's origins. Use your knowledge of Greek or Latin roots, for example, to build meaning. The words *formation* and *reformation* contain the Latin root *form,* which means "shape." *Formation* is the shape in which something is arranged. *Reformation* is a change in the shape of an idea or institution.

Analyze the Text's Structure

Just as you organize a story about your weekend to highlight the most important parts, authors will organize their writing to stress their key ideas. Analyzing text structure can help you tap into this organization. In a social studies text, the author frequently uses one of the structures listed in the chart at right to organize information. Learn to identify structures in texts and you'll remember text information more effectively.

Analyze the Author's Purpose

Different reading materials are written with different goals, or purposes. For example, this book is written to teach you about world history. The technical manual that accompanies computer software is written to teach readers how to use the product. In a newspaper, some articles will be written to inform readers about news events, while editorials will be written to persuade readers to accept a particular view about those events.

Structures for Organizing Information

Compare and Contrast Here, an author highlights similarities and differences between two or more ideas, cultures, processes, people, etc. Look for clue words such as *on the other hand* or *similarly*.

Sequence Here, an author recounts the order in which events occurred or steps were taken. History is often told in chronological sequence but can also involve flashbacks from later times to earlier times. Look for sequence words such as *initially*, *later*, and *ultimately*.

Cause and Effect Here, an author highlights the impact of one event on another or the effects of key events. Cause and effect is critical to understanding history because events in one time often strongly influence those in later times. Look for clue words such as *because*, *so*, or *as a result*.

An author's purpose influences not only how the material is presented but also how you read it. Thus you must identify the purpose, whether it is stated directly or merely suggested. If it is not directly stated, use clues in the text—such as opinion words in an editorial—to identify the author's purpose.

Distinguish Between Facts and Opinions/Recognize Bias

It's important to read actively, especially when reading informational texts. Decide whether information is factual—which means it can be proven—or if it includes opinions or bias—that is, people's views or evaluations.

Anytime you read material that conveys opinions, such as an editorial, keep an eye out for author bias. This bias might be revealed in the use of emotionally charged words or faulty logic. For example, the newspaper editorial below includes factual statements (in blue) and opinion statements (in red). Underlined words are emotionally charged words—they'll get a rise out of people. Faulty logic (in green) may include circular reasoning that returns to its beginning and either/or arguments that ignore other possibilities.

Editorial

In 1993, the people of Brazil voted to keep their government a republic rather than revert to a monarchy. Voters chose between the two options in a special election. Clearly, anyone who favored monarchy was a reactionary dinosaur who maliciously wanted to undermine Brazil's progress. The republican format allows Brazilians to vote for their leaders directly. As a result, our brilliant leader Fernando Henrique Carlosa spearheaded life-saving reforms to Brazil's dying and antiquated economic system. In a monarchy, this would be impossible.

Identify Evidence

Read critically. Don't accept an author's conclusion automatically. Identify and evaluate the author's evidence. Does it justify the conclusion in quantity and content? An author may present facts to support a claim, but there may be more to the story than facts. For example, what evidence does the writer of the editorial above present to support the claim that a monarch could not help Brazil's economy? Perhaps a monarch would use his or her more centralized authority to achieve more sweeping and rapid reforms.

Evaluate Credibility

After you evaluate evidence, check an author's credentials. Consider his or her level of experience and expertise about the topic. Is he or she likely to be knowledgeable *and* objective about the topic? Evaluating credibility is especially important with sites you may visit on the Internet. Ask the following questions to determine if a site and its author are reliable.

- Who sponsors the Web site? Is it a respected organization, a discussion group of individuals, or a single person?

- What is the source of the Web site's information? Does the site list sources for facts and statements?

- Does the Web site creator include his or her name and credentials?

- Is the information on the Web site balanced and objective or biased to reflect only one point of view?

- Can you verify the Web site's information using two other sources, such as an encyclopedia or news agency?

- Is the information current? Is there a date on the Web site to show when it was created or last updated?

Strategies for After Reading

Evaluate Understanding

Evaluate how well you understand what you've read.

- Go back to the questions you asked yourself before reading. Try to answer each of them.
- Check the predictions you made and revise them if appropriate.
- Draw a conclusion about the author's evidence and credibility.
- Check meanings of unfamiliar words in the dictionary to confirm your definitions.

Recall Information

Before moving on to new material, you should be able to answer the following questions fully:

- What is the text about?
- What is the purpose of the text?
- How is the text structured?

You should also be able to place the new information in the context of your prior knowledge of the topic.

Writing Handbook

 SSWHRC1d(B)

Writing is one of the most powerful communication tools you will use for the rest of your life. Research shows that writing about what you read actually helps you learn new information and ideas. A systematic approach to writing—including prewriting, drafting, revising, and proofing—can help you write better, whether you're writing an essay or a research paper.

Narrative Essay

Narrative writing tells a story, often about a personal experience. In social studies, this story might be a narrative essay that recounts how a recent or historical event affected you or your family.

❶ Prewriting

Choose a topic. The focus of your essay should be an experience of significance to you. Use these ideas as a guide.

- **Look at photos** that show you and/or your family. Perhaps you attended a political rally or visited an important historical monument.

- **Scan the news** in print or through electronic media. Consider how current events relate to you and your family.

- **Brainstorm** with family or friends about recent events. How did you respond to these events? Jot down ideas like the ones below.

Connections to History This Year
— trip to art museum: Renaissance painters
— historical books: World War II Africa
— mock debate: Vietnam War

Consider audience and purpose.

- Keep your **audience's** knowledge and experience level in mind. Make sure you provide any necessary background information.

- Choose a **purpose** as well. If you want to entertain, include humorous details. To convey how the experience changed you, you might share more serious insights.

Gather details. Collect the facts and details you need to tell your story.

- **Research** any background about the historical event that readers might need to know about.

- **List details** about your own experience as it relates to the event.

❷ Drafting

Identify the climax, or most interesting part of your story. Then logically organize your story into a beginning, middle, and end. Narratives are usually told in chronological order.

Open strongly with an engaging sentence, such as the one below, that will catch your reader's attention.

Use sensory details, such as sights, sounds, or smells, to make the story vivid for readers. Describe people's actions and gestures. Pinpoint and describe locations.

Write a conclusion that sums up the significance of the event or situation you have experienced.

> I never expected to find myself arguing to support America's role in Vietnam. Our recent mock debate on the Vietnam War gave me new insight about this complex time in my nation's history. **Research took me inside the perspective of those who supported the War and its goals.** On the day of the debate, my hands were covered in sweat and my heart pounded as I stood to explain this currently unpopular position.

Strong opening engages the reader.

Insight or significance tells the reader what this event means to you.

Sensory details help the reader envision the experience.

❸ Revising

Add dialogue or description. Dialogue, or conveying a person's thoughts or feelings in his or her own words, can make a narrative more effective. Look for places where the emotions are especially intense. In the model, this might be when the writer's opponents respond to the debate position.

First Draft	Revised Original
At the debate, my hands were wet and my heart beat fast.	On the day of the debate, my hands were covered in sweat and my heart pounded.

Revise word choice. Replace general words with more specific, colorful ones. Choose vivid action verbs, precise adjectives, and specific nouns to convey your meaning. Look at the example above. Notice how much more effective the revised version is at conveying the experience.

Read your draft aloud. Listen for grammatical errors and statements that are unclear. Revise your sentences as necessary.

❹ Publishing and Presenting

Share by reading aloud. Highlight text you want to emphasize and then read your essay aloud to the class. Invite and respond to questions.

21st Century Skills

SKILLS HANDBOOK

Expository Writing

Expository writing explains ideas or information in detail. The strategies on these pages examine each of several expository writing styles.

① Prewriting

Choose a topic. In social studies, the focus of your writing might be explaining a historical process, comparing and contrasting cultural trends, explaining causes and effects of current events, or exploring problems societies have faced and the solutions they have sought. These ideas are a guide.

- **Ask questions.** For process writing, consider the question *how*. Think about *how* people in history have accomplished their goals, such as building a giant monument. Identify the steps and procedures involved.

> **Question:** How did great thinkers of the 1600s change people's view of the world?
>
> **Answer:** They developed the scientific method.

- **Create a compare/contrast grab bag.** With a small group, write on separate slips of paper examples from each category: ideas, cultures, or time periods. Mix the slips in a bag and choose two. Compare and contrast the two ideas, cultures, or time periods.

- **Interview** someone who made a major change in lifestyle, such as moving from one culture to another. Find out how and why the person did this. Understanding *why* is the basis of any cause and effect essay.

- **Take a mental walk.** Study a map and envision taking a tour of the region. Think about problems each area you visit might face, such as armed conflict, natural disaster, or governmental change. Choose a problem and suggest solutions for it.

Consider audience and purpose. Consider how much your readers know about the problem, comparison, event, or process you will address. Suit your writing to your audience's knowledge or plan to give explanations of unfamiliar terms and concepts.

Gather details. Collect the facts and details you need to write your essay.

Research the topic. Use books, the Internet, or interviews of local experts. List facts, details, and other evidence related to your topic. Also consider your personal experience. For example, you might know about a process from personal experience or have witnessed the effects of a historic legal decision.

Create a graphic organizer. For cause-and-effect or problem-solution essays, use a two-column chart. Process writing can be listed as a bulleted list of steps. A Venn diagram can help you compare and contrast.

World War I
- new weapons used: machine guns, poison gas, submarines
- 8.5 million military deaths

- fought by two powerful alliances
- began in Europe, then spread

World War II
- new weapon used: atomic bomb
- 20 million military deaths

Identify causes and effects. List possible explanations for events. Remember that many events result from multiple causes. Identify effects both large and small. Note that some events may have effects that in turn cause other events. Look for causes and effects in all your expository essays. For example, in a process explanation, one step often causes the next.

Fine-tune your ideas. For a problem-solution essay, decide what you will suggest as a solution. Keep your solution narrow to be achievable in cost, effort, and timing. Make sure no one has tried it before, or if it has been tried and it failed, address the failure.

❷ Drafting

Match structure to purpose. Typically, process writing and cause-and-effect writing are written in sequence order. Problem-solution essays benefit from block organization, which presents the entire problem and proposes a solution. For compare/contrast essays, you can organize by subject or by point.

By subject: Discuss the events and outcomes of World War I, and then compare and contrast these with those of World War II.

By point: Introduce a category, such as use of new weapons. Relate both wars to this category, comparing or contrasting them along the way.

Give background. To discuss events from history, first orient the reader to time and place. Choose the important facts but don't overwhelm the reader with detail. If you need to, return to prewriting to narrow your topic further.

Elaborate for interest and emphasis. Give details about each point in your essay. For example, add facts that make the link between events so that a cause-and-effect relationship is clear. Also, readers will support proposed solutions more if your details clearly show how these solutions will solve the stated problem. Use facts and human experiences to make your essay vivid.

Connect to today. Even when you write about historical events, you may find links to today. Explore these links in your essay.

Mexico's population underwent great change during the mid- twentieth century. Population shifted from rural areas to urban areas. The nation's society went from largely agricultural to largely industrial and urban. Urban populations exploded, with Mexico City alone growing from 1.5 million people in 1940 to nearly 20 million later in the century. These changes resulted from several causes.
Identify the topic to orient readers.

First, land reform begun in the 1930s failed. The millions of acres redistributed by then–President Lázaro Cárdenas proved arid and unproductive. Second, the rural population was growing rapidly. This placed increased demands on the land. The land became even more depleted and unproductive. Finally, several Mexican governments in turn shifted their attention from the small rural peasant farmer toward larger scale farming operations.
Chronological order walks readers through the cause-effect sequence.
Elaboration supports the relationship you are highlighting.

Mexico's shifting population and changing economic patterns yielded new problems for its leaders by late in the twentieth century.
Connection to today tells readers why this matters to them.

---

❸ Revising

Add transition words. Make cause-and-effect relationships clear with words such as *because, as a result,* and *so*. To compare or contrast ideas, use linking words, such as *similarly, both, equally* or *in contrast, instead, yet*. Use words such as *first, second, next,* and *finally* to help readers follow steps in a process. Look at the following examples. In the revised version, a reader knows the correct order in which to perform the steps.

First Draft	Revised
Scientists form an educated guess called a hypothesis. They test that hypothesis with an experiment.	<u>Next,</u> scientists form an educated guess called a hypothesis. <u>Then,</u> they test that hypothesis with an experiment.

Remember purpose. Shape your draft so that it answers the question or thesis you began with. For a problem-solution essay—in which your purpose is to sell your solution—that means anticipating opposing arguments and responding to them. For cause-and-effect, you want to stress the way one event leads to the next. Always tell readers *why* they should care about your topic.

Review organization. Confirm that your ideas flow in a logical order. Write main points on index cards. Reorganize these until you are satisfied that the order best strengthens your essay.

Add details. Make sure you haven't left out any steps in your essay, and don't assume readers will make the connections. For example, you might forget to state explicitly that a process must be repeated in order to produce accurate results. Add more background if necessary for clarity.

Revise sentences and words. Look at your sentence length. Vary it to include both short and long sentences. Then scan for vague words, such as *good*. Replace them with specific and vibrant words, such as *effective*. Use technical terms only when necessary, and then define them.

Peer review. Ask a peer to read your draft. Is it clear? Can he or she follow your ideas? Revise areas of confusion.

❹ Publishing and Presenting

Collect in a class manual. Contribute your process explanation to a class manual of *History How-To's*.

Submit to a library. Find a specialized library, such as a presidential library. Mail your essay to the library's publications or public relations department.

Seek publication. If your historical events or issues are local, seek publication in a local historical magazine or contact a historical society. You might speak to their members.

Mail to an advocacy group. Find a local, national, or international organization that is concerned with your topic. Send them your essay and ask for comments on its ideas. Make sure to include a self-addressed stamped envelope and a note explaining your essay and offering thanks for its review.

Research Writing

① Prewriting

Choose a topic. Often, a teacher will assign your research topic. You may have flexibility in choosing your focus or you may have the opportunity to completely define your topic. These ideas are a guide.

- **Catalog scan.** Using a card or electronic catalog, search for topics that interest you. When a title looks promising, find the book on the shelves. Libraries usually use the Dewey Decimal Classification system to group research materials by subject, so you should find other books on similar subjects nearby. You can use them all to decide on your final topic.

- **Notes review.** Review your social studies notes from the last month or so. Jot down topics that you found interesting. Then repeat the process with your other classes. For example, you might find a starting point for research into the Scientific Revolution from a math theorem.

- **Social studies categories game.** With a group, brainstorm categories in social studies. For example, you might list key world leaders or important wars. Within each category, take turns adding subtopics. The chart below looks at different transportation topics.

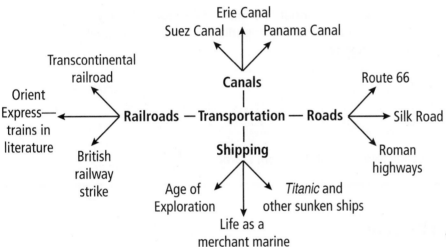

You can use sources such as newspapers to get ideas.

Analyze the audience. Your research and your paper should be strongly influenced by the audience. How much will readers know about this topic and how much will you have to teach them?

Gather details. Collect the facts and details you need to write your paper. Use resources beyond the typical history books. Look at nonfiction books such as memoirs or collections of letters. Also look at magazine and newspaper articles. Consider news magazines, as well as those focused on topics such as history or travel. You may find interviews with experts on your topic or travel articles about a region that interests you. Search the Internet, starting with online encyclopedias, news organizations, and history Web sites.

Organize evidence and ideas. Use note cards to record information and to help you organize your thoughts. Start with a general thesis statement in mind. Then begin reading and taking notes. Write a heading at the top of each note card to group it under a subtopic. Note a number or title to identify the information source. In the examples below, the number 3 is used. Use the same number for an additional source card containing the bibliographic information you will need.

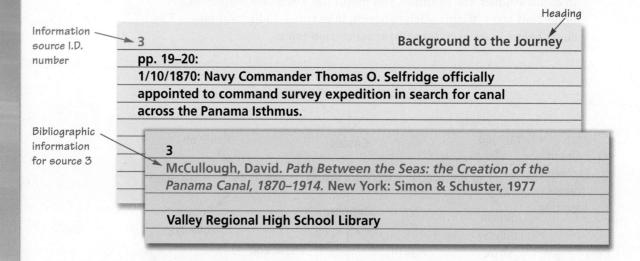

Heading

Information source I.D. number

3   **Background to the Journey**

pp. 19–20:

1/10/1870: Navy Commander Thomas O. Selfridge officially appointed to command survey expedition in search for canal across the Panama Isthmus.

Bibliographic information for source 3

3

McCullough, David. *Path Between the Seas: the Creation of the Panama Canal, 1870–1914.* New York: Simon & Schuster, 1977

Valley Regional High School Library

❷ Drafting

Fine-tune your thesis. Review your notes to find relationships between ideas. Shape a thesis that is supported by the majority of your information, then check that it is narrow enough to address thoroughly in the allotted time and space. Remember, you can fine-tune your thesis further as you draft or even when you revise.

Organize to fit your purpose. Do you want to persuade readers of a particular position about your topic, compare and contrast aspects of the topic, or show a cause-and-effect relationship? Organize appropriately—for example, by looking at parts of a whole to examine events leading to building and completing the Panama Canal.

Make an outline. Create an outline in which you identify each topic and subtopic in a single phrase. You can then turn these phrases into sentences and later into the topic sentences of your draft paragraphs. Study the example at the top of the next page to see how to do this well.

Write by paragraph. Write an introduction, at least three body paragraphs, and a conclusion. Address a subtopic of your main topic in each body paragraph. Support all your statements with the facts and details you gathered.

Building the Panama Canal

Outline

I. Introduction

II. Why the Canal Was Built

III. How the Canal Was Built
   A. Physical Challenges
   B. Medical Challenges

IV. Conclusion

Introduction

Ever since Christopher Columbus first explored the Isthmus of Panama, the Spanish had been looking for a water route through it. They wanted to be able to sail west from Spain to Asia without sailing around South America. However, it was not until 1914 that the dream became a reality.

Conclusion

It took eight years and more than 70,000 workers to build the Panama Canal. It remains one of the greatest engineering feats of modern times.

An outline helps you structure your information.

Each body paragraph looks at a part of the whole topic.

The introduction puts the topic in a context of time and place. The entire paragraph conveys the thesis: Building the Panama Canal was a dream that took centuries to achieve.

The conclusion recaps key points and leaves readers with a final statement to remember.

❸ Revising

Add detail. Mark points where more details would strengthen your statements. Look at the following examples. Notice the added details in the revised version. When adding facts, make certain that they are accurate.

First Draft	Revised
The Navy excursion was a huge undertaking. Supplies were gathered to support the team for many months.	The Navy excursion was a huge undertaking. Supplies were gathered to support the team for many months, including more than 600 pairs of shoes, 100 miles of telegraph wire, 2,500 pounds of coffee, and 10,000 pounds of bread! (McCullough 20).

Make the connection for readers. Help readers find their way through your ideas. First, check that your body paragraphs and the information within them flow in a logical sequence. If they do not, revise to correct this. Then add transition words to link ideas and paragraphs.

Give credit. Check that you have used your own words or given proper credit for borrowed words. You can give credit easily with parenthetical notes. These include the author's last name and the relevant page number from the source. For example, you could cite the note card here as (McCullough 19–20).

❹ Publishing and Presenting

Plan a conference. Gather a group of classmates and present your research projects. You may each wish to create visual materials to accompany your presentations. After you share your papers, hold a question and answer session.

Persuasive Essay

Persuasive writing supports an opinion or position. In social studies, persuasive essays often argue for or against positions on historical or current issues.

❶ Prewriting

Choose a topic. Choose a topic that provokes an argument and has at least two sides. Use these ideas as a guide.

- **Round-table discussion.** Talk with classmates about issues you have studied recently. Outline pro and con positions about these issues.
- **Textbook flip.** Scan the table of contents or flip through the pages of your textbook. Focus on historical issues that engage your feelings.
- **Make connections.** Relate current events to history. Develop a position for or against a situation of importance today using historical evidence.

Narrow your topic.

- **Cover part of the topic** if you find too many pros and cons for a straightforward argument.
- **Use looping.** Write for five minutes on the general topic. Circle the most important idea. Then write for five minutes on that idea. Continue looping until the topic is manageable.

Consider your audience. Choose arguments that will appeal to the audience for your writing and that are likely to persuade them to agree with your views.

Gather evidence. Collect the evidence to support your position convincingly.

- **Identify pros and cons.** Use a graphic organizer like the one below to list points on both sides of the issue.

Position: Education is key to improving life in developing nations.	
Pro	**Con**
• Education allows people to get higher-paying jobs. • With more money, people can help boost the economy. • With education, people can better handle disease and disaster.	• Building new schools may cost more than the government has available for education. • Some countries have other large problems to handle, such as serious diseases.

- **Interview** adults who have lived or worked in developing nations. What do they think? Ask them for reasons to support their views.
- **Research** to get your facts straight. Read articles or books about life in developing nations.

❷ Drafting

State your thesis. Clearly state your position, as in this example:

> Education is the key to revitalizing developing nations. Once many people are educated, many other problems can be solved.

Use your introduction to provide a context for the issue. Tell your readers when and why the issue arose, and identify the important people involved.

Sequence your arguments. Open or close with your strongest argument. If you close with the strongest argument, open with the second-best argument.

Acknowledge opposition. State, and then refute, opposing arguments.

Use facts and details. Include quotations, statistics, or comparisons to build your case. Include personal experiences or reactions to the topic, such as those a family member might have shared when interviewed.

Write a conclusion that restates your thesis and closes with a strong, compelling argument.

Many people living in developing nations want to improve life in their countries. They want the people to have everything they need, such as food and clean water, electricity, medicines, and even fun items like televisions and bicycles. Education is the key to revitalizing developing nations. Once many people are educated, many other problems can be solved.

Education allows people to get higher-paying jobs. With more money, people can help boost the economy. As well, education is an added tool people can use to deal with other problems. It's true that building new schools costs a lot. And in some places, people face many other major problems such as serious diseases. But education will only help them handle these issues....

Background orients readers.

Thesis identifies your main argument.

Supporting argument clarifies your thesis.

Opposing argument, noted and refuted, adds to your position.

Revising

Add information. Extra details can generate interest in your topic. For example, add a quotation from a news article that assesses the role of education in a developing nation or a poor area.

Review arguments. Make sure your arguments are logically sound and clearly developed. Avoid faulty logic such as circular reasoning (arguing a point by merely restating it differently). Evidence is the best way to support your points. Look at the following examples. Notice how much more effectively the revised version supports the argument.

First Draft	Revised
Education allows people to make more money, which is helpful.	Education allows people to get higher-paying jobs. With more money, people can help boost the economy.

Use transition words to guide readers through your ideas.

- To show contrast: *however, although, despite*
- To point out a reason: *since, because, if*
- To signal conclusion: *therefore, consequently, so, then*

4 Publishing and Presenting

Persuasive Speech. Many persuasive essays are delivered orally. Prepare your essay as a speech, highlighting words for emphasis and adding changes in tone, volume, or speed.

Biographical Writing

❶ Prewriting

Choose a topic. Biographical writing tells the story of a real person's life. For social studies, you should focus on the life of an important historical or current figure. The following ideas are a guide.

- **Find a hero.** Think about a person from history whom you admire—for example, a world leader, a great thinker, or an inventor. Remember to choose someone about whom information is easily available.

- **Name game.** On an index card, write the name of a person in the news today. Write a sentence or phrase explaining what makes this person interesting to you, as on the examples below. With a group, shuffle all the cards and then take turns drawing topics. If you like, trade your topic with a friend.

Martin Luther
He thought the Bible—not the pope—should guide a person's actions.

Wangari Maathai
She thinks preserving the environment can improve people's lives.

- **Table of Contents scan.** Your history book lists the short biographies that are included in the text. Scan this listing in the book's Table of Contents for three possible subjects. Read the biography of each subject before you make a final choice.

Focus your approach. Decide how you want to approach your subject. For example, you could emphasize the person's influence on historical events, or you could show how personal experiences affected his or her achievements.

Gather details. Collect the facts and details you need to write your paper. Use the research methods for gathering information explained on page SH14. In particular, check biographical source materials in the reference section of the library.

Isolate episodes. As you learn about your subject, focus on the particular episodes that seem to be most important. Then learn more about the events surrounding these episodes and take notes on them, as in the example below.

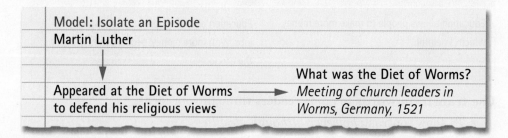

Model: Isolate an Episode
Martin Luther

	What was the Diet of Worms?
Appeared at the Diet of Worms to defend his religious views	*Meeting of church leaders in Worms, Germany, 1521*

Focus your fact-gathering. Your goal is to bring this person's life to readers—to share facts and opinions relating to that life and respond to them with your own conclusions. As you determine the main points you wish to make about this person, find facts to support your assertions. Make sure to give enough factual background for readers to appreciate your points.

❷ Drafting

Focus your essay. In a single paper, you will probably need to focus on an aspect of your subject's life or on a quick overview of major events in that life.

Organize important events. Choose the events you will discuss, and then order them in a logical way. Biographies are usually organized chronologically.

Reveal your subject. Include direct description of your subject, which allows you to convey information quickly. Balance this with quotations or examples of the person's actions, which lend color and authenticity to your essay.

Open strongly. Get readers' attention immediately with an engaging quotation, an interesting fact about your subject, or an anecdote that sets the tone.

"Here I stand, I cannot do otherwise." Martin Luther spoke these words at the Diet of Worms in 1521. The Diet, a conference of religious leaders, had summoned Luther to explain his controversial religious views.

Martin Luther was born in 1483 into a German family. Raised a Catholic, Luther entered a monastery after experiencing a religious calling. He became both devout and committed to strict observance. Over time, this approach brought him into conflict with the Church. For example, Luther felt that the Catholic Church should not sell indulgences, or guarantees of good grace after death.

Luther developed new ideas about the Church and its leadership. At the core were his beliefs that people should have a direct relationship to the Bible and that the Church and the pope stood in the way of this. In his 95 Theses, Luther called for widespread reforms in the Catholic Church and later in the German government. Because his views were contrary to accepted beliefs, Luther was called in front of the Diet of Worms. He refused to back down, so the Church expelled him in 1521.

A quote gets the readers attention and quickly establishes the subject's personality.

The biography will focus on this aspect of Luther's life.

Chronological organization helps readers see the development of Luther's ideas.

The conclusion brings the biography back to its initial anecdote.

❸ Revising

Examine word choice. Bring your subject to life with vivid adjectives, specific verbs, and precise nouns. Then link your chronological organization with words that show sequence. The draft above uses dates as well as phrases such as *over time* to show the sequence of Luther's life and religious growth.

Make connections for readers. For example, the sentence below connects Luther's life to current times by linking it to the modern Lutheran Church.

Although Luther himself never called for a new church, today the Protestant branch named for him claims more than 5 million members in America alone.

Give credit. Cite sources for any facts, statistics, or quotations you include. If several pieces of information in a paragraph come from a single source, you may cite the source once at the end of the paragraph. Always check with your teacher for specific bibliographic requirements.

❹ Publishing and Presenting

Create a biographical character. Use what you've learned about this person's life to appear as that person. If you wish, wear a costume. Explain who you are and what is most important to you. Ask and answer questions.

Writing for Assessment

Assessment writing differs from all other writing that you do. You have fewer choices as a writer, and you almost always face a time limit. In social studies, you'll need to write both short answers and extended responses for tests. While these contrast in some ways, they share many requirements.

1 Prewriting

Choose a topic. Short-answer questions seldom offer a topic choice. For extended response, however, you may have a choice of more than one question. Use the following strategies to help you navigate that choice.

- **Examine the question.** To choose a question you can answer effectively, analyze what each question is asking. Use key words such as those listed below to help you choose topics and respond to short-answer questions in which the topic is given.

Key Words	What You Need in an Answer
Explain	Give a clear, complete account of how something works or why something happened.
Compare/Contrast	Show how two or more things are alike and different.
Define	Give examples to explain meaning.
Argue, Convince, Support, Persuade	Take a position on an issue and present strong reasons to support your side of the issue.
Summarize	Provide the most important elements of a subject.
Evaluate/Judge	Assign a value or explain an opinion.
Interpret	Support a thesis with examples from the text.

Notice in the examples below that the key words are underlined:

Short answer: Describe one way that Chief Joseph showed his military expertise.

Extended response: According to the author of this article, Chief Joseph was both a peace chief and a military genius. Use information from the article to support this conclusion.

- **Plot your answer.** After choosing a question, quickly plot the answer in your mind. Do you have the information to answer this question? If the answer is *no*, try another question.

Measure your time. Your goal is to show the instructor that you've mastered the material. To stay focused on this goal, divide your time: one-quarter on prewriting; half on drafting; one-quarter on revising. For short-answer questions, determine how much of the overall test time you can spend on each question. Don't spend more than that.

Gather details. Organize the facts and details you need to write your answer. For short-answer questions, this usually involves identifying exactly what information is required.

Use a graphic organizer. For extended response, divide your topic into subtopics that fit the type of question. Jot down facts and details for each. For the question on Chief Joseph, the following organizer would be effective:

Chief Joseph of the Nez Percé
Peace Chief
• traded peacefully with white settlers (1)
• reluctantly went to war (2)
• famous speech, "I will fight no more forever." (3)
Military Genius
• won battles with fewer warriors than opposing troops had (a)
• avoided capture for many months (b)
• led his people more than 1,000 miles (c)
• knew when to surrender for the good of his people (c)

❷ Drafting

Choose an organization that fits the question. With a short-answer question, write one to three complete sentences. With extended response, you'll need more elaborate organization. For the question on Chief Joseph, organize your points by importance within each subtopic. For a summary or explanation, use chronological order. For compare/contrast, present similarities first, then differences.

Open and close strongly. Start your answer by restating the question or using its language to state your position. This helps you focus and shows the instructor that you understand the question. Finish with a strong conclusion that restates your position. For short answer, include some language from the question in your response.

One way that Chief Joseph showed his military expertise was by defeating U.S. Army troops despite having fewer warriors than they had.

Support your ideas. Each paragraph should directly or indirectly support your main idea. Choose facts that build a cohesive argument. The numbered sentences in the draft below show how this writer organized support.

The opening restates the question and presents the main idea.

The writer uses information from the graphic organizer, in order of importance.

The writer supports the second subtopic.

The conclusion recaps the main idea and again uses the question's language.

Chief Joseph was both a peace chief and a military genius. He was a peace chief because he traded peacefully with white settlers for many years. (1) He went to war reluctantly after the government ordered his people to move to a reservation. (2) When he finally surrendered, he said in a famous speech, "I will fight no more forever." (3) Chief Joseph was also a military genius. He fought off U.S. Army forces with fewer warriors than they had, (a) and he avoided capture for many months. (b) He led his people more than 1,000 miles (c) before he made the decision to surrender. Chief Joseph will long be remembered for his dual roles as peace chief and military genius.

❸ Revising

Examine word choice. Replace general words with specific words. Add transitions where these improve clarity. Read the following examples. The revised version shows the relative importance of the writer's supporting evidence.

First Draft	Revised
Chief Joseph was both a peace chief and a military genius. He was a peace chief because he traded peacefully with white settlers for many years. He went to war reluctantly...	Chief Joseph was both a peace chief and a military genius. He was a peace chief for several reasons. First, he traded peacefully with white settlers for many years. Second, he went to war reluctantly...

Check organization. Make sure your introduction includes a main idea and defines subtopics. Review each paragraph for a single main idea. Check that your conclusion summarizes the information you've presented.

❹ Publishing and Presenting

Edit and proof. Check spelling, grammar, and mechanics. Make sure that tenses match, that subjects agree with verbs, and that sentences are not too long. Finally, confirm that you have responded to all the questions you were asked to answer.

Writing Rubric

Use this chart, or rubric, to evaluate your writing.

SAT

SCORE OF 6

An essay in this category is **outstanding**, demonstrating **clear and consistent mastery**, although it may have a few minor errors. A typical essay

- effectively and insightfully develops a point of view on the issue and demonstrates outstanding critical thinking, using clearly appropriate examples, reasons, and other evidence to support its position
- is well organized and clearly focused, demonstrating clear coherence and smooth progression of ideas
- exhibits skillful use of language, using a varied, accurate, and apt vocabulary
- demonstrates meaningful variety in sentence structure
- is free of most errors in grammar, usage, and mechanics

SCORE OF 5

An essay in this category is **effective**, demonstrating **reasonably consistent mastery**, although it will have occasional errors or lapses in quality. A typical essay

- effectively develops a point of view on the issue and demonstrates strong critical thinking, generally using appropriate examples, reasons, and other evidence to support its position
- is well organized and focused, demonstrating coherence and progression of ideas
- exhibits facility in the use of language, using appropriate vocabulary
- demonstrates variety in sentence structure
- is generally free of most errors in grammar, usage, and mechanics

SCORE OF 4

An essay in this category is **competent**, demonstrating **adequate mastery**, although it will have lapses in quality. A typical essay

- develops a point of view on the issue and demonstrates competent critical thinking, using adequate examples, reasons, and other evidence to support its position
- is generally organized and focused, demonstrating some coherence and progression of ideas
- exhibits adequate but inconsistent facility in the use of language, using generally appropriate vocabulary
- demonstrates some variety in sentence structure
- has some errors in grammar, usage, and mechanics

SCORE OF 3

An essay in this category is **inadequate**, but demonstrates **developing mastery**, and is marked by **one or more** of the following weaknesses:

- develops a point of view on the issue, demonstrating some critical thinking, but may do so inconsistently or use inadequate examples, reasons, or other evidence to support its position
- is limited in its organization or focus, but may demonstrate some lapses in coherence or progression of ideas
- displays developing facility in the use of language, but sometimes uses weak vocabulary or inappropriate word choice
- lacks variety or demonstrates problems in sentence structure
- contains an accumulation of errors in grammar, usage, and mechanics

SCORE OF 2

An essay in this category is **seriously limited**, demonstrating **little mastery**, and is flawed by **one or more** of the following weaknesses:

- develops a point of view on the issue that is vague or seriously limited, demonstrating weak critical thinking, providing inappropriate or insufficient examples, reasons, or other evidence to support its position
- is poorly organized and/or focused, or demonstrates serious problems with coherence or progression of ideas
- displays very little facility in the use of language, using very limited vocabulary or incorrect word choice
- demonstrates frequent problems in sentence structure
- contains errors in grammar, usage, and mechanics so serious that meaning is somewhat obscured

SCORE OF 1

An essay in this category is **fundamentally lacking**, demonstrating **very little** or **no mastery**, and is severely flawed by one or more of the following weaknesses:

- develops no viable point of view on the issue, or provides little or no evidence to support its position
- is disorganized or unfocused, resulting in a disjointed or incoherent essay
- displays fundamental errors in vocabulary
- demonstrates severe flaws in sentence structure
- contains pervasive errors in grammar, usage, or mechanics that persistently interfere with meaning

SCORE OF 0

Essays not written on the essay assignment will receive a score of zero.

Analyze the Five Themes of Geography

The five themes of geography are tools you can use to analyze geographic information given in photographs, charts, maps, and text.

- **Location** answers the question "Where is it?" The answer might be an absolute location, such as 167 River Lane, or a relative location, such as six miles west of Mill City.

- **Regions** are areas that share at least one common feature. Climate, culture, and government are features that can be used to define a region.

- **Place** identifies natural and human features that make a place different from other places. Landforms, climate, plants, animals, people, culture, and languages are features that can be used to identify a specific place.

- **Movement** answers the question "How do people, goods, and ideas move from place to place?"

- **Human-Environment Interaction** focuses on the relationship between people and the environment. Humans often make changes to the environment, and the environment often affects how humans live.

Use the photograph and steps that follow to analyze the five themes of geography.

The Nile River in Egypt

Read supporting information such as a caption or key. Use this information and your own knowledge of the world to determine location and region.

Analyze the content. Consider the elements of the visual or text to develop ideas about region, place, movement, and human-environment interaction.

Practice and Apply the Skill

Use the photograph above to answer the following questions:

1. How might you describe the relative location of the fields of crops?

2. What is the climate region shown here? How do you know?

3. What elements in the scene identify this specific place?

4. How do you think people, goods, and ideas move to and from this place?

5. How have the people of this area changed their environment?

Understand Latitude and Longitude

Geographers divide the globe along imaginary horizontal lines called parallels of latitude. They measure these parallels in degrees (°) north or south of the Equator, which itself is a line of latitude. Geographers also divide the globe along imaginary vertical lines called meridians of longitude. They measure these meridians in degrees east or west of the Prime Meridian, a line of longitude running through Greenwich, England. All meridians intersect at the North Pole and the South Pole. Together, the lines of latitude and longitude form a grid that gives an absolute location for every place on Earth. Use the globes and the steps that follow to understand latitude and longitude.

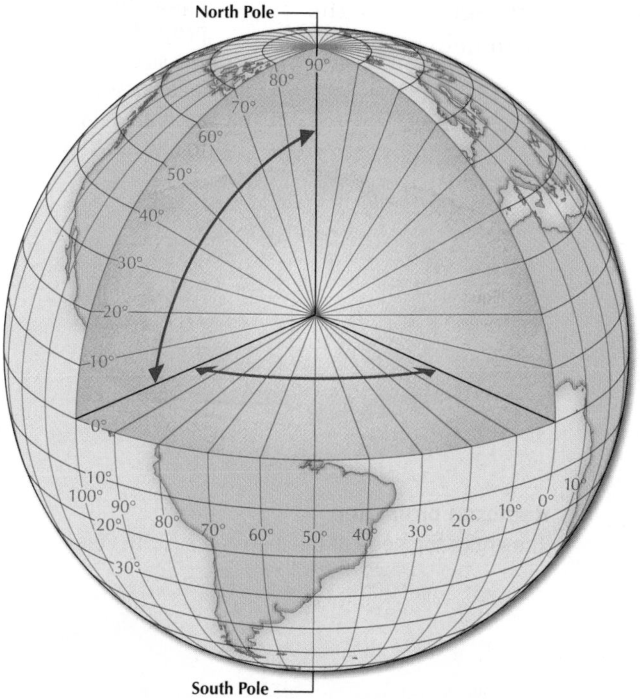

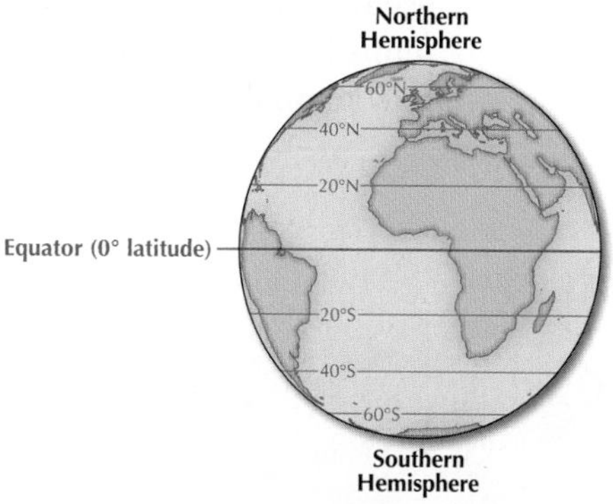

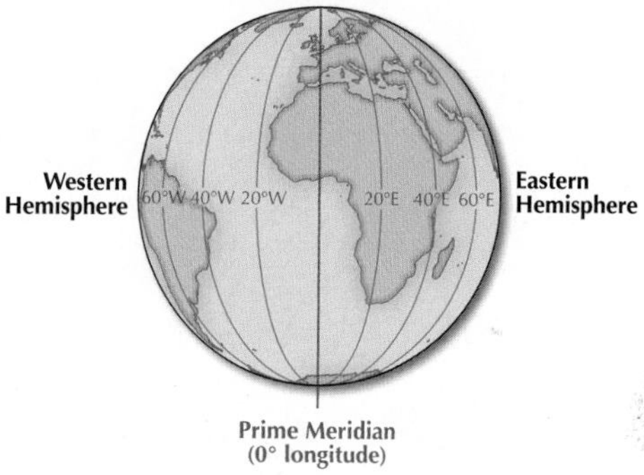

Study purpose. Study the two main globes to understand why geographers divide the globe into parallels and meridians. Study the two smaller globes to understand the role of the Equator and the Prime Meridian as starting points for measuring parallels and meridians.

Read labels and captions. Read the labels and captions to understand how to determine the latitude and longitude of a given location, as well as to identify which hemispheres it sits in.

Identify absolute location. You can use lines of latitude and longitude together to identify the absolute location of any spot on Earth.

Practice and Apply the Skill

Use the text and globes above to answer the following questions:

1. Which part of the location 67° N, 55° E represents the longitude?
2. What line of latitude lies halfway from the Equator to the North Pole?
3. Do lines of latitude ever intersect one another? Explain.
4. If you followed the 70° W line of longitude north to the North Pole and then continued on the same line south, what line of longitude would you be on? (Hint: The globe, like a circle, has a total of 360 degrees.)

Analyze Map Projections

Because maps are flat, they cannot show the correct size and shape of every feature on Earth's curved surface. Mapmakers must shrink some places and stretch others. Different types of map projections distort Earth's surface in different ways. Mapmakers choose the projection that has the least distortion for the information they are presenting.

Same-shape map projections such as the Mercator projection accurately show the shapes of landmasses. However, they distort sizes and distances. Equal-area map projections show the correct size of landmasses but distort shapes, especially at the edges of a map. The Robinson projection keeps the size and shape relationships of most continents and oceans but distorts the size of the polar regions. Use the maps below and the steps that follow to help you learn how to analyze map projections.

Equal-area projection
The sizes of landmasses are accurate relative to one another.

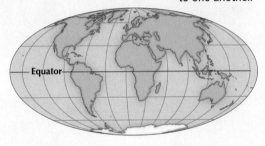

Mercator projection

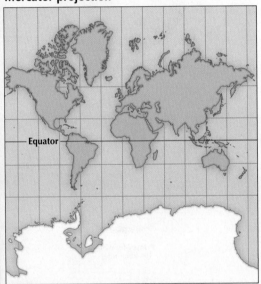

The greatest distortion is at the far northern and southern latitudes.

Robinson projection
The entire top edge of the map is the North Pole.

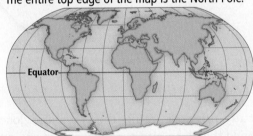

The entire bottom edge of the map is the South Pole.

Identify each projection. Study the appearance of each type of projection.

Read labels and captions. Read the labels and captions to understand the important details of each projection.

Compare the maps. Compare the shape of the maps and then the shapes of landmasses on them. Last, compare the amount of curvature of the lines of latitude and longitude on the maps.

Practice and Apply the Skill

Use the maps above to answer the following questions:

1. If you wanted to plot a course to sail from one port to another on the most direct route, which map projection would work best? Why?

2. Which map shows the most accurate relative size of Antarctica, the white region on each map? Why?

3. How do the grid lines on the Mercator projection vary from a globe's?

4. Why do you think many maps in this book use the Robinson projection?

Read Maps

Maps can show many different kinds of information. A physical map represents what a region looks like by showing its major physical features, such as mountains and plains. A political map focuses on elements related to government, such as nations, borders, and cities. Special-purpose maps provide information on a specific subject—for example, land use, population distribution, or trade routes. Road maps and weather maps are two kinds of special purpose maps.

Mapmakers provide clues to help you read maps and gather the information they offer. Use the map below and the steps that follow to practice reading a map.

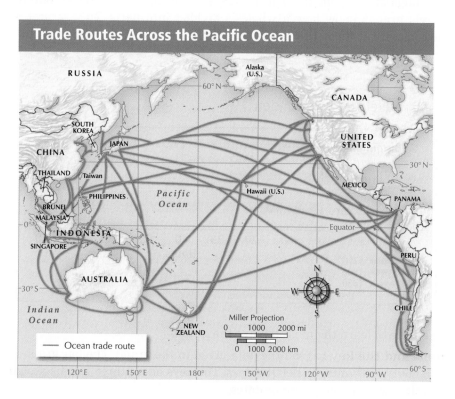

Read the title. The title tells you the subject of the map.

Read the key. The key explains the symbols, lines, and colors and the map.

Use the scale bar and compass rose. Use the scale bar to determine distances between places on the map. Use the compass rose to determine the relative directions of places on the map.

Practice and Apply the Skill

Use the map above to answer the following questions.

1. What is the purpose of this map? What part of the world does it show?
2. What do the blue lines represent?
3. How many trade routes go through New Zealand?
4. When goods travel from the United States to Australia, in what direction do they travel?
5. What generalization could you make about trade across the Pacific Ocean based on this map?

Critical Thinking
About Texts, Visuals, and Media Sources

Analyze Graphic Data

The study of history requires that you think critically about the text you're reading as well as any visuals or media sources. This section of the Skills Handbook will allow you to practice and apply some important skills for critical thinking.

Graphs show numerical facts in picture form. Bar graphs and line graphs compare things at different times or places, such as changes in school enrollment. Circle graphs show how a whole is divided into parts. To interpret a graph, look closely at its features. Use the graphs below and the steps that follow to practice analyzing graphic data.

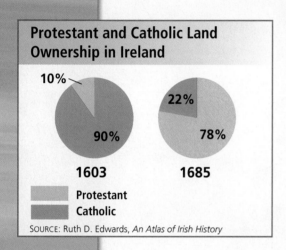

Protestant and Catholic Land Ownership in Ireland

10%
90%
1603

22%
78%
1685

Protestant
Catholic

SOURCE: Ruth D. Edwards, *An Atlas of Irish History*

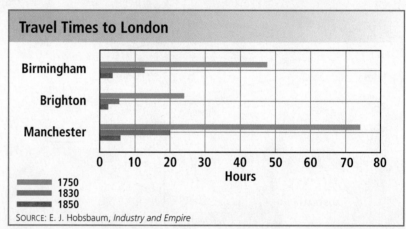

Travel Times to London

Birmingham
Brighton
Manchester

0 10 20 30 40 50 60 70 80
Hours

1750
1830
1850

SOURCE: E. J. Hobsbaum, *Industry and Empire*

Read the title to learn the main topic of the graph.

Use labels and the key to read the data given in the graph. The bar graph is labeled in hours, with intervals of 10 hours. The keys on all three graphs assign different colors to different groups or dates.

Interpret the graph. Look for interesting patterns in the data. Look at changes over time or compare information for different groups.

Practice and Apply the Skill

Use the graphs above to answer the following questions:

1. What is the title of the bar graph? What is its topic?

2. Which cities show the longest travel times to London, and in which years? What does this tell you about changes in transportation?

3. What color on the circle graphs shows Catholic land ownership? How did Irish land ownership change over time? What might explain this change?

4. Could the information in the circle graph be shown as a bar graph? Explain.

Analyze Images

Television, film, the Internet, and print media all carry images that seek to convey information or influence attitudes. To respond, you must develop the ability to understand and interpret visuals. Use the photograph below and the steps that follow to practice analyzing images.

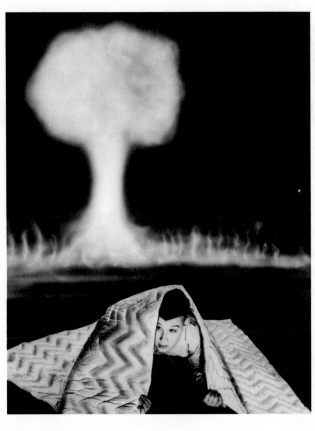

In the 1950s, people everywhere worried about nuclear attack. This 1954 image advertised a bogus "radiation-resistant" blanket.

Identify the content. Look at all parts of the image and determine which are most important.

Note emotions. Study facial expressions and body positions. Consider the emotions they may suggest.

Read captions/credits. Gather information about the image, such as when it was produced.

Study purpose. Consider who might have created this image. Decide if the purpose was to entertain, inform, or persuade.

Consider context. Determine the context in which the image was created—in this case, the Cold War between the United States and the Soviet Union.

Respond. Decide if a visual's impact achieves its purpose—to inform, to entertain, or to persuade.

Practice and Apply the Skill

Use the photograph above to answer the following questions:

1. What are the three main images in this photograph?

2. What feelings are conveyed by the boy's facial expression?

3. What do you think the photograph's purpose is?

4. When was this image produced? How did historical context influence its production?

Analyze Timelines

Timelines show the order in which events occur as well as the amount of time that passes between events. To understand a timeline, study its labels and captions carefully. Use the timeline below and the steps that follow to practice analyzing timelines

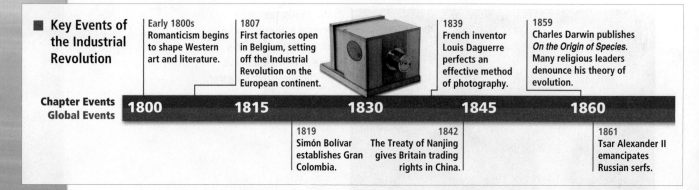

■ **Key Events of the Industrial Revolution**

Early 1800s Romanticism begins to shape Western art and literature.

1807 First factories open in Belgium, setting off the Industrial Revolution on the European continent.

1839 French inventor Louis Daguerre perfects an effective method of photography.

1859 Charles Darwin publishes *On the Origin of Species.* Many religious leaders denounce his theory of evolution.

Chapter Events
Global Events

| 1800 | 1815 | 1830 | 1845 | 1860 |

1819 Simón Bolívar establishes Gran Colombia.

1842 The Treaty of Nanjing gives Britain trading rights in China.

1861 Tsar Alexander II emancipates Russian serfs.

Identify time units. Find the main time units of the timeline. Determine how much time is represented by the entire timeline.

Read each entry. Read each of the entries on the timeline. Connect each entry to the events before and after it.

Look for patterns among the events shown. Determine if any of the entries fall into a common category. Think about whether the events might be causes and/or effects.

Practice and Apply the Skill

Use the timeline above to answer the following questions.

1. What is the most recent event on the timeline? When did it take place?

2. When did the first factories open in Belgium?

3. How many years after the first factories opened did Louis Daguerre perfect his method of photography?

4. What happened in 1859?

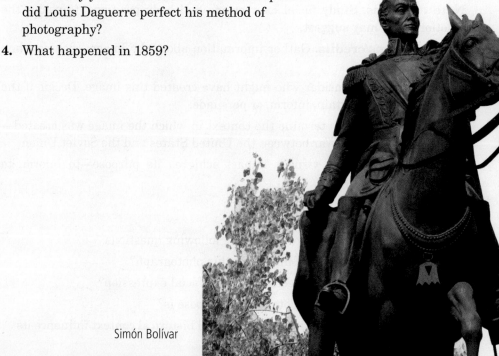

Simón Bolívar

Analyze Primary Sources

Primary sources include official documents and firsthand accounts of events or visual evidence such as photographs, paintings, and political cartoons. Such sources provide valuable information about the past. Use the excerpt below and the steps that follow to learn to analyze primary sources.

The following excerpt is a translation from *The Satires,* a series of poems written in Latin by Juvenal about life in Rome in the first century A.D. In this excerpt, Juvenal recounts a friend's reasons for moving away from Rome.

> **Primary Source**
>
> ❝Since at Rome there is no place for honest pursuits, no profit to be got by honest toil—my fortune is less to-day than it was yesterday. . . .
>
> What shall *I* do at Rome? I can not lie; if a book is bad, I can not praise it and beg a copy. I know not the motions of the stars. . . . no one shall be a thief by my co-operation. . . .
>
> Who, now-a-days, is beloved except the confidant of crime. . .?❞
>
> —Juvenal, *The Satires of Juvenal, Persius, Sulpicia, and Lucilius*

Read the headnote, caption, or attribution line. Determine the source's historical context—who wrote it, when, and why.

Read the primary source. Identify and define unfamiliar words. Then look for the writer's main point.

Identify facts and opinions. Facts can be proven. Opinions reflect a person's views or feelings. Use opinion clues to help: exaggeration, phrases such as "I think," or descriptive words such as "gorgeous."

Identify bias and evaluate credibility. Consider whether the author's opinions suggest bias. Evaluate other factors that might lead to author bias, such as his or her previous experiences. Decide if the author knows enough to be credible and was objective enough to be reliable. Determine whether the source might be propaganda, that is, material published to promote a policy, idea, or cause.

Practice and Apply the Skill

Political cartoons reflect an artist's observations about events of the time. They often use symbols to represent things or exaggeration to make a point. Use the cartoon at right to answer the following questions.

1. Who is the author of this primary source?
2. What does the bulldozer represent?
3. What is exaggerated in this cartoon?
4. What opinion is the cartoonist expressing?
5. Do you think the cartoonist's opinion is valid? Why or why not?

This cartoon by Arcadio Esquivel of Costa Rica comments on environmental destruction.

Compare Viewpoints

A person's viewpoint is shaped by subjective influences such as feelings, prejudices, and past experiences. Two politicians will recommend different policies to address the same problem. Comparing such viewpoints will help you understand issues and form your own views. The excerpts below offer two different views on the purpose of education. Use the excerpts and the steps that follow to learn about comparing viewpoints.

King Henri Christophe of Haiti set up schools for outstanding students. He believed these schools would secure Haiti's new and hard-won freedom. In 1817, he wrote:

Primary Source

66To form good citizens we must educate our children. From our national institutions will proceed a race of men capable of defending by their knowledge and talents those rights so long denied by tyrants. It is from these sources that light will be diffused among the whole mass of the population.99

—Henri Christophe, 1817

Leo Tolstoy, a Russian aristocrat of the late 1800s, became a famous novelist as a young man. As he grew older, he increasingly focused on social issues in his writing. In 1902, he wrote:

Primary Source

66You can take a puppy and feed him, and teach him to carry something, and enjoy the sight of him; but it is not enough to rear and bring up a man, and teach him Greek: he has to be taught to live, that is, to take less from others, and give more.99

—Leo Tolstoy, 1902

Identify the authors. Determine when and where the authors lived.

Examine the viewpoints. Identify the author's main idea and evaluate his or her supporting arguments. Determine whether the arguments are logical and the evidence is sufficient to support the main idea. Confirm that the evidence is valid by doing research if necessary.

Determine the author's frame of reference. Consider how the author's attitudes, beliefs, and past experiences might affect his or her viewpoint.

Recognize facts and opinions. Identify which statements are opinions and which are facts. Opinions represent the author's viewpoint.

Evaluate each viewpoint's validity. Decide whether the viewpoints are based on facts and/or reasonable arguments. Consider whether or not you agree with the viewpoints.

Practice and Apply the Skill

Use the excerpts above to answer the following questions.

1. Who are the authors of these two documents? Where and when did each one live?
2. What is each man's main argument about education? What evidence or supporting arguments does each provide?
3. How might each man's frame of reference affect his viewpoint?
4. How does Tolstoy's phrase "he has to be taught to live" signal an opinion?
5. Are these two viewpoints based on reasonable arguments? Explain.

Synthesize Information

Just as you might ask several friends about a movie before deciding to see it, you can combine information from different sources to develop a fuller understanding of any topic. This process, called synthesizing, will help you become better informed. Study the documents below about developments in the 1400s and 1500s. Then use the steps that follow to learn to synthesize information.

Document A

This caravel helped Europeans sail across and into the wind.

Document B

Improved Technology

Several improvements in technology helped Europeans navigate the vast oceans of the world. Cartographers, or mapmakers, created more accurate maps and sea charts. European sailors learned to use the astrolabe, an instrument developed by the ancient Greeks and perfected by the Arabs, to determine their latitude at sea.

Europeans also designed larger and better ships. The Portuguese developed the caravel, which combined the square sails of European ships with Arab lateen, or triangular, sails. Caravels also adapted the sternpost rudder and numerous masts used on Chinese ships. The new rigging made it easier to sail across or even into the wind.

Document C

Hardships on the Uncharted Sea

In his journal, Italian sailor Antonio Pigafetta detailed the desperate conditions Magellan's sailors experienced as they crossed the Pacific Ocean:

Primary Source

66 We remained three months and twenty days without taking in provisions or other refreshments, and we only ate old biscuit reduced to powder, and full of grubs, and stinking from the dirt which the rats had made on it. . . . we drank water that was yellow and stinking. We also ate the ox hides which were under the main-yard [and] were very hard on account of the sun, rain, and wind. . . . 99

—Journal of Antonio Pigafetta

Identify thesis statements. Before you can synthesize, you must understand the thesis, or main idea, of each source.

Compare and contrast. Analyze how the information and ideas in the sources are the same or different. When several sources agree, the information is more reliable and thus more significant.

Draw conclusions and generalize. Look at all the information. Use it to draw conclusions that form a single picture of the topic. Make a generalization, or statement that applies to all the sources.

Practice and Apply the Skill

Use the documents above to answer the following questions.

1. What is the main idea of each source?

2. Which sources support the idea that European sailors became better equipped to sail the seas?

3. What view does Antonio Pigafetta contribute to the topic?

4. Draw a conclusion about European ocean exploration in the early 1500s.

Analyze Cause and Effect

One of a historian's main tasks is to understand the causes and effects of the event he or she is studying. Study the facts below, which are listed in random order. Then use the steps that follow to learn how to analyze cause and effect.

In the 1980s and 1990s, the Soviet Union underwent a major change in its economy and government. As a result, the Soviet Union ceased to exist. This list shows key elements in that change.

- Low output of crops and consumer goods
- Soviets want to ensure influence in neighboring Afghanistan, so they invade that nation in 1979
- Soviet Union breaks up into 15 republics after its central government collapses
- Changeover to market economy in Russia
- Ethnic and nationalist movements to achieve independence from Soviet Union
- Cold War with United States leads to high military spending
- Food and fuel shortages
- Rise to power of Mikhail Gorbachev in 1985
- Russian republic approves a new constitution
- Baltic states of Estonia, Latvia, and Lithuania demonstrate for independence
- Cold War ends

Identify the central event. Determine to what event or issue all the facts listed relate.

Locate clue words. Use words such as *because, so,* and *due to* to spot causes and effects.

Identify causes and effects. Causes precede the central event and contribute to its occurrence. Effects come after the central event. They occur or emerge as a result of it.

Consider timeframe. Decide if causes have existed for a long period of time or emerged just prior to the central event. Short-term causes are usually single or narrowly defined events. Long-term causes usually arise from ongoing conditions.

Make recommendations. Use what you've learned to suggest actions or make predictions.

Practice and Apply the Skill

Use the list above to answer the following questions:

1. Which item on the list describes the central event whose causes and effects can be determined?
2. Name three facts that are long-term causes.
3. Name three facts that are probably short-term causes.
4. Name three facts that were most likely effects of the central event.

Problem Solving and Decision Making

You will face many problems in your life, from disputes with friends to how to vote on issues facing your nation. You will be most likely to find solutions if you make decisions in a logical way. Study the situation outlined below. Then use the steps that follow to learn the skills of problem solving and decision making.

A Problem for Japan and China

In the 1800s, Japan and China faced a problem. Industrialized nations had developed machinery and weapons that were superior to those that the Japanese and Chinese had. Some industrialized nations used their new power to demand special trading privileges in Asia.

Options for Japan and China

Option	Advantages	Disadvantages
1. Give in to demands of the industrialized powers.	• Avoid conflict. •	• Native merchants lose profits to foreigners.
2. Give in to demands, but also build modern machines and weapons.	• •	• •
3. Refuse the demands and reject much of the new technology.	• •	• •

The Decisions
- The Japanese government decided to follow option 2.
- The Chinese government decided to follow option 3.

Effects of the Decisions
- Japan quickly became a modern industrial and military power. Although it demilitarized after suffering defeat in World War II, it remains one of the world's leading industrial powers.
- China was weakened by a century of conflict with Great Britain and other major powers, and was invaded and occupied by Japan. Foreign nations gained special privileges in China. Today, China is still struggling to become a leading industrial power.

Identify the problem. You cannot solve a problem until you examine it and understand it.

Gather information and identify options. Most problems have many solutions. Identify as many solution options as possible.

Consider advantages and disadvantages. Analyze each option by predicting benefits and drawbacks.

Decide on and implement the solution. Pick the option with the most desirable benefits and least important drawbacks.

Evaluate the decision. After time, reexamine your solution. If necessary, make a new decision.

Practice and Apply the Skill

Use information from the box above to answer the following questions:

1. What problem did China and Japan face? What caused this problem?
2. Describe an option that Japan or China could have chosen other than those in the list.
3. Identify two advantages and two disadvantages for options 2 and 3.
4. Why do you think China and Japan chose the options they did?

Draw Inferences and Conclusions

Text and artwork may not contain all the facts and ideas you need to understand a topic. You may need to add information from your own experience or knowledge, or use information that is implied but not directly stated in the text or artwork. Study the biography below. Then use the steps that follow to learn how to draw inferences and conclusions.

BIOGRAPHY

James Watt

How did a clever Scottish engineer become the "Father of the Industrial Revolution"? After repairing a Newcomen steam engine, James Watt (1736–1819) had become fascinated with the idea of improving the device. Within a few months, he knew he had a product that would sell. Still, Watt lacked the money needed to produce and market it.

Fortunately, he was able to form a partnership with the shrewd manufacturer Matthew Boulton. They then founded Soho Engineering Works in Birmingham, England, to manufacture steam engines. Watt's version of the steam engine shown here had a separate condensing chamber and was patented in 1769. Eventually, a measure of mechanical and electrical power, the watt, would be named for James Watt. **How might the Industrial Revolution have been different if Watt had not found a business partner?**

Study the facts. Determine what facts and information the text states.

Summarize information. Confirm your understanding of the text by briefly summarizing it.

Ask questions. Use *who, what, when, where, why,* and *how* questions to analyze the text and learn more. For example, you might compare and contrast, or look for causes or effects.

Add your own knowledge. Consider what you know about the topic. Use this knowledge to evaluate the information.

Draw inferences and conclusions. Use what you learned from the text and your own knowledge to draw inferences and conclusions about the topic.

Practice and Apply the Skill

Use the biography above to answer these questions.

1. Who is discussed in the biography? When did he live?

2. Briefly summarize the text.

3. How do Watt's accomplishments still have an impact on our lives today?

4. Why do you think Watt wanted to improve a technology that already existed?

Use the Internet for Research

The Internet is a valuable research tool that provides links to millions of sources of information created by businesses, governments, schools, organizations, and individuals all over the world. Follow the steps to learn how you could use the Internet to research the European Renaissance.

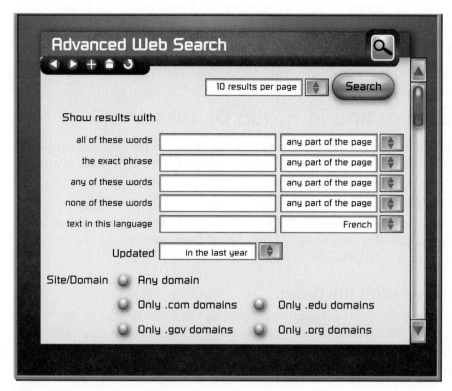

Sample search engine

Begin a search. Use search engines on the Internet to help you find useful Web sites. Type in key words that briefly summarize your topic. Use *and* between words to find documents containing all your keywords. Use *or* between words to find documents containing any one of several keywords.

Find reliable information. Universities, museums, libraries, and government agencies are usually the most reliable and useful for social studies research. The URLs for education sites end in *.edu,* government sites in *.gov,* and not-for-profit organization sites in *.org.* Read each site summary and choose those most likely to be reliable. Click on links to access individual sites.

Evaluate Web sites. Explore each Web site. Note its sponsor and when it was last updated.

Use advanced searches. Try advanced search options. Limit by date or type of site, such as educational institutions. Try new or different key words if you still don't get what you need.

Practice and Apply the Skill

Use a computer connected to the Internet to answer the following questions:

1. What key words might you use to learn about the European Renaissance? Type them into a search engine Web site and see what results you get.

2. Which of the first ten sites that came up in your search is most likely to be reliable? Why?

3. Who is the sponsor of the site you chose? What does this suggest about its quality or its possible bias?

Speaking and Listening

Speaking and listening are forms of communication you use every day. In certain situations, however, specific skills and strategies can increase the effectiveness of your communication. The strategies offered in this section will help you improve both your speaking and listening skills.

Participating in Group Discussions

A group discussion is an informal meeting of people that is used to openly discuss ideas and topics. You can express your views and hear those of others.

Identify Issues

Before you speak, identify the issues and main points you want to address. Incorporate what you already know about these issues into your views. Then find the best words to convey your ideas effectively.

Interact With the Group

As with persuasive writing, in a discussion it helps to accept the validity of opposing views, then argue your position. Always acknowledge the views of others respectfully, but ask questions that challenge the accuracy, logic, or relevance of those views.

Debating

A debate is a formal argument about a specific issue. Explicit rules govern the procedure of a debate, with each debater or team given an allotted time to make arguments and respond to opposing positions. You may also find yourself arguing a position you don't personally hold.

Prepare Your Arguments

If you support a position, use your existing knowledge of it to direct your research. If you personally oppose an assigned position, use that knowledge to identify likely opposing arguments. Generate an outline and then number note cards to highlight key information for each of your main points.

Avoid Common Pitfalls

Stay focused on your arguments. Be aware of words that may reveal bias, such as *unpatriotic.* Speak assertively, but avoid getting overly emotional. Vary the pitch and tone of your voice to keep listeners engaged. Try to speak actively, rather than just reading aloud, and use eye contact and gestures to emphasize your message.

Giving an Oral or Multimedia Presentation

An oral or multimedia presentation provides an audience with information through a variety of media.

Choose Media

If you are limited to speaking only, focus your time on developing a presentation that engages listeners. If you can include other media, consider what kind of information each form of media conveys most effectively.

Maps	Graphs/charts	Pictures	Diagrams	Audio/video
Clarify historical or geographical information	Show complicated information in an accessible format	Illustrate objects, scenes, or other details	Show link between parts and a whole or a process	Brings the subject to life and engages audience

Generate Text

Gather information using library and online sources. Develop your most important ideas in the body of your presentation. Back up assertions with solid facts and use multimedia examples to illustrate key points.

Present With Authority

Practice your presentation to gain comfort with the text and the presentation sequence. Experiment with the timing of how to include multimedia elements. Make sure you have the necessary equipment and know how to use it.

Active Listening

Active listening is a key component of the communication process. Like all communication, it requires your engaged participation.

Focus Your Attention on Ideas

Look at and listen to the speaker. Think about what you hear and see. Which ideas are emphasized or repeated? What gestures or expressions suggest strong feelings? Can you connect the speaker's ideas to your own experiences?

Listen to Fit the Situation

Active listening involves matching your listening to the situation. Listen critically to a speech given by a candidate for office. Listen empathetically to the feelings of a friend. Listen appreciatively to a musical performance.

Ask Questions

Try to think of questions while you're listening. Look at these examples:

Open-ended	Closed	Fact
Why do you think it is so important for young people to vote?	Do you support the current voting age of 18?	How many people aged 18–25 voted in the most recent election?

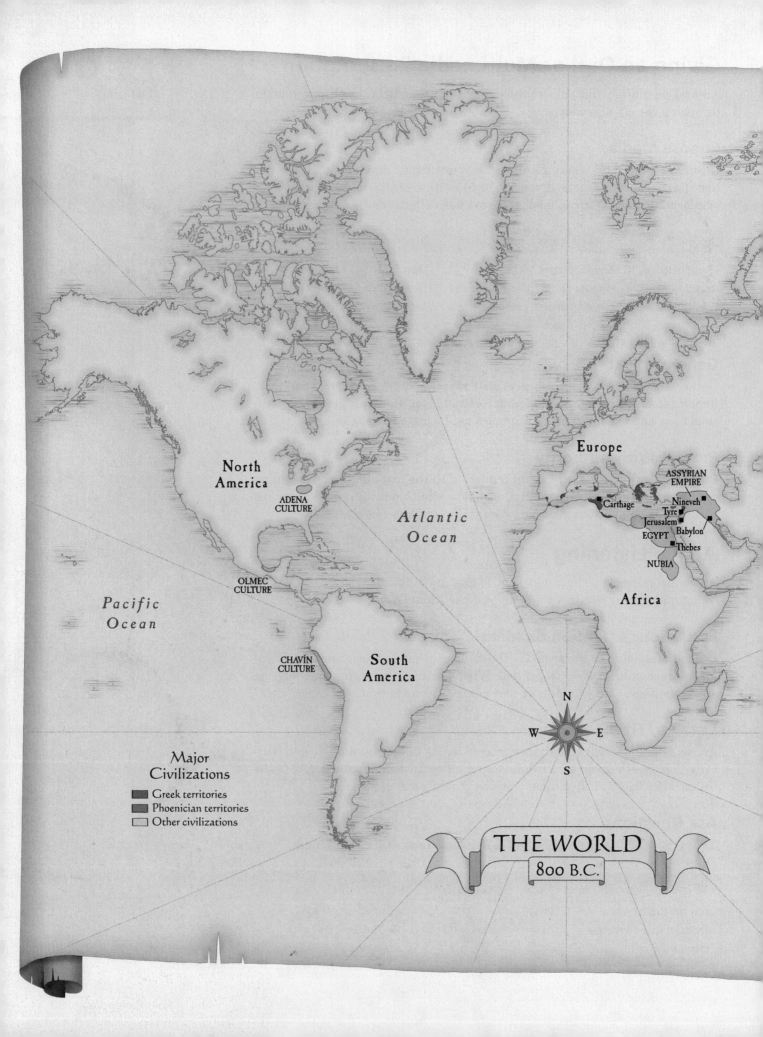

North
America

ADENA
CULTURE

OLMEC
CULTURE

CHAVÍN
CULTURE

South
America

*Pacific
Ocean*

*Atlantic
Ocean*

Europe

ASSYRIAN
EMPIRE

Carthage

Nineveh
Tyre
Jerusalem
Babylon
EGYPT
Thebes

NUBIA

Africa

Major
Civilizations

Greek territories
Phoenician territories
Other civilizations

N
W   E
S

THE WORLD
800 B.C.

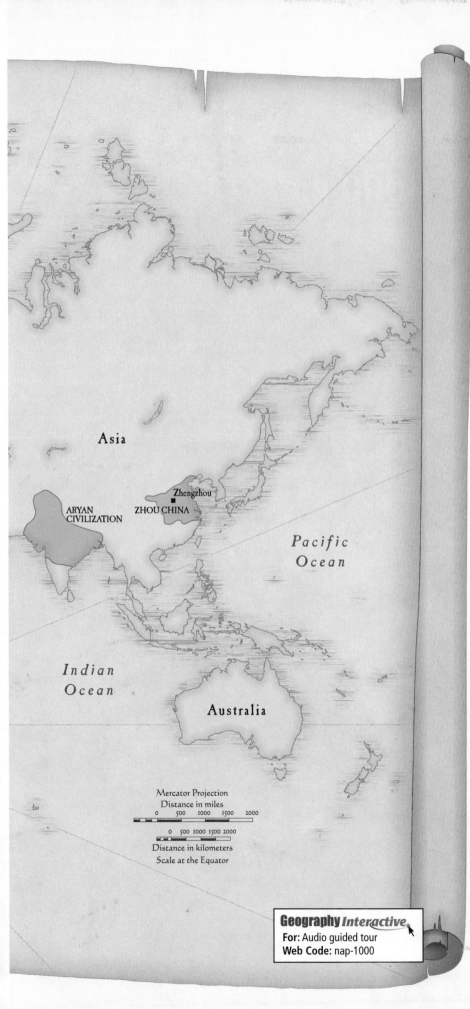

Asia

Zhengzhou

ARYAN
CIVILIZATION

ZHOU CHINA

Pacific
Ocean

Indian
Ocean

Australia

Mercator Projection
Distance in miles
0   500 1000 1500 2000

0   500 1000 1500 2000
Distance in kilometers
Scale at the Equator

Geography *Interactive*
For: Audio guided tour
Web Code: nap-1000

Early Civilizations

Prehistory– A.D. 1570

CHAPTER

Foundations of Civilization
Prehistory–3000 B.C.

Discovering the Ancient Past

British archaeologist Howard Carter described his discovery of the tomb of ancient Egypt's King Tutankhamen like this:

> 66 Three thousand, four thousand years maybe, have passed and gone since human feet last trod [walked on] the floor on which you stand, and yet . . . you feel it might have been but yesterday. . . . [You feel] the exhilaration of discovery, the fever of suspense, the almost overmastering impulse, born of curiosity, to break down seals and lift the lids of boxes, the thought—pure joy to the investigator—that you are about to add a page to history. 99

Listen to the Witness History audio to hear more about Carter's discovery.

◄ Howard Carter (left) carefully cleans the golden coffin of King Tutankhamen soon after discovering it in 1922.

King Tutankhamen's funeral mask

Ancient cave painting from Altamira, Spain

 Performance Standards

Chapter Focus Question: What was life like in early times, and how did it change as civilizations began to develop?

Section 1
Understanding Our Past SSWH1, SSWHRC1c

Section 2
Turning Point:
The Neolithic Revolution
SSWH1a

Section 3
Beginnings of Civilization
SSWH1a

Ancient Mesopotamian dog statue

Use the ☑ **Quick Study Timeline** at the end of this chapter to preview chapter events.

 Concept Connector ONLINE

To explore Essential Questions related to this chapter, go to PHSchool.com
Web Code: nad-0107

WITNESS HISTORY ◀))) AUDIO

A Clue From the Past

Mary Leakey spent her career studying the earliest ancestors of humans. In 1978, in Laetoli, Tanzania, she uncovered a remarkable and unique remnant of the early ancestors of humans—their footprints, preserved over time in volcanic ash. As Leakey studied the pattern of the footprints, she imagined how they might have been created:

❝ At one point, . . . the traveler stops, pauses, turns to the left to glance at some possible threat or irregularity, then continues to the north. This motion, so intensely human, transcends time. Three million seven hundred thousand years ago, a remote ancestor— just as you or I—experienced a moment of doubt. ❞

Focus Question What have scholars learned about the ancestors of humans, and how have they done so?

An anthropologist studying the Laetoli footprints (at left); a 2-million-year-old skull (top right)

Understanding Our Past

 Performance Standards

- **SSWH1** Analyze complex societies in the ancient Mediterranean.
- **SSWHRC1c** Explore understanding of new words in subject area texts.

Terms, People, and Places

prehistory	Mary Leakey
historian	Louis Leakey
artifact	Olduvai Gorge
anthropology	technology
culture	Donald Johanson
archaeology	

Note Taking

Reading Skill: Summarize As you read, use a concept web like the one below to identify the types of scholars who study the past and summarize what each type does.

By about 5,000 years ago, groups of people in different parts of the world had begun to keep written records. The invention and use of writing marked the beginning of recorded history. However, humans and their ancestors had lived on Earth for thousands upon thousands of years before the recording of history began. We call the long period of time before people invented writing **prehistory.**

Studying the Historical Past

Historians are scholars who study and write about the historical past. Historians often learn details of the past from **artifacts,** or objects made by humans. Clothing, coins, artwork, and tombstones are all types of artifacts. However, historians rely even more on written evidence, such as letters or tax records. Although it is often hard to find thorough written records from early times, those that exist offer us a narrative of events, as well as names and dates. Historians of the recent past also study such evidence as photographs or films.

Like a detective, a historian must evaluate all evidence to determine if it is reliable. Do records of a meeting between two officials tell us exactly what was said? Who was taking notes? Was a letter writer really giving an eyewitness report or just passing on rumors? Could the letter be a forgery? Historians try to find the answers to questions like these. They then interpret the evidence, or explain what it means. Often, a historian's goal is to determine the causes of a certain development or event, such as a war or an economic collapse. By explaining why things occurred in the past, historians can help us understand what happens today and what may happen in the future.

Generally, historians try to give a straightforward account of events. However, sometimes their personal experiences, cultural backgrounds, or political opinions bias their interpretations. Other times, historians disagree with one another about what the evidence proves. Such differences can lead to lively debates.

 Checkpoint   What kinds of evidence do historians use to study the past?

Investigating Prehistory

About 150 years ago, scholars began studying the period of prehistory. They hoped to learn about the origins and development of people and their societies. Today, we call this field of study **anthropology.**

Anthropology Modern anthropologists specialize in certain areas of their field. For example, some study the bones of our ancestors to understand how human physical traits have changed over time. Other anthropologists focus on the characteristics of human cultures from both the past and present. In anthropology, **culture** refers to the way of life of a society, which includes its beliefs, values, and practices. Culture is handed down from one generation to the next through learning and experience.

Archaeology Within the field of anthropology, a specialized branch exists called archaeology (ahr kee AHL uh jee). **Archaeology** is the study of past people and cultures through their material remains. These remains include buildings and artifacts such as tools, weapons, pottery, clothing, and jewelry. Archaeologists find and analyze artifacts to learn about life during prehistory as well as during historical times. This helps them draw conclusions about the beliefs, values, and activities of our ancestors. However, most archaeologists agree that the story of the past is never fully known. Since archaeologists make new discoveries frequently, at times they must revise their theories in light of the new evidence.

Mycenaean pottery from about 1350 B.C.

Dating Material Remains

Relative Dating Methods

For artifacts such as pottery that change in style over time, archaeologists can group similar artifacts and then order the groups in a series from earliest style to latest style.	Archaeologists can create a chronology of artifacts based on the fact that, in general, older artifacts are found in lower levels of the site than newer ones.	When the ages of geological features at the site are known, archaeologists can use these dates to help determine the ages of material remains found near them.

Absolute Dating Methods

Because scientists know that bones lose chemical elements at a certain rate, archaeologists can determine whether or not bones found near each other were buried at the same time.	Because the age of a tree can be determined by studying the inside of its trunk, archaeologists can determine fairly accurate ages for structures built from wood.	All living things contain carbon-14, a radioactive element that decays at a set rate. Archaeologists can use carbon-14 levels to date the remains of once-living items such as bones, wood, and ash.

Chart Skills Relative dating means determining whether material remains are older or newer than one another. Absolute dating means determining exact ages. *How might you determine the ages of ten pots found buried under the floor of a wooden structure?*

Archaeologists at Work Finding ancient artifacts can be difficult, but archaeologists have devised many useful means of doing so. In the 1800s and early 1900s, archaeologists would pick a likely place, called a site, and begin digging. The farther down they dug, the older the artifacts they found. Some of the objects, which had been buried for very long periods of time, crumbled as soon as they were removed from the ground. Today, archaeologists and others who work with them take great care to preserve such fragile artifacts.

Once archaeologists have found artifacts, they analyze them. One <u>technique</u> is to mark the location of each type of artifact found on a map of the site. After studying the map, an archaeologist may be able to tell what activities people took part in at different locations within the site. An area full of rabbit bones, for example, might suggest the workplace of a cook. Archaeologists also need to find out how old the artifacts are.

Vocabulary Builder
<u>technique</u>—(tek NEEK) *n.* procedure, skill, or art used in a particular task

● **INFOGRAPHIC**

Piecing the Past Together

Many objects, monuments, or structures that archaeologists find have fallen apart over the course of time. To understand what the remains represent, an archaeologist must figure out how to piece them together correctly and then analyze their form and location. Sometimes this means fitting a building back together brick by brick; other times, it means carefully digging a skeleton out of the ground and studying the items found directly around it. The possibilities of what archaeologists might find and where they will find them are quite numerous, so they use careful procedures and their well-trained eyes to solve as best they can whatever puzzles they encounter.

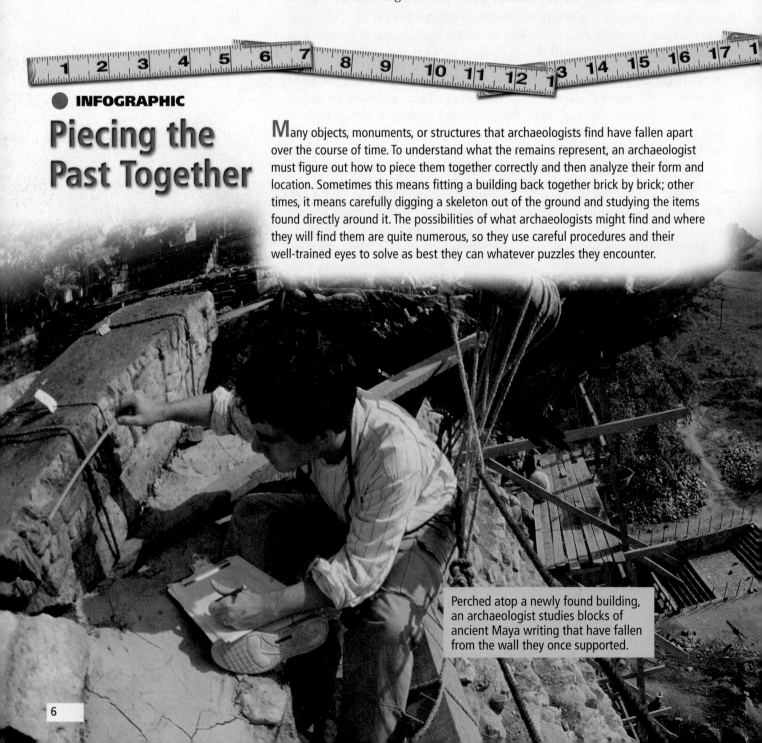

Perched atop a newly found building, an archaeologist studies blocks of ancient Maya writing that have fallen from the wall they once supported.

Geologists, or experts on earth science, can help with this task by determining the age of rocks located near archaeological sites. In addition, botanists and zoologists—experts on plants and on animals—examine seeds and animal bones to learn about the diets of our ancestors. Experts on climate determine what conditions our ancestors faced on the plains of Africa or in ice-covered parts of Europe. Biologists analyze human bones as well as bloodstains found on old stone tools and weapons.

In addition to working with experts in various fields, archaeologists today use many modern innovations to study their findings. Computers help them store and sort data or develop accurate maps of archaeological sites. Aerial photographs help archaeologists to better see the layout of land and structures once lived in by past people. Techniques for measuring radioactivity aid scientists in determining the age of objects.

✓ **Checkpoint** What types of evidence do anthropologists and archaeologists study to learn about prehistory?

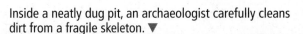

Before

In the late 1800s, archaeologists began excavating this hillside in Copán, Honduras, across which lay scattered building stones inscribed with Maya writing.

After

Today, instead of seeing a hillside, visitors to Copán marvel at a 63-step stairway reconstructed by archaeologists to look as it did when used by the ancient Maya.

Inside a neatly dug pit, an archaeologist carefully cleans dirt from a fragile skeleton. ▼

Thinking Critically

1. **Analyze Information** Which of the various aspects of archaeological work do these images represent?
2. **Draw Conclusions** What challenges do you think archaeologists faced in piecing together the stairway in Copán?

Reading Skill: Summarize As you read, keep track of the key details scholars have learned about different hominid groups by completing a summary table like the one below. Look for dates, innovations, and other details about each hominid group.

Hominids	
Group	**Summary**
Australopithecines	

Discoveries in Africa and Beyond

Before the 1950s, anthropologists knew little about early humans and their ancestors. Prehistoric groups did not have cities, countries, organized central governments, or complex inventions, so clues about them were hard to find. However, archaeologists in East Africa started uncovering ancient footprints, bones, and tools. With these first key discoveries, scholars began to form a picture of life during prehistory.

Ancient Clues Found in East Africa In the 1930s, anthropologists **Mary Leakey** and **Louis Leakey** started searching for clues to the human past in a deep canyon in Tanzania called **Olduvai Gorge** (OHL duh vy). Geologists have dated the bottom layers of Olduvai Gorge to an age of 1.7 to 2.1 million years. As the Leakeys searched the sides of the gorge, they found very ancient tools chipped from stone. Although these tools looked simple, with jagged edges and rough surfaces, they showed that whoever had made them had learned to develop technologies to help them survive. **Technology** refers to the skills and tools people use to meet their basic needs and wants. More recent stone tools proved more sophisticated—both smooth and polished—but the older ones were exciting to the Leakeys. They felt there must be evidence of the makers of those tools in Olduvai Gorge as well.

BIOGRAPHY

Mary Leakey

Mary Leakey (1913–1996) was born in London, England. During her childhood, she traveled throughout Europe and visited numerous prehistoric sites, which increased her interest in the fields of archaeology and geology. Because of her natural artistic talent, Leakey began working as an illustrator at archaeological sites during her teenage years. In particular, she focused on drawing Stone Age tools. Through this work, she met Louis Leakey, whom she married in 1936. Together they spent 30 years digging for early humans in East Africa. Mary Leakey found many remains that have become key to our understanding of early hominids. **How did Mary Leakey become interested in studying the ancient past?**

Louis Leakey

Louis Leakey (1903–1972) was born in Kenya, where his English parents lived with the Kikuyu people. Leakey was initiated as a Kikuyu warrior at age 13 and continued to speak the Kikuyu language for many years after leaving Kenya. Leakey moved to England to attend Cambridge University, where he studied anthropology. Afterward, he returned to East Africa to search for the remains of early humans. He and his wife, Mary, found many tools, bones, and other artifacts. In later life, he traveled all over the world, lecturing and raising funds for new research projects. Leakey's enthusiasm inspired a generation of anthropologists. **Why might someone devote his or her life to studying early humans?**

In 1959, after more than two decades of searching, Mary Leakey found a skull embedded in ancient rock at Olduvai Gorge. After careful testing, the Leakeys concluded that the skull belonged to an early hominid. Hominids, a group that includes humans and their closest relatives, all walk upright on two feet. Humans are the only hominids that live today.

Additional evidence of early hominids was found in 1974 by anthropologist **Donald Johanson.** In Ethiopia, Johanson found many pieces of a single hominid skeleton, which was dated to at least 3 million years ago. For the first time, archaeologists had enough of one skeleton to piece together and really look at an early hominid. Johanson named his historic find "Lucy" after a Beatles' song. Studying Lucy's skeleton, Johanson could see that she was an upright walker who was about 4 feet (1.2 meters) tall.

Donald Johanson was with another researcher, Tom Gray, when he began finding pieces of Lucy's skeleton. How would you describe Johanson's reaction to their discovery?

Primary Source

66 [Gray] picked it up. It was the back of a small skull. A few feet away was part of a femur: a thighbone.... We stood up, and began to see other bits of bone on the slope: a couple of vertebrae, part of a pelvis—all of them hominid. An unbelievable, impermissible thought flickered through my mind. Suppose all these fitted together? Could they be parts of a single, extremely primitive skeleton? No such skeleton had ever been found—anywhere.

'Look at that,' said Gray. 'Ribs.'

A single individual?

'I can't believe it,' I said. 'I just can't believe it.' 99

—Donald Johanson AUDIO

Donald Johanson at work in Ethiopia

Evidence of Early Hominid Groups As of today, scientists and anthropologists have discovered and studied numerous remains and artifacts of hominids. From this work, they have established that a number of different groups of hominids lived over the course of several million years. They call the earliest group of hominids australopithecines (aw stray loh PITH uh synz). Lucy and the hominids who left their footprints in Laetoli were australopithecines. All the australopithecines lived in Africa. Anthropologists think that they may have lived there as early as 7 million years ago.

About 2 million years ago, a group of hominids emerged that anthropologists call *Homo habilis*. Scholars gave the group this name, which means "handy man," because they thought these were the first hominids to make stone tools. Since the discovery of *Homo habilis*, anthropologists have uncovered even older stone tools—2.6 million years in age—but they have not determined which hominids created them. By studying many stone tools, anthropologists have concluded that *Homo habilis* used their tools for purposes such as cutting, scraping, chopping, or sawing plants, animals, and wood.

Another group of hominids, called *Homo erectus,* also appeared around 2 million years ago. They were given their name, which means "upright man," because their skeletons show that they were fully upright walkers. *Homo erectus* were notable for having larger brains and bones and smaller teeth than other hominids. They also showed a greater range of capabilities. For example, *Homo erectus* are thought to be the first hominids to learn how to use fire. They also pioneered a new form of stone tool, called a hand ax, that could be used as the earlier tools were but also worked for digging, shattering stone or bone, and boring holes into hard surfaces. *Homo erectus* remains have been found in Asia and Europe, making scholars think they were the first hominids to migrate out of Africa.

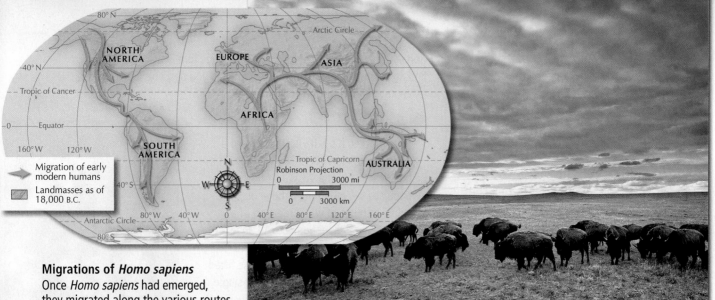

Migrations of *Homo sapiens*
Once *Homo sapiens* had emerged, they migrated along the various routes shown on the map. Many of these routes followed the paths of large herd animals such as bison. *What do you think was the benefit to* Homo sapiens *of following large herd animals?*

First Finds of Humans Around the World Scientists think that between 250,000 and 100,000 years ago, *Homo erectus* disappeared and a new group of hominids emerged. This new group, called *Homo sapiens,* is the group to which modern humans belong. There is some dispute over where *Homo sapiens* first lived. Many scholars think the archaeological and scientific evidence supports the "Out of Africa" theory, which says that *Homo sapiens* first lived in Africa and then migrated into other areas of the world. Other scientists think that *Homo erectus* developed into *Homo sapiens* around the same time in different parts of the world.

Either way, scholars think that two groups of *Homo sapiens* soon arose—Neanderthals and the earliest modern humans. Early modern humans eventually spread all over the world, while Neanderthals lived mostly in Europe and western Asia. Sometime between 50,000 and 30,000 years ago, the Neanderthals disappeared, leaving early modern humans as the only hominids on Earth.

 Checkpoint What have anthropologists learned about the use of tools during prehistory?

SECTION 1

Assessment

Progress Monitoring *Online*
For: Self-quiz with vocabulary practice
Web Code: naa-0111

Terms, People, and Places

1. For each term, person, or place listed at the beginning of the section, write a sentence explaining its significance.

Note Taking

2. **Reading Skill: Summarize** Use your completed concept web and table to answer the Focus Question: What have scholars learned about the ancestors of humans, and how have they done so?

Comprehension and Critical Thinking

3. **Express Problems Clearly** What types of obstacles do historians have to overcome to give a straightforward account of events? How do you think they might do this?

4. **Analyze Information** In what ways do archaeologists work with new technologies and other scholars in their work?

5. **Synthesize Information** Describe the story that anthropologists think the bones and tools they have discovered reveal about prehistory.

● Writing About History

Quick Write: Explore a Topic Choose a specific topic from this section and write a series of questions that you could use to direct your research for a report on it. For example, on the topic of Olduvai Gorge, you could ask the following:

- Why did the Leakeys decide to investigate this particular site?
- Have any discoveries other than the ones described in the text been made at Olduvai Gorge?

Egyptian wooden model of an agricultural scene from about 2000 B.C.

WITNESS HISTORY 🔊 AUDIO

The World's First Revolution

❝ For hundreds of thousands of years, [man] had lived on wild foods, as a hunter and gatherer. . . . The revolutionary step forward was the discovery that wild grains could be cultivated and made more productive, and wild animals herded and their products made constantly available. With this discovery, the growth of fixed settlements became possible. . . . From this, all civilisation is derived. ❞

—Kathleen Kenyon, archaeologist

Focus Question How was the introduction of agriculture a turning point in prehistory?

Turning Point:
The Neolithic Revolution

Performance Standards

• **SSWH1a** Describe religious and economic development of Mesopotamian societies.

Terms, People, and Places

Old Stone Age	animism
Paleolithic Period	Neolithic Revolution
New Stone Age	domesticate
Neolithic Period	Çatalhüyük
nomad	Jericho

Note Taking

Reading Skill: Summarize Use the chart below to summarize the eras of prehistory before and after the introduction of agriculture.

Eras of Prehistory	
Life Before Farming	**Life After Farming**
•	•
•	•
•	•

Based on the evidence gathered by anthropologists over many years, scholars have divided prehistory into different eras. They call the long period from at least 2 million B.C. to about 10,000 B.C. the **Old Stone Age,** or **Paleolithic Period.** They refer to the period from about 10,000 B.C. until the end of prehistory as the **New Stone Age,** or **Neolithic Period.** During both eras, people created and used various types of stone tools. However, during the New Stone Age, people began to develop new skills and technologies that led to dramatic changes in their everyday lives.

Skills and Beliefs of the Old Stone Age

Early modern humans lived toward the end of the Old Stone Age. Researchers have pieced together evidence left by early modern humans to paint a picture of what daily life was like for them. Early modern people were **nomads,** or people who move from place to place to find food. Typically, about 20 or 30 people lived together in small bands, or groups. They survived by hunting and by gathering food. In general, men hunted or fished. Women and children gathered berries, fruits, nuts, grains, roots, or shellfish. This food kept the band alive when game animals were scarce.

Humans Develop Strategies for Survival Early people depended heavily on their environment for food and shelter. They also found ways to adapt their surroundings to their needs. As hominids had throughout the Stone Age, early humans made tools

Techniques for Making Stone Tools

Archaeologists have discovered vast quantities of stone tools and artifacts related to their creation. Hominids made many early tools from stones such as flint that are relatively easy to shape by chipping off flakes of the stone. Once chipped, these stones have very sharp edges. Even stone tools from locations very far apart were made in similar sizes and shapes and with similar techniques.

Chopper

Flake

Oldowan Choppers and Flakes*

2.6–1.2 million years ago
Toolmakers chipped a few flakes off a stone to create a sharp-edged chopper. They often also used the flakes for scraping and cutting.

Acheulian Hand Axes

1.5 million–200,000 years ago Toolmakers chipped flakes off both sides of a stone and then shaped it into an oval with two straight, sharp edges.

Flake

Levallois Axes*

200,000–35,000 years ago
Toolmakers chipped sharp edges all around a stone. Then they knocked off one large flake that was thick in the center and sharp all around.

*Images are about 60 percent of actual size.

Creating any type of stone tool required patience, skill, strength, and a number of other tools.

Using a hard stone, the toolmaker strikes flakes off another stone to create the rough shape of an Acheulian ax.

The toolmaker uses a piece of bone to carefully refine the tool's shape.

Using a small chisel, the toolmaker chips the final flakes off the stone.

Thinking Critically

1. **Make Comparisons** How were the Acheulian hand axes and the Levallois axes similar? How were they different?
2. **Make Inferences** What can we infer about hominids communication skills from the stone tools they made?

and weapons out of the materials at hand—stone, bone, or wood. They built fires for cooking and used animal skins for clothing. At some point, early modern humans developed spoken language, which allowed them to cooperate during the hunt and perhaps discuss plans for the future.

Some Old Stone Age people also learned to travel across water, which helped them spread into new places. For example, people boated from Southeast Asia to Australia at least 40,000 years ago, most likely using rafts or canoes. They may have stopped for years at islands along the way, but in between they would have had to boat across as much as 40 miles (64 kilometers) of open ocean.

Clues About Early Religious Beliefs Toward the end of the Old Stone Age, people began to leave evidence of their belief in a spiritual world. About 100,000 years ago, some people began burying their dead with great care. Some anthropologists think that this practice suggests a belief in life after death. Old Stone Age people may have believed the afterlife would be similar to life in this world and thus provided the dead with tools, weapons, and other needed goods to take with them.

Many scholars think that our ancestors believed the world was full of spirits and forces that might reside in animals, objects, or dreams. Such beliefs are known as **animism.** In Europe, Australia, and Africa, cave or rock paintings vividly portray animals such as deer, horses, and buffaloes. Some cave paintings show people, too. The paintings often lie deep in caves, far from a band's living quarters. Some scholars think cave paintings were created as part of animist religious rituals.

✓ **Checkpoint** What skills did Old Stone Age people develop in order to adapt their surroundings to their needs?

The New Stone Age Begins With Farming

The New Stone Age began about 12,000 years ago (or about 10,000 B.C.), when nomadic people made a breakthrough that had far-reaching effects—they learned to farm.

The Neolithic Revolution By producing their own food, people no longer needed to roam in search of animals, fish, or plants. For the first time, they could remain in one place throughout the year. As a result, early farmers settled the first permanent villages. They also developed entirely new skills and technologies. This transition from nomadic life to settled farming brought about such dramatic changes in way of life that it is often called the **Neolithic Revolution.**

Vocabulary Builder
transition—(tran ZISH un) *n.* process of undergoing a change from one stage to another

People Domesticate Plants and Animals These early farmers were the first humans to **domesticate** plants and animals—that is, to raise them in a controlled way that makes them best suited to human use. Plant domestication may have begun with food gatherers realizing that seeds scattered on the ground would produce new plants the next year. Animal domestication may have begun with people deciding to round up the animals they usually hunted. They could then use the animals as they always had—for food and skins—as well as to provide other benefits, such as milk or eggs.

Evidence shows that people began to farm in different parts of the world at different times, and that they did not domesticate all the same plants or animals in each place. The dog was probably the first animal to be domesticated, at least 15,000 years ago. People brought domesticated dogs wherever they migrated. From about 8000 B.C. to 6000 B.C., people in western Asia and northern Africa domesticated goats, sheep, pigs, and cattle; and people in South America domesticated llamas and alpacas. Around the same time—from about 10,000 B.C. to 6000 B.C.—people in West Africa and Southeast Asia domesticated yams, in China millet and rice, in Central America and Mexico squash, and in the Middle East barley, chickpeas, peas, lentils, and wheat.

World's First Domesticated Animal
About 10,000 years after people first domesticated dogs, people in some cultures began depicting dogs in their artwork. Around 2000 B.C., an artist from Mesopotamia created this stone sculpture of a dog, which is covered in ancient writing.

✓ **Checkpoint** What major lifestyle changes did farming allow people to make?

The inhabitants might use the upper floor to store crops such as wheat and apples.

Many houses included a shrine. It was decorated with bulls' horns and sometimes wall paintings. A burial often lay sheltered beneath the shrine floor.

Food was prepared in a small clay oven or over a hearth.

At Home in Çatalhüyük
Archaeologists have studied the ruins of Çatalhüyük to learn about the village's houses. They think people entered a house through a hole in its roof. *Based on the illustration, what evidence do you think archaeologists used to learn about the interior of the houses?*

The Neolithic Revolution Brings Dramatic Change

Once the Neolithic Revolution had begun, no greater change in the way people lived took place until the Industrial Revolution of the late 1700s. Settled farming led to the establishment of the first villages and to significant advances in technology and culture. As you will read in the next section, these advances eventually led to a new stage of development—the emergence of cities and civilizations.

Earliest Villages Established Archaeologists have unearthed the remains of some of the first Neolithic villages, including **Çatalhüyük** (chah TAHL hyoo YOOK) in modern-day Turkey and **Jericho** (JEHR ih koh), which still exists today as an Israeli-controlled city. Jericho was built between 10,000 and 9000 B.C. Although the village was tiny—about the size of a few soccer fields—a few thousand people lived in it. The village was surrounded by a huge wall, which suggests that it had a government or leader who was able to organize a large construction project. Çatalhüyük seems to have developed around 7000 B.C. and may have had a population as large as 6,500 people. The village covered about three times more land than Jericho and included hundreds of rectangular mud-brick houses, all connected and all about the same size.

Settled People Change Their Ways of Life Like their Paleolithic ancestors, early farmers probably divided up the work by gender and age. Still, important differences began to emerge. In settled farming communities, men came to dominate family, economic, and political life. Heads of families, probably older men, formed a council of elders and made decisions about when to plant and harvest. When food was scarce, warfare increased, and some men gained prestige as warriors. These elite warriors asserted power over others in society.

Settled people had more personal property than nomadic people. In addition, some settled people accumulated more possessions than their neighbors, so differences in wealth began to appear.

Villagers Invent New Technologies To farm successfully, people had to develop new technologies. Like farmers today, they had to find ways to protect their crops and measure out enough seed for the next year's harvest. They also needed to measure time accurately to know when to plant and harvest. Eventually, people would use such measurements to create the first calendars. As well, many farmers learned to use animals such as oxen or water buffalo to plow the fields.

Archaeological evidence shows that some villages had separate workshops where villagers made tools, including smooth, polished ax heads and chipped arrowheads. In some parts of the world, Neolithic people learned to weave cloth from animal hair or vegetable fibers. Many Neolithic people began using clay to create pottery for cooking and storage. Archaeologists have learned about life during this period from finds such as "the Iceman"—the body of a Neolithic man found preserved in snow in the European Alps alongside various tools and belongings.

Technologies were not invented everywhere at the same time. Knowledge of some traveled slowly from one area to another, perhaps taking thousands of years to spread across continents. Other technologies were invented separately in different parts of the world and showed varying degrees of similarity.

 Checkpoint What new technologies did people invent as a result of agriculture?

SECTION **2 Assessment**

Progress Monitoring _Online_
For: Self-quiz with vocabulary practice
Web Code: naa-0121

Terms, People, and Places

1. What do many of the key terms listed at the beginning of the section have in common? Explain.

Note Taking

2. **Reading Skill: Summarize** Use your completed chart to answer the Focus Question: How was the introduction of agriculture a turning point in prehistory?

Comprehension and Critical Thinking

3. **Predict Consequences** How do you think the development of spoken language influenced people's development of skills and religious beliefs?

4. **Determine Relevance** How are our lives today affected by the Neolithic Revolution that occurred 11,000 years ago?

5. **Make Comparisons** How was settled village life different from nomadic life? Consider population size, social status, and technology in your answer.

● **Writing About History**
Quick Write: Gather Information
Choose a topic from this section to write a research report about and gather sources related to it. Your sources may include books, magazines, and the Internet. For example, on the topic of cave paintings, you might locate the following:

- a magazine article that describes and shows photographs of the paintings in a particular cave
- a book that compares Stone Age cave paintings from different regions

Paleolithic Cave Art

The surviving examples of the first human art date from the end of the Paleolithic Period, from roughly 30,000 to 12,000 B.C. Examples have been discovered in about 250 caves in southern France and northern Spain. A few caves containing art have also been found in Italy, Siberia, southern and eastern Africa, and Australia. Cave paintings, which often cover entire walls, are a common form of Paleolithic cave art. Paleolithic people also engraved drawings on cave walls and carved the stone when it was soft enough.

Sculpture
Paleolithic carved sculpture such as this clay bison has only been found in caves in France. On some of the sculptures, traces of pigment can still be found, indicating that they were once painted.

Wall Paintings
Many of the Paleolithic cave paintings found so far show large animals such as horses, bison, bulls, and deer. Lions, bears, seals, and owls appear occasionally. The animals are usually painted in pigments made from minerals such as hematite, kaolin, and charcoal.

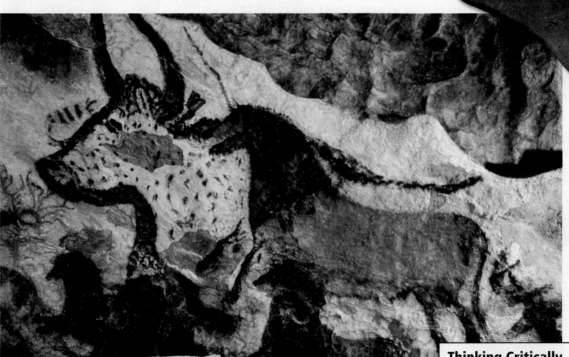

Cave Lamp
Paleolithic artists created light in the caves by burning animal fat in lamps like this one.

Hematite

Kaolin

Charcoal

Thinking Critically
1. **Make Generalizations** What might the fact that Paleolithic people created art on cave walls tell you about their skills and experiences?
2. **Express Problems Clearly** What challenges do you think people face today when trying to locate Paleolithic cave art?

Ancient Mesopotamian carving of a carpenter at work

The Daily Grind Begins

The development of the first civilizations brought about a major change in daily life. Instead of everyone working on a few major tasks necessary for day-to-day survival, such as farming and hunting, people in early civilizations developed and perfected many new trades. A carpenter like the one shown at left might spend his day shaping wooden furniture, while his wife might weave fabrics and sell them in a local market.

Focus Question How did the world's first civilizations arise and develop?

Beginnings of Civilization

 Performance Standards

• **SSWH1a** Describe religious and cultural development of Mesopotamian societies.

Terms, People, and Places

surplus	pictograph
traditional economy	scribe
civilization	cultural diffusion
steppe	city-state
polytheistic	empire
artisan	

Note Taking

Reading Skill: Summarize As you read, create a chart showing the different phases of the development of civilizations. Summarize each phase using details from the text.

The Development of Civilizations		
Rise of Cities and Civilizations	**Features of Civilizations**	**Changes Over Time**
•	•	•
•	•	•

The establishment of villages such as Çatalhüyük and Jericho symbolized a huge step in human development. Societies were becoming more organized, and people's technological innovations were becoming increasingly complex. Soon would follow a momentous change in human existence—the development of civilizations.

First Cities and Civilizations Arise

The earliest civilizations to develop were all situated near major rivers. These rivers provided a regular water supply and a means of transportation. The animals that flocked to the rivers to drink were a source of food. Perhaps most important, conditions in the river valleys favored farming. Floodwaters spread silt—tiny bits of rock and dirt from the river bottom—across the valleys, renewing the soil and keeping it fertile.

In such rich conditions, farmers were able to produce **surpluses** of food, or more than was necessary. These surpluses allowed them to feed growing populations and to store food for the future. Thus they were able to produce enough food to support increasingly large populations. As populations expanded, some villages swelled into the world's first cities. In these cities, some of the people were able to work at jobs other than farming. This was a radical departure from the traditional economies of the Stone Age. A **traditional economy** relies on habit, custom, or ritual and tends not to change over time. As you will read, in cities, many aspects of life were dramatically different than they had been before.

EUROPE

ASIA

Shang China

Egypt

Sumer

Indus civilization

AFRICA

Equator

Indian Ocean

Atlantic Ocean

Miller Projection
0   500   1000   1500 mi
0   500 1000 1500 km

Egypt, 2575–2130 B.C.
Indus civilization, 2600–1900 B.C.
Shang China, 1766–1122 B.C.
Sumer, 3300–1900 B.C.

Tropic of Capricorn

AUSTRALIA

0°

30°S

0°   60°E   90°E

Egypt
Mediterranean Sea
Nile Delta
Giza
Memphis
Libyan Desert
Nile River
Thebes
Red Sea
Nubian Desert

Miller Projection
0   200 mi
0   200 km

Sumer
Tigris River
Euphrates River
Uruk
Ur
Arabian Desert
Persian Gulf

Miller Projection
0   200 mi
0   200 km

Indus Civilization
Hindu Kush
Indus River
Harappa
Mohenjo-Daro
HIMALAYAS
Northern Plain
Thar Desert
Ganges R.
Arabian Sea
Vindhya Mts.
Narmada River

Miller Projection
0   250 mi
0   250 km

Shang China
Huang River
Anyang
Huang River
Wei River
Luoyang
Zhengzhou
Yellow Sea
Chang River
East China Sea

Miller Projection
0   300 mi
0   300 km

Map Skills The world's earliest civilizations arose in fertile river valleys in Africa and Asia.

1. **Locate** (a) Sumer (b) Mohenjo-Daro (c) Chang River (d) Giza

2. **Region** Locate the Indus civilization. What types of natural features surround the region? Name one feature of each type.

3. **Make Comparisons** How did the four River Valley Civilizations compare to one another in size? In time frame? How might you explain Sumer's small size based on the comparison of time frames?

River Valley Civilizations The rise of cities was the main feature of civilization. A **civilization** is a <u>complex</u>, highly organized social order. The world's first civilizations arose independently in a number of river valleys. These River Valley Civilizations include Sumer, between the Tigris and Euphrates rivers in the Middle East; Egypt, along the Nile River; the Indus civilization, along the Indus River in India; and the Shang civilization, along the Huang (hwahng) River, or Yellow River, in China. You will read in depth about each of these River Valley Civilizations in later chapters.

Vocabulary Builder
<u>complex</u>—(kahm PLEKS) *adj.* made up of many interrelated parts

First Civilizations in the Americas Unlike the first civilizations in Asia and Africa, the first civilizations in the Americas arose away from river valleys. Major civilizations emerged in the highlands of Peru, Mexico, and Central America, where people learned to farm on the sides of mountains or to fill in swamps with land for farming. You will read about the achievements of civilizations such as the Inca, the Olmec, and the Maya in a later chapter.

Life Away From Cities Away from the first cities, many people continued to hunt, gather food, or live in farming villages. On some less fertile lands or on sparse, dry grasslands called **steppes,** nomadic herders tended cattle, sheep, goats, or other animals. Because the lands did not have abundant water or grass, these nomads had to keep moving to find new pasture.

 Checkpoint In what ways were river valleys ideal locations for civilizations to develop?

Basic Features That Define Civilization

What did the early civilizations that arose in different parts of the world have in common? While cities are the main feature of civilization, historians distinguish several other basic features of most early civilizations. Seven of the major features are (1) organized governments, (2) complex religions, (3) job specialization, (4) social classes, (5) arts and architecture, (6) public works, and (7) writing.

Organized Governments Councils of elders or chiefs ruled many of the world's farming villages. However, in cities, more powerful organized governments arose to oversee large-scale efforts that benefited the people. For example, as cities grew, their residents required a steady supply of food. A central government could coordinate the production of large amounts of food. In addition, farmers near rivers needed to control flooding and channel waters to the fields. A well-organized government could bring people together for projects such as building dikes, digging canals, and carving out irrigation ditches.

Many rulers also relied on royal officials to help them govern by issuing laws, collecting taxes, and organizing systems of defense. Over time, governments became more complex, and separate departments often evolved to oversee different functions of government. In many early cases, priests probably had the greatest power in government. In others, warrior kings emerged as the main political leaders. Often, they claimed that their right to rule came from the gods, and they passed their power on from father to son. Thus, many political rulers gained religious power as well.

Complex Religions Most ancient people were **polytheistic,** which means they believed in many gods. People appealed to sun gods, river goddesses, and other gods that they believed controlled natural forces or human activities such as birth or war.

In early religions, priests and worshipers sought to gain the favor of the gods through complex rituals such as ceremonies, dances, prayers, and hymns. To ensure divine help, people built temples and sacrificed animals, crops, or sometimes other humans to the gods. Sacrifices and other ceremonies required the full-time attention of priests, who had special training and knowledge.

Job Specialization The lives of city dwellers differed from those of nomads. Urban people developed so many new crafts that a single individual could not master all the skills needed to make tools, weapons, or other goods. For the first time, individuals began to specialize in certain jobs. Some became **artisans,** or skilled craftspeople, and made pottery or finely carved or woven goods. Among the crafts developed in cities, metalworking was particularly important. People learned to make tools and weapons, first out of copper and later out of bronze, a more durable mixture of copper and tin.

Cities had other specialists, too. Bricklayers built city walls. Soldiers defended these walls. Merchants sold goods in the marketplace. Singers, dancers, and storytellers entertained on public occasions. Such specialization made people dependent on others for their various needs.

Social Classes In cities, social organization became more complex. People were ranked according to their jobs. Such ranking led to the growth of social classes. Priests and nobles usually occupied the top level of an ancient society. Next came a small class of wealthy merchants, followed by artisans. Below them came the vast majority of people—peasant farmers who lived in the surrounding villages and produced food for the city.

In many civilizations, slaves occupied the lowest social level. Slaves sometimes came from poor families who sold family members into slavery to pay their debts. Others became slaves as punishment for crimes or were prisoners captured in war. Because male captives were often killed, women and children made up the largest number of slaves in some societies.

Arts and Architecture The arts and architecture of ancient civilizations expressed the talents, beliefs, and values of the people who created them. Temples and palaces often dominated the city landscape. Many rulers may have ordered such buildings to be constructed in order to remind people of the strength and power of their government and religion. The skilled workers who built these massive buildings decorated them with wall paintings, statues of gods, goddesses, or rulers, and other stunning pieces of design work.

Basic Features of Civilizations	
Feature	**Description**
Cities	Population centers that are notably larger and more organized than towns or villages and that support the other features of civilizations
Organized Governments	Structured governments that coordinate large-scale projects such as food production or construction, establish laws, and organize defense systems
Complex Religions	Systems of religious beliefs that usually include rituals and worship of one or more gods and/or goddesses
Job Specialization	System in which there are different types of jobs and each worker focuses on one particular type
Social Classes	Ranked groups within society that are determined by job or economic standing
Arts and Architecture	Various types of artwork and buildings that express the talents, beliefs, and values of people in a society
Public Works	Large-scale and often costly projects that benefit the city and its people
Writing	Structured writing systems used initially by governments or religious leaders to record important information

Chart Skills The basic features of civilizations help show how early civilizations differed from smaller farming societies and nomadic lifestyles. *Which features of civilizations do you think most affected the daily lives of average people?*

Bridges: Then and Now

Today, bridges span countless waterways, ravines, highways, and other areas around the world that people need to pass over. Their construction requires solid leadership, thorough planning, and often immense resources. In ancient times, such public works projects could only be undertaken once civilizations had established organized governments and developed the mathematical and engineering knowledge needed to construct bridges that would remain standing over time.

▲ **600 B.C.** The oldest stone bridge still standing today was constructed under the rule of Assyrian King Sennacherib. It spans a small river in Jerwan, Iraq.

▲ **A.D. 600** Chinese Emperor Yang Ti oversaw the construction of the An Ji Bridge. It was the first of its kind, called an open-spandrel arched bridge.

◄ **1992** Like the dramatic Alamillo Bridge built in Seville, Spain, many modern-day bridges are suspension bridges supported by strong cables.

Thinking Critically

1. **Draw Conclusions** Why would ancient societies have valued bridges?
2. **Recognize Sufficient Evidence** What evidence would archaeologists need to learn how ancient bridges were built?

Public Works Strong rulers also ordered vast public works to be built. Such projects included irrigation systems, roads, bridges, and defensive walls. These public works projects were meant to benefit the city by protecting it from attack, ensuring its food supply, or enhancing the reputation of its ruler. The projects were often quite costly, requiring a great deal of human labor and sometimes resulting in the loss of lives during construction.

Writing Of the earliest civilizations, some but not all developed a critical skill—writing. The first writing systems were established in different places and at different times, in many cases with no contact among the different groups who created them. Thus the earliest writing systems varied in appearance, structure, and purpose. Some were first used in temples, where priests needed to record amounts of grain collected, accurate information about the seasons, and precise rituals and prayers. Other writing systems were first used on public monuments, where rulers spelled out their greatest achievements as a means of advertising their power to the people. Archaeologists have found masses of ancient writings, some on clay tablets or vases, others on stone statues, and yet others on the walls of buildings.

The first step people made toward developing writing was to use **pictographs** (also called pictograms), or simple drawings that look like the objects they represent. Later, they developed complex writing systems including symbols that represent words, syllables, or letters. As writing grew more complex, only specially trained people called **scribes** could read and write. Scribes kept records for priests, rulers, and merchants. Only a few societies permitted women to become scribes, an occupation that could lead to political power.

Comparing Nomadic Life and Civilizations Nomadic cultures differed from civilizations in their social organization—that is, they did not exhibit many of the characteristics of civilization. The people did not build cities, and their governments were simpler than those of civilizations. However, nomadic peoples often excelled in arts and sciences. For example, many groups developed sophisticated traditions in oral poetry, music, weaving, jewelry making, and animal raising.

 Checkpoint What roles did governments play in early civilizations?

Civilizations Change Over Time

Ancient civilizations changed in many ways over the centuries. Among the chief causes of change were shifts in the physical environment and interactions among people. Among the major results was the expansion of cities into larger political entities.

Environment Affects People's Lives Like their Stone Age ancestors, people living in early civilizations depended heavily on the physical environment. They needed ample rain and fertile soil to be able to produce crops. Resources such as stone, timber, or metals were also essential. Significant changes in the environment could have an immediate impact on people's lives.

At times, a sudden, drastic event would devastate a community. An earthquake or the eruption of a volcano could wipe out an entire civilization. Farming the same land too much could destroy soil fertility, and rivers could become too salty. Cities would then suffer famine, and survivors would be forced to move away.

If people used up nearby timber or ran out of other building resources, they would have to find ways to adapt to this scarcity. They might, for example, trade with people in areas where such resources were readily available. Or they might use alternate building materials such as reeds.

Cause and Effect

Causes

- Neolithic people learn to farm. → Hunters and gatherers settle into farming communities. → Some farmers settle in river valleys, where the soil is very fertile. → New technologies improve farming. → Food surpluses support growing populations. → The first cities are built in fertile valleys.

Rise of River Valley Civilizations

Effects

- Complex forms of government develop.
- Arts become more elaborate.
- Job specialization leads to social classes.
- People invent writing.
- Early civilizations conquer neighboring lands.

Connections to Today

- Archaeologists continue to discover rich stores of information about Neolithic people and early civilizations.
- In the modern day, people continue to live along rivers, in both villages and large cities.

Analyze Cause and Effect A series of different factors caused the rise of River Valley Civilizations. *Which cause do you think led most directly to job specialization? Why?*

Culture Changes Hands and Changes Shape Another major source of change for people living in ancient times was **cultural diffusion,** the spread of ideas, customs, and technologies from one people to another. Cultural diffusion occurred through migration, trade, and warfare.

As famine, drought, or other disasters led people to migrate, they interacted with others whose lives differed from their own. As a result, people often shared and adapted the customs of others. Trade, too, introduced people to new goods or better methods of producing them. In ancient times, skills such as working with bronze and writing, as well as religious beliefs, passed from one society to another. Warfare also brought change. Often, victorious armies forced their way of life upon the people they defeated. On other occasions, the victors incorporated the ways of a conquered people into their society.

Cities Grow Into City-States As ancient rulers gained more power, they conquered territories beyond the boundaries of their cities. This expansion led to the rise of the **city-state,** a political unit that included a city and its surrounding lands and villages. Rulers, nobles, and priests often controlled the land outside the city and forced peasants to give them some of the crops they grew on it. In some places, a <u>significant</u> portion of each harvest went to support the government and temples.

First Empires Are Established Rival leaders often battled for power. Sometimes, ambitious rulers conquered many cities and villages, creating the first empires. An **empire** is a group of states or territories controlled by one ruler. For the conquered people, defeat was painful and often cruel. At the same time, empire building also brought benefits. It helped end war between neighboring communities and created common bonds among people. As you will soon read, many impressive civilizations and powerful empires developed all over the world and left a lasting legacy behind them.

✔ **Checkpoint** How have different types of challenges encouraged peoples and civilizations to change over time?

With Empires Come Warfare
One of the most powerful empires of ancient history was that of Alexander the Great. Here, Darius III of Persia leads his troops into a ferocious—but losing—battle against Alexander.

Vocabulary Builder
<u>significant</u>—(sig NIF uh kint) *adj.* relatively large in amount

SECTION 3 Assessment

Progress Monitoring *Online*
For: Self-quiz with vocabulary practice
Web Code: naa-0131

Terms, People, and Places

1. Place each of the terms listed at the beginning of the section into one of the following categories: government, culture, economy, geography, or technology. Write a sentence for each term explaining your choice.

Note Taking

2. **Reading Skill: Summarize** Use your completed chart to answer the Focus Question: How did the world's first civilizations arise and develop?

Comprehension and Critical Thinking

3. **Make Comparisons** How were the conditions under which early civilizations developed in Asia and Africa different from those of the Americas?

4. **Synthesize Information** In early civilizations, how did religion influence government and social classes?

5. **Identify Central Issues (a)** Give three examples of cultural change in early civilizations. **(b)** Give two examples of cultural diffusion today.

● **Writing About History**

Quick Write: Make an Outline Choose a topic from this section and make an outline of a research report about it. In your outline, include main ideas and details that support them. For example, on the topic of the invention of writing, you might include these main ideas in your outline:

- Writing was a major achievement of early civilizations.
- The first known writing system was developed in Mesopotamia.
- Writing was first used for different reasons in different civilizations.

CHAPTER 1

Quick Study Guide

GA SSWH1a

Progress Monitoring *Online*
For: Self-test with vocabulary practice
Web Code: naa-0141

■ Scholars Who Study the Past

Historians	Anthropologists/Archaeologists
Study and write about the people and events of history	Study the origins and developments of people and their societies during prehistory and history; study physical and cultural traits of people
Primarily analyze written records; also analyze artifacts	Primarily analyze artifacts and material remains; also analyze written records
Evaluate the evidence using reasonable judgments and the work of other scholars	Evaluate the evidence using reasonable judgments, modern innovations, and the work of other types of scholars
Interpret and explain the evidence	Interpret and explain the evidence
Sort out disagreements over the evidence and change theories in light of new evidence	Sort out disagreements over the evidence and change theories in light of new evidence

■ Hominid Groups Over Time

Hominid Group	Earliest Known Evidence
Australopithecines	7 million years ago
Homo habilis	2 million years ago
Homo erectus	2 million years ago
Homo sapiens • Neanderthals • Early modern humans	250,000–100,000 years ago

■ Key Stages of Human Development

Old Stone Age
- creation of stone, bone, and wood tools and weapons
- use of fire
- spoken language
- ability to travel across water in boats
- belief in a spiritual world
- creation of cave paintings
- burial of the dead

New Stone Age
- farming and domestication of plants and animals
- settling of permanent villages
- dominance of family, economic, and political life by men
- gaining of prestige by warriors
- appearance of differences in wealth
- creation of first calendars
- more elaborate tools and new technologies

Rise of Civilizations
- production of surpluses of food
- expansion of populations
- development of cities, civilizations, and governments
- government oversight of large-scale projects
- belief in polytheistic religions
- job specialization
- development of social classes
- development of arts and architecture
- invention of writing systems
- expansion of some cities into city-states and empires
- cultural diffusion

■ Key Events of Prehistory

2 million B.C.
Early human ancestors have begun making and using simple stone tools.

7 million B.C.	**2 million B.C.**	**100,000 B.C.**

7 million B.C.
By this time, the earliest ancestors of modern humans may live in Africa.

100,000 B.C.
The earliest modern humans, called *Homo sapiens*, begin to spread throughout the world.

Concept Connector

Essential Question Review

To connect prior knowledge with what you have learned in this chapter, answer the questions below in your Concept Connector journal. Use the journal in the Reading and Note Taking Study Guide to record your answers (or go to www.phschool.com **Web Code**: nad-0107). In addition, record information about the following concepts:

- Technology: Paleolithic stone tools
- Geography's Impact: rivers and the rise of civilization

1. **Migration** Populations of both *Homo erectus* and *Homo sapiens* eventually migrated into various parts of the world. Additionally, migration was a regular part of life for nomads during the periods of prehistory and history. What factors do you think contributed to the migrations of early people? Think about the following:
   - sources of food
   - climate changes
   - environmental events
   - competition among groups of people

2. **Geography's Impact** Create a chart that compares the ways that Stone Age hominids adapted the environment to their needs to the ways that Neolithic farmers adapted the environment to their needs.

3. **Economic Systems** How did the ways in which goods were produced and distributed change as civilization developed?

■ Connections to Today

1. **Geography's Impact: The History of Cities** Just as the first cities were built in river valleys because of the benefits they offered, many of today's major cities were also built in advantageous locations. Some cities—such as St. Louis, Missouri; London, England; and Delhi, India—do lie along rivers. Other cities—such as New York, New York; Cape Town, South Africa; Rio de Janeiro, Brazil; and Lisbon, Portugal—sit alongside the open ocean. Yet others rise up from the rare low ground amidst mountain ranges. Conduct research on three major world cities to find out why they were built in their particular locations. Write a few paragraphs explaining your findings.

2. **Technology: The Computer Revolution** The introduction of farming during the New Stone Age is considered the world's first technological revolution. During the twentieth century, the computer revolutionized life as well. Early computers were enormous machines, but by the 1970s, they began to be built smaller, and by the 1990s, many households owned at least one personal computer. In addition, the Internet and numerous small electronic devices soon made personal computing a basic part of life for many people. Computers also revolutionized work life, as many industries came to rely on computers to power their operations. Considering the various ways in which computers have changed daily life, what similarities and differences do you see between the impact of the Neolithic Revolution and that of the computer revolution?

40,000 B.C.
By this time, people have traveled across the ocean by boat from Southeast Asia to Australia.

9000 B.C.
People learn to grow their own crops and begin settling in permanent farming villages.

History Interactive
For: Interactive timeline
Web Code: nap-0141

40,000 B.C. — **9000 B.C.** — **3000 B.C.**

30,000 B.C.
Early people begin painting animals on the walls of caves.

3200 B.C.
The world's first civilizations begin to develop in river valleys.

Chapter Assessment

Terms, People, and Places

Choose the italicized term in parentheses that best completes each sentence.

1. The way of life of a society is its *(technology/culture)*.
2. *(Mary Leakey/Donald Johanson)* gave the name Lucy to an australopithecine skeleton.
3. The *(Paleolithic Period/Neolithic Period)* lasted from at least 2 million B.C. to about 10,000 B.C.
4. *(Çatalhüyük/Jericho)* was a tiny Neolithic village surrounded by a huge wall.
5. A highly organized social order is a *(steppe/civilization)*.
6. People who believe in many gods are *(scribes/polytheistic)*.
7. A group of states or territories controlled by one ruler is a(n) *(empire/city-state)*.

Main Ideas

Section 1 (pp. 4–10)

8. In what part of the world did the earliest hominids live?
9. For what purposes did hominids create stone tools?

Section 2 (pp. 11–16)

10. How did Old Stone Age people find food?
11. What change marked the beginning of the New Stone Age? In what ways did this change alter people's way of life?

Section 3 (pp. 17–23)

12. In which four river valleys did early civilizations emerge?
13. List the eight basic features of most early civilizations.

Chapter Focus Question

14. What was life like in early times, and how did it change as civilizations began to develop?

Critical Thinking

15. **Analyze Cartoons** How does this cartoon reflect the challenges that archaeologists face when interpreting the evidence that they find?

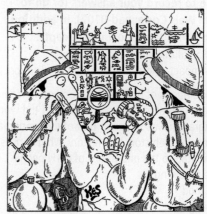

"Don't be ridiculous Caruthers, you must have mistranslated it. How can it possibly say, KingRamases @www.ram2.com?"

16. **Draw Inferences** Many scholars interpret evidence such as cave paintings and burials as indications of early people's beliefs. How do you think material remains help show people's feelings and thoughts?
17. **Make Comparisons** Think about the ways of life of both early nomads and early farmers. How do you think geography affected each group in both positive and negative ways?
18. **Predict Consequences** Before writing systems were invented, people had to share and remember ideas, customs, and technology by word of mouth. How do you think writing eventually changed this?
19. **Recognize Cause and Effect** Which feature(s) of civilization do you think most allowed empires to develop?

● Writing About History

In this chapter's three Section Assessments, you developed skills for writing a research report.

Writing a Research Report The period of prehistory includes many fascinating topics related to the development of early humans and civilizations. Write a research report on one of the following topics: discoveries at Olduvai Gorge, cave painting, the Neolithic Revolution, early writing systems. Be sure to describe some of the evidence that anthropologists and archaeologists have gathered and explain what it tells us about the topic. Consult page SH13 of the Writing Handbook for additional help.

Prewriting

• Choose the topic that interests you most and take notes about the evidence scholars have found and what they think it means.

• Create a set of questions about the topic and gather additional resources that will help you answer those questions.

Drafting

• Develop a working thesis and choose information to support it.
• Make an outline organizing the report.
• Write an introduction explaining why the topic is interesting. Then write the body of the text and a conclusion.

Revising

• Use the guidelines for revising your report on page SH15 of the Writing Handbook.

Prepare for the GHSGT

Who Were These Tiny Hominids?

When anthropologists make new finds, they are not always sure exactly what they have discovered. As you study the reports below of researchers finding the remains of tiny hominids, consider the challenges of determining the meaning of ancient evidence.

Document A

"Scientists have discovered a new species of ancient human that lived 18,000 years ago on an island east of the Java Sea—a pre-historic hunter. . . . These "little people" stood about three feet tall and had heads the size of grapefruit. . . . The research team . . . described the remains—a fairly complete skull, the jawbone and much of the skeleton—as those of a 30-year-old woman. . . . The team also found . . . the remains of between five and seven people in all."

—Guy Gugliotta, **washingtonpost.com,** October 28, 2004

Document B

"So what was this strange creature, and what was it doing on [the island of] Flores? The [researchers] have had to make diffi-cult choices in deciding how to classify the creature, although it is clear that this person was definitely not a modern human. The small brain size and the hip-bone shape might favour classifica-tion as an australopithecine, whereas the size and shape of the skull might suggest a primitive form of *H. erectus.* Given the unique combination of features, the [researchers] have decided to give the specimen a new name: *Homo floresiensis.*"

—Chris Stringer, **news@nature.com,** October 27, 2004

Document C

"The researchers estimate that the tiny people lived on [the island of] Flores from about 95,000 years ago until at least 13,000 years ago. The scientists base their theory on charred bones and stone tools found on the island. The [tools] were apparently used to hunt big game. . . . The Flores people used fire in hearths for cooking and hunted stegodon, a primitive dwarf elephant found on the island. . . . Almost all of the stegodon bones associated with the human artifacts are of juveniles [youths], suggesting the tiny humans selectively hunted the smallest stegodons."

—Hillary Mayell, **nationalgeographic.com,** October 27, 2004

Document D

An adult *Homo floresiensis* skull (left) beside an adult modern human skull (right)

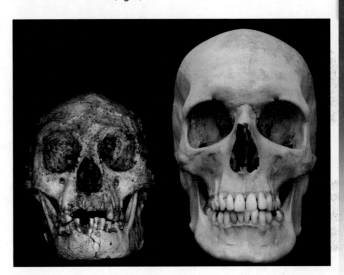

Analyzing Documents

Use your knowledge of prehistory and Documents A, B, C, and D to answer questions 1–4.

1. Documents B and C describe the discovery of
   A modern human remains.
   B australopithecine remains.
   C *Homo erectus* remains.
   D *Homo floresiensis* remains.

2. Which is NOT a theory that researchers have expressed about the tiny hominids whose remains were found on Flores?
   A The tiny hominids lived at least 13,000 years ago.
   B The tiny hominids were juveniles.
   C The tiny hominids had small heads and brains.
   D The tiny hominids hunted dwarf elephants.

3. Which is the most accurate conclusion that can be drawn from Document D about the relative sizes of *Homo floresiensis* and modern human adults?
   A Modern human adults have larger bodies than *Homo floresiensis* adults.
   B Modern human adults have larger skulls than *Homo floresiensis* adults.
   C The modern human skull pictured is larger than the *Homo floresiensis* skull pictured.
   D The *Homo floresiensis* skull pictured is older than the modern human skull pictured.

4. **Writing Task** Which information given in Documents A, B, C, and D seems the most reliable to you? Which seems the least reliable? Use your knowledge and specific information from these documents to support your opinion.

Ancient Middle East and Egypt

3200 B.C.–500 B.C.

Expanding Empires, Elite Troops

As the world's first civilizations and empires arose, military power became one of the defining aspects of success. The Persian rulers who controlled a vast empire relied on a large army that included a famous and elite branch of troops. The Greek historian Herodotus described these troops as follows:

66 This corps was known as the Immortals, because it was invariably kept up to strength; if a man was killed or fell sick, the vacancy he left was filled at once, so that the total strength of the corps was never less—and never more— than 10,000. 99

Listen to the Witness History audio to hear more about ancient Persia.

◀ The archers that emerge from the walls of the palace of Persian ruler Darius I in Susa are thought to represent the Immortals.

An ancient coin from the Persian empire

A musical instrument called a lyre from ancient Sumer

 Performance Standards

Chapter Focus Question What distinct characteristics did the early civilizations and empires of the Middle East and Egypt develop?

Section 1
City-States of Ancient Sumer
SSWH1a, SSWH1e

Section 2
Invaders, Traders, and Empire Builders
SSWH1a, SSWH1c, SSWH1d, SSWH1e

Section 3
Kingdom on the Nile
SSWH1b

Section 4
Egyptian Civilization
SSWH1b, SSWH1e

Section 5
Roots of Judaism
SSWH1c, SSWH2d

Use the ✔ **Quick Study Timeline** at the end of this chapter to preview chapter events.

The blue glass drinking vessel of an ancient Egyptian king

 Concept **Connector** ONLINE

To explore Essential Questions related to this chapter, go to PHSchool.com
Web Code: nad-0207

Sumerian depiction of a man playing a lyre (above); Sumerian lyre (right)

Ancient Times, Ancient Tunes

Music may be one of the most difficult artistic forms of early civilizations for us to find evidence of because the songs themselves leave no physical trace. But in the ruins of Sumer, the world's first civilization, archaeologists have turned up both musical instruments and artwork showing musicians playing them. Although we may never know how Sumerian music sounded, we do know that even in the world's first cities, musicians filled the air with song.

Focus Question What were the characteristics of the world's first civilization?

City-States of Ancient Sumer

 Performance Standards

• **SSWH1a** Describe religious, cultural, and economic development of Mesopotamian societies.

• **SSWH1e** Explain cuneiform writing.

Terms, People, and Places

Fertile Crescent   hierarchy
Mesopotamia   ziggurat
Sumer   cuneiform
The Epic of Gilgamesh

Note Taking

Reading Skill: Identify Main Ideas Use this concept web to record the main idea of each section of text that follows a red heading.

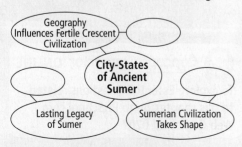

A number of early civilizations arose in the **Fertile Crescent,** a region of the Middle East named for its rich soils and golden wheat fields. Over time, nomadic herders, ambitious invaders, and traders easily overcame the region's few natural barriers. As a result, the region became a crossroads where people and ideas met and mingled. Each new group that arrived made its own contributions to the history of the region.

Geography Influences Fertile Crescent Civilization

The Fertile Crescent curves from the Persian Gulf to the eastern coast of the Mediterranean Sea. Within the Fertile Crescent lies a region that the ancient Greeks later named **Mesopotamia,** which means "between the rivers." Mesopotamia is the area of land between the Tigris and Euphrates rivers, which flow from the highlands of modern-day Turkey through Iraq into the Persian Gulf. Around 3300 B.C., the world's first civilization developed in southeastern Mesopotamia, in a region called **Sumer.**

Organizing for Floods and Irrigation Control of the Tigris and Euphrates was key to developments in Mesopotamia. The rivers frequently rose in terrifying floods that washed away topsoil and destroyed mud-brick villages. The Mesopotamian narrative poem *The Epic of Gilgamesh,* which was first told orally in Sumer, describes a great flood that destroys the world. Archaeologists have indeed found evidence that catastrophic floods occurred regularly in the ancient days of the Fertile Crescent.

To survive and to protect their farmland, villagers along the riverbanks had to work together. Even during the dry season, the rivers had to be controlled in order to channel water to the fields. Temple priests or royal officials provided the leadership that was necessary to <u>ensure</u> cooperation. They organized villagers to work together on projects such as building dikes to hold back floodwaters and irrigation ditches to carry water to their fields.

Sumerians Build Thriving Cities The Sumerians had few natural resources, but they made the most of what they did have. They lacked building materials such as timber or stone, so they built with clay and water. They used the clay to make bricks, which they shaped in wooden molds and dried in the sun. These bricks were the building blocks for some of the world's first great cities, such as Ur and Uruk.

Trade brought riches to Sumerian cities. Traders sailed along the rivers or risked the dangers of desert travel to carry goods to distant regions. Although it is unclear where and when the wheel was invented, the Sumerians may have made the first wheeled vehicles. Archaeologists have found goods from as far away as Egypt and India in the rubble of Sumerian cities.

✔ **Checkpoint** What geographic characteristics made the Fertile Crescent a good place for civilization to develop?

Vocabulary Builder

<u>ensure</u>—(en SHOOR) *v.* to make sure that something will happen

Geography *Interactive*
For: Audio guided tour
Web Code: nap-0211

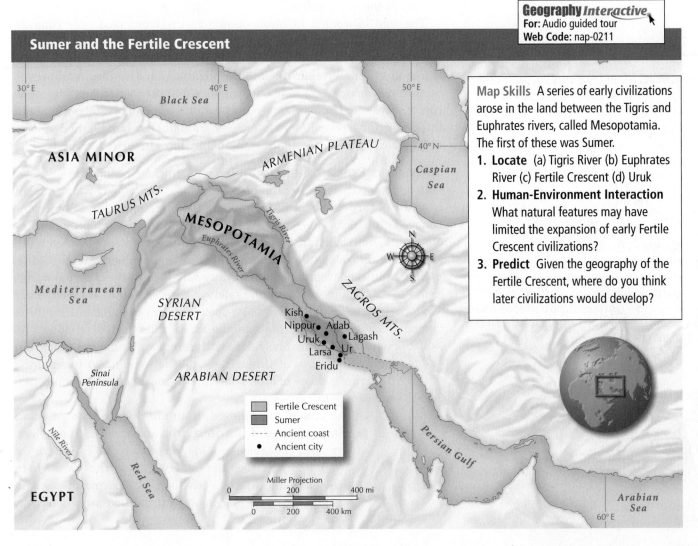

Sumer and the Fertile Crescent

Map Skills A series of early civilizations arose in the land between the Tigris and Euphrates rivers, called Mesopotamia. The first of these was Sumer.

1. **Locate** (a) Tigris River (b) Euphrates River (c) Fertile Crescent (d) Uruk
2. **Human-Environment Interaction** What natural features may have limited the expansion of early Fertile Crescent civilizations?
3. **Predict** Given the geography of the Fertile Crescent, where do you think later civilizations would develop?

Fertile Crescent
Sumer
Ancient coast
Ancient city

Miller Projection
0   200   400 mi
0   200   400 km

Sumerian Civilization Takes Shape

Within a few hundred years of its beginning, Sumer included at least 12 separate city-states. Rival city-states often battled for control of land and water. For protection, people turned to war leaders. Over time, the practice of rule by war leaders <u>evolved</u> into hereditary rule.

Complex Government Unfolds In each city-state, the ruler was responsible for maintaining the city walls and the irrigation systems. He led its armies in war, enforced the laws, and employed scribes to carry out functions such as collecting taxes and keeping records. The ruler was seen as the chief servant of the gods and led ceremonies meant to please them.

Sumerians Structure Their Society Each Sumerian city-state had a distinct social **hierarchy** (HY ur ahr kee), or system of ranking groups. The highest class included the ruling family, leading officials, and high priests. A small middle class was made up of lesser priests, scribes, merchants, and artisans. Artisans who practiced the same trade, such as weavers or carpenters, often lived and worked on the same street.

The majority of people were peasant farmers, and they formed the lowest level of society. Some had their own land, but most worked land belonging to the king or to temples. Sumerians also owned slaves. Most slaves had been captured in war. Some, though, had sold themselves into slavery to pay their debts.

The role of women in Mesopotamian society changed over time. In Sumer, goddesses were highly honored in religious practice. Perhaps because of the importance of female deities, women held a higher social standing in Sumer than in later civilizations of the region. However, Sumerian women never held legal rights equal to those of men. But some rulers' wives had supervisory powers, and a number wrote songs about their husbands, revealing to later scholars that they had learned writing and music. On rare occasion, a woman may have inherited property.

Sumerians Practice Religion Like most ancient peoples, the Sumerians were polytheistic, worshiping many gods. These gods were thought to control every aspect of life, especially the forces of nature. Sumerians believed that gods and goddesses behaved like ordinary people—they ate, drank, married, and raised families. Although the gods favored truth and justice, they were also responsible for causing violence and suffering.

Sumerians believed their highest duty was to keep these divine beings happy and, by doing so, ensure the safety of their city-state. Each city built a **ziggurat** (ZIG oo rat), a large, stepped platform thought to have been topped by a temple dedicated to the city's chief god or goddess. As well, Sumerians celebrated holy days with ceremonies and processions. In one ritual, the king went through a symbolic wedding to Inanna, the life-giving goddess of love. This rite was meant to ensure a prosperous new year.

The Sumerians believed in an afterlife. In their view, all people lived after death in a grim underworld from which there was no release. One character in *The Epic of Gilgamesh* describes the underworld as "the place where they live on dust, their food is mud, / . . . and they see no light, living in blackness / on the door and door-bolt, deeply settled dust."

Temple to the Gods
Priests and priestesses could climb stairs to the top of the ziggurat to perform rituals and prayers. The people watched from below. They also prayed and offered sacrifices of animals, grain, and wine to win the favor of the gods.

1 The Sumerians sometimes pressed tokens into the surface of a clay envelope before placing them within it, perhaps to indicate its contents.

Cuneiform Develops in Stages

Around 8000 B.C., Sumerians began using differently shaped clay tokens to represent various items of exchange, such as sheep, bread, or oil. To record economic transactions, they placed the tokens inside clay envelopes often shaped like balls. Around 3500 B.C., Sumerians began to press the tokens into clay tablets to make signs. They also started marking the clay using a sharp tool called a stylus. Around 3200 B.C., they created a true writing system that included symbols that represented words or syllables.

2 A scribe listed quantities of various commodities on this clay tablet using both token impressions and a stylus.

Cuneiform Symbol			
Meaning	Mountain	Orchard	Fish

SOURCE: Stephen Bertman, *Handbook to Life in Ancient Mesopotamia*

3 Scribes wrote cuneiform on both sides of a tablet, which was small enough to hold in one hand.

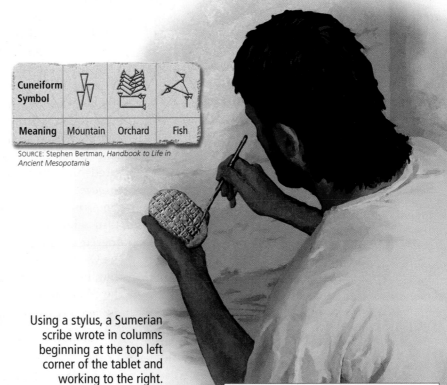

Using a stylus, a Sumerian scribe wrote in columns beginning at the top left corner of the tablet and working to the right.

Thinking Critically

1. **Draw Inferences** How do you think the use of clay shaped the writing system the Sumerians developed?
2. **Make Comparisons** How did cuneiform writing allow Sumerians to communicate more effectively than they could using tokens and clay envelopes?

Sumerians Invent Writing By 3200 B.C., Sumerians had invented the earliest known writing. It was later called **cuneiform** (kyoo NEE uh fawrm), from the Latin word *cuneus* for "wedge," because scribes wrote by making wedge-shaped marks on clay tablets. Cuneiform grew out of a system of pictographs used to record goods brought to temple storehouses. Later, the Sumerians developed symbols to represent more complicated thoughts. As their writing evolved, the Sumerians used it to record not only economic exchanges but also myths, prayers, laws, and business contracts.

Sumerian scribes had to go through years of difficult schooling to acquire their skills. Discipline was strict. Untidy copying or talking in class could be punished by caning. Students who did well often learned about religion, mathematics, and literature as well.

✓ **Checkpoint** How was Sumerian society structured?

The Story of the Stars

Mesopotamian astronomers were the first to associate many constellations with the shapes we know them for today. It was they who saw the lion in the stars we now call Leo and the scorpion in those we call Scorpio. *How do you think ancient notions of the night sky were passed on over so much time?*

▲ Leo

▲ Scorpio

Lasting Legacy of Sumer

Beginning around 2500 B.C., armies of conquering peoples swept across Mesopotamia and overwhelmed the Sumerian city-states. By 1900 B.C., the Sumerian civilization had been replaced by other civilizations and empires that you will read about in the next section.

However, Sumer left behind a lasting legacy. Newcomers to the region adopted many ideas and innovations from the Sumerians. For example, the Akkadians, Babylonians, and Assyrians adapted cuneiform so it could be used with their own languages. These peoples then helped spread Sumerian learning across the Middle East.

Over the centuries, Sumerian scholars had begun to develop astronomy and mathematics. They studied the skies and recorded the movements of planets and stars. They also established a number system based on six, dividing the hour into 60 minutes and the circle into 360 degrees, as we still do today. The Babylonians later built on this Sumerian learning to develop basic algebra and geometry, to create accurate calendars, and to predict eclipses of the sun and moon. Later peoples also elaborated on Sumerian oral narratives, such as *The Epic of Gilgamesh*, which was written down in cuneiform by both the Akkadians and the Babylonians.

In addition, by means of the various peoples who conquered the Middle East, Sumerian knowledge passed on to the Greeks and Romans. As you will read in later chapters, they, in turn, had a powerful impact on the development of the Western world.

✔ **Checkpoint**   What advances did the Sumerians make in mathematics and astronomy?

Progress Monitoring *Online*
For: Self-quiz with vocabulary practice
Web Code: naa-0211

SECTION 1

Assessment

Terms, People, and Places

1. For each term, person, or place listed at the beginning of the section, write a sentence explaining its significance.

Note Taking

2. **Reading Skill: Identify Main Ideas** Use your completed concept web to answer the Focus Question: What were the characteristics of the world's first civilization?

Comprehension and Critical Thinking

3. **Draw Inferences** Sumerians faced significant geographic challenges, such as floods. How do you think facing these challenges played a role in the formation of a strong government?

4. **Determine Relevance** How might the invention of cuneiform writing have strengthened Sumerian government and religious practices?

5. **Analyze Information** Describe ways in which later peoples built on Sumerian learning. Would this have been possible without the invention of writing?

● **Writing About History**

Quick Write: Determine the Purpose When you write a biographical essay, start by determining its purpose. For example, your purpose might be to bring attention to someone who is not well known. Another purpose might be to describe the achievements that made someone very famous. Make a list of people about whom you could write an essay for either of these purposes, or for another purpose you may want to explore.

The Epic of Gilgamesh

The Epic of Gilgamesh may date from about 2000 B.C. Many different versions of it have been found, but all are missing many lines. Thus a "standard version" has been compiled from the many versions. The result is a collection of tales about a hero named Gilgamesh, who may have been a real-life king of the Sumerian city of Uruk. In this excerpt, Gilgamesh listens to Utnapishtim (ut nuh PISH tim), a man given immortality by the gods, and is tempted to believe in eternal life. However, he comes to realize that death is the fate of all people.

Artists have depicted scenes from *The Epic of Gilgamesh* for thousands of years. About 2,500 years ago, a Persian artist created this gold plate (above) showing Gilgamesh fighting two lions. A modern-day American artist created this print (below) revealing the snake carrying away Gilgamesh's plant.

Utnapishtim said to him, to Gilgamesh: . . .
   "A secret of the gods let me tell you.
There is a plant. Its roots go deep, like the boxthorn;
its spike [thorn] will prick your hand like a bramble.
If you get your hands on that plant, you'll have everlasting life."

Gilgamesh, on hearing this, . . . bound heavy stones to his feet;
they dragged him down into the abyss[1] and he saw the plant.
He seized the plant, though it cut into his hand;
he cut the heavy stones from his feet;
the sea cast him up onto its shore.

Gilgamesh said to Urshanabi the Boatman:
"Urshanabi, this is the plant . . . by which a man can get
   life within. . . .
Its name is The-Old-Man-Will-Be-Made-Young.
I too will eat it, and I will return to what I was in my youth." . . .

Gilgamesh saw a pool of cool water.
He went down into it and bathed in the water.
A snake smelled the fragrance of the plant.
It came up through the water and carried the plant away.
As it turned it threw off its skin.

That day Gilgamesh sat down weeping.
Over his face the tears flowed.
He took the hand of Urshanabi the Boatman.
"For whom, Urshanabi, do my arms toil[2]?
For whom has the blood of my heart dried up?
I have not won any good for myself;
it's the lion-of-the ground [snake] that has won good fortune."

1. abyss (uh BIS) *n.* something that is immeasurably deep
2. toil (toyl) *vi.* to work long and hard

Thinking Critically

1. **Summarize** Why does Gilgamesh pick the plant that Utnapishtim has described? What does he want it to do for him?
2. **Analyze Literature** Which physical characteristic of a snake makes it work well as the character who ends up benefiting from the plant?

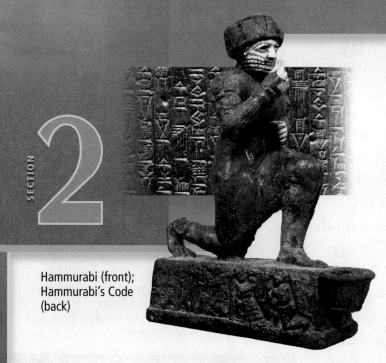

Hammurabi (front); Hammurabi's Code (back)

WITNESS HISTORY 🔊 AUDIO

Establishing the Law

To establish the law of the land, Babylonian king Hammurabi set the law in stone and placed it in public view. He began the law code with a statement of his authority:

66 Then [the gods] Anu and Bel called by name me, Hammurabi, the exalted prince, who feared God, to bring about the rule of righteousness in the land . . . so that the strong should not harm the weak; so that I should rule over the [people] and enlighten the land, to further the well-being of mankind. 99

Focus Question How did various strong rulers unite the lands of the Fertile Crescent into well-organized empires?

Invaders, Traders, and Empire Builders

 Performance Standards

- **SSWH1a** Describe Hammurabi's Code.
- **SSWH1c** Describe Zoroastrianism.
- **SSWH1d** Describe Phoenicians' impact on the Mediterranean World.
- **SSWH1e** Explain the Phoenician alphabet.

Terms, People, and Places

Sargon	barter economy
Hammurabi	money economy
codify	Zoroaster
civil law	colony
criminal law	alphabet
Nebuchadnezzar	

Note Taking

Reading Skill: Identify Main Ideas Use a table like this one to record the main idea of each section of text that follows a red heading.

Red Heading	Main Idea
First Empires Arise in Mesopotamia	
Conquests Bring New Empires and Ideas	

Through thousands of years of war and peace, the peoples of the Middle East built great empires and made long-lasting innovations. The region became a vital crossroads where warriors and traders met, clashed, and mingled. Many of the beliefs and ideas of the ancient Middle East survived to shape our modern world.

First Empires Arise in Mesopotamia

Again and again through time, nomadic peoples or ambitious warriors descended on the rich cities of the Fertile Crescent. While many invaders simply looted and burned, some stayed to rule. Powerful leaders created large, well-organized empires, bringing peace and prosperity to the region.

Sargon Builds the First Empire About 2300 B.C., **Sargon,** the ruler of Akkad, invaded and conquered the neighboring city-states of Sumer. He continued to expand his territory, building the first empire known to history. He appointed local rulers, each of whom served as king of the land he oversaw. However, the world's first empire did not last long. After Sargon's death, other invaders swept into the wide valley between the rivers, tumbling his empire into ruin.

Hammurabi Brings Babylon to Power In time, the Sumerian city-states revived, and they resumed their power struggles. Eventually, however, new conquerors followed in Sargon's footsteps and imposed unity over the Fertile Crescent. About

1790 B.C., **Hammurabi** (hah muh RAH bee), king of Babylon, brought much of Mesopotamia under the control of his empire.

Hammurabi's most ambitious and lasting contribution was his publication of a set of laws known as Hammurabi's Code. Most of the laws had been around since Sumerian times, but Hammurabi wanted to ensure that everyone in his empire knew the legal principles his government would follow. He had artisans carve nearly 300 laws on a stone pillar for all to see. Hammurabi's Code was the first important attempt by a ruler to **codify**, or arrange and set down in writing, all the laws that would govern a state.

Establishing Civil Law One section of Hammurabi's Code codified **civil law.** This branch of law deals with private rights and matters, such as business contracts, property inheritance, taxes, marriage, and divorce. Much of Hammurabi's civil code was designed to protect the powerless, such as slaves or women. Some laws, for example, allowed a woman to own property and pass it on to her children. Another law spelled out the rights of a married woman, saying that if she was found to be blameless for the problems between herself and her husband, she could leave the marriage. If she were found to be at fault, however, the law instructed that she be thrown in the river.

In general, Babylonian civil law gave a husband both legal authority over his wife and a legal duty to support her. The code also gave a father nearly unlimited authority over his children. The Babylonians believed that an orderly household was necessary for a stable empire.

Defining Crime and Punishment Hammurabi's Code also addressed **criminal law.** This branch of law deals with offenses against others, such as robbery, assault, or murder. Earlier traditions often permitted victims of crimes or their families to take the law into their own hands. By setting out specific punishments for specific offenses, Hammurabi's Code limited personal vengeance and encouraged social order.

By today's standards, the punishments in Hammurabi's Code often seem cruel, following the principle of "an eye for an eye and a life for a life." For example, if a house collapsed because of poor construction and the owner died as a result, the house's builder could be put to death. Still, such a legal code imposed more social order than existed when individuals sought their own justice.

Other Accomplishments Made by Hammurabi Although most famous for his code of laws, Hammurabi took other steps to successfully unite his empire. He improved the system of irrigation, organized a well-trained army, and ordered many temples to be repaired. To encourage religious unity across his empire, he promoted Marduk, the patron god of Babylon, over older Sumerian gods. In time, Marduk became the chief god of Babylonian worship.

✔ **Checkpoint** How do civil law and criminal law differ?

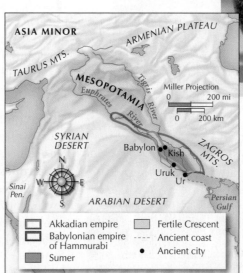

Civilizations Expand
As new civilizations took control of Fertile Crescent lands, their empires expanded but stayed near the two large rivers. Many elements of shared culture existed among these civilizations, including worship of Marduk (above), who became the region's chief god.

MAP:
ASIA MINOR
ARMENIAN PLATEAU
TAURUS MTS.
MESOPOTAMIA
Euphrates
Tigris River
Miller Projection
0   200 mi
0   200 km
SYRIAN DESERT
Babylon • Kish
Uruk •
Ur •
ZAGROS MTS.
Sinai Pen.
ARABIAN DESERT
Persian Gulf
N W E S

Akkadian empire
Babylonian empire of Hammurabi
Sumer
Fertile Crescent
---- Ancient coast
• Ancient city

Conquests Bring New Empires and Ideas

Later empires shaped the Middle East in different ways. Some conquerors, such as the Hittites, brought new skills to the region's people. Other conquerors uprooted the peoples they defeated, which had the side effect of spreading to new regions the ideas of those forced to move.

Hittites Learn the Secret of Ironworking The Hittites pushed out of Asia Minor into Mesopotamia in about 1400 B.C. They brought with them a major advancement—the knowledge of how to extract iron from ore. The tools and weapons they made with iron were harder and had sharper edges than those made out of bronze or copper. Because iron was plentiful, the Hittites were able to arm more people at less expense.

The Hittites tried to keep this valuable technology secret. But as their empire collapsed in about 1200 B.C., Hittite ironsmiths migrated to serve customers elsewhere. The new knowledge thus spread across Asia, Africa, and Europe, ushering in the Iron Age.

Assyrian Warriors Expand Ancient Knowledge The Assyrians, who lived on the upper Tigris, also learned to forge iron weapons. They had established an empire by about 1350 B.C., and by 1100 B.C., they began expanding their empire across Mesopotamia. Over the course of 500 years, they earned a reputation for being among the most feared warriors in history.

Historians are unsure why warfare was so central to Assyrian culture. Was it to keep others from attacking, or to please their god Assur by bringing wealth to the region? Whatever the reason, Assyrian rulers boasted of their conquests. One told of capturing Babylon. He proclaimed, "The city and its houses, from top to bottom, I destroyed and burned with fire."

Despite their fierce reputation, Assyrian rulers encouraged a well-ordered society. They used riches from trade and war loot to pay for splendid palaces in their well-planned cities. They were also the first rulers to develop extensive laws regulating life within the royal household. For example, women of the palace were confined to secluded quarters and had to wear veils when they appeared in public.

At Nineveh (NIN uh vuh), King Assurbanipal (ahs ur BAH nee pahl) founded one of the world's first libraries. There, he kept cuneiform tablets that he ordered scribes to collect from all over the Fertile Crescent. Those tablets have offered modern scholars a wealth of information about the ancient Middle East.

Nebuchadnezzar Revives Babylon In 612 B.C., shortly after Assurbanipal's death, neighboring peoples joined forces to crush the once-dreaded Assyrian armies. In their absence, Babylon—which a king named Nabopolassar had reestablished as a power in 625 B.C.—quickly revived under its aggressive and ruthless second king, **Nebuchadnezzar** (neb yuh kud NEZ ur). The new Babylonian empire stretched from the Persian Gulf to the Mediterranean Sea.

Rebuilding Babylon
When Nebuchadnezzar became king, he had much of Babylon rebuilt in glorious fashion. The Ishtar Gate (below) is famous for its now faded blue bricks and animals depicting various gods. *Why might Nebuchadnezzar have erected such a substantial gateway to the city and in honor of the gods?*

● **INFOGRAPHIC**

HITTITES REFINE THE HORSE-DRAWN CHARIOT

Technological advances such as the use of iron to build powerful weapons were key to the success of conquering empires. From the Hittites, other peoples picked up the use of iron and began building new tools and weapons. In the same manner, the Hittites modified a military technology invented by others—the horse-drawn chariot—to increase their own firepower capabilities.

▲ A Hittite warrior

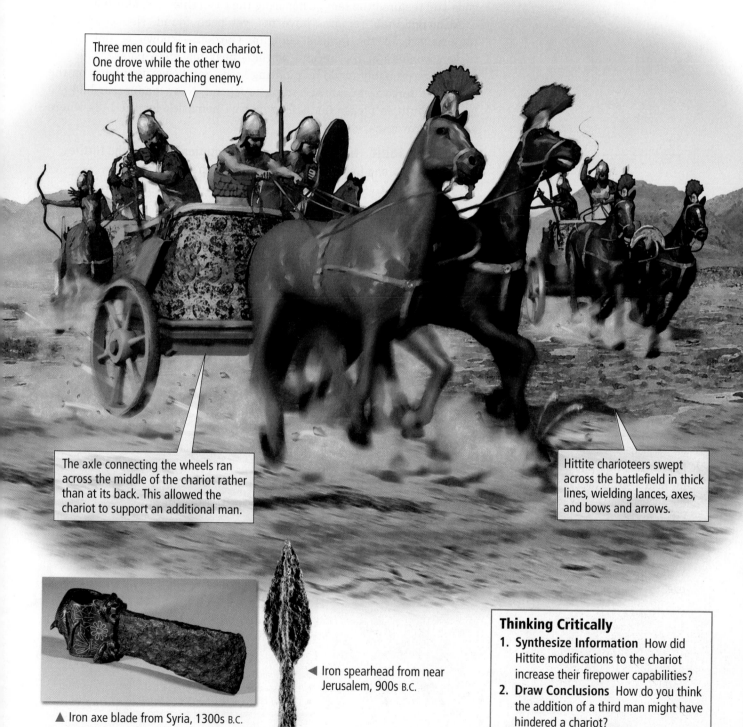

Three men could fit in each chariot. One drove while the other two fought the approaching enemy.

The axle connecting the wheels ran across the middle of the chariot rather than at its back. This allowed the chariot to support an additional man.

Hittite charioteers swept across the battlefield in thick lines, wielding lances, axes, and bows and arrows.

◀ Iron spearhead from near Jerusalem, 900s B.C.

▲ Iron axe blade from Syria, 1300s B.C.

Thinking Critically

1. **Synthesize Information** How did Hittite modifications to the chariot increase their firepower capabilities?
2. **Draw Conclusions** How do you think the addition of a third man might have hindered a chariot?

After nearly a thousand years of the city facing decline and destruction, Nebuchadnezzar oversaw the rebuilding of the canals, temples, walls, and palaces of Babylon. During his reign, the city became one of the largest and most highly regarded in the history of ancient Mesopotamia.

Nebuchadnezzar surrounded Babylon with a defensive moat and a brick wall that was 85 feet (26 meters) thick. Nine solid gateways dedicated to important gods allowed people to pass through the wall. The most famous one today, the Ishtar Gate, was made of bricks glazed bright blue and covered in lions representing the goddess Ishtar, dragons representing the god Marduk, and bulls representing the god Hadad. At the center of the city, Nebuchadnezzar enlarged and decorated the city's ziggurat to the gods and restored the temple honoring the city's chief god, Marduk.

Although their remains have not yet been found, Nebuchadnezzar may have built the famous Hanging Gardens—known as one of the "seven wonders of the ancient world"—near his main palace. The gardens were probably made by planting trees and flowering plants on the steps of a huge ziggurat. According to legend, Nebuchadnezzar had the gardens built to please his wife, who was homesick for the hills where she had grown up.

✔ **Checkpoint** Name a significant contribution made by the Hittites, Assyrians, and Babylonians after each group's conquest in the Middle East.

Assyria, Persia, and the Phoenician Colonies

Map Skills The Assyrians and Persians built huge empires in the ancient Middle East. The Phoenicians, on the other hand, had a relatively small homeland but established trade and colonies throughout the Mediterranean world.

1. **Locate** (a) Assyrian empire (b) Persepolis (c) Phoenicia (d) Carthage
2. **Movement** What information on the map supports the claim that the Phoenicians were skilled sailors?
3. **Analyze Information** Study the locations of the Persian capitals. Were they well placed for rule over the entire empire?

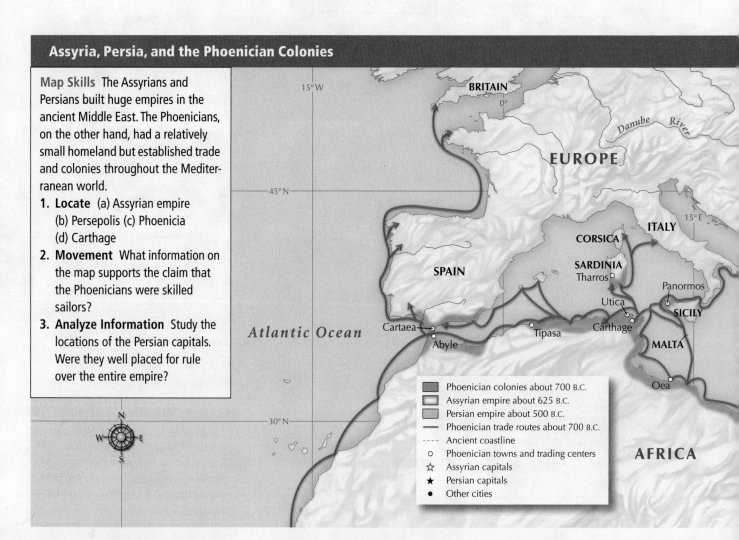

The Persians Establish a Huge Empire

The thick walls built by Nebuchadnezzar failed to hold back new conquerors. In 539 B.C., Babylon fell to the Persian armies of Cyrus the Great. Cyrus and his <u>successors</u> went on to build the largest empire yet seen. The Persians eventually controlled a wide sweep of territory that stretched from Asia Minor to India, including present-day Turkey, Iran, Egypt, Afghanistan, and Pakistan. In general, Persian kings pursued a policy of tolerance, or acceptance, of the people they conquered. The Persians respected the customs of the diverse groups in their empire.

Darius Unites Many Peoples The real unification of the Persian empire was accomplished under the emperor Darius I, who ruled from 522 B.C. to 486 B.C. Darius set up a bureaucracy, or a system of government through departments and subdivisions administered by officials who follow set rules. The Persian bureaucracy became a model for later rulers. Darius divided the empire into provinces, each called a satrapy and headed by a governor called a satrap. Each satrapy had to pay taxes based on its resources and wealth. Special officials visited each satrapy to check on the satraps.

Darius adapted laws from the peoples he conquered and, like Hammurabi, drew up a single code of laws for the empire. To encourage unity, he had hundreds of miles of roads built or repaired. Roads made it easier to communicate with different parts of the empire.

Geography *Interactive*

For: Audio guided tour
Web Code: nap-0221

Vocabulary Builder

<u>successor</u>—(suk SES ur)
n. somebody or something that follows another and takes up the same position

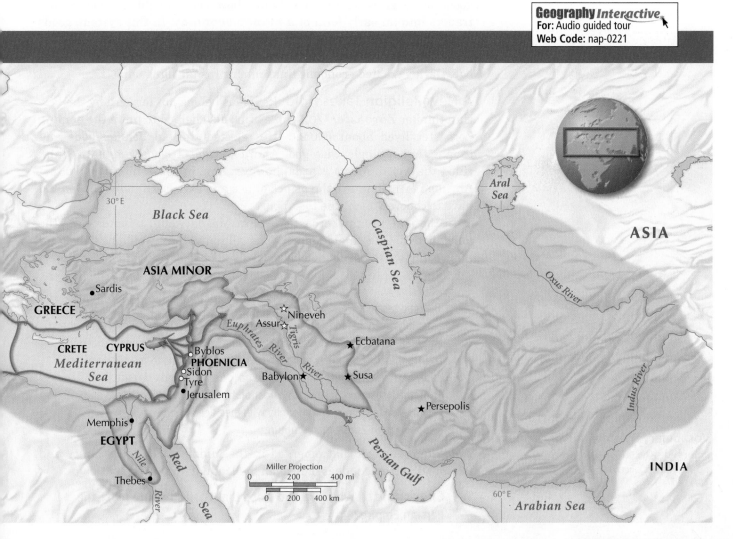

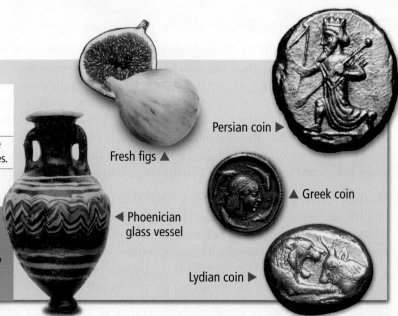

Money and Economics

Benefits of a Money Economy

- Exchanges are simplified because only one party is purchasing items rather than two.
- Comparison of items being considered for purchase is simplified because all items are given exact values.
- Money can be kept for use at a later time, whereas barter items such as live animals may not last.

Chart Skills Barter economies, in which Phoenician glassware might be traded for Israeli figs, continued to exist throughout the world. But money economies developed quickly as well, thanks to the benefits they offered to the exchange process. **What advantages did a money economy offer?**

Fresh figs ▲

Persian coin ▶

◀ Phoenician glass vessel

▲ Greek coin

Lydian coin ▶

Improving Economic Life To improve trade, Darius set up a common set of weights and measures. He also encouraged the use of coins, which the Lydians of Asia Minor had first introduced. Most people continued to be part of the **barter economy,** which means they exchanged one set of goods or services for another. Coins, however, brought merchants and traders into an early form of a **money economy.** In this system, goods and services are paid for through the exchange of some token of an agreed value, such as a coin or a bill. By setting up a single Persian coinage, Darius created economic links among his far-flung subjects.

A New Religion Takes Hold Religious beliefs put forward by the Persian thinker **Zoroaster** (ZOH ruh as tur) also helped to unite the empire. Zoroaster lived about 600 B.C. He rejected the old Persian gods and taught that a single wise god, Ahura Mazda (AH hoo ruh MAHZ duh), ruled the world. Ahura Mazda, however, was in constant battle against Ahriman (AH rih mun), the prince of lies and evil. Each individual would have to choose which side to support.

In the end, taught Zoroaster, Ahura Mazda would triumph over the forces of evil. On a final judgment day, all individuals would be judged for their actions, as described below:

Primary Source

❝ Then the assembly . . . will meet , that is, all men of this earth will stand. In that assembly, every person will see his own good deeds and evil deeds. The righteous will be as conspicuous [obvious] amongst the wicked as a white sheep among the black. . . . They will then [carry] the righteous to the abode of harmony [heaven], and cast the wicked back to the wicked existence [hell]. . . . Then [the last savior] Soshyant by order of the Creator will give reward and recompense to all men in conformity with their deeds.❞
—*Bundahishn,* Zoroastrian scripture

Vocabulary Builder

emerged—(ee MURJD) *vi.* arose, appeared, or occurred

Two later religions that emerged in the Middle East, Christianity and Islam, also stressed ideas of heaven, hell, and a final judgment day.

✓ **Checkpoint** What are two steps that Darius took to unite the Persian Empire?

Contributions of Phoenician Sea Traders

While powerful rulers subdued large empires, many small states of the ancient Middle East made their own contributions to civilization. The Phoenicians (fuh NISH unz), for example, gained fame as both sailors and traders. They occupied a string of cities along the eastern Mediterranean coast, in the area that today is Lebanon and Syria.

Expanding Manufacturing and Trade The coastal land, though narrow, was fertile and supported farming. Still, because of their location near the sea, the resourceful Phoenicians became best known for manufacturing and trade. They made glass from coastal sand. From a tiny sea snail, they produced a widely admired purple dye, called "Tyrian purple" after the city of Tyre.

Phoenicians traded with people all around the Mediterranean Sea. To promote trade, they set up colonies from North Africa to Sicily and Spain. A **colony** is a territory settled and ruled by people from another land. A few Phoenician traders braved the stormy Atlantic and sailed as far as Britain. There, they exchanged goods from the Mediterranean for tin.

Establishing an Alphabet Historians have called the Phoenicians "carriers of civilization" because they spread Middle Eastern civilization around the Mediterranean. One of the most significant Phoenician contributions to culture was their alphabet. Unlike cuneiform, in which symbols represent syllables or whole words, an **alphabet** is a writing system in which each symbol represents a single basic sound, such as a consonant or vowel.

Phoenician traders developed an alphabetic system of 22 symbols that stood for consonant sounds. Later, the Greeks adapted the Phoenician alphabet and added symbols for the vowel sounds. From this Greek alphabet came the letters in which this book is written—that is, the alphabet we use today.

Sculpture of a Phoenician trading ship from about 100 B.C.

✔ **Checkpoint** How has the Phoenician development of an alphabet been a lasting contribution to civilization?

SECTION **2 Assessment**

Progress Monitoring *Online*
For: Self-quiz with vocabulary practice
Web Code: naa-0221

Terms, People, and Places

1. For each term, person, or place listed at the beginning of the section, write a sentence explaining its significance.

Note Taking

2. **Reading Skill: Identify Main Ideas** Use your completed table to answer the Focus Question: How did various strong rulers unite the lands of the Fertile Crescent into well-organized empires?

Comprehension and Critical Thinking

3. **Demonstrate Reasoned Judgment** What do you think was the most important achievement of Sargon? Of Hammurabi? Why?

4. **Draw Inferences** How do you think the Persian policy of tolerance helped the empire grow so large?

5. **Draw Conclusions** One effect of warfare and conquest was that knowledge and beliefs spread among different peoples. How else did people of the ancient Middle East spread their ideas?

● **Writing About History**

Quick Write: Gather Information
Choose a person from this section about whom you want to write a biographical essay and list important facts about him. You may want to use the Internet or the library to gather information about the person. Include details such as when and where he was born, what he did in his life, and what he did that most interests you.

Ancient Egyptian wall painting of a man hunting birds in the marshes of the Nile

WITNESS HISTORY 🔊 AUDIO

The Gift of the Nile

Every year, as the Nile River flooded its banks, the people of ancient Egypt sang a hymn of praise. They honored the river for nourishing the land and filling their storehouses with food:

❝ But all is changed for mankind when
  [the Nile] comes. . . .
If [the Nile] shines, the earth is joyous,
every stomach is full of rejoicing,
every spine is happy,
every jaw-bone crushes [its food]. ❞
—Hymn to the Nile

Focus Question How did the Nile influence the rise of the powerful civilization of Egypt?

Kingdom on the Nile

 Performance Standards

• **SSWH1b** Describe the relationship of religion and authority in Ancient Egypt.

Terms, People, and Places

cataract	vizier
delta	Hatshepsut
dynasty	Thutmose III
pharaoh	Ramses II
bureaucracy	

Note Taking

Reading Skill: Identify Supporting Details
Use an outline like this one to record the main idea of each section of the text that follows a red heading. Include at least two supporting details for each main idea.

```
I.
  A.
  B.
II.
  A.
  B.
```

The fertile lands of the Nile Valley attracted Stone Age farmers. People migrated there from the Mediterranean area, from hills and deserts near the Nile, and from other parts of Africa. In time, a powerful civilization emerged that depended heavily on the control of river waters.

Geography Helps Shape Egypt

"Egypt," said the ancient Greek historian Herodotus, "is wholly the gift of the Nile." Without the Nile, Egypt would be just the barren desert that surrounds the river. But while the desert protected Egypt from invasion, it also limited where people could settle.

In ancient times, as today, farming villages dotted the narrow band of land watered by the Nile. Beyond the rich, irrigated "Black Land," generally no more than 10 miles wide, lay the "Red Land," a sun-baked desert that stretches across North Africa. Farmers took advantage of the fertile soil of the Nile Valley to grow wheat and flax, a plant whose fibers were used for clothing.

Yearly Floods Bring Benefits The Nile rises in the highlands of Ethiopia and the lakes of central Africa. Every spring, the rains in this interior region send water racing down streams that feed the Nile River. In ancient times, Egyptians eagerly awaited the annual flood. It soaked the land with life-giving water and deposited a layer of rich silt.

People had to cooperate to control the Nile's floods. Under the direction of early governments, they built dikes, reservoirs, and irrigation ditches to channel the rising river and store water for the dry season.

Uniting Two Regions Ancient Egypt had two distinct regions, Upper Egypt in the south and Lower Egypt in the north. Upper Egypt stretched from the Nile's first **cataract,** or waterfall, to within 100 miles of the Mediterranean Sea. Lower Egypt covered the delta region where the Nile empties into the Mediterranean. A **delta** is a triangular area of marshland formed by deposits of silt at the mouth of some rivers.

About 3100 B.C., Menes, the king of Upper Egypt, united the two regions. He founded Egypt's first capital at Memphis, a site near where the Nile empties into its delta. Menes and his successors used the Nile as a highway linking north and south. They could send officials or armies to towns along the river. The Nile thus helped make Egypt one of the world's first unified states.

The river also served as a trade route. Egyptian merchants traveled up and down the Nile in sailboats and barges, exchanging the products of Africa, the Middle East, and the Mediterranean region.

✔️ **Checkpoint** How did the yearly floods of the Nile influence life in ancient Egypt?

World's Longest River
As the world's longest river, the Nile extends about another 3,600 miles south of its first cataract, which you can see on the map. Egyptians today continue to rely on the river (above) to provide water for agriculture as well as for transportation. *Do you think Egypt was the only civilization to arise along the Nile? Why or why not?*

The Old Kingdom Forms

Scholars divide the history of ancient Egypt into three main periods: the Old Kingdom (about 2575 B.C.–2130 B.C.), the Middle Kingdom (about 1938 B.C.–1630 B.C.), and the New Kingdom (about 1539 B.C.–1075 B.C.). Although power passed from one **dynasty,** or ruling family, to another, the land generally remained united.

A Strong Government Takes Hold During the Old Kingdom, Egyptian kings, later called **pharaohs** (FEHR ohz), organized a strong, centralized state. Pharaohs held absolute power and played key roles in government and religion. Egyptians believed each pharaoh was a god. However, the pharaohs were also seen as human. People expected their pharaohs to behave morally and judged the pharaohs for their deeds.

Pharaohs of the Old Kingdom ruled by means of a **bureaucracy**—a system of government that includes departments and levels of authority. The pharaoh depended on a **vizier** (vih ZEER), or chief minister, to supervise the government. Under the vizier, various departments looked after tax collection, farming, and the all-important irrigation system. Thousands of scribes carried out the vizier's instructions.

Below the pharaoh, aristocrats, or nobles, were powerful locally. Beneath the aristocracy and a small middle class of merchants and scribes, most Egyptians were peasants, or poor farmers.

Ptah-hotep (ptah HOH tep), who lived around 2450 B.C. in Egypt, was a vizier to a pharaoh who took an interest in training young officials. Based on his vast experience of government, he wrote a book, *Instructions of the Vizier Ptah-hotep,* in which he emphasized the importance of being humble and honest, obedient to one's father and superiors, and fair in dealing with other officials of all ranks.

The Great Pyramids Are Built During the Old Kingdom, Egyptian pharaohs built many necropolises (neh KRAHP uh lis iz), or cemeteries, containing majestic pyramids in the areas surrounding Memphis. Today, the best known are the Great Pyramids that still stand at Giza. Tombs within the pyramids were considered homes in which the deceased would live for eternity. Because Egyptians believed in an afterlife, they preserved the bodies of their dead rulers and provided them with everything they would need in their new lives. Building each of the pyramids took so long that often a pharaoh would begin to build his tomb as soon as he came to power.

 Checkpoint How was Egyptian government structured during the Old Kingdom?

The Turbulent Middle Kingdom

Power struggles, crop failures, and the cost of building the pyramids all contributed to the collapse of the Old Kingdom. Then, after more than a century of disunity, new pharaohs reunited the land, ushering in a new era, the Middle Kingdom.

The Middle Kingdom was a turbulent period. The Nile did not rise as regularly as it had in the past. Corruption and rebellions were common. Still, strong rulers did organize a large drainage project, creating vast new stretches of arable, or farmable, land. During this period, the central state ended the powers and privileges of the regional aristocrats. In addition, Egyptian armies occupied part of Nubia (also known as Kush), a gold-rich land to the south. Traders also had greater contacts with the peoples of the Middle East and the Mediterranean island of Crete.

About 1700 B.C., foreign invaders called the Hyksos (HIK sohs) occupied the Nile delta region. Although the Hyksos took over the governance of Egypt, there was little conflict between the new rulers and the Egyptian people. The Hyksos awed the Egyptians with their horse-drawn war chariots. In time, the Egyptians mastered this new military technology. The Hyksos, in turn, were impressed by Egyptian civilization. They soon adopted Egyptian customs, beliefs, and even names. Finally, after more than 100 years of Hyksos rule, new Egyptian leaders arose and established the New Kingdom.

 Checkpoint In what ways was the Middle Kingdom turbulent?

New Kingdom Egypt Grows Strong

During the years of New Kingdom, a number of powerful and ambitious pharaohs created a large empire. At its height around 1450 B.C., the Egyptian empire reached as far north as Syria and the Euphrates River. The New Kingdom proved to be an age of conquest that brought Egyptians into greater contact with peoples in southwestern Asia as well as other parts of Africa.

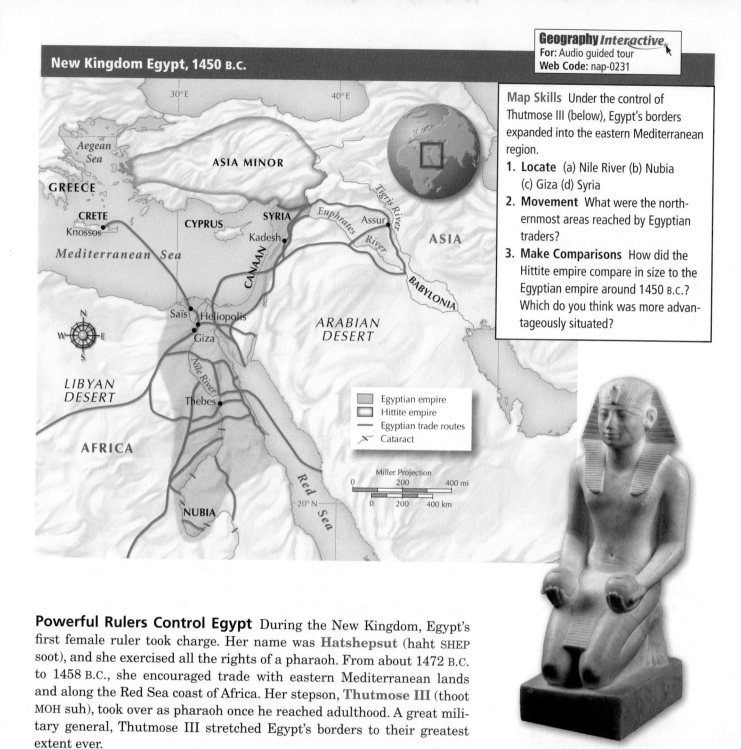

Geography *Interactive*
For: Audio guided tour
Web Code: nap-0231

Map Skills Under the control of Thutmose III (below), Egypt's borders expanded into the eastern Mediterranean region.

1. **Locate** (a) Nile River (b) Nubia (c) Giza (d) Syria
2. **Movement** What were the northernmost areas reached by Egyptian traders?
3. **Make Comparisons** How did the Hittite empire compare in size to the Egyptian empire around 1450 B.C.? Which do you think was more advantageously situated?

Legend:
- Egyptian empire
- Hittite empire
- Egyptian trade routes
- Cataract

Miller Projection

New Kingdom pharaoh
Thutmose III

Powerful Rulers Control Egypt During the New Kingdom, Egypt's first female ruler took charge. Her name was **Hatshepsut** (haht SHEP soot), and she exercised all the rights of a pharaoh. From about 1472 B.C. to 1458 B.C., she encouraged trade with eastern Mediterranean lands and along the Red Sea coast of Africa. Her stepson, **Thutmose III** (thoot MOH suh), took over as pharaoh once he reached adulthood. A great military general, Thutmose III stretched Egypt's borders to their greatest extent ever.

Much later, **Ramses II** (RAM seez) became pharaoh of the New Kingdom. He ruled for 66 years, from 1279 B.C. to 1213 B.C., and during that time pushed Egyptian control northward again as far as Syria. He may be the best known of the Egyptian rulers because he boasted of his conquests on numerous temples and monuments, although his greatest reported victory may not actually have taken place.

Egypt Battles With Its Neighbors During the reign of Ramses II, Egypt fought a number of fierce battles against the Hittites of Asia Minor. After years of fighting, the Egyptians and the Hittites signed a peace treaty, the first such document in history known to have survived. It declared that Egypt and the Hittites "shall be at peace and in brotherhood forever."

BIOGRAPHY

Hatshepsut

Hatshepsut (?1540 B.C.–?1457 B.C.) was the daughter of the pharaoh Thutmose I, the wife and widow of Thutmose II, and the stepmother of Thutmose III. Like some earlier Egyptian queens, she began ruling in the name of a male heir—her stepson—who was too young to take the throne. However, she later took the bold step of declaring herself pharaoh and won the support of key officials. Because Egyptians thought of their rulers as male, she wore a false beard as a sign of authority.

For herself and her father, Hatshepsut had constructed a magnificent funeral temple on the walls of which she left behind a record of her reign. Carvings depict a construction project as well as an expedition she sent down the Red Sea coast of Africa, which brought back ivory, spices, and incense. **For what reasons do you think Hatshepsut wanted to leave a record of her accomplishments?**

Vocabulary Builder

<u>displaced</u>—(dis PLAYSD) *vt.* took the place of somebody or something

To the south of Egypt, Nubia had developed along the Nile. For centuries, Egyptians traded or fought with their southern neighbor. From Nubia, they acquired ivory, cattle, and slaves. During the New Kingdom, Egypt conquered Nubia. Ramses II used gold from Nubia to pay charioteers in his army. Nubians served in Egyptian armies and left their mark on Egyptian culture. Much Egyptian art of this period shows Nubian soldiers, musicians, or prisoners.

Egypt Declines After 1100 B.C., Egyptian power slowly declined. Invaders, such as the Assyrians and the Persians, conquered the Nile region. In 332 B.C., the last Egyptian dynasty ended as the Greeks took control. In 30 B.C., Roman armies <u>displaced</u> the Greeks. Each new conqueror was eager to add the fertile Nile Valley to a growing empire.

 Checkpoint What role did Egyptian conquest of others play during Egypt's New Kingdom?

SECTION

3 Assessment

Progress Monitoring *Online*
For: Self-quiz with vocabulary practice
Web Code: naa-0231

Terms, People, and Places

1. What do the key people listed at the beginning of the section have in common? Explain.

Note Taking

2. **Reading Skill: Identify Supporting Details** Use your completed outline to answer the Focus Question: How did the Nile influence the rise of the powerful civilization of Egypt?

Comprehension and Critical Thinking

3. **Summarize** How did the Nile play a crucial role in uniting Egypt?

4. **Analyze Information** What knowledge did Egyptians gain from their conquerors the Hyksos? How do you think this helped them later on?

5. **Draw Conclusions** What types of information about ancient Egypt can we learn from colossal monuments such as the Great Pyramids or the building projects of Hatshepsut and Ramses II?

● **Writing About History**

Quick Write: Draw Conclusions Choose a person from this section about whom you want to write a biographical essay and draw conclusions about his or her personality traits. Consider the person's actions and what they tell you about his or her personality. You may want to use the Internet or the library to gather more information about the person.

Building the Pyramids

Building an Egyptian pyramid was costly and required great planning. For example, the pharaoh Khufu built the first and largest of the pyramids at Giza. Thousands of farmers worked on the pyramid (shown below) when not planting or harvesting crops. They had no iron tools or wheeled vehicles. To complete the pyramid, workers quarried millions of huge limestone blocks. They transported the cut stones on barges along the Nile and then pulled them on sleds up a long ramp to and around the pyramid.

Broken remain of an ancient Egyptian A-frame, used to ensure that walls being constructed were level

Great Pyramid of Khufu: Fascinating Facts*

Height	481 feet (146.5 meters)
Type of stone	Mostly limestone and some granite
Distance from limestone quarry to Great Pyramid	500 yards
Number of cut stones used	2.3 million
Average weight of one cut stone	2.5 tons
Average weight of largest cut stone	40 tons
Total weight of Great Pyramid	6 million tons
Length of construction	20–30 years
Size of workforce	20,000–30,000 workers, skilled and unskilled
Types of workers	Construction workers, carpenters, water carriers, toolmakers, potters, overseers, scribes, cooks, bakers, butchers, physicians, priests

* All figures except the Great Pyramid's height are estimated values.

SOURCES: Encyclopedia Britannica Online; NOVA Online; Kevin Jackson and Jonathan Stamp, *Building the Great Pyramid*; Tim McNeese, *The Pyramids of Giza*

Thinking Critically

1. **Identify Ideologies** What Egyptian beliefs made it seem reasonable to spend so many resources and years building pyramids?
2. **Draw Conclusions** Based on the information given here, why do you think the Giza pyramids built after Khufu's were not as large as his?

Amon-Re was associated with both the sun (shown atop his head at right) and the ram (far right).

The Greatest of Gods

In ancient Egypt, the people of each city tended to worship one god in particular over all others. In time, however, the god Amon-Re became revered as the greatest of the gods. Most importantly, people believed the pharaohs received their right to rule from Amon-Re. They said of him, "Far away he is as one who sees, near he is as one who hears." Therefore even the pharaohs had to be careful of their actions, for Amon-Re's judgment could not only alter their lives but also put their leadership in jeopardy.

Focus Question How did religion and learning play important roles in ancient Egyptian civilization?

Egyptian Civilization

 Performance Standards

- **SSWH1b** Describe the relationship of religion and authority in Ancient Egypt.
- **SSWH1e** Explain hieroglyphics.

Terms, People, and Places

Amon-Re	hieroglyphics
Osiris	papyrus
Isis	decipher
Akhenaton	Rosetta Stone
mummification	

Note Taking

Reading Skill: Identify Supporting Details Use a chart to record the main idea of each section of text that follows a red heading. Include at least two supporting details for each main idea.

Egyptian Civilization			
Red Heading	Main Idea	Supporting Detail	Supporting Detail

Religious beliefs about gods, values, and life after death affected the daily lives of ancient Egyptians. In addition, scribes used one of the world's earliest forms of writing to record information, and scholars and artists made advances in science, art, and literature.

Religion Shapes Life in Ancient Egypt

Today, much of what we know about Egyptian religion comes from inscriptions on monuments and wall paintings in tombs. These inscriptions describe Egyptians appealing to the divine forces that they believed ruled this world and the afterlife.

Chief Gods and Goddesses In the sun-drenched land of Egypt, the chief god was the sun god. During the Old Kingdom, Egyptians worshipped a sun god named Re (ray). By the Middle Kingdom, Egyptians associated Re with another god, Amon (AH mun), and called this great lord of the gods **Amon-Re.** The pharaohs, whom Egyptians viewed as gods as well as kings, were believed to receive their right to rule from Amon-Re.

Most Egyptians related more to the god **Osiris** (oh SY ris) and the goddess **Isis** (EYE sis), whose story touched human emotions such as love and jealousy. According to mythology, Osiris ruled Egypt until his jealous brother, Set, killed him. Set then cut Osiris into pieces, which he tossed all over Egypt. Osiris' wife, Isis, saved him. She reassembled his body and brought him back to life. Because Osiris could no longer rule over the living, he became god of the dead and judge of souls seeking admission to the afterlife.

To Egyptians, Osiris was especially important because, in addition to ruling over the underworld, he was also god of the Nile. In that role, he controlled the annual flood that made the land fertile. Isis had special appeal for women, who believed that she had first taught women to grind corn, spin flax, weave cloth, and care for children. Like Osiris, Isis promised the faithful that they would have life after death.

A Pharaoh Tries to Reshape Religion About 1380 B.C., a young pharaoh named Amenhotep IV (ah mun HOH tep) challenged the powerful priests of Amon-Re. He devoted his life to the worship of Aton, a minor god. The pharaoh took the name **Akhenaton** (ah keh NAH tun), meaning "he who serves Aton." He ordered priests to worship only Aton and to remove the names of other gods from their temples.

Akhenaton's <u>radical</u> ideas had little success. Priests of Amon-Re and of other gods resisted such revolutionary changes. The people, too, were afraid to abandon their old gods in favor of Aton. Nobles also deserted the pharaoh because he neglected his duty of defending the empire. After Akhenaton's death, priests of the old gods reasserted their power.

✔ **Checkpoint** Which details about the Egyptian gods show the importance of agriculture to Egyptian society?

Vocabulary Builder

radical—(RAD ih kul) *adj.* favoring or making economic, political, or social changes of a sweeping or extreme nature

How Egyptians Viewed the Afterlife

As you have read, Egyptians believed that Osiris and Isis had promised them eternal life after death. Belief in the afterlife affected all Egyptians, from the highest noble to the lowest peasant.

Proving Oneself to Osiris The Egyptians believed that each soul had to pass a test to win eternal life. First, the dead soul would be ferried across a lake of fire to the hall of Osiris. Then, the dead person's heart would be weighed against the feather of truth. Those Osiris judged to be sinners would be fed to the crocodile-shaped Eater of the Dead. Worthy souls would enter the Happy Field of Food, where they would live forever in bliss. To survive the dangerous journey through the underworld, Egyptians relied on the *Book of the Dead*. It contained spells, charms, and formulas for the dead to use in the afterlife.

The *Book of the Dead* (page shown at left) includes the Negative Confession below, which the dead could use to prove his or her worthiness to Osiris. *What sorts of crimes does the confession say one has not committed?*

> **Primary Source**
>
> ❝I have caused none to feel pain. I have made [no man] to weep. I have not committed murder. . . . I have not stolen from the orchards; nor have I trampled down the fields. . . . I have not turned back water at its springtide. . . . I am pure. I am pure. I am pure.❞
> —*Book of the Dead*
>
> ◀)) AUDIO

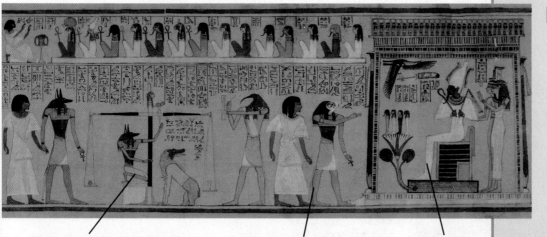

The god Anubis weighs Hunefer's heart against a feather.

The god Horus leads Hunefer to Osiris for judgment.

Osiris

History *Interactive*
For: Interactive infographic
Web Code: nap-0241

Mummification

The ancient Egyptians made a science out of mummifying the dead. Skilled embalmers extracted the brain of the dead person through the nostrils and removed most of the internal organs. They then filled the body cavity with linen and a drying powder, sprinkled spices on the body, and rubbed a mixture that kept out moisture into the skin. Later they wrapped the body in strips of linen. This costly process took months to complete.

Mummies were often laid to rest ▼ inside a nest of coffins. King Tutankhamen's coffins, shown here, were made of gold and wood and highly decorated.

◄ Mummification preserves bodies so well that even thousands of years later, they look lifelike when unwrapped.

Thinking Critically

1. **Determine Relevance** What does mummification tell us about ancient Egyptian religious views?
2. **Predict Consequences** Which fields of science do you think mummification helped the Egyptians learn about?

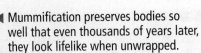

▲ Once removed from the body, the internal organs were also mummified. They were then stored in jars and placed within the tomb of the deceased.

Preparing the Dead for the Afterlife Egyptians believed that the afterlife would be much like life on Earth. As a result, they buried their dead with everything they would need for eternity. To give a soul use of its body in the afterlife, Egyptians perfected skills in **mummification** (mum uh fih KAY shun), the preservation of dead bodies by embalming them and wrapping them in cloth. At first, mummification was a privilege reserved for rulers and nobles. Eventually, ordinary Egyptians also won the right to mummify their dead, including beloved pets.

Evidence Found in the Tomb of Tutankhamen During the New Kingdom, many pharaohs were buried in a desolate valley known as the Valley of the Kings. Their tombs, known to be filled with fantastic riches, were a temptation to robbers in ancient times. As a result, most royal tombs were stripped of their treasures long ago. In 1922, however, British archaeologist Howard Carter unearthed the tomb of the young pharaoh Tutankhamen (toot ahng KAH mun), who was the son-in-law of Akhenaton. The tomb had remained almost untouched for more than 3,000 years. Its treasures have provided scholars a wealth of evidence about Egyptian civilization.

The body of the 18-year-old "King Tut" had been placed in a solid-gold coffin, nested within richly decorated outer coffins. Today, the dazzling array of objects found in the tomb fills several rooms in the Egyptian Museum in Cairo. The treasures include chariots, weapons, furniture, jewelry, toys, and games. Tutankhamen was only a minor king. We can only imagine what treasures must have filled the tombs of great pharaohs like Thutmose III or Ramses II.

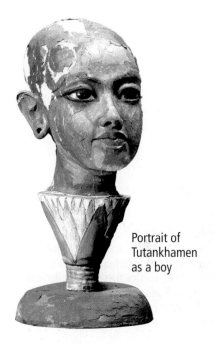

Portrait of Tutankhamen as a boy

✔ **Checkpoint** How did mummification reflect Egyptian beliefs about the afterlife?

Egyptians Organize Their Society

Like other early civilizations, Egypt had its own class system. As both a god and an earthly leader, the pharaoh stood at the top of society, along with the royal family. Directly under the pharaoh were government officials and the high priests and priestesses, who served the gods and goddesses. Next came a tiny class of merchants, scribes, and artisans. They provided for the needs of the rich and powerful. The bottom layer of society was the largest—made up of peasants who worked the land.

Most People Were Farmers Most Egyptians were peasant farmers. Many were slaves. Men and women spent their days working the soil and repairing the dikes. One ancient record describes the life of a typical Egyptian peasant. "When the water is full he irrigates [the fields] and repairs his equipment. He spends the day cutting tools for cultivating barley, and the night twisting ropes."

In the off-season, peasant men were expected to serve the pharaoh, laboring to build palaces, temples, and tombs. Besides working in the fields, women also spent much time raising children, collecting water, and preparing food.

Changes to Social Structure During the New Kingdom, social classes became more fluid as trade and warfare increased. Trade offered new opportunities to the growing merchant class. Foreign conquests brought riches to Egypt, which in turn meant more business for artisans.

These skilled craftworkers made fine jewelry, furniture, and fabrics for the palaces and tombs of pharaohs and nobles.

Egyptian Women Enjoyed Higher Status Egyptian women generally enjoyed a higher status and greater independence than women elsewhere in the ancient world. For example, Ramses II declared, "The foot of an Egyptian woman may walk where it pleases her and no one may deny her." Under Egyptian law, women could inherit property, enter business deals, buy and sell goods, go to court, and obtain a divorce.

Although there were often clear distinctions between the occupations of women and men, women's work was not confined to the home. Women manufactured perfume and textiles, managed farming estates, and served as doctors. Women could also enter the priesthood, especially in the service of goddesses. Despite their many rights and opportunities, few women learned to read and write. Even if they did, they were excluded from becoming scribes or holding government jobs.

✔ **Checkpoint** Which social class grew in size as a result of trade and warfare?

Egyptians Make Advances in Learning

Learned scribes played a central role in Egyptian society. Some kept records of ceremonies, taxes, and gifts. Others served government officials or the pharaoh. Scribes also acquired skills in mathematics, medicine, and engineering. With skill and luck, a scribe from a poor family might become rich and powerful.

Keeping Written Records Like people in other early civilizations, the ancient Egyptians developed writing. In fact, they developed multiple writing systems. The first was **hieroglyphics** (hy ur oh GLIF iks), a system in which symbols or pictures called hieroglyphs represent objects, concepts, or sounds. The Egyptians used hieroglyphs to record important economic, administrative, and royal information. Often, priests and scribes carved hieroglyphs in stone. Such inscriptions on temples and other monuments are records of Egyptian culture that have endured for thousands of years.

Around the time that hieroglyphics came into use, scribes also developed hieratic (hy ur AT ik) writing, a simpler script for everyday use. The hieratic script was a cursive form of writing created by simplifying the shapes of the hieroglyphs. Over time, hieratic script was replaced by a similar one called demotic. The Egyptians also learned to make a paperlike writing material from **papyrus** (puh PY rus), a plant that grows along the banks of the Nile. (Paper would

Simplified Writing
Because hieroglyphs took a lot of time and care to write, Egyptian scribes also developed the cursive hieratic and demotic scripts for quicker use. *How much do the cursive forms of each symbol resemble their equivalent hieroglyphs?*

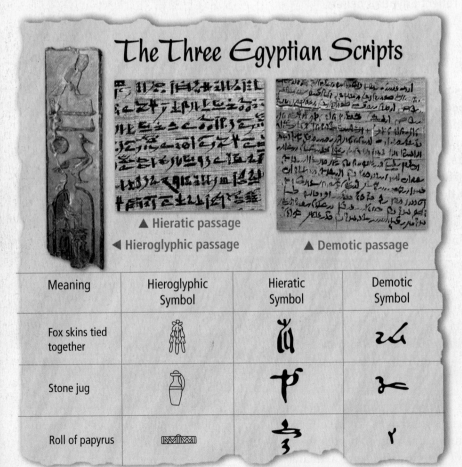

The Three Egyptian Scripts

▲ Hieratic passage

◄ Hieroglyphic passage

▲ Demotic passage

Meaning	Hieroglyphic Symbol	Hieratic Symbol	Demotic Symbol
Fox skins tied together			
Stone jug			
Roll of papyrus			

not be invented until about A.D. 100, in China.) Writing cursive scripts with reed pens and ink on the smooth surface of papyrus strips was much easier than chiseling words onto stone. When writing official histories, however, scribes continued to carve hieroglyphs.

The Clues of the Rosetta Stone After ancient Egypt declined, the meanings of ancient hieroglyphs were lost. Not until the early 1800s did a French scholar, Jean Champollion (zhahn shahm poh LYOHN), unravel the then mysterious writings on Egypt's great monuments. Champollion did so by **deciphering,** or figuring out the meaning of, passages written on the **Rosetta Stone.** This flat, black stone presents the same passage carved in hieroglyphics, demotic script, and Greek. By comparing the three versions, Champollion worked out the meanings of many hieroglyphs. As a result of that breakthrough, scholars could begin to read the thousands of surviving records from ancient Egypt.

Furthering Science and Mathematics The ancient Egyptians accumulated a vast store of knowledge in fields such as medicine, astronomy, and mathematics. Like most doctors until recent times, Egyptian physicians believed in various kinds of magic. However, they learned a great deal about the human body through their knowledge of mummification. They also became skilled at observing symptoms, diagnosing illnesses, and finding cures.

Doctors also performed complex surgical operations, which we know about today because they are described on papyrus scrolls that survived through time. Many plant parts that Egyptian doctors prescribed as medicines—such as anise, castor beans, and saffron—are still used today for various purposes.

Egyptian priest-astronomers studied the heavens, mapping constellations and charting the movements of the planets. With this knowledge, they developed a calendar that included 12 months of 30 days each as well as 5 days added at the end of each year. With a few changes, this ancient Egyptian calendar became the basis for our modern calendar.

Egyptians developed mathematics partly in response to practical problems that they faced. Flooding Nile waters forced Egyptians to redraw the boundaries of their fields each year. To do this, scholars developed geometry in order to survey the land. Egyptian engineers also used geometry to calculate the exact size and location of each block of stone to be used in construction of a pyramid or temple. Huge projects such as building pyramids required considerable skills in design and engineering.

✓ **Checkpoint** Describe three advances in learning made by the ancient Egyptians.

Ancient Medicine
Art and artifacts like the ones below have also given us clues about the medical knowledge of the ancient Egyptians. An Old Kingdom wall carving (below top) shows a wounded man walking on crutches to meet a doctor. The skillfully shaped artificial toe (below bottom) was discovered on a mummy from the New Kingdom. *What medical skills do these pieces reveal?*

Egyptians Develop Arts and Literature

The Egyptians left behind them a rich legacy of art and literature. Statues, paintings, poems, and tales have given us a wealth of information about ancient Egyptian viewpoints and values.

Egyptian Arts The arts of ancient Egypt included statues, wall paintings in tombs, and carvings on temples. Some show everyday scenes of trade, farming, family life, or religious ceremonies. Others boast of victories in battle.

Painting and sculpture styles remained almost unchanged for thousands of years. Artists always presented gods and pharaohs as much larger than other figures—size indicated the subject's importance, not his or her real size. Also, artists usually depicted people with their heads and limbs in profile but their eyes and shoulders facing the viewer.

Statues often showed people in stiff, standard poses. Some human figures have animal heads that represent special qualities. The Sphinx that crouches near the Great Pyramids at Giza portrays an early pharaoh as a powerful lion-man. Egyptians also erected many stone buildings and monuments, mostly tombs and temples.

Egyptian Literature The oldest Egyptian literature includes hymns and prayers to gods, proverbs, and love poems. Other writings tell of royal victories in battle or, like Ptah-hotep's book, give practical advice.

In Egypt, as in other early societies, folk tales were popular, especially *The Tale of Sinuhe*. It relates the wanderings of Sinuhe (SIN oo hay), an Egyptian official forced to flee into what is now Syria. He fights his way to fame among the desert people, whom the Egyptians consider uncivilized. As he gets older, Sinuhe longs to return home. The story ends happily when the pharaoh welcomes him back to court. *The Tale of Sinuhe* helps us see how Egyptians viewed both themselves and the people of the surrounding desert.

✓ **Checkpoint** What art forms were common in ancient Egypt?

Colorful Variety of Art
Ancient Egyptian artists created a great variety of colorful and intricate pieces of art, such as Thutmose III's blue glass drinking vessel (above right), the lifelike bust of Akhenaton's wife Nefertiti (above left), and Tutankhamen's decorative pectoral jewelry (right).

SECTION 4 Assessment

Progress Monitoring *Online*
For: Self-quiz with vocabulary practice
Web Code: naa-0241

Terms, People, and Places

1. What do three of the key names listed at the beginning of the section have in common? Explain.

Note Taking

2. **Reading Skill: Identify Supporting Details** Use your completed chart to answer the Focus Question: How did religion and learning play important roles in ancient Egyptian civilization?

Comprehension and Critical Thinking

3. **Predict Consequences** Egyptians believed that their pharaohs received the right to rule from Amon-Re. How do you think replacing him with the god Aton would have affected the authority of the pharaohs?

4. **Make Comparisons** How do the Book of the Dead and the tomb of Tutankhamen offer different types of information about Egyptian views of the afterlife?

5. **Summarize** What jobs were Egyptian women allowed to hold? What jobs were they not allowed to hold?

6. **Analyze Information** Considering the materials that ancient Egyptians used to create their writing and art, what do you think are the challenges of locating examples of them today?

● **Writing About History**
Quick Write: Write an Introduction
Choose a person from ancient Egypt about whom you want to write a biographical essay and write an introduction. Be sure to include a thesis statement that explains who the person was and why he or she is worth learning about. Try to find an anecdote or quotation to use to set the tone for your essay.

Moses

The One God of Judaism

❝I am the LORD your God, who brought you out of the land of Egypt, out of the house of bondage. You shall have no other gods before Me.❞
—Exodus 20:2–3

In the Hebrew Bible, God speaks these words to Moses to explain a belief that set the Israelites apart from all other people of the ancient world at that time. Instead of worshiping many gods, the Israelites prayed to just one God for guidance and protection.

Focus Question How did the worship of only one God shape Judaism?

Roots of Judaism

 Performance Standards

- **SSWH1c** Explain the development of monotheism of the ancient Hebrews.
- **SSWH2d** Explain patriarchal family.

Terms, People, and Places

monotheistic	Solomon
Torah	patriarchal
Abraham	Sabbath
covenant	prophet
Moses	ethics
David	Diaspora

Note Taking

Reading Skill: Identify Supporting Details Use a chart to record the main idea of each section of text that follows a red heading. Include at least two supporting details for each main idea.

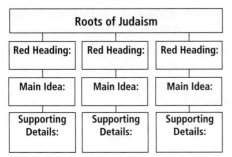

The present-day nation of Israel lies at the far western end of the Fertile Crescent, on the eastern coast of the Mediterranean Sea. About 4,000 years ago, the ancient Israelites developed the religion of Judaism, which became a defining feature of their culture. Today, Judaism is one of the world's major faiths.

The Ancient Israelites Shape a Unique Belief System

The beliefs of the ancient Israelites, also called the Hebrews, differed in basic ways from those of nearby peoples. The Israelites were **monotheistic,** believing that there was only one God. At the time, all other peoples worshiped many gods. A few religious leaders, such as the Egyptian pharaoh Akhenaton, spoke of a single powerful god. However, such ideas did not have the lasting impact that Israelite beliefs did.

The Israelites believed in an all-knowing, all-powerful God who was present everywhere. In their views, history and faith were interconnected. Each event reflected God's plan for the people of Israel. As a result, they recorded events and laws in the **Torah** (TOH ruh), their most sacred text. The Torah includes the first five books of the Hebrew Bible—that is, the books of Genesis, Exodus, Leviticus, Numbers, and Deuteronomy. The Hebrew Bible includes a total of 24 books. Additional laws and customs written down much later make up another important text, the Talmud.

✔ **Checkpoint** How did the beliefs of ancient Israelites differ from those of other nearby peoples?

The Dead Sea Scrolls

The oldest known texts of the Hebrew Bible were discovered in 1947 in a region along the northwest shore of the Dead Sea. They were written about 2,000 years ago on papyrus scrolls and bound in leather and copper. At some point, the Dead Sea Scrolls were stored carefully in clay jars and tucked away in a series of caves near Qumran, where an unsuspecting young shepherd happened upon them one day.

The caves of Qumran (above); a clay storage jar (top left); and one of the aged scrolls (bottom left)

◀ Many of the scrolls were so worn by time and weather that they had broken into many fragments, which had to be pieced back together carefully to be read.

Thinking Critically

1. **Determine Relevance** Why do you think the Dead Sea Scrolls were considered an important find?
2. **Draw Conclusions** Why might someone have decided to store these scrolls in a cave?

The Ancient Israelites

According to the Torah, a man named **Abraham** lived near Ur in Mesopotamia. About 2000 B.C., he and his family migrated, herding their sheep and goats into a region called Canaan (KAY nun). Abraham is considered the father of the Israelite people.

God Makes a Covenant With the Israelites The Israelites believed that God had made the following **covenant,** or promise and agreement, with Abraham:

> 66 You shall be the father of a multitude of nations. . . . I will make nations of you, and kings shall come forth from you. And I will establish my covenant between me and you and your descendants after you throughout their generations for an everlasting covenant, to be God to you and to your descendants after you. And I will give to you, and to your descendants after you, the land of your sojournings [short stay], all the land of Canaan. . . . 99
> —Genesis 17:4–8

God's covenant with Abraham included two declarations that became the basis of two key beliefs of Judaism. First, God declared that He would have a special relationship with Abraham and his descendants. The Israelites believed that God had chosen them to fulfill certain obligations and duties in the world. Second, God declared that Canaan would one day belong to the Israelites. As a result, the Israelites viewed Canaan as their "promised land."

An Israelite named **Moses** later renewed God's covenant with the Israelites. Genesis tells that a famine forced many Israelites to migrate to Egypt. There, they were eventually enslaved. In the book of Exodus, Moses tells the Israelites that in return for faithful obedience to God, God will lead them out of bondage and into the promised land. In time, Moses led the Israelites in their exodus, or departure, from Egypt. After 40 years, they reached Canaan, although Moses died just before they arrived.

The Kingdom of Israel Established By 1000 B.C., the Israelites had set up the kingdom of Israel. The Torah tells of twelve separate tribes of Israel that had feuded up until this time. Then **David,** the strong and wise second king of Israel, united these tribes into a single nation.

According to the Torah, David's son **Solomon** followed him as king. Solomon <u>undertook</u> the task of turning the city of Jerusalem into an impressive capital. Jerusalem was praised for its splendid temple dedicated to God, which David had begun constructing and Solomon completed. Solomon also won fame for his wisdom and understanding. Additionally, he tried to increase Israel's influence around the region by negotiating with powerful empires in Egypt and Mesopotamia.

Vocabulary Builder
undertook—(un dur TOOK) *vt.* began to do something

Israel Suffers Division and Conquest Solomon's building projects required such high taxes and so much forced labor that revolts erupted after he died about 922 B.C. The kingdom then split into Israel in the north and Judah in the south.

The Israelites remained independent for 200 years but eventually fell to more powerful peoples. In 722 B.C., the Assyrians conquered Israel. In 586 B.C., Babylonian armies captured Judah. Nebuchadnezzar destroyed the great temple and forced many of those he defeated into exile in Babylon. This period of exile, called the Babylonian Captivity, lasted about 50 years.

In 539 B.C., the Persian ruler Cyrus the Great conquered Babylon and soon freed the Israelites. Since most of them had come from the kingdom of Judah, they became known as Jews. Many Jews returned to Judah where they rebuilt a smaller version of Solomon's temple. However, like other groups in the region, they lived under Persian rule.

✔ **Checkpoint** According to the Torah, where did the Israelites go once they left Egypt? What was special to them about this place?

Judaism Teaches About Law and Morality

From early times, the concept of law was central to the Israelites. The Torah includes many laws and is thus often referred to as the Books of the Law. Some of the laws deal with everyday matters such as cleanliness and food preparation. Others define criminal acts. The Torah also establishes moral principles.

Israelite society was **patriarchal,** which means that men held the greatest legal and moral authority. A family's oldest male relative was the head of the household and arranged marriages for his daughters.

Women had fewer legal rights than men. Still, in early times, a few outstanding women, such as the judge Deborah, won great honor.

The Ten Commandments as a Guide At the heart of Judaism are the Ten Commandments, a set of laws that Jews believe God gave to them through Moses. The first four commandments stress religious duties toward God, such as keeping the Sabbath, a holy day for rest and worship. The rest address conduct toward others. They include "Honor your father and mother," "You shall not murder," and "You shall not steal."

Teaching an Ethical Worldview Often in Jewish history, spiritual leaders emerged to interpret God's will. These prophets, such as Isaiah and Jeremiah, reminded the Jewish people of their duties.

The prophets also taught a strong code of ethics, or moral standards of behavior. They urged both personal morality and social justice, calling on the rich and powerful to protect the poor and weak. All people, they said, were equal before God. Unlike many ancient societies in which the ruler was seen as a god, Jews saw their leaders as fully human and bound to obey God's law.

Jews Maintain Their Beliefs Over Time and Place For a 500-year period that began with the Babylonian Captivity, many Jews left Judah and moved to different parts of the world. This spreading out of the Jewish people was called the Diaspora (dy AS pur uh). Some Jews were exiled, others moved to farther reaches of the empires that controlled their land, and yet others moved because of discontent with political rulers. Wherever Jews settled, many maintained their identity as a people by living in close-knit communities and obeying their religious laws and traditions. These traditions helped them survive centuries of persecution, or unfair treatment inflicted on a particular group of people, which you will read about in later chapters.

Today, Judaism is considered a major world religion for its unique contribution to religious thought. It influenced both Christianity and Islam, two other monotheistic faiths that also arose in the Middle East. Jews, Christians, and Muslims alike honor Abraham, Moses, and the prophets, and they all teach the ethical worldview developed by the Israelites. In the West, this shared heritage of Jews and Christians is known as the Judeo-Christian tradition.

 Checkpoint How did the prophets help Jews uphold the law?

SECTION 5 Assessment

Progress Monitoring Online
For: Self-quiz with vocabulary practice
Web Code: naa-0251

Terms, People, and Places

1. What do many of the key terms and people listed at the beginning of the section have in common? Explain.

Note Taking

2. **Reading Skill: Identify Supporting Details** Use your completed chart to answer the Focus Question: How did the worship of only one God shape Judaism?

Comprehension and Critical Thinking

3. **Recognize Ideologies** Which events recorded in the Torah reflect the Israelite belief that God had a plan for the people of Israel?

4. **Summarize** At which points in its early history was Israel unified, divided, or ruled by outsiders?

5. **Categorize** What types of laws does Judaism uphold?

● **Writing About History**

Quick Write: Present Evidence Choose a person from ancient Israel about whom you want to write a biographical essay and present interesting biographical evidence about him or her. Start by writing a thesis statement that explains why you think this person is important. Then write a paragraph summarizing facts, details, and examples from the person's life that support the thesis statement.

Psalm 23

The Psalms are a collection of 150 religious hymns. These songs reflect the Israelites' belief in God as the powerful savior of Israel. Many of the psalms praise the faithfulness of God to each of his people. In Psalm 23, the speaker describes his faith in God's protection and celebrates the Israelites' sense of a special relationship with a loving God.

Scribes hand-wrote Hebrew Bibles from right to left on long scrolls of parchment. Medieval scribes copied religious texts and decorated the pages, as in this version of Psalm 23 from about A.D. 1280.

The LORD is my shepherd,
I shall not want;

he makes me lie down in green pastures.
He leads me beside still waters;

he restores my soul.
He leads me in paths of righteousness for his name's sake.

Even though I walk through the valley of the shadow of death,
I fear no evil;
for thou art with me;
thy rod and thy staff,
they comfort me.

Thou preparest a table before me in the presence of my enemies;
thou anointest[1] my head with oil, my cup overflows.

Surely goodness and mercy shall follow me all the days of my life;
and I shall dwell in the house of the LORD for ever.

1. **anointest** (uh NOYNT ist) *v.* to rub into a part of the body as part of a religious ceremony

Scribes still hand-write scriptures today.

Thinking Critically

1. **Analyze Information** List two lines from the song that reflect the writer's sense that he is protected by God.
2. **Analyze Literature** Why do you think the writer describes God as a shepherd?

Quick Study Guide

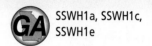

GA SSWH1a, SSWH1c, SSWH1e

Progress Monitoring *Online*
For: Self-test with vocabulary practice
Web Code: naa-0261

■ Key Civilizations

Civilization	Time Period	Notable Rulers
Sumer	3200 B.C.–1900 B.C.	
Egypt	Old Kingdom 2575 B.C.–2130 B.C. Middle Kingdom 1938 B.C.–1630 B.C. New Kingdom 1539 B.C.–1075 B.C.	Hatshepsut Thutmose III Ramses II
Akkad	2300 B.C.–2150 B.C.	Sargon
Babylon	Old 1790 B.C.–1595 B.C. New 626 B.C.–539 B.C.	Hammurabi Nebuchadnezzar
Hittite	1650 B.C.–1200 B.C.	
Assyria	1350 B.C.–609 B.C.	Assurbanipal
Israel	1000 B.C.–586 B.C.	David Solomon
Persia	539 B.C.–323 B.C.	Cyrus the Great Darius I

■ Key Innovations

Sumer: social hierarchy; cuneiform writing; advances in astronomy and mathematics
Egypt: bureaucracy; pyramids; peace treaty; mummification; social hierarchy; hieroglyphic, hieratic, and demotic writing; papyrus; advances in medicine, astronomy, and mathematics; 365-day calendar
Babylon: legal code; advances in astronomy and mathematics
Hittites: iron working
Assyrians: legal regulation of royal household; libraries
Israel: monotheistic religion, Judaism
Persians: government organized into provinces with governors; roads; common set of weights and measures; use of coins and money economy; new religion of Zoroaster
Phoenicians: Tyrian purple dye; alphabet

■ Key Causes of Rise and Fall of Civilization

- Leadership able to coordinate control of rivers (Sumer, Egypt)
- Wealth gained from economic pursuits such as trade (Sumer, Persia, Phoenicia, Egypt) }
- Conquest of existing states (Akkad, Babylon, Assyria, Persia)
- Unification of existing regions (Persia, Egypt, Israel)

→ **Rise of Civilization**

- Conquest by others (Sumer, Akkad, Assyria, Babylon, Egypt, Israel)

→ **Fall of Civilization**

■ The Rise of Civilization

3300 B.C.
City-states flourish in Sumer.

2575 B.C.
Egypt's Old Kingdom begins.

2300 B.C.
Sargon, the ruler of Akkad, conquers Sumer.

Chapter Events
World Events

3500 B.C.   **3000 B.C.**   **2500 B.C.**

2600 B.C.
Cities are built in the Indus Valley of South Asia.

Concept Connector

? Essential Question Review

To connect prior knowledge with what you have learned in this chapter, answer the questions below in your Concept Connector journal. Use the journal in the Reading and Note Taking Study Guide to record your answers (or go to www.phschool.com **Web Code:** nad-0207). In addition, record information about the following concepts:

• Geography's Impact: Tigris and Euphrates rivers

1. **Technology** Ancient Egyptians and peoples of Mesopotamia made both large and small advances in technology that helped shape their civilizations. Select three technological advances and explain the impact they had on the civilization.

2. **Belief Systems** Compare the religious beliefs of the ancient Sumerians, Persians, Egyptians, and Israelites. How did religion influence the relationship and behavior of people in these societies?

3. **Empire** Darius I is credited with unifying the peoples of the large Persian empire built by Cyrus the Great. To accomplish this, he set up a system of government called a bureaucracy. What were some of the other policies Darius I used to unite an empire that stretched from Asia Minor to India? Think about the following:
   • government
   • culture
   • transportation
   • the economy

4. **Cultural Diffusion** Give specific examples of how the rise and fall of empires contributed to cultural diffusion.

■ Connections to Today

1. **Economic Systems: Money in the World Today** The establishment of a money economy by the Persians allowed the many peoples living within the vast empire to exchange goods more easily because they shared a common currency. Today, many countries have their own unique coins and bills, so all people within each country use the same money. To sell goods or services in another country, however, people must exchange their own money for the equivalent amount of the other country's money. Do you think there should be one common world currency? Explain your answer.

2. **Geography's Impact: A Dam on the Nile** Like their ancient ancestors, modern Egyptians rely on the Nile. Nearly all Egyptians live on the 4 percent of land closest to the Nile's shores. Since 1970, when Egypt completed construction of the Aswan High Dam across the Nile, people have had year-round access to water for farming and drinking. The dam also generates half the country's electricity. However, it prevents the Nile's rich silt from reaching farmland downstream. Compare the ways in which the Nile has served as a challenge and a resource in ancient times and today.

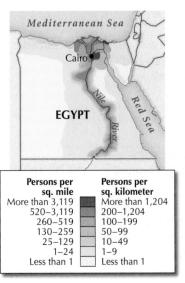

Persons per sq. mile	Persons per sq. kilometer
More than 3,119	More than 1,204
520–3,119	200–1,204
260–519	100–199
130–259	50–99
25–129	10–49
1–24	1–9
Less than 1	Less than 1

History *Interactive*
For: Interactive timeline
Web Code: nap-0261

1790s B.C.
Hammurabi, the king of Babylon, issues the first written law code.

1100 B.C.
The Assyrians expand across Mesopotamia.

1000 B.C.
The kingdom of Israel is established, and Israelite beliefs evolve into a major religion, Judaism.

522 B.C.
Darius begins to unify the Persian empire.

2000 B.C.   1500 B.C.   1000 B.C.   500 B.C.

2000 B.C.
The kingdom of Nubia develops along the Nile River in East Africa.

1766 B.C.
The Shang dynasty of China emerges.

1150 B.C.
The Olmecs build the first civilization in the Americas.

750 B.C.
Greek city-states such as Athens begin to develop.

509 B.C.
The Roman republic is founded.

Chapter Assessment

Terms, People, and Places

Match the following terms with the definitions below.

ziggurat	Hatshepsut
Torah	Osiris
prophet	colony
Zoroaster	codify
delta	dynasty
Fertile Crescent	ethics

1. moral standards of behavior
2. Egyptian god of the underworld
3. a territory ruled by outsiders
4. to arrange and set down in writing
5. the most sacred text in Judaism
6. triangular area of marshland at the mouth of some rivers
7. large, stepped platform
8. ruling family
9. Egypt's first female ruler
10. a region of the Middle East with rich soil and wheat fields
11. spiritual leader who interprets God's will
12. Persian founder of a new religion

Main Ideas

Section 1 (pp. 30–35)
13. Describe Sumer's social hierarchy.
14. How was the development of writing in Sumer influenced by economic needs?

Section 2 (pp. 36–43)
15. Explain the significance of Hammurabi's Code.
16. How did the knowledge of iron working help both the Hittites and the Assyrians to expand?

Section 3 (pp. 44–49)
17. Describe the government bureaucracy of Old Kingdom Egypt.

Section 4 (pp. 50–56)
18. Describe three gods or goddesses who were important to ancient Egyptians. How did Akhenaton try to change their roles?
19. Name an achievement the ancient Egyptians made in each of the following fields: medicine, astronomy, and mathematics.

Section 5 (pp. 57–61)
20. What did the Israelites believe God's covenant required of them?
21. How does the Torah reflect the Israelites' respect for the law?

Chapter Focus Question
22. What distinct characteristics did the early civilizations and empires of the Middle East and Egypt develop?

Critical Thinking

23. **Make Comparisons** Compare the views about the afterlife of the Sumerians, the ancient Egyptians, and Zoroaster. Point out similarities and differences.
24. **Recognize Cause and Effect** How did an Egyptian religious practice—mummification—affect the field of medicine?
25. **Analyze Information** Consider the separate inventions of writing in Sumer and in Egypt. Why do you think that, in both cases, writing continued to change in form and in use over time?
26. **Demonstrate Reasoned Judgment** Many ancient peoples, including the Babylonians, Assyrians, and Israelites, lived in societies guided by well-established laws. Do you think that having a code of laws is an essential aspect of civilization? Why or why not?
27. **Synthesize Information** Conquest by different leaders was a constant theme of life in the lands of the ancient Middle East and Egypt. In what ways did leaders unite the often distant and culturally different lands that they ruled?

● Writing About History

In this chapter's five Section Assessments, you developed skills for writing a biographical essay.

Writing a Biographical Essay Write a biographical essay on one of the following people: Nebuchadnezzar, Darius I, Hatshepsut, Solomon, or any other person mentioned in the chapter.

Prewriting
- Decide which person from the chapter interests you most. You may choose someone whose actions you admire or someone who seems particularly unique and interesting to you.
- Decide whether you want to focus more on the historical events the person took part in or on details of the person's life.
- Do research to gather facts and details about the actions or life of the person.

Drafting
- Develop a focus for your essay and choose information to support that focus.
- Make an outline organizing the events or details in a logical way, such as chronologically.
- Write an introduction, a body, and a conclusion. Be sure to use direct descriptions, quotations, and anecdotes.

Revising
- Use the guidelines for revising your report on page SH19 of the Writing Handbook.

Prepare for the GHSGT

War in the Ancient Middle East

Military campaigns were conducted frequently in the ancient Middle East. Scribes and artists often recorded their leaders' victories on monuments. The following documents reveal that these early wars were both devastating and widespread.

Document A

". . . [My troops] were like lions roaring upon the mountaintops. The chariotry consisted of runners, of picked men, of every good and capable chariot-warrior. The horses were quivering in every part of their bodies, prepared to crush the foreign countries under their hoofs. . . . Those who reached my frontier, . . . their heart and their soul are finished forever and ever. Those who came forward together on the sea, the full flame was in front of them at the river-mouths, while a stockade of lances surrounded them on the shore. . . . I have made the lands turn back from (even) mentioning Egypt; for when they pronounce my name in their land, then they are burned up."

—From Pharaoh Ramses III of Egypt

Document B

"In the eighteenth year of my rule I crossed the Euphrates for the sixteenth time. [King] Hazael of Damascus put his trust upon his numerous army and called up his troops in great number. . . . I fought with him and inflicted a defeat upon him, killing with the sword 16,000 of his experienced soldiers. I took away from him 1,121 chariots, 470 riding horses as well as his camp. . . . I followed him and besieged him in Damascus, his royal residence. I cut down his gardens. . . . I marched as far as the mountains of Hauran, destroying, tearing down and burning innumerable towns, carrying booty away from them which was beyond counting. I marched as far as the mountains of Ba'li-ra'si . . . and erected there a stela [stone pillar] with my image as king."

—From King Shalmaneser III of Assyria

Document C
Soldiers of Ramses III in Battle

Document D
Soldiers of Shalmaneser III in Battle

Analyzing Documents

Use your knowledge of ancient warfare and Documents A, B, C, and D to answer questions 1–4.

1. Documents A and B are told from the point of view of
   A a victim of an ambush.
   B the ally of a conquering ruler.
   C the enemy of a conquering ruler.
   D the leader of a successful campaign.

2. What did the narrator of Document B do in the mountains of Ba'li-ra'si after he conquered the king of Damascus?
   A conquer a great city
   B set up a monument showing his image
   C chase the enemies' leader
   D receive tribute from the conquered people

3. Which can you learn from Documents C and D?
   A who won each battle shown
   B how many men fought in each battle
   C where each battle took place
   D what weapons the soldiers used in battle

4. **Writing Task** Consider that inscriptions and artwork were two different means for rulers to tell their people about their conquests. What motives would have led the rulers to have such documents created? Do you think such documents serve as reliable records of historical events? Use your knowledge and specific information from these documents to support your opinion.

A Life-Size Legacy

China's first emperor, who took power in 221 B.C., later built a tomb that astonished archaeologists when they uncovered it more than 2,000 years later. He had buried himself with a life-size clay army of 6,000 soldiers and horses. The Chinese historian Sima Qian described the construction of the tomb:

66 The labourers . . . built models of palaces, pavilions, and offices and filled the tomb with fine vessels, precious stones, and rarities. . . . With quicksilver [mercury] the various waterways of the empire . . . were created and made to flow and circulate mechanically. With shining pearls the heavenly constellations were depicted above, and with figures of birds in gold and silver and of pine trees carved of jade the earth was laid out below. 99

Listen to the Witness History audio to hear more about this remarkable tomb.

◄ Artists constructed each soldier by hand, so that no two are identical.

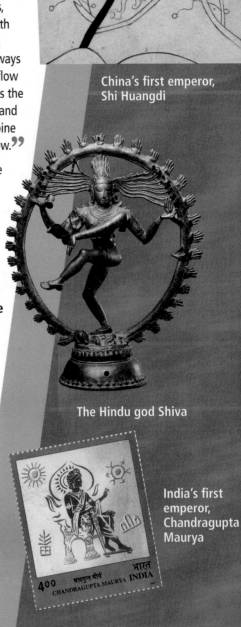

China's first emperor, Shi Huangdi

The Hindu god Shiva

 Performance Standards

Chapter Focus Question In what ways did the civilizations and empires of ancient India and China lay long-lasting social and political foundations?

Section 1
Early Civilizations of India and Pakistan
SSWH2a

Section 2
Hinduism and Buddhism SSWH2b

Section 3
Powerful Empires of India SSWH2a

Section 4
Rise of Civilization in China SSWH2c, SSWH2d, SSWH2e

Section 5
Strong Rulers Unite China SSWH2b, SSWH2c, SSWH2d, SSWHRC1c

India's first emperor, Chandragupta Maurya

Use the ☑ **Quick Study Timeline** at the end of this chapter to preview chapter events.

❓ Concept Connector ONLINE

To explore Essential Questions related to this chapter, go to PHSchool.com Web Code: nad-0307

Indus clay figurine

Indus stone bust, possibly of a priest or ruler

WITNESS HISTORY 🔊 AUDIO

Forgotten Civilization Discovered

❝ Not often has it been given to archaeologists . . . to light upon the remains of a long-forgotten civilisation. It looks, however, at this moment, as if we were on the threshold of such a discovery in the plains of the Indus.

Up to the present our knowledge of Indian antiquities [ancient history] has carried us back hardly further than the third century [B.C.]. Of the long ages before the coming of the Greeks and the rise of the Maurya dynasty; of the birth and growth of civilisation in the great river basins . . . archaeology has given us but the faintest glimmerings. ❞
—Sir John Marshall, Director General of Archaeology in India, 1924

Focus Question How have scholars learned about India's first two civilizations, the Indus and the Aryan?

Early Civilizations of India and Pakistan

 Performance Standards

• **SSWH2a** Describe development of Indian civilization.

Terms, People, and Places

subcontinent	Mohenjo-Daro	Indra
plateau	veneration	brahman
monsoon	Vedas	mystic
Harappa	rajah	acculturation

N*o*te Taking

Reading Skill: Recognize Sequence Keep track of the sequence of important events in early India by recording them in the order they occurred.

Date	Event

In the early 1900s, archaeologists digging in the Indus River valley of Pakistan made some startling discoveries. They unearthed bricks, small clay seals, figurines, and other artifacts dissimilar in style to any they had seen before. The archaeologists soon realized they had uncovered a civilization that had flourished 4,500 years earlier. It had been unknown to the world ever since.

Geography of the Indian Subcontinent

The Indus Valley is located in the region known as South Asia, or the Indian subcontinent. A **subcontinent** is a large landmass that juts out from a continent. The Indian subcontinent is a huge peninsula extending into the Indian Ocean. Today, it includes three of the world's ten most populous countries—India, Pakistan, and Bangladesh—as well as the island nation of Sri Lanka (sree LAHNG kuh) and the mountain nations of Nepal and Bhutan.

\Towering, snow-covered mountain ranges mark the northern border of the subcontinent, including the Hindu Kush and the Himalayas. These mountains limited contacts with other lands, leaving India's distinct culture to develop on its own. However, the mountains were not a complete barrier. Steep passes through the Hindu Kush served as gateways to migrating and invading peoples for thousands of years.

Natural Features Define Regions The Indian subcontinent is divided into three major zones: the fertile Gangetic Plain in the north, the dry Deccan plateau, and the coastal plains on either side of the Deccan.

The Gangetic Plain lies just south of the Himalayas. This fertile region is watered by mighty rivers: the Indus, which gives India its name, the Ganges (GAN jeez), and the Brahmaputra (brah muh POO truh). These rivers and their tributaries carry melting snow from the mountains to the plains, making agriculture possible.

The Deccan is a **plateau**, or raised area of level land, that juts into the Indian Ocean. Much of it lacks the melting snows that feed the rivers of the north and provide water for irrigation. As a result, parts are arid, agriculturally unproductive, and sparsely populated.

The coastal plains are separated from the Deccan by low-lying mountain ranges, the Eastern and Western Ghats. Rivers and heavy seasonal rains provide water for farmers. Also, from very early times, people in this region used the seas for fishing and as highways for trade.

Monsoons Affect Climate A defining feature of life in the Indian subcontinent is the **monsoons**, or seasonal winds that regularly blow from a certain direction for part of the year. In October, the winter monsoons blow from the northeast, bringing hot, dry air that withers crops. In mid-June, the summer monsoons blow from the southwest. They pick up moisture over the Indian Ocean and drench the land with downpours.

The monsoons have shaped Indian life. Each year, people welcome the rains that are desperately needed to water the crops. If the rains are late, famine and starvation may occur. However, if the rains are too heavy, rushing rivers will unleash deadly floods.

✓ **Checkpoint** How has geography affected where people live in the Indian subcontinent?

Geography *Interactive*
For: Audio guided tour
Web Code: nap-0311

Indus Civilization

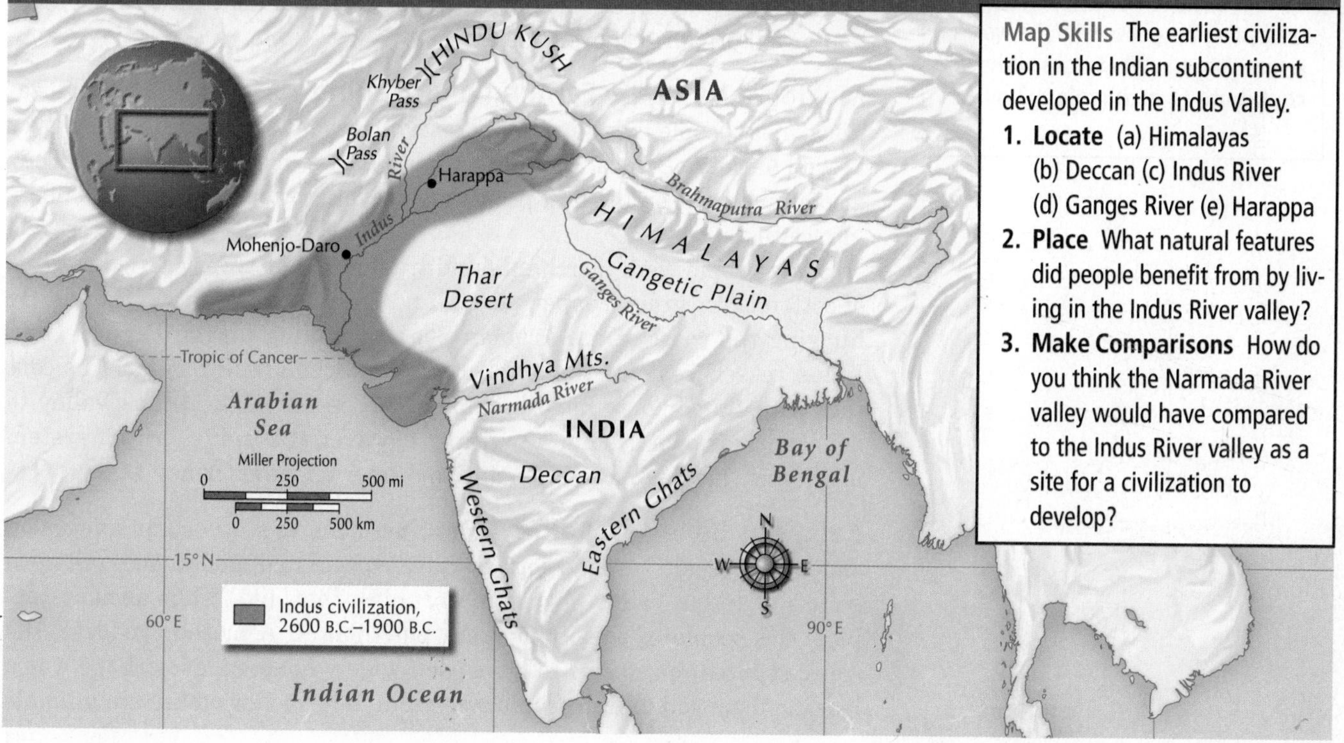

Map Skills The earliest civilization in the Indian subcontinent developed in the Indus Valley.
1. **Locate** (a) Himalayas (b) Deccan (c) Indus River (d) Ganges River (e) Harappa
2. **Place** What natural features did people benefit from by living in the Indus River valley?
3. **Make Comparisons** How do you think the Narmada River valley would have compared to the Indus River valley as a site for a civilization to develop?

Mortimer Wheeler

Much of what we know about Indus civilization comes from the work of Sir Mortimer Wheeler (1890–1976), who directed the excavations of Harappa and Mohenjo-Daro in the 1940s. Previously, Wheeler had led one of England's first university archaeology departments, run a museum, and headed the first archaeological excavation to use trained volunteers rather than untrained laborers.

As well, through publications and frequent appearances on popular radio and television shows, Wheeler inspired thousands of people to visit his research sites. Indeed, Wheeler succeeded in fascinating the public with the work of archaeologists. **What did Wheeler contribute to archaeology?**

Indus Civilization Rises and Falls

About 2600 B.C., the earliest South Asian civilization emerged in the Indus River valley, in present-day Pakistan. The Indus civilization flourished for about 700 years. However, only since the 1920s have its once-prosperous cities emerged beneath the archaeologists' picks and shovels.

Archaeologists have investigated numerous Indus sites. Unfortunately, they have not yet turned up any names of kings or queens, tax records, literature, or accounts of famous victories. The written remains of Indus civilization are found only rarely, usually on small clay seals that do not include any long passages. Still, we do know that the Indus Valley civilization covered the largest area of any civilization until the rise of Persia more than 1,000 years later. We know, too, that its cities rivaled those of Sumer.

Well-Planned Cities Reveal Organized Government Archaeologists' investigations in recent years have led them to believe that at least five large cities may have been prominent during the course of the civilization's history. A few hundred smaller sites have also been studied. Since their discovery in the 1920s, the Indus cities of **Harappa** and **Mohenjo-Daro** (moh HEN joh DAH roh) have been considered possible twin capitals of the civilization or cities that ruled the area one after the other. Both were large, some three miles in circumference. Each was dominated by a massive hilltop structure whose exact purpose is unknown. Each city also included a huge warehouse used for storage.

A notable feature of Mohenjo-Daro and a few smaller sites is how carefully planned they were. Mohenjo-Daro was laid out in an organized pattern, with long, wide main streets and large rectangular blocks. Most of its houses were built with baked clay bricks of a standard size. At Harappa and other Indus sites, mud and unbaked bricks were also common building materials. In addition, Indus houses had complex plumbing systems, with baths, drains, and water chutes that led into sewers beneath the streets. Indus merchants used a uniform system of weights and measures. From such evidence, archaeologists have concluded that these Indus cities had a well-organized government.

Making a Living by Farming and Trading As in other early civilizations, most people living in the Indus civilization were farmers. They grew a wide variety of crops, including wheat, barley, melons, and dates. They also may have been the first people to cultivate cotton and weave its fibers into cloth.

Some people were merchants and traders. Their ships carried cargoes of cotton cloth, grain, copper, pearls, and ivory combs to distant lands. By hugging the coast of the Arabian Sea and sailing up the Persian Gulf, Indus vessels reached the cities of Sumer. Scholars think that this contact with Sumer may have prompted the people of the Indus Valley to develop their own system of writing; however, the Indus writing system is unique, showing no relationship to Sumerian cuneiform.

Religious Beliefs Develop From clues such as statues and images on small clay seals, archaeologists have speculated about the religious beliefs of Indus Valley people. Many think that, like other ancient peoples, the people of the Indus were polytheistic. A mother goddess, the source of creation, seems to have been widely honored, as perhaps was a leading male god. Indus people also seem to have viewed certain animals as sacred, including the buffalo and the bull. Some scholars think these early practices influenced later Indian beliefs, especially the **veneration** of, or special regard for, cattle.

Indus Civilization Declines By 1900 B.C., the quality of life in the Indus Valley was declining. Crude pottery replaced the finer works of earlier days. The use of writing halted. Mohenjo-Daro was entirely abandoned. The populations of the other Indus cities and towns also dwindled to small numbers.

Scholars do not know for sure what happened to the Indus civilization, but they have offered several explanations for its decline. They once thought that invaders attacked and overran the cities of the Indus, but this now seems unlikely. Some suggest that damage to the local environment was a factor. Possibly too many trees were cut down to fuel the ovens of brick makers. Tons of river mud found in the streets of Mohenjo-Daro suggest a major flood. Other evidence points to a devastating earthquake. Today scholars think that some of these events may have worked together to bring an end to Indus civilization.

✔ **Checkpoint** What evidence shows that Indus civilization included a well-organized government?

The Remnants of Indus Civilization

Archaeologists have considered numerous explanations for how the Indus civilization ended, but most agree that there was likely not one single cause. While people did continue to live in the Indus Valley, the basic features of civilization dwindled away as they returned to simpler ways of life. Read the primary source at right. *What types of evidence did archaeologists stop finding after the Indus civilization's decline?*

▲ The Indus people carved seals with writing and depictions of animals.

The ruins of Mohenjo-Daro still stand today. ▼

▲ The Indus people developed standardized cubic weights to measure the masses of various objects.

Primary Source

❝The Indus Civilization remains an historical enigma [puzzle]. A remarkably uniform [culture], distributed over a vast geographical area, utterly disappears without an apparent successor. Cities, writing, the high achievement of their crafts, the use of standardized weights, long distance trade with the Gulf, and their exceptional system of urban sanitation simply disappear from the South Asian social landscape. [These were] replaced by what had existed before: regionally distinctive cultures inhabiting small villages with a limited scattering of modest sized towns that [were] wholly distinctive from that of the Indus Civilization.❞
—Carl Lamberg-Karlovsky, archaeologist

Aryan Civilization Develops During the Vedic Age

During the centuries between 2000 B.C. and 1500 B.C., waves of nomadic peoples migrated slowly with their herds of cattle and horses from Central Asia. They traveled through the mountain passes into northwestern India.

Aryans Emerge in India These nomads belonged to one of many groups of speakers of Indo-European languages who migrated across Europe and Asia. The nomads intermarried with local peoples to form a group who called themselves Aryans. Through **acculturation,** or the blending of two or more cultures, the Aryans combined the cultural traditions of the nomads with those of earlier Indian peoples.

The early Aryans in India built no cities and left behind very little archaeological evidence. Most of what we know about them comes from the **Vedas,** a collection of hymns, chants, ritual instructions, and other religious teachings. Aryan priests memorized and recited the Vedas for a thousand years before they ever wrote down these sacred teachings. This period, from 1500 B.C. to 500 B.C., is often called the Vedic Age.

In the Vedas, the Aryans appear as warriors who fought in chariots with bows and arrows. They loved food, drink, music, chariot races, and dice games. These nomadic herders valued cattle, which provided them with food and clothing. Later, when they became settled farmers, families continued to measure their wealth in cows and bulls.

From Nomadic Life to Farming Gradually, the Aryans gave up their nomadic ways and settled into villages to cultivate crops and breed cattle. From local farmers, the Aryans learned to raise crops. They also took up other skilled crafts.

In time, the Aryans spread eastward to colonize the heavily forested Ganges basin. By about 800 B.C., they learned to make tools out of iron. Equipped with iron axes and weapons, restless pioneers carved farms and villages out of the rain forests of the northeast.

Aryan tribes were led by chiefs who were called **rajahs.** A rajah, who was often the most skilled war leader, had been elected to his position by an assembly of warriors. As he ruled, he considered the advice of a council of elders made up of the heads of families. Rajahs often fought with one another to control trade and territory across the Gangetic Plain.

Some rajahs became powerful hereditary rulers, extending their influence over many villages.

Aryans Structure Society From the Vedas, we learn that the Aryans divided their society into ranked groups based on occupation. The highest group was made up of the Brahmins, or priests. Next came the Kshatriyas (kuh SHAT ree yuhz), or warriors. The third group, the Vaisyas (VYS yuz), included herders, farmers, artisans, and merchants. The Aryans separated people who had little or no Aryan heritage into a fourth group, the Sudras (SOO druz). This group included farmworkers, servants, and other laborers. The lowest social group, the dalits (DAH lits), was considered outside of the caste system. These people did work that others wouldn't, such as making leather from animal skins.

The gods' creation of the universe is described in the *Rig Veda.* It says they divided the body of Purusha, the first man, into four parts to create the four social groups of ancient India. Which parts of the body became the warriors?

Primary Source

66 When they divided Purusha, in how many different portions did they arrange him? What became of his mouth, what of his two arms? What were his two thighs and his two feet called?

His mouth became the Brahmin; his two arms were made into the Rajanya [Kshatriya]; his two thighs the Vaisya; from his two feet the Sudra was born.99

—*Rig Veda,* "Hymn of Man"

Aryan Religious Beliefs Develop

The Aryans were polytheistic. They worshiped gods and goddesses who <u>embodied</u> natural forces such as sky, sun, storm, and fire. The chief Aryan deity was fierce **Indra,** the god of war. Indra's weapon was the thunderbolt, which he used not only to destroy demons but also to announce the arrival of rain, so vital to Indian life. Other major gods included Varuna, the god of order and creation, and Agni, the god of fire and the messenger who communicated human wishes to the gods. The Aryans also honored animal deities, such as monkey and snake gods.

Brahmins offered sacrifices of food and drink to the gods. Through the correct rituals and prayers, the Aryans believed, they could call on the gods for health, wealth, and victory in war.

As the lives of the Aryans changed, so, too, did their beliefs. Some religious thinkers were moving toward the notion of **brahman,** a single spiritual power that existed beyond the many gods of the Vedas and that resided in all things. There was also a move toward mysticism. **Mystics** are people who seek direct communion with divine forces. Aryan mystics practiced meditation and yoga, spiritual and bodily disciplines designed to enhance the attempt to achieve direct contact with the divine. The religions that emerged in India after the Vedic Age were influenced by both mysticism and the notion of brahman.

✔ **Checkpoint** How were Aryan society and government structured?

Vocabulary Builder

<u>embodied</u>—(em BAH deed) *vt.* gave a visible form to something abstract

Communing With the Divine
Below, a young woman in China practices yoga, which is popular around the world today. At left, a 1,500-year-old Indian sculpture shows a Hindu man seated in a traditional meditation pose. Meditation, too, is still practiced by many people. *Why do you think these disciplines have appealed to people for so long?*

Epic Literature Tells About Aryan Life

By 500 B.C., Indian civilization consisted of many rival kingdoms. Archaeologists have learned that cities were growing rapidly at this time as people left the countryside to practice skilled crafts. By this time, too, the written language, Sanskrit, that priests had used to write sacred texts began to flourish in literary usage.

The Aryans maintained a strong oral tradition as well. They continued to memorize and recite ancient hymns, as well as two long epic poems, the *Mahabharata* (muh hah BAH rah tuh) and the *Ramayana* (rah MAH yuh nuh). Like the Sumerian *Epic of Gilgamesh*, the Indian epics mix history, mythology, adventure, and religion.

***Mahabharata* Tells of Warfare and Religion** The *Mahabharata* is India's greatest epic. Through its nearly 100,000 verses, we hear echoes of the battles that rival Aryan tribes fought to gain control of the Ganges region. Five royal brothers, the Pandavas, lose their kingdom to their cousins. After a great battle that lasts 18 days, the Pandavas regain their kingdom and restore peace to India. One episode, a lengthy poem known as the *Bhagavad-Gita* (BUG uh vud GEE tuh), reflects important Indian religious beliefs about the immortality of the soul and the value of performing one's duty. In its verses, the god Krishna instructs Prince Arjuna on the importance of duty over personal desires and ambitions.

***Ramayana* Teaches Values of Behavior** The *Ramayana* is much shorter but equally memorable. It recounts the fantastic deeds of the daring hero Rama and his beautiful bride Sita. Early on, Sita is kidnapped by the demon-king Ravana. The rest of the story tells how Rama finally rescues Sita with the aid of the monkey general Hanuman.

Like the Aryan religion, these epics evolved over thousands of years. Priest-poets added new morals to the tales to teach different lessons. For example, they pointed to Rama as a model of virtue or as an ideal king. Likewise, Sita came to be honored as an ideal woman who remained loyal and obedient to her husband through many hardships.

 Checkpoint What types of values are revealed in Indian epics?

SECTION 1 Assessment

Terms, People, and Places

1. Place each of the key terms at the beginning of the section into one of the following categories: politics, culture, or geography. Write a sentence for each term explaining your choice.

Note Taking

2. **Reading Skill: Recognize Sequence**
Use your completed chart to answer the Focus Question: How have scholars learned about India's first two civilizations, the Indus and the Aryan?

Comprehension and Critical Thinking

3. **Analyze Information** Describe two ways in which geography and climate have influenced the people of the Indian subcontinent.

4. **Recognize Sufficient Evidence** What types of evidence do you think archaeologists should look for to explain how the Indus civilization declined and became unknown to the world for 4,000 years?

5. **Draw Conclusions** How reliably do you think epic literature tells us about Aryan life?

● Writing About History

Quick Write: Draft a Main Idea On some essay tests, you may be asked to choose one of several topics to write about. You may find it easiest to select the topic for which you can most quickly develop a main idea statement. Choose one of the following topics and draft a main idea statement for it:
• the decline of the Indus civilization
• the role(s) of the Vedas in Aryan history
• the nature of Aryan religious beliefs

The *Mahabharata*

An epic of the ancient Aryans, the *Mahabharata* has served as a major source of social and religious doctrine for India for many hundreds of years. Indian storytellers still recite segments of the 100,000 stanzas to entertain and instruct village audiences. This excerpt tells of the rewards the god Indra bestows upon a dutiful king, Vasu, who upholds the law of the gods.

GA SSWH2a, SSWHRC1b

▲ A central theme of the *Mahabharata* is battle between feuding families. Here we see two of the victors, Arjuna and Krishna, preparing to fight.

*I*ndra said:

May never on earth, O lord of this earth, the Law be confused! Protect it, for the upheld Law holds up all the world. Guard the this-worldly Law, forever on guard and attentive; if yoked[1] to the Law, you shall win the blessed worlds of eternity. You standing on earth have become the dear friend of me standing in heaven—now possess . . . a country that is the udder of earth, abounding in cattle and holy, of stable [climate], with wealth and rice aplenty, protected by the skies. . . . It is a country beyond all others, with riches and jewels and all good things. . . .

The country people are accustomed to the Law, quite content and upright. No lies are spoken there even in jest, let alone in earnest. Sons are devoted to their elders there; they do not divide off from their fathers. Cows are never yoked to the cart, and even lean cows yield plenty. All the classes abide by[2] their own Law, in this land. . . .

This large celestial[3] crystalline chariot in the sky, which it is the God's privilege to enjoy, this airborne chariot will come to you as my gift. Among all mortals you alone shall stand upon a grand and sky-going chariot, and indeed, you will ride there above, like a God come to flesh! And I give you this garland Vaijayanti, woven of lotuses that never fade, which shall sustain you in battle, never hurt by swords. That shall be your mark of distinction here, sovereign of men—grand, rich, unmatched, and renowned[4] as "Indra's Garland"!

▲ Indra

1. **yoked** (yohkd) *vt.* joined or linked forcibly
2. **abide by** (uh BYD by) *vi.* to accept and submit to
3. **celestial** (suh LES chul) *adj.* belonging to, suitable for, in, or typical of heaven
4. **renowned** (rih NOWND) *adj.* well known or famous

Thinking Critically
1. **Identify Central Issues** What seems to be the king's most important function, and why do you think it is so significant?
2. **Synthesize Information** What rewards does Indra say Vasu will receive for pleasing the gods?

A woman prays in the Ganges (right). The colors of marigolds floating in the water (left) have symbolic meaning.

WITNESS HISTORY 🔊 AUDIO

River Waters Bring Salvation

❝ Thus said the God of Fire:—Now I shall describe the sanctity of the river Ganges, which imparts to men enjoyment of earthly cheers in this life and salvation in the next. The countries which the Ganges meanders through should be deemed as hallowed [holy] grounds. The river Ganges is the earthly door to salvation to men who long for emancipation [freedom] from this prison house of life. . . . Hundreds, nay thousands, of impious [immoral] persons become sinless and pure, by seeing, touching, or drinking of the river Ganges. ❞
—*Agni Puranam*, a Hindu sacred text

Focus Question In what ways were religion and society intertwined in ancient India?

Hinduism and Buddhism

GA **Performance Standards**

• **SSWH2b** Explain the development and impact of Hinduism and Buddhism on India and the world.

Terms, People, and Places

atman	caste
moksha	Siddhartha Gautama
reincarnation	Four Noble Truths
karma	Eightfold Path
dharma	nirvana
ahimsa	sect

Note Taking

Reading Skill: Recognize Sequence Keep track of the development of Hinduism and Buddhism by filling in a flowchart like the one below with important stages, in the order they occurred.

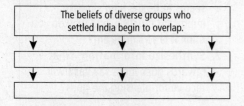

The beliefs of diverse groups who settled India begin to overlap.

Thousands of years ago, two major religions—Hinduism and Buddhism—emerged in ancient India. The ethical and spiritual messages of both religions profoundly shaped Indian civilization.

The Beliefs of Hinduism Develop

Unlike most major religions, Hinduism has no single founder and no single sacred text. Instead, it grew out of the overlapping beliefs of the diverse groups who settled India. The process probably began when the Aryans added the gods of the Indus civilization to their own. Later people brought other gods, beliefs, and practices. As a result, Hinduism became one of the world's most complex religions, with countless gods and goddesses and many forms of worship existing side by side. Despite this diversity, all Hindus share certain basic beliefs.

One Force Underlies Everything "God is one, but wise people know it by many names." This ancient proverb reflects the Hindu belief that everything is part of the unchanging, all-powerful spiritual force called brahman. Hindus worship a variety of gods who give concrete form to brahman. The most important Hindu gods are Brahma, the Creator; Vishnu, the Preserver; and Shiva, the Destroyer. Each can take many forms, human or animal, to represent the various aspects of brahman with which he is associated. Some Hindus also worship various forms of the powerful goddess Shakti. She is both kind and cruel, a creator and a destroyer.

Sacred Texts Reveal Hindu Beliefs Over many hundreds of years, Hindu teachings were recorded in the sacred texts of the Vedas. The Upanishads (oo PAN ih shadz) are a section of the Vedas that address mystical questions related to Hinduism. These sacred texts use vivid images to examine complex ideas about the human soul and the connectedness of all life. In addition, literary works such as the *Bhagavad-Gita* were also revered for their representations of Hindu beliefs.

Achieving Moksha Is the Goal of Life To Hindus, every person has an essential self, or **atman** (AHT mun). Some view it as the same as brahman and others as a form of brahman. The ultimate goal of existence, Hindus believe, is achieving **moksha** (MAHK shuh), or union with brahman. To do that, individuals must free themselves from selfish desires that separate them from brahman. Most people cannot achieve moksha in one lifetime, but Hindus believe in **reincarnation,** or the rebirth of the soul in another bodily form. Reincarnation allows people to continue working toward moksha through several lifetimes.

In each existence, Hindus believe, a person can come closer to achieving moksha by obeying the law of karma. **Karma** refers to all the actions of a person's life that affect his or her fate in the next life. To Hindus, all existence is ranked. Humans are closest to brahman. Then come animals, plants, and objects like rocks or water. People who live virtuously earn good karma and are reborn at a higher level of existence. Those who do evil acquire bad karma and are reborn into suffering at a lower level of existence. In Indian art, this cycle of death and rebirth is symbolized by the image of the wheel.

To escape the wheel of fate, Hinduism stresses the importance of **dharma** (DAHR muh), the religious and moral duties of an individual. These duties vary according to class, occupation, gender, and age. Another key moral principle of Hinduism is **ahimsa** (uh HIM sah), or nonviolence. To Hindus, all people and things are aspects of brahman and therefore deserve to be respected. Many Hindus try to follow the path of ahimsa.

Key Hindu Gods

▲ Brahma, the Creator

▲ Vishnu, the Preserver

▲ Shiva, the Destroyer

Artisans covered each Hindu temple with masterful carvings, including depictions of the various forms of the god to whom a temple was dedicated. This temple at Somnathpur honors Vishnu.

Jainism Develops From Hinduism About 500 B.C., the teacher Mahavira (mah hah VEE ruh) founded Jainism (JY niz um), a religion that grew out of Hindu traditions and that is still practiced today. Mahavira rejected the idea that Brahmin priests alone could perform certain sacred rites. Jain teachings emphasize meditation, self-denial, and an extreme form of ahimsa. To avoid accidentally killing a living thing, even an insect, Jains carry brooms to sweep the ground in front of their feet.

✓ **Checkpoint** How do the Hindu gods relate to brahman?

The Caste System Shapes India

As you read in Section 1, the Aryans divided society into four groups. Non-Aryans held the lowest jobs. During the Vedic Age, class divisions moved more toward reflecting social and economic roles than ethnic differences between Aryans and non-Aryans. As these changes occurred, they led to a more complex system of castes, or social groups into which people are born and which can rarely be changed.

Complex Rules Uphold the Caste System Caste was closely linked to Hindu beliefs. To Hindus, people in different castes were different species of beings. A high-caste Brahmin, for example, was purer and therefore closer to moksha than someone from a lower caste. To ensure spiritual purity, a web of complex caste rules governed every aspect of life—for example, where people lived, what they ate, how they dressed, and how they earned a living. Rules forbade marrying outside one's caste or eating with members of another caste. High-caste people had the strictest rules to protect them from the spiritually polluted, or impure, lower castes. Because they had jobs such as digging graves, cleaning streets, or turning animal hides into leather, some people were considered so impure that they were called "untouchables."

For the untouchables, today called dalits, life was harsh and restricted. Other castes feared that contact with an untouchable could spread pollution. Untouchables had to live apart and to sound a wooden instrument called a clapper to warn of their approach.

Caste Affects the Social Order Despite its inequalities, caste ensured a stable social order. People believed that the law of karma determined their caste. While they could not change their status in this life, they could reach a higher state in a future life by faithfully fulfilling the duties of their present caste.

The caste system gave many people a sense of identity and interdependence. Each caste had its own occupation and its own leaders. Caste members cooperated to help one another. In addition, each caste had its own special role in Indian society as a whole. Although strictly separated, different castes depended on one another for their basic needs. A lower-caste carpenter, for example, built the home of a higher-caste scholar. The caste system also adapted to changing conditions.

Over time, many additional castes and subcastes evolved. As people migrated into the subcontinent, they formed new castes. Other castes grew out of new occupations and religions. This flexibility allowed people with diverse customs to live side by side in relative harmony. By modern times, there were thousands of major castes and subcastes.

✓ **Checkpoint** How did caste provide a sense of order in society?

THE LIFE OF THE BUDDHA

Central to Buddhism is the idea that one must live a moral life. Over the centuries, as many Buddhists have strived to do this, they have taken lessons from the life and actions of the Buddha, Siddhartha Gautama. Reminders of the Buddha's traits and actions abound in Asia and throughout the world in the form of sculpture both colossal and small, paintings, and literature. A few climactic scenes from the Buddha's life are repeated consistently in this art.

▲ **Gaining Awareness** In this illustration, Prince Gautama sees a dead man for the first time. From this and other journeys out of the palace, Gautama was inspired to abandon his life of privilege—a model many Buddhists attempt to follow.

Meditating This large bronze Buddha sits in a classic meditation pose—with legs crossed and hands resting face up in his lap. Buddhists believe that like Gautama, they can achieve enlightenment through meditation. ▶

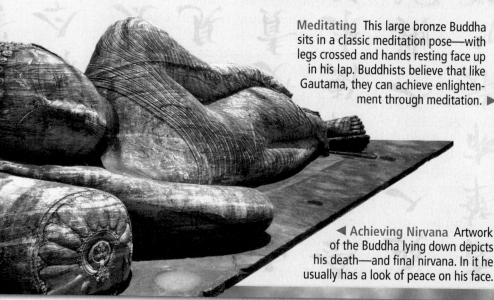

◀ **Achieving Nirvana** Artwork of the Buddha lying down depicts his death—and final nirvana. In it he usually has a look of peace on his face.

Thinking Critically

1. **Make Generalizations** Why do you think Buddhists find it important to tell the story of the Buddha's life in art?
2. **Recognize Ideologies** Which of the basic beliefs of Buddhism are revealed in the Buddha sculptures shown here?

Key Teachings of the Buddha

In the foothills of the Himalayas, a reformer appeared named **Siddhartha Gautama** (sih DAHR tuh gow TUH muh). His teachings eventually spread across Asia to become the core beliefs of one of the world's most influential religions, Buddhism.

From Boy to Buddha Gautama's early life is known mostly through various religious writings and literature. He was born a prince about 563 B.C. According to tradition, his mother dreamed that a radiant white elephant descended to her from heaven. Signs such as this led a prophet to predict that the boy would someday become a wandering holy man. To prevent that—in hopes of his son one day becoming a ruler—Gautama's father kept him in the family's palaces, surrounded by comfort and luxury. At age 16, Gautama married a beautiful woman and enjoyed a happy life.

At age 29, Gautama's life changed. One day he took a ride beyond the palace gardens and saw an old man. On following rides, he also saw a sick person and a dead body. For the first time, Gautama became aware of human suffering. Deeply disturbed, he bade farewell to his family and left the palace, never to return. He set out to discover "the realm of life where there is neither suffering nor death."

Gautama wandered for years, seeking answers from Hindu scholars and holy men whose ideas failed to satisfy him. He fasted and meditated. At some point, he took a seat under a large tree, determined to stay there until he understood the mystery of life. Throughout the night, legend tells, evil spirits tempted Gautama to give up his meditations, but he fended them off. When he rose, he believed he understood the cause of and cure for suffering and sorrow. He was no longer Gautama; he had become the Buddha, or "Enlightened One."

Following the Four Noble Truths The Buddha spent the rest of his life teaching others what he had learned. In his first sermon after reaching enlightenment, he explained the **Four Noble Truths** that lie at the heart of Buddhism:

1. All life is full of suffering, pain, and sorrow.
2. The cause of suffering is nonvirtue, or negative deeds and mindsets such as hatred and desire.
3. The only cure for suffering is to overcome nonvirtue.
4. The way to overcome nonvirtue is to follow the Eightfold Path.

Vocabulary Builder
aspiration—(as puh RAY shun) *n.* desire or ambition to achieve something

The Buddha described the **Eightfold Path** as "right views, right aspirations, right speech, right conduct, right livelihood, right effort, right mindfulness, and right contemplation." The first two steps involved understanding the Four Noble Truths and committing oneself to the Eightfold Path. Next, a person had to live a moral life, avoiding evil words and actions. Through meditation, a person might at last achieve enlightenment. For the Buddhist, the final goal is **nirvana,** or union with the universe and release from the cycle of rebirth.

The Buddha saw the Eightfold Path as a middle way between a life devoted to pleasure and one based on harsh self-denial. He stressed moral principles such as honesty, charity, and kindness to all living creatures.

Comparing Buddhism and Hinduism Buddhism grew from the same traditions as Hinduism. Both Hindus and Buddhists stressed nonviolence and believed in karma, dharma, and a cycle of rebirth. Yet the religions differed in several ways. Instead of focusing on the priests, formal rituals, and many gods of Hinduism, the Buddha urged each person to seek enlightenment through meditation. Buddhists also rejected the caste system, offering the hope of nirvana to all regardless of birth.

✔ **Checkpoint** What did Gautama hope to learn when he left home?

Buddhism Spreads Beyond India

The Buddha attracted many disciples, or followers, who accompanied him as he preached across northern India. Many men and women who accepted the Buddha's teachings set up monasteries and convents for meditation and study. Some Buddhist monasteries grew into major centers of learning.

Map Skills Missionaries and merchants spread Buddhism to many parts of Asia. It still thrives there today—though it is not practiced much in India.

1. Locate (a) India (b) China (c) Sri Lanka (d) Korea

2. Movement How did Buddhism spread to Japan?

3. Synthesize Information Looking at both maps, which arrows on the large map do you think represent the spread of Theravada Buddhism?

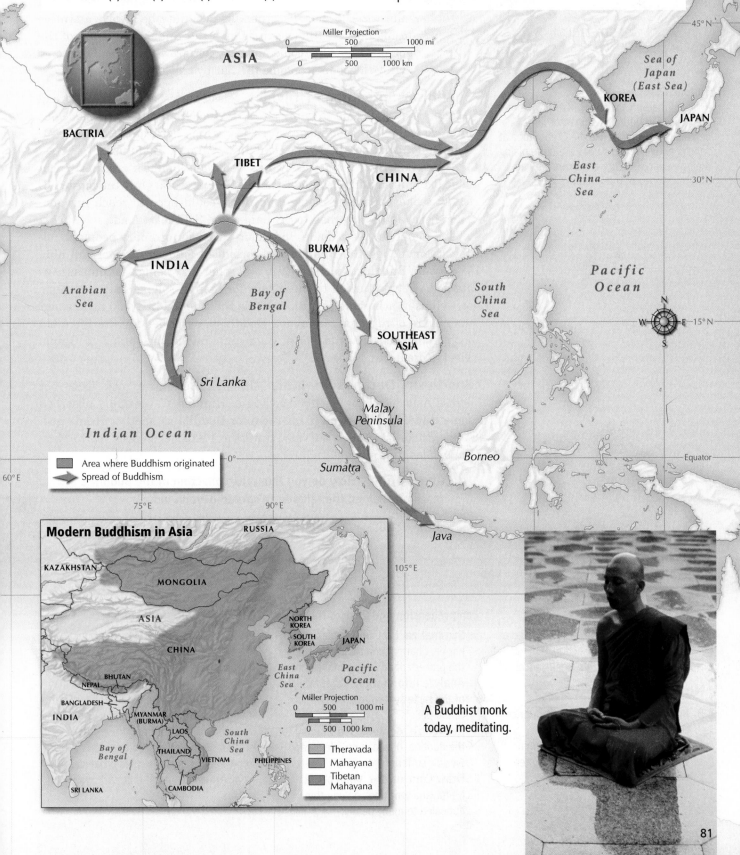

A Buddhist monk today, meditating.

81

Collecting the Buddha's Teachings Legend holds that at age 80, the Buddha ate spoiled food. As he lay dying, he told his disciples, "Decay is inherent in all things. Work out your own salvation with diligence." After the Buddha's death, his followers collected his teachings into the *Tripitaka*, or "Three Baskets of Wisdom." One of the "baskets" includes sayings like this one, which echoes the Hindu emphasis on duty: "Let a man, after he has discerned his own duty, be always attentive to his duty. " Other sayings give the Buddha's version of the golden rule: "Overcome anger by not growing angry. Overcome evil with good. Overcome the liar by truth."

Buddhist Stupas
Relics of the Buddha and other holy people are housed in Buddhist stupas, or large dome-shaped shrines like the Great Stupa at Sanchi, above. While stupas are quite plain, their gateways feature elaborate carvings that tell stories of the Buddha's life.

Buddhism Spreads and Divides Missionaries and traders spread Buddhism across India to many parts of Asia. Gradually, Buddhism split into two major **sects**, or subgroups. These were Theravada (thehr uh VAH duh) Buddhism and Mahayana (mah huh YAH nuh) Buddhism.

Theravada Buddhism closely followed the Buddha's original teachings. It required a life devoted to hard spiritual work. Only the most dedicated seekers, such as monks and nuns, could hope to reach nirvana. The Theravada sect spread to Sri Lanka and Southeast Asia.

The Mahayana sect made Buddhism easier for ordinary people to follow. Even though the Buddha had forbidden followers to worship him, Mahayana Buddhists pictured him and other holy beings as compassionate gods. People turned to these gods for help in solving daily problems as well as in achieving salvation. While the Buddha had said little about the nature of nirvana, Mahayana Buddhists described an afterlife filled with many heavens and hells. Mahayana Buddhism spread to China, Tibet, Korea, and Japan.

Buddhism Declines in India Although Buddhism took firm root across Asia, it slowly declined in India. Hinduism eventually absorbed some Buddhist ideas and made room for Buddha as another Hindu god. A few Buddhist centers survived until the 1100s, when they fell to Muslim armies that invaded India.

✓ **Checkpoint** How do you think the collecting of the Buddha's teachings helped the religion to spread beyond India?

Terms, People, and Places
1. For each term, person, or place listed at the beginning of the section, write a sentence explaining its significance.

Note Taking

2. **Reading Skill: Recognize Sequence** Use your completed flowchart to answer the Focus Question: In what ways were religion and society intertwined in ancient India?

Comprehension and Critical Thinking
3. **Summarize** Explain the roles of karma, dharma, and reincarnation in the process of achieving moksha.
4. **Analyze Information** What aspects of the caste system relate to basic Hindu beliefs?
5. **Recognize Ideologies** According to the Buddha, how can people escape worldly suffering?
6. **Draw Conclusions** What about Mahayana teachings do you think appealed to many people?

● **Writing About History**

Quick Write: Gather Details On some essay tests, you may be asked to compare and contrast two topics that you have studied. Before you write a response, you may find it useful to gather details related to the two topics and create a graphic organizer to compare and contrast those details. Gather details about Hinduism and Buddhism and create a graphic organizer to compare and contrast them.

In This Chapter SSWH2b(A), SSWH2b(B)

Belief systems can influence not only rules of conduct and social structure but also art and architecture. Hinduism, Buddhism, Confucianism, and Daoism are all belief systems that originated in India or China in ancient times. The painting of the Buddha (right) is in the Jokhang Temple in Tibet. For centuries, the temple has attracted millions of monks and pilgrims, who carry prayer wheels and chant sacred mantras.

Throughout History

- **First century B.C.** Jewish teachings stress religious duties and ethical conduct.

- **500–1500 A.D.** The Christian church gains political power in Europe.

- **600s** Arabs are united under Islam.

- **1600s** Puritans stress education so people can read the Bible.

- **1700s–1800s** Religious groups in the United States and Britain fight to end slavery.

- **2000s** Religious differences affect the politics of nations and the world.

Continuing Today

Today, billions of people identify themselves as belonging to a specific religion or belief system. The extent of religious influence in a given country varies, however. In a theocracy, such as Iran, religious leaders make sure that laws conform to Islamic teachings.

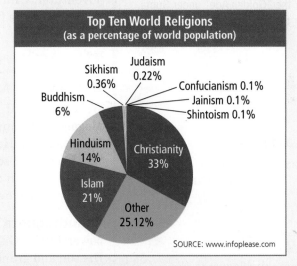

Top Ten World Religions
(as a percentage of world population)

- Sikhism 0.36%
- Judaism 0.22%
- Confucianism 0.1%
- Jainism 0.1%
- Shintoism 0.1%
- Buddhism 6%
- Hinduism 14%
- Islam 21%
- Christianity 33%
- Other 25.12%

SOURCE: www.infoplease.com

21st Century Skills

❓ TRANSFER Activities

1. Analyze Throughout history, how has religion affected society?

2. Draw Conclusions Why does what people believe affect what they do?

3. Transfer Complete a Web quest in which you analyze the influence of religion on a specific country; record your thoughts in the Concept Connector Journal; and learn to make a video. Web Code nah-0308

The *Arthashastra* was written for India's first emperor, Chandragupta Maurya, who is still honored today.

Behavior Fit For a King

❝In the happiness of his subjects lies [a king's] happiness, in their welfare his welfare. He shall not consider as good that which pleases him but treat as beneficial to him whatever pleases his subjects.❞
—*Arthashastra*, a Maurya handbook on governance

According to Hindu teachings, a ruler's duties included maintaining peace and order by enforcing laws, resisting invaders, and encouraging economic growth. Those who successfully achieved those goals became some of India's great rulers.

Focus Question In what ways did Maurya and Gupta rulers achieve peace and order for ancient India?

Powerful Empires of India

 Performance Standards

- **SSWH2a** Describe the rise and fall of the Maurya Empire, the "Golden Age" under Gupta, and India under the emperor Ashoka.

Terms, People, and Places

Chandragupta Maurya	golden age
dissent	decimal system
Asoka	joint family
missionary	dowry

Note Taking

Reading Skill: Recognize Sequence Use a timeline to record the sequence of important events that occurred during the Maurya and Gupta periods.

321 B.C.

Northern India was often a battleground where rival rajahs fought for control of the rich Ganges valley. But in 321 B.C., a young adventurer, **Chandragupta Maurya** (chun druh GUP tuh MOWR yuh), forged the first Indian empire.

The Maurya Empire Creates a Strong Government

We know about Chandragupta largely from reports written by Megasthenes (muh GAS thuh neez), a Greek ambassador to the Maurya court. He described the great Maurya capital at Pataliputra. It boasted schools and a library as well as splendid palaces and temples. An awed Megasthenes reported that the wall around the city "was crowned with 530 towers and had 64 gates."

Chandragupta Forges an Empire Chandragupta first gained power in the Ganges valley. He then conquered northern India. His son and grandson later pushed south, adding much of the Deccan to their empire. From 321 B.C. to 185 B.C., the Maurya dynasty ruled over a vast, united empire.

Chandragupta maintained order through a well-organized bureaucracy. Royal officials supervised the building of roads and harbors to benefit trade. Other officials collected taxes and managed state-owned factories and shipyards. People sought justice in royal courts. Chandragupta's rule was effective but harsh. A brutal secret police force reported on corruption, crime, and **dissent**— that is, ideas that opposed those of the government. Fearful of his many enemies, Chandragupta had specially trained women warriors guard his palace.

Asoka Rules by Moral Example The most honored Maurya emperor was Chandragupta's grandson, **Asoka** (uh SOH kuh). A few years after becoming emperor in 268 B.C., Asoka fought a long, bloody war to conquer the Deccan region of Kalinga. Then, horrified at the slaughter—more than 100,000 people are said to have died—Asoka turned his back on further conquests. He converted to Buddhism, rejected violence, and resolved to rule by moral example.

True to the Buddhist principle of respect for all life, Asoka stopped eating most meats and limited Hindu animal sacrifices. He sent **missionaries,** or people sent on a religious mission, to spread Buddhism across India and to Sri Lanka. By doing so, he paved the way for the spread of Buddhism throughout Asia. Although Asoka promoted Buddhism, he also preached tolerance for other religions.

Asoka had stone pillars set up across India, offering moral advice and promising a just government. Asoka's rule brought peace and prosperity and helped unite the diverse peoples within his empire. He built hospitals and Buddhist shrines. To aid transportation, he built roads and rest houses for travelers. "I have had banyan trees planted on the roads to give shade to people and animals," he noted. "I have planted mango groves, and I have had [wells] dug and shelters erected along the roads."

Division and Disunity Set In

After Asoka's death, Maurya power declined. By 185 B.C., the unity of the Maurya empire was shattered as rival princes again battled for power across the Gangetic Plain.

In fact, during its long history, India has seldom remained united for long. In ancient times, as today, the subcontinent was home to many peoples. Although northern India shared a common civilization, fierce local rivalries kept it divided. Meanwhile, distance and cultural differences separated the peoples of the north and the peoples of the Deccan in the south. Adding to the turmoil, foreigners frequently pushed through mountain passes into northern India. The divided northern kingdoms often proved incapable of resisting these conquerors.

✔ **Checkpoint** How did Chandragupta organize Maurya government?

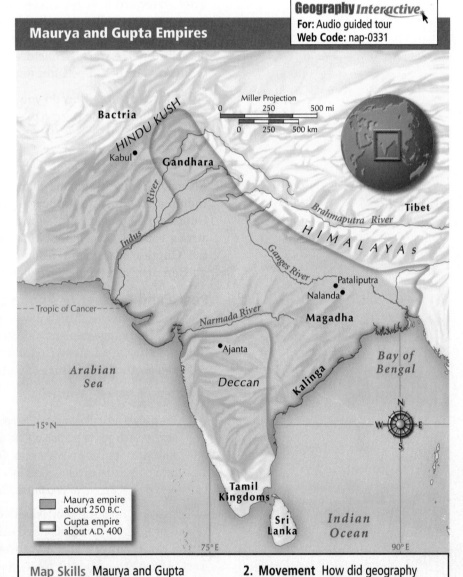

Geography *Interactive*
For: Audio guided tour
Web Code: nap-0331

Maurya and Gupta Empires

Bactria

HINDU KUSH

Kabul

Gandhara

Miller Projection
0   250   500 mi
0   250   500 km

Tibet

Brahmaputra River

HIMALAYAS

Indus

Ganges River

Pataliputra

Nalanda

- - Tropic of Cancer - -

Narmada River

Magadha

Ajanta

Arabian Sea

Deccan

Kalinga

Bay of Bengal

15° N

Tamil Kingdoms

Maurya empire about 250 B.C.
Gupta empire about A.D. 400

Sri Lanka

Indian Ocean

75° E   90° E

Map Skills Maurya and Gupta emperors were able to unite much of India under their rule.

1. **Locate** (a) Ganges River (b) Indus River (c) Tamil Kingdoms (d) Hindu Kush (e) Nalanda

2. **Movement** How did geography limit the northward expansion of both empires?

3. **Analyze Information** What region of the Indian subcontinent remained separate from both the Maurya and the Gupta empires?

Kingdoms Arise Across the Deccan

Like the Gangetic Plain, the Deccan was divided into many kingdoms after the decline of Maurya power. Each kingdom had its own capital with magnificent temples and bustling workshops. The peoples of the Deccan were Dravidians with very different languages and traditions from the peoples of the north. Over the centuries, Hindu and Buddhist traditions and Sanskrit writings drifted south and blended with local cultures. Deccan rulers generally tolerated all religions as well as the many foreigners who settled in their busy ports.

In the Tamil kingdoms, which occupied much of the southernmost part of India, trade was important. Tamil rulers improved harbors to support overseas trade. Tamil merchants sent spices, fine textiles, and other luxuries westward to eager buyers in the Roman empire. And as the Roman empire declined, Tamil trade with China increased.

The Tamil kingdoms left a rich and diverse literature. Tamil poets described fierce wars, heroic deeds, and festive occasions, along with the ordinary routines of peasant and city life.

 Checkpoint How do you think trade helped link the separate kingdoms of the Deccan?

The Guptas Bring About a Golden Age

Although many kingdoms flourished in the Deccan, the most powerful Indian states rose to its north. About 500 years after the Mauryas, the Gupta dynasty again united much of India. Gupta emperors organized a strong central government that promoted peace and prosperity. Under the Guptas, who ruled from A.D. 320 to about 540, India enjoyed a **golden age,** or period of great cultural achievement.

Peace and Prosperity Abound Gupta rule was probably looser than that of the Mauryas. Much power was left in the hands of individual villages and city governments elected by merchants and artisans. Faxian (FAH shyahn), a Chinese Buddhist monk who visited India in the 400s, reported on the mild nature of Gupta rule:

> **Primary Source**
>
> 66 The people are numerous and happy; . . . only those who cultivate the royal land have to pay [a portion of] the grain from it. . . . The king governs without . . . corporal punishments. Criminals are simply fined, lightly or heavily, according to the circumstances [of each case]. 99
> —Faxian, *A Record of Buddhistic Kingdoms*

Trade and farming flourished across the Gupta empire. Farmers harvested crops of wheat, rice, and sugar cane. In cities, artisans produced cotton cloth, pottery, and metalware for local markets and for export to East Africa, the Middle East, and Southeast Asia. The prosperity of Gupta India contributed to a flowering in the arts and learning.

Indians Make Advances in Learning Under Gupta rule, students were educated in religious schools. However, in Hindu and Buddhist centers, learning was not limited to religion and philosophy. The large Buddhist monastery-university at Nalanda, which attracted students from many parts of Asia, taught mathematics, medicine, physics, languages, literature, and other subjects.

GOLDEN AGE IN THE ARTS

Gupta artists may be best known for the magnificent sculpture that they carved on stone temples for the rajahs who sponsored an immense flowering in the arts. Such buildings were literally covered with carvings of mostly religious subjects. In addition, the golden age of the Gupta dynasty encompassed other arts, including painting, music, dance, and literature. Regarded as highly now as they were when created, the Gupta arts influenced artistic styles in later Indian societies as well as in many other parts of Asia.

Music Musicians often ▲ entertained in Gupta courts. This terracotta tile shows a musician playing a lyre.

◀ **Sculpture** Scenes from Indian religious myths abound in Gupta sculpture. This one depicts the Hindu god Vishnu (center top) rescuing from a serpent a man who was cursed into the form of an elephant.

▼ **Painting** Famous Gupta murals decorate a series of cave temples carved into rock cliffs at Ajanta, in western India. The vibrant paintings, such as this one showing divine musicians, recall Buddhist stories and legends.

Dance Dancers have performed Indian classical dances since a few centuries before the Gupta era up through the present day. Each movement of the arms, hands, and eyes carries particular meaning. ▶

Thinking Critically

1. **Synthesize Information** What role did religion play in the arts of Gupta India? What role do you think the arts played in religion?
2. **Make Comparisons** Compare the subject matter of the three pieces of art shown here. What is similar? What is different?

Performed for Centuries
The Indian play *Shakuntala* has been re-enacted for centuries. In this scene from a modern-day performance, Shakuntala, her husband, and her son reunite at the end of the play, with gods watching over them. *What about this play might appeal to people throughout time?*

Indian advances in mathematics had a wide impact on the rest of the world. Gupta mathematicians devised the system of writing numbers that we use today. (However, these numerals are now called "Arabic" numerals because Arabs carried them from India to the Middle East and Europe.) Indian mathematicians also originated the concept of zero and developed the **decimal system** of numbers based on ten digits, which we still use today.

By Gupta times, Indian physicians were using herbs and other remedies to treat illness. Surgeons were skilled in setting bones and in simple surgery to repair injuries. It seems that doctors also began vaccinating people against smallpox about 1,000 years before this practice was used in Europe.

Expanding India's Literature During Gupta times, many fine writers added to the rich heritage of Indian literature. They collected and recorded fables and folk tales in the Sanskrit language. In time, Indian fables were carried west to Persia, Egypt, and Greece.

The greatest Gupta poet and playwright was Kalidasa. His most famous play, *Shakuntala* (shahk oon TAH luh), tells the story of a king who marries the lovely orphan Shakuntala. Under an evil spell, the king forgets his bride. After many plot twists, he finally recovers his memory and is reunited with her.

The Gupta Empire Declines Eventually, Gupta India declined under the pressure of weak rulers, civil war, and foreign invaders. From central Asia came the White Huns, a nomadic people who overran the weakened Gupta empire, destroying its cities and trade. Once again, India split into many kingdoms. It would see no other great empire like those of the Mauryas or Guptas for almost 1,000 years.

✔ **Checkpoint** How did religion influence learning and the arts in Gupta India?

Family and Village Life Shape Indian Society

Most Indians knew nothing of the dazzling courts of the Mauryas or Guptas. The vast majority were peasants who lived in the villages that dotted the Indian landscape. In Indian society, everyday life revolved around the rules and duties associated with caste, family, and village.

Joint Family Structure The ideal family was a **joint family,** in which parents, children, and their offspring shared a common dwelling. Indian families were patriarchal—the father or oldest male in a family headed the household. Adult sons continued to live with their parents even after they married and had children. (A daughter would go to live with her husband and his family.) Often only the wealthy could afford such large households. Still, even when they did not share the same house, close ties linked brothers, uncles, cousins, and nephews.

A father was thought to have wisdom and experience, and he enjoyed great authority. Even so, his power was limited by sacred laws and tradition. Usually, he made decisions after consulting his wife and other family members. Property belonged to the whole family.

The Family Performs Certain Duties The family performed the essential function of training children in the traditions and duties of their castes. Thus family interests came before individual wishes. Children worked with older relatives in the fields or at a family trade. While still young, a daughter learned that as a wife she would be expected to serve and obey her husband and his family. A son learned the rituals to honor the family's ancestors. Such rites linked the living and the dead, deepening family bonds across the generations.

For parents, an important duty was arranging good marriages for their children, based on caste and family interests. Marriage customs varied. In northern India, for example, a bride's family commonly provided a **dowry,** or payment to the bridegroom, and financed the costly wedding festivities. After marriage, the daughter left her home and became part of her husband's family.

Role of Women Changes Over Time In early Aryan society, women seem to have enjoyed a higher <u>status</u> than in later times. Aryan women even composed a few Vedic hymns. However, attitudes and customs affecting women varied across India and changed over time. By late Gupta times, upper-class women were increasingly restricted to the home. When they went outside the home, they were supposed to cover themselves from head to foot. Lower-class women, however, labored in the fields or worked at spinning and weaving.

Women were thought to have shakti, a creative energy that men lacked. In marriage, a woman's shakti helped to make the husband complete. Still, shakti might also be a destructive force. A husband's duty was to channel his wife's energy in the proper direction. Women had few rights within the family and society. Their primary duties were to marry and raise children.

For a woman, rebirth into a higher existence was gained through devotion to her husband. Often, a widow was expected to join her dead husband on his funeral fire. In this way, a widow became a sati, or "virtuous woman." Some widows accepted this painful death as a noble duty that wiped out their own and their husbands' sins. Other women bitterly resisted the custom.

Vocabulary Builder

<u>status</u>—(STAT us) *n.* social standing or prestige

 With the monsoon, the tempo of life and death increases. Almost overnight grass begins to grow and leafless trees turn green. . . . While the monsoon lasts, the showers start and stop without warning. The clouds fly across, dropping their rain on the plains as it pleases them, till they reach the Himalayas. . . . Lightning and thunder never cease.
—Khushwant Singh,
Train to Pakistan   ◆)) AUDIO

A family escapes the floodwaters caused by the monsoons, which still bring both hardship and needed rain to people in India today.

Typical Village Structure

Typical Village Structure Throughout India's history, the village was at the heart of daily life. The size of villages varied, from a handful of people to hundreds of families. A typical village included a cluster of homes made of earth or stone. Beyond these dwellings stretched the fields, where farmers grew wheat, rice, cotton, sugar cane, or other crops according to region.

Each village included people of different castes who performed the necessary tasks of daily life. It ran its own affairs based on caste rules and traditions and faced little outside interference as long as it paid its share of taxes. A village headman and council made decisions. The council included the most respected people of the village. In early times, women served on the council. As Hindu law began to place greater restrictions on women, they were later excluded. The headman and council organized villagers to cooperate on vital local projects such as building irrigation systems and larger regional projects like building roads and temples.

Agriculture and Trade Shape Life In most of India, farming depended on the rains brought by the summer monsoons. Too much or too little rain meant famine. Landlords owned much of the land. Farmers who worked the land had to give the owner part of the harvest. Often, what remained was hardly enough to feed the farmers and their families.

Villages usually produced most of the food and goods that they needed. However, they relied on trade for some essentials, such as salt and spices, as well as various manufactured goods. People regularly interacted with others from nearby villages while attending weddings, visiting relatives, or shopping at marketplaces. This continual interchange was crucial in the establishment of common ideas across the subcontinent.

✓ **Checkpoint** Describe the structure of a typical Indian family.

SECTION 3 Assessment

Terms, People, and Places

1. For each term, person, or place listed at the beginning of the section, write a sentence explaining its significance.

Note Taking

2. **Reading Skill: Recognize Sequence** Use your completed timeline to answer the Focus Question: In what ways did Maurya and Gupta rulers achieve peace and order for ancient India?

Comprehension and Critical Thinking

3. **Make Comparisons** Compare the approaches of Chandragupta and Asoka to ruling the Maurya empire.

4. **Analyze Information** Describe three achievements of the Gupta period that made it a golden age.

5. **Recognize Ideologies** How did the roles played by family and village in Indian life reveal the value of placing the needs of the community or group above those of the individual?

● **Writing About History**

Quick Write: Gather Details On some essay tests, you may be asked to defend a position about a topic that you have studied. Before you write a response, you may find it useful to gather details that support your position and organize them in an outline. Gather details and write an outline defending your position on the following topic: What was the most important way in which religion influenced life in ancient India?

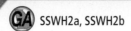

Asoka's Edicts

During his rule of Maurya India, Asoka converted to Buddhism, rejected violence, and resolved to rule by moral example. The messages he published on stone pillars across India pronounced moral edicts, or commands, and described the just actions of his government. The following are excerpts from several of the pillars.

▲ Asoka

All men are my children. Just as I seek the welfare and happiness of my own children in this world and the next, I seek the same things for all men.

It is difficult to achieve happiness, either in this world or in the next, except by intense love of Dharma, intense self-examination, intense obedience, intense fear [of sin], and intense enthusiasm. Yet as a result of my instruction, regard for Dharma and love of Dharma have increased day by day and will continue to increase. . . . For these are the rules: to govern according to Dharma, to administer justice according to Dharma, to advance the people's happiness according to Dharma, and to protect them according to Dharma.

The faiths of others all deserve to be honored for one reason or another. By honoring them, one exalts[1] one's own faith and at the same time performs a service to the faith of others. By acting otherwise, one injures one's own faith and also does disservice to that of others. . . . Therefore concord[2] alone is commendable.

Whatever good deeds I have done the people have imitated, and they have followed them as a model. In doing so, they have progressed and will progress in obedience to parents and teachers, in respect for elders, in courtesy to priests and ascetics[3], to the poor and distressed, and even to slaves and servants.

There is no gift that can equal the gift of Dharma. . . . If one acts in this way, one achieves . . . happiness in this world and infinite merit in the world to come.

I have commanded this edict on Dharma to be inscribed so that it may last forever and so that my descendants may conform to it.

1. **exalt** (eg ZAWLT) *vt.* raise up
2. **concord** (KAHN kawrd) *n.* friendly relations or peace
3. **ascetic** (uh SET ik) *n.* someone who chooses a life of self-denial

▲ Many of Asoka's pillars, such as this one in Vaishali, India, were erected in places where people often congregated.

Thinking Critically
1. **Identify Central Issues** What are the major themes in these edicts?
2. **Predict Consequences** In what ways do you think Asoka's edicts may have contributed to the peace and prosperity of the Maurya empire?

Emperor Yu

WITNESS HISTORY ◀)) AUDIO

The Rewards of Devotion

In very ancient times, relates a Chinese legend, floodwaters rose to the top of the highest hills. Yu, a hard-working official, labored for a decade to drain the waters, not going home once to see his family. As a reward for his selfless efforts, the emperor appointed Yu the next ruler of China.

❝ The emperor said, 'Come, Yu. The inundating [flooding] waters filled me with dread, [but then] you realized all that you represented, and accomplished your task—thus showing your superiority to other men. . . . I see how great is your virtue, how admirable your vast achievements.'❞
—*Books of Yu*

Focus Question What characteristics defined the civilization that developed in China under its early rulers?

Rise of Civilization in China

 Performance Standards

- **SSWH2c** Describe the development of Chinese civilization under Zhou.
- **SSWH2d** Explain the diffusion of Confucianism to Southeast Asia.
- **SSWH2e** Explain how the Indian Subcontinent affected movement and ideas.

Terms, People, and Places

loess
clan   philosophy
dynastic cycle   filial piety
feudalism   oracle bone
Confucius   character
Laozi   calligraphy

Note Taking

Reading Skill: Recognize Sequence Keep track of the sequence of events in early China by making an outline of the events in the order they occurred.

```
I.
  A.
  B.
II.
  A.
  B.
```

The legend of Yu offers insights into early China. The Chinese depended so much on rivers for irrigation and transportation that they highly valued the ability to control floodwaters and to develop irrigation systems. The legend also shows how much the Chinese prized devotion to duty. Both themes played a key role in the development of Chinese civilization.

Geography Influences Civilization

Long distances and physical barriers separated China from Egypt, the Middle East, and India. This isolation contributed to the Chinese belief that China was the center of the earth and the sole source of civilization. These beliefs in turn led the ancient Chinese to call their land Zhongguo (jahng gwoh), or the Middle Kingdom.

Geographic Barriers Set China Apart To the west and southwest of China, brutal deserts and high mountain ranges—the Tian Shan (tyen shahn) and the Himalayas—blocked the easy movement of people. To the southeast, thick rainforests divided China from Southeast Asia. To the north awaited a forbidding desert, the Gobi. To the east lay the vast Pacific Ocean.

Despite these formidable barriers, the Chinese did have contact with the outside world. They traded with neighboring people and, in time, Chinese goods reached the Middle East and beyond. More often, the outsiders whom the Chinese encountered were nomadic invaders. Such conquerors, however, were usually absorbed into the advanced Chinese civilization.

China Includes Varied Regions As the Chinese expanded over an enormous area, their empire came to include many regions. The Chinese heartland lay along the east coast and the valleys of the Huang, or Yellow, River and the Chang River. In ancient times, as today, these fertile farming regions supported the largest populations. Then, as now, the rivers provided water for irrigation and served as transportation routes.

Beyond the heartland are the outlying regions of Xinjiang (shin jyahng) and Mongolia. These regions have harsh climates and rugged terrain. Until recent times, they were mostly occupied by nomads and subsistence farmers. Nomads repeatedly attacked and plundered Chinese cities. At times, however, powerful Chinese rulers conquered or made alliances with the people of these regions and another outlying region, Manchuria. China also extended its influence over the Himalayan region of Tibet, which the Chinese called Xizang (shih dzahng).

Settling Along the "River of Sorrows" Chinese history began in the Huang River valley, where Neolithic people learned to farm. As in other places, the need to control the flow of the river through large water projects probably led to the rise of a strong central government and the founding of what is sometimes called the Yellow River civilization.

The Huang River got its name from the **loess,** or fine windblown yellow soil, that it carries eastward from Siberia and Mongolia. Long ago, the Huang River earned a bitter nickname, "River of Sorrows." As loess settles to the river bottom, it raises the water level. Chinese peasants labored constantly to build and repair dikes to prevent the river from overflowing. If the dikes broke, floodwaters burst over the land. Such disasters destroyed crops and brought mass starvation.

✓ **Checkpoint** In what different ways did people live in ancient China?

Geography *Interactive*
For: Audio guided tour
Web Code: nap-0341

Shang and Zhou Civilizations

Map Skills Today, China extends west from the Pacific Ocean deep into central Asia. Its first civilizations existed in the eastern part of the modern-day country.

1. **Locate** (a) Chang River (b) Gobi (c) Huang River (d) Anyang
2. **Place** What physical features acted as obstacles to contact outside China?
3. **Draw Inferences** In which directions from China do you think it was easiest for the Chinese to make contact with other people? Why?

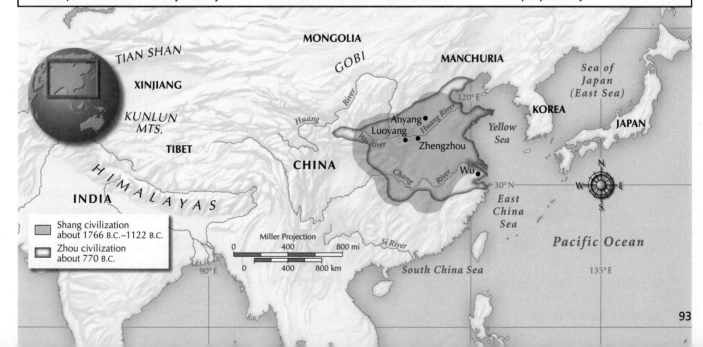

Shang artists were famous for their bronze works, such as the mask and vessel shown here.

Vocabulary Builder

interacted—(in tur AKT ed) *vi.* was involved in communication, work, or social activity with someone else

China Begins to Take Shape Under the Shang Dynasty

About 1766 B.C., the first Chinese dynasty for which scholars have found solid evidence arose in a corner of northern China. This dynasty, the Shang, would dominate the region until about 1122 B.C.

Formation of Government Archaeologists have uncovered some of the large palaces and rich tombs of Shang rulers. The evidence indicates that from their walled capital city at Anyang, the Shang emerged to drive off nomads from the northern steppes and deserts. Shang kings probably controlled only a small area. Loyal princes and local nobles governed most of the land. They were likely the heads of important **clans,** or groups of families who claim a common ancestor.

In one Shang tomb, archaeologists discovered the burial place of Fu Hao (foo how), wife of the Shang king Wu Ding. Artifacts show that she owned land and helped to lead a large army against invaders. This evidence suggests that noblewomen may have had considerable status during the Shang period.

Social Classes Develop As in other early civilizations, the top level of Shang society included the royal family and a class of noble warriors. Shang warriors used leather armor, bronze weapons, and horse-drawn chariots. They may have learned of chariots from other Asian peoples with whom they interacted.

Early Chinese cities supported a class of artisans and merchants. Artisans produced goods for nobles, including bronze weapons, silk robes, and jade jewelry. Merchants exchanged food and crafts made by local artisans for salt, certain types of shells, and other goods not found in northeastern China.

The majority of people in Shang China were peasants. They clustered together in farming villages. Many lived in thatch-roofed pit houses whose earthen floors were dug several feet below the surrounding ground. Peasants led grueling lives. All family members worked in the fields, using stone tools to prepare the ground for planting or to harvest grain. When they were not in the fields, peasants had to repair the dikes. If war broke out between noble families, the men had to fight alongside their lords.

✓ **Checkpoint** How was China governed during the Shang dynasty?

The Zhou Dynasty Further Defines China

In 1122 B.C., the battle-hardened Zhou (joh) people marched out of their kingdom on the western frontier to overthrow the Shang. They set up the Zhou dynasty, which lasted until 256 B.C.

Receiving the Mandate of Heaven To justify their rebellion against the Shang, the Zhou promoted the idea of the Mandate of Heaven, or the divine right to rule. The cruelty of the last Shang king, they declared, had so outraged the gods that they had sent ruin on him. The gods then passed the Mandate of Heaven to the Zhou, who "treated the multitudes of the people well."

The Chinese later expanded the idea of the Mandate of Heaven to explain the **dynastic cycle,** or the rise and fall of dynasties. As long as a dynasty provided good government, it enjoyed the Mandate of Heaven. If the rulers became weak or corrupt, the Chinese believed that heaven would withdraw its support. Floods, famine, or other catastrophes were signs that a dynasty had lost the favor of heaven. In the resulting chaos, an ambitious leader might seize power and set up a new dynasty. His success and strong government showed the people that the new dynasty had won the Mandate of Heaven. The dynastic cycle would then begin again.

Establishing a Feudal State The Zhou rewarded their supporters by granting them control over different regions. Thus, under the Zhou, China developed into a feudal state. **Feudalism** (FYOOD ul iz um) was a system of government in which local lords governed their own lands but owed military service and other forms of support to the ruler.

In theory, Zhou kings ruled China for more than 850 years. For about 250 of those years, they actually did enjoy great power and prestige. After the 800s B.C., however, feudal lords exercised the real power and profited from the lands worked by peasants within their domains.

Spurring Economic Growth During the Zhou period, China's economy grew. Knowledge of ironworking reached China in the 600s B.C. As iron axes and ox-drawn iron plows replaced stone, wood, and bronze tools, farmers produced more food. Peasants also began to grow new crops, such as soybeans. Some feudal lords organized large-scale irrigation works, making farming even more productive.

History Interactive
For: Interactive diagram
Web Code: nap-0342

Dynastic Rule in China

Dynasties ruled China for most of its history until 1912. The Chinese believed that dynasties could gain or lose the Mandate of Heaven, depending on how wisely an emperor ruled. A Zhou emperor is shown here in his chariot. *According to the diagram, how did a new dynasty try to repair the problems left by an aging dynasty?*

Dynasties of China

Dynasty	Dates
Shang	1766 B.C.–1122 B.C.
Zhou	1122 B.C.–256 B.C.
Qin	221 B.C.–206 B.C.
Han	202 B.C.–A.D. 220
Sui	A.D. 581–A.D. 618
Tang	A.D. 618–A.D. 907
Song	A.D. 960–A.D. 1279
Ming	A.D. 1368–A.D. 1644
Qing	A.D. 1644–A.D. 1911

The Dynastic Cycle

The New Dynasty
• Restores peace
• Appoints loyal officials
• Redistributes land to peasants
• Builds canals, irrigation systems, and roads
• Repairs defensive walls

After several generations, the new dynasty becomes an aging dynasty.

The Aging Dynasty
• Neglects government duties
• Ignores corrupt officials
• Loses control of the provinces
• Imposes heavy taxes to pay for luxuries
• Allows defensive walls to decay

New dynasty claims the Mandate of Heaven.

Aging dynasty loses the Mandate of Heaven.

Problems
• Floods, famine, earthquakes
• Invasions
• Armed bandits in the provinces
• Peasant revolts

Commerce expanded, too. The Chinese began to use money for the first time. Chinese copper coins were made with holes in the center so that they could be strung on cords. This early form of a money economy made trade easier. Merchants also benefited from new roads and canals that feudal lords constructed.

Economic expansion led to an increase in China's population. People from the Huang River heartland advanced into central China and soon began to farm the immense Chang River basin. As well, feudal nobles expanded their territories and encouraged peasants to settle in the conquered territories.

Zhou Dynasty Ends By 256 B.C., China was a large, wealthy, and highly developed center of civilization. Yet the Zhou dynasty was too weak to control feudal lords who ignored the emperor and battled one another in savage wars. Out of these wars rose a ruthless leader who was determined to impose political unity. His triumphs brought an end to the Zhou dynasty and ushered in the Qin (chin) dynasty, which you will read about in the next section.

✔ **Checkpoint** Explain three ways that China expanded during the Zhou dynasty.

Religious Beliefs Develop in Early China

By Shang times, the Chinese had developed complex religious beliefs, many of which continued to be practiced for thousands of years. The early Chinese prayed to many gods and nature spirits. Chief among them was the supreme god, Shang Di (shahng dee). The king was seen as the link between the people and Shang Di.

Gods as great as Shang Di, the Chinese believed, would not respond to the pleas of mere mortals. Only the spirits of the greatest people, such as the ancestors of the king, could possibly get the ear of the gods. Thus, the prayers of rulers and nobles to their ancestors were thought to serve the community as a whole, ensuring such benefits as good harvests or victory in war.

At first, only the royal family and other nobles had ancestors important enough to influence the gods. Gradually, other classes shared in these rituals. The Chinese called on the spirits of their ancestors to bring good fortune to the family. To honor their ancestors' spirits, they offered them sacrifices of food and other necessities. When westerners reached China, they mistakenly called this practice "ancestor worship."

✔ **Checkpoint** What did early Chinese communities do to ensure good harvests?

Two Major Belief Systems Take Root in Zhou China

During the late Zhou period, when war and social changes were disrupting old ways of life, new belief systems developed that would form the basis of China's culture and government for centuries to come. Thinkers such as **Confucius** (known by the Chinese as Kong Fuzi) and **Laozi** (LOW dzuh) put forward ideas on how to restore social order and maintain harmony with nature.

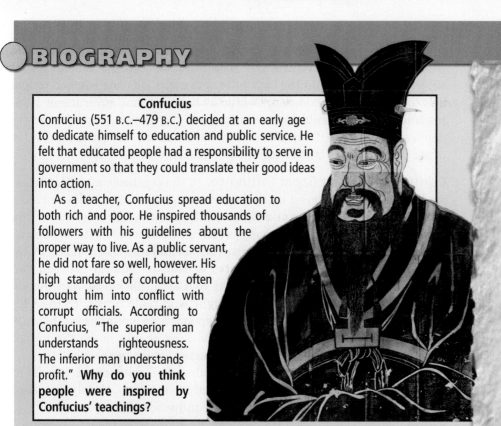

Confucius

Confucius (551 B.C.–479 B.C.) decided at an early age to dedicate himself to education and public service. He felt that educated people had a responsibility to serve in government so that they could translate their good ideas into action.

As a teacher, Confucius spread education to both rich and poor. He inspired thousands of followers with his guidelines about the proper way to live. As a public servant, he did not fare so well, however. His high standards of conduct often brought him into conflict with corrupt officials. According to Confucius, "The superior man understands righteousness. The inferior man understands profit." **Why do you think people were inspired by Confucius' teachings?**

The Master said, If out of the three hundred *Songs* I had to take one phrase to cover all my teaching, I would say ëLet there be no evil in your thoughts.'

Tzu-kung asked about the true gentleman. The Master said, He does not preach what he practices till he has practiced what he preaches.

The Master said, Yu, shall I teach you what knowledge is? When you know a thing, to recognize that you know it, and when you do not know a thing, to recognize that you do not know it. That is knowledge.

—*Analects*

Confucius Spreads His Wisdom Confucius was born in 551 B.C. to a noble but poor family. A brilliant scholar, Confucius hoped to become an adviser to a local ruler. He studied ancient texts to learn the rules of conduct that had guided the ancestors. For years, he wandered from court to court talking to rulers about how to govern. Unable to find a permanent government position, he turned to teaching. As his reputation for wisdom grew, he attracted many students. Like two other influential thinkers who lived about the same time—Siddhartha Gautama in India and Socrates in Greece—Confucius never wrote down his ideas. Rather, his students collected many of his sayings in the *Analects*.

Unlike the Buddha, Confucius took little interest in spiritual matters such as salvation. Instead, he developed a **philosophy,** or system of ideas, that was concerned with worldly goals, especially those of ensuring social order and good government.

Five Relationships Shape Behavior Confucius taught that harmony resulted when people accepted their place in society. He stressed five key relationships: ruler to subject, parent to child, husband to wife, elder brother to younger brother, and friend to friend. Confucius believed that, except for friendship, none of these relationships were equal. For example, he felt that older people were superior to younger ones and men were superior to women.

According to Confucius, everyone had duties and responsibilities. Superiors should care for their inferiors and set a good example, while inferiors owed loyalty and obedience to their superiors. Correct behavior, Confucius believed, would bring order and stability. Confucius put **filial piety,** or respect for parents, above all other duties. Other Confucian values included honesty, hard work, and concern for others. "Do not do to others," he declared, "what you do not wish yourself."

Confucius also taught that it was a ruler's responsibility to provide good government. In return, the people would be respectful and loyal subjects. Confucius said the best ruler was a virtuous one who led people by good example. In addition, Confucius believed that government leaders and officials should be well educated. "By nature, men are pretty much alike," he said. "It is learning and practice that set them apart." He urged rulers to take the advice of wise, educated men.

Confucianism Has Great Influence In the centuries after Confucius died, his ideas influenced many aspects of Chinese life. Chinese rulers relied on Confucian ideas and chose Confucian scholars as officials. The Confucian emphasis on filial piety bolstered traditional customs such as reverence for ancestors. Confucianism also introduced a long-lasting Chinese belief that the universe reflected a delicate balance between two forces, yin and yang. Yin was linked to Earth, darkness, and female forces, while yang stood for heaven, light, and male forces. To the Chinese, the well-being of the universe depended on maintaining balance between yin and yang. For example, the king should make the proper sacrifices to heaven while also taking practical steps to rule well.

As Chinese civilization spread, hundreds of millions of people in Korea, Japan, and Vietnam accepted Confucian beliefs. Nearly one third of the world's population came under the influence of these ideas.

To show the harmony of yin and yang, the Chinese have traditionally depicted them as two halves of a circle, one dark and one light.

Daoism Teaches Harmony With Nature Laozi, or "Old Master," is said to have lived at the time of Confucius and to have founded a philosophy called Daoism (DOW iz um). Although little is known about Laozi, he has been credited with writing the *Dao De Jing* (dow duh jing), or *The Way of Virtue*, a book that had enormous influence on Chinese life.

Unlike Confucianism, Daoism was not concerned with bringing order to human affairs. Instead, Daoists sought to live in harmony with nature. Laozi stressed that people should look beyond everyday cares to focus on the Dao, or "the way" of the universe. The Dao, he explained, was hard to understand fully or put into words. Thus he taught, "Those who know the Dao do not speak of it. Those who speak of it do not know it." To know the Dao, one should reject conflict and strife. Daoists stressed the simple ways of nature and the virtue of yielding. Water, they pointed out, does not resist, but rather yields to outside pressure—yet it is an unstoppable force.

Many Daoists turned from the "unnatural" ways of society. Some became hermits, artists, or poets. Daoists viewed government as unnatural and, therefore, the cause of many problems. "If the people are difficult to govern," Laozi declared, "it is because those in authority are too fond of action." To Daoists, the best government was one that governed the least.

Confucianism and Daoism Change and Blend Although scholars kept to Daoism's original teachings, the philosophy also evolved into a popular religion with gods, goddesses, and magical practices. Chinese peasants turned to Daoist priests for charms to protect them from unseen forces. In addition, people gradually blended Confucian and Daoist teachings. Although the two belief systems differed, people took beliefs and practices from each. Confucianism showed them how to behave. Daoism influenced their view of the natural world.

 Checkpoint Explain the different ways in which Confucianism and Daoism taught that people should live their lives.

Achievements Abound in Early China

The people of Shang and Zhou China are known for numerous cultural achievements. For example, Shang astronomers studied the movement of planets and recorded eclipses of the sun. Their findings helped them develop an accurate calendar with $365\frac{1}{4}$ days. In addition, the Chinese also improved the art and technology of bronze-making, producing stunning bronze weapons and ritual vessels covered with intricate decorations.

Discovering the Secret of Silk-making By 2640 B.C., the Chinese had made a discovery with extremely long-lasting impact: they had learned how to make silk thread from the cocoons of silkworms. Soon, the Chinese were cultivating both silkworms and the mulberry trees on which they fed. Women did the laborious work of tending the silkworms and processing the cocoons into thread. They then wove silk threads into a smooth cloth that was colored with brilliant dyes.

Only royalty and nobles could afford robes made from this luxurious silk. In time, silk became China's most valuable export. To protect their control of this profitable trade item, the Chinese kept the process of silk-making a secret for many hundreds of years.

INFOGRAPHIC The Secrets of Making Silk

Long viewed as a luxurious fabric, silk was a special commodity manufactured only in China for many hundreds of years. The ancient Chinese could not have begun to produce the fine fabric had they not discovered the special relationship between a tiny creature—the silkworm (above)—and a small tree—the mulberry. Silkworms were so important to the Chinese that they used jade, a precious stone, to carve their likeness.

▲ This Chinese painting shows women weaving silk threads after unwinding them from the cocoons.

▼ Swath of silk fabric, about 2,000 years old

The silkworm is actually a caterpillar. As it spins a cocoon (below), it produces a thin fiber—silk. But it won't produce any silk if it hasn't feasted on the leaves of a mulberry tree (at left). ▼

Thinking Critically
1. **Determine Relevance** Why do you think the Chinese kept the technology of making silk secret for so long?
2. **Draw Inferences** How does silk-making show that even highly developed civilizations can be reliant on the environment?

The Chinese have written with characters such as these (at top) since the time of their invention through to today. A calligrapher might use a brush like this one (above).

Establishing a Complex System of Writing Written Chinese took shape at least 4,000 years ago, if not earlier. Some of the oldest examples are found on **oracle bones.** These are animal bones or turtle shells on which Shang priests wrote questions addressed to the gods or to the spirit of an ancestor. Priests then heated each bone or shell until it cracked. They believed that by interpreting the pattern of cracks, they could provide answers or advice from the ancestors.

Over time, a writing system evolved that includes tens of thousands of **characters,** or written symbols. Each character represents a whole word or idea. To write a character requires a number of different brush or pen strokes. In the past century, the Chinese have simplified their characters, but Chinese remains one of the most difficult languages to learn to read and write. A person must memorize several thousand characters to read a newspaper. By contrast, languages such as English or Arabic, which are based on an alphabet, contain only about two dozen symbols that represent basic sounds.

Although it was complex, this written language fostered unity in early China. People in different parts of China often could not understand one another's spoken language, but they all used the same system of writing. Not surprisingly, in earlier times, only the well-to-do could afford the years of study needed to master the skills of reading and writing. Working with brush and ink, Chinese scholars later turned writing into an elegant art form called **calligraphy.**

Creating the First Books Under the Zhou, the Chinese made the first books. They bound thin strips of wood or bamboo together and then carefully drew characters on the flat surface with a brush and ink. Among the greatest Zhou works is the lovely *Book of Songs*. Many of its poems describe such events in the lives of farming people as planting and harvesting. Others praise kings or describe court ceremonies. The book also includes tender or sad love songs.

 Checkpoint For what purpose did writing begin in China?

SECTION 4 Assessment

Progress Monitoring *Online*
For: Self-quiz with vocabulary practice
Web Code: naa-0341

Terms, People, and Places

1. Place each of the key terms at the beginning of the section into one of the following categories: politics, culture, or geography. Write a sentence for each term explaining your choice.

Note Taking

2. **Reading Skill: Recognize Sequence** Use your completed chart to answer the Focus Question: What characteristics defined the civilization that developed in China under its early rulers?

Comprehension and Critical Thinking

3. **Summarize** What geographic challenges did China's early rulers face when trying to unite China or make alliances with peoples outside of China?

4. **Synthesize Information** What were the characteristics of the Shang and Zhou government and social structure?

5. **Analyze Information** What aspects of Confucianism and Daoism do you think contributed to their long-lasting influence?

6. **Draw Inferences** How do the various cultural developments of early China still affect the lives of people today?

● **Writing About History**

Quick Write: Gather Details On some essay tests, you may be asked to show causes and effects. Before you write a response, you may find it useful to gather details about the topic, and then create a graphic organizer to sort out the causes and related effects. Gather details about China's isolation during its early history. Then create a graphic organizer that presents the causes of the isolation and predicts its effects.

Shi Huangdi

Records of the
Grand Historian

WITNESS HISTORY 🔊 AUDIO

A New Age In China

Sima Qian (sih MAH chen), who served later Chinese emperors as Grand Historian, recounted an inscription on a monument built by the first Qin emperor to praise his own deeds:

❝The Emperor . . . rectified [put right] the laws, by which all things are regulated, human affairs are clarified, and fathers and sons united.

Being sagacious [wise], intelligent, benevolent, and righteous, he manifested [made clear to see] the Way [the Dao] and reason . . .

All things receive his favor, and live peacefully in their own abode [house].❞
—*Records of the Grand Historian*

Focus Question How did powerful emperors unite much of China and bring about a golden age of cultural achievements?

Strong Rulers Unite China

 Performance Standards

- **SSWH2b** Explain development and impact of Hinduism on India.
- **SSWH2c** Describe development of Chinese civilization under Qin.
- **SSWH2d** Explain the examination system.
- **SSWHRC1c** Demonstrate understanding of contextual vocabulary.

Terms, People, and Places

Shi Huangdi
Wudi
monopoly
expansionism

civil servant
warlord
acupuncture

Note Taking

Reading Skill: Recognize Sequence Keep track of the sequence of important events in the Qin and Han periods by recording them in a chart like this one in the order they occurred.

Date	Event

From his base in western China, the powerful ruler of the state of Qin rose to unify all of China. An ancient Chinese poet and historian described how Zheng (jeng) crushed all his rivals: "Cracking his long whip, he drove the universe before him, swallowing up the eastern and the western Zhou and overthrowing the feudal lords."

In 221 B.C., Zheng proclaimed himself **Shi Huangdi** (shur hwahng dee), or "First Emperor." Although his methods were brutal, he ushered in China's classical age—a term historians use when a civilization sets patterns in government, philosophy, religion, science, and the arts that serve as a framework for later cultures.

Shi Huangdi Unifies China

Shi Huangdi was determined to end the divisions that had splintered Zhou China. He spent nearly 20 years conquering most of the warring states. Then, imposing punishments for failure, he built the strong, authoritarian Qin government.

Legalism Establishes Harsh Rule Shi Huangdi centralized power with the help of Legalist advisers. Legalism was based on the teachings of Hanfeizi (hahn fay dzuh), who had died in 233 B.C. According to Hanfeizi, "the nature of man is evil. His goodness is acquired." Greed, he declared, was the motive for most actions and the cause of most conflicts. Hanfeizi insisted that the only way to achieve order was to pass strict laws and impose harsh punishments for crimes.

A Chinese artist captured Shi Huangdi's harsh approach in this painting, in which Legalists execute scholars as books burn in the foreground.

To Legalists, strength, not goodness, was a ruler's greatest virtue. "The ruler alone possesses power," declared Hanfeizi, "wielding it like lightning or like thunder." Many feudal rulers chose Legalism as the most effective way to keep order. Shi Huangdi made it the official policy of the Qin government. He then moved harshly against his critics. He tortured, killed, or enslaved many who opposed his rule. Hardest hit were the feudal nobles and Confucian scholars who loathed his laws.

To end dissent, Shi Huangdi approved a ruthless campaign of book burning, ordering the destruction of all writings other than manuals on topics such as medicine and agriculture. Laws such as these were so cruel that later generations despised Legalism. Yet Legalist ideas survived for hundreds of years in laws that forced people to work on government projects and punished those who shirked their duties. Indeed, the policy of enslaving people as punishment for crimes lasted through most of the following dynasty, though only a very small percentage of Chinese were enslaved.

Unity Imposed Shi Huangdi also abolished feudalism, which required little allegiance from local rulers to the central government. He replaced the feudal states with 36 military districts and appointed loyal officials to administer them. Shi Huangdi forced noble families to live in his capital at Xianyang (shyahn yahng), where he could monitor them. He distributed the lands of the displaced nobles to peasants. Still, peasants had to pay high taxes to support Shi Huangdi's armies and building projects.

To promote unity, the First Emperor standardized weights and measures and replaced the diverse coins of the Zhou states with Qin coins. He also had scholars create uniformity in Chinese writing. Workers repaired and extended roads and canals to strengthen the transportation system. A new law even required cart axles to be the same width so that wheels could run in the same ruts on all Chinese roads.

Constructing the Great Wall Shi Huangdi's most remarkable and costly achievement was the Great Wall. In the past, individual feudal states had built walls to defend their lands against raiders. Shi Huangdi ordered the walls to be joined. Hundreds of thousands of laborers worked for years through bitter cold and burning heat. They pounded earth and stone into a mountainous wall almost 25 feet high and topped with a wide brick road. Many workers died in the harsh conditions.

Over the centuries, the wall was extended and rebuilt many times. Eventually, it snaked for thousands of miles across northern China. While the wall did not keep invaders out of China, it did demonstrate the emperors' ability to mobilize China's vast resources. The Great Wall became an important symbol to the Chinese people, dividing and protecting their civilized world from the nomadic bands north of the wall.

Qin Dynasty Collapses When Shi Huangdi died in 210 B.C., anger over heavy taxes, forced labor, and cruel policies exploded into revolts. As Qin power officially collapsed in 206 B.C., Gao Zu (gow dzoo), an illiterate peasant leader, defeated rival armies and founded the new Han dynasty four years later.

 Checkpoint What kind of government did Legalists favor?

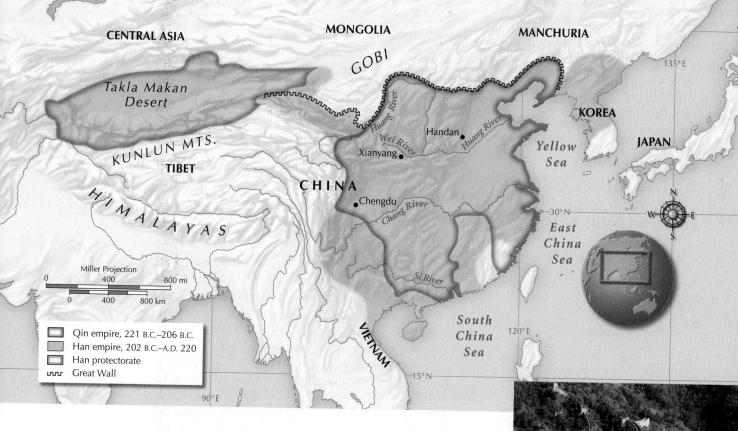

Qin and Han Empires

Map Skills Under the Qin and Han dynasties, Chinese rule expanded significantly, as did the Great Wall (pictured below).

1. **Locate** (a) Great Wall (b) Qin empire (c) Han empire (d) Chengdu (e) Takla Makan Desert
2. **Place** What natural barriers helped protect China from invaders?
3. **Draw Conclusions** How did the Great Wall's placement relate to the extent of the empires? What does this tell you about where invaders came from?

CENTRAL ASIA

MONGOLIA

MANCHURIA

GOBI

Takla Makan Desert

KUNLUN MTS.

TIBET

HIMALAYAS

Huang River

Wei River

Handan

Huang River

Xianyang

CHINA

Chengdu

Chang River

Si River

VIETNAM

KOREA

JAPAN

Yellow Sea

East China Sea

South China Sea

135° E

30° N

120° E

15° N

90° E

Miller Projection

| 0 | 400 | 800 mi |
| 0 | 400 | 800 km |

- ☐ Qin empire, 221 B.C.–206 B.C.
- ☐ Han empire, 202 B.C.–A.D. 220
- ☐ Han protectorate
- ⎐ Great Wall

The Han Dynasty Strengthens China

As emperor, Gao Zu set about restoring order and justice to his empire. Although he continued earlier efforts to unify China, he lowered taxes and eased Legalist policies. In a key move, he appointed Confucian scholars as advisors. His policies created strong foundations for the Han dynasty, which lasted from 202 B.C. until A.D. 220.

Emperor Wudi Makes Improvements The most famous Han emperor, **Wudi** (woo dee), took China to new heights. During his long reign from about 141 B.C. to 87 B.C., he strengthened the government and economy. Like Gao Zu, he chose officials from Confucian "men of wisdom and virtue." To train scholars, he set up an imperial university at Xian (shyahn).

Wudi furthered economic growth by improving canals and roads. He had granaries set up across the empire so the government could buy grain when it was abundant and sell it at stable prices when it was scarce. He reorganized finances and imposed a government monopoly on iron and salt. A **monopoly** is the complete control of a product or business by one person or group. The sale of iron and salt gave the government a source of income other than taxes on peasants.

66 Southeast of Ta-hsia [Bactria] is the kingdom of Shen-tu [India]. 'When I was in Ta-hsia,' Chang Ch'ien [Zhang Qian] reported, 'I saw bamboo canes from Ch'iung and cloth made in the [Chinese] province of Shu. When I asked the people how they had gotten such articles, they replied, 'Our merchants go to buy them in the markets of Shen-tu.' Shen-tu, they told me, lies several thousand *li*[1] southeast of Ta-hsia. The people cultivate the land and live much like the people of Ta-shia. The region is said to be hot and damp. The inhabitants ride elephants when they go into battle. The kingdom is situated on a great river. . . .

Thus the emperor learned of . . . great states rich in unusual products whose people cultivated the land and made their living in much the same way as the Chinese. 99

—*Records of the Grand Historian*

1 A *li* is an ancient Chinese measurement equal to about one third of a mile.

Zhang Qian Explores Outside China

Sima Qian's *Records of the Grand Historian* includes the accounts of Zhang Qian, a diplomat whom Emperor Wudi sent on various journeys to establish contact with peoples outside the Han empire. Zhang traveled as far as India and the eastern edge of the Roman empire. The information he brought back about the rich kingdoms he had seen led to the founding of the Silk Road, the legendary trade network that connected China and the western empires.

Wudi followed a policy of **expansionism,** or expanding a country's territory, by increasing the amount of land under Chinese rule. He fought many battles to expand China's borders and to drive nomadic peoples beyond the Great Wall. Chinese armies added outposts in Manchuria, Korea, northern Vietnam, Tibet, and Central Asia. Soldiers, traders, and settlers slowly spread Chinese influence across these areas.

Silk Road Links China to the West The emperor Wudi opened up a network of trade routes, later called the Silk Road, that would link China and the West for centuries. During the Han period, new foods such as grapes, figs, cucumbers, and walnuts flowed into China from western Asia. Lucky traders might return to China bearing furs from Central Asia, muslin from India, or glass from Rome. At the same time, the Chinese sent large quantities of silk westward to fill a growing demand for the prized fabric.

Eventually, the Silk Road stretched for 4,000 miles, linking China to the Fertile Crescent in the Middle East. Few traders covered the entire distance, however; instead, goods were relayed in stages from one set of traders to another. At the western end, trade was controlled by various peoples, including the Persians.

China Selects Scholar-Officials Han emperors made Confucianism the official belief system of the state. They relied on well-educated scholars to run the bureaucratic government. A scholar-official was expected to match the Confucian ideal of a gentleman. He would be courteous and dignified and possess a thorough knowledge of history, music, poetry, and Confucian teachings.

Founding the Civil Service System Han emperors adopted the idea that **civil servants**—that is, officials in the government—should win their positions by merit, rather than through family ties as had occurred

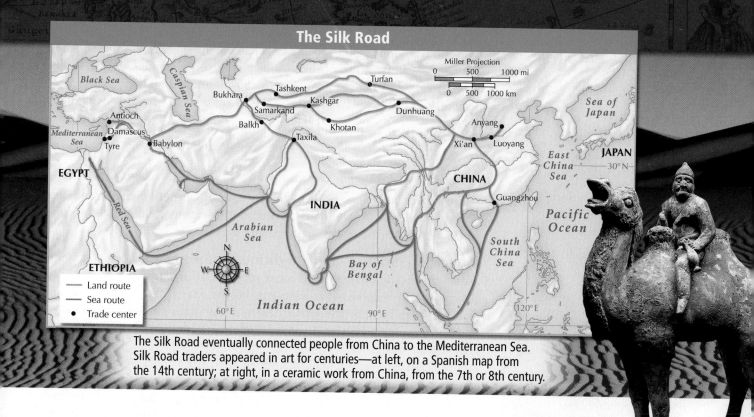

The Silk Road

The Silk Road eventually connected people from China to the Mediterranean Sea. Silk Road traders appeared in art for centuries—at left, on a Spanish map from the 14th century; at right, in a ceramic work from China, from the 7th or 8th century.

in the past. In the Han civil service system, a young man would start in a clerical job. Once he proved his abilities, he would move up in local government. If he continued to excel, he would eventually be recruited into the civil service and might be tested on his knowledge of government policy. Essential to his studies were the Five Classics, a collection of histories, poems, and handbooks <u>compiled</u> by Confucius and others that served as a guide to conduct for about 2,000 years.

Much later, in the 580s, the Sui dynasty set up a formal system of civil service exams, which were given at the local, provincial, and national levels. In theory, any man could take the exams. In practice, only those who could afford years of study, such as the sons of wealthy landowners or officials, could hope to succeed. Occasionally, a village or wealthy family might pay for the education of a brilliant peasant boy. If he passed the exams and obtained a government job, he, his family, and his clan all enjoyed immense prestige and moved up in society. Confucian teachings about filial piety and the superiority of men prevented women from taking the civil service exam. As a result, women were excluded from government jobs.

The civil service system remained in use until 1912. It put men trained in Confucian thought at every level of government and created an enduring system of values. Dynasties rose and fell, but Confucian influence survived.

Han Empire Overthrown As the Han dynasty aged, signs of decay appeared. Court intrigues undermined emperors who could no longer control powerful **warlords,** or local military rulers. Weak emperors let canals and roads fall into disrepair. Burdened by heavy taxes and crushing debt, many peasants revolted. Thousands of rebellious peasants abandoned their villages and fled to the mountains. There they joined secret groups of bandits known by colorful names like the "Red Eyebrows" and the "Green Woodsmen."

Thinking Critically
1. **Synthesize Information** How were people in Ta-hsia able to buy goods from the Chinese province of Shu?
2. **Analyze Information** How do you think the knowledge Zheng gained helped establish the Silk Road?

Vocabulary Builder
<u>compiled</u>—(kum PYLD) *vt.* created by gathering things together

In A.D. 220, ambitious warlords overthrew the last Han emperor. After 400 years of unity, China broke up into several kingdoms. Adding to the disorder, invaders poured over the Great Wall and set up their own states. In time, many of these newcomers were absorbed into Chinese civilization.

✔ **Checkpoint** How did Han emperors further economic growth?

Achievements of the Han Golden Age

The Han period was one of the golden ages of Chinese civilization. Han China made such tremendous advances in so many fields that the Chinese later called themselves "the people of Han."

Advancing Science and Medicine Han scientists wrote texts on chemistry, zoology, botany, and other subjects. Han astronomers carefully observed and measured movements of the stars and planets, which enabled them to improve earlier calendars and invent better timekeeping devices. One scientist invented a simple seismograph to detect and measure earthquakes.

The scientist Wang Chong disagreed with the widely held belief that comets and eclipses showed heaven's anger. "On the average, there is one moon eclipse about every 180 days," he wrote, "and a solar eclipse about every 41 or 42 months. Eclipses . . . are not caused by political action." Wang Chong argued that no scientific theories should be accepted unless they were supported by proof.

Chinese physicians diagnosed diseases, developed anesthetics, and experimented with herbal remedies and other drugs. Many doctors promoted the use of **acupuncture.** In this medical treatment, developed about 2500 B.C., the doctor inserts needles into the skin at specific points to relieve pain or treat various illnesses.

Forging Ahead With Technology and Engineering In its time, Han China was the most technologically advanced civilization in the world. Cai Lun (ky loon), an official of the Han court, invented a method for making paper out of wood pulp. His basic method is still used to manufacture paper today. The Chinese also pioneered advanced methods of shipbuilding and invented the rudder to steer. Other practical inventions included bronze and iron stirrups, fishing reels, wheelbarrows, and suspension bridges. Some of these ideas moved west slowly, reaching Europe hundreds of years later.

Expanding the Arts The walled cities of Han China boasted splendid temples and palaces amid elegant parks. Although these wooden buildings have not survived, Han poets and historians have described their grandeur. In addition, artisans produced delicate jade and ivory carvings and fine ceramic figures. Bronze-workers and silk-makers improved on earlier techniques and set high standards for future generations.

Lessons for Women, a handbook of behavior written by Ban Zhao (bahn jow) around A.D. 100, carefully spells out the proper behavior for women and men. Ban Zhao favored equal education for boys and girls. However, she stressed that women should be obedient, respectful, and submissive. "Let a woman modestly yield to others," she advised. "Let her respect others."

✔ **Checkpoint** What sorts of achievements made the Han period a golden age?

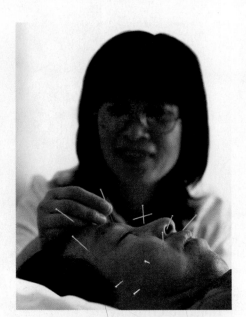
Acupuncturists like this woman place needles in specific spots on the body to treat each ailment.

The Chinese Accept Buddhism

By A.D. 100, missionaries and merchants had spread Mahayana Buddhism from India into China. At first, the Chinese had trouble with the new faith. For example, Chinese tradition valued family loyalty, while Buddhism honored monks and nuns who gave up the benefits of family life for a life of solitary meditation.

Despite obstacles such as this, Buddhism became increasingly popular, especially in times of crisis. Its great appeal was the promise of escape from suffering. Mahayana Buddhism offered the hope of eternal happiness and presented the Buddha as a compassionate, merciful god. Through prayer, good works, and devotion, anyone could hope to gain salvation. Neither Daoism nor Confucianism emphasized this idea of personal salvation.

By A.D. 400, Buddhism had spread throughout China. Buddhist monasteries became important centers of learning and the arts. Buddhism absorbed many Confucian and Daoist traditions. Chinese Buddhist monks stressed filial piety and honored Confucius.

✓ **Checkpoint** Why did Buddhism appeal to many people in China?

Looking Ahead

Shi Huangdi, Gao Zu, Wudi, and later Han rulers forged a vast and varied land into a united China. Han rulers created an empire roughly the size of the continental United States. During this period, Chinese officials established the system of administration that would survive until 1912. In coming centuries, China would undergo great changes. It would break up and be painfully reassembled over and over. On the whole, however, Chinese civilization would flourish. After periods of disunity, in A.D. 581 a new dynasty, the Sui, would turn to Confucian scholars to revive the days of Han greatness.

In Mahayana Buddhism, people hope to become *bodhisattvas*, or enlightened people, who help others gain salvation. The *bodhisattva* of compassion and mercy (above), called Kuan-yin in China, is one of the most popular.

SECTION 5 Assessment

Progress Monitoring Online
For: Self-quiz with vocabulary practice
Web Code: naa-0351

Terms, People, and Places

1. For each term, person, or place listed at the beginning of the section, write a sentence explaining its significance.

Note Taking

2. **Reading Skill: Recognize Sequence** Use your completed chart to answer the Focus Question: How did powerful emperors unite much of China and bring about a golden age of cultural achievements?

Comprehension and Critical Thinking

3. **Summarize** What were three steps Shi Huangdi took to unify China?

4. **Demonstrate Reasoned Judgment** What aspects of the civil service system do you think allowed it to last for such a great length of time?

5. **Determine Relevance** Select three achievements made during the Han period and describe why you think they were significant advancements.

● Writing About History

Quick Write: Draft a Quick Outline On some essay tests, you will not be given much time to write an essay. Drafting a quick outline can help you save time as you write your response. Write a quick outline of a response to one of the following essay topics:

- the role of Legalism in Qin government
- the importance of the Silk Road
- the greatest cultural achievements of the Han

Quick Study Guide

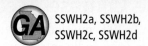 SSWH2a, SSWH2b, SSWH2c, SSWH2d

Progress Monitoring *Online*
For: Self-test with vocabulary practice
Web Code: naa-0361

■ Eras of Civilization

India		China	
Indus civilization	2600 B.C. to 1900 B.C.	Shang dynasty	1766 B.C. to 1122 B.C.
Aryan civilization	1500 B.C. to ?	Zhou dynasty	1122 B.C. to 256 B.C.
Maurya empire	321 B.C. to 185 B.C.	Qin dynasty	221 B.C. to 206 B.C.
Gupta empire	A.D. 320 to A.D. 550	Han dynasty	202 B.C. to A.D. 220

■ Unification of China

Cause and Effect	
Long-Term Causes	**Immediate Causes**
• Confucian ideas dominate education. • China's isolation permits development without much outside interference. • A common system of writing evolves.	• Zheng conquers the eastern and western Zhou and overthrows the feudal lords. • Zheng proclaims himself Shi Huangdi ("First Emperor").

Unification of China	
Immediate Effects	**Long-Term Effects**
• Shi Huangdi abolishes feudalism. • Shi Huangdi standardizes weights and measures and money. • The government cracks down on dissenters. • Shi Huangdi supervises work on the Great Wall.	• China makes advances in government and trade. • Confucian-educated officials hold most government jobs. • Its common culture helps China survive upheavals.

■ Religions Founded in India

Hinduism
• Originated with the Aryans
• Ultimate goal: moksha, or union with brahman
• Achieve moksha by following laws of karma and dharma through various cycles of life

• Karma
• Dharma
• Reincarnation

Buddhism
• Founded by Siddhartha Gautama, the Buddha
• Ultimate goal: nirvana, or union with the universe
• Achieve nirvana by following the Four Noble Truths and the Eightfold Path; follow karma and dharma along the way

■ Philosophies Founded in China

Confucianism	Daoism
• Founded by Confucius • Focuses on worldly goals of ensuring social order and good government • Stresses accepting one's place in society and behaving correctly • Views government as responsible for setting a good example for people and for being run by well-educated people	• Possibly founded by Laozi • Focuses on living in harmony with nature • Stresses simple ways of nature and the virtue of yielding • Views government as unnatural and as a body that should govern the people as little as possible

■ Expansion of Civilization

2600 B.C.
Civilization arises on the Indian subcontinent in the Indus River valley.

2000 B.C.
Civilization emerges along China's river valleys.

Chapter Events
World Events

3500 B.C.

2500 B.C.

3200 B.C.
Civilization begins in Sumer.

2700 B.C.
Egypt's Old Kingdom is established.

Concept Connector

 Essential Question Review

To connect prior knowledge with what you have learned in this chapter, answer the questions below in your Concept Connector journal. Use the journal in the Reading and Note Taking Study Guide to record your answers (or go to www.phschool.com **Web Code**: nad-0307). In addition, record information about the following concepts:

- Cultural Diffusion: decimal system, Hinduism, and Buddhism
- Migration: Indo-European migrations
- Impact of the Individual: Confucius

1. **Political Systems** After the Shang Dynasty was overthrown, the Zhou Dynasty established a feudal state in China. What is feudalism? How did feudal lords contribute to China's economic growth during this period? How did feudalism contribute to the downfall of the Zhou Dynasty?

2. **Belief Systems** Compare the views of ancient Egyptians and ancient Indians about the results of a person's actions during his or her lifetime. Think about the following:
   - the role of the god Osiris
   - the concepts of karma, dharma, and reincarnation
   - the Eightfold Path

   How do you think each of these views helped establish a set of morals by which people could lead their daily lives?

3. **Trade** How was the trade network of the Phoenicians similar to the Silk Road in its impact on economics and culture? For each trade network, think about the following:
   - its geographic extent
   - the various civilizations it involved
   - the trade items exchanged along it
   - instances of cultural diffusion that occurred because of it

■ **Connections to Today**

1. **Economic Systems: The Use of Monopolies** When Han emperor Wudi established the first monopolies in China's history, he hoped the resulting lack of competition would ensure the government a reliable new source of income. In many economic systems today, however, monopolies are banned or carefully controlled so that competition is always possible. Both the United States and Great Britain have passed laws to severely limit monopolies. What do you think are the advantages and the disadvantages of monopolies? Why might monopolies have been viewed differently in ancient times than in the world today? Study the political cartoon below to start generating ideas.

History *Interactive*

For: Interactive timeline
Web Code: nap-0361

| 1650 B.C. China's first known dynasty, the Shang, is established. | 1500 B.C. The Aryans establish a civilization and Hinduism in India. | 566 B.C. Siddhartha Gautama, the founder of Buddhism, is born. | 321 B.C. India's first empire, the Maurya, begins. | A.D. 320 The Gupta empire begins a golden age in India. |

1500 B.C. 500 B.C. A.D. 500

| 1500 B.C. The Olmecs build the first civilization in the Americas. | 509 B.C. The Roman republic is founded. | 460 B.C. The Age of Pericles begins in Greece. | A.D. 250 Maya city-states flourish in Mexico and Central America. | A.D. 476 The western Roman empire collapses. |

Chapter Assessment

Terms, People, and Places

Complete each sentence by choosing the correct answer from the terms below. You will not use all the terms.

brahman	golden age
monopoly	warlord
rajah	reincarnation
filial piety	dowry
dynastic cycle	karma
feudalism	atman

1. The chiefs who led Aryan tribes were called _____.
2. In Hinduism, the essential self is called _____.
3. A _____ is a period of great cultural achievements.
4. _____ means respect for one's parents.
5. The rise and fall of Chinese dynasties is called the _____.
6. The complete control of a product or business by one person or group is a _____.

Main Ideas

Section 1 (pp. 68–75)

7. What documents from the Aryan written tradition tell us about Aryan society?

Section 2 (pp. 76–83)

8. In Hinduism, what is a person's ultimate goal? What is it in Buddhism?

Section 3 (pp. 84–91)

9. How did caste rules affect the daily lives of Indians during Maurya and Gupta times?

Section 4 (pp. 92–100)

10. Summarize the roles of the Mandate of Heaven and the dynastic cycle in China.
11. Describe two cultural achievements made in early China.

Section 5 (pp. 101–107)

12. How did Shi Huangdi centralize power in China? How did Wudi then expand China's power?

Chapter Focus Question

13. In what ways did the civilizations and empires of ancient India and China lay long-lasting social and political foundations?

Critical Thinking

14. **Synthesize Information** Describe two aspects of Indian society that began in Aryan times and have lasted until the present day.
15. **Make Comparisons** What similarities and differences exist between Hindu and Buddhist teachings about the way that a person should live?
16. **Geography and History** Monsoons greatly affected life in India in early times. How might their effect be similar or different today?
17. **Analyze Information** Consider two major achievements made in ancient China—Shi Huangdi's expansion of the Great Wall and Wudi's opening up the Silk Road. How did each affect China's relationship with the outside world?
18. **Draw Inferences** Compare the initial intention of feudalism with its resulting effect on the Zhou dynasty. Under what circumstances might feudalism have been more successful?
19. **Demonstrate Reasoned Judgment** Confucianism lay at the foundations of the Chinese civil service system, which lasted for 2,000 years. What about Confucianism do you think led to such a stable administrative structure?
20. **Analyzing Visuals** What types of information can scholars learn from studying Indus artifacts such as the seal and cubic weights shown on page 71?

● Writing About History

In this chapter's five Section Assessments, you developed skills for writing an essay on a test.

Writing for Assessment To prepare for a test about ancient India and China, write an essay responding to one of the following topics.

(1) Explain two key cultural achievements of ancient India or China.
(2) Compare the belief systems developed in ancient India to those developed in ancient China.
(3) Argue which approach to governing taught in ancient India or ancient China is the best.

Consult page SH20 of the Writing Handbook for additional help.

Prewriting

- Choose a topic by examining each question and determining which you are best able to answer.
- Decide how to divide your time between prewriting, drafting, and revising.
- Gather details related to the topic and use a graphic organizer to organize them.

Drafting

- Choose a logical strategy for organizing the points you will make, such as chronologically.
- Write an opening for the essay that restates the question and a conclusion that recaps your points.
- Select facts that support the main idea of your essay.

Revising

- Use the guidelines for revising your essay on page SH22 of the Writing Handbook.

Prepare for the GHSGT

Three Paths in Chinese Philosophy

The Chinese philosophies established in ancient times laid out varied approaches to living and governing. The documents below illustrate some of the differences among Daoist, Confucian, and Legalist advice on governance.

Document A

"Refrain from exalting [praising] the worthy,
　　So that the people will not scheme and contend;
Refrain from prizing rare possessions,
　　So that the people will not steal;
Refrain from displaying objects of desire,
　　So that the people's hearts will not be disturbed.

Therefore a sage [wise one] rules his people thus:
　　He empties their minds,
　　　　And fills their bellies;
　　He weakens their ambitions,
　　　　And strengthens their bones.

He strives always to keep the people innocent of knowledge and desires, and to keep the knowing ones from meddling."

—From the **Dao De Jing**

Document B

"Behave when away from home as though you were in the presence of an important guest. Deal with the common people as though you were officiating [presiding] at an important sacrifice. Do not do to others what you would not want others to do to you, then there will be no dissatisfaction either in the state or at home. . . .

　　Lead the people by laws and regulate them by penalties, and the people will try to keep out of jail, but will have no sense of shame. Lead the people by virtue and restrain them by the rules of decorum [social expectations], and the people will have a sense of shame, and moreover will become good."

—From the **Analects** of Confucius

Document C

". . . rewards should be rich and certain so that the people will be attracted by them; punishments should be severe and definite so that the people will fear them; and laws should be uniform and steadfast so that the people will be familiar with them. Consequently, the sovereign [ruler] should show no wavering in bestowing reward and grant no pardon in administering punishments, and he should add honor to rewards and disgrace to punishments—when this is done, then both the worthy and the unworthy will want to exert themselves. . ."

—From the writings of Hanfeizi

Document D

Chinese Imperial Dragon

The dragon was the symbol of the Chinese emperor.

Analyzing Documents

Use your knowledge of history and Documents A, B, C, and D to answer questions 1–4.

1. According to the *Dao De Jing,* a wise ruler governs well by
   A displaying power and wealth.
   B promoting education.
   C holding up some people as most worthy.
   D feeding and supporting the people.

2. How does Confucius say rulers should treat common people?
   A with harsh but just punishments and occasional rewards
   B with the same respect they would show at an important ceremony
   C with the same distrust and fear they feel toward rivals
   D with disinterest

3. Which words best describe Hanfeizi's approach to governance?
   A kind, compassionate, fair
   B decent, modest, unassuming
   C direct, strict, unwavering
   D sly, methodical, devious

4. **Writing Task** Suppose you had to advise an ancient Chinese ruler. What advice would you give, and which philosophy would you base it on? Use Documents A, B, and C along with information from the chapter to write your answer.

4 Ancient Greece
1750 B.C.–133 B.C.

The Highest Good

The independent sovereignty of the city-state was the basic political structure of ancient Greece. Although the governments that ruled the city-states were varied and numerous, the goals these communities strived to attain were similar as described in *Politics* by the great philosopher Aristotle.

❝Every State is a community of some kind, and every community is established with a view to some good; for mankind always act in order to obtain that which they think good. But, if all communities aim at some good, the state or political community, which is the highest of all, and which embraces all the rest, aims at good in a greater degree than any other, and at the highest good.❞

Listen to the Witness History audio to hear more about Greek government and philosophy.

◀ Men voting under the watchful eye of the Greek goddess Athena

The Greek philosopher Aristotle

Sixth century B.C. bronze helmet

Relief tile depicting Plato and his student Aristotle

GA Performance Standards

Chapter Focus Question What enduring traditions and institutions did Greek culture extend to most of the Western world?

Section 1
Early People of the Aegean
SSWH1d, SSWH3a, SSWH3c

Section 2
The Rise of Greek City-States
SSWH3a, SSWH3c, SSWH3d

Section 3
Conflict in the Greek World
SSWH3a, SSWH3c

Section 4
The Glory That Was Greece
SSWH3b, SSWH3c

Section 5
Alexander and the Hellenistic Age
SSWH3b, SSWH3c

Use the ☑ **Quick Study Timeline** at the end of this chapter to preview chapter events.

 Concept Connector ONLINE

To explore Essential Questions related to this chapter, go to PHSchool.com
Web Code: nad-0407

Greek amphora, or storage pot, depicting the kidnapping of Europa

WITNESS HISTORY 🔊 AUDIO

Zeus Kidnaps Europa

Europa, the beautiful daughter of the king of Phoenicia, was gathering flowers when she saw a bull quietly grazing with her father's herds. The bull was actually Zeus, king of all the Greek gods, who had fallen in love with her. When Europa reached up to place flowers on his horns, he suddenly bounded into the air and carried the weeping princess far across the Mediterranean Sea to the island of Crete. Eventually, Europa married the king of Crete and gave her name to a new continent—Europe.

Focus Question How did the Minoans and Mycenaeans shape early Greek civilizations?

Early People of the Aegean

 Performance Standards

- **SSWH1d** Describe early trading networks in Eastern Mediterranean.
- **SSWH3a** Compare the Greek polis, the Roman Republic, and the Roman Empire.
- **SSWH3c** Analyze contributions of Hellenistic and Roman culture.

Terms, People, and Places

Knossos	Trojan War
shrine	strait
fresco	Homer

Note Taking

Reading Skill: Identify Main Ideas Create a table like the one below. Then, use the table to record the main ideas relating to the groups of people discussed in the section.

Minoans	Mycenaeans	Dorians
•	•	•
•	•	•

The island of Crete (kreet) was the cradle of an early civilization that later influenced Greeks living on the European mainland. The people of Crete, however, had absorbed many ideas from the older civilizations of Egypt and Mesopotamia. Europa's mythic journey from Phoenicia to Crete suggests this movement of ideas from east to west.

Minoans Trade and Prosper

Washed by the warm waters of the Aegean (ee JEE un) Sea, Crete was home to a brilliant early civilization. We do not actually know what the people who built this civilization called themselves. However, the British archaeologist who unearthed its ruins called them Minoans after Minos, a legendary king of Crete. Minoan civilization reached its height, or greatest success, between 1600 B.C. and 1500 B.C.

The success of the Minoans was based on trade, not conquest. Minoan traders set up outposts throughout the Aegean world. From their island home in the eastern Mediterranean, they crossed the seas to the Nile Valley and the Middle East. Through contact with Egypt and Mesopotamia, they acquired ideas and technology in fields such as writing and architecture that they adapted to their own culture.

Minoan Art at Knossos The rulers of this trading empire lived in a vast palace at **Knossos** (NAHS us). It housed rooms for the royal family, banquet halls, and working areas for artisans. It also included religious **shrines**, areas dedicated to the honor of gods and goddesses.

The walls of the palace at Knossos were covered with colorful **frescoes,** watercolor paintings done on wet plaster. These frescoes tell us much about Minoan society. Leaping dolphins reflect the importance of the sea to the Minoan people. Religious images indicate that the Minoans worshiped the bull as well as a mother goddess. Other frescoes show young men and women strolling through gardens or jumping through the horns of a charging bull. The paintings also suggest that women appeared freely in public and may have enjoyed more rights than women in most other ancient civilizations.

Minoan Civilization Disappears By about 1400 B.C., Minoan civilization had vanished. Archaeologists are not sure of the reasons for its disappearance. A sudden volcanic eruption on a nearby island may have rained flaming death on Knossos. Or perhaps an earthquake may have destroyed the palace, followed by an immense wave that drowned the inhabitants of the island. However, it is certain that invaders played some role in the destruction of Minoan civilization. These intruders were the Mycenaeans (my suh NEE unz), the first Greek-speaking people of whom we have a written record.

✔ **Checkpoint**   How does the art at Knossos reflect Minoan culture?

Trade and War in Mycenae

Like the Aryans who spread across India, the Mycenaeans spoke an Indo-European language. They conquered the Greek mainland before overrunning the island of Crete.

Sea Trade Brings Wealth Mycenaean civilization dominated the Aegean world from about 1400 B.C. to 1200 B.C. Like the Minoans, the Mycenaeans were sea traders. They reached out beyond the Aegean to Sicily, Italy, Egypt, and Mesopotamia. The Mycenaeans learned many skills from the Minoans, including the art of writing. They, too, absorbed Egyptian and Mesopotamian customs, many of which they passed on to later Greeks.

The Mycenaeans lived in separate city-states on the mainland. In each, a warrior-king built a thick-walled fortress from which he ruled the surrounding villages. Wealthy rulers amassed treasure, including fine gold ornaments that archaeologists have unearthed from their tombs.

Life Near the Sea
This detail from an ancient Minoan fresco decorates the wall of a house located on the Greek island of Thera. *How do the scene depicted above and the daggers below reflect the importance of the sea to the Minoan and Mycenaean civilizations?*

A Mycenaean dagger and sheath with inlaid depictions of sea creatures, *c.* 1200 B.C.

The Trojan Horse
The story of the Trojan horse had great significance to ancient Greeks. The image of the horse was often used by Greek artisans to decorate their work, such as this relief on the neck of a seventh-century B.C. amphora. *Why do you think the ancient Greeks would memorialize the Trojan War in their art?*

The Trojan War The Mycenaeans are best remembered for their part in the **Trojan War,** which took place around 1250 B.C. The conflict may have had its origins in economic rivalry between Mycenae and Troy, a rich trading city in present-day Turkey, that controlled the vital **straits,** or narrow water passages, connecting the Mediterranean and Black seas.

In Greek legend, however, the war had a more romantic cause. When the Trojan prince, Paris, kidnaps Helen, the beautiful wife of a Greek king, the Mycenaeans sail to Troy to rescue her. For the next 10 years, the two sides battle until the Greeks finally seize Troy and burn the city to the ground.

For centuries, most people regarded the Trojan War as pure legend. Then, in the 1870s, a wealthy German businessman, Heinrich Schliemann (HYN rik SCHLEE mahn), set out to prove that the legend was rooted in fact. As Schliemann excavated the site of ancient Troy, he found evidence of fire and war dating to about 1250 B.C. Though most of the details remain lost in legend, modern scholars now agree that the Trojan War was an actual event.

 Checkpoint How did trade shape Mycenaean society?

Homer and the Great Legends of Greece

Not long after their victory over Troy, the Mycenaens themselves came under attack from sea raiders and also from another Greek-speaking people, the Dorians, invading from the north. As Mycenaean power faded, their people abandoned the cities and trade declined. People forgot many skills, including the art of writing. From the end of the Mycenaean civilization in about 1100 B.C. until about 900 B.C., Greek civilization seemed to step backward.

Much of what we know about the Trojan War and life during this period comes from two great epic poems, the *Iliad* and the *Odyssey.* These epics may have been the work of many people, but they are credited to the poet **Homer,** who probably lived about 750 B.C. According to tradition, Homer was a blind poet who wandered from village to village, singing of heroic deeds. Like the great Indian epics, Homer's tales were passed on orally for generations before they were finally written down.

The *Iliad,* full as it is of gods, goddesses, and even a talking horse, is our chief source of information about the Trojan War. At the start of the poem, Achilles (uh KIL eez), the mightiest Greek warrior, has withdrawn from battle because he has been unfairly treated and insulted by his commander. The war soon turns against the Greeks, but Achilles stubbornly refuses to listen to pleas that he rejoin the fighting. Only after his best friend is killed does Achilles return to battle.

The *Odyssey* tells of the many struggles of the Greek hero Odysseus (oh DIS ee us) on his return home to his faithful wife, Penelope, after the fall of Troy. On his long voyage, Odysseus encounters a sea monster, a race of one-eyed giants, and a beautiful sorceress who turns men into swine.

The *Iliad* and *Odyssey* reveal much about the values of the ancient Greeks. The heroes display honor, courage, and eloquence, as when Achilles rallies his troops:

Vocabulary Builder
eloquence—(EL uh kwens)
n. a manner of speech that is vivid and persuasive

66 Every man make up his mind to fight
And move on his enemy! Strong as I am,
It's hard for me to face so many men
And fight with all at once. . . .
And yet I will! 99
—Homer, *Iliad*

For almost 3,000 years, the epics of Homer have inspired European writers and artists.

✓ **Checkpoint**   What do Homer's epics reveal about Greek culture?

Looking Ahead

After the Dorian invasions, the land of Greece passed several centuries in obscurity. The people lived in small isolated villages and had few contacts with the outside world. Over time they made the stories about Crete and Mycenae a part of their heritage, and they built upon the legacy of those and other civilizations to forge a new, Greek civilization. When it emerged, this Greek civilization would not only dominate the region, it would ultimately extend the influence of Greek culture over most of the Western world.

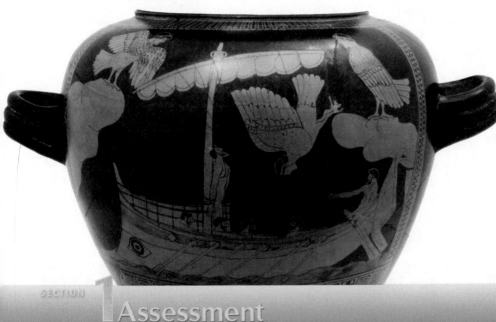

Hero of the *Odyssey*
Odysseus was admired for his cleverness. Here, he outwits the siren, whose song lures sailors to their doom. In order to hear their song and yet survive, Odysseus fills his crew's ears with beeswax. Then, he has himself tied to the ship's mast so he can hear the siren's song without endangering the ship or his crew.

Progress Monitoring *Online*
For: Self-quiz with vocabulary practice
Web Code: naa-0411

SECTION 1 **Assessment**

Terms, People, and Places

1. For each term, person, or place listed at the beginning of the section, write a sentence explaining its significance.

Note Taking

2. **Reading Skill: Identify Main Ideas** Use your completed table to answer the Focus Question: How did the Minoans and Mycenaens shape early Greek civilizations?

Comprehension and Critical Thinking

3. **Determine Relevance** How did trade contribute to the development of the Minoan and Mycenaean cultures?

4. **Draw Inferences** What values of the ancient Greeks are found in the poems of Homer?

5. **Demonstrate Reasoned Judgment** Do you think the epics of Homer are a reliable source of information about the history of the ancient Greeks? Why or why not?

● **Writing About History**

Quick Write: Write a Thesis Statement Review the section and think of how early people of the Aegean contributed to Greek civilization. Write a thesis statement that expresses your thought. Remember that a thesis statement should provide the main idea for an essay.

Battling soldiers in phalanx formation

WITNESS HISTORY 🔊 AUDIO

For the People's Good

Tyrtaeus, a Spartan poet in the 600s B.C., wrote elegies that praised and encouraged bravery and honor on the Spartan battlefields. Here, while championing courage in the phalanx, Tyrtaeus captures the essence of how the Greeks held the city-state, or *polis,* above all else.

66 This is the common good, for the *polis* and the whole *demos* [the people], when a man stands firm in the front ranks without flinching and puts disgraceful flight completely from his mind, making his soul and spirit endure and with his words encourages the man stationed next to him.99

Focus Question How did government and culture develop as Greek city-states grew?

The Rise of Greek City-States

GA **Performance Standards**

- **SSWH3a** Compare the Greek polis, the Roman Republic, and the Roman Empire.
- **SSWH3c** Analyze contributions of Hellenistic and Roman culture and contributions of women in Hellenistic and Roman culture.
- **SSWH3d** Describe polytheism in the Greek and Roman world.

Terms, People, and Places

polis	phalanx
acropolis	Sparta
citizen	Athens
monarchy	democracy
aristocracy	tyrant
oligarchy	legislature

Note Taking

Reading Skill: Identify Supporting Details
Create an outline to record the main ideas and supporting details described in this section.

> I. Geography Shapes Greece
>   A. Landscape defines political boundaries
>   1.
>   2.
>   B. Life by the sea
>   1.
>   2.

The Mediterranean and Aegean seas were as central to the development of Greek civilization as the Nile was to the Egyptians. The ancient Greeks absorbed many ideas and beliefs from the older civilizations of Mesopotamia and Egypt. At the same time, they developed their own unique ways. In particular, the Greeks developed new ideas about how best to govern each individual Greek *polis* (POH lis), or city-state.

Geography Shapes Greece

As you have read, the earliest civilizations rose in fertile river valleys. There, strong rulers organized irrigation works that helped farmers produce food surpluses needed to support large cities. A very different set of geographic conditions influenced the rise of Greek civilization.

Landscape Defines Political Boundaries Greece is part of the Balkan peninsula, which extends southward into the eastern Mediterranean Sea. Mountains divide the peninsula into isolated valleys. Beyond the rugged coast, hundreds of rocky islands spread toward the horizon.

The Greeks who farmed the valleys or settled on the scattered islands did not create a large empire such as that of the Egyptians or Persians. Instead, they built many small city-states, cut off from one another by mountains or water. Each included a city and its surrounding countryside. Greeks fiercely defended the independence of their small city-states, and endless rivalry frequently led to war.

Life by the Sea While mountains divided Greeks from one another, the seas provided a vital link to the world outside. With its hundreds of bays, the Greek coastline offered safe harbors for ships. The Greeks became skilled sailors and carried cargoes of olive oil, wine, and marble to parts throughout the eastern Mediterranean. They returned not only with grains and metals but also with ideas, which they adapted to their own needs. For example, the Greeks adapted the Phoenician alphabet to meet their needs. The resulting alphabet in turn became the basis for all later Western alphabets.

By 750 B.C., rapid population growth forced many Greeks to leave their own overcrowded valleys. With fertile land limited, the Greeks expanded overseas. Gradually, a scattering of Greek colonies took root all around the Mediterranean from Spain to Egypt. Wherever they traveled, Greek settlers and traders carried their ideas and culture.

✔ **Checkpoint** How did the sea contribute to Greek commerce?

Governing the City-States

As their world expanded after 750 B.C., the Greeks evolved a unique version of the city-state, which they called the polis. The polis was made up of a major city or town and its surrounding countryside. Typically, the city itself was built on two levels. On the top of a hill stood the **acropolis** (uh KRAH puh lis), or high city, with its great marble temples dedicated to different gods and goddesses. On flatter ground below lay the walled main city with its marketplace, theater, public buildings, and homes.

The population of each city-state was fairly small, which helped the **citizens,** or free residents, share a sense of responsibility for its triumphs and defeats. In the warm climate of Greece, free men spent much time outdoors in the marketplace, debating issues that affected their lives. The whole community joined in festivals honoring the city's special god or goddess. The rights of citizens were unequal, however; and male landowners held all the political power.

Development of the Alphabet

Phoenician	Greek	Roman
≮	A	A
⟁	B	B
◁	△	D
⟩	K	K
∠	∧	L
⟨	N	N

Chart Skills Our alphabet comes to us from the Phoenicians by way of the Greeks. The word *alphabet* itself comes from the first two Greek letters, *alpha* and *beta*. *Describe how the modern letter* L *has changed over time.*

Geography of Ancient Greece

Geography *Interactive*
For: Audio guided tour
Web Code: nap-0421

Mycenaen world about 1300 B.C.
Centers of ancient Greek civilization
Gold
Silver
Iron
Marble
Timber

Axiós River
Mt. Olympus
40° N
PINDUS MTS.
Piniós River
Miller Projection
0   50   100 mi
0   50   100 km
Delphi
GREECE
Corinth
Olympia   Mycenae
Peloponnesus
Sparta
Athens
Aegean Sea
ASIA MINOR
Ephesus
Milos
Rhodes
Crete
Mediterranean Sea
36° N
N W E S
20° E   24° E   28° E

Map Skills Ancient Greek civilization was shaped by rugged mountainous terrain and the surrounding seas. These geographic features worked as both a barrier and a link.
1. **Locate** (a) Greece (b) Crete (c) Mycenae (d) Athens (e) Sparta (f) Aegean Sea (g) Peloponnesus
2. **Region** How did the geography of Greece present obstacles to unity?
3. **Analyze Information** How did the geography of Greece differ from that of other ancient civilizations?

Types of Government Evolve

Between 750 B.C. and 500 B.C., different forms of government evolved in Greece. At first, the ruler of the polis, like those in the river valley empires, was a king. A government in which a hereditary ruler exercises central power is a **monarchy.** Slowly, however, power shifted to a class of noble landowners. Because only they could afford bronze weapons and chariots, these nobles were also the military defenders of the city-states. At first these landowners defended the king. In time, however, they won power for themselves. The result was an **aristocracy,** or rule by a hereditary landholding elite.

As trade expanded, a new middle class of wealthy merchants, farmers, and artisans emerged in some cities. They challenged the landowning nobles for power and came to dominate some city-states. The result was a form of government called an **oligarchy.** In an oligarchy, power is in the hands of a small, wealthy elite.

New Warfare Methods Shape Greece Changes in military technology increased the power of the middle class. By about 650 B.C., iron weapons replaced bronze ones. Since iron was cheaper, ordinary citizens could afford iron helmets, shields, and swords. Meanwhile, a new method of fighting emerged—the **phalanx,** a massive tactical formation of heavily armed foot soldiers. It required long hours of drill to master. Shared training created a strong sense of unity among the citizen-soldiers.

By putting the defense of the city-state in the hands of ordinary citizens, the phalanx reduced class differences. The new type of warfare, however, led the two most influential city-states—Athens and Sparta—to develop very different ways of life. While Sparta stressed military virtues and stern discipline, Athens glorified the individual and extended political rights to more citizens.

✓ **Checkpoint** How was a city-state shaped by its citizenry?

Sparta: A Warrior Society

Dorian invaders from the north conquered Laconia, in the southern part of the Peloponnesus (pel uh puh NEE sus). The Dorians settled here and built the city-state of **Sparta.** The invaders turned the conquered people into state-owned slaves, called helots, and made them work the land. Because the helots greatly outnumbered their rulers, the Spartans set up a brutal system of strict control.

The Spartan government included two kings and a council of elders who advised the monarchs. An assembly made up of all citizens approved major decisions. Citizens were male, native-born Spartans over the age of 30. The assembly also elected five ephors, or officials, who ran day-to-day affairs.

Daily Life Ruled by Discipline From childhood, a Spartan prepared to be part of a military state. Officials examined every newborn, and sickly children were abandoned to die. Spartans wanted future soldiers and the future mothers of soldiers to be healthy.

At the age of seven, boys began training for a lifetime in the military. They moved into barracks, where they were toughened by a coarse diet, hard exercise, and rigid discipline. This strict and harsh discipline made Spartan youths excellent soldiers. To develop cunning and supplement their diet, boys were even encouraged to steal food. If caught, though, they were beaten severely.

Spartan Education

An Athenian historian explains the system of education set up by Lycurgus, the Spartan lawgiver:

❝ Instead of softening the boys' feet with sandals, he required them to harden their feet by going without shoes. He believed that if this habit were cultivated, it would enable them to climb hills more easily and descend steep inclines with less danger, and that a youth who had accustomed himself to go barefoot would leap and jump and run more nimbly than a boy in sandals. And instead of letting them be pampered in the matter of clothing, he introduced the custom of wearing one garment throughout the year, believing that they would thus be better prepared to face changes of heat and cold. ❞

—Xenophon, *Constitution of the Lacedaemonians*

Describe the Spartan student dress code. What was its purpose? 🔊)) AUDIO

At the age of 20, a man could marry, but he continued to live in the barracks for another 10 years and to eat there for another 40 years. At the age of 30, after further training, he took his place in the assembly.

Women of Sparta Girls, too, had a rigorous upbringing. As part of a warrior society, they were expected to produce healthy sons for the army. They therefore were required to exercise and strengthen their bodies.

Like other Greek women, Spartan women had to obey their fathers or husbands. Yet under Spartan law, they had the right to inherit property. Because men were occupied with war, some women took on responsibilities such as running the family's estate.

Sparta Stands Alone The Spartans isolated themselves from other Greeks. They looked down on trade and wealth, forbade their own citizens to travel, and had little use for new ideas or the arts. While other Greeks admired the Spartans' military skills, no other city-state imitated their rigorous way of life. "Spartans are willing to die for their city," some suggested, "because they have no reason to live."

✔ **Checkpoint** Why was discipline important to Spartans?

Athens Evolves Into a Democracy

Athens was located in Attica, just north of the Peloponnesus. As in many Greek city-states, Athenian government evolved from a monarchy into an aristocracy. By 700 B.C., landowners held power. They chose the chief officials, judged major court cases, and dominated the assembly.

Demands for Change Under the aristocracy, Athenian wealth and power grew. Yet discontent spread among ordinary people. Merchants and soldiers resented the power of the nobles. They argued that their service to Athens entitled them to more rights. Foreign artisans, who produced many of the goods that Athens traded abroad, were resentful that foreigners were barred from becoming citizens. Farmers, too, demanded change. During hard times, many farmers were forced to sell their land to nobles. A growing number even sold themselves and their families into slavery to pay their debts.

As discontent spread, Athens moved slowly toward **democracy**, or government by the people. As you will see, the term had a different meaning for the ancient Greeks than it has for us today.

Solon Reforms Government Solon, a wise and trusted leader, was appointed archon (AHR kahn), or chief official, in 594 B.C. Athenians gave Solon a free hand to make needed reforms. He outlawed debt slavery and freed those who had already been sold into slavery for debt. He opened high offices to more citizens, granted citizenship to some foreigners, and gave the Athenian assembly more say in important decisions.

Solon introduced economic reforms as well. He encouraged the export of wine and olive oil. This policy helped merchants and farmers by increasing demand for their products.

Despite Solon's reforms, citizenship remained limited, and many positions were open only to the wealthy. Continued and widespread unrest

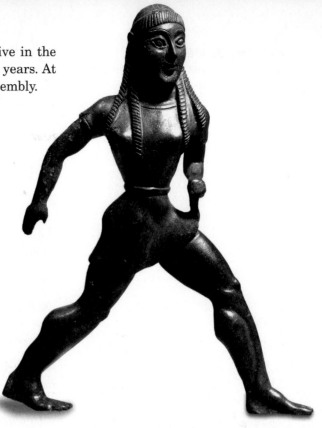

Spartan Fitness
The Spartans put great emphasis on the strength and agility of the human body. The sculpture above shows a Spartan woman exercising, a task rarely expected of other Greek women.

Vocabulary Builder
imposing—(im POHZ ing) *vt.* placing or
setting something compulsory upon

led to the rise of **tyrants,** or people who gained power by force. Tyrants often won support from the merchant class and the poor by <u>imposing</u> reforms to help these groups. Although Greek tyrants often governed well, the word *tyrant* has come to mean a vicious and brutal ruler.

Citizens Share Power and Wealth

The Athenian tyrant Pisistratus (py SIS truh tus) seized power in 546 B.C. He helped farmers by giving them loans and land taken from nobles. New building projects gave jobs to the poor. By giving poor citizens a greater voice, he further weakened the aristocracy.

In 507 B.C., another reformer, Cleisthenes (KLYS thuh neez), broadened the role of ordinary citizens in government. He set up the Council of 500, whose members were chosen by lot from among all citizens over the age of 30. The council prepared laws considered by the assembly and supervised the day-to-day work of government. Cleisthenes made the assembly a genuine **legislature,** or lawmaking body, that debated laws before deciding to approve or reject them. All male citizens were members of the assembly and were expected to participate.

A Limited Democracy

By modern standards, Athenian democracy was quite limited. Only citizens could participate in government, and citizenship was restricted to landowning men. Women were excluded along with merchants and people whose parents were not citizens. So were the tens of thousands of Athenian slaves who lacked political rights as well as personal freedom, although it was their labor that gave citizens the time to participate in government. Still, Athens gave more people a say in decision making than any other ancient civilization.

Women in Athens

As in other Greek city-states, women in Athens had no share in political life. According to Aristotle, "the man is by nature fitter for command than the female just as an older person is superior to a younger, more immature person." Although some men disagreed, most Greeks accepted the view that women must be guided by men.

Women played their most significant public role in religion. Their participation in sacred processions and ceremonies was considered essential for the city's well-being. In well-to-do Athenian homes, women managed the entire household. They spun and wove, cared for their children, and prepared food, but lived a secluded existence and were rarely seen in public. Their slaves or children were sent to buy food and to fetch water from the public well. Poorer women worked outside the home, tending sheep or working as spinners, weavers, or potters.

Educating the Youth

Unlike girls, who received little or no formal education, boys attended school if their families could afford it. Besides learning to read and write, they studied music, memorized poetry, and studied public speaking because, as citizens in a democracy, they would have to voice their views. Although they received military training and participated in athletic contests, unlike Sparta, which put military training above all else, Athens encouraged young men to explore many areas of knowledge.

Checkpoint How was democracy limited in Athens?

Athenian Education
This drinking cup from 480 B.C. illustrates some of the subjects studied by Athenian boys, including instruction in speech and playing the lyre. *How does this image demonstrate the differences between the Athenian and Spartan systems of education?*

Forces for Unity

Strong local identification, an independent spirit, and economic rivalry led to fighting among the Greek city-states. Despite these divisions, Greeks shared a common culture. They spoke the same language, honored the same ancient heroes, participated in common festivals, and prayed to the same gods.

Mythology and Religion Like most other ancient people, the Greeks were polytheistic, believing in more than one deity. According to their myths, or traditional stories that explain the ways of nature or the gods, the gods lived on Mount Olympus in northern Greece. In Greek myths, the most powerful Olympian was Zeus (zoos), who presided over the affairs of gods and humans. His children included Ares (EHR eez), god of war, and Aphrodite (af ruh DY tee), goddess of love. His daughter Athena (uh THEE nuh), goddess of wisdom, gave her name to Athens.

Greeks honored their gods with temples and festivals, which included processions, sacrifices, feasts, plays, choral singing, and athletic competitions. Greeks consulted oracles, who were priests or priestesses through whom the gods were thought to speak. However, some Greek thinkers came to believe that the universe was regulated not by the gods but by natural laws.

Greek View of Foreigners As trade and colonies expanded, the Greeks came in contact with people from foreign lands with different languages and customs. Greeks called them *barbaroi*, people who did not speak Greek, and felt superior to them. The English word *barbarian* comes from this Greek term. These "barbarians" even included the Phoenicians and Egyptians, from whom the Greeks borrowed important ideas and inventions. This sense of uniqueness and superiority would help the Greeks when they were threatened by the mightiest power in the Mediterranean world—the Persian empire.

Ruins of the Sanctuary of Athena at the Tholos Temple in Delphi

✔ **Checkpoint** What factors united the city-states of Greece?

SECTION 2 Assessment

Terms, People, and Places

1. What do each of the key terms listed at the beginning of the section have in common? Explain.

Note Taking

2. **Reading Skill: Identify Supporting Details** Use your completed outline to answer the Focus Question: How did government and culture develop as Greek city-states grew?

Comprehension and Critical Thinking

3. **Summarize** How did geography influence the development of Greece?

4. **Synthesize Information** Why do you think the three different forms of government evolved over time?

5. **Draw Conclusions** (a) In what ways was Athenian democracy limited? (b) Despite such limits, Athens is still admired as an early model of democracy. Why do you think this is the case?

● **Writing About History**

Quick Write: Choose a Topic A persuasive essay supports an opinion or position. Suppose you are given the assignment to write a persuasive essay about ancient Greece. Review this section and select three possible topics for your essay. Your topics might be about democracy, the rights of citizens, or political systems. Then write a brief summary for each topic and describe what arguments you could make to support it in a persuasive essay.

Miltiades, Athenian victor at Marathon

WITNESS HISTORY 🔊 AUDIO

Athens Demands Action

As the Persian invaders grew dangerously close, the Athenian generals were split between going into battle or waiting for Spartan reinforcements. To break the deadlock, the Athenian general Miltiades approached Callimachus, the commander-in-chief, and pleaded that a decision must be made.

❝ Callimachus, it is up to you, *right now*, to enslave Athens or to make her free. . . . Athens is in the most perilous moment of her history. . . . If we fight now, why then we can survive this battle. . . . It hangs on your decision—*now*. If you vote with me, your fatherland will be free . . . , but if you choose . . . not to fight, then the opposite of all good . . . will fall to you. ❞

Focus Question How did war with invaders and conflict among Greeks affect the city-states?

Conflict in the Greek World

 Performance Standards

- **SSWH3a** Compare the Greek polis, the Roman Republic, and the Roman Empire.
- **SSWH3c** Analyze contributions of Hellenistic and Roman culture.

Terms, People, and Places

alliance
Pericles
direct democracy
stipend
jury
ostracism

Note Taking

Reading Skill: Identify Supporting Details
Make a table like the one below. Then, use the table to record the supporting details as they relate to the main ideas discussed in the section.

Persian Wars	Athenian Democracy	Peloponnesian War
• Athens is victorious at Marathon.	•	• Greeks resent Athenian domination.
•	•	•

Like the Athenian generals, divided on whether or not to go into battle, the Greek city-states were often at odds with one another. Yet, when the Persians threatened them, the Greeks briefly put aside their differences to defend their freedom.

The Persian Wars

As you have read, the Persians conquered a huge empire stretching from Asia Minor to the border of India. Their subjects included the Greek city-states of Ionia in Asia Minor. Though under Persian rule, these Ionian city-states were largely self-governing. Still, they resented their situation.

In 499 B.C., Ionian Greeks rebelled against Persian rule. Athens sent ships to help them. As the historian Herodotus wrote some years later, "These ships were the beginning of mischief both to the Greeks and to the barbarians."

Athenians Win at Marathon The Persians soon crushed the rebel cities. However, Darius I was furious at the role Athens played in the uprising. In time, Darius sent a huge force across the Aegean to punish Athens for its interference. The mighty Persian army landed near Marathon, a plain north of Athens, in 490 B.C. The Athenians asked for help from neighboring Greek city-states, but received little support.

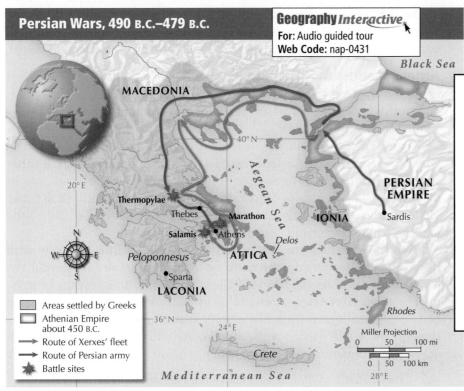

Persian Wars, 490 B.C.–479 B.C.

Geography *Interactive*
For: Audio guided tour
Web Code: nap-0431

Black Sea

MACEDONIA

40° N

20° E

Thermopylae

Thebes

Marathon

Salamis
Athens

Delos

Peloponnesus
ATTICA

Sparta
LACONIA

36° N

24° E

Crete

Mediterranean Sea

28° E

Aegean Sea

IONIA

Sardis

PERSIAN
EMPIRE

Rhodes

Miller Projection
0   50   100 mi
0   50   100 km

Areas settled by Greeks
Athenian Empire about 450 B.C.
Route of Xerxes' fleet
Route of Persian army
Battle sites

Map Skills When the Persian empire attacked Greece, the Greek city-states briefly joined forces to defend their independence.
1. **Locate** (a) Athens (b) Sparta (c) Marathon (d) Thermopylae (e) Salamis
2. **Movement** Describe the routes of the Persian army and navy toward the city-state of Athens.
3. **Making Inferences** Why do you think Xerxes' fleet hugged the Greek coastline instead of sailing directly across the Aegean Sea?

The Persians greatly outnumbered Athenian forces. Yet the invaders were amazed to see "a mere handful of men coming on at a run without either horsemen or archers." The Persians responded with a rain of arrows, but the Greeks rushed onward. They broke through the Persian line and engaged in fierce hand-to-hand combat. Overwhelmed by the fury of the assault, the Persians hastily retreated to their ships.

The Athenians celebrated their triumph. Still, the Athenian leader, Themistocles (thuh MIS tuh kleez), knew the victory at Marathon had bought only a temporary lull in the fighting. He urged Athenians to build a fleet of warships and prepare other defenses.

Greek City-States Unite Darius died before he could mass his troops for another attack. But in 480 B.C., his son Xerxes (ZURK seez) sent a much larger force to conquer Greece. By this time, Athens had persuaded Sparta and other city-states to join in the fight against Persia.

Once again, the Persians landed in northern Greece. A small Spartan force guarded the narrow mountain pass at Thermopylae (thur MAHP uh lee). Led by the great warrior-king Leonidas (lee AHN ih dus), the Spartans held out heroically against the enormous Persian force, but were defeated in the end. The Persians marched south and burned Athens. The city was empty, however. The Athenians had already withdrawn to safety.

The Greeks now put their faith in the fleet of ships that Themistocles had urged them to build. The Athenians lured the Persian navy into the narrow strait of Salamis (SAHL uh mis). Then, Athenian warships, powered by rowers, drove into the Persian boats with underwater battering rams. On the shore, Xerxes watched helplessly as his mighty fleet sank.

A relief illustrating the Athenian battle with the Persians at Marathon

The next year, the Greeks defeated the Persians on land in Asia Minor. This victory marked the end of the Persian invasions. In a brief moment of unity, the Greek city-states had saved themselves from the Persian threat.

Athens Leads the Delian League Victory in the Persian Wars increased the Greeks' sense of their own <u>uniqueness</u>. The gods, they felt, had protected their superior form of government—the city-state—against invaders from Asia.

Athens emerged from the war as the most powerful city-state in Greece. To continue to defend against Persia, it organized with other Greek city-states an **alliance,** or a formal agreement between two or more nations or powers to cooperate and come to one another's defense. Modern scholars call this alliance the Delian League after Delos, the location where the league held meetings.

From the start, Athens dominated the Delian League. It slowly used its position of leadership to create an Athenian empire. It moved the league treasury from the island of Delos to Athens, using money contributed by other city-states to rebuild its own city. When its allies protested and tried to withdraw from the league, Athens used force to make them remain. Yet, while Athens was enforcing its will abroad, Athenian leaders were championing political freedom at home.

 Checkpoint What factors led to the Persian defeat?

The Age of Pericles and Direct Democracy

The years after the Persian Wars from 460 B.C. to 429 B.C. were a golden age for Athens under the able statesman **Pericles** (PEHR uh kleez). Because of his wise and skillful leadership, the economy thrived and the government became more democratic.

Athenian Democracy Periclean Athens was a **direct democracy.** Under this system, citizens take part directly in the day-to-day affairs of government. By contrast, in most democratic countries today, citizens participate in government indirectly through elected representatives.

By the time of Pericles, the Athenian assembly met several times a month. A Council of 500, selected by lot, conducted daily government business. Pericles believed that all citizens, regardless of wealth or social class, should take part in government. Athens therefore began to pay a **stipend,** or fixed salary, to men who participated in the Assembly and its governing Council. This reform enabled poor men to serve in government.

In addition, Athenians also served on juries. A **jury** is a panel of citizens who have the authority to make the final judgment in a trial. Unlike a modern American trial jury, which is usually made up of 12 members, an Athenian jury might include hundreds or even thousands of jurors. Citizens over 30 years of age were chosen by lot to serve on the jury for a year.

Athenian citizens could also vote to banish, or send away, a public figure whom they saw as a threat to their democracy. This process was called **ostracism** (AHS truh siz um). The person with the largest number of votes cast against him was ostracized, meaning that that individual would have to live outside the city, usually for a period of 10 years.

Culture Thrives in Athens Athens prospered during the Age of Pericles. With the empire's riches, Pericles directed the rebuilding of the Acropolis, which the Persians had destroyed. With the help of an

ATHENIAN DEMOCRACY

The Athenians called their political system *demokratia*, which means "rule by the people." In a democracy, the people hold supreme political authority and government is conducted only by and with the consent of the people. By the 6th century B.C., ordinary citizens of Athens could participate fully in government. Some of the most basic principles of modern democracies originated in Athens—including majority rule, civic debate, impartial juries, and the rule of law.

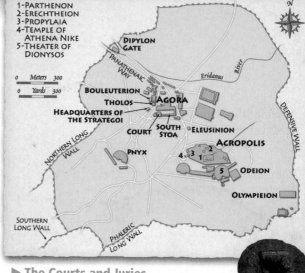

1-PARTHENON
2-ERECHTHEION
3-PROPYLAIA
4-TEMPLE OF ATHENA NIKE
5-THEATER OF DIONYSOS

► The Courts and Juries
Athenian courts enforced and interpreted the laws passed by the ecclesia. Juries were large to prevent corruption. A solid disc was a vote for innocence. A disk with a hole was a vote for guilt.

The Boule, or Council of 500
Day-to-day decisions and the agenda for the ecclesia were made by a Council of 500 known as the boule. The boule met at the bouleuterion (see map above) and members slept nearby in the Tholos in order to be able to respond to emergencies. Members of the council were chosen by lot from the entire citizenry and served for one year.

▼ The Ecclesia
The assembly of all citizens of Athens, the ecclesia met about three times a month outside the city on Pnyx hill (below). Here, citizens would gather to debate important issues (left) and would vote on laws. Once a year, citizens could vote to ostracize, or exile, someone by writing their name on an ostrakon (above left).

Geography *Interactive*
For: Interactive map skills
Web Code: nap-0432

Thinking Critically
1. **Identify Main Ideas** Why is Athens's system of government described as a "direct democracy" as opposed to an "indirect democracy"?
2. **Make Comparisons** How does Athenian democracy compare to the democratic system of the United States?

educated foreign-born woman named Aspasia (as PAY shuh), Pericles turned Athens into the cultural center of Greece. They encouraged the arts through public festivals, dramatic competitions, and building programs. Such building projects increased Athenians' prosperity by creating jobs for artisans and workers.

✔ **Checkpoint** Describe Pericles's influence on Athens.

The Peloponnesian War

Many Greeks outside Athens resented Athenian domination. Before long, the Greek world was split into rival camps. To counter the Delian League, Sparta and other enemies of Athens formed the Peloponnesian League. In 431 B.C., warfare broke out between Athens and Sparta. This conflict, which became known as the Peloponnesian War, soon engulfed all of Greece. The fighting would last for 27 years.

Sparta Defeats Athens Despite its riches and powerful navy, Athens faced a serious geographic disadvantage. Because Sparta was inland, Athens could not use its navy to attack. Sparta's powerful army, however, had only to march north to attack Athens. When the Spartan troops came near, Pericles allowed people from the countryside to move inside the city walls. The overcrowded conditions led to a terrible plague that killed many Athenians, including Pericles himself.

As the war dragged on, each side committed savage acts against the other. Sparta even allied itself with Persia, the longtime enemy of the Greeks. Finally, in 404 B.C., with the help of the Persian navy, the Spartans captured Athens. The victors stripped the Athenians of their fleet and empire. However, Sparta rejected calls from its allies to destroy Athens.

Greek Dominion Declines The Peloponnesian War ended Athenian domination of the Greek world. The Athenian economy eventually revived and Athens remained the cultural center of Greece. However, its spirit and vitality declined. Meanwhile, as Greeks battled among themselves, a new power rose in Macedonia (mas uh DOH nee uh), a kingdom to the north of Greece. By 359 B.C., its ambitious ruler stood poised to conquer the quarrelsome Greek city-states.

✔ **Checkpoint** How did conflict lead to the decline of Athens?

Armor of the Hoplites
The Greek hoplite was named after his unique shield, the *hoplon*. These heavily armored soldiers were usually men from the middle class who could afford to purchase the armor and weapons.

Progress Monitoring *Online*
For: Self-quiz with vocabulary practice
Web Code: naa-0431

SECTION **3** Assessment

Terms, People, and Places

1. For each term, person, or place listed at the beginning of the section, write a sentence explaining its significance.

Note Taking

2. **Reading Skill: Identify Supporting Details** Use your completed table to answer the Focus Question: How did war with invaders and conflict among Greeks affect the city-states?

Comprehension and Critical Thinking

3. **Summarize** How did the Persian Wars affect the Greek city-states?

4. **Analyze Information** How did Pericles contribute to Athenian greatness?

5. **Demonstrate Reasoned Judgement** Do you think the process of ostracism is fair or unfair? Explain.

6. **Recognize Cause and Effect** How did the growth of Athenian power lead to war?

● **Writing About History**

Quick Write: Organize Evidence Write an opening paragraph that introduces a persuasive essay arguing for or against Athenian direct democracy. The paragraph should include a thesis statement reflecting the position you will prove and should indicate what the essay will discuss. Remember that an opening paragraph should grab the reader's attention and make the topic sound interesting.

The Funeral Oration of Pericles

This excerpt from Thucydides' *History of the Peloponnesian War* records a speech made by the Athenian leader Pericles in honor of those who died fighting Sparta in the first year of the war (431 B.C.). In the speech, Pericles describes the superior qualities of Athenian democracy as compared with life in Sparta. This speech is one of the most famous defenses of democracy of all time.

Marble bust of the great Athenian statesman Pericles

For our government is not copied from those of our neighbors; we are an example to them rather than they to us. Our constitution is named a democracy because it is in the hands not of the few but of the many. But our laws secure equal justice for all in their private disputes, and our public opinion welcomes and honors talent in every branch of achievement, not for any sectional reason but on grounds of excellence alone. And as we give free play to all in our public life, so we carry the same spirit into our daily relations with one another. . . .

We are lovers of beauty without extravagance[1], and lovers of wisdom without unmanliness. Wealth to us is not mere material for vainglory[2] but an opportunity for achievement; and poverty we think it no disgrace to acknowledge but a real degradation[3] to make no effort to overcome. Our citizens attend both to public and private duties, and do not allow absorption[4] in their own various affairs to interfere with their knowledge of the city's. We differ from other states in regarding the man who holds aloof[5] from public life not as 'quiet' but as useless; we decide or debate, carefully and in person, all matters of policy, holding not that words and deeds go ill together but that acts are foredoomed to failure when undertaken undiscussed. For we are noted for being at once adventurous in action and most reflective beforehand. Other men are bold in ignorance, while reflection will stop their onset. But the bravest are surely those who have the clearest vision of what is before them, glory and danger alike, and yet notwithstanding[6] go out to meet it. . . . In a word I claim that our city as a whole is an education to Greece, and that her members yield to none, man by man, for independence of spirit, many-sidedness of attainment[7], and complete self-reliance in limbs and brain.

1. **extravagance** (ek STRAV uh guns) *n.* excess
2. **vainglory** (VAYN glawr ee) *n.* vanity, excessive pride
3. **degradation** (deg ruh DAY shun) *n.* decline to a low or demoralized state
4. **absorption** (ab SAWRP shun) *n.* entire occupation of the mind
5. **aloof** (uh LOOF) *adj.* removed, distant
6. **notwithstanding** (naht with STAND ing) *adv.* nevertheless, however
7. **attainment** (uh TAYN munt) *n.* accomplishment

Thinking Critically

1. **Analyze Information** How does Pericles define *democracy*?
2. **Synthesize Information** What does Pericles say it takes for a person to be a good citizen?

The great philosopher Aristotle

Aristotle Meditates on Thought

Aristotle is considered one of the greatest philosophers of all time. After studying under Plato for twenty years, Aristotle eventually became a teacher himself. His interests varied greatly and he studied numerous subjects including biology, political theory, and logic. In *Metaphysics,* Aristotle theorized on the nature of divine thinking:

❝It is of itself that the divine thought thinks (since it is the most excellent of things), and its thinking is a thinking on thinking.❞

Focus Question How did Greek thinkers, artists, and writers explore the nature of the universe and people's place in it?

The Glory That Was Greece

 Performance Standards

• **SSWH3b** Identify the ideas and impact of Aristotle, Plato, and Socrates.

• **SSWH3c** Analyze contributions of Hellenistic and Roman culture.

Terms, People, and Places

philosopher	Aristotle
logic	Parthenon
rhetoric	tragedy
Socrates	comedy
Plato	Herodotus

Note Taking

Reading Skill: Identify Supporting Details
Make a concept web similar to the one below. Then use the diagram to record the supporting details of the Greek achievements discussed in the section. Add circles as necessary.

Even in the midst of wars and political turmoil, Greeks had confidence in the power of the human mind. Driven by curiosity and a belief in reason, Greek thinkers, artists, and writers explored the nature of the universe and the place of people in it. To later admirers, Greek achievements in the arts represented the height of human development in the Western world. They looked back with deep respect on what one poet called "the glory that was Greece."

Philosophers: Lovers of Wisdom

As you have read, some Greek thinkers challenged the belief that events were caused by the whims of gods. Instead, they used observation and reason to find causes for events. The Greeks called these thinkers **philosophers,** meaning "lovers of wisdom."

Greek philosophers explored many subjects, from mathematics and music to **logic,** or rational thinking. Through reason and observation, they believed, they could discover laws that governed the universe. Much modern science traces its roots to the Greek search for such principles.

Debating Morality and Ethics Some Greek philosophers were interested in ethics and morality. They debated such questions as what was the best kind of government and what standards should rule human behavior.

In Athens, the Sophists questioned accepted ideas. To them, success was more important than moral truth. They developed skills in **rhetoric,** the art of skillful speaking. Ambitious men could use clever and persuasive rhetoric to advance their careers. The turmoil of the Peloponnesian War led many young Athenians to follow the Sophists. Older citizens, however, accused the Sophists of undermining traditional Greek values.

Socrates Questions Tradition One outspoken critic of the Sophists was **Socrates,** an Athenian stonemason and philosopher. Most of what we know about Socrates comes from his student **Plato.** Socrates himself wrote no books. Instead, he passed his days in the town square asking people about their beliefs. Using a process we now call the Socratic method, he would pose a series of questions to a student or passing citizen, and challenge them to examine the implications of their answers. To Socrates, this patient examination was a way to help others seek truth and self-knowledge. To many Athenians, however, such questioning was a threat to accepted values and traditions.

When he was about 70 years old, Socrates was put on trial. His enemies accused him of corrupting the city's youth and failing to respect the gods. Standing before a jury of 501 citizens, Socrates offered a calm and reasoned defense. But the jurors condemned him to death. Loyal to the laws of Athens, Socrates accepted the death penalty. He drank a cup of hemlock, a deadly poison.

Plato Envisions A Perfect Society The execution of Socrates left Plato with a lifelong distrust of democracy. He fled Athens for 10 years. When he returned, he set up a school called the Academy. There, he taught and wrote about his own ideas. Like Socrates, Plato emphasized the importance of reason. Through rational thought, he argued, people could discover unchanging ethical values, recognize perfect beauty, and learn how best to organize society.

In his book *The Republic*, Plato described his vision of an ideal state. He rejected Athenian democracy because it had condemned Socrates just as it tended to other excesses. Instead, Plato argued that the state should regulate every aspect of its citizens' lives in order to provide for their best interests. He divided his ideal society into three classes: workers to produce the necessities of life, soldiers to defend the state, and philosophers to rule. This elite class of leaders would be specially trained to ensure order and justice. The wisest of them, a philosopher-king, would have the ultimate authority.

Plato thought that, in general, men surpassed women in mental and physical tasks, but that some women were superior to some men. Talented women, he said, should be educated to serve the state. The ruling elite, both men and women, would take military training together and raise their children in communal centers for the good of the republic.

Aristotle Pursues the Golden Mean Plato's most famous student, **Aristotle,** developed his own ideas about government. He analyzed all forms of government, from monarchy to democracy, and found good and bad examples of each. Like Plato, he was suspicious of democracy, which he thought could lead to mob rule. In the end, he favored rule by a single strong and virtuous leader.

Aristotle also addressed the question of how people ought to live. In his view, good conduct meant pursuing the "golden mean," a moderate course between the extremes. He promoted reason as the guiding force for learning. He set up a school, the Lyceum, for the study of all branches

BIOGRAPHY

Socrates
Contrasting with his glorified image in Jacques-Louis David's painting *The Death of Socrates* (above), to most Athenians, Socrates (469 B.C.–399 B.C.) was not an impressive figure. Tradition tells us that his clothes were untidy and he made a poor living. But young men loved to watch him as he questioned citizens and led them to contradict themselves.

Many Athenians felt that Socrates was annoying, but Plato had a different view of his teacher. He called Socrates "the wisest, justest, and best of all I have ever known." As for Socrates himself, he knew what he was doing. When he was put on trial, he told the jury, "All day long and in all places I am always fastening upon you, stirring you and persuading you and reproaching you. You will not easily find another like me."

Socrates said, "The unexamined life is not worth living." How did his actions support this idea?

of knowledge. He left writings on politics, ethics, logic, biology, literature, and many other subjects. When the first European universities evolved some 1,500 years later, their courses were based largely on the works and ideas of Aristotle.

✓ **Checkpoint** Why might some of the philosophers' ideas be a threat to Greek tradition?

Idealism in Architecture and Art

Plato argued that every object on Earth had an ideal form. The work of Greek artists and architects reflected a similar concern with balance, order, and beauty.

Monumental Architecture Greek architects sought to convey a sense of perfect balance to reflect the harmony and order of the universe. The most famous example of Greek architecture is the **Parthenon,** a temple dedicated to the goddess Athena. The basic plan of the Parthenon is a

INFOGRAPHIC

ART AND ARCHITECTURE OF ANCIENT GREECE

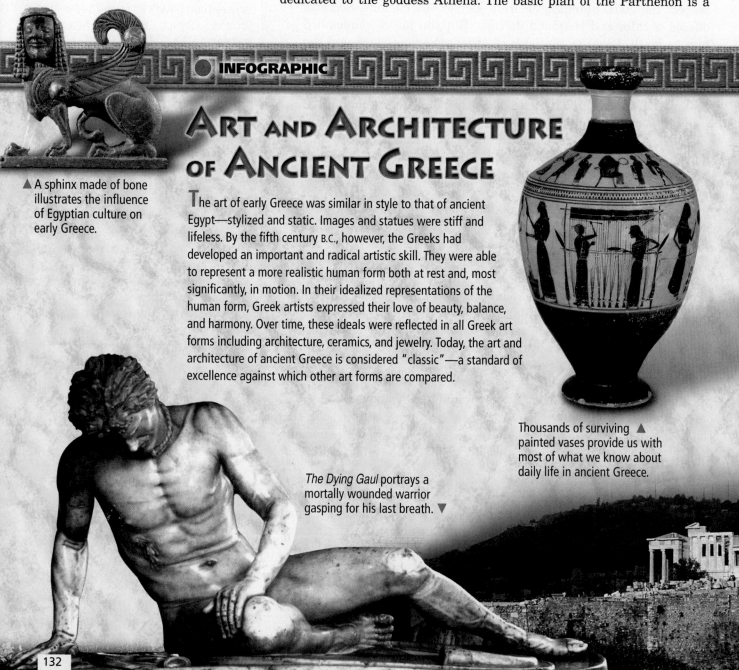

▲ A sphinx made of bone illustrates the influence of Egyptian culture on early Greece.

The art of early Greece was similar in style to that of ancient Egypt—stylized and static. Images and statues were stiff and lifeless. By the fifth century B.C., however, the Greeks had developed an important and radical artistic skill. They were able to represent a more realistic human form both at rest and, most significantly, in motion. In their idealized representations of the human form, Greek artists expressed their love of beauty, balance, and harmony. Over time, these ideals were reflected in all Greek art forms including architecture, ceramics, and jewelry. Today, the art and architecture of ancient Greece is considered "classic"—a standard of excellence against which other art forms are compared.

Thousands of surviving ▲ painted vases provide us with most of what we know about daily life in ancient Greece.

The Dying Gaul portrays a mortally wounded warrior gasping for his last breath. ▼

simple rectangle, with tall columns supporting a gently sloping roof. The delicate curves and placement of the columns add dignity and grace.

Greek architecture has been widely admired for centuries. Today, many public buildings throughout the world have incorporated Greek architectural elements, such as columns, in their designs.

Artists Craft Lifelike Human Forms Early Greek sculptors carved figures in <u>rigid</u> poses, perhaps imitating Egyptian styles. By 450 B.C., Greek sculptors had developed a new style that emphasized more natural forms. While their work was lifelike, it was also idealistic. That is, sculptors carved gods, goddesses, athletes, and famous men in a way that showed human beings in their most perfect, graceful form.

The only Greek paintings to survive are on pottery. They offer intriguing views of every day Greek life. Women carry water from wells, warriors race into battle, and athletes compete in javelin contests. Each scene is designed to fit the shape of the pottery.

✔ **Checkpoint** How did Greek art reflect the idea of an ideal form?

Vocabulary Builder
<u>rigid</u>—(RIJ id) *adj.* stiff; unbending; severe

Nike of Samothrace, also ▶ known as *Winged Victory*, reflects the artist's amazing ability to create a sense of power, movement, and grace in a work of stone.

The Greek ideals ▲ of balance and beauty are even apparent in this gold sprig of leaves and flowers.

Built over a fifteen-year period at the direction of Pericles, the Parthenon epitomizes the Greek ideals of balance and order. ▼

Thinking Critically
1. **Synthesize Information** Study the photograph of the Parthenon. What kinds of modern buildings were influenced by its architecture? Why do you think this is so?
2. **Draw Conclusions** Why do you think the ability to portray movement was important in the development of Greek art?

133

Greek Literature

In literature, as in art, the ancient Greeks developed their own style. To later Europeans, Greek styles were a model of perfection. They admired what they called the "classical style," referring to the elegant and balanced forms of traditional Greek works of art.

Greek literature began with the epic poems of Homer, whose stirring tales inspired later writers. In later times, the poet Sappho sang of love and of the beauty of her island home, while the poetry of Pindar celebrated the victors in athletic contests.

Tragic Drama Perhaps the most important Greek contribution to literature was in the field of drama. The first Greek plays evolved out of religious festivals, especially those held in Athens to honor the god of fertility and wine, Dionysus (dy uh NY sus). Plays were performed in large outdoor theaters with little or no scenery. Actors wore elaborate costumes and stylized masks. A chorus sang or chanted comments on the action taking place on stage. Greek dramas were often based on popular myths and legends. Through these familiar stories, playwrights discussed moral and social issues or explored the relationship between people and the gods.

The greatest Athenian playwrights were Aeschylus (ES kih lus), Sophocles (SAH fuh kleez), and Euripides (yoo RIP ih deez). All three wrote **tragedies,** plays that told stories of human suffering that usually ended in disaster. The purpose of tragedy, the Greeks felt, was to stir up and then relieve the emotions of pity and fear. For example in his play *Oresteia* (aw res TEE uh), Aeschylus showed a powerful family torn apart by betrayal, murder, and revenge. Audiences saw how even the powerful could be subject to horrifying misfortune and how the wrath of the gods could bring down even the greatest heroes.

In *Antigone* (an TIG uh nee), Sophocles explored what happens when an individual's moral duty conflicts with the laws of the state. Antigone is a young woman whose brother has been killed leading a rebellion. King Creon forbids anyone to bury the traitor's body. When Antigone buries her brother anyway, she is sentenced to death. She defiantly tells Creon that duty to the gods is greater than human law:

Primary Source

66 For me, it was not Zeus who made that order. . . .
Nor did I think your orders were so strong
that you, a mortal man, could overrun
the gods' unwritten and unfailing laws. 99
—Sophocles, *Antigone*

Like Sophocles, Euripides survived the horrors of the Peloponnesian War. That experience probably led him to question many accepted ideas of his day. His plays suggested that people, not the gods, were the cause of human misfortune and suffering. In *The Trojan Women,* he stripped war of its glamour by showing the suffering of women who were victims of the war.

Theatrical Masks
Greek masks, with their exaggerated facial features, enabled those sitting far from the stage to recognize the characters. A small mouthpiece inside the mask helped project the actor's voice.

Greek Comedy Some Greek playwrights wrote **comedies,** humorous plays that mocked people or customs. Almost all the surviving Greek comedies were written by Aristophanes (a rih STAHF uh neez). In *Lysistrata,* he shows the women of Athens banding together to force their husbands to end a war against Sparta. Unlike tragedy which focused on events of the past, comedies ridiculed individuals of the day, including political figures, philosophers, and prominent members of society. Through ridicule, comic playwrights sharply criticized society, much as political cartoonists do today.

✔ **Checkpoint** How was drama used to influence Greek society?

Vocabulary Builder
bias—(BI uhs) *n.* a mental leaning; prejudice; slant

Recording Events as History

The Greeks also applied observation, reason, and logic to the study of history. **Herodotus** is often called the "Father of History" in the Western world because he went beyond listing names of rulers or the retelling of ancient legends. Before writing *The Persian Wars,* Herodotus visited many lands, collecting information from people who remembered the actual events he chronicled. In fact, Herodotus used the Greek term *historie*, which means inquiry, to define his work. Our *history* comes from this word, but its definition has evolved today to simply mean the recording and study of past events.

Herodotus cast a critical eye on his sources, noting bias and conflicting accounts. However, despite this special care for detail and accuracy, his writings reflected his own view that the war was a clear moral victory of Greek love of freedom over Persian tyranny. He even invented conversations and speeches for historical figures.

Another historian Thucydides, who was a few years younger than Herodotus, wrote about the Peloponnesian War, a much less happy subject for the Greeks. He had lived through the war and vividly described the war's savagery and corrupting influence on all those involved. Although he was an Athenian, he tried to be fair to both sides.

Both writers set standards for future historians. Herodotus stressed the importance of research. Thucydides showed the need to avoid bias.

✔ **Checkpoint** Why is Herodotus considered the "Father of History"?

Herodotus, the "Father of History"

Progress Monitoring *Online*
For: Self-quiz with vocabulary practice
Web Code: naa-0441

4 Assessment

Terms, People, and Places

1. For each term, person, or place listed at the beginning of the section, write a sentence explaining its significance.

Note Taking

2. **Reading Skill: Identify Supporting Details** Use your completed concept web to answer the Focus Question: How did Greek thinkers, artists, and writers explore the nature of the universe and people's place in it?

Comprehension and Critical Thinking

3. **Make Generalizations** (a) Why did Plato reject democracy? (b) Describe the ideal form of government set forth in Plato's *Republic.*

4. **Summarize** What standards of beauty did Greek artists follow?

5. **Analyze Information** (a) How were Greek plays performed? (b) What were the topics of Greek poetry and plays?

6. **Identify Central Issues** Why do you think research and avoiding bias is important to the writing of history?

● **Writing About History**

Quick Write: Write a Thesis Statement
Suppose you are writing a persuasive essay using Plato's ideas about what constitutes a perfect society to persuade the reader that Athenian democracy was imperfect. Based on what you have read, write a thesis statement for your essay.

Aristotle: *Politics*

The Greek philosopher Aristotle (384 B.C.–322 B.C.) was suspicious of democracy, which he thought could lead to mob rule. Instead, Aristotle favored rule by a single strong and virtuous leader. In this excerpt from his *Politics,* Aristotle outlines the forms of government and discusses the strengths and weaknesses of each form. Besides describing the ideal state, Aristotle also writes about practical matters relating to the preservation and improvement of government.

The Greek philosopher Aristotle

Thinking Critically

1. **Summarize** How does Aristotle describe constitutional government?
2. **Analyze Information** What do you think Aristotle means when he states that "man is by nature a political animal"?

First, let us consider what is the purpose of a state, and how many forms of government there are by which human society is regulated. We have already said, in the first part of this treatise[1]. . . that man is by nature a political animal. And therefore, men, even when they do not require one another's help, desire to live together . . . and are also brought together by their common interests . . . well-being . . . is certainly the chief end, both of individuals and of states. . . .

The conclusion is evident: that governments which have a regard to the common interest are constituted[2] in accordance with strict principles of justice, and are therefore true forms; but those which regard only the interest of the rulers are all defective and perverted forms, for they are despotic[3], whereas a state is a community of freemen. . . .

Of forms of government in which one rules, we call that which regards the common interests kingship or royalty; that in which more than one, but not many, rule, aristocracy; and it is so called, either because the rulers are the best men, or because they have at heart the best interests of the state and of the citizens. But when the citizens at large administer the state for the common interest, the government is called by the generic[4] name—a constitution. . . .

Of the above-mentioned forms, the perversions are as follows: of royalty, tyranny; of aristocracy, oligarchy; of constitutional government, democracy. For tyranny is a kind of monarchy which has in view the interest of the monarch only; oligarchy has in view the interest of the wealthy; democracy, of the needy; none of them the common good of all.

1. **treatise** (TREET is) *n.* a written argument
2. **constituted** (KAHN stuh too ted) *vt.* made or composed of
3. **despotic** (des PAHT ik) *adj.* characteristic of a tyrant or absolute ruler
4. **generic** (juh NEHR ik) *adj.* relating to a group, general

Alexander the Great
at the Battle of Issus

Alexander Shares the Rewards

A young man named Alexander inherited the Macedonian empire from his father, Philip II. Alexander proceeded to extend the empire to epic proportions. However, he did not do it alone. Here, in a speech attributed to him, Alexander rallies his troops to continue the quest of expanding the empire.

66 I could not have blamed you for being the first to lose heart if I . . . had not shared in your exhausting marches and your perilous campaigns. . . . You and I . . . have shared the labor and shared the danger, and the rewards are for us all. . . . whoever wishes to return home will be allowed to go. . . . I will make those who stay the envy of those who return. 99

Focus Question How did Alexander the Great expand his empire and spread Greek culture throughout the realm?

Alexander and the Hellenistic Age

GA **Performance Standards**

- **SSWH3b** Describe the diffusion of Greek culture by Alexander the Great.
- **SSWH3c** Analyze scientific contributions and contributions of women in Hellenistic and Roman culture.

Terms, People, and Places

Alexander the Great	Pythagoras
Philip II	heliocentric
assassination	Archimedes
assimilate	Hippocrates
Alexandria	

Note Taking

Reading Skill: Identify Supporting Details As you read this section, make an outline to keep track of the important main ideas and supporting details of the empire of Alexander the Great.

I. The Empire of Alexander the Great
  A. Philip II conquers Greece
    1.
    2.
  B. Alexander takes Persia
    1.
    2.

In 338 B.C., Athens fell to the Macedonian army. Athens and the other Greek city-states lost their independence. Yet the disaster ushered in a new age in which Greek culture spread from the Mediterranean to the borders of India. The architect of this new era was the man who would eventually become known to history as **Alexander the Great.**

The Empire of Alexander the Great

To the Greeks, the rugged, mountainous kingdom of Macedonia was a backward, half-civilized land. The rulers of this frontier land, in fact, were of Greek origin and kept ties to their Greek neighbors. As a youth, **Philip II** had lived in Thebes and had come to admire Greek culture. Later, he hired Aristotle as a tutor to his young son Alexander.

Philip II Conquers Greece When Philip II gained the throne in 359 B.C., he dreamed of conquering the prosperous city-states to the south. He built a superb and powerful army. Through threats, bribery, and diplomacy, he formed alliances with many Greek city-states. Others he conquered. In 338 B.C., when Athens and Thebes joined forces against him, Philip II defeated them at the battle of Chaeronea (kehr uh NEE uh). He then brought all of Greece under his control.

Philip had a still grander dream—to conquer the Persian empire. Before he could achieve that plan, though, he was assassinated at

Miller Projection

0   200   400 mi
0   200   400 km

Danube River

Black Sea

MACEDONIA

Dardanelles

CAUCASUS MTS.

Aral Sea

Jaxartes River

Oxus River

Caspian Sea

Troy

Gordium

Athens

ASIA MINOR

Issus

Tigris River

Thapsacus

Ecbatana

Euphrates River

Alexandria

Alexandropolis

Alexandria

Alexandria

HINDU KUSH

Nicaea

Bucephala

Mediterranean Sea

Tyre

Damascus

Jerusalem

Babylon

Susa

PERSIA

Indus River

Alexandria

PALESTINE

Gaza

Alexandria

Memphis

Alexander's death, 323 B.C.

River

Alexandria

Persepolis

Alexandria

Alexandria
Alexandria
Alexandria

Nile River

Red Sea

Persian Gulf

Alexandria

Alexandria

N
W   E
S

Arabian Sea

20° N

40° E

60° E

70° E

Macedonia, 336 B.C.

Alexander's empire at its height, 323 B.C.

Route of Alexander, 334 B.C.–323 B.C.

Towns founded by Alexander and his followers

Other cities

Although eventually stopped short from achieving his goal, Alexander once described the limitless size he envisioned his empire would one day reach:

Primary Source

" Our ships will sail round from the Persian Gulf to Libya as far as the Pillars of Hercules, whence all Libya to the eastward will soon be ours, and all Asia too, and to this empire there will be no boundaries but what God Himself has made for the whole world. "

A youthful image of the powerful Alexander the Great (top) and the revered leader's profile on a gold coin minted in Macedonia (bottom)

Map Skills The ambitions of Alexander the Great led him to conquer lands across an expansive area.

1. **Locate** (a) Mediterranean Sea (b) Arabian Sea (c) Indus River (d) Nile River (e) Euphrates River (f) Babylon

2. **Region** Locate the map entitled *Assyria, Persia, and the Phoenician Colonies,* which appears in an earlier chapter. (a) Which of the empires was largest? (b) Which parts of Alexander's empire had not been part of the Persian empire?

3. **Predicting Consequences** Judging from this map, do you think Alexander's empire would be difficult to keep united? Explain your reasoning.

his daughter's wedding. **Assassination** is the murder of a public figure, usually for political reasons. Philip's queen, Olympias, then outmaneuvered his other wives and children to put her own son, Alexander, on the throne.

Alexander Takes Persia Alexander was only 20 years old. Yet he was already an experienced soldier who shared his father's ambitions. With Greece subdued, he began organizing the forces needed to conquer Persia. By 334 B.C., he had enough ships to cross the Dardanelles, the strait separating Europe from Asia Minor.

Persia was no longer the great power it had once been. The emperor Darius III was weak, and the provinces were often in rebellion against him. Still, the Persian empire stretched more than 2,000 miles from Egypt to India.

Alexander won his first victory against the Persians at the Granicus River. He then moved from victory to victory, marching through Asia Minor into Palestine and south to Egypt before turning east again to take Babylon in 331 B.C. Other cities followed. But before Alexander could capture Darius, the Persian emperor was murdered.

Advance Into India With much of the Persian empire under his control, the restless Alexander headed farther east. He crossed the Hindu Kush into northern India. There, in 326 B.C., his troops for the first time faced soldiers mounted on war elephants. Although Alexander never lost a battle, his soldiers were tired of the long campaign and refused to go farther east. Reluctantly, Alexander agreed to turn back. After a long and difficult march, they reached Babylon, where Alexander began planning a new campaign.

Alexander's Early Death Before he could set out again, the thirty-two-year-old fell victim to a sudden fever. As Alexander lay dying, his commanders asked to whom he left his immense empire. "To the strongest," he is said to have whispered.

In fact, no one leader proved strong enough to succeed Alexander. Instead, after years of disorder, three generals divided up the empire. Macedonia and Greece went to one general, Egypt to another, and most of Persia to a third. For the next 300 years, their descendants competed for power over the lands Alexander had conquered.

✔ **Checkpoint** Why was Alexander the Great able to conquer the Persian empire?

The Legacy of Alexander

Although Alexander's empire soon crumbled following his premature death, he had unleashed changes that would ripple across the Mediterranean world and the Middle East for centuries. His most lasting achievement was the spread of Greek culture.

Cultures Combine Across his far-flung empire, Alexander founded many new cities, most of them named after him. The generals who succeeded him founded still more. Greek soldiers, traders, and artisans settled these new cities. From Egypt to the borders of India, they built Greek temples, filled them with Greek statues, and held athletic contests as they had in Greece. Local people **assimilated,** or absorbed, Greek ideas. In turn, Greek settlers adopted local customs.

Greek Artistic Influence
Alexander's conquests helped spread Greek culture throughout the empire. The influence of the assimilated culture is frequently found in art such as this sitting Buddha who is portrayed here with flowing robes in the classical Greek style.

Scientific Advances in the Hellenistic Age

The vast size of Alexander's empire and his encouragement of scholarship brought many advances in science and mathematics. Throughout Alexander's empire, ideas and theories were exxchanged and improved upon. A great research institute and library were built in the Egyptian city of Alexandria. Scholars from all regions converged on the city to conduct research and discuss their theories with the best minds of the day. The city became the largest center of learning and scholarship during the Hellenistic Age, which lasted from the death of Alexander to about A.D. 100.

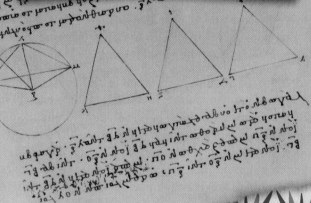

An engraver's depiction of the Library of ▶ Alexandria (top), which is estimated to have had up to 700,000 scrolls, perhaps including the works of Euclid (bottom right).

Alexander had encouraged a blending of eastern and western cultures when he had married a Persian woman and urged his soldiers to follow his example. He had also adopted many Persian customs, including Persian dress. Gradually, after his death, a vital new culture emerged that blended Greek, Persian, Egyptian, and Indian influences. This Hellenistic civilization would flourish for several centuries.

Alexandria: The Cultural Capital At the very heart of the Hellenistic world stood the city of **Alexandria,** Egypt. Located on the sea lanes between Europe and Asia, its markets boasted a wide range of goods, from Greek marble to Arabian spices to East African ivory. A Greek architect had drawn up plans for the city, which would become home to almost a million people. Among the city's marvelous sights was the Pharos, an enormous lighthouse that soared 440 feet into the air.

Alexander and his successors encouraged the work of scholars. The rulers of Alexandria built the great Museum as a center of learning. The Museum boasted laboratories, lecture halls, and a zoo. Its library had thousands of scrolls representing the accumulated knowledge of the ancient world. Unfortunately, the library was later destroyed in a fire.

New Roles for Women Paintings, statues, and legal codes show that women were no longer restricted to their homes during the Hellenistic period. More women learned to read and write. Some became philosophers

Vocabulary Builder

accumulate—(uh KYOOM yoo layt) vt. to gather together or collect over a period of time

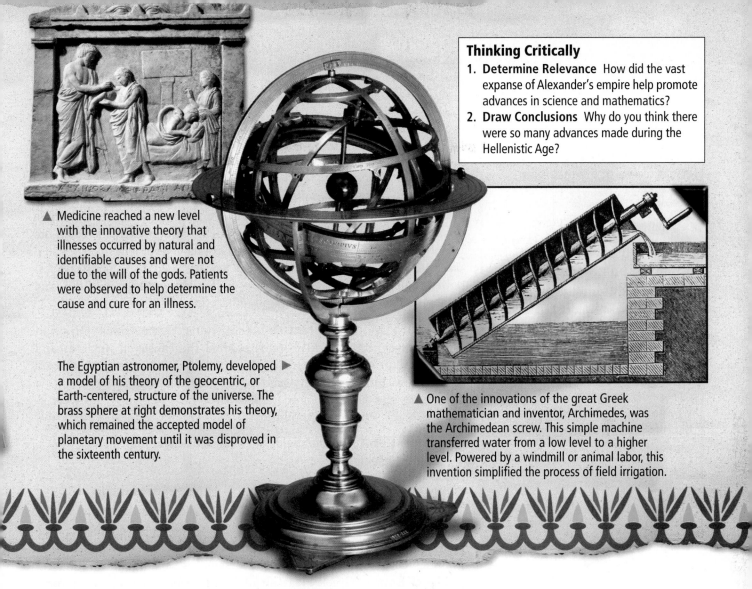

Thinking Critically
1. **Determine Relevance** How did the vast expanse of Alexander's empire help promote advances in science and mathematics?
2. **Draw Conclusions** Why do you think there were so many advances made during the Hellenistic Age?

▲ Medicine reached a new level with the innovative theory that illnesses occurred by natural and identifiable causes and were not due to the will of the gods. Patients were observed to help determine the cause and cure for an illness.

The Egyptian astronomer, Ptolemy, developed ▶ a model of his theory of the geocentric, or Earth-centered, structure of the universe. The brass sphere at right demonstrates his theory, which remained the accepted model of planetary movement until it was disproved in the sixteenth century.

▲ One of the innovations of the great Greek mathematician and inventor, Archimedes, was the Archimedean screw. This simple machine transferred water from a low level to a higher level. Powered by a windmill or animal labor, this invention simplified the process of field irrigation.

or poets. Royal women held considerable power, working alongside husbands and sons who were the actual rulers. In Egypt, the able and clever queen Cleopatra VII came to rule in her own right.

✔ **Checkpoint** How did Alexander encourage the blending of cultures?

Hellenistic Arts and Sciences

The cities of the Hellenistic world employed armies of architects and artists. Temples, palaces, and other public buildings were much larger and grander than the buildings of classical Greece. The <u>elaborate</u> new style reflected the desire of Hellenistic rulers to glorify themselves as godlike.

New Philosophies Political turmoil during the Hellenistic age contributed to the rise of new schools of philosophy. The most influential was Stoicism. Its founder, Zeno, urged people to avoid desires and disappointments by accepting calmly whatever life brought. Stoics preached high moral standards, such as the idea of protecting the rights of fellow humans. They taught that all people, including women and slaves, though unequal in society, were morally equal because all had the power of reason. Stoicism later influenced many Roman and Christian thinkers.

Advances in Math and Astronomy During the Hellenistic age, scholars built on earlier Greek, Babylonian, and Egyptian knowledge. In

Vocabulary Builder
<u>elaborate</u>—(ee LAB uh rit) *adj.* developed in great detail; highly ornamented

The methods ancient Greek doctors used to diagnose disease are so unlike those of today that scholars find many ancient Greek medical writings difficult to decipher. However, the ancient Greek code of ethics—the Hippocratic oath—is still used by medical professionals today.

❝I will use my power to help the sick to the best of my ability and judgment; I will abstain from harming or wronging any man by it. . . .

Whatever I see or hear, professionally, or privately, which ought not to be divulged, I will keep secret . . .

If, therefore, I observe this oath and do not violate it, may I prosper both in my life and in my profession, earning good repute among all men for all time.❞

Why do you think the Hippocratic oath has continued through the centuries as a guide to doctors?

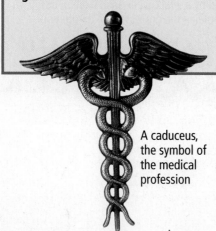

A caduceus, the symbol of the medical profession

mathematics, **Pythagoras** (pih THAG uh rus) derived a formula to calculate the relationship between the sides of a right triangle. Euclid (YOO klid) wrote *The Elements,* a textbook that became the basis for modern geometry.

Using mathematics and careful observation, the astronomer Aristarchus (a ris TAHR kus) argued that the Earth rotated on its axis and orbited the sun. This theory of a **heliocentric,** or sun-centered, solar system was not accepted by most scientists until almost 2,000 years later. Another Hellenistic astronomer, Eratosthenes, (eh ruh TAHS thuh neez), showed that the Earth was round and accurately calculated its circumference.

The most famous Hellenistic scientist, **Archimedes** (ahr kuh MEE deez), applied principles of physics to make practical inventions. He mastered the use of the lever and pulley and boasted, "Give me a lever long enough and a place to stand on, and I will move the world." Then, to demonstrate the power of his invention, Archimedes used it to draw a ship over the land before a crowd of awed spectators.

Improving Medical Practice About 400 B.C., the Greek physician **Hippocrates** (hih PAH kruh teez) studied the causes of illnesses and looked for cures. The Hippocratic oath attributed to him set ethical standards for doctors. Greek physicians swore to "help the sick according to my ability and judgment but never with a view to injury and wrong." Doctors today still take a similar oath.

✔ **Checkpoint** In what fields did Hellenistic civilization make advancements?

Looking Ahead

With its conquest of Asia Minor in 133 B.C., Rome replaced Greece as the dominant power in the Mediterranean world. However, the Greek legacy remains. Greek works in the arts and sciences set a standard for later people of Europe. Greek ideas about law, freedom, justice, and government continue to influence political thinking to the present day. These achievements were especially remarkable because they were produced by a scattering of tiny city-states whose rivalries left them too weak to defend themselves from conquest. Later, you will learn how the Greek legacy influenced the civilizations of Rome and of Western Europe.

SECTION 5 Assessment

Progress Monitoring *Online*
For: Self-quiz with vocabulary practice
Web Code: naa-0451

Terms, People, and Places

1. For each term, person, or place listed at the beginning of the section, write a sentence explaining its significance.

Note Taking

2. **Reading Skill: Identify Supporting Details** Use your completed outline to answer the Focus Question: How did Alexander the Great expand his empire and spread Greek culture throughout the realm?

Comprehension and Critical Thinking

3. **Summarize** What was the extent of Alexander's vast empire and how did he acquire it?

4. **Synthesize Information** How did Alexander's conquests lead to a new civilization?

5. **Recognize Ideologies** What new ideas did the Stoics introduce?

6. **Draw Conclusions** Why do you think the Hippocratic oath is considered a medical advance?

● **Writing About History**

Quick Write: Organize Evidence In organizing a persuasive essay, one should often save the strongest argument for last. For practice, write a concluding paragraph for a persuasive essay from the perspective of a conquered person who either supports or opposes the assimilation of Greek ideas and culture.

Golden Age of Greek Drama

The ancient Greeks loved going to plays. During the golden age of Greek drama—the 400s B.C.—almost every Greek city had an open-air theater. Enthusiastic audiences filled the stone benches to watch comedies and tragedies performed by two or three actors and a chorus. Many of the techniques developed in these Greek theaters have influenced dramatic productions from ancient times though Shakespeare's era to our own day.

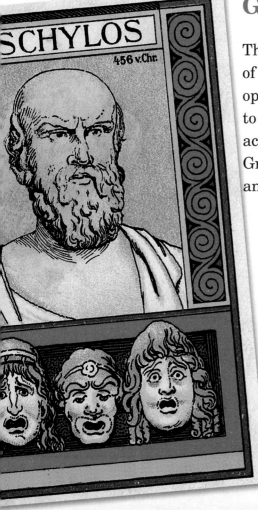

◀ The poster, left, shows Greek playwright Aeschylus and three theatrical masks.

▲ In this modern production of Aeschylus's tragedy *The Persians*, the actors wear character masks like the ones Greek actors would have worn.

The actors performed on the **stage** and on the **skene** (skay NAY), a building directly behind the stage. The roof of the skene could represent the heavens.

The audience sat in the **theatron** (THAY ah tran), or "viewing place." The ruins of this Greek theater are in Sicily.

The **orchestra**, or "dancing place," was a round, level place where the chorus performed. There was often an altar in the center.

Thinking Critically

1. **Draw Inferences** How do you think wearing masks affected the way actors showed their characters emotions?

2. **Connect to Today** Which Greek theater terms and techniques are still used today?

CHAPTER 4

Quick Study Guide

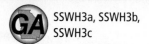 **GA** SSWH3a, SSWH3b, SSWH3c

Progress Monitoring *Online*
For: Self-test with vocabulary practice
Web Code: naa-0461

■ Major Conflicts in Ancient Greece

Conflict	Participants	Reason	Victor
Trojan War	Mycenae and Troy	Economic rivalry	Mycenaeans
Persian War	Greek city-states and Persia	Halt the spread of the Persian empire	Greek city-states
Peloponnesian War	Athens and Sparta (spread to all of Greece)	Resentment of Athenian domination and disagreement on form of government	Sparta and allies

■ Key Political Leaders

Leader	Accomplishments
Solon	Athenian archon who introduced reforms making the government more democratic and the economy more profitable
Pisistratus	Athenian tyrant who gave poor citizens a voice in government and weakened the aristocracy
Cleisthenes	Athenian leader who created the Council of 500 and made the assembly a legislature
Pericles	Athenian statesman who instituted direct democracy in Athens, increased participation in government, provided salaries for government employees, and encouraged the cultural development of Athens
Philip II	Macedonian king who conquered Greece
Alexander the Great	Macedonian leader who conquered an empire stretching from Greece to India and encouraged the spread of Greek culture throughout his empire

■ Important Cultural Figures of Greece

Individual	Achievement
Philosophy	
Socrates	Sought truth and self-knowledge; Socratic method
Plato	Favored the rule of a philosopher-king; wrote *The Republic*
Aristotle	Promoted the idea of the ìgolden mean ”; wrote *Politics*
Zeno	Founder of Stoicism
Literature	
Homer	Poet; wrote the *Iliad* and the *Odyssey*
Aeschylus	Tragic playwright; wrote the *Oresteia*
Sophocles	Tragic playwright; wrote *Antigone*
Euripides	Tragic playwright; wrote *The Trojan Women*
Aristophanes	Comic playwright; wrote *Lysistrata*
History	
Herodotus	Historian; encouraged research in histories; wrote *The Persian Wars*
Thucydides	Historian; promoted unbiased writing of histories
Mathematics and Science	
Pythagoras	Developed the formula for the relationship among the sides of a right triangle known as the Pythagorean theorem
Euclid	Developed the basis for modern geometry; wrote *The Elements*
Aristarchus	Theorized that the solar system is heliocentric
Eratosthenes	Determined that the Earth is round and calculated its circumference
Archimedes	Mastered the lever and pulley
Hippocrates	Developed a code of ethics for medical practitioners

■ Key Events in Ancient Greece

1600 B.C.
Minoan civilization at its height

594 B.C.
Solon appointed archon.

460 B.C.
Age of Pericles marks the height of democracy in Athens.

Chapter Events
World Events

1600 B.C.   **600 B.C.**   **500 B.C.**

800 B.C.
Olmec civilization disappearing in present-day Mexico

539 B.C.
Persian empire is founded.

500 B.C.
Nok civilization in West Africa is on the rise.

Concept Connector

Essential Question Review

To connect prior knowledge with what you have learned in this chapter, answer the questions below in your Concept Connector journal. Use the journal in the Reading and Note Taking Study Guide to record your answers (or go to www.phschool.com **Web Code: nad-0407**). In addition, record information about the following concepts:

- Geography's Impact: the Aegean and Mediterranean seas
- Conflict: the Persian War
- Political Systems: Oligarchy

1. **Trade** The culture and economy of ancient Greece were greatly influenced by trade. However, Greece was not the first civilization to be defined by its trade with others. Compare and contrast the system of trade in ancient Greece and Phoenicia. For each group, think about the following:
   - the form of travel used and the routes taken
   - the range of territory reached by each group
   - the building and settlement of towns
   - contact with other groups and cultural diffusion

2. **Science** Learning and study were important priorities in both ancient Greece and in ancient China. Each society made numerous scientific contributions that still affect us today. Compare the achievements made by each society in astronomy and medicine. How do you think these advances impact us today?

3. **Cultural Diffusion** The Phoenician alphabet was borrowed and modified by the Greeks. That alphabet was then borrowed and adapted by the Romans. As you know, this evolution of the alphabet led to the version we use today. How do you think the alphabet spread among these cultures? Why do you think this alphabet more than any other form of ancient writing is still used in most Western cultures today?

Connections To Today

1. **Cooperation: Alliances of the 21st Century** Throughout history, nations have joined together to form alliances like the Delian League in Greece. Conduct research on one of the following organizations: the League of Nations, the European Union, the North Atlantic Treaty Organization (NATO), the United Nations, the African Union, the Association of Southeast Asian Nations, the Organization for Economic Cooperation and Development, or the League of Arab States. Then write a summary about it. Be sure to include the original reason for the creation of the group, the year it was created, the organization's main purpose or goals, and the number and names of the member nations.

2. **Culture: Architecture** The style of architecture developed by the ancient Greeks has influenced architecture for over 2,000 years. During the Renaissance, the Greek style, called the "classical" style, was revived and was perceived as the perfect form of architecture. The style is still frequently used today. Recently, the Ronald Reagan Building (below) in Washington, D.C., was built in this style. Conduct research to identify three additional buildings that have been influenced by the classical Greek style. Create a poster with images of the buildings, include a brief description of its location and purpose, and explain why you think the classical Greek style of architecture was used.

| 431 B.C. Peloponnesian War begins. | 331 B.C. Alexander the Great conquers the Persian empire. | 323 B.C. The Hellenistic Age begins. | | 133 B.C. Dominance in the Mediterranean passes from Greece to Rome. |

400 B.C.   300 B.C.   200 B.C.

| 450 B.C. Roman Republic publishes its legal code. | 321 B.C. The Maurya dynasty begins in India. | 221 B.C. Shi Huangdi unites China. | **History Interactive** **For:** Interactive timeline **Web Code:** nap-0461 |

Chapter Assessment

Terms, People, and Places

Complete each sentence by choosing the correct answer from the list of terms below. You will not use all of the terms listed.

fresco	rhetoric
aristocracy	Aristotle
tyrant	tragedy
alliance	logic
direct democracy	Plato
Pericles	strait

1. A system of government in which a large number of citizens take part in the day-to-day affairs is called a(n) _____.
2. _____ set up the Lyceum, a school for the study of all branches of knowledge.
3. The art of skillful speaking is known as _____.
4. _____ believed that all men should take part in government regardless of wealth or class.
5. A play that tells a story of human suffering is known as a(n) _____.
6. A(n) _____ is a watercolor painting done on wet plaster.
7. A government ruled by a hereditary landholding elite is known as a(n) _____.
8. In ancient Greece, someone who gained power by force was known as a(n) _____.

Main Ideas

Section 1 (pp. 114–117)
9. How did trade affect the development of early Greek civilizations?

Section 2 (pp. 118–123)
10. How did the systems of government and education differ between Athens and Sparta?

Section 3 (pp. 124–129)
11. What were the results of the Persian Wars?
12. How did the leadership of Pericles affect the government and culture of Athens?

Section 4 (pp. 130–136)
13. Why were some of the ideas of ancient Greek philosophers considered a threat to Greek society and tradition?
14. What was the design objective of the art and architecture of ancient Greece?

Section 5 (pp. 137–143)
15. What was the extent of Alexander's empire, and why was he able to conquer such an extended area?
16. What were some of the cultural achievements of the Hellenistic period?

Chapter Focus Question
17. What enduring traditions and institutions did Greek culture extend to most of the Western world?

Critical Thinking

18. **Geography and History** What role did the Mediterranean and Aegean seas play in the development of the culture of ancient Greece?
19. **Recognize Cause and Effect** Identify two immediate and two long-term causes of the Peloponnesian War. Why might it be said that all Greeks lost the Peloponnesian War?
20. **Make Comparisons** How was the form of government outlined in Plato's *Republic* similar to and different from the government of Sparta?
21. **Draw Inferences** How did Athenian culture stress the importance of the individual?
22. **Recognize Ideologies** Why do you think many Greeks condemned the ideas of the Sophists?
23. **Draw Conclusions** Would you agree that Alexander deserved to be called "the Great"? Why or why not?

● Writing About History

In this chapter's five Section Assessments, you developed skills for writing a persuasive essay.

Writing a Persuasive Essay The cultures of ancient Athens and Sparta were quite different from each other. Their rivalry frequently led to conflict between the two city-states. Although they joined forces to defeat the Persians, their differences eventually led to the Peloponnesian War. Write a persuasive essay from the point of view of an Athenian statesmen in which you try to prevent war by persuading the Spartan leadership of the benefits of direct democracy. Consult page SH16 of the Writing Handbook for additional help.

Prewriting
• Make a list of what you believe to be the strongest arguments of the Athenian statesman.

• Organize the arguments on your list from weakest to strongest.

Drafting
• Write a thesis statement clearly stating the position that you will prove.
• Sequence your arguments so that you open or close with your strongest argument.
• Write a conclusion that restates your thesis and closes with a strong argument.

Revising
• Review your arguments to make sure that you have explained them logically and clearly.
• Use the guidelines for revising your essay on page SH17 of the Writing Handbook.

Politics and Philosophy in Ancient Greece

Philosophy flourished under Athenian democracy. In their search for the best form of government, the best leaders, and the perfect society, Greek philosophers created works that have influenced thinkers for ages. These "lovers of wisdom" used reason to guide their quest for truth, as the documents below show.

Document A

"[Justice] is not a matter of external behavior, but of the inward self and of attending to all that is, in the fullest sense, a man's proper concern. The just man does not allow the several elements in his soul to usurp one another's functions; he is indeed one who sets his house in order, by self-mastery and discipline coming to be at peace with himself, and bringing into tune those . . . parts. . . . Only when he has linked these parts together in well-tempered harmony . . . will he be ready to go about whatever he may have to do, whether it be making money . . . or business transactions, or the affairs of state. In all these fields when he speaks of just and honorable conduct, he will mean the behavior that helps to produce and to preserve this habit of mind; and by wisdom he will mean the knowledge which presides over such conduct. Any action which tends to break down this habit will be for him unjust: and the notions governing it he will call ignorance and folly.

That is perfectly true, Socrates.

Good, said I. I believe we should not be thought altogether mistaken, if we claimed to have discovered the just man and the just state, and wherein their justice consists."

—Plato's **Republic,** quoting Socrates

Document B

"The legislator should always include the middle class in his government; if he makes laws oligarchical, to the middle class let him look; if he makes them democratical, he should equally by his laws try to attach this class to the state. There only can the government ever be stable where the middle class exceeds one or both of the others, and in that case there will be no fear that the rich will unite with the poor against the rulers. . . . There comes a time when out of a false good there arises a true evil, since the encroachments of the rich are more destructive to the constitution than those of the people."

—**Politics,** Aristotle

▲ Plato and Aristotle in a detail from the sixteenth century "School of Athens" fresco by Raphael

Document C

"[F]or the truth is that you can have a well-governed society only if you can discover for your future rulers a better way of life than being in office; then only will power be in the hands of men who are rich, not in gold, but in the wealth that brings happiness, a good and wise life. All goes wrong when, starved for lack of anything good in their own lives, men turn to public affairs hoping to snatch from thence the happiness they hunger for. They set about fighting for power and this internecine [mutually destructive] conflict ruins them and their country. The life of true philosophy is the only one that looks down upon offices of state; and access to power must be confined to men who are not in love with it."

—**Republic,** Plato

Analyzing Documents

Use your knowledge of Greek philosophy and Documents A, B, and C to answer the questions below.

1. According to Socrates (Document A), a just state depends on
   A scientific truth and reason.
   B the harmony and discipline of the individual.
   C the stability of the elected government.
   D wisdom, education and wealth.

2. According to Plato (Document C), which group of people would make the best rulers?
   A artists
   B rich aristocrats
   C philosophers
   D soldiers

3. According to Aristotle (Document B), why is the middle class necessary for a stable government?
   A to give rich people allies
   B to offer hope to poor people
   C to contribute a reasonable tax base
   D to balance the rich and the poor

4. **Writing Task** Greek philosophers held a deep interest in politics. What does this reflect about Greek society? Base your response on these documents and information provided in the chapter.

CHAPTER

5 Ancient Rome and the Rise of Christianity

509 B.C.–A.D. 476

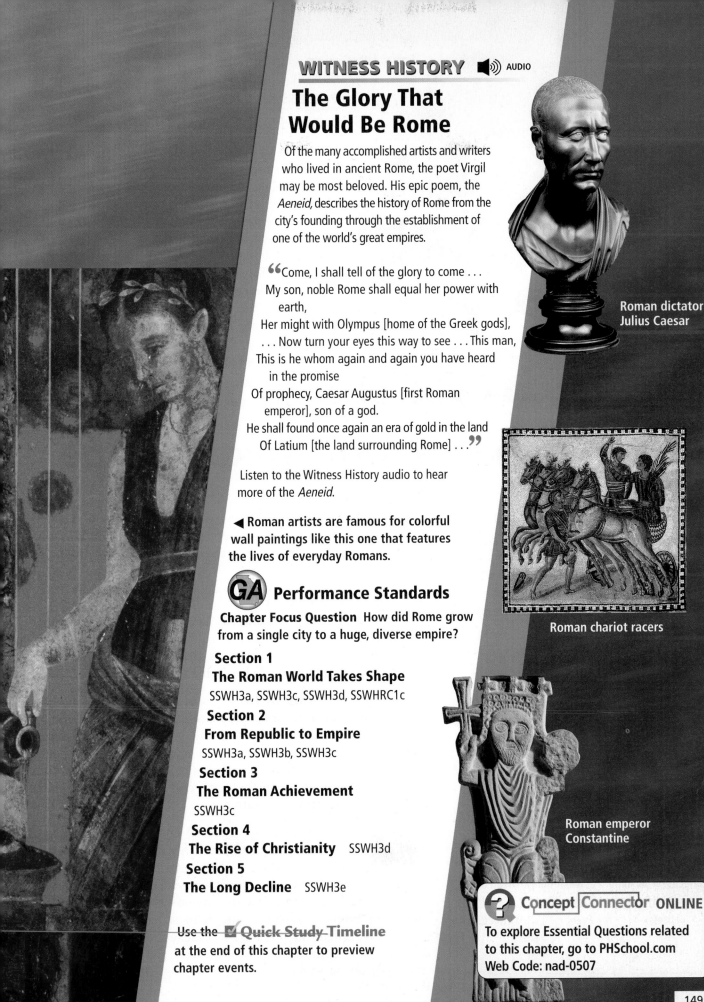

The Glory That Would Be Rome

Of the many accomplished artists and writers who lived in ancient Rome, the poet Virgil may be most beloved. His epic poem, the *Aeneid,* describes the history of Rome from the city's founding through the establishment of one of the world's great empires.

❝Come, I shall tell of the glory to come . . .
My son, noble Rome shall equal her power with earth,
Her might with Olympus [home of the Greek gods],
. . . Now turn your eyes this way to see . . . This man,
This is he whom again and again you have heard in the promise
Of prophecy, Caesar Augustus [first Roman emperor], son of a god.
He shall found once again an era of gold in the land
Of Latium [the land surrounding Rome] . . .❞

Listen to the Witness History audio to hear more of the *Aeneid*.

◀ Roman artists are famous for colorful wall paintings like this one that features the lives of everyday Romans.

Roman dictator Julius Caesar

Roman chariot racers

Roman emperor Constantine

GA Performance Standards

Chapter Focus Question How did Rome grow from a single city to a huge, diverse empire?

Section 1
The Roman World Takes Shape
SSWH3a, SSWH3c, SSWH3d, SSWHRC1c

Section 2
From Republic to Empire
SSWH3a, SSWH3b, SSWH3c

Section 3
The Roman Achievement
SSWH3c

Section 4
The Rise of Christianity   SSWH3d

Section 5
The Long Decline   SSWH3e

Use the ☑ Quick Study Timeline at the end of this chapter to preview chapter events.

? Concept Connector ONLINE

To explore Essential Questions related to this chapter, go to PHSchool.com
Web Code: nad-0507

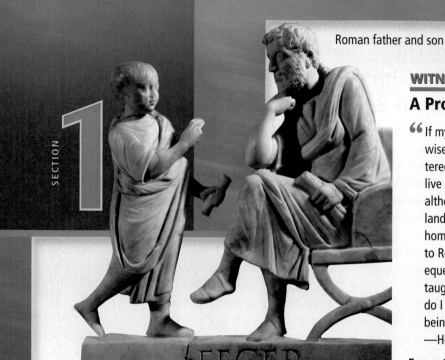

Roman father and son

WITNESS HISTORY 🔊 AUDIO

A Proud Son Speaks of His Father

❝ If my character is flawed by a few minor faults, but is otherwise decent and moral, if you can point out only a few scattered blemishes on an otherwise immaculate surface, . . . if I live a virtuous life, . . . my father deserves all the credit. For although he was a poor man, with only an infertile plot of land, he was not content to send me to [the school in his home town]. . . . My father had the courage to take his boy to Rome, to have him taught the same skills which any equestrian [rider of horses] or senator would have his sons taught. . . . I could never be ashamed of such a father, nor do I feel any need, as many people do, to apologize for being a freedman's [former slave's] son.❞
—Horace, Roman poet

Focus Question What values formed the basis of Roman society and government?

The Roman World Takes Shape

 Performance Standards

- **SSWH3a** Compare the Greek polis, the Roman Republic, and the Roman Empire.
- **SSWH3c** Analyze contributions of women in Hellenistic and Roman culture.
- **SSWH3d** Describe polytheism in the Greek and Roman world.
- **SSWHRC1c** Explore understanding of new words in subject area texts.

Terms, People, and Places

Etruscans	plebeian
republic	tribune
patrician	veto
consul	legion
dictator	

Note Taking

Reading Skill: Identify Causes and Effects For each red heading, fill in a cause-and-effect chart like the one below to identify the cause(s) and the effect(s) of an important event that you read about.

Cause(s)	→	Event	→	Effect(s)

Rome began as a small city in Italy and became a ruler of the Mediterranean and beyond. The story of the Romans and how they built a world empire begins with the land in which they lived.

Roman Civilization Arises in Italy

The Italian peninsula is centrally located in the Mediterranean Sea, and the city of Rome sits toward the center of Italy. This location would benefit the Romans as they expanded—first within Italy and then into the lands bordering the Mediterranean.

Unifying the Lands of Italy Because of its geography, Italy proved much easier to unify than Greece. Unlike Greece, Italy is not broken up into small, isolated valleys. In addition, the Apennine Mountains, which run down the length of the Italian peninsula, are less rugged than the mountains of Greece. Finally, Italy has broad, fertile plains in the north and the west. These plains supported the growing population.

Early Peoples Settle Italy By about 800 B.C., the ancestors of the Romans, called the Latins, migrated into Italy. The Latins settled along the Tiber River in small villages scattered over seven low-lying hills. There, they herded and farmed. Their villages would in time grow together into Rome, the city on seven hills. Legend held that twin brothers, Romulus and Remus, had founded the city. Romans regarded this tale highly because the twins were said to be sons of a Latin woman and the war god Mars, lending the Romans a divine origin.

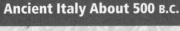
Ancient Italy About 500 B.C.

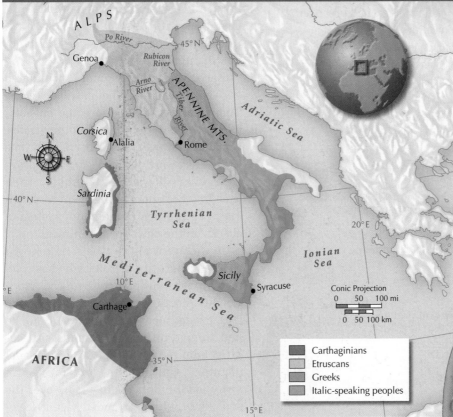

Carthaginians
Etruscans
Greeks
Italic-speaking peoples

Map Skills At the time the state of Rome was founded, the Romans' many neighbors on the Italian peninsula included other speakers of Italic languages such as Latin.

1. **Locate** (a) Rome (b) Apennine Mountains (c) Mediterranean Sea (d) Carthage (e) Tiber River
2. **Region** Based on this map, which group would you think most influenced the Romans? Explain.
3. **Make Generalizations** What do you think are some advantages and disadvantages of living near a variety of different peoples?

The Romans shared the Italian peninsula with other peoples. Among them were Greek colonists whose city-states dotted southern Italy and the **Etruscans,** who lived mostly north of Rome. The origins of the Etruscan civilization are uncertain. One theory says they migrated from Asia Minor, while another suggests they came from the Alps. What is certain is that, for a time, the Etruscans ruled much of central Italy, including Rome itself.

The Romans learned much from Etruscan civilization. They adapted the alphabet that the Etruscans had earlier acquired from the Greeks. The Romans also learned from the Etruscans to use the arch in construction, and they adapted Etruscan engineering techniques to drain the marshy lands along the Tiber. As well, the Romans adopted some Etruscan gods and goddesses and merged them with Roman deities.

The Roman god Jupiter, whose traits resembled those of Tinia, an important Etruscan god

✔ **Checkpoint** How did geography influence the origins and expansion of Rome?

The Romans Establish a Republic

The Romans drove out their Etruscan ruler in 509 B.C. This date is traditionally considered to mark the founding of the Roman state, which would last for 500 years. The Romans established their state with a form of government called in Latin a *res publica,* or "that which belongs to the people." In this form of government, which today we call a **republic,** the people chose some of the officials. A republic, Romans thought, would prevent any individual from gaining too much power.

THE ROMAN *CURSUS HONORUM*

In 180 B.C., the Romans enacted a law that formalized the career path of Roman officials. Called the *cursus honorum*, this path dictated that men hold particular offices in a certain order and assigned age requirements to these offices. Previously, Roman men could fill the offices in any order and do so at any age, as long as they had already completed a period of military service. The *cursus honorum* became the foundation of a Roman political system in which politicians advanced based on merit and experience rather than popularity, influence, or class.

Censor (2)
- Patricians only originally; as of 339 B.C., one had to be plebeian; must have held consulship first
- Maintained the official list of Roman citizens; held much authority
- No minimum age

Consul (2)
- Patricians only originally; as of 367 B.C., one had to be plebeian; must have held praetorship first
- Served as joint head of state; could veto other consul
- Minimum age of 42 for plebeians and 40 for patricians

Praetor (8 by 100 B.C.)
- Patricians only originally; as of 337 B.C., plebeians eligible; must have held quaestorship first
- Served as legal officers with broad authority in government; stood in for consuls when they were away
- Minimum age set at 39

Tribune of the Plebs (10)
- Plebeians only; usually held quaestorship first
- Presided over plebeian assembly and advocated for plebeian demands
- No minimum age

Aedile (4 by 366 B.C.)
- Plebeians only originally; as of 366 B.C., 2 new offices open to plebeians and patricians; must have held quaestorship first
- Oversaw care of the city, distribution of grain, public games
- Minimum age 36

Quaestor (20 by 82 B.C.)
- Patricians only originally; as of 421 B.C., plebeians eligible
- Oversaw finances in treasury and military
- Minimum age set at 30 in 82 B.C.

Thinking Critically
1. **Draw Conclusions** Why do you think at least one of the censors had to be a plebeian?
2. **Predict Consequences** In what ways might the *cursus honorum* have changed politics in Rome?

Structuring the Republic In the early republic, the senate made the laws and controlled the government. Originally, its 300 members were all **patricians,** or members of the land-holding upper class.

Each year, the senators nominated two **consuls** from the patrician class. Their job was to supervise the business of government and command the armies. Consuls, however, could serve only one term. They were also expected to approve each other's decisions. By limiting their time in office and making them responsible to each other, Rome had a system of checks on the power of government.

In the event of war, the senate might choose a **dictator,** or ruler who has complete control over a government. Each Roman dictator was granted power to rule for six months. After that time, he had to give up power. Romans particularly admired Cincinnatus as a model dictator. Cincinnatus organized an army, led the Romans to victory over the attacking enemy, attended victory celebrations, and returned to his farmlands—all within 15 days.

Plebeians Fight for Their Rights At first, all government officials were patricians. **Plebeians** (plih BEE unz), the farmers, merchants, and artisans who made up most of the population, had the legal rights of citizenship but little influence. Plebeian demands for power shaped politics in the early republic.

In time, the plebeians gained the right to elect their own officials, called **tribunes,** to protect their interests. The tribunes could **veto,** or block, laws that they felt were harmful to plebeians. Little by little, plebeians forced the senate to choose plebeians as consuls and to admit plebeians as members of the senate itself. These changes made Rome's government more democratic.

Another breakthrough for the plebeians came in 450 B.C., when the government oversaw the inscription of the laws of Rome on 12 tablets, which were set up in the Forum, Rome's marketplace. Plebeians had protested that citizens could not know what the laws were because they were not written down. The Laws of the Twelve Tables made it possible for the first time for plebeians to appeal a judgment handed down by a patrician judge.

Romans Leave a Lasting Legacy Although the senate still <u>dominated</u> the government, the common people had gained access to power and won safeguards for their rights without having to resort to war or revolution. More than 2,000 years later, the framers of the United States Constitution would adapt such Roman ideas as the senate, the veto, and checks on political power.

✔ **Checkpoint** How did the membership of the senate change over time?

Vocabulary Builder
<u>dominated</u>—(DAHM uh nayt id) *vt.* had authority over

Characterizing Roman Society

The family was the basic unit of Roman society. Under Roman law, the male head of the household—usually the father—had absolute power in the family. He enforced strict discipline and demanded total respect for his authority. His wife was subject to his authority and was not allowed to administer her own affairs. The ideal Roman woman was loving, dutiful, dignified, and strong.

The Role of Women Changes Over Time Roman women played a larger role in society than did Greek women. They could own property, and, in later Roman times, women from all classes ran a variety of businesses, from small shops to major shipyards. Those who made their fortunes earned respect by supporting the arts or paying for public festivals. However, most women worked at home, raising their families, spinning, and weaving.

Over the centuries, Roman women gained greater freedom and influence. Patrician women went to the public baths, dined out, and attended the theater or other forms of public entertainment with their husbands. Some women, such as Livia and Agrippina the Younger, had highly visible public roles and exercised significant political influence.

Romans Educate Most Children Girls and boys from the upper and lower classes learned to read and write. By the later years of the republic, many wealthy Romans hired private tutors, often Greeks, to educate their children. Children memorized major events in Roman history. Boys who wanted to pursue political careers studied rhetoric.

Roman Mythology and Religion The Romans believed in numerous gods and goddesses, many of whom they adapted from Greek religion. Roman mythology was also similar to that of the Greeks. Like the Greek god Zeus, the Roman god Jupiter ruled over the sky and the other gods. According to Roman myths, his wife Juno, like the Greek goddess Hera, protected marriage. Romans also prayed to Neptune, god of the sea, whose powers were the same as those of the Greek god Poseidon. On the battlefield, they turned to Mars, the god of war.

The Roman calendar was full of feasts and other celebrations to honor the gods and goddesses and to ensure divine favor for the city. As loyal citizens, most Romans joined in these festivals, which inspired a sense of community. Throughout Rome, dozens of temples housed statues of the gods. In front of these temples, Romans took part in ritual activities such as worshipping the gods and asking for divine assistance.

✔ **Checkpoint** What social rights did Roman women have?

The Roman Republic Grows

As Rome's political and social systems evolved at home, its armies expanded Roman power across Italy. Roman armies conquered first the Etruscans and then the Greek city-states in the south. By about 270 B.C., Rome controlled most of the Italian peninsula.

Citizen-Soldiers Make Up the Roman Army Rome's success was due to skillful diplomacy and to its loyal, well-trained army. The basic military unit was the **legion,** each of which included about 5,000 men. As in Greece, Roman armies consisted of citizen-soldiers who originally fought without being paid and had to supply their own weapons. Eventually, they received a small stipend, or payment, but their main compensation was always a share of the spoils of victory. Roman citizens often made good soldiers because they were brought up to value loyalty, courage, and respect for authority.

To ensure success, Roman commanders mixed rewards with harsh punishment. Young soldiers who showed courage in action won praise and gifts. If a unit fled from battle, however, one out of every ten men from the disgraced unit was put to death.

Rome Is Just With Conquered Lands Rome generally treated its defeated enemies with justice. Conquered peoples had to acknowledge Roman leadership, pay taxes, and supply soldiers for the Roman army. In return, Rome let them keep their own customs, money, and local government.

To a few privileged groups among the conquered people, Rome gave the highly prized right of full citizenship. Others became partial citizens, who were allowed to marry Romans and carry on trade in Rome. As a result of such generous policies, most conquered lands remained loyal to Rome even in troubled times.

Maintaining the State To protect its conquests, Rome posted soldiers throughout the land. It also built a network of all-weather military roads to link distant territories to Rome. As trade and travel increased, local peoples incorporated Latin into their languages and adopted many Roman customs and beliefs. Slowly, Italy began to unite under Roman rule.

✓ **Checkpoint** How did the Romans treat the people they conquered?

During the time of the late republic, praetorians (above), or bodyguards, began protecting army generals. Later, they would become an elite guard for Roman emperors.

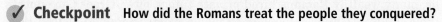

SECTION 1

Assessment

Progress Monitoring *Online*
For: Self-quiz with vocabulary practice
Web Code: naa-0511

Terms, People, and Places

1. What do many of the key terms listed at the beginning of the section have in common? Explain.

Note Taking

2. **Reading Skill: Identify Causes and Effects** Use your completed cause-and-effect chart to answer the Focus Question: What values formed the basis of Roman society and government?

Comprehension and Critical Thinking

3. **Summarize** Describe the cultural setting in which Rome developed.

4. **Identify Central Issues** In both Roman politics and Roman society, equality was prized. Describe an example of Romans achieving political or social equality.

5. **Recognize Cause and Effect** What were two reasons for Rome's success in expanding its power across Italy?

● Writing About History

Quick Write: Take Notes for Comparison
Take notes on the government of the Roman republic, including details about its structure and functions. Then make a list of other governments in history to which you could compare the Roman republic.

Golden bracelet of a wealthy Roman

Roman laborers hard at work crushing grapes

WITNESS HISTORY 🔊 AUDIO

A Plea for Reform

While the republic grew in size, everyone did not benefit from the new wealth. Addressing a group of plebeians, the Roman tribune Tiberius Gracchus described an injustice he saw in Roman society:

❝ The wild beasts that roam over Italy . . . have every one of them a cave or lair to lurk in; but the men who fight and die for Italy enjoy the common air and light, indeed, but nothing else; . . . they fight and die to support others in wealth and luxury, and though they are styled [referred to as] masters of the world, they have not a single clod of earth that is their own.❞
—*Plutarch's Lives*

Focus Question What factors led to the decline of the Roman republic and the rise of the Roman empire?

From Republic to Empire

Performance Standards

- **SSWH3a** Compare the Greek polis, the Roman Republic, and the Roman Empire.
- **SSWH3b** Identify the impact of Julius Caesar and Augustus Caesar.
- **SSWH3c** Analyze contributions of Hellenistic and Roman culture.

Terms, People, and Places

imperialism	Julius Caesar
latifundia	Augustus
Tiberius Gracchus	census
Gaius Gracchus	Hadrian

Note Taking

Reading Skill: Recognize Multiple Causes As you read, fill in a chart like the one below with factors that led to the decline of the Roman republic and the rise of the Roman empire.

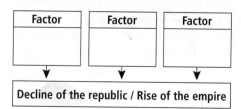

Factor	Factor	Factor

↓ ↓ ↓

Decline of the republic / Rise of the empire

After gaining control of the Italian peninsula, Rome began to build an empire around the Mediterranean Sea. This expansion created conflicts in Roman society that weakened and finally crushed the republic. Out of the rubble, however, rose the Roman empire and a new chapter in Rome's long history.

Rome Grows Through Conquest

Rome's conquest of the Italian peninsula brought it into contact with Carthage, a city-state on the northern coast of Africa. Settled by North Africans and Phoenician traders, Carthage ruled over an empire that stretched across North Africa and the western Mediterranean, including parts of Spain. As Rome expanded westward, conflict between these two powers became inevitable.

Rome Fights Carthage in the Punic Wars Between 264 B.C. and 146 B.C., Rome fought three wars against Carthage. They are called the Punic Wars, from *Punicus*, the Latin word for Phoenician. In the First Punic War, Rome defeated Carthage and won the islands of Sicily, Corsica, and Sardinia.

The Carthaginians sought revenge in the Second Punic War. In 218 B.C., the Carthaginian general Hannibal led his army, including dozens of war elephants, on an epic march across the Pyrenees, through France, and over the Alps into Italy. The trek cost Hannibal one third of his army. But with it he surprised the Romans, who had expected an invasion from the south. For 15 years, Hannibal and his army moved across Italy, winning battle after battle.

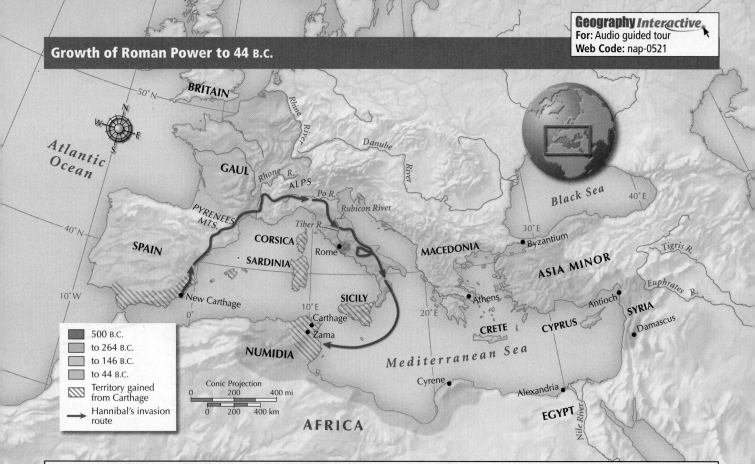

Atlantic Ocean

BRITAIN

50°N

GAUL

Rhine River

Danube

ALPS

Rhone R.

Po R.

Rubicon River

PYRENEES MTS.

Tiber R.

40°N

SPAIN

CORSICA

Rome

SARDINIA

40°E

Black Sea

30°E

Byzantium

MACEDONIA

ASIA MINOR

Tigris R.

Euphrates R.

10°W

New Carthage

0°

10°E

SICILY

Carthage

Zama

Athens

20°E

CRETE

CYPRUS

Antioch

SYRIA

Damascus

NUMIDIA

Mediterranean Sea

Cyrene

Alexandria

Nile River

EGYPT

AFRICA

■	500 B.C.
■	to 264 B.C.
■	to 146 B.C.
■	to 44 B.C.
▨	Territory gained from Carthage
→	Hannibal's invasion route

Conic Projection
0   200   400 mi
0   200   400 km

Map Skills Although Hannibal (below) posed a challenge, the Roman republic gradually gained control of lands around the Mediterranean Sea through conquest and diplomacy.

1. **Locate** (a) Spain (b) Gaul (c) Asia Minor (d) Macedonia (e) Pyrenees Mountains
2. **Region** During what period did Asia Minor come under Roman control?
3. **Synthesize Information** What does this map tell you about the outcome of the Punic Wars with Carthage, which lasted from 264 B.C. to 146 B.C.?

The Carthaginians failed to capture Rome itself, however. In the end, the Romans outflanked Hannibal by sending an army to attack Carthage. Hannibal returned to defend his homeland, where the Romans defeated him at last. Carthage gave up all its lands outside of Africa. Nevertheless, many Romans still saw Carthage as a rival and wanted revenge for the terrible destruction that Hannibal's army had brought to Italy. For years, the senator Cato ended every speech he made with the words "Carthage must be destroyed."

Finally, in the Third Punic War, Rome completely destroyed Carthage. Survivors were killed or sold into slavery. The Romans poured salt over the earth so that nothing would grow there again. The Romans were now masters of the western Mediterranean.

Ruling the Mediterranean "The Carthaginians fought for their own preservation and the sovereignty of Africa," observed a Greek witness to the fall of Carthage; "the Romans, for supremacy and world domination." The Romans were committed to a policy of **imperialism,** or establishing control over foreign lands and peoples. While Rome fought Carthage in the west, it was also expanding into the eastern Mediterranean. There, Romans confronted the Hellenistic rulers who had divided up the empire of Alexander the Great.

Sometimes to defend Roman interests, sometimes simply for plunder, Rome launched a series of wars in the area. One by one, Macedonia, Greece, and parts of Asia Minor surrendered and became Roman provinces. Other regions, such as Egypt, allied with Rome. By 133 B.C., Roman power extended from Spain to Egypt. Truly, the Romans were justified in calling the Mediterranean *Mare Nostrum*, or "Our Sea."

The Impact at Home Conquests and control of busy trade routes brought incredible riches into Rome. Generals, officials, and traders amassed fortunes from loot, taxes, and commerce. A new class of wealthy Romans emerged. They built lavish mansions and filled them with luxuries imported from the east. Wealthy families bought up huge farming estates, called **latifundia.** As Romans conquered more and more lands, they forced people captured in war to work as slaves on the latifundia. By the last days of the republic, around a third of Italy's people lived in slavery.

The widespread use of slave labor hurt small farmers, who were unable to produce food as cheaply as the latifundia could. The farmers' problems grew when huge quantities of grain pouring in from the conquered lands drove down grain prices. Many farmers fell into debt and had to sell their land.

In despair, landless farmers flocked to Rome and other cities looking for jobs. There, they joined an already restless class of unemployed people. As the gap between rich and poor widened, angry mobs began to riot. In addition, the new wealth led to increased corruption. Greed and self-interest replaced the virtues of the early republic, such as simplicity, hard work, and devotion to duty.

Making Attempts at Reforms Two young plebeians, brothers named **Tiberius** and **Gaius Gracchus** (GAY us GRAK us), were among the first to attempt reform. Tiberius, elected a tribune in 133 B.C., called on the state to distribute land to poor farmers. Gaius, elected a tribune ten years later, sought a wider range of reforms, including the use of public funds to buy grain to feed the poor. The reforms of the Gracchus brothers angered the senate, which saw them as a threat to its power. The brothers and thousands of their followers were killed in waves of street violence set off by senators and their hired thugs.

✓ **Checkpoint** What challenges did Rome face while building an empire around the Mediterranean Sea?

Slavery in Ancient Rome
Rome relied heavily on the labor of slaves, especially for public works projects and agriculture. Many people, like the two here wearing chains (above), were enslaved after being taken captive in combat. For identification, slaves often had to wear a collar (inset) with the master's name and address inscribed on it.

The Roman Republic Declines

Unable to resolve its problems peacefully, Rome plunged into a series of civil wars. At issue was who should hold power—the senate, which wanted to govern as it had in the past, or popular political leaders, who wanted to weaken the senate and enact reforms.

The turmoil sparked slave uprisings at home and revolts among Rome's allies. Meanwhile, the old legions of Roman citizen-soldiers became professional armies whose first loyalty was to their commanders. This often

happened because commanders provided them with more benefits—such as parcels of captured land—than the state did. Once rival commanders had their own armies, they could march into Rome to advance their ambitions.

Julius Caesar the Dictator Out of this chaos emerged **Julius Caesar,** an ambitious military commander. For a time, Caesar and another brilliant general, Pompey, dominated Roman politics.

In 58 B.C., Caesar set out with his army to make new conquests. After nine years of fighting, he completed the conquest of Gaul—the area that is now France and Belgium. Fearful of Caesar's rising fame, Pompey persuaded the senate to order Caesar to disband his army and return to Rome. Caesar defied the order. Swiftly and secretly, he led his army across the Rubicon River into northern Italy and headed toward Rome. Once again, civil war erupted across the Roman world.

Caesar crushed Pompey and his supporters. He then swept around the Mediterranean, suppressing rebellions. "Veni, vidi, vici"—"I came, I saw, I conquered"—he announced after one victory. Later, returning to Rome, he forced the senate to make him dictator. Although he maintained the senate and other features of the republic, he was in fact the absolute ruler of Rome.

Caesar Makes Reforms Between 48 B.C. and 44 B.C., Caesar pushed through a number of reforms intended to deal with Rome's many problems. He launched a program of public works to employ the jobless and gave public land to the poor. He also reorganized the government of the provinces and granted Roman citizenship to more people. Caesar's most lasting reform was the introduction of a new calendar based on that of the Egyptians. The Roman calendar, later named the Julian calendar, was used in western Europe for more than 1,600 years. With minor changes, it is still our calendar today.

Caesar Killed, War Follows Caesar's enemies worried that he planned to make himself king of Rome. To save the republic, they plotted against him. In March of 44 B.C., as Caesar arrived in the senate, his enemies stabbed him to death.

The death of Julius Caesar plunged Rome into a new round of civil wars. Mark Antony, Caesar's chief general, and Octavian, Caesar's grandnephew,

Vocabulary Builder

suppressing—(suh PRES ing) *vt.* using force to put an end to something joined forces to hunt down the murderers. The two men soon quarreled, however, setting off a bitter struggle for power. In 31 B.C., Octavian finally defeated Antony and his powerful ally, Queen Cleopatra of Egypt.

✓ **Checkpoint** What central issue sparked the warfare that eventually led to the decline of Rome?

The Age of the Roman Empire Dawns

The senate gave the triumphant Octavian the title of **Augustus,** or Exalted One, and declared him princeps, or first citizen. Although he was careful not to call himself king, a title that Romans had hated since Etruscan times, Augustus exercised absolute power and named his successor, just as a king would do.

Under Augustus, who ruled until A.D. 14, the 500-year-old republic came to an end. Romans did not know it at the time, but a new age had dawned—the age of the Roman empire.

Augustus Builds a Stable Government Through firm but moderate policies, Augustus laid the foundation for a stable government. He left the senate in place and created an efficient, well-trained civil service to enforce its laws. High-level jobs were open to men of talent, regardless of their class. In addition, he cemented the allegiance of cities and provinces to Rome by allowing them a large amount of self-government.

Augustus also undertook economic reforms. To make the tax system more fair, he ordered a **census,** or population count, of the empire so there would be records of all who should be taxed. He set up a postal service and issued new coins to make trade easier. He put the jobless to work building roads and temples and sent others to farm the land.

The government that Augustus organized functioned well for 200 years. Still, a serious problem kept arising: Who would rule after an emperor died? Romans did not accept the idea of power passing automatically from father to son. As a result, the death of an emperor often led to intrigue and violence.

Emperors Vary Not all Augustus' successors were great rulers. Some were weak and incompetent. Two early emperors, Caligula and Nero, were considered evil and perhaps insane. Caligula, for example, appointed his favorite horse as consul. Nero viciously persecuted Christians and was even blamed for setting a great fire that destroyed much of Rome.

Between A.D. 96 and A.D. 180, the empire benefited from the rule of a series of "good emperors." **Hadrian,** for example, codified Roman law, making it the same for all provinces. He also had soldiers build a wall across Britain to hold back attackers from the non-Roman north.

Marcus Aurelius, who read philosophy while leading wars, was close to being Plato's ideal of a philosopher-king. His *Meditations* show his commitment to duty: "Hour by hour resolve firmly . . . to do what comes to hand with correct and natural dignity."

Comparing Structures of Government	
Roman Republic	**Roman Empire**
Highest Official(s)	
Two consuls • annually elected • held equal power **Dictator** • appointed in times of emergency • held office for 6 months only	**Emperor** • inherited power • served for life • if served well, was worshipped as a god after death
Governing Bodies	
Senate • issued advisory decrees to magistrates and people • in practice, held enormous power • had about 300 members **Popular Assemblies** • two assemblies: centuriate (military), tribal (nonmilitary) • elected magistrates, held legislative power, made key decisions	**Senate** • issued binding decrees, acted as a high court, elected magistrates • in practice, held little power as compared to the emperor • had about 600 members

Chart Skills Given the differences in these two structures of government, why do you think the senate held less power in the empire than it did in the republic?

The Pax Romana Brings Prosperity The 200-year span that began with Augustus and ended with Marcus Aurelius is known as the period of the *Pax Romana*, or "Roman Peace." During that time, Roman rule brought peace, order, unity, and prosperity to lands stretching from the Euphrates River in the east to Britain in the west, an area roughly equal in size to the continental United States.

During the Pax Romana, Roman legions maintained and protected the roads, and Roman fleets chased pirates from the seas. Trade flowed freely to and from distant lands. Egyptian farmers supplied Romans with grain. From other parts of Africa came ivory and gold, as well as lions and other wild animals to be used for public entertainment. From India came spices, cotton, and precious stones. Trade caravans traveled along the great Silk Road, bringing silk and other goods from China. People, too, moved easily within the Roman empire, spreading ideas and knowledge, especially the advances of the Hellenistic east.

The Distraction of Entertainment Throughout the empire, rich and poor alike loved spectacular forms of entertainment. At the Circus Maximus, Rome's largest racecourse, chariots thundered around an oval course, making dangerously tight turns at either end. Fans bet feverishly on their favorite teams—the Reds, Greens, Blues, or Whites—and successful charioteers were hailed as heroes.

Gladiator contests were even more popular. Many gladiators were slaves who had been trained to fight. In the arena, they battled one another, either singly or in groups. Crowds cheered a skilled gladiator, and a good fighter might even win his freedom. But if a gladiator made a poor showing, sometimes the crowd turned thumbs down, a signal that he should be killed.

During the Pax Romana, the general prosperity hid underlying social and economic problems. To the emperors who paid for them with taxes they collected from the empire, these amusements were a way to pacify the city's restless mobs. In much the same spirit, the government provided free grain to feed the poor. Critics warned against this policy of "bread and circuses," but few listened.

This Roman mosaic shows charioteers ready to race at the Circus Maximus.

✔ **Checkpoint** How did Augustus lay the foundation for stable government in the Roman empire?

SECTION

2 Assessment

Progress Monitoring *Online*
For: Self-quiz with vocabulary practice
Web Code: naa-0521

Terms, People, and Places

1. For each term, person, or place listed at the beginning of the section, write a sentence explaining its significance.

Note Taking

2. **Reading Skill: Recognize Multiple Causes** Use your completed chart to answer the Focus Question: What factors led to the decline of the Roman republic and the rise of the Roman empire?

Comprehension and Critical Thinking

3. **Make Comparisons** Compare the positive and negative results of conquest for Rome. Which do you think had the most impact?

4. **Predict Consequences** Do you think the reforms Caesar enacted would have been enough to maintain the Roman republic, had he not been killed?

5. **Analyze Information** How do you think the founders of the Roman republic would have viewed the government of the Roman empire?

● **Writing About History**

Quick Write: Make a Venn Diagram Use what you have read in this section and the previous one to make a Venn diagram comparing the Roman republic and the Roman empire. Consider different aspects of their structures such as who held the most power and who could take part in government.

Cicero launches an attack in the Senate.

WITNESS HISTORY 🔊 AUDIO

Safety Under the Law

Marcus Tullius Cicero was a philosopher, politician, and passionate defender of law. As the republic declined, he often attacked ambitious men such as Julius Caesar. When Caesar came to power by force, one might have expected Cicero to be in danger. But Caesar forgave Cicero, noting that it was "more glorious to have enlarged the limits of the Roman mind than the boundaries of Roman rule."

Focus Question How did advances in arts, learning, and the law show the Romans' high regard for cultural and political achievements?

The Roman Achievement

 Performance Standards

- **SSWH3c** Analyze contributions of Hellenistic and Roman culture, its contributions to law, and its scientific contributions.

Terms, People, and Places

Virgil	engineering
satirize	aqueduct
mosaic	Ptolemy

Note Taking

Reading Skill: Understand Effects The Romans prized cultural and political achievement. As you read, use a concept web like the one below to list developments that show the effects of achievements like these.

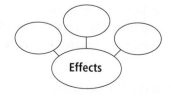

Effects

Through war and conquest, Roman generals carried the achievements of Roman civilization to distant lands. Yet the civilization that developed was not simply Roman. Rather, it blended Greek, Hellenistic, and Roman achievements.

Romans Write Literature, History, and Philosophy

In its early days, Rome absorbed ideas from Greek colonists in southern Italy, and it continued to borrow heavily from Greek culture after it conquered Greece. To the Romans, Greek art, literature, philosophy, and scientific genius represented the height of cultural achievement. Their admiration never wavered, leading the Roman poet Horace to note, "Greece has conquered her rude conqueror."

The Romans adapted Greek and Hellenistic achievements, just as the Greeks had once absorbed ideas from Egypt and the Fertile Crescent. The blending of Greek, Hellenistic, and Roman traditions produced what is known as Greco-Roman civilization. Trade and travel during the Pax Romana helped spread this vital new civilization.

Poets Write With Respect and Humor In the field of literature, the Romans owed a great debt to the Greeks. Many Romans spoke Greek and imitated Greek styles in prose and poetry. Still, the greatest Roman writers used Latin to create their own literature.

In his epic poem the *Aeneid,* **Virgil** tried to show that Rome's past was as heroic as that of Greece. He linked his epic to Homer's work by telling how Aeneas escaped from Troy to found Rome. Virgil wrote the *Aeneid* soon after Augustus came to power. He hoped it would arouse patriotism and help unite Rome after years of civil wars.

Other poets used verse to **satirize,** or make fun of, Roman society. Horace's satires were gentle, using playful wit to attack human folly. Those of Juvenal and Martial were more biting. Martial's poems, for example, were so harsh that he had to use fictitious names to protect himself from retribution.

Historians Tell the Story of Rome Roman historians pursued their own theme—the rise and fall of Roman power. Like the poet Virgil, the historian Livy sought to arouse patriotic feeling and restore traditional Roman virtues by recalling images of Rome's heroic past. In his history of Rome, Livy recounted tales of great heroes such as Horatius and Cincinnatus.

Another historian, Tacitus, wrote bitterly about Augustus and his successors, who, he felt, had destroyed Roman liberty. He admired the simple culture of the Germans who lived on Rome's northern frontier and would later invade the empire.

Romans Adapt Greek Philosophy Romans borrowed much of their philosophy from the Greeks. The Hellenistic philosophy of Stoicism impressed Roman thinkers such as the emperor Marcus Aurelius. Stoics stressed the importance of duty and acceptance of one's fate. They also showed concern for the well-being of all people, an idea that would be reflected in the Christian teachings you will read about in Section 4.

✓ **Checkpoint**   How did Roman writers promote patriotism?

Roman Art and Architecture Develops

To a large degree, Roman art and architecture were based on Greek and Etruscan models. However, as with literature, the Romans made adaptations to develop their own style.

Creating Expressive Art Like the Greeks before them, Roman sculptors stressed realism, portraying their subjects with every wart and vein in place. The Romans also broke new ground by focusing on revealing an individual's character. A statue of a soldier, a writer, or an emperor might capture an expression of smugness, discontent, or haughty pride.

Some Roman sculpture, however, was idealistic. For example, sculptors transformed Augustus, who was neither handsome nor imposing, into a symbol of power and leadership.

Romans used works of art to beautify their homes. Examples of these works were preserved in Pompeii, a city buried by the volcanic eruption of Mount Vesuvius in A.D. 79. Artists depicted scenes from Roman literature and daily life in splendid frescoes and mosaics. A **mosaic** is a picture made from chips of colored stone or glass.

Advancing Architecture While the Greeks aimed for simple elegance in architecture, the Romans emphasized grandeur. Immense palaces, temples, and stadiums stood as mighty monuments to Roman power and dignity.

The Romans also improved on existing structural devices such as columns and arches. Utilizing concrete as a building material, they developed the rounded dome as a roof for large spaces. The most famous domed structure is the Pantheon, a temple that honors the many Roman gods. It still stands in Rome today.

✓ **Checkpoint**   How did Roman architecture differ from Greek architecture?

In this passage, Livy (shown below) comments on the importance of studying history. In what ways does he say we can learn from history?

Primary Source

❝ . . . in history you have a record of the infinite variety of human experience plainly set out for all to see; and in that record you can find for yourself and your country both examples and warnings: fine things to take as models, base things, rotten through and through, to avoid.❞
—Livy, *The History of Rome*

Vocabulary Builder
utilizing—(YOOT ul lyz ing) *vt.* making use of something

REMNANTS OF ROMAN DAILY LIFE

When trying to learn about everyday people in ancient times, scholars often face two challenges. First, time has worn away at the remnants of the past, leaving investigators much less to study than once existed. Second, usually those most able to commission texts or art were the political and social elite; often little remains to shed light on the lives of other classes. In ancient Rome, however, a traumatic event—the eruption of Mount Vesuvius in A.D. 79—perfectly preserved many artifacts. In the ash and mud that buried cities such as Herculaneum and Pompeii, archaeologists have found records of all aspects of Roman daily life.

Many Romans played music at home. This fresco shows a woman playing the cithara, or lyre. ▼

◀ Theater was popular in ancient Rome. In this mosaic, actors begin to don costumes and masks before a play.

As Mount Vesuvius erupted, some 18 feet of volcanic debris fell on Pompeii. Many people died trying to escape. In the mid-1800s, archaeologist Guiseppe Fiorelli poured plaster into cavities in the ash that were left behind once bodies decayed. Like this one, the plaster casts he created show vividly the desperate struggle to flee the eruption. ▼

Thinking Critically

1. **Synthesize Information** What are some aspects of Roman daily life that these artifacts reveal to us?

2. **Determine Relevance** Why do you think Fiorelli thought it important to create plaster casts of the victims?

▼ Pompeiiís remains tell us about a variety of Roman professions. The oven and grain mills of a bakery still stand in Pompeii (below), and a petrified loaf of bread (left) was found nearby.

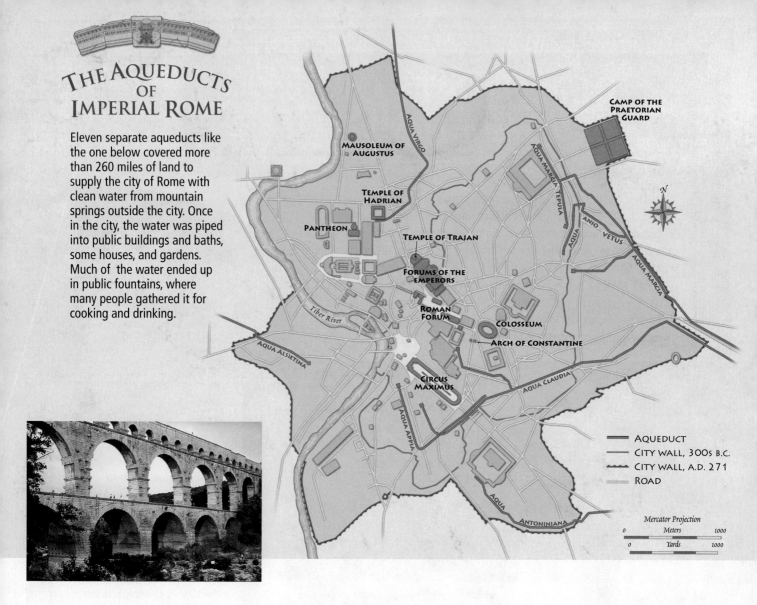

THE AQUEDUCTS OF IMPERIAL ROME

Eleven separate aqueducts like the one below covered more than 260 miles of land to supply the city of Rome with clean water from mountain springs outside the city. Once in the city, the water was piped into public buildings and baths, some houses, and gardens. Much of the water ended up in public fountains, where many people gathered it for cooking and drinking.

CAMP OF THE PRAETORIAN GUARD

MAUSOLEUM OF AUGUSTUS

TEMPLE OF HADRIAN

PANTHEON

TEMPLE OF TRAJAN

FORUMS OF THE EMPERORS

ROMAN FORUM

COLOSSEUM

ARCH OF CONSTANTINE

CIRCUS MAXIMUS

Tiber River

AQUA VIRGO

AQUA MARCIA TEPULA

AQUA ANIO VETUS

AQUA MARCIA

AQUA ALSIETINA

AQUA APPIA

AQUA CLAUDIA

AQUA ANTONINIANA

AQUA

▬▬	AQUEDUCT
——	CITY WALL, 300s B.C.
·····	CITY WALL, A.D. 271
═══	ROAD

Mercator Projection

Meters 0 — 1000
Yards 0 — 1000

Romans Apply Science and Mathematics for Practical Use

The Romans excelled in **engineering**, which is the application of science and mathematics to develop useful structures and machines. Roman engineers built roads, bridges, and harbors throughout the empire. Roman roads were so solidly built that many of them were still used long after the fall of the empire. Roman engineers also built many immense **aqueducts,** or bridgelike stone structures that carried water from the hills into Roman cities. The wealthy had water piped in, and almost every city boasted public baths. Here, people gathered not only to wash themselves but also to hear the latest news and exchange gossip.

The Romans generally left scientific research to the Greeks, who were by that time citizens of the empire. In Alexandria, Egypt, Hellenistic scientists exchanged ideas freely. It was there that astronomer-mathematician **Ptolemy** (TAHL uh mee) proposed his theory that the Earth was the center of the universe, a mistaken idea that was accepted in the Western world for nearly 1,500 years.

The Greek doctor Galen advanced the frontiers of medical science by insisting on experiments to prove a conclusion. Galen compiled a medical encyclopedia summarizing what was known in the field at the time. It remained a standard text for more than 1,000 years.

Although the Romans did little original research, they did put science to practical use. They applied geography to make maps and medical knowledge to help doctors improve public health. Like Galen, they collected knowledge into encyclopedias. Pliny the Elder, a Roman scientist, compiled volumes on geography, zoology, botany, and other topics, all based on other people's works.

✔ **Checkpoint** Who in the Roman empire engaged in scientific research? Who put science to practical use?

New Law Codes Protect the Empire

"Let justice be done," proclaimed a Roman saying, "though the heavens fall!" Probably the greatest legacy of Rome was its commitment to the rule of law and to justice. During the Roman empire, the rule of law fostered unity and stability. Many centuries later, the principles of Roman law would become the basis for legal systems throughout the world, including that of the United States.

Two Codes Become One During the republic, Rome developed a system of law, known as the civil law, that applied to its citizens. As Rome expanded, however, it ruled many foreigners who were not covered under the civil law. Gradually, a second system of law, known as the law of nations, emerged. It applied to all people under Roman rule, both citizens and non-citizens. Later, when Rome extended citizenship across the empire, the two systems merged.

Leaving a Legal Legacy As Roman law developed, certain basic principles evolved. Many of these principles are familiar to Americans today. An accused person was presumed innocent until proven guilty. The accused was allowed to face the accuser and offer a defense against the charge. Guilt had to be established "clearer than daylight," using solid evidence. Judges were allowed to interpret the laws and were expected to make fair decisions. Penalties, however, varied according to social class, and lower-class defendants could be treated more harshly.

✔ **Checkpoint** What were the basic principles of Roman law?

SECTION **3** Assessment

Progress Monitoring *Online*
For: Self-quiz with vocabulary practice
Web Code: naa-0531

Terms, People, and Places

1. For each term, person, or place listed at the beginning of the section, write a sentence explaining its significance.

Note Taking

2. **Reading Skill: Understand Effects** Use your completed concept web to answer the Focus Question: How did advances in arts, learning, and the law show the Romans' high regard for cultural and political achievements?

Comprehension and Critical Thinking

3. **Make Generalizations** How did Greek culture influence the development of Roman civilization?

4. **Synthesize Information** How did Romans use science and mathematics to improve life in the empire?

5. **Determine Relevance** Give two examples of how Roman principles of law affect life in the United States today.

● **Writing About History**

Quick Write: Write an Introduction Prepare for a compare-and-contrast essay about Roman writers and artists by writing an introductory paragraph. Include brief mention of the different types of writing and arts the Romans practiced as well as the overall focus of each type.

Renaissance painter Raphael depicted the cross appearing above Constantine (right); the fish and the cross (far right) were early Christian symbols.

WITNESS HISTORY ◀)) AUDIO

Roman Emperor Accepts Christianity

The Roman empire was tolerant of different religions, but it was almost 300 years before a Roman emperor fully supported the new religion of Christianity. Legend has it that the emperor Constantine—just before battle—saw a cross in the sky along with the words "By this you shall conquer." He had his troops mark their shields with a Christian symbol. After winning the battle, he fully embraced Christianity.

Focus Question How did Christianity emerge and then spread to become the official religion of the Roman empire?

The Rise of Christianity

 Performance Standards

• **SSWH3d** Describe the start and spread of Christianity in the Roman world.

Early in the Pax Romana, a new religion, Christianity, arose in a distant corner of the Roman empire. At first, Christianity was one of many religions practiced in the empire. But the new faith grew rapidly, and throughout the A.D. 380s and 390s it was gradually made the official religion of the Roman empire. As it gained strength and spread through the empire, Christianity reshaped Roman beliefs. When the Roman empire fell, the Christian Church took over much of its role, becoming the central institution of Western civilization for nearly 1,000 years.

Early Empire Includes Diverse Religions

Within the culturally diverse Roman empire, various religious beliefs coexisted. Jupiter, Mars, Juno, and other traditional Roman gods remained important. However, a growing number of people looked elsewhere for spiritual fulfillment.

Terms, People, and Places

messiah	bishop
apostle	patriarch
Paul	pope
martyr	heresy
Constantine	Augustine
clergy	

Note Taking

Reading Skill: Understand Effects As you read, fill in a chart like the one below with factors that allowed the rise of Christianity and its establishment as the official religion of the Roman empire.

Causes	Effects
•	• Rise of Christianity
•	• Establishment of Christianity as empireís official religion
•	

Rome Tolerates Diversity Some people turned to the so-called mystery religions, which emphasized secret rituals and promised special rewards. One of the most popular of these was the cult of Isis, which started in Egypt and offered women equal status with men. Roman soldiers favored the cult of the Persian god Mithras, who championed good over evil and offered life after death.

Generally, Rome tolerated the varied religious traditions of its subjects. As long as citizens showed loyalty by honoring Roman gods and acknowledging the divine spirit of the emperor, the government allowed them to worship other gods as they pleased. Because most people were polytheistic, they were content to worship the Roman gods along with their own.

Divisions Arise in Judea By 63 B.C., the Romans had conquered Judea, where most Jews of the time lived. To avoid violating the Jewish belief in one God, the Romans excused Jews from worshiping Roman gods. Among the Jewish people themselves, however, religious ferment was creating deep divisions. During the Hellenistic age, many Jews absorbed Greek customs and ideas. Concerned about the weakening of their religion, Jewish conservatives rejected these influences and called for strict obedience to Jewish laws and traditions.

While most Jews were reluctantly willing to live under Roman rule, others, called Zealots, were not. They called on Jews to revolt against Rome and reestablish an independent state. Some Jews believed that a **messiah,** or anointed king sent by God, would soon appear to lead their people to freedom.

A Jewish Rebellion Is Defeated In A.D. 66, discontent flared into rebellion. Four years later, Roman forces crushed the rebels, captured Jerusalem, and destroyed the Jewish temple. When revolts broke out again in the next century, Roman armies leveled Jerusalem. Thousands of Jews were killed in the fighting, and many others were enslaved and transported to various parts of the empire. Faced with the destruction that resulted from the rebellions, growing numbers of Jews decided to leave Judea.

Although the Jewish people were defeated in their efforts to regain political independence, they survived in scattered communities around the Mediterranean. Over the centuries, Jewish religious teachers called rabbis extended and preserved the Jewish law, and Judaism survived.

The Limits of Toleration
The Romans' destruction of Jerusalem's temple in A.D. 70 (above left) was a massive assault against revolt. Three years later, rebellion against Rome ended with the siege of Masada (above right), a mountaintop fortress at which nearly 1,000 Jews may have taken their own lives to avoid being killed by Romans. *Why would a government only believe in toleration to a certain point?*

✓ **Checkpoint** What was Rome's policy toward most of the religions in the empire?

Jesus Proclaims His Teachings

As turmoil engulfed the Jews in Judea, a new religion, Christianity, arose among them. It began among the followers of a Jew named Jesus. Almost all the information we have about the life of Jesus comes from the Gospels, the first four books of the New Testament of the Christian Bible. Early Christians attributed the writing of these accounts to four followers of Jesus—Matthew, Mark, Luke, and John.

Primary Source

f Blessed are the meek, for they shall inherit the earth.
Blessed are those who hunger and thirst for righteousness, for they shall be satisfied.
Blessed are the merciful, for they shall obtain mercy.
Blessed are the pure in heart, for they shall see God.
Blessed are the peacemakers, for they will be called sons of God. ™

—Matthew 5:5–9

Jesus Begins Preaching Jesus was born about 4 B.C. in Bethlehem, near Jerusalem. According to the Gospels, he was a descendant of King David of Israel. The Gospels say an angel told Jesus' mother, Mary, that she would give birth to the messiah. "He will be great," said the angel, "and will be called the Son of the Most High God."

Growing up in the small town of Nazareth, Jesus worshiped God and followed Jewish law. As a young man, he may have worked as a carpenter. At the age of 30, the Gospels relate, he began preaching to villagers near the Sea of Galilee. Large crowds gathered to hear his teachings, especially when word spread that he had performed miracles of healing. Jesus often used parables, or short stories with simple moral lessons, to communicate his ideas. He recruited 12 of his disciples, or close followers, to help him in his mission. He called these 12 the **apostles,** a name that in Greek means "a person sent forth." After three years, Jesus and his disciples went to Jerusalem to spread his message there.

Jesus Teaches New Beliefs Jesus' teachings were firmly rooted in Jewish tradition. Jesus believed in one God and accepted the Ten Commandments. He preached obedience to the laws of Moses and defended the teachings of the Jewish prophets. However, Jesus also preached new beliefs. According to his followers, he called himself the Son of God. Many people believed he was the long-anticipated messiah. Jesus proclaimed that his mission was to bring spiritual salvation and eternal life to anyone who believed in him.

Echoing the teachings of Judaism, Jesus emphasized God's love and taught the need for justice, morality, and service to others. According to Jesus, a person's major duties were to observe the Jewish command to "love the Lord your God with all your heart" and to "love your neighbor as yourself." Jesus also emphasized the importance of forgiveness.

Condemned to Death According to the Gospels, Jesus traveled to Jerusalem near the time of the Jewish festival of Passover, a celebration of the exodus from Egypt. To the Roman authorities, Jesus was a threat because his speeches could inflame those eager to end Roman rule.

The Gospels state that Jesus was betrayed by one of his disciples. He was then arrested by the Romans, tried, and condemned to death by crucifixion. In this method of execution, which the Romans often used, a person was nailed or bound to a cross and left to die. Jesus' crucifixion threw his disciples into confusion. But then rumors spread through Jerusalem that Jesus was not dead at all. The Gospels report that his disciples saw and talked with Jesus, who had risen from death. The Gospels go on to say that Jesus, after commanding his disciples to spread his teachings to all people, ascended into heaven.

✔ **Checkpoint** What are the main ideas of Jesus' message?

The Message of Christianity Spreads

After Jesus' death, the apostles and other disciples did spread his message. At first, they preached only among the Jews of Judea. Some Jews accepted the teaching that Jesus was the messiah, or the Christ, from the Greek word for "anointed one." Soon, they were called Christians.

Spread of Christianity to A.D. 476

BRITAIN

GERMANY

20°E

Atlantic Ocean

GAUL

EUROPE

Milan

50°N

40°N

10°W

SPAIN

ITALY

Rome

SARDINIA

SICILY

0°

Carthage

GREECE

Thessalonica

Philippi

Athens

Corinth

Ephesus

Colossae

CRETE

Black Sea

Constantinople

ASIA MINOR

GALATIA

Antioch

SYRIA

Mediterranean Sea

Jerusalem

Alexandria

EGYPT

Red Sea

AFRICA

Christian areas, A.D. 325
Christian areas added by A.D. 476
Boundary of Roman empire, A.D. 476
Paul's first journey
Paul's second journey
Paul's third journey
Paul's journey to Rome

Conic Projection
0   200   400 mi
0   200   400 km

Gradually, these disciples went to preach in Jewish communities throughout the Roman world. According to tradition, the apostle Peter established Christianity in the city of Rome itself. But **Paul,** a Jew from Asia Minor, played the most influential role in spreading Christianity.

Paul Spreads Christianity Paul had never met Jesus. In fact, he had been among those who persecuted Jesus' followers. But one day Paul had a vision of Jesus speaking to him. He immediately joined the Christians and decided to spread Jesus' teachings to gentiles, or non-Jews.

Until this time, Christianity had remained a sect within Judaism. The work of missionaries like Paul set Christianity on the road to becoming a world religion. A tireless traveler, Paul journeyed around the Mediterranean and set up churches in Asia Minor and Greece. In letters to the Christian communities, he explained difficult doctrines, judged disputes, and expanded Christian teachings, emphasizing that Jesus had sacrificed his life out of love for humankind. Paul asserted that those who believed Jesus was the son of God and <u>complied</u> with his teachings would achieve salvation, or eternal life. His letters became part of the New Testament.

Christians Are Oppressed Rome's tolerant attitude toward religion was not extended to Christianity. Roman officials found the Christians disloyal to Rome because they refused to honor the emperor with sacrifices or ask the traditional gods to protect the Roman state. When Christians met in secret to avoid persecution, rumors spread that they were engaged in evil practices.

Map Skills Aided by the work of Paul and other missionaries, Christianity gradually spread across the Roman empire.
1. **Locate** (a) Jerusalem (b) Ephesus (c) Antioch (d) Constantinople (e) Alexandria
2. **Movement** In what areas did Paul travel on his first journey?
3. **Analyze Information** How did the extent of Christianity in A.D. 325 compare to that in A.D. 476? Was there a significant difference?

Vocabulary Builder

complied—(kum PLYD) *vi.* obeyed or conformed to something

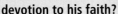

In times of trouble, persecution increased. Some Roman rulers, such as Nero, used Christians as scapegoats, blaming them for social or economic ills. Christians who were killed in times of persecution became known as **martyrs,** or people who suffer or die for their beliefs. According to tradition, both Peter and Paul were martyred in Rome during the reign of Nero.

The Message Appeals to Many Despite the attacks, Christianity continued to spread throughout the Roman world. Jesus had welcomed all people, especially the lowly, the poor, and the oppressed. These people found comfort in his message of love, as well as in his teachings of equality, dignity, and the promise of a better life beyond the grave.

As they did their work, Christian missionaries like Paul used ideas from Plato, the Stoics, and other Greek thinkers to explain Jesus' message. A religion that incorporated the discipline and moderation of Greek philosophy appealed in particular to educated Romans. The unity of the Roman empire also eased the work of missionaries. Christians traveled along Roman roads and across the Mediterranean Sea, which was protected by Roman fleets. Early Christian documents were usually written in Greek or Latin, languages that many people across the empire understood.

Even persecution brought new converts. Observing the willingness of Christians to die for their religion, people were impressed by the strength of Christians' belief. "The blood of the martyrs is the seed of the [Christian] Church," noted one Roman.

Rome Embraces Christianity The persecution of Christians finally ended in A.D. 313, when the emperor **Constantine** issued the Edict of Milan. It granted freedom of worship to all citizens of the Roman empire. By the end of the century, the emperor Theodosius (thee uh DOH shus) had made Christianity the official religion of the Roman empire and repressed the practice of other faiths. The church grew in power and developed its own bureaucracy alongside that of the empire.

✔ **Checkpoint** What factors enabled Christianity to spread throughout the Roman empire?

The Early Christian Church Develops

Early Christian communities shared a common faith in the teachings of Jesus and a common way of worship. Only gradually, however, did these scattered communities come together as a structured Church.

Joining the Church To join the Christian community, a person had to be baptized, or blessed with holy water. Christians believed that through the rite of baptism their sins were forgiven by the grace of God. Members of the community were considered equals, and they addressed each other as "brother" or "sister." Each Sunday, Christians gathered for a ceremony of thanksgiving to God. The baptized ate bread and drank wine in a sacred rite called the Eucharist. They did this in memory of Jesus, whose last supper was described in the Gospels.

Many women welcomed Christianity's promise that in the Church "there is neither Jew nor Greek . . . neither slave nor free . . . neither male nor female." In early Christian communities, women served as teachers and administrators. Later, women were barred from any official role in the Church. Like men, however, they continued to work as missionaries sent out by the Church to convert people to Christianity both within the Roman empire and beyond.

Structuring the Clergy Only men were eligible to become members of the Christian **clergy,** or the group of people who conduct Christian services. Each Christian community and its clergy were grouped together as a diocese. Every diocese had its own priest. Over the priest presided a **bishop,** a high Church official responsible for everyone in his diocese. Bishops traced their spiritual authority to the apostles, and through the apostles, to Jesus himself. In the early Christian Church, all bishops were considered equal successors of the apostles.

Gradually, the bishops of the most important cities in the Roman empire—Rome, Antioch, Alexandria, Jerusalem, and Constantinople—gained greater authority. These bishops took on the honorary title of **patriarch** and exercised authority over other bishops in their area. The Christian Church thus developed into a hierarchy, or organization in which officials are arranged according to rank.

Differences Arise Within the Church As the rituals and structure of the Church became more defined, rivalry among the patriarchs developed. In the Latin-speaking west, bishops of Rome, who came to be called **popes,** began to claim authority over all other bishops. In the Greek-speaking east, where the other four patriarchs lived, the patriarchs felt that the five should share spiritual authority as equals.

The emergence of **heresies,** or beliefs said to be contrary to official Church teachings, also caused division. To end disputes over questions of faith, councils of Church leaders met to decide official Christian teachings.

Scholars Further Define Christianity Early Christians produced an abundance of works defining Christian theology. The word *theology* is Greek and means "talk or discourse about God." Two leading scholars of the early Church were Clement and Origen. Both worked as teachers in Egypt, in Alexandria, a major center of learning in the Roman world. Perhaps the greatest of the early Church scholars was **Augustine,** bishop of Hippo in North Africa. He combined Christian doctrine with Greco-Roman learning, especially the philosophy of Plato.

✔ **Checkpoint** How was the early Christian clergy organized?

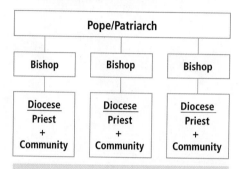

The Christian Clergy

Chart Skills Over time the structure of the Christian church developed into a hierarchy. *What are some positive and negative elements that may arise from this type of organizational structure?*

SECTION 4 **Assessment**

Progress Monitoring *Online*
For: Self-quiz with vocabulary practice
Web Code: naa-0541

Terms, People, and Places

1. What do each of the key people listed at the beginning of the section have in common? Explain.

Note Taking

2. **Reading Skill: Understand Effects** Use your completed chart to answer the Focus Question: How did Christianity emerge and then spread to become the official religion of the Roman empire?

Comprehension and Critical Thinking

3. **Identify Central Issues** Why were many Jews unhappy under Roman rule even though the Romans were tolerant of their religion?

4. **Synthesize Information** What were three basic teachings of Jesus?

5. **Summarize** What practices and organizational structures helped establish the early Christian Church?

● **Writing About History**

Quick Write: Make an Outline To prepare for an essay comparing the experiences of Jews and of Christians in the Roman empire, make an outline identifying key points of comparison. Include details under each key point.

GA SSWH3d,
SSWHRC1b

First Letter to the Corinthians

Around A.D. 51, Paul founded a Christian community in the thriving commercial city of Corinth. After his departure, he wrote two letters to the newly converted Christians to encourage and guide them in their faith. In this excerpt from Paul's First Letter to the Corinthians, Paul declares that, for a Christian, love is more important than any other quality.

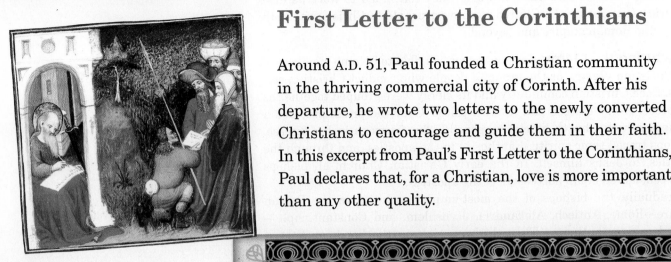

Paul writing one of his epistles, or letters

If I speak in the tongues of men and of angels, but have not love, I am a noisy gong or a clanging cymbal. And if I have prophetic[1] powers and understand all mysteries and all knowledge, and if I have all faith, so as to remove mountains, but have no love, I am nothing. If I give away all I have, and if I deliver my body to be burned, but have not love, I gain nothing.

Love is patient and kind; love is not jealous or boastful; it is not arrogant or rude. Love does not insist on its own way; it is not irritable or resentful; it does not rejoice at wrong, but rejoices in the right. Love bears all things, believes all things, hopes all things, endures all things.

Love never ends; as for prophecies, they will pass away; as for tongues, they will cease; as for knowledge, it will pass away. For our knowledge is imperfect and our prophecy is imperfect; but when the perfect comes, the imperfect will pass away. When I was a child, I spoke like a child, I thought like a child, I reasoned like a child; when I became a man, I gave up childish ways. For now we see in a mirror dimly, but then face to face. Now I know in part; then I shall understand fully, even as I have been fully understood. So faith, hope, love abide, these three; but the greatest of these is love.

Thinking Critically

1. **Analyze Literature** Paul uses repetition of words and phrases throughout this letter. What purpose does this serve?
2. **Draw Conclusions** What does Paul mean when he says that love "endures all things"?

1. **prophetic** (pruh FET ik) *adj.* able to predict events

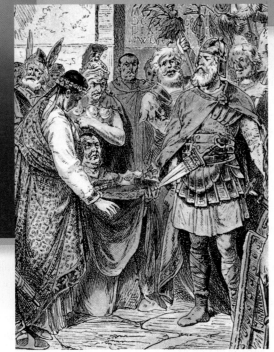

The western Roman empire came to an end in 476, when the emperor gave up his crown.

A plaque from an invader's shield

WITNESS HISTORY ◀)) AUDIO

The Exhausted Empire

After 300 years of empire, Rome was weakening due to various causes. The oppressive government and corrupt upper class generated hostility among those who suffered in the weak economy. When invaders came from the north and east, the empire's days were numbered. The Roman writer Salvian noted the mood of the Roman people:

❝ In the districts taken over by the barbarians, there is one desire among all the Romans, that they should never again find it necessary to pass under Roman jurisdiction [authority].❞
—Salvian, *On the Governance of God*

Focus Question How did military, political, social, and economic factors combine to cause the fall of the western Roman empire?

The Long Decline

GA Performance Standards

- **SSWH3e** Analyze factors leading to the collapse of Western Roman Empire.

Terms, People, and Places

Diocletian
inflation
Constantinople
Huns
mercenary

Note Taking

Reading Skill: Recognize Multiple Causes As you read, complete a chart like the one below by filling in the causes of the fall of the western Roman empire.

Causes of the Fall of the Western Roman Empire			
Military:	Social:	Political:	Economic:
•	•	•	•
•	•	•	•

After ruling the Mediterranean for hundreds of years, the Roman empire faced threats from inside and outside. Economic problems, foreign invasions, and a decline in traditional values were undermining stability and security.

The Roman Empire Divides

After the death of the emperor Marcus Aurelius in 180, the golden age of the Pax Romana ended. For the next 100 years, political and economic turmoil rocked the Roman empire.

Political Violence Becomes Common During this period, a disruptive political pattern emerged. Again and again, emperors were overthrown by political intriguers or ambitious generals who seized power with the support of their troops. Those who rose to the imperial throne in this way ruled for just a few months or years until they, too, were overthrown or assassinated. In one 50-year period, at least 26 emperors reigned. Only one died of natural causes. Political violence and instability had become the rule.

Social and Economic Problems Arise At the same time, the empire was shaken by disturbing social and economic trends. High taxes to support the army and the bureaucracy placed heavy burdens on business people and small farmers. Farmland that had been over-cultivated for too long lost its productivity.

Many poor farmers left their land and sought protection from wealthy landowners. Living on large estates, they worked for the landowners and farmed small plots for themselves. Although technically free, they were not allowed to leave the land.

Emperor Diocletian Shares Power In 284, the emperor **Diocletian** (dy uh KLEE shun) set out to restore order. To better handle the challenge of governing the huge empire, he divided it into two parts. He kept control of the wealthier eastern part for himself and appointed a co-emperor, Maximian, to rule the western provinces.

Diocletian also took steps to end the empire's economic decay. To slow **inflation,** or the rapid rise of prices, he fixed the prices of many goods and services. Other laws forced farmers to remain on the land. In cities, sons were required to follow their fathers' occupations. These rules were meant to ensure steady production of food and other goods.

Emperor Constantine Makes Further Reforms In 312, the talented general Constantine gained the throne. As emperor, Constantine continued Diocletian's reforms. In addition, he took two steps that changed the course of European history. First, as you have read, Constantine granted toleration to Christians. Second, he established a new capital at the centuries-old city of Byzantium, which he renamed **Constantinople.** With this "New Rome," Constantine made the eastern empire the center of power.

Improvements Prove Temporary The reforms of Diocletian and Constantine had mixed results. They revived the economy, and by increasing the power of government, they helped hold the empire together for another century. Still, the reforms failed to stop the long-term decline. In the end, internal problems combined with attacks from outside to bring the empire down.

✓ Checkpoint How do you think Rome's unstable government affected the economy?

INFOGRAPHIC

Redefining the Empire

By the 200s, the days of the empire were numbered. Diocletian and Constantine undertook numerous reforms to help keep it alive. Although they could not stop the decline, Diocletian and Constantine redefined the empire both politically and religiously. The effects of their changes would last well beyond the official ìfall of Rome. " While the western empire would face failure, the eastern empire would maintain power for another thousand years as the Byzantine empire.

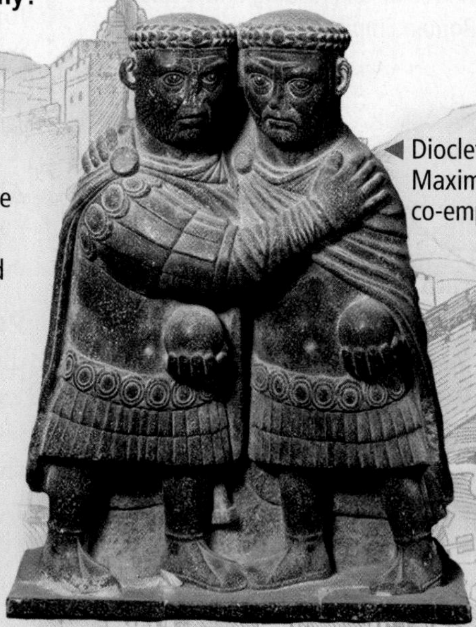

◀ Diocletian and Maximian, the co-emperors

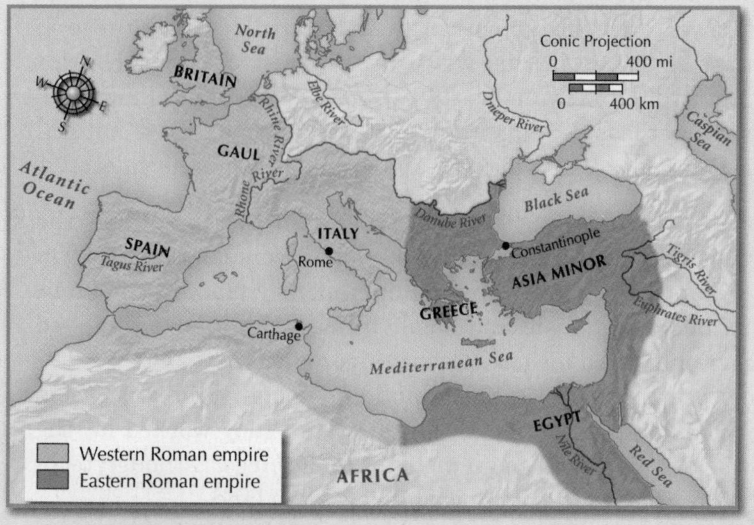
North Sea
BRITAIN
Elbe River
Rhine River
GAUL
Rhone River
Atlantic Ocean
SPAIN
Tagus River
ITALY
Rome
Carthage
Danube River
Black Sea
Constantinople
ASIA MINOR
GREECE
Tigris River
Euphrates River
Mediterranean Sea
EGYPT
Nile River
Red Sea
AFRICA
Dnieper River
Caspian Sea
Conic Projection
0 400 mi
0 400 km
Western Roman empire
Eastern Roman empire

Political Reforms

Diocletian's division of the empire into eastern and western halves (at left) made the huge territory more manageable to oversee. When Constantine later moved the capital from Rome to Constantinople (background image), he set the eastern empire on a path to long-lasting power. Previously called Byzantium, Constantinople would thrive as the capital of the Byzantine empire until 1453.

Invaders Threaten the Roman Empire

For centuries, Rome had faced attacks from the Germanic peoples who lived east of the Rhine and north of the Danube rivers. When Rome was powerful, the legions on the frontiers were successful in holding back the invaders. Some of the Germanic peoples who lived along the borders learned Roman ways and became allies of the Romans.

Migrating Nomads Attack As early as 200, wars in East Asia set off a chain of events that would eventually overwhelm Rome, thousands of miles to the west. Those wars sent a nomadic people, the **Huns,** migrating from central Asia toward eastern Europe, which they reached by 370. These skilled riders fought fierce battles to dislodge the Germanic peoples in their path. The Visigoths, Ostrogoths, and other Germanic peoples crossed into Roman territory seeking safety.

With the empire in decline, Roman legions were hard pressed to halt the invaders. Under pressure from attacks, the Roman empire surrendered first Britain, then France and Spain. It was only a matter of time before foreign invaders marched into Italy and took over Rome itself.

Rome Is Sacked In 378, when a Roman army tried to turn back the Visigoths at Adrianople, it suffered a stunning defeat. Roman power was fading. New waves of invaders were soon hammering at Rome's borders, especially in the west. In 410, the Visigoth general Alaric overran Italy and plundered the city of Rome. Meanwhile, a Germanic people called the Vandals moved through Gaul and Spain into North Africa. Gradually, Germanic groups occupied more and more of the western Roman empire.

Religious Reforms

Before Constantine came to power, many Roman emperors had persecuted Christians, arresting or executing them. Diocletian had been among the most brutal persecutors. This painting shows the Christian martyr Lucy being burned under his reign (an ordeal she is said to have survived).

Growth of Christianity in the Roman Empire

Year	Number of Christians*
0	0
50	1,400
100	7,530
150	40,496
200	217,795
250	1,171,356
300	6,299,832
350	33,882,008

*Numbers are estimates.
SOURCE: Rodney Stark, *The Rise of Christianity*

Whether Constantine (above) fueled Christianity's growth or its growth fueled his acceptance is not known. What is clear is that in the 300s, Christianity was thriving in the empire. It would underlie social and cultural developments for centuries onward.

Thinking Critically

1. **Make Comparisons** Compare the short-term and long-term effects of Diocletian's division of the empire.
2. **Synthesize Information** How do you think the acceptance of Christianity changed life in the empire?

What Kind of Downfall?

Historians have long held that the "fall of Rome" was an important historical event, but they argue over many details. **Critical Thinking** *What about Rome's end most surprises Gibbons? How does Brown differ with Gibbons on this point?*

Argument for an Enduring Rome	Argument for a Ruined Rome
The Roman empire lasted a lot longer than its supposed date of collapse.... Things don't change overnight in a big, lazy empire. The life of the cities remained much more vigorous than was thought; the classics continued to be taught with great intensity and a real feeling that they were still relevant. Even after the official end of the empire, as late as 476 A.D., many of the social structures we associate with the empire endured. —Historian Peter Brown	[T]he decline of Rome was the natural and inevitable effect of immoderate [excessive] greatness. Prosperity ripened the ... decay; the causes of destruction multiplied with the extent of conquest; and as soon as time or accident had removed the artificial supports, the stupendous fabric yielded to the pressure of its own weight. The story of its ruin is simple and obvious; and instead of inquiring *why* the Roman empire was destroyed, we should rather be surprised that it had subsisted so long. —Historian Edward Gibbons

For Rome, the worst was yet to come. Starting in 434, the Hun leader Attila embarked on a savage campaign of conquest across much of Europe. Christians called Attila the "scourge of God" because they believed his attacks were a punishment for the sins of humankind. The Hun invasion sent still more Germanic peoples fleeing into the lands of the Roman empire.

Finally, in 476, Odoacer (oh doh AY sur), a Germanic leader, ousted the emperor in Rome. Later, historians referred to that event as the "fall" of Rome. By then, however, the Roman empire had already lost many of its territories, and Roman power in the west had ended.

✔ **Checkpoint**   How did the Hun invasion weaken the Roman empire?

Many Problems Cause Rome to Fall

The passing of Rome's power and greatness was a major turning point in the history of Western civilization. Why did Rome "fall"? Modern historians identify a number of interrelated causes.

Military Attacks Perhaps the most obvious cause of Rome's fall was the invasions. Still, these attacks were successful partly because Roman legions of the late empire lacked the discipline and training from which earlier Roman armies had benefited. To meet its need for soldiers, Rome hired **mercenaries,** or foreign soldiers serving for pay, to defend its borders. Many were Germanic warriors who, according to some historians, felt little loyalty to Rome.

Political Turmoil Political problems also contributed to Rome's decline. First, as the government became more oppressive and authoritarian, it lost the support of the people. Growing numbers of corrupt officials undermined loyalty, too. So did frequent civil wars over succession to the imperial throne. Again and again, rival armies battled to have their commanders chosen as emperor. Perhaps most important, dividing the empire at a time when it was under attack may have weakened it beyond repair. The richer eastern Roman empire did little to help the west.

Economic Weakness Economic problems were widespread in the empire. Heavier and heavier taxes were required to support the vast government bureaucracy and huge military establishment. At the same time, reliance on slave labor discouraged Romans from exploring new technology. The wealth of the empire dwindled as farmers abandoned their land and the middle classes sank into poverty. Some scholars have suggested that climate change was yet another reason for reduced agricultural productivity. In addition, the population itself declined as war and epidemic diseases swept the empire.

Social Decay For centuries, worried Romans pointed to the decline in values such as patriotism, discipline, and devotion to duty on which the empire was built. The need to replace citizen-soldiers with mercenaries testified to the decline of patriotism. The upper class, which had once provided leaders, devoted itself to luxury and <u>prestige</u>. Besides being costly, providing "bread and circuses" may have undermined the self-reliance of the masses.

Did Rome Fall? Although we talk of the "fall" of Rome, the Roman empire did not disappear from the map in 476. An emperor still ruled the eastern Roman empire, which continued to exist for another 1,000 years under the name of the Byzantine empire.

The phrase "the fall of Rome" is, in fact, shorthand for a long, slow change from one way of life to another. Roman civilization survived the events of 476. In Italy, people continued to live much as they had before, though under new rulers. Many still spoke Latin and obeyed Roman laws.

Over the following centuries, however, Germanic customs and languages replaced much of Roman culture. Old Roman cities crumbled, and Roman roads disappeared. Still, the Christian Church preserved elements of Roman civilization. In later chapters, you will read how Roman and Christian traditions gave rise to medieval civilization in western Europe.

✔ **Checkpoint** What social problems contributed to the decline of the Roman empire?

Vocabulary Builder

<u>prestige</u>—(pres TEEZH) *n.* the power to impress or influence because of success or wealth

Assessment

Progress Monitoring *Online*
For: Self-quiz with vocabulary practice
Web Code: naa-0551

Terms, People, and Places

1. For each term, person, or place listed at the beginning of the section, write a sentence explaining its significance.

Note Taking

2. **Reading Skill: Recognize Multiple Causes** Use your completed chart to answer the Focus Question: How did military, political, social, and economic factors combine to cause the fall of the western Roman empire?

Comprehension and Critical Thinking

3. **Summarize** Describe the crisis that afflicted the Roman empire after the Pax Romana ended. How did Diocletian try to resolve the crisis?

4. **Express Problems Clearly** How did the successes of invaders such as the Huns reveal the fading power of the Roman empire?

5. **Identify Central Issues** What features of the western Roman empire survived after the year 476?

● **Writing About History**

Quick Write: Write a Conclusion
Compare the various factors that led to the "fall" of Rome. Write a conclusion paragraph for an essay explaining which factors you think played the greatest role.

THE FALL OF ROME

Many factors contributed to the fall of Rome, but perhaps none is as vivid and dramatic as the military plundering of the capital and its surrounding territory by invading groups. Although the Roman armies fought hard to defend their lands, aggressive leaders and fierce warriors wreaked havoc on all regions of the western Roman empire and parts of the east.

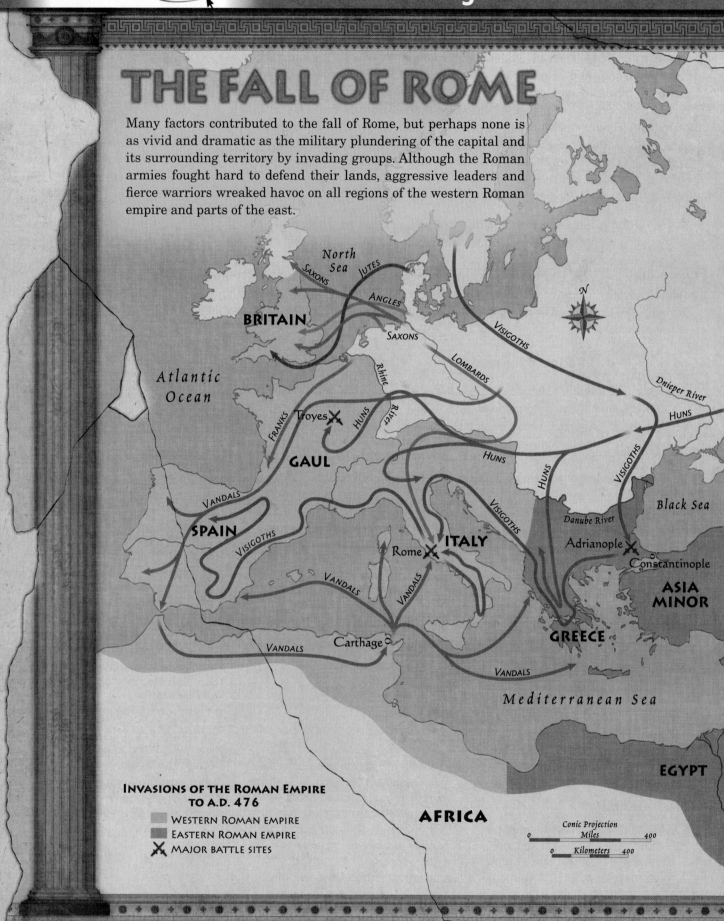

North Sea

JUTES

Saxons

ANGLES

VISIGOTHS

BRITAIN

Saxons

LOMBARDS

Dnieper River

Atlantic Ocean

Rhine

HUNS

FRANKS

Troyes ✗

HUNS

River

HUNS

VISIGOTHS

GAUL

HUNS

HUNS

Black Sea

VANDALS

VISIGOTHS

Danube River

SPAIN

VISIGOTHS

ITALY

Adrianople ✗

Rome ✗

Constantinople

VANDALS

VANDALS

ASIA MINOR

Carthage

GREECE

VANDALS

Mediterranean Sea

VANDALS

EGYPT

INVASIONS OF THE ROMAN EMPIRE TO A.D. 476

WESTERN ROMAN EMPIRE

EASTERN ROMAN EMPIRE

✗ MAJOR BATTLE SITES

AFRICA

Conic Projection

Miles

0 ——— 400

0 ——— 400

Kilometers

378
At Adrianople, the Visigoths slay the
Roman emperor Valens and much of his army.

441
Attila, king of the Huns, begins
assaults along the northeastern
borders of the Roman empire.

451
The Romans and
Visigoths push back
Attila and his troops.

476
The German king Odoacer overthrows
the Roman emperor Romulus Augustulus
and becomes king of Italy, thus finalizing
the "fall of Rome."

400

425

450

500

375

402
The Roman general Stilicho
defeats the Visigoths and
their leader, Alaric.

420
Gunderic, king of the Vandals
and the Alanis, defeats the
Romans and the Goths.

475

455
The Vandals and Alani,
led by Gaiseric, capture
and ransack Rome.

410
Alaric plunders Rome. Roman troops
withdraw from Britain and Gaul.

406
The Vandals pillage Gaul.

Ostrogothic helmet ▶

HUNS

Caspian Sea

Tigris River

Euphrates River

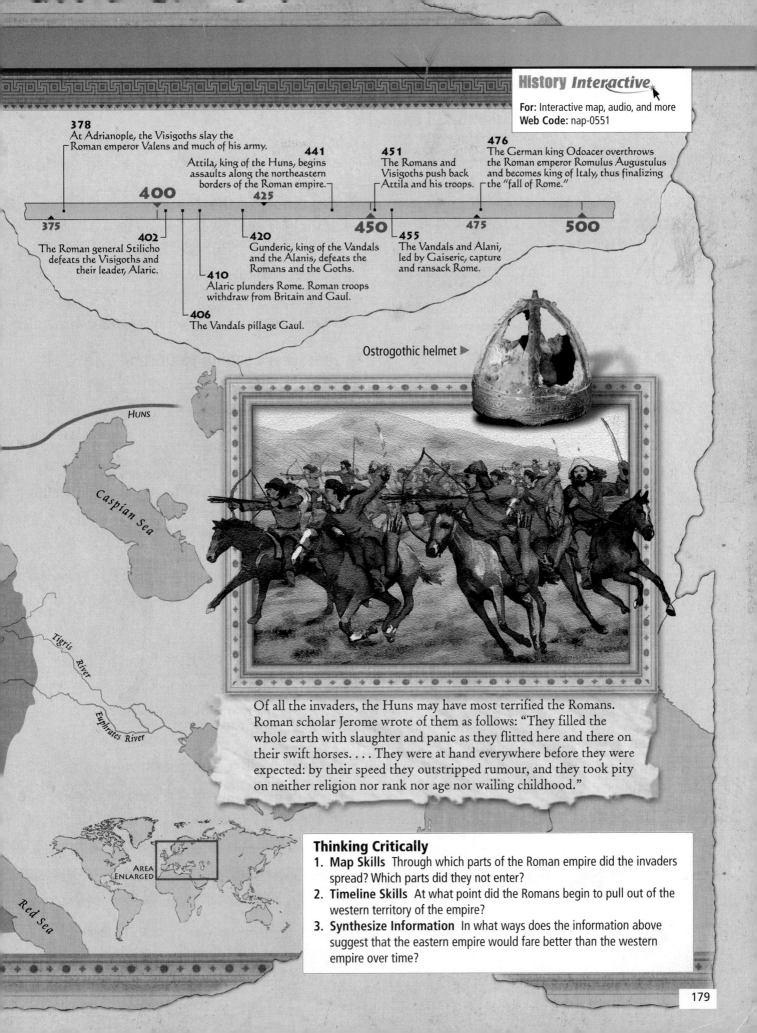

Of all the invaders, the Huns may have most terrified the Romans.
Roman scholar Jerome wrote of them as follows: "They filled the
whole earth with slaughter and panic as they flitted here and there on
their swift horses. . . . They were at hand everywhere before they were
expected: by their speed they outstripped rumour, and they took pity
on neither religion nor rank nor age nor wailing childhood."

AREA
ENLARGED

Red Sea

Thinking Critically

1. **Map Skills** Through which parts of the Roman empire did the invaders
   spread? Which parts did they not enter?
2. **Timeline Skills** At what point did the Romans begin to pull out of the
   western territory of the empire?
3. **Synthesize Information** In what ways does the information above
   suggest that the eastern empire would fare better than the western
   empire over time?

CHAPTER 5

Quick Study Guide

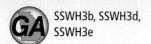 SSWH3b, SSWH3d, SSWH3e

Progress Monitoring *Online*
For: Self-test with vocabulary practice
Web Code: naa-0561

■ Roman Rulers Who Made History

Ruler	Dates	Key Accomplishments
Julius Caesar	100 B.C.(?)–44 B.C.	• Attempted to make reforms to help save the ailing republic • Made himself absolute ruler
Octavian/ Augustus	63 B.C.–A.D. 14	• Declared Exalted One and first citizen by the Senate • First ruler of the Pax Romana
Marcus Aurelius	A.D. 121–A.D. 180	• Last great emperor of the Pax Romana
Diocletian	A.D. 245–A.D. 316	• Divided the empire into two parts, eastern and western
Constantine	A.D. 280 (?)–A.D. 337	• Moved Roman power eastward by building a new capital at Constantinople • Granted toleration to Christians through the Edict of Milan

■ Key Roles in Early Christianity

Individual/Function	Role
Jesus	Jesus taught a new faith, which came to be called Christianity. He recruited followers and spread his message widely.
Apostles	These 12 men were close followers of Jesus. They spread Christianity after his death.
Paul	Through his teachings and writings, Paul spread Christianity throughout the Roman empire.
Missionaries	These religious teachers traveled with the sole purpose of spreading Christianity.
Priests	These leaders of Christian communities formed the majority of the church clergy.
Bishops	These church officials ranked over the priests. Each served an area called a diocese. They were considered the successors of the apostles.
Patriarchs	These men were bishops of major cities and exercised authority over other bishops in their area.

■ Governors of the Republic

Senate—patricians, served for life and made laws for Rome
Consuls—patricians, elected by Senate to supervise the running of Rome
Dictators—patricians, elected by Senate on occasions of war
Tribunes—plebeians, elected by plebeians to guard the interests of plebeians
Citizen-soldiers—citizens, served in the Roman military

■ Pressures Leading to Decline

Military • Germanic invasions • Weakened Roman army	**Economic** • Heavy taxes • Population decline
Political • Oppressive government • Corrupt officials • Divided empire	**Social** • Erosion of traditional values • Weakened Roman army • "Bread and circuses"

ROMAN EMPIRE

■ The Rise of Rome

Chapter Events
World Events

500 B.C.

250 B.C.

509 B.C.
The Romans establish a republic.

218 B.C.
The Carthaginian general Hannibal invades Italy during the Punic Wars.

460 B.C.
The Age of Pericles begins in Athens.

321 B.C.
The Maurya dynasty begins in India.

221 B.C.
Shi Huangdi unites China.

Concept Connector

? Essential Question Review

To connect prior knowledge with what you have learned in this chapter, answer the questions below in your Concept Connector journal. Use the journal in the Reading and Note Taking Study Guide to record your answers (or go to www.phschool.com **Web Code:** nad-0507). In addition, record information about the following concepts:

- Cultural Diffusion: Spread of Roman culture
- Belief Systems: Christianity
- Democracy: Roman citizenship

1. **Empire** The Romans were committed to a policy of imperialism, or establishing control over foreign lands and peoples. By 133 B.C., the Romans were calling the Mediterranean *Mare Nostrum,* or "Our Sea." Why did most of these conquered lands remain loyal to Rome? How did local peoples respond to Roman rule? How did the Roman Empire maintain control over its conquests?

2. **Conflict** The Roman policy of imperialism created an empire, but led to conflict within the Republic. Describe the impact that imperialism had on the Roman Republic and explain how the results of imperialism led to a series of civil wars. Focus on the following:
   - new wealth
   - agriculture
   - reform

3. **Political Systems** The Romans established a form of government called a *res publica,* or "that which belongs to the people." Today, this form of government is called a republic. Why did Romans choose this form of government? Explain how the Roman senate became more democratic over time. Think about the following:
   - plebeians
   - tribunes
   - veto

■ Connections to Today

1. **Dictatorship** During the Roman republic, the Senate was given the power to establish a dictator who could rule for just six months at a time. The need for such absolute leadership was seen as a solution to the problem of war or internal crisis—that is, it was seen as a temporary solution to a dire situation. Through the course of history, however, dictators have often seized power, rather than been given it, and many of them have ruled their countries for years or even decades on end. In the past few decades, dictators have controlled countries such as North Korea, Chile, and Iraq. Conduct research on a recent dictator of a country anywhere in the world and write a summary of how and why he or she took power.

2. **Advances in Technology: Communication** The sprawling system of Roman roads (see below) was crucial in unifying the Roman empire. New technologies often shape communication and, therefore, society. Today, communication is being revolutionized by the Internet. How are the effects of the Internet similar to those of Rome's well-built system of roads? How might the Internet and Roman roads be similar in their impact on culture and trade?

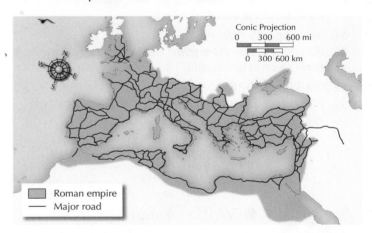

Conic Projection

Roman empire
— Major road

A.D. **27**
The Roman republic ends. Augustus founds the Roman empire.

A.D. **284**
Diocletian divides the Roman empire into two parts.

A.D. **312**
The capital of the Roman empire moves eastward to Constantinople.

A.D. **392**
Christianity becomes the official Roman religion.

A.D. **476**
Odoacer, a Germanic leader, unseats the last Roman emperor.

A.D. **1**

A.D. **250**

A.D. **500**

A.D. **300**
The Maya golden age begins in Mexico and Central America.

A.D. **323**
The Hellenistic Age begins, and Greek culture spreads.

A.D. **350s**
Axum, located in Ethiopia, conquers Nubia.

History *Interactive*
For: Interactive timeline
Web Code: nap-0561

Chapter Assessment

Terms, People, and Places

Choose the italicized term in parentheses that best completes each sentence.

1. The application of science and mathematics to develop useful structures is called *(aqueducts/engineering)*.
2. A person who dies or suffers for his or her beliefs is a *(martyr/apostle)*.
3. The senate gave *(Octavian/Julius Caesar)* the title of Augustus, or "Exalted One."
4. Men elected by the senate to supervise the business of the government were called *(consuls/plebeians)*.
5. *(Patricians/Mercenaries)* were foreign soldiers serving in the Roman army for pay.
6. A *(legion/mosaic)* is a picture made from chips of colored stone or glass.
7. Beliefs that were contrary to official Church teachings were called *(heresies/latifundia)*.
8. The rapid rise of prices is called *(inflation/census)*.

Main Ideas

Section 1 (pp. 150–154)
9. What values of the Roman republic were revealed in the establishment of the role of tribune?

Section 2 (pp. 155–160)
10. How did Augustus' rise to power mark a significant change in Rome's form of government?

Section 3 (pp. 161–165)
11. How did the concept of Greco-Roman civilization come into existence?
12. What were three important principles of Roman law?

Section 4 (pp. 166–171)
13. How did Christianity spread through the Roman empire?

Section 5 (pp. 173–177)
14. Describe three reasons for the fall of the Roman empire.

Chapter Focus Question
15. How did Rome grow from a single city to a huge, diverse empire?

Critical Thinking

16. **Geography and History** How did both Greece and Rome benefit from their location on the Mediterranean Sea?
17. **Identify Point of View** "History," said Cicero, "illuminates reality, vitalizes memory, provides guidance in daily life, and brings us tidings of antiquity." How do you think the works of Roman historians like Livy and Tacitus illustrate Cicero's point of view?
18. **Draw Conclusions** What were some possible negative consequences of following the Roman policy of "bread and circuses"?
19. **Analyze Information** Give two examples of how the principles of law developed by Rome affect life in the United States today.
20. **Analyze Visuals** Look back at the photograph of a Roman aqueduct on page 164. Why do you think the construction of aqueducts can be called a major accomplishment of Roman civilization?
21. **Recognize Cause and Effect** What were the causes and effects of the division of the Roman empire into two parts?
22. **Draw Conclusions** Some emperors persecuted Christians for their refusal to make sacrifices to the emperor or to honor Roman gods. Why do you think emperors considered this refusal a threat to the empire?

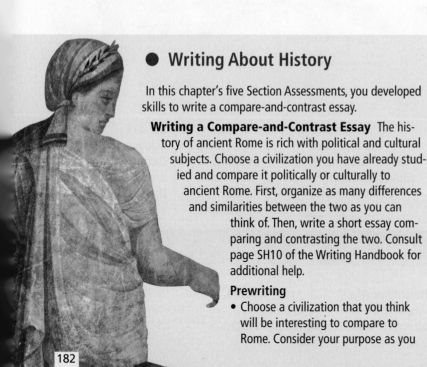

● Writing About History

In this chapter's five Section Assessments, you developed skills to write a compare-and-contrast essay.

Writing a Compare-and-Contrast Essay The history of ancient Rome is rich with political and cultural subjects. Choose a civilization you have already studied and compare it politically or culturally to ancient Rome. First, organize as many differences and similarities between the two as you can think of. Then, write a short essay comparing and contrasting the two. Consult page SH10 of the Writing Handbook for additional help.

Prewriting
- Choose a civilization that you think will be interesting to compare to Rome. Consider your purpose as you

make this decision—are there influences on or legacies left by the two civilizations that make them particularly interesting to compare and contrast?
- Gather details of the similarities and differences between Rome and the other civilization. Create a graphic organizer to organize these details.

Drafting
- Write an attention-grabbing introduction that defines how and why you are comparing and contrasting the two civilizations.
- Give details about each point of comparison/contrast and use parallel structure to cover similar points for the two cases.

Revising
- Use the guidelines for revising your report on page SH12 of the Writing Handbook.

Prepare for the GHSGT

Julius Caesar: Father of the Roman Empire

Julius Caesar has been called the father of the Roman empire and the most influential man in European history. After Caesar's assassination, his nephew Octavian declared him a god. The documents below are just a few of many impressions of him that writers, historians, and artists have left behind for centuries.

Document A

"There is a story that while he was crossing the Alps he came to a small village with hardly any inhabitants and altogether a miserable-looking place. His friends were laughing and joking about it, saying: 'No doubt here too one would find people trying hard to gain office, and here too there are struggles to get the first place [in government] and jealous rivalries among the great men.' Caesar then said to them in all seriousness: 'As far as I am concerned, I would rather be the first man here than the second in Rome.'"

—From **Life of Caesar** by Plutarch

Document B

"O mighty Caesar, dost thou lie so low?
Are all thy conquests, glories, triumphs, spoils,
Shrunk to this little measure? Fare thee well.
I know not, gentlemen, what you intend,
Who else must be let blood, who else is rank.
If I myself, there is no hour so fit
As Caesar's death's hour, nor no instrument
Of half that worth as those your swords, made rich
With the most noble blood of all this world."

—Mark Antony, upon discovering Caesar's murder;
From **The Tragedy of Julius Caesar**
by William Shakespeare

Document C

"In eloquence and warlike achievements, he equaled at least, if he did not surpass, the greatest of men. . . . Cicero, in recounting to Brutus the famous orators, declares, 'that he does not see that Caesar was inferior to any one of them'; and says, 'that he had an elegant, splendid, noble, and magnificent vein of eloquence.'"

—From **The Lives of the Twelve Caesars**
by Suetonius

Document D

Julius Caesar

Analyzing Documents

Use your knowledge of history and Documents A, B, C, and D to answer questions 1–4.

1. Which side of Caesar does Plutarch's anecdote reveal?
   A his drive to be the best
   B his desire to serve Rome
   C his wish to reach high spiritual levels
   D his interest in having many areas of achievement

2. According to Shakespeare's Mark Antony, Caesar was
   A cunning, cruel, and ambitious.
   B weak, foolish, and condescending.
   C honorable, noble, and great.
   D humble, kind, and compassionate.

3. What about Caesar did Cicero admire?
   A that he was a cunning strategist
   B that he was a practical and realistic leader
   C that he was a humble and kind man
   D that he was an engaging and talented speaker

4. **Writing Task** Julius Caesar was murdered more than 2,000 years ago. Why has he continued to be a figure of interest through modern times?

6 Civilizations of the Americas
Prehistory–A.D. 1570

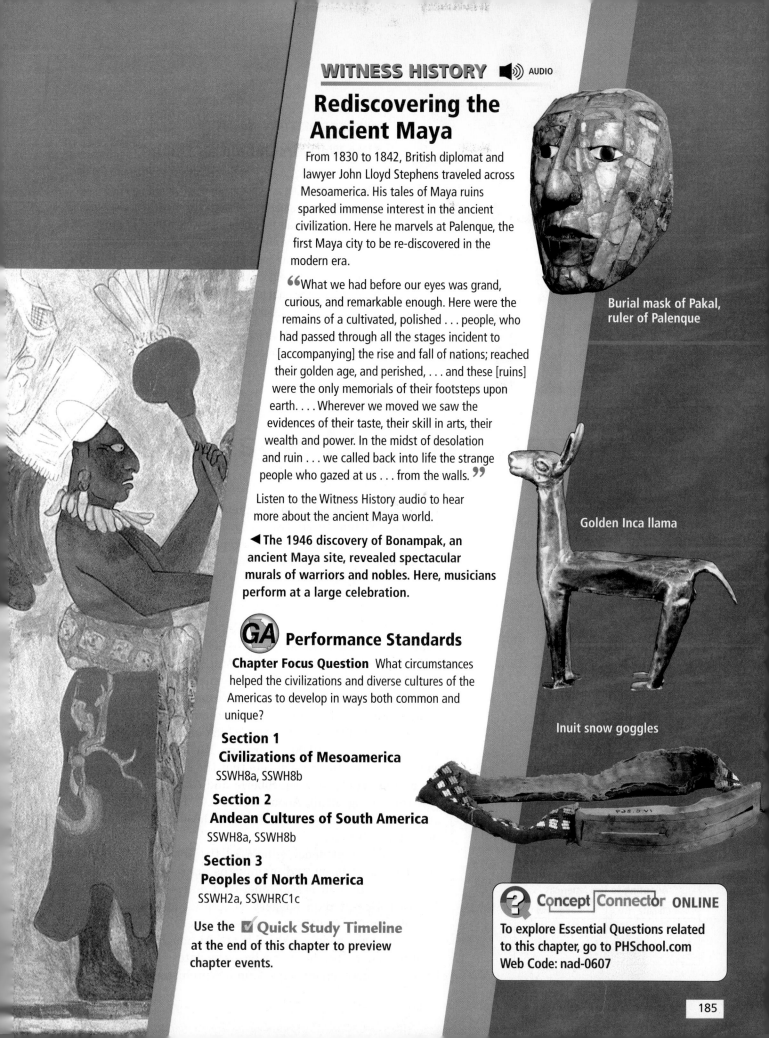

Rediscovering the Ancient Maya

From 1830 to 1842, British diplomat and lawyer John Lloyd Stephens traveled across Mesoamerica. His tales of Maya ruins sparked immense interest in the ancient civilization. Here he marvels at Palenque, the first Maya city to be re-discovered in the modern era.

❝What we had before our eyes was grand, curious, and remarkable enough. Here were the remains of a cultivated, polished . . . people, who had passed through all the stages incident to [accompanying] the rise and fall of nations; reached their golden age, and perished, . . . and these [ruins] were the only memorials of their footsteps upon earth. . . . Wherever we moved we saw the evidences of their taste, their skill in arts, their wealth and power. In the midst of desolation and ruin . . . we called back into life the strange people who gazed at us . . . from the walls. ❞

Listen to the Witness History audio to hear more about the ancient Maya world.

◀ The 1946 discovery of Bonampak, an ancient Maya site, revealed spectacular murals of warriors and nobles. Here, musicians perform at a large celebration.

Burial mask of Pakal, ruler of Palenque

Golden Inca llama

Inuit snow goggles

GA Performance Standards

Chapter Focus Question What circumstances helped the civilizations and diverse cultures of the Americas to develop in ways both common and unique?

Section 1
Civilizations of Mesoamerica
SSWH8a, SSWH8b

Section 2
Andean Cultures of South America
SSWH8a, SSWH8b

Section 3
Peoples of North America
SSWH2a, SSWHRC1c

Use the ☑ **Quick Study Timeline** at the end of this chapter to preview chapter events.

? Concept Connector ONLINE

To explore Essential Questions related to this chapter, go to PHSchool.com
Web Code: nad-0607

Aztec eagle warrior

WITNESS HISTORY 🔊)) AUDIO

Elite Warriors Uphold an Empire

Among the Aztecs, a force of fierce soldiers emerged to aid the ruler in maintaining an empire. The most highly regarded fighters were eagle and jaguar warriors, who wore costumes resembling the honored animals for whom they were named (a tradition in other cultures of the Americas as well). Indeed, Aztec warfare served both a political purpose—defending the empire—and a ritual one. It was the gods whom the Aztec rulers believed granted them the right to rule. Sacrificing humans—the captives of battle—was the leading way to appeal to the gods.

Focus Question What factors encouraged the rise of powerful civilizations in Mesoamerica?

Civilizations of Mesoamerica

 Performance Standards

• **SSWH8a** Explain the rise and fall of the Olmec, Mayan, and Aztec Empires.

• **SSWH8b** Compare cultures of the Americas.

Terms, People, and Places

Mesoamerica	Tenochtitlán
maize	chinampas
Olmecs	tribute
stela	Teotihuacán
Valley of Mexico	

Note Taking

Reading Skill: Compare and Contrast Use a chart like the one below to take notes on similarities and differences in how early people adapted to climate and geography in different parts of the Americas.

Adapting to the Americas	
Climate	**Geography**
•	•
•	•
•	•

The Americas include two continents, North America and South America. Within these two geographic regions lies a cultural region called **Mesoamerica,** which is made up of Mexico and Central America. Some of the earliest civilizations in the Americas developed in Mesoamerica.

People Settle in the Americas

Sometime between 12,000 and 10,000 years ago, most scholars believe, people first arrived in the Americas. Scholars are still trying to understand the details of how this great migration occurred. Originally, it was believed that people came from Asia and entered through Alaska. This migration is thought to have taken place near the end of the last Ice Age, which lasted from about 100,000 years ago to about 10,000 years ago. During the ice age, so much water froze into thick ice sheets that the sea level dropped, exposing a land bridge between Siberia and Alaska in the area that is now the Bering Strait. About 10,000 B.C., Earth's climate warmed and the ice melted. As a result, water levels rose and covered the Bering land bridge.

The earliest evidence supported the theory that hunters followed herds of bison and mammoths across the land bridge and then south through North America, Central America, and South America. Recent data suggest something different—that people migrated to parts of the Americas much earlier and along coastal routes, perhaps paddling small boats. Although neither theory has been proved, researchers now base the dates of migration into the Americas mostly on evidence found at prehistoric sites.

Geography *Interactive*
For: Audio guided tour
Web Code: nap-0611

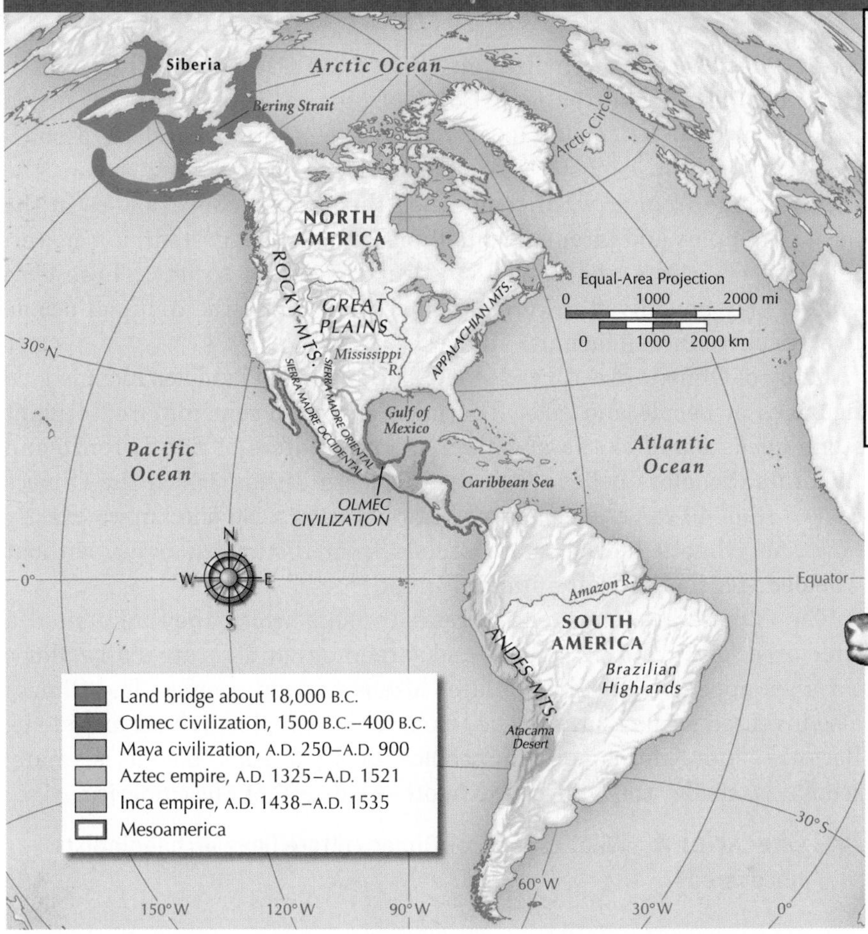

Map Skills The descendants of the first Americans spread throughout the Americas, establishing both small settlements and large civilizations.

1. **Locate** (a) Bering Strait (b) Gulf of Mexico (c) Amazon River (d) Rocky Mountains
2. **Location** Which culture bordered the Gulf of Mexico and the Caribbean Sea?
3. **Draw Inferences** In what types of environments did the Inca live? The Aztecs?

Map legend:
- Land bridge about 18,000 B.C.
- Olmec civilization, 1500 B.C.–400 B.C.
- Maya civilization, A.D. 250–A.D. 900
- Aztec empire, A.D. 1325–A.D. 1521
- Inca empire, A.D. 1438–A.D. 1535
- Mesoamerica

The Inca were famous for their goldwork, such as this figurine of a llama.

Adapting to New Environments

The first Americans faced a variety of environments in which they could settle. For example, great mountain chains—the Rockies, the eastern and western Sierra Madre, and the Andes—dominate the western Americas. In addition, through the continents flow two of the world's four longest rivers, the Amazon of South America and the Mississippi of North America. Far to the north and south of the continents, people learned to survive in icy, treeless lands. Closer to the Equator, people settled in the hot, wet climate and dense vegetation of the Amazon rain forest. Elsewhere, hunters adapted to deserts like the Atacama of Chile, woodlands like those in eastern North America, and the fertile plains of both continents.

People Begin to Farm and Build Villages

In the Americas, as elsewhere, the greatest adaptation occurred when people learned to domesticate plants and animals. These changes took place slowly between about 8500 B.C. and 2000 B.C. In Mesoamerica, Neolithic people cultivated a range of crops, including beans, sweet potatoes, peppers, tomatoes, squash, and **maize**—the Native American name for corn. People in South America cultivated crops such as maize and cassava and domesticated llamas and other animals valued for their wool. By 3000 B.C. in parts of South America and 1500 B.C. in parts of Mesoamerica, farmers had settled in villages. Populations then expanded, and some villages eventually grew into the great early cities of the Americas.

✓ **Checkpoint** How did early Americans adapt to different environments?

Civilization Arises With the Olmecs

The earliest American civilization, that of the **Olmecs,** emerged in the tropical forests along the Gulf Coast of Mexico. The civilization lasted from about 1500 B.C. to 400 B.C. Compared to other civilizations, archaeologists know little about the Olmecs. They do not know where the Olmecs came from or what they called themselves. But evidence in the form of temples and large and small pieces of art suggests that a powerful class of priests and nobles stood at the top of society. These elite groups may have lived in ceremonial centers, while the common people lived in surrounding farming villages.

Much of Olmec art is carved stone. The smallest examples include jade figurines of people and gods. The most dramatic remains are 14 giant stone heads found at the major ceremonial centers of San Lorenzo and La Venta. Scholars believe that these colossal heads, which the Olmecs carved from 40-ton stones, are portraits of rulers. No one knows exactly how the Olmecs moved these stones from distant quarries without wheeled vehicles or draft animals.

The Olmecs also engaged in trade, through which they influenced a wide area. The grinning jaguars and serpents that decorate many Olmec carvings appear in the arts of later Mesoamerican peoples. The Olmecs also invented a calendar, and they carved hieroglyphic writing into stone. Because later Mesoamerican peoples adopted such advances, many scholars consider the Olmecs the "mother culture" of Mesoamerica.

✔ **Checkpoint** What aspects of Olmec culture have archaeologists uncovered?

The Maya Build Widespread Civilization

Among the peoples the Olmecs influenced were the Maya. By 300 B.C., the Maya were building large cities, such as El Mirador in Guatemala. By about A.D. 250, the Maya golden age—known as the Classic Period—began, with city-states flourishing from the Yucatán Peninsula in southern Mexico through much of Central America.

Agriculture Thrives Before the Maya developed large population centers, they lived scattered across the land. They developed two farming methods that allowed them to thrive in the tropical environment. In many areas, farmers burned down forests and then cleared the land in order to plant on it. After a few years, the fields were no longer fertile. The Maya would then abandon these lands until they could be used once again. In the meantime, farmers would burn and clear new lands for farming. In addition, along the banks of rivers, Maya farmers built raised fields to lift crops up above the annual floodwaters. These methods allowed the Maya to produce enough maize and other crops to support rapidly growing cities.

Powerful City-States Emerge The Maya cities that developed before and during the Classic Period never formed an empire. Instead, individual and powerful city-states evolved. The smaller city-states ruled over the people living directly within and near their borders. The largest ones reigned over neighboring areas as well—often requiring nearby cities to show allegiance to their kings and to participate in their ritual activities. Over the course of hundreds of years, many different city-states held

Colossal Olmec head from La Venta

Note Taking

Reading Skill: Compare and Contrast
Use a Venn diagram to keep track of key similarities and differences among the cultures of Mesoamerica.

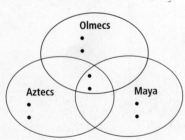

Cities of the Maya Realm

Map labels:

Gulf of Mexico

Dzibilchaltún
Chichén Itzá · Coba
Uxmal · Kabah
Jaina · Sayil · Labna
Santa Rosa Xtampak'
Etzna
20° N

Comalcalco

Becan · Xpuhil
Río Bec · Cerros
Calakmul · El Palmar
El Mirador · Nakbe
Palenque · Uaxactun · Nak'um
Tonina · Piedras Negras · El Perú · Tikal · Yaxha · Naranjo
Yaxchilan
Bonampak · Seibal · Caracol
Altar de Sacrificios · Dos Pilas
Pusilha
88° W
16° N

Quirigua

Izapa · Copán · Kaminaljuyu
Monte Alto

Pacific Ocean

96° W · 92° W

Miller Projection
0   50   100 mi
0   50   100 km

Caribbean Sea

Legend:
- Extent of Maya civilization
- ● Key Maya city, 300 B.C.–A.D. 250
- ○ Key Maya city, A.D. 250–A.D. 900

Geography *Interactive*
For: Interactive map
Web Code: nap-0612

Map Skills Many Maya cities were hidden for centuries beneath tropical overgrowth. The archaeologists who uncovered them have learned that numerous powerful governments once ruled the area.

1. **Locate** (a) Tikal (b) Calakmul (c) Copán (d) Palenque (e) Piedras Negras
2. **Region** How did the geography of the Maya region differ from north to south?
3. **Make Generalizations** Some Maya cities existed only in the earlier era shown on the map, some only in the later era, and some in both. Why might the lifespan of a Maya city have varied?

---

power, with warfare and trade a constant theme of life among them. Cities such as Palenque, Copán, and Piedras Negras all carried great influence in their time, but the largest and most supreme power resided in the rulers of Tikal and Calakmul.

While the Maya were not united politically, city-states maintained regular contact through a system of economic exchange, which generated much wealth. Traders carried valuable cargoes long distances by sea and along roads made of packed earth. Trade goods included items of daily use—such as honey, salt, and cotton—and nonessential but prized items such as feathers, jade, and jaguar pelts. These goods might have been used in ceremonies or to show status.

Structuring Society Each Maya city had its own ruler, who was usually male. Maya records and carvings show that women occasionally governed on their own or in the name of young sons. Nobles served many functions in support of the ruler. Some were military leaders, while others managed public works, collected taxes, and enforced laws. Scribes, painters, and sculptors were also very highly respected. Merchants may have formed a middle class in society, though the wealthiest and most powerful merchants were certainly nobles.

The majority of the Maya were farmers. They grew maize, beans, and squash—the basic food crops of Mesoamerica—as well as fruit trees, cotton, and brilliant tropical flowers. To support the cities, farmers paid taxes in food and worked on construction projects. Some cities also included a population of slaves, who generally were commoners who had been captured in war.

✔ **Checkpoint** How did the Maya political structure differ from an empire?

Powerful Maya rulers included Yax Pac of Copán (above, receiving the staff of leadership from the city's first ruler) and Pakal of Palenque (who wore the jade burial mask at left).

Cultural Life of the Maya

The cultural life of the Maya included impressive advances in learning and the arts. In addition, the Maya developed a complex polytheistic religion that influenced their cultural life as well as their spiritual beliefs. Many Maya today maintain elements of the traditional religion established by the ancient Maya, such as the belief that each person's spirit is associated with a particular animal.

Sculptors Leave a Legacy in Stone The cities of the Maya are known today for their towering temples and palaces built from stone. Temples rested on pyramid-shaped platforms that were often quite large. Atop the temples, priests performed rites and sacrifices, while the people watched from the plazas below. Some temples also served as burial places for rulers, nobles, and priests. Palaces may have been used as royal residences as well as locations for meetings, courts, and other governmental activities.

The Maya placed elaborately carved sculpture on many of their buildings. They also sculpted tall stone monuments, each of which is called a **stela** (STEE luh). These carvings preserve striking images of nobles, warriors in plumed headdresses, and powerful rulers. They also represent the Maya gods, including the creator god Itzamna (et SAHM nah), the rain god Chac (chakh), and the sun god K'inich Ajaw (keen EECH ah HOW).

Scribes Record Historical Events The Maya also developed a hieroglyphic writing system, which scholars did not decipher until recent decades. Maya scribes carved inscriptions on stelae that include names of rulers, mentions of neighboring city-states, and dates and descriptions of events. They also wrote about astronomy, rituals, and other religious matters in books made of bark paper. Spanish conquerors later burned most of these books, considering any works that were written by non-Christians to be unacceptable. Three books, however, were taken to Europe and have survived into the present.

Priests Develop Astronomy and Mathematics Maya priests needed to measure time accurately in order to hold ceremonies at the correct moment. As a result, many priests became expert mathematicians and astronomers. They developed an accurate 365-day solar calendar as well as a 260-day ritual calendar. Maya priests also invented a numbering system that included place values and the concept of zero.

Maya Civilization Declines About A.D. 900, the Maya abandoned many of their cities. In the Yucatán Peninsula, cities flourished for a few more centuries, but there, too, the Maya eventually stopped building them. By the time the Spanish arrived in the 1500s, the Maya mostly lived in farming villages. Archaeologists do not know for sure why Maya civilization declined, although theories abound. For example, frequent warfare may have taken its toll on society, or overpopulation could have led to over-farming and exhaustion of the soil.

Throughout the region, however, the remoteness of their jungle and mountain locations allowed many Maya to survive the encounter with the Spanish. Today, more than two million Maya people live in Guatemala and southern Mexico.

✔ **Checkpoint** What do Maya arts and writing tell us about their religion and history?

Photographs From the Past
British archaeologist Alfred P. Maudslay won fame in the late 1800s for his sharp and stunning photographs of Maya ruins, such as this stela showing a ruler from the city of Quirigua.

The Common Culture of Mesoamerica

In addition to the societies you are reading about in this section, numerous others arose in Mesoamerica between the time of the Olmecs and the arrival of Spanish explorers in the 1500s. While each developed individual traits that set it apart from the other groups, they all shared various cultural elements. For example, both the Maya and the Aztecs used the complicated "calendar round," which combined days from a 260-ritual calendar and a 365-solar calendar to form 52-year cycles similar in cultural importance to our centuries.

Writing
All Mesoamerican societies that developed writing used a hieroglyphic system. The level of complexity varied from group to group, however. The Zapotec (back) and the Maya (front) systems were the most advanced.

Architecture
Throughout the region, architecture varied in style and decoration. However, the stepped pyramid prevailed as a basic shape of buildings in all cultures, from the small temple at the Toltec capital at Tula (above) to this enormous structure (right) at the Maya city of Tikal.

Sport and Ritual Although rules varied in the famous Mesoamerican ballgame, the basic format stayed the same. Players competed on an **I**-shaped ballcourt with sloped walls, like the Zapotec court below. They wore thick padding (as on the Maya ballplayer figurine above) to avoid injury as they tried to knock a solid rubber ball down the court and through a small hoop. The challenging game carried great ritual importance, representing the movements of the moon and sun. Sometimes, the losing team would be sacrificed to keep these heavenly bodies in motion (as shown at right).

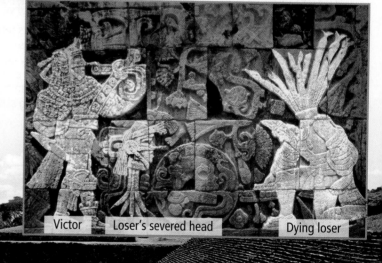

Victor   Loser's severed head   Dying loser

Thinking Critically
1. **Draw Inferences** In what ways do you think these societies passed elements of culture to one another?
2. **Determine Relevance** How might learning about the shared elements of culture help scholars understand each Mesoamerican society?

The Aztec Empire Forms in Mexico

Sometime shortly after about A.D. 1200, bands of nomadic people from the north migrated into the **Valley of Mexico,** which lies in the high plateau of central Mexico. These people identified themselves as separate tribes, such as the Mexica (may SHEE kah), from whom Mexico gets it name. All the tribes spoke one language—Nahuatl (NAH hwaht el)—and believed their origins began in the same legendary birthplace, Aztlan. Together, these tribes are known as the Aztecs.

The Aztecs Settle in the Valley of Mexico In A.D. 1325, the Aztecs founded their capital city, **Tenochtitlán** (teh nawch tee TLAHN). According to Aztec legend, the gods had told the Aztecs to search for an eagle holding a snake in its beak and perching atop a cactus. When they saw this sign, they would know where to build their capital. Indeed, they finally saw the sign on a swampy island in Lake Texcoco (tesh KOH koh), and there they built their city. Today, Mexico City sits atop this same site.

As their population grew, the Aztecs found <u>ingenious</u> ways to create more farmland in their lake environment. They built **chinampas,** artificial islands made of mud piled atop reed mats that were anchored to the shallow lake-bed with willow trees. On these "floating gardens," the Aztecs raised maize, squash, and beans. They gradually filled in parts of the lake and created canals for transportation. Wide stone causeways linked Tenochtitlán to the mainland.

Vocabulary Builder

<u>ingenious</u>—(in JEEN yus) *adj.* clever, original, and effective

Tenochtitlán: Building an Island City

The Aztecs built causeways to connect Tenochtitlán to the rural settlements of the mainland. After the Spanish invaded in the 1500s, they drew a map of the city (at left). Although not to scale, it shows the causeways and dense buildings of the large capital. The diagram (below) shows how the chinampas were built. *What engineering skills must the Aztecs have used to build the city?*

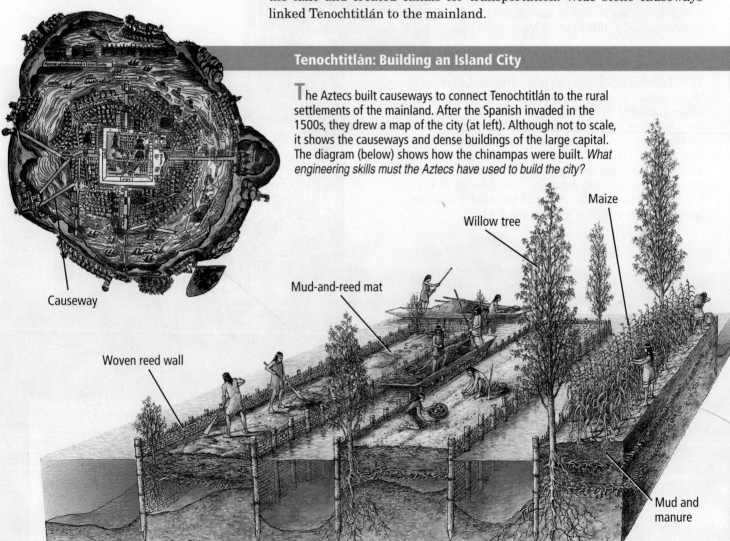

Causeway

Maize

Willow tree

Mud-and-reed mat

Woven reed wall

Mud and manure

The Empire Expands In the 1400s, the Aztecs greatly expanded their territory. Through a combination of fierce conquests and shrewd alliances, they spread their rule across most of Mexico, from the Gulf of Mexico in the east to the Pacific Ocean in the west. By 1517, the Aztec empire numbered an estimated five to six million people.

✓ **Checkpoint** What are some advantages and disadvantages of building a city on an island in a lake?

Aztec Society Takes Shape

War brought immense wealth as well as power to the Aztec empire. **Tribute,** or payment from conquered peoples, helped the Aztecs turn their capital into a magnificent city. From its temples and royal palaces to its zoos and floating gardens, Tenochtitlán seemed a city of wonders. It was also the center of a complex, well-ordered empire.

Structuring Government and Society Unlike the Maya city-states, each of which had its own king, the Aztec empire had a single ruler. A council of nobles, priests, and military leaders elected the emperor, whose primary function was to lead in war. Below him, nobles served as officials, judges, and governors of conquered provinces. Next came the warriors, who could rise to noble status by performing well on the battlefield. The priests were a class apart. They performed rituals to please the gods and prevent droughts or other disasters.

A powerful middle class included long-distance traders, who ferried goods across the empire and beyond. With goods from the highlands such as weapons, tools, and rope, they bartered for tropical products such as jaguar skins and cocoa beans.

The majority of people were commoners who farmed the land. At the bottom of society were serfs and slaves, who were mostly prisoners of war or debtors. Despite their low status, slaves' rights were clearly established by law. For example, slaves could own land and buy their freedom.

Religion and Mythology Influence Culture The Aztecs believed in many gods, including Huitzilopochtli (weets ee loh POHCH tlee), whom they revered as the patron god of their people. His temple towered above central Tenochtitlán. The Aztecs also worshipped Quetzalcoatl (ket sahl koh AHT el), the feathered serpent who reigned over earth and water, plus the other powerful gods of an earlier culture that had been centered at the city of Teotihuacán (tay oh tee wah KAHN).

Teotihuacán had dominated life in the Valley of Mexico from about A.D. 200 to A.D. 750. The city was well planned, with wide roads, massive temples, and large apartment buildings to house its population of perhaps 200,000. Along the main avenue, the enormous Pyramid of the Sun and the Pyramid of the Moon rose majestically toward the sky.

Citizens of Teotihuacán worshiped gods such as Quetzalcoatl and Tlaloc (TLAH lohk), the rain god. After Teotihuacán fell, possibly to invaders, its culture survived and greatly influenced later peoples of Mesoamerica. The Aztecs, for example, believed that the gods had created the world multiple times. In their mythology, it was in Teotihuacán that the gods created the world in which the Aztecs lived.

Representations of Tlaloc (left) and Quetzalcoatl (right)

In this translation from an Aztec text, Nanahuatzin's bravery is underscored as he proves willing to sacrifice himself where another god, the moon, was not.

Primary Source

❝ It is said that when the [sun] was made, . . . there was fasting for four days. It is said that the moon would be the sun. And when four days were completed, it is said, the [sun] was made during the night. . . . a very great fire was laid . . . into which was to leap, was to fall the moon—where he was to gain renown, glory: by which he would become the sun. And the moon thereupon went in order to leap into the fire. But he did not dare do it; he feared the fire. Then all the gods shouted, they said: "When [is this to be], O gods? Let the sun stop!" But little [Nanahuatzin] had already dared; he thereupon had leaped into the fire. Thus he became the sun.

And the moon, when he was deprived of the renown, the glory, was much shamed. ❞

—Fray Bernardino de Sahagún, *General History of the Things of New Spain*

In Aztec mythology, the gods frequently sacrificed themselves for the good of the people. They believed a god named Nanahuatzin (nah nah WAHTS een) had sacrificed himself to become the sun. To give the sun strength to rise each day, the Aztecs offered human sacrifices. Most of the victims were prisoners of war, who were plentiful because the Aztecs carried on almost continuous warfare.

Aztec Knowledge Expands Priests were the keepers of Aztec knowledge. They recorded laws and historical events in the Aztec hieroglyphic writing system. Some priests ran schools. Others used their knowledge of astronomy and mathematics to foretell the future. The Aztecs, like the Maya, developed a 260-day ritual calendar and a 365-day solar calendar.

Like many other ancient peoples, the Aztecs believed that illness was a punishment from the gods. Still, Aztec priests used herbs and other medicines to treat fevers and wounds. Aztec physicians could set broken bones and treat dental cavities. They also prescribed steam baths as cures for various ills, a therapy still in use today.

✔ **Checkpoint** How was Aztec society structured?

Looking Ahead

The Aztecs developed a sophisticated and complex culture. But among many of the peoples they conquered, discontent festered and rebellion often flared up. At the height of Aztec power, word reached Tenochtitlán that pale-skinned, bearded men had landed on the east coast. When the armies from Spain arrived, they found ready allies among peoples who were ruled by the Aztec empire. In a later chapter, you will read about the results of the encounter between the Aztecs and the newcomers from far-off Spain.

SECTION 1 Assessment

Progress Monitoring *Online*
For: Self-quiz with vocabulary practice
Web Code: naa-0611

Terms, People, and Places

1. For each term, person, or place listed at the beginning of the section, write a sentence explaining its significance.

Note Taking

2. **Reading Skill: Compare and Contrast** Use your completed chart and Venn diagram to answer the Focus Question: What factors encouraged the rise of powerful civilizations in Mesoamerica?

Comprehension and Critical Thinking

3. **Recognize Sufficient Evidence** What types of evidence do you think archaeologists need in order to know for certain when people populated the Americas?

4. **Analyze Information** How do you think archaeologists use public buildings, monuments, and artwork to trace the influence of earlier civilizations, such as the Olmecs, on later people?

5. **Make Comparisons** Compare the Aztec and Maya civilizations. What characteristics do they share the most? In what way(s) do they differ the most?

● **Writing About History**

Quick Write: Choose a Topic When you write a narrative essay, start by choosing a topic. Suppose you want to write a narrative from the perspective of an ancient Maya person. Make a list of topics that interest you, such as a day in the life of a Maya sculptor or an account of a battle between two rival Maya city-states. You may want to do research in books and on the Internet before you settle on a topic.

On Inca roads, couriers (right) often carried quipus (far right), or recording devices.

WITNESS HISTORY ◀)) AUDIO

Impressive Inca Roads

❝In human memory, I believe that there is no account of a road as great as this, running through deep valleys, high mountains, banks of snow, torrents of water, living rock, and wild rivers. . . . In all places it was clean and swept free of refuse, with lodgings, storehouses, Sun temples, and posts along the route. Oh! Can anything similar be claimed for Alexander [the Great] or any of the [other] powerful kings who ruled the world. . . ?❞
—Pedro Cieza de León, Spanish explorer admiring the Inca road system in the 1500s

Focus Question What characterized the cultures and civilizations that developed in the Andes?

Andean Cultures of South America

Performance Standards

- **SSWH8a** Explain the rise and fall of the Inca empire.
- **SSWH8b** Compare cultures of the Americas.

Terms, People, and Places

Chavín	Pachacuti Inca Yupanqui
Moche	Sapa Inca
adobe	Cuzco
Nazca	quipu
Huari	ayllu
Tiahuanaco	Inti

Note Taking

Reading Skill: Contrast Contrast the cultures of the early peoples of the Andes with that of the Inca. Use a chart like the one below to organize relevant details about each culture as you read.

Chavín	
Location	
Unique achievements	

The first cultures of South America developed in the Andean region along the western edge of the continent. This region includes a variety of climates and terrains. The narrow coastal plain is a dry, lifeless desert crossed by occasional rivers. Further inland, the snow-capped Andes Mountains rise steeply, leveling off into high plateaus that bake by day and freeze at night. East of the Andes, dense jungles stretch from Peru into Brazil.

Cultures Develop in the Andes

Thousands of years ago, people settled in fishing villages along the desert coast of Peru and Chile. Gradually they expanded inland, farming the river valleys that run up into the highland plateaus. Using careful irrigation, they grew maize, cotton, squash, and beans. On mountain slopes, they cultivated potatoes, eventually producing 700 varieties. On high plateaus, they domesticated the llama and the alpaca. Eventually, they built large ceremonial centers and developed skills in pottery and weaving.

Chavín Culture Unifies a Region Archaeologists have pieced together a chronology of various cultures that left their mark on the Andean region over the course of 2,000 years. The earliest of these was the **Chavín** (chah VEEN) culture, named for ruins at Chavín de Huantar (chah VEEN day WAHN tahr). There, in about 900 B.C., people built a huge temple complex. Archaeologists are not sure of the Chavín political structure, but they think the culture's religion unified people throughout northern and central Peru. Chavín arts and religion continued to influence later peoples of Peru as well.

The Moche Build a Culture Between A.D. 100 and A.D. 700, the Moche (MOH chay) people—named after their most famous city—forged a civilization along the arid north coast of Peru. Skilled Moche farmers developed methods for fertilizing the soil and used canals to irrigate the land. Their leaders built roads and organized networks of relay runners to carry messages, ideas that another Andean civilization, the Inca, would later adopt.

At the city of Moche, builders constructed the largest adobe structure in the ancient Americas. Adobe is a mixture of clay and plant fibers that becomes hard as it dries in the sun. Moche artisans perfected skills in textile production, goldworking, and woodcarving and produced ceramic vessels in lifelike imitation of people and animals.

Cultures of the Southern Andes Many other Andean cultures emerged, and some left behind intriguing clues about their lives and beliefs. Between about 200 B.C. and A.D. 600 along the southern coast of Peru, the Nazca (NAHS kah) people etched geoglyphs in the desert. A geoglyph is a figure or line made on Earth's surface by clearing away rocks and soil. The Nazca geoglyphs include straight lines that run for miles as well as giant birds, whales, and other animals. Most researchers think that the geoglyphs carried some sort of spiritual meaning.

The city of Huari (WAH ree) developed east of the Nazca culture. It controlled much of Peru's mountain and coastal areas. At the same time, a powerful city, Tiahuanaco (tee ah wah NAH koh), developed on the southern shores of Lake Titicaca, in modern-day Bolivia. It reigned over parts of modern-day Argentina, Chile, and Peru. Many of the same artistic styles appear at Huari and Tiahuanaco, leading scholars to think that these two southern powers shared religious or trade affiliations.

✔ **Checkpoint** What was unique about the Nazca culture of the Andes?

Cultures of the Andes
For more than 2,000 years, cultures of varying sizes developed in the Andean region. Although not all as powerful as the Inca, most left behind fascinating clues to their skills and interests—such as this Moche laughing-man vessel (top right) and Nazca spider geoglyph (bottom right). *In the region of which earlier culture did the Inca build Cuzco?*

Pacific Ocean

Equator 0°

10°S

Chan Chan
Moche
Chavín de Huantar

Equal-Area Projection
0   250   500 mi
0   250   500 km

Huari
Cuzco

Tiahuanaco

20°S

30°S

Chavín culture,
900 B.C.–200 B.C.

Paracas culture,
600 B.C.–350 B.C.

Nazca culture,
200 B.C.–A.D. 500

Moche culture,
A.D. 100–A.D. 700

Huari culture,
A.D. 650

Tiahuanaco culture,
A.D. 700

Chimú culture,
A.D. 1475

Inca empire,
A.D. 1525

90°W   80°W

Inca Rulers Maintain a Large Empire

The most powerful of the Andean civilizations—the Inca civilization—came into being in the 1100s with the founding of its first dynasty. For the next three centuries, the Inca civilization stood out no more than any other. But in 1438, a historic change occurred. **Pachacuti Inca Yupanqui** (pahch ah KOO tee ING kuh yoo PANG kee), a skilled warrior and leader, proclaimed himself **Sapa Inca,** or emperor.

From his small kingdom at Cuzco in a high mountain valley, Pachacuti set out on a campaign of conquest. Once he subdued neighboring peoples, he enlisted them in his armies. His son, emperor Topa Inca Yupanqui, continued the expansion. With **Cuzco** as its capital, the resulting empire stretched more than 2,500 miles along the Andes, from Ecuador in the north to Chile in the south.

The Emperor Rules Over All The Sapa Inca held absolute power. Claiming to be divine, the son of the sun itself, he was also the empire's religious leader. Gold, considered the "sweat of the sun," served as his symbol. His queen, the Coya, carried out important religious duties and sometimes governed in his absence.

The Sapa Inca laid claim over all the land, herds, mines, and people of his empire. Thus the people had no personal property, so there was little demand for items for barter or sale. As a result, trade did not play a major role in the Inca economy. Instead, the Sapa Inca kept the people fed and public works projects staffed using a labor tax. Periodically, he would call upon men of a certain age to serve as laborers for short periods, perhaps a few months. By so doing, he could access millions of laborers at once.

Inca rulers ran an efficient government. Nobles ruled the provinces along with local chieftains whom the Inca armies had conquered. Below them, officials carried out the day-to-day business of enforcing laws and organizing labor. Specially trained officials kept records on a **quipu,** a collection of colored strings that were knotted in different ways to represent various numbers. Scholars think that the Inca, who never invented a writing system, may have used quipus to record economic, bureaucratic, religious, and other information.

Uniting the Empire To unite their empire, the Inca imposed their language, Quechua (KECH wuh), and their religion on the people they conquered. They also created one of history's great road <u>networks</u>. At its greatest extent, it wound about 14,000 miles through mountains and deserts, passing through an area inhabited by almost 10 million people. Hundreds of bridges spanned rivers and deep gorges. Steps were cut into steep slopes and tunnels dug through hillsides. The expanse of the Inca road system was unmatched in the early Americas.

The roads allowed armies and news to move rapidly throughout the empire. At stations set regular distances apart, runners waited to carry messages. Relays of runners could carry news of a revolt swiftly from a distant province to the capital. Inca soldiers stood guard at outposts throughout the empire. Within days of an uprising, they would be on the move to crush the rebels. Ordinary people were restricted from using the roads at all.

BIOGRAPHY

Pachacuti

Growing up, Pachacuti Inca Yupanqui (1391?–1473?) did not seem destined to rule the Inca people. True, his father, Viracocha, was their king. But Viracocha had chosen another son—Urcon—as his successor.

According to Inca sagas, one day the army of a powerful neighboring people, the Chanca, threatened to sweep down on Cuzco. With the Chanca army quickly approaching, Viracocha and Urcon withdrew from Cuzco to a nearby fort. Pachacuti remained to defend the city, commanding the army and inspiring his warriors on to a stunning victory. Pachacuti then set himself up as king of Cuzco, eventually reuniting the entire Inca state under his rule. **What traits and skills must Pachacuti have needed to become emperor?**

Vocabulary Builder

<u>network</u>—(NET wurk) *n.* a widely distributed group of things that work together as a unit or system

Cuzco as Capital All roads led through Cuzco. People from all the culture groups ruled by the empire lived in the city. Members of a given group lived in a particular part of the city and wore the traditional clothing and practiced the traditional crafts of their region of origin. In the heart of the city stood the great Temple of the Sun, its interior walls lined with gold. Like Inca palaces and forts, the temple was made of enormous stone blocks, each polished and carved to fit exactly in place without mortar used to secure it. Inca engineers were so precise that many of their buildings have survived severe earthquakes.

✓ **Checkpoint** Describe three ways that the Inca united their empire.

Daily Life of the Inca

The Inca strictly regulated the lives of millions of people within their empire. The leaders of each Inca village, called an **ayllu** (EYE loo), carried out government orders. They assigned jobs to each family and organizing the community to work the land. Government officials arranged marriages to ensure that men and women were settled at a certain age.

Farming the Land Inca farmers expanded step terraces built by earlier Andean peoples. They carved out flat strips of land on steep hillsides and built stone walls to hold the land in place. The terraces the Inca created kept rains from washing away the soil and made farming possible in places where naturally flat land was scarce.

Farmers spent part of each year working land for their community, and part working land for the emperor and the temples. The government allotted part of each harvest to specific groups of people or for particular purposes. It stored the rest in case of disasters such as famine.

Mastering Metalwork and Weaving The Inca were some of the most skilled metalworkers in the Americas. They learned to work and alloy, or blend, copper, tin, bronze, silver, and gold. While they employed copper

The Heights of Inca Stonework
Machu Picchu is the most impressive example of Inca stonework. Built high in the Andes, the large complex of buildings sits at an elevation of more than 7,000 feet. Agricultural terraces line the surrounding hillsides. *What challenges do you think the Inca faced when building in such a location?*

and bronze for useful objects, they reserved precious metals for statues of gods and goddesses, eating utensils for the nobles, and decoration.

The Inca also mastered the art of weaving, a practice passed down to them from earlier Andean peoples. They raised cotton and sheared the wool from llamas and alpacas to create colorful textiles to be worn as clothing or as adornments, such as belts and bags.

Medical Advances The Inca developed important medical practices, including surgery on the human skull. In such operations, they cleaned the area to be operated on and then gave the patient a drug to make him or her unconscious—procedures similar to the modern use of antiseptics and anesthesia. The Inca also used medical procedures to mummify the dead.

Religion and Ritual The Inca worshipped many gods linked to the forces of nature. People offered food, clothing, and drink to the guardian spirits of the home and the village. Each month had its own festival, from the great ripening and the dance of the young maize to the festival of the water. Festivals were celebrated with ceremonies, sports, and games.

A powerful class of priests served the gods. Chief among the gods was **Inti,** the sun god. His special attendants, the "Chosen Women," were selected from each region of the empire. During years of training, they studied the mysteries of the religion, learned to prepare ritual food and drink, and made the elaborate wool garments worn by the Sapa Inca and the Coya. After their training, most Chosen Women continued to serve Inti. Others joined the Inca's court or married nobles.

✔ **Checkpoint** How did the Inca excel in the arts and in medicine?

Looking Ahead

At its height, the Inca civilization was a center of learning and political power. But in 1525, the emperor Huayna Capac (WY nuh kah PAHK) died suddenly of illness. Civil war broke out over which of his sons would reign next, weakening the empire at a crucial moment—the eve of the arrival of Spanish invaders.

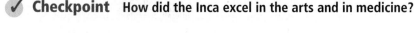

SECTION 2 Assessment

Progress Monitoring *Online*
For: Self-quiz with vocabulary practice
Web Code: naa-0621

Terms, People, and Places

1. Place each of the key terms at the beginning of the section into one of the following categories: culture, economy, and technology.

Note Taking

2. **Reading Skill: Contrast** Use your completed chart to answer the Focus Question: What characterized the cultures and civilizations that developed in the Andes?

Comprehension and Critical Thinking

3. **Demonstrate Reasoned Judgment** Why do you think that many separate cultures developed in the Andes before the Inca?

4. **Draw Conclusions** Explain three ways in which you think the Inca system of roads strengthened the empire.

5. **Identify Points of View** From the point of view of the Inca people, what might be some advantages of having an absolute ruler? What might be some disadvantages?

● **Writing About History**

Quick Write: Gather Details When you write a narrative essay, you often need to gather details about your topic. Suppose you want to write a narrative about the life of the Sapa Inca. Conduct research to find descriptions of the Sapa Inca's life and illustrations of artifacts that related to his rule. You may want to research a particular Sapa Inca, such as Pachacuti.

In This Chapter SSWHRC1a

Because they lived in vastly different geographic areas, early Americans interacted with their environment in a variety of ways. Mayan farmers burned rain forests to clear the land. High in the Andes, Incas carved out roads to tie their empire together (right) and built terraces to farm. Desert dwellers, like the Hohokam, built irrigation systems.

Throughout History

3200 B.C. Early civilizations begin to develop in river valleys.

1300 B.C. Divided by mountains and water, Greeks live in separate city-states.

1800s A.D. European nations compete to control Africa and its rich resources.

1800s The United States expands westward across the continent.

2000s Oil reserves in the Middle East make the region strategically important.

Continuing Today

Despite modern technology, geography still plays an important role in human activities. This woman is laying down hay barriers to hold back advancing desert sands.

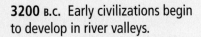 **21st Century Skills**

? TRANSFER Activities

1. Analyze How has geography influenced history?

2. Predict What geographic issues might affect how people live in the future?

3. Transfer Complete a Web quest analyzing the impact of geography; record your thoughts in the Concept Connector Journal; and learn to make a video. Web Code nah-0608

The Haida people believe a raven released the first people from a clam shell.

WITNESS HISTORY 🔊 AUDIO

Birth of Diverse Cultures

66 For a long time everyone spoke the same language, but suddenly people began to speak in different tongues. Kulsu [the Creator], however, could speak all of the languages, so he called his people together and told them the names of the animals in their own language, taught them to get food, and gave them their laws and rituals. Then he sent each tribe to a different place to live . . . 99
—Creation myth of the Maidu people of California

Focus Question What factors contributed to the growth of diverse cultures in North America?

Peoples of North America

GA **Performance Standards**

• **SSWH2a** Describe development of Indian civilization.

• **SSWHRC1a** Explore understanding of new words in subject area texts.

Terms, People, and Places

Mesa Verde	earthwork
pueblo	Cahokia
Pueblo Bonito	potlatch
kiva	Iroquois League

Note Taking

Reading Skill: Compare and Contrast As you read, outline the experiences and achievements of Native American groups in each culture area discussed. Then compare and contrast the details you have recorded for the various culture areas.

I. Southwest
  A. Environment
    1.
    2.
  B. Settlement type
    1.
    2.

Hundreds of Native American cultural groups lived in North America before A.D. 1500 and the arrival of Europeans. Based on the environments in which people lived, scholars have categorized them into ten culture areas: Arctic, Subarctic, Northwest Coast, California, Great Basin, Plateau, Southwest, Plains, Southeast, and Northeast. In each area, people adapted to geographic conditions that influenced their ways of life.

Peoples Adapt to the Desert Southwest

For millennia, Native American groups lived by hunting, fishing, and gathering wild plants. After farming spread north from Mesoamerica, many people raised corn and other food crops. Some people farmed so successfully that they built large permanent settlements. Some of the earliest farming cultures arose in what is today the southwestern United States.

The Hohokam Farm in the Desert Perhaps as long ago as 300 B.C., fields of corn, beans, and squash bloomed in the desert of present-day Arizona, near the Salt and Gila rivers. These fields were planted by a people later called the Hohokam, or "Vanished Ones," by their descendants, the Pima and the Papago. To farm in the desert, the Hohokam built a complex irrigation system that included numerous canals. The canals carried river water to fields as far as several miles away. The Hohokam also built temple mounds and ball courts similar in appearance to those of Mesoamerica. Evidence indicates that, for unknown reasons, the Hohokam left their settlements sometime during the A.D. 1400s.

Geography *Interactive*
For: Audio guided tour
Web Code: nap-0631

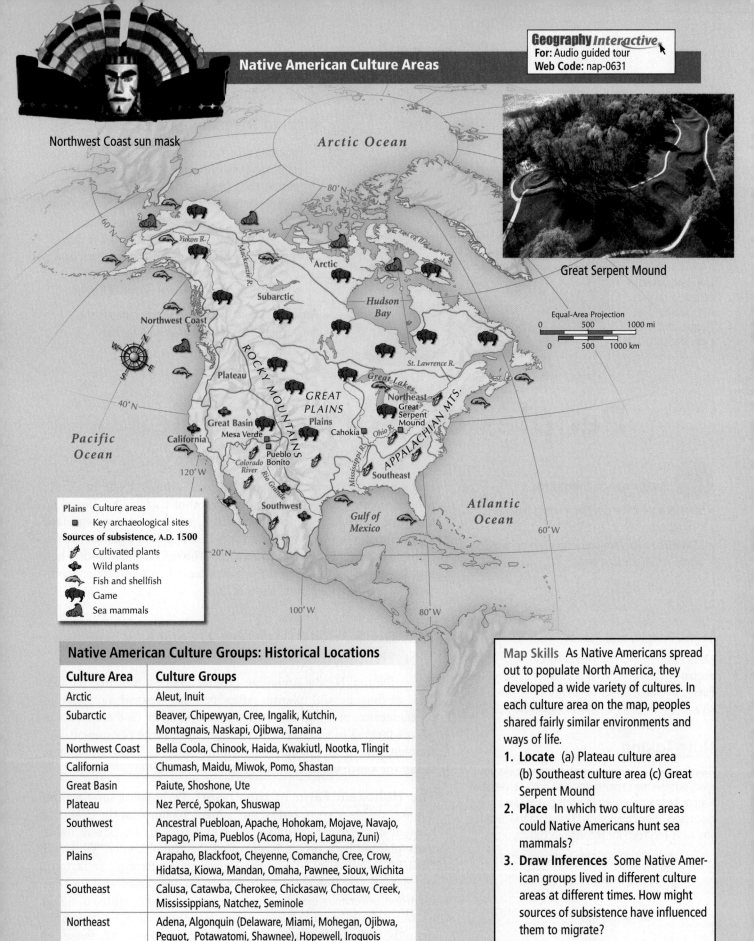

Northwest Coast sun mask

Great Serpent Mound

Arctic Ocean

80° N

60° N

Yukon R.

Mackenzie R.

Arctic

Subarctic

Hudson Bay

Northwest Coast

St. Lawrence R.

Plateau

ROCKY MOUNTAINS

Great Lakes

Northeast

Great Serpent Mound

40° N

GREAT PLAINS

Great Basin

Plains

Cahokia

Ohio R.

APPALACHIAN MTS.

Mesa Verde

Pacific Ocean

California

Pueblo Bonito

Colorado River

120° W

Mississippi R.

Southeast

Rio Grande

Southwest

Gulf of Mexico

Atlantic Ocean

60° W

20° N

100° W

80° W

Equal-Area Projection
0   500   1000 mi
0   500   1000 km

Plains Culture areas
■ Key archaeological sites
Sources of subsistence, A.D. 1500
🌾 Cultivated plants
🌿 Wild plants
🐟 Fish and shellfish
🦬 Game
🦭 Sea mammals

Native American Culture Groups: Historical Locations

Culture Area	Culture Groups
Arctic	Aleut, Inuit
Subarctic	Beaver, Chipewyan, Cree, Ingalik, Kutchin, Montagnais, Naskapi, Ojibwa, Tanaina
Northwest Coast	Bella Coola, Chinook, Haida, Kwakiutl, Nootka, Tlingit
California	Chumash, Maidu, Miwok, Pomo, Shastan
Great Basin	Paiute, Shoshone, Ute
Plateau	Nez Percé, Spokan, Shuswap
Southwest	Ancestral Puebloan, Apache, Hohokam, Mojave, Navajo, Papago, Pima, Pueblos (Acoma, Hopi, Laguna, Zuni)
Plains	Arapaho, Blackfoot, Cheyenne, Comanche, Cree, Crow, Hidatsa, Kiowa, Mandan, Omaha, Pawnee, Sioux, Wichita
Southeast	Calusa, Catawba, Cherokee, Chickasaw, Choctaw, Creek, Mississippians, Natchez, Seminole
Northeast	Adena, Algonquin (Delaware, Miami, Mohegan, Ojibwa, Pequot, Potawatomi, Shawnee), Hopewell, Iroquois (Cayuga, Erie, Huron, Mohawk, Onandaga, Oneida, Seneca, Tuscarora), Micmac, Winnebago

Map Skills As Native Americans spread out to populate North America, they developed a wide variety of cultures. In each culture area on the map, peoples shared fairly similar environments and ways of life.

1. **Locate** (a) Plateau culture area (b) Southeast culture area (c) Great Serpent Mound

2. **Place** In which two culture areas could Native Americans hunt sea mammals?

3. **Draw Inferences** Some Native American groups lived in different culture areas at different times. How might sources of subsistence have influenced them to migrate?

Ancestral Puebloans Build Cliff Dwellings and Pueblos About A.D. 100, Ancestral Puebloans lived in what is today the Four Corners region of Arizona, New Mexico, Colorado, and Utah. Within a few hundred years, they were building villages, some inside caves and some outside.

Between A.D. 1150 and A.D. 1300, the Ancestral Puebloans (also known as Anasazi) built their famous cliff residences. Using hand-cut stone blocks, they constructed housing <u>complexes</u> on cliffs along canyon walls. Such cliffs offered protection from raiders. The largest of these cliff dwellings, at **Mesa Verde** (MAY suh VEHR dee) in present-day Colorado, included more than 200 rooms. People climbed ladders to reach their fields on the flatlands above or the canyon floor below.

The Ancestral Puebloans also built freestanding villages, which were similar in structure to the cliff dwellings. These communities, which the Spanish later called **pueblos** (PWEB lohs), were made of multi-floor houses that were connected to one another by doorways and ladders.

Remains of **Pueblo Bonito,** the largest such pueblo, still stand in New Mexico. The huge complex consisted of 800 rooms that could have housed about 3,000 people. Builders used stone and adobe bricks to erect a crescent-shaped compound rising five stories high. In the center of the great complex lay a plaza. There, the Ancestral Puebloans dug their **kiva** (KEE vuh), a large underground chamber used for religious ceremonies and political meetings. In the kiva, they carved out a small hole in the floor, which represented the birthplace of the tribe. They also painted the walls with geometric designs and scenes of ritual or daily life.

In the late 1200s, a long drought forced the Ancestral Puebloans to abandon their dwellings. Attacks by Navajos and Apaches—peoples from the north—may have contributed further to their decline. However, Ancestral Puebloan traditions survived among several groups of descendants. Known collectively as Pueblo Indians, many of these groups continue to live in the southwestern United States today.

 Checkpoint What types of technological advances did early peoples of the Southwest make?

Vocabulary Builder

<u>complex</u>—(KAHM pleks) *n.* a whole composed of various interrelated parts

Cliff Palace, the largest dwelling at Mesa Verde, may have housed 250 people.

Cultures Develop in the East

Far to the east of the Ancestral Puebloans, in the Mississippi and Ohio river valleys, other farming cultures emerged after about 1000 B.C. They, too, left behind impressive constructions from which we can learn a great deal about their lives.

The Adena and Hopewell Build With Earth Both the Adena and the later Hopewell people of the Northeast are known for giant **earthworks** that they built for various purposes by heaping earth in piles and shaping them. Some of the earthworks were large burial mounds, others served as platforms for structures such as temples, and still others served as defensive walls. Mounds were usually cone-shaped, oval, or formed into the shape of an animal. The Adena's Great Serpent Mound in Ohio wriggles and twists in the shape of a snake for almost a quarter of a mile.

Some of the objects found in the Hopewell mounds show that traders extended their influence over a wide area. They acquired goods such as conch shells from the Gulf of Mexico, grizzly bear teeth and obsidian from the Rocky Mountains, and copper from the Great Lakes region. Skilled artisans then hammered and shaped the copper into fine ornaments.

The Mississippians Build Bigger By A.D. 800, these early eastern cultures had disappeared. A new people, whom today we refer to as the Mississippians, gained influence in the Southeast region. As their culture spread, the Mississippians built clusters of earthen mounds and ever larger towns and ceremonial centers.

The greatest Mississippian center, **Cahokia** in present-day Illinois, housed as many as 20,000 people by about A.D. 1100. Cahokia boasted 120 mounds, atop some of which sat the homes of rulers and nobles. The largest mound probably had a temple on its summit, where priests and rulers offered prayers and sacrifices to the sun.

The Natchez Carry on the Traditions The Mississippians left no written records, and their cities disappeared after Europeans reached the area. Their traditions, however, survived among the Natchez people, who are known for their worship of the sun. They called their ruler, who held absolute power, the Great Sun. He and his family lived on the top of pyramid mounds. Society was divided into castes, the highest group was called the suns.

✔️ **Checkpoint** What aspects of cultural life do the earthworks built by the Adena and Hopewell people reveal?

Unique Cultures Develop in Different Geographic Regions

Distinct ways of life developed in each Native American culture area. Here, we examine three cultures areas—the Arctic, the Northwest Coast, and the Eastern Woodlands—in which varied climates and natural environments helped unique cultures develop.

The Inuit Live in a Frozen World In the far northern stretches of Canada, the Inuit (IN oo it; often called the Eskimo) adapted to the harsh climate of the Arctic. By about 2000 B.C., they had settled there, using the resources of the frozen land to survive. Small bands lived by hunting and fishing. Seals and other sea mammals provided them with food, skins for clothing, bones for needles and tools, and oil for cooking. The Inuit paddled kayaks in open waters or used dog sleds to transport goods across the ice. In some areas, the Inuit constructed igloos, or dome-shaped homes made from snow and ice. In others, they built sod dwellings that were partly underground.

Adapting to the Arctic
The Inuit built kayaks with wood or whale bone, over which they stretched oiled animal skins to keep out water. As they paddled through icy waters on the hunt for seals (below right), they wielded harpoons and other weapons and wore snow goggles (below left) to protect their eyes from the glare. *How did the Inuit overcome the challenges of living in the harsh Arctic climate?*

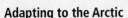

Thriving in a Land of Plenty
The peoples of the Northwest Coast lived in an environment far richer in natural resources than the Inuit did. Rivers teemed with salmon, and the Pacific Ocean offered a supply of other fish and sea mammals. Hunters tracked deer, wolves, and bears in the forests. In this land of plenty, people built large permanent villages with homes made of wood. They traded their surplus goods, gaining wealth that was then shared in a ceremony called **potlatch.** At this ceremony, which is still practiced in Canada and the Northwest coast of the United States today, a person of high rank and wealth distributes lavish gifts to a large number of guests. By accepting the gifts, the guests acknowledge the host's high status.

The Iroquois Join Together On the other side of the continent, the Northeast was home to numerous Native American groups. Many of these spoke the Iroquois (IHR uh kwoy) language, shared similar traditions, and were known collectively as the Iroquois. Typically, the Iroquois cleared land and built villages in the forests. While women farmed, men hunted and frequently fought wars against rival groups.

According to Iroquois tradition, the prophet Dekanawidah (deh kan ah WEE dah) urged these rivals to stop their constant wars. In the late 1500s, he became one of the founders of the unique political system known as the **Iroquois League.** This was an alliance of five Iroquois groups—the Mohawk, Oneida, Onondaga, Cayuga, and Seneca—who were known as the Five Nations. The Iroquois League did not always succeed in keeping the peace. Still, it was the best-organized political group north of Mexico. Member nations governed their own villages but met jointly in a council when they needed to address larger issues. Only men sat on the council, but each clan had a "clan mother" who could name or remove members of the council.

The Iroquois League emerged at the same time that Europeans arrived in the Americas. Just as encounters with Europeans would topple the Aztec and Incan empires, so too would they take a fearful toll on the peoples of North America.

✔ **Checkpoint** How did geography influence the Inuit way of life?

SECTION 3 Assessment

Terms, People, and Places
1. For each term, person, or place listed at the beginning of the section, write a sentence explaining its significance.

Note Taking
2. **Reading Skill: Compare and Contrast** Use your completed outline to answer the Focus Question: What factors contributed to the growth of diverse cultures in North America?

Comprehension and Critical Thinking
3. **Draw Conclusions** What challenges do you think the Ancestral Puebloans faced when constructing cliff dwellings? Consider location and natural resources.
4. **Categorize** Many of the earthen mounds built in the Southeast are similar in construction. What types of evidence do you think archaeologists looked for to establish the different purposes of these mounds?
5. **Analyze Information** What role do you think language played in enabling the political structure of the Iroquois?

● **Writing About History**
Quick Write: Write the Climax A narrative essay should include a climax—that is, the high point of the story that a reader will find most gripping. Suppose you want to write a narrative from the perspective of a member of one of the Native American groups you have read about in this section. Write a climax to the story you would tell of this person's life.

Primary Source

In about 1570, Dekanawidah persuaded warring Iroquois nations to form a confederacy, or an alliance for a common purpose. What benefits do you think a confederacy offered?

" I, Dekanawidah, and the confederate lords now uproot the tallest pine tree and into the cavity [hole] thereby made we cast all weapons of war. Into the depths of the earth . . . we cast all weapons of strife [conflict]. We bury them from sight forever and plant again the tree. Thus shall all Great Peace be established and hostilities shall no longer be known between the Five Nations but only peace to a united people. "

—The Constitution of the Five Nations

Quick Study Guide

GA SSWH8b

Progress Monitoring Online
For: Self-test with vocabulary practice
Web Code: naa-0641

■ Civilizations of Mesoamerica and South America

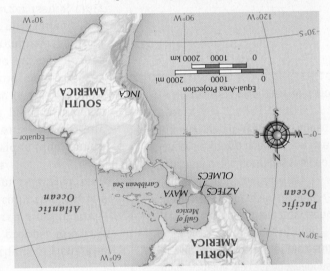

■ Key Sites of the Americas

North America
Mesa Verde—largest Ancestral Puebloan cliff dwelling
Pueblo Bonito—largest Ancestral Puebloan pueblo
Great Serpent Mound—large Adena earthwork
Cahokia—largest Mississippian center

Mesoamerica
La Venta, San Lorenzo—major Olmec ceremonial centers
Tikal, Calakmul—largest, most powerful Maya cities
Tenochtitlán—Aztec capital; future site of Mexico City
Teotihuacán—pre-Aztec city of religious importance to the Aztecs

South America
Chavín de Huantar—center of Chavín culture
Moche—center of Moche culture; site of the largest adobe structure in the Americas
Cuzco—capital of Inca empire

■ Cultures of North America

Culture Area	Culture Groups
Arctic	Aleut, Inuit
Subarctic	Beaver, Chipewyan, Cree, Ingalik, Kutchin, Montagnais, Naskapi, Ojibwa, Tanaina
Northwest Coast	Bella Coola, Chinook, Haida, Kwakiutl, Nootka, Tlingit
California	Chumash, Maidu, Miwok, Pomo, Shastan
Great Basin	Paiute, Shoshone, Ute
Plateau	Nez Percé, Spokan, Shuswap
Southwest	Ancestral Puebloan, Apache, Hohokam, Mojave, Navajo, Papago, Pima, Pueblos
Plains	Arapaho, Blackfoot, Cheyenne, Comanche, Cree, Crow, Hidatsa, Kiowa, Mandan, Omaha, Pawnee, Sioux, Wichita
Southeast	Calusa, Catawba, Cherokee, Chickasaw, Choctaw, Creek, Mississippians, Natchez, Seminole
Northeast	Adena, Algonquin, Hopewell, Iroquois, Micmac, Winnebago

■ The Rise of American Civilizations

1500 B.C.
The Olmecs establish the first American civilization.

900 B.C.
A huge temple complex emerges at Chavín de Huantar in Peru.

300 B.C.
The Maya are building large cities in Central America.

Chapter Events
World Events

1500 B.C.	1000 B.C.	500 B.C.

1122 B.C.
The Zhou dynasty begins its rule over China.

750 B.C.
Greek city-states such as Athens begin to develop.

200 B.C.
Axum begins to build a large trade network.

Concept Connector

❓ Essential Question Review

To connect prior knowledge with what you have learned in this chapter, answer the questions below in your Concept Connector journal. Use the journal in the Reading and Note Taking Study Guide to record your answers (or go to www.phschool.com **Web Code:** nad-0607). In addition, record information about the following concepts:

- People and the Environment: farming methods, the building of Tenochtitlán, geoglyphs, cliff dwellings, earthworks
- Empire: Aztec, Inca
- Science: Inca surgery

1. **Political Systems** The Aztecs spread their rule across most of Mexico. The Inca were the most powerful of the Andean civilizations. Describe similarities in the governments of these two cultures. Think about the roles of the following:
   - heads of state
   - nobles
   - priests

2. **Geography's Impact** Compare the geographic environments in which civilizations developed in India, Rome, South America, and Mesoamerica. How did natural features such as rivers, seas, mountains, valleys, and rain forests affect different aspects of civilization? Think about the following:
   - trade and economics
   - protection from attack
   - cultural diffusion
   - cooperation

3. **Cooperation** In the 1500s, a unique political system known as five Iroquois groups formed the Iroquois League. The five allied Iroquois groups were known as the Five Nations. What did these five Iroquois nations have in common? Why did they form an alliance? Suggest other ways that an alliance might have benefited the members of the Iroquois League.

■ Connections to Today

1. **Migration** Scholars trying to determine when and how the first people migrated to the Americas have not relied on archaeological evidence alone. Scientists have studied the genetic diversity of Native Americans today, which gives clues about how long ago their ancestors arrived in the Americas. Linguists have also studied the diversity of languages that Native Americans speak today to gain similar information about how long people have lived in the Americas. Do you think scholars can use these types of non-archaeological data to determine whether the first people arrived in the Americas by walking over land or traveling by boat? What other types of evidence might be useful to help answer the question?

2. **Geography's Impact** When the Aztecs founded Tenochtitlán, they modified the nearby environment in various ways—for example, by building chinampas and canals and filling in parts of the lake to expand the city. The same area is less supportive of a large modern city. In the same spot, more than 18 million people inhabit Mexico City. The surrounding mountains trap pollution from sources such as vehicle exhaust and factory smoke. Thus a cloud of smog hangs permanently over Mexico City. How can people influence the environment in both positive and negative ways? Research the situation in other modern cities, such as Los Angeles and Milan, to help you answer.

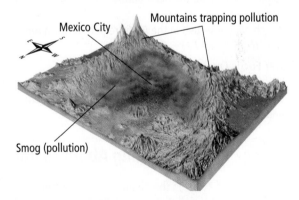

Mexico City

Mountains trapping pollution

Smog (pollution)

A.D. 100	A.D. 1100	A.D. 1325	A.D. 1438	A.D. 1500s
Ancestral Puebloans settle in the American Southwest.	The Mississippian center of Cahokia thrives.	The Aztecs found their capital at Tenochtitlán in Mexico.	Pachacuti founds the Inca empire in Peru.	The Iroquois League forms in the eastern United States.

A.D. 500   **A.D. 1000**   **A.D. 1500**

A.D. 622	A.D. 800	A.D. 1556
The Muslim prophet Muhammad leaves Mecca.	Charlemagne is crowned Holy Roman emperor by Pope Leo III.	Akbar begins his rule of Mughal India.

History *Interactive*

For: Interactive timeline
Web Code: nap-0641

Chapter Assessment

Terms, People, and Places

1. How did the Aztecs build **chinampas?** For what purpose?
2. From whom did the Aztecs collect **tribute?**
3. Describe what you might see on a Maya **stela.**
4. What is **adobe?** What did Moche people build with it?
5. Describe a **quipu.** What do scholars think the Inca may have used quipus for?
6. What was an Inca **ayllu?**
7. How were Ancestral Puebloan **kivas** constructed? What did each one represent?
8. What is a **potlatch?** In what culture area of North America was it originally practiced?
9. What was the **Iroquois League?** What was its main goal?

Main Ideas

Section 1 (pp. 186–194)
10. In which parts of the Americas did villages first arise? When?
11. Name three advances in learning made by the Maya.
12. Describe the social structure of the Aztec empire.

Section 2 (pp. 195–200)
13. Describe the control the Sapa Inca had over the government and over the Inca people.

Section 3 (pp. 201–205)
14. How were the Ancestral Puebloans innovative in their building of dwellings?
15. What purposes did the giant earthworks of the Adena and Hopewell people serve?
16. Which people settled in the Arctic region of North America? How did they live?

Chapter Focus Question
17. What circumstances helped the civilizations and diverse cultures of the Americas to develop in ways both common and unique?

Critical Thinking

18. **Geography and History** How do the land-bridge and coastal theories of how people migrated in the Americas differ? How does the time frame of the migration change depending on the theory?
19. **Make Comparisons** How were the farming methods developed by the Maya, the Aztecs, and the Inca different? How were they similar?
20. **Predict Consequences** With the arrival of Europeans in the 1500s, peoples of the Americas would face the threat of conquest by outsiders. Which peoples would you expect to fare the best against attack? Consider location in relation to other groups of people as well as natural features, language, and political organization as you answer.

21. **Synthesize Information** How was the role of trade in Inca society unique as compared to trade in the Maya and Aztec societies? Why?
22. **Analyzing Visuals** This page from an Aztec book shows a symbolic representation of Tenochtitlán. What parts of the image do you think represent Lake Texcoco and the canals the Aztec built? What Aztec legend does the bird in the center of the page represent?

● Writing About History

In this chapter's three Section Assessments, you developed skills to write a narrative essay.

Writing a Narrative Essay Write a narrative essay telling a story about one of the cultures of the Americas. If you have visited any of these cultures, write the story of your visit, including your impressions. Otherwise, write about the life of a historical individual or a fictional character from the Americas. Consult page SH8 of the Writing Handbook for additional help.

Prewriting
- Choose a culture to write about that you have visited or that interests you most.
- Choose a purpose for your essay. For example, you might want to share your own feelings about an experience or highlight a certain aspect of a culture that you think deserves attention.
- Gather details related to your essay topic.

Drafting
- Identify the climax, or most important part, of your story. Then decide what will happen in the beginning, middle, and end of the essay.
- Write an opening for the essay that will grab a reader's interest.
- Use many details to make the story vivid. Include dialogue when possible to convey your thoughts or those of your character.
- Write a conclusion that summarizes the significance of the experience to you or to the character.

Revising
- Use the guidelines for revising your essay on page SH9 of the Writing Handbook.

Prepare for the GHSGT

Aztec Training and Education

In Aztec society, a person's place in society was based on rank and family as well as ability. All children received an education that prepared them for a life of hard work. Most men labored in the fields, in trades and crafts, or on public works. Women worked hard in the home and learned the important skill of weaving. The process of educating Aztec youths was complex, as the documents below illustrate.

Document A

"First: thou art to be one who riseth from sleep. One who holdeth vigil through the night. Thou art not to give thyself excessively to sleep, lest . . . thou wilt be named a heavy sleeper . . . a dreamer. . . .

And second, thou art to be prudent in thy travels; peacefully, quietly, tranquilly, deliberately art thou to go. . . .

Third: thou art to speak very slowly, very deliberately. . . .

Fourth: thou art to pretend not to dwell upon that which is done, that which is performed. Especially art thou to . . . forsake evil. . . ."

—A nobleman's advice to his son, from ***General History of the Things of New Spain*** by Fray Bernardino de Sahagún

Document B

"[A]t fifteen . . . youths might enter either the *calmecac*, a temple or monastery in which they were entrusted to priests, or the school called the *telpochcalli*, 'the house of the young men', which was run by masters chosen from among the experienced warriors. . . . In theory the *calmecac* was kept for the sons and daughters of the dignitaries, but the children of the trading class were also admitted."

—From ***Daily Life of the Aztecs*** by Jacques Soustelle

Document C

Aztec girls grinding maize and learning to weave, from the Codex Mendoza, a 16th century Aztec book

Document D

"But even those who inherited high rank had to prove themselves and validate their status. Diplomatic skills or prowess on the battlefield could promote upward mobility. But, the close ties of family and lineage—the reality of birthright—were the fundamental cement of Mexica society."

—From ***The Aztecs*** by Brian M. Fagan

Analyzing Documents

Use your knowledge of history and Documents A, B, C, and D to answer questions 1–4.

1. Document A advises against
   A speaking freely.
   B traveling too often.
   C sleeping too much.
   D doing good.

2. What is the main point of Document B?
   A The Aztecs only educated youths from trading families.
   B Aztec higher education involved training by priests or warriors.
   C *Calmecacs* were temples or monasteries where children of noble and trade families could receive higher education.
   D The Aztecs provided higher education to only the most talented youths.

3. Based on Document D, how might youths who were not of noble birth advance themselves?
   A by marrying into a noble family
   B by training in the best schools
   C by a stroke of good fortune
   D by pursuing a career in trade

4. **Writing Task** Consider the advice of a nobleman in Document A. How might an aspiring Aztec tradesman advise his son or daughter? Use the information from these documents along with what you know from the chapter to answer this question.

Arctic Ocean

SCOTTISH
KINGDOMS ENGLISH
IRISH KINGDOMS
KINGDOMS
WALES Aachen
Europe
CHARLEMAGNE'S
EMPIRE
CHRISTIAN Rome Constantinople
SPAIN
MUSLIM BYZANTINE EMPIRE
STATES
ABBASID CALIPHATE Baghdad
Jerusalem
Mecca
GHANA NUBIAN
STATES
Axum
Africa AXUM

North
America

EARLY
MISSISSIPPIAN
CULTURES

ANASAZI
CULTURE

Atlantic
Ocean

Teotihuacán
Tikal
MAYA
CIVILIZATION

Pacific
Ocean

Bantu

Peoples

ANDEAN
CULTURES
Tiahuanaco

South
America

N
W E
S

The
WORLD
A.D. 800

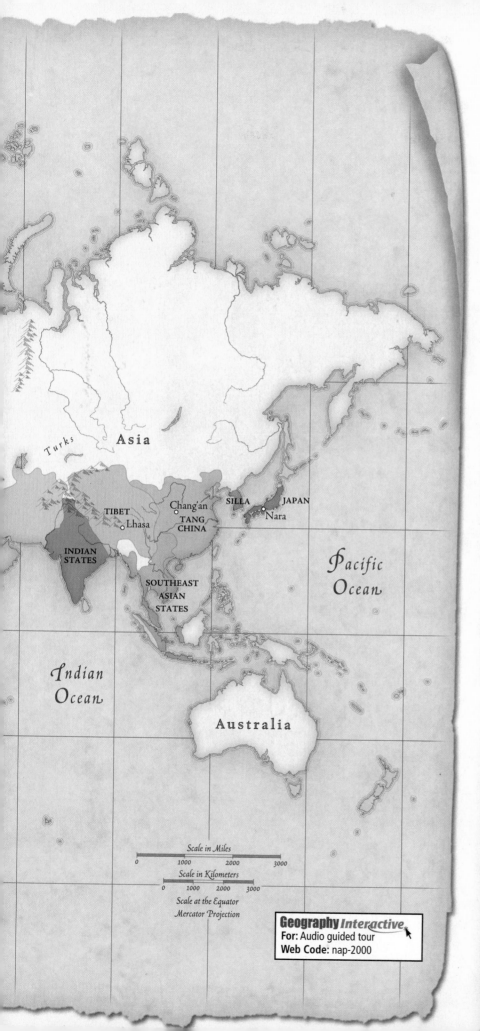

Turks

Asia

TIBET
Lhasa

Chang'an
TANG
CHINA

SILLA

JAPAN
Nara

INDIAN
STATES

SOUTHEAST
ASIAN
STATES

Pacific
Ocean

Indian
Ocean

Australia

Scale in Miles
0   1000   2000   3000

Scale in Kilometers
0   1000   2000   3000

Scale at the Equator
Mercator Projection

Geography *Interactive*
For: Audio guided tour
Web Code: nap-2000

UNIT

2

Regional Civilizations

730 B.C.– A.D. 1650

The Rise of Europe

500–1300

Tests of Skill and Courage

❝[A]lmost every fortnight tournaments were held. . . . [O]nce they had reached the field: all [the knights] did was lower their lances. You could see horses galloping on, lances flying into pieces, shields hacked to bits and men falling from saddles. . . . [Y]ou would have heard blows coming from swords, . . . helmets ringing and resounding; some grabbed at bridles to take men prisoner, whilst others, to defend themselves, smote with maces and swords.❞

Tournaments, or mock battles between knights, were often dangerous tests of skill and courage. Listen to the Witness History audio to hear more of this description, which was written in 1226.

◄ A medieval king and his court watch a tournament.

Medieval coat of arms

 Performance Standards

Chapter Focus Question How did feudalism, the manor economy, and the Church shape life in Western Europe as the regions slowly developed a new medieval culture?

A Frankish ornament in gold from the early Middle Ages

Section 1
The Early Middle Ages
SSWH7a

Section 2
Feudalism and the Manor Economy SSWH7a

Section 3
The Medieval Church
SSWH7b, SSWH7c

Section 4
Economic Recovery Sparks Change
SSWH7d

Use the ☑ **Quick Study Timeline** at the end of this chapter to preview chapter events.

A guild emblem

 Concept Connector ONLINE

To explore Essential Questions related to this chapter, go to PHSchool.com
Web Code: nad-0707

King Clovis (right); a
Frankish cross from
the 400s (above)

WITNESS HISTORY 🔊 AUDIO

A King Converts to Christianity

In A.D. 496, Clovis, warrior king of the Franks, was
engaged in a ferocious battle. According to the
Chronicle of St. Denis,

❝ He looked up to heaven humbly, and spoke
thus, 'Most mighty God, whom my queen
Clothilde worships and adores with heart and
soul, I pledge Thee perpetual service unto Thy
faith, if only Thou givest me now the victory
over mine enemies.' Instantly . . . his men
were filled with burning valor, and a great fear
smote his enemies, so that they turned the
back and fled.❞

Focus Question How did Germanic tribes divide
Western Europe into small kingdoms?

The Early Middle Ages

Performance Standards

• **SSWH7a** Explain the importance of
Charlemagne.

Terms, People, and Places

Clovis	battle of Tours
medieval	Charlemagne
Franks	Magyars
Charles Martel	Vikings

Note Taking

Reading Skill: Identify Main Ideas Keep track
of the important characteristics of early medieval
Europe in a table. Look for the main idea under each
red heading and write it in the second column.

Early Medieval Europe	
Heading	**Main Idea**
Western Europe in Decline	
The Rise of the Germanic Kingdoms	
The Age of Charlemagne	
Europe After Charlemagne	

King **Clovis** won this battle—and many others. The kingdom he
established was one of many Germanic kingdoms that replaced
the unifying force of the Roman empire in Western Europe.

Western Europe in Decline

At its height, the Roman empire included much of Western
Europe. Rome unified the region and spread classical ideas, the
Latin language, and Christianity to the tribal peoples of Western
Europe. The Germanic peoples who settled in Europe and con-
quered Rome would later build on these traditions.

After the collapse of Rome, Western Europe entered a period of
political, social, and economic decline. From about 500 to 1000, it
was politically divided, rural, and largely cut off from advanced civilizations in the Middle East, China, and India. Waves of invaders
swept across the region, trade slowed to a trickle, towns emptied,
and classical learning virtually ceased. For those reasons, this
period in Europe has sometimes been called the Dark Ages.

Today, historians recognize that this period was not "dark."
Greco-Roman, Germanic, and Christian traditions slowly blended,
creating a new civilization. Much later, this period between
ancient times and modern times—roughly from 500 to 1500—
would be called the Middle Ages. Its culture would be called
medieval civilization, from the Latin words for "middle age."

✔ **Checkpoint** Describe Western Europe after the collapse of
the western Roman empire.

The Rise of the Germanic Kingdoms

The Germanic tribes that conquered parts of the Roman empire included the Goths, Vandals, Saxons, and Franks. Their culture was very different from that of the Romans. They were mostly farmers and herders, so they had no cities or written laws. Instead, they lived in small communities governed by unwritten customs. Kings were elected by tribal councils. Warriors swore loyalty to the king in exchange for weapons and a share in the plunder taken from conquered people. Between 400 and 700, these Germanic tribes carved Western Europe into small kingdoms.

The Franks Extend Their Power One of these kingdoms was that of the Franks. In 486, Clovis, king of the Franks, conquered the former Roman province of Gaul, which later became the kingdom of France. He ruled his new lands according to Frankish custom but preserved much of the Roman legacy. Clovis took an important step when he converted to Christianity, the religion of his subjects in Gaul. Not only did he earn their support, but he also gained a powerful ally in the pope, leader of the Christian Church of Rome.

A Muslim Empire Threatens Europe As the Franks and other Germanic peoples carved up Europe, a new power was emerging across the Mediterranean. The religion of Islam began in Arabia in the 600s. From there, Muslims, or believers in Islam, created a new civilization and built a huge and expanding empire.

Leaders of the Church and of Christian kingdoms became alarmed when Muslim armies overran Christian lands from Palestine to North Africa to present-day Spain. When a Muslim army crossed into France, **Charles Martel** rallied Frankish warriors. At the **battle of Tours** in 732, Christian warriors triumphed. To them, the victory was a sign that God was on their side. Muslims advanced no farther into Western Europe, although they continued to rule most of what is now Spain. This nearby Muslim presence remained a source of anxiety to many European Christian leaders. In time, however, medieval Europeans would trade with Muslims, whose learning in many areas exceeded their own.

✔ **Checkpoint** How did the Germanic tribes govern their kingdoms?

The Age of Charlemagne

In 768, the grandson of Charles Martel became king of the Franks. He briefly united Western Europe when he built an empire reaching across what is now France, Germany, and part of Italy. Also named Charles, he became known as **Charlemagne** (SHAHR luh mayn), or Charles the Great.

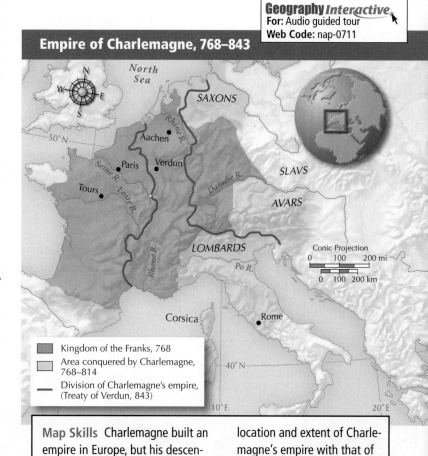

Empire of Charlemagne, 768–843

Legend:
- Kingdom of the Franks, 768
- Area conquered by Charlemagne, 768–814
- Division of Charlemagne's empire, (Treaty of Verdun, 843)

Map Skills Charlemagne built an empire in Europe, but his descendants were unable to hold it together.
1. **Locate** (a) the Frankish kingdom in 768 (b) Charlemagne's empire in 814 (c) Tours
2. **Compare** Look at a map of the Roman empire. Compare the location and extent of Charlemagne's empire with that of Rome.
3. **Predicting Consequences** What might be one result of the division of Charlemagne's empire? Explain.

The Age of Charlemagne	
Heading	**Main Idea**
A New Emperor of the Romans	
Creating a Unified Christian Empire	
A Revival of Learning	

Vocabulary Builder
<u>unify</u>—(YOO nuh fy) *v.* to combine into one

Charlemagne spent much of his 46-year reign fighting Muslims in Spain, Saxons in the north, Avars and Slavs in the east, and Lombards in Italy. His conquests reunited much of the old western Roman empire.

A New Emperor of the Romans In 799, Pope Leo III asked Charlemagne for help against rebellious nobles in Rome. The delegation that Charlemagne sent to Rome arrested Leo's opponents. On Christmas Day in the year 800, the pope showed his gratitude by placing a crown on Charlemagne's head and proclaiming him Emperor of the Romans.

This ceremony would have enormous significance. A Christian pope had crowned a Germanic king successor to the Roman emperors. In doing so, Pope Leo III revived the ideal of a united Christian community, which came to be called Christendom. At the same time, he also sowed the seeds for desperate power struggles between future popes and Germanic emperors.

The pope's action also outraged the emperor of the eastern Roman empire in Constantinople. While the western Roman empire had been collapsing, the eastern empire had continued to flourish. The eastern emperor saw himself as the sole Roman ruler. In the long run, the crowning of Charlemagne deepened the split between the eastern and western Christian worlds.

Creating a Unified Christian Empire Charlemagne strove to create a united Christian Europe. Working closely with the Church, he helped spread Christianity to the conquered peoples on the fringes of his empire. Missionaries converted many Saxons and Slavs.

Like other Germanic kings, Charlemagne appointed powerful nobles to rule local regions. To keep control of these provincial rulers, he sent out officials called *missi dominici* (MIH see daw mih NEE chee) to check on roads, listen to grievances, and see that justice was done. Charlemagne instructed the *missi* to "administer the law fully and justly in the case of the holy churches of God and of the poor, of wards and of widows, and of the whole people."

A Revival of Learning Charlemagne regarded education as another way to <u>unify</u> his kingdom. He could read but not write. Still, as a ruler, he saw the need for officials to keep accurate records and write clear reports. Charlemagne set out to revive Latin learning throughout his empire and encouraged the creation of local schools. He also wanted to revive the glory of Rome at his court at Aachen (AH kun). He brought many of the best scholars of Europe to the Palace School there.

✓ **Checkpoint** How did Charlemagne unify Europe?

The Palace School at Aachen

Charlemagne brought a respected scholar, Alcuin (AL kwin) of York, to direct the Palace School. Alcuin created a curriculum that included grammar, rhetoric, logic, arithmetic, geometry, music, and astronomy. Charlemagne, his family, his nobles, and his nobles' sons were all taught there, and it became a center of learning and lively discussion. Alcuin's system would become the educational model for medieval Europe.

Alcuin also hired scholars to copy ancient manuscripts, including the Bible and Latin works of history and science. In this way, the school preserved past knowledge for future generations.

Europe After Charlemagne

After Charlemagne died in 814, his son Louis I took the throne. Later, Louis' sons battled for power. Finally, in 843, Charlemagne's grandsons drew up the Treaty of Verdun, which split the empire into three regions.

Charlemagne's Legacy Although his empire did not remain intact, Charlemagne still left a lasting legacy. He extended Christian civilization into northern Europe and furthered the blending of Germanic, Roman, and Christian traditions. He also set up strong, efficient governments. Later medieval rulers looked to his example when they tried to strengthen their own kingdoms.

New Waves of Invasions Charlemagne's heirs faced new waves of invasions. Despite the victory at Tours, Muslim forces still posed a threat to Christian Europe. In the late 800s, they conquered Sicily, which became a thriving center of Muslim culture. Not until the 900s, when power struggles erupted in the Middle East, did Muslim attacks finally subside.

Geography *Interactive*
For: Audio guided tour
Web Code: nap-0712

Invasions of Europe, 700–1000

Map Skills Between 700 and 1000, Western Europe was battered by invaders.

1. **Locate** (a) France (b) Germany (c) Scandinavia (d) Hungary (e) Muslim-controlled lands

2. **Movement** Describe the invasion routes of the (a) Magyars, (b) Vikings, and (c) Muslims.

3. **Draw Inferences** Note which invaders built settlements. What can you infer about these groups from the fact that they settled in regions they raided?

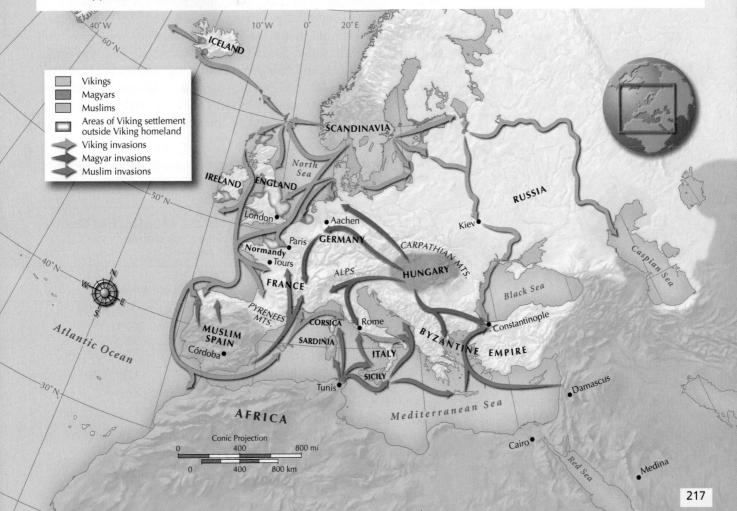

Viking Warship
This painting of a Viking warship with a prow in the shape of a mythical beast was done by an Anglo-Saxon artist around 1025. *What aspect of the ship does the artist emphasize? What does this suggest about the Anglo-Saxon reaction to the Vikings?*

About 900, a new wave of nomadic people, the **Magyars** settled in present-day Hungary. From there, they overran eastern Europe and moved on to plunder Germany, parts of France, and Italy. Finally, after about 50 years, they were pushed back into Hungary.

Raiders From the North The **Vikings** broke the last threads of unity in Charlemagne's empire. At home in Scandinavia—a northern region that now includes Norway, Sweden, and Denmark—the Vikings were independent farmers ruled by land-owning chieftains. They were also expert sailors. Starting in the late 700s, they burst out of Scandinavia, looting and burning communities along the coasts and rivers of Europe.

Viking sailors were not just destructive raiders. They were also traders and explorers who sailed around the Mediterranean Sea and across the Atlantic Ocean. Around the year 1000, they set up a short-lived Viking colony in North America. Vikings opened trade routes that linked northern Europe to Mediterranean lands. They also settled in England, Ireland, northern France, and parts of Russia, where they mixed with the local populations.

✓ **Checkpoint** Describe the invasions of Europe that took place after Charlemagne's death.

Progress Monitoring *Online*
For: Self-quiz with vocabulary practice
Web Code: naa-0711

SECTION 1 Assessment

Terms, People, and Places

1. For each term, person, or place listed at the beginning of the section, write a sentence explaining its significance.

Note Taking

2. **Reading Skill: Identify Main Ideas** Use your completed charts to answer the Focus Question: How did Germanic tribes divide Western Europe into small kingdoms?

Comprehension and Critical Thinking

3. **Recognize Cause and Effect** How did the collapse of the western Roman empire affect Western Europe?

4. **Summarize** How did the Franks create a kingdom in Western Europe, and what external threat did it face?

5. **Analyze Information** What made Charlemagne a successful leader?

6. **Express Problems Clearly** What happened to Charlemagne's empire after he died? Why?

● **Writing About History**

Quick Write: Explore a Topic Choose one person or group discussed in this section and write a series of questions that you could use to write a research report. For example, for the Vikings you could ask the following:

• What were Viking communities in Scandinavia like?

• What kind of community did the Vikings set up in North America?

A monarch knights a young man on the battlefield.

WITNESS HISTORY 🔊 AUDIO

Being Knighted on the Battlefield

A young man of good family has been trained in warfare. He has proven himself in battle, bravely assisting the knight he serves. Now, as another battle looms, his knightly master tells the young squire to kneel. The knight strikes the young man on the shoulder with the flat of his sword or his glove, and says "I make you knight." As his sponsor, the older knight also presents the young man with a sword and spurs. Now the young man is ready to fight for his lord. He has achieved a place of both honor and responsibility in the medieval world: he has become a knight.

Focus Question How did feudalism and the manor economy emerge and shape medieval life?

Feudalism and the Manor Economy

 Performance Standards

• **SSWH7a** Explain the manorial and feudalism systems.

Terms, People, and Places

feudalism	tournament
vassal	chivalry
feudal contract	troubadour
fief	manor
knight	serf

Note Taking

Reading Skill: Identify Main Ideas Use a flowchart to keep track of the main ideas of this section. Write the main idea of each red heading in the appropriate box.

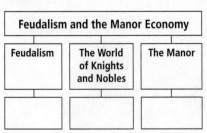

Feudalism and the Manor Economy

Feudalism	The World of Knights and Nobles	The Manor

Not all squires were knighted in battle. Others went through elaborate public ceremonies in which their responsibilities were carefully spelled out. Medieval society was a network of mutual obligations. Even kings and nobles exchanged vows of loyalty and service before witnesses. These vows were part of a new political and economic system that governed European life during the Middle Ages.

Feudalism Develops

In the face of invasions by Vikings, Muslims, and Magyars, kings and emperors were too weak to maintain law and order. People needed protection for themselves, their homes, and their lands. In response to this basic need for protection, a decentralized political and economic structure evolved, known as feudalism. **Feudalism** was a loosely organized system of rule in which powerful local lords divided their landholdings among lesser lords. In exchange, these lesser lords, or **vassals,** pledged service and loyalty to the greater lord. The way feudalism was put into practice varied from place to place and changed over time.

Mutual Obligations The political and economic relationship between lords and vassals was based on the exchange of land for loyalty and military service. It was established by custom and tradition and by an exchange of pledges known as the **feudal contract.** Under this system, a powerful lord granted his vassal a **fief** (feef), or estate. Fiefs ranged from a few acres to hundreds of square miles. In addition to the land itself, the fief included peasants to work the land, as well as any towns or buildings on it.

As part of this agreement, the lord promised to protect his vassal. In return, the vassal pledged loyalty to his lord. He also agreed to provide the lord with 40 days of military service each year, certain money payments, and advice.

A Structured Society All <u>aristocrats</u> had a place in this structure of power. Below the monarch were powerful lords, such as dukes and counts, who held the largest fiefs. Each of these lords had vassals, and these vassals in turn had their own vassals. In many cases, the same man was both vassal and lord—vassal to a more powerful lord above him and lord to a less powerful vassal below him.

Because vassals often held fiefs from more than one lord, relationships between them grew very complex. A vassal who had pledged loyalty to several lords could have serious problems if his overlords quarreled with each other. What was he to do if both demanded his aid? To solve this problem, a vassal usually had a liege lord to whom he owed his first loyalty.

✔ **Checkpoint**   What was the relationship between lords and vassals?

The World of Knights and Nobles

For medieval nobles, warfare was a way of life. Rival lords battled constantly for power. Many nobles began training in boyhood for a future occupation as a **knight,** or mounted warrior.

Vocabulary Builder
<u>aristocrats</u>—(uh RIS tuh krats) *n.*
members of the nobility

● **INFOGRAPHIC**

DEFENDING A CASTLE

Castles were made for defense. They were large complexes where many people and their supplies could hold out for long periods. They had strong, thick stone walls. A drawbridge over the castle moat—a ditch filled with water—could be raised in case of attack.

One way to capture a castle was by siege: the enemy would surround the castle and wait until the defenders' food ran out and they had to surrender. But soldiers could also attack by going over, through, or under the castle's defenses. Some attackers filled in the moat with stones or tunneled under the walls to weaken them until they collapsed. More often, they shot flaming arrows or hurled large stones over the walls. Some tried to go over the walls or to break down the gates.

Motte and Bailey Castle
This early type of castle was developed in the 800s. A keep, or tower, was built on a hill called a motte. A wooden bridge connected the motte to the bailey, a courtyard surrounded by a fence.

Battering Ram
Inside this hut on wheels was a huge log which soldiers used to break down the thick castle gate.

Catapult
A type of catapult called a trebuchet (TREB yoo shet) could hurl stones weighing 600 pounds (270 kilograms) as far as 1,000 feet (300 meters).

Knights and Warfare At the age of seven, a boy slated to become a knight was sent away to the castle of his father's lord. There, he learned to ride and fight. He also learned to keep his armor and weapons in good condition. Training was difficult and discipline was strict. Any laziness was punished with an angry blow or even a severe beating.

With his training finished, the youth was dubbed a knight, often in a public ceremony. His knight master or lord said words like these: "In the name of God, Saint Michael, and Saint George, I dub thee knight; be brave and loyal." Then the young knight took his place beside other warriors.

Knights usually fought on horseback using swords, axes, and lances, which were long poles. They wore armor and carried shields for protection. Other soldiers fought on foot using daggers, spears, crossbows, and longbows. In addition to actual warfare, knights engaged in mock battles called **tournaments.**

Castles and Defense During the early Middle Ages, powerful lords fortified their homes to withstand attack. The strongholds gradually became larger and grander. By the 1100s, monarchs and nobles owned sprawling stone castles with high walls, towers, and drawbridges over wide moats. They were not merely homes for the lords; they were also fortresses. The knights who defended the castle also lived there. In time of war, the peasants in the nearby villages would take refuge within the castle walls. Wars often centered on seizing castles that commanded strategic river crossings, harbors, or mountain passes.

History Interactive
For: An interactive activity
Web Code: nap-0721

Hooks and Ladders
The castle's defenders used poles with hooks to push away attackers' ladders. They also showered the enemy with hot oil and flaming arrows.

Siege Tower
If attackers could span the moat, they would roll this huge tower up to the castle walls. Then they faced hand-to-hand combat at the top.

Thinking Critically
1. **Express Problems Clearly** What were some of the drawbacks of using a castle for defense?
2. **Draw Inferences** What technologies developed in response to castle defenses?

Eleanor of Aquitaine

Eleanor (1122–1204), daughter of the Duke of Aquitaine, inherited her father's lands when he died in 1137. When she was only 15, she married the heir to the French throne. Eleanor had considerable influence over her husband, King Louis VII, and even accompanied him on the Second Crusade, wearing armor and riding on horseback alongside male crusaders.

When Louis ended his marriage to Eleanor, she regained control of Aquitaine. In 1152, she married another king, Henry II of England, and again became active in politics. In 1173, Eleanor aided several of her sons in an attempt to overthrow Henry. When the revolt failed, Henry had Eleanor imprisoned. After Henry died, her son Richard (known as "the Lion-Heart") became king of England. Richard freed his mother, and she later ruled in his place while he went on a crusade to the Holy Land. **How did Eleanor expand the usual role of medieval women?**

ENGLAND

Atlantic Ocean

FRANCE

Aquitaine

Noblewomen: Restrictions and Power Noblewomen played active roles in this warrior society. While her husband or father was off fighting, the "lady of the manor" took over his duties. She supervised vassals, managed the household, and performed necessary agricultural and medical tasks. Sometimes she might even have to go to war to defend her estate. A few medieval noblewomen took a hand in politics. For example, Eleanor of Aquitaine was a leading force in European politics for more than 50 years.

Women's rights to inheritance were restricted under the feudal system, although women did sometimes inherit fiefs. Land usually passed to the eldest son in a family. A woman frequently received land as part of her dowry, and fierce marriage negotiations swirled around an unmarried or widowed heiress. A widow retained her land.

Like their brothers, the daughters of nobles were sent to friends or relatives for training. Before her parents arranged her marriage, a young woman was expected to know how to spin and weave and how to supervise servants. A few learned to read and write. In her role as wife, a noblewoman was expected to bear many children and be dutiful to her husband.

Chivalry: Romance and Reality In the later Middle Ages, knights adopted a code of conduct called **chivalry.** Chivalry required knights to be brave, loyal, and true to their word. In warfare, they had to fight fairly. For example, a knight agreed not to attack another knight before the opponent had a chance to put on his armor. Warriors also had to treat a captured knight well or even release him if he promised to pay his ransom. Chivalry had limits, though. Its elaborate rules applied to nobles only, not to commoners.

But chivalry also dictated that knights protect the weak, and that included both peasants and noblewomen. In theory, if not always in practice, chivalry placed women on a pedestal. **Troubadours,** or wandering musicians, sang about the brave deeds of knights and their devotion to their lady loves. Their songs became the basis for epic stories and poems. Few real knights could live up to the ideals of chivalry, but they did provide a standard against which a knight's behavior could be measured.

 Checkpoint How was warfare central to life in the Middle Ages?

Manors Support Feudalism

The heart of the feudal economy was the **manor,** or lord's estate. Most manors included one or more villages and the surrounding lands. Peasants, who made up the majority of the population in medieval society, lived and worked on the manor.

Most peasants on a manor were **serfs,** bound to the land. Serfs were not slaves who could be bought and sold. Still, they were not free. They could not leave the manor without the lord's permission. If the manor was granted to a new lord, the serfs went along with it.

Lords and Peasants: Mutual Obligations

Peasants and their lords were tied together by mutual rights and obligations. Peasants had to work several days a week farming the lord's lands. They also repaired his roads, bridges, and fences. Peasants had to ask the lord's permission to marry. Peasants paid the lord a fee when they inherited their father's acres or when they used the local mill to grind grain. Other payments fell due at Christmas and Easter. Peasants had little opportunity to use money, so they paid with products such as grain, honey, eggs, or chickens.

In return for their labor and other payments, peasants had the right to farm some land for themselves. They were also entitled to their lord's protection from raids or warfare. Although they could not leave the manor freely, they also could not be forced off it. In theory, at least, they were guaranteed food, housing, and land. This system supported the nobility, making feudalism possible.

A Self-Sufficient World

During the early Middle Ages, the manor was generally self-sufficient. That is, the peasants who lived there produced almost everything they needed, from food and clothing to simple furniture and tools. Most peasants never ventured more than a few miles from their village. They had no schooling and no knowledge of a larger world outside.

A typical manor included cottages and huts clustered close together in a village. Nearby stood a water mill to grind grain, a church, and the lord's manor house. The fields surrounding the village were divided into narrow strips. Each family had strips of land in different fields so that good land and bad land were shared evenly.

Beyond the fields for growing crops, there were pastures for animals and meadows that provided hay. The forests that lay beyond the cleared land—and all the animals in them—were usually reserved for the use of the lord.

Life on the Manor

The lord of the manor and his family lived in relative luxury. As the illustration below shows, nobles had a variety of foods and were waited on by servants when they dined. Notice the lord's home, or demesne, in the medieval diagram at the right and compare it with the village homes of the peasants who worked his land.

Back-Breaking Labor
These peasants use sickles to harvest grain under the watchful eye—and cane—of the lord's official. A medieval sickle is shown above (right) along with a billhook for maintaining hedges. *What does the illustration suggest about peasant life?*

Peasant Life For most peasants, life was harsh. Men, women, and children worked long hours, from sunup to sundown. During planting season, a man might guide an ox-drawn plow through the fields while his wife walked alongside, urging the ox on with a pointed stick. Children helped in the fields, planting seeds, weeding, and taking care of pigs or sheep. In late winter, when the harvest was gone and new crops had not yet ripened, hunger was common. Disease took a heavy toll, and few peasants lived beyond the age of 35.

The peasant family ate a simple diet of black bread with vegetables such as cabbage, turnips, or onions. They seldom had meat—that was reserved for the lord. Peasants who poached, or illegally killed wild game on their lord's manor, risked harsh punishment. If they lived near a river, peasants might add fish to their diet. At night, the family and their livestock—cows, chickens, pigs, or sheep—slept together in their hut.

Still, peasants found occasions to celebrate, such as marriages and births. Welcome breaks came at Christmas and Easter, when peasants had a week off from work. At these times, people might butcher an animal for a feast. There would also be dancing and rough sports, from wrestling to ball games.

✔ **Checkpoint** How did the manor system work?

Progress Monitoring *Online*
For: Self-quiz with vocabulary practice
Web Code: naa-0721

SECTION 2 Assessment

Terms, People, and Places

1. For each term, person, or place listed at the beginning of the section, write a sentence explaining its significance.

Note Taking

2. **Reading Skill: Identify Main Ideas** Use your completed flowchart to answer the Focus Question: How did feudalism and the manor economy emerge and shape medieval life?

Comprehension and Critical Thinking

3. **Analyze Information** How did a lord benefit from giving his lands away as fiefs?

4. **Make Comparisons** Compare the rights and obligations of noblemen and noblewomen during the Middle Ages.

5. **Draw Conclusions** How did the manor serve the needs of the early Middle Ages?

● **Writing About History**

Quick Write: Develop a Thesis and Choose Supporting Information Choose a group discussed in this section. Write a sentence expressing your view of this group's place in medieval society. Jot down some information to support your statement. Revise this working thesis as you learn more. For example, you might begin with this thesis:

Peasants did most of the work but derived few benefits from the manor system.

On Pilgrimage

In the Middle Ages, most Western Europeans were devout Christians, and many of them went on pilgrimages to visit holy places. The medieval writer Geoffrey Chaucer noted that, when spring comes,

❝ Then people long to go on pilgrimages . . .
In England, down to Canterbury they wend
To seek the holy blissful martyr, quick
To give his help to them when they were sick. ❞
—Geoffrey Chaucer, *The Canterbury Tales*

Focus Question How did the Church play a vital role in medieval life?

Stained-glass illustration of pilgrims to Canterbury and a pilgrim badge (upper right) showing the saint Thomas Becket

The Medieval Church

 Performance Standards

- **SSWH7b** Describe political impact of Christianity and Pope Gregory VII.
- **SSWH7c** Explain role of church in medieval society.

Terms, People, and Places

sacrament	excommunication
Benedictine Rule	interdict
secular	friar
papal supremacy	St. Francis of Assisi
canon law	

Note Taking

Reading Skill: Identify Main Ideas Copy this concept web. As you read, fill in the main idea of each red heading. Add circles to record main ideas for the boldfaced headings.

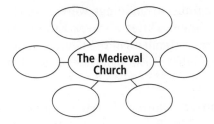

Pilgrimages were only one way that medieval Christians showed their devotion to their faith. The Church and its teachings were central to medieval life. It took centuries for Christian missionaries to spread their faith across Europe. But in time, the Roman Church emerged as the most powerful force in the region. Religion shaped the everyday lives of Christian Europeans, and the Church hierarchy came to exert considerable economic and political power.

The Church Dominates Medieval Life

During the early Middle Ages, the Church's most important achievement was converting the diverse peoples of Western Europe to Christianity. In 597, Pope Gregory I sent St. Augustine to convert the Anglo-Saxons in England. From Britain, later missionaries went back to the continent to spread their faith among Germanic tribes. By the late Middle Ages, Western Europe had become a Christian civilization. Anyone who did not belong to the church community was viewed with suspicion.

The Role of the Parish Priest Christian rituals and faith were part of the fabric of everyday life. In villages, the priest of the parish, or local region, was often the only contact people had with the Church. The priest celebrated the mass and administered the **sacraments,** the sacred rites of the Church. Christians believed that participation in the sacraments would lead them to salvation, or everlasting life with God. Priests also preached the teachings of the Church and explained the Bible, which was in Latin only. They guided people on moral issues and offered assistance to the sick and needy. In the later Middle Ages, some parish priests ran schools.

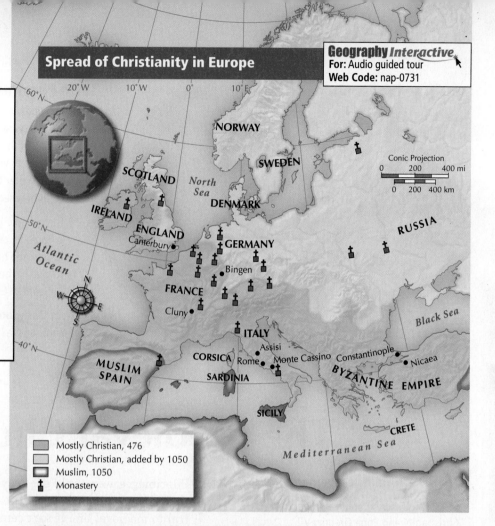

Spoken of Christianity in Europe

Geography *Interactive*
For: Audio guided tour
Web Code: nap-0731

Map Skills Missionaries helped spread Christianity throughout medieval Europe.

1. **Locate** (a) Canterbury (b) Rome (c) Cluny (d) Assisi
2. **Region** (a) Name three areas of Europe that became Christian between 476 and 1050. (b) Which areas of Europe came under Muslim control?
3. **Apply Information** (a) How does this map indicate the sequence of events? (b) What can you conclude about the spread of Christianity from this map?

Conic Projection

| Mostly Christian, 476 |
| Mostly Christian, added by 1050 |
| Muslim, 1050 |
| Monastery |

The Importance of the Village Church

The church was a social center as well as a place of worship because it was often the largest public building in a village. Daily life revolved around the Christian calendar, which included many holidays, such as Easter, and local holy days dedicated to saints. The main events of each person's life took place at the church. Baptism marked entrance into the community, marriages were performed on the church steps, and the dead were buried in the churchyard.

Villages took pride in their church buildings and decorated them with care. In later medieval times, prosperous communities built stone churches rather than wooden ones. Some churches housed relics, which could be possessions or remains of saints. Many people made pilgrimages, or religious journeys, to pray before the relics. The Church required Christians to pay a tithe, or tax equal to a tenth of their income. In the early Middle Ages, the tithe supported the local parish. Later, increasing amounts of money were sent to Rome.

The Rise of Cathedrals

Bishops, who supervised parish priests, managed larger churches called cathedrals. By the 1100s, communities used new technology to build huge cathedrals in the ornate, buttressed form known as the Gothic style. These magnificent buildings were a source of pride to the communities that built them. Cities all over Europe competed to build grander, taller cathedrals. Members of the Church contributed money, labor, and skills to help build these monuments glorifying their god.

Church Attitudes Toward Women

Church <u>doctrine</u> taught that men and women were equal before God. But on Earth, women were

Vocabulary Builder

<u>doctrine</u>—(DAHK trin) *n.* something taught as the principle of a religion

viewed as weak and easily led into sin. Thus, they needed the guidance of men. At the same time, the Church offered a view of the ideal woman in Mary, whom the Church believed to be the modest and pure mother of Jesus. Many churches were dedicated to the "mother of God" and "queen of heaven." Men and women asked Mary to pray to God on their behalf.

On the one hand, the Church tried to protect women. It set a minimum age for marriage. Church courts could fine men who seriously injured their wives. Yet they often punished women more harshly than men for similar offenses.

✓ Checkpoint What role did the Church play in the daily lives of medieval Christians?

Monasteries and Convents

During the early Middle Ages, some men and women withdrew from worldly life to the monastic life. They became monks and nuns. Behind the walls of monasteries and convents, they devoted their entire lives to spiritual goals.

Monastic Life: The Benedictine Rule About 530, a monk named Benedict organized the monastery of Monte Cassino in central Italy. He created rules to regulate monastic life. In time, the **Benedictine Rule** was used by monasteries and convents across Europe.

● **INFOGRAPHIC**

Life in a Monastery

▲ The ivory carving above shows monks at work in the scriptorium.

Monasteries were not only places where monks lived and prayed, they were also places of work and study. Many monasteries, or abbeys, housed self-contained communities that grew their own food and made many of the objects they used. Monks worked in the fields, in workshops, and in scriptoria, or writing rooms, where they copied and decorated manuscripts. Music was important to monastic life; and chants marked the canonical hours, or religious divisions, of the day.

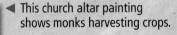

◄ This church altar painting shows monks harvesting crops.

▲ This picture of monks singing is in the center of the letter "C" in an illuminated manuscript.

Thinking Critically
1. **Make a Reasoned Judgment** Which of these activities do you think was most useful to medieval society as a whole? Explain.
2. **Make Comparisons** How were monasteries like manors?

An Educated Woman
Hildegard of Bingen was from a noble family. She founded an abbey, wrote plays, and composed music. ◀))) AUDIO

Under the Benedictine Rule, monks and nuns took three vows. The first was obedience to the abbot or abbess who headed the monastery or convent. The second was poverty, and the third was chastity, or purity. Each day was divided into periods for worship, work, and study. Benedict required monks to work in the fields or at other physical tasks. As part of their labor, monks and nuns cleared and drained land and experimented with crops. Because they developed better agricultural methods, they helped improve the economy of the Middle Ages, which was based on farming.

Service and Scholarship In a world without hospitals or schools, monasteries and convents often provided basic health and educational services. Monks and nuns looked after the poor and sick and set up schools for children. They gave food and lodging to travelers, especially to Christian pilgrims traveling to holy shrines. Some monks and nuns became missionaries. These missionaries spread Christianity throughout western and central Europe during the early Middle Ages.

Monasteries and convents also performed a vital role in keeping learning alive. Their libraries contained Greek and Roman works, which monks and nuns copied as a form of labor. Educated monks and nuns also wrote and taught Latin, which was the language of the church and educated people. In Britain, the Venerable Bede wrote the earliest known history of England.

Opportunities for Women Although women could not become priests, many did enter convents. There, capable women could escape the limits of society. In the 1100s, Abbess Hildegard of Bingen composed religious music and wrote books on many subjects. Because of her mystical visions, popes and rulers sought her advice.

In the later Middle Ages, the Church withdrew rights that nuns had once enjoyed, such as preaching the Gospels, and placed most independent convents under the control of Church officials. It frowned on too much learning for women, preferring them to accept Church authority.

✓ **Checkpoint** Describe monastic life according to Benedictine Rule.

Church Power Grows

In the centuries after the fall of Rome, the Church hierarchy carved out a unique position in Western Europe. It not only controlled the spiritual life of Christians but gradually became the most powerful **secular,** or worldly, force in medieval Europe.

The Church's Role in Society During the Middle Ages, the pope was the spiritual leader of the Western Christian Church, based in Rome. Declaring themselves representatives of God on Earth, medieval popes eventually claimed **papal supremacy,** or authority over all secular rulers, including kings and emperors. The pope headed an army of churchmen who supervised church activities. High clergy, such as bishops and archbishops, were usually nobles. Like other feudal lords, they had their own territories and armies. The pope himself held vast lands in central Italy, later called the Papal States. Some monasteries also held large tracts of land, which gave them considerable economic and political power.

Church officials were closely linked to secular rulers. Churchmen were often highly educated, so feudal rulers appointed them to government positions. In addition, Church officials were often relatives of secular rulers.

Religious Authority and Political Power The medieval Christian Church was dedicated to the worship of God. At the same time, Christians believed that all people were sinners and that many were doomed to eternal suffering. To avoid the tortures of hell, one had to do good works, believe in Christ, and participate in the sacraments. Because the Church administered the sacraments and could deny them as a punishment, it had absolute power in religious matters.

The Church developed its own body of laws, known as **canon law,** as well as its own courts. Canon law, based on religious teachings, governed many aspects of life, including wills, marriages, and morals. Anyone who disobeyed Church law faced a range of penalties. The most severe and terrifying was **excommunication.** Those who were excommunicated could not receive the sacraments or a Christian burial, which condemned them to hell for eternity. A powerful noble who opposed the Church could face the **interdict,** an order excluding an entire town, region, or kingdom from receiving most sacraments and Christian burial. Even the strongest ruler gave in rather than face the interdict, which usually caused revolts by the common people.

A Force for Peace The Church tried to use its great authority to end warfare among nobles. It declared periods of temporary peace known as the Truce of God. It demanded that fighting stop between Friday and Sunday each week and on religious holidays. Such efforts may have contributed to the decline of warfare in Europe during the 1100s.

✓ **Checkpoint** How did the Church gain secular power?

Corruption and Reform

The very success of the Church brought problems. As its wealth and power grew, discipline weakened. Pious Christians left their wealth and lands to monasteries and convents, leading some monks and nuns to ignore their vows of poverty. Some clergy lived in luxury. Priests could marry, but some spent more time on family matters than on religious duties, and some even treated the priesthood as a family inheritance. Throughout the Middle Ages, there were calls for reform in the Church.

Two Movements for Reform In the early 900s, Abbot Berno set out to reform his monastery of Cluny in eastern France. First, he revived the Benedictine Rule of obedience, poverty, and chastity. Then, he refused to allow nobles or bishops to interfere in monastery affairs. Instead, Cluny was placed under the direct protection of the pope. Over the next 200 years, many monasteries and convents copied these reforms.

In 1073, Gregory VII, a former monk, became pope and began another push for reform. He wanted to limit secular influence on the Church. Gregory insisted that the Church alone choose Church officials such as bishops. That policy eventually sparked a bitter battle of wills with the German emperor. Gregory also outlawed marriage for priests and prohibited simony (SY muh nee), the selling of Church offices.

New Preaching Orders **Friars,** monks who did not live in isolated monasteries, took a different approach to reform. They traveled around Europe's growing towns, preaching to the poor. The first order of friars, the Franciscans, was founded by a wealthy Italian now known as **St. Francis of Assisi.** Giving up his comfortable life, he devoted himself to preaching

BIOGRAPHY

St. Francis of Assisi
Famous stories about St. Francis of Assisi (1181?–1226) tell of him preaching to the birds and convincing a wolf to stop attacking townspeople if they, in turn, would feed the wolf. St. Francis regarded all nature as the mirror of God, and he called animals his brothers and sisters.

St. Francis came from a wealthy family and had been a fun-loving and worldly young man. Then, in his mid-20s, he heard a voice speak to him while he was praying. He gave up his wealth to "walk in the footsteps," or example, of Jesus. He was soon joined by a small group of followers—the first Franciscan friars—and together they lived a life of service to the poor and the sick. The Church made him a saint in 1228. **What great changes did St. Francis make in his life?**

the Gospels and teaching by his own examples of good works. The Franciscan order preached poverty, humility, and love of God. St. Dominic, a Spanish priest, founded the Dominican order of friars. Dominicans dedicated themselves to teaching official Christian beliefs in order to combat heresies, religious doctrines that differed from church teachings.

Women also supported the reform movement. Some became Dominican nuns and others joined the Poor Clares, linked to the Franciscans. Often these orders welcomed only well-born women whose families gave a dowry, or gift, to the church. Another group, the Beguines, welcomed poor women who could not be accepted by other religious orders.

✓ **Checkpoint** How did monks contribute to the reform of the Church?

Jews in Medieval Europe

In the Middle Ages, Jewish communities existed all across Europe. Jews flourished in present-day Spain, where Muslim rulers were tolerant of both Jews and Christians. Spain became a center of Jewish culture and scholarship, and Jews served as officials in Muslim royal courts. In other parts of Western Europe, Christians and Jews lived side by side in relative peace for centuries. Early German kings gave educated Jews positions at court. Many rulers in northern Europe valued and protected Jewish communities, although they taxed them heavily.

By the late 1000s, Western Europe had become more christianized, and prejudice against Jews increased. When faced with disasters they could not understand, such as illness or famine, Christians often blamed Jews. Jews were not part of the parish structure that regulated Christian lives. Therefore, they had little interaction with the Christians who were suspicious of a culture they did not understand. As the Church grew in power, it issued orders forbidding Jews to own land or practice most occupations. Yet popes and rulers still turned to educated Jews as financial advisers and physicians. In response to growing persecution, thousands of Jews migrated to Eastern Europe. There, rulers welcomed the newcomers' skills and knowledge. Jewish communities thrived in Eastern Europe until modern times.

✓ **Checkpoint** How were Jews treated in medieval Europe?

Preserving Jewish Culture
In spite of living in predominantly Christian areas, Jews celebrated their own religious holidays during the Middle Ages. This 1300s menorah, or Hanukkah lamp, is from France. *Why do you think it might have been difficult for Jews to continue these celebrations?*

Progress Monitoring *Online*
For: Self-quiz with vocabulary practice
Web Code: naa-0731

SECTION **3** Assessment

Terms, People, and Places

1. What do the key terms listed at the beginning of this section have in common? Explain.

Note Taking

2. **Reading Skill: Identify Main Ideas** Use your completed concept web to answer the Focus Question: How did the Church play a vital role in medieval life?

Comprehension and Critical Thinking

3. **Synthesize Information** How did monks and nuns contribute to medieval life?

4. **Recognize Cause and Effect** (a) How did the Church increase its secular power? (b) How did riches and power lead to Church abuses and then to reforms?

5. **Draw Conclusions** Why did attitudes toward Jews change in medieval Europe?

● **Writing About History**

Quick Write: Write an Introduction
Write a working thesis statement about a person or group discussed in this section. Then use a quotation or dramatic event to grab your audience's attention and introduce your thesis. For example, a paper on Abbess Hildegard might begin with her words to a ruler:

"Take care the Highest King does not strike you down because of the blindness that prevents you from governing justly."

A Boy Learns a Trade

In the Middle Ages, boys were apprenticed by legal agreements such as this one:

> 66 I, Peter Borre, in good faith and without guile, place with you, Peter Feissac, weaver, my son Stephen, for the purpose of learning the trade or craft of weaving, to live at your house, and to do work for you . . . for four continuous years, promising you by this agreement to take care that my son does the said work, . . . will neither steal nor take anything away from you, nor fleen or depart from you for any reason, until he has completed his apprenticeship. 99
> —French apprenticeship agreement, 1248

Focus Question How did changes in agriculture and trade lead to the growth of towns and commerce?

A master blacksmith (above) brightens the flame while apprentices (at right) hammer the iron.

Economic Recovery Sparks Change

 Performance Standards

• **SSWH7d** Describe how trade led to the growth of towns and cities.

Terms, People, and Places

charter	middle class
capital	guild
partnership	apprentice
tenant farmer	journeyman

Note Taking

Reading Skill: Identify Main Ideas Outline the main ideas of this section. Use Roman numerals for the main idea of each red heading. Use capital letters for the main ideas of the black headings.

Economic Recovery Sparks Change

I. 1000s—agricultural revolution changed Europe
  A. New technologies allowed farmers to grow more crops.
  B.
II.

Like the earlier granting of fiefs, apprenticeship agreements laid out mutual obligations. The French apprenticeship agreement quoted above goes on to say, "And I, the said Peter Feissac, promise you, Peter Borre, that I will teach your son faithfully and will provide food and clothing for him." Enormous changes had to occur in medieval Europe before apprenticeship agreements became commonplace. And these changes began in agriculture.

An Agricultural Revolution

Changes in Europe by 1000 set the foundation for economic prosperity. It began in the countryside, where peasants adopted new farming technologies that made their fields more productive. The result was an agricultural revolution that transformed Europe.

Technology Improves Farming By the 800s, peasants were using iron plows that carved deep into the heavy soil of northern Europe. These plows were an improvement over wooden plows, which were designed for light Mediterranean soils rather than heavier northern soils. Also, a new kind of harness allowed peasants to use horses rather than oxen to pull the plows. Faster-moving horses could plow more land in a day than oxen could, so peasants could enlarge their fields and plant more crops.

Production and Population Grow Other changes brought more land into use. Lords who wanted to boost the incomes of their

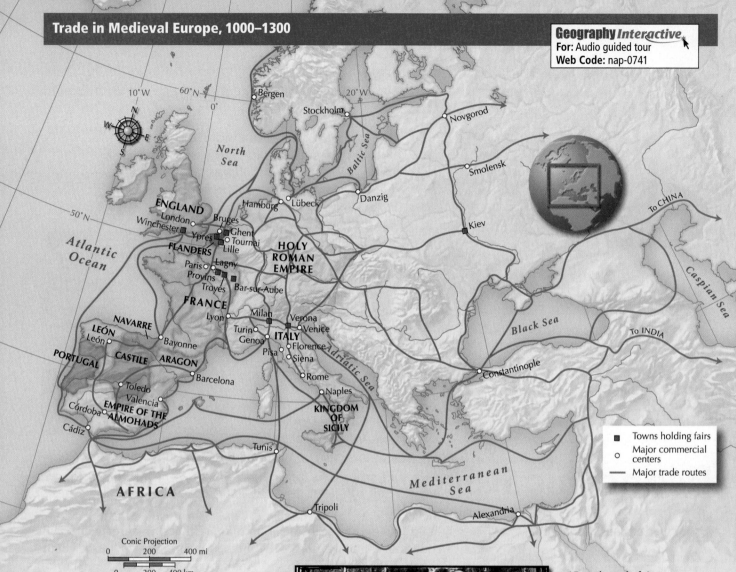

Towns holding fairs
Major commercial centers
Major trade routes

◀ French trade fair, fourteenth century

▲ Byzantine earrings, sixth century

Map Skills As trade revived in medieval Europe, trade routes multiplied and many towns hosted trade fairs.

1. **Locate** (a) Constantinople (b) Adriatic Sea (c) Venice (d) Flanders (e) London (f) Baltic Sea

2. **Region** In which areas were there (a) clusters of commercial centers? (b) clusters of trade fairs? (c) many converging trade routes?

3. **Draw Inferences** Why do you think many of these trade routes avoided overland travel and went by sea or river? What does this suggest about travel during this time?

Trade Fairs: Fun and Profit

Before the onset of widespread travel, traders and their customers did business at local trade fairs. These fairs took place each year near navigable rivers or where busy trade routes met. People from the surrounding villages, towns, and castles flocked to the fairs. Peasants traded farm goods and animals and enjoyed the antics of jugglers, acrobats, or even dancing bears. Nobles, wealthy churchmen, and well-off townspeople bought luxury goods such as fine swords, sugar, and silks.

manors had peasants clear forests, drain swamps, and reclaim wasteland for farming and grazing. Peasants also adopted a new way of rotating crops: the three-field system. They planted one field with grain; a second with legumes, such as peas and beans; and the third they left unplanted. The legumes restored fertility to the soil and added protein to the peasants' diet. The new method left only one third of the land unplanted, rather than half. All these improvements allowed farmers to produce more food. With more food available, the population began to grow. Between about 1000 and 1300, the population of Europe almost tripled.

✔ **Checkpoint** Why did agricultural production improve?

The Revival of Trade and Travel

As Europe's population grew, other changes also took place. In the 1100s, feudal warfare and foreign invasions declined. People felt safer, and began to travel more. The crusaders brought luxury goods back to Europe from the Middle East. Wealthy nobles desired goods that could not be produced on manors. Peasants needed iron for farm tools. Traders began to crisscross Europe to meet the growing demand for goods.

Trade Routes Expand Enterprising traders formed merchant companies that traveled in armed caravans for safety. They followed regular trade routes, many of which had hardly been used for centuries. Along these routes, merchants exchanged local goods for those from remote markets in the Middle East and farther east into Asia.

In Constantinople, merchants bought Chinese silks, Byzantine gold jewelry, and Asian spices. They shipped these goods by sea to Venice, where traders loaded their wares onto pack mules and headed north to Flanders. There, other traders bought the goods at trade fairs and sent them to England and lands along the Baltic Sea. Northern Europeans paid for these goods with products such as honey, furs, cloth, tin, and lead.

In the 1200s, German towns along the Baltic Sea formed the Hanseatic League, an association to protect their trading interests, which dominated trade in Northern Europe for more than 150 years. It took action against robbers and pirates, built lighthouses, and trained ships' pilots.

The Growth of Towns and Cities Many trade fairs closed in the autumn, when the weather made roads impassable. Merchants might wait out the winter near a castle or in a town. These settlements attracted artisans who made goods that merchants could sell. Slowly, these small centers of trade and handicraft became the first medieval cities. Some boasted populations of 10,000, and by the fourteenth century, a few topped 100,000. Europe had not seen towns of this size since Roman times. The richest cities emerged in northern Italy and Flanders—the two ends of the profitable north-south trade route. Both areas were centers of the wool trade and had prosperous textile industries.

To protect their interests, the merchants who set up a new town asked the local lord, or the king himself, for a **charter.** This written document set out the rights and privileges of the town. In return, merchants paid the lord or the king a large sum of money, a yearly fee, or both. Most charters also had a clause, popular with runaway serfs, that declared that anyone who lived in the town for one year and one day was free.

In the late 900s, a monk named Richer set out with a guide from Rheims to Chartres, where he planned to continue his studies. He described the journey:

Primary Source

66 We reached the bridge before the town but could barely see it in the rainy night. I became even more anxious because the bridge had so many holes and large gaps that the citizens of Meaux could hardly cross it in the daytime, much less in the dark—and in a storm! . . .[W]e faced a difficult path over the bridge. As we went, the messenger put his shield over the smaller holes for the horses. He used planks for the larger gaps. At times he would be bending over, now standing up, now running here and there in order to keep the horses calm and safe. 99
—Richer of Rheims AUDIO

Why were roads and bridges in such poor condition at this time?

Although charters (below) varied from place to place, they almost always granted townspeople the right to choose their own leaders and control their own affairs. At the left, a town in Flanders receives its charter.

Meanwhile, as Europe's population grew, manors became overcrowded, and lords often allowed peasants to buy their freedom and move to towns.

✓ **Checkpoint**   How and why did medieval towns and cities grow?

A Commercial Revolution

As trade revived, the use of money increased. In time, the need for **capital,** or money for investment, <u>stimulated</u> the growth of banking houses. Merchants also extended credit to one another. That is, they arranged to delay payment for goods for a certain set time.

The Beginnings of Modern Business   To meet the needs of the changing economy, Europeans developed new ways of doing business. Groups of merchants joined together in **partnerships.** They pooled their funds to finance a large-scale venture that would have been too costly for any individual trader. This practice made capital more easily available. It also reduced the risk for any one partner because no one had to invest all his or her capital in the company.

Later, merchants developed a system of insurance to help reduce business risks. For a small fee, an underwriter insured the merchant's shipment. If the shipment was lost or destroyed, the underwriter paid the merchant most of its value. If the goods arrived safely, the merchant lost only the insurance payment.

Europeans adopted some practices from the Muslim merchants with whom they traded. These traders had developed methods of using credit rather than cash in their business. European versions included letters of credit and bills of exchange. For example, a merchant would deposit

Vocabulary Builder
<u>stimulated</u>—(STIM yuh layt ed) *v.* made more active

money with a banker in his home city. The banker would issue a bill of exchange, which the merchant could exchange for cash in a distant city. The merchant could thus travel without carrying gold coins, which were easily stolen.

Society Begins to Change These new business practices were part of a commercial revolution that transformed the medieval economy. Slowly, they also reshaped medieval society. For example, the use of money undermined serfdom. Feudal lords needed money to buy fine goods. As a result, many peasants began selling farm products to townspeople and paying rent to their lord in cash rather than in labor. By 1300, most peasants in Western Europe were either **tenant farmers,** who paid rent for their land, or hired farm laborers.

During the Middle Ages, the Church forbade Christians to lend money at interest. As a result, many Jews who were barred from other professions became moneylenders. Although moneylenders played an essential role in the growing medieval economy, their success led to resentment and a rise in anti-Jewish prejudice.

✓ **Checkpoint** Describe three changes of the commercial revolution.

The Rise of the Middle Class

In towns, the old social order of nobles, clergy, and peasants gradually changed. By the year 1000, merchants, traders, and artisans formed a new social class. In status, this class ranked between nobles and peasants, so it was called the **middle class.** Nobles and the clergy despised the new middle class. To nobles, towns were a disruptive influence beyond their control. To the clergy, the profits that merchants and bankers made from usury (YOO zhuh ree), or lending money at interest, were immoral.

The Role of Guilds In medieval towns, the middle class gained economic and political power. First, merchants and artisans formed associations known as **guilds.** Merchant guilds appeared first. They dominated town life, passing laws and levying taxes. They also decided whether to spend funds to pave the streets with cobblestones or make other town improvements.

In time, artisans came to resent the powerful merchants. They organized craft guilds. Each guild represented workers in one occupation, such as weavers, bakers, or goldsmiths. In some towns, struggles between craft guilds and the wealthier merchant guilds led to riots.

Guild members cooperated to protect their own economic interests. To prevent competition, they limited guild membership. No one except guild members could work in any trade. Guilds made rules to protect the quality of their goods, regulate hours of labor, and set prices. Guilds also provided social services. They operated schools and hospitals, looked after the needs of their members, and provided support for the widows and orphans of their members.

Becoming a Guild Member Becoming a guild member took many years of hard work. At the age of seven or eight, a child might become an **apprentice,** or trainee, to a guild master. The apprentice usually spent seven years learning the trade. The guild master paid no wages, but was required to give the apprentice food and housing. Few apprentices ever became guild masters unless they were related to one. Most worked for guild members as **journeymen,** or salaried workers. Journeymen often

Medieval Advertising
These guild emblems from 1602 are similar to those used by medieval guilds to represent their crafts. From the top: guild emblems for eyeglass-makers, armorers, barbers, and bakers. *Why do you think the emblems use both pictures and words?*

accused masters of keeping their wages low so that they could not save
enough to open a competing shop.

Women and the Guilds Women worked in dozens of crafts. A woman
often engaged in the same trade as her father or husband and might
inherit his workshop if he died. Because she knew the craft well, she
kept the shop going and sometimes became a guild master herself. Young
girls became apprentices in trades such as ribbonmaking and papermaking. Women dominated some trades and even had their own guilds. In
Paris, they far outnumbered men in the profitable silk and wool guilds. A
third of the guilds in Frankfurt were composed entirely of women.

✔ **Checkpoint** Why were guilds important in town life?

Town and City Life

Medieval towns and cities were surrounded by high, protective walls. As
a city grew, space within the walls filled to overflowing, and newcomers
had to settle in the fields outside the walls. Because of overcrowding, city
dwellers added second and third stories to their houses and shops.
Therefore, a typical medieval city was a jumble of narrow streets lined
with tall houses. Upper floors extended outward over the streets below,
making them dim even in daytime. Fire was a constant threat.

In the largest cities, a great cathedral or a splendid guild hall might
tower above humbler residences. Almost all cities and towns had a
church with a steeple that could be seen for miles. Around the church,
people usually lived in neighborhoods with people of similar backgrounds. This meant that guild members, such as butchers, lived in the
same area.

During the day, streets echoed with the cries of hawkers selling their
wares and porters grumbling under heavy loads. At night, the unlit
streets were deserted. Even a rich town had no garbage collection or
sewer system. Residents simply flung their wastes into the street. Some
larger cities passed laws to promote better sanitary conditions, such as
one requiring butchers to dump their garbage on the edge of town. Still,
towns remained filthy, smelly, noisy, and crowded—a perfect breeding
ground for disease.

✔ **Checkpoint** What were medieval cities like?

SECTION 4 Assessment

Terms, People, and Places

1. What do many of the key terms listed at
the beginning of this section have in
common? Explain.

Note Taking

2. **Reading Skill: Identify Main Ideas**
Use your completed outline to answer
the Focus Question: How did changes in
agriculture and trade lead to the growth
of towns and commerce?

Comprehension and Critical Thinking

3. **Recognize Cause and Effect** What
were two effects of the agricultural
revolution of the Middle Ages?

4. **Draw Conclusions** Why was the
revival of trade so important?

5. **Summarize** How did the emergence
of a middle class affect European life?
Explain.

6. **Draw Inferences** What were the
advantages and disadvantages of living
in a medieval city?

● **Writing About History**

Quick Write: Credit Sources Use a
library or the Internet to find three reliable
sources of information about a group discussed in this section. Include at least one
primary source. Use the guidelines in the
Writing Handbook to write bibliography
entries for your sources.

SSWHRC1b

The Canterbury Tales by Geoffrey Chaucer

In *The Canterbury Tales* (1387–1400), Geoffrey Chaucer presents a portrait of medieval English society. The *Tales* are a series of poems that focus on 29 men and women who are on a pilgrimage to the tomb of St. Thomas Becket in Canterbury. To help pass the time, they tell stories to one another. The detailed descriptions of each character provide a sharp look at three classes of society as they were developing in the 1200s and 1300s: nobles, the middle class, and peasants. In the passages below, Chaucer describes a noble knight, a wealthy merchant, and a humble plowman, or farmworker.

Geoffrey Chaucer (1343?–1400)

A knight

A merchant

There was a Knight, a most distinguished man,
Who from the day on which he first began
To ride abroad had followed chivalry,
Truth, honor, generousness, and courtesy.
He had done nobly in his sovereign's war
And ridden into battle, no man more,
As well in Christian as heathen places,
And ever honored for his noble graces[1]. . . .

There was a Merchant with a forking beard
And motley[2] dress; high on his horse he sat,
Upon his head a Flemish beaver hat
And on his feet daintily buckled boots. . . .
He was expert at currency exchange.
This estimable[3] Merchant so had set
His wits to work, none knew he was in debt,
He was so stately[4] in negotiation,
Loan, bargain, and commercial obligation. . . .

There was a Plowman with him there, his brother.
He was an honest worker, good and true,
Living in peace and perfect charity. . . .
For steadily about his work he went
To thrash his corn, to dig or to manure
Or make a ditch; and he would help the poor
For love of Christ and never take a penny
If he could help it, and, as prompt as any,
He paid his tithes in full when they were due. . . .

1. **graces** (GRAYS iz) *n.* decency, thoughtfulness, and manners
2. **motley** (MAHT lee) *adj.* of many colors
3. **estimable** (ES tuh muh bul) *adj.* deserving respect
4. **stately** (STAYT lee) *adj.* dignified

Thinking Critically

1. **Identify Point of View** Which of these characters does Chaucer seem to disapprove of? How can you tell?
2. **Analyze Literature** What qualities do the knight and the plowman have in common? How do they show these qualities?

Quick Study Guide

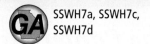 SSWH7a, SSWH7c, SSWH7d

Progress Monitoring *Online*
For: Self-test with vocabulary practice
Web Code: naa-0751

■ Why Did Europe Decline?

- The western Roman empire collapsed.
- Invaders swept across the region.
- Trade, travel, towns, and learning all decreased.
- Germanic kingdoms carved up a once-unified empire.

■ Key Figures in the Rise of Europe

- Clovis, *King of the Franks, who converted to Christianity*
- Charles Martel, *leader of the Franks at the battle of Tours*
- Charlemagne, *emperor who united much of Western Europe into a Christian kingdom*
- Eleanor of Aquitaine, *politically influential wife of King Louis VII of France and later of King Henry II of England, and mother of King Richard, the Lion-heart*
- Benedict, *monk who instituted the Benedictine Rule for monastic life*
- St. Francis of Assisi, *founder of Franciscan order of friars*

■ Feudalism and the Manor System

FEUDALISM		THE MANOR SYSTEM	
Lord to Vassal ↔	Vassal to Lord	Lord of Manor to Peasants ↔	Peasants to Lord
• Fief (land, buildings, workers) • Protection	• Loyalty • Military service • Certain fees • Advice	• Use of land for farming • Protection • Could not be forced off land	• Money or crops as rent • Labor on lord's lands • Certain fees

■ Role of the Church

Daily Life	Economic Power	Political Power
• Mass • Sacraments • Religious calendar • Aid to needy • Moral guidance	• Owned large tracts of land • People willed riches to Church • Agricultural and commercial activity in monasteries	• Papal supremacy • Threat of excommunication, interdict • Raised own armies • Clergy served in governments • Moral authority

■ Rise of Towns and the Middle Class

Agricultural Revolution	→	Revival of Trade	→	Towns and the Middle Class
• Production increases. • Population grows.		• Warfare decreases. • Travel becomes safer. • Desire for foreign goods increases. • Trade fairs develop. • Towns and cities grow.		• As towns grow, merchants gain power. • Guilds form and become powerful. • Modern business practices develop. • The middle class gains power. • Trade and commerce gain importance.

■ The Rise of Europe

500s
Germanic tribes such as the Franks dominate Western Europe, carving the region into small kingdoms.

732
At the battle of Tours, Christian armies stop the Muslim advance into Europe.

800
Charlemagne is crowned emperor by the pope and begins to unite much of Western Europe into a Christian empire.

Chapter Events
Global Events

500	600	700	800

527
Justinian begins his rule of the Byzantine Empire.

600s
Maya civilization thrives in the Americas.

622
The Muslim prophet Muhammad leaves Mecca, signaling the beginning of the religion of Islam.

Concept Connector

 Essential Question Review

To connect prior knowledge with what you have learned in this chapter, answer the questions below in your Concept Connector journal. Use the journal in the Reading and Note Taking Study Guide to record your answers (or go to www.phschool.com **Web Code:** nad-0707). In addition, record information about the following concepts:

• **Geography's Impact:** Vikings

1. **Empire** During his long reign, Charlemagne built an empire that stretched across the present-day nations of France, Germany, and part of Italy. How did Charlemagne gain control of a vast empire? How was he able to maintain control over his empire?

2. **Trade** During the 1100s, travel and trade became easier throughout Europe. Write a paragraph explaining how the following factors affected trade in Europe:
   • population growth
   • decrease in foreign invasions
   • safety of travel
   • trade routes
   • banks

3. **Political Systems** The feudal system was based on exchanges of land and serfs for loyalty and military service. Explain how the Agricultural Revolution and the revival of trade and travel led to the end of the feudal system. Think about the following:
   • population
   • charters
   • money

■ Connections to Today

1. **Cooperation: The European Union** The Romans and Charlemagne attempted to unify Western Europe. Later in the Middle Ages, the Holy Roman Empire and the Church clashed over control of the region. When European nation-states developed, they became economic and military rivals. Now, however, there is an effort to unite Europe through cooperation rather than conquest. The European Union was established in 1993, and a common currency called the euro came into use in 1999. The photo below shows a produce stand in Spain at the time of transition to the euro. Notice that the prices are displayed in both the old Spanish currency and the euro. Research and write a brief report on the European Union and the euro. Discuss their history and how well they have succeeded in unifying Europe.

2. **Economic Systems: Banking** You have read that medieval merchants extended credit to one another, and about early forms of letters of credit and bills of exchange. Do research to find out more about these early banking practices. Then investigate how they are used today. Write a brief report comparing these banking practices then and now.

900s	1000s	1200s	
Viking raiders plunge much of Europe into disorder, contributing to the emergence of European feudalism.	**The European economy begins to recover. The growth of trade and towns are signs of this revival.**	**The Dominican and Franciscan orders of Christian friars are founded.**	**History Interactive** For: Interactive timeline Web Code: nap-0751

900   **1000**   **1100**   **1200**

960	**1100s**	**1230**
The Song dynasty is founded in China.	**Feudalism develops in Japan.**	**Sundiata founds the empire of Mali in West Africa.**

Chapter Assessment

Terms, People, and Places

Choose the italicized term in parentheses that best completes each sentence.

1. The king of the Franks who conquered Gaul and converted to Christianity was (*Clovis/Charles Martel*).
2. Scandinavian raiders from the north were (*Magyars/Vikings*).
3. When a lord inherited a manor, he also gained control of the (*knights/serfs*) who worked on it.
4. The sacred rites of the church are called (*sacraments/canon law*).
5. Popes claimed (*excommunication/papal supremacy*), giving them authority over kings and emperors.
6. Monks who traveled around Europe preaching to the poor were called (*friars/secular*).
7. A (*charter/capital*) set out the rights and privileges of a town.
8. Medieval merchants joined together in (*charters/partnerships*) to reduce financial risk.

Main Ideas

Section 1 (pp. 214–218)
9. How were the Germanic tribes governed?
10. Why did Charlemagne's empire break up after his death?

Section 2 (pp. 219–224)
11. Describe the mutual obligations that emerged under feudalism.
12. How did medieval manors function?

Section 3 (pp. 225–230)
13. What role did the Church play in daily life?
14. How did the Church gain secular power?

Section 4 (pp. 231–237)
15. What were the effects of improvements in agriculture?
16. What led to the growth of towns?
17. What was the commercial revolution?

Chapter Focus Question
18. How did feudalism, the manor economy, and the Church shape life in Western Europe as the region slowly developed a new medieval culture?

Critical Thinking

19. **Recognize Cause and Effect** Why did the collapse of the western Roman empire lead to a new age in Western Europe?
20. **Draw Conclusions** Why was Charlemagne important even though his empire collapsed after his death?
21. **Make Comparisons** Compare and contrast the manor economy with the kind of economy that developed in towns during the commercial revolution.
22. **Synthesize Information** Why was the pope a powerful figure in medieval Europe?
23. **Recognize Cause and Effect** What social changes were caused by the commercial revolution? Explain why.
24. **Predict Consequences** How do you think the existence of a powerful Muslim empire on the fringes of Europe will affect the later Middle Ages? Explain why.

● Writing About History

In this chapter's four Section Assessments, you developed skills for writing a research report.

Writing a Research Report The Middle Ages produced a civilization very different from our own. Write a research report about one aspect of medieval civilization. To choose your topic, focus first on a group that interests you, such as knights, noblewomen, serfs, apprentices, monks, or merchants. Consult the Writing Handbook for additional help.

Prewriting
• Choose the group that interests you most and write a series of questions that reflect what you would like to learn about that group.
• Gather more resources and narrow your topic to one or two of the questions you listed.

Drafting
• Develop a working thesis and choose information from your sources to support it.
• Make an outline to organize your report.
• Write an introduction, body, and conclusion. Choose an interesting anecdote or quotation for your introduction or conclusion.

Revising
• Use the guidelines for revising your report on page SH15 of the Writing Handbook.

Prepare for the GHSGT

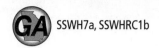

The Many Faces of Charlemagne

Medieval documents have provided historians with considerable detailed information about the life and reign of Charlemagne. The author of Document A was Charlemagne's personal biographer, who was a student of Alcuin at the Palace School at Aachen. Document C was written by the Monk of Saint Gall at the request of the royal family about 70 years after Charlemagne's death.

Document A

"Charles spent much time . . . in learning rhetoric [logic] and dialectic, and especially astronomy, from Alcuin. He learnt, too, the art of reckoning [mathematics], and . . . scrutinized most carefully the course of the stars. He tried also to learn to write, and for this purpose used to carry with him . . . tablets and writing-sheets that he might in his spare moments accustom himself to the formation of letters. But he made little advance in this strange task, which was begun too late in life."

—From *The Life of Charlemagne* by Einhard

Document B

◄ This image of Charlemagne was painted by a German artist in the 1500s.

Document C

"Once when he was on a journey Charlemagne came unheralded [unannounced] to a certain town which lies on the seashore in Southern Gaul. While he sat eating his supper incognito [in disguise], a raiding-party of Northmen [Vikings] made a piratical attack on the harbour of this town. As their ships came in sight, some said that they were . . . merchants. . . . Charlemagne in his wisdom knew better. From the build of the ships and their speed through the water he recognized them as enemies rather than merchants. 'Those ships are not loaded with goods,' he said to his men. 'They are loaded with savage enemies.' . . . [His men] rushed off to the ships at full speed, each striving to be the first to reach them. They were not successful. As soon as the Northmen learned that the man whom they were accustomed to call Charles the Hammer was in the neighbourhood, they sailed away at incredible speed."

—From *Charlemagne* by Notker the Stammerer, the Monk of Saint Gall

Document D

This image of Charlemagne on the battlefield was created about 1215. It is at the cathedral in Aachen, Germany, where Charlemagne is buried. ▼

Analyzing Documents

Use your knowledge of Charlemagne and Documents A, B, C, and D to answer questions 1–4.

1. The description of Charlemagne in Document A reveals that he
   A did not care about mathematics.
   B tried hard to educate himself.
   C was a great scholar.
   D was a poor student.

2. Which of the following statements best reflects what the author of Document C wants to convey about Charlemagne?
   A Both his men and his enemies feared him.
   B He was a knowledgeable and powerful military leader.
   C He was wise and willing to take personal risks.
   D He was powerful but has poor judgment.

3. Documents B and C best support the statement that
   A later Europeans admired Charlemagne.
   B Charlemagne was a great king.
   C Charlemagne was admired during his lifetime.
   D all Europeans admire Charlemagne.

4. **Writing Task** Think about the people who created the documents above and their possible motives for portraying Charlemagne. How reliable do you think the documents are? Write about at least two of the documents. Consider which details are probably reliable, how the documents provide insight into Charlemagne's character, and how they might be exaggerations.

Joan of Arc Fights for France

May 5, 1429—The French have been trying to drive the English out of France since 1337. Now a new leader, Joan of Arc, is turning the tide of the Hundred Years' War. She writes a letter to the enemy:

66You, men of England, who have no right to be in this Kingdom of France, the King of Heaven entreats and orders you through me, Joan the Maiden, to abandon your fortresses and go back to your own country; or I will make a disturbance such as will be eternally remembered.99

Listen to the Witness History audio to hear more about the great disturbance she created.

◄ Joan of Arc enters Orleans.

Joan of Arc's coat of arms

GA Performance Standards

Chapter Focus Question How did changing economic and social conditions, wars, and the growing power of monarchs begin to build the framework for the modern nation-state?

German imperial crown

Section 1
Royal Power Grows
SSWH7a

Section 2
The Holy Roman Empire and the Church
SSWH7b, SSWH7c

Section 3
The Crusades and the Wider World
SSWH5e, SSWH9c

Section 4
Learning and Culture Flourish
SSWH5e

Medieval inkwell and pen

Section 5
A Time of Crisis
SSWH7c

Use the ☑ **Quick Study Timeline** at the end of this chapter to preview chapter events.

 Concept Connector ONLINE

To explore Essential Questions related to this chapter, go to PHSchool.com
Web Code: nad-0807

German imperial crown

A lord pledges fealty to his king.

WITNESS HISTORY ◀》 AUDIO

A Struggle for Royal Authority

Medieval monarchs could not always count on the loyalty of their nobles and churchmen.

❝A.D. 1137 King Stephen . . . seized Alexander, bishop of Lincoln, and the Chancellor Roger, his nephew, and threw [them] into prison till they gave up their castles. . . . They had done him homage, and sworn oaths, but they no truth maintained. They were all forsworn, and forgetful of their troth [loyalty]; for every rich man built his castles, which they held against [the king]; and they filled the land full of castles.❞
—*The Anglo-Saxon Chronicle*

Focus Question How did monarchs in England and France expand royal authority and lay the foundations for united nation-states?

Royal Power Grows

 Performance Standards

• **SSWH7a** Explain the manorial and feudalism systems.

As medieval monarchs struggled to exert royal authority over nobles and churchmen, they slowly built the framework for the European nation-states of today. Nation-states are regions that share a government and that are independent of other states. Each of these nations developed differently, and a monarch's success in establishing power could have consequences for centuries.

Monarchs, Nobles, and the Church

During the early Middle Ages, as you have read, monarchs in Europe stood at the head of society but had limited power. Nobles and the Church had as much power as monarchs. In some cases, they were more powerful than monarchs. Both nobles and the Church had their own courts, collected their own taxes, and fielded their own armies. They jealously guarded their rights and privileges against any effort by monarchs to increase royal authority.

During the High Middle Ages—about 1000 to 1300—the balance of power started to shift. Monarchs used various means to centralize power. They expanded the royal domain and set up systems of royal justice that undermined feudal and Church courts. They organized government bureaucracies, developed tax systems, and built standing armies. Monarchs also strengthened ties with the townspeople of the middle class. Townspeople, in turn, supported royal rulers, who could impose the peace and unity that were needed for successful trade.

Terms, People, and Places

William the Conqueror	Magna Carta
common law	due process of law
jury	habeas corpus
King John	Parliament
	Louis IX

Note Taking

Reading Skill: Identify Causes Keep track of how royal power increased and decreased by using a cause-effect chart like the one below.

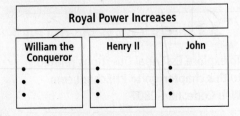

Royal Power Increases

William the Conqueror	Henry II	John
•	•	•
•	•	•
•	•	•

✓ **Checkpoint** What groups gained and lost power?

English Kings Strengthen Their Power

During the 400s and 500s, a group of Germanic tribes known as the Angles and Saxons, or Anglo-Saxons, conquered most of the Roman colony of Britain. The country became known as England. Despite Viking invasions in the 800s, a unified English kingdom emerged. In 1066, however, King Edward of England died without an heir. A council of nobles chose Edward's brother-in-law Harold to rule. But William, Duke of Normandy, in France, a tough descendant of Vikings, also claimed the English throne. He was related to King Edward, who, William claimed, had promised him the throne. The answer to the rival claims lay on the battlefield.

William of Normandy Conquers England William raised an army and won the backing of the pope. He then sailed across the English Channel to England. At the Battle of Hastings, William and his Norman knights triumphed over Harold. **William the Conqueror,** as he was now called, became king of England on Christmas Day 1066.

Although William's French-speaking nobles dominated England, the country's Anglo-Saxon population survived. Over the next 300 years, there was a gradual blending of Norman French and Anglo-Saxon customs, languages, and traditions.

Expanding Royal Power Now that William had conquered England, he set out to impose his control over the land. Like other feudal monarchs, he granted fiefs to the Church and to his Norman lords, or barons, but he also kept a large amount of land for himself. He monitored who built castles and where. He required every vassal to swear first allegiance to him rather than to any other feudal lord.

To learn about his kingdom, William had a complete census taken in 1086. The result was the *Domesday Book* (pronounced "doomsday"), which listed every castle, field, and pigpen in England. As the title suggests, the survey was as thorough and inevitable as doomsday, believed to be God's final day of judgment that no one could escape. Information in the Domesday Book helped William and later English monarchs build an efficient system of tax collection. William's successors also created the royal exchequer, or treasury, to collect taxes, fees, fines, and other dues.

Developing a Unified Legal System In 1154, an energetic, well-educated king, Henry II, inherited the throne. He broadened the system of royal justice by expanding accepted customs into law. He then sent out traveling justices to enforce these royal laws. The decisions of the royal courts became the foundation of English **common law,** a legal system based on custom and court rulings. Unlike local feudal laws, common law applied to all of England. In time, people brought their disputes to royal courts rather than to those of nobles or the Church. Because royal courts charged fees, the exchequer benefited from the growth of royal justice.

Under Henry II, England also developed an early jury system. When traveling justices visited an area, local officials collected a **jury,** or group of men sworn to speak the truth. These early juries determined which cases should be brought to trial and were the ancestors of today's grand jury. Later, another jury evolved that was composed of 12 neighbors of an accused person. It was the ancestor of today's trial jury.

Conflict With the Church Henry's efforts to extend royal power led to a bitter dispute with the Church over the issue of legal authority.

BIOGRAPHY

William the Conqueror

From the time he became Duke of Normandy at age seven, William the Conqueror's (1028–1087) life and position were in constant danger, mostly from jealous relatives. Four of his guardians were murdered—one in the very room in which William slept.

After William was knighted at the age of 15, he sought the help of his liege lord, Henry I of France, to put down rebellions by his barons. At 20, he led an army to defeat a rebellious cousin. His continuing efforts to gain power included putting pressure on Edward, the English king, to declare him heir to the English throne. **How did William's experience as duke prepare him to be a powerful king of England?**

Henry claimed the right to try clergy in royal courts. Thomas Becket, the archbishop of Canterbury and once a close friend of Henry, fiercely opposed the king on this issue. The conflict simmered for years.

At last, Henry's fury exploded. "What cowards I have brought up in my court," he cried. "Who will rid me of this meddlesome priest?" Four hotheaded knights took Henry at his word. In 1170, they murdered the archbishop in his own cathedral. Henry denied any part in the attack. Still, to make peace with the Church, he eased his attempts to regulate the clergy. Meanwhile, Becket was honored as a martyr and declared a saint. Pilgrims flocked to his tomb at Canterbury, where miracles were said to occur.

✔ **Checkpoint** How did William and Henry II increase royal power?

Evolving Traditions of Government

Later English rulers repeatedly clashed with nobles and the Church as they tried to raise taxes or to impose royal authority over traditional feudal rights. Out of those struggles evolved traditions of government that would have great influence on the modern world.

King John Makes Powerful Enemies A son of Henry II, **King John** was a clever, cruel, and untrustworthy ruler. During his reign, he faced three powerful enemies: King Philip II of France, Pope Innocent III, and his own English nobles. He lost his struggles with each.

Ever since William the Conqueror, Norman rulers of England had held vast lands in France. In 1205, John suffered a setback when he lost a war with Philip II and had to give up lands in Anjou and Normandy.

Next, John battled with Innocent III over selecting a new archbishop of Canterbury. When John rejected the pope's nominee, the pope excommunicated him. Innocent also placed England under the interdict—the papal order that forbade Church services in an entire kingdom. Even the strongest ruler was likely to give in to that pressure. To save himself and his crown, John had to accept England as a fief of the papacy and pay a yearly fee to Rome.

The Magna Carta Finally, John angered his own nobles with oppressive taxes and other abuses of power. In 1215, a group of rebellious barons cornered John and forced him to sign the **Magna Carta,** or great charter. This document contained two very important ideas that would shape English government in the future. First, it asserted that the nobles had certain rights. Over time, these rights were extended to all English citizens. Second, the Magna Carta made it clear that the monarch must obey the law.

Besides protecting their own privileges, the barons included provisions that recognized the legal rights of townspeople and the Church. Two of the most significant were in a clause protecting freemen from arbitrary arrest, imprisonment, and other legal actions, except "by legal judgment of his peers or by the law of the land." This clause formed the basis of the right we know today as **due process of law.**

Note Taking

Use a Venn diagram like the one below to show the similar and different ways royal power developed in England and France.

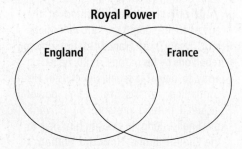

Royal Power

England   France

English nobles presented the Magna Carta to King John at Runnymede, a field along the Thames River. Why did King John agree to the Magna Carta?

Primary Source

❝ King John, when he saw that he was deserted by almost all, so that out of his regal superabundance of followers he scarcely retained seven knights, was much alarmed lest the barons would attack his castles and reduce them without difficulty, as they would find no obstacle to their so doing. . . . Accordingly, at the time and place pre-agreed on [Runnymede], the king and nobles . . . began a long discussion about terms of peace and aforesaid liberties. . . . King John, seeing that he was inferior in strength to the barons, without raising any difficulty, granted the underwritten laws and liberties, and confirmed them by his charter.❞

—Roger of Wendover

 AUDIO

Evolution of English Government

1066 Norman Conquest William, Duke of Normandy, defeats King Harold of the Anglo-Saxons at Hastings.

1086 *Domesday Book* King William uses this census, or survey of people and property, as a basis for taxation.

1160s–1180s Common Law Henry II uses accepted customs to lay the foundation for the English legal system.

1215 Magna Carta King John approves this document limiting royal power and extending rights to nobles and freemen.

1295 Model Parliament King Edward I expands Parliament to include representatives of common people as well as lords and clergy.

Chart Skills Which of the milestones above increased the power of the monarchy? Which limited the monarch's power? Explain your answers.

Model Parliament

The king presides over nobles and clergy, above. Representatives from towns and counties met separately.

A King Edward I   **D** Clergy

B Archbishops   **E** Barons (Lords)

C Kings of Scotland and Wales   **F** Judges

It is also seen as the basis for the right of **habeas corpus,** the principle that no person can be held in prison without first being charged with a specific crime. Habeas corpus was later clarified and defined in the Petition of Right (1628) and the Habeas Corpus Act (1679).

The king also agreed not to raise new taxes without first consulting his Great Council of lords and clergy. Many centuries later, American colonists would claim that those words meant that any taxation without representation was unjust. In 1215, though, neither the king nor his lords could have imagined such an idea.

The Development of Parliament In keeping with the Magna Carta, English rulers often called on the Great Council for advice. During the 1200s, this council evolved into **Parliament,** which later became England's legislature. As Parliament acquired a larger role in government, it helped unify England.

In 1295, King Edward I summoned Parliament to approve money for his wars in France. "What touches all," he declared, "should be approved by all." He had representatives of the "common people" join with the lords and clergy. The "commons" included two knights from each county and representatives of the towns. Much later, this assembly became known as the Model Parliament because it set up the framework for England's legislature. In time, Parliament developed into a two-house body: the House of Lords with nobles and high clergy and the House of Commons with knights and middle-class citizens. Over the centuries, Parliament gained the crucial "power of the purse": the right to approve any new taxes. With that power, Parliament could insist that the monarch meet its demands before voting for taxes. In this way, it could limit the power of the monarch.

✔ **Checkpoint** How was the power of the English king limited?

Successful Monarchs in France

Unlike William the Conqueror in England, monarchs in France did not rule over a unified kingdom. The successors to Charlemagne had little power over a patchwork of French territories ruled by powerful nobles.

The Capetian Kings In 987, these nobles elected Hugh Capet, the count of Paris, to fill the vacant French throne. They may have chosen him because they thought he was too weak to pose a threat to them. Hugh's own lands around Paris were smaller than those of many of his vassals.

Nevertheless, Hugh and his heirs slowly increased royal power. First, they made the throne hereditary, passing it from father to son. The Capetian dynasty lasted for 300 years, making the kingdom more stable. Next, they added to their lands by playing rival nobles against each other. They also won the support of the Church.

Perhaps most important, the Capetians built an effective bureaucracy. Government officials collected taxes and imposed royal law over the king's lands. By establishing order, they increased their prestige and gained the backing of the new middle class.

Philip Augustus Extends French Power In 1179, Philip II became king of France. Called Philip Augustus, he was a shrewd and able ruler. Instead of appointing nobles to fill government positions, Philip paid middle-class officials who would owe their loyalty to him. He granted charters to many new towns and introduced a new national tax.

Philip also quadrupled royal land holdings. Through trickery, diplomacy, and war, he gained control of English-ruled lands in Normandy, Anjou, and elsewhere. He then began to take over southern France. When he sent his knights to help the pope suppress a heretical group called the Albigensians (al buh JEN see unz) in the south, he was able to add this vast area to his domain. Before his death in 1223, Philip had become the most powerful ruler in Europe.

Vocabulary Builder

domain—(doh MAYN) *n.* territory under one ruler

Geography *Interactive*
For: Audio guided tour
Web Code: nap-0811

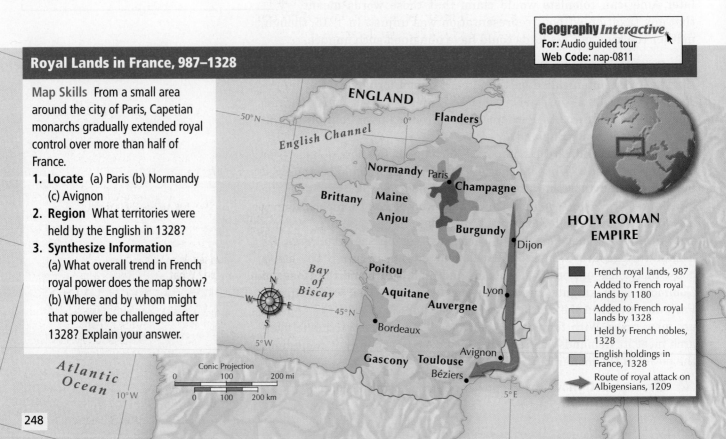

Royal Lands in France, 987–1328

Map Skills From a small area around the city of Paris, Capetian monarchs gradually extended royal control over more than half of France.

1. **Locate** (a) Paris (b) Normandy (c) Avignon
2. **Region** What territories were held by the English in 1328?
3. **Synthesize Information** (a) What overall trend in French royal power does the map show? (b) Where and by whom might that power be challenged after 1328? Explain your answer.

Legend:
- French royal lands, 987
- Added to French royal lands by 1180
- Added to French royal lands by 1328
- Held by French nobles, 1328
- English holdings in France, 1328
- Route of royal attack on Albigensians, 1209

Louis IX, King and Saint In 1226, Louis IX became King of France. A deeply religious man, Louis persecuted heretics, or those who held beliefs contrary to Church teachings. He also persecuted Jews and led French knights in two Crusades, or wars against Muslims. Within 30 years of his death, the Church declared him a saint.

Louis did much to improve royal government. Like Charlemagne, he sent out roving officials to check on local administrators. He expanded the royal courts, outlawed private wars, and ended serfdom in his personal domain. To ensure justice, he even heard cases himself. His enormous personal prestige helped create a strong national feeling among his subjects. By the time of his death in 1270, France was emerging as an efficient centralized monarchy.

Clashing With the Pope Louis's grandson, Philip IV, ruthlessly extended royal power. To raise cash, he tried to collect new taxes from the clergy. These efforts led to a clash with Pope Boniface VIII. Declaring that "God has set popes over kings and kingdoms," the pope forbade Philip to tax the clergy without papal consent. Philip threatened to arrest any clergy who did not pay. As their quarrel escalated, Philip sent troops to seize Boniface. The pope escaped, but he died soon afterward.

Shortly after, in 1305, a Frenchman was elected pope. Four years later, he moved the papal court to Avignon (ah vee NYOHN), just outside the southern border of France, where French rulers could exercise more control over it. Eventually, this move led to a crisis in the Church when another pope was elected in Rome. The rival popes each claimed to be the true leader of the Church.

Forming the Estates General During this struggle with the pope, Philip rallied French support by setting up the Estates General in 1302. This body had representatives from all three estates, or classes of French society: clergy, nobles, and townspeople. Although later French kings consulted the Estates General, it never gained the power of the purse or otherwise served as a balance to royal power.

✔ **Checkpoint** Describe how two French kings increased royal power.

Louis IX Leads a Crusade
The forces of King Louis IX attack Damietta, a city in Egypt. *What can you tell about medieval weapons and warfare from this painting?*

Section 1 Assessment

Progress Monitoring Online
For: Self-quiz with vocabulary practice
Web Code: naa-0811

Terms, People, and Places

1. What do many of the key terms listed at the beginning of the section have in common? Explain.

Note Taking

2. **Reading Skill: Identify Causes** Use your completed graphic organizers to answer the Focus Question: How did monarchs in England and France expand royal authority and lay the foundations for united nation-states?

Comprehension and Critical Thinking

3. **Analyze Information** How were nobles and the Church obstacles for monarchs who wanted more power?

4. **Summarize** How did William increase royal power in England?

5. **Draw Conclusions** Explain the importance of (a) the Magna Carta and (b) the Model Parliament.

6. **Synthesize Information** Describe the power struggle between French kings and the pope.

● **Writing About History**

Quick Write: Define a Topic Choose a central event or trend from this section. Ask yourself: What happened? When did it begin? What led up to it? What followed? Brainstorm causes and effects. For the growth of royal power in England, you might ask:

• How did William the Conqueror increase royal power?
• How did the nobles react to King John's abuse of power?

Magna Carta

In 1215, a group of barons, or lords, forced King John of England to put his royal seal on the Magna Carta. The barons were tired of the king's military campaigns and heavy taxes. Principles in the Magna Carta shape modern English law and government and influence governments around the world. Below are excerpts from 5 of the 63 articles of this important document.

1. We have also granted to all the freemen of our Kingdom, for us and our heirs, forever, all the underwritten Liberties, to be enjoyed and held by them and their heirs, from us and from our heirs.

12. No scutage [tax] nor aid shall be imposed in our kingdom, unless by the common council of our kingdom; excepting to redeem[1] our person, to make our eldest son a knight, and once to marry our eldest daughter, and not for these, unless a reasonable aid shall be demanded.

14. And also to have the common council of the kingdom, to assess and aid, otherwise than in the three cases aforesaid: and for the assessing of scutages, we will cause to be summoned the Archbishops, Bishops, Abbots, Earls, and great Barons, individually by our letters. And besides, we will cause to be summoned in general by our Sheriffs and Bailiffs[2], all those who hold of us in chief, at a certain day, that is to say at the distance of forty days (before their meeting), at the least, and to a certain place; and in all the letters of summons, we will express the cause of the summons; and the summons being thus made, the business shall proceed on the day appointed, according to the counsel of those who shall be present, although all who have been summoned have not come.

39. No freeman shall be seized, or imprisoned . . . nor will we condemn him, nor will we commit him to prison, excepting by the legal judgment of his peers, or by the laws of the land.

40. To none will we sell, to none will we deny, to none will we delay right of justice.

---

1. redeem (ri DEEM) *v.* to recover ownership of by paying a certain amount of money

2. bailiff (BAY lif) *n.* an official in England who collected taxes and acted as magistrate

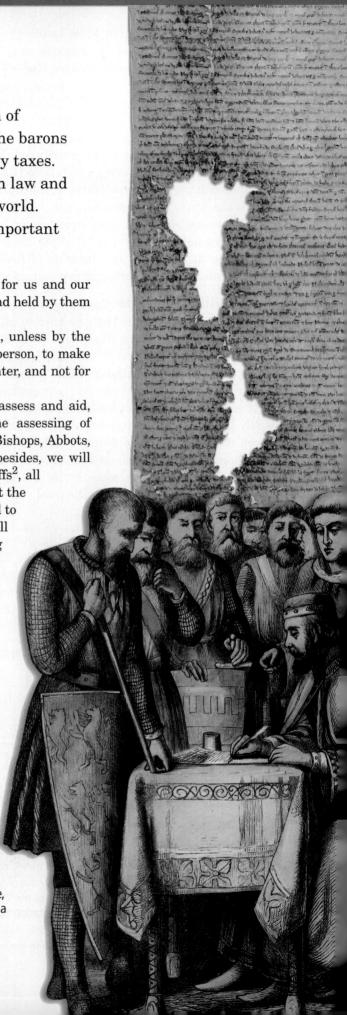

► King John approving the Magna Carta at Runnymede, and the Magna Carta itself (above)

Thinking Critically

1. **Draw Inferences** Who is not included in the membership of the general council, as described in Article 14? What can you infer from this omission?

2. **Make Generalizations** What do Articles 39 and 40 suggest about abuse of power at this time? Explain your reasoning.

Henry IV humbling himself before Pope Gregory VII

Holy Roman emperor's jewel-encrusted orb and cross

WITNESS HISTORY 🔊 AUDIO

An Emperor Begs Forgiveness

In 1076 Henry IV, emperor of the vast Holy Roman Empire, knelt in the snow outside an Italian castle. Inside was Pope Gregory VII, who had excommunicated Henry. Gregory described the event in a letter:

❝ Wretchedly with bare feet and clad in wool, [Henry] continued for three days to stand before the gate of the castle. Nor did he desist from imploring with many tears . . . until he had moved all . . . present . . . to such pity and depth of compassion. . . . Finally, won by the persistence of his suit . . . we . . . received him into the favor of communion and into the lap of the Holy Mother Church. ❞

Focus Question How did explosive conflicts between monarchs and popes affect the balance of power in Europe?

The Holy Roman Empire and the Church

GA Performance Standards

• **SSWH7b** Describe political impact of Pope Gregory VII and of King Henry IV of Germany.

• **SSWH7c** Explain role of church in medieval society.

Terms, People, and Places

Holy Roman Empire	lay investiture
Henry IV	Frederick Barbarossa
Pope Gregory VII	Pope Innocent III

Note Taking

Reading Skill: Understand Effects Complete a table to record the actions of Holy Roman emperors and popes and the effects of their actions.

Pope or Emperor	Actions	Effects
Otto I	• Cooperated with Church	• Pope crowned Otto emperor
Gregory VII		

During the early Middle Ages, the Church spread its influence and increased its power across Europe. Meanwhile, monarchs also became more powerful. By 1077, explosive conflicts had arisen between secular rulers and Church officials. The longest and most destructive struggle pitted popes against the rulers of the **Holy Roman Empire,** who ruled vast lands from Germany to Italy.

The Holy Roman Empire

In the early Middle Ages, Charlemagne brought much of present-day France and Germany under his rule. After his death, the empire dissolved into a number of separate states. In time, the dukes of Saxony extended their power over neighboring German lands. In 936, Duke Otto I of Saxony took the title King of Germany.

Otto I Becomes Emperor Like Charlemagne, Otto I worked closely with the Church. He appointed bishops to top government jobs. He also took an army into Italy to help the pope defeat rebellious Roman nobles. In 962, a grateful pope crowned Otto emperor. Later, Otto's successors took the title Holy Roman emperor—"holy" because they were crowned by the pope, and "Roman" because they saw themselves as heirs to the emperors of ancient Rome.

Emperors Struggle for Control German emperors claimed authority over much of central and eastern Europe as well as parts of France and Italy. In fact, the real rulers of these lands were the emperor's vassals— hundreds of nobles and Church officials. For German emperors, the challenge was to control their vassals. It was a challenge they never met.

Another challenge for the emperors involved the appointment of Church officials. Here, they <u>confronted</u> the power of the popes. Like other monarchs, the Holy Roman emperors often decided who would become bishops and abbots within their realm. At the same time, popes tried to end such interference in the Church from secular rulers.

✔ **Checkpoint** Describe the Holy Roman Empire.

The Feud Between Pope and Emperor

In 1054 **Henry IV** was crowned king of Germany; later he also became Holy Roman emperor. At that time, **Gregory VII** was pope. During their reigns, the conflict between monarchs and the Church erupted.

Gregory VII Causes Controversy Many medieval Europeans admired Pope Gregory VII, who instituted many Church reforms. At the same time, his policies aroused hatred and contempt. Gregory wanted to make the Church independent of secular rulers, so he banned the practice of **lay investiture.** Under this practice, the emperor or another lay person (a person who is not a member of the clergy) "invested," or presented, bishops with the ring and staff that symbolized their office. Only the pope, said Gregory, had the right to appoint and install bishops in office.

Henry IV Responds Pope Gregory's ban brought an angry response from the Holy Roman emperor, Henry IV. He argued that bishops held their lands as royal fiefs. Since he was their overlord, Henry felt entitled to give them the symbols of office. The feud heated up as the two men exchanged insulting letters. Meanwhile, rebellious German princes undermined Henry by supporting the pope.

The Struggle Intensifies In 1076, Gregory excommunicated Henry, freeing his subjects from their allegiance to the emperor. The pope then headed north to crown a new emperor. Faced with revolts, Henry was forced to make peace. In January 1077, he presented himself to the pope as a repentant sinner. Gregory knew that Henry was just trying to save his throne. Still, as a priest, the pope had no choice but to forgive a confessed sinner. He lifted the order of excommunication, and Henry quickly returned to Germany to subdue his rebellious nobles. He also took revenge on Gregory by leading an army to Rome and forcing the pope into exile.

A Compromise: The Concordat of Worms The struggle over investiture dragged on for almost 50 years. Finally, in 1122, both sides accepted a treaty known as the Concordat of Worms (vawrmz). This treaty declared that the Church had the sole power to elect and invest bishops with spiritual authority. The emperor, however, still invested them with fiefs.

✔ **Checkpoint** Describe the feud between the pope and the emperor.

Scenes from the Life of Pope Gregory
A medieval drawing shows Henry driving Gregory from Rome (top). Other scenes include Gregory excommunicating Henry (bottom left) and Gregory on his deathbed (bottom right).

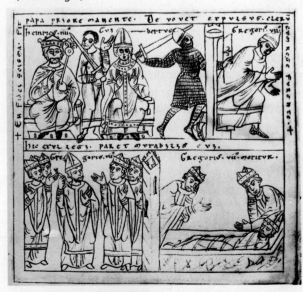

The Struggle for Italy

Although the investiture struggle was over, new battles were soon raging between popes and emperors. During the 1100s and 1200s, ambitious German emperors sought to control Italy. As they did so, they came into conflict with popes and with the wealthy cities of northern Italy.

German Emperors Try to Subdue Italy The Holy Roman emperor Frederick I, called **Frederick Barbarossa,** or "Red Beard," dreamed of building an empire from the Baltic to the Adriatic. For years, he fought to bring the wealthy cities of northern Italy under his control. With equal energy, they resisted. By joining forces with the pope in the Lombard League, they finally managed to defeat Barbarossa's armies.

Barbarossa did succeed, however, in arranging a marriage between his son Henry and Constance, heiress to Sicily and southern Italy. That move entangled German emperors even more deeply in Italian affairs. Barbarossa's grandson, Frederick II, was raised in southern Italy. An able and arrogant leader, he pursued his ambitions in Italy, clashing repeatedly and unsuccessfully with several popes. Like his grandfather, Frederick also tried but failed to subdue the cities of northern Italy.

Effects on Germany and Italy While Frederick II was involved in Italy, German nobles grew more independent. The Holy Roman Empire survived, but remained a patchwork of feudal states. Unlike France and England, Germany would not become a nation-state for another 600 years. Southern Italy and Sicily also faced centuries of upheaval. There, popes turned to the French to overthrow Frederick's heirs. A local uprising against French rule in Sicily led to 200 years of chaos as French and Spanish rivals battled for power. The region that had once been a thriving center of culture was left in ruins.

✔ **Checkpoint**   What obstacles did German emperors face in Italy?

Frederick Barbarossa Goes to War
About to embark on a Crusade, Frederick Barbarossa (at left, with red cape over armor) carries an unsheathed sword and an orb with a cross. *How do these two objects symbolize his goals in the Crusade?*

Church Power Reaches Its Height

In the 1200s, the Church reached the peak of its political power. Reforming popes like Gregory VII claimed the right to depose kings and emperors. Gregory's successors greatly expanded papal power.

Papal Supremacy In 1198, the powerful Pope Innocent III took office. As head of the Church, Innocent III claimed supremacy over all other rulers. The pope, he said, stands "between God and man, lower than God but higher than men, who judges all and is judged by no one." Innocent III clashed with all the powerful rulers of his day, and usually won. As you have read, when King John of England dared to appoint an archbishop of Canterbury without the pope's approval, Innocent excommunicated the king and placed his kingdom under interdict. Innocent ordered the same punishment for France when Philip II tried unlawfully to annul, or invalidate, his marriage.

In 1209, Innocent, aided by Philip II, launched a brutal crusade, or holy war, against the Albigensians in southern France. The Albigensians were a religious group regarded as heretics by the Church because they rejected central Catholic beliefs and rituals. Knights from all over western Europe took part. Tens of thousands of people were slaughtered in the Albigensian Crusade.

Saint Francis of Assisi kneels before Pope Innocent III, who approves the rules of the Franciscan order.

Innocent strengthened papal power within the Church as well. He extended the Papal States, reformed the Church courts, and changed the way that Church officials were chosen. Finally, he called a council that issued decrees that justified the pope's new power.

Looking Ahead After Innocent's death, popes continued to claim supremacy. During this period, though, the French and English monarchies grew stronger. In 1296, Philip IV of France successfully challenged Pope Boniface VIII on the issue of taxing the clergy. After Philip engineered the election of a French pope, the papacy entered a period of decline.

✓ **Checkpoint** How did Innocent III embody the Church's political power?

SECTION 2 Assessment

Progress Monitoring *Online*
For: Self-quiz with vocabulary practice
Web Code: naa-0821

Terms, People, and Places

1. Place each of the key terms at the beginning of this section into one of the following categories: politics, culture, or geography. Write a sentence for each term explaining your choice.

Note Taking

2. **Reading Skill: Understand Effects** Use your completed table to answer the Focus Question: How did explosive conflicts between monarchs and popes affect the balance of power in Europe?

Comprehension and Critical Thinking

3. **Synthesize Information** Why was the power of German emperors limited?
4. **Determine Relevance** What was the significance of the conflict between Pope Gregory VII and Emperor Henry IV?
5. **Recognize Cause and Effect** How did conflicts between popes and emperors affect Italy?
6. **Analyze Information** How did Pope Innocent III assert the power of the Church?

● **Writing About History**

Quick Write: Narrow Your Topic After exploring a topic, narrow your focus by deciding whether to concentrate on economic, social, political, or cultural elements, or a combination. If your topic is the excommunication of Henry IV, you could choose
- political events leading up to the event
- short-term political effects
- long-term political and social effects
Choose a topic from the section and list three ways in which you could narrow it for a cause-and-effect essay.

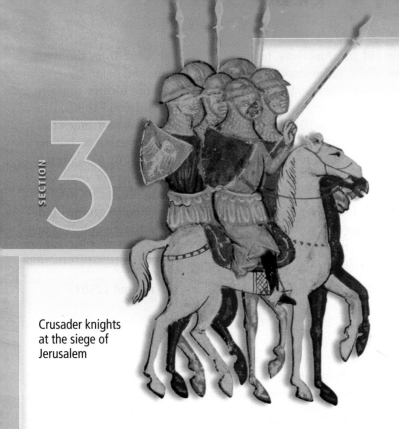

Crusader knights at the siege of Jerusalem

Crusaders Capture Jerusalem

❝ The Franks entered the city magnificently at the noonday hour. . . . With trumpets sounding and with everything in an uproar, exclaiming, 'Help, God!' they vigorously pushed into the city, and straightaway raised the banner on the top of the wall. All the heathen, completely terrified, changed their boldness to swift flight through the narrow streets of the quarters. . . . Nowhere was there a place where the Saracens could escape the swordsmen. . . . What more shall I tell? Not one of them was allowed to live. ❞
—Fulcher of Chartres

Focus Question How did the Crusades change life in Europe and beyond?

The Crusades and the Wider World

Performance Standards

- **SSWH5e** Describe how the Crusades impacted the Islamic World and Europe.
- **SSWH5f** Analyze the relationship between Judaism, Christianity and Islam.

Terms, People, and Places

Crusades	Reconquista
Holy Land	Ferdinand and Isabella
Pope Urban II	Inquisition

Note Taking

Reading Skill: Identify Causes and Effects
Track causes of the Crusades in the top ovals and effects in the lower ones of a concept web like this one.

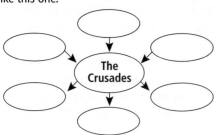

Fulcher of Chartres was just one of thousands of Europeans who took part in a series of wars known as the **Crusades.** In these wars, which began in 1096, Christians battled Muslims for control of lands in the Middle East. As they streamed eastward over the next 200 years, Western Europeans learned that the world was much larger than they had ever dreamed. Their encounters outside Europe would serve to accelerate the pace of change at home.

The World in 1050

In 1050, as Western Europe was just emerging from a period of isolation, many other civilizations were thriving elsewhere. The religion of Islam had given rise to a brilliant civilization that stretched from present-day Spain to India, and Muslim traders and scholars spread goods and ideas even farther.

India was a land of thriving cities where Hindu and Buddhist traditions flourished, and wealthy princes built stunning temples and palaces. In East Asia, under the Tang and Song dynasties, China's culture flourished and influenced neighboring peoples. Meanwhile, the Soninke people of West Africa were building the great trading empire of Ghana.

Across the Atlantic, in Central America, the Maya had cleared rain forests and built cities with towering temples. In the Andes of South America, Native Americans were building a great empire.

The civilizations of the Americas, however, remained apart from the contacts that were taking place among Africans, Europeans, and Asians.

Closer to Western Europe, the Byzantine empire—the former eastern Roman empire—was generally prosperous and united. In the 1050s, the Seljuk Turks invaded the Byzantine empire. The Turks had migrated from Central Asia into the Middle East, where they converted to Islam. By 1071, the Seljuks had overrun most Byzantine lands in Asia Minor (present-day Turkey). The Seljuks also extended their power over the **Holy Land,** that is, Jerusalem and other places in Palestine where Christians believe Jesus lived and preached. Other Muslim groups had controlled this region in the past, but invasions by the Seljuk Turks threatened the Byzantine empire. The conflict prevented Christian pilgrims from traveling to the Holy Land.

 Checkpoint   What civilizations were flourishing around 1050?

The Crusades

The Byzantine emperor Alexius I urgently asked **Pope Urban II** for Christian knights to help him fight the Muslim Turks. Although Roman popes and Byzantine emperors were longtime rivals, Urban agreed.

Called to War At the Council of Clermont in 1095, Urban incited bishops and nobles to action. "From Jerusalem and the city of Constantinople comes a grievous report," he began. "An accursed race . . . has violently invaded the lands of those Christians and has depopulated them by pillage and fire." Urban then called for a crusade to free the Holy Land:

> **Primary Source**
>
> 66 Both knights and footmen, both rich and poor . . . [must] strive to help expel [the Seljuks] from our Christian lands before it is too late. . . . Christ commands it. Remission of sins will be granted for those going thither. 99
> —Fulcher of Chartres, *Chronicle of the First Crusade*

"God wills it!" roared the assembly. By 1096, thousands of knights were on their way to the Holy Land. As the crusading spirit swept through Western Europe, armies of ordinary men and women inspired by fiery preachers left for the Holy Land, too. Few returned. Religious zeal was not the only factor that motivated the crusaders. Many knights hoped to win wealth and land. Some crusaders sought to escape troubles at home. Others yearned for adventure.

The pope, too, had mixed motives. Urban hoped to increase his power in Europe and perhaps heal the schism, or split, between the Roman and Byzantine churches. In 1054, the two branches of Christianity had divided after disputes over beliefs and authority. Urban also hoped that the Crusades would set Christian knights to fighting Muslims instead of one another.

Fighting a Losing Battle Only the First Crusade came close to achieving its goals. After a long and bloody campaign, Christian knights captured Jerusalem in 1099. They capped their victory with a massacre of Muslim and Jewish residents of the city.

The Crusades continued, off and on, for over 200 years. The crusaders divided their captured lands into four small states, called crusader states. The Muslims repeatedly sought to destroy these Christian states, prompting Europeans to launch new crusades. In 1187, Jerusalem fell to the Muslims.

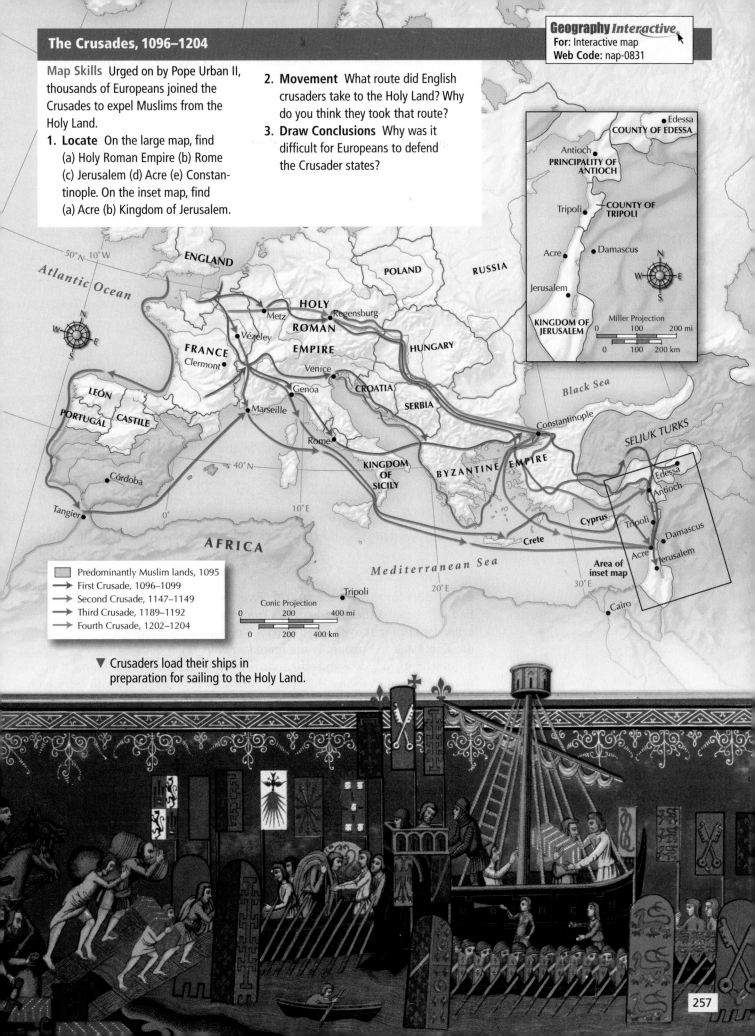

The Crusades, 1096–1204

Geography *Interactive*
For: Interactive map
Web Code: nap-0831

Map Skills Urged on by Pope Urban II, thousands of Europeans joined the Crusades to expel Muslims from the Holy Land.

1. **Locate** On the large map, find (a) Holy Roman Empire (b) Rome (c) Jerusalem (d) Acre (e) Constantinople. On the inset map, find (a) Acre (b) Kingdom of Jerusalem.

2. **Movement** What route did English crusaders take to the Holy Land? Why do you think they took that route?

3. **Draw Conclusions** Why was it difficult for Europeans to defend the Crusader states?

Inset map labels:
Edessa
COUNTY OF EDESSA
Antioch
PRINCIPALITY OF ANTIOCH
Tripoli
COUNTY OF TRIPOLI
Acre — Damascus
Jerusalem
KINGDOM OF JERUSALEM
Miller Projection
0 100 200 mi
0 100 200 km

Large map labels:
50°N 10°W
Atlantic Ocean
ENGLAND
POLAND
RUSSIA
Metz
Regensburg
HOLY ROMAN EMPIRE
Vézelay
FRANCE
Clermont
HUNGARY
Venice
CROATIA
SERBIA
Genoa
LEÓN
PORTUGAL
CASTILE
Marseille
Rome
KINGDOM OF SICILY
BYZANTINE EMPIRE
Black Sea
Constantinople
SELJUK TURKS
Córdoba
40°N
Edessa
Antioch
Cyprus
Tripoli
Damascus
Acre
Jerusalem
Tangier
0°
10°E
AFRICA
Crete
Mediterranean Sea
Area of inset map
Tripoli
20°E
30°E
Cairo

Legend:
Predominantly Muslim lands, 1095
First Crusade, 1096–1099
Second Crusade, 1147–1149
Third Crusade, 1189–1192
Fourth Crusade, 1202–1204
Conic Projection
0 200 400 mi
0 200 400 km

▼ Crusaders load their ships in preparation for sailing to the Holy Land.

By 1187, the Muslim leader Saladin had retaken Jerusalem from the Christian crusaders. King Richard I tried to persuade Saladin to return the city to the Christians. Saladin refused, saying:

❝ To us Jerusalem is as precious . . . as it is to you, because it is the place from where our Prophet [Muhammad] made his journey by night to heaven. . . . Do not dream that we will give it up to you. ❞ 🔊 AUDIO

However, because he recognized how important it was to Christians to be able to visit the sacred sites of their religion, Saladin did reopen Jerusalem to Christian pilgrims. **What does Saladin's response to King Richard's demands show about him?**

The victor was the able Muslim leader Salah al-Din, known to Europeans as Saladin. On the Third Crusade, Europeans failed to retake Jerusalem. After negotiations, though, Saladin did reopen the holy city to Christian pilgrims.

Europeans also mounted crusades against other Muslim lands, especially in North Africa. All ended in defeat. During the Fourth Crusade, the crusaders were diverted from fighting Muslims to fighting other Christians. After helping merchants from the northern Italian city of Venice defeat their Byzantine trade rivals in 1204, crusaders captured and looted Constantinople, the Byzantine capital.

Meanwhile, Muslim armies overran the crusader states. By 1291, they had captured the last Christian outpost, the port city of Acre. As in Jerusalem 200 years earlier, the victors massacred their enemies. This time, the victims were Christians.

✔ **Checkpoint**   How successful were the Crusades?

The Impact of the Crusades

The Crusades left a bitter legacy of religious hatred. In the Middle East, both Christians and Muslims committed appalling atrocities in the name of religion. In Europe, crusaders sometimes turned their religious fury against Jews, massacring entire communities.

The crusaders arrived in the Middle East at a time when various Muslim regimes were struggling among themselves for control of the region. These groups rallied together to fight the invaders, and, under Saladin, began to reunify the region from Egypt to Syria.

Though the crusaders failed to keep control of the Holy Land, the Crusades did have significant effects on life in Europe. These wars helped to quicken the pace of changes that were already underway.

European Economies Expand   Even before the Crusades, Europeans had developed a taste for luxuries from the Byzantine empire. Returning crusaders brought even more fabrics, spices, and perfumes from the Middle East back to Europe. Trade increased and expanded.

Merchants in Venice and other northern Italian cities had built large fleets to carry crusaders to the Holy Land. Now they used those fleets to carry on trade in such goods as sugar, cotton, and rice with the Middle East.

The Crusades further encouraged the growth of a money economy. To finance a journey to the Holy Land, nobles needed money. They therefore allowed peasants to pay rents in money rather than in grain or labor. Peasants began to sell their goods in towns to earn money, a practice that helped to undermine serfdom.

Effects on Monarchs and the Church   The Crusades helped to increase the power of monarchs. These rulers won new rights to collect taxes in order to support the Crusades. Some rulers, such as the French king Louis IX and the English king Richard I, called the Lion-Heart, led Crusades, which added greatly to their prestige.

Enthusiasm for the Crusades brought papal power to its greatest height. This period of enhanced prestige was short-lived, however. As you have read, popes were soon involved in bitter power struggles with monarchs. Also, the Crusades did not end the split between the Roman and Byzantine churches as Pope Urban had hoped. Instead, Byzantine resentment against the West hardened as a result of the Fourth Crusade, during which crusaders had conquered and looted Constantinople.

A Wider Worldview Evolves Contacts with the Muslim world led Christians to realize that millions of people lived in regions they had never even known existed. Soon, a few curious Europeans had left to explore far-off places such as India and China.

In 1271, a young Venetian, Marco Polo, set out for China with his merchant father and uncle. After many years in China, he returned to Venice and wrote a book about the wonders of Chinese civilization. Doubting Europeans wondered if he had really gone to China. To them, his tales of a government-run mail service and black stones (coal) that were burned to heat homes were unbelievable.

The experiences of crusaders and of travelers like Marco Polo expanded European horizons. They brought Europe into a wider world from which it had been cut off since the fall of Rome. In the 1400s, a desire to trade directly with India and China would lead Europeans to a new age of exploration.

✓ **Checkpoint** Summarize the effects of the Crusades.

Prayer beads like these are used by people of many faiths. ▶

▲ A Muslim woman kneels in prayer (above left); Christian pilgrims carry a cross through the streets (above right).

◀ A Jewish pilgrim prays at the Western Wall.

● **INFOGRAPHIC**

JERUSALEM

Today Jews, Christians, and Muslims still consider Jerusalem sacred. Despite continued disputes—and violence—over control of the city, pilgrims still visit holy places. Christians come to the Church of the Holy Sepulcher, believed to be the site of Jesus' resurrection. Equally sacred to Muslims is the Dome of the Rock, from which the Prophet Muhammad is believed to have ascended to heaven. And Jewish pilgrims still pray at the Western Wall, all that remains of the city's ancient temple, Judaism's holiest site.

Medieval map of Jerusalem ▶

Thinking Critically
1. **Analyze Visuals** What do the people in the three photos have in common?
2. **Make Comparisons** How is Jerusalems situation today similar to its situation at the time of the Crusades?

The Reconquista

The crusading spirit continued after the European defeat at Acre, especially in the Iberian peninsula. North African Muslims, called Moors, had conquered most of present-day Spain in the 700s. However, several tiny Christian kingdoms in the north slowly expanded their borders and sought to take over Muslim lands. Their campaign to drive Muslims from the peninsula became known as the **Reconquista**, or "reconquest."

Christians Conquer Spain The first real success of these Christian warriors came in 1085, when they captured the city of Toledo. During the next 200 years, Christian forces pushed slowly and steadily southward. By 1140, the Christian kingdom of Portugal had been established, and by 1300, Christians controlled the entire Iberian Peninsula except for Granada. Muslim influences remained strong, though, and helped shape the arts and literature of Christian Spain. In 1469, the marriage of Ferdinand of Aragon and Isabella of Castile created the unified state called Spain. Using their combined forces, **Ferdinand and Isabella** made a final push against the Muslim stronghold of Granada. In 1492, Granada fell. The Reconquista was complete.

Vocabulary Builder

diverse—(dih VURS) *adj.* varied; different

Spain Expels Non-Christians Ferdinand and Isabella wanted to impose unity on their <u>diverse</u> peoples. Isabella was determined to bring religious as well as political unity to Spain. Under Muslim rule, Spanish Christians, Jews, and Muslims lived in relative peace, allowed to worship as they chose. Isabella ended that tolerance. With the support of the **Inquisition,** a Church court set up to try people accused of heresy, Isabella launched a brutal crusade. Jews and Muslims who had been forced to convert to Christianity could be tried by the Inquisition. If found guilty of practicing their religions, they could be turned over to the secular authorities for punishment. Many who refused to conform to Church teachings were burned at the stake.

The queen achieved religious unity, but at a high price. More than 150,000 people—mostly Muslims and Jews—fled Spain. Many of these exiles were skilled, educated people who had contributed much to Spain's economy and culture.

✔ **Checkpoint** What was the Reconquista?

SECTION 3 Assessment

Progress Monitoring *Online*
For: Self-quiz with vocabulary practice
Web Code: naa-0831

Terms, People, and Places

1. For each term, person, or place listed at the beginning of the section, write a sentence explaining its significance.

Note Taking

2. **Reading Skill: Identify Causes and Effects** Use your completed concept web to answer the Focus Question: How did the Crusades change life in Europe and beyond?

Comprehension and Critical Thinking

3. **Draw Conclusions** Why was the invasion of the Byzantine empire by the Turks significant?

4. **Recognize Cause and Effect** Explain three reasons why Europeans joined the Crusades.

5. **Determine Relevance** How did the Crusades accelerate change in Europe?

6. **Demonstrate Reasoned Judgment** Do you think unity in Spain was worth the costs of the Reconquista? Explain.

● **Writing About History**

Quick Write: Organize Your Essay After defining your topic, use a graphic organizer to organize your information. For example, for the Crusades you might:

- use a flowchart to show events leading up to the First Crusade.
- use a cause-effect chart to show social, economic, and political effects.

Fill in your main ideas for each category in your graphic organizer and use it as a framework for your essay.

CONFLICT

When, if ever, should people go to war?

In This Chapter **GA** SSWH5f

During the Middle Ages, people repeatedly chose to deal with their differences by waging war. Conflicts over power, territory, and beliefs sparked both the Crusades and the Reconquista (right). Like many other wars, they sowed the seeds of future discord.

Throughout History

- **264 B.C.–146 B.C.** Romans fight Carthage for control of the western Mediterranean.

- **711 A.D.** Muslim forces spread Arab rule into Spain.

- **1756–1763** In the Seven Years' War, Britain and France struggle for global power

- **1861** Conflict over slavery leads to the American Civil War.

- **1914** A series of alliances pull European nations into World War I.

- **1961** Eritrea begins a 30-year struggle for independence from Ethiopia.

Continuing Today

The origin of many conflicts today can be traced to the past. Long-standing rivalries make it hard to gain or maintain lasting peace in many parts of the globe.

Conflicts in the World Today

21st Century Skills

? TRANSFER Activities

1. **Analyze** Why have nations gone to war in the past?

2. **Evaluate** List in order of importance what you consider to be just causes for war. Explain the reason for your choices.

3. **Transfer** Complete a Web quest analyzing the reasons why states do or don't go to war; record your thoughts in the Concept Connector Journal; and learn to make a video. Web Code nah-0808

SECTION 4

Medieval scholars at the University of Paris

Medieval inkwell and pen

Life in a Medieval University

Although some university students were scolded for fooling around rather than studying, this father had the opposite worry:

❝ They tell me that, unlike everyone else, you get out of bed before the first bell sounds in order to study, that you are the first into the classroom and the last to leave it. And that when you get back home you spend the whole day going over what you were taught in your lessons. . . . Many people make themselves permanently ill through excessive study; some of them die, and others . . . waste away day after day.❞
—Boncompagno da Signa

Focus Question What achievements in learning, literature, and the arts characterized the High and late Middle Ages?

Learning and Culture Flourish

 Performance Standards

- **SSWH5e** Describe how the Crusades impacted the Islamic World and Europe.
- **SSWH9c** Explain the ideas of Dante.

Terms, People, and Places

scholasticism	Geoffrey Chaucer
Thomas Aquinas	Gothic style
vernacular	flying buttresses
Dante Alighieri	illumination

N̲o̲te Taking

Reading Skill: Recognize Multiple Causes
Keep track of the many causes of the cultural and intellectual flowering of the Middle Ages by completing a flowchart like the one below.

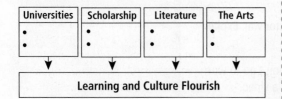

In spite of the problems of students studying too much—or sometimes too little—medieval universities brought prestige and profit to the cities in which they were located. Local merchants provided students with housing, food, clothing, and entertainment. But students could also create problems for university communities. The priest Jacques de Vitry complained, "They were always fighting and engaging in scuffles." Who were these students, and why did universities begin to spring up in the 1100s?

Medieval Universities Emerge

By the 1100s, Europe was experiencing dynamic changes. A more reliable food supply and the growth of trade and towns were signs of increased prosperity.

The Need for Educated People Grows As economic and political conditions improved in the High Middle Ages, the need for education expanded. The Church wanted better-educated clergy. Royal rulers also needed literate men for their growing bureaucracies. By acquiring an education, the sons of wealthy townspeople might hope to qualify for high positions in the Church or with royal governments.

By the 1100s, schools had sprung up around the great cathedrals to train the clergy. Some of these cathedral schools evolved into the first universities. They were organized like guilds, with charters to protect the rights of members and established standards for training.

As early as the 900s, the Italian city of Salerno had a respected medical school. Later, Bologna's university—founded in 1158—became famous for legal studies. Paris and Oxford founded their universities in the later 1100s. Soon, other cities rushed to organize universities. Students often traveled from one university to another to study different subjects, seeking food and lodging from whatever patrons they could find to support them.

Student Life University life offered few comforts. A bell wakened students at about 5 A.M. for prayers. Students then attended classes until 10 A.M., when they had their first meal of the day. Afternoon classes continued until 5 P.M. Students usually ate a light supper and then studied until bedtime. Because at first medieval universities did not have permanent buildings, classes were held in rented rooms or in the choir loft of a church. Students sat for hours on hard benches as the teacher dictated and then explained Latin texts. Students were expected to memorize what they heard.

A program of study covered the seven liberal arts: arithmetic, geometry, astronomy, music, grammar, rhetoric, and logic. There were separate programs for the further study of law, medicine, and theology. To show mastery of a subject, students took an oral exam. Earning a degree as a bachelor of arts took between three and six years. Only after several more years of study could a man qualify to become a master of arts and a teacher. Theology was the longest course of study.

Women and Education Women were not allowed to attend universities. And so, for the most part, they were also deprived of the mental stimulation that was an important part of university life. Without a university education, women could not become doctors, lawyers, or church officials.

There were educated women, however. Some girls received good educations in convents, and girls from noble families attended classes at Notre Dame de Paris, located in the French capital. Some nuns became scholars and writers. The writer Christine de Pisan (duh pee ZAHN) examined the issue of women's education. In *The City of Ladies,* she asks Lady Reason whether women are less capable of learning and understanding, as men insist. Lady Reason replies:

Primary Source

❝ If it were customary to send daughters to school like sons, and if they were then taught the same subjects, they would learn as thoroughly and understand the subtleties of all arts and sciences as well as sons.❞
—Christine de Pisan

Still, men continued to look on educated women as oddities. Most medieval men felt that women should pursue their "natural" gifts at home—raising children, managing the household, doing needlework—and leave books and writing to men.

✔ **Checkpoint** What was university life like in medieval Europe?

Europeans Acquire "New" Learning

Universities received a further boost from an explosion of knowledge that reached Europe in the High Middle Ages. Many of the "new" ideas had originated in ancient Greece but had been lost to Western Europeans after the fall of Rome.

BIOGRAPHY

Christine de Pisan
Christine de Pisan (1364?–1430?) was more educated than most men of her time. Her father, a physician and astronomer in the French court, saw that she received an excellent education. She spoke French, Italian, and possibly Latin as well.

Christine married at 15. When her husband died 10 years later, she supported herself and her three children by writing. Her first works were poems of lost love dedicated to her husband. Her writing was supported by lords and monarchs.

Because of her desire to comment on social issues, Christine gradually switched her focus from poetry to prose. She described women's place in medieval society and promoted women's rights and accomplishments. **Why do you think Christine began to write about women's issues?**

Medieval Innovation in Europe

Many technological innovations that still affect our daily lives were either invented or adapted by Europeans during the Middle Ages.

The invention of the escapement mechanism allowed a clock to measure hours of equal length regardless of the times of sunrise and sunset. These clocks regulated when church bells rang to mark the divisions of the day. ▼

In the 1200s, the first buttons were used as ornaments and sold by jewelers. Once their practical use was discovered, less expensive buttons allowed garments to have adjustable necklines and detachable sleeves. ▼

The invention of eyeglasses was particularly welcome to medieval monks who copied manuscripts. In fact, a 1313 document attributes this innovation to a Dominican friar from Italy. ▶

A series of innovations ▶ improved medieval farming—and the food supply. The iron plow was more efficient. A new harness allowed a change from oxen to faster horsepower.

Vocabulary Builder

initiated—(ih NISH ee ayt ed) *vt.* started; introduced

Muslim Scholarship Advances Knowledge Muslim scholars had translated the works of Aristotle and other Greek thinkers into Arabic. Their translations and knowledgeable commentaries on these ancient texts spread across the Muslim world. In Muslim Spain, Jewish and Christian scholars translated these works into Latin, the language of Christian European scholars. In the 1100s, when these new translations reached Western Europe, they <u>initiated</u> a revolution in the world of learning.

Christian Scholars Struggle With New Ideas The writings of the ancient Greeks posed a challenge to Christian scholars. Aristotle taught that people should use reason to discover basic truths. Christians, however, accepted many ideas on faith. They believed that the Church was the final authority on all questions. How could they use the logic of Aristotle without undermining their Christian faith?

Some Christian scholars tried to resolve the conflict between faith and reason. Their method, known as **scholasticism,** used reason to support Christian beliefs. Scholastics studied the works of the Muslim philosopher Averroës (uh VEER uh weez) and the Jewish rabbi Maimonides (my MAHN uh deez). These thinkers, too, used logic to resolve the conflict between faith and reason.

The writings of these philosophers influenced the famous scholastic **Thomas Aquinas** (uh KWY nus). In a monumental work, *Summa theologica,* Aquinas concluded that faith and reason exist in harmony. Both lead to the same truth, that God rules over an orderly universe. Aquinas thus brought together Christian faith and classical Greek philosophy.

New Approaches to Science and Mathematics Scientific works, translated from Arabic and Greek, also reached Europe from Spain and the Byzantine empire. Christian scholars studied Hippocrates on medicine and Euclid on geometry, along with works by Arab scientists. They saw, too, how Aristotle had used observation and experimentation to study the physical world. Yet science made little real progress in Europe in the Middle Ages because most scholars still believed that all true knowledge must fit with Church teachings. It would take many centuries before Christian thinkers changed the way they viewed the physical world.

During this period, Europeans adopted Hindu-Arabic numerals, which were much easier to use than the cumbersome system of Roman numerals that had been traditional throughout Europe for centuries. In time, the use of Arabic numerals (as they are commonly called) allowed both scientists and mathematicians to make extraordinary advances in their fields.

✔ **Checkpoint** Describe the new learning of medieval Europe.

Medieval Literature

While Latin remained the written language of scholars and churchmen, new writings began to appear in the **vernacular,** or the everyday languages of ordinary people, such as French, German, and Italian. These writings captured the spirit of the High and late Middle Ages. Medieval literature included epics, or long narrative poems, about knights and chivalry as well as tales of the common people.

Heroic Epics Captivate Across Europe, people began writing down oral traditions in the vernacular. French pilgrims traveling to holy sites loved to hear the *chansons de geste,* or "songs of heroic deeds." The most popular was the *Song of Roland,* written around 1100, which praises the courage of one of Charlemagne's knights. A true chivalric hero, Roland loyally sacrifices his life out of a sense of honor. Spain's great epic, *Poem of the Cid,* tells the story of Rodrigo Díaz de Vivar, a bold and fiery Christian lord who fought both with and against Muslim forces. His nickname, *El Cid,* comes from the Arabic word for "lord."

Dante's *Divine Comedy* "In the middle of the journey of life, I found myself in a dark wood, where the straight way was lost." So begins the *Divine Comedy* written in the early 1300s by the Italian poet **Dante Alighieri** (DAHN tay ah leeg YEH ree). The poem takes the reader on an imaginary journey into hell and purgatory, where souls await forgiveness. Finally, in the third section, Dante describes a vision of heaven.

"Abandon all hope, ye that enter here" is the warning Dante receives as he approaches hell. There, he talks with people from history who tell how they earned a place in hell. Humor, tragedy, and the endless medieval quest for religious understanding are all ingredients in Dante's poem. His journey summarizes Christian ethics, showing how people's actions in life determine their fate in the afterlife.

Near the end of the French epic poem the *Song of Roland,* the great hero, Count Roland, has been wounded in battle. Now he "feels death coming over him." Why does the author include the angels bearing Roland's soul to heaven?

Primary Source

❝ Count Roland lay stretched out beneath a pine;
He turned his face toward the land of Spain,
Began to remember many things now:
How many lands, brave man, he had conquered;
And he remembered: sweet France, the men of his line,
Remembered Charles, his lord, who fostered him:
Cannot keep, remembering, from weeping, sighing;
But would not be unmindful of himself:
He confesses his sins, prays God for mercy.
Then he held out his right glove to his Lord:
Saint Gabriel took the glove from his hand.
He held his head bowed down upon his arm,
He is gone, his two hands joined, to his end.
Then God sent him his angel Cherubin
And Saint Michael, angel of the sea's Peril;
And with these two there came Saint Gabriel:
They bear Count Roland's soul to Paradise. ❞

 AUDIO

Chaucer's *Canterbury Tales* In the *Canterbury Tales*, the English writer Geoffrey Chaucer describes a band of pilgrims traveling to Saint Thomas Becket's tomb. In brilliant word portraits, he sketches a range of characters, including a knight, a plowman, a merchant, a miller, a monk, and a nun. Each character tells a story to entertain the group. Whether funny, romantic, or bawdy, each tale adds to our picture of medieval life.

✔ **Checkpoint** **Describe three works of medieval literature.**

Architecture and Art

"In the Middle Ages," wrote French author Victor Hugo, "men had no great thought that they did not write down in stone." Those "writings" were the great buildings of the Middle Ages. With riches from trade and commerce, townspeople, nobles, and monarchs indulged in a flurry of building. Their greatest achievements were the towering stone cathedrals that served as symbols of their wealth and religious devotion.

From Romanesque to Gothic In the year 1000, monasteries and towns were building solid stone churches that reflected Roman influences. These Romanesque churches looked like fortresses with thick walls and towers. Typically, the roof of a Romanesque church was a barrel vault, a long tunnel of stone that covered the main part of the structure. It was heavy, supported by massive walls with no windows or only tiny slits of windows for fear of weakening the support for the roof. As a result, the interior of a Romanesque church was dark and gloomy.

About 1140, Abbot Suger wanted to build a new abbey church at St. Denis near Paris. He hoped that it "would shine with wonderful and uninterrupted light." There, builders developed what became known as the Gothic style of architecture. Its most important feature was the **flying buttresses,** or stone supports that stood outside the church. These supports allowed builders to construct higher, thinner walls and leave space for large stained-glass windows. Gothic churches soared to incredible heights. Their graceful spires and tall windows carried the eye upward to the heavens. "Since their brilliance lets the splendor of the True Light pass into the church," declared a medieval visitor, "they enlighten those inside."

Making Art in Stone and Glass As churches rose, stonemasons carved sculptures to decorate them both inside and out. In addition to scenes from the Bible and the lives of the saints, sculptors included lifelike forms of plants and animals. They also carved whimsical or frightening images of mythical creatures such as dragons and unicorns.

Stained glass rose window in Notre Dame Cathedral, Paris

HAROLD: HIC APPREHENDIT: VVIDO: HA

At the same time, other skilled craft workers created stained-glass windows that added to the splendor of Gothic churches. These artisans stained small pieces of glass in glowing colors. They then set the pieces in thin lead frames to create pictures depicting the life of Jesus, a biblical event, or other religious themes. These religious pictures helped educate the many people who were unable to read.

Paintings, Manuscripts, and Tapestries Churches also contained religious paintings called altarpieces. The purpose of these paintings, and similar ones that wealthy people had in their homes, was to symbolize religious ideas. In this Gothic style, religious figures were not meant to look like real people in real settings but rather to inspire devotion.

In the 1300s and 1400s, the Gothic style was also applied to the artistic decoration of books, known as **illumination.** Since the early Middle Ages, monks, nuns, and other skilled artisans had illuminated books with intricate designs and miniature paintings of biblical scenes and daily life. They often featured brilliant colors and decorative detail. Artists decorated prayer books known as Books of Hours with depictions of towns and castles, knights and ladies, and peasants in the fields.

Medieval artists also created "paintings" in thread. Stone castles were drafty and cold. Tapestries, or woven wall hangings, were hung in castle rooms and halls to add color and warmth. One of the most famous, the Bayeux Tapestry, is really a huge embroidery 231 feet long. Its 70 scenes depict the Norman Conquest of England, and historians have used it to learn about that event.

✔ **Checkpoint** Describe the artistic works found in medieval churches.

The Bayeux Tapestry
This section of the famous Bayeux Tapestry shows Harold, who became the last Anglo-Saxon king of England, with his fleet. Harold was killed in the Battle of Hastings in 1066.

SECTION 4
Assessment

Progress Monitoring *Online*
For: Self-quiz with vocabulary practice
Web Code: naa-0841

Terms, People, and Places
1. What do the key terms and people listed at the beginning of the section have in common? Explain.

Note Taking
2. **Reading Skill: Recognize Multiple Causes** Use your completed flowchart to answer the Focus Question: What achievements in learning, literature, and the arts characterized the High and late Middle Ages?

Comprehension and Critical Thinking
3. **Predict Consequences** How might universities that drew students from many lands affect European life in the future? Explain your answer.
4. **Analyze Information** How did new knowledge pose a challenge to Christian scholars?
5. **Synthesize Information** Why were heroic epics in the vernacular popular with medieval Europeans?
6. **Identify Central Issues** How was religion central to the art and architecture of the Middle Ages?

● **Writing About History**
Quick Write: Write a Thesis Statement
Your thesis statement expresses your idea about your topic. It might state the most important cause of an event or that multiple causes were at work, or it might emphasize effects. Refer to your graphic organizer to formulate statements such as:
- Changing economic, political, and social conditions led to the emergence of universities.
- Muslim scholarship had far-reaching effects on European philosophy, science, and mathematics.

The Gothic Cathedral

The Gothic cathedral was the crowning achievement of medieval architecture. Flying buttresses allowed for thinner walls with large windows that flooded the churches with light. Tall spires reached for the heavens and dominated the landscape. European cities competed to build the largest, grandest cathedrals. Notre Dame de Paris, shown here, was begun in 1163. It took artisans almost two centuries to complete it.

Vaulted Ceilings
Pointed arches called vaults form a strong skeleton on which the roof material is laid. This view looks up at Notre Dame's vaulted ceiling.

Gargoyles
Imaginatively carved figures serve as waterspouts to drain water from the roof. Later, the term *gargoyle* included other grotesque carvings on Gothic churches.

Flying Buttresses
These stone arches carry much of the weight of the roof, so thick stone walls are no longer needed.

Thinking Critically
1. **Synthesize Information** How did new technology allow Gothic cathedrals to "soar to the heavens" and be flooded with light?
2. **Draw Conclusions** What does the time and effort required to build Gothic cathedrals reveal about medieval culture?

◄ Lead crosses used in mass graves of plague victims

Stained-glass window depicting fear of the plague, Canterbury Cathedral, England ▼

WITNESS HISTORY 🔊 AUDIO

The Black Death Approaches

❝We see death coming into our midst like black smoke, a plague which cuts off the young, a rootless phantom which has no mercy or fair countenance. Woe is me. . . . It is an ugly eruption that comes with unseemly haste. It is a grievous ornament that breaks out in a rash. The early ornaments of black death.❞
—Jevan Gethin

The disease called the plague, or the Black Death, reached the British Isles from mainland Europe in 1348, spreading fear and then sickness and death. The Welsh poet who wrote these words died of the plague in 1349.

Focus Question How did the combination of plague, upheaval in the Church, and war affect Europe in the 1300s and 1400s?

A Time of Crisis

 Performance Standards

• **SSWH7c** Explain role of church in medieval society.

Terms, People, and Places

Black Death   schism
epidemic   longbow
inflation

Note Taking

Reading Skill: Recognize Causes and Effects Keep track of the spread of the Black Death and its effects in a flowchart like this one. Use the middle box to describe what life was like during the plague.

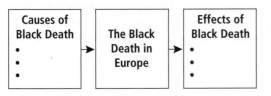

To Europeans in the mid-1300s, the end of the world seemed to have come. First, widespread crop failures brought famine and starvation. Then, plague and war ravaged populations. Europe eventually recovered from these disasters. Still, the upheavals of the 1300s and 1400s marked the end of the Middle Ages and the beginning of the early modern age.

The Black Death: A Global Epidemic

In the autumn of 1347, a fleet of Genoese trading ships loaded with grain left the Black Sea port of Caffa and set sail for Messina, Sicily. By midvoyage, sailors were falling sick and dying. Soon after the ships tied up at Messina, townspeople, too, began to fall sick and die. Within months, the disease that Europeans called the **Black Death** was raging through Italy. By 1348, it had reached Spain and France. From there, it ravaged the rest of Europe. One in three people died—a death rate worse than in any war in history.

The Plague Spreads from Asia The sickness was bubonic plague, a disease spread by fleas carried by rats. Bubonic plague had broken out before in Europe, Asia, and North Africa but had subsided. One strain, though, had survived in Mongolia. In the 1200s, Mongol armies conquered much of Asia, probably setting off the new **epidemic,** or outbreak of rapid-spreading disease.

In the pre-modern world, rats infested ships, towns, and even the homes of the rich and powerful, so no one took any notice of them. In the early 1300s, rats spread the plague in crowded Chinese cities, which killed about 35 million people there. Fleas jumped from those rats to infest the clothes and packs of traders traveling west. As a result, the disease quickly spread from Asia to the Middle East and then to Europe.

Normal Life Breaks Down In Europe, the plague brought terror and bewilderment, as people had no way to stop the disease. Some people turned to magic and witchcraft for cures. Others plunged into wild pleasures, believing they would soon die anyway. Still others saw the plague as God's punishment. They beat themselves with whips to show that they repented their sins. Normal life broke down as people fled cities or hid in their homes to avoid contracting the plague from neighbors and relatives.

Some Christians blamed Jews for the plague, charging unjustly that they had poisoned the wells to cause the disease. In the resulting hysteria, thousands of Jews were slaughtered.

The Economy Suffers As the plague kept recurring in the late 1300s, the European economy plunged to a low ebb. When workers and employers died, production declined. Survivors demanded higher wages. As the cost of labor soared, **inflation,** or rising prices, broke out too. Landowners and merchants pushed for laws to limit wages. To limit rising costs, landowners converted croplands to land for sheep raising, which required less labor. Villagers forced off the land looked for work in towns. There, guilds limited opportunities for advancement.

Coupled with the fear of the plague, these restrictions sparked explosive revolts. Angry peasants rampaged in England, France, Germany, and elsewhere. In the cities, artisans fought for more power, usually without success. Revolts erupted on and off through the 1300s and 1400s. The plague had spread death and social unrest. It would take western Europe more than 100 years to fully recover from its effects.

✓ **Checkpoint** How did the Black Death affect Europe?

Upheaval in the Church

The late Middle Ages brought spiritual crisis, scandal, and division to the Roman Catholic Church. Many priests and monks died during the plague. Their replacements faced challenging questions. Survivors asked, "Why did God spare some and kill others?"

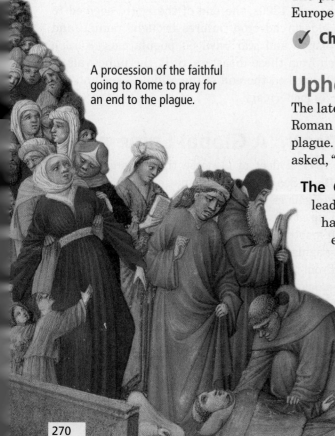

A procession of the faithful going to Rome to pray for an end to the plague.

The Church Splits The Church was unable to provide the strong leadership needed in this desperate time. In 1309, Pope Clement V had moved the papal court to Avignon outside the border of southern France. It remained there for about 70 years under French domination. In Avignon, popes reigned over a lavish court. Critics lashed out against the worldly, pleasure-loving papacy, and anticlerical sentiment grew. Within the Church itself, reformers worked for change.

In 1378, reformers elected their own pope to rule from Rome. French cardinals responded by choosing a rival pope. For decades, there was a **schism,** or split, in the Church. During this schism, two and sometimes even three popes claimed to be the true "vicar of Christ."

A Church council at Constance, Germany, finally ended the crisis in 1417 by removing authority from all three popes and electing a compromise candidate. Pope Martin V returned the papacy to Rome.

Responding to New Heresies As the moral authority of the Church weakened, popular preachers began to call for change. In England, John Wycliffe, an Oxford professor, attacked corruption in Church. Wycliffe insisted that the Bible, not the Church, was the source of Christian truth. His followers began translating the Bible into English so that people could read it themselves rather than rely on the clergy to interpret it. Czech students at Oxford carried Wycliffe's ideas to Bohemia—today's Czech Republic. There, Jan Hus led the call for reforms, supported by his followers, known as Hussites.

The Church responded by persecuting Wycliffe and his followers and suppressing the Hussites. Hus was tried for preaching heresy—ideas contrary to Church teachings. Found guilty, he was burned at the stake in 1415. The ideas of Wycliffe and Hus survived, however. A century later, other reformers took up the same demands.

✔ **Checkpoint** Describe the threats to Church power.

The Hundred Years' War

On top of the disasters of famine, plague, and economic decline came a long, destructive war. Between 1337 and 1453, England and France engaged in a series of conflicts, known as the Hundred Years' War.

French and English Rivalry Grows English rulers had battled for centuries to hold onto the French lands of their Norman ancestors. But French kings were intent on extending their own power in France. When Edward III of England, whose mother had been a French princess, claimed the French crown in 1337, war erupted anew between these rival powers.

Note Taking

Reading Skill: Recognize Causes and Effects Keep track of the Hundred Years' War by completing a flowchart. List causes of the war in the first box, and put effects in the last box. Use the middle box to record major events that occurred during the war.

Causes	Hundred Years' War	Effects
• • •	→ • • • →	• •

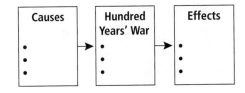

Geography *Interactive*
For: Audio guided tour
Web Code: nap-0851

The Hundred Years' War, 1337–1453

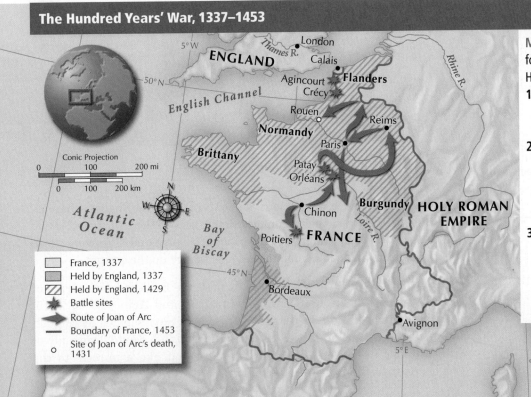

Conic Projection

0   100   200 mi
0   100   200 km

Atlantic Ocean

Bay of Biscay

ENGLAND
London
Calais
Agincourt
Crécy
Flanders
Rouen
Normandy
Reims
Paris
Brittany
Patay
Orléans
Chinon
Burgundy
Poitiers
FRANCE
Bordeaux
HOLY ROMAN EMPIRE
Avignon
English Channel
Thames R.
Rhine R.
Loire R.
5°W
50°N
45°N
5°E
N S E W

France, 1337
Held by England, 1337
Held by England, 1429
Battle sites
Route of Joan of Arc
Boundary of France, 1453
Site of Joan of Arc's death, 1431

Map Skills The English and French fought for control of France in the Hundred Years' War.

1. **Locate** (a) Normandy (b) Crécy (c) Poitiers (d) Agincourt (e) Calais
2. **Place** (a) What regions of France did England gain between 1337 and 1429? (b) What city in France was still under English control in 1453?
3. **Make Comparisons** (a) How were the boundaries of France different in 1453 than in 1337? (b) How did the Hundred Years' War change Europe?

271

INFOGRAPHIC

NEW WEAPONS TURN THE TIDE

New military technology not only turned the tide of the Hundred Years' War but also changed warfare itself. Early in the war, English soldiers equipped with a powerful new weapon overpowered their French counterparts. An English archer with a longbow could shoot three arrows in the time it took a French archer with his crossbow to fire just one. Arrows from the powerful six-foot longbow could pierce all but the heaviest armor. The French responded by using cannons, which could smash castle walls. Cannons helped the French capture English-held castles and drive the English from Normandy.

Weapons

Weapons in the medieval painting correspond to those in the photos.

A Crossbow

B Longbow

C Cannon

Thinking Critically

1. **Analyze Visuals** Find the longbows and crossbows in the medieval painting above. Which side seems to be winning? Explain.
2. **Draw Inferences** How might cannons be used in this battle?

England and France were also rivals for control of the English Channel, the waterway between their countries. Each also wanted to control trade in the region. Once fighting started, economic rivalry and a growing sense of national pride made it hard for either side to give up the struggle.

The English Win Early Victories At first, the English won a string of victories—at Crécy in 1346, Poitiers in 1356, and Agincourt in 1415. They owed much of their success to the new **longbow** wielded by English archers. For a time, it looked as though England would bring all of France under its control. Then, in what seemed like a miracle to the French, their fortunes were reversed.

Joan of Arc Fights for France In 1429, a 17-year-old peasant woman, Joan of Arc, appeared at the court of Charles VII, the uncrowned king of France. She told him that God had sent her to save France. Desperate, Charles <u>authorized</u> her to lead an army against the English.

To Charles's amazement, Joan inspired the battered and despairing French troops to fight anew. In one astonishing year, she led the French to several victories and planted the seeds for future triumphs.

Joan paid for success with her life. She was taken captive by allies of the English and turned over to her enemies for trial. To discredit her, the English had Joan tried for witchcraft. She was convicted and burned at the stake. Much later, however, the Church declared her a saint.

The execution of Joan rallied the French, who saw her as a martyr. After Joan's death, the French took the offensive. With a powerful new weapon, the cannon, they attacked English-held castles. By 1453, the English held only the port of Calais in northwestern France.

Impact of the Hundred Years' War The Hundred Years' War set France and England on different paths. The war created a growing sense of national feeling in France and allowed French kings to expand their power. On the other hand, during the war, English rulers turned repeatedly to Parliament for funds, which helped that body win the "power of the purse." Power in English government began to swing towards Parliament. While the loss of French lands shattered English dreams of a continental empire, English rulers turned to new trading ventures overseas.

The Hundred Years' War brought many changes to the late medieval world. Castles and armored knights were doomed to disappear because their defenses could not stand up to the more deadly firepower of the longbow and the cannon. Society was changing. Monarchs needed large armies, not feudal vassals, to fight their wars. More and more, they turned to hired soldiers to do their fighting.

As Europe recovered from the Black Death, the population expanded, and manufacturing grew. These changes led to increased trade. Italian cities flourished as centers of trade and shipping. Europeans borrowed and developed new technologies. This recovery set the stage for further changes during the Renaissance, the Reformation, and the Age of Exploration.

✔ **Checkpoint** Summarize the events of the Hundred Years' War.

Vocabulary Builder

authorized—(AW thur ezd) *vt.* gave official power to

SECTION 5 Assessment

Progress Monitoring *Online*
For: Self-quiz with vocabulary practice
Web Code: naa-0851

Terms, People, and Places

1. For each term, person, or place listed at the beginning of the section, write a sentence explaining its significance.

Note Taking

2. **Reading Skill: Recognize Causes and Effects** Use your completed flowcharts to answer the Focus Question: How did the combination of plague, upheaval in the Church, and war affect Europe in the 1300s and 1400s?

Comprehension and Critical Thinking

3. **Recognize Cause and Effect** What were three effects of the Black Death on late medieval Europe?

4. **Draw Inferences** How did the pope's move to Avignon and the establishment of a rival pope in Rome affect Church authority and power?

5. **Make Comparisons** Compare the effects of the Hundred Years' War on France and on England.

● **Writing About History**

Quick Write: Gather Evidence Gather examples and details to support your thesis. For example, you can support the thesis "Joan of Arc was a cause of French success in the Hundred Years' War" with general facts such as "she led the French to victories and her martyrdom inspired the French soldiers," and so on. Use specific details such as particular battles she led and quotations from soldiers to support your general statements.

THE BLACK DEATH

"Wretched, terrible, destructive year, the remnants of the people alone remain." That description of 1349 was found on a hand-carved sign only months after the bubonic plague reached England. Between 1347 and 1353, the plague, or the Black Death, killed one third of the population of Europe—more than 25 million people.

The plague was caused by bacteria carried by fleas that lived on rats. The epidemic probably originated in China, where infected fleas got into the packs of merchants traveling west. Merchant ships carried the plague from busy Black Sea ports to Sicily. Spreading outward in waves of terror, the Black Death soon ravaged most of Europe.

Flea-covered rats thrived in filthy medieval cities, and the disease spread quickly. Within hours, victims developed egg-sized lumps under their arms. Fever, vomiting, and black spots caused by internal bleeding followed. Once victims started spitting blood, death was certain.

As the disease raced through towns, many people fled to the countryside. Others hid in their homes. The death toll was so high that gravediggers used carts to collect corpses as they walked the streets calling "Bring out your dead!"

So many farm workers died that crops rotted in the fields. Shortages led to demands for higher wages and peasant revolts. Buildings and roads fell to ruin. And survivors lived in fear of the return of the plague, which recurred in waves through the 1600s.

▶ Outbreaks of the plague continued for centuries. To ward off infections, this doctor from the 1600s wears a leather mask with glass eyes and a long beak filled with herbs and spices.

◀ In crowded medieval cities, houses were close together, and residents threw garbage and human waste into the streets. Rats and fleas were commonplace in the homes of both the rich and the poor.

▼ In the Middle Ages, rats were great travelers. They thrived on ships and moved from port to port—bringing their fleas with them. Fleas that had bitten infected rats then bit people, spreading disease.

274

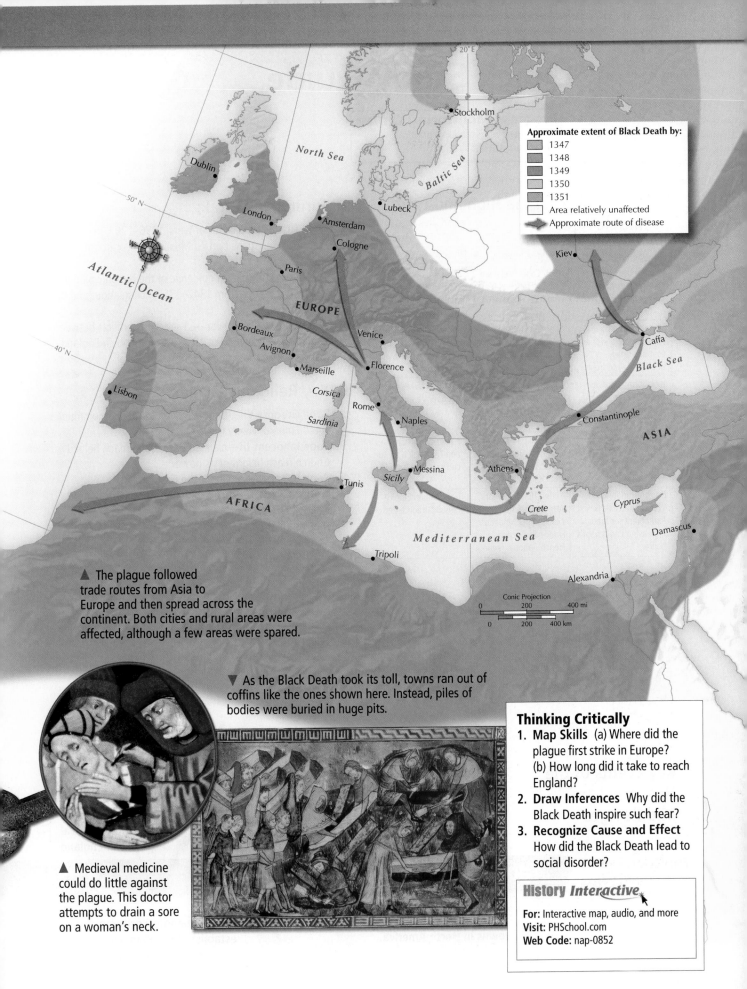

Approximate extent of Black Death by:
- 1347
- 1348
- 1349
- 1350
- 1351
- Area relatively unaffected
- Approximate route of disease

North Sea

Stockholm

Baltic Sea

Dublin

London

Lübeck

Amsterdam

Cologne

Paris

EUROPE

Atlantic Ocean

50° N

40° N

Bordeaux

Avignon

Venice

Marseille

Florence

Corsica

Rome

Sardinia

Naples

Lisbon

Messina

Sicily

Tunis

Athens

AFRICA

Tripoli

Crete

Mediterranean Sea

Kiev

Caffa

Black Sea

Constantinople

ASIA

Cyprus

Damascus

Alexandria

20° E

Conic Projection

0   200   400 mi

0   200   400 km

▲ The plague followed trade routes from Asia to Europe and then spread across the continent. Both cities and rural areas were affected, although a few areas were spared.

▼ As the Black Death took its toll, towns ran out of coffins like the ones shown here. Instead, piles of bodies were buried in huge pits.

▲ Medieval medicine could do little against the plague. This doctor attempts to drain a sore on a woman's neck.

Thinking Critically

1. **Map Skills** (a) Where did the plague first strike in Europe? (b) How long did it take to reach England?
2. **Draw Inferences** Why did the Black Death inspire such fear?
3. **Recognize Cause and Effect** How did the Black Death lead to social disorder?

History *Interactive*

For: Interactive map, audio, and more
Visit: PHSchool.com
Web Code: nap-0852

Quick Study Guide

 SSWH7b

Progress Monitoring *Online*
For: Self-test with vocabulary practice
Web Code: naa-0861

■ Power Shifts in the High and Late Middle Ages

England	France	Holy Roman Empire
William the Conqueror consolidates royal power, limiting power of lords.	Hugh Capet is elected king by French nobles who feel he is weak.	Otto is crowned Holy Roman emperor, but nobles and Church officials wield power.
Henry II strengthens royal courts, and tries to make clergy accountable to them.	Capetian kings make throne hereditary, take lands from nobles, build a bureaucracy.	Henry IV is excommunicated by Pope Gregory VII, and then forgiven.
King John approves Magna Carta, limiting monarch's power.	Louis IX improves royal government, ends serfdom, creates strong national feeling.	Henry IV forces Pope Gregory VII into exile.
Parliament develops under Edward I.	After Philip IV clashes with Pope Boniface, French monarchs gain more control over popes.	Frederick Barbarossa and Frederick II try to conquer Italy but fail.
During Hundred Years' War, monarchs ask Parliament for funds, increasing Parliament's power.	During Hundred Years' War, English are expelled from most of France, increasing French national feeling.	Holy Roman Empire remains fragmented.

■ Turmoil in Europe

The Crusades—a series of wars, 1096–1204, in which European Christians battled Muslims for control of the Holy Land

The Black Death—an epidemic of the bubonic plague that swept Europe from 1347–1353, killing about one third of the population

The Hundred Years War—a series of conflicts between England and France from 1337–1453, in which England lost control of most of its territory in France

■ Key Religious Leaders

Pope Gregory VII—banned lay investiture, excommunicated Emperor Henry IV

Pope Innocent III—claimed papal supremacy, helped Church reach height of its power

Pope Urban II—called for the First Crusade

Thomas Becket—Archbishop of Canterbury, opposed Henry II on power of courts to try clergy, murdered by Henry's knights

Thomas Aquinas—scholar who used scholasticism to reconcile faith and reason

■ Key Events of the High and Late Middle Ages

European Events
Global Events

1000

1066
William the Conqueror completes the Norman Conquest of England.

1096
Christians launch the First Crusade.

1100

1215
King John approves the Magna Carta limiting royal power in England.

1200

1000s
The Anasazi build pueblo towns in North America.

1192
Minamoto Yoritomo establishes the Kamakura shogunate in Japan.

Concept Connector

 Essential Question Review

To connect prior knowledge with what you have learned in this chapter, answer the questions below in your Concept Connector journal. Use the journal in the Reading and Note Taking Study Guide to record your answers (or go to www.phschool.com **Web Code:** nad-0807).

1. **Conflict** By 1071, Seljuk Turks, who were Muslim, had gained control of the Holy Land. Other Muslim groups had controlled this region in the past. Why did the pope call for a crusade to expel the Seljuk Turks from the Holy Land? Think about the following:
   - pilgrimages
   - the Byzantine empire
   - the pope's motives

2. **Democracy** In 1295, King Edward I summoned Parliament to approve money for his wars in France. "What touches all should be approved by all," he declared. What did King Edward mean? What did he do to ensure that all of the English people were heard? How would Edward's actions affect the power of the monarch?

3. **Human Rights** During the Reconquista, Christian forces drove the Muslims out of Spain. Under Muslim rule, Spanish Christians, Muslims, and Jews had been allowed to worship as they chose. Why were Spanish Jews and Muslims denied freedom of worship after the Reconquista? What role did the Church play in denying religious freedom? What happened to Spanish Muslims and Jews who practiced their religion during this period?

■ Connections to Today

1. **Conflict: The Holy City of Jerusalem** A battleground since ancient times, the city of Jerusalem is still fought over today. It is a holy city to Jews, Christians, and Muslims, and all three groups have claimed it. Today it is the capital of Israel, the Jewish state, but it is also claimed by the Muslim Palestinians as the capital of the state they hope to establish. Research disputes over Jerusalem since 1948, when the state of Israel was established. Then compare today's disputes to those of the Middle Ages.

2. **Advances in Science: Epidemics** At the time of the Black Death, science provided little insight into the cause, spread, or treatment of disease. Today, in spite of advances in science, the world still suffers from epidemics. In 1918, troop ships carried influenza back and forth between the European battlefields of World War I and the United States. The flu eventually spread worldwide, killing as many as 25 million people. More recently, SARS (severe acute respiratory syndrome) has spread quickly and been carried internationally by airplane travelers. The Chinese officials pictured above are wearing masks to protect themselves from SARS. Research an epidemic that occurred after 1900. Write a brief report comparing its cause, spread, and treatment to those of the Black Death.

History Interactive
For: Interactive timeline
Web Code: nap-0861

1337
The Hundred Years' War between England and France begins.

1347
The Black Death breaks out in Italy.

1431
After leading French troops to victory, Joan of Arc is executed by the English.

1492
King Ferdinand and Queen Isabella complete the Reconquista in Spain.

1300   1400   1500

1300s
The kingdom of Benin is established in West Africa.

1368
The Ming dynasty is established in China.

1453
Ottoman Turks capture Constantinople.

1462
The reign of Ivan the Great begins in Russia.

Chapter Assessment

Terms, People, and Places

Complete each sentence by choosing the correct answer from the list of terms below. You will not use all of the terms.

Frederick Barbarossa	Inquisition
common law	lay investiture
epidemic	schism
habeas corpus	scholasticism
illumination	vernacular

1. _____ is based on custom and court rulings.
2. Pope Gregory banned _____ in order to strengthen the power of the Church.
3. The _____ was part of Queen Isabella's effort to rid Spain of Jews, Muslims, and heretics.
4. _____ used reason to support Christian beliefs.
5. Dante wrote *The Divine Comedy* in the _____ rather than in Latin.
6. The _____ of manuscripts was often done by monks.
7. _____ tried unsuccessfully to conquer Italy.
8. Rival popes caused a _____ in the Church.

Main Ideas

Section 1 (pp. 244–250)
9. How did the monarchs of England and France consolidate their power?

Section 2 (pp. 251–254)
10. Why were the Holy Roman emperors unsuccessful in unifying their empire?

Section 3 (pp. 255–261)
11. How did the Crusades affect the economy and outlook of Europeans?

Section 4 (pp. 262–268)
12. How did changing economic and social conditions lead to the emergence of universities and to new kinds of philosophy and literature?

Section 5 (pp. 269–275)
13. How did war and plague cause major changes in medieval Europe?

Chapter Focus Question
14. How did changing economic and social conditions, wars, and the growing power of monarchs begin to build the framework for the modern nation-state?

Critical Thinking

15. **Predict Consequences** How do you think the lack of a document like the Magna Carta will affect the development of French government?
16. **Demonstrate Reasoned Judgment** Who do you think had a better "case": Gregory VII or Henry IV? Explain and support your position.
17. **Draw Inferences** How did the rise of vernacular literature reflect a change in education and literacy in medieval Europe?
18. **Make Comparisons** How were the Crusades and the Reconquista similar? How were they different?
19. **Analyzing Visuals** Use the medieval illustration of the Model Parliament in Section 1 to explain the relative importance and power of the different groups in English society.
20. **Geography and History** Review the map "Trade in Medieval Europe" in Chapter 7 and the map "Spread of the Black Death" in this chapter. How might trade routes and the spread of the epidemic be linked?

● Writing About History

In this chapter's five Section Assessments, you developed skills for writing an expository essay.

Writing an Expository Essay: Cause and Effect Write an expository essay analyzing the causes or effects of one of the major events or trends of the High and Late Middle Ages: the Norman Conquest, the Magna Carta, the Reconquista, the preaching of John Wycliffe, the invention of the longbow. Consult page SH10 of the Writing Handbook for additional help.

Prewriting
• Do online or library research to find accounts of each of the topics listed above.

• Choose an event that interests you and brainstorm its causes and effects.
• Define and focus your topic. Use a graphic organizer.

Drafting
• Write a thesis statement and choose supporting information.
• Decide how to organize your writing: chronologically, by order of importance, or by categories of causes and effects.
• Write an introduction to present your thesis, a body to support your evidence, and a conclusion.

Revising
• Use the guidelines for revising your essay on page SH12 of the Writing Handbook.

Prepare for the GHSGT

Richard the Lion-heart, King and Crusader

Richard I, king of England from 1189 to 1199, spent only six months in England during his reign. The rest of the time he was at war abroad, most famously as one of the leaders of the Third Crusade. His daring as a warrior gained him the nickname "Lionheart," by which he is still referred to today. On his way home from the Holy Land, Richard was held for ransom by Emperor Henry IV of the Holy Roman Empire. It took his mother, Eleanor of Aquitaine, a year to raise the money to free him.

Document A

"Some . . . advised the king against engaging such a large army, as he then only had around fifty knights with him. Yet their trepidation [fear] only made him more courageous. Putting spur to horse, he charged into the enemy, broke through and scattered their battleline, destroying them. . . . When this was over the king put out an edict by public crier. All the locals who wanted peace could freely come and go, unhindered by his people, and enjoy guaranteed liberty."

—From ***Itinerarium Peregrinorum et Gesta Regis Ricardi,*** eyewitness account of the Third Crusade

Document B

"Yet to the sad 'tis comfort to complain
Friends I have many, and promises abound;
Shame will be theirs; if, for winters twain,
Unransom'd, I still bear a tyrant's chain.
Full well they know, my lords and nobles all . . .
Ne'er did I slight my poorest vassal's call . . .
They know this well who now are rich and strong . . .
That far from them, in hostile bonds I strain."

—poem by King Richard I, written while imprisoned by Holy Roman Emperor Henry IV

Document C

"[King Richard I of England] is one of the most romantic figures of all English history. . . . Richard has become the very epitome [symbol] of chivalry, the knight fighting bravely for his kingdom, his church, and his lady with ax, shield, and horse. . . . That in actual history, [he] does not quite measure up to the standards of his own legend does not dull his allure [appeal]. He was a brilliant military mind and a fearsome general . . . in single combat he was unrivaled in bravery and recklessness. . . . Richard is remembered for his bravado [daring] and cunning—and his extravagance. He is not remembered for his compassion, his tact, or his restraint."

—From ***Warriors of God,*** by James Reston, Jr., 2001

Document D

Richard the Lionheart

Analyzing Documents

Use your knowledge of medieval Europe and the Crusades and Documents A, B, C, and D to answer questions 1–4.

1. According to Document A, Richard I
   A bravely but foolishly rushed at the enemy when he was outnumbered.
   B was a good commander who stayed in the background.
   C was a brave conqueror and town crier.
   D was an impressive warrior and compassionate conqueror.

2. Which of the following statements BEST summarizes Reston's view of Richard the Lion-heart?
   A Although he was a brave warrior, he does not measure up to his own legend.
   B He was compassionate and tactful.
   C He is a truly heroic figure worthy of his reputation.
   D His legend leaves out his good qualities.

3. What do the creators of Documents A and D want to convey about Richard I?
   A his bravery and compassion
   B his bravery and skill as a poet
   C his bravery and skill as a warrior
   D his greatness as a Christian ruler

4. **Writing Task** Which of the documents above are most reliable, and why? How does each one help you understand Richard's character? Write your own description of Richard's character, using at least three of the documents to support your thesis.

9 The Byzantine Empire, Russia, and Eastern Europe

330–1613

Justinian Reforms the Law

At the beginning of his reign, the Byzantine emperor Justinian realized that the laws—inherited from ancient Rome—were long and confusing. He created a commission to collect, organize, and revise them into a body of law called the *Corpus Juris Civilis*, known as Justinian's Code. In the introduction, Justinian explains the basis of the law code:

66 The precepts of the law are these: to live honestly, to injure no one, and to give every man his due. The study of law consists of two branches, law public and law private. The former relates to the welfare of the Roman State; the latter to the advantage of the individual citizen. Of private law then we may say that it is of threefold origin, being collected from the precepts of nature, from those of the law of nations, or from those of the civil law of Rome. 99

Listen to the Witness History audio to hear more about Justinian's Code.

◄ This mosaic from a Byzantine church in Italy shows the emperor Justinian.

Emperor Constantine I

Gold cross showing the Virgin Mary

Russian necklace

 Performance Standards

Chapter Focus Question How did the Byzantine Empire preserve the heritage of Greece and Rome and help to shape the cultures of Russia and Eastern Europe?

Section 1
The Byzantine Empire
SSWH4a, SSWH4b, SSWH4c, SSWH4e

Section 2
The Rise of Russia
SSWH4b, SSWH4d

Section 3
Shaping Eastern Europe   SSWH5f

Use the ☑ **Quick Study Timeline** at the end of this chapter to preview chapter events.

 Concept Connector ONLINE

To explore Essential Questions related to this chapter, go to PHSchool.com
Web Code: nad-0907

Cross and chain

Depiction of the church of the Holy Apostles in Constantinople

WITNESS HISTORY 🔊 AUDIO

A Sovereign City

In 1203, when the Crusaders arrived at Constantinople, they were amazed by its splendor:

❝ [T]hose who had never seen Constantinople opened wide eyes now; for they could not believe that so rich a city could be in the whole world, when they saw her lofty walls and her stately towers wherewith she was encompassed, and these stately palaces and lofty churches, so many in number as no man might believe who had not seen them, and the length and breadth of this town which was sovereign over all others. ❞
—Villehardouin, a French Crusader

Focus Question What made the Byzantine empire rich and successful for so long, and why did it finally crumble?

The Byzantine Empire

Performance Standards

- **SSWH4a** Analyze importance of Justinian and Theodora.
- **SSWH4b** Describe impact of Byzantium on Moscow and the Russian Empire.
- **SSWH4c** Explain the Great Schism of 1054 CE.
- **SSWH4e** Explain Ottoman role in the Byzantine decline and Constantinople's capture.

Terms, People, and Places

Constantinople
Justinian
Justinian's Code
autocrat
Theodora
patriarch
icon
Great Schism

Note Taking

Reading Skill: Recognize Sequence Keep track of the sequence of events in the Byzantine empire in a table.

The Byzantine Empire	
330	Constantinople becomes the capital of the eastern Roman empire.

Constantinople sat at a crossroads of land and sea routes, and its great wealth came from trade. In addition to encouraging trade, its leaders constructed strong defenses for their city. As the cities of the western Roman empire crumbled, Constantinople remained secure and prospered. With its high walls and golden domes, it stood as the proud capital of the Byzantine empire.

Constantine Creates a "New Rome"

You have read that as German invaders pounded the Roman empire in the west, the Roman emperor Constantine and his successors shifted their base to the eastern Mediterranean. Constantine rebuilt the Greek city of Byzantium and then renamed it after himself—Constantinople. In 330, he made Constantinople the new capital of the empire. From this "New Rome," roads fanned out to the Balkans, to the Middle East, and to North Africa. In time, the eastern Roman empire became known as the Byzantine empire.

Constantinople Grows The vital center of the empire was Constantinople. The city was located on the shores of the Bosporus, a strait that links the Mediterranean and Black seas. Constantinople had an excellent harbor and was guarded on three sides by water. Emperors after Constantine built an elaborate system of land and sea walls to bolster its defenses.

Equally important, Constantinople commanded key trade routes linking Europe and Asia. For centuries, the city's favorable location made it Europe's busiest marketplace. There, merchants sold silks from China, wheat from Egypt, gems from India, spices from Southeast Asia, and furs from Viking lands in the north.

At the center of the city, Byzantine emperors and empresses lived in glittering splendor. Dressed in luxurious silk, they attended chariot races at the Hippodrome arena. Crowds cheered wildly as rival charioteers careened around and around in their vehicles. The spectacle was another reminder of the city's glorious Roman heritage.

Blending of Cultures After rising to spectacular heights, the Byzantine empire eventually declined to a small area around Constantinople itself. Yet it was still in existence nearly 1,000 years after the fall of the western Roman empire. As the heir to Rome, it promoted a brilliant civilization that blended ancient Greek, Roman, and Christian influences with other traditions of the Mediterranean world.

✔ **Checkpoint** Why did Constantinople become a rich and powerful city?

Constantine embarked on an ambitious building program to improve his new capital. Byzantium had been a walled city, but the new imperial buildings and growing population required a new set of walls outside the old, tripling the size of the city.

Primary Source

66 [Constantine] enlarged the city formerly called Byzantium, and surrounded it with high walls; likewise he built splendid dwelling houses . . . He erected all the needed edifices [for a great capital]—a hippodrome, fountains, porticoes [covered walkways] and other beautiful adornments.99
—Sozomen, Church historian, *circa* 450

Byzantium Flourishes Under Justinian

The Byzantine empire reached its peak under the emperor **Justinian,** who ruled from 527 to 565. Justinian was determined to revive ancient Rome by recovering lands that had been overrun by invaders. Led by the brilliant general Belisarius, Byzantine armies reconquered North Africa, Italy, and the southern Iberian peninsula. However, the fighting exhausted Justinian's treasury and weakened his defenses in the east. Moreover, the victories were only temporary. Justinian's successors would lose the bitterly contested lands, one after the other.

The Great City Is Rebuilt Justinian left a more lasting monument in the structures of his capital. In 532, riots and a devastating fire swept Constantinople. Many buildings were destroyed and many lives were lost. To restore Roman glory, Justinian launched a program to make Constantinople grander than ever. His great triumph was rebuilding the church of Hagia Sophia (AH yee uh suh FEE uh), which means "Holy Wisdom." Its immense, arching dome improved on earlier Roman buildings. The interior glowed with colored marble and embroidered silk curtains. Seeing this church, the emperor recalled King Solomon's temple in Jerusalem. "Glory to God who has judged me worthy of accomplishing such a work as this!" Justinian exclaimed. "O Solomon, I have surpassed you!"

Justinian's Code Has Far-Reaching Effects Even more important than expanding the empire and rebuilding its capital was Justinian's reform of the law. Early in his reign, he set up a commission to collect, revise, and organize all the laws of ancient Rome. The result was the *Corpus Juris Civilis,* or "Body of Civil Law," popularly known as **Justinian's Code.** This massive collection included laws passed by Roman assemblies or decreed by Roman emperors, as well as the legal writings of Roman judges and a handbook for students.

Vocabulary Builder

temporary—(TEM puh rehr ee) *adj.*
lasting for or relating to a limited time

Hagia Sophia

Hagia Sophia, or "Holy Wisdom," stands at a cultural and geographic crossroads. Istanbul—once called Constantinople—is located where Europe meets Asia and Islam meets Christianity. Justinian ordered the construction of Hagia Sophia in 532, after the previous church was destroyed in riots. Since then, the dome has been rebuilt and the building repaired. Despite warfare and invasions, Hagia Sophia has remained intact, a prize for whoever controlled the city. It has served as a cathedral of Eastern Orthodox Christianity, a Roman Christian cathedral, and an Islamic mosque. Since 1935, it has been a museum. The modern interior reflects the Christian and Muslim heritage of the building. Islamic artists avoid using human or animal figures, while Byzantine artists were famous for their mosaics of religious figures, such as the one above.

Round plaques decorated with calligraphy were added between 1847 and 1849. This one shows Muhammad's name.

pendentives

These towers, called minarets, were built after the building became a mosque. Mosque officials, called muezzins, call Muslims to prayer from the minarets.

The dome rises 184 feet from the floor. The architects used a technique that was new in the 500s to support this huge dome. Triangular supports called pendentives were inserted in the corners of the square, which supported the weight of the dome on the square base.

Thinking Critically

1. **Synthesize Information** Explain the significance of Constantinople.
2. **Draw Inferences** Why was Hagia Sophia turned into a museum?

Justinian's Code had an impact far beyond the Byzantine empire. By the 1100s, it had reached Western Europe. There, monarchs modeled their laws on its principles, which helped them to strengthen and centralize their power. Centuries later, the code also guided legal thinkers who began to put together the international law in use today.

Justinian Rules With Absolute Power Justinian used the law to <u>unify</u> the empire under his control. He ruled as an **autocrat,** or sole ruler with complete authority. The Byzantine emperor also had power over the Church. He was deemed Christ's co-ruler on Earth. As a Byzantine official wrote, "The emperor is equal to all men in the nature of his body, but in the authority of his rank he is similar to God, who rules all." Unlike feudal monarchs in Western Europe, he combined both political power and spiritual authority. His control was aided by his wife, **Theodora.** A shrewd politician, she served as advisor and co-ruler to Justinian and even pursued her own policies.

Economic and Military Strength Is Second to None The Byzantine empire flourished under a strong central government, which exercised strict control over a prosperous economy. Peasants formed the backbone of the empire, working the land, paying taxes, and providing soldiers for the military. In the cities of the empire, trade and industry flourished. While the economy of Western Europe struggled and use of money declined, the Byzantine empire preserved a healthy money economy. The bezant, the Byzantine gold coin stamped with the emperor's image, circulated from England to China.

At the same time, the Byzantines built one of the strongest military forces in the world. Soldiers, ships, and sailors protected the empire, and fortifications protected its capital. The Byzantines also relied on a secret weapon called Greek fire, a liquid that probably contained petroleum. Thrown toward an enemy, it would ignite on contact, and its fire could not be put out with water. For centuries, Greek fire was an effective and terrifying weapon of the Byzantine navy.

The Empire's Fortunes Change In the centuries after Justinian, the empire faced successive attacks by Persians, Slavs, Vikings, Huns, and Turks. These attacks were largely unsuccessful. The empire thus served as a buffer for Western Europe, especially in preventing the spread of Muslim conquest. Beginning in the 600s and 700s, however, Arab armies gradually gained control of much of the Mediterranean world. Still, Constantinople itself withstood their attack, and the Byzantines held on to their heartland in the Balkans and Asia Minor.

✔ **Checkpoint** Describe Justinian's accomplishments.

Byzantine Christianity

Christianity was as influential in the Byzantine empire as it was in Western Europe. But the way Christianity was practiced differed in the two regions. Over time, these differences became more distinct and caused increasing friction.

BIOGRAPHY

Empress Theodora
From humble beginnings as the daughter of a bear keeper at Constantinople's Hippodrome, Theodora (497–548) rose to become Justinian's wife, advisor, and co-ruler. A shrewd, tough, and sometimes ruthless politician, Theodora did not hesitate to challenge the emperor and pursue her own policies.

Theodora's most dramatic act came during a revolt in 532. "Emperor, if you wish to flee, well and good; you have the money, the ships are ready, the sea is clear," said Theodora calmly. "But I shall stay," she concluded. "I accept the ancient proverb: Royal purple is the best burial sheet." Theodora's courageous words inspired Justinian to remain in Constantinople and crush the revolt that threatened his power. **How did Theodora contribute to the greatness of the empire?**

Vocabulary Builder
<u>unify</u>—(YOO nuh fy) v. to bring people or things together to form a single unit or entity

Geography *Interactive*
For: Audio guided tour
Web Code: nap-0912

Byzantine empire, 527–565
Byzantine empire, about 1020
Byzantine empire, 1360

Miller Projection

0   200   400 mi

0   200   400 km

Map Skills The Byzantine empire reached its greatest size by 565. By 1000, it had lost much of its territory to invading armies.

1. **Locate** (a) Constantinople (b) Rome (c) Jerusalem
2. **Describe** Describe the extent of the Byzantine empire in 1020.
3. **Draw Inferences** What does the extent of the empire in 565 suggest about the rule of Justinian?

East and West Differ Since early Christian times, differences had emerged over Church leadership. Although the Byzantine emperor was not a priest, he controlled Church affairs and appointed the **patriarch,** or highest Church official, in Constantinople. Byzantine Christians rejected the pope's claim to authority over all Christians.

Unlike priests in Western Europe, the Byzantine clergy kept their right to marry. Greek, not Latin, was the language of the Byzantine Church. As in the Roman Church, the chief Byzantine holy day was Easter, celebrated as the day Jesus rose from the dead. However, Byzantine Christians placed somewhat less emphasis on Christmas—the celebration of the birth of Jesus—compared to Christians in the West.

The Church Divides During the Middle Ages, the two branches of Christianity drew farther apart. A dispute over the use of **icons,** or holy images, contributed to the split. Many Byzantine Christians used images of Jesus, the Virgin Mary, and the saints in their worship. In the 700s, however, a Byzantine emperor outlawed the veneration of icons, saying it violated God's commandment against worshiping "graven images."

The ban set off violent battles within the empire. From the west, the pope joined in the dispute by condemning the Byzantine emperor. Although a later empress eventually restored the use of icons, the conflict left great resentment against the pope in the Byzantine empire.

In 1054, other controversies provoked a schism, or split, between eastern and western Christianity, known as the **Great Schism.** The Byzantine church became known as the Eastern, or Greek, Orthodox

Church. The western branch became known as the Roman Catholic Church. The pope and the patriarch excommunicated each other. Thereafter, contacts between the two churches were guarded and distant. They treated each other as rivals rather than as branches of the same faith.

✓ **Checkpoint** Why did the Eastern and Western churches differ?

The Empire Suffers Crisis and Collapse

By the time of the schism, the Byzantine empire was in decline. Struggles over succession, court intrigues, and constant wars undermined its strength. As in Western Europe, powerful local lords gained control of large areas. As the empire faltered, its enemies advanced. The Normans conquered southern Italy. Even more serious, the Seljuk Turks advanced across Asia Minor. The Seljuks had been a nomadic people in central Asia. They converted to Islam in their migrations westward.

The Crusades Lead to Plunder In the 1090s, the Byzantine emperor called for Western help to fight the Seljuks, whose attacks blocked the pilgrimage routes to Jerusalem. The result was the First Crusade. During later crusades, however, trade rivalry sparked violence between the Byzantine empire and Venice, a city-state in northern Italy. In 1204, Venetian merchants persuaded knights on the Fourth Crusade to attack Constantinople. For three days, crusaders burned and plundered the city, sending much treasure westward. Western Christians ruled Constantinople for 57 years. Although a Byzantine emperor reclaimed the capital in the 1260s, the empire never recovered. Venetian merchants had gained control of Byzantine trade, draining the wealth of the empire. But there was an even more threatening foe—the increasingly powerful Ottoman Turks, who soon controlled most of Asia Minor and the Balkans.

Constantinople Falls to the Turks In 1453, Ottoman forces surrounded the city of Constantinople. They brought cannons to attack the city's walls. The Byzantine defenders had stretched a huge chain across the harbor to protect against invasion by sea, but the Turks hauled their ships overland and then launched them into the harbor. After a siege lasting two months, the Turks stormed Constantinople's broken walls. It is said that when the last Byzantine emperor was offered safe passage, he replied, "God forbid that I should live an emperor without an empire." He chose instead to die fighting.

Forces led by Ottoman ruler Mehmet II entered the city in triumph. The ancient city was renamed Istanbul and became the capital of the Ottoman empire. Hagia Sophia was turned into an Islamic house of worship, and Istanbul soon emerged as a great center of Muslim culture.

✓ **Checkpoint** How was the Byzantine empire destroyed?

The Byzantine Heritage

Although Byzantine power had faded long before, the fall of Constantinople marked the end of an age. To Europeans, the empire had stood for centuries as the enduring symbol of Roman civilization. Throughout the Middle Ages, Byzantine influence radiated

Turks Take Constantinople
The nineteenth-century painting below shows the Turks entering Constantinople after defeating Byzantine forces.

Byzantine Art
The religious icon above is typical of Byzantine art. Notice that both eyes of each person are shown. An evil person was depicted in profile, with only one eye showing.

across Europe. Even the Ottoman conquerors adapted features of Byzantine government, social life, and architecture.

What was the Byzantine heritage? For 1,000 years, the Byzantines built on the culture of the Hellenistic world. Byzantine civilization blended Christian religious beliefs with Greek science, philosophy, arts, and literature. The Byzantines also extended Roman achievements in engineering and law.

Unique Contributions in the Arts Byzantine artists made unique contributions, especially in religious art and architecture, that influenced Western styles from the Middle Ages to the present. Icons, designed to evoke the presence of God, gave viewers a sense of personal contact with the sacred. Mosaics brought scenes from the Bible to life. In architecture, Byzantine palaces and churches blended Greek, Roman, Persian, and other Middle Eastern styles.

The World of Learning Byzantine scholars preserved the classic works of ancient Greece and Rome. In addition, they produced their own great books, especially in the field of history.

Like the Greek historians Herodotus and Thucydides, Byzantine historians were mostly concerned with writing about their own times. Procopius, an advisor to the general Belisarius, chronicled the Byzantine campaign against Persia. In his *Secret History,* Procopius savagely criticized Justinian and Theodora. He called the emperor "both an evil-doer and easily led into evil . . . never of his own accord speaking the truth." Anna Comnena is considered by many scholars to be the Western world's first important female historian. In the *Alexiad,* she analyzed the reign of her father, Emperor Alexius I. Comnena's book portrayed Latin crusaders as greedy barbarians.

As the empire tottered in the 1400s, many Greek scholars left Constantinople to teach at Italian universities. They took valuable Greek manuscripts to the West, along with their knowledge of Greek and Byzantine culture. The work of these scholars contributed to the European cultural flowering that became known as the Renaissance.

✓ **Checkpoint** Describe Byzantine contributions to art and learning.

Progress Monitoring *Online*
For: Self-quiz with vocabulary practice
Web Code: naa-0911

SECTION 1 **Assessment**

Terms, People, and Places
1. For each term, person, or place listed at the beginning of the section, write a sentence explaining its significance.

Note Taking
2. **Reading Skill: Recognize Sequence** Use your completed table to answer the Focus Question: What made the Byzantine empire rich and successful for so long, and why did it finally crumble?

Comprehension and Critical Thinking
3. **Categorize** Which of Justinian's achievements do you think had the most impact on his empire's greatness? Explain your answer.
4. **Make Comparisons** Compare Byzantine Christianity and Western Christianity at the time of the schism.
5. **Demonstrate Reasoned Judgment** Why was the Byzantine empire so important to Western Europe? Explain.

● **Writing About History**
Quick Write: Gather Information
Choose a person you read about in this section, and use at least two reliable library or Internet sources to find out information about him or her. Create a timeline showing the most important events in that person's life. Choose several of those events and ask questions about them, such as the following:
• What led to this event?
• What was the result of this event?

A Russian necklace

Prince Yuri Dolgoruky
of Moscow

WITNESS HISTORY 🔊 AUDIO

The Third Rome

In Russia, a patriotic monk saw a special meaning in the fall of Constantinople in 1453. Now, he declared, Moscow was the "third Rome," the successor to the Roman and Byzantine empires:

❝ [T]he third Rome . . . shines like the sun . . . throughout the whole universe. . . . [T]wo Romes have fallen, and the third one stands, and a fourth one there shall not be.❞
—Philotheos, quoted in *Tsar and People* (Cherniavsky)

Focus Question How did geography and the migrations of different peoples influence the rise of Russia?

The Rise of Russia

 Performance Standards

- **SSWH4b** Describe impact and effects of Byzantium on Moscow and the Russian empire and culture on Tsar Ivan III and Kiev.
- **SSWH4d** Analyze role of Chinggis Khan in developing the Mongol Empire and analyze the impact of the Mongols on Russia, China, and the West.

Terms, People, and Places

steppe	Ivan the Great
Kiev	tsar
Cyrillic	Ivan the Terrible
Golden Horde	

Note Taking

Reading Skill: Recognize Sequence Make a timeline to keep track of the sequence of events in the rise of Russia between the 700s and 1613. The sample below will help you get started. Add events as you read.

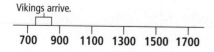

Vikings arrive.

700   900   1100   1300   1500   1700

As Western Europe was developing its distinctive medieval civilization, Russian culture took a different path in the east. Connecting Europe and Asia, it became a center of power in its own right. One reason Russia developed differently from Western Europe was its unique geography.

Geography's Influence

Russia lies across the vast Eurasian plain that stretches from Europe to the borders of China. Although mapmakers use the Ural Mountains to mark the boundary between Europe and Asia, these ancient mountains were long ago worn away to wooded hills. They posed no great obstacle to migration.

Three Regions Three broad zones with different climates and resources helped shape early Russian life. The northern forests supplied lumber for building and fuel. Fur-bearing animals attracted hunters, but poor soil and a cold, snowy climate hindered farming. Farmers did settle in a band of fertile land farther south. This second region, which today includes the country of Ukraine, was home to Russia's first civilization.

A third region, the southern **steppe,** is an open, treeless grassland. It offered splendid pasture for the herds and horses of nomadic peoples. With no natural barriers, the steppe was a great highway along which streams of nomads migrated. From Asia, they spread into Europe, settling and conquering new territory.

Rivers Link Russia and Byzantium Russia's network of rivers, running from north to south, provided transportation for both people and goods. They linked early Russians to the advanced Byzantine world in the south. During the early Middle Ages, Russians turned in this direction rather than to Western Europe, which was a fragmented, frontier territory after the fall of the Roman empire.

✔ **Checkpoint** How did geography affect Russian settlement and growth?

Kiev Grows Strong

The city of **Kiev,** the capital of present-day Ukraine, was the center of the first Russian state. Its culture and growth were the result of a mixing of two distinct peoples.

Vikings Settle Among Slavs During Roman times, Slavic peoples lived in a region extending from present-day Poland and Belarus into Ukraine. During the 500s and 600s, they spread east into present-day Russia and south toward the Byzantine Empire. They had a simple political organization and were organized into clans. They lived in small villages, farming and trading along the rivers that ran between the Baltic and the Black seas.

In the 700s and 800s, Vikings steered their long ships out of Scandinavia. These Vikings, whom the Russians called Varangians, traveled south along the rivers, trading with and collecting tribute, or forced payment, from the Slavs. They also conducted a thriving trade with Constantinople. Located at the heart of this vital trade network was the city of Kiev.

Russians traditionally date the origins of their country to 862, when Rurik, a prince of a Varangian tribe called the Rus (roos), began his rule of Novgorod in the north. After Rurik's death, Rus lands expanded to include Kiev, which became their capital. The Rus princes lent their name to the growing principality of Russia.

The Byzantines Gain Influence Trade first brought Kiev into the Byzantine orbit. In the 800s, Constantinople sent Christian missionaries to convert the Slavs. About 863, two Greek brothers, Cyril and Methodius, adapted the Greek alphabet so they could translate the Bible into the Slavic tongue. This **Cyrillic** (suh RIL ik) alphabet became the written script that is still used today in Russia, Ukraine, Serbia, and Bulgaria.

In 957, Princess Olga of Kiev converted to Byzantine Christianity. During the reign of her grandson Vladimir, the new religion spread widely. After his own conversion, Vladimir married the sister of a Byzantine emperor. He made Orthodox Christianity the religion of the Rus and began to align his kingdom politically and culturally with the Byzantine empire. Soon, Russians adopted aspects of Byzantine culture, such as art, music, and architecture. Byzantine domes evolved into the onion-shaped domes typical of Russian churches.

Princes Secure Power Kiev gained strength under Vladimir and his son, Yaroslav the Wise. Both won military victories and spread Christianity. Yaroslav set up close ties

Byzantine Missionaries
The icon below shows Cyril and Methodius, Greek missionaries who spread Christianity among the Slavs.

between church and state. Russian rulers, like the Byzantine emperor, eventually controlled the Church, making it dependent on them for support. The Russian Orthodox Church became a pillar of state power.

In addition to giving legal status to the Church, Yaroslav had many religious texts translated into the Slavic language. He made improvements to the city and issued a written law code. However, Kiev declined after his death as rival families battled for the throne.

✔ **Checkpoint** Why did Kiev become an important city?

The Mongols Rule Russia

In the early 1200s, a young leader united the nomadic Mongols of central Asia. As his mounted bowmen overran lands from China to eastern Europe, he took the title Genghis Khan (GENG is kahn), or "World Emperor."

The Golden Horde Advances Between 1236 and 1241, Batu, the grandson of Genghis, led Mongol armies into Russia. Known as the **Golden Horde** because of the color of their tents, these invaders looted and burned Kiev and other Russian towns. So many inhabitants were killed, declared a Russian historian, that "no eye remained to weep for the dead." From their capital on the Volga, the Golden Horde ruled Russia for more than 150 years. Areas that were not directly controlled by the Mongols suffered destructive raids from Mongol armies.

Although they were fierce conquerors, the Mongols were generally not meddlesome rulers. Russian princes had to acknowledge the Mongols as their overlords and pay heavy tribute. But as long as the tribute was paid, the Mongols left the Russian princes to rule without much other interference.

The Mongols Exert Influence Historians have long debated how Mongol rule affected Russia. Although the Mongols converted to Islam, they <u>tolerated</u> the Russian Orthodox Church, which grew more powerful during this period. The Mongol conquest also brought peace to the huge swath of land between China and Eastern Europe, and Russian merchants benefited from new trade routes across this region.

In addition, the absolute power of the Mongols served as a model for later Russian rulers. Russian princes developed a strong desire to centralize their own power without interference from nobles, the clergy, or wealthy merchants. Perhaps most important, Mongol rule cut Russia off from contacts with western Europe at a time when Europeans were making rapid advances in the arts and sciences.

✔ **Checkpoint** Describe Mongol rule of Russia.

Vocabulary Builder

tolerated—(TAHL ur ayt ed) *v.* recognized and did not suppress the different beliefs or practices of other people

St. Basil's Cathedral in Moscow, Russia

Moscow Takes the Lead

During the Mongol period, the princes of Moscow steadily increased their power. Their success was due in part to the city's location near important river trade routes. They also used their positions as tribute collectors for the Mongols to subdue neighboring towns. When the head of the Russian Orthodox Church made Moscow his capital, the city became not just Russia's political center, but its religious center as well.

As Mongol power declined, the princes of Moscow took on a new role as patriotic defenders of Russia against foreign rule. In 1380, they rallied other Russians and defeated the Golden Horde at the battle of Kulikovo (koo lih KOH vuh). Although the Mongols continued their terrifying raids, their strength was much reduced.

The Success of Ivan the Great A driving force behind Moscow's successes was Ivan III, known as **Ivan the Great.** Between 1462 and 1505, he brought much of northern Russia under his rule. He also recovered Russian territory that had fallen into the hands of neighboring Lithuania.

Mongol armor

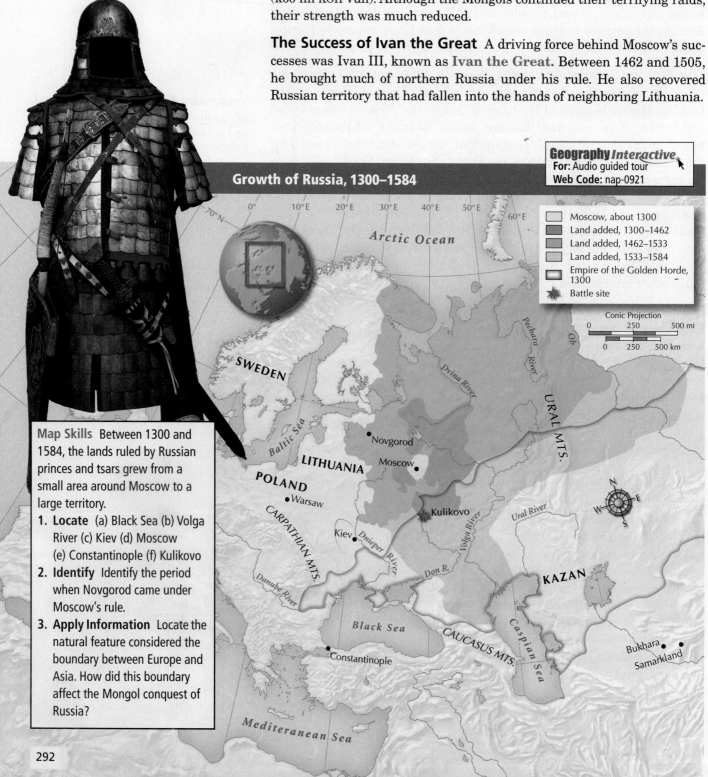

Growth of Russia, 1300–1584

Map Legend:
- Moscow, about 1300
- Land added, 1300–1462
- Land added, 1462–1533
- Land added, 1533–1584
- Empire of the Golden Horde, 1300
- Battle site

Conic Projection
0   250   500 mi
0   250   500 km

Map Skills Between 1300 and 1584, the lands ruled by Russian princes and tsars grew from a small area around Moscow to a large territory.

1. **Locate** (a) Black Sea (b) Volga River (c) Kiev (d) Moscow (e) Constantinople (f) Kulikovo
2. **Identify** Identify the period when Novgorod came under Moscow's rule.
3. **Apply Information** Locate the natural feature considered the boundary between Europe and Asia. How did this boundary affect the Mongol conquest of Russia?

Ivan built the framework for absolute rule. He tried to limit the power of the *boyars*, or great landowning nobles. After he married a niece of the last Byzantine emperor, Ivan adopted Byzantine court rituals to emphasize Russia's role as the heir to Byzantine power. Like the Byzantine emperors, he used a double-headed eagle as his symbol and sometimes referred to himself as **tsar,** the Russian word for Caesar. In 1504, a Russian church council echoed Byzantine statements, declaring, "By nature, the tsar is like any other man, but in power and office he is like the highest God."

Ivan the Terrible Establishes Absolute Rule In 1547, Ivan IV, grandson of Ivan the Great, became the first Russian ruler officially crowned tsar. He further centralized royal power by limiting the privileges of the old boyar families and granting land to nobles in exchange for military or other service. At a time when the manor system was fading in Western Europe, Ivan IV introduced new laws that tied Russian serfs to the land.

About 1560, Ivan IV became increasingly unstable. He trusted no one and became subject to violent fits of rage. In a moment of madness, he even killed his own son. He organized the *oprichniki* (ah PREECH nee kee), agents of terror who enforced the tsar's will. Dressed in black robes and mounted on black horses, they slaughtered rebellious boyars and sacked towns where people were suspected of disloyalty. Their saddles were decorated with a dog's head and a broom, symbols of their constant watchfulness to sweep away their master's enemies.

The tsar's awesome power, and the ways he used it, earned him the title **Ivan the Terrible.** When he died in 1584, he left a land seething with rebellion. But he had introduced Russia to a tradition of extreme absolute power that would shape Russian history well into the twentieth century.

✔ **Checkpoint** How did Ivan III and Ivan IV establish authoritarian power?

Ivan the Terrible

"I grew up on the throne," explained Ivan the Terrible (1530–1584) of his unhappy childhood. His father, Vasily, died when Ivan was only three years old. Intelligent, well-read, and religious, young Ivan was crowned tsar at age 17.

Although Ivan had long been a harsh ruler, his behavior became increasingly unstable after his wife died. Prone to violence, he crushed any opposition, real or imagined. He had thousands of people in the city of Novgorod killed because he feared a plot against him. Almost every noble family was affected by his murders. "I have surpassed all sinners," he confessed in his will. **How do you think a reign like Ivan's affected Russian life?**

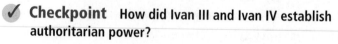

SECTION 2 **Assessment**

Progress Monitoring *Online*
For: Self-quiz with vocabulary practice
Web Code: naa-0921

Terms, People, and Places

1. Place each of the key terms at the beginning of the section into one of the following categories: government, culture, or geography. Write a sentence for each term explaining your choice.

Note Taking

2. **Reading Skill: Recognize Sequence** Use your completed timeline to answer the Focus Question: How did geography and the migrations of different peoples influence the rise of Russia?

Comprehension and Critical Thinking

3. **Recognize Cause and Effect** How did Russia's geography affect its early history?

4. **Determine Relevance** How important was Byzantine influence on Russia? Explain your answer.

5. **Synthesize Information** How did Mongol rule influence Russia's economy and political structure?

6. **Analyze Information** How did a tradition of absolute rule develop in Russia?

● **Writing About History**

Quick Write: Write a Thesis Statement
Use a reliable library or Internet source to list the important events in the life of someone you read about in this section. Describe the personality traits that person displayed in his or her life. Write a thesis statement that presents your conclusion about his or her personality and actions. For example, you might say that Ivan the Terrible was a harsh and unstable ruler.

Silver brooch

King Milutin of Serbia

WITNESS HISTORY  AUDIO

A Fragmented Region

In 965, Ibrahim-Ibn-Yaqub, a Jewish traveler from Moorish Spain, visited Eastern Europe:

66 The lands of the Slavs stretch from the Syrian Sea to the Ocean in the north. . . . They comprise numerous tribes, each different from the other. . . . If not for the disharmony amongst them, caused by the multiplication of factions and by their fragmentation into clans, no people could match them for strength. . . . The Slavs wage war with the Byzantines, with the Franks and Langobards, and with other peoples . . . with varying success. 99

Focus Question How did geography and ethnic diversity contribute to the turmoil of Eastern European history?

Shaping Eastern Europe

GA Performance Standards

• **SSWH5f** Analyze the relationship between Judaism, Christianity and Islam.

Terms, People, and Places

Balkan Peninsula   diet
ethnic group   Golden Bull of 1222

Note Taking

Reading Skill: Recognize Multiple Causes As you read, notice the conditions and events that led to the diversity of peoples and cultures in Eastern Europe. Keep track of these causes by filling in a concept web like the one below. Add ovals as needed.

The history of Eastern Europe has been marked by migration, foreign conquest, war, and revolution. Along with the Slavs described by Ibrahim-Ibn-Yaqub, the region is home to a diverse mix of peoples who have often battled with each other and with foreigners. At the same time, this diverse mix of peoples has greatly enriched the culture of the region.

Geography Shapes Eastern Europe

Eastern Europe has been both a buffer and a crossroads. It is a wide swath of territory lying between German-speaking Central Europe to the west and the largest Slavic nation, Russia, to the east. It reaches from the chilly waters of the Baltic Sea, down across the plains of Poland and Hungary, and then through the mountainous **Balkan Peninsula.** This roughly triangular arm of land, often called simply the Balkans, juts southward into the warm Mediterranean.

Much of the region lies on the great European Plain that links up with the steppes of southern Russia. Its main rivers, such as the Danube and the Vistula (VISH chuh luh), flow either south into the Black Sea or north into the Baltic Sea. Goods and cultural influences traveled along these river routes. As a result, the Balkans in the south felt the impact of the Byzantine empire and, later, the Muslim Ottoman empire. In contrast, northern regions bordering Germany and the Baltic Sea forged closer links to Western Europe. The eastern part of the region felt the strong influence of Russia.

✓ **Checkpoint** How did its rivers affect Eastern Europe?

Migrations Contribute to Diversity

Eastern Europe's geography has contributed to its cultural diversity. The ease of migration through the region encouraged many different peoples to seek new homes there. Some neighboring groups sought to influence or <u>dominate</u> the region. As a result, Eastern Europe now includes a wealth of languages and cultures.

Ethnic Groups Settle in Eastern Europe and the Balkans In the early Middle Ages, the Slavs spread out from a region centered on present-day Belarus. The West Slavs filtered into present-day Poland and the Czech and Slovak republics. The South Slavs occupied the Balkans. The Balkans were peopled by various other ethnic groups as well. (An **ethnic group** is a group of people who share the same language and cultural heritage.)

Vocabulary Builder

<u>dominate</u>—(DAHM uh nayt) *v.* to have control, power, or authority over somebody or something

● **INFOGRAPHIC**

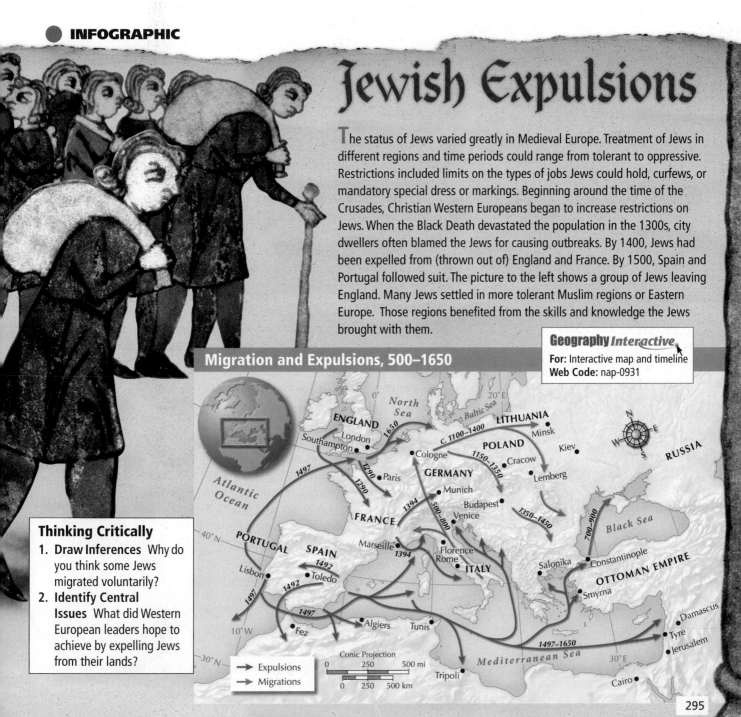

Jewish Expulsions

The status of Jews varied greatly in Medieval Europe. Treatment of Jews in different regions and time periods could range from tolerant to oppressive. Restrictions included limits on the types of jobs Jews could hold, curfews, or mandatory special dress or markings. Beginning around the time of the Crusades, Christian Western Europeans began to increase restrictions on Jews. When the Black Death devastated the population in the 1300s, city dwellers often blamed the Jews for causing outbreaks. By 1400, Jews had been expelled from (thrown out of) England and France. By 1500, Spain and Portugal followed suit. The picture to the left shows a group of Jews leaving England. Many Jews settled in more tolerant Muslim regions or Eastern Europe. Those regions benefited from the skills and knowledge the Jews brought with them.

Geography *Interactive*
For: Interactive map and timeline
Web Code: nap-0931

Migration and Expulsions, 500–1650

Thinking Critically
1. **Draw Inferences** Why do you think some Jews migrated voluntarily?
2. **Identify Central Issues** What did Western European leaders hope to achieve by expelling Jews from their lands?

Expulsions
Migrations

Waves of Asian peoples migrated into Eastern Europe, among them the Huns, Avars, Bulgars, Khazars, and Magyars. Vikings and other Germanic peoples added to the mix.

Christians and Muslims Influence the Region Powerful neighboring states exercised strong cultural and religious influences on Eastern Europe. Byzantine missionaries spread Eastern Orthodox Christianity and Byzantine culture throughout the Balkans. German knights and missionaries from the West brought Roman Catholic Christianity to Poland, Hungary, the Czech area, and the western Balkans. In the 1300s, the Ottomans invaded the Balkans, bringing Islam into pockets of that region.

Jewish Settlers Migrate to Poland In the early Middle Ages, there were thriving Jewish communities in Muslim Spain. Jews had also migrated to Western Europe. Although educated Jews sometimes held important government and scholarly posts, Christians often blamed Jews for hard times and natural disasters. Western European Christians launched brutal attacks on Jewish communities, particularly during the Crusades and the Black Death. Monarchs in England, France, and Spain even expelled Jews from their lands. Faced with persecution or expulsion, many Jews fled east in the late Middle Ages. Eastern Europe became a refuge for many Jewish settlers.

In 1264, Prince Boleslaw of Cracow issued a charter protecting the liberties of Jews, and Polish kings continued a policy of toleration toward Jews for the next 500 years. As a result, Jewish villages sprang up in Poland and other sparsely populated areas of Eastern Europe. Jewish merchants and scholars contributed to the economic and cultural development of Poland during this period.

✓ **Checkpoint** How did three major religions come to Eastern Europe?

Three Early Kingdoms Develop

During the Middle Ages, Eastern Europe included many kingdoms and small states. Sometimes empires absorbed national groups. Alliances or royal marriages might bind others together. A look at the kingdoms of Poland, Hungary, and Serbia will demonstrate these shifting fortunes.

Poland Enjoys Greatness Missionaries brought Roman Catholicism to the West Slavs of Poland in the 900s. Within a century, the first Polish king was crowned. To survive, Poland often had to battle Germans, Russians, and Mongols.

The marriage of Queen Jadwiga (yahd VEE gah) to Duke Wladyslaw Jagiello (vwah DIS wahf yahg YEH loh) of Lithuania in 1386 ushered in Poland's greatest age. Poland-Lithuania was the largest state in Europe, stretching from the Baltic to the Black Sea. Unlike in Russia or most of Western Europe, however, political power in Poland gradually shifted from the monarch to the nobles. They met in a **diet,** or assembly, where

Note Taking

Reading Skill: Recognize Sequence As you read, fill in important events in the history of these countries in a chart like the one below.

Important Events		
Poland	Hungary	Serbia

Duke Jagiello (below) and Queen Jadwiga (right) of Poland

the vote of a single noble could block the passage of a law. This *liberum veto,* or "free veto," made it hard for the government to take decisive action.

Without a strong central government, Poland-Lithuania declined. It enjoyed a final moment of glory in 1683 when the Polish king Jan Sobieski (yahn soh BYEH skee) broke the Ottoman siege of Vienna. In the next century, however, Poland and Lithuania were gobbled up by ambitious neighbors and disappeared from the map.

The Magyars Rule Hungary The Magyars, who had raided Europe from the Asian steppes, eventually settled in Hungary. Like the West Slavs of Poland, they adopted Roman Catholicism. During the Middle Ages, Magyar rulers also controlled present-day Slovakia, Croatia, and parts of Romania. Like King John of England, the Hungarian king was forced to sign a charter recognizing nobles' rights. Known as the **Golden Bull of 1222,** it strictly limited royal power.

The Mongols overran Hungary in 1241, killing as much as half its population. These invaders soon withdrew, so the Mongol invasion did not have the lasting impact on Hungary that it had on Russia. The expansion of the Ottoman Turks, though, ended Hungarian independence in 1526.

The Serbs Establish a Balkan Kingdom Some of the South Slavs who settled the Balkans became the ancestors of the Serbs. Early Serb leaders recognized Byzantine authority, and by the late 800s, most Serbs had accepted Orthodox Christianity. In the late 1100s, they set up their own state, which reached its height in the 1300s under Stefan Dusan (STEH vahn DOO shahn). Dusan also encouraged Byzantine culture, even modeling his law code on that of Justinian.

Dusan's successors lacked his political gifts, however, and Serbia could not withstand the advance of Ottoman Turks. At the battle of Kosovo in 1389, Serbs fought to the death, a memory still honored by their descendants more than 600 years later.

✔ **Checkpoint** How did each kingdom lose its independence?

Stefan Dusan (1308–1355)
As king, Dusan based his law code on the Byzantine example, but he also attacked the empire he admired. He took Albania, Macedonia, and other lands from the Byzantines.

Terms, People, and Places

1. For each term, person, or place listed at the beginning of the section, write a sentence explaining its significance.

Note Taking

2. **Reading Skill: Recognize Multiple Causes** Use your completed concept web to answer the Focus Question: How did geography and ethnic diversity contribute to the turmoil of Eastern European history?

Comprehension and Critical Thinking

3. **Determine Relevance** How did geography affect the development of Eastern Europe?

4. **Identify Central Issues** How did Eastern Europe become home to so many ethnic groups?

5. **Make Comparisons** How were the histories of Poland and Hungary similar? How were they different?

● **Writing About History**

Quick Write: Write an Introduction Research someone you read about in this section, and write a thesis statement expressing an idea about that person's life. Group information that supports your thesis statement into categories, such as actions that show bravery, actions that show religious devotion, or actions that show power. Include specific facts to support these points. Write a paragraph supporting your thesis statement and major points.

CHAPTER 9

Quick Study Guide

 SSWH4b

Progress Monitoring Online
For: Self-test with vocabulary practice
Web Code: naa-0941

■ Religions in Eastern Europe

Region	Religion
Byzantine empire	Eastern Orthodox Christianity
Russia	Eastern Orthodox Christianity
Poland	Roman Catholicism Many Jewish settlements
Czech area	Roman Catholicism
Hungary	Roman Catholicism
The Balkans	Serbs: Eastern Orthodox Christianity Croats: Roman Catholicism Slovenes: Eastern Orthodox Christianity Bosnians: Islam

■ Key Political Leaders

Byzantine empire

- Constantine established Constantinople (named for himself) as the capital of the eastern Roman empire; converted to Christianity
- Justinian, emperor during the Byzantine empire's golden age

Russia

- Rurik, Rus prince who ruled Novgorod
- Princess Olga of Kiev, converted to Christianity
- Yaroslav the Wise, presided over golden age in Kiev
- Ivan the Great, expanded Russia and centralized power
- Ivan the Terrible, tsar who established absolute power

Eastern Europe

- Queen Jadwiga, queen of Poland, joint ruler of Poland-Lithuania
- Duke Wladislaw Jagiello, Lithuanian duke, joint ruler of Poland-Lithuania
- Stefan Dusan, ruler of Serbia

■ The Byzantine Empire, Eastern Europe, and Russia in 1300

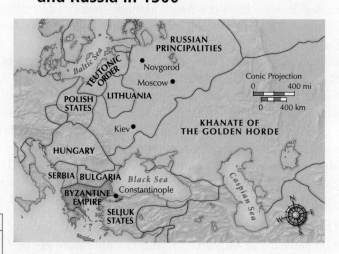

■ Key Events in the Byzantine Empire, Eastern Europe, and Russia

330
Constantinople becomes the capital of the Eastern Roman empire.

527
Justinian begins his rule of the Byzantine empire.

862
Rurik begins his rule of Novgorod, establishing the Rus dynasty.

Chapter Events
Global Events

300

600

900

622
Muhammad makes a journey, known as the hijra, from Mecca to Yathrib.

800
Pope Leo III crowns Charlemagne emperor of the Romans.

Concept Connector

Essential Question Review

To connect prior knowledge with what you have learned in this chapter, answer the questions below in your Concept Connector journal. Use the journal in the Reading and Note Taking Study Guide to record your answers (or go to www.phschool.com **Web Code**: nad-0907). In addition, record information about the following concepts:

- Empire: the Byzantine empire
- Belief Systems: the Great Schism

1. **Cultural Diffusion** Byzantine rulers thought of their empire as the successor to the Roman empire. Like the Romans before them, the Byzantines spread their culture across a wide expanse of Europe. Compare how the two empires spread their cultures. Think about the following:
   - language and learning
   - religion
   - art and architecture
   - political ideas
   - where their culture spread
   - how their culture spread

2. **Geography's Impact** Rivers have played a central role in the development of civilization. Compare how rivers affected development of Russia and Eastern Europe with one of the following ancient civilizations: Egypt, Mesopotamia, India, and China. Think about the following:
   - migration
   - trade
   - cultural diffusion

3. **Trade** One of the earliest trading centers was Phoenicia, an ancient culture of sea traders. Compare Phoenician trade with that of Kiev. Consider the following in your answer:
   - method of transportation
   - relationship with trading partners
   - effect on expansion

■ Connections to Today

1. **Dictatorship: A Russian Tradition** The Russian tsars established a tradition of absolute dictatorship that continued under Soviet premiers. After the collapse of communism and the breakup of the Soviet Union, Russia set up a democratic government. Today, however, many people fear that Russia is again turning to autocratic rule. Research Soviet rulers such as Joseph Stalin and Nikita Khrushchev and a modern leader such as Vladimir Putin. Compare their rules to those of Ivan the Great and Ivan the Terrible.

2. **Conflict: Balkan Boiling Pot** Throughout the 1990s, violence exploded in the Balkans. In 1992, Eastern Orthodox Serbs, Bosnian Muslims, and Catholic Croats fought a bloody civil war in Bosnia. In 1998, Christian Serbs and Muslims of Albanian heritage clashed in Kosovo. These wars echo ethnic struggles that have gone on for more than 600 years in the Balkans as different ethnic and religious groups have dispersed throughout the region. Even when forced to live together, the different groups have remained independent. Instead of blending together, ethnic and cultural differences in the Balkan region have continued to simmer and occasionally boil over. Research a conflict in the Balkans that occurred after 1900. Describe the conflict and its causes.

History *Interactive*
For: Interactive timeline
Web Code: nap-0941

1236–1241	1386	1453	1462
Mongol armies called the Golden Horde conquer Russia.	Poland-Lithuania becomes the largest state in Europe.	Constantinople falls to the Turks.	Ivan the Great begins his reign in Russia.

1200   1500

1076	1324	1556
Pope Gregory VII excommunicates King Henry IV of Germany.	Mansa Musa, ruler of Mali, makes a pilgrimage to Mecca.	Akbar becomes ruler of the Mughal empire in India.

Chapter Assessment

Terms, People, and Places

Match the following definitions with the terms listed below.

autocrat	Kiev
patriarch	Golden Horde
icon	ethnic group
steppe	Golden Bull of 1222

1. a large group of people who share the same language and cultural heritage
2. open, treeless grassland
3. highest church official in the Eastern Orthodox Church
4. sole ruler with complete authority
5. Mongol armies that invaded Russia
6. charter limiting royal power signed by the Hungarian king
7. holy image of a saint or other religious figure
8. center of the first Russian state

Main Ideas

Section 1 (pp. 282–288)
9. Summarize how the Byzantine empire became rich and successful.
10. Describe the schism between the Orthodox Church and the Church in Rome.

Section 2 (pp. 289–293)
11. How did the Rus, other Viking groups, and the Byzantine empire affect the rise of Kiev?
12. What were the effects of the Mongol rule of Russia?
13. Describe the achievements of Ivan the Great.

Section 3 (pp. 294–297)
14. How did the Balkans become home to such a diverse mix of peoples?
15. How did Poland-Lithuania become the largest state in Europe?

Chapter Focus Question

16. How did the Byzantine empire preserve the heritage of Greece and Rome and help to shape the cultures of Russia and Eastern Europe?

Critical Thinking

17. **Draw Conclusions** The Byzantine empire preserved part of the heritage of the Roman empire. Why was this important?
18. **Synthesize Information** Why was Justinian such a successful ruler?
19. **Analyze Visuals** What aspects of Constantinople appear most prominent in this map? Why does the artist emphasize those?

20. **Test Conclusions** (a) Patriotic Russians called Moscow the third Rome. Why do you think they did so? (b) Do you think Moscow was truly the heir to Rome? Why or why not?
21. **Analyze Information** How did absolute power develop in Russia?
22. **Geography and History** How did the location and geographic features of the Balkans affect its history?
23. **Recognize Cause and Effect** Why did many Jews migrate to Eastern Europe?

● Writing About History

In this chapter's three Section Assessments, you developed skills for writing a biographical essay.

Writing a Biographical Essay Many fascinating people helped shape the fortunes of Russia and the Byzantine Empire. Write a biographical essay about one of the following in which you present a conclusion about the personality, actions, and importance of the person: Justinian, Theodora, Ivan the Great, or Ivan the Terrible. Consult page SH18 of the Writing Handbook for additional help.

Prewriting
• Do online or library research to read accounts of each of the people listed above.

• Choose the person who interests you most and gather information about him or her.
• Make a timeline of important events in the person's life and draw conclusions about his or her personality and importance.

Drafting
• Write a thesis statement that presents your conclusion about the person.
• Write an introduction presenting your thesis statement and two or three major points that support your conclusion.
• Use specific facts to support your main points in the body of your essay, and sum up in your conclusion.

Revising
• Use the guidelines for revising your essay on page SH19 of the Writing Handbook.

Prepare for the GHSGT

Constantinople: "The Great City"

The Byzantines called Constantinople "The Great City" and "The New Rome." By the time of Constantine, Rome was in steep decline. Byzantium—renamed Constantinople—became the capital of Constantine's empire and a center of governmental, religious, and economic life. The city inspired both praise and condemnation, as the documents below illustrate.

Document A

"The focal point of Constantine's new city was the *Milion,* or the First Milestone. It consisted of four triumphal arches forming a square and supporting a cupola [dome], above which was set the most venerable [revered] Christian relic of all—the True Cross itself, sent back by the Empress Helena from Jerusalem a year or two before. From it all the distances in the Empire were measured; it was, in effect the centre of the world."

—*A Short History of Byzantium*, by John Julius Norwich, 1997

Document B

"The city itself is squalid and fetid and in many places harmed by permanent darkness, for the wealthy overshadow the streets with buildings and leave these dirty, dark places to the poor and to travelers; there murders and robberies and other crimes . . . are committed. . . . In every respect she exceeds moderation; for, just as she surpasses other cities in wealth, so, too, does she surpass them in vice."

—From *Journey of Louis VII to the East (1147)* by Odo of Deuil, a monk who accompanied the French king on the Second Crusade

Document C

This nineteenth-century painting shows the Byzantine emperor receiving European troops into Constantinople.

Document D

"It is a busy city, and merchants come to it from every country by sea or land, and there is none like it in the world except Bagdad, the great city of Islam. . . . Wealth like that of Constantinople is not to be found in the whole world. Here also are men learned in all the books of the Greeks, and they eat and drink every man under his vine and his fig tree . . . No Jews live in the city, for they have been placed behind an inlet of the sea. An arm of the sea of Marmora shuts them in on the one side, and they are unable to go out except by way of the sea, when they want to do business with the inhabitants."

—*Itinerary* (1160s), by Benjamin of Tudela, a Jewish traveler

Analyzing Documents

Use your knowledge of the Byzantine empire, Russia, and Eastern Europe and Documents A, B, C, and D to answer questions 1–4.

1. Constantine's placement of the relic given by Empress Helena, as described in Document A, suggests that the
   A power of the Byzantine Empire had shifted to the holy city of Jerusalem.
   B holy city of Jerusalem was still the center of civilization.
   C focus of the Christian world would shift to the East.
   D Byzantine rulers had opposed the crusaders who had reclaimed Jerusalem for Christianity.

2. According to Document B, Constantinople's wealth and grandeur
   A helped to eliminate poverty and crime.
   B were the result of highly supervised trading.
   C led to greater literacy and appreciation for the arts.
   D existed side by side with poverty and crime.

3. Document D shows that religious toleration
   A extended to all faiths in ancient Constantinople.
   B was limited in ancient Constantinople.
   C was a founding principle of the city, thanks to Constantine.
   D derived from a strong economic foundation.

4. **Writing Task** Write a letter home from a visitor to ancient Constantinople, describing "the Great City." Use these documents along with information from the chapter in your letter.

Muslims at the Kaaba

In the Arabian town of Mecca, the marketplace echoed with the sounds of buyers and sellers bargaining. One corner, though, was hushed. There, a husky man spoke to a handful of followers:

“The righteous man is he who believes in God and the Last Day, in the angels and the Book [Scriptures] and the prophets; who, though he loves it dearly, gives away his wealth to kinsfolk, to orphans, to the destitute, to the traveller in need, and to beggars. . . . Such are the true believers.”
—The Quran

Some bowed their heads, moved by Muhammad's words. Many merchants were infuriated, however. Muhammad's words condemned the many gods that pilgrims came to worship in Mecca. The pilgrim trade would be disrupted, and profits ruined! Listen to the Witness History audio to hear more about Muhammad.

 ◄ A modern Muslim pilgrim in Mecca, the holy city of Islam

Mughal emperors Jahangir, Akbar, and Shah Jahan

An astrolabe

GA Performance Standards

Chapter Focus Question Who was Muhammad, and how did his teachings lead to the rise and spread of Islam?

Section 1
The Rise of Islam   SSWH5a, SSWH5f

Section 2
Building a Muslim Empire
SSWH5a, SSWH5c, SSWH5f

Section 3
Muslim Civilization's Golden Age   SSWH5b, SSWH5d

Section 4
India's Muslim Empires
SSWH5a, SSWH12a, SSWH12b

Section 5
The Ottoman and Safavid Empires
SSWH4e, SSWH12a

Use the ☑ **Quick Study Timeline** at the end of this chapter to preview chapter events.

The Quran

 Concept Connector ONLINE

To explore Essential Questions related to this chapter, go to PHSchool.com
Web Code: nad-1007

Muslims at Mount Hira

◀)) AUDIO

Messenger of God

During the month of Ramadan, as Muhammad sat meditating in a cave on Mount Hira, an angel in the form of a man came to him. The angel said, "Recite!" Muhammad said, "What shall I recite?" The angel overwhelmed Muhammad in an embrace, and then released him and said again, "Recite!" Muhammad repeated, "What shall I recite?" and again the angel overwhelmed him in an embrace. This happened a third time, after which the angel said, "Recite in the name of your Lord who created—created man from clots of blood." According to Muslim belief, on this and several other occasions, Muhammad heard the angel Gabriel calling him to be the messenger of God.

Focus Question What messages, or teachings, did Muhammad spread through Islam?

Muhammad's name, written in calligraphy

The Rise of Islam

GA Performance Standards

- **SSWH5a** Explain the origin of Islam and the growth of the Islamic Empire.
- **SSWH5f** Analyze the relationship between Judaism, Christianity and Islam.

Terms, People, and Places

Bedouins	Kaaba
Muhammad	Quran
Mecca	mosque
Yathrib	hajj
hijra	jihad
Medina	Sharia

Note Taking

Reading Skill: Recognize Sequence On a sheet of paper, draw a timeline like the one below and label the main events described in this section.

The religion of Islam, whose followers are called Muslims, emerged in the Arabian Peninsula. This region of southwestern Asia is mostly desert, yet it was home to many Arab tribes in the A.D. 500s. Nomadic herders called **Bedouins** (BED oo inz) moved through the desert to reach seasonal pasturelands for their camels, goats, and sheep. Competition for water and grazing land often led to warfare. Bedouins also traded with settled Arab tribes in oasis towns and protected the caravan trading routes.

Muhammad Becomes a Prophet

Muhammad was born in the oasis town of Mecca around A.D. 570. **Mecca** was a bustling market town at the crossroads of several caravan routes. It was also a thriving pilgrimage center. Many Arabs came to pray at the Kaaba, an ancient temple that housed statues of pagan gods and goddesses. The pilgrims helped make Mecca's merchants wealthy. All weapons had to be laid down near the temple, making Mecca a safe and peaceful place to do business.

Arabia's deserts and trade centers shaped Muhammad's early life. In his youth, he worked as a shepherd among the Bedouins. Later, he led caravans across the desert and became a successful merchant. When he was about 25, Muhammad married Khadija (ka DEE jah), a wealthy widow who ran a prosperous caravan business. Muhammad became known for his honesty in business and was a devoted husband and father.

Muhammad Becomes God's Messenger Muhammad was troubled by the moral ills of Meccan society, especially greed. He often went to a cave in the hills near Mecca to meditate. According to Muslim belief, when he was about 40 years old he heard the voice of the angel Gabriel calling him to be the messenger of God. Muhammad was terrified and puzzled. How could he, an illiterate merchant, become the messenger of God? Khadija encouraged him to accept the call. She became the first convert to the faith called Islam, from the Arabic word that means "to submit to God." Muhammad devoted his life to spreading Islam. He urged Arabs to give up their worship of pagan gods and submit to the one true God. In Arabic, the word for God is *Allah*.

The Hijra: A Turning Point At first, few people listened to Muhammad's teachings. His rejection of traditional Arab gods angered Mecca's merchants, who feared that neglect of their idols would disrupt the pilgrim trade. In 622, faced with the threat of murder, Muhammad and his followers left Mecca for **Yathrib**, a journey known as the **hijra** (hih JY ruh). Later, Yathrib was renamed **Medina**, or "city of the Prophet," and 622 became the first year of the Muslim calendar.

The hijra was a turning point for Islam. In Medina, Muslim converts welcomed Muhammad and agreed to follow his teachings. They became a community of Muslims, or *umma*. Loyalty to the umma was based on Islam instead of old family rivalries. Muhammad created rules that governed and united Muslims and brought peace among the clans of Medina. As his reputation grew, thousands of Arabs adopted Islam. Meanwhile, Meccan leaders grew more hostile toward the Muslims. After Muslims attacked several caravans, the Meccans prepared for war.

After fighting battles with the Meccans, Muhammad triumphantly returned to Mecca in 630. He destroyed the idols in the **Kaaba**, the temple that he believed Abraham had built to worship the one true God. He rededicated the Kaaba to Allah, and it became the most holy place in Islam. For the next two years, Muhammad worked to unite the Arabs under Islam. Muhammad died in 632, but the faith that he proclaimed continued to spread. Today, Islam is one of the world's major religions.

✓ **Checkpoint** How did Muhammad become the prophet of Islam?

The photograph below shows Medina as it appears today. The illustration shows both Medina (left) and Mecca (right) in 1160. *What evidence do you see that Medina is an important pilgrimage site?*

Teachings of Islam

Like Judaism and Christianity, Islam is monotheistic, based on belief in one God. The **Quran** (koo RAHN), the sacred text of Islam, teaches that God is all-powerful and compassionate. It also states that people are responsible for their own actions. Islam does not require priests to <u>mediate</u> between the people and God. Muslims believe that God had sent other prophets, including Abraham, Moses, and Jesus, but that Muhammad was the last and greatest prophet.

Muslims Study the Quran To Muslims, the Quran contains the sacred word of God as revealed to Muhammad. It is the final authority on all matters discussed in the text. The Quran teaches about God's will and provides a guide to life. Its ethical standards emphasize honesty, generosity, and social justice. It sets harsh penalties for crimes such as stealing or murder. According to the Quran, each individual will stand before God on the final judgment day to face either eternal punishment in hell or eternal bliss in paradise.

Muslims believe that the Quran is the direct, unchangeable word of God. Because the meaning and poetic beauty of the Quran reside in its original language, all Muslims, including converts to Islam, learn Arabic. This shared language has helped unite Muslims from many regions throughout the world.

Muslims Follow Duties All observant Muslims perform five basic duties, known as the Five Pillars of Islam. The first is to make a declaration of faith. The second is to pray five times daily. After a ritual washing, Muslims face the holy city of Mecca to pray. Although Muslims may pray anywhere, they often gather in houses of worship called masjids or **mosques.** A mosque official called a muezzin (myoo EZ in) calls the faithful to prayer.

The third pillar is to give charity to the poor. The fourth is to fast from sunrise to sunset during the holy month of Ramadan—the month in which Muhammad received his first revelations from God. The fifth pillar is to make the **hajj,** or pilgrimage to Mecca, if a person is able. Pilgrims participate in ceremonies commemorating the actions of Muhammad, Abraham, and Abraham's family. Their simple attire symbolizes the abandonment of the material world for the sake of God.

Another duty is **jihad,** or struggle in God's service. Jihad is usually a personal duty for Muslims, who focus on overcoming immorality within themselves. At other times, jihad may be interpreted as a holy war to defend Islam and the Muslim community, much like the Crusades to defend Christianity. However, just holy war may be declared only by the community, not by an individual Muslim or small group.

"People of the Book" Muslims, Jews, and Christians worship the same God. The Quran teaches that Islam is God's final and complete revelation, while Hebrew scriptures and the Christian Bible contain portions of earlier revelations. Muslims consider Jews and Christians to be "People of the Book," spiritually superior to polytheistic idol worshipers. Although there have been exceptions, the People of the Book have historically enjoyed religious freedom in many Muslim societies.

✔ **Checkpoint** What are the duties required of Muslims?

Vocabulary Builder

<u>mediate</u>—(MEE dee ayt) *v.* to act as a go-between

Note Taking

Reading Skill: Identify Main Ideas Copy the web diagram below. As you read, fill in the outer ovals with the teachings of Islam.

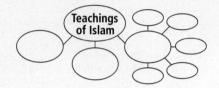

THE FIVE PILLARS OF ISLAM

All observant Muslims perform five individual duties, known as the Five Pillars of Islam. These are based on Muhammad's example. The photograph below shows pilgrims praying at the Kaaba, the most important temple of Islam. Whenever Muslims pray, they face the Kaaba, which is located in Mecca. Find Mecca on the map and then read about the Five Pillars of Islam.

1. Declaration of Faith

The Muslim profession of faith is called the *shahada*. It states, "There is no god but God, Muhammad is the messenger of God." Muslims believe that God had sent other prophets, including Abraham, Moses, and Jesus, but that Muhammad was the last and greatest prophet.

2. Daily Prayer

Muslims pray five times each day. After a ritual washing, they face Mecca and perform specific actions as they pray.

3. Alms for the Poor

Muslims care for others by giving charity to the poor. In some Muslim countries, money is collected in the form of a tax called the *zakat*. Other Muslims give individual donations.

4. Fast During Ramadan

Muslims fast from sunrise to sunset during the holy month of Ramadan. The sick and very young children are not required to fast. The children below are celebrating the end of Ramadan.

5. Hajj

Muslims who are physically and financially able must make a pilgrimage to pray at the Kaaba in Mecca at least once. More than two million Muslims visit Mecca each year for this purpose. Pilgrims wear simple garments that erase cultural and class differences so that all stand equal before God.

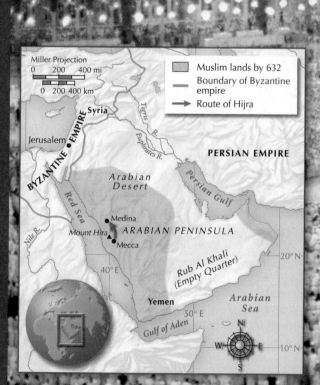

Miller Projection

0   200   400 mi

0   200 400 km

Muslim lands by 632
Boundary of Byzantine empire
→ Route of Hijra

Jerusalem • BYZANTINE EMPIRE

Syria

Tigris R.

Euphrates R.

PERSIAN EMPIRE

Arabian Desert

Red Sea

Nile R.

Persian Gulf

● Medina

Mount Hira ▲

● Mecca

ARABIAN PENINSULA

Rub Al Khali (Empty Quarter)

Yemen

Arabian Sea

40° E

50° E

20° N

10° N

Gulf of Aden

N W E S

Thinking Critically

1. **Summarize** Describe the Five Pillars of Islam.
2. **Draw Inferences** Why do Muslims perform the Five Pillars?

Islamic Law Court
In this painting, a man and his son seek a decision before a judge, who is seated. *What does this picture suggest about the judge's status within the legal system?*

Vocabulary Builder
affirm—(uh FURM) *v.* to judge as valid

Islam: A Way of Life

Islam is both a religion and a way of life. Its teachings shape the lives of Muslims around the world. Islamic law governs daily life, and Muslim traditions determine ethical behavior and influence family relations.

Sharia—Islamic System of Law Over time, Muslim scholars developed the Sharia, a body of law that includes interpretation of the Quran, examples of behavior from Muhammad's life, and Muslim traditions. Similar to Jewish law, the Sharia regulates moral conduct, family life, business practices, government, and other aspects of individual and community life. It does not separate religion from criminal or civil law, but applies religious principles to all legal situations. Just as the Quran unifies Muslim beliefs, the Sharia unites Muslims under a common legal framework.

Impact of Islam on Women Before Islam, the position of women in Arab society varied. In some communities, women were active in religion, trade, or politics. As in most societies at that time, however, most women had limited rights. Arab women could not inherit property and had to obey a male guardian. Among a few tribes, unwanted daughters were sometimes killed at birth.

Islam extended rights and protection to women by affirming the spiritual equality of all Muslims. The Quran teaches that "Whoever does right, whether male or female, and is a believer, all such will enter the Garden." The Quran prohibited the killing of daughters, granted women an inheritance, and allowed women to reject a marriage offer. Islam also encouraged education for men and women so that all Muslims could study the Quran.

Although spiritually equal under Islam, men and women had different roles and rights. For example, women inherited less than men and had a more difficult time getting a divorce. As Islam spread, Muslims adopted practices of conquered peoples. For example, the practices of veiling upper-class women and secluding them in a separate part of the home were Persian customs. The Quran says that women should dress modestly, which has been interpreted in multiple ways. Still, women's lives varied according to region and class. In rural areas, peasant women often needed to work and did not wear a veil, but took care to dress modestly.

 Checkpoint How did Islam affect Muslim women?

Progress Monitoring *Online*
For: Self-quiz with vocabulary practice
Web Code: naa-1011

Terms, People, and Places
1. For each term, person, or place listed at the beginning of the section, write a sentence explaining its significance.

Note Taking
2. **Reading Skill: Recognize Sequence and Identify Main Ideas** Use your completed timeline and web diagram to answer the Focus Question: What messages, or teachings, did Muhammad spread through Islam?

Comprehension and Critical Thinking
3. **Identify Point of View** Why were merchants in Mecca at first opposed to Muhammad's teachings?
4. **Determine Relevance** Why do Muslims consider Mecca sacred?
5. **Recognize Ideologies** How do the Quran and Sharia guide Muslims?
6. **Draw Inferences** Which aspects of Islam would have appealed to the poor, enslaved, and isolated—many of the first Muslim converts? Explain.

● Writing About History
Quick Write: Choose a Topic Compare and contrast one tradition of Islam (religious holidays, for example) to a similar tradition within Judaism and/or Christianity. First, choose a topic to compare and contrast. To do so, write a list of the categories from which you can choose a topic to research for both religions. Refer to this list as you collect the facts and details you need to write a compare-and-contrast essay.

The Quran

The Quran, the holy scriptures of Islam, contains 114 *suras*, or chapters, which are divided into verses. Muslims believe that the Quran is the word of God as revealed to Muhammad. They also believe that God instructed Muhammad to arrange the chapters into the order in which they appear. The following excerpts from the Quran tell Muslims how to be righteous and faithful. They also encourage believers to fast and observe the holy month of Ramadan.

Righteousness does not consist in whether you face towards the East or the West. The righteous man is he who believes in God and the Last Day, in the angels and the Book [Scriptures] and the prophets; who, though he loves it dearly, gives away his wealth to kinsfolk, to orphans, to the destitute, to the traveller in need and to beggars, and for the redemption[1] of captives; who attends to his prayers and renders the alms[2] levy; who is true to his promises and steadfast in trial and adversity and in times of war. Such are the true believers; such are the God–fearing. —The Quran 2:177

Believers, fasting is decreed for you as it was decreed for those before you; perchance you will guard yourselves against evil. Fast a certain number of days, but if any one among you is ill or on a journey, let him fast a similar number of days later; and for those that cannot endure it there is a penance ordained: the feeding of a poor man. He that does good of his own accord shall be well rewarded; but to fast is better for you, if you but knew it.

In the month of Ramadan the [Quran] was revealed, a book of guidance for mankind with proofs of guidance distinguishing right from wrong. Therefore whoever of you is present in that month let him fast. But he who is ill or on a journey shall fast a similar number of days later on.

God desires your well-being, not your discomfort. He desires you to fast the whole month so that you may magnify God and render thanks to Him for giving you His guidance. —The Quran 2:183–185

At the top, the intricate pattern of this Quran illustration echoes the calligraphy at the center, and, below, a young woman reads the Quran.

The wide borders on the pages of this Quran ensure that the reader's fingers will not touch the sacred text.

Thinking Critically

1. **Summarize Information** According to the excerpt above, to whom should righteous people give their wealth?
2. **Analyze Information** In which situation can a righteous person avoid fasting during Ramadan?
3. **Apply Information** How does this passage from the Quran support the Five Pillars of Islam?

1. redemption (rih DEMP shun) *n.* freedom from enslavement or captivity by payment of ransom
2. alms (ahmz) *n.* charity given freely to the poor

Muslim soldiers pitching a tent

WITNESS HISTORY ◀)) AUDIO

Nomadic Raids

❝ For centuries nomadic Arab tribes had been in the habit of making raids or razzias on other tribes. The usual aim was to drive off the camels or other livestock of the opponents. The favorite plan was to make a surprise attack with overwhelming force on a small section of the other tribe. In such circumstances it was no disgrace to the persons attacked if they made their escape; and so in many razzias there was little loss of life. . . . From the standpoint of the Muslims, the crossing of the straits of Gibraltar in 711 was . . . one more in a series of raiding expeditions which had been pushing ever farther afield. . . . After experiencing one or more such raiding expeditions the inhabitants of the countries traversed usually surrendered and became protected allies. ❞
—from *The Influence of Islam on Medieval Europe*, by W. Montgomery Watt

Focus Question How did Muhammad's successors extend Muslim rule and spread Islam?

Building a Muslim Empire

 Performance Standards

- **SSWH5a** Explain the origin of Islam and the growth of the Islamic Empire.
- **SSWH5c** Explain the reasons for the split between Sunni and Shia Muslims.
- **SSWH5f** Analyze the relationship between Judaism, Christianity and Islam.

Terms, People, and Places

Abu Bakr	Umayyads
caliph	Abbasids
Sunni	Baghdad
Shiite	minaret
Sufis	sultan

Note Taking

Reading Skill: Recognize Sequence Copy the timeline below. As you read, fill in the timeline with major events concerning the spread of Islam and the rise and fall of Muslim empires.

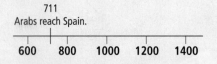

711
Arabs reach Spain.

600   800   1000   1200   1400

The death of Muhammad plunged his followers into grief. Muhammad had been a pious man and a powerful leader. No one else had ever been able to unify so many Arab tribes. Could the community of Muslims survive without him?

Early Challenges to Islam

Muslims faced a problem when Muhammad died because he had not named a successor to lead the community. Eventually, they agreed that **Abu Bakr** (uh BOO BAK ur), Muhammad's father-in-law and an early convert to Islam, should be the first **caliph,** or successor to Muhammad. Abu Bakr sternly told the faithful, "If you worship Muhammad, Muhammad is dead. If you worship God, God is alive."

Arabs Unite Under Islam Abu Bakr faced an immediate crisis. The loyalty of some Arab tribal leaders had been dependent on Muhammad's personal command. They refused to follow Abu Bakr and withdrew their loyalty to Islam. After several battles with the wavering tribes, Abu Bakr succeeded in reuniting the Muslims, based on their allegiance to Islam. Once reunited, the Muslims set out on a remarkable series of military campaigns. They began by converting the remaining Arab tribes to Islam, which ended warfare between Arabs and united them under one leader.

Early Victories Under the first four caliphs, the Arab Muslims marched from victory to victory against two great empires on their borders. The Byzantines and Persians had competed with each other over control of lands in the Middle East. Once the Arabs united, they surprised their neighbors, conquering great portions of the Byzantine empire and defeating the Persians entirely. First, they took the provinces of Syria and Palestine from the Byzantines, including the cities of Damascus and Jerusalem. Then, they captured the weakened Persian empire and swept into Byzantine Egypt.

✓ **Checkpoint** How did Muslims overcome early challenges to Islam?

Divisions Emerge Within Islam

When Muhammad died, Muslims disagreed about who should be chosen to be the leader of the community. The split between **Sunni** (SOO nee) and **Shiite** (SHEE yt) Muslims had a profound impact on later Islamic history.

Sunnis and Shiites One group of Muslims felt that Muhammad had designated his son-in-law, Ali, to be his successor. They were called Shiites, after *shi'at Ali*, or followers of Ali. Shiites believe that the true successors to Muhammad are the descendants of Ali and Muhammad's daughter, Fatima. They believe that these descendants, called Imams, are divinely inspired religious leaders, who are empowered to interpret the Quran and the actions of Muhammad. Another group felt that any good Muslim could lead the community, since there could be no prophet after Muhammad. This group soon divided and fought among themselves as well as with others over issues of who could be defined as a "good" Muslim.

The majority of Muslims eventually compromised around the view that the successor to Muhammad should be a pious male Muslim from Muhammad's tribe. This successor is called a caliph and is viewed as a political leader of the religious community, without any divine or prophetic functions. The compromise group, which forms the majority of Muslims in the world today, are known as Sunnis, since they follow the custom of the community, or *sunna*. The Sunni believe that inspiration comes from the example of Muhammad as recorded by his early followers.

Note Taking

Reading Skill: Compare and Contrast
Copy the Venn diagram below. As you read, fill in the diagram with points on which Sunni and Shiite Muslims agree and differ.

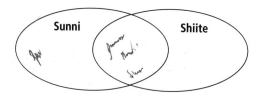

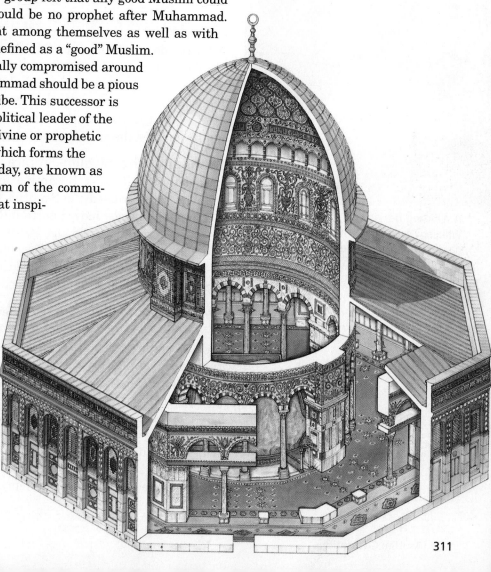

The Dome of the Rock
The Dome of the Rock in Jerusalem is the oldest surviving Islamic building. Construction began soon after Muslims captured Jerusalem. According to Muslim teaching, Muhammad ascended to heaven from the rock inside this building. *Why was it important for Muslims to build in Jerusalem?*

Like the <u>schism</u> between Roman Catholic and Eastern Orthodox Christians, the division between Sunni and Shiite Muslims has survived to the present day. Members of both branches of Islam believe in the same God, look to the Quran for guidance, and follow the Pillars of Islam. However, Sunnis and Shiites differ in such areas as religious practice, law, and daily life. Today, about 90 percent of Muslims are Sunni. Most Shiites live in Iran, Lebanon, Iraq, and Yemen. The Shiite branch itself has further split into several different subgroups.

Over the centuries, the division between Sunnis and Shiites was sometimes a source of conflict. When Sunni rulers held power, they often favored other Sunnis and deprived Shiites of wealth and power. When Shiites gained power, Sunnis often stood to lose. This sometimes bitter rivalry remains a source of tension in the Middle East today.

Sufis In both the Sunni and Shiite branches of Islam, a group called the **Sufis** emerged. Sufis are Muslim <u>mystics</u> who sought communion with God through meditation, fasting, and other rituals. Sufis were respected for their piety and some were believed to have miraculous powers.

Like Christian monks and nuns, some Sufis helped spread Islam by traveling, preaching, and being good examples to others. They carried the faith to remote villages, where they blended local traditions and beliefs into Muslim culture.

✔ **Checkpoint** Describe differences between Sunni and Shiite Muslims.

Umayyad Caliphs Build an Empire

After the death of Ali, a powerful Meccan clan set up the **Umayyad** (oo MY ad) caliphate, a dynasty of Sunni caliphs that ruled the Muslim empire until 750. From their capital at Damascus in Syria, they directed the spectacular conquests that extended Arab rule from Spain and Morocco in the west to the Indus River Valley in the east. Their conquests enabled the spread of Islam and Muslim civilization.

A Whirling Dervish
Whirling Dervishes are Sufi mystics who dance as a form of prayer.

Expanding the Muslim Empire From Egypt, Arab Muslim armies moved west, defeating Byzantine forces across North Africa. In 711, Muslim forces crossed the Strait of Gibraltar and conquered Spain. In 731, a Muslim army moved north into France to settle new areas. There, Frankish forces defeated the Muslims at the battle of Tours. Muslims ruled parts of Spain for centuries, but advanced no farther into Europe. Elsewhere, Muslim forces besieged the Byzantine capital of Constantinople, but failed to take the well-defended city.

Reasons for Muslim Success Several factors can explain the series of Muslim victories. One factor was the weakness of the Byzantine and Persian empires. The longtime rivals had fought each other to exhaustion. Many people also welcomed the Arabs as liberators from harsh Byzantine or Persian rule. Another factor was the Arabs' bold, efficient fighting methods. The Bedouin camel and horse cavalry mounted aggressive and mobile offensives that overwhelmed more traditional armies.

Under the first four caliphs, Muslims knitted a patchwork of competing tribes into a unified state. Belief in Islam and the desire to glorify the new religion spurred the Muslim armies to victory. As the empire expanded, the rulers created an orderly system of administration.

Treatment of Conquered People The advancing Arabs brought many people under their rule. These Arabs imposed certain restrictions and a special tax on non-Muslims, but allowed Christians, Jews, and Zoroastrians to practice their own faiths and follow their own religious customs within those restrictions. Early Umayyads did not attempt to convert these "People of the Book," because the tax supported the Arab troops who settled in conquered areas. As Muslim civilization developed, many Jews and Christians played key roles as officials, doctors, and translators. Muslim leaders wisely prohibited looting and destruction of conquered lands, ensuring continued wealth and prosperity for the empire in the form of tribute and taxes. However, the rulers also urged Arab settlers to stay separate from the native populations, which created an Arab upper class throughout the empire.

In time, many non-Muslims converted to Islam. Some converted to gain political or economic advantages. However, many were drawn to Islam's simple and direct message, and they saw its triumph as a sign of God's favor. Many of the nomadic peoples in North Africa and Central Asia chose Islam immediately. Unlike some religions, Islam had no religious hierarchy or class of priests. In principle, it emphasized the equality of all believers, regardless of race, gender, class, or wealth. In later centuries, Turkish and Mongol converts helped spread Islam far across Asia.

Decline of the Umayyad Caliphate As military victories and negotiation expanded the Muslim empire, the Umayyads faced numerous problems. First, Arabs had to adapt from living in the desert to ruling large cities and huge territories. In many ways, the caliphs ruled like powerful tribal leaders, rather than kings with large bureaucracies. To govern their empire, the Umayyads often relied on local officials. Although they helped govern the empire, non-Arabs often did not have the same privileges that Arabs had, even if they converted to Islam.

While conquests continued, vast wealth flowed into Umayyad hands. When conquests slowed in the 700s, economic tensions increased between wealthy Arabs and those who had less. In addition, more and more resources were used to support the caliphs' luxurious lifestyle. By the eighth century, many Muslims criticized the court at Damascus for abandoning the simple ways of the early caliphs. Shiites considered the Umayyad caliphs to be illegitimate rulers of the Islamic community.

Unrest also grew among non-Arab converts to Islam, who had fewer rights than Arabs.

✓ **Checkpoint** What are three reasons for the success of Muslim conquests?

Rise of the Abbasids

Discontented Muslims found a leader in Abu al-Abbas, descended from Muhammad's uncle. With strong support from Shiite and non-Arab Muslims, he captured Damascus in 750. Soon after, he had members of the defeated Umayyad family killed. Only one survived, escaping to Spain. Abu al-Abbas then founded the **Abbasid** (uh BAS id) dynasty, which lasted until 1258.

Changes Under the Abbasids The Abbasid dynasty tried to create an empire based on the equality of all Muslims. The new rulers halted the large military conquests, ending the dominance of the Arab military class. Under the early Abbasids, the empire of the caliphs reached its greatest wealth and power, and Muslim civilization flourished. Under the Abbasids, Islam became a more diverse religion because discrimination against non-Arab Muslims ended. Official policy encouraged conversion to Islam and treated all Muslims equally. The Abbassids created a more sophisticated bureaucracy and encouraged learning.

The Abbasids also moved the capital from Damascus to Baghdad, a small market town on the banks of the Tigris river. This move into Persian territory allowed Persian officials to hold important offices in the caliph's government. It also allowed Persian traditions to influence the development of the caliphate. Although these traditions strongly influenced Arab culture, Islam remained the religion of the empire and Arabic its language. The most important official was known as the vizier, or the head of the bureaucracy, a position that had existed in Persian government.

Splendors of Baghdad The second Abbasid caliph, al-Mansur, chose **Baghdad** as the site of his new capital. The walls formed a circle, with the caliph's palace in the center. Poets, scholars, philosophers, and entertainers from all over the Muslim world flocked to the Abbasid court. Under the Abbasids, Baghdad exceeded Constantinople in size and wealth. Visitors no doubt felt that Baghdad deserved its title "City of Peace, Gift of God, Paradise on Earth."

The city was beautiful, with many markets, gardens, the palace, and mosques. Domes and **minarets** (min uh RETS), slender towers of the mosques, loomed overhead. Five times each day, muezzins climbed to the tops of the minarets and called the faithful to prayer. Merchants sold goods from Africa, Asia, and Europe. The palace of the caliph bustled with activity.

Muslim Culture in Spain The surviving member of the Umayyad family had fled to Spain and established an independent Muslim state. There, Muslim rulers presided over brilliant courts, where the arts and

Spread of Islam

Geography *Interactive*
For: Interactive map
Web Code: nap-1021

Map Skills In less than 150 years, Muslim rule spread from Arabia across southwest Asia and North Africa and into Europe.

1. **Locate** (a) Damascus (b) Baghdad (c) Persia (d) Cairo (e) Constantinople (f) Córdoba (g) Tours

2. **Region** During what period did Spain come under Muslim rule?

3. **Apply Information** How might the spread of Islam have contributed to Muslim success in trade?

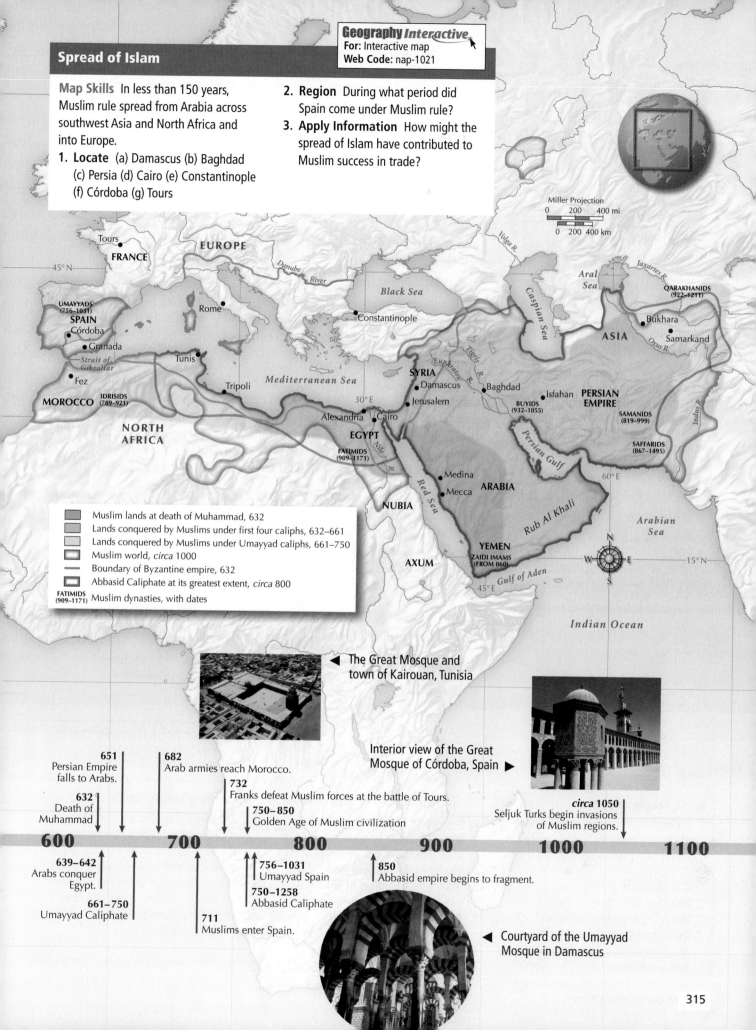

Miller Projection

0   200   400 mi

0   200   400 km

Legend:
- Muslim lands at death of Muhammad, 632
- Lands conquered by Muslims under first four caliphs, 632–661
- Lands conquered by Muslims under Umayyad caliphs, 661–750
- Muslim world, *circa* 1000
- Boundary of Byzantine empire, 632
- Abbasid Caliphate at its greatest extent, *circa* 800
- **FATIMIDS (909–1171)** Muslim dynasties, with dates

Map labels:
Tours, FRANCE, EUROPE, 45° N, Danube River, Rome, Black Sea, Constantinople, Volga R., Aral Sea, Jaxartes R., QARAKHANIDS (922–1211), Bukhara, Samarkand, ASIA, Caspian Sea, Oxus R., UMAYYADS (756–1031), SPAIN, Córdoba, Granada, Strait of Gibraltar, Tunis, Fez, MOROCCO, IDRISIDS (789–921), Tripoli, Mediterranean Sea, 30° E, SYRIA, Damascus, Jerusalem, Euphrates R., Tigris R., Baghdad, Isfahan, BUYIDS (932–1055), PERSIAN EMPIRE, SAMANIDS (819–999), SAFFARIDS (867–1495), Indus R., 60° E, NORTH AFRICA, Alexandria, Cairo, EGYPT, Nile R., FATIMIDS (909–1171), Persian Gulf, NUBIA, Red Sea, Medina, Mecca, ARABIA, Rub Al Khali, Arabian Sea, AXUM, YEMEN, ZAIDI IMAMS (FROM 860), Gulf of Aden, 45° E, 15° N, Indian Ocean

◄ The Great Mosque and town of Kairouan, Tunisia

Interior view of the Great Mosque of Córdoba, Spain ►

Timeline:

651 Persian Empire falls to Arabs.

632 Death of Muhammad

682 Arab armies reach Morocco.

732 Franks defeat Muslim forces at the battle of Tours.

750–850 Golden Age of Muslim civilization

circa 1050 Seljuk Turks begin invasions of Muslim regions.

600   700   800   900   1000   1100

639–642 Arabs conquer Egypt.

661–750 Umayyad Caliphate

711 Muslims enter Spain.

756–1031 Umayyad Spain

750–1258 Abbasid Caliphate

850 Abbasid empire begins to fragment.

◄ Courtyard of the Umayyad Mosque in Damascus

The Great Mosque
The photo above shows the outside of the mosque in Córdoba, Spain. A picture of the inside appears on the previous page. It was built around 785.

learning thrived. In general, they were more tolerant of other religions than were Christian rulers of the time. At centers of learning, such as the city of Córdoba, rulers employed Jewish officials and welcomed Christian scholars to study science and philosophy. Architects built grand buildings, such as the Alhambra, a fortified palace in Granada. Its lovely gardens, reflecting pools, and finely decorated marble columns mark a high point of Muslim civilization in Spain. Muslim rule endured in parts of Spain until 1492.

✓ **Checkpoint** How did Islam become a more universal faith?

The Muslim Empire Declines

The Abbasids never ruled Spain, and starting about 850, their control over the rest of the Muslim empire fragmented. In Egypt and elsewhere, independent dynasties ruled states that had been part of a unified empire. As the caliph's power faded in some regions, Shiite rulers came to power. Between 900 and 1400, a series of invasions added to the chaos.

Seljuk Turks Take Control In the 900s, Seljuk Turks migrated into the Middle East from Central Asia. They adopted Islam and built a large empire across the Fertile Crescent. By 1055, a Seljuk **sultan,** or ruler, controlled Baghdad, but he kept the Abbasid caliph as a figurehead. As the Seljuks pushed into Asia Minor, they threatened the Byzantine empire. The conflict prevented Christian pilgrims from traveling to Jerusalem, leading Pope Urban II to call for the First Crusade in 1095.

Mongols Sweep Across Central Asia In 1216, Genghis Khan led the Mongols out of Central Asia across southwest Asia. Mongol armies returned again and again. In 1258, Hulagu, the grandson of Genghis, burned and looted Baghdad, killing the last Abbasid caliph. Later, the Mongols adopted Islam as they mingled with local inhabitants. In the late 1300s, another Mongol leader, Timur the Lame, or Tamerlane, led his armies into the Middle East. Though he was a Muslim, Tamerlane's ambitions led him to conquer Muslim as well as non-Muslim lands. His armies overran southwest Asia before invading Russia and India.

✓ **Checkpoint** What caused the Abbasid dynasty to decline?

Progress Monitoring Online
For: Self-quiz with vocabulary practice
Web Code: naa-1021

SECTION 2 **Assessment**

Terms, People, and Places
1. For each term, person, or place listed at the beginning of the section, write a sentence explaining its significance.

Note Taking
2. **Reading Skill: Recognize Sequence** Use your completed timelines to answer the Focus Question: How did Muhammad's successors extend Muslim rule and spread Islam?

Comprehension and Critical Thinking
3. **Recognize Ideologies** How did the issue of heredity cause the division of Islam into Sunni and Shiite Muslims?
4. **Analyze Information** How did the Umayyads' treatment of non-Muslims and non-Arabs affect their empire?
5. **Recognize Cause and Effect** Why did the empire of the Abbasid caliphs decline and eventually break up?

● Writing About History
Quick Write: Explore a Topic Many Bedouins visited Baghdad during the reign of Harun al-Rashid. Write a paragraph through their eyes in which you describe how life in Baghdad differs from nomadic life in the desert. Give details about each point of comparison to make your essay more accessible to readers.

Aristotle educates Muslim scholars (foreground); a Greek medical text translated into Arabic (background)

WITNESS HISTORY ◀)) AUDIO

Inspiration from Aristotle

One night, Caliph al-Mamun had a vivid dream. There in his chambers he came upon a balding, blue-eyed stranger sitting on the low couch.

"Who are you?" the caliph demanded.

"Aristotle," the man replied.

The caliph was delighted. He plied the great Greek philosopher with questions about ethics, reason, and religion. After al-Mamun awoke, his dream inspired him to action. He had scholars collect the great works of the classical world and translate them into Arabic. By 830, the caliph had set up the "House of Wisdom," a library and university in Baghdad. During the Abbasid period, scholars made advances in a variety of fields.

Focus Question What achievements did Muslims make in economics, art, literature, and science?

Muslim Civilization's Golden Age

 Performance Standards

- **SSWH5b** Identify and assess the economic impact of Muslim trade routes.
- **SSWH5d** Identify the contributions of Islamic scholars in medicine.

Terms, People, and Places

social mobility	Ibn Khaldun
Firdawsi	al-Khwarizmi
Omar Khayyám	Muhammad al-Razi
calligraphy	Ibn Sina
Ibn Rushd	

Note Taking

Reading Skill: Categorize Copy the chart below. As you read, fill in the categories of the advances made during the golden age of Muslim civilization.

Muslim Achievements	
Economics	
Arts	
Literature	
Philosophy	
Sciences	

Under the Abbasids, Muslim civilization absorbed traditions from many cultures. In the process, a flourishing new civilization arose in cities from Baghdad to Córdoba. It incorporated all the people who lived under Muslim rule, including Jews and Christians. The great works produced by scholars of the Abbasid period shaped Muslim culture and civilization. Through contacts in Spain and Sicily, Christian European scholars began to study Muslim philosophy, art, and science. Muslim scholars also reintroduced knowledge of Greco-Roman civilization to later Europeans.

Social and Economic Advances

Muslim rulers united diverse cultures, including Arab, Persian, Egyptian, African, and European. Later, Mongols, Turks, Indians, and Southeast Asians joined the Muslim community. Muslim civilization absorbed and blended many of their traditions.

Muslims Build an International Trade Network Merchants were honored in Muslim culture, in part because Muhammad had been a merchant. A traditional collection of sayings stated:

Primary Source

❝ I commend the merchants to you, for they are the couriers of the horizon and God's trusted servants on Earth. ❞
—Sayings of the Prophet

Between 750 and 1350, merchants built a vast trading network across Muslim lands and beyond. Camel caravans—the "ships of the desert"—crossed the Sahara into West Africa. Muslim, Jewish, and Christian traders traveled the Silk Road toward China and were a vital link in the exchange of goods between East Asia and Europe. Monsoon winds carried Arab ships from East Africa to India and southeast Asia. Some traders made great fortunes.

Trade spread products, technologies, knowledge, and culture. Muslim merchants introduced an Indian number system to the Western world, where they became known as Arabic numerals. Traders also carried sugar from India and papermaking from China, introducing Islam to many new regions. As more people converted and learned Arabic, a common language and religion helped the global exchange grow and thrive.

Extensive trade and a money economy led Muslims to pioneer new business practices. They created partnerships, bought and sold on credit, formed banks to change currency, and invented the ancestors of today's bank checks. The English word *check* comes from the Arabic word *sakk*. Bankers developed a sophisticated system of accounting. They opened branch banks in all major cities, so that a check written in Baghdad might be cashed in Cairo.

A Muslim Market and Its Wares
At bottom, Muslim merchants sold local goods and goods from distant lands. Persian weavers were known for their beautiful carpets, such as the one shown above.

Manufactured Goods Are Highly Valued As in medieval Europe, handicraft manufacturing in Muslim cities was typically organized by guilds. The heads of the guilds, chosen by their members, often had the authority to regulate prices, weights and measures, methods of production, and the quality of the product. Most labor was done by wage workers. Muslim artisans produced a wealth of fine goods. Steel swords from Damascus, leather goods from Córdoba, cotton textiles from Egypt, and carpets from Persia were highly valued. Workshops also turned out fine glassware, furniture, and tapestries.

Agriculture Thrives Outside the cities, agriculture flourished across a wide variety of climates and landforms. Both Umayyad and Abbasid rulers took steps to preserve and extend agricultural land. Small farming communities in desert areas faced a constant scarcity of water. To improve farm output, the Abbasids organized massive irrigation projects and drained swamplands between the Tigris and Euphrates rivers. In addition to crops raised for food, farmers cultivated sugar cane, cotton, medicinal herbs, and flowers that were sold in far-off markets. Farmers began to grow crops that came from different regions.

The deserts continued to support nomads who lived by herding. Still, nomads and farmers shared economic ties. Nomads bought dates and grain from settled peoples, while farming populations acquired meat, wool, and hides from the nomads. Pastoral groups also provided pack animals and guides for the caravan trade.

Social Structure and Slavery Muslim society in the eighth and ninth centuries was more open than that of medieval Christian Europe. Muslims enjoyed a certain degree of **social mobility,** the ability to move up in social class. People could improve their social rank through religious, scholarly, or military achievements.

As in many earlier societies, slavery was a common institution in Muslim lands, though Islamic law encouraged the freeing of slaves as an act of charity. Slaves were often from conquered lands because Muslims were not supposed to enslave other Muslims. Some slaves bought their freedom, often with the help of charitable donations or even state funds. However, if non-Muslim slaves converted to Islam, they did not automatically become free. A female slave who bore a child by her Muslim owner gained freedom upon her master's death. Children born of a slave mother and free father were also considered freeborn.

Most slaves worked as household servants, while some were skilled artisans. To help break down the tribal system, Abbasid caliphs also created a class of Turkish slave-soldiers who were loyal only to the caliph. Often educated in Islamic law and government, some of these men rose to high positions in the government, such as vizier. This set the stage for the Turks to become powerful later in the Abbasid era.

✓ **Checkpoint** What business practices were pioneered by merchants in Muslim lands?

Muslim Art, Literature, and Architecture

Muslim art and literature reflected the diverse traditions of the various peoples who lived under Muslim rule, including Greeks, Romans, Persians, and Indians. As in Christian Europe and Hindu India, religion shaped the arts and literature of Muslim civilization. The great work of Islamic literature was the Quran itself. Because the Quran strictly banned the worship of idols, Muslim religious leaders forbade artists to portray God or human figures in religious art, giving Islamic art a distinctive style.

Poetry and Tales of Adventure Long before Muhammad, Arabs had a rich tradition of oral poetry. In musical verses, poets chanted the dangers of desert journeys, the joys of battle, or the glories of their clans. Their most important themes—chivalry and the romance of nomadic life—recurred in Arab poetry throughout the centuries. Later Arab poets developed elaborate formal rules for writing poetry and explored both religious and worldly themes. The poems of Rabiah al-Adawiyya expressed Sufi mysticism and encouraged the faithful to worship God selflessly without hope of reward. "If I worship Thee in hope of Paradise / Exclude me from Paradise," she wrote in one prayer poem.

Persians also had a fine poetic tradition. **Firdawsi** (fur DOW see) wrote in Persian using Arabic script. His masterpiece, the *Shah Namah,* or *Book of Kings,* tells the history of Persia. **Omar Khayyám** (OH mahr ky AHM), famous in the Muslim world as a scholar and an astronomer, is best known for *The Rubáiyát* (roo by AHT). In this collection of four-line stanzas, Khayyám meditates on fate and the fleeting nature of life:

Primary Source

“ The Moving Finger writes; and having writ,
Moves on; nor all your Piety nor Wit
Shall lure it back to cancel half a line,
Nor all your Tears wash out a word of it. ”
—Omar Khayyám, *The Rubáiyát*

A Hero's Super Powers
The illustration above is from Firdawsi's *Shah Namah*, which tells the story of many Persian heroes—among them, Rustam. Why was Rustam's strength both an advantage and a disadvantage?

Primary Source

“ The tale is told that Rustam had at first
Such strength bestowed by Him who giveth all
That if he walked upon a rock his feet
Would sink therein. Such [power] as that
Proved an abiding trouble, and he prayed
To God in bitterness of soul to [diminish]
His strength that he might walk like other men. ”
—Firdawsi, *Shah Namah*

BIOGRAPHY

Ibn Rushd (Averroës)

While growing up in Spain, Muslim scholar Ibn Rushd (1126–1198)—known to Europeans as Averroës—was interested in almost every subject and profession. He focused first on medicine and became chief physician to the Muslim ruler in Spain. Later, he studied astronomy and wrote several important books on the subject. Ibn Rushd also studied law, became a famous judge, and wrote a digest of Islamic law.

Ibn Rushd is best known as a philosopher. Muslims, Jews, and Christians alike have studied his commentaries on Aristotle for centuries. For part of his life, however, Ibn Rushd lived in exile outside Spain because some Muslim religious leaders felt that his writings contradicted the teachings of Islam. **What role did Ibn Rushd play in increasing the knowledge of people during the Middle Ages?**

Arab writers also prized the art of storytelling. Along with ancient Arab tales, they gathered and adapted stories from Indian, Persian, Greek, Jewish, Egyptian, and Turkish sources. The best-known collection is *The Thousand and One Nights,* a group of tales narrated by a fictional princess. They include romances, fables, adventures, and humorous anecdotes, many set in Harun al-Rashid's Baghdad. Later versions filtered into Europe, where children heard about "Aladdin and His Magic Lamp" or "Ali Baba and the Forty Thieves."

Religious Buildings Domed mosques and high minarets dominated Muslim cities. Adapted from Byzantine buildings, domes and arches became symbolic of Muslim architecture. For example, the Dome of the Rock in Jerusalem was built around 688. Inside, the walls and ceilings of mosques were decorated with elaborate abstract, geometric patterns. In addition, Muslim artists perfected skills in **calligraphy,** the art of beautiful handwriting. They worked the flowing Arabic script, especially verses from the Quran, into decorations on buildings.

Nonreligious Art Some Muslim artists painted human and animal figures in nonreligious art. Arabic scientific works, including those on the human body, were often lavishly illustrated. Literary works sometimes showed stylized figures. Later Persian, Turkish, and Indian artists excelled at painting miniatures to illustrate books of poems and fables.

✓ **Checkpoint** What elements characterized Muslim art?

Muslims Seek Knowledge

Although Muhammad could neither read nor write, his respect for learning inspired Muslims to make great advances in philosophy, history, mathematics, and the sciences. Both boys and girls received elementary education, which emphasized reading and writing. Muslims needed these skills to study the Quran. Institutions of higher learning included schools for religious instruction and for the study of Islamic law.

Centers of Learning Al-Mamun and later caliphs established Baghdad as the greatest Muslim center of learning. Its libraries attracted well paid and highly respected scholars. Other cities, like Cairo, Córdoba, and Timbuktu were also known as centers of learning. In these places, scholars made advances in philosophy, mathematics, medicine, and other fields. They also preserved the learning of earlier civilizations by translating ancient Persian, Sanskrit, and Greek texts into Arabic.

Philosophy and History Muslim scholars translated the works of the Greek philosophers, as well as many Hindu and Buddhist texts. Scholars tried to harmonize Greek ideas about reason with religious beliefs based on divine revelation. In Córdoba, the philosopher **Ibn Rushd**—known in Europe as Averroës—put all knowledge except the Quran to the test of reason. His writings on Aristotle were translated into Latin and influenced Christian scholastics in medieval Europe.

Another Arab thinker, **Ibn Khaldun** (IB un kal DOON), set standards for the scientific study of history. He stressed economics and social structure as causes of historical events. He also warned about common causes of error in historical writing, such as bias, exaggeration, and overconfidence in the accuracy of sources. Ibn Khaldun urged historians to trust sources only after a thorough investigation.

Muslim Advances in Astronomy

During the Muslim Golden Age, scientists and mathematicians in Muslim regions made great advances in the field of astronomy. At observatories from Baghdad to Central Asia, astronomers studied eclipses, observed Earth's rotation, and calculated the circumference of Earth to within a few thousand feet. When overland trade along the Silk Road became disrupted in the 1400s, new navigation tools paved the way for seafaring explorers like Christopher Columbus.

A Greek invention, the astrolabe is ▲ a projection of the sky as seen from a specific position on earth. Muslim astronomers added more information to it and made it more accurate.

The quadrant was an early navigation instrument. By measuring the height of a star, sailors could determine their latitude. ▶

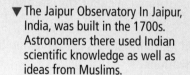

◀ An astronomical illustration

▼ The Jaipur Observatory In Jaipur, India, was built in the 1700s. Astronomers there used Indian scientific knowledge as well as ideas from Muslims.

▲ The picture above shows astronomers at a Turkish observatory with their instruments. What tools are they using?

Thinking Critically

1. **Analyze Information** What evidence do you see that astronomers were respected?
2. **Draw Inferences** What were some benefits of advances in astronomy?

Origin of Arabic Numerals		
Eastern Muslim Regions	Western Muslim Regions	Modern Western
۱	۱	1
۲	2	2
۳	۳	3
۴	۶	4
۵	۷	5
۶	6	6
۷	۱	7
۸	8	8
۹	9	9
۰	0	0

Arabic numerals originally developed in India and changed as traders introduced them to Muslim lands and, eventually, to Europe.

Mathematics One of the greatest Muslim mathematicians was **al-Khwarizmi** (al KWAHR iz mee). He pioneered the study of algebra (from the Arabic word *al-jabr*). In the 800s, he wrote a book that was translated into Latin and became a standard mathematics textbook in Europe. Like many scholars of the time, al-Khwarizmi contributed to other fields too. He developed a set of astronomical tables based on Greek and Indian discoveries.

Medicine Building on the knowledge of the ancient Greeks, Muslims made remarkable advances in medicine and public health. Under the caliphs, physicians and pharmacists had to pass a test before they could practice their professions. The government set up hospitals, where injured people could get quick treatment at a facility similar to today's emergency room. Physicians traveled to rural areas to provide healthcare to those who could not get to a city, while others regularly visited jails.

One of the most original medical thinkers was **Muhammad al-Razi,** head physician at Baghdad's chief hospital. He wrote many books on medicine, including a pioneering study of measles and smallpox. He also challenged accepted medical practices. Treat the mind as well as the body, he advised young doctors. He theorized that if doctors were hopeful with their patients, recovery would be faster.

The famous Persian physician **Ibn Sina** (IB un SEE nah) was known in Europe as Avicenna. By the age of 16, he was a doctor to the Persian nobility. His great work was the *Canon on Medicine*, a huge encyclopedia of what the Greeks, the Arabs, and he himself had learned about diagnosing and treating diseases. The book includes many prescriptions, made with such ingredients as mercury from Spain, myrrh from East Africa, and camphor from India.

Other Muslim surgeons developed a way to treat cataracts, drawing fluid out of the lenses with a hollow needle. For centuries, surgeons around the world used this method to save patients' eyesight. Arab pharmacists were the first to mix bitter medicines into sweet-tasting syrups and gums. Eventually, European physicians began to attend Muslim universities in Spain. Arabic medical texts were translated into Latin and the works of Avicenna and al-Razi became the standard medical textbooks at European schools for 500 years.

✓ **Checkpoint** How did Muslim scholars preserve and build on the learning of earlier civilizations?

 SECTION **3** Assessment

Terms, People, and Places

1. For each term, person, or place listed at the beginning of the section, write a sentence explaining its significance.

Note Taking

2. **Reading Skill: Categorize** Use your completed chart to answer the Focus Question: What achievements did Muslims make in economics, art, literature, and science?

Comprehension and Critical Thinking

3. **Summarize** How could slaves gain their freedom in Muslim society?

4. **Recognize Cause and Effect** How did business methods of Muslim merchants encourage trade and industry?

5. **Make Generalizations** What were the central themes of Muslim literature and Arab poetry?

6. **Determine Relevance** How did Ibn Khaldun improve the study and writing of history?

● **Writing About History**

Quick Write: Use Parallel Structure Compare or contrast at least three similarities or differences between Muslim society under the Abbasids and European society in the early Middle Ages. Discuss the points about each subject in the same order. For example, you could contrast the attitude toward merchants first in Muslim society and then in European society. Use similar sentence structures to emphasize the points being compared.

Islamic Art

GA SSWH12b

Most Islamic art shares distinctive characteristics. One reason for this was the prohibition on depicting humans or animals in religious art. As a result, many Muslims use a style known as arabesque, which focuses on floral and geometric shapes. Other artists created an elaborate style of calligraphy, turning the words themselves into works of art.

Flowering Patterns ▶
The arabesque appears in rugs, textiles, and glassware. The arabesque style has religious purposes, among them to show the infinity of God and the unity of Islam. Even the areas that are left empty are carefully planned to project a feeling of weightlessness.

Patterns of Glass and Stone ▼
Many mosques in the Muslim world are decorated with elaborate mosaics—thousands of small pieces of colored glass, ceramic, and stone tiles arranged to create decorative patterns and arabesques. An artist patiently fits the pieces tightly together into a concrete surface, slightly tilting each piece so that it catches the light.

▲ The Art of Beautiful Writing
Calligraphers want to make both words and the writing of them works of art. Like great European artists, gifted calligraphers were honored in Muslim society and have been studied by scholars worldwide. Some of the most elaborate examples, such as the Quran page from the 1700s above, use calligraphy to reinforce the sacred nature of the text. The fifteenth-century inkwell at left shows calligraphic designs worked in metal.

Thinking Critically
1. **Recognize Ideologies** Why did Islam prohibit the depiction of people or animals in religious art?
2. **Determine Relevance** Why would the visual elements of light and space be important artistically for the interior of mosques?

Akbar rides an elephant.

WITNESS HISTORY 🔊 AUDIO

Akbar the Great

Thirteen-year-old Akbar had grown up learning to hunt, run, and fight. Raised in the rugged country of Afghanistan, he never found the time to read and write. Now it was the year 1556, his father was dead, and the boy became *padshah*—"ruler of the empire." Under the guidance of his regent, Akbar immediately began seizing territory lost after his father's death. To seek knowledge, he had books read aloud to him. To promote unity between the Muslims and Hindus in his empire, he married a Hindu princess.

Akbar's father had foretold a bright future for his son, and Akbar fulfilled that prophecy. Many historians view Akbar as the greatest ruler in Indian history.

Focus Question How did Muslim rule affect Indian government and society?

India's Muslim Empires

 Performance Standards

- **SSWH5a** Explain the origin of Islam and the growth of the Islamic Empire.
- **SSWH12a** Describe the Mughal Empire's borders when Babur and Akbar ruled.
- **SSWH12b** Explain how Muslim empires influenced religion, law, and the arts.

Terms, People, and Places

sultan	Mughal
Delhi	Akbar
rajah	Nur Jahan
Sikhism	Shah Jahan
Babur	Taj Mahal

Note Taking

Reading Skill: Identify Supporting Details
Copy the outline below. As you read, finish it following the organization in the example.

> I. The Delhi Sultanate
>   A. The Sultan of Delhi Defeats the Hindus
>   1.
>   2.

The arrival of Islam brought changes to India as great as those caused by the Aryan migrations 2,000 years earlier. As Muslims mingled with Indians, each civilization absorbed elements from the other.

The Delhi Sultanate

After the Gupta empire fell in about 550, India again fragmented into many local kingdoms. Rival princes battled for control of the northern plain. Despite power struggles, Indian culture flourished. Hindu and Buddhist rulers spent huge sums to build and decorate magnificent temples. Trade networks linked India to the Middle East, Southeast Asia, and China.

The Sultan of Delhi Defeats the Hindus Although Arabs conquered the Indus Valley in 711, they advanced no farther into the subcontinent. Then around 1000, Muslim Turks and Afghans pushed into India. They were fierce warriors with a tradition of conquest. Sultan Mahmud of Ghazni pillaged much of the north, but he did not settle there. In the late 1100s, though, the **sultan**, or Muslim ruler, of Ghur defeated Hindu armies across the northern plain and made **Delhi** his capital. From there, his successors organized a sultanate, or land ruled by a sultan. The Delhi sultanate, which lasted from 1206 to 1526, marked the start of Muslim rule in northern India.

Why did the Muslim invaders triumph? They won on the battlefield in part because Muslim mounted archers had far greater mobility than Hindu forces, who rode slow-moving war elephants. Also, Hindu princes wasted resources battling one another instead of uniting against a common enemy. In some places, large numbers of Hindus, especially from low castes, converted to Islam. In the Hindu social system, people were born into castes, or social groups, from which they could not change.

Muslim Rule Changes Indian Government and Society Muslim rule brought changes to Indian government and society. Sultans introduced Muslim traditions of government. Many Turks, Persians, and Arabs migrated to India to serve as soldiers or officials. Trade between India and Muslim lands increased. During the Mongol raids of the 1200s, many scholars and adventurers fled from Baghdad to India, bringing Persian and Greek learning. The newcomers helped create a brilliant civilization at Delhi, where Persian art and architecture flourished.

The Sultans Lose Power In 1398, Tamerlane invaded India. He plundered the northern plain and smashed into Delhi. "Not a bird on the wing moved," reported stunned survivors. Thousands of artisans were enslaved to build Tamerlane's capital at Samarkand. Delhi, an empty shell, slowly recovered. The sultans no longer controlled a large empire, however, and northern India again fragmented, this time into rival Hindu and Muslim states.

✓ **Checkpoint** What changes did Muslim rule bring to Indian government and society?

Geography *Interactive*
For: Audio guided tour
Web Code: nap-1041

Delhi Sultanate and Mughal Empire

Map Skills Two Muslim dynasties ruled much of the Indian subcontinent. The Delhi sultanate lasted more than 300 years before the Mughal dynasty replaced it.
1. **Locate** (a) Delhi (b) Hindu Kush (c) Ganges River
2. **Movement** Describe Tamerlane's route into India.

3. **Applying Information** Use the map of Asia in the Atlas and Geography Handbook to identify the present-day countries that now occupy the lands of the Mughal empire.

Tamerlane's forces invade India. ▼

Miller Projection
0   200   400 mi
0   200   400 km

HINDU KUSH

Lahore

Delhi

Agra

Indus R.

HIMALAYAS

Ganges R.

Brahmaputra R.

Tropic of Cancer

Narmada R.

Arabian Sea

DECCAN PLATEAU

Bay of Bengal

☐ Delhi sultanate about 1300
➤ Route of Tamerlane's invasion, 1398
☐ Mughal empire, 1526
☐ Lands added to the empire by 1605
☐ Lands added to the empire by 1707
☐ Taj Mahal

Goa (Portuguese)

Indian Ocean

60°E   75°E   90°E

Muslims and Hindus Clash

At its worst, the Muslim conquest of northern India inflicted disaster on Hindus and Buddhists. The widespread destruction of Buddhist monasteries contributed to the drastic decline of Buddhism as a major religion in India. During the most violent <u>onslaughts</u>, many Hindus were killed. Others may have converted to escape death. In time, though, relations became more peaceful.

Vocabulary Builder

<u>onslaught</u>—(AHN slawt) *n.* a vigorous attack

Hindu-Muslim Differences The Muslim advance brought two utterly different religions and cultures face to face. Hinduism was an ancient religion that had evolved over thousands of years. Hindus recognized many sacred texts and prayed before statues representing many gods and goddesses. Islam, by contrast, was a newer faith with a single sacred text. Muslims were devout monotheists who saw the statues and carvings in Hindu temples as false gods.

Hindus accepted differences in caste status and honored Brahmans as a priestly caste. Muslims taught the equality of all believers before God and had no religious hierarchy. Hindus celebrated religious occasions with music and dance, a practice not found in Muslim worship.

A Blending of Cultures Eventually, the Delhi sultans grew more tolerant of their Hindu subjects. Some Muslim scholars argued that behind the many Hindu gods and goddesses was a single god. Hinduism was thus accepted as a monotheistic religion. As a protected subject group, Hindus were allowed to practice their religion as long as they paid a poll tax. Some sultans even left **rajahs,** or local Hindu rulers, in place.

During the Delhi sultanate, a growing number of Hindus converted to Islam. Some lower-caste Hindus preferred Islam because it rejected the caste system. Other converts came from higher castes. They chose to adopt Islam either because they accepted its beliefs or because they served in the Muslim government. Indian merchants were attracted to Islam in part because of the strong trade network across Muslim lands.

Indian Muslims also absorbed elements of Hindu culture, such as marriage customs and caste ideas. Urdu, a new language, combined Persian, Arabic, and the Indian language spoken in Delhi. Local artisans

A Sikh man prays (below left) and a statue of the Hindu god Ganesh (below right)

Sikhism: A Blend of Religious Beliefs

Islam	Hinduism
• Belief in one God	• Belief in many gods, all part of Brahman
• Religious and moral duties defined in Five Pillars	• Emphasis on religious and moral duties, or dharma
• Belief in Heaven and Hell, and a Day of Judgment	• Belief in a cycle of birth, death, and rebirth
• No priests; all believers are religious equals	

Sikhism
- Belief in the "Unity of God"
- Belief in reincarnation
- Rejection of caste

Chart Skills This chart shows some teachings of Hinduism, Islam, and Sikhism. *Which teachings of Sikhism are similar to those of Hinduism? Which teachings of Sikhism are similar to those of Islam?*

applied Persian art styles to Indian subjects. Indian music and dance reappeared at the courts of the sultan.

An Indian holy man, Nanak, sought to blend Islamic and Hindu beliefs. He preached "the unity of God, the brotherhood of man, the rejection of caste, and the futility of idol worship." His teachings led to the rise of a new religion, **Sikhism** (SEEK iz um), in northern India. The Sikhs later organized into military forces that clashed with the powerful Mughal rulers of India.

✔ **Checkpoint** How did Muslim and Hindu cultures clash and then blend?

Mughal India

In 1526, Turkish and Mongol armies again poured through mountain passes into India. At their head rode **Babur** (BAH bur), who claimed descent from Genghis Khan and Tamerlane. Babur was a military genius, poet, and author of a detailed book of memoirs.

Babur Founds the Mughal Dynasty Just north of Delhi, Babur met a huge army led by the sultan Ibrahim. "I placed my foot in the stirrup of resolution and my hands on the reins of confidence in God," recalled Babur. His force was small but had cannons, which he put to good use:

Primary Source

❝ The sun had mounted spear-high when the onset began, and the battle lasted till midday, when the enemy was completely broken and routed. By the grace and mercy of Almighty God, this difficult affair was made easy to me, and that mighty army . . . was crushed in the dust.❞
—Babur, *Memoirs*

In little time, Babur swept away the remnants of the Delhi sultanate and set up the **Mughal** dynasty, which ruled from 1526 to 1857. (*Mughal* is the Persian word for "Mongol.") The map in this section shows you that Babur and his heirs conquered an empire that stretched from the Himalayas to the Deccan Plateau.

Akbar the Great The chief builder of the Mughal empire was Babur's grandson **Akbar.** During his long reign, from 1556 to 1605, he created a strong central government, earning the title Akbar the Great.

Akbar was a leader of unusual abilities. Although a Muslim, he won the support of Hindu subjects through his policy of toleration. He opened government jobs to Hindus of all castes and treated Hindu princes as his partners in ruling the vast empire. Akbar ended the tax on non-Muslims, and he married a Hindu princess.

Akbar could not read or write, but he consulted leaders of many faiths, including Muslims, Hindus, Buddhists, and Christians. Like the early Indian leader Asoka, he hoped to promote religious harmony through tolerance. By recognizing India's diversity, Akbar placed Mughal power on a firm footing.

Akbar strengthened his empire in other ways as well. To improve government, he used paid officials in place of

Akbar (center) with his son, Jahangir, and grandson, Shah Jahan

The Taj Mahal
Shah Jahan began construction on this tomb for his wife in 1632, a year after her death. It took 22,000 workers about 20 years to complete the structure.

Vocabulary Builder
usurp—(yoo SURP) *v.* to seize and hold by force without legal right

hereditary officeholders. He modernized the army, encouraged international trade, standardized weights and measures, and introduced land reforms.

Akbar's Successors Akbar's son Jahangir (juh HAHN geer) was a weaker ruler than his father. He left most details of government in the hands of his wife, **Nur Jahan.** Fortunately, she was an able leader whose shrewd political judgment was matched only by her love of poetry and royal sports. She was the most powerful woman in Indian history until the twentieth century.

The high point of Mughal literature, art, and architecture came with the reign of **Shah Jahan,** Akbar's grandson. When his wife, Mumtaz Mahal, died at age 39 after having borne 14 children, Shah Jahan was distraught. "Empire has no sweetness," he cried, "life itself has no relish left for me now." He had a stunning tomb built for her, the **Taj Mahal** (tahzh muh HAHL). Designed by a Persian architect, it has spectacular white domes and graceful minarets mirrored in clear blue reflecting pools. Verses from the Quran adorn its walls, and pleasant gardens surround the entire structure. The Taj Mahal stands as perhaps the greatest monument of the Mughal empire.

Shah Jahan planned to build a twin structure to the Taj Mahal as a tomb for himself. However, before he could do so, his son Aurangzeb usurped the throne in 1658. Shah Jahan was kept imprisoned until he died several years later.

✔ **Checkpoint** What policies did Akbar follow to strengthen his empire?

Looking Ahead

In the late 1600s, the emperor Aurangzeb rejected Akbar's tolerant policies and resumed persecution of Hindus. Economic hardships increased under heavy taxes, and discontent sparked revolts against Mughal rule. This climate of discontent helped European traders gain a foothold in the once powerful Mughal empire.

SECTION **4** Assessment

Progress Monitoring *Online*
For: Self-quiz with vocabulary practice
Web Code: naa-1041

Terms, People, and Places
1. For each term, person, or place listed at the beginning of the section, write a sentence explaining its significance.

N̲o̲t̲e̲ Taking
2. **Reading Skill: Identify Supporting Details** Use your completed outline to answer the Focus Question: How did Muslim rule affect Indian government and society?

Comprehension and Critical Thinking
3. **Recognize Cause and Effect** Why were the founders of the Delhi sultanate able to conquer northern India?
4. **Analyze Information** How did relations between Hindus and Muslims evolve over time?
5. **Predict Consequences** Rulers after Akbar rejected the policy of toleration of other religious beliefs. How do you think this rejection of toleration affected relations between Hindus and Muslims?

⬤ **Writing About History**

Quick Write: Add Transition Words Write two paragraphs comparing the major beliefs of Islam and Hinduism. Use comparison or contrast linking words—such as *similarly, in the same way, in contrast,* and *instead*—to connect your ideas as well as to highlight similarities and differences.

◀ Mehmet II

Constantinople Falls

When Mehmet II became Ottoman sultan in 1451, his goal was to conquer Constantinople, which was all that was left of the once mighty Byzantine empire. The Ottoman fleet was anchored near the city walls. The Byzantines sought help from the pope and European princes as Mehmet's grip tightened. In 1453, Mehmet began a 54-day siege of Constantinople. He used every means to break through the ancient walls of the city, including commissioning a 27-foot cannon hauled overland by oxen. As the walls were bombarded, the defenders quickly repaired them. Time, however, was running out. Constantinople fell to the Ottomans, who made the city their capital.

Focus Question What were the main characteristics of the Ottoman and Safavid empires?

▲ Constantinople under attack by Ottoman Turks

SECTION 5

The Ottoman and Safavid Empires

 Performance Standards

- **SSWH4e** Explain Ottoman role in the Byzantine decline and Constantinople's capture.
- **SSWH12a** Describe the Ottoman Empire's borders when Suleyman the Magnificent ruled; describe the Safavid Empire's border when Shah Abbas I ruled.

Terms, People, and Places

Ottomans	shah
Istanbul	Shah Abbas
Suleiman	Isfahan
janizary	Qajars
Safavid	Tehran

Note Taking

Reading Skill: Synthesize Information Copy this table. As you read, fill in key characteristics of the Ottoman and Safavid empires.

Characteristics	Ottomans	Safavids
Capital		
Dates		
Strongest ruler		
Extent of empire		
Type of Islam		
Relationship with Europe		

While the Mughals ruled India, two other dynasties—the Ottomans and Safavids—dominated the Middle East and parts of Eastern Europe. All three empires owed much of their success to new weapons that changed warfare. Cannons, and later, muskets, gave greater firepower to ordinary foot soldiers, thus reducing the importance of mounted warriors. The new military technology helped the Ottomans and Safavids create strong central governments. As a result, this period from about 1450 to 1650 is sometimes called "the age of gunpowder empires."

The Ottoman Empire Expands

Like the Seljuks, the **Ottomans** were a Turkish-speaking nomadic people who had migrated from Central Asia into northwestern Asia Minor. In the 1300s, they spread across Asia Minor and into Eastern Europe's Balkan Peninsula.

Constantinople Falls to the Ottomans Ottoman expansion threatened the crumbling Byzantine empire. After several failed attempts to capture Constantinople, Mehmet II finally succeeded in 1453. In a surprise move, the Ottomans hauled ships overland and launched them into the harbor outside Constantinople. After a nearly two-month siege, Ottoman cannons finally blasted gaps in the great defensive walls of the city, and it became the new capital of the Ottoman empire. From Constantinople (renamed **Istanbul**), the Ottoman Turks continued their conquests for the next 200 years.

Suleiman the Magnificent The Ottoman empire enjoyed a golden age under the sultan Suleiman (soo lay MAHN), who ruled from 1520 to 1566. His people called him "the Lawgiver," while Europeans called him Suleiman the Magnificent. A brilliant general, Suleiman modernized the army and conquered many new lands. He extended Ottoman rule eastward into the Middle East, and also into Kurdistan and Georgia in the Caucasus Mountain region. In the west, Suleiman advanced deeper into Europe through diplomacy and warfare. In 1529, his armies besieged the Austrian city of Vienna, sending fear through Western Europe.

Although they failed to take Vienna, the Ottomans ruled the largest, most powerful empire in both Europe and the Middle East for centuries. At its height, the empire stretched from Hungary to Arabia and Mesopotamia and across North Africa. Suleiman felt justified in claiming to be the rightful heir of the Abbasids and caliph of all Muslims. To the title of "Emperor," he added the symbolic name of "Protector of the Sacred Places" (Mecca and Medina).

✔ **Checkpoint** What technology and techniques enabled Suleiman to extend Ottoman rule?

Ottoman Culture

Suleiman was a wise and capable ruler. He strengthened the government of the rapidly growing empire and improved its system of justice. As sultan, Suleiman had absolute power, but he ruled with the help of a grand vizier and a council. A huge bureaucracy supervised the business of government, and the powerful military kept the peace. Ottoman law was based on the Sharia, supplemented by royal edicts. Government officials worked closely with religious scholars who interpreted the law.

Society Is Organized Into Classes Ottoman society was divided into classes, each with its appointed role. At the top were "men of the sword"—soldiers who guarded the sultan and defended the state—and "men of the pen"—scientists, lawyers, judges, and poets. Below them were "men of negotiation," such as merchants, tax collectors, and artisans who carried out trade and production. Finally, there were "men of husbandry," or farmers and herders who produced food for the community.

The Ottomans ruled diverse peoples of many religions. The men of the sword and men of the pen were almost all Muslims, but the other classes included non-Muslims. The people were organized into millets, or religious communities. These included Muslims, Greek Christians, Armenian Christians, and Jews. Each millet had its own leaders who were responsible for education and some legal matters. The Jewish millets included many Jews who had been expelled from Spain in 1492. They brought international banking connections with them, plus a new technology for making cloth that helped the Ottoman empire finance its expansion.

Janizaries—The Elite Force Like earlier Muslim empires, the Ottomans recruited officers for the army and government from among the huge populations of conquered peoples in their empire. The Ottomans levied a "tax" on Christian families in the Balkans, requiring them to turn over their young sons for government service.

Suleiman the Magnificent
The picture above shows the sultan Suleiman and his viziers, or advisors.

Vocabulary Builder
edict—(EE dikt) *n.* an order or command having the force of law

The boys were converted to Islam and put into rigorous military training at the palace school. The best soldiers won a prized place in the **janizaries** (JAN ih sehr eez), the elite force of the Ottoman army. The brightest students received special education to become government officials. They might serve as judges, poets, or even grand vizier.

Like the boys, non-Muslim girls from eastern Europe served as slaves in wealthy Muslim households. There, they might be accepted as members of the household. Some of the enslaved girls were freed after the death of their masters.

An Ottoman soldier on horseback

Literature and the Arts

The arts blossomed under Suleiman. Ottoman poets adapted Persian and Arab models to produce works in Turkish. Influenced by Persian artistic styles, Ottoman painters produced detailed miniatures and illuminated manuscripts.

The royal architect Sinan, a janizary military engineer, designed hundreds of mosques and palaces. He compared his most famous building, the Selimiye Mosque at Edirne, to the greatest church of the Byzantine empire. "With God's help and the Sultan's mercy," Sinan wrote, "I have succeeded in building a dome for the mosque which is greater in diameter and higher than that of Hagia Sophia."

Decline of the Ottomans

After Suleiman's death in 1566, the Ottoman empire began a slow decline. Suleiman had killed two of his most able sons because he suspected them of treason. His son and successor Selim II left most of the governing to his ministers, and government bureaucracy became corrupt.

By the 1700s, European advances in both commerce and military technology were leaving the Ottomans behind. Russia and other European powers captured Ottoman lands, while local rulers in North Africa and elsewhere broke away from Ottoman control. Able sultans tried to revive Ottoman power with limited success.

✓ **Checkpoint** What were the four divisions of Ottoman society?

The Janizary Corps
The soldiers below wear the dress of the sultan's soldiers.

Ottoman and Safavid Empires, 1453–1629

Map Skills At its greatest extent, the Ottoman empire stretched across three continents. At about the same period, the Safavid empire controlled most of what is today Iran.

1. **Locate** (a) Istanbul (b) Black Sea (c) Isfahan (d) Hungary

2. **Movement** Into what regions did the Ottoman empire expand under Suleiman?

3. **Recognize Point of View** How do you think Russians felt about the expansion of the Ottoman and Safavid empires? Explain.

RUSSIA

Aral Sea

EUROPE

Vienna

AUSTRIA

HUNGARY

FRANCE

45°N

Danube River

Black Sea

ASIA

Caspian Sea

SPAIN

0°

Istanbul

ASIA MINOR

Tehran

ALGERIA

GREECE

15°E

Mediterranean Sea

30°E

Euphrates River

Tigris River

Damascus

Baghdad

PERSIA

Isfahan

Tripoli

Jerusalem

60°E

TRIPOLI

Cairo

EGYPT

Persian Gulf

AFRICA

Nile River

Medina

ARABIA

15°N

Mecca

Red Sea

45°E

Indian Ocean

N
W E
S

Miller Projection

0   200   400 mi

0   200   400 km

- ▉ Ottoman empire, 1453
- ▉ Lands added, 1453–1520
- ▉ Lands added under Suleiman, 1520–1566
- ▉ Safavid empire at death of Shah Abbas the Great, 1629

A Center of Persian Culture Under Shah Abbas, Isfahan flourished. The shah welcomed artists, poets, and scholars to the court. Palace workshops produced magnificent porcelains, clothes, and rugs. Abbas liked to walk the streets of Isfahan in disguise, mingling with the crowds in bazaars. Amid the cries of street vendors and swarms of traders and customers, he asked people about their problems. If he heard stories of corruption, he punished the guilty.

Early 1300s
Ottoman Turks spread into Balkan Peninsula

1453
Constantinople falls to Ottoman Turks

1588–1629
Reign of Shah Abbas

1722
Safavid ruler abdicates

1300   **1400**   **1500**   **1600**   **1700**

1451–1481
Reign of Mehmet II

1520–1566
Reign of Suleiman

1629–1722
Decline of the Safavid empire

1453 Ottoman dates
1722 Safavid dates

The Safavid Empire

By the early 1500s, the **Safavid** (sah FAH vid) dynasty had united an empire in Persia (present-day Iran). Sandwiched between two expansionist powers—Mughal India and the Ottoman empire—the Safavids often engaged in warfare. Religion played a role in the conflict. The Safavids were Shiite Muslims who enforced their beliefs in their empire. The Ottomans were Sunni Muslims who despised the Shiites as heretics.

Abbas the Great The Safavid king was called the **shah.** The best-known, **Shah Abbas** the Great, revived the glory of ancient Persia. From 1588 to 1629, he centralized the government and created a powerful military force modeled on the Ottoman janizaries. Abbas used a mixture of force and diplomacy against the Ottomans. He also sought alliances with European states that had reason to fear Ottoman power.

To strengthen the economy, Abbas reduced taxes on farmers and herders and encouraged the growth of industry. Unlike earlier Safavids, Abbas tolerated non-Muslims and valued their economic contributions. He built a new capital at **Isfahan** (is fah HAHN), which became a center of the international silk trade. Armenians controlled the trade, so Abbas brought thousands of Armenians to Isfahan. He had a settlement built for these Christians just outside the capital, where they governed themselves.

The Safavid Empire Declines Safavid glory slowly faded after the death of Shah Abbas and under continuing pressure from Ottoman armies. Shiite scholars also challenged the authority of the shah by stressing their own authority to interpret law and determine government policy. They encouraged persecution of religious minorities, pushing Sunni Afghans to rebel. The rebels defeated imperial armies, captured Isfahan, and forced the last Safavid ruler to abdicate in 1722.

In the late 1700s, a new dynasty, the **Qajars** (kuh JAHRZ), won control of Iran. They made **Tehran** their capital and ruled until 1925. Still, the Safavids left a lasting legacy. They established Shiism firmly in Iran and gave Persians a strong sense of their own identity.

> ✔ **Checkpoint**   How did Shah Abbas revive the glory of ancient Persia?

Vocabulary Builder

<u>sagacious</u>—(suh GAY shus) *adj.* having good judgment

In 1604, a Carmelite missionary visited the Persian court. The monk recorded his observations of Shah Abbas the Great. According to Abbas, how does his style of leadership differ from that of Christian rulers?

Primary Source

❝He is <u>sagacious</u> in mind, likes fame and to be esteemed: he is courteous in dealing with everyone and at the same time very serious. For he will go through the public streets, eat from what they are selling there and . . . speak at ease freely with the lower classes . . . or will sit down beside this man or that. He says that is how to be a king, and that the king of Spain and other Christians do not get any pleasure out of ruling, because they are obliged to comport themselves with so much pomp and majesty.❞

—*A Chronicle of the Carmelites in Persia* ◀))) AUDIO

SECTION 5 Assessment

Progress Monitoring *Online*
For: Self-quiz with vocabulary practice
Web Code: naa-1051

Terms, People, and Places

1. For each term, person, or place listed at the beginning of the section, write a sentence explaining its significance.

Note Taking

2. **Reading Skill: Synthesize Information** Use your completed table to answer the Focus Question: What were the main characteristics of the Ottoman and Safavid empires?

Comprehension and Critical Thinking

3. **Summarize** Describe the extent of the Ottoman empire at its height.
4. **Analyze Information** How did Suleiman govern the Ottoman empire?
5. **Explain** What policies did Abbas the Great use to strengthen the Safavid empire?
6. **Draw Conclusions** Why do you think Ottoman and Safavid rulers allowed some religious toleration?

● Writing About History

Quick Write: Revise Word Choice
Compare and contrast Suleiman the Magnificent with Shah Abbas the Great by examining their contributions and the effects they had on their respective empires. As you write, choose specific verbs and adjectives that highlight similarities or differences. For example, *flourished* contrasts with *grew* to emphasize the extent to which a particular culture or location developed.

Quick Study Guide

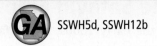

GA SSWH5d, SSWH12b

Progress Monitoring *Online*
For: Self-test with vocabulary practice
Web Code: naa-1061

■ Key Muslim Empires

Empire	Muhammad and First Successors (632–661)	Umayyad (661–750) (756–1031 in Spain)	Abbasid (750–1258)	Mughal (1526–1857)	Ottomans (late 1200s–1922)	Safavids (early 1500s–1722)
Key Leader(s)	• Muhammad • Abu Bakr • Umar • Ali	• Mu'awiyah	• Abu al-Abbas • al-Mansur • Harun al-Rashid	• Babur • Akbar • Jahangir • Shah Jahan • Aurangzeb	• Mehmet II • Suleiman • Selim II	• Shah Abbas
Capital	Mecca	Damascus (Córdoba in Spain)	Baghdad	Delhi, Agra	Istanbul	Isfahan

■ Spread of the Arab Empire

Cause and Effect

Long-Term Causes	Immediate Causes
• Weakness of Byzantine and Persian empires • Economic and social changes in Arabia	• Tribes of Arabia unified by Islam around a central message • Wide acceptance of religious message of Islam • Easy acceptance of social ideas of Islam, such as equality among believers

Spread of Islam

Immediate Effects	Long-Term Effects
• Islam spreads from the Atlantic coast to the Indus River valley • Centers of learning flourish in Cairo, Córdoba, and elsewhere	• Muslim civilization emerges • Linking of Europe, Asia, and Africa through Muslim trade network • Arabic becomes shared language of Muslims • Split between Sunnis and Shiites

■ Five Pillars of Islam

- Make the declaration of faith: "There is no god but God, Muhammad is the messenger of God."
- Pray five times per day, facing Mecca.
- Give alms (charity) to the poor.
- Fast from sunrise to sunset during Ramadan.
- Make the hajj, or pilgrimage to Mecca, if physically and financially able.

■ Key Muslim Scholars

- Firdawsi—writer and poet, *Shah Namah (Book of Kings)*
- Omar Khayyám—scholar, astronomer, poet, *The Rubáiyát*
- Ibn Rushd (Averroës)—philosopher, physician, astronomer, judge
- Ibn Khaldun—philosopher and historian
- al-Khwarizmi—mathematician, astronomer, pioneered algebra
- Muhammad al-Razi—physician
- Ibn Sina (Avicenna)—physician, *Canon on Medicine*

■ Key Events of Muslim Civilization

622 Muhammad and his followers journey from Mecca to Medina.

750 Abu al-Abbas establishes the Abbasid dynasty.

900 Arabs complete the conquest of Sicily.

Muslim Events
Global Events

600

800

1000

732 Muslims are defeated at the battle of Tours, halting Islam's advance into Western Europe.

802 Jayavarman is crowned god-king of the Khmer empire in Cambodia.

982 Eric the Red establishes the first Viking colonies in Greenland.

Concept Connector

Essential Question Review

To connect prior knowledge with what you have learned in this chapter, answer the questions below in your Concept Connector journal. Use the journal in the Reading and Note Taking Study Guide to record your answers (or go to www.phschool.com **Web Code:** nad-1007). In addition, record information about the following concepts:

- Cultural Diffusion: Spread of Islam
- Empire: Abbasid Empire
- Empire: Mughal Empire

1. **Belief Systems** Muhammad said, "Know ye that every Muslim is a brother to every other Muslim and that ye are now one brotherhood." How might this idea have increased the appeal of Islam to conquered peoples?

2. **Empire** After they captured Constantinople, the Ottoman Turks continued their conquests. The period from 1450 to 1650 is sometimes called "the age of gunpowder empires," because new military technology helped the Ottomans and the Safavids build their empires. What factors led to the decline of the Ottoman empire?

3. **Impact of the Individual** Choose one leader from the chart Key Muslim Empires in the Quick Study Guide of this chapter. Write a paragraph explaining how the leader expanded or changed the empire and Islam.

Connections to Today

1. **Belief Systems** Islam is the religion of nearly one-fifth of the world's population, with millions of Muslims making the hajj, or pilgrimage, to Mecca each year. Research to learn more about the hajj, including when it occurs, the various actions that pilgrims are required to perform, and what those actions symbolize. Include information about what the government of Saudi Arabia does to prepare the city of Mecca for the millions of Muslims who arrive annually to fulfill one of the Pillars of Islam.

2. **Cultural Diffusion** Akbar the Great spoke eloquently about the diversity he found in his land: "O God, in every temple I see people that seek You. In every language I hear spoken, people praise You. If it be a mosque, people murmur the holy prayer. If it be a Christian church, they ring the bell for love of You. . . . It is You whom I seek from temple to temple." Should a nation encourage diversity? Or can lack of unity weaken the fabric of a society? As an American, you live in a highly diverse society. Write a statement in which you identify and explain two advantages and two disadvantages this diversity brings to American society.

History Interactive
For: Interactive timeline
Web Code: nap-1061

1099
Christian crusaders capture Jerusalem from the Muslims.

1206
Muslims set up the Delhi sultanate in northern India.

1453
Mehmet II and the Ottomans capture Constantinople.

1520
Suleiman the Magnificent rules the Ottoman empire.

1588
Shah Abbas the Great begins reign of Safavid empire in Persia.

1200

1400

1600

1066
William of Normandy defeats Harold at the Battle of Hastings and becomes king of England.

1279
The Mongols gain control of China.

1347
The Black Death devastates Europe.

1503
Leonardo da Vinci paints the *Mona Lisa*.

1558
Elizabeth I becomes queen of England.

Chapter Assessment

Terms, People, and Places

Match the following terms with the definitions listed below.

mosque	rajah
caliph	jihad
calligraphy	minaret
janizary	Sufi
shah	sultan
Quran	Sharia

1. Islamic law
2. successor to Muhammad
3. struggle in God's service
4. Islamic house of worship
5. elite force of the Ottoman army
6. authority or ruler in the Turkish empires
7. art of beautiful handwriting
8. Hindu ruler
9. a Muslim mystic
10. king in Safavid empire

Main Ideas

Section 1 (pages 304–309)
11. What are the Five Pillars of Islam?
12. Who are the "People of the Book," and how did Muslims regard them?

Section 2 (pages 310–316)
13. Who was the first caliph, and how did he reunite the Arabs?
14. How did Muslims treat conquered peoples?

Section 3 (pages 317–323)
15. Describe three business practices introduced by Muslim traders.
16. What medical advances were made by Muslim physicians?

Section 4 (pages 324–328)
17. Why did many Hindus convert to Islam during the Delhi sultanate?
18. How did Akbar's rule affect life in India?

Section 5 (pages 329–333)
19. What were the four social divisions in the Ottoman empire?
20. How did Abbas the Great strengthen the Safavid economy and encourage trade?

Chapter Focus Question
21. Who was Muhammad, and how did his teachings lead to the rise and spread of Islam?

Critical Thinking

22. **Analyze Information** In what ways was traditional Bedouin society different from the society that was formed under Islam?
23. **Draw Conclusions** Muhammad taught that "the ink of the scholar is holier than the blood of the martyr." What do you think he meant? How might this attitude have contributed to the development of Muslim civilization?
24. **Recognize Cause and Effect** Do you think there would have been a split between Sunni and Shiites if Muhammad had designated a successor before he died? Explain.
25. **Geography and History** How do you think the geography of the Middle East might have helped Muslims spread the teachings of Islam throughout the region?
26. **Make Inferences** Do you think Ottoman policies encouraged Christians in the empire to be loyal or disloyal to their Muslim rulers? Explain.
27. **Predict Consequences** How do you think Safavid shahs might have been able to halt or slow the decline of their empire after the reign of Abbas the Great?

● Writing About History

In this chapter's five Section Assessments, you developed skills for writing a compare-and-contrast essay.

Expository Essay: Compare and Contrast Akbar the Great is considered by historians to be the greatest ruler in Indian history. The reign of his great-grandson Aurangzeb, in contrast, is highly controversial. Although often criticized because of his intolerance toward Hindus, Aurangzeb attempted to eliminate many social evils. Research the two rulers and then write a compare-and-contrast essay on their respective reigns.

Prewriting
• Write a list of the various categories you wish to compare and contrast. Refer to this list as you collect facts and details.

Drafting
• Discuss the points about each subject in the same order. For example, you could write about Akbar's view toward scholars first, followed by Aurangzeb's view. Use similar sentence structures to emphasize the points being compared.
• Give vivid and descriptive details about each point of comparison to make your essay more accessible to readers.
• Use comparison or contrast linking words—such as *similarly, in the same way, in contrast,* and *instead*—to connect your ideas as well as to highlight similarities and differences.

Revising
• Use the guidelines for revising your essay on page W22 of the Writing Handbook.

Prepare for the GHSGT

Muslim Trade Networks

In the eighth century A.D., Arab armies spread Islam across North Africa and deep into Asia. Muslim traders advanced in their wake, taking control of established trade routes on both continents. Pilgrims followed these same routes on the annual *hajj* to Mecca, eastward from Africa and westward from Asia. Trade and religion united this vast empire, as the documents below illustrate.

Document A

"Under the Abbasids, the center of the Moslem world was the city of Baghdad (Gift of God), founded by Caliph al-Mansur in 762 on the west bank of the Tigris. . . . The site was not chosen by inadvertence, for the Moslems had taken over the existing long-distance networks that had operated in the East for centuries. . . . if the pilgrimage caravans made only one round trip a year in the prescribed season, it was the traders who, as always, kept the Silk Road active all the year round. By the ninth century, some Arab traders had pushed overland to China."

—From *The Silk Road* by Irene M. Franck and David M. Brownstone

Document B

A muezzin calls Muslims to prayer in Urumqi, China.

Document C

"The speed of the Arab conquest of North Africa had been made possible because of the way the Arabs treated the desert as a highway rather than an obstacle. . . . [Control of the Sahara] gave the Arab conquerors immediate control of the inland caravan routes, which had previously been controlled by independent tribal powers . . . These inland routes were put to immediate use by merchants, messengers, military reinforcements and Mecca-bound pilgrims, for they were less dangerous than maritime travel."

—From *A Traveller's History of North Africa* by Barnaby Rogerson

Document D

African and Arab Muslims on a merchant ship

Analyzing Documents

Use your knowledge of Muslim civilizations and Documents A, B, C, and D to answer questions 1–4.

1. According to Document A, one reason the Abbasids chose Baghdad as their capital was the city's
   A religious significance to pilgrims.
   B lack of merchants.
   C location near the Silk Road.
   D strategic location for Arab armies.

2. Documents B and D support the statement that
   A All Muslims are Arabs.
   B All Arabs are Muslim.
   C Muslims are ethnically diverse.
   D Muslims only traded over land.

3. According to Document C, the Arabs did not consider the Sahara an obstacle. Why?
   A The Sahara is vast, hot, and dry.
   B The Arabs knew that their enemies would get lost there.
   C The Arabs liked traveling on large, hot highways.
   D The Arabs were used to traveling in the desert.

4. **Writing Task** In what sense did the Muslim trade routes make up a true "network"? Use these documents and information from the chapter to form your answer.

337

Bronze plaque of Benin warriors in their battle dress

Merchants at the Royal Court of Benin

By the late 1400s, merchants from Europe arrived at the Royal Court of Benin in West Africa in search of slaves, pepper, stone beads, cloth, and ivory.

The intricate detail on this West African saltcellar reveals the value of the salt it held.

66After [the king of Benin] had . . . [asked] the cause of their coming into the country, they answered . . . that they were merchants, traveling [to] his country for exchange of wares. . . . The king . . . having . . . a certain storehouse . . . of pepper, willed them to look upon the same, and . . . to bring him a sight of such merchandise as they had brought with them. . . . when they were returned and the wares seen, the king grew to this end with the merchants to provide in 30 days the loading of all their ships with pepper. . . . and thereupon sent the country [to] gather pepper. . . . So that within . . . 30 days, they had gathered fourscore tons of pepper.**99**

Listen to the Witness History audio to hear more about trade in medieval Africa.

 ◄ **Bronze plaque of Benin warriors in their battle dress**

Illustrated Arabic manuscript from the fifteenth century

GA **Performance Standards**

Chapter Focus Question How did trade influence the development of the kingdoms and trading states of Africa?

Section 1
Early Civilizations of Africa
SSWH5a, SSWH6a

Section 2
Kingdoms of West Africa
SSWH6b

Section 3
Kingdoms and Trading States of East Africa SSWH5d, SSWH6a, SSWH6d, SSWH6e

Section 4
Societies in Medieval Africa
SSWH5d, SSWH6b, SSWH6c, SSWH6e

Use the ☑ **Quick Study Timeline** at the end of this chapter to preview chapter events.

Shields were used for ceremonial as well as defensive purposes.

 Concept Connector ONLINE

To explore Essential Questions related to this chapter, go to PHSchool.com
Web Code: nad-1107

Twelfth-century illustration of a traveling caravan

A lone traveler traversing the vast Sahara

WITNESS HISTORY 🔊 AUDIO

Danger in the Desert

In 1325 a young Moroccan named Ibn Battuta began his pilgrimage to Mecca. This expedition led to a journey throughout Asia and Africa that lasted more than 30 years. Here, Battuta describes the dangers of crossing the Sahara.

❝ That desert . . . make[s] sport of him [the traveler] and disorder[s] his mind, so that he loses his way and perishes. For there is no visible road or track . . . nothing but sand blown hither and thither by the wind. You see hills of sand in one place, and afterwards you will see them moved to quite another place. ❞

Focus Question How did geography and natural resources affect the development of early societies throughout Africa?

Early Civilizations of Africa

 Performance Standards

- **SSWH5a** Explain the origin of Islam and the growth of the Islamic Empire.
- **SSWH6a** Identify Bantu migration patterns and contribution to agriculture.

Terms, People, and Places

Sahara	Bantu
savanna	Nubia
cataract	Meroë
desertification	

Note Taking

Reading Skill: Identify Causes and Effects As you read this section, make an outline like the one below to keep track of the important effects caused by Africa's geography and natural resources.

> I. The influence of geography
>   A. Geographic patterns
>   1.
>   2.
>   B. Resources spur trade
>   1.
>   2.

The vast and perilous **Sahara,** the largest desert in the world, is just one geographic feature in the great variety of African landscapes. For thousands of years, the geographic features of this huge continent have played a major role in its development.

The Influence of Geography

Africa is the second largest continent. Its size and location contribute to its wide range of climates, vegetation, and terrains. This variety has greatly influenced the diversity of culture found in Africa.

Geographic Patterns As shown on this section's map, Africa's vegetation regions create wide bands that stretch across the continent. Along the Equator is a band of tropical rain forest. Moving north and south from this band are the continent's largest and most populated regions, the **savannas,** or grassy plains. Beyond the savannas lie the great African deserts. These vegetation regions affect how people live and how they make a living.

Africa's geographic features also influenced cultural development by acting as barriers or highways to easy movement of people, goods, and ideas. In addition to the deserts and rain forests, Africa's high plateau interior and rivers with **cataracts,** or waterfalls, hindered easy movement. While on the other hand, the Great Rift Valley served as an interior passageway and the Mediterranean and Red seas provided overseas trade routes to regions in southwest Asia and present-day Europe.

Resources Spur Trade Since ancient times, Africa's mineral wealth has spurred trade across the continent. Salt, gold, iron, and copper were particularly valuable items to early trade and brought great wealth and power to African trading cities. Trade also linked Africa to other continents.

Initially hindered by the vast deserts, early trade greatly expanded with the introduction of a new form of transportation from Asia—the camel. By A.D. 200, these "ships of the desert" had revolutionized trade across the Sahara. Although early traders had made the difficult desert crossing in horse-drawn chariots, camel caravans created new trade networks. Camels could carry heavy loads and plod 20 or 30 miles a day, often without water. The caravans brought great profits to merchants on both sides of the Sahara.

✓ **Checkpoint** What geographic features limited movement in Africa and what made them obstacles?

People and Ideas Migrate

Archaeologists have uncovered evidence that Africa was the home of the earliest ancestors of modern people. In spite of geographic barriers, various members of these groups migrated all over Africa and beyond.

The Sahara Dries Out In Africa, as elsewhere, Paleolithic people developed skills as hunters and food gatherers. By 5500 B.C., Neolithic farmers had learned to cultivate the Nile Valley and to domesticate animals. As farming spread across North Africa, Neolithic villages even appeared in the Sahara, which was then a well-watered area. Ancient rock paintings have been found that show a Sahara covered with rich grasslands and savanna.

About 2500 B.C., a climate change slowly dried out the Sahara. As the land became parched, the desert spread. This process of **desertification** devoured thousands of acres of cropland and pastureland. The Sahara's desertification prompted migration, as people were forced to seek new areas to maintain their ways of life.

The Bantu Migrations Over thousands of years, migrations contributed to the rich diversity of cultures in Africa. Scholars have traced these migrations by studying language patterns. They have learned, for example, that West African farmers and herders migrated to the south and east between about 1000 B.C. and A.D. 1000. Like the Indo-European peoples of Europe and Asia, these West African peoples spoke a variety of languages deriving from a single common language. The root language is called **Bantu,** which gives this movement its name— the Bantu migrations.

As they migrated into southern Africa, the Bantu-speakers spread their skills in farming, ironworking, and domesticating animals. Some existing cultures merged with those of the Bantu-speakers wherever they settled. The influence of the Bantu-speakers is still found in the languages of the region today.

✓ **Checkpoint** How did migration affect the development of African cultures?

The Great Rift Valley
Extending approximately 4,000 miles from Southwest Asia through East Africa, the Great Rift Valley is the longest rift, or deep trench, on Earth's surface. Although many of Africa's highest mountains border the valley, this relatively low and flat corridor was an important passageway for early migrating groups in Africa. *Why do you think the Great Rift Valley would be ideal to travel through?*

Africa's Vegetation

Map Skills Africa consists of four major vegetation regions. These regions affected where and how people lived.

1. **Locate** (a) the Sahara Desert (b) the Great Rift Valley (c) the Congo River (d) the Mediterranean Sea (e) the Nile River (f) the Red Sea

2. **Movement** Why do you think the Bantu-speakers migrated south in the pattern described instead of north?

3. **Predict Consequences** Using the information provided in the map, predict three areas where you think a trade settlement would most likely develop. Explain your reasoning.

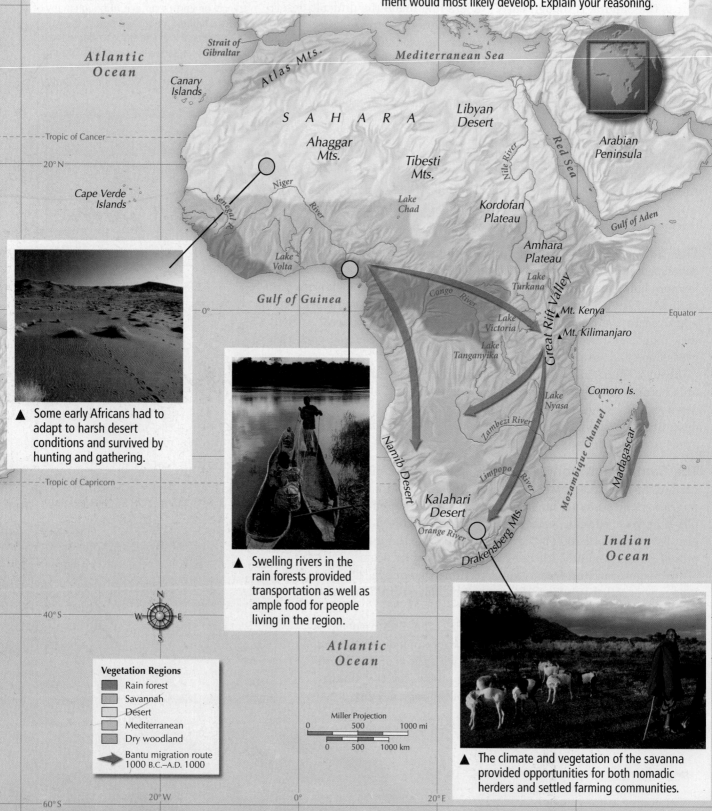

▲ Some early Africans had to adapt to harsh desert conditions and survived by hunting and gathering.

▲ Swelling rivers in the rain forests provided transportation as well as ample food for people living in the region.

▲ The climate and vegetation of the savanna provided opportunities for both nomadic herders and settled farming communities.

Vegetation Regions
- Rain forest
- Savannah
- Desert
- Mediterranean
- Dry woodland
- → Bantu migration route 1000 B.C.–A.D. 1000

Miller Projection
0   500   1000 mi
0   500   1000 km

Nubia Flourishes Along the Nile

About 2700 B.C. the great civilization of Egypt was growing along the northern banks of the Nile. At the same time, as shown on the map in the next section, another African civilization was taking shape to the south. On a wide band of fertile land on the upper Nile, the ancient kingdom of **Nubia,** also called Kush, was flourishing in present-day Sudan.

Nubia Rivals Egypt Trade led to contact between Nubia and Egypt. It also led to rivalry as both powers desired to control trade in the region. By 1500 B.C., Nubia was under Egyptian control and remained so for almost 500 years. As a result, Nubians adapted many Egyptian traditions. They modeled palaces and pyramids on Egyptian style and worshiped Egyptian deities.

By 1100 B.C., Egyptian control was declining and Nubia gained its independence. In fact, about 730 B.C., the Nubian king Piankhi (PYAHN kee) actually conquered Egypt. In 670 B.C., however, Nubia was invaded by the Assyrians from Southwest Asia. Unable to match the superior iron weapons of these invaders, the Nubian armies were forced to retreat from Egypt and returned to the south.

Meroë Masters Trade and Iron By 500 B.C., Assyrian invaders had forced Nubian rulers to move their capital from Napata to **Meroë** (MEHR oh ay). Meroë eventually commanded both the Nile's north-south trade route and the east-west trade route from the Red Sea to North Africa. Along this wide trade network, Nubia sent gold, ivory, animal skins, perfumes, and enslaved people to the Mediterranean world and Southwest Asia. Meroë's location was a major reason for its development into a successful center of trade.

Equally important, however, was the region's resources. Meroë was rich in iron ore. Fueled by the region's large quantities of timber, the smelting furnaces of Meroë produced the iron tools and weaponry needed to feed, control, and defend the kingdom. Today, giant heaps of iron waste remain as evidence of ancient Meroë's industry.

Splendor and Decline Although Nubia absorbed much from Egypt, Nubian culture later followed its own course. For example, after gaining independence from Egypt, Nubians worshiped their own gods, including Apedemak, a lion-headed warrior god. At Meroë, artistic styles reflected a greater sense of freedom than did Egyptian styles. Nubians also created their own system of writing, using an alphabet instead of hieroglyphics. Unfortunately, the Nubian alphabet has yet to be deciphered and still remains a mystery.

After the joint reign of King Natakamani and Queen Amanitere in the first century A.D., the splendor of Nubia's golden age dimmed. Finally, about A.D. 350, Nubia was overwhelmed by King Ezana's armies from the kingdom of Axum to its south.

✔ **Checkpoint** How did conquest affect the development of Nubia?

Cultural Exchange
The Nubian bronze of the Egyptian god Amun (top), was worshipped by some Nubians after they conquered Egypt. The rings with seals (bottom) were found among the funerary treasure of the Meroë queen Amanichaheto. *How do these artifacts illustrate the cultural exchange between Egypt and Nubia?*

Arabic Influences Scholarship
Arabic books with beautifully illustrated title pages such as the one above may have been used by students at early North African universities.

Vocabulary Builder
utilized—(YOOT il yzd) *vt.* put to practical use

Outside Influences Affect North Africa

The Nile was not the only waterway that influenced the development of civilizations in Africa. Early African civilizations also had strong ties to the regions across the Mediterranean and Red seas.

Phoenicians Build Carthage As Nubia was thriving along the Nile, Carthage was rising as a great North African power. Founded by Phoenician traders as a port on the Mediterranean coast, Carthage came to dominate western Mediterranean trade. From 800 B.C. to 146 B.C., it forged an empire that stretched from present-day Tunisia, Algeria, and Morocco to southern Europe. As you have read, however, territorial and trade rivalries between Rome and Carthage eventually led to a series of conflicts called the Punic Wars. At the end of the Third Punic War, the Romans literally burned Carthage to the ground.

Rome Rules North Africa After defeating Carthage, Rome gained control of the narrow strip of North Africa between the Mediterranean coast and the Sahara. There, they built roads, dams, aqueducts, and cities. The Romans developed and <u>utilized</u> North Africa's farmlands as a granary—a region that produces much grain—to feed the Roman empire. North Africa also provided soldiers for the Roman army, including Septimius Severus who would later become an emperor of Rome.

Under Roman rule, Christianity spread to the cities of North Africa. In fact, St. Augustine, the most influential Christian thinker of the late Roman Empire, was born in present-day Algeria. From A.D. 395 to A.D. 430, Augustine was bishop of Hippo, a city located near the ruins of ancient Carthage.

Islam Spreads Into Africa In the 690s, Muslim Arabs conquered and occupied the cities of North Africa. By the early 700s, they had successfully conquered the Berbers, a largely nomadic North African people. Under Arab rule, Islam eventually replaced Christianity as the dominant religion of North Africa, and Arabic replaced Latin as its language. Muslim civilization blossomed in cities such as Cairo, Fez, and Marrakesh, which became famous for their mosques and universities. Over time, Muslim traders from North Africa carried Islam into West Africa.

✔ **Checkpoint** How did trade cause change in North Africa?

Progress Monitoring *Online*
For: Self-quiz with vocabulary practice
Web Code: naa-1111

Terms, People, and Places
1. For each term, person, or place listed at the beginning of the section, write a sentence explaining its significance.

Note Taking
2. **Reading Skill: Identify Causes and Effects** Use your completed outline to answer the Focus Question: How did geography and natural resources affect the development of early societies throughout Africa?

Comprehension and Critical Thinking
3. **Recognize Cause and Effect** How did its geography affect movement in Africa?
4. **Determine Relevance** How did the Bantu migrations contribute to Africa's cultural diversity?
5. **Draw Conclusions** Why did the kingdom of Nubia prosper?
6. **Identify Central Issues** What factors motivated outsiders to conquer regions of North Africa?

● **Writing About History**
Quick Write: Understanding Chronology Using the information provided in this section, make a timeline of the events described. Make sure that you place each event in chronological order.

Concept Connector

THE ESSENTIAL ?

CULTURAL DIFFUSION

How does cultural diffusion occur?

In This Chapter

GA SSWH6a

During their migration, Bantu-speaking peoples from West Africa slowly diffused, or spread, their language over much of the African continent. Language, religion, and cultural traits have moved along the way of migrations, trade routes, and invading armies. Travelers changed and were changed by the cultures with whom they came in contact.

Throughout History

1200 A.D. Migration of Hittite ironsmiths spreads technology of weapon making.

586 B.C. Exiled Jews take their laws and traditions to other lands.

600s–700s A.D. Arab armies carry Muslim culture to conquered lands.

1455 The printing press speeds the exchange of ideas.

1800s Imperialism spreads Western influence in Africa and Asia.

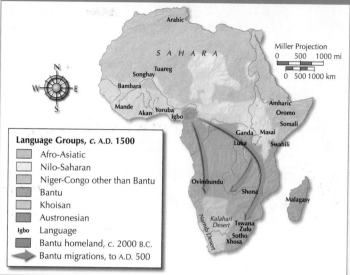

Language and the Bantu Migrations

Language Groups, c. A.D. 1500
- Afro-Asiatic
- Nilo-Saharan
- Niger-Congo other than Bantu
- Bantu
- Khoisan
- Austronesian
- Igbo — Language
- Bantu homeland, c. 2000 B.C.
- Bantu migrations, to A.D. 500

Miller Projection
0   500   1000 mi
0   500 1000 km

Continuing Today

American culture has had a major impact around the world. The popularity of baseball has spread from the United States around the world, leading to a World Baseball Classic.

21st Century Skills

 TRANSFER Activities

1. **Analyze** How are methods of cultural diffusion similar?

2. **Evaluate** What are some costs and benefits of cultural diffusion?

3. **Transfer** Complete a Web quest in which you analyze how cultures diffuse today; record your thoughts in the Concept Connector Journal; and learn to make a video. Web Code nah-1108

The Value of Salt

In 1526, Hassan ibn Muhammad, also known as Leo Africanus, published an account of his travels through North and West Africa. Here he describes the value of goods traded in Gao, a city in the African kingdom of Mali:

❝ It is a wonder to see what plenty of merchandise is daily brought hither, and how costly and sumptuous [lavish] all things be. Horses bought in Europe for ten ducats [coins] are here sold again for forty. . . . and spices are sold at a high rate: but of all other commodities salt is most extremely dear [expensive].❞

Focus Question How did the kingdoms of West Africa develop and prosper?

Slabs of salt being readied for market

Kingdoms of West Africa

 Performance Standards

- **SSWH6b** Describe the development and decline of Mali and Songhai; describe the pilgrimage of Mansa Musa to Mecca.

Terms, People, and Places

surplus
commodity
Ghana
Sundiata

Mali
Mansa Musa
Songhai

N**ote** Taking

Reading Skill: Identify Causes and Effects
As you read this section, look for clues that signal cause and effect. Then use a flowchart like the one below to record your findings.

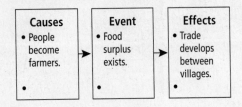

Causes	Event	Effects
• People become farmers.	• Food surplus exists.	• Trade develops between villages.
•	•	

Trading centers like that of the city of Gao developed over time throughout Africa as trade extended beyond village borders. Some of these medieval cities became wealthy international commercial centers. Between 800 and 1600, several powerful kingdoms won control of these prosperous cities and their trade.

Trade in the Sahara

Salt was rare in many regions of Africa. It was, however, important to human health. This combination made it highly prized as a trade item. The earliest development of trade in the region, however, was tied to another important development—agriculture.

Surplus Leads to Trade As the Sahara dried out, some Neolithic people migrated southward into the savanna, an area of grasslands that was good for farming. By A.D. 100, settled agricultural villages were expanding, especially along the Senegal and Niger rivers and around Lake Chad. This expansion from farming villages to towns was due, in part, to the development of trade.

Farming villages began to produce a **surplus,** that is, more than they needed. They began to trade their surplus food for products from other villages. Gradually, a trade network linked the savanna to forest lands in the south and then funneled goods across the Sahara to civilizations along the Mediterranean and in Southwest Asia. From West Africa, caravans crossed the Sahara carrying leather goods, kola nuts, cotton cloth, and enslaved people. From North Africa, Arab and Berber merchants brought silk, metal, beads, and horses.

Trading Gold for Salt Two products, gold and salt, dominated the Sahara trade. Gold was widely available in the area of present-day Ghana, Nigeria, and Senegal. It was found in the soil along rivers in various forms, including gold nuggets and dust. Experts today estimate that between A.D. 500–1600 about eight tons of gold were exported annually from West Africa.

In exchange, West Africans traded for an equally important **commodity**, or valuable product—salt. People need salt in their diet, especially in hot, tropical areas, to replace salt lost in perspiration. Salt was also important for its use in food preservation. The Sahara had an abundance of salt. At Taghaza, in the central Sahara, people even built homes out of blocks of salt. But in the savanna, several hundred miles south, salt was scarce. In fact, when caravans reached the kingdom of Ghana, merchants would pay one pound of gold for one pound of salt.

As farming and trade prospered, cities developed on the northern edges of the savanna. Soon strong monarchs arose, gained control of the most profitable trade routes, and built powerful kingdoms.

✓ **Checkpoint** How did farming lead to the development of cities?

Ghana: The Land of Gold

By A.D. 800, the rulers of the Soninke people were able to unite many farming villages and create the kingdom of **Ghana.** (The present-day country of Ghana is not the same as this ancient kingdom. Modern Ghana chose the name to celebrate Africa's rich heritage.) The ancient kingdom of Ghana was located in the fertile, broad "V" made by the Niger and Senegal rivers in present-day Mali. From there, the king controlled gold-salt trade routes across West Africa. The two streams of trade met in the marketplaces of Ghana, where the king collected tolls on all goods entering or leaving his land. So great was the flow of gold that Arab writers called Ghana "the land of gold."

Cities of Splendor The capital of Ghana was Kumbi Saleh, which was made up of two separate walled towns some six miles apart. The first town was dominated by the royal palace, which was surrounded by a complex of domed buildings. Here, in a court noted for its wealth and splendor, the king of Ghana presided over elaborate ceremonies. To his people, he was a godlike figure who administered justice and kept order. In the second town of Kumbi Saleh, prosperous Muslim merchants from north of the Sahara lived in luxurious stone buildings. Lured by the gold wealth of Ghana, these merchants helped make Kumbi Saleh a bustling center of trade.

Vocabulary Builder
administer—(ad MIN is tur) *vt.* to manage or direct

Weights of Gold
In the 1400s, a system of using standardized weights in the form of brass figures, such as the one above, to weigh the gold dust currency was developed in West Africa. The brass figures also served a cultural purpose by representing local proverbs or truisms. The gold dust currency was used to purchase items such as spices similar to those below. *Why do you think having standardized weights was important in trade?*

Equestrian figure from Mali ▶

BIOGRAPHY

Sundiata

Soon after defeating Sumanguru, the ruler who had spared him from execution, Sundiata (?–1255) gained control of Kumbi Saleh, the capital of Ghana. Over the next two decades, Sundiata then proceeded to expand his power and the Mali empire. In addition to his military leadership, he was renowned for his administrative and law-making skills. Even now his leadership is still felt as elements of his legal system still govern the Malinke people today.

Sundiata, whose achievements are legendary, is celebrated as a great hero in West African oral traditions. In fact, West African griots, or storytellers, have passed down the epic of Sundiata from memory for hundreds of years. **Why do you think Sundiata's accomplishments are still celebrated today?**

Vocabulary Builder

tolerance—(TAHL ur uns) *n.* a fair and objective attitude toward opinions and practices which differ from one's own

Influence of Islam Muslim merchants brought their Islamic faith with them to the kingdom of Ghana. The king employed Muslims as counselors and officials, gradually incorporating some of their military technology and ideas about government. Muslims also introduced their written language, coinage, and business methods. Although Islam spread slowly at first, in time, a few city dwellers adopted the religion. However, most of the Soninke people continued to follow their own traditional beliefs.

About 1050, the Almoravids (al muh RAH vuds), pious Muslims of North Africa, launched a campaign to take control of Ghana's trade routes. They eventually overwhelmed Ghana, but were unable to maintain control over their extended empire for long. In time, Ghana was swallowed up by a rising new power, the West African kingdom of Mali.

✔ **Checkpoint** What effect did trade have on the West African kingdom of Ghana?

The Kingdom of Mali

Amid the turmoil of Ghana's collapse, the Mandinka people on the upper Niger suffered a bitter defeat by a rival leader. Their king and all but one of his sons were executed. According to tradition, the survivor was **Sundiata,** a sickly boy regarded as too weak to be a threat. By 1235, however, Sundiata had crushed his enemies, won control of the gold trade routes, and founded the empire of **Mali.**

Mansa Musa Rules Mali *Mali* is an Arab version of the Mandinka word that means "where the king dwells." The *mansas,* or kings of Mali, expanded their influence over the gold-mining regions to the south and the salt supplies of Taghaza. Where caravan routes crossed, towns like Timbuktu mushroomed into great trading cities.

The greatest ruler of the kingdom of Mali was **Mansa Musa** (MAHN sah MOO sah), who came to the throne in about 1312. He expanded Mali's borders westward to the Atlantic Ocean and pushed northward to conquer many cities. During his 25-year reign, Mansa Musa worked to ensure peace and order in his empire. He converted to Islam and based his system of justice on the Quran. However, in order to ensure prosperity and peace in his kingdom, he did not impose Islam on the people, but promoted religious freedom and tolerance.

The Hajj of Mansa Musa In 1324, Mansa Musa fulfilled one of the Five Pillars of Islam by making the hajj, or pilgrimage, to Mecca. Through his pilgrimage, Mansa Musa showed his devotion to Islam. He also forged new diplomatic and economic ties with other Muslim states. In addition, he brought back scholars, architects, and teachers who helped promote Islamic education in Mali. In fact, an Islamic university was built in Timbuktu, which attracted students from far and wide. This movement of wealth, people, and ideas increased Mali's renown.

✔ **Checkpoint** What did Mansa Musa accomplish during his reign over the kingdom of Mali?

Trans-Saharan Trade

People of West Africa traded among themselves for many centuries. By about the 400s, this regional trade system had grown into an extensive trans-Saharan trade system connecting much of Africa. Traveling along these desert routes was long as well as dangerous. It could take over three months to cross the desert. To make the investment worth the trip, large caravans with over 1,000 camels were assembled. Control of these trade routes led to rivalry and conquest, and over the centuries powerful African kingdoms rose and fell.

The wealth of the Mali empire was renown as shown in this detail from a 1325 world map depicting Mansa Musa offering gold to a trader. ▼

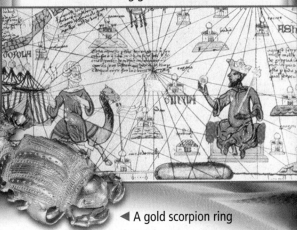

◄ A gold scorpion ring

African Kingdoms and Trading States, 1000 B.C. –A.D. 1600

Geography Interactive
For: Interactive map
Web Code: nap-1121

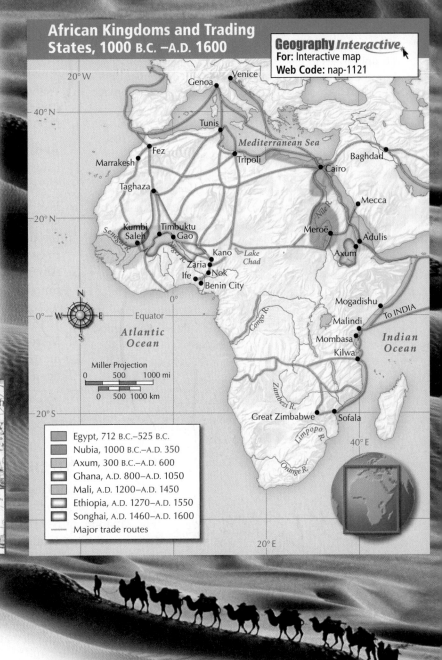

Legend:
- Egypt, 712 B.C.–525 B.C.
- Nubia, 1000 B.C.–A.D. 350
- Axum, 300 B.C.–A.D. 600
- Ghana, A.D. 800–A.D. 1050
- Mali, A.D. 1200–A.D. 1450
- Ethiopia, A.D. 1270–A.D. 1550
- Songhai, A.D. 1460–A.D. 1600
- Major trade routes

A New Empire in Songhai

In the 1400s, disputes over succession weakened Mali. Subject peoples broke away, and the empire shriveled. By the 1460s, the wealthy trading city of Gao (gow) had become the capital of the emerging West African kingdom of **Songhai** (SAWNG hy).

Extending the Empire Songhai developed on the fertile region at the bend of the Niger River in present-day Mali and Niger. Between 1464 and 1492, the soldier-king Sonni Ali built the largest state that had ever existed in West Africa. Sonni Ali brought trade routes and wealthy cities like Timbuktu under his control. Unlike the rulers of Mali, he did not adopt Islam, but instead followed traditional religious beliefs.

Soon after Sonni Ali's death in 1492, however, the emperor Askia Muhammad set up a Muslim dynasty. He further expanded the territory of Songhai and improved the government. To run the empire more efficiently, he set up a bureaucracy with separate departments for farming, the military, and the treasury. Each was supervised by officials appointed by the emperor.

Thinking Critically

1. **Draw Conclusions** Why do you think West and East Africa saw a series of kingdoms develop within the same general areas?
2. **Analyze Information** How was southern Africa connected to the trans-Saharan trade system?

By the 1400s, Timbuktu had become a leading center of learning. The city drew some of the best scholars from all over the Muslim world. In his book, *History and Description of Africa*, Leo Africanus described the intellectual life of the city:

❝ Here [in Timbuktu] are great store of doctors, judges, priests, and other learned men, that are bountifully maintained at the king's cost and charges. And hither are brought diverse manuscript or written books out of Barbarie [North Africa], which are sold for more money than any other merchandise. ❞

How does this description reflect the value of knowledge in Timbuktu?

▲ Sankore Mosque, also known as the University of Timbuktu

Like Mansa Musa, Askia Muhammad made a pilgrimage to Mecca that led to stronger ties with the wider Muslim world. Scholars from Muslim lands flocked to Askia Muhammad's court at Gao. In towns and cities across Songhai, he built mosques and opened schools for the study of the Quran.

Armies Invade From the North Although Songhai continued to prosper after Askia Muhammad's death in 1528, disputes over succession led to frequent changes in leadership. In 1549, Askia Daud became emperor, and the empire experienced a period of relative peace. After his death in 1582, succession disputes recurred and led to civil war. At this time of unrest, the sultan of Morocco, Ahmad al-Mansur, sent his armies south to seize the Songhai gold and salt mines. By 1591, these invaders, using gunpowder weapons, conquered the empire.

Like the Almoravids who conquered Ghana, the Moroccans were unable to rule an empire that stretched across the Sahara. Their control over the region weakened, but the glory of Songhai could not be restored.

✔ **Checkpoint** How did Askia Muhammad help shape the empire of Songhai?

Smaller Societies of West Africa

Although smaller than the great kingdoms of Ghana, Mali, and Songhai, other societies flourished in West Africa in the period from 500 to 1500. The kingdom of Benin (beh NEEN) developed in the rain forest, while the fertile northern lands of modern-day Nigeria were home to the Hausa (HOW suh) people. As in the larger kingdoms, farming and trading were also key to the success and prosperity of these societies.

The Forest Kingdom of Benin South of the savanna, Benin rose in the rain forests of the Guinea coast. The forest peoples built farming villages and traded pepper and ivory—and later, slaves—to their neighbors in the savanna.

The rulers of Benin organized their kingdom in the 1300s. Their *oba*, or king, was a political, judicial, and religious leader. Still, much power was spread among other figures, including the queen mother and a council of hereditary chiefs.

A three-mile-long wall surrounded the capital, Benin City. There, a great palace was decorated with elaborate brass plaques and sculptures. According to tradition, artisans from Ife (EE fay), a neighboring forest society, had taught the people of Benin how to cast bronze and brass. Benin sculptors developed their own unique style for representing the human face and form. Their works depicted warriors, queen mothers, and the oba himself. Later they showed helmeted and bearded Portuguese merchants, who began to arrive in growing numbers in the 1500s.

Walled City-States of the Hausa Conflict and invasion were frequent events in West Africa. For protection, the Hausa built walls around their villages. By the 1300s, the Hausa had built a number of independent clay-walled cities. Over time, these cities expanded into thriving

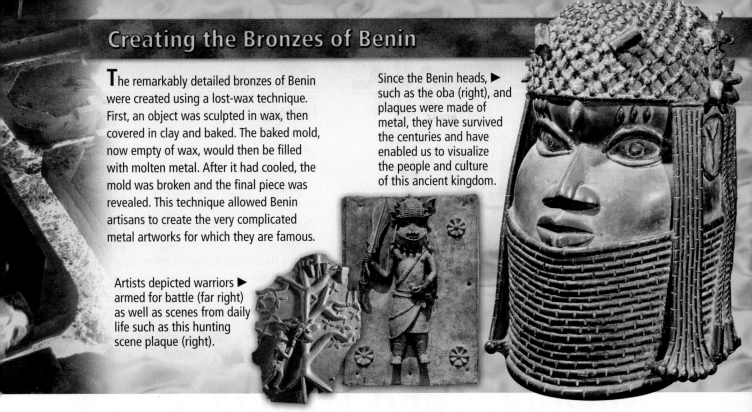

Creating the Bronzes of Benin

The remarkably detailed bronzes of Benin were created using a lost-wax technique. First, an object was sculpted in wax, then covered in clay and baked. The baked mold, now empty of wax, would then be filled with molten metal. After it had cooled, the mold was broken and the final piece was revealed. This technique allowed Benin artisans to create the very complicated metal artworks for which they are famous.

Since the Benin heads, ▶ such as the oba (right), and plaques were made of metal, they have survived the centuries and have enabled us to visualize the people and culture of this ancient kingdom.

Artists depicted warriors ▶ armed for battle (far right) as well as scenes from daily life such as this hunting scene plaque (right).

commercial centers where cotton weavers and dyers, leatherworkers, and other artisans produced goods for sale. Merchants traded with Arab and Berber caravans from north of the Sahara. Hausa goods were sold as far away as North Africa and southern Europe.

Kano was the most prosperous Hausa city-state. Its walls, over 12 miles in circumference and up to 50 feet high, protected a population of more than 30,000. Kano's greatest king, Muhammad Rumfa, was a Muslim, as were many of the city's merchants and officials. During his reign, Arabic script influenced the Hausa writing system, and Islamic law greatly influenced government.

Many Hausa rulers were women, such as Amina of the city-state of Zazzau, which is located in present-day Nigeria. In the late 1500s, she conquered Kano and other regions, expanding the boundary of Zaria as far as the Niger River. Under Amina, the Hausa came to dominate many Saharan trade routes.

✔ **Checkpoint** How did other cultures influence the development of Benin and the Hausa city-states?

Progress Monitoring *Online*
For: Self-quiz with vocabulary practice
Web Code: naa-1121

SECTION 2 Assessment

Terms, People, and Places

1. For each term, person, or place listed at the beginning of the section, write a sentence explaining its significance.

Note Taking

2. **Reading Skill: Identify Causes and Effects** Use your completed flowchart to answer the Focus Question: How did the kingdoms of West Africa develop and prosper?

Comprehension and Critical Thinking

3. **Recognize Cause and Effect** How did the gold-salt trade develop between West Africa and North Africa?

4. **Make Comparisons** How was the reign of Mansa Musa similar to that of Askia Muhammad?

5. **Draw Conclusions** Why do you think the walls surrounding Benin City and the Hausa city-states contributed to their success in trade?

● **Writing About History**

Quick Write: Gather Details Choose one of the kingdoms from this section and create a list of details about the kingdom in chronological order. Make sure to include how one event led to or was influenced by the subsequent event.

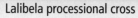

Lalibela processional cross

Page from a 15th-century Ethiopian illuminated Gospel

WITNESS HISTORY ◀)) AUDIO

Divine Intervention

Traditionally, the ancient rulers of Ethiopia commemorated their conquests by having a description of their victories inscribed on stone. In the transcription of his conquest of Nubia, King Ezana acknowledged that his success had divine assistance:

66 May the Lord of Heaven make my kingdom strong! And as He has this day conquered my enemy for me may He conquer for me wherever I go. . . . I will rule the people with righteousness and justice, and will not oppress them. . . . I have set up this throne by the might of the Lord of Heaven.99

Focus Question What influence did religion and trade have on the development of East Africa?

Kingdoms and Trading States of East Africa

 Performance Standards

- **SSWH5d** Identify the contributions of Islamic scholars in geography.
- **SSWH6a** Identify Bantu migration patterns and contribution to agriculture.
- **SSWH6d** Analyze religious syncretism in early African societies.
- **SSWH6e** Analyze role of geography and resources in trans-Saharan trade.

Terms, People, and Places

Axum	King Lalibela
Adulis	Swahili
Ethiopia	Great Zimbabwe

Note Taking

Reading Skill: Understand Effects As you read the section, create a flowchart like the one below to keep track of the effects that trade caused on societies in East Africa.

Effects of Trade on East African Societies

Axum	Ethiopia	Coastal City-States	Great Zimbabwe
• Christianity brought to region	•	• Swahili language developed	•
•	•	•	•

After 100 B.C., the kingdom of Axum expanded across the northern Ethiopian highlands. By about A.D. 1, Axum gained control of the Red Sea coast in present-day Eritrea. By controlling the Red Sea trade with Rome and Persia, the kingdom of Axum grew rich.

Axum: Center of Goods and Ideas

Located to the southeast of Nubia, **Axum** extended from the mountains of present-day Ethiopia to the sun-bleached shores of the Red Sea in present-day Eritrea. The peoples of Axum were descended from African farmers and people from the Middle East who brought Jewish traditions through Arabia. This merging of cultures gave rise to a unique written and spoken language, Geez.

Trade Brings Wealth The kingdom of Axum profited from the strategic location of its two main cities, the port of **Adulis** on the Red Sea and the upland capital city of Axum (see the map in the previous section). By A.D. 400, the kingdom commanded a triangular trade network that connected Africa, India, and the Mediterranean world.

A great variety of goods and enslaved people funneled in and out of the markets of these two cities. From the interior of Africa, traders brought ivory, animal hides, and gold to the markets of Axum. Goods from farther south along the African coast came to the harbor of Adulis on the Red Sea. There, the markets offered iron, spices, precious stones, and cotton cloth from India and other lands beyond the Indian Ocean. Ships carried these goods up the Red Sea, where they collected goods from Europe and countries along the Mediterranean.

Axum Converts to Christianity In these great centers of international trade, Greek, Egyptian, Arab, and Jewish merchants mingled with traders from Africa, India, and other regions. As elsewhere, ideas spread along with goods. By the 300s, Christianity had reached the region. After converting to the new religion, King Ezana made Christianity the official religion of Axum. As the religion took hold among the people, older temples were replaced with Christian churches decorated with intricately designed biblical murals and religious images painted on wood panels.

At first, Christianity strengthened the ties between Axum, North Africa, and the Mediterranean world. In the 600s, however, Islam began spreading across North Africa and other regions surrounding Axum. Many African rulers embraced this new faith, creating strong cultural ties across much of the continent. Axum, which remained Christian, was now isolated from its own trade network—by distance from Europe and by religion from many former trading partners. Civil war and economic decline combined to weaken Axum, and the kingdom slowly declined.

✓ **Checkpoint** How did the spread of religion affect the kingdom of Axum?

Ethiopia: A Christian Outpost

Though Axum's political and economic power faded, its cultural and religious influence did not disappear. This legacy survived among the peoples of the interior uplands, in what is today northern Ethiopia. Although Axum's empire was only a portion of the present-day nation, when referring to their kingdom as a whole, the Axumite kings frequently used **Ethiopia,** which was a term the Greeks used for the region.

An Isolated Ethiopia Medieval Ethiopia was protected by rugged mountains, and the descendants of the Axumites were able to maintain their independence for centuries. Their success was due in part to the <u>unifying</u> power of their Christian faith, which gave them a unique sense of identity and helped establish a culture distinct from that of neighboring peoples.

One example of Ethiopia's distinct culture is the unique churches of Lalibela. In the early 1200s, **King Lalibela** came to power in Ethiopia. During his reign, he directed the building of eleven remarkable churches, which were actually carved from ground level downward into the solid rock of the mountains. These amazing structures still exist today and illustrate the architectural and artistic skill of the craftsmen who created them.

Despite their isolation, Ethiopian Christians kept ties with the Holy Land. In fact, some made pilgrimages to Jerusalem. They also were in touch with Christian communities in Egypt. Over time, Ethiopian Christianity absorbed many local customs. Traditional East African music and dance were adapted, and their influence is still felt in Ethiopian church services today. In addition, the services are still conducted in the ancient language of Geez.

Sculpted Churches
Beta Ghiorgis (House of George) is one of the Lalibela solid rock churches created during the thirteenth century. A trench was dug to create a solid block of rock, which was then sculpted and carved into to create the interior and exterior of this cross-shaped church.

Vocabulary Builder
<u>unify</u>—(YOO nuh fy) *vt.* to form into a single unit

Ibn Battuta Witnesses a Unique Trading Tradition

Moroccan *qadi*, or judge, Ibn Battuta (1304–*c*.1368) was born in Tangier to a Berber family of the Muslim faith. After he completed his education at the age of 21, Battuta decided to make the hajj, or Muslim pilgrimage to Mecca. What started as a reasonably challenging trek for the period became one of the great journeys of medieval times. During nearly 30 years of travel, Battuta visited much of Southwest Asia, West Africa, southern Russia, India, and China. Along the way he gained fame and wealth and met kings, sheiks, and holy men—including the Byzantine emperor and the sultan of Delhi—as well as ordinary people. In this excerpt from his book, the *Rihlah*, or *Travels*, Battuta describes the unique trading tradition of Mogadishu.

◄ Ibn Battuta in Egypt

66On leaving Zayla we sailed for fifteen days and came to Maqdashaw [Mogadishu], which is an enormous town. Its inhabitants are merchants.... When a vessel reaches the port, it is met by *sumbuqs*, which are small boats, in each of which are a number of young men, each carrying a covered dish containing food. He presents this to one of the merchants on the ship saying "This is my guest," and all the others do the same. Each merchant on disembarking goes only to the house of the young man who is his host..... The host then sells his goods for him and buys for him, and if anyone buys anything from him at too low a price, or sells to him in the absence of his host, the sale is regarded by them as invalid.99

—*Ibn Battuta*
from the **Rihlah**

Judaism in Ethiopia The kings of Ethiopia claimed descent from the Israelite king Solomon and the queen of Sheba. This belief was recorded in an ancient Ethiopian book called *The Glory of Kings* and reinforced by the fact that Ethiopians observe some of the Jewish holidays and dietary laws. Some Ethiopians practiced Judaism not the predominant Christianity. These Ethiopian Jews lived in the mountains of Ethiopia until the late 1900s, when most evacuated to Israel due to famine and persecutions.

 Checkpoint How did the geographic isolation of medieval Ethiopia shape its culture?

East African City-States

While Axum declined, a string of commercial cities—including Kilwa, Mogadishu, Mombasa, and Sofala—gradually arose along the East African coast. Since ancient times, Phoenician, Greek, Roman, and Indian traders had visited this region. Under the protection of local African rulers, Arab and Persian merchants set up Muslim communities beginning in the 600s. Port cities, as well as offshore islands such as Lamu and Zanzibar were ideally located for trade with Asia. As a result, Asian traders and immigrants from as far away as Indonesia soon added to the rich cultural mix.

Trading Centers Flourish By the 600s, sailors had learned that the annual monsoon winds could carry sailing ships between India and Africa. On the East African coast, rulers took advantage of the opportunities for trade that these winds provided. They welcomed ships from Arabia, Persia, and China. Traders acquired ivory, leopard skins, iron,

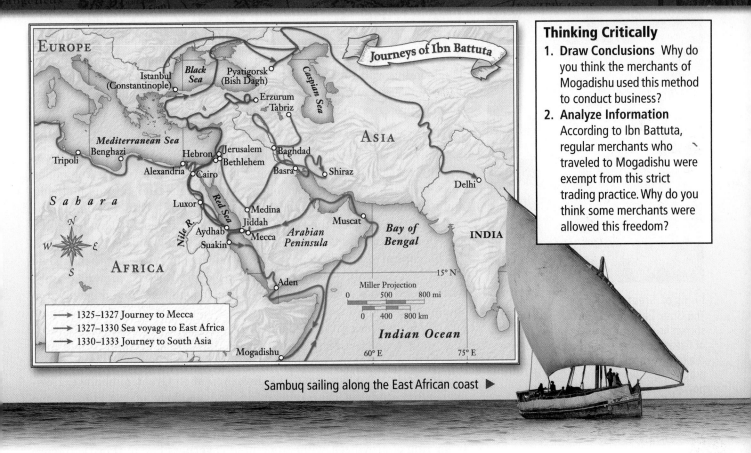

Journeys of Ibn Battuta

Legend:
→ 1325–1327 Journey to Mecca
→ 1327–1330 Sea voyage to East Africa
→ 1330–1333 Journey to South Asia

Sambuq sailing along the East African coast ▶

Thinking Critically
1. **Draw Conclusions** Why do you think the merchants of Mogadishu used this method to conduct business?
2. **Analyze Information** According to Ibn Battuta, regular merchants who traveled to Mogadishu were exempt from this strict trading practice. Why do you think some merchants were allowed this freedom?

copper, gold, and enslaved people from the interior of Africa, as well as from coastal regions. From India, Southeast Asia, and China came cotton cloth, silk, spices, porcelain, glassware, and swords.

Trade was not only beneficial to the merchants; it also helped local rulers build strong, independent city-states. Although they competed for trade, relations between the city-states were generally peaceful. A Muslim visitor described Kilwa, the most successful city-state, as "one of the most beautiful and well-constructed towns in the world." Its royal palace still stands on cliffs that today overlook the ocean. The <u>complex</u> consists of courtyards, terraces, and nearly 100 rooms. Built of coral and cut stone, the structure is evidence of the old city's splendor.

Trade Shapes Swahili The successful East African international trade system led to the emergence of a vibrant culture and a new language both known as **Swahili.** By the 1000s, many East African coastal cities had not only grown in wealth but also in size. Traders from the Middle East and Asia began to settle permanently in flourishing trading cities such as Kilwa.

As more settlers arrived, the local East African culture absorbed cultural elements from these new residents. For example, the architecture of private houses and palaces illustrated a blend of East African and Arabic designs that created unique and elegant Swahili buildings and furniture. In addition, over time many Arabic words were absorbed into the local Bantu-based language. In fact, the term *swahili* comes from an Arabic word meaning "of the coast." The language itself was eventually written in Arabic script.

Vocabulary Builder

<u>complex</u>—(KAHM pleks) *n.* a group of connected buildings that form a single whole

✔ **Checkpoint** How did trade influence the city-states of East Africa?

The Stone Houses of Great Zimbabwe

To the south and inland from the coastal city-states, massive stone ruins sprawl across rocky hilltops near the great bend in the Limpopo River. The looming walls, large palace, and cone-shaped towers were once part of the powerful and prosperous capital of a great inland empire. Today, these impressive ruins are known as **Great Zimbabwe.**

Inland Capital of Trade The word *zimbabwe* comes from a Bantu-based word that means "stone houses." In fact, Great Zimbabwe was built by a succession of Bantu-speaking peoples who settled in the region between 900 and 1500. These newcomers brought iron, mining methods, and improved farming skills. Early settlers raised cattle and built stone enclosures to protect their livestock. In time, these settlers improved their building methods and erected large walls and palaces.

The capital probably reached its height about 1300. By then, it had tapped nearby gold resources and created profitable commercial links with coastal cities such as Sofala. Archaeologists have found beads from India and porcelain from China, showing that Great Zimbabwe was part of a trade network that reached across the Indian Ocean. In addition, they have found artifacts that indicate that Great Zimbabwe had artisans skilled in making jewelry and weaving cotton cloth.

Very little is known about the government in Great Zimbabwe. However, after studying the architecture and artifacts of the ruins, some scholars have suggested that the ruler was a god-king who presided over a large court. Below the king, a central bureaucracy may have ruled an inner ring of provinces, while appointed governors had authority in more distant villages. Although there is much about Great Zimbabwe that remains unknown, as archaeologists continue their research, we are learning more about how the capital and empire developed.

Zimbabwe Falls to Ruins By 1500, Zimbabwe was in decline. Some scholars suggest that the population had grown too great. Civil war and dwindling trade probably contributed as well. By then, Portuguese traders were pushing inland to find the region's source of gold. They failed to discover the gold mines, but their attempts further weakened the small states that formed in the region as Zimbabwe declined.

 Checkpoint How do the ruins of Great Zimbabwe reflect the capital's former prosperity?

Ruins of Great Zimbabwe
The Great Enclosure, a portion of which is shown here, is one of the two major ruins of Great Zimbabwe. Archaeologists believe the enclosures did not serve any military purpose, but were built to display the ruler's power. However, much about Great Zimbabwe is still being debated.

SECTION 3 Assessment

Progress Monitoring *Online*
For: Self-quiz with vocabulary practice
Web Code: naa-1131

Terms, People, and Places
1. For each term, person, or place listed at the beginning of the section, write a sentence explaining its significance.

Note Taking
2. **Reading Skill: Understand Effects** Use your completed flowchart to answer the Focus Question: What influence did religion and trade have on the development of East Africa?

Comprehension and Critical Thinking
3. **Synthesize Information** Why did Ethiopia become increasingly isolated from its neighbors over the centuries?
4. **Draw Inferences** Why did the language of Swahili emerge in the East African city-states?
5. **Test Conclusions** What evidence suggests that Great Zimbabwe was a center of trade?

Writing About History
Quick Write: Use Sensory Details Choose one of the locations from this section. Suppose you are a merchant or traveler entering the city for the first time. What sights and sounds do you encounter? Write a letter to your family that describes your experiences from the moment you enter the city until you reach your final destination there.

A Mossi woman from present-day Burkina Faso

Cultural Variety

Ibn Battuta traveled widely throughout Africa and Asia. His travels included more than visits to the capitals and large trading cities. He also visited small African communities where he learned of the great variety of cultures and societies that had developed on the continent.

❝The women [of the Massufa tribe] are shown more respect than the men. The state of affairs amongst these people is indeed extraordinary. . . . no one claims descent from his father, but on the contrary from his mother's brother. A person's heirs are his sister's sons, not his own sons. This is a thing which I have seen nowhere in the world. . . .❞

Focus Question What factors influenced the development of societies in Africa?

SECTION 4

Societies in Medieval Africa

GA **Performance Standards**

- **SSWH5d** Identify the contributions of Islamic scholars in geography.
- **SSWH6b** Describe the role of Sundiata.
- **SSWH6c** Describe trans-Saharan trade in gold, salt, and slaves.
- **SSWH6d** Analyze religious syncretism in early African societies.

Terms, People, and Places

nuclear family	lineage
patrilineal	consensus
matrilineal	griot

Note Taking

Reading Skill: Recognize Multiple Causes As you read this section, create a concept web like the one below to keep track of the factors that influenced the development of African societies.

Considering Africa's immense size, it is not surprising that Ibn Battuta came across new cultures. Factors such as Africa's varied geography, diverse climates, and later migration and trade played major roles in how early societies developed throughout the continent.

As you have read, throughout the world the Neolithic Revolution led to the beginning of settled farming communities located in areas with fertile soil and proximity to water. These farming settlements grew as surpluses increased, enabling artisans to develop specialized skills.

Advancements in transportation, such as the use of the camel, increased a community's reach beyond its borders, and this exchange allowed villages to grow into towns. Extended trade brought additional wealth, leading to the creation of individual states and kingdoms. Throughout Africa, communities varied in size, environment, and economics. However, each society, including the kingdoms you read about earlier in this chapter, developed around four common elements—family, government, religion, and art.

Family Patterns

In medieval Africa, as elsewhere, the family was the basic unit of society. Patterns of family life varied greatly depending on the culture of the group. In some small societies, for example, the basic family unit was the **nuclear family,** or parents and children living and working together as a unit. In other communities, family units included the extended family—parents, children, and several generations such as grandparents and uncles—who lived and worked close together to ensure the success of the group.

Kinship Family organization varied in other ways. Some families were **patrilineal.** In these families, important kinship ties such as inheritance were passed through the father's side. Other families, such as the one described by Ibn Battuta, were **matrilineal,** with inheritance traced through the mother's side. In some cultures, one spouse would move to the other spouse's village and join his or her parents' family.

Matrilineal cultures forged strong ties between brothers and sisters. Brothers were expected to protect their sisters, and sons were expected to help their mother's brothers whenever needed.

Extended Lineages Each family belonged to a **lineage,** or group of households who claimed a common ancestor. Several lineages formed a clan that traced its descent to an even more remote and often legendary ancestor. Belonging to a particular family, lineage, or clan gave people a sense of community with shared responsibilities to that community.

An individual's place in some medieval African societies was also determined by a system of age grades. An age grade included all girls or boys born in the same year. Each age grade had particular responsibilities and privileges. As they moved up from one age grade to another, children began to take part in village activities, which created social ties beyond the family.

✓ **Checkpoint** How did kinship help identify an individual's place in his or her society?

African Culture Expressed in Art

Considering the variety of African cultures, it is understandable that each group developed its own individual artistic tradition. The designs on many objects as well as the materials used to create them reflect the artists' beliefs, culture, and environment. For example, the wooden Mende slit drum (left) from West Africa was both a musical instrument and a symbolic sculpture used in ceremonies and rituals. Even many everyday objects were created with such care for detail that they could be considered works of art.

◄ These two East African shields are made from readily available materials: A Maasai shield made of cattle hide (left), and an Ethiopian shield made from a hippopotamus hide (bottom).

An ivory ornamental mask most likely worn around the neck of the Benin oba. The figures at the top are representations of Portuguese traders and symbolized Benin's alliance with and control over them. ►

Political Patterns

Most medieval African farming peoples lived in tightknit communities and helped one another in tasks such as clearing the land, planting, and harvesting. As communities grew, the need for a form of government arose. Throughout Africa, political patterns varied, depending in part on the size and culture of the community.

Power Sharing Unlike the large kingdoms, smaller medieval African societies were often organized with power shared among a number of people rather than centralized in the hands of a single leader. In some villages, a chief had a good deal of authority, but in many others, elders made the major decisions. In some places, especially in parts of West Africa, women took the dominant role in the marketplace or acted as official peacemakers in the village.

Villages often made decisions by a process known as **consensus,** or general agreement. In open discussions, people whose opinions were valued voiced their views before a final agreement was reached. Because of the experience and wisdom of older men and women, their opinions usually carried the greatest weight.

In villages that were part of a large kingdom such as Songhai, decisions made at a distant court had to be obeyed. These villagers, therefore, had to pay taxes and provide soldiers to the central, and frequently distant, government.

The gold nugget, ▶ shells, and horns on a healer's charm necklace (right) were believed to have magical healing properties.

This West African Dogon ▶ dancer is wearing a grass and shell costume and mask created for the dama funerary ceremony. During the dama, a masked dance is performed symbolizing the end of the mourning period.

▼ The elephant at the base of this West African stool identifies that it was used only by the king of the Asante.

Thinking Critically

1. **Draw Conclusions** How does the Dogon dancer's costume help identify the group's location? Explain.
2. **Synthesize Information** Why do you think symbolism was important in medieval African societies?

Limited Power Another form of government developed when many villages were grouped into districts and provinces that were governed by officials appointed by a king. The kingdom of Kongo, which flourished around A.D. 1500 in central Africa, is an example. There, each village still had its own chief. Taxes were collected through local governors either in goods or in cowrie shells, a common African currency. Unlike rulers of larger West African states who maintained strong standing armies, the kings of Kongo could only call upon men to fight in times of need. In fact, the king was actually chosen by a group of electors and had to govern according to traditional laws. It might seem as though a king wielded absolute power; however, in some societies like the kingdom of Kongo, the monarch's power was somewhat limited.

 Checkpoint How was ruling power shared in some of the smaller African societies?

Religious Beliefs

As you have read, religion played an important role in the development of medieval African societies. Religious beliefs that existed before the arrival of Islam and Christianity were varied and complex. Like the Hindus or ancient Greeks and Romans, some Africans worshiped many gods and goddesses. They identified the forces of nature with divine spirits and tried to influence those forces through rituals and ceremonies.

Many African peoples believed that a single, unknowable supreme being stood above all the other gods and goddesses. This supreme being was the creator and ruler of the universe and was helped by the lesser spirits, who were closer to the people. Some African peoples believed, like the Chinese, that the spirits of their ancestors could help, warn, or punish their descendants on Earth. Just as Christians in medieval Europe called on the saints for help, medieval Africans turned to the spirits of their departed ancestors.

By A.D. 1000, both Christianity and Islam had spread to many regions of Africa. Those who adopted these religions often associated the God of the Christians and Muslims with their traditional supreme being. In this way, Christianity and Islam in Africa absorbed many local practices and beliefs.

 Checkpoint Describe the religious beliefs in medieval Africa.

Traditions in Art and Literature

African artistic traditions extend far back in time to the ancient rock paintings of the Sahara, which were created by about 1000 B.C., and the over 4,000-year-old pyramids of Egypt and Nubia. More recently, but still about 1,000 years ago, the rock churches of Ethiopia and the palace of Great Zimbabwe were built. These accomplishments bear lasting witness to the creative power of these early and medieval civilizations.

Creative Arts African artists worked in many materials including gold, ivory, wood, bronze, and cloth. They created many decorative items such as woven cloth, inscribed jugs and bowls, or jewelry simply for their beauty. Even so, art usually served social and religious purposes as well.

Art strengthened bonds within the community and linked the makers and the users of the work. Patterns used to decorate textiles, baskets,

Vocabulary Builder
complex—(kahm PLEKS) *adj.* made up of different parts connected in a way that is hard to understand

swords, and other objects had important meanings or special messages that the artisan or owner wanted to convey. Often, they identified an object as the work of a particular clan or the possession of royalty. One example is kente cloth, a traditional West African textile woven of silk and cotton. When it was made in bright gold and blue colors, the symbols of power, only the ruling elite and the wealthy were allowed to wear it.

In medieval Africa, as elsewhere, much art was closely tied to religion. Statues and other objects were used in religious rites and ceremonies. In some rituals, for example, leaders wore elaborately carved masks decorated with cowrie shells or grass. Once the mask was in place, both the wearer and the viewers could feel the presence of the spiritual force it represented.

Literature Early and medieval African societies preserved their histories and values through both written and oral literature. Ancient Egypt, Nubia, and Axum left written records of their past. Later, Arabic provided a common written language in those parts of Africa influenced by Islam. African Muslim scholars gathered in cities such as Timbuktu and Kilwa. Documents in Arabic offer invaluable evidence about the law, religion, and history of the time.

Oral traditions date back many centuries. In West Africa, **griots** (GREE ohz), or professional storytellers recited ancient stories such as the Sundiata epic. The griots preserved both histories and traditional folk tales in the same way that the epics of Homer or Aryan India were passed orally from generation to generation. The histories praised the heroic deeds of famous ancestors or kings. The folk tales, which blended fanciful stories with humor and sophisticated word play, taught important moral lessons. Oral literature, like religion and art, thus encouraged a sense of community and common values within the medieval societies of Africa.

Language of Drums
Not all "oral tradition" is spoken. The talking drums of western and central Africa are used to communicate important information such as messages and announcements as well as traditional texts such as prayers and eulogies for historic individuals. *Why do you think the sound of a drum could be more powerful than the spoken word?*

✓ **Checkpoint** How did African societies preserve their history?

SECTION **4** Assessment

Progress Monitoring *Online*
For: Self-quiz with vocabulary practice
Web Code: naa-1141

Terms, People, and Places
1. For each term, person, or place listed at the beginning of the section, write a sentence explaining its significance.

Note Taking
2. **Reading Skill: Recognize Multiple Causes** Use your completed concept web to answer the Focus Question: What factors influenced the development of societies in Africa?

Comprehension and Critical Thinking
3. **Recognize Cause and Effect** How did an individual's lineage affect his or her life in African societies?
4. **Demonstrate Reasoned Judgment** Do you think consensus is a fair or unfair method of decision making? Explain the reasons for your answer.
5. **Determine Relevance** How was art connected to religion in African cultures?
6. **Identify Central Issues** Why do you think art, literature, and religion inspired a sense of unity within medieval African communities?

● **Writing About History**
Quick Write: Creating Dialogue Select two individuals, such as an elder and a tribal chief or an uncle and nephew, from the topics discussed in this section and create a dialogue between them placing yourself as one of the characters. Make sure that the dialogue generally relates to one of the main subjects of the section such as government or family ties.

Quick Study Guide

Progress Monitoring *Online*
For: Self-test with vocabulary practice
Web Code: naa-1142

■ Major African Kingdoms and Trading States

Kingdom or State	Date	Location	Religion	Economic Base
Egypt	2575 B.C.–1075 B.C.	North Africa	Local religion	Trade
Nubia	1100 B.C.–A.D. 350	Northeast Africa	Local religion	Trade and iron ore
Ghana	800–1050	West Africa	Local religion and Islam	Gold
Mali	1235–1400s	West Africa	Local religion and Islam	Gold and salt
Songhai	1460–1591	West Africa	Local religion and Islam	Trade
Benin	1300s–1500s	West Africa	Local religion	Pepper, ivory, and slaves
Axum	350–600s	East Africa	Christianity	Trade
Great Zimbabwe	1300s–1500s	East Africa	Unknown	Trade

■ Important Ancient and Medieval African Rulers

Ruler	Kingdom	Accomplishment
Piankhi	Nubia	Conquered Egypt and brought it under Nubian control
Sundiata	Mali	Defeated Sumanguru and founded the empire of Mali
Mansa Musa	Mali	Expanded Mali's borders and based justice system on the Quran
Askia Muhammad	Songhai	Expanded Songhai's territory and improved the government by setting up bureaucracies
Amina	Hausa city-states	Gained control of many Saharan trade routes
King Ezana	Axum	Made Christianity the official religion and defeated Nubia
King Lalibela	Ethiopia	Sponsored the building of the Lalibela churches

■ Key Events in Ancient and Medieval Africa

730 B.C.
Nubia conquers Egypt.

500s B.C.
Meroë becomes Nubian captial and controls North African trade routes.

Chapter Events
Global Events

1000 B.C.   **500 B.C.**   **A.D. 1**

500s B.C.
In India, the sacred Hindu texts are recorded.

460 B.C.
The Age of Pericles begins in Athens.

218 B.C.
Hannibal crosses the Alps to attack Rome during the Second Punic War.

Concept Connector

Essential Question Review

To connect prior knowledge with what you have learned in this chapter answer the questions below in your Concept Connector journal. Use the journal in the Reading and Note Taking Study Guide to record your answers (or go to www.phschool.com **Web Code:** nad-1107).

1. **Migration** By 5500 B.C., Neolithic farmers had cultivated the Nile Valley and domesticated animals. Villages even appeared in the Sahara, which was then a well-watered area. What prompted migration from the Sahara? Do you think ancient Africa's mineral wealth, early trade, and "ships of the desert" might have affected migration patterns? Why or why not?

2. **Geography's Impact** As in Africa, the cultures and early history of Eastern Europe were heavily influenced by the region's geography. Compare and contrast the impact geography had on cultural development in Eastern Europe and Africa. For each region, think about the following:
   • geographic passageways and waterways
   • barriers to easy movement and access to new ideas
   • cultural links to other regions

3. **Trade** Like the Greeks before them and the Vikings after them, East African traders used their nautical skills to reach distant lands, gaining access to goods and ideas. How did this ability to trade shape not only the economy but also the culture of East Africa? How did the trade affect inland Africa?

■ Connections to Today

1. **Geography's Impact: Desertification** Parts of the Sahara were once well-watered areas with rivers that supported forests and grasslands as well as people. Beginning about 2500 B.C. and continuing today, the desert has been gradually spreading. In fact, during the early 1970s a long drought in the Sahel extended the Sahara as much as 60 miles in some areas, and the resulting famine led to the loss of almost 100,000 lives. Desertification is difficult to reverse and is considered not only a major environmental problem in Africa but a serious social and economic problem as well. However, efforts are being made to address the issue. The following African countries are heavily affected by desertification: Burkina Faso, Chad, Gambia, Ghana, Mali, Mauritania, Nigeria, Niger, Senegal, and Sudan. Select one of these nations and then conduct research on how desertification is affecting that country and what the country is doing to address the problem.

2. **Trade: Trade in the 21st Century** As you have read, the extent of medieval African trade was far-reaching. Each region provided commodities to the world that were indigenous and frequently unique to that region. The farther away a trader transported a commodity, the more its value would increase. Considering today's advances in agriculture, manufacturing, and transportation, write a one-page essay on the similarities and differences between medieval trade and trade in the twenty-first century.

History Interactive
For: Interactive timeline
Web Code: nap-1141

A.D. 300s	A.D. 600s	A.D. 800s	A.D. 1200s	A.D. 1324	A.D. 1500s
Axum gains control of an extensive trade network.	Islam spreads to North Africa.	Kingdom of Ghana controls West African gold-salt trade routes.	Lalibela churches built in Ethiopia.	Mansa Musa completes his hajj to Mecca.	The kingdom of Kongo flourishes in central Africa.

500   1000   1500

A.D. 300s	A.D. 668	A.D. 1347	A.D. 1492
Maya civilization flourishes in Mexico and Central America.	The Silla dynasty unites Korea.	The Black Death begins to ravage Europe.	Christopher Columbus sails the Atlantic and reaches the Caribbean.

Chapter Assessment

Terms, People, and Places

Choose the italicized term in parentheses that best completes each sentence.

1. The most populated vegetation region in Africa is the (*Sahara, savanna*).
2. (*Adulis, Axum*) was a prosperous trading port in East Africa.
3. Some medieval African societies made political decisions using a process of (*griot, consensus*).
4. An important (*commodity, surplus*) in medieval African trade was salt.
5. A (*patrilineal, matrilineal*) family passes inheritance through the father's side.
6. (*Bantu, Swahili*) is a root language used by scholars to understand early African migration patterns.
7. (*Mansa Musa, King Lalibela*) based his system of justice on the Quran.
8. The kingdom of (*Ghana, Nubia*) was greatly influenced by its proximity to Egypt.

Main Ideas

Section 1 (pp. 340–345)
9. How did the environment affect the development of societies in Africa?
10. Describe the effects of trade on the cities of North Africa.

Section 2 (pp. 346–351)
11. Summarize how agriculture led to the development of prosperous trading centers.
12. What influence did Islam have on the large kingdoms of West Africa?

Section 3 (pp. 352–356)
13. What factors led to the isolation of Ethiopia from its neighbors?
14. How did trade bring about a blend of cultures in the city-states of East Africa?

Section 4 (pp. 357–361)
15. How did kinship ties influence daily life in medieval Africa?
16. How can artistic traditions identify a community and its environment?

Chapter Focus Question
17. How did trade influence the development of the kingdoms and trading states of Africa?

Critical Thinking

18. **Draw Conclusions** Why do you think the king of Ghana collected tolls on goods entering or leaving his kingdom?
19. **Synthesize Information** What primary factors attracted invaders to the great cities and kingdoms of Africa? Why did these invasions often succeed?
20. **Make Comparisons** Compare and contrast the consequences of adopting a new religion for the kingdoms of Mali and Axum.
21. **Geography and History** How did the geography of Africa affect the value of trade goods?
22. **Make Comparisons** How was the kingdom of Kongo's system of government similar to that of the government of the United States? How was it different?
23. **Distinguish False From Accurate Images** How do trading kingdoms and city-states contradict the misconceptions that many people have of medieval Africa?

● Writing About History

In this chapter's four Section Assessments, you developed skills for writing a narrative.

Writing a Narrative African oral historians brought the events of the past to life through their engaging and entertaining stories in order to ensure that important people and events were remembered. Write a narrative that could be recounted aloud about a specific event involving one of the following: Saharan trade, Timbuktu, Mansa Musa, King Ezana, Lalibela, Amina. Consult page SH8 of the Writing Handbook for additional help.

Prewriting
• Choose the topic or event that interests you most and take notes about the people and locations involved.

• Collect the facts and details you will need to tell your story, including any historic background your listeners might need to know about the historic event.

Drafting
• Identify the climax of the story and then organize the story in chronological order.
• Make sure to engage your audience with a dramatic opening and include sensory details.
• Write a conclusion that sums up the significance of the event.

Revising
• Use the guidelines for revising your narrative on page SH9 of the Writing Handbook.

Prepare for the GHSGT

Mansa Musa, King of Mali

From 1312 until 1337, Mansa Musa ruled the West African kingdom of Mali. During his reign, the gold trade in the kingdom expanded as did the amount of territory under Mali's control. The wealth of the kingdom and Mansa Musa's power and generosity became legendary following his pilgrimage to Mecca in 1324. In fact, it is said that he spent so lavishly during his hajj that the value of gold actually fell in Egypt. Mansa Musa's renown spread throughout Africa to Europe and Southwest Asia, as the excerpts and map below demonstrate.

Document A

"We belong to a house which hands on the kinship by inheritance. The king [Abobakar II] who was my predecessor did not believe that it was impossible to discover the furthest limit of the Atlantic Ocean and wished vehemently to do so. . . ."

"Then that Sultan got ready 2,000 ships, 1,000 for himself and the men whom he took with him, and 1,000 for water and provisions. He left me to deputize for him and embarked on the Atlantic Ocean with his men. That was the last we saw of him and all those who were with him, and so, I became king in my own right."

—Mansa Musa, quoted by Ibn Amir Hajib

Document B

"[Mansa Musa] and all those with him . . . were well-dressed, grave, and dignified. He was noble and generous and performed many acts of charity and kindness. He had left his country with 100 loads of gold which he spent during his Pilgrimage on the tribes who lay along his route. . . . As a consequence he needed to borrow money in Egypt and pledged his credit with the merchants at a very high rate of gain so they made 700 dinars profit on 300. Later he paid them back amply. He sent to me 500 mithqals of gold by way of honorarium."

—Ibn Amir Hajib

Document C

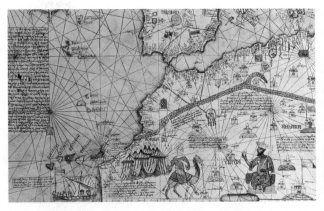

Detail of West Africa from a fourteenth-century Spanish world map showing Mansa Musa offering gold to a trader.

Document D

From the beginning of my coming to stay in Egypt I heard talk of the arrival of this sultan Musa on his Pilgrimage. . . . I asked the emir Abu . . . and he told me . . . "When I [the emir] went out to meet him . . . he did me extreme honor and treated me with the greatest courtesy. . . . Then he forwarded to the royal treasury many loads of unworked native gold and other valuables. I tried to persuade him to go up to the Citadel to meet the sultan, but he refused persistently. . . . I realized that the audience was repugnant to him because he would be obliged to kiss the ground and the sultan's hand. . . . so I kept on at him till he agreed.

"[In the sultan's presence Mansa Musa] said 'I make obeisance to God who created me!' then he prostrated himself and went forward to the sultan. The sultan half rose to greet him and sat him by his side."

—Al 'Umari

Analyzing Documents

Use your knowledge of Mansa Musa, the kingdom of Mali, and Documents A, B, C, and D to answer questions 1–4.

1. According to Document A, Mansa Musa became king after his predecessor
   A was killed in a battle.
   B lost favor with religious leaders.
   C left on a sea voyage.
   D was assassinated by an ally of Mansa Musa.

2. The Catalan Atlas, Document C, features Mansa Musa so prominently to
   A provide a reference point for the kingdom of Mali.
   B show that Mansa Musa is the region's monarch.
   C enhance the decorative elements of the map.
   D emphasize the wealth, power, and importance of Mansa Musa.

3. Which qualities of Mansa Musa does Document D show?
   A cruelty and deceit
   B kindness and compassion
   C compassion and generosity
   D generosity and faith

4. **Writing Task** Why is Mansa Musa's rule known as "the Golden Age of Mali"? Use documents from this page along with information from the chapter in your response.

Kublai Khan's Fleet

Although the Mongols dominated much of Asia in the 1200s, they were never able to conquer Japan. Kublai Khan's fleet attempted to invade Japan twice—in 1274 and 1281—but a kamikaze, or "divine wind," helped destroy his fleet both times. Over 700 years later, archaeologists found artifacts and a shipwreck from the Mongol fleet in Imari Bay, Japan. Listen to the Witness History audio to hear more about this exciting discovery.

66 Stepping off the dock into the waters of Imari Bay, I swam to the bottom, . . . [and] suddenly I saw the wreck. . . . Clusters of timbers and artifacts suggested that a ship, or ships, had crashed into the shore and been ripped apart. There were armor fragments, a pottery bowl decorated with calligraphy, and wood with what seemed like fresh burn marks. My heart started to pound when I swam up to one object and realized it was an intact Mongol helmet. 99
—J.P. Delgado, *Archaeology,* January/February 2003

◀ In this illustrated scroll created in the 1290s, the Japanese defeat Kublai Khan's fleet with help from a kamikaze.

 Performance Standards

Chapter Focus Question How did China's culture develop and influence its neighbors in East and Southeast Asia?

Section 1
Two Golden Ages of China   SSWH2c, SSWH2d, SSWH11b

Section 2
The Mongol and Ming Empires   SSWH4d, SSWH10a

Section 3
Korea and Its Traditions   SSWH2d

Section 4
The Emergence of Japan and the Feudal Age   SSWH2d, SSWH11a, SSWH11b, SSWH14a

Section 5
Diverse Cultures of Southeast Asia
SSWH2d

Use the ☑ **Quick Study Timeline** at the end of this chapter to preview chapter events.

Passport, Yuan dynasty

Buddha made of celadon, Korea

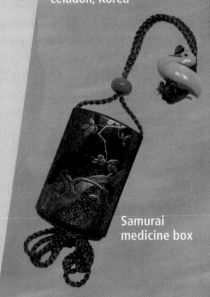
Samurai medicine box

 Concept Connector ONLINE
To explore Essential Questions related to this chapter, go to PHSchool.com
Web Code: nad-1207

Empress Wu Zhao

WITNESS HISTORY 🔊 AUDIO

The Only Female Emperor in China

Many people in China had reason to distrust Empress Wu Zhao (woo jow). From a lowly place at court, she had risen to a position of influence with the emperor. After his death, she ruthlessly took power into her own hands. She even unseated her own sons from the throne. She declared herself "Son of Heaven," the age-old title of China's emperors. No other woman had ever dared do such a thing!

Focus Question Describe the political, economic, and cultural achievements of the Tang and Song dynasties.

Two Golden Ages of China

 Performance Standards

- **SSWH2c** Describe development of Chinese civilization under Zhou.
- **SSWH2d** Explain the examination system, the status of peasants and merchants, and the patriarchal family.
- **SSWH11b** Analyze how population growth impacted Chinese social structure.

Terms, People, and Places

Tang dynasty	Song dynasty
Tang Taizong	gentry
tributary state	dowry
land reform	pagoda

Note Taking

Reading Skill: Compare and Contrast Create a Venn diagram to take notes on the Tang and Song dynasties. Include information that applies to both dynasties where the circles overlap.

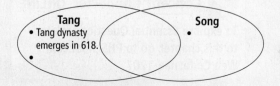

In the late 600s, Wu Zhao became the only woman to rule China in her own name. Her strong rule helped guide China through one of its most brilliant periods. At a time when Europe was fragmented into many small feudal kingdoms, two powerful dynasties—the Tang and the Song—restored unity in China.

The Tang Dynasty Reunifies China

After the Han dynasty collapsed in 220, China broke apart and remained divided for nearly 400 years. Yet China escaped the decay that disrupted Western Europe after the fall of Rome. Farm production expanded and technology slowly improved. Buddhism spread, while learning and the arts continued to flourish. Even Chinese cities survived.

Although invaders stormed northern China, they often adopted Chinese civilization rather than demolishing it. Meanwhile, various dynasties rose and fell in the south. During the brief Sui (swee) dynasty (589–618), the emperor Sui Wendi reunited the north and south. But China was not restored to its earlier glory until the emergence of the **Tang dynasty** in 618.

The Tang Build an Empire The first Tang emperor, Li Yuan (lee yoo AHN), was a general under the Sui dynasty. When the Sui began to crumble, Li Yuan's ambitious 16-year-old son, Li Shimin, urged him to lead a revolt. Father and son crushed all rivals and established the Tang dynasty. Eight years later, Li Shimin <u>compelled</u> his aging father to step down and mounted the throne himself, taking the name **Tang Taizong** (ty DZUNG). A brilliant general, government reformer, historian, and master of the calligraphy brush, Tang Taizong would become China's most admired emperor.

Later Tang rulers carried empire-building to new heights, conquering territories deep into Central Asia. Chinese armies forced the neighboring lands of Vietnam, Tibet, and Korea to become **tributary states.** That is, while these states remained self-governing, their rulers had to acknowledge Chinese supremacy and send regular tribute to the Tang emperor. At the same time, students from Korea and Japan traveled to the Tang capital to learn about Chinese government, law, and arts.

The Government and Economy Grow

Tang rulers, such as Empress Wu Zhao, helped restore the Han system of uniform government throughout China. They rebuilt the bureaucracy and enlarged the civil service system to recruit talented officials trained in Confucian philosophy. They also set up schools to prepare male students for the exams and developed a flexible new law code.

Tang emperors instituted a system of **land reform** in which they broke up large agricultural holdings and redistributed the land to peasants. This policy strengthened the central government by weakening the power of large landowners. It also increased government revenues, since the peasants who farmed their own land would be able to pay taxes.

The Tang Dynasty Declines

Like earlier dynasties, the Tang eventually weakened. Later Tang emperors lost territories in Central Asia to the Arabs. Corruption, high taxes, drought, famine, and rebellions all contributed to the downward swing of the dynastic cycle. In 907, a rebel

Vocabulary Builder

<u>compelled</u>—(kum PELD) *v.* forced to do something

The Tang Dynasty
The Western Market (below left) of the Tang dynasty specialized in foreign goods. Tang Taizong (below right) is considered one of the greatest monarchs in the history of China. *What led to the decline of the Tang Dynasty?*

Technology of Tang and Song China

In addition to the advances shown below, the Chinese developed a smallpox vaccine, invented a spinning wheel, and pioneered the use of arches in bridge building. In time, many of these developments traveled westward. Modernized versions of most of these inventions are still widely used today. **How could one of the inventions shown here have aided the spread of Chinese civilization to other lands?**

Gunpowder, 850 ▲
The earliest form of gunpowder was made from a mixture of saltpeter, sulfur, and charcoal, all found in abundance in China. It was first used in fireworks and later in weapons. Song forces were the first to use a cannon (shown above), according to historical records.

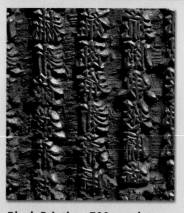

Block Printing, 700s, and ▲
Movable Type, 1040s
Block printing, developed during the Tang dynasty, involved carving a full page of characters onto a wooden block (above). China improved on this printing process during the Song dynasty by inventing movable type, in which precut characters were combined to form a page.

◀ **Mechanical Clock, 700s**
The Chinese learned of water-powered clocks from Middle Easterners. Mechanical clocks used a complex series of wheels, shafts, and pins, turning at a steady rate, to tell exact time.

general overthrew the last Tang emperor. This time, however, the chaos following the collapse of a dynasty did not last long.

✔ **Checkpoint**   How did the Tang dynasty reunify China?

The Song Dynasty

In 960, a scholarly general named Zhao Kuangyin reunited much of China and founded the **Song** (sung) **dynasty.** The Song ruled for 319 years, slightly longer than the Tang, but they controlled less territory than the Tang. The Song also faced the constant threat of invaders in the north. In the early 1100s, the battered Song retreated south of the Huang River. There, the southern Song continued to rule for another 150 years. As you will learn, however, in the late 1200s invaders from the north called the Mongols attacked and overthrew the Song.

Despite military setbacks, the Song period was a time of great achievement. China's wealth and culture dominated East Asia even when its armies did not. Under the Song, the Chinese economy expanded because of improved farming methods and open border policy. The latter allowed a new type of faster-growing rice to be imported from Southeast Asia. Farmers were now able to produce two crops a year, one of rice and one of a cash crop to sell. The rise in productivity created surpluses, allowing more people to pursue commerce, learning, or the arts.

Through China's history, a system of canals had been built that encouraged internal trade and transportation. The Grand Canal, completed during the Sui dynasty, linked the Huang River to the Chang River. As a result, food grown in the south could be shipped to the capital in the north. The Grand Canal reached its peak during the Song dynasty, when thousands of tons of grain were shipped to northern China each year.

Under both the Tang and Song, foreign trade flourished. Merchants arrived from India, Persia, and Arabia. Chinese merchants carried goods to Southeast Asia in exchange for spices and special woods. Song porcelain has been found as far away as East Africa. To improve trade, the government issued paper money. China's cities, which had been mainly centers of government, now prospered as centers of trade.

✓ **Checkpoint** How was the Song dynasty able to continue its prosperity despite threats from the north?

China's Ordered Society

Under the Tang and Song, China was a well-ordered society. At its head was the emperor, whose court was filled with aristocratic families. The court supervised a huge bureaucracy, from which officials fanned out to every part of China. China's two main social classes were the gentry and the peasantry.

The Gentry Value Education As in previous dynasties, the scholar-official class formed the top stratum of society. Most scholar-officials at court came from the gentry, or wealthy landowning class. They alone could afford to spend years studying the Confucian classics in order to pass the grueling civil service exam. When not in government service, the gentry often served in the provinces as allies of the emperor's officials.

The Song scholar-gentry valued learning more than physical labor. They supported a revival of Confucian thought. New schools of Confucian philosophers emphasized social order based on duty, rank, and proper behavior. Although corruption and greed existed among civil servants, the ideal Confucian official was a wise, virtuous scholar who knew how to ensure harmony in society.

Peasants Work the Land Most Chinese were peasants who worked the land, living on what they produced. Drought and famine were a constant threat, but new tools and crops did improve the lives of many peasants. To add to their income, some families produced handicrafts such as baskets or embroidered items. They carried these products to nearby market towns to sell or trade for salt, tea, or iron tools.

Peasants lived in small, largely self-sufficient villages that managed their own affairs. "Heaven is high," noted one Chinese saying, "and the emperor far away." Peasants relied on one another rather than the government. When disputes arose, a village leader and council of elders put pressure on the parties to resolve the problem. Only if such efforts failed did villagers take their disputes to the emperor's county representative.

In China, even peasants could move up in society through education and government service. If a bright peasant boy received an education and passed the civil service examinations, both he and his family rose in status. Slaves in early China, however, did not have such opportunities. As in many other parts of the world, slavery played a role in early China, though a limited one.

Merchants Have Lowest Status In market towns and cities, some merchants acquired wealth. Still, according to Confucian tradition, merchants had an even lower social status than peasants since their riches came from the labor of others. An ambitious merchant, therefore, might buy land and educate one son to enter the ranks of the scholar-gentry.

Pair of shoes for a woman with bound feet in China

The Confucian attitude toward merchants affected economic policy. Some rulers favored commerce but sought to control it. They often restricted where foreign merchants could live and even limited the activities of private traders. Still, Chinese trade flourished during Song times.

The Status of Women Women had higher status in Tang and early Song times than they did later. Within the home, women were called upon to run family affairs. A man's wife and his mother had great authority, managing servants and family finances. Still, families valued boys more than girls. When a young woman married, she became a part of her husband's family. She could not keep her **dowry,** the payment that a woman brings to a marriage, and could never remarry.

Women's subordinate position was reinforced in late Song times when the custom of foot binding emerged. The custom probably began at the imperial court but later spread to the lower classes. The feet of young girls were bound with long strips of cloth, producing a lily-shaped foot about half the size of a foot that was allowed to grow normally. Tiny feet and a stilted walk became a symbol of nobility and beauty. Foot binding was extremely painful, yet the custom survived. Even peasant parents feared that they could not find a husband for a daughter with large feet.

Not all girls in China had their feet bound. Peasants who needed their daughters to work in the fields did not accept the practice. Yet most women did have to submit to foot binding. Women with bound feet often could not walk without help. Thus, foot binding reinforced the Confucian tradition that women should remain inside the home.

✓ **Checkpoint**   How did most Chinese people live?

The Tang and Song Develop a Rich Culture

A prosperous economy supported the rich culture of Tang and Song China. Although their splendid royal palaces were long ago destroyed, many paintings, statues, temples, and ceramics have survived.

Artists Paint Harmony Along with poetry, painting and calligraphy were essential skills for the scholar-gentry. In both of these crafts, artists sought balance and harmony through the mastery of simple strokes and lines. The Song period saw the triumph of Chinese landscape painting. Steeped in the Daoist tradition, painters sought to capture the spiritual essence of the natural world. "When you are planning to paint," instructed a Song artist, "you must always create a harmonious relationship between heaven and earth."

Misty mountains and delicate bamboo forests dominated Chinese landscapes. Yet Chinese painters also produced realistic, vivid portraits of emperors or lively scenes of city life.

Architecture and Porcelain Buddhist themes dominated sculpture and influenced Chinese architecture. The Indian stupa evolved into the graceful Chinese **pagoda,** a multistoried temple with eaves that curve up at the corners. Chinese sculptors created striking statues of the Buddha. These statues created such a strong impression that many people today picture the Buddha as a Chinese god rather than an Indian holy man.

A CHINESE HOUSE

◄ The ideal woman during the Tang dynasty was sophisticated and wore head ornaments, combs, and powders. Like this woman, Tang women piled their hair high upon their heads.

This residence is typical of those owned by imperial or wealthy families. ▼

Dwellings during the Tang and Song dynasties ranged from caves to round tents to palaces. Ideally, all types of Chinese homes were built facing south so that they received warmth from the sun in the winter. Wealthy families lived in compounds that consisted of groups of buildings separated by a varying number of courtyards as shown in the painting below. Each structure within the compound had a distinct purpose for such things as ancestor worship, a library, or a music hall. Covered walkways, or porticos, joined the buildings. Atop the compound, expensive rooftops made of sloping tiles had terra cotta animals and dragons that adorned the ridges and eaves. Grand gardens with hills, ponds, rare flowers, twisted pine trees, and stones were an important part of the finest homes. The building and gardens together produced an overall harmonious effect.

Features of the Home

A Roofs were the most expensive and striking feature of the home. The finest homes had roofs with upturned edges and colorful tiles painted yellow, pale green, or jade green.

B Most houses included enclosed shaded courtyards.

C Each pavilion had a special purpose, whether for banquets or for playing music.

D Houseguests stayed in rooms located along the outer edge of the compound.

Thinking Critically

1. **Draw Inferences** According to the images shown here, what can you say about the status of women during this time?
2. **Synthesize Information** How does this compound illustrate the belief of the Tang and Song that a harmonious relationship should exist between home and gardens?

李白

宇太白丑夢長庚入懷而生
如草見之日此謫此人供奉翰林
過華陰縣今貴供云曾用電
巾拭睡衛手調美刀七肌靴貴
妃捧硯天子殿前矣是鳥草唸蟾
更宗勝斯令為湘

Li Bo, Chinese poet

The Chinese perfected techniques in making porcelain, a shiny, hard pottery that was prized as the finest in the world. They developed beautiful glazes to decorate vases, tea services, and other objects that Westerners would later call "chinaware." Artists also produced porcelain figures of camels, elegant court ladies playing polo, and bearded foreigners newly arrived from their travels on the Silk Road.

Chinese Writing Prose and poetry flowed from the brushes of Tang and Song writers. Scholars produced works on philosophy, religion, and history. Short stories that often blended fantasy, romance, and adventure made their first appearance in Chinese literature.

Among the gentry, poetry was the most respected form of Chinese literature. Confucian scholars were expected to master the skills of poetry. We know the names of some 200 major and 400 minor Tang and Song poets. Their works touched on Buddhist and Daoist themes as well as on social issues. Many poems reflected on the shortness of life and the immensity of the universe.

Probably the greatest Tang poet was Li Bo (lee boh). A zestful lover of life and freedom, he moved about from one place to another for most of his life. He wrote some 2,000 poems celebrating harmony with nature or lamenting the passage of time. A popular legend says that Li Bo drowned when he tried to embrace the reflection of the moon in a lake.

More realistic and less romantic were the poems of Li Bo's friend Du Fu. His verses described the horrors of war or condemned the lavishness of the court. A later poet, Li Qingzhao (lee ching jow), described the experience of women left behind when loved ones went off to war. Her poems reflect a time when invasion threatened to bring the brilliant Song dynasty to an end.

 Checkpoint What themes did Tang and Song arts and literature address?

Progress Monitoring _Online_
For: Self-quiz with vocabulary practice
Web Code: naa-1211

SECTION 1 Assessment

Terms, People, and Places

1. For each term, person, or place listed at the beginning of the section, write a sentence explaining its significance.

Note Taking

2. **Reading Skill: Compare and Contrast** Use your completed diagram to answer the Focus Question: Describe the political, economic, and cultural achievements of the Tang and Song dynasties.

Comprehension and Critical Thinking

3. **Draw Conclusions** In what ways did the rise of the Tang dynasty unify and benefit China?

4. **Determine Relevance** What was the significance of the Grand Canal to the Song dynasty?

5. **Recognize Ideologies** (a) Describe the social structure of China under the Tang and Song dynasties. (b) How did the social structure reflect Confucian traditions?

6. **Analyze Information** What ideas and traditions shaped Chinese paintings?

● **Writing About History**

Quick Write: Make a Cause-Effect Tree To make a cause-and-effect tree, choose either the Tang or Song dynasty and write its name in the center of a piece of paper. Above the dynasty's name, write the causes that led to its downfall.

TRADE

What are the intended and unintended effects of trade?

In This Chapter SSWH2d

As routes became safer, trade along the ancient Silk Road increased. Merchants traveled in both directions between China and the Mediterranean Sea. Along with porcelain, silk, and spices came religion, art, architecture, and ideas. For more than a thousand years, the network of trade routes helped shape the tastes and cultures of people in much of Asia and Europe.

Throughout History

600s B.C. Greek traders bring goods and the Phoenician alphabet back to Greece.

1400s A.D. The search for a new trade route to Asia brings Europeans to the Americas.

1500s–1800s Slave trade enriches merchants but destroys African societies.

1700s New crops from the Americas boost farm output in China.

1850s–1860s Western demands for trade lead to modernization of Japan.

Continuing Today

Trade involves the movement of goods. Sometimes, unexpected cargo goes along for the ride. One invasive species, the zebra mussel, arrived in the United States in the bilge tank of an East European cargo ship. Zebra mussels clog water intake pipes and upset the ecosystem of the Great Lakes region.

21st Century Skills

 TRANSFER Activities

1. **Analyze** How has trade had more than just economic impact?

2. **Evaluate** What limits, if any, should there be on trade?

3. **Transfer** Complete a Web quest in which you investigate the pros and cons of free trade; record your thoughts in the Concept Connector Journal; and learn to make a video. Web Code nah-1208

Mongolian archer
on horseback

Mongol warrior's boots

2

WITNESS HISTORY ◀)) AUDIO

Warriors on Horseback

The Mongols were tough warriors who lived in the saddle and were considered the most skilled riders in the world. The Italian traveler Marco Polo described Mongol battle tactics:

❝ They keep hovering about the enemy, discharging their arrows first from one side and then from the other. . . . Their horses are so well broken-in to quick changes of movement, that upon the signal given, they instantly turn in any direction, and by these rapid maneuvers many victories have been obtained. ❞
—Marco Polo, *A Description of the World*

Focus Question What were the effects of the Mongol invasion and the rise of the Ming dynasty on China?

The Mongol and Ming Empires

 GA **Performance Standards**

- **SSWH4d** Analyze the spread of the Mongol Empire; the role of Chinggis (Gennghis) Khan in developing the Mongol Empire; the impact of the Mongols on Russia, China, and the West.
- **SSWH10a** Explain the role of Zheng He.

Terms, People, and Places

steppe
Genghis Khan
Kublai Khan
Yuan dynasty

Marco Polo
Ming dynasty
Zheng He

Note Taking

Reading Skill: Recognize Sequence Create a timeline like the one below to record important events as you read this section.

Mongols advance
into China.

| c. 1200 | 1279 | 1368 | 1405 |

About 1200, the Mongols burst out of Central Asia to conquer an empire stretching across Asia and Europe. In the process, they overran Song China and imposed Mongol rule on its people.

Mongol Armies Build an Empire

The Mongols were a nomadic people who grazed their horses and sheep on the **steppes,** or vast, treeless plains, of Central Asia. Rival Mongol clans spent much of their time warring with one another. In the early 1200s, however, a brilliant Mongol chieftain united these warring tribes. This chieftain took the name **Genghis Khan,** meaning "Universal Ruler." Under his leadership, Mongol forces conquered a vast empire that stretched from the Pacific Ocean to Eastern Europe.

Mongols Invade China Genghis Khan imposed strict military discipline and demanded absolute loyalty. His highly trained, mobile armies had some of the most skilled horsemen in the world. Genghis Khan had a reputation for fierceness. He could order the massacre of an entire city. Yet he also could be generous, rewarding the bravery of a single fighter.

Mongol armies conquered the Asian steppe lands with some ease, but as they turned on China, they encountered the problem of attacking walled cities. Chinese and Turkish military experts taught them to use cannons and other new weapons. The Mongols and Chinese launched missiles against each other from metal tubes filled with gunpowder. This use of cannons in warfare would soon spread westward to Europe.

Genghis Khan did not live to complete the conquest of China. His heirs, however, continued to expand the Mongol empire. For the next 150 years, they <u>dominated</u> much of Asia. Their furious assaults toppled empires and spread destruction from southern Russia through Muslim lands in Southwest Asia to China. Protected by steep mountain ranges, India avoided invasion, but the Mongols arrived in China, devastated the flourishing province of Sichuan (see chwahn), and annihilated its great capital city of Chengdu.

Vocabulary Builder

<u>dominated</u>—(DAHM ih nayt id) *v.* ruled or controlled with power

Rulers Establish Order and Peace Once conquest was completed, the Mongols were not oppressive rulers. Often, they allowed conquered people to live much as they had before—as long as they regularly paid tribute to the Mongols.

Genghis Khan had set an example for his successors by ruling conquered lands with toleration and justice. Although the Mongol warrior had no use for city life, he respected scholars, artists, and artisans. He listened to the ideas of Confucians, Buddhists, Christians, Muslims, Jews, and Zoroastrians.

In the 1200s and 1300s, the sons and grandsons of Genghis Khan established peace and order within their domains. Today, many historians refer to this period of order as the *Pax Mongolica,* or Mongol Peace.

Political stability set the stage for economic growth. Under the protection of the Mongols, who now controlled the great Silk Road, trade flourished across Eurasia. According to a contemporary, Mongol rule meant that people "enjoyed such a peace that a man might have journeyed from the land of sunrise to the land of sunset with a golden platter upon his head without suffering the least violence from anyone."

Cultural exchanges increased as foods, tools, inventions, and ideas spread along the protected trade routes. From China, the use of gunpowder moved westward into Europe. Techniques of papermaking also reached parts of Europe, and crops and trees from the Middle East were carried into East Asia.

✓ **Checkpoint** How did the Mongol Empire change once conquest was over?

China Under Mongol Rule

Although Genghis Khan had subdued northern China, the Mongols needed nearly 70 more years to conquer the south. Genghis Khan's grandson, **Kublai Khan** (KOO bly KAHN), finally toppled the last Song emperor in 1279. From his capital at Khanbaliq, present-day Beijing, Kublai Khan ruled all of China as well as Korea and Tibet.

An All-Mongol Government Kublai Khan tried to prevent the Mongols from being absorbed into Chinese civilization as other conquerors of China had been. He decreed that only Mongols could serve in the military. He also reserved the highest government jobs for

BIOGRAPHY

Genghis Khan
Originally called Temüjin, Genghis Khan (c. 1162–1227) was renowned for being ruthless, determined, and courageous. When Temüjin was nine years old, a rival Mongol clan poisoned his father. At the age of 15, Temüjin was taken prisoner. For the rest of his life, he never forgot the humiliation of being locked in a wooden collar and paraded before his enemies.

When he regained his freedom, Temüjin wandered among drifting clans. He took revenge on the clan that had imprisoned him and in time, became supreme ruler of all the Mongols. Once despised, Genghis Khan would be admired and feared across two continents. **How might Temüjin's experiences have motivated him to unite the Mongol clans?**

Marco Polo

Marco Polo ▶
Polo

Marco Polo (1254–1324) was a traveler and adventurer from Venice. In 1295, he returned home after a sojourn of 25 years in Asia where he had served the Chinese emperor Kublai Khan for 17 years. In 1298, Marco Polo was imprisoned during a war with the city-state of Genoa. It was at this time that he dictated his tales to a fellow prisoner, and they were subsequently published as *The Travels of Marco Polo*. This excerpt (facing page) is from Marco Polo's description of Kublai Khan's palace.

▼ Marco Polo at the Court of Kublai Khan, 1375

Mongols or for other non-Chinese officials whom he employed. Still, because there were too few Mongols to control so vast an empire, Kublai allowed Chinese officials to continue to rule in the provinces.

Under Mongol rule, an uneasy mix of Chinese and foreign customs developed. Kublai adopted a Chinese name for his dynasty, the **Yuan** (yoo AHN), and turned Khanbaliq into a Chinese walled city. At the same time, he had Arab architects design his palace, and many rooms reflected Mongol steppe dwellings. Kublai rebuilt and extended the Grand Canal to his new capital, which made the shipment of rice and other goods easier. He also welcomed many foreigners to his court, including the African Muslim world traveler Ibn Battuta.

Marco Polo Writes About China The Italian merchant **Marco Polo** was one of many visitors to China during the Yuan dynasty. Although there is some debate on whether Marco Polo reached China, most historians acknowledge that he did indeed reach Cathay (northern China). In 1271, Polo left Venice with his father and uncle. He crossed Persia and Central Asia to reach China. He then spent 17 years in Kublai's service. Finally, he returned to Venice by sea, visiting Southeast Asia and India along the way.

In his writings, Marco Polo left a vivid account of the wealth and splendor of China. He described the royal palace of Kublai Khan (see Traveler's Tale) and also described China's efficient royal mail system,

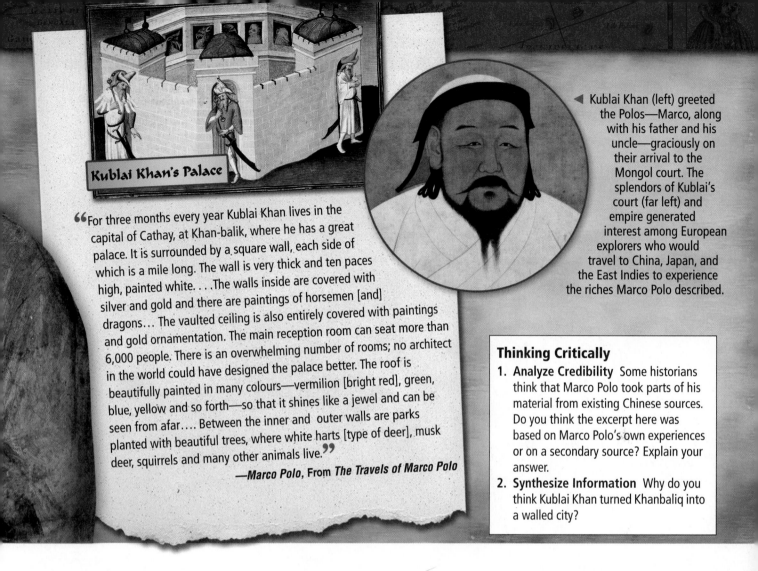

Kublai Khan's Palace

"For three months every year Kublai Khan lives in the capital of Cathay, at Khan-balik, where he has a great palace. It is surrounded by a square wall, each side of which is a mile long. The wall is very thick and ten paces high, painted white. . . .The walls inside are covered with silver and gold and there are paintings of horsemen [and] dragons… The vaulted ceiling is also entirely covered with paintings and gold ornamentation. The main reception room can seat more than 6,000 people. There is an overwhelming number of rooms; no architect in the world could have designed the palace better. The roof is beautifully painted in many colours—vermilion [bright red], green, blue, yellow and so forth—so that it shines like a jewel and can be seen from afar…. Between the inner and outer walls are parks planted with beautiful trees, where white harts [type of deer], musk deer, squirrels and many other animals live."

—*Marco Polo*, From *The Travels of Marco Polo*

◀ Kublai Khan (left) greeted the Polos—Marco, along with his father and his uncle—graciously on their arrival to the Mongol court. The splendors of Kublai's court (far left) and empire generated interest among European explorers who would travel to China, Japan, and the East Indies to experience the riches Marco Polo described.

Thinking Critically
1. **Analyze Credibility** Some historians think that Marco Polo took parts of his material from existing Chinese sources. Do you think the excerpt here was based on Marco Polo's own experiences or on a secondary source? Explain your answer.
2. **Synthesize Information** Why do you think Kublai Khan turned Khanbaliq into a walled city?

with couriers riding swift ponies along the empire's well-kept roads. Furthermore, he reported that the city of Hangzhou was 10 or 12 times the size of Venice, one of Italy's richest city-states. In the next centuries, Polo's reports sparked European interest in the riches of Asia.

Mongols Continue Outside Contact As long as the Mongol empire prospered, contacts between Europe and Asia continued. The Mongols tolerated a variety of beliefs. The pope sent Christian priests to Beijing, while Muslims set up their own communities in China. Meanwhile, some Chinese products moved toward Europe. They included gunpowder, porcelain, and playing cards.

✔ **Checkpoint** How did Kublai Khan organize Mongol rule in China?

The Ming Restore Chinese Rule

The Yuan dynasty declined after the death of Kublai Khan, which occurred in 1294. Most Chinese despised the foreign Mongol rulers. Confucian scholars retreated into their own world, seeing little to gain from the barbarians. Heavy taxes, corruption, and natural disasters led to frequent uprisings. Finally, Zhu Yuanzhang (dzoo YOO AHND zahng), a peasant leader, forged a rebel army that toppled the Mongols and pushed them back beyond the Great Wall. In 1368, he founded a new Chinese dynasty, which he called the **Ming,** meaning brilliant.

The Mongol Empire

Map Skills At its height, the Mongol empire was the largest in the world up to that time.

1. **Locate** (a) Beijing (b) Venice (c) Hangzhou

2. **Region** Describe what happened to the Mongol empire between 1227 and 1294.

3. **Make Comparisons** What countries would Marco Polo pass through if he made his journey today?

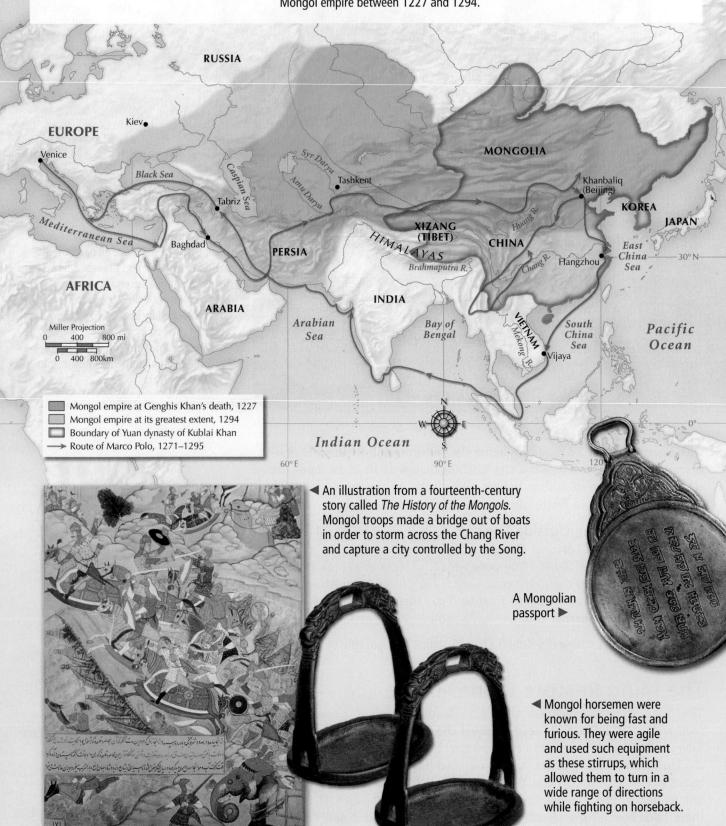

RUSSIA

Kiev

EUROPE

Venice

Black Sea

Caspian Sea

Tabriz

Syr Darya

Amu Darya

Tashkent

MONGOLIA

Khanbaliq
(Beijing)

KOREA

JAPAN

Mediterranean Sea

Baghdad

PERSIA

HIMALAYAS

**XIZANG
(TIBET)**

Brahmaputra R.

CHINA

Huang R.

Chang R.

Hangzhou

*East
China
Sea*

30° N

AFRICA

ARABIA

INDIA

*Arabian
Sea*

*Bay of
Bengal*

VIETNAM

Mekong R.

Vijaya

*South
China
Sea*

*Pacific
Ocean*

Miller Projection
0   400   800 mi
0   400 800km

Indian Ocean

60° E

90° E

120

0°

■	Mongol empire at Genghis Khan's death, 1227
□	Mongol empire at its greatest extent, 1294
□	Boundary of Yuan dynasty of Kublai Khan
→	Route of Marco Polo, 1271–1295

◀ An illustration from a fourteenth-century story called *The History of the Mongols*. Mongol troops made a bridge out of boats in order to storm across the Chang River and capture a city controlled by the Song.

A Mongolian
passport ▶

◀ Mongol horsemen were known for being fast and furious. They were agile and used such equipment as these stirrups, which allowed them to turn in a wide range of directions while fighting on horseback.

Early Ming rulers sought to reassert Chinese greatness after years of foreign rule. They initially moved the capital to Nanjing, which they felt possessed more characteristics of the Chinese, but eventually moved it back to present-day Beijing. The Ming restored the civil service system, and Confucian learning again became the road to success. The civil service exams became more rigorous than ever. A board of censors watched over the bureaucracy, rooting out corruption and disloyalty.

The Economy Grows Economically, Ming China was immensely productive. The fertile, well-irrigated plains of eastern China supported a population of more than 100 million. In the Chang River valley, peasants produced huge rice crops. Better methods of fertilizing helped to improve farming. Reshaping the landscape helped as well. Some farmers cut horizontal steps called terraces into steep hillsides to gain soil in which to grow crops. In the 1500s, new crops reached China from the Americas, especially corn and sweet potatoes.

Chinese cities, such as Nanjing, were home to many industries, including porcelain, paper, and tools. The Ming repaired the extensive canal system that linked various regions, made trade easier, and allowed cities to grow. New technologies increased output in manufacturing. Better methods of printing, for example, led to the production of a flood of books.

Culture Flourishes Ming China also saw a revival of arts and literature. Ming artists developed their own styles of landscape painting and created brilliant blue and white porcelain. Ming vases were among the most valuable and popular Chinese products exported to the West.

Confucian scholars continued to produce classical poetry. At the same time, new forms of popular literature to be enjoyed by the common people began to emerge. Ming writers composed novels, including *The Water Margin* about an outlaw gang that tries to end injustice by corrupt officials. Ming writers also produced the world's first detective stories.

 Checkpoint How did Ming rulers restore a previous style of Chinese government?

Chinese Fleets Sail the Seas

Early Ming rulers proudly sent Chinese fleets into distant waters to show the glory of their government. The most extraordinary of these overseas ventures were the voyages of the Chinese admiral and diplomat **Zheng He** (jeng he).

Zheng He and His Fleets Starting in 1405, Zheng He commanded the first of seven expeditions. He departed at the head of a fleet of 62 huge ships and over 200 smaller ones, carrying a crew of about 28,000 sailors. The largest ships measured 400 feet long. The goal of each expedition was to promote trade and collect tribute from lesser powers across the western seas.

Between 1405 and 1433, Zheng He explored the coasts of Southeast Asia and India and the entrances to the Red Sea and the Persian Gulf. He also visited many ports in East Africa. In the wake of these expeditions, Chinese merchants settled in Southeast Asia and India and became a permanent presence in their trading centers. Exotic animals, such as giraffes, were imported from foreign lands as well. The voyages also showed local rulers the power and strength of the Chinese empire.

Zheng He set up an engraved stone tablet listing the dates, places, and achievements of his voyages. The tablet proudly proclaimed that the Ming had unified the "seas and continents" even more than the Han and Tang had done. What was the relevance of Zheng He's overseas expeditions?

Primary Source

66 The countries beyond the horizon and from the ends of the earth have all become subjects. . . . We have traversed immense waterspaces and have beheld in the ocean huge waves like mountains rising sky high, and we have set eyes on barbarian regions far away . . . while our sails loftily unfurled like clouds day and night continued their course, traversing those savage waves as if we were treading on a public thoroughfare. 99

—Zheng He, quoted in *The True Dates of the Chinese Maritime Expeditions in the Early Fifteenth Century* (Duyvendak)

Exploration Ends In 1435, the year Zheng He died, the Ming emperor suddenly banned the building of seagoing ships. Later, ships with more than two masts were forbidden. Zheng He's huge ships were retired and rotted away.

Why did China, with its advanced naval technology, turn its back on overseas exploration? Historians are not sure. Some speculate that the fleets were costly and did not produce profit. Also, Confucian scholars at court had little interest in overseas ventures and commerce. To them, Chinese civilization was the most successful in the world. They wanted to preserve its ancient traditions, which they saw as the source of stability. In fact, such rigid loyalty to tradition would eventually weaken China and once again leave it prey to foreign domination.

Fewer than 60 years after China halted overseas expeditions, the explorer Christopher Columbus would sail west from Spain in search of a sea route to Asia. As you will see, this voyage made Spain a major power and had a dramatic impact on the entire world. We can only wonder how the course of history might have changed if the Chinese had continued the explorations they had begun under the Ming.

✓ **Checkpoint** What occurred in 1435 that changed China's relationship with the rest of the world?

Progress Monitoring *Online*

For: Self-quiz with vocabulary practice
Web Code: naa-1221

SECTION 2 Assessment

Terms, People, and Places

1. For each term, person, or place listed at the beginning of the section, write a sentence explaining its significance.

Note Taking

2. **Reading Skill: Recognize Sequence** Use your completed timeline to answer the Focus Question: What were the effects of the Mongol invasion and the rise of the Ming dynasty on China?

Comprehension and Critical Thinking

3. **Synthesize Information** How did the Mongol conquests promote trade and cultural exchanges?

4. **Recognize Cause and Effect** Describe one effect of each of the following on China: (a) the Mongol invasion (b) the expulsion of the Mongols (c) the rise of the Ming dynasty

5. **Draw Conclusions** How did the Ming emperors try to restore Chinese culture?

● Writing About History

Quick Write: Provide Elaboration To illustrate each cause and effect of your essay, you should have supporting details, facts, and examples. List as many specific details as you can about the Mongol invasion of China. Then write a paragraph using the details you listed to explain the effects of the invasion.

Buddha statues
made of celadon

WITNESS HISTORY 🔊 AUDIO

The Power of Ideas

Buddhism was brought to the Korean peninsula from China in the fourth century. It influenced Korea greatly, and its effects were seen in both culture and politics. Here, a Korean writer discusses Buddhism:

66 If you teach people to rely on this teaching [Buddhism] and practice it, then their minds can be corrected, and their bodies can be cultivated. You can regulate your family, you can govern the state, and you can bring peace to all the world. 99
—Gihwa, *The Exposition of the Correct*

Focus Question How are Korea's history and culture linked to those of China and Japan?

Korea and Its Traditions

 Performance Standards

• **SSWH2d** Explain the status of peasants and merchants.

Terms, People, and Places

Silla dynasty	King Sejong
Koryo dynasty	hangul
celadon	literacy rate
Choson (Yi) dynasty	

N̲o̲te **Taking**

Reading Skill: Categorize Draw a concept web like the one shown below. As you read the section, fill in the blank circles with relevant information about Korea. Add more circles as needed.

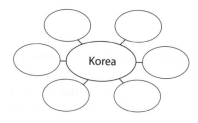

As early as Han times, Korea's larger neighbor to the north—China—was an influence. However, although Koreans absorbed many Chinese traditions, they also maintained a separate and distinct culture.

Geography of the Korean Peninsula

Korea is located on a peninsula that juts south from the Asian mainland and points toward Japan. At the northern end of the peninsula, mountains and the Yalu River separate Korea from China.

Living Among Mountains and Seas An early visitor once compared Korea's landscape to "a sea in a heavy gale." Low but steep mountains cover nearly 70 percent of the Korean peninsula. The most important range is the T'aebaek (ta bak). It runs from north to south along the eastern coast, with smaller chains branching off to form hilly areas. Because farming is difficult on the mountains, most people live along the western coastal plains, Korea's major farming region.

Korea has a 5,400-mile coastline with hundreds of good harbors. In addition, the offshore waters feature thousands of islands. Since early times, Koreans have depended upon seafood for most of the protein in their diet. Today, South Korea has one of the largest fishing industries in the world.

Location Affects Korea Korea's location on China's eastern border has played a key role in its development. From its powerful

Korea's Three Kingdoms

Geography *Interactive*
For: Audio guided tour
Web Code: nap-1231

CHINA
Paektu Mt.
Conic Projection
0 50 100 mi
0 50 100km
Yalu River
NANGNIM RANGE
Taedong River
40° N
N
S
E
W
Korea Bay
KOREA
Imjin River
T'AEBAEK RANGE
East Sea (Sea of Japan)
Kaesong
Han R.
Yellow Sea
SOBAEK RANGE
Puyo
Kyongju
36° N
124° E
132° E
Korea Strait
JAPAN
128° E
Kingdoms, A.D. 300–A.D. 600
Koguryo
Paekche
Silla
Capital city

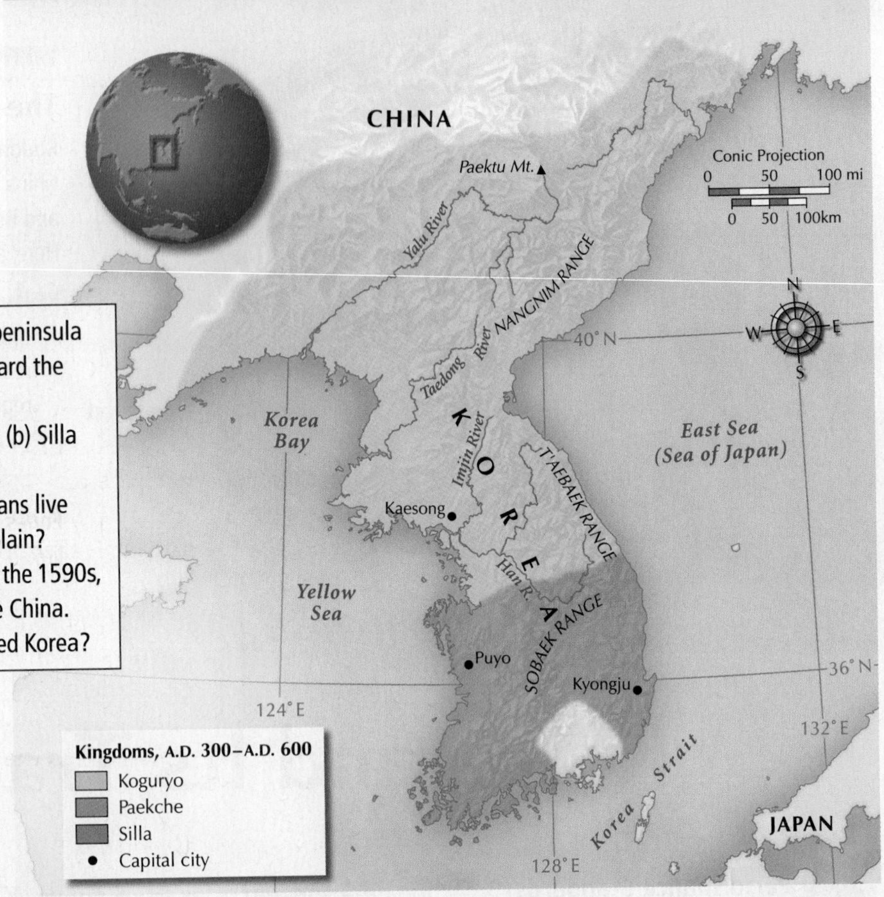

Map Skills Korea occupies a peninsula that juts south from China toward the islands of Japan.

1. **Locate** (a) T'aebaek Range (b) Silla (c) East Sea (Sea of Japan)
2. **Region** Why do most Koreans live along the western coastal plain?
3. **Predict Consequences** In the 1590s, Japan made plans to invade China. How might this have affected Korea?

mainland neighbor, Korea received many cultural and technological influences. At various times in history, China extended political control over the Korean peninsula. Korea has also served as a cultural bridge linking China and Japan. Koreans have, from early times, adapted and transformed Chinese traditions before passing them on to the Japanese.

Vocabulary Builder
evolved—(ee VAHLVD) *v.* developed gradually

The earliest Koreans probably migrated southeastward from Siberia and northern Manchuria during the Stone Age. They evolved their own ways of life before the first wave of Chinese influence reached the peninsula during the Han dynasty. In 108 B.C., the Han emperor, Wudi, invaded Korea and set up a military colony there. From this outpost, Confucian traditions and Chinese ideas about government, as well as Chinese writing and farming methods, spread to Korea.

✓ **Checkpoint** **How did the relative location of the Korean peninsula influence the development of Korean civilization?**

Development of the Silla and Koryo Dynasties

Between 100 B.C. and A.D. 676, powerful local rulers forged three separate kingdoms: Koguryo in the north, Paekche in the southwest, and Silla in the southeast. Although they shared the same language and cultural background, the three kingdoms often warred with one another or with China. Still, Chinese influences continued to arrive. Missionaries spread Mahayana Buddhism, which took root among the rulers and nobles. Korean monks then traveled to China and India to learn more about Buddhism. They brought home the arts and learning of China.

Backed by the Tang emperor, the Silla kingdom defeated Paekche and Koguryo in 676 and united Korea. From this time until 1910, Korea had only three unified dynasties. The Unified Silla ruled from 668 to 935, the Koryo ruled from 918 to 1392, and the Choson ruled from 1392 to 1910.

Silla Dynasty Unites Kingdoms Under the **Silla dynasty,** Korea prospered and the arts flourished. Silla civilization was among the most advanced in the world. Buddhism grew to become a powerful force, and hundreds of Buddhist temples were built. A brisk trade was conducted with China. Chinese culture, written language, and political institutions continued to be extremely important influences on Korea.

Much of this great cultural and technical flowering centered at the Silla capital, Kyongju, which was modeled on the Tang capital at Chang'an. Kyongju was renowned as the "city of gold," where the aristocracy pursued a life of high culture and extravagance. Medicine, astronomy, metal casting, sculpture, and textile manufacturing reached especially high levels.

In 682, the Silla set up a national Confucian academy to train high officials and later instituted a civil-service examination modeled on that of China. But in China, even a peasant could win political influence by passing the exam. In Korea, only aristocrats were permitted to take the test. Eventually, conflicts between peasants and the aristocrats led to the overthrow of the Silla dynasty.

The Koryo Dynasty The **Koryo dynasty,** from which the modern word Korea is derived, replaced the Silla in 918. A new capital was established at Songak, present-day Kaesong.

Confucianism and Buddhism were both influential and widespread during this time. Koreans used woodblock printing from China to produce a flood of Buddhist texts. Later, Korean inventors took the Chinese invention one step further and created movable metal type to print large numbers of books. Koreans also improved on other Chinese inventions. They learned to make porcelain from China, and then perfected the technique for making **celadon,** or porcelain with an unusual blue-green glaze. Korean celadon vases and jars were prized throughout Asia. In the 1200s, when

The Pulguksa Temple, completed during the Silla dynasty, is considered to be the most famous Buddhist temple in Korea.

During the Silla dynasty, Buddhism expanded and beautiful temples, such as the Pulguksa Temple shown here, were constructed. This oath is from an early Korean document:

Primary Source

66 Hereafter we will worship the Buddha and revere the clergy. If we break this oath, may heaven strike us dead. 99

The Korean Alphabet

Hangul (bottom), the Korean writing system, is fairly simple to learn and was developed to replace the complicated Chinese system (top). Notice that like Chinese, however, hangul is made up of a sequence of symbols that are relatively square-shaped. Hangul is now used for nearly all written communications in both North and South Korea. *Why did Korea want its own system of writing?*

▲ Chinese characters

무궁화미용실

▲ Hangul characters

the Mongols overran Korea and destroyed many industries, the secret of making celadon was lost forever.

✔ **Checkpoint**   **What were the achievements of the Koryo dynasty?**

The Choson Dynasty Rules for Over 500 Years

The Mongols invaded Korea between 1231 and the 1250s. In 1258, the Koryo made peace with the Mongols, but a lack of tax income weakened the kingdom. In 1392, the brilliant Korean general Yi Song-gye (yee sung gyeh) overthrew them and set up the **Choson dynasty.** This was the last and longest-lived of Korea's three dynasties. General Yi reduced Buddhist influence and set up a government based upon Confucian principles.

Korea Creates Alphabet   In 1443, Korea's most celebrated ruler, **King Sejong,** decided to replace the complex Chinese system of writing. "The language of this land," he noted, "is different from China's." Sejong had experts develop **hangul,** the Korean phonetic alphabet that uses symbols to represent the sounds of spoken Korean.

Although Confucian scholars and Koreans of the upper classes rejected hangul at the outset, its use quickly spread. Hangul was easier for Koreans to use than the thousands of characters of written Chinese. Its use led to an extremely high **literacy rate,** or percentage of people who can read and write.

Japan Invades   In the 1590s, an ambitious Japanese ruler decided to invade China by way of Korea. Japanese armies landed and for years looted and burned across the peninsula. To stop the invaders at sea, the Korean Admiral Yi Sun-shin, one of Korea's great heroes, used "turtle ships," so named because they were armored and shaped like turtles. The ships were able to sail right into the Japanese fleet. After six years, the Japanese armies withdrew from Korea. As they left, however, they carried off many Korean artisans to introduce their skills to Japan.

✔ **Checkpoint**   **How did Korea preserve its own identity under the Choson dynasty?**

SECTION 3 Assessment

Progress Monitoring *Online*
For: Self-quiz with vocabulary practice
Web Code: naa-1231

Terms, People, and Places

1. What do each of the key terms listed at the beginning of the section have in common? Explain.

Note Taking

2. **Reading Skill: Categorize** Use your completed concept web to answer the Focus Question: How are Korea's history and culture linked to those of China and Japan?

Comprehension and Critical Thinking

3. **Make Generalizations** Why might Korea's location be considered strategic to other countries?

4. **Synthesize Information** Give two examples of how Koreans adapted or modified Chinese ideas under the Silla or Koryo dynasty?

5. **Analyze Information** Today, Hangul Day is a holiday in South Korea. Why do you think Koreans celebrate the creation of their alphabet?

● **Writing About History**

Quick Write: Create a Flowchart
Organize the information in this chapter by creating a flowchart. The chart should show either the course of Korean unification and the sequence of dynasties or the influences on Korean civilization. Remember that a flowchart connects information to show a relationship between the different pieces of information.

Prince Shotoku depicted on a wall hanging and on a 1000 yen note

WITNESS HISTORY 🔊 AUDIO

The Importance of Harmony

Prince Shotoku of Japan's ruling Yamato clan wanted to create an orderly society. In 604, he outlined ideals of behavior for both the royal court and ordinary people. "Harmony should be valued," he wrote, "and quarrels avoided." Shotoku's words reflected a strong Confucian influence about social order. As he stated:

> 66 Everyone has his biases, and few men are far-sighted. Therefore some disobey their lords and fathers and keep up feuds with their neighbors. But when the superiors are in harmony with each other and inferiors are friendly, then affairs are discussed quietly and the right view of matters prevails. 99

Focus Question What internal and external factors shaped Japan's civilization, and what characterized Japan's feudal age?

The Emergence of Japan and the Feudal Age

 Performance Standards

- **SSWH2d** Explain the diffusion of Confucianism to Southeast Asia.
- **SSWH11a** Describe the policies of Oda Nobunaga.
- **SSWH11b** Analyze how population growth impacted Japanese social structure.
- **SSWH14a** Compare Louis XIV, Peter the Great and Tokugawa Ieyasu's absolutism.

Terms, People, and Places

archipelago	kana
tsunami	samurai
Shinto	bushido
selective borrowing	Zen

Note Taking

Reading Skill: Categorize Fill in a table like the one shown below with examples of internal and external factors that shaped Japan's civilization.

Influences on Japan	
Internal Factors	**External Factors**
• geography	•
•	•

Like Korea, Japan felt the powerful influence of Chinese civilization early in its history. At the same time, the Japanese continued to maintain their own distinct culture.

Geography Sets Japan Apart

Japan is located on an **archipelago** (ahr kuh PEL uh goh), or chain of islands, about 100 miles off the Asian mainland and east of the Korean peninsula. Its four main islands are Hokkaido, Honshu, Kyushu, and Shikoku.

Seas Protect Japan Japan is about the size of Montana, but four-fifths of its land are too mountainous to farm. As a result, most people settled in narrow river valleys and along the coastal plains. A mild climate and sufficient rainfall, however, helped Japanese farmers make the most of the limited arable land.

The surrounding seas have both protected and isolated Japan. The country was close enough to the mainland to learn from Korea and China, but too far away for the Chinese to conquer. Japan thus had greater freedom to accept or reject Chinese influences than did other East Asian lands. At times, the Japanese sealed themselves off from foreign influences, choosing to go their own way. The seas that helped Japan preserve its identity also served as

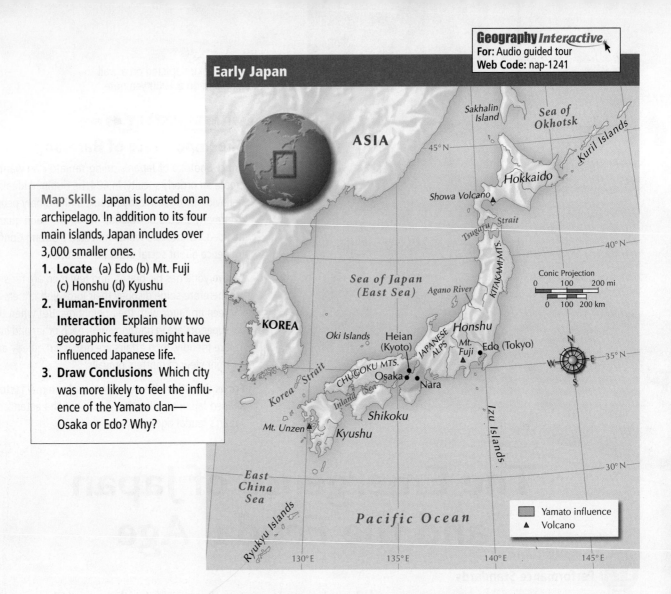

Early Japan

Geography *Interactive*
For: Audio guided tour
Web Code: nap-1241

Map Skills Japan is located on an archipelago. In addition to its four main islands, Japan includes over 3,000 smaller ones.

1. **Locate** (a) Edo (b) Mt. Fuji (c) Honshu (d) Kyushu
2. **Human-Environment Interaction** Explain how two geographic features might have influenced Japanese life.
3. **Draw Conclusions** Which city was more likely to feel the influence of the Yamato clan—Osaka or Edo? Why?

trade routes. The Inland Sea was an especially important link among various Japanese islands. The seas also offered plentiful food resources and the Japanese developed a thriving fishing industry.

Forces of Nature The Japanese came to fear and respect the dramatic forces of nature. Japan lies in a region known as the Ring of Fire, which is made up of a chain of volcanoes that encircle the Pacific Ocean. This region is therefore subject to frequent volcanic activity and earthquakes. Underwater earthquakes can launch killer tidal waves, called **tsunamis,** which sweep over the land without warning, wiping out everything in their path.

✓ **Checkpoint** How did the sea help Japan preserve its identity?

Early Traditions

The people we know today as the Japanese probably migrated from the Asian mainland more than 2,000 years ago. They slowly pushed the earlier inhabitants, the Ainu, onto the northernmost island of Hokkaido.

The Yamato Clan Claims Power Early Japanese society was divided into *uji*, or clans. Each *uji* had its own chief and a special god or goddess who was seen as the clan's original ancestor. Some clan leaders were women, suggesting that women enjoyed a respected position in society.

By about A.D. 500, the Yamato clan came to dominate a corner of Honshu, the largest Japanese island. For the next 1,000 years, the Yamato Plain was the heartland of Japanese government. The Yamato set up Japan's first and only dynasty. They claimed direct descent from the sun goddess, Amaterasu, and chose the rising sun as their symbol. Later Japanese emperors were revered as living gods. While this is no longer the case, the current Japanese emperor still traces his roots to the Yamato clan.

A Religion of Nature Early Japanese clans honored kami, or superior powers that were natural or divine. The worship of the forces of nature became known as **Shinto,** meaning "the way of kami." Although Shinto has not evolved into an international religion like Christianity, Buddhism, or Islam, its traditions survive to the present day in Japan. Hundreds of Shinto shrines dot the Japanese countryside. Though simple in design, they are generally located in beautiful, natural surroundings. Shinto shrines are dedicated to special sites or objects such as mountains or waterfalls, ancient gnarled trees, or even oddly shaped rocks.

The Korean Connection The Japanese language is distantly related to Korean but completely different from Chinese. From early on, Japan and Korea were in continuous contact with each other. Korean artisans and metalworkers settled in Japan, bringing sophisticated skills and technology. Japanese and Korean warriors crossed the sea in both directions to attack each other's strongholds. Some of the leading families at the Yamato court claimed Korean ancestors.

Missionaries from Korea had introduced Buddhism to Japan in the 500s. With it came knowledge of Chinese writing and culture that sparked a sustained period of Japanese interest in Chinese civilization.

✔ **Checkpoint** How did the Yamato clan influence future Japanese government?

Japan Looks to China

In the early 600s, Prince Shotoku of the Yamato clan decided to learn about China directly instead of through Korean sources. He sent young nobles to study in China. Over the next 200 years, many Japanese students, monks, traders, and officials visited the Tang court.

The Japanese Visit China Each visitor to China spent a year or more there—negotiating, trading, but above all studying. The visitors returned to Japan eager to spread Chinese thought, technology, and arts. They also imported Chinese ideas about government. Japanese rulers adopted the title "Heavenly Emperor" and claimed absolute power. They strengthened the central government, set up a bureaucracy, and adopted a law code similar to that of China. Still, the new bureaucracy had little real authority beyond the royal court. Out in the countryside, the old clans remained strong.

In 710, the Japanese emperor built a new capital at Nara, modeled on the Tang capital at Chang'an. There, Japanese nobles spoke Chinese and dressed in Chinese fashion. Their cooks prepared Chinese dishes and served food on Chinese-style pottery. Tea drinking, along with an elaborate tea ceremony, was imported from China. Japanese officials and scholars used Chinese characters to write official histories. Tang music and dances became very popular, as did gardens designed using Chinese influences.

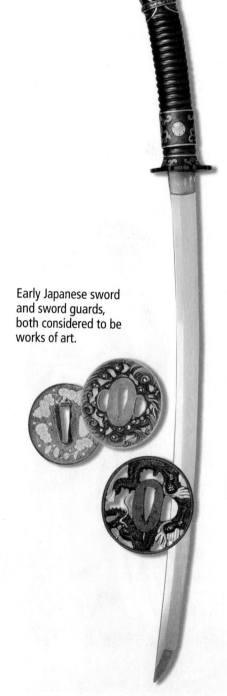

Early Japanese sword and sword guards, both considered to be works of art.

As Buddhism spread, the Japanese adopted pagoda architecture. Buddhist monasteries grew rich and powerful. Confucian ideas and ethics also took root. They included an emphasis on filial piety, the careful management of relationships between superior and inferior, and respect for learning.

Selective Borrowing Preserves Culture In time, the initial enthusiasm for everything Chinese died down. The Japanese kept some Chinese ways but discarded or modified others. This process is known as **selective borrowing.** Japan, for example, never accepted the Chinese civil service examination to choose officials based on merit. Instead, they maintained their tradition of inherited status through family position. Officials were the educated sons of nobles.

By the 800s, as Tang China began to decline, the Japanese court turned away from its model. After absorbing all they could from China, the Japanese spent the next 400 years digesting and modifying these cultural borrowings to produce their own unique civilization. The Japanese asserted their identity by revising the Chinese system of writing and adding **kana,** or phonetic symbols representing syllables. Japanese artists developed their own styles.

 Checkpoint How did Japan seek out Chinese influences?

The Heian Period

This blending of cultures took place from 794 to 1185. During this time, the imperial capital was in Heian (hay ahn), present-day Kyoto. There, emperors performed traditional religious ceremonies, while wealthy court families like the Fujiwara wielded real power. The Fujiwara married their daughters to the heirs to the throne, thus ensuring their authority.

Women Shape the Court At the Heian court, an elegant and sophisticated culture blossomed. Noblewomen and noblemen lived in a fairy-tale atmosphere of beautiful pavilions, gardens, and lotus pools. Elaborate rules of etiquette governed court ceremony. Courtiers dressed with extraordinary care in delicate, multicolored silk. Draping one's sleeve out a carriage window was a fine art.

Although men at court still studied Chinese, women were forbidden to learn the language. Despite these restrictions, it was Heian women who produced the most important works of Japanese literature of the period.

In the 900s, Sei Shonagon, a lady-in-waiting to the empress during the Heian period, wrote *The Pillow Book*. In a witty series of anecdotes and personal observations, she provides vivid details of court manners, amusements, decor, and dress. In one section, Shonagon discusses the importance of keeping up a good appearance at court:

Primary Source

66 Nothing can be worse than allowing the driver of one's ox-carriage to be poorly dressed. It does not matter too much if the other attendants are shabby, since they can remain at the rear of the carriage; but the drivers are bound to be noticed and, if they are badly turned out, it makes a painful impression. 99
—Sei Shonagon, *The Pillow Book*

Lady Murasaki Writes the World's First Novel The best-known Heian writer was Murasaki Shikibu. Her monumental work, *The Tale of Genji*, was the world's first full-length novel.

The Tale of Genji recounts the adventures and loves of the fictional Prince Genji and his son. In one scene, Genji moves with ease through the festivities at an elaborate "Chinese banquet." After dinner, "under the great cherry tree of the Southern court," the entertainment begins. The main event of the evening is a Chinese poetry contest. Genji and other guests are given a "rhyme word," which they must use to compose a poem in Chinese. Genji's poem is the hit of the banquet.

Elegant though they are, the Heian poems and romances are haunted by a sense of sadness. The writers lament that love does not last and the beauty of the world is soon gone. Perhaps this feeling of melancholy was prophetic. While noble men and women strolled through manicured gardens, clouds of rebellion and civil war were gathering.

✔ **Checkpoint**   How did women influence culture at the Heian court?

Warriors Establish Feudalism

Feudal warfare swept Japan in the 1400s. Disorder continued through the following century. Yet, despite the turmoil, a new Japanese culture arose. While the emperor presided over the splendid court at Heian, rival clans battled for control of the countryside. Local warlords and even some Buddhist temples formed armed bands loyal to them rather than to the central government. As these armies struggled for power, Japan evolved a feudal system. As in the feudal world of medieval Europe, a warrior aristocracy dominated Japanese society.

In theory, the emperor stood at the head of Japanese feudal society. In fact, he was a powerless, though revered, figurehead. Real power lay in the hands of the shogun, or supreme military commander. Minamoto Yoritomo was appointed shogun in 1192. He set up the Kamakura shogunate, the first of three military dynasties that would rule Japan for almost 700 years.

The Ways of the Warriors Often the shogun controlled only a small part of Japan. He distributed lands to vassal lords who agreed to support him with their armies in time of need. These great warrior lords were later called daimyo (DY myoh). They, in turn, granted land to lesser warriors called **samurai,** meaning "those who serve." Samurai were the fighting aristocracy of a war-torn land.

Like medieval Christian knights in Europe, samurai were heavily armed and trained in the skills of fighting. They also developed their own code of values. Known as **bushido,** or the "way of the warrior," the code emphasized honor, bravery, and absolute loyalty to one's lord.

Noblewomen Lose Ground At first, some noblewomen in Japanese feudal society trained in the military arts. A few even became legendary warriors. At times, some noblewomen supervised their family's estates.

As the age of the samurai progressed, however, the position of women declined steadily. When feudal warfare increased, inheritance was limited to sons. Unlike the European ideal of chivalry, the samurai code did not set women on a pedestal. The wife of a warrior had to accept the same hardships as her husband and owed the same loyalty to his overlord.

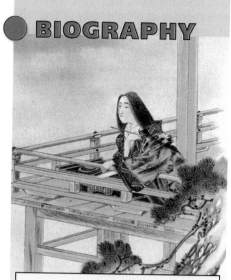

BIOGRAPHY

Murasaki Shikibu
"If only you were a boy, how happy I would be!" said Murasaki Shikibu's father. Although he was praising her intelligence, he was also revealing how Japan valued men over women. Growing up, Murasaki Shikibu (978[?]–1014[?]) studied with her brother. This fact was probably kept secret, because learning by girls was considered improper.

After the death of her husband, she went to the imperial court as a lady-in-waiting. There, as Lady Murasaki, she penned the world's first full-length novel, *The Tale of Genji*, a story of the Heian age that has been celebrated for more than a thousand years. **What personal qualities can you infer that Lady Murasaki possessed?**

WITNESS HISTORY VIDEO

Watch *The Samurai of Japan* on the **Witness History Discovery School**™ video program to learn about the samurai.

Discovery SCHOOL

Oda Nobunaga was a Japanese warrior who ended years of fighting by uniting half of Japan under his rule. Although he failed to bring all of Japan together his attempt at unification laid the groundwork for future success.

Peasants, Artisans, and Merchants Far below the samurai in the social hierarchy were the peasants, artisans, and merchants. Peasants, who made up 75 percent of the population, formed the backbone of feudal society in Japan. Peasant families cultivated rice and other crops on the estates of samurai. Some peasants also served as foot soldiers in feudal wars. On rare occasions, an able peasant soldier might rise through the ranks to become a samurai himself.

Artisans, such as armorers and swordmakers, provided necessary goods for the samurai class. Merchants had the lowest rank in Japanese feudal society. However, as you will see, their status gradually improved.

Japan Holds Off Mongols During the feudal age, most fighting took place between rival warlords, but the Mongol conquest of China and Korea also threatened Japan. When the Japanese refused to accept Mongol rule, Kublai Khan launched an invasion from Korea in 1274. A fleet carrying 30,000 troops arrived, but shortly afterwards a typhoon wrecked many Mongol ships and drove the invaders back to the mainland.

In 1281, the Mongols landed an even larger invasion force, but again a typhoon destroyed much of the Mongol fleet. The Japanese credited their miraculous delivery to the kamikaze (kah muh KAH zee), or divine winds. The Mongol failure reinforced the Japanese sense that they were a people set apart who enjoyed the special protection of the gods.

 Checkpoint What was bushido and why was it important?

The Tokugawas Unite Japan

The Kamakura shogunate crumbled in the aftermath of the Mongol invasions. A new dynasty took power in 1338, but the level of warfare increased after 1450. To defend their castles, daimyo gave arms to peasants as well as to samurai, which led to even more ruthless fighting. A saying of the time declared, "The warrior does not care if he's called a dog or beast. The main thing is winning."

Gradually, several powerful warriors united large parts of Japan. The first was Oda Nobunaga who by his death in 1582 had unified Japan's central region. By 1590, the brilliant general Toyotomi Hideyoshi (hee day YOH shee), a commoner by birth, had brought most of Japan under his control. He then tried, but failed, to conquer Korea and China. In 1600, the daimyo Tokugawa Ieyasu (toh koo gah wah ee AY ah soo) defeated his rivals to become master of Japan. Three years later, he was named shogun. The Tokugawa shogunate would go on to rule Japan until 1868.

Central Government Imposed The Tokugawa shoguns were determined to end feudal warfare. They maintained the outward forms of feudal

Feudal Society in Japan

Emperor
Held highest rank in society but had no political power

Shogun
Actual ruler

Daimyo
Large landowners

Samurai
Warriors loyal to daimyo

Peasants
Three-fourths of the population

Merchants
Lowest status but gradually gained influence

Artisans
Made swords and armor for the samurai class

Chart Skills The organizational chart above illustrates the social levels of feudal society in Japan. *According to the chart, who occupied the lowest position? How does the chart show this?*

CODE OF THE SAMURAI

"If you think of saving your life," it was said, "you had better not go to war at all." The true samurai was supposed to have no fear of death. Samurai prepared for hardship by going hungry or walking barefoot in the snow. For a samurai, it was said, "when his stomach is empty, it is a disgrace to feel hungry." A samurai who betrayed the code of bushido was expected to commit seppuku, or ritual suicide, rather than live without honor. Bushido covered nearly every aspect of a samurai's life, including how to walk, bow, and hold chopsticks. It was also important for a warrior to balance his life by engaging in such activities as writing poetry, painting, or reading Japanese literature. In the 1400s, samurai warlord Hojo Soun advised his samurai followers, "Hold literary skills in your left hand, martial skills in your right."

A Japanese ▶ family emblem

▼ Two samurai warriors duel in this woodblock print. The samurai wore colorful, patterned pants and robes under their armor. As weapons and armor progressed throughout the centuries, the sword and spear replaced the bow and arrows of the early samurai.

◀ Samurai warriors wore helmets with horns or antlers and fierce-looking masks to scare off the enemy. Their body armor was made of metal or leather scales that were tied together with string.

Thinking Critically

1. **Draw Conclusions** What might be the advantages and disadvantages of the type of armor used by a samurai?
2. **Synthesize Information** How did the rules that governed the samurai affect their way of life?

society but imposed central government control on all Japan. For this reason, their system of government is called centralized feudalism.

The Tokugawas created a unified, orderly society. To control the daimyo, they required these great lords to live in the shogun's capital at Edo (present-day Tokyo) every other year. A daimyo's wife and children had to remain in Edo full time, giving the shogun a powerful check on the entire family. The shogun also forbade daimyo to repair their castles or marry without permission.

Zen Gardening
Zen beliefs shaped Japanese culture in many ways. At Zen monasteries, upper-class men learned to express devotion to nature in such activities as landscape gardening. *How did Zen gardening reflect Zen values?*

New laws fixed the old social order rigidly in place and upheld a strict moral code. Only samurai were allowed to serve in the military or hold government jobs. They were expected to follow the traditions of bushido. Peasants had to remain on the land. People in lower classes were forbidden to wear luxuries such as silk clothing.

The Economy Booms While the shoguns tried to hold back social change, the Japanese economy grew by leaps and bounds. With peace restored to the countryside, agriculture improved and expanded. New seeds, tools, and the use of fertilizer led to a greater output of crops.

Food surpluses supported rapid population growth. Towns sprang up on the lands around the castles of daimyo. Edo grew into a booming city, where artisans and merchants flocked to supply the needs of the daimyo and their families.

Trade flourished within Japan. New roads linked castle towns and Edo. Each year, daimyo and their servants traveled to and from the capital, creating a demand for food and services along the route. In the cities, a wealthy merchant class emerged. In accordance with Confucian tradition, merchants had low social status. Japanese merchants, however, were able to gain influence by lending money to daimyo and samurai. Sometimes, merchants further improved their social position by arranging to marry their daughters into the samurai class.

✓ **Checkpoint** How did the Tokugawas set up centralized feudalism?

Zen Buddhism Shapes Culture

During Japan's feudal age, a Buddhist sect from China won widespread acceptance among samurai. Known in Japan as **Zen,** it emphasized self-reliance, meditation, and devotion to duty.

Zen had seemingly contradictory traditions. Zen monks were great scholars, yet they valued the uncluttered mind and <u>stressed</u> the importance of reaching a moment of "non-knowing." Zen stressed compassion for all, yet samurai fought to kill. In Zen monasteries, monks sought to experience absolute freedom, yet rigid rules were in place.

Vocabulary Builder
<u>stressed</u>—(stresd) *vt.* emphasized

Zen Buddhists believed that people could seek enlightenment through meditation and through the precise performance of everyday tasks. For example, the elaborate rituals of the tea ceremony reflected Zen values of peace, simplicity, and love of beauty. Zen reverence for nature also influenced the development of fine landscape paintings.

✔ **Checkpoint** How was Zen Buddhism similar to bushido?

Artistic Traditions Change

Cities such as Edo and Osaka were home to an explosion in the arts and theater. At stylish entertainment quarters, sophisticated nobles mixed with the urban middle class. Urban culture emphasized luxuries and pleasures and differed greatly from the feudal culture that had dominated Japan for centuries.

New Drama Develops In the 1300s, feudal culture had produced Noh plays performed on a square, wooden stage without scenery. Men wore elegant carved masks while a chorus chanted important lines to musical accompaniment. The action was slow, and each movement had a special meaning. Many Noh plays presented Zen Buddhist themes, emphasizing the need to renounce selfish desires. Others recounted fairy tales or the struggles between powerful feudal lords.

In the 1600s, towns gave rise to a popular new form of drama called Kabuki. Kabuki was influenced by Noh plays, but it was less refined and included comedy or melodrama. Puppet plays, known as bunraku, were also enormously popular in towns. A narrator told a story while handlers silently manipulated near-life-sized puppets. Bunraku plays catered to popular middle-class tastes.

Painting and Printmaking Japanese paintings often reflected the influence of Chinese landscape paintings, yet Japanese artists developed their own styles. On magnificent scrolls, painters boldly recreated historical events, such as the Mongol invasions.

In the 1600s, the vigorous urban culture produced a flood of colorful woodblock prints to satisfy middle-class tastes. Some woodblock artists produced humorous prints. Their fresh colors and simple lines give us a strong sense of the pleasures of town life in Japan.

✔ **Checkpoint** What new art forms catered to the growing middle class?

SECTION 4 Assessment

Progress Monitoring *Online*
For: Self-quiz with vocabulary practice
Web Code: naa-1241

Terms, People, and Places

1. For each term, person, or place listed at the beginning of the section, write a sentence explaining its significance.

Note Taking

2. **Reading Skill: Categorize** Use your completed table to answer the Focus Question: What internal and external factors shaped Japan's civilization, and what characterized Japan's feudal age?

Comprehension and Critical Thinking

3. **Make Comparisons** How was the Japanese development of kana similar to the Korean development of hangul?

4. **Analyze Information** How did the Japanese preserve their own identity and culture?

5. **Recognize Causes and Effects** Describe three results of the centralized feudalism imposed by the Tokugawas.

● **Writing About History**

Quick Write: Write a Thesis Statement and Introduction Review this section by thinking about cause and effect relationships in Japanese history. Write a thesis statement and introductory paragraph for an essay that discusses a cause and effect in ancient Japan. Remember that an introduction should map out what the essay will discuss.

Kabuki Theater

An *onnagata*, or actor who plays the part of a woman ▼

Kabuki is one of the most popular styles of traditional Japanese theater. Kabuki emerged in towns in the early 1600s and was less refined than the Noh plays that had previously been performed for feudal audiences. While actors in Noh plays use slow movements to tell a story, Kabuki actors often use lively and exaggerated movements. Although a woman named Okuni was credited with creating Kabuki, women have been banned from playing Kabuki roles for most of the theater's 400-year history.

▼ The first Kabuki plays were staged in a dry riverbed in Kyoto and featured female casts and dancing. A 1629 edict barred women from acting in Kabuki plays. With women banned from Kabuki, men known as *onnagata* played female roles. The *onnagata* achieved their impersonations with the help of elaborate costumes and make-up. Today, Kabuki artists perform a repertoire of about 300 plays involving everything from tragedies to light family comedies.

As Kabuki developed, ▶ various acting styles emerged. One of the best known was the *aragoto* or "rough business" style, which emphasized aggressiveness and masculinity. Actors employing this style would often strike an exaggerated pose known as a *mie*, which involved crossing the eyes and making a dramatic face.

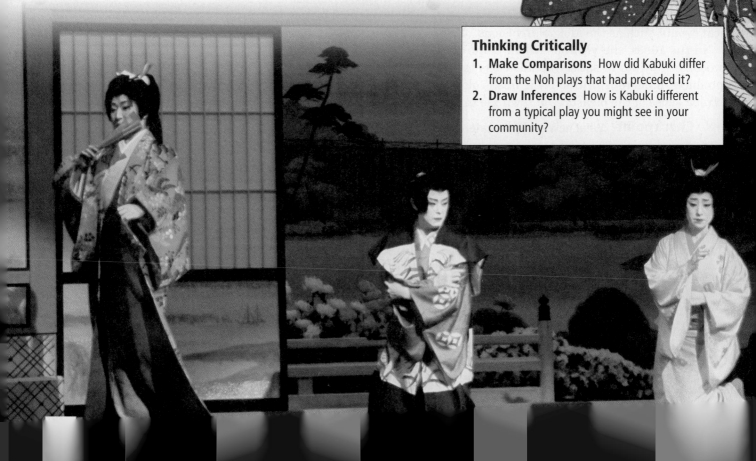

Thinking Critically
1. **Make Comparisons** How did Kabuki differ from the Noh plays that had preceded it?
2. **Draw Inferences** How is Kabuki different from a typical play you might see in your community?

Burmese statue of
King Anawrahta

WITNESS HISTORY 🔊 AUDIO

Buddhism in Burma

According to the chronicles of early Burma (modern Myanmar), King Anawrahta converted to Theravada Buddhism due to the influence of a monk named Shin Arahan.

66 'Preach [to] me somewhat—yea, but a little—of the Law preached by the Lord, the Master!' And Shin Arahan preached the Law, beginning with the things not to be neglected. . . . Then the king's heart was full of faith, steadfast, and immovable; faith sank into him as oil filtered a hundred times soaks into cotton. 99
—*The Glass Palace Chronicle of the Kings of Burma*

Focus Question How was Southeast Asia affected by the cultures of both China and India?

Diverse Cultures of Southeast Asia

 Performance Standards

• **SSWH2d** Explain the impact of Confucianism on Chinese culture.

Terms, People, and Places

matrilineal
stupa
paddy

Note Taking

Reading Skill: Summarize As you read the section, prepare an outline like the one below to summarize the diverse characteristics of Southeast Asia.

> I. Geography of Southeast Asia
>   A. Location
>   1. Mainland set apart by mountains and plateaus
>   2.
>   B. Trade routes in the southern seas

Buddhism was one of many exports from India that had a profound effect on the peoples of Southeast Asia. Located between China and India, the region known today as Southeast Asia was strongly influenced by both of these powerful neighbors. Even so, the distinct cultures of Southeast Asia retained their own unique identities.

Geography of Southeast Asia

Southeast Asia is made up of two major regions. The first, mainland Southeast Asia, includes several peninsulas that jut south between India and China. Today, this region is home to Myanmar, Thailand, Cambodia, Laos, Vietnam, and part of Malaysia. The second region, island Southeast Asia, consists of more than 20,000 islands scattered between the Indian Ocean and the South China Sea. It includes the present-day nations of Indonesia, Singapore, Brunei (broo NY), and the Philippines.

Separated by Mountains The mainland is separated from the rest of Asia by mountains and high plateaus. Still, traders and invaders did push overland into the region. Mountains also separate the four main river valleys of Southeast Asia—the Irrawaddy (ihr uh WAH dee), Chao Phraya (chow PRY uh), Mekong, and Red. These river valleys were home to early civilizations.

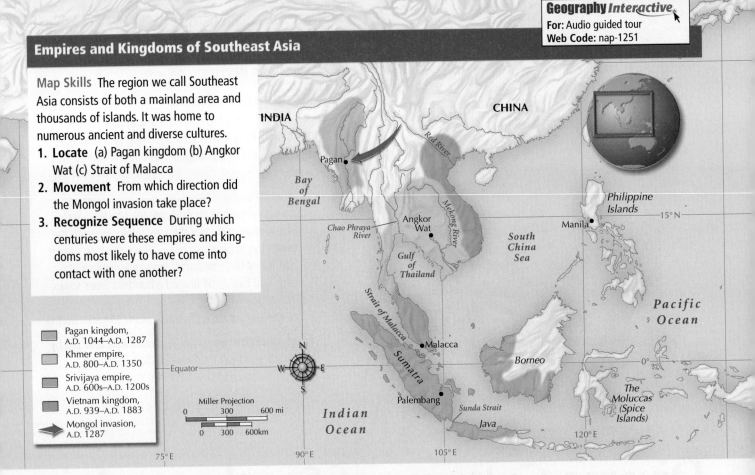

Empires and Kingdoms of Southeast Asia

Map Skills The region we call Southeast Asia consists of both a mainland area and thousands of islands. It was home to numerous ancient and diverse cultures.

1. **Locate** (a) Pagan kingdom (b) Angkor Wat (c) Strait of Malacca
2. **Movement** From which direction did the Mongol invasion take place?
3. **Recognize Sequence** During which centuries were these empires and kingdoms most likely to have come into contact with one another?

Pagan kingdom, A.D. 1044–A.D. 1287

Khmer empire, A.D. 800–A.D. 1350

Srivijaya empire, A.D. 600s–A.D. 1200s

Vietnam kingdom, A.D. 939–A.D. 1883

Mongol invasion, A.D. 1287

Miller Projection

INDIA

CHINA

Red River

Pagan

Bay of Bengal

Chao Phraya River

Angkor Wat

Mekong River

Gulf of Thailand

Strait of Malacca

Sumatra

Malacca

Palembang

Sunda Strait

Java

Indian Ocean

South China Sea

Borneo

Manila

Philippine Islands

Pacific Ocean

The Moluccas (Spice Islands)

Geography Interactive
For: Audio guided tour
Web Code: nap-1251

Island Southeast Asia has long been of strategic importance. All seaborne trade between China and India had to pass through either the Malacca or Sunda straits. Whoever commanded these straits controlled rich trade routes.

Trade Routes in the Southern Seas The monsoons, or seasonal winds, shaped trading patterns in the southern seas. Ships traveled northeast in summer and southwest in winter. Between seasons, while waiting for the winds to shift, merchants harbored their vessels in Southeast Asian ports, which became important centers of trade and culture. Soon, an international trade network linked India, Southeast Asia, and China to East Africa and the Middle East. Originally, the key product of Southeast Asia was spices, and only a fraction of those traded in the region made their way to the markets in Europe.

Early Traditions The peoples of Southeast Asia developed their own cultures before Indian or Chinese influences shaped the region. At Bang Chiang in Thailand, archaeologists have found jars and bronze bracelets at least 5,000 years old. This evidence is challenging old theories about when civilization began in the region.

Over the centuries, diverse ethnic groups speaking many languages settled in Southeast Asia. Living in isolated villages, they followed their own religious and cultural patterns. Many societies were built around the nuclear family rather than the extended families of India and China.

Women had greater equality in Southeast Asia than elsewhere in Asia. Female merchants took part in the spice trade, gaining fame for their skill in bargaining, finance, and languages. In some port cities, they gained enough wealth and influence to become rulers. **Matrilineal** descent, or inheritance through the mother, was an accepted custom in Southeast Asia. Women also had some freedom in choosing or divorcing their marriage partners. Even after Indian and Chinese influences arrived, women retained their traditional rights.

✓ **Checkpoint** How did geography make Southeast Asia strategically important?

Indian Culture Spreads to Southeast Asia

Indian merchants and Hindu priests filtered into Southeast Asia, slowly spreading their culture. Later, Buddhist monks and scholars introduced Theravada beliefs. Following the path of trade and religion came the influence of writing, law, government, art, architecture, and farming.

Indian Influence Reaches Its Peak In the early centuries A.D., Indian traders settled in Southeast Asian port cities in growing numbers. They gave presents to local rulers and married into influential families. Trade brought prosperity as merchants exchanged products such as cotton cloth, jewels, and perfume for raw materials such as timber, spices, and gold.

In time, local Indian families exercised considerable power. Also, people from Southeast Asia visited India as pilgrims or students. As these contacts increased, Indian beliefs and ideas won widespread acceptance. Indian influence reached its peak between 500 and 1000.

Indians Bring Islam Long after Hinduism and Buddhism took root in Southeast Asia, Indians carried a third religion, Islam, into the region. By the 1200s, Muslims ruled northern India. From there, traders spread Islamic beliefs and Muslim culture throughout the islands of Indonesia and as far east as the Philippines. Today, Indonesia has the largest Muslim population of any nation in the world. Arab merchants, too, spread the new faith. The prevalence of Islam in lands surrounding the Indian Ocean contributed to the growth of a stable, thriving trade network.

✓ **Checkpoint** What changes occurred as India increased contact with Southeast Asia?

New Kingdoms and Empires Emerge

The blend of Indian influences with local cultures in time produced a series of kingdoms and empires in Southeast Asia. Some of these would rival those of India.

The Shwezigon Pagoda
King Anawrahta made the Pagan kingdom a Buddhist center and had many stupas and pagodas built. Shown here are the elaborate interior columns at the famous Shwezigon Pagoda. *What does this pagoda suggest about the importance of Buddhism?*

Angkor Wat
Angkor was the capital of the Khmer empire for more than 500 years. Built during this time were many impressive complexes of buildings. The most famous is Angkor Wat (above right), which still stands today in Cambodia. Inside, the temple walls are covered with detailed bas-relief carvings (above). *What does Angkor Wat reveal about the strength of the Khmer empire?*

The Pagan Kingdom Arises

The kingdom of Pagan (puh GAHN) arose in the fertile rice-growing Irrawaddy Valley in present-day Myanmar. In 1044, King Anawrahta (an ow RAHT uh) united the region. He is credited with bringing Buddhism to the Burman people. Buddhism had reached nearby cultures long before, but Anawrahta made Pagan a major Buddhist center. He filled his capital city with magnificent **stupas,** or dome-shaped shrines, at about the same time that people in medieval Europe were beginning to build Gothic cathedrals.

Pagan flourished for some 200 years after Anawrahta's death, but fell in 1287 to conquering Mongols. When the Burmans finally threw off foreign rule, they looked back with pride to the great days of Pagan.

The Khmer Empire

Indian influences also helped shape the Khmer (kuh MEHR) empire, which reached its peak between 800 and 1350. Its greatest rulers controlled much of present-day Cambodia, Thailand, and Malaysia. The Khmer people adapted Indian writing, mathematics, architecture, and art. Khmer rulers became pious Hindus. Like the princes and emperors of India, they saw themselves as god-kings. Most ordinary people, however, preferred Buddhism.

In the 1100s, King Suryavarman II (sur yuh VAHR mun) built the great temple complex at Angkor Wat. The ruins that survive today, though overgrown with jungle and pocked by the bullets of recent wars, are among the most impressive in the world. Hundreds of carved figures tell Hindu myths and glorify the king. Although the images of Vishnu, Shiva, and the Buddha reflect strong Indian influence, the style is uniquely Khmer.

Srivijaya Empire Flourishes

In Indonesia, the trading empire of Srivijaya (sree wih JAW yuh) flourished from the 600s to the 1200s. Srivijaya controlled the Strait of Malacca, which was vital to shipping. Both Hinduism and Buddhism reached this island empire. As elsewhere in Southeast Asia, however, the local people often blended Indian beliefs into their own forms of worship based on nature spirits.

Later, Islam spread to Sumatra, Java, and other islands. Local rulers adopted the new religion, which cemented commercial links with other Muslim trading centers around the Indian Ocean.

✓ **Checkpoint** How did India influence the Pagan kingdom and the Khmer and Srivijaya empires?

Vietnam Emerges

In most of Southeast Asia, Indian influence outweighed Chinese influence. Indian traditions spread mostly through trade rather than conquest. China, however, sent military forces to conquer the neighboring state of Annam (now the northern part of Vietnam). The heart of northern Vietnam was the Red River delta, around present-day Hanoi. There, the river irrigated fertile rice **paddies,** or fields, which provided food for a growing population.

Chinese Domination In 111 B.C., Han armies conquered the region, and China remained in control for the next 1,000 years. During that time, the Vietnamese absorbed Confucian ideas. They adopted the Chinese civil service system and built a government bureaucracy similar to that found in China. Vietnamese nobles adopted the custom of speaking and writing the Chinese language. Unlike the rest of Southeast Asia, where Theravada Buddhism had the strongest <u>impact</u>, Vietnam adopted Mahayana beliefs from China. Daoism also helped shape Vietnamese society.

Vocabulary Builder
<u>impact</u>—(IM pakt) *n.* effect

The Vietnamese Preserve Their Identity Despite these powerful Chinese influences, the Vietnamese preserved a strong sense of their separate identity. In A.D. 39, two noble sisters, Trung Trac and Trung Nhi, led an uprising that briefly drove the Chinese occupiers from the land. They tried to restore a simpler form of government based on ancient Vietnamese traditions. To this day, the Trung sisters are remembered as great martyrs and heroes. Finally in 939, as the Tang dynasty collapsed in China, Vietnam was able to break free from China. Thereafter, the Vietnamese turned back repeated Chinese efforts to re-conquer their land, but they still remained a tributary state of China for years to come.

✓ **Checkpoint** How did China influence Vietnam?

SECTION **5** Assessment

Progress Monitoring Online
For: Self-quiz with vocabulary practice
Web Code: naa-1251

Terms, People, and Places
1. For each term, person, or place listed at the beginning of the section, write a sentence explaining its significance.

Note Taking
2. **Reading Skill: Summarize** Use your completed outline to answer the Focus Question: How was Southeast Asia affected by the cultures of both China and India?

Comprehension and Critical Thinking
3. **Analyze Information** How did geography make Southeast Asia of strategic importance?
4. **Make Comparisons** How did the spread of Indian influence differ from the spread of Chinese influence in Southeast Asia?
5. **Identify Central Issues** How did Vietnam retain its own identity despite adapting much of China's culture?

● **Writing About History**
Quick Write: Gather Evidence to Support Thesis Statement Write a thesis statement on the impact of India on Southeast Asia. Review the section and list facts that support the thesis statement.

Quick Study Guide

 SSWH2d

■ Cultural Achievements of the Tang and Song Dynasties

- **Calligraphy** Artists sought balance and harmony through the mastery of simple strokes and lines.
- **Chinese landscape painting** Painters sought to capture the spiritual essence of nature.
- **Porcelain** The Chinese perfected skills in making porcelain that would be prized around the world.
- **Architecture** Pagodas, influenced by Indian Buddhism, graced the landscape.
- **Literature** Writers created short stories and thousands of poems.

■ The Mongol and Ming Empires

c.1200: Mongols unite warring tribes and begin conquering China.	Genghis Khan builds the Mongol empire by taking land from Russia to China.	1279: Kublai Khan topples last Song emperor.
Kublai Khan expands the empire to its largest size. Mongols attempt to run the empire without the Chinese, with some success.	1368: Chinese peasant leader pushes out Mongols and founds the Ming dynasty.	Ming rule reasserts a Chinese government. The economy booms during a period of cultural flowering and overseas exploration.

■ China's Influence on Its Neighbors

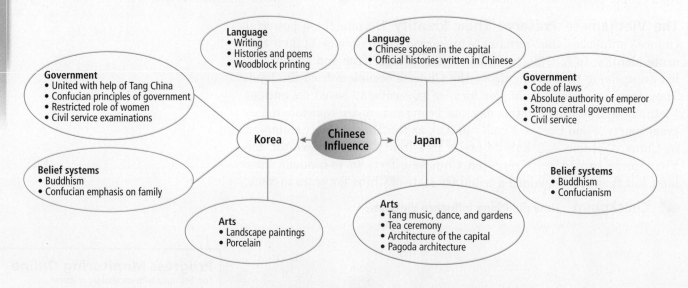

Government
- United with help of Tang China
- Confucian principles of government
- Restricted role of women
- Civil service examinations

Language
- Writing
- Histories and poems
- Woodblock printing

Language
- Chinese spoken in the capital
- Official histories written in Chinese

Government
- Code of laws
- Absolute authority of emperor
- Strong central government
- Civil service

Belief systems
- Buddhism
- Confucian emphasis on family

Korea ← Chinese Influence → Japan

Belief systems
- Buddhism
- Confucianism

Arts
- Landscape paintings
- Porcelain

Arts
- Tang music, dance, and gardens
- Tea ceremony
- Architecture of the capital
- Pagoda architecture

■ Events From 500–1650

500s	618	668	794	960
Buddhism is introduced to Japan.	The Tang dynasty begins in China.	Silla rulers unite Korea.	The Japanese royal court moves to Heian.	The Song dynasty is founded in China.

Chapter Events
Global Events

500	700	900

527
Justinian becomes ruler of the Byzantine empire.

800
Charlemagne is crowned emperor by the pope.

Concept Connector

Essential Question Review

To connect prior knowledge with what you have learned in this chapter, answer the questions below in your Concept Connector journal. Use the journal in the Reading and Note Taking Study Guide to record your answers (or go to www.phschool.com **Web Code**: nad-1207). In addition, record information about the following concepts:

- Technology: printing press
- Technology: gunpowder
- Trade: Chinese trade in southern China and up coast

1. **Empire** Tang rulers carried empire building to new heights, conquering Vietnam, Tibet, and Korea. Within China, Tang emperors instituted a system of land reform. How did foreign conquests and land reform strengthen the economy and the Tang empire? Think about:
   - tributary states
   - education
   - central government

2. **Geography's Impact** A nation's geography can determine its culture and even its government. Geography shaped how Japanese people lived, much as it determined how Mesopotamians lived between the Tigris and Euphrates rivers. Describe the impact of geography in Japan and in Mesopotamia. Think about the following:
   - ways of living
   - natural disasters
   - trade

3. **Cultural Diffusion** When Kublai Khan established his capital in what is now Beijing, he decreed that only Mongols could serve in the military. What might have been the outcome if he had allowed Chinese soldiers to serve?

■ Connections to Today

1. **Economics: Rapid Growth in China** During the Ming dynasty, China's economy grew rapidly. Agriculture, trade, and manufacturing created much wealth. Today, China is going through another economic boom. Find articles about China in newspapers or news magazines. Gather statistics that demonstrate how China's economy is expanding. Write a paragraph about China's economy.

2. **Political Systems: A Peninsula Divided** Korean unity lasted almost 1,300 years. But today, the Korean peninsula is again divided into hostile camps. While North Korea is a communist country, South Korea is a democracy. Both North and South Korea want to reunify Korea. Both have massed soldiers and equipment along the border between them. The United States is South Korea's most powerful ally. North Korea maintains close ties to Communist China and has worked to develop nuclear weapons. As a result, Korea is one of the world's hot spots. The Korean War was fought there (1950–1953), and there is a fear that the troubled Korean Peninsula may be the site of more bloodshed. How is today's division of Korea different from that of the early kingdoms?

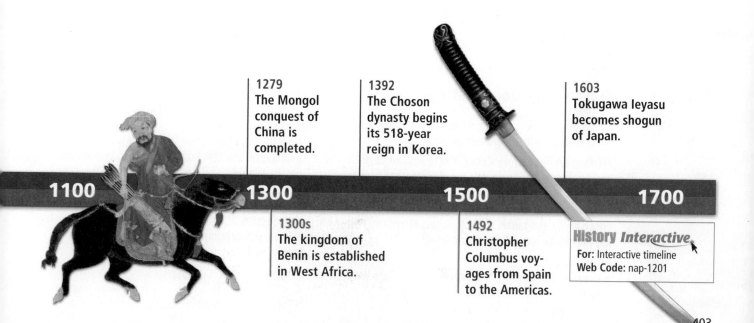

1279
The Mongol conquest of China is completed.

1392
The Choson dynasty begins its 518-year reign in Korea.

1603
Tokugawa Ieyasu becomes shogun of Japan.

1100   1300   1500   1700

1300s
The kingdom of Benin is established in West Africa.

1492
Christopher Columbus voyages from Spain to the Americas.

History Interactive
For: Interactive timeline
Web Code: nap-1201

Chapter Assessment

Terms, People, and Places

Match the following terms with the definitions below. You will not use all the terms.

literacy rate	stupa
land reform	Marco Polo
hangul	Kublai Khan
archipelago	pagoda
samurai	matrilineal

1. dome-shaped shrine
2. percentage of people who can read or write
3. the Mongol leader who unseated the last Song emperor
4. chain of islands
5. breakup of large agricultural holdings for redistribution among peasants
6. alphabet that uses symbols to represent the sounds of spoken Korean
7. multistoried Buddhist temple with its origins in India
8. member of the warrior class in Japanese feudal society

Main Ideas

Section 1 (pp. 368–375)
9. How did Tang rulers carry empire building to new heights?

Section 2 (pp. 376–382)
10. What impact did Mongol rule have on Asia?

Section 3 (pp. 383–386)
11. Describe the location of Korea in relation to China and Japan.

Section 4 (pp. 387–396)
12. How has Japan's island geography affected its history?
13. How did life in Japan change under the Tokugawas?

Section 5 (pp. 397–401)
14. Identify two early traditions of people in Southeast Asia.

Chapter Focus Question
15. How did China's culture develop and influence its neighbors in East and Southeast Asia?

Critical Thinking

16. **Draw Conclusions** How might a map of China before the Tang dynasty differ from a map of China afterward? Give two examples.
17. **Synthesize Information** How was the Mongol period both destructive and constructive?
18. **Analyze Information** (a) Describe the Japanese practice of selective borrowing. (b) What are some of the benefits and disadvantages of borrowing from other cultures?
19. **Geography and History** In what ways are the geographies of Japan and Korea similar? What similar effects has geography had on these nations?
20. **Make Comparisons** How were the kingdoms and empires in Southeast Asia similar and different?
21. **Analyzing Visuals** Ming dynasty artisans created a unique form of blue and white porcelain, as shown here. How does this vase build on earlier Chinese achievements?

● Writing About History

In this chapter's five Section Assessments, you developed skills to write an expository essay.

Writing an Expository Essay The regions of East and Southeast Asia were influenced by neighboring countries such as China and India. Write an expository essay to compare and contrast the ways China influenced Korea and Japan. Consult page SH10 of the Writing Handbook for additional help.

Prewriting
• Draw a Venn diagram to compare and contrast the cultures of Korea and Japan as influenced by China.

Remember to list common factors in the shared center of the diagram.

Drafting
• Now that you have identified points of comparison and contrast, decide how you want to present the details. Would it make more sense to use subject-by-subject organization or point-by-point organization?
• Write a thesis statement and an attention-grabbing introduction.
• Provide elaboration to fully develop your points of comparison and contrast.

Revising
• Use the guidelines for revising your report on page SH12 of the Writing Handbook.

Prepare for the GHSGT

Shinto: "The Way of the Spirits"

Shinto originated in prehistoric times. At the heart of Shinto is the belief in spirit beings that govern the natural world. Many shrines and festivals are dedicated to these kami. Over the centuries, Confucianism, Daoism, and especially Buddhism, influenced Shinto. The native religion absorbed elements of these foreign religions, while remaining uniquely Japanese, as the documents here illustrate.

Document A

▼ People walk through a wooden torii, or tall shrine gate, in front of the Meiji Shinto Shrine, Japan.

Document B

"At this time the heavenly deities, all with one command, said to the two deities Izanagi-nö-mikötö and Izanami- nö-mikötö: 'Complete and solidify this drifting land!'

Giving them the Heavenly Jeweled Spear, they entrusted the mission to them. Thereupon, the two deities stood on the Heavenly Floating Bridge and, lowering the jeweled spear, stirred with it. They stirred the brine with a churning-churning sound; and when they lifted up [the spear] again, the brine dripping down from the tip of the spear piled up and became an island. This was the island Onögörö."

—From *Kojiki*, an ancient Shinto text

Document C

"Speaking in general, it may be said that kami signifies, in the first place, the deities of heaven and earth that appear in the ancient records and also the kami spirits of the shrines where they are worshipped. . . . It also includes such objects as birds, beasts, trees, plants, seas, mountains, and so forth. In ancient usage, anything whatsoever which was outside the ordinary, which possessed superior power, or which was awe-inspiring was called kami. . . . It is needless to say that among human beings who are called kami the successive generations of sacred emperors are all included."

—Motoori Norinaga (1730–1801), a great Japanese scholar

Document D

"The Japanese pray to kami (deities) for longevity, health, wealth, fame, and all other world benefits, while they turn to *hotoke* (Buddha) for their personal religious salvation."

—Luis de Almeida, a Portuguese Jesuit visitor, 1565

Analyzing Documents

Use your knowledge of Shinto and Documents A, B, C, and D to answer the questions below.

1. The people in Document A are most likely visiting the shrine to
   A attend a funeral.
   B visit relatives.
   C pray to the kami and worship.
   D ensure good karma.

2. What does the legend in Document B describe?
   A the creation of Japan
   B the creation of the Japanese people
   C the gift of rice from the kami to the Japanese people
   D the gift of fire from the kami to the Japanese people

3. According to Document C, the emperors of Japan are
   A spirits of the shrines.
   B objects in nature.
   C kami.
   D deities of heaven and earth.

4. In what ways is Shinto a unique religion? Use these documents along with information from the chapter in your answer. (Hint: You may compare Shinto to a religion with which you are familiar.)

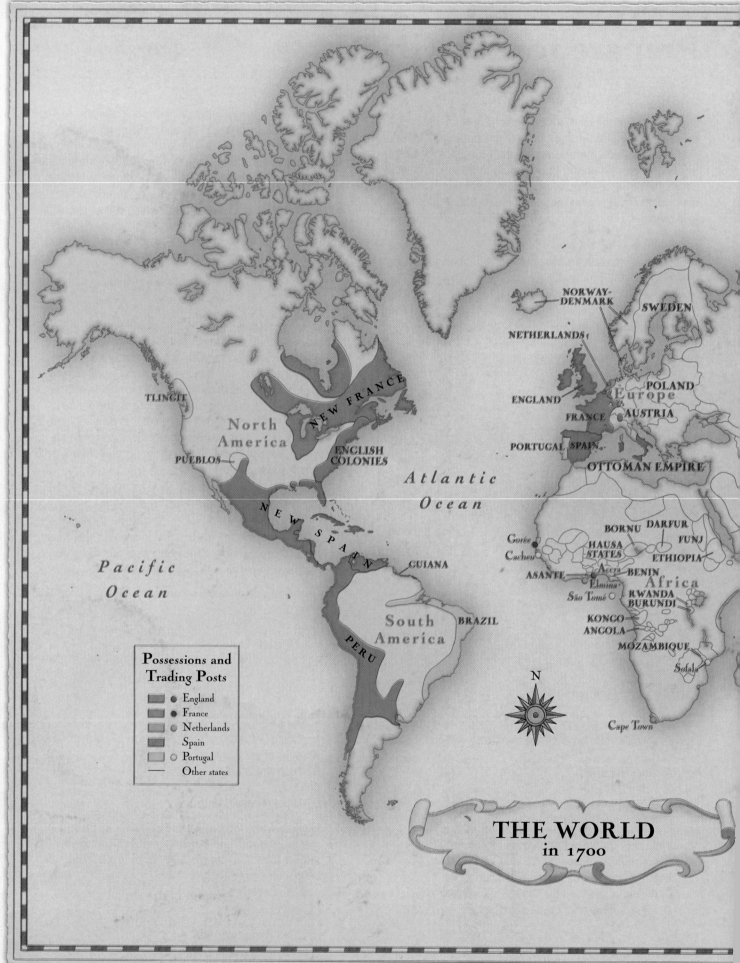

THE WORLD
in 1700

**Possessions and
Trading Posts**

- England
- France
- Netherlands
- Spain
- Portugal
- Other states

North America

TLINGIT

PUEBLOS

NEW FRANCE

ENGLISH COLONIES

NEW SPAIN

Pacific Ocean

Atlantic Ocean

GUIANA

South America

BRAZIL

PERU

N

Europe

NORWAY-DENMARK

SWEDEN

NETHERLANDS

ENGLAND

POLAND

FRANCE

AUSTRIA

PORTUGAL SPAIN

OTTOMAN EMPIRE

Gorée
Cacheu

BORNU DARFUR

HAUSA STATES

FUNJ

ETHIOPIA

ASANTE

Accra

BENIN

Elmina

Africa

São Tomé

RWANDA
BURUNDI

KONGO
ANGOLA

MOZAMBIQUE

Sofala

Cape Town

RUSSIAN EMPIRE

Asia

CHINESE
EMPIRE

PERSIAN
EMPIRE

MUGHAL
EMPIRE
　Bombay
Goa
Madras
SIAM
Cochin　Pondicherry
CEYLON

BURMA

Deshima　JAPAN

Macao
PHILIPPINE
ISLANDS
ANNAM

Pacific
Ocean

Indian
Ocean

Bourbon

DUTCH EAST INDIES
PORTUGUESE
TIMOR

Australia

Mercator Projection
0 　　1,000 　　2,000 miles

0 　1,000 　2,000 kilometers
Scale at the Equator

Geography *Interactive*
For: Audio guided tour
Web Code: nap-3000

Painting a Renaissance Marvel

For four years, painter and sculptor Michelangelo stood on top of a high scaffold, painting the enormous ceiling of the Sistine Chapel in Rome. He hadn't wanted to take the job, but the pope had insisted. Michelangelo wrote a poem about the work:

“My belly is shoved up under my chin . . .
My beard faces skyward and the back of my neck is wedged into my spine . . .
My face is richly carpeted with a thick layer of paint from my brush . . .
I don't want to be here and I'm no painter.”

Listen to the Witness History audio to hear more about Michelangelo's work and how it came to symbolize the great period of cultural rebirth that transformed Europe.

◄ An art restorer uses computer technology to restore a portion of the frescoes in the Sistine Chapel.

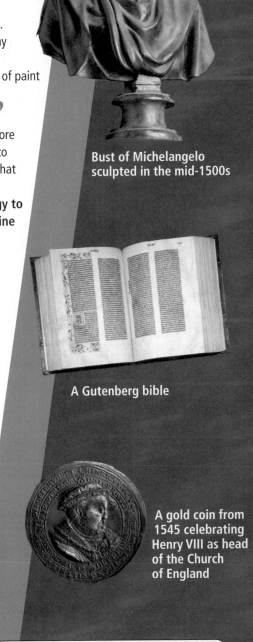

Bust of Michelangelo sculpted in the mid-1500s

A Gutenberg bible

A gold coin from 1545 celebrating Henry VIII as head of the Church of England

GA Performance Standards

Chapter Focus Question How did the Renaissance shape European art, thought, and religion?

Section 1
The Renaissance in Italy
SSWH9a, SSWH9b, SSWH9c

Section 2
The Renaissance in the North
SSWH9c, SSWH9c, SSWH9g

Section 3
The Protestant Reformation
SSWH9d

Section 4
Reformation Ideas Spread
SSWH9e, SSWH9f

Section 5
The Scientific Revolution
SSWH13a

Use the **Quick Study Timeline** at the end of this chapter to preview chapter events.

Concept Connector ONLINE

To explore Essential Questions related to this chapter, go to PHSchool.com
Web Code: nad-1307

Vasari designed the Uffizi Gallery in Florence, which houses his self-portrait.

A detail from the Uffizi

WITNESS HISTORY ◀)) AUDIO

An Artist Becomes a Biographer

In 1546, a young artist named Giorgio Vasari dined at the Cardinal's residence in Rome. The conversation turned to the amazing artistic achievement of Renaissance Italy. Vasari decided to record a tribute to all the important Italian artists who had contributed to this remarkably creative time period. Four years later, Vasari published his book *Lives of the Most Eminent Painters, Sculptors, and Architects.* A true "Renaissance man"— he was an able painter and architect as well as a writer—Vasari also became a biographer and historian of his era.

Focus Question What were the ideals of the Renaissance, and how did Italian artists and writers reflect these ideals?

The Renaissance in Italy

 Performance Standards

- **SSWH9a** Explain changes that contributed to rise of Florence.
- **SSWH9b** Identify Leonardo da Vinci's artistic and scientific achievements and the meaning of "Renaissance man;" Identify Michelangelo's achievements.
- **SSWH9c** Explain the ideas of Petrach.

Terms, People, and Places

humanism	Leonardo
humanities	Michelangelo
Petrarch	Raphael
Florence	Baldassare Castiglione
patron	Niccolò Machiavelli
perspective	

Note Taking

Reading Skill: Identify Main Ideas As you read, create an outline like the one below to record main ideas about the Italian Renaissance.

> I. What was the Renaissance?
> A. A changing worldview
> 1.
> 2.
> B. A spirit of adventure

A new age had dawned in Western Europe, given expression by remarkable artists and thinkers. Europeans called this age the Renaissance, meaning "rebirth." It began in the 1300s and reached its peak around 1500. The Renaissance marked the transition from medieval times to the early modern world.

What Was the Renaissance?

The Renaissance was a time of creativity and great change in many areas—political, social, economic, and cultural. It marked a slow shift from an agricultural to an urban society, in which trade assumed greater importance than in the past. It was also a time when creative thinking and new technology let people <u>comprehend</u> and describe their world more accurately.

A New Worldview Evolves During the Renaissance, creative minds set out to transform their own age. Their era, they felt, was a time of rebirth after what they saw as the disorder and disunity of the medieval world.

Renaissance thinkers had a reawakened interest in the classical learning of Greece and Rome, which medieval scholars had preserved. They continued to use Latin as the language of the Church as well as for scholarship. Yet they produced new attitudes toward culture and learning. Medieval scholars had focused more on religious beliefs and spirituality. In contrast, Renaissance thinkers explored the richness and variety of human experience in the here and now. At the same time, society placed a new emphasis on individual achievement. Indeed, the Renaissance ideal was a person with talents in many fields.

A Spirit of Adventure The Renaissance supported a spirit of adventure and a wide-ranging curiosity that led people to explore new worlds or to reexamine old ones. Navigators who sailed across the ocean, scientists who looked at the universe in new ways, and writers and artists who experimented with new forms and techniques all shared that spirit. In part, that spirit of adventure came from a new view of man himself. As Italian thinker Pico della Mirandola asserted in 1486: "To [man] it is granted to have whatever he chooses, to be whatever he wills."

Expressing Humanism At the heart of the Italian Renaissance was an intellectual movement known as **humanism.** Humanists studied the classical culture of Greece and Rome, but used that study to increase their understanding of their own times. Though most humanists were pious Christians, they focused on worldly subjects rather than on the religious issues that had occupied medieval thinkers. Humanists believed that education should stimulate the individual's creative powers. They emphasized the **humanities**—subjects such as grammar, rhetoric (the study of using language effectively), poetry, and history—that had been taught in ancient Greek and Roman schools.

Francesco **Petrarch** (PEE trahrk), a Florentine who lived in the 1300s, was an early Renaissance humanist, poet, and scholar. He assembled a library of Greek and Roman manuscripts in monasteries and churches. In later years his efforts and those of others encouraged by his example enabled the works of Cicero, Homer, and Virgil to again become known to Western Europeans.

 Checkpoint What were the main characteristics of the Renaissance?

Italy: Cradle of the Renaissance

The Renaissance began in Italy. Over the next hundred years it spread to the rest of Europe, eventually transforming the entire Western world. Italy was the place where the Renaissance <u>emerged</u> for several reasons.

Italy's History and Geography Renaissance thinkers had a new interest in ancient Rome. Italy had been the center of the Roman empire, and people could study its art and architecture. The Roman Catholic Church, based in Rome, supported many artists and scholars.

Italy's location on the Mediterranean Sea also encouraged trade with the Muslim world just across the sea. Ships carrying a variety of goods docked at Italy's many ports. Banking, manufacturing, and merchant networks developed to support trade. Italian merchants led the growth of trade across Europe during the late Middle Ages. Trade provided the wealth that fueled Italy's Renaissance.

Trade routes also carried new ideas that were important in shaping the Renaissance. Muslim scholars had preserved and developed the scientific and technical knowledge of ancient Greece and Rome, which had been forgotten in medieval Europe. Contact through trade gave Italy access to the Muslim world's wealth of knowledge.

Michelangelo's *David*
Michelangelo sculpted his masterpiece *David* out of a block of marble left over from another sculpture. Completed in 1504, the statue was commissioned to express the power and strength of Florence.

Vocabulary Builder
<u>comprehend</u>—(kahm pree HEND) *v.* understand; take in
<u>emerge</u>—(ee MURJ) *v.* develop; rise from; become known

Italian Bankers
This painting from the 1400s depicts a typical scene in an Italian banking house. *How is the wealth of the banker shown in this image?*

Italy's Vibrant City-States Unlike the kingdoms of most of the rest of Europe, Italy was divided into many small city-states. Each Italian city-state was controlled by a powerful family and dominated by a wealthy and powerful merchant class. These merchant families exerted both political and economic leadership, and their interest in art and emphasis on personal achievement helped to shape the Italian Renaissance.

The Medici (MED uh chee) family of **Florence,** for example, ranked among the richest merchants and bankers in Europe. Cosimo de' Medici gained control of the Florentine government in 1434, and the family continued as uncrowned rulers of the city for many years. Cosimo's grandson Lorenzo, known as "the Magnificent," represented the Renaissance ideal. A clever politician, he held Florence together during difficult times in the late 1400s. He was also a generous **patron,** or financial supporter, of the arts. At Lorenzo's invitation, poets and philosophers frequently visited the Medici palace. Artists learned their craft by sketching ancient Roman statues displayed in the Medici gardens.

The Medicis' great wealth and influence transformed Florence. Perhaps more than any other city, it came to symbolize the energy and brilliance of the Italian Renaissance. Like the ancient city of Athens, it produced a dazzling number of gifted poets, artists, architects, scholars, and scientists in a relatively short span of time.

✔ **Checkpoint** Why was Italy a favorable setting for the Renaissance?

Renaissance Art Flowers

The Renaissance attained its most glorious expression in its paintings, sculpture, and architecture. Wealthy patrons, popes, and princes played a major role in this artistic flowering. Ordinary people—who were beginning to appreciate human experiences not related to the Church—also played a role.

Reflecting Humanist Thought Renaissance art reflected the ideas of humanism. Like artists of the Middle Ages, Renaissance artists portrayed religious themes. However, they often set religious figures such as Jesus and Mary against classical Greek or Roman backgrounds. Painters also produced portraits of well-known figures of the day, reflecting the humanist interest in individual achievement. Renaissance artists studied ancient Greek and Roman works and revived many classical forms. The sculptor Donatello, for example, created a life-size statue of a soldier on horseback. It was the first such figure done since ancient times.

Using New Artistic Techniques Roman art had been very realistic, but in medieval times art became much more stylized. Renaissance painters returned to the realism of classical times by developing new techniques for representing both humans and landscapes. In particular, the rules of **perspective** allowed Renaissance artists to create realistic art. By making distant objects smaller than those close to the viewer, artists could paint scenes that appeared three-dimensional.

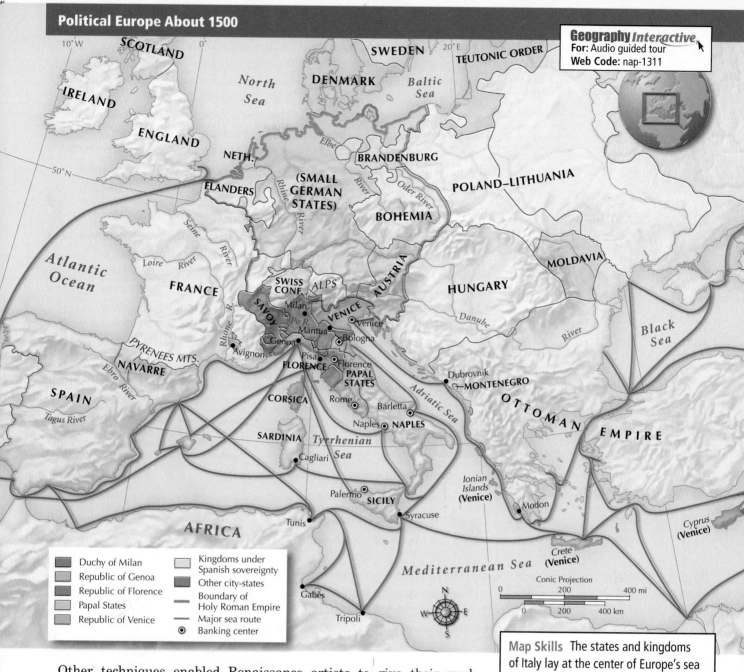

Political Europe About 1500

Geography *Interactive*
For: Audio guided tour
Web Code: nap-1311

SCOTLAND

IRELAND

ENGLAND

SWEDEN

DENMARK

TEUTONIC ORDER

North Sea

Baltic Sea

NETH.

BRANDENBURG

FLANDERS

(SMALL GERMAN STATES)

POLAND–LITHUANIA

BOHEMIA

Atlantic Ocean

FRANCE

SWISS CONF.

ALPS

AUSTRIA

HUNGARY

MOLDAVIA

Milan

SAVOY

VENICE

Venice

Mantua

Bologna

Genoa

Pisa

Danube

FLORENCE

Florence

PAPAL STATES

Dubrovnik

MONTENEGRO

Black Sea

PYRENEES MTS.

NAVARRE

Avignon

Rome

CORSICA

Adriatic Sea

OTTOMAN

EMPIRE

SPAIN

Tagus River

Ebro River

Loire River

Seine River

Rhône R.

Po R.

Rhine River

Elbe

Oder River

River

Barletta

Naples

NAPLES

SARDINIA

Tyrrhenian Sea

Cagliari

Palermo

SICILY

Ionian Islands (Venice)

Modon

Syracuse

Cyprus (Venice)

AFRICA

Tunis

Crete (Venice)

Mediterranean Sea

Gabès

Tripoli

Conic Projection

0   200   400 mi

0   200   400 km

N W E S

Legend

- Duchy of Milan
- Republic of Genoa
- Republic of Florence
- Papal States
- Republic of Venice
- Kingdoms under Spanish sovereignty
- Other city-states
- —— Boundary of Holy Roman Empire
- —— Major sea route
- ⊙ Banking center

Map Skills The states and kingdoms of Italy lay at the center of Europe's sea trade.

1. **Locate** (a) Florence (b) Palermo (c) Crete
2. **Identify** Which republic controlled Crete? Which kingdom controlled Sicily?
3. **Apply Information** Why were so many banking centers located in Italy?

Other techniques enabled Renaissance artists to give their work energy and realism. Renaissance painters used shading to make objects look round and real, and new oil paints to reflect light. Painters and sculptors also studied human anatomy and drew from observing live models. As a result, they were able to portray the human body much more accurately than medieval artists had done.

Architecture: A "Social Art" Architecture was transformed in Renaissance Italy. Architect Leon Alberti described architecture as a "social art," meant to blend beauty with utility and improvement of society. Architects rejected the Gothic style of the late Middle Ages as disorderly. Instead, they adopted the columns, arches, and domes that had been favored by the Greeks and Romans. For the cathedral in Florence, Filippo Brunelleschi (broo nay LAYS kee) created a majestic dome, which he modeled on the dome of the Pantheon in Rome. Like other Renaissance artists, Brunelleschi was multitalented. He studied art and sculpture with Donatello and was an accomplished engineer, inventing many of the machines used to construct his dome.

Leonardo da Vinci Artist **Leonardo** da Vinci (duh VIN chee) (1452–1519) had an endless curiosity that fed a genius for invention. He made sketches of nature and of models in his studio, and dissected corpses to learn how bones and muscles work. As a result, Leonardo's paintings grip people with their realism. The *Mona Lisa* is a portrait of a woman whose mysterious smile has baffled viewers for centuries. *The Last Supper,* showing Jesus and his apostles on the night before the crucifixion, is both a moving religious painting and a masterpiece of perspective. Because Leonardo experimented with a new type of paint, much of *The Last Supper* decayed over the years. However, it has recently been restored.

Leonardo thought of himself as an artist. Yet his talents and accomplishments ranged over many areas, including botany, anatomy, optics, music, architecture, and engineering. He made sketches for flying machines and undersea boats centuries before the first airplane or submarine was actually built. Though most of his paintings are lost today, his many notebooks survive as a testament to his genius and creativity.

Michelangelo Artist **Michelangelo** Buonarroti (1475–1564), like Leonardo, had many talents—he was a sculptor, engineer, painter, architect, and poet. Michelangelo has been called a "melancholy genius" because his work reflects his many life-long spiritual and artistic struggles. In his twenties, he created marble masterpieces such as *David* and the

● **INFOGRAPHIC**

The Discovery of Perspective

Before the 1400s, artists did not know how to create perspective, or the technique of showing distant objects on flat surfaces the way the eye actually sees them. The discovery of perspective revolutionized art. Using simple geometry, Renaissance artists could for the first time reproduce what their eyes actually saw.

Brunelleschi is credited with inventing perspective. His many studies (left) helped him design Florence's Duomo, completed in 1436. At 185 feet (56 m) high, it was the largest domed structure built since A.D. 125. ▶

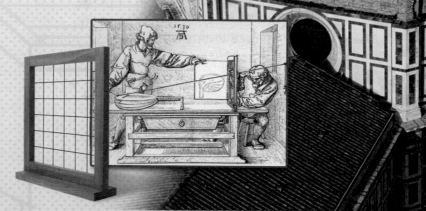

Artist Leon Alberti refined Brunelleschi's ideas. ▶
He wrote books explaining the rules of perspective, and developed the "perspective net" (right). To show perspective, the artist looks over an eyepiece and through the net at a model (far right). Then he reproduces the outlines of the model on paper with grids corresponding to those on the net.

Pietà. The *Pietà* captures the sorrow of the Biblical Mary as she cradles her dead son Jesus on her knees. Michelangelo's heroic statue of *David*, the Biblical shepherd who killed the giant Goliath, recalls the harmony and grace of ancient Greek tradition.

One of Michelangelo's greatest projects was painting a series of huge murals to decorate the ceiling of the Sistine Chapel in Rome. The enormous task, which took four years to complete and left the artist partially crippled, depicted the biblical history of the world from the Creation to the Flood. Michelangelo was also a talented architect. His most famous design was for the dome of St. Peter's Cathedral in Rome. It served as a model for many later structures, including the United States Capitol building in Washington, D.C.

Raphael A few years younger than Michelangelo, **Raphael** (rah fah EL) (1483–1520) was widely admired both for his artistic talent and "his sweet and gracious nature." Raphael studied the works of the great masters but developed his own style of painting that blended Christian and classical styles. He is probably best known for his tender portrayals of the Madonna, the mother of Jesus. In *The School of Athens,* Raphael pictured an imaginary gathering of great thinkers and scientists, including Plato, Aristotle, Socrates, and the Arab philosopher Averroës. With typical Renaissance self-confidence, Raphael included the faces of Michelangelo, Leonardo—and himself.

✓ **Checkpoint** How were Renaissance ideals reflected in the arts?

History Interactive

For: Interactive *The Last Supper*
Web Code: nap-1312

Leonardo eagerly explored perspective in his mural *The Last Supper.* He uses converging lines, like those shown below, to create a vanishing point. This vanishing point draws the viewer's eye to the space above Jesus, and gives the painting the illusion of space and depth. ▶

Thinking Critically
1. **Apply Information** Why was the invention of perspective necessary for artists to achieve realism in painting?
2. **Analyze Visuals** What other techniques bring the eye to the central figure of Jesus in *The Last Supper?*

Writing for a New Society

Italian writers reflected the trademark Renaissance curiosity and interest in the humanities. Humanists and historians wrote works of philosophy and scholarship. Other writers developed a literature of guidebooks to help ambitious men and women who wanted to achieve success in the Renaissance world.

In the mid-1500s, Giorgio Vasari wrote a biography of Leonardo da Vinci, whose self-portrait is shown here. Why is Leonardo da Vinci described today as an ideal "Renaissance man"?

Primary Source

❝ Sometimes, in supernatural fashion, beauty, grace, and talent are united beyond measure in one single person. . . . This was seen by all mankind in Leonardo da Vinci . . . so great was his genius, and such its growth, that to whatever difficulties he turned his mind, he solved them with ease. In him was great bodily strength . . . with a spirit and courage ever royal and magnanimous; and the fame of his name so increased, that not only in his lifetime was he held in esteem, but his reputation became even greater among posterity after his death. ❞ AUDIO

Castiglione's Ideal Courtier The most widely read of these handbooks was *The Book of the Courtier.* Its author, **Baldassare Castiglione** (kahs teel YOH nay), describes the manners, skills, learning, and virtues that a member of the court should have. Castiglione's ideal courtier was a well-educated, well-mannered aristocrat who mastered many fields, from poetry to music to sports.

Castiglione's ideal differed for men and women. The ideal man, he wrote, is athletic but not overactive. He is good at games, but not a gambler. He plays a musical instrument and knows literature and history but is not arrogant. The ideal woman offers a balance to men. She is graceful and kind, lively but reserved. She is beautiful, "for outer beauty," wrote Castiglione, "is the true sign of inner goodness."

Machiavelli's Successful Prince Niccolò Machiavelli (mahk ee uh VEL ee) wrote a guide for rulers on how to gain and maintain power. Unlike ancient writers such as Plato, Machiavelli did not discuss leadership in terms of high ideals. Instead, his book *The Prince* looked at real rulers in an age of ruthless power politics. Machiavelli stressed that the end justifies the means. He urged rulers to use whatever methods were necessary to achieve their goals.

Machiavelli saw himself as an enemy of oppression and corruption, but critics attacked his cynical advice. (In fact, the term "Machiavellian" came to refer to the use of deceit in politics.) Later students of government, however, argued that Machiavelli provided a realistic look at politics. His work continues to spark debate because it raises important ethical questions about the nature of government and the use of power.

✔ **Checkpoint** How did Renaissance writings express realism?

Section 1 Assessment

Progress Monitoring *Online*
For: Self-quiz with vocabulary practice
Web Code: naa-1311

Terms, People, and Places

1. For each term, person, or place listed at the beginning of the section, write a sentence explaining its significance.

Note Taking

2. **Reading Skill: Identify Main Ideas** Use your completed outline to answer the Focus Question: What were the ideals of the Renaissance, and how did Italian artists and writers reflect these ideals?

Comprehension and Critical Thinking

3. **Make Generalizations** How was the Renaissance worldview different from that of the Middle Ages?
4. **Summarize** In what ways did Italian city-states encourage the Renaissance?
5. **Synthesize Information** How did humanism influence Renaissance painting and sculpture?
6. **Recognize Ideologies** Why were nature and human nature important to Renaissance artists and writers?

● **Writing About History**

Quick Write: Generate Arguments Consider the following thesis statement for a persuasive essay: Renaissance Italy produced some of the greatest writers and thinkers that the world has ever known. Next, generate a number of arguments that support that thesis. Rank your arguments in order of importance.

The Prince by Niccolò Machiavelli

Florentine Niccolò Machiavelli (1469–1527) served in the government as a diplomat for fourteen years before becoming a full-time writer and scholar. In 1513, he used his experience in politics and his studies of ancient Roman history to write a book called *The Prince*. In this book, Machiavelli combined his personal experience of politics with his knowledge of the past to offer a guide to rulers on how to gain and maintain power.

A portrait of Niccolò Machiavelli painted in the late 1500s

Here the question arises: is it better to be loved than feared, or vice versa? I don't doubt that every prince would like to be both; but since it is hard to accommodate these qualities, if you have to make a choice, to be feared is much safer than to be loved. For it is a good general rule about men, that they are ungrateful, fickle[1], liars and deceivers, fearful of danger and greedy for gain. While you serve their welfare, they are all yours, offering their blood, their belongings, their lives, and their children's lives, as we noted above—so long as the danger is remote. But when the danger is close at hand, they turn against you. Then, any prince who has relied on their words and has made no other preparations will come to grief; because friendships that are bought at a price, and not with greatness and nobility of soul, may be paid for but they are not acquired, and they cannot be used in time of need. People are less concerned with offending a man who makes himself loved than one who makes himself feared: the reason is that love is a link of obligation which men, because they are rotten, will break any time they think doing so serves their advantage; but fear involves dread of punishment, from which they can never escape.

Still, a prince should make himself feared in such a way that, even if he gets no love, he gets no hate either; because it is perfectly possible to be feared and not hated, and this will be the result if only the prince will keep his hands off the property of his subjects or citizens, and off their women. When he does have to shed blood, he should be sure to have a strong justification and manifest[2] cause; but above all, he should not confiscate[3] people's property, because men are quicker to forget the death of a father than the loss of a patrimony[4]. Besides, pretexts[5] for confiscation are always plentiful; it never fails that a prince who starts living by plunder can find reasons to rob someone else. . . .Returning to the question of being feared or loved, I conclude that since men love at their own inclination but can be made to fear at the inclination of the prince, a shrewd prince will lay his foundations on what is under his own control, not on what is controlled by others.

1. **fickle** (FIK ul) *adj.* changeable
2. **manifest** (MAN uh fest) *adj.* clear; plain to see
3. **confiscate** (KAHN fis kayt) *v.* to seize or take

4. **patrimony** (PA truh moh nee) *n.* property or inheritance
5. **pretexts** (PREE teksts) *n.* excuses; false reasons

Thinking Critically

1. **Summarize Information** Why does Machiavelli believe that it is better for a prince to be feared than to be loved?
2. **Make Comparisons** Reread the section of the text titled Castiglione's Ideal Courtier. Is Machiavelli's description of an ideal prince consistent with that of Castiglione's courtier? Why or why not?

417

An Expanding World

❝All the world is full of knowing men, of most learned schoolmasters, and vast libraries; and it appears to me as a truth, that neither in Plato's time, nor Cicero's . . . there was ever such conveniency for studying, as we see at this day there is.❞
—François Rabelais, 1532

Scholars and artists throughout northern Europe in the 1500s lived in an exciting time. The newly invented printing press made the world seem smaller. All over Europe, the world of knowledge was expanding in ways that would have been unthinkable in medieval times.

Focus Question How did the Renaissance develop in northern Europe?

A modern artist depicts Gutenberg and his printing press; at top right is a Bible Gutenberg printed *circa* 1455.

The Renaissance in the North

 Performance Standards

- **SSWH9c** Explain the main characteristics of humanism and the ideas of Erasmus.
- **SSWH9g** Explain the importance of Guttenberg and the printing press.

Terms, People, and Places

Johann Gutenberg   Erasmus
Flanders   Thomas More
Albrecht Dürer   utopian
engraving   Shakespeare
vernacular

Note Taking

Reading Strategy: Identify Main Ideas Keep track of the main ideas of the section by creating a chart like the one below. Add boxes to complete the chart.

Renaissance in the North		
Printing Revolution	Artists and Writers	Humanists

As the Renaissance began to flower in Italy, northern Europe was still recovering from the ravages of the Black Death. But by the 1400s, the cities of the north began to enjoy the economic growth—and the wealth—needed to develop their own Renaissance.

The Printing Revolution

An astounding invention aided the spread of the Renaissance. In about 1455, **Johann Gutenberg** (GOOT un burg) of Mainz, Germany, printed the first complete edition of the Bible using a printing press with movable type. A printing revolution had begun that would transform Europe. Before the printing press, there were only a few thousand books in all of Europe. These books had been slowly copied out by hand. By 1500, according to some estimates, 15 to 20 million volumes had been produced on printing presses.

The printing revolution brought immense changes. Printed books were cheaper and easier to produce than hand-copied works. With books more readily available, more people learned to read. Readers gained access to a broad range of knowledge, from medicine and law to mining. As printing presses were established in Italy and other parts of Europe, printed books exposed educated Europeans to new ideas and new places.

✔ **Checkpoint** What was the impact of the printing press?

Northern Renaissance Artists

The northern Renaissance began in the <u>prosperous</u> cities of **Flanders,** a region that included parts of present-day northern France, Belgium, and the Netherlands. Flanders was a thriving center of trade for northern Europe. From Flanders, the Renaissance spread to Spain, France, Germany, and England.

Flemish Painters In the 1400s, Jan van Eyck was one of the most important Flemish painters. Van Eyck's portrayals of townspeople as well as religious scenes abound in rich, realistic details. In the 1500s, Flemish painter Pieter Bruegel (BROY gul) used vibrant colors to portray lively scenes of peasant life, earning him the nickname "Peasant Bruegel." Bruegel also addressed religious and classical themes, but he set them against a background of common people.

In the 1600s, Peter Paul Rubens blended the realistic tradition of Flemish painters like Bruegel with the classical themes and artistic freedom of the Italian Renaissance. As a scholar and humanist, Rubens had a wide knowledge of mythology, the Bible, and classical history. Many of his enormous paintings portray these themes.

Dürer: "Leonardo of the North" German painter **Albrecht Dürer** (DYOOR ur) was one of the first northern artists to be profoundly affected by Renaissance Italy. In 1494, he traveled to Italy to study the Italian masters. He soon became a pioneer in spreading Renaissance ideas to northern Europe. At the same time, his own methods influenced artists in Italy. Because of his wide-ranging interests, which extended far beyond art, he is sometimes called the "Leonardo of the North."

Dürer's important innovation was to apply the painting techniques he had learned in Italy to **engraving.** In engraving, an artist etches a design on a metal plate with acid. The artist then uses the plate to make prints. Dürer had studied engraving in his goldsmith father's workshop and perfected the technique. Many of Dürer's engravings and paintings portray religious upheaval, one of the northern Renaissance's most powerful themes.

✓ **Checkpoint** What themes did northern Renaissance artists explore?

Northern Humanists and Writers

Northern European humanists and writers also helped spread Renaissance ideas. Humanist scholars stressed education and classical learning, hoping to bring about religious and moral reform. Though humanist scholars wrote mainly in Latin, other writers began writing in the **vernacular,** or everyday language of ordinary people. This appealed to a new, middle class audience who lived in northern towns and cities.

Erasmus: Making Humanism Popular The Dutch priest and humanist Desiderius **Erasmus** (ih RAZ mus), born in 1466, was one of the most important scholars of the age. He wrote texts on a number of subjects and used his knowledge of classical languages to produce a new Greek edition of the Bible.

Vocabulary Builder

<u>prosperous</u>—(PRAHS pur us) *adj.* successful; wealthy

Dürer, Artist and Gentleman
In Germany artists were viewed merely as skilled craftsmen, prompting Dürer to comment that "[In Italy] I am a gentleman, at home I am a parasite." He worked hard to change that view, learning languages and court manners to promote himself. Dürer painted this self-portrait in 1498 when he was 26 years old. *Judging from the painting, how did Dürer view his own importance?*

Northern European artists eagerly pursued realism in their art. The new technique of oil painting allowed them to produce strong colors and a hard surface that could survive the centuries. They also used oils to achieve depth and to create realistic details. Artists placed a new emphasis on nature, recording in their art what they actually saw. Land-scapes became a major theme, not just the backdrop to human activities.

▲ Pieter Bruegel the Elder is best known for his scenes of daily life. In *Winter Landscape With Skaters and a Bird Trap,* every detail—from the bare trees to the people walking on ice—conveys the white and frozen reality of northern Europe in winter.

Erasmus helped spread Renaissance humanism to a wider public. He called for a translation of the Bible into the vernacular. He scorned those who ". . . don't want the holy scriptures to be read in translation by the unlearned . . . as if the chief strength of the Christian religion lay in people's ignorance of it. . . ." To Erasmus, an individual's chief duties were to be open-minded and to show good will toward others. As a priest, he was disturbed by corruption in the Church and called for reform.

Sir Thomas More's Ideal Society Erasmus's friend, the English humanist Sir **Thomas More,** also pressed for social reform. In *Utopia,* More describes an ideal society in which men and women live in peace and harmony. No one is idle, all are educated, and justice is used to end crime rather than to eliminate the criminal. Today, the word **utopian** has come to describe any ideal society often with the implication that such a society is ultimately impractical.

Rabelais's Comic Masterpiece The French humanist François Rabelais (rab uh LAY) had a varied career as a monk, physician, Greek scholar, and author. In *Gargantua and Pantagruel,* he chronicles the adventures of two gentle giants. On the surface, the novel is a comic tale of travel and war. But Rabelais uses his characters to offer opinions on religion, education, and other serious subjects. Like More and Erasmus, Rabelais was deeply religious, but had doubts about the organized church.

Shakespeare Writes for All Time The towering figure of Renaissance literature was the English poet and playwright William **Shakespeare.** Between 1590 and 1613, he wrote 37 plays that are still performed around the world. Fellow playwright and poet Ben Jonson correctly predicted at the time that Shakespeare ". . . was not of an age, but for all time."

◄ Oils made from linseed, walnuts, or poppies were mixed with colored pigments to make oil paint. Oil paints have two qualities that allow them to achieve realism— they can blend together, thus creating more realistic colors, and they reflect light, adding depth and glow.

▲ Jan van Eyck refined and spread the technique of oil painting. In *Portrait of Giovanni Arnolfini and His Wife*, van Eyck layered oil paints to create the shimmering fabrics the couple wore.

▲ Albrecht Dürer kept extensive notebooks on nature. He used his avid curiosity and his keen powers of observation to paint amazingly realistic pictures of plants and animals.

Thinking Critically

1. **Analyze Images** What realistic details appear in van Eyck's painting?
2. **Compare and Contrast** Compare these paintings with the Cranach woodcut in Section 3. How do the artists' intentions differ?

Shakespeare's genius was in expressing universal themes in everyday, realistic settings. His work explores Renaissance ideals such as the complexity of the individual and the importance of the classics. At the same time, his characters speak in language that common people can understand and appreciate. Shakespeare's love of words also vastly enriched the English language. More than 1,700 words appeared for the first time in his works.

✔ **Checkpoint** What Renaissance ideas did Shakespeare's work address?

SECTION 2 **Assessment**

Progress Monitoring *Online*
For: Self-quiz with vocabulary practice
Web Code: naa-1321

Terms, People, and Places

1. What do the key people listed at the beginning of the section have in common? Explain.

Note Taking

2. **Reading Skill: Identify Main Ideas** Use your completed chart to answer the Focus Question: How did the Renaissance develop in northern Europe?

Comprehension and Critical Thinking

3. **Predict Consequences** What impact would the printing press have on religious reform movements of the 1500s?
4. **Analyze Information** How did northern Renaissance artists blend Italian Renaissance ideas with their own?
5. **Identify Point of View** How did Erasmus's training as a priest sharpen his critique of the Church?
6. **Synthesize Information** What factors encouraged the use of the vernacular in literature in Renaissance society?

● **Writing About History**

Quick Write: Generate Arguments List a number of arguments that could be used to oppose your thesis in a persuasive essay. For example, reread the thesis statement in the Section 1 Quick Write. Then use the information from Section 2 to generate arguments opposing your thesis. Be sure to cite important northern European artists and technological developments. Organizing your arguments into a pro-and-con chart can be helpful.

Shakespeare's Globe Theatre

In his play *As You Like It*, William Shakespeare wrote that "all the world's a stage." When it came to showcasing his own work, however, the playwright chose the Globe Theatre. In 1599, when the English people were increasingly eager for plays and other sorts of entertainment, Shakespeare and his company of actors built the Globe on the south bank of London's Thames River. The three-story, open-air theater could seat 3,000 people and had a stage more than 40 feet wide. Shakespeare wrote many of his plays—including *Hamlet, Macbeth,* and *Othello*—specifically to be performed at the Globe Theatre. Twenty of Shakespeare's plays were performed there during his lifetime. During a performance of his play *Henry VII* in 1613, onstage cannon fire ignited the theater's thatched roof and destroyed the building.

▲ William Shakespeare

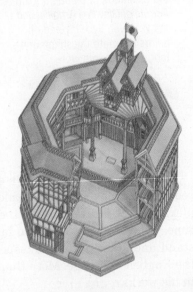

The 1997 reconstruction of the Globe Theatre (below) is faithful to the original. Wealthy theatergoers in the seventeenth century sat in galleries along the theater's walls. Poorer people bought cheap seats on the ground in front of the stage.

The center of the theater was open to the sky. Because the theater had no interior lights, plays were performed in the afternoon to let in as much light as possible.

The theater's round shape meant that the audience surrounded the stage on three sides. The stage was not curtained off, further drawing the audience into the action. ▶

Thinking Critically

1. **Draw Inferences** What are the advantages and disadvantages of staging productions in an open-air theater like the Globe?
2. **Synthesize Information** What about Shakespeare's plays drew people from all social classes to the theater?

Luther is shown tacking his 95 Theses to a church door in Wittenberg. At top right is a print block from a printing press.

A Monk Rebels

❝ I have cast the die. . . . I will not reconcile myself to them [the Roman Catholic Church] for all eternity. . . . Let them condemn and burn all that belongs to me; in return I will do as much for them. . . . Now I no longer fear, and I am publishing a book in the German tongue about Christian reform, directed against the pope, in language as violent as if I were addressing the Antichrist.❞
—Martin Luther, 1520

Focus Question How did revolts against the Roman Catholic Church affect northern European society?

The Protestant Reformation

 Performance Standards

• **SSWH9d** Analyze the impact of the Protestant Reformation and the ideas of Martin Luther and John Calvin.

Terms, People, and Places

indulgences	John Calvin
Martin Luther	predestination
Wittenberg	Geneva
Charles V	theocracy
diet	

Note Taking

Reading Skill: Identify Main Ideas Use a concept web like the one below to record main ideas about the Reformation. Add circles as necessary.

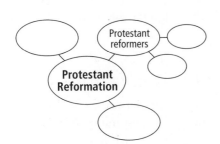

In the 1500s, the Renaissance in northern Europe sparked a religious upheaval that affected Christians at all levels of society. Northern European calls for church reform eventually unleashed forces that would shatter Christian unity. This movement is known as the Protestant Reformation.

Background to the Reformation

Many northern Europeans faced a great deal of uncertainty in their lives. As in Renaissance Italy, most people were poor and life could be violent. Fixed medieval economies were giving way to more uncertain urban, market-based economies, and wealth was distributed unequally. Renaissance humanist ideas found fertile ground in this uncertain society. Spread by the printing press, humanist ideas such as a return to classical education and an emphasis on social reform quickly took root. Many people looked for ways to shape a society that made more sense to them. Increasingly, they used humanist ideas to question a central force in their lives—the Church.

Church Abuses Beginning in the late Middle Ages, the Church had become increasingly caught up in worldly affairs. Popes competed with Italian princes for political power. They fought long wars to protect the Papal States against invasions by secular rulers. They plotted against powerful monarchs who tried to seize control of the Church within their lands. The Church also fought to expand its own interests.

Analyzing Art

Protestant Art German artist Lucas Cranach the Elder expressed his views of Protestantism (left panel) and Catholicism (right panel) in this woodcut made in 1545. He wrote that the work was meant to show the difference between the "true religion" and the "false idolatrous teaching."

A Angels float peacefully in the sky above Luther.

B A preaching Martin Luther is shown as having a direct connection to God above.

C A Catholic clergyman sells indulgences.

D The pope counts bags of money.

1. According to Cranach, which of the religions shown is the "true religion"?
2. Find another detail in the painting that expresses the artist's opinion.

Like other Renaissance rulers, popes led lavish lives, supported the arts, and hired artists to beautify churches. To finance such projects, the Church increased fees for services such as marriages and baptisms. Some clergy also sold **indulgences.** According to Church teaching, an indulgence was a lessening of the time a soul would have to spend in purgatory, a place where souls too impure to enter heaven atoned for sins committed during their lifetimes. In the Middle Ages, the Church had granted indulgences only for good deeds. By the late 1400s, however, indulgences could be bought with money.

Many Christians protested such practices, especially in northern Europe. Christian humanists such as Erasmus urged a return to the simple ways of the early Christian church. They stressed Bible study and rejected what they saw as the worldliness of the Church.

Early Revolts Against the Church Long before the Protestant Reformation, a few thinkers protested against the Church more strongly. In England in the 1300s, John Wycliffe launched a systematic attack against the Church, using sermons and writings to call for change. After his death, his followers met secretly to keep alive the movement he started. Jan Hus, born about 40 years after Wycliffe in what is now the Czech Republic, led a reform movement for which he was executed.

✔ **Checkpoint** What factors set the stage for the Protestant Reformation?

Martin Luther: Catalyst of Change

In 1517, protests against Church abuses erupted into a full-scale revolt. The man who triggered the revolt was a German monk and professor of theology named **Martin Luther.**

As a young man, Luther prayed and fasted and tried to lead a holy life. He once remarked that "... if ever a monk got into heaven by monkery, so should I also have gotten there." Still, he found himself growing disillusioned with what he saw as Church corruption and worldliness. At last, an incident in the town of Wittenberg prompted him to take action.

Writing the 95 Theses In 1517, a priest named Johann Tetzel set up a pulpit on the outskirts of **Wittenberg,** in Germany. He offered indulgences to any Christian who contributed money for the rebuilding of the Cathedral of St. Peter in Rome. Tetzel claimed that purchase of these indulgences would assure entry into heaven not only for the purchasers but for their dead relatives as well.

To Luther, Tetzel's actions were the final outrage, because they meant that poor peasants could not get into heaven. He drew up 95 Theses, or arguments, against indulgences. Among other things, he argued that indulgences had no basis in the Bible, that the pope had no authority to release souls from purgatory, and that Christians could be saved only through faith. In accordance with the custom of the time, he may have posted his list on the door of Wittenberg's All Saints Church.

Igniting a Firestorm Almost overnight, copies of Luther's 95 Theses were printed and distributed across Europe, where they stirred furious debate. The Church called on Luther to recant, or give up his views. Luther refused. Instead, he developed even more radical new doctrines. Before long, he was urging Christians to reject the authority of Rome. He wrote that the Church could only be reformed by secular, or non-Church, authorities.

In 1521, Pope Leo X excommunicated Luther. Later that year, the new Holy Roman emperor, **Charles V,** summoned Luther to the **diet** at the city of Worms. The word diet, or assembly of German princes, comes from a Middle English word meaning "a day for a meeting." Luther went, expecting to defend his writings. Instead, the emperor simply ordered him to give them up. Luther again refused to recant.

Charles declared Luther an outlaw, making it a crime for anyone in the empire to give him food or shelter. Still, Luther had many powerful supporters and thousands hailed him as a hero. They accepted his teachings and, following his lead, renounced the authority of the pope.

Vocabulary Builder
radical—(RAD ih kul) *adj.* extreme; calling for change
doctrine—(DAHK trin) *n.* practice; teaching

BIOGRAPHY

Martin Luther
"I am rough, boisterous, stormy, and altogether warlike," concluded Martin Luther (1483–1546). Luther's strong personality allowed him to take on the powerful Catholic Church. As a monk, Luther closely studied the Bible and came to believe that only its words—and not the pope or the Catholic Church—should dictate a person's actions.

When he appeared at the Diet of Worms, Luther (right) was 37 years old. Though depressed and fearful about the confrontation, he is said to have affirmed, "Here I stand, I cannot do otherwise." When he refused to retract his statements, an order was given to destroy his books. Yet his influence grew, leading to a deep division within Christianity and the founding of a new church that took his name. **Why did Luther refuse to retract his statements?**

Comparing Catholicism, Lutheranism, and Calvinism

	Catholicism	Lutheranism	Calvinism
Salvation	Salvation is achieved through faith and good works.	Salvation is achieved through faith.	God alone predetermines who will be saved.
Sacraments	Priests perform seven sacraments, or rituals—baptism, confirmation, marriage, ordination, communion, anointing the sick, and repentance.	Accepts some of the sacraments, but rejects others because rituals cannot erase sin—only God can.	Accepts some of the sacraments, but rejects others because rituals cannot erase sin—only God can.
Head of Church	Pope	Elected councils	Council of elders
Importance of the Bible	Bible is one source of truth; Church tradition is another.	Bible alone is source of truth.	Bible alone is source of truth.
How Belief Is Revealed	Priests interpret the Bible and Church teachings for the people.	People read and interpret the Bible for themselves.	People read and interpret the Bible for themselves.

Chart Skills *Who was the head of the Lutheran church? Why was this an important difference from the organization of the Catholic Church?*

Luther's Teachings At the heart of Luther's teachings were several beliefs, shown in the chart at left. All Christians, he said, have equal access to God through faith and the Bible. Like Erasmus and other humanist scholars, Luther wanted ordinary people to be able to read and study the Bible, so he translated parts of it into German. He also wanted every town to have a school so that all children could learn to read the Bible. Luther wanted to change other church practices. He banned indulgences, confession, pilgrimages, and prayers to saints. He simplified the elaborate ritual of the mass and instead emphasized the sermon. And he permitted the clergy to marry.

Luther's Ideas Spread The new printing presses spread Luther's writings throughout Germany and Scandinavia, prompting him to declare that "Printing was God's highest act of grace." Fiery preachers denounced Church abuses. By 1530, the Lutherans were using a new name, Protestant, for those who "protested" papal authority.

Many clergy saw Luther's reforms as the answer to Church corruption. A number of German princes, however, embraced Lutheran beliefs for more selfish reasons. Some saw Lutheranism as a way to throw off the rule of both the Church and the Holy Roman emperor. Others welcomed a chance to seize Church property in their territories, and use it for their own purposes. Still other Germans supported Luther because of feelings of national loyalty. They were tired of German money going to support churches and clergy in Italy.

The Peasants' Revolt Many peasants also took up Luther's banner. They hoped to gain his support for social and economic change. In 1524, a Peasants' Revolt erupted across Germany. The rebels called for an end to serfdom and demanded other changes in their harsh lives. However, Luther strongly favored social order and respect for political authority. As the Peasants' Revolt grew more violent, Luther denounced it. With his support, nobles suppressed the rebellion, killing tens of thousands of people and leaving thousands more homeless.

The Peace of Augsburg During the 1530s and 1540s, Charles V tried to force Lutheran princes back into the Catholic Church, but with little success. Finally, after a number of brief wars, Charles and the princes reached a settlement. The Peace of Augsburg, signed in 1555, allowed each prince to decide which religion—Catholic or Lutheran—would be followed in his lands. Most northern German states chose Lutheranism. The southern German states remained largely Catholic.

 Checkpoint How did Luther's teachings affect people and society in northern Europe?

Switzerland's Reformation

Swiss reformers also challenged the Catholic Church. Ulrich Zwingli, a priest and an admirer of Erasmus, lived in the Swiss city of Zurich. Like Luther, he stressed the importance of the Bible and rejected elaborate church rituals. Many of his ideas were adopted by Zurich's city council. The other reformer was **John Calvin,** who would profoundly affect the direction of the Reformation.

Calvin was born in France and trained as a priest and lawyer. In 1536, he published a widely-read book that set forth his religious beliefs and explained how to organize and run a Protestant church. Calvin shared many of Luther's beliefs. But he put forth a number of ideas of his own. He preached **predestination,** the idea that God had long ago determined who would gain salvation. To Calvinists, the world was divided into two kinds of people—saints and sinners. Calvinists tried to live like saints, believing that only those who were saved could live truly Christian lives.

In 1541, Protestants in the Swiss city-state of **Geneva** asked Calvin to lead their community. Calvin set up a **theocracy,** or government run by church leaders. Calvin's followers in Geneva came to see themselves as a new "chosen people" entrusted by God to build a truly Christian society. Calvinists stressed hard work, discipline, thrift, honesty, and morality. Citizens faced fines or other harsher punishments for offenses such as fighting, swearing, laughing in church, or dancing. To many Protestants, Calvinist Geneva seemed like a model community.

Reformers from all over Europe visited Geneva and then returned home to spread Calvin's ideas. By the late 1500s, Calvinism had taken root in Germany, France, the Netherlands, England, and Scotland. This new challenge to the Roman Catholic Church set off bloody wars of religion across Europe. In Germany, Catholics and Lutherans opposed Calvinists. In France, wars raged between French Calvinists and Catholics. Calvinists in the Netherlands avoided persecution by preaching in the remote countryside. In England, some Calvinists sailed to the Americas in the early 1600s to escape persecution at home. In Scotland, a Calvinist preacher named John Knox led a religious rebellion, overthrowing the Catholic queen.

✔ **Checkpoint** How were Calvin's ideas put into practice?

A Calvinist Church, 1564
The Calvinist belief in simplicity is reflected in the design of this church. No images other than scriptures and coats of arms decorate the church, and the preacher's pulpit is the center of focus.

SECTION **3 Assessment**

Progress Monitoring *Online*
For: Self-quiz with vocabulary practice
Web Code: naa-1331

Terms, People, and Places

1. For each term, person, or place listed at the beginning of the section, write a sentence explaining its significance.

Note Taking

2. **Reading Skill: Identify Main Ideas** Use your completed concept web to answer the Focus Question: How did revolts against the Roman Catholic Church affect northern European society?

Comprehension and Critical Thinking

3. **Synthesize Information** Why did the sale of indulgences become a critical issue during the Renaissance but not during the Middle Ages?

4. **Compare Points of View** How did Luther's ideas differ from those expressed by the Catholic Church?

5. **Draw Inferences** How might Luther have felt about the Calvinist theocracy in Geneva?

● **Writing About History**

Quick Write: Choose Strongest Argument Consider this thesis statement: The Reformation was the most important event in European history. List possible arguments for a persuasive essay that supports this thesis. Review each one and choose the strongest. Make sure that factual points in the text support your argument.

Painter Hans Holbein shows Henry VIII as a commanding and regal king. A gold medal (top right) celebrates King Henry as the head of the Church of England.

WITNESS HISTORY 🔊 AUDIO

A King Speaks Out

Henry VIII, the Catholic king of England, was deeply disturbed by Luther's teachings. In 1521 he wrote to the pope to express his displeasure.

❝ . . . we believe that no duty is more incumbent on a Catholic sovereign than to preserve and increase the Catholic faith . . . so when we learned that the pest of Martin Luther's heresy had appeared in Germany and was raging everywhere . . . we bent all our thoughts and energies on uprooting [those heresies] in every possible way. . . . ❞

Just a few years later, Henry would break with the Catholic Church and set England on the path to becoming a Protestant country.

Focus Question How did the Reformation bring about two different religious paths in Europe?

Reformation Ideas Spread

 Performance Standards

- **SSWH9e** Describe the Counter Reformation at the Council of Trent and the Jesuits' role in the Counter Reformation.
- **SSWH9f** Describe the English Reformation and the roles of Henry VIII and Elizabeth I.

Terms, People, and Places

sect	compromise
Henry VIII	Council of Trent
Mary Tudor	Ignatius of Loyola
Thomas Cranmer	Teresa of Avila
Elizabeth	ghetto
canonize	

Note Taking

Reading Skill: Identify Main Ideas As you read about the spread of the Protestant Reformation, record the main ideas in a flowchart like this one below. Add more boxes as necessary.

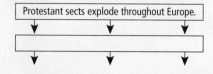

Throughout Europe, Catholic monarchs and the Catholic Church fought back against the Protestant challenge by taking steps to reform the Church and to restore its spiritual leadership of the Christian world. Still, Protestant ideas continued to spread.

An Explosion of Protestant Sects

As the Reformation continued, hundreds of new Protestant **sects,** or religious groups that had broken away from an established church, sprang up. Many of these followed variations on the teachings of Luther, Calvin, and Zwingli. Some sects, however, had ideas that were even more radical—such as rejecting infant baptism. Infants, they argued, are too young to understand what it means to accept the Christian faith. They became known as Anabaptists.

A few Anabaptist sects sought radical social change as well. Some wanted to abolish private property. Others sought to speed up the coming of God's day of judgment by violent means. When radical Anabaptists took over the city of Munster in Germany, even Luther advised his supporters to join Catholics in suppressing the threat to the traditional order. Most Anabaptists, however, were peaceful. They called for religious toleration and separation of church and state. Despite harsh persecution, these groups influenced Protestant thinking in many countries. Today, the Baptists, Mennonites, and Amish all trace their religious ancestry to the Anabaptists.

✔ **Checkpoint** Who were the Anabaptists?

The English Reformation

In England, religious leaders like John Wycliffe had called for Church reform as early as the 1300s. By the 1520s, some English clergy were exploring Protestant ideas. The break with the Catholic Church, however, was the work not of religious leaders but of King **Henry VIII.**

Henry VIII Seeks an Annulment At first, Henry VIII stood firmly against the Protestant revolt. The pope even awarded him the title "Defender of the Faith" for a pamphlet that he wrote denouncing Luther.

In 1527, however, an issue arose that set Henry at odds with the Church. After 18 years of marriage, Henry and his Spanish wife, Catherine of Aragon, had only one surviving child, **Mary Tudor.** Henry felt that England's stability depended on his having a male heir. He had already fallen in love with a young noblewoman named Anne Boleyn, who served the Queen. He hoped that if he married her she would bear him a son. Because Catholic law does not permit divorce, he asked the pope to annul, or cancel, his marriage. Popes had annulled royal marriages before. But this pope refused. He did not want to offend the Holy Roman emperor Charles V, Catherine's nephew.

Breaking With the Church Henry was furious. Spurred on by his advisors, many of whom leaned toward Protestantism, he decided to take over the English church. Guided by his chancellor Thomas Cromwell, he had Parliament pass a series of laws. They took the English church from the pope's control and placed it under Henry's rule. At the same time, Henry appointed **Thomas Cranmer** archbishop of the new church. Cranmer annulled the king's marriage, and in 1533 Henry married Anne Boleyn. Soon, Anne gave birth to a daughter, **Elizabeth.**

In 1534, Parliament passed the Act of Supremacy, making Henry "the only supreme head on Earth of the Church of England." Many loyal Catholics refused to accept the Act of Supremacy and were executed for treason. Among them was the great English humanist Sir Thomas More, who served in Henry's government but tried to resign in protest. More was later **canonized,** or recognized as a saint, by the Catholic Church.

Strengthening the Church of England Between 1536 and 1540, royal officials investigated Catholic convents and monasteries. Claiming that they were centers of immorality, Henry ordered them closed. He then confiscated, or seized, their lands and wealth. Henry shrewdly granted some of these lands to nobles and other high-ranking citizens. He thus secured their support for the Anglican Church, as the new Church of England was called. Despite these actions, Henry was not a religious radical. He rejected most Protestant doctrines. Aside from breaking away from Rome and allowing use of the English Bible, he kept most Catholic forms of worship.

Religious Turmoil When Henry died in 1547, he had only one surviving son—despite having married six times. Nine-year-old Edward VI inherited the throne. The young king and his advisors were devout Protestants and took steps to make England a truly Protestant country. Under Edward, Parliament passed new laws bringing Protestant reforms to England. Thomas Cranmer drew up the Protestant *Book of Common Prayer,* which became required reading in all of the country's church services. Though it outlined a moderate form of Protestant service, it sparked uprisings. These uprisings were harshly suppressed.

BIOGRAPHY

Elizabeth I

The life of Elizabeth I (1533–1603) did not start favorably. When she was only two years old her mother, Anne Boleyn, was beheaded so that her father, Henry VIII, could remarry. The young princess grew up in isolation. Still, Henry VIII was affectionate to his daughter and saw to it that she received a rigorous education. Even as a teenager she was well-respected for her sharp mind, fluency in languages, and understanding of philosophy and theology.

Under the reign of her half-sister Mary Tudor, Elizabeth became both a rallying symbol for Protestants and a target for Catholics. Though arrested and imprisoned, she survived her sister to become queen of England at age 25. The well-loved Elizabeth used her talents to unify England, expand its international power, and encourage a period of great artistic flowering. **Why do you think the period under Elizabeth's reign is now called the Elizabethan Age?**

When Edward died in his teens, his half-sister Mary Tudor became queen. She was determined to return England to the Catholic faith. Under Queen Mary hundreds of English Protestants, including Archbishop Cranmer, were burned at the stake for heresy.

The Elizabethan Settlement On Mary's death in 1558, the throne passed to 25-year-old Elizabeth, the daughter of Henry VIII and Anne Boleyn. For years, Elizabeth had survived court intrigues, including the religious swings under Edward and Mary. As queen, Elizabeth had to determine the future of the Church of England. Moving cautiously at first, she slowly enforced a series of reforms that over time came to be called the Elizabethan settlement.

The queen's policies were a **compromise,** or acceptable middle ground, between Protestant and Catholic practices. The Church of England preserved much Catholic ritual, and it kept the hierarchy of bishops and archbishops. Unlike Henry, the queen did not call herself "supreme head" of the church, but she reaffirmed that the monarch was the "supreme governor" over spiritual matters in England. At the same time, Elizabeth restored a version of the *Book of Common Prayer,* accepted moderate Protestant doctrine, and allowed English to replace Latin in church services. Her sensible compromises, which satisfied most Catholics and Protestants, largely ended decades of religious turmoil.

During a long reign, Elizabeth used all her skills to restore unity to England. Even while keeping many Catholic traditions, she made England a firmly Protestant nation. After her death, England faced new religious storms. But it escaped the endless religious wars that tore apart France and many other European states during the 1500s.

✔ **Checkpoint** Why was the Church of England established?

Major Events of the English Reformation

1521 Henry VIII writes to the pope to condemn Luther's teachings.

King Henry the eyght.

1529 Parliament begins passing laws to make Henry VIII head of the church in England.

1533 Henry VIII divorces Catherine of Aragon and marries Anne Boleyn.

1534 Parliament passes the Act of Supremacy.

The Catholic Reformation

As the Protestant Reformation swept across northern Europe, a vigorous reform movement took hold within the Catholic Church. Led by Pope Paul III, it is known as the Catholic Reformation, or the Counter-Reformation. During the 1530s and 1540s, the pope set out to revive the moral authority of the Church and roll back the Protestant tide. He also appointed reformers to end corruption within the papacy itself. They and their successors led the Catholic Reformation for the rest of the century.

Council of Trent To establish the direction that reform should take, the pope called the **Council of Trent** in 1545. Led by Italian cardinal Carlo Borromeo, the council met off and on for almost 20 years. The council reaffirmed the traditional Catholic views that Protestants had challenged. It declared that salvation comes through faith and good works. According to the council, the Bible, while a major source of religious truth, is not the only source. The council also took steps to end abuses in the Church. It provided stiff penalties for worldliness and corruption among the clergy. It also established schools to create a better-educated clergy who could challenge Protestant teachings.

Empowering the Inquisition Pope Paul strengthened the Inquisition to fight Protestantism. As you have read, the Inquisition was a Church court set up during the Middle Ages. The Inquisition used secret testimony, torture, and execution to root out heresy. It also prepared the *Index of Forbidden Books*, a list of works considered too immoral or irreligious for Catholics to read. The list included books by Luther and Calvin, as well as earlier works by Petrarch and other humanists.

1547 Henry VIII dies; his son Edward VI becomes king and begins making Protestant reforms.

1553 Edward VI dies; Mary Tudor ▶ becomes queen and restores Catholic doctrines.

1558 Mary Tudor dies; Elizabeth I becomes queen and unifies England with the Elizabethan Settlement.

Analyze Information
Because of Henry VIII's determination to obtain a divorce, Catholic England had become a solidly Protestant nation by 1600. *How long did it take Henry VIII to become head of the Church of England?*

Major European Religions About 1600

Legend:
- Mainly Roman Catholic
- Mainly Anglican
- Mainly Lutheran
- Mainly Calvinist
- Areas of Muslim minorities
- Mainly Orthodox Christian
- Boundary of Holy Roman Empire

Note: Not all minority religious groups are shown. Jews were dispersed throughout Europe.

Conic Projection
0   200   400 mi
0   200 400 km

Map Skills By 1600, the spread of Protestantism had transformed Catholic Europe.

1. **Locate** (a) London (b) Wittenberg (c) Rome
2. **Identify** Identify the religion practiced in each of the locations above.
3. **Understand Main Ideas** Explain why most people in each region were practicing that religion by 1600.

Geography *Interactive*
For: Audio guided tour
Web Code: nap-1341

Vocabulary Builder

rigorous—(RIG ur us) *adj.* strict; thorough

Founding the Jesuits In 1540, the pope recognized a new religious order, the Society of Jesus, or Jesuits. The order was founded by **Ignatius of Loyola,** a Spanish knight raised in the crusading tradition. After his leg was shattered in battle, he found comfort reading about saints who had overcome mental and physical torture. Vowing to become a "soldier of God," Ignatius drew up a strict program for the Jesuits. It included spiritual and moral discipline, <u>rigorous</u> religious training, and absolute obedience to the Church. Led by Ignatius, the Jesuits embarked on a crusade to defend and spread the Catholic faith worldwide.

To further the Catholic cause, Jesuits became advisors to Catholic rulers, helping them combat heresy in their lands. They set up schools that taught humanist and Catholic beliefs and enforced discipline and obedience. Daring Jesuits slipped into Protestant lands in disguise to minister to Catholics. Jesuit missionaries spread their Catholic faith to distant lands, including Asia, Africa, and the Americas.

Teresa of Avila As the Catholic Reformation spread, many Catholics experienced renewed feelings of intense faith. **Teresa of Avila** symbolized this renewal. Born into a wealthy Spanish family, Teresa entered a convent in her youth. Finding convent routine not strict enough, she established her own order of nuns. They lived in isolation, eating and sleeping very little and dedicating themselves to prayer and meditation.

Impressed by her spiritual life, her superiors in the Church asked Teresa to reorganize and reform Spanish convents and monasteries. Teresa was widely honored for her work, and after her death the Church canonized her. Her spiritual writings rank among the most important Christian texts of her time, and are still widely read today.

Legacy of the Catholic Reformation By 1600, the majority of Europeans remained Catholic. Tireless Catholic reformers, like Francis de Sales in France, had succeeded in bringing back Protestant converts. Moreover, renewed piety found expression in literature and art. Across Catholic Europe, charity flourished and church abuses were reduced.

Still, Protestantism had gained a major foothold on the continent. The Reformation and the Catholic Reformation stirred up intense feeling and debate. Religious conflict played into heated disagreements about government, which would erupt into war throughout much of Europe. At the end, Europe would remain—and still remains today—divided by differing interpretations of Christianity.

✔ **Checkpoint** What was the outcome of the Catholic Reformation?

Widespread Persecution

During this period of heightened religious passion, persecution was widespread. Both Catholics and Protestants fostered intolerance and persecuted radical sects like the Anabaptists, people they thought were witches, and Jews.

Conducting Witch Hunts Between 1450 and 1750, tens of thousands of women and men died as victims of witch hunts. Those accused of being witches, or agents of the devil, were usually women. Most victims of the witch hunts died in the German states, Switzerland, and France, all centers of religious conflict. When the wars of religion came to an end, the persecution of witches also declined.

Scholars have offered various reasons for this persecution, but most agree that it had to do with people's twin beliefs in Christianity and magic. Most people believed that among them were witches who practiced magical deeds, often with the aid of the devil. Thus witches were seen as anti-Christian. Because witches often behaved in non-traditional ways, many people accused of witchcraft were often social outcasts, such as beggars. Midwives and herbalists were also targeted.

Persecuting Jews For many Jews in Italy, the early Renaissance had been a time of relative prosperity. While Spain had expelled its Jews in 1492, Italy allowed them to remain. Still, pressure remained strong on Jews to convert. In 1516, Venice ordered Jews to live in a separate quarter of the city called the **ghetto.** Other Italian cities soon followed.

During the Reformation, restrictions on Jews increased. At first, Luther hoped that Jews would be converted to his teachings. When they did not convert, he called for them to be expelled from Christian lands and for their synagogues to be burned. In time, some German princes did expel Jews. In the 1550s, Pope Paul IV placed added restrictions on Jews. Even Emperor Charles V, who supported toleration of Jews in the Holy Roman Empire, banned them from Spanish territories and new American colonies. From the early 1500s on, many Jews migrated to the Mediterranean parts of the Ottoman Empire and to the Netherlands.

✔ **Checkpoint** Why were Jews and other people persecuted?

Teresa of Avila wrote a book in 1610 describing her work with reforming Catholic convents and monasteries.

Primary Source

❝ At about this time there came to my notice the harm and havoc that were being wrought in France by these Lutherans and the way in which their unhappy sect was increasing. . . . I wept before the Lord and entreated Him to remedy this great evil. I felt that I would have laid down a thousand lives to save a single one of all the souls that were being lost there. And, seeing that I was a woman, and a sinner . . . I determined to do the little that was in me. . . . ❞

SECTION 4 Assessment

Progress Monitoring *Online*
For: Self-quiz with vocabulary practice
Web Code: naa-1341

Terms, People, and Places

1. Place each of the key terms at the beginning of this section into one of the following categories: politics, culture, economy, or geography. Write a sentence for each term explaining your choice.

Note Taking

2. **Reading Skill: Identify Main Ideas** Use your completed flowchart to answer the Focus Question: How did the Reformation bring about two different religious paths in Europe?

Comprehension and Critical Thinking

3. **Identify Point of View** Why were the Anabaptists considered to be radical?

4. **Understand Sequence** How did reforms cause England to become a Protestant country?

5. **Recognize Ideologies** Why might the Catholic Church have found the ideas of Ignatius to be particularly relevant to the Catholic Reformation?

6. **Make Comparisons** Why did witch hunting decline with the end of the religious wars, while persecution of Jews did not?

● **Writing About History**

Quick Write: Decide on an Organizational Strategy Write a thesis statement for a persuasive essay about the spread of the Reformation. List your supporting arguments, from strongest to weakest. Then make an outline that shows where your arguments will appear and how they relate to your thesis statement. You may want to save your strongest argument for the last paragraph of body text before your conclusion.

WITNESS HISTORY ◀)) AUDIO

Mountains on the Moon

In 1609, Italian astronomer Galileo Galilei heard of a new Dutch invention, the telescope. It was designed to help people see distant enemy ships. Galileo was interested for another reason—he wondered what would happen if he trained a telescope on the night sky. So he built his own telescope for this purpose. When he pointed it at the sky, he was amazed. The new telescope allowed him to see mountains on the moon, fiery spots on the sun, and four moons circling the planet Jupiter. "I did discover many particulars in Heaven that had been unseen and unheard of until this our age," he later wrote.

Focus Question How did discoveries in science lead to a new way of thinking for Europeans?

An 1800s artist imagines Galileo at work, peering into the sky. Galileo's telescope is shown at top right.

The Scientific Revolution

GA Performance Standards

• **SSWH13a** Explain how Copernicus', Galileo's, Kepler's, and Newton's contributions changed Europe's worldview.

Terms, People, and Places

Nicolaus Copernicus	scientific method
heliocentric	hypothesis
Tycho Brahe	Robert Boyle
Johannes Kepler	Isaac Newton
Galileo	gravity
Francis Bacon	calculus
René Descartes	

Note Taking

Reading Skills: Identify Main Ideas Use a table like the one below to record information about important people of the Scientific Revolution.

Thinkers of the Scientific Revolution	
Nicolaus Copernicus	Developed sun-centered universe theory

The Renaissance and the Reformation facilitated the breakdown of the medieval worldview. In the mid-1500s, a profound shift in scientific thinking brought about the final break with Europe's medieval past. Called the Scientific Revolution, this movement pointed toward a future shaped by a new way of thinking about the physical universe. At the heart of the Scientific Revolution was the assumption that mathematical laws governed nature and the universe. The physical world, therefore, could be known, managed, and shaped by people.

Changing Views of the Universe

Until the mid-1500s, Europeans' view of the universe was shaped by the theories of the ancient writers Ptolemy and Aristotle. More than 1,000 years before the Renaissance, they had taught that Earth was the center of the universe. Not only did this view seem to agree with common sense, it was accepted by the Church. In the 1500s and 1600s, however, people began to question this view.

Copernicus Challenges Ancient Astronomy In 1543, Polish scholar **Nicolaus Copernicus** (koh PUR nih kus) published *On the Revolutions of the Heavenly Spheres.* In it, he proposed a **heliocentric,** or sun-centered, model of the universe. The sun, he said, stands at the center of the universe. Earth is just one of several planets that revolve around the sun.

Most experts rejected this revolutionary theory. In Europe at the time, all scientific knowledge and many religious teachings were based on the arguments developed by classical thinkers. If Ptolemy's reasoning about the planets was wrong, people believed, then the whole system of human knowledge might be called into question. But in the late 1500s, the Danish astronomer **Tycho Brahe** (TEE koh BRAH uh) provided evidence that supported Copernicus's theory. Brahe set up an astronomical observatory. Every night for years, he carefully observed the sky, accumulating data about the movement of the heavenly bodies.

After Brahe's death, his assistant, the brilliant German astronomer and mathematician **Johannes Kepler,** used Brahe's data to calculate the orbits of the planets revolving around the sun. His calculations supported Copernicus's heliocentric view. At the same time, however, they showed that each planet does not move in a perfect circle, as both Ptolemy and Copernicus believed, but in an oval-shaped orbit called an ellipse.

Galileo's "Heresies" Scientists from many different lands built on the foundations laid by Copernicus and Kepler. In Italy, **Galileo** Galilei assembled an astronomical telescope. As you have read, he observed that the four moons of Jupiter move slowly around that planet—exactly, he realized, the way Copernicus said that Earth moves around the sun.

Galileo's discoveries caused an uproar. Other scholars attacked him because his observations <u>contradicted</u> ancient views about the world. The Church condemned him because his ideas challenged the Christian teaching that the heavens were fixed in position to Earth, and perfect.

In 1633, Galileo was tried before the Inquisition, and for the rest of his life he was kept under house arrest. Threatened with death unless he withdrew his "heresies," Galileo agreed to state publicly in court that Earth stands motionless at the center of the universe. Legend has it that as he left the court he muttered, "And yet it moves."

✔ **Checkpoint** Why was Copernicus's theory seen as radical?

A New Scientific Method

Despite the opposition of the Church, by the early 1600s a new approach to science had emerged, based upon observation and experimentation. During the Renaissance, the works of the ancient Greek <u>philosopher</u> Plato were rediscovered. Plato taught that man should look beyond simple appearances to learn nature's truths. He believed that mathematics, one of the greatest human achievements, was the key to learning these truths. His teachings were rediscovered by Renaissance scientists and helped shape people's view of the physical world.

Views of the Moon
Galileo sketched the views of the moon he saw through his telescope in 1609 (left). Pictures of the moon taken through a modern telescope (right) look remarkably similar.

Vocabulary Builder
<u>contradict</u>—(kahn truh DIKT) v. to go against

Vocabulary Builder
<u>philosopher</u>—(fih LAHS uh fur) n. a person who is an expert in the study of knowledge

Bacon and Descartes: Revolutionary Thinkers The new scientific method was really a revolution in thought. Two giants of this revolution were the Englishman **Francis Bacon** and the Frenchman **René Descartes** (day KAHRT). Each devoted himself to understanding how truth is determined. Both Bacon and Descartes, writing in the early 1600s, rejected Aristotle's scientific assumptions. They also challenged the scholarly traditions of the medieval universities that sought to make the physical world fit in with the teachings of the Church. Both argued that truth is not known at the beginning of inquiry but at the end, after a long process of investigation.

Bacon and Descartes differed in their methods, however. Bacon stressed experimentation and observation. He wanted science to make life better for people by leading to practical technologies. Descartes emphasized human reasoning as the best road to understanding. In his *Discourse on Method* (1637), he explains how he decided to discard all traditional authorities and search for provable knowledge. Left only with doubt, he concluded that doubt was the only thing he could not question, and that in order to doubt he had to exist as a rational, thinking being. Therefore he made his famous statement, "I think, therefore I am."

A Step-by-Step Process Over time, a step-by-step process of discovery evolved that became known as the **scientific method.** The scientific method required scientists to collect and accurately measure data. To explain the data, scientists used reasoning to propose a logical **hypothesis,** or possible explanation. They then tested the hypothesis with further observation or experimentation. Mathematical calculations were used to convert the observations and experiments into scientific laws. After reaching a conclusion, scientists repeated their work at least once—and usually many times—to confirm and refine their hypotheses or formulate better ones.

Diagram Skills The scientific method, still used today, is based on careful observation and measurement of data. *Why is Step 7 an important part of the process?*

✔ **Checkpoint** How did Bacon and Descartes each approach the new scientific method?

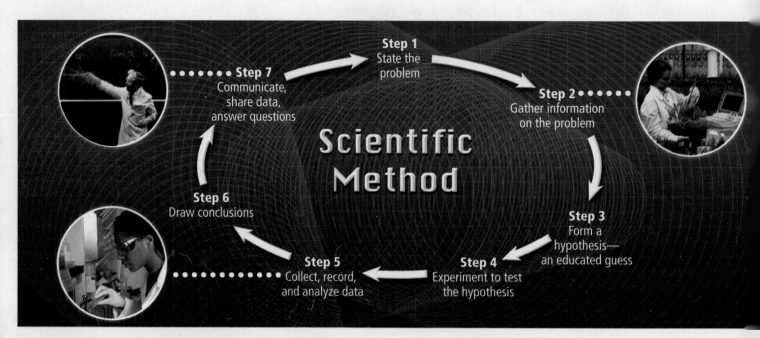

Scientific Method

Step 1 State the problem

Step 2 Gather information on the problem

Step 3 Form a hypothesis— an educated guess

Step 4 Experiment to test the hypothesis

Step 5 Collect, record, and analyze data

Step 6 Draw conclusions

Step 7 Communicate, share data, answer questions

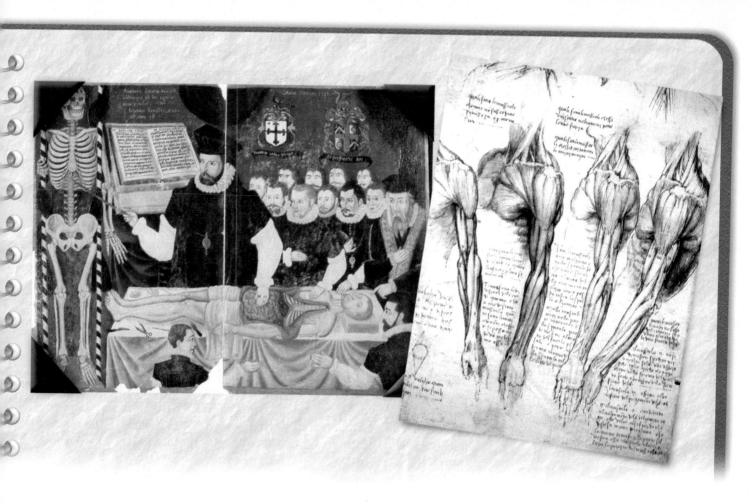

Breakthroughs in Medicine and Chemistry

The 1500s and 1600s saw dramatic changes in many branches of science, especially medicine and chemistry. The rapid changes in science and technology that began in this period still continue to this day.

Exploring the Human Body Medieval physicians relied on the works of the ancient physician Galen. Galen, however, had made many errors, in part because he had limited knowledge of human anatomy. During the Renaissance, physicians made new efforts to study the human body. In 1543, Andreas Vesalius (vuh SAY lee us) published *On the Structure of the Human Body,* the first accurate and detailed study of human anatomy. Vesalius used whatever means he could to increase his knowledge of anatomy. He used friendships with people of influence to get invitations to autopsies. He also autopsied bodies that he himself obtained—counting on friends in the local government to look the other way.

In the early 1540s, French physician Ambroise Paré (pa RAY) developed a new and more effective ointment for preventing infection. He also developed new surgical techniques, introduced the use of artificial limbs, and invented several scientific instruments. Then in the early 1600s, William Harvey, an English scholar, described the circulation of the blood for the first time. He showed how the heart serves as a pump to force blood through veins and arteries. Later in the century, the Dutch inventor Anton van Leeuwenhoek (LAY wun hohk) perfected the microscope and became the first human to see cells and microorganisms. These pioneering scientists opened the way for further discoveries.

Human Anatomy
Renaissance artists and scientists, determined to learn how things really worked, studied nature with great curiosity. In the 1400s, Leonardo drew the muscles of the human arm with amazing accuracy (right). Renaissance doctors learned much about human anatomy from dissections (left). *How does this painting from the 1500s reflect the advances in scientific thinking?*

Transforming Chemistry The branch of science now called chemistry was in medieval times called alchemy. Alchemists believed that any substance could be transformed into any other substance, and many of them tried unsuccessfully to turn ordinary metals into gold. With the advances of the Scientific Revolution, the experiments of alchemists were abandoned. However, some of their practices—especially the manipulation of metals and acids—set the stage for modern chemistry.

In the 1600s, English chemist **Robert Boyle** refined the alchemists' view of chemicals as basic building blocks. He explained all matter as being composed of tiny particles that behave in knowable ways. Boyle distinguished between individual elements and chemical compounds, and explained the effect of temperature and pressure on gases. Boyle's work opened the way to modern chemical analysis of the composition of matter.

✔ **Checkpoint** How did Boyle transform the science of chemistry?

Isaac Newton Links the Sciences

As a student in England, **Isaac Newton** devoured the works of the leading scientists of his day. By age 24, he had formed a brilliant theory to explain why the planets moved as they did. According to one story, Newton saw an apple fall from a tree. He wondered whether the force that pulled that apple to Earth might not also control the movements of the planets. In the next 20 years, Newton perfected his theory. Using mathematics, he showed that a single force keeps the planets in their orbits around the sun. He called this force **gravity.**

In 1687, Newton published a book explaining the law of gravity and other workings of the universe. Nature, argued Newton, follows uniform laws. All motion in the universe can be measured and described mathematically. To many, Newton's work seemed to link the sciences just as gravity itself bound the universe together.

For more than 200 years, Newton's laws held fast. In the early 1900s, startling new theories of the universe called some of his ideas into question. Yet his laws of motion and mechanics continue to have many practical uses. For example, **calculus**—a branch of mathematics partially developed by Newton and used to explain his laws—is still applied today.

✔ **Checkpoint** How did Newton use observations of nature to explain the movements of the planets?

SECTION 5
Assessment

Progress Monitoring Online
For: Self-quiz with vocabulary practice
Web Code: naa-1351

Terms, People, and Places
1. What do all of the key people listed at the beginning of this section have in common? Explain.

Note Taking
2. **Reading Skill: Identify Main Ideas** Use your completed table to answer the Focus Question: How did discoveries in science lead to a new way of thinking for Europeans?

Comprehension and Critical Thinking
3. **Recognize Ideologies** Why did the theories of Copernicus and Galileo threaten the views of the Church?
4. **Make Generalizations** In what ways did the scientific method differ from earlier approaches to learning?
5. **Recognize Cause and Effect** What impact did Renaissance ideas have on medicine?
6. **Synthesize Information** How did Newton use the ideas of Plato?

● **Writing About History**

Quick Write: Write a Conclusion Write a conclusion to a persuasive essay about the Scientific Revolution. Your conclusion should restate a thesis statement, supported by one or two strong arguments. You may want to end your essay with a quotation. For example, you could use the Pope quotation to support a thesis that Newton's ideas were the most important of the Scientific Revolution.

Concept Connector

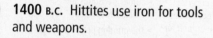

SCIENCE AND TECHNOLOGY

What are the benefits and costs of science and technology?

In This Chapter **GA** SSWH13a

Science and religion clashed during the Scientific Revolution as new theories and discoveries conflicted with traditional views. Galileo was tried and imprisoned by the Inquisition (right) for claiming that Earth revolved around the sun.

Throughout History

- **1400 B.C.** Hittites use iron for tools and weapons.

- **850 A.D.** Chinese develop explosives used in fireworks and guns.

- **1700s** New farming methods raise output but displace workers.

- **1800s** Industrialization increases standards of living and pollution.

- **2000s** The Internet leads to increased communication and computer-based fraud.

Continuing Today

Nuclear energy generates electrical power without the carbon emissions of fossil fuels. However, environmentalists (below) are among those who warn of the dangers of nuclear waste and the possibility of the accidental release of radioactive ions into the atmosphere.

TRANSFER Activities

1. **Analyze** Why do science and technology have both costs and benefits?

2. **Evaluate** Does science have a greater potential for helping society, or for hurting society? Why?

3. **Transfer** Complete a Web quest in which you identify a successful innovator; record your thoughts in the Concept Connector Journal; and learn to make a video. Web Code nah-1308

Quick Study Guide

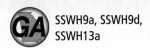 SSWH9a, SSWH9d, SSWH13a

Progress Monitoring *Online*
For: Self-test with vocabulary practice
Web Code: naa-1361

■ Major Themes of the Renaissance

- Importance of classical learning
- Emphasis on the individual
- Adventurous spirit and willingness to experiment
- Focus on realism in art and literature
- Questioning of traditional religious ideas

■ Important Figures of the Scientific Revolution

Person	Achievement	Date
Nicolaus Copernicus	Developed the sun-centered model of the universe	1543
Tycho Brahe and Johannes Kepler	Built astronomical observatory to calculate the planetal orbits; supported Copernicusís views	Late 1500s
Galileo Galilei	Developed telescope to view the planets and confirmed Copernicus's theory	1600
Francis Bacon	Called for new scientific method	Early 1600s
René Descartes	Developed new philosophy of human reasoning	Early 1600s
Isaac Newton	Developed laws of gravity and motion; invented calculus	Late 1600s
Robert Boyle	Identified basic building blocks of matter, opening the way for modern chemistry	Late 1600s

■ Causes and Effects of the Protestant Reformation

Cause and Effect	
Long-Term Causes	**Immediate Causes**
• Roman Catholic Church becomes more worldly. • Humanists urge a return to simple religion. • Shift to more uncertain, urban-based economies causes people to look for society that makes more sense to them. • Monarchs and other leaders question the pope's authority and wealth.	• Johann Tetzel sells indulgences in Wittenberg. • Martin Luther posts 95 Theses. • Luther translates the Bible into German. • The printing press spreads reform ideas. • Calvin and other reformers preach against Roman Catholic traditions.

The Protestant Reformation	
Immediate Effects	**Long-Term Effects**
• Peasants' Revolt • Catholic Reformation • Strengthening of the Inquisition • Luther's calls for Jewish expulsion result in Jewish migration to Eastern Europe	• Religious wars in Europe • Founding of Lutheran, Calvinist, Anglican, Presbyterian, and other Protestant churches • Weakening of Holy Roman Empire • Increased anti-Semitism

■ Key Events of the Renaissance and the Reformation

1300s
The Renaissance begins in the city-states of Italy.

1434
The Medici family gains control of Florence's government.

Chapter Events
World Events

| 1300 | 1350 | 1400 |

1324
Mansa Musa makes hajj.

1368
The Ming dynasty is founded in China.

1450
The kingdom of Songhai emerges in West Africa.

Concept Connector

 Essential Question Review

To connect prior knowledge with what you have learned in this chapter, answer the questions below in your Concept Connector journal. Use the journal in the Reading and Note Taking Study Guide to record your answers (or go to www.phschool.com **Web Code:** nad-1307).

1. **Cultural Diffusion** The Renaissance that emerged in Italy and northern Europe from about 1300 to 1500 and the flowering of Muslim civilization under the Abbasid dynasty from about 750 to 850 are both described as golden ages. Why were these periods in history considered golden ages? How and why did the ideas of Islam and the Renaissance spread?

2. **Science** During the Scientific Revolution, there were many advances in science, mathematics, philosophy and medicine. These developments challenged existing ideas and changed how people looked at the world. How were the ideas of the Scientific Revolution a break from the past? How do these changes affect our understanding of the world today?

■ **Connections to Today**

1. **Technology: The Communications Revolution** During the Renaissance, new technology like the printing press revolutionized life. Consider the various impacts that the printing press had during the Renaissance, in areas ranging from literacy to religion. Then choose a modern technology that has had a comparable effect. Write two paragraphs explaining why the technology you chose is as important in terms of its impact today as the printing press was in Renaissance times.

Gutenberg invents the paper jam

2. **Science: Its Global Impact** The Scientific Revolution transformed technology, government, economy, and society in Europe. Use of the scientific method allowed Europeans to improve farming techniques and ways of manufacturing goods. It helped them to improve mapmaking and navigation techniques and to sail across oceans. European governments found that these changes increased their income and their power, and so many of them supported scientific research. As you will read in the next two chapters, Europe's improved sea power, military technology, and economic might allowed it to conquer parts of Africa and Asia and most of the Americas. Considering these developments, explain how the world today is different from the world before the Scientific Revolution.

History Interactive
For: Interactive timeline
Web Code: nap-1361

1456
The Gutenberg printing press produces the first printed Bible.

1512
Michelangelo completes the Sistine Chapel frescoes.

1517
Martin Luther posts his 95 Theses.

1534
English Parliament passes the Act of Supremacy.

King Henry the eyght.

1633
Galileo is tried before the Inquisition for his theories.

1500   **1550**   **1600**

1453
Constantinople falls to the Ottoman Turks.

1492
Christopher Columbus reaches the Caribbean islands.

1532
Spanish forces defeat the Incan empire of South America.

1620
Pilgrims found the Plymouth Colony in Massachusetts.

Chapter Assessment

Terms, People, and Places

Complete each sentence by choosing the correct answer from the list of terms below. You will not use all of the terms.

patron	indulgence	ghetto
humanism	predestination	heliocentric
vernacular	compromise	hypothesis
utopian		

1. Lorenzo de' Medici was a _____ of the Florentine arts.
2. Rabelais and Shakespeare wrote in the _____ to appeal to the common people.
3. Calvin's belief in _____ set him apart from Catholics.
4. Elizabeth's sensible _____ helped keep England unified in the face of religious conflict.
5. Copernicus's _____ theory of the universe challenged the accepted teachings of the Church.

Main Ideas

Section 1 (pp. 410–417)
6. How did the new Renaissance worldview shape the work of Italian Renaissance artists and writers?

Section 2 (pp. 418–422)
7. What was the role of the printing press in spreading Renaissance ideas?
8. How did northern European artists and writers apply Renaissance ideas in their work?

Section 3 (pp. 423–427)
9. How did the Renaissance open the door to the Protestant Reformation?

Section 4 (pp. 428–433)
10. Why did the Church respond with its Catholic Reformation?

Section 5 (pp. 434–439)
11. How were the scientists of the Scientific Revolution influenced by Renaissance ideas?

Chapter Focus Question
12. How did the Renaissance shape European art, thought, and religion?

Critical Thinking

13. **Geography and History** How did Italy's geography encourage the spread of the Renaissance?
14. **Analyze Information** In what ways was the Renaissance a break with medieval times? In what ways was it a continuation of medieval times?
15. **Predict Consequences** Under what circumstances are religious beliefs likely to inspire anger or violence?
16. **Analyze Visuals** What Renaissance theme does the bas-relief below express?

17. **Test Conclusions** The Renaissance and Scientific Revolution are often described as eras of human progress. Evaluate whether this is an accurate description.
18. **Recognize Cause and Effect** Why did England escape the kinds of religious wars that tore apart other European nations?
19. **Synthesize Information** An English author wrote, "The preaching of sermons is speaking to a few of mankind, but printing books is talking to the whole world." How does this statement suggest a relationship between two of the key events discussed in this chapter?

● Writing About History

In this chapter's five Section Assessments, you developed skills for writing a persuasive essay.

Writing a Persuasive Essay European history from 1300 to the 1600s was a time of great change, discovery, and religious upheaval. Write a persuasive essay that presents your position on either the Renaissance, the Reformation, or the Scientific Revolution.

Prewriting
• Choose a topic and decide what your main position will be.
• Think of arguments that both support and oppose your position.
• Gather evidence that supports your position.

Drafting
• State your position in a thesis statement.
• Organize your arguments into a draft outline.
• Write the introduction, body text, and closing arguments. Be sure to support your arguments with a variety of points, including facts, comparisons, and statistics.

Revising
• Use the guidelines for revising your report on page SH17 of the Writing Handbook.

Prepare for the GHSGT

The Impact of the Printing Press

In a time when new ideas and discoveries were commonplace, the invention of the printing press was no less than astonishing in its impact. Documents A, B, and D describe the spread of printing during the Renaissance. Document C, written by a historian in the 1500s, describes its impact at the time.

Document A

"In 1455 all Europe's printed books could have been carried in a single wagon. Fifty years later, the titles ran to tens of thousands, the individual volumes to millions. Today, books pour off presses at the rate of 10,000 million *a year.* That's some 50 million tons of paper. Add in 8,000 to 9,000 daily newspapers, and the Sundays, and the magazines, and the figure rises to 130 million tons . . . It would make a pile 700 meters [2,297 feet] high—four times the height of the Great Pyramid."

—From ***Gutenberg: How One Man Remade the World with Words*** by John Man

Document B

"Printing spread from Mainz to Strasbourg (1458), Cologne (1465), Augsburg (1468), Nuremberg (1470), Leipzig (1481), and Vienna (1482). German printers, or their pupils, introduced the 'divine' art to Italy in 1467, Switzerland and Bohemia in 1468, France and the Netherlands in 1470, Spain, England, Hungary, and Poland between 1474 and 1476, Denmark and Sweden in 1482–1483. By 1500 the presses had issued about six million books in approximately forty thousand editions, more books, probably, than had been produced in western Europe since the fall of Rome . . . Now individuals could afford to own books, where before they had normally been owned almost exclusively by institutions—monasteries, cathedral chapters, and colleges."

—From ***The Foundation of Early Modern Europe, 1460–1559*** by Eugene F. Rice, Jr.

Document C

"As if to offer proof that God has chosen us to accomplish a special mission, there was invented in our land a marvelous new and subtle art, the art of printing. This opened German eyes even as it is now bringing enlightenment to other countries. Each man became eager for knowledge, not without feeling a sense of amazement at his former blindness."

—From ***Address to the Estates of the Empire*** by Johann Sleidan

Document D

The Spread of Printing in Renaissance Europe

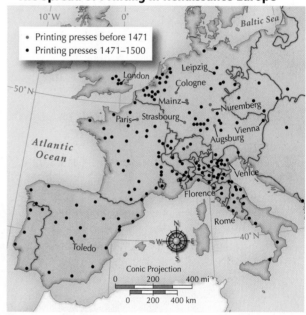

Analyzing Documents

Use your knowledge of the Renaissance and Documents A, B, C, and D to answer questions 1–4.

1. According to Document B, the increased supply and lower cost of books had what effect?
   A More people became teachers.
   B More people became printers.
   C More people bought books.
   D More people bought printing presses.

2. What information about printing can be found only on Document D?
   A specific dates when printing presses were introduced
   B areas where the concentration of printing presses was densest
   C numbers of printing presses introduced into selected cities
   D countries where printing presses were introduced

3. What does German historian Sleidan, in Document C, imply is the *most important* role of the printing press?
   A spreading the Protestant religion
   B teaching German history to other countries
   C Making books cheaper
   D giving Germans more knowledge

4. **Writing Task** How did the invention of the printing press affect the spread of the Reformation? Use specific evidence from the documents above, along with information from this chapter, to support your answer.

14 The Beginnings of Our Global Age: Europe, Africa, and Asia

1415–1796

Around the World and Into History

In 1519, a fleet of five Spanish ships with more than 250 crew sailed from Spain. Ferdinand Magellan, the captain, had been commissioned to sail around the Americas to the Spice Islands. Three years later, a single battered ship limped back into a Spanish harbor. On board were just 18 malnourished, skeletal sailors, so weak they could barely walk. Magellan and all but one of the ship's officers had perished. The survivors told an amazing tale. One recorded in his journal:

66 From the time we left that bay . . . until the present day, we had sailed 14,460 leagues [nearly 60,000 miles], and furthermore had completed the circumnavigation of the world from east to west. 99

Listen to the Witness History audio to hear more about this historic voyage.

 ◀ A Portuguese painting from 1522 tells the story of the martyrdom of Ursula, a medieval Catholic saint. The religious story and the sailing ships in the background express the themes of the age of exploration.

GA Performance Standards

Chapter Focus Question How did European voyages of exploration lead to European empires in the Eastern Hemisphere?

Section 1
The Search for Spices   SSWH10a, SSWH10c

Section 2
Turbulent Centuries in Africa   SSWH6c

Section 3
European Footholds in South and Southeast Asia   SSWH10a, SSWH10c, SSWH14d

Section 4
Encounters in East Asia   SSWH11a

Use the ☑ **Quick Study Timeline** at the end of this chapter to preview chapter events.

A pottery dish in the Muslim Spanish style shows a *nao*, a light sailing ship developed in the 1400s.

African statue of a Portuguese soldier

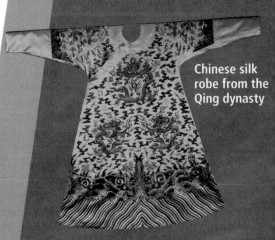

Chinese silk robe from the Qing dynasty

 Concept Connector ONLINE

To explore Essential Questions related to this chapter, go to PHSchool.com
Web Code: nad-1407

The Search Is On

Cinnamon, pepper, nutmeg, cloves . . . these and other spices were a vital part of the world economy in the 1400s. Because the spice trade was controlled by Arab merchants and traders, Europeans didn't know how to get the spices they desperately wanted. Even when Europeans learned that spice plants could be obtained in Asia, they didn't have a hope of growing them in Europe. As an Indonesian ruler boasted to a European trader,

66 You may be able to take our plants, but you will never be able to take our rain. 99

Europeans knew that the only way they could take control of the spice trade would be to establish sea routes to Asia—at any cost.

Focus Question How did the search for spices lead to global exploration?

A French traveler in the 1400s illustrated workers harvesting pepper in southern India; a clove plant is shown at left.

The Search for Spices

GA **Performance Standards**

- **SSWH10a** Explain the role of da Gama, Columbus, and Magellan.
- **SSWH10c** Explain the role of improved technology in European exploration.

Terms, People, and Places

Moluccas
Prince Henry
cartographer
Vasco da Gama
Christopher Columbus

Line of Demarcation
Treaty of Tordesillas
Ferdinand Magellan
circumnavigate

Note Taking

Reading Skill: Identify Causes and Effects
Examine the text for clues that signal cause and effect. Then use a flowchart like this one to record major causes and effects of European exploration.

Throughout history, groups of people—from the ancient Greeks to Muslim Arabs and the Vikings of Scandinavia—had explored the seas, trading and migrating over long distances. The European sailors of the 1400s began a dramatic new period of exploration.

Motivations for Exploring the Seas

Europeans traded with Asians long before the Renaissance. The Crusades introduced Europeans to many luxury goods from Asia, carried on complex overland routes through the Mongol empire of the 1200s and 1300s. The Black Death and the breakup of the Mongol empire disrupted that trade. By the 1400s, though, Europe's population was growing, along with its demand for trade goods. The most valued items were spices, used to preserve food, add flavor to meat, and make medicines and perfumes. The chief source of spices was the **Moluccas,** an island chain in present-day Indonesia, which Europeans then called the Spice Islands.

In the 1400s, Arab and Italian merchants controlled most trade between Asia and Europe. Muslim traders brought prized goods to eastern Mediterranean ports, and Italian traders carried them to European markets. Europeans outside Italy knew that it would be more profitable to gain direct access to Asia. They were also driven by Renaissance curiosity to seek new lands.

✓ **Checkpoint** What factors encouraged European exploration?

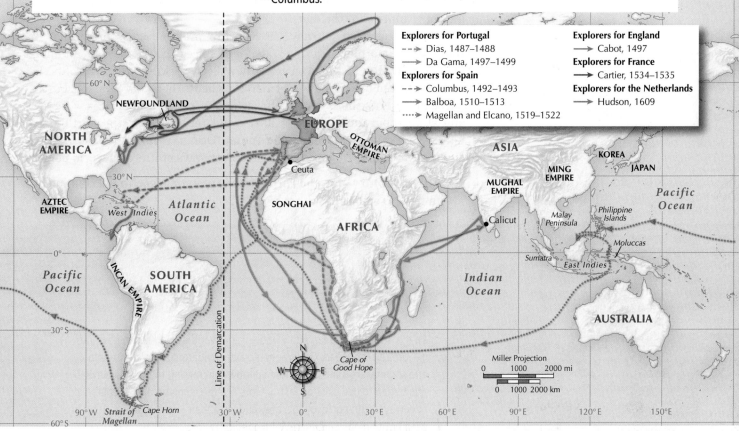

Early Voyages of European Exploration, 1487–1609

Map Skills Spain, England, France, and the Netherlands quickly followed Portugal's lead in exploring the world by ship.

1. **Locate** (a) West Indies (b) East Indies (c) Line of Demarcation (d) Strait of Magellan
2. **Describe** Describe the route of Columbus.
3. **Draw Inferences** Why do you think explorers from different countries followed similar routes?

Explorers for Portugal
- - -→ Dias, 1487–1488
——→ Da Gama, 1497–1499

Explorers for Spain
- - -→ Columbus, 1492–1493
——→ Balboa, 1510–1513
·······→ Magellan and Elcano, 1519–1522

Explorers for England
——→ Cabot, 1497

Explorers for France
——→ Cartier, 1534–1535

Explorers for the Netherlands
——→ Hudson, 1609

Portugal Sails East

Prince Henry led the way in sponsoring exploration for Portugal, a small nation next to Spain. First, Prince Henry's navigators discovered and claimed the Madeira and Azores islands to the west and southwest of Portugal. By 1415, Portugal had expanded into Muslim North Africa, seizing the port of Ceuta (SYOO tah) on the North African coast.

Mapping the African Coast Prince Henry saw great promise in Africa. The Portuguese could convert Africans—most of whom practiced either Islam or tribal religions—to Christianity. He also believed that in Africa he would find the sources of riches the Muslim traders controlled.

Finally, Prince Henry hoped to find an easier way to reach Asia, which meant going around Africa. The Portuguese felt that with their expert knowledge and technology, they could accomplish this feat. At Sagres, in southern Portugal, Henry gathered scientists, **cartographers,** or mapmakers, and other experts. They redesigned ships, prepared maps, and trained captains and crews for long voyages. Henry's ships then slowly worked their way south to explore the western coast of Africa.

Henry died in 1460, but the Portuguese continued their quest. In 1488, Bartholomeu Dias rounded the southern tip of Africa. Despite the turbulent seas around it, the tip became known as the Cape of Good Hope because it opened the way for a sea route to Asia.

Seeking India In 1497, Portuguese navigator **Vasco da Gama** followed in Dias's footsteps, leading four ships around the Cape of Good Hope. Da Gama, however, had plans to go farther. After a ten-month voyage, da Gama reached the great spice port of Calicut on the west coast of India. On the long voyage home, the Portuguese lost half their ships, and many sailors died of hunger, thirst, and scurvy, a disease caused by a lack of vitamin C in the diet.

Despite the hard journey, the venture proved highly profitable. In India, da Gama had acquired a cargo of spices that he sold at an enormous profit. He quickly outfitted a new fleet, seeking greater profits. In 1502, he forced a treaty on the ruler of Calicut. Da Gama then left Portuguese merchants there whose job was to buy spices when prices were low and store them until the next fleet could return. Soon, the Portuguese had seized key ports around the Indian Ocean, creating a vast trading empire. Da Gama's voyages confirmed Portugal's status as a world power.

✓ **Checkpoint** How did Portuguese exploration lead to the creation of a trading empire?

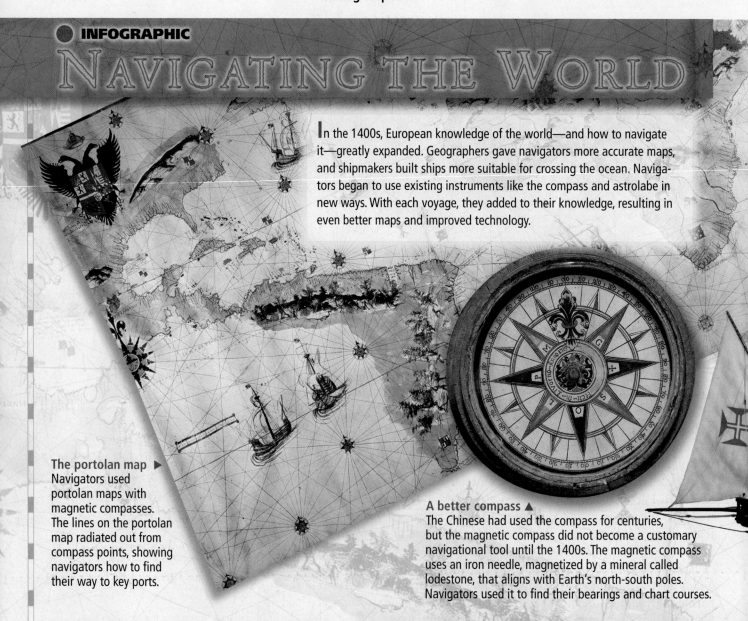

● INFOGRAPHIC

NAVIGATING THE WORLD

In the 1400s, European knowledge of the world—and how to navigate it—greatly expanded. Geographers gave navigators more accurate maps, and shipmakers built ships more suitable for crossing the ocean. Navigators began to use existing instruments like the compass and astrolabe in new ways. With each voyage, they added to their knowledge, resulting in even better maps and improved technology.

The portolan map ▶
Navigators used portolan maps with magnetic compasses. The lines on the portolan map radiated out from compass points, showing navigators how to find their way to key ports.

A better compass ▲
The Chinese had used the compass for centuries, but the magnetic compass did not become a customary navigational tool until the 1400s. The magnetic compass uses an iron needle, magnetized by a mineral called lodestone, that aligns with Earth's north-south poles. Navigators used it to find their bearings and chart courses.

Columbus Sails West

News of Portugal's successes spurred other people to look for a sea route to Asia. An Italian navigator from Genoa, named **Christopher Columbus,** wanted to reach the East Indies—a group of islands in Southeast Asia, today part of Indonesia—by sailing west across the Atlantic. Like most educated Europeans, Columbus knew that Earth was a sphere. A few weeks sailing west, he reasoned, would bring a ship to eastern Asia. His plan made sense, but Columbus greatly underestimated Earth's size. And he had no idea that two continents lay in his path.

Reaching Faraway Lands Portugal refused to sponsor him, but Columbus persuaded Ferdinand and Isabella of Spain to finance his voyage. To increase their <u>authority</u>, the Spanish rulers had taken radical measures, including expelling Jews from Spain. They hoped their actions would strengthen Catholicism. However, the loss of some of Spain's most affluent and cultured people weakened the nation. The rulers hoped Columbus's voyage would bring wealth and prestige.

Vocabulary Builder

<u>authority</u>—(uh THAWR uh tee) *n.* the power to give commands and enforce obedience

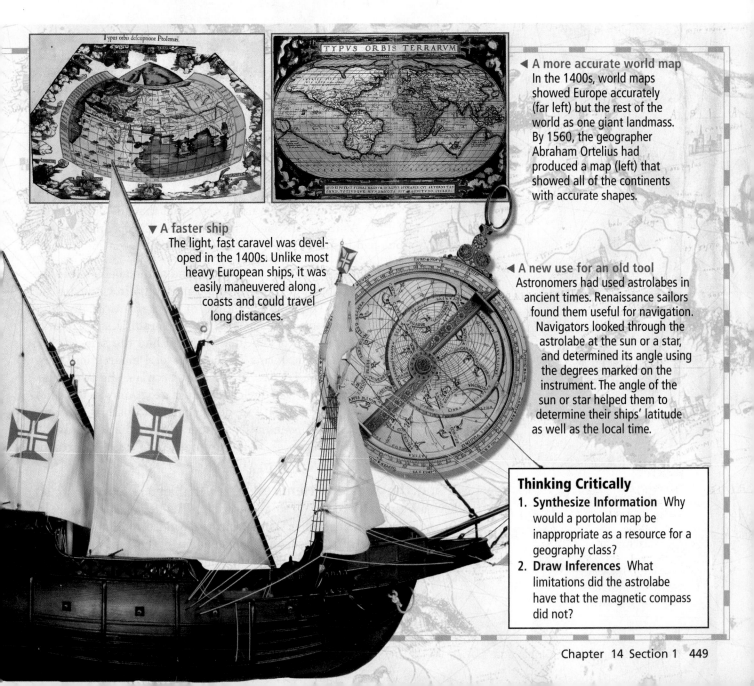

◄ **A more accurate world map** In the 1400s, world maps showed Europe accurately (far left) but the rest of the world as one giant landmass. By 1560, the geographer Abraham Ortelius had produced a map (left) that showed all of the continents with accurate shapes.

▼ **A faster ship** The light, fast caravel was developed in the 1400s. Unlike most heavy European ships, it was easily maneuvered along coasts and could travel long distances.

◄ **A new use for an old tool** Astronomers had used astrolabes in ancient times. Renaissance sailors found them useful for navigation. Navigators looked through the astrolabe at the sun or a star, and determined its angle using the degrees marked on the instrument. The angle of the sun or star helped them to determine their ships' latitude as well as the local time.

Thinking Critically
1. **Synthesize Information** Why would a portolan map be inappropriate as a resource for a geography class?
2. **Draw Inferences** What limitations did the astrolabe have that the magnetic compass did not?

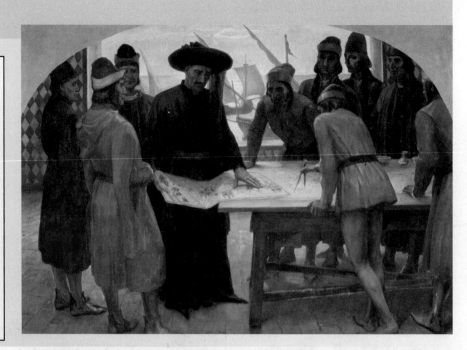

Henry the Navigator

All of the European explorers owed a debt to Prince Henry (1394–1460), whose Christian faith, curiousity, and national pride ushered in the great age of European exploration. The English nicknamed Henry "the Navigator." Yet Henry himself, who sponsored and encouraged navigators, geographers, and merchants, never traveled the seas. Henry's work required financial risks, and his enthusiasm motivated his navigators to take great personal risks. Henry also inspired generations of later explorers. **What characteristics does the artist ascribe to Henry (center figure in black)?**

On August 3, 1492, Columbus sailed west with three small ships, the *Niña*, the *Pinta*, and the *Santa María*. Although the expedition encountered good weather and a favorable wind, no land came into sight for many weeks. Provisions ran low, and the crew became anxious. Finally, on October 12, land was spotted.

Columbus spent several months cruising the islands of the Caribbean. Because he thought he had reached the Indies, he called the people of the region "Indians." In 1493, he returned to Spain to a hero's welcome. In three later voyages, Columbus remained convinced that he had reached the coast of East Asia. Before long, though, other Europeans realized that Columbus had found a route to previously unknown continents.

Dividing the Globe in Half In 1493 Ferdinand and Isabella appealed to the Spanish-born Pope Alexander VI to support their claim to the lands of the new world. The pope set a **Line of Demarcation,** dividing the non-European world into two zones. Spain had trading and exploration rights in any lands west of the line. Portugal had the same rights east of the line. The specific terms of the Line of Demarcation were agreed to in the **Treaty of Tordesillas,** signed between the two countries in 1494. The actual line was unclear, because geography at the time was imprecise. However, the treaty made it obvious to both Spain and Portugal—and to other European nations, eager to defy what they saw as Spain and Portugal's arrogance—that they needed to build their own empires quickly.

Naming the Western Hemisphere An Italian sea captain named Amerigo Vespucci wrote a journal describing his voyage to Brazil. In 1507, a German cartographer named Martin Waldseemüller used Vespucci's descriptions of his voyage to publish a map of the region, which he labeled "America." Over time, the term "Americas" came to be used for both continents of the Western Hemisphere. The islands Columbus had explored in the Caribbean became known as the West Indies.

✓ **Checkpoint** How did Columbus influence the Treaty of Tordesillas?

The Search for a Direct Route Continues

Though Europeans had claimed vast new territories, they had not yet found a direct route to Asia. The English, Dutch, and French explored the coast of North America unsuccessfully for a "northwest passage," or a route from the Atlantic Ocean to the Pacific through the Arctic islands. Meanwhile, in 1513 the Spanish adventurer Vasco Núñez de Balboa, helped by local Indians, hacked a passage westward through the tropical forests of Panama. From a ridge on the west coast, he gazed at a huge body of water. The body of water that he named the South Sea was in fact the Pacific Ocean.

On September 20, 1519, a minor Portuguese nobleman named **Ferdinand Magellan** set out from Spain with five ships to find a way to reach the Pacific. Magellan's ships sailed south and west, through storms and calms and tropical heat. At last, his fleet reached the coast of South America. Carefully, they explored each bay, hoping to find one that would lead to the Pacific. In November 1520, Magellan's ships entered a bay at the southern tip of South America. Amid brutal storms, rushing tides, and unpredictable winds, Magellan found a passage that later became known as the Strait of Magellan. The ships emerged into Balboa's South Sea. Magellan renamed the sea the Pacific, from the Latin word meaning *peaceful*.

Their mission accomplished, most of the crew wanted to return to Spain the way they had come. Magellan, however, insisted that they push on across the Pacific to the East Indies. Magellan underestimated the size of the Pacific. Three more weeks, he thought, would bring them to the Spice Islands. Magellan was wrong. For nearly four months, the ships plowed across the uncharted ocean. Finally, in March 1521, the fleet reached the Philippines, where Magellan was killed. On September 8, 1522, nearly three years after setting out, the survivors— one ship and 18 sailors—reached Spain. The survivors had been the first people to **circumnavigate,** or sail around, the world. Antonio Pigafetta, one of the few survivors of the expedition, observed: "I believe of a certainty that no one will ever again make such a voyage."

✔ **Checkpoint** What was the significance of Balboa's discovery?

SECTION 1 Assessment

Progress Monitoring Online
For: Self-quiz with vocabulary practice
Web Code: naa-1411

Terms, People, and Places

1. For each term, person, or place listed at the beginning of the section, write a sentence explaining its significance.

Note Taking

2. **Reading Skill: Identify Causes and Effects** Use your completed flowchart to answer the Focus Question: How did the search for spices lead to global exploration?

Comprehension and Critical Thinking

3. **Recognize Cause and Effect** How did the Renaissance motivate European explorers?

4. **Recognize Ideologies** How did Prince Henry's Christian faith shape his role as a sponsor of exploration?

5. **Identify Alternatives** If Columbus had understood the real geography of the world, would he still have made his voyage? Why or why not?

6. **Predict Consequences** What effect might Magellan's circumnavigation of the world have on English, Dutch, and French explorers?

● **Writing About History**

Quick Write: Gather Information
Choose one of the following people from this section for a biographical essay: Prince Henry, Christopher Columbus, or Ferdinand Magellan. Gather information about the person you chose. Note events that were both directly and indirectly influenced by this person.

Error

Error

Chapter 14 Section 1   451

A Benin ivory carving (right) depicts a Portuguese sailor in a ship. Iron weights (top) were used in western Africa to weigh gold.

WITNESS HISTORY ◀)) AUDIO

Great Seabirds Arrive

A Portuguese captain named Alvise Cadamosto reached West Africa in the mid-1400s. He described the reaction of the West Africans to the sight of his ship:

❝ It is said that the first time they saw sails . . . they believed they were great seabirds with white wings, which were flying and had come from some strange place. . . . Some thought the ships were fishes, others that they were ghosts that went by night, at which they were terrified. ❞
—Alvise Cadamosto, 1455

Focus Question What effects did European exploration have on the people of Africa?

Turbulent Centuries in Africa

Performance Standards

• **SSWH6c** Describe trans-Saharan trade in gold, salt, and slaves.

Terms, People, and Places

Mombasa	Osei Tutu
Malindi	monopoly
plantation	Oyo empire
Affonso I	Cape Town
missionary	Boers
Asante kingdom	

Note Taking

Reading Skill: Identify Effects As you read, record effects of European exploration in Africa in a chart like the one below.

```
        Effects of European Exploration
       ┌──────────┬──────────┬──────────┐
   European      Slave      New African
   Footholds     Trade        States
```

European encounters with Africa had occurred for hundreds of years. Yet the European explorers who arrived in the 1400s brought great and unforeseen changes to Africa's peoples and cultures.

Portugal Gains Footholds

As you have read, the Portuguese who explored Africa's coasts in the 1400s were looking for a sea route to Asia that bypassed the Mediterranean. They also wanted to buy goods directly from their source, rather than trading through Arab middlemen.

The Portuguese began carrying out their strategy in West Africa, building small forts to collect food and water and to repair their ships. They also established trading posts to trade muskets, tools, and cloth for gold, ivory, hides, and slaves. These were not colonies peopled by settlers. Instead, the Portuguese left just enough men and firepower to defend their forts.

From West Africa, the Portuguese sailed around the continent. They continued to establish forts and trading posts, but they also attacked existing East African coastal cities such as **Mombasa** and **Malindi,** which were hubs of international trade. With cannons blazing, they expelled the Arabs who controlled the East African trade network and took over this thriving commerce for themselves. Each conquest added to their growing trade empire.

Over the next two centuries, some Portuguese explorers managed to reach parts of present-day Congo, Zambia, and Zimbabwe, establishing limited trade. In general, however, the Portuguese did not venture far from the coasts. They knew little about Africa's interior, and they lacked accurate maps or other resources to help them explore there. Furthermore, Africans in the interior, who wanted to control the gold trade, resisted such exploration. As a result of all these factors, when the Portuguese empire declined in the 1600s, the Portuguese did not leave a strong legacy in Africa.

✔ **Checkpoint** Why did the Portuguese establish a presence mainly along the African coast?

The African Slave Trade Explodes

In the 1500s and 1600s, Europeans began to view slaves as the most important item of African trade. Slavery had existed in Africa, as elsewhere around the world, since ancient times. Egyptians, Greeks, Romans, Persians, Indians, and Aztecs often enslaved defeated foes. The English word *slave* comes from the large number of Slavs taken from southern Russia to work as unpaid laborers in Roman times.

The Arab empire also used slave labor, often captives from East Africa. In the Middle East, enslaved Africans often worked on farming estates. Others became artisans, soldiers, or merchants. Some rose to prominence in the Muslim world even though they were slaves.

Europeans Enter the Slave Trade Portuguese traders quickly joined the profitable slave trade, followed by other European traders. Europeans bought large numbers of slaves to perform labor on their **plantations**—large estates run by an owner or an owner's overseer—in the Americas and elsewhere. Rich Europeans also bought slaves as exotic household servants. By the 1500s, European participation had encouraged a much broader Atlantic slave trade.

Europeans seldom went into Africa's interior to take part in slave raids. Instead, they relied on African rulers and traders to seize captives in the interior and bring them to coastal trading posts and forts. There, the captives were exchanged for textiles, metalwork, rum, tobacco, weapons, and gunpowder. Over the next 300 years, the slave trade grew into a huge and profitable business to fill the need for cheap labor. Each year, traders shipped tens of thousands of enslaved Africans across the Atlantic to work on sugar, rice, tobacco, and other plantations in the Americas. These slaves were considered to be property, and they had no hope of bettering their situations.

African Leaders Resist Some African leaders tried to slow down or stop the transatlantic slave trade. But in the end, the system that supported the trade was simply too strong for them. An early voice raised against the slave trade was that of **Affonso I,** ruler of Kongo in west-central Africa. As a young man, Affonso had been tutored by Portuguese **missionaries,** who hoped to convert Africans to Christianity.

A Valuable Commodity
Since ancient times, gold was a valuable trade good in western Africa. Beginning in the 1500s, it became an important part of the slave trade. Europeans melted down African gold jewelry like the pieces above to make gold coins.

A Portuguese observer described the first ship of African slaves arriving in Portugal in 1444 from West Africa. Judging from the writer's words, what was his opinion of what he saw?

Primary Source

❝ Some kept their heads low and their faces bathed in tears, looking at each other . . . others struck themselves in the face and threw themselves to the ground; and others sang sad songs—although we did not understand their words, the sound told of their great sorrow. . . . The mothers threw themselves flat on the ground. They were beaten but they refused to give up their children. ❞
—From *Chronicle of the Discovery and Conquest of Guinea*

 AUDIO

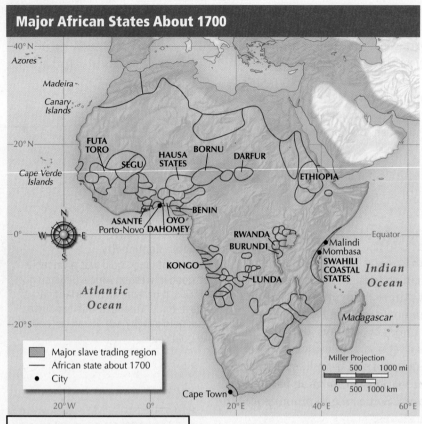

Major African States About 1700

- Major slave trading region
- African state about 1700
- City

Miller Projection
0   500   1000 mi
0 500 1000 km

Map Skills By about 1700, many of Africa's states and kingdoms were involved in the slave trade.
1. **Locate** (a) Malindi (b) Kongo (c) Asante (d) Bornu
2. **Describe** Which states were part of a major slave trading region?
3. **Synthesize Information** In general, where were most slave trading regions located? Explain.

Geography *Interactive*
For: Audio guided tour
Web Code: nap-1421

Vocabulary Builder

dominate—(DAHM uh nayt) *v.* to rule or control by superior power

Vocabulary Builder

unified—(YOO nuh fyd) *v.* combined into one

After becoming king in 1505, he called on the Portuguese to help him develop Kongo as a modern Christian state. But he became alarmed as more and more Portuguese came to Kongo each year to buy slaves. Affonso wanted to maintain contact with Europe but end the slave trade. His appeal failed, and the slave trade continued.

In the late 1700s, another African ruler tried to halt the slave trade in his lands. He was the almany (from the Arabic words meaning "religious leader") of Futa Toro, in present-day Senegal. Since the 1500s, French sea captains had bought slaves from African traders in Futa Toro. In 1788, the almany forbade anyone to transport slaves through Futa Toro for sale abroad. However, the inland slave traders simply worked out a new route to the coast. Sailing to this new market, the French captains easily purchased the slaves that the almany had prevented them from buying in Futa Toro.

 Checkpoint How did the African slave trade expand?

New African States Arise

The slave trade had major effects on African states in the 1600s and 1700s. In West Africa, for example, the loss of countless numbers of young women and men resulted in some small states disappearing forever. At the same time, there arose new states whose way of life depended on the slave trade. The rulers of these powerful new states waged war against other Africans to <u>dominate</u> the slave trade.

The Asante Kingdom The **Asante kingdom** (uh SAHN teh) emerged in the area occupied by present-day Ghana. In the late 1600s, an able military leader, **Osei Tutu,** won control of the trading city of Kumasi. From there, he conquered neighboring peoples and <u>unified</u> the Asante kingdom. The Asante faced a great challenge in the Denkyera, a powerful neighboring enemy kingdom. Osei Tutu realized that in order to withstand the Denkyera, the people of his kingdom needed to be firmly united. To do this, he claimed that his right to rule came from heaven, and that people in the kingdom were linked by spiritual bonds. This strategy paid off when the Asante defeated the Denkyera in the late 1600s.

Under Osei Tutu, government officials, chosen by merit rather than by birth, supervised an efficient bureaucracy. They managed the royal monopolies on gold mining and the slave trade. A **monopoly** is the exclusive control of a business or industry. The Asante traded with Europeans on the coast, exchanging gold and slaves for firearms. They also played rival Europeans against one another to protect themselves. In this way, they built a wealthy, powerful state.

The Oyo Empire The Oyo empire arose from successive waves of settlement by the Yoruba people of present-day Nigeria. It began as a relatively small forest kingdom. Beginning in the late 1600s, however, its leaders used wealth from the slave trade to build up an impressive army. The Oyo empire used the army to conquer the neighboring kingdom of Dahomey. At the same time, it continued to gain wealth by trading with European merchants at the port city of Porto-Novo.

✓ **Checkpoint** What caused some African states to grow?

The European Presence Expands

Following the Portuguese example, by the 1600s several European powers had established forts along the western coast of Africa. As Portuguese power declined in the region, British, Dutch, and French traders took over their forts. Unlike the Portuguese, they established permanent footholds throughout the continent.

In 1652, Dutch immigrants arrived at the southern tip of the continent. They built **Cape Town,** the first permanent European settlement, to supply ships sailing to or from the East Indies. Dutch farmers, called **Boers,** settled around Cape Town. Over time, they ousted, enslaved, or killed the people who lived there. The Boers held a Calvinist belief that they were the elect, or chosen, of God. They looked on Africans as inferiors and did not respect their claims to their own land. In the 1700s, Boer herders and ivory hunters began to push north from the Cape Colony. Their migrations would eventually lead to battle with several African groups.

By the mid-1600s, the British and French had both reached present-day Senegal. The French established a fort in the region around 1700. In the late 1700s, stories about British explorers' search for the source of the Nile River sparked an interest in Africa among Europeans, especially the French and British. In 1788, the British established the African Association, an organization that sponsored explorers to Africa. Over the next century, European exploration of Africa would explode.

✓ **Checkpoint** How did the European presence in Africa expand?

Elmina Castle
European traders called the places where they held and traded slaves "castles." Built by the Portuguese in 1482, Elmina Castle in present-day Ghana was used as a base for trading slaves, gold, and imported European products.

SECTION 2 Assessment

Progress Monitoring *Online*
For: Self-quiz with vocabulary practice
Web Code: naa-1421

Terms, People, and Places

1. What do many of the key terms and people listed at the beginning of the section have in common? Explain.

Note Taking

2. **Reading Skill: Identify Effects** Use your completed chart to answer the Focus Question: What effects did European exploration have on the people of Africa?

Comprehension and Critical Thinking

3. **Determine Relevance** How did the Portuguese strategy of building forts instead of permanent colonies affect Portugal's history in Africa?

4. **Recognize Cause and Effect** How did Europeans change the nature of African slavery?

5. **Analyze Information** Why did the Asante and Oyo need to trade with Europeans to maintain power?

6. **Predict Consequences** Would the Europeans have taken the same course in Africa if the people there had been Christian like themselves?

● Writing About History

Quick Write: Write a Thesis Statement Write a thesis statement that will support a biographical essay about either Osei Tutu or Affonso I. Remember that the facts and events you cite in your essay should support your thesis statement. For example, the following thesis statement is not supported by the facts in the text: Affonso I was instrumental in slowing the slave trade in Africa.

King Affonso I:
Letter to King John III of Portugal

In 1490, the Portuguese converted the son of a Kongo king to Christianity and then helped him take his father's throne. The new king, born Nzinga Mbemba, was renamed Affonso. King Affonso soon realized that his relationship with Portugal had extremely negative consequences, as can be seen from his letter to King John III of Portugal in 1526. In this letter, the king of Kongo appeals to the king of Portugal to end the slave trade.

▲ A Congolese brass and wood crucifix dating from the 1500s blends Christian and traditional African symbols.

Sir, Your Highness of Portugal should know how our Kingdom is being lost in so many ways. This is caused by the excessive freedom given by your officials to the men and merchants who are allowed to come to this Kingdom to set up shops with goods and many things which have been prohibited by us. Many of our vassals, whom we had in obedience, do not comply[1] because they have the things in greater abundance than we ourselves. It was with these things that we had them content and subjected under our jurisdiction[2], so it is doing a great harm not only to the service of God, but to the security and peace of our Kingdoms and State as well.

And we cannot reckon how great the damage is, since the mentioned merchants are taking every day our natives, sons of the land and the sons of our noblemen and vassals and our relatives. The thieves and men of bad conscience grab them wishing to have the things and wares of this Kingdom which they are ambitious of; they grab them and get them to be sold. And so great, Sir, is the corruption and licentiousness[3] that our country is being completely depopulated, and your Highness should not agree with this nor accept it as in your service. And to avoid it we need from those your Kingdoms no more than some priests and a few people to teach in schools, and no other goods except wine and flour for the holy sacrament.

That is why we beg of Your Highness to help and assist us in this matter, commanding your factors[4] that they should not send here either merchants or wares, because it is our will that in these kingdoms there should not be any trade of slaves nor outlet for them. Concerning what is referred to above, again we beg of Your Highness to agree with it otherwise we cannot remedy such an obvious damage.

▲ King John III of Portugal

1. **comply** (kum PLY) *v.* agree to a request
2. **jurisdiction** (joor is DIK shun) *n.* area of authority or power
3. **licentiousness** (ly SEN shus nis) *n.* lack of morality
4. **factors** (FAK turs) *n.* agents

Thinking Critically

1. **Identify Causes** What does King Affonso believe has caused his vassals to become disobedient?

2. **Analyze Information** What specifically does King Affonso say he still needs from the Portuguese?

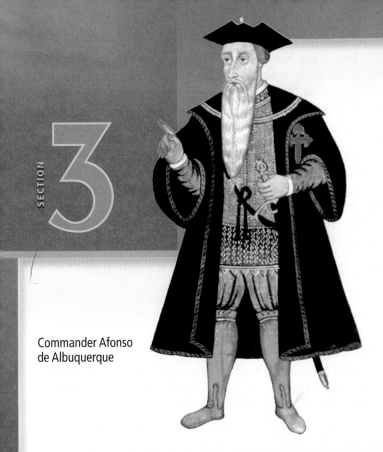

Commander Afonso
de Albuquerque

WITNESS HISTORY 🔊 AUDIO

Gunfire Over Malacca

In 1511, a Portuguese fleet commanded by Afonso de Albuquerque (AL buh kur kee) dropped anchor off Malacca, a rich Islamic trading port that controlled the sea route linking India, Southeast Asia, and China. The fleet remained at anchor for several weeks before opening fire. According to a Malaysian account:

❝The cannon balls came like rain. And the noise of the cannon was as the noise of thunder in the heavens and the flashes of fire of their guns were like flashes of lightning in the sky: and the noise of their matchlocks [guns] was like that of groundnuts [peanuts] popping in the frying pan.❞
—From the *Malay Annals*

Focus Question How did European nations build empires in South and Southeast Asia?

European Footholds in South and Southeast Asia

 Performance Standards

- **SSWH10a** Explain the roles of explorers and conquistadors.
- **SSWH10c** Explain role of improved technology in European exploration.
- **SSWH14d** Analyze the spread of the Mongol Empire.

Terms, People, and Places

Afonso de Albuquerque	Dutch East India Company
Mughal empire	sovereign
Goa	Philippines
Malacca	sepoys
outpost	

Note Taking

Reading Skill: Identify Causes and Effects As you read this section, fill in a chart like the one below with the causes and effects of European exploration in South and Southeast Asia.

Portugal	Netherlands	Spain	Britain
•	•	•	•
•	•	•	•

Portugal was the first European power to gain a foothold in Asia. The Portuguese ships were small in size and number, but the firepower of their shipboard cannons was unmatched. In time, this superior firepower helped them win control of the rich Indian Ocean spice trade and build a trading empire in Asia.

Portugal Builds an Eastern Empire

After Vasco da Gama's voyage, the Portuguese, under **Afonso de Albuquerque's** command, burst into the Indian Ocean. By that time, Muslim rulers, originally from central Asia, had established the **Mughal empire** throughout much of India. The southern regions of India, however, were still controlled by a patchwork of local princes. The Portuguese won these princes to their side with promises of aid against other Europeans. With these southern footholds, Albuquerque and the Portuguese hoped to end Muslim power and turn the Indian Ocean into a "Portuguese lake."

A Rim of Trading Outposts In 1510, the Portuguese seized the island of **Goa** off the coast of India, making it their major military and commercial base. Albuquerque burned coastal towns and crushed Arab fleets at sea. The Portuguese took the East Indies port of **Malacca** in 1511, massacring the city's Muslims.

In less than 50 years, the Portuguese had built a trading empire with military and merchant **outposts,** or distant areas under their control, rimming the southern seas. They used the cities they had seized on the east coast of Africa to resupply and repair their ships. For most of the 1500s, Portugal controlled the spice trade between Europe and Asia.

A Limited Impact Despite their sea power, the Portuguese lacked resources and faced too much resistance to make great inroads into the region. They made harsher efforts to convert local people to Christianity than they had in Africa, attacking Muslims and destroying Hindu temples. Still, by 1600 the Portuguese had converted fewer than a million people to Christianity. The conversion rate was especially low among Asian Muslims.

✓ **Checkpoint**   How did the Portuguese control the spice trade?

Rise of the Dutch

The Dutch were the first Europeans to challenge Portuguese domination of Asian trade. The land we know today as the Netherlands included a group of provinces and prosperous trading cities on the North Sea. In the early 1500s it was part of the Holy Roman Empire, but later the Protestant northern provinces won independence. The independent Netherlands entered vigorously into competition for overseas influence.

Building a Mighty Sea Power In 1599, a Dutch fleet returned to Amsterdam from Asia after more than a year's absence. It carried a cargo of pepper, cloves, and other spices. The success of this voyage led to a frenzy of overseas activity. Soon Dutch warships and trading vessels had made the Netherlands a leader of European commerce. Dutch power set up colonies and trading posts around the world. With their <u>strategic</u> settlement at Cape Town, the Netherlands had a secure foothold in the region.

A Powerful Dutch Company In 1602, a group of wealthy Dutch merchants formed the **Dutch East India Company.** From the beginning, this company had an unusual amount of power. Unlike Portuguese and Spanish traders, whose expeditions were tightly controlled by government, the Dutch East India Company had full **sovereign** powers. With its power to build armies, wage war, negotiate peace treaties, and govern overseas territory, it came to dominate the region.

Vocabulary Builder

<u>strategic</u>—(struh TEE jik) *adj.* important to carrying out a plan of action

Different Perspectives
A European artist (right) shows the king of Sri Lanka and a Dutch explorer meeting as equals. In the Indian painting to the left, Europeans are shown as vassals bringing gifts to India's ruler. *How did European and Asian artists bring their own perspectives to early encounters?*

Asserting Dutch Dominance In 1641, the Dutch captured Malacca from the Portuguese and opened trade with China. Soon they were able to enforce a monopoly in the Spice Islands, controlling shipments to Europe as well as much of the trade within Southeast Asia. Like the Portuguese, the Dutch used military force to further their trading goals. Yet they forged closer ties with local rulers than the Portuguese had. Many Dutch merchants married Asian women.

In the 1700s, the growing power of England and France contributed to the decline of the Dutch trading empire in the East. Still, the Dutch maintained an empire in Indonesia until the 1900s.

 Checkpoint How did the Dutch build up a strong presence in Southeast Asia?

Symbols of the Dutch Empire
The Dutch painting *Jacob Mathieusen and His Wife* (*c.* 1650) shows a senior official in the Dutch East India Company overlooking the Dutch fleet in Batavia, Indonesia. A slave holds a parasol, an Asian symbol of power. *How can you tell that the artist was European?*

Spain Seizes the Philippines

While the Portuguese and Dutch set up bases on the fringes of Asia, Spain took over the **Philippines**. Magellan had claimed the archipelago for Spain in 1521. Within about 50 years, Spain had conquered and colonized the islands, renaming them for the Spanish king Philip II. Unlike most other peoples of Southeast Asia, the Filipinos were not united. As a result, they could be conquered more easily.

In the spirit of the Catholic Reformation, Spanish priests set out to convert the Filipino people to Christianity. Later, missionaries from the Philippines tried to spread Catholic teachings in China and Japan.

The Philippines became a key link in Spain's overseas trading empire. The Spanish shipped silver mined in Mexico and Peru across the Pacific to the Philippines. From there, they used the silver to buy goods in China. In this way, large quantities of American silver flowed into the economies of East Asian nations.

 Checkpoint Why was Spain able to conquer the Philippines easily?

Mughal India and European Traders

For two centuries, the Mughal empire had enjoyed a period of peace, strength, and prosperity. European merchants were dazzled by India's splendid Mughal court and its many luxury goods.

A Center of Valuable Trade Mughal India was the center of the valuable spice trade. It was also the world leader in textile manufacturing, exporting large quantities of silk and cotton cloth. The Mughal empire was larger, richer, and more powerful than any kingdom in Europe. When Europeans sought trading rights, Mughal emperors saw no threat in granting them. The Portuguese—and later the Dutch, English, and French—thus were permitted to build forts and warehouses in Indian coastal towns.

A Great Empire Shatters Over time, the Mughal empire weakened. Conflicts between Hindu and Muslim princes rekindled. Years of civil war drained Mughal resources. Rulers then increased taxes, sparking rebellions. Corruption became widespread, and the central government collapsed. As Mughal power faltered, French and English traders fought for power. Like the Dutch, both the British and the French had established East India companies. These companies made alliances with local officials and independent rajahs, or local chiefs. Each company organized its own army of **sepoys,** or Indian troops.

By the mid-1700s, the British and the French had become locked in a bitter struggle for global power. The fighting involved both nations' lands in Asia and the Americas. In India, the British East India Company used an army of British troops and sepoys to drive out the French. The company then forced the Mughal emperor to recognize its right to collect taxes in the northeast. By the late 1700s, it had used its great wealth to dominate most of India.

 Checkpoint How did Britain gain control of India?

Princes and warriors from India gather at a reception for British officers

SECTION **3** Assessment

Terms, People, and Places

1. For each term, person, or place listed at the beginning of the section, write a sentence explaining its significance.

Note Taking

2. **Reading Skill: Identify Causes and Effects** Use your completed flowchart to answer the Focus Question: How did European nations build empires in South and Southeast Asia?

Comprehension and Critical Thinking

3. **Draw Inferences** You read that the Portuguese did not attempt to conquer inland territory. What does that tell you about their assessment of the inland empires?

4. **Analyze Information** Why did the leaders of the Netherlands give so much power to the Dutch East India Company?

5. **Identify Central Issues** What about the location of the Philippines made it a valuable asset for Spain?

6. **Identify Assumptions** The Mughal empire gave trading rights to several European countries. What assumptions about the power of those countries does this show?

● **Writing About History**

Quick Write: Present Evidence to Support a Thesis Write a biographical essay about Afonso de Albuquerque. First, think of a thesis statement that describes the main points you want to make. Then write the main body text, referring frequently to your thesis statement. The details in a biographical essay should directly support your main point. For example, if your thesis is that Albuquerque was a violent man, you would include details about his takeover of Malacca.

Progress Monitoring Online
For: Self-quiz with vocabulary practice
Web Code: naa-1431

A Chinese watercolor portrays Matteo Ricci with European objects, including a model of the universe. A geography book that Ricci translated into Chinese is shown at the top.

A Jesuit in China

In 1583, a young Jesuit priest arrived in China. He had studied Chinese and immediately impressed Chinese rulers with his fluency as well as his knowledge of European science. Matteo Ricci recognized that the Chinese would not accept a European religion "unless it be seasoned with an intellectual flavoring." In his nearly 30 years in China, Ricci translated five European books into Chinese. Ricci adopted Chinese dress and established friendships with Confucian scholars. When he died in 1610 at age 58, he was buried near the emperor. Much of Europe's knowledge about China came from Ricci's writings.

Focus Question How were European encounters in East Asia shaped by the worldviews of both Europeans and Asians?

Encounters in East Asia

Performance Standards

• **SSWH11a** Describe the policies of Oda Nobunaga.

Terms, People, and Places

Macao	Qing
Guangzhou	Qianlong
Matteo Ricci	Lord Macartney
Manchus	Nagasaki

Note Taking

Reading Skill: Understand Effects Fill in a chart like the one below with effects of European contacts in East Asia.

Portuguese ships first reached China from their base in Malacca in 1514. To the Chinese, the Portuguese, like other foreigners, were barbarians. Europeans, by contrast, wrote enthusiastically about China. In 1590, a visitor described Chinese artisans "cleverly making devices out of gold, silver and other metals," and wrote with approval: "They daily publish huge multitudes of books."

European Contact With Ming China

European interest in China and other parts of East Asia continued to grow. The Ming, however, had no interest in Europe—since, as a Ming document proclaimed, "our empire owns the world."

The Ming Limit Trade The Portuguese wanted Chinese silks and porcelains, but had little to offer in exchange. European textiles and metalwork were inferior to Chinese products. The Chinese therefore demanded payment in gold or silver. The Ming eventually allowed the Portuguese a trading post at **Macao** near Canton, present-day **Guangzhou** (GWAHNG joh). Later, they let Dutch, English, and other Europeans trade with Chinese merchants. Foreigners could trade only at Canton under the supervision of <u>imperial</u> officials. When each year's trading season ended, they had to sail away.

Seeking Converts Portuguese missionaries arrived in China along with the traders. In later years the Jesuits—from Spain, Italy, and Portugal—arrived. Most Jesuits had a broad knowledge of many subjects, and the Chinese welcomed the chance to learn about Renaissance Europe from these scholars. The brilliant Jesuit priest **Matteo Ricci** (mah TAY oh REE chee) made a particularly strong impression on the Chinese. Still, Ricci and other priests had little success spreading their religious beliefs in China. They did, however, become important sources of information for Europeans who knew little about China.

✓ **Checkpoint**   Why did Ming China demand that Europeans pay for goods with gold or silver?

The Manchu Conquest

By the early 1600s, the aging Ming dynasty was decaying. Revolts erupted, and Manchu invaders from the north pushed through the Great Wall. The **Manchus** ruled a region in the northeast, Manchuria, that had long been influenced by Chinese civilization. In 1644, victorious Manchu armies seized Beijing and made it their capital.

● **INFOGRAPHIC**

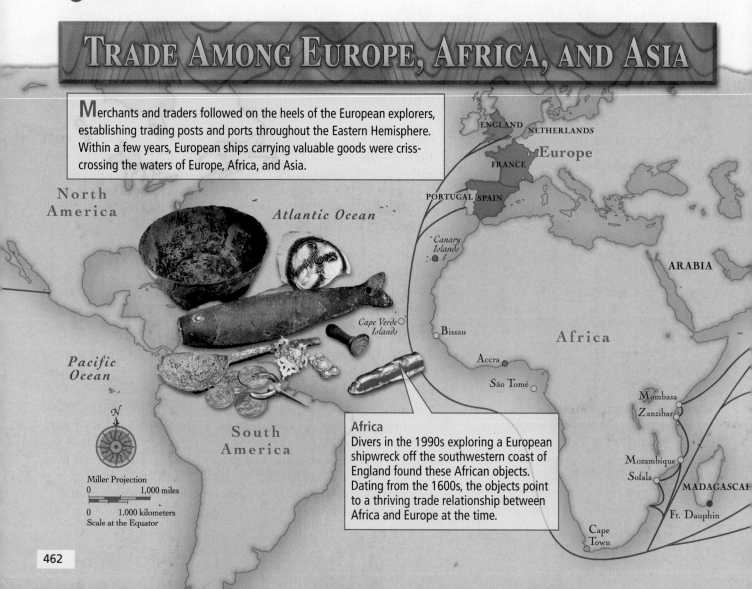

TRADE AMONG EUROPE, AFRICA, AND ASIA

Merchants and traders followed on the heels of the European explorers, establishing trading posts and ports throughout the Eastern Hemisphere. Within a few years, European ships carrying valuable goods were criss-crossing the waters of Europe, Africa, and Asia.

Africa
Divers in the 1990s exploring a European shipwreck off the southwestern coast of England found these African objects. Dating from the 1600s, the objects point to a thriving trade relationship between Africa and Europe at the time.

Miller Projection
0   1,000 miles

0   1,000 kilometers
Scale at the Equator

Founding the Qing Dynasty The Manchus set up a new dynasty called the **Qing** (ching). The Manchus won the support of Chinese scholar-officials because they adopted the Confucian system of government. For each top government position, the Qing chose two people, one Manchu and one Chinese. Local government remained in the hands of the Chinese, but Manchu troops stationed across the empire ensured loyalty.

Two rulers oversaw the most brilliant age of the Qing. Kangxi (kahng shee), who ruled from 1661 to 1722, was an able administrator and military leader. He extended Chinese power into Central Asia and promoted Chinese culture. Kangxi's grandson **Qianlong** (chyahn lung) had an equally successful reign from 1736 to 1796. He expanded China's borders to rule the largest area in the nation's history. Qianlong retired after 60 years because he did not want to rule longer than his grandfather had.

Spreading Peace and Prosperity The Chinese economy expanded under both emperors. New crops from the Americas, such as potatoes and corn, had been introduced into China. These crops boosted farm output, which in turn contributed to a population boom. China's population rose from 140 million in 1740 to over 300 million by 1800. The silk, cotton, and porcelain industries expanded. Internal trade grew, as did the demand for Chinese goods from all over the world.

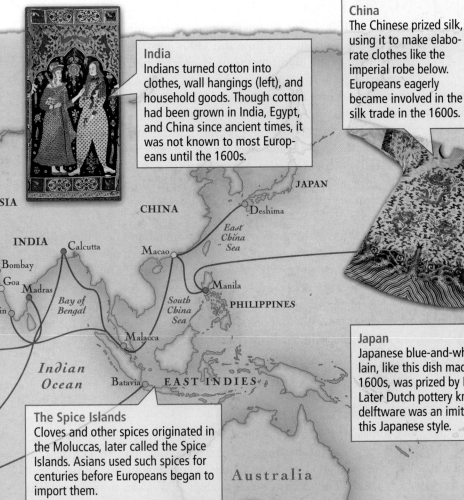

India
Indians turned cotton into clothes, wall hangings (left), and household goods. Though cotton had been grown in India, Egypt, and China since ancient times, it was not known to most Europeans until the 1600s.

China
The Chinese prized silk, using it to make elaborate clothes like the imperial robe below. Europeans eagerly became involved in the silk trade in the 1600s.

Japan
Japanese blue-and-white porcelain, like this dish made in the 1600s, was prized by Europeans. Later Dutch pottery known as delftware was an imitation of this Japanese style.

The Spice Islands
Cloves and other spices originated in the Moluccas, later called the Spice Islands. Asians used such spices for centuries before Europeans began to import them.

Ports controlled by
- England ○ Netherlands ● Spain
- France ○ Portugal — Trade routes

History *Interactive*
For: Interactive trade routes
Web Code: nap-1431

Thinking Critically
1. **Analyze Information** Which European country most likely monopolized the Indian cotton trade?
2. **Make Predictions** What impact would important goods like cotton have on European struggles for power in the Americas?

463

Emperor Qianlong wrote a letter to King George III denying Britain's request for more trading rights and permanent ambassadors. How does Emperor Qianlong's language express his view that China is superior to Britain?

Primary Source

"As to your entreaty to send one of your nationals . . . to my Celestial Court, this request is contrary to all usage of my dynasty and cannot possibly be entertained. . . .

I have but one aim in view, namely, to maintain a perfect governance and to fulfill the duties of the State: strange and costly objects do not interest me. . . . Our dynasty's majestic virtue has penetrated unto every country under Heaven, and Kings of all nations have offered their costly tribute by land and sea. As your Ambassador can see for himself, we possess all things. I set no value on objects strange or ingenious, and have no use for your country's manufactures."

Rejecting Contact With Europeans The Qing maintained the Ming policy of restricting foreign traders. Still, Europeans kept pressing to expand trade to cities other than Guangzhou. In 1793, **Lord Macartney** arrived in China at the head of a British diplomatic mission. He brought samples of British-made goods to show the Chinese the advantages of trade with Westerners. The Chinese, who looked on the goods as rather crude products, thought they were gifts offered as tribute to the emperor.

Further misunderstandings followed. Macartney insisted on an audience with the emperor. The Chinese told Macartney he would have to perform the traditional kowtow, touching his head to the ground to show respect to the emperor. Macartney refused. He also offended the Chinese by speaking of the natural superiority of the English. The negotiations faltered.

At the time, Qianlong's attitude seemed justified by China's successes. After all, he already ruled the world's greatest empire. Why should he negotiate with a nation as distant as Britain? In the long run, however, his policy proved disastrous. In the 1800s, China would learn that its policy of ignoring Westerners and their technology would have undesired consequences.

✔ **Checkpoint** How did the Qing respond to Britain's diplomatic mission?

Korea Chooses Isolation

Before the 1500s, Korean traders had far-reaching contacts across East Asia. A Korean map from the 1300s accurately outlines lands from Japan to the Mediterranean. Koreans probably acquired this knowledge from Arab traders who came to Korea.

In 1592, and again in 1597, the Japanese invaded Korea. The Japanese were driven out in 1598, but the invasions proved disastrous for Korea. Villages were burned to the ground, famine and disease became widespread, and the population decreased. Then, in 1636, before the country was fully recovered, the Manchus invaded Korea. When the Manchus set up the Qing dynasty in China, Korea became a tributary state. It was run by its own government but forced to acknowledge China's supremacy.

Devastated by the two invasions, Korean rulers adopted a policy of isolation, excluding foreigners except the Chinese and a few Japanese. When European sailors were shipwrecked on Korean shores, they were imprisoned and held as spies. Although Korea had few contacts with much of the world for almost 250 years, Koreans on tribute missions brought back maps as well as books on scientific discoveries. This was also a great age for Korean arts and literature.

✔ **Checkpoint** Why did Korea become isolated?

Foreign Traders in Japan

Unlike the Chinese or Koreans, the Japanese at first welcomed Westerners. In 1543, the Portuguese reached Japan, followed by the Spanish, Dutch, and English. They arrived at a turbulent time, when Japanese daimyo were struggling for power. The daimyo quickly adopted Western firearms which may have helped the Tokugawa shoguns centralize power and impose order.

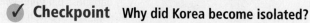

Jesuits, such as the Spanish priest Francis Xavier, found the Japanese curious about Christianity. A growing number of Japanese adopted the new faith. The Japanese also welcomed the printing press the Jesuits brought. The Tokugawa shoguns, however, grew increasingly hostile toward foreigners. After learning that Spain had seized the Philippines, they may have seen the newcomers as threats. They also worried that Japanese Christians—who may have numbered as many as 300,000—owed their <u>allegiance</u> to the pope, rather than to Japanese leaders. In response, the Tokugawas expelled foreign missionaries. They brutally persecuted Japanese Christians, killing many thousands of people.

By 1638, the Tokugawas had turned against European traders as well. Japan barred all European merchants and forbade Japanese to travel abroad. To further their isolation, they outlawed the building of large ships, thereby ending foreign trade. In order to keep informed about world events, they permitted just one or two Dutch ships each year to trade at a small island in **Nagasaki** harbor.

Japan remained isolated for more than 200 years. Art and literature flourished, and internal trade boomed. Cities grew in size and importance, and some merchant families gained wealth and status. By the early 1700s, Edo (present-day Tokyo) had a million inhabitants, more than either London or Paris.

Bringing Trade and Christianity

This 1600s decorative screen shows Japanese people meeting a Portuguese ship carrying European goods and missionaries. *Did the presence of missionaries help or hurt European-Japanese trade relations?*

Vocabulary Builder

allegiance—(uh LEE juns) *n.* loyalty or devotion to a cause or person

✓ **Checkpoint**   **Why did the Tokugawas turn against Europeans?**

SECTION 4 Assessment

Progress Monitoring *Online*
For: Self-quiz with vocabulary practice
Web Code: naa-1441

Terms, People, and Places

1. Place each of the key terms, people, or places listed at the beginning of the section into one of the following categories: politics, culture, government, or geography. Write a sentence for each term explaining your choice.

Note Taking

2. **Reading Skill: Understand Effects** Use your completed chart to answer the Focus Question: How were European encounters in East Asia shaped by the worldviews of both Europeans and Asians?

Comprehension and Critical Thinking

3. **Analyze Credibility** Reread the quotation from the Ming document on page 461. Do you think its characterization of China is credible? Explain.

4. **Draw Inferences** What do Qing China's trade policies with Europeans in the 1700s tell you about the state of the Qing economy?

5. **Make Comparisons** Why did both Japan and Korea respond to increased foreign contact by going into isolation?

6. **Synthesize Information** Why did Japan allow limited contact with the Dutch, but not with the Spanish or Portuguese?

● **Writing About History**

Quick Write: Write a Conclusion Write a sentence to conclude a biographical essay about Matteo Ricci. Read the information about Ricci in this section. Then construct a broad summary sentence that covers the main point you want to make about his life. For example, if your thesis is that Ricci believed Chinese culture to be superior to European culture, you would include that point in your summary sentence.

Quick Study Guide

 SSWH10a, SSWH11a

Progress Monitoring *Online*
For: Self-test with vocabulary practice
Web Code: naa-1451

■ Causes of European Exploration

- Desire for Asian luxury goods such as spices, gold, and silks
- Motivation to spread Christianity
- Strategic need to gain more direct access to trade
- Desire to gain glory for country
- Renaissance curiosity to explore new lands
- Competition with other European countries

■ European Footholds in the Eastern Hemisphere

Country	Date	Foothold	Reason for Interest
Portugal	1502	Calicut, India	Spices
Portugal	1510	Goa, India	Military and commercial base
Portugal	1511	Malacca, Southeast Asia	Center of sea trade
Spain	1521	The Philippines	Center of sea trade
Portugal	1589	Mombasa, East Africa	Hub of international trade
Netherlands	1652	Cape Town, southern Africa	Strategic port for repairing and resupplying ships
Great Britain	1757	Northeastern India	Spices, trade goods

■ Important European Explorers

Explorer	Accomplishment
Vasco da Gama (Portugal)	Sailed around Cape of Good Hope; established ports on Indian Ocean
Christopher Columbus (Spain)	Sailed west across Atlantic Ocean to Caribbean
Vasco Núñez de Balboa (Spain)	Crossed Panama, reaching Pacific Ocean
Ferdinand Magellan (Spain)	Circumnavigated the globe

■ Major Asian Dynasties and Empires

Ruler	Location	Description	European Contact
Mughal empire	India	Major trading empire	After two centuries of peace and prosperity, civil war between Muslim and Hindu princes weakened empire; European powers took control in 1700s
Ming dynasty	China	Prosperous dynasty that had sponsored overseas exploration	Allowed some trade with Europeans and sought out European learning; revolts in the 1600s led to overthrow by the Manchus
Qing dynasty	China	Powerful dynasty that expanded China's borders and promoted Chinese culture	Increasingly restricted European trading rights
Choson dynasty	Korea	Chinese-influenced Confucian state	Had few contacts with the outside world except for China and Japan
Tokugawa shogunate	Japan	Powerful warrior kingdom	Welcomed Europeans at first but then expelled missionaries and most traders

■ Europe, Africa, and Asia 1415–1796

1492 Christopher Columbus reaches the Caribbean.

1498 Portuguese explorer Vasco da Gama rounds Africa and reaches India.

1522 Magellan's expedition circumnavigates the globe.

Chapter Events
Global Events

1450	1500	1550

1453 The Ottoman Turks take Constantinople, ending the Byzantine empire.

1500 The kingdom of Kongo thrives in Africa.

1556 Akbar begins the Mughal reign in India.

Concept Connector

Essential Question Review

To connect prior knowledge with what you have learned in this chapter, answer the questions below in your Concept Connector journal. Use the journal in the Reading and Note Taking Study Guide to record your answers (or go to www.phschool.com Web Code: nad-1407). In addition, record information about the following concepts:

- Technology: the compass
- Trade: Dutch trading empire; Indian trade in Southeast Asia

1. **Empire** With the founding of the Qing Empire, the Manchus established one of China's most successful dynasties. Identify policies the Qing Dynasty used to gain the support of the Chinese people and explain how these policies helped the Qing to expand their empire.

2. **Conflict** As the French and British began to establish global empires in the 1600s and 1700s, they frequently came into conflict. Review the Causes of European Exploration on the opposite page. Then create a list of factors that would cause conflict between two European countries pursuing global empires during this period. Consider military, economic, and political goals.

3. **Trade** As trade brought different nations into greater contact with one another from the 1400s to the 1700s, there were both winners and losers. What were some of the costs and benefits of international trade in this era? How did some states demonstrate their resistance to this expanded contact? Consider the impact on the following:
   - economics
   - politics
   - society

Connections to Today

1. **Trade: The Dutch Trading Empire** In the 1500s, the Dutch began establishing an overseas trade empire in Southeast Asia, using the tools of sea power and monopolistic trade policies. Today, the Dutch are not known for their sea power or overseas domination, yet the strong economy of the Netherlands still depends heavily on trade. Research Dutch trade, including its global rank in exports, the number and types of companies owned by the Dutch in the United States, and the role of multinational companies in the economy of the Netherlands. Write two paragraphs summarizing the importance of trade to the Netherlands today.

2. **Technology: The Compass** European exploration would not have been possible without the compass. The compass allowed navigators to find direction accurately, rather than relying on the sun, stars, and moon. Consider the events and discoveries that the compass made possible. Then think of recent technological inventions that have had profound impacts on the world today. Which technology do you consider to be equivalent in its impact to the compass? Why?

1602 The Dutch establish the Dutch East India Company.

1641 The Dutch take Malacca from the Portuguese.

1736 China's emperor Qianlong begins his reign.

History Interactive
For: Interactive timeline
Web Code: nap-1451

1600   **1650**   **1700**   **1750**

1603 The Tokugawas come to power in Japan.

1642 The English Civil War begins.

1756 The Seven Years' War breaks out between Britain and France.

Chapter Assessment

Terms, People, and Places

1. Define **cartographer**. How did Prince Henry encourage the work of cartographers?
2. Write a sentence or two that shows why scurvy was a problem for sailors who **circumnavigated** the globe.
3. What was the role of European **plantations** in the growth of slavery?
4. Define **outpost**. Why were European outposts important in the development of overseas empires?
5. Why did European trading companies organize armies of **sepoys** in India?
6. How did the Asante kingdom use **monopolies** to keep its power?

Main Ideas

Section 1 (pp. 446–451)
7. How did European interest in the spice trade lead to the discovery of new routes and lands?

Section 2 (pp. 452–456)
8. How did new sea routes lead to an expanded European presence in Africa?
9. What legacy did the Portuguese leave in Africa?

Section 3 (pp. 457–460)
10. How did Portugal gain dominance of the spice trade?
11. How did the Dutch use their foothold in Cape Town to develop an overseas trade empire?
12. What effect did European trade have on the Mughal empire?

Section 4 (pp. 461–465)
13. Summarize European attempts to establish trade and missions in East Asia.
14. Why were East Asians generally resistant to European trade and ideas?

Chapter Focus Question
15. How did European voyages of exploration lead to European empires in the Eastern Hemisphere?

Critical Thinking

16. **Predict Consequences** What might have happened if Asian explorers, rather than Europeans, had first reached the Americas?
17. **Geography and History** How did Japan's geography allow the Tokugawas to maintain a long period of isolation?
18. **Draw Conclusions** Did missionaries hurt or help European attempts to establish trade in Asia? Explain your answer.
19. **Analyze Visuals** The woodcut below was made in 1555 by a Swedish geographer. What does it tell you about European knowledge of the world before the age of exploration?

20. **Recognize Cause and Effect** How did competition among European countries affect overseas exploration and conquest?

● Writing About History

In this chapter's four Section Assessments, you developed skills for writing a biographical essay.

Writing a Biographical Essay Many great Europeans, Africans, and Asians shaped the history of our global age. Write about one of the following important people in a biographical essay: Ferdinand Magellan, Affonso I, Afonso de Albuquerque, Emperor Qianlong, or Matteo Ricci. Consult page SH18 of the Writing Handbook for additional help.

Prewriting
• Choose the person who interests you the most. Take notes about this person and his role in shaping the age of global exploration.

• Draw conclusions about the person you have chosen. Think about how you can turn these conclusions into main points for your essay.

Drafting
• Write an introduction and a thesis statement. Your thesis statement should summarize the main point you want to make about the person you chose.
• Write the body text, introducing details and evidence that support your thesis statement. Then write a conclusion.

Revising
• Use the guidelines for revising your essay on page SH19 of the Writing Handbook.

Prepare for the GHSGT

Why Did Europeans Explore the Seas?

In the 1400s, Europeans began to embark on long and dangerous voyages to unknown destinations. Why did this age of exploration begin? In Documents A and B, a contemporary observer and a modern-day historian describe the impetus behind these early expeditions.

Document A

"The discovery of the new Western World followed, as an incidental consequence, from the long struggle of the nations of Europe for commercial supremacy and control of the traffic with the East. In all these dreams of the politicians and merchants, sailors and geographers, who pushed back the limits of the unknown world, there is the same glitter of gold and precious stones, the same odour of far-fetched spices."

—Sir Walter Raleigh, 1509

Document B

"The starting point for the European expansion out of the Mediterranean and the Atlantic continental shelf had nothing to do with, say, religion or the rise of capitalism—but it had a great deal to do with pepper. . . . . [Pepper] comprised more than half of all the spice imports into Italy over a period of more than a century. No other single spice came within one-tenth of the value of pepper. . . . However, since about 1470 the Turks had been impeding the overland trade routes east from the Mediterranean. As a result the great Portuguese, Italian, and Spanish explorers all sailed west or south in order to reach the Orient. The Americas were discovered as a by-product in the search for pepper."

—From *Seeds of Change* by Henry Hobhouse

This page from a sixteenth-century book about navigation depicts England's Queen Elizabeth in the ship at the right. ▶

Document C

◀ This fifteenth-century painting depicts Henry the Navigator, standing at right in round black hat. A Portuguese prince, Henry did much to advance maritime exploration and the fields of navigation and cartography.

Document D

Analyzing Documents

Use your knowledge of European exploration and Documents A, B, C, and D to answer questions 1–4.

1. Documents A and B both make the point that the discovery of new lands was motivated by
   A religious fanaticism.
   B adventurous dreams.
   C wanting to make money.
   D Renaissance ideals.

2. What motivation for exploration is implied in Document C?
   A the search for spices
   B the desire to please king or country
   C the desire to spread Christianity
   D both B and C

3. What does Document D suggest about how European monarchs viewed exploration?
   A They saw it as vitally important to their nations.
   B They viewed exploration as interesting but unnecessary.
   C They saw it as important but not worth spending money on.
   D They had no opinion on exploration.

4. **Writing Task** Using information from the chapter, assess the various motivations for exploration. Are there any that are not shown in these documents? Choose the motivation you think was the most compelling for Europeans. Use specific evidence from the chapter and documents to support your argument.

The Beginnings of Our Global Age: Europe and the Americas

1492–1750

A Heavenly City

By the 1400s, the Aztec city of Tenochtitlán was one of the largest and most well-planned cities in the world. Aztec wealth had provided clean streets, beautiful gardens, and overflowing storehouses. An Aztec poem written in the early 1500s expressed the writer's pride in the great city:

❝Proudly stands the city of Mexico— Tenochtitlán.
Here no one fears to die in war . . .
Keep this in mind, oh princes . . .
Who could attack Tenochtitlán?
Who could shake the foundation of heaven?❞

Just a few years after this poem was written, Tenochtitlán would fall to an unknown invader from far away. Listen to the Witness History audio to hear more about the end of the Aztec empire.

◄ Contemporary Mexican artist Diego Rivera depicts the Totonacs, Indians who were conquered by the Aztecs and later joined the Spanish.

Aztec feather shield made during the time of Moctezuma

 GA **Performance Standards**

Chapter Focus Question How did European colonization of the Americas shape global economies and societies?

Section 1
Conquest in the Americas
SSWH10a

Section 2
Spanish and Portuguese Colonies in the Americas
SSWH10b

Section 3
Struggle for North America
SSWH10a, SSWH10b, SSWH10c

Section 4
The Atlantic Slave Trade
SSWH10b, SSWHRC1c

Section 5
Effects of Global Contact
SSWH10b

Use the ☑ **Quick Study Timeline** at the end of this chapter to preview chapter events.

Portuguese colonial carving made from brazilwood

Canadian powder horn showing fur trading routes

 Concept **Connector** **ONLINE**

To explore Essential Questions related to this chapter, go to PHSchool.com
Web Code: nad-1507

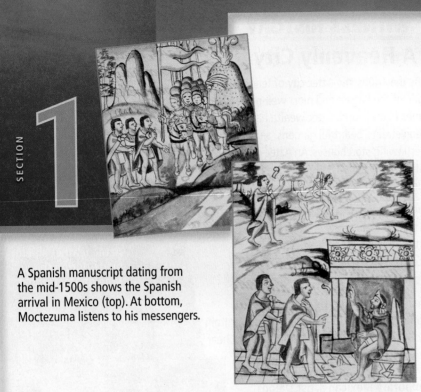

A Spanish manuscript dating from the mid-1500s shows the Spanish arrival in Mexico (top). At bottom, Moctezuma listens to his messengers.

WITNESS HISTORY 🔊 AUDIO

Moctezuma Hears Strange News

In 1519, the Aztec ruler Moctezuma heard an astounding report from his messengers. They described unusual people who had just arrived in the region—people with white skin and yellow hair, clad completely in iron, who rode "deer" as tall as a house and had dogs with burning yellow eyes. According to a Spanish translation of native accounts, "When Moctezuma heard this, he was filled with terror. It was as if his heart grew faint, as it shrank; he was overcome by despair."

Focus Question How did a small number of Spanish conquistadors conquer huge Native American empires?

Conquest in the Americas

 Performance Standards

- **SSWH10a** Explain the roles of explorers and conquistadors and da Gama.

Terms, People, and Places

conquistador
immunity
Hernán Cortés
Tenochtitlán
Malinche

alliance
Moctezuma
Francisco Pizarro
civil war

Note Taking

Reading Skill: Recognize Sequence Keep track of the sequence of events that led to European empires in the Americas by completing a chart like the one below.

Spain Establishes An Empire		
Columbus	**Cortés**	**Pizarro**
• Columbus arrives in the West Indies. •	• •	• •

In 1492, explorer Christopher Columbus landed in the Caribbean islands that are now called the West Indies. The wave of exploration he spurred in the Americas would have drastic, far-reaching consequences for the people who already lived there.

First Encounters in the Americas

Columbus's first meeting with Native Americans began a cycle of encounter, conquest, and death that would be repeated throughout the Western Hemisphere.

Meeting the Taínos When Columbus first arrived in the West Indies, he encountered the Taíno (TY noh) people. The Taínos lived in villages and grew corn, yams, and cotton, which they wove into cloth. They were friendly and open toward the Spanish. Columbus noted that they were "generous with what they have, to such a degree as no one would believe but he who had seen it."

Despite this friendly reception, the Spanish treated the Taíno harshly. Columbus's men assaulted Taíno men and women, claimed their land for Spain, and seized some to take back to the Spanish king. The Spanish killed any Taínos who dared to resist. Columbus later required each Taíno to give him a set amount of gold. Any Taíno who failed to deliver was tortured or killed.

Columbus's encounter was repeated by a wave of Spanish **conquistadors** (kahn KEES tuh dawrz), or conquerors, who soon arrived in the Americas. They first settled on the islands of Hispaniola (now the Dominican Republic and Haiti), Cuba, and Puerto Rico.

Throughout the region, the conquistadors seized the Native Americans' gold ornaments and then made them pan for more gold. At the same time, the Spanish forced the Native Americans to convert to Christianity.

Guns, Horses, and Disease Although Spanish conquistadors only numbered in the hundreds as compared to millions of Native Americans, they had many advantages. Their guns and cannons were superior to the Native Americans' arrows and spears, and European metal armor provided them with better protection. They also had horses, which not only were useful in battle and in carrying supplies, but also frightened the Native Americans, who had never seen a horse.

Most importantly, an invisible invader—disease—helped the conquistadors take control of the Taínos and other Native Americans. Europeans unknowingly carried diseases such as smallpox, measles, and influenza to which Native Americans had no **immunity,** or resistance. These diseases spread rapidly and wiped out village after village. As a result, the Native American population of the Caribbean islands declined by as much as 90 percent in the 1500s. Millions of Native Americans died from disease as Europeans made their way inland.

 Checkpoint How did Spanish conquistadors treat the Taínos?

Cortés Conquers Mexico

From the Caribbean, Spanish explorers probed the coasts of the Americas. They spread stories of empires rich in gold, but they also told of fierce fighting people. Attracted by the promise of riches as well as by religious zeal, a flood of adventurers soon followed.

Cortés Advances on the Aztecs Among the earliest conquistadors was **Hernán Cortés.** Cortés, a landowner in Cuba, heard of Spanish expeditions that had been repelled by Indians. He believed that he could succeed where none had before. In 1519, he landed on the coast of Mexico with about 600 men, 16 horses, and a few cannons. He began an inland trek toward **Tenochtitlán** (teh nawch tee TLAHN), the capital of the Aztec empire. A young Indian woman named **Malinche** (mah LEEN chay), called Doña Marina by the Spanish, served as his translator and advisor. Malinche knew both the Maya and Aztec languages, and she learned Spanish quickly.

Malinche told Cortés that the Aztecs had gained power by conquering other groups of people. The Aztecs sacrificed thousands of their captives to the Aztec gods each year. Many conquered peoples hated their Aztec overlords, so Malinche helped Cortés arrange **alliances** with them. They agreed to help Cortés fight the Aztecs.

Moctezuma Faces a Dilemma Meanwhile, messengers brought word about the Spanish to the Aztec emperor **Moctezuma** (mahk tih ZOO muh). Terrified, he wondered if the leader of the pale-skinned, bearded strangers might be Quetzalcoatl (ket sahl koh AHT el), an Aztec god-king who had long ago vowed to return from the east. Because Moctezuma did not know for sure if Cortés was a god, he did not know how to respond to the news. He sent gifts of turquoise, feathers, and other goods with religious importance, but urged the strangers not to continue to Tenochtitlán.

Cortés, however, had no intention of turning back. He was not interested in the Aztec religious objects, but was extremely interested in the gold and silver ornaments that Moctezuma began sending him.

This passage from a Maya book written in the 1500s describes life before the arrival of the Spanish. What does the writer say was the main effect of Europeans on the Maya?

 Primary Source 🔊 AUDIO

66 There was then no sickness;
They had then no aching bones;
They had then no high fever;
They had then no smallpox;
They had then no burning chest. . .
At that time the course of humanity was orderly.
The foreigners made it otherwise when they arrived here.99

Malinche Shapes History
Malinche's parents sold her as a slave when she was a child, believing that she was born under an unlucky star. Despite her unfortunate beginning, she left a major mark on the history of the Americas.

Traveler's Tales
EYEWITNESS ACCOUNT

Díaz Sets the Record Straight

Bernal Díaz del Castillo was a Spanish soldier who came to Cuba in 1514. In 1519, he accompanied Hernán Cortés on his conquest of the Aztecs. More than 40 years later, Díaz wrote his *True History* because he felt other accounts of the conquest—written by historians who had not been there—were inaccurate. He insisted that as an eyewitness of events he was a better historical source. For example, Díaz was there when Moctezuma took Cortés to the top of the great temple to look at Tenochtitlán, his magnificent capital city on the lake.

Cortés became more determined than ever to reach Tenochtitlán. Fighting and negotiating by turns, Cortés led his forces inland toward the capital. At last, the Spanish arrived in Tenochtitlán, where they were dazzled by the grandeur of the city.

Tenochtitlán Falls to the Spanish Moctezuma welcomed Cortés to his capital. However, relations between the Aztecs and Spaniards soon grew strained. The Spanish scorned the Aztecs' religion and sought to convert them to Christianity. At the same time, as they remained in the city, they saw more of the Aztec treasure. They decided to imprison Moctezuma so they could gain control of the Aztecs and their riches.

Cortés <u>compelled</u> Moctezuma to sign over his land and treasure to the Spanish. In the meantime, a new force of Spanish conquistadors had arrived on the coast to challenge Cortés. In the confusion that followed—with various groups of Spanish, Aztecs, and Native Americans all fighting for control—the Aztecs drove the Spanish from the city. More than half of the Spanish were killed in the fighting, as was Moctezuma.

Cortés retreated to plan an assault. In 1521, in a brutal struggle, Cortés and his Indian allies captured and demolished Tenochtitlán. The Spanish later built Mexico City on the ruins of Tenochtitlán. As in the Caribbean, disease had aided their cause. Smallpox had spread among the Aztecs from the 1519 encounter, decimating the population.

Vocabulary Builder
compel—(kum PEL) *v.* to force

✓ **Checkpoint** What impact did the Aztecs' religious beliefs have on Cortés's approach to Tenochtitlán?

> 66When we saw so all those cities and villages built in the water, and other great towns on dry land, and that straight and level causeway leading toward [Tenochtitlán], we were astounded. These great towns and [pyramids] and buildings rising from the water, all made of stone, seemed like an enchanted vision... Indeed, some of our soldiers asked whether it was not all a dream.... It was all so wonderful that I do not know how to describe this first glimpse of things never heard of, seen or dreamed of before.99

> 66We turned back to the great market and the swarm of people buying and selling. The mere murmur of their voices was loud enough to be heard more than three miles away. Some of our soldiers who had been in many parts of the world, in Constantinople, in Rome, and all over Italy, said that they had never seen a market so well laid out, so large, so orderly, and so filled with people.99

> — *Bernal Díaz del Castillo*
> from ***The True History of the Conquest of New Spain***

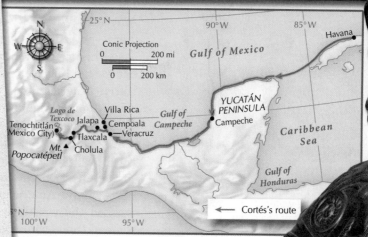

Hernán Cortés ▶

Thinking Critically

1. **Draw Inferences** Why do you think Díaz included the opinions of "some of our soldiers"?
2. **Make a Reasoned Judgment** Do you agree with Díaz that the best historical accounts are written by people who participated in or witnessed the events? Explain your answer.

Pizarro Takes Peru

Cortés's success inspired other adventurers, among them Spaniard **Francisco Pizarro** (pee SAHR oh). Pizarro was interested in Peru's Inca empire, which was reputed to have even more riches than the Aztecs. Pizarro arrived in Peru in 1532, just after the Incan ruler Atahualpa (ah tah WAHL puh) had won the throne from his brother in a bloody **civil war.** A civil war is fought between groups of people in the same nation.

Pizarro's secretary described Atahualpa as

Primary Source

> 66a man of thirty years, good-looking and poised, somewhat stout, with a wide, handsome, and ferocious face, and the eyes flaming with blood . . .99
> —Francisco de Xerez

Atahualpa refused to become a Spanish vassal or convert to Christianity. In response, Pizarro, aided by Indian allies, captured him and slaughtered thousands of Inca. The Spanish demanded a huge ransom for the ruler. The Inca paid it, but the Spanish killed Atahualpa anyway.

Despite continuing resistance, Pizarro and his followers overran the Incan heartland. He had superior weapons, and the Inca were weakened by European diseases. From Peru, Spanish forces surged across Ecuador and Chile. Before long, Spain had added much of South America to its growing empire. Pizarro himself was killed by a rival Spanish faction a few years after he established the city of Lima.

✓ **Checkpoint** What factors encouraged Spanish success in Peru?

Effects of the Spanish Conquistadors

The Spanish conquistadors accomplished a major victory in the Americas. Within a few decades, a few hundred European soldiers—helped by superior weapons, horses, and especially disease—had conquered millions of Native Americans. The Spanish had seized huge quantities of valuable goods. And they had used Native American labor to establish silver mines in Peru and Mexico to finance their new empire. In the 1500s and early 1600s, treasure fleets sailed each year to Spain or the Spanish Philippines loaded with gold and silver. With this wealth, Spain became Europe's greatest power.

The effect on Native Americans, however, was quite different. Some Native Americans believed that the disasters they suffered marked the world's end. As tens of thousands of Indians died, some of the bewildered and demoralized survivors felt that their gods were less powerful than the god of their conquerors. They therefore stopped resisting. Many Native Americans converted to Christianity in the hopes that their suffering would end.

Yet many Indians continued to resist the Spanish in any way they could. For centuries, the Maya fought Spanish rule in Mexico and Central America. Long after the death of Atahualpa, revolts erupted among the Inca. And throughout the Americas, Indians resisted European influences by preserving aspects of their own culture, including language, religious traditions, and clothing. In time, Native American culture came to influence the culture of Latin America.

The early encounters between the Spanish conquistadors and Native Americans had long-lasting impacts that reached far beyond these two groups. By establishing an empire in the Americas, Spain dramatically changed the pattern of global encounter set in motion with the first European exploration of Africa. For the first time, much of the world was now connected by sea routes, on which traveled ships carrying goods, people, and ideas.

✔ **Checkpoint** In what ways did Native Americans resist Europeans?

Sunken Treasure
Spanish ships sunk in the waters off Cuba's coast hundreds of years ago still yield gold and silver treasure to divers today. A craftsman of mixed Spanish and Native American ancestry made these ceremonial weapons in 1631.

SECTION 1 Assessment

Terms, People, and Places

1. What do each of the key terms listed at the beginning of the section have in common? Explain.

Note Taking

2. **Reading Skill: Recognize Sequence** Use your completed chart to answer the Focus Question: How did a small number of Spanish conquistadors conquer huge Native American empires?

Comprehension and Critical Thinking

3. **Determine Relevance** Which factor was the most important in aiding Spanish success in the Americas?

4. **Summarize Information** How did Cortés gain control of Tenochtitlán?

5. **Recognize Cause and Effect** How did the Incan civil war affect the Spanish outcome in Peru?

6. **Identify Alternatives** How might the history of Europeans in the Americas have been different if the Indians had not been killed by European diseases?

● Writing About History

Quick Write: List Things to Compare When you write an expository essay comparing and contrasting two things, you first need to decide which things are useful to compare. List several people, places, or activities from this section to compare. The things you choose should be appropriate for comparison. For example, comparing Malinche and Columbus would not make sense because their roles and purposes were so different from one another.

A 1584 drawing of slaves laboring at the Potosí silver mine, Bolivia

WITNESS HISTORY 🔊 AUDIO

A Missionary Protests

❝ Everything that has happened since the marvellous discovery of the Americas . . . seems to overshadow all the deeds of famous men past, no matter how heroic, and to silence all talk of other wonders of the world. Prominent amid the aspects of this story which have caught the imagination are the massacres of innocent peoples. . . . ❞
—Friar Bartolomé de Las Casas, 1542

Focus Question How did Spain and Portugal build colonies in the Americas?

Spanish and Portuguese Colonies in the Americas

Performance Standards

• **SSWH10b** Define the Columbian Exchange and its economic and cultural impact.

Terms, People, and Places

viceroy	creole
encomienda	mestizo
Bartolomé de Las Casas	mulatto
peon	privateer
peninsular	

Note Taking

Reading Skill: Recognize Sequence Use a flowchart like this one to keep track of the steps the Spanish took to establish an overseas empire. Add boxes as necessary.

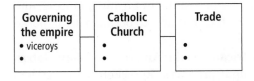

A flood of Spanish settlers and missionaries followed the conquistadors to Spain's new empire. Wherever they went they established colonies, claiming the land and its people for their king and Church. When there was resistance, the newcomers imposed their will by force. Over time, however, a new culture emerged that reflected European, Native American, and African traditions.

Ruling the Spanish Empire

By the mid-1500s, Spain claimed a vast empire stretching from California to South America. In time, it divided these lands into four provinces, including New Spain (Mexico) and Peru.

Governing the Provinces Spain was determined to maintain strict control over its empire. To achieve this goal, the king set up the Council of the Indies to pass laws for the colonies. He also appointed **viceroys,** or representatives who ruled in his name, in each province. Lesser officials and audiencias (ow dee EN see ahs), or advisory councils of Spanish settlers, helped the viceroy rule. The Council of the Indies in Spain closely monitored these colonial officials to make sure they did not assume too much authority.

Spreading Christianity To Spain, winning souls for Christianity was as important as gaining land. The Catholic Church worked with the government to convert Native Americans to Christianity.

Cultural Blending
Encounters with Native Americans, or stories about such encounters, influenced Spanish and Portuguese artists. This painting dating from the early 1500s places a Biblical story—the adoration of the Magi—in the Americas, with Native American figures.

Vocabulary Builder
drastic—(DRAS tik) *adj.* severe; having a strong effect

Church leaders often served as royal officials and helped to regulate the activities of Spanish settlers. As Spain's American empire expanded, Church authority expanded along with it.

Franciscans, Jesuits, and other missionaries baptized thousands of Native Americans. They built mission churches and worked to turn new converts into loyal subjects of the Catholic king of Spain. They also introduced European clothing, the Spanish language, and new crafts such as carpentry and locksmithing. Where they could, the Spanish missionaries forcibly imposed European culture over Native American culture.

Controlling Trade To make the empire profitable, Spain closely controlled its economic activities, especially trade. The most valuable resources shipped from Spanish America to Spain were silver and gold. Colonists could export raw materials only to Spain and could buy only Spanish manufactured goods. Laws forbade colonists from trading with other European nations or even with other Spanish colonies.

When sugar cane was introduced into the West Indies and elsewhere, it quickly became a profitable resource. The cane was refined into sugar, molasses, and rum. Sugar cane, however, had to be grown on plantations, large estates run by an owner or the owner's overseer. And plantations needed large numbers of workers to be profitable.

Encomienda—A System of Forced Labor At first, Spanish monarchs granted the conquistadors **encomiendas** (en koh mee EN dahs), the right to demand labor or tribute from Native Americans in a particular area. The conquistadors used this system to force Native Americans to work under the most brutal conditions. Those who resisted were hunted down and killed. Disease, starvation, and cruel treatment caused drastic declines in the Native American population.

The encomienda system was used in the mines as well as on plantations. By the 1540s, tons of silver from the Potosí region of Peru and Bolivia filled Spanish treasure ships. Year after year, thousands of Native Americans were forced to extract the rich ore from dangerous shafts deep inside the Andes Mountains. As thousands of Indians died from the terrible conditions, they were replaced by thousands more.

A Spanish Priest Speaks Out A few bold priests, like **Bartolomé de Las Casas** (bahr toh loh MAY deh lahs KAHS ahs), condemned the evils of the encomienda system. In vivid reports to Spain, Las Casas detailed the horrors that Spanish rule had brought to Native Americans and pleaded with the king to end the abuse.

Prodded by Las Casas, Spain passed the New Laws of the Indies in 1542. The laws forbade enslavement and abuse of Native Americans, but Spain was too far away to enforce them. Many Native Americans were forced to become **peons,** workers forced to labor for a landlord in order to pay off a debt. Landlords advanced them food, tools, or seeds, creating debts that workers could never pay off in their lifetime.

Bringing Workers From Africa To fill the labor shortage, Las Casas urged colonists to import workers from Africa. He believed that Africans were immune to tropical diseases and had skills in farming, mining, and metalworking. Las Casas later regretted that advice because it furthered the brutal African slave trade.

The Spanish began bringing Africans to the Americas as slave laborers by the 1530s. As demand for sugar products skyrocketed, the settlers imported millions of Africans as slaves. They were forced to work as field hands, miners, or servants in the houses of wealthy landowners. Others became skilled artists and artisans. Within a few generations, Africans and their American-born descendants greatly outnumbered European settlers throughout the Americas. In the cities, some enslaved Africans earned enough money to buy their freedom. Others resisted slavery by rebelling or running away.

✔ **Checkpoint**   What was the encomienda system?

Colonial Society and Culture

In Spanish America, the mix of diverse peoples gave rise to a new social structure. The blending of Native American, African, and European peoples and traditions resulted in a culture distinct to the Americas.

Cultural Blending   Although Spanish culture was dominant in the cities, the blending of diverse traditions changed people's lives throughout the Americas. Settlers learned Native American styles of building, ate foods native to the Americas, and traveled in Indian-style canoes. Indian artistic styles influenced the newcomers. At the same time, Europeans taught their religion to Native Americans. They also introduced animals, especially the horse, thereby transforming the lives of many Native Americans. Africans contributed to this cultural mix with their farming methods, cooking styles, and crops. African drama, dance, and song heightened Christian services. In Cuba, Haiti, and elsewhere, Africans forged new religions that blended African and Christian beliefs.

A Spanish Cathedral
A group of Tzotzil Maya women gather in front of the Cathedral of San Cristóbal in Chiapas, Mexico. The church was originally built in 1528. *How can you tell that the church is a vital part of life in the town?*

A Changing Population

The population of Spanish America changed dramatically within a century, as the two pie charts illustrate. Artist Miguel Cabrera showed this diversity in a 1700s painting of a single family made up of a Spanish father, a Native American mother, and a mestizo daughter.

Population of Spanish America

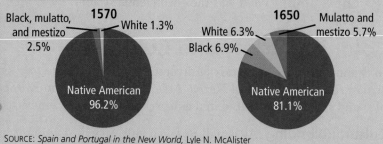

1570
Black, mulatto, and mestizo 2.5%
White 1.3%
Native American 96.2%

1650
White 6.3%
Black 6.9%
Mulatto and mestizo 5.7%
Native American 81.1%

SOURCE: *Spain and Portugal in the New World,* Lyle N. McAlister

Chart Skills Study the pie graphs. Which group increased the most between 1570 and 1650? Notice that the 1650 graph includes a category that the 1570 graph does not. Explain why this is so.

A Layered Society Spanish colonial society was made up of distinct social classes. At the top were **peninsulares** (peh neen soo LAH rayz), people born in Spain. (The term *peninsular* referred to the Iberian Peninsula, on which Spain is located.) Peninsulares filled the highest positions in both colonial governments and the Catholic Church. Next came **creoles,** American-born descendants of Spanish settlers. Creoles owned most of the plantations, ranches, and mines.

Lower social groups reflected the mixing of populations. They included **mestizos,** people of Native American and European descent, and **mulattoes,** people of African and European descent. Native Americans and people of African descent formed the lowest social classes.

Lively Towns and Cities Spanish settlers generally lived in towns and cities. The population of Mexico City grew so quickly that by 1550 it was the largest Spanish-speaking city in the world. Colonial cities were centers of government, commerce, and European culture. Around the central plaza, or square, stood government buildings and a Spanish-style church. Broad avenues and public monuments symbolized European power and wealth. Cities were also centers of intellectual and cultural life. Architecture and painting, as well as poetry and the exchange of ideas, flourished in Spanish cities in the Americas.

Emphasizing Education To meet the Church's need for educated priests, the colonies built universities. The University of Mexico was established as early as 1551. A dozen Spanish American universities were already educating young men long before Harvard was founded in 1636 as the first college in the 13 English colonies.

Women wishing an education might enter a convent. One such woman was Sor Juana Inés de la Cruz (sawr HWAN uh ee NES deh lah krooz). Refused admission to the University of Mexico because she was female, Juana entered a convent at around the age of 18. There, she devoted herself to study and the writing of poetry. She earned a reputation as one of the greatest poets ever to write in the Spanish language.

✔ **Checkpoint** What was the role of the Church in colonial education?

N̲o̲te Taking

Compare and Contrast Complete a Venn diagram like this one to compare and contrast the Spanish and Portuguese empires in the Americas.

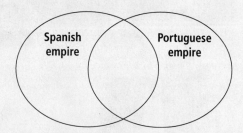

Spanish empire

Portuguese empire

Beyond the Spanish Empire

A large area of South America remained outside the Spanish empire. By the Treaty of Tordesillas in 1494, Portugal claimed its empire in the east, Brazil.

Settling Brazil As in the Spanish empire, the Native Americans who lived in Brazil—the Tupian Indians—had been largely wiped out by disease. In the 1530s, Portugal began to issue grants of land to Portuguese nobles, who agreed to develop the land and share profits with the crown. Landowners sent settlers to build towns, plantations, and churches.

Unlike Spain's American colonies, Brazil offered no instant wealth from silver or gold. However, early settlers cut and exported brazilwood. The Portuguese named the colony after this wood, which was used to produce a valuable dye. Soon they turned to plantation agriculture and raising cattle. Like the Spanish, the Portuguese forced Indians and Africans to clear land for plantations. As many as four million Africans were sent to Brazil. As in Spanish America, a new culture emerged in Brazil that blended European, Native American, and African elements.

Challenging Portugal and Spain In the 1500s, the wealth of the Americas helped make Spain the most powerful country in Europe, with Portugal not far behind. The jealous English and Dutch shared the resentment that French king Francis I felt when he declared, "I should like to see Adam's will, wherein he divided the Earth between Spain and Portugal."

To get around those countries' strict control over colonial trade, smugglers traded illegally with Portuguese and Spanish colonists. In the Caribbean and elsewhere, Dutch, English, and French pirates preyed on treasure ships from the Americas. Some pirates, called **privateers,** even operated with the approval of European governments. Other European explorers continued to sail the coasts of the Americas, hunting for gold and other treasure, as well as a northwest passage to Asia.

Smuggling Brazilwood
A panel carved from brazilwood in the 1550s shows French privateers illegally cutting Portuguese brazilwood and storing it on their boats.

✔ **Checkpoint** What was Brazil's economy based on?

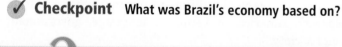

SECTION 2 Assessment

Progress Monitoring *Online*
For: Self-quiz with vocabulary practice
Web Code: naa-1521

Terms, People, and Places

1. Place each of the key terms at the beginning of the section into one of the following categories: culture, government, or economics. Write a sentence for each term explaining your choice.

Note Taking

2. **Reading Skill: Recognize Sequence** Use your completed flowchart and Venn diagram to answer the Focus Question: How did Spain and Portugal build colonies in the Americas?

Comprehension and Critical Thinking

3. **Identify Alternatives** How might the Spanish have solved the problem of finding a dependable labor supply without the use of slavery?

4. **Analyze Information** How did the mix of peoples in Spanish America result in a new social structure?

5. **Make Comparisons** In what ways were the Spanish and Portuguese empires in the Americas similar? In what ways were they different?

6. **Draw Inferences** Why did some European monarchs support the illegal activities of privateers?

● Writing About History

Quick Write: Make a Venn Diagram When you write an essay comparing and contrasting two things, you first need to make clear how they are similar and different. A graphic organizer can help you outline similarities and differences. Choose two people, places, or events from the section. Then create a Venn diagram that you can use to compare and contrast them. Refer to the Venn diagram at the beginning of the section as an example.

A statue of Samuel de Champlain

A Piece of the Past

In 1867, a Canadian farmer of English descent was cutting logs on his property with his fourteen-year-old son. As they used their oxen to pull away a large log, a piece of turf came up to reveal a round, yellow object. The elaborately engraved object they found, dated 1603, was an astrolabe that had belonged to French explorer Samuel de Champlain. This astrolabe was a piece of the story of the European exploration of Canada and the French-British rivalry that followed.

Focus Question How did European struggles for power shape the North American continent?

Struggle for North America

 Performance Standards

- **SSWH10a** Explain the role of Samuel de Champlain.
- **SSWH10c** Explain the role of improved technology in European exploration.

Terms, People, and Places

New France   compact
revenue   French and Indian War
Pilgrims   Treaty of Paris

Note Taking

Reading Skill: Recognize Sequence Create a timeline like the one below to record the sequence of important events in the struggle for North America.

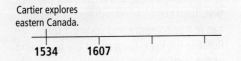

Cartier explores
eastern Canada.

1534   1607

In the 1600s, France, the Netherlands, England, and Sweden joined Spain in settling North America. North America did not yield vast treasure or offer a water passage to Asia, as they had hoped. Before long, though, the English and French were turning large profits. By 1700, France and England controlled large parts of North America. Their colonies differed from each other and from those of Spanish America in terms of language, government, resources, and society.

Building New France

By the early 1500s, French fishing ships were crossing the Atlantic each year to harvest rich catches of cod off Newfoundland, Canada. Within 200 years, the French had occupied or claimed nearly half of North America.

Explorers and Missionaries French claims in Canada—which the French called **New France**—quietly grew while French rulers were distracted by wars at home in Europe. In 1534, Jacques Cartier (zhahk kahr tee AY) began exploring the coastline of eastern Canada, eventually discovering the St. Lawrence River. Traveling inland on the river, he claimed much of present-day eastern Canada for France. Jesuits and other missionaries soon followed the explorers. They advanced into the wilderness, trying with little success to convert the Native Americans they met to Christianity.

Furs, Trapping, and Fishing French explorers and fur traders gradually traveled inland with the help of Native American allies, who sought support against rival Native American groups. Eventually, France's American empire reached from Quebec to the Great Lakes and down the Mississippi River to Louisiana and the Gulf of Mexico.

The population of New France, however, grew slowly. The first permanent French settlement was not established until 1608, when Samuel de Champlain established a colony in Quebec. Wealthy landlords bought huge tracts, or areas of land, along the St. Lawrence River. They sought settlers to farm the land, but the harsh Canadian climate, with its long winters, attracted few French peasants.

Many who went to New France soon abandoned farming in favor of the more profitable fur trapping and trading. They faced a hard life in the wilderness, but the soaring European demand for fur ensured good prices. Fishing was another industry that supported settlers, who exported cod and other fish to Europe.

An Empire Slowly Expands In the late 1600s, the French king Louis XIV set out to strengthen royal power and boost **revenues,** or income, from taxes from his overseas empire. He appointed officials to oversee economic activities in New France. He also sent soldiers and more settlers—including women—to North America. Louis, however, who was Catholic, prohibited Protestants from settling in New France. By the early 1700s, French forts, missions, and trading posts stretched from Quebec to Louisiana, and the population was growing. Yet the population of New France remained small compared to that of the English colonies that were expanding along the Atlantic coast.

✔ **Checkpoint** Why did French settlers abandon farming in favor of fur trapping and trading?

BIOGRAPHY

Jacques Cartier
In 1534, Jacques Cartier (1491–1557) sailed to North America on behalf of France. His commission was to find spices, gold, and a passage to Asia. Cartier found none of these things, despite several attempts, and ended his career in relative obscurity.

During his own lifetime, no one guessed the impact that Cartier's voyages would have. In his thousand-mile trek into Canada's interior, he staked France's later claim to a huge amount of North American territory. His legacy also lives on in the Canadian place names he coined such as the St. Lawrence River and the name Canada—derived from an Iroquois word meaning "village" or "settlement." **Why were Cartier's discoveries undervalued at the time?**

The English Colonies

In 1497, a Venetian navigator known by the English name John Cabot found rich fishing grounds off Newfoundland, which he claimed for England. Later English navigators continued to search for a northwest passage to Asia, with no success. In the 1600s, England concentrated on establishing colonies along the Atlantic seaboard—the coast of the present-day eastern United States.

Establishing the First Colonies The English built their first permanent colony at Jamestown, Virginia, in 1607. Although the colony was meant to bring wealth and profit, in the early years of the colony many settlers died of starvation and disease. The rest survived with the help of friendly Native Americans. The colony finally made headway when the settlers started to grow and export tobacco, a plant that had been cultivated by Native Americans for thousands of years.

In 1620, another group of English settlers landed at Plymouth, Massachusetts. They were **Pilgrims**, or English Protestants who rejected the Church of England. They sought religious freedom rather than commercial profit. Before coming ashore, they signed the Mayflower Compact, in which they set out guidelines for governing their North American colony. A **compact** is an agreement among people. Today, we see this document as an important early step toward self-government.

Many Pilgrims died in the early years of the Plymouth colony. Local Native Americans, however, taught them to grow corn and helped them survive in the new land. Soon, a new wave of English Protestant immigrants arrived to establish the Massachusetts Bay Colony.

The English Colonies Grow In the 1600s and 1700s, the English established additional colonies. Some, like Virginia and New York, were commercial ventures, organized for profit. Others, like Massachusetts, Pennsylvania, and Maryland, were set up as havens for persecuted religious groups. Still others, like Georgia and South Carolina, were gifts from English kings to loyal supporters.

Settlers in all of the colonies spent the early years just struggling to survive. They quickly abandoned dreams of finding riches like the Spanish gold and silver. However, over time they learned to create wealth by using the resources native to their surroundings. In New England, prosperous fishing, timber, and shipbuilding industries grew. In the middle colonies, farmers grew huge quantities of grain on the abundant land. In the South, colonists found that cash crops such as rice and tobacco grew well in the warm climate. They therefore developed a plantation economy to grow these crops. As in New Spain, the colonists imported African slaves to clear land and work the plantations. In several colonies, especially in the South, enslaved Africans and their descendants would eventually outnumber people of European descent.

Governing the Colonies Like the rulers of Spain and France, English monarchs asserted control over their American colonies. They appointed royal governors to oversee colonial affairs and had Parliament pass laws to regulate colonial trade. Yet, compared with settlers in the Spanish and French colonies, English colonists enjoyed a large degree of self-government. Each colony had its own representative assembly, elected by propertied men, that advised the governor and made decisions on local issues.

The tradition of consulting representative assemblies grew out of the English experience. Beginning in the 1200s, Parliament had begun to play an important role in English affairs. Slowly, too, English citizens had gained certain legal and political rights. England's American colonists expected to enjoy the same rights. When colonists later protested British policies in North America, they viewed themselves as "freeborn Englishmen" who were defending their traditional rights.

✓ **Checkpoint** For what reasons were the English colonies established?

A Fanciful View
An English play promised that "... gold is more plentiful there [Virginia] than copper is with us.... and as for rubies and diamonds, they go forth on holy days and gather them by the seashore." *Does this photo of the re-creation of the Jamestown colony support the playwright's views?*

European Land Claims in the Americas, About 1700

NORTH AMERICA

INUIT
KUTCHIN
KASKA
INUIT
TLINGIT
CREE
OJIBWA
SIOUX
UTE
NOMADIC PLAINS CULTURES
COMANCHE
PUEBLO
APACHE
NOMADIC HUNTERS
WOODLAND CULTURES

Canada

English Colonies

Pacific Ocean

40° N
20° N

Equal-Area Projection
0   500   1000 mi
0   500   1000 km

Viceroyalty of New Spain

Atlantic Ocean

Guiana
CARIBANA
MANOA
SHUAR
ARUAC
NOMADIC HUNTERS
GÊ
GUARANI

SOUTH AMERICA

Brazil

Viceroyalty of Peru

NOMADIC HUNTERS

140° W   120° W   60° W   40° W
0°
40° S

Legend:
- England
- France
- Spain
- Portugal
- Netherlands
- *UTE* Native culture

▲ A Chippewa beadwork bag reflects the influence of the French nuns who taught the Native Americans how to embroider.

▼ Europeans used American gold and silver to make dishes like this Portuguese platter dating from the 1500s.

▼ A coat of arms from the time the Dutch briefly controlled the colony of New Netherland (New York) shows the importance of the beaver to the colony's trade.

New Encounters

As Europeans explored the Americas, claiming lands for their monarchs, they encountered diverse groups of Native Americans who already lived there. Europeans and Native Americans both relied on the resources of the land they inhabited. Though the groups often clashed, they influenced each other in many ways.

▲ English settlers made chests like this one out of native American oak, using traditional English patterns.

Map Skills Within a hundred years or so, European exploration of the Americas had led to huge land claims by various countries.

1. **Locate** (a) Brazil (b) English colonies (c) Peru (d) New Spain
2. **Describe** What geographical factor do all of the European land claims share? Why is this so?
3. **Draw Conclusions** Why do you think the boundaries of the European land claims end as illustrated on the map?

485

Struggling for Power

By the 1600s, Spain, France, England, and the Netherlands all had colonies in North America. They began to fight—both in the colonies and around the world—to protect and expand their interests.

Competing for Colonies By the late 1600s, French claims included present-day Canada as well as much of the present-day central United States. The Spanish had moved north, making claims to present-day Texas and Florida. Meanwhile, the English and Dutch maintained colonies along the East Coast. Native Americans throughout the colonies entered the conflict, hoping to play the Europeans against one another. Competition was also fierce in the Caribbean, as European nations fought to acquire the profitable sugar-producing colonies. By the 1700s, the French and English Caribbean islands, worked by enslaved Africans, had surpassed the whole of North America in exports to Europe.

Bitter Rivalry Turns to War During the 1700s, Britain and France emerged as powerful rivals. They clashed in Europe, North America, Africa, and Asia. In North America, war between the two powers erupted in 1754. Called the **French and Indian War**, it raged until 1763. It also turned into a worldwide struggle known as the Seven Years' War, which spread to Europe in 1756 and then to India and Africa.

During the war, British soldiers and colonial troops launched a series of campaigns against the French in Canada and on the Ohio frontier. At first, France won several victories. Then, in 1759, British troops launched an attack on Quebec, the capital of New France. The British scaled steep cliffs along the river and captured the city. Although the war dragged on until 1763, the British had <u>prevailed</u> in Canada.

The 1763 **Treaty of Paris** officially ended the worldwide war and ensured British dominance in North America. France was forced to cede Canada and its lands east of the Mississippi River to Britain. It handed the Louisiana Territory over to Spain. However, France regained the rich sugar-producing islands in the Caribbean and the slave-trading outposts in Africa that the British had seized during the war.

✓ **Checkpoint** Why was the French and Indian War fought?

Progress Monitoring Online
For: Self-quiz with vocabulary practice
Web Code: naa-1531

Vocabulary Builder

<u>prevail</u>—(pree VAYL) *v.* to succeed; to triumph

Living Languages

A sign in British Columbia—written in both English and the local Indian language—shows how Native American influence lingers long after the Americas became British.

SECTION **3** Assessment

Terms, People, and Places

1. For each term, person, or place listed at the beginning of the section, write a sentence explaining its significance.

Note Taking

2. **Reading Skill: Recognize Sequence** Use your completed timeline to answer the Focus Question: How did European struggles for power shape the North American continent?

Comprehension and Critical Thinking

3. **Make Comparisons** Why did New France grow slowly compared with Spanish and English colonies?

4. **Identify Central Issues** Why did the English colonies have a large degree of self-government?

5. **Make Generalizations** How did Britain come to dominate North America?

6. **Draw Inferences** Why did Native American groups side with European powers rather than join together to oppose them?

● **Writing About History**

Quick Write: Write a Thesis Statement Once you have chosen the things you will compare and contrast in your essay, you must write a thesis statement. Your thesis statement should address clearly how the things you are comparing relate similarly or differently to your topic. For example, your thesis statement might focus on how the French and the English took different paths in establishing colonies in the Americas.

This portrait of Olaudah Equiano dates from the 1780s. The iron shackles shown at the right were used to bind slaves during the slave trade.

WITNESS HISTORY 🔊 AUDIO

Forced Into Slavery

❝ The first object which saluted my eyes when I arrived on the coast was the sea, and a slave ship which was then riding at anchor and waiting for its cargo. These filled me with astonishment, which was soon converted into terror when I was carried on board.❞

So wrote Olaudah Equiano. In the 1750s, when he was 11 years old, Equiano was seized from his Nigerian village by slave traders. He was then transported as human cargo from West Africa to the Americas.

Focus Question How did the Atlantic slave trade shape the lives and economies of Africans and Europeans?

The Atlantic Slave Trade

Performance Standards

- **SSWH10b** Define the Columbian Exchange and its economic and cultural impact.
- **SSWHRC1c** Explore understanding of new words in subject area texts.

Terms, People, and Places

Olaudah Equiano   Middle Passage
triangular trade   mutiny

Note Taking

Reading Skill: Recognize Sequence Use a flowchart like the one below to record the events that led to millions of Africans being shipped to the Americas.

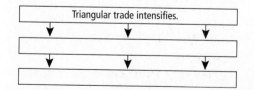

Triangular trade intensifies.

Vocabulary Builder

<u>commodity</u>—(kuh MAHD uh tee) *n.* anything bought and sold

Enslaved Africans like **Olaudah Equiano** formed part of an international trade network that arose during the 1500s. The Spanish were the first major European partners in the slave trade, buying slaves to labor in Spain's South American empire. As other European powers established colonies in the Americas, the slave trade—and with it the entire international trade network—intensified.

Triangular Trade Across the Atlantic

The Atlantic slave trade formed one part of a three-legged international trade network known as **triangular trade.** This was a triangle-shaped series of Atlantic trade routes linking Europe, Africa, and the Americas.

Shipping People and Goods Triangular trade worked in the following way. On the first leg, merchant ships brought European goods—including guns, cloth, and cash—to Africa. In Africa, the merchants traded these goods for slaves. On the second leg, known as the **Middle Passage,** the slaves were transported to the Americas. There, the enslaved Africans were exchanged for sugar, molasses, and other products manufactured at plantations owned by Europeans.

On the final leg, merchants carried sugar, molasses, cotton, and other American goods such as furs, salt fish, and rum made from molasses. These goods were shipped to Europe, where they were traded at a profit for the European <u>commodities</u> that merchants needed to return to Africa.

Industries and Cities Thrive Triangular trade was immensely profitable for many people. Merchants grew wealthy. Even though there were risks such as losing ships at sea, the money to be made from valuable cargoes usually outweighed the risks. Certain industries that supported trade thrived. For example, a shipbuilding industry in New England grew to support the shipping industry. Other colonial industries, such as fishing, raising tobacco, and processing sugar, became hugely successful.

Thriving trade led to successful port cities. European cities such as Nantes, France, and Bristol, England, grew prosperous because of triangular trade. In North America, even newly settled towns such as Salem, Massachusetts, and Newport, Rhode Island, quickly grew into thriving cities. Even though few slaves were imported directly to the northern cities, the success of the port cities there was made possible by the Atlantic slave trade.

✔ **Checkpoint** How did triangular trade affect colonial economies?

● INFOGRAPHIC

The Middle Passage: A Forced Journey

A historic drawing shows how slaves were packed into tiny spaces in the ship's hold. ▼

The Middle Passage was a crucial part of triangular trade (inset map). Most slaves did not tell about their passage—many died, and those who survived faced lives of bondage in the Americas. But some Europeans recorded their impressions about the slave trade. And a few remarkable slaves learned to read and write, making their stories part of history.

History Interactive
For: Interactive triangular trade
Web Code: nap-1541

A slave "castle" in Ghana ▼

❝When we arrived at the castle, I saw [my kidnapper] take a gun, a piece of cloth, and some lead [to trade] for me... when a vessel arrived to conduct us away to the ship, there was nothing to be heard but the rattling of chains, smacking of whips, and the groans and cries of our fellow-men.... And when we found ourselves at last taken away, death was more preferable than life.❞

—*Nigerian slave Ottobah Cugoano, 1787*

Horrors of the Middle Passage

To merchants, the Middle Passage was just one leg of triangular trade. For enslaved Africans, the Middle Passage was a horror.

The Trek to the Ships The terrible journey began before the slave ships set sail. Most Africans were taken from inland villages. After they were enslaved, they were forced to march to coastal ports. Men, women, and children were bound with ropes and chains, often to one another, and forced to walk distances as long as a thousand miles. They might be forced to carry heavy loads, and often the men's necks were encircled with thick iron bands.

Many captives died along the way. Others tried to escape, and were often quickly recaptured and brutally punished. Those who survived the march were <u>restrained</u> in coastal holding pens and warehouses in slave shipping ports such as Elmina, Ghana, or Gorée, Senegal. They were held there until European traders arrived by ship.

Vocabulary Builder

restrain—(rih STRAYN) *v.* to keep under control; to keep from action

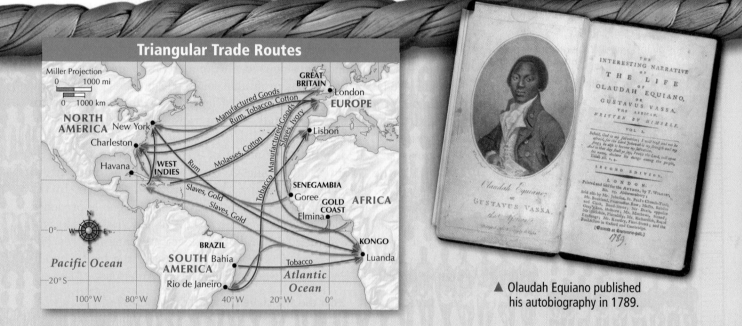

Triangular Trade Routes

Miller Projection
0   1000 mi
0   1000 km

NORTH AMERICA — New York, Charleston, Havana
WEST INDIES
SOUTH AMERICA — BRAZIL, Bahia, Rio de Janeiro
Pacific Ocean
Atlantic Ocean
GREAT BRITAIN — London
EUROPE — Lisbon
SENEGAMBIA — Goree
GOLD COAST — Elmina
AFRICA
KONGO — Luanda

Manufactured Goods
Rum, Tobacco, Cotton
Slaves, Ivory
Tobacco, Manufactured Goods
Molasses, Cotton
Rum
Slaves, Gold
Slaves, Gold
Tobacco

▲ Olaudah Equiano published his autobiography in 1789.

> ❝This work is so hard that any slave, newly put to it, in the course of a month becomes so weak that often he is totally unfit for labour. If he falls back behind the rest, the driver keeps forcing him up with the whip.❞
>
> —Ashton Warner, early 1800s

An 1823 painting shows slaves laboring on the island of Antigua. ▶

Thinking Critically

1. **Map Skills** What were slaves exchanged for in the West Indies?
2. **Draw Inferences** Why are there so few first-person slave narratives?

489

Seventy Gold-Coast SLAVES

SLAVERY ADVERTISEMENT.

William Cowper wrote the following poem in the 1700s. How does he use irony to express his disapproval of the slave trade?

Primary Source

❝I own I am shocked at the purchase of slaves,
And fear those who buy them and sell them are knaves;
What I hear of their hardships, their tortures and groans,
Is almost enough to draw pity from stones.
I pity them greatly, but I must be mum,
For how could we do without sugar and rum?❞

Aboard the "Floating Coffins" Once purchased, Africans were packed below the decks of slave ships, usually in chains. Hundreds of men, women, and children were crammed into a single vessel for voyages that lasted from three weeks to three months. The ships faced many perils, including storms at sea, raids by pirate ships, and **mutinies,** or revolts, by the captives.

Disease was the biggest threat to the lives of the captives and the profit of the merchants. Of the slaves who died, most died of dysentery. Many died of smallpox. Many others died from apparently no disease at all. Whatever the cause, slave ships became "floating coffins" on which up to half the Africans on board died from disease or brutal mistreatment.

Some enslaved Africans resisted, and others tried to seize control of the ship and return to Africa. Suicide, however, was more common than mutiny. Many Africans believed that in death they would be returned to their home countries. So they hanged themselves, starved themselves, or leapt overboard.

 Checkpoint How did enslaved Africans resist captivity?

Impact of the Atlantic Slave Trade

The slave trade brought enormous wealth to merchants and traders, and provided the labor that helped profitable colonial economies grow. Yet the impact on Africans was devastating. African states and societies were torn apart. The lives of individual Africans were either cut short or forever brutalized.

Historians still debate the number of Africans who were directly involved in the Atlantic slave trade. In the 1500s, they estimate about 2,000 enslaved Africans were sent to the Americas each year. In the 1780s, when the slave trade was at its peak, that number approached 80,000 a year. By the mid-1800s, when the overseas slave trade was finally stopped, an estimated 11 million enslaved Africans had reached the Americas. Another 2 million probably died under the brutal conditions of the Middle Passage between Africa and the Americas.

Checkpoint How did the slave trade affect Africans?

SECTION 4 Assessment

Progress Monitoring *Online*
For: Self-quiz with vocabulary practice
Web Code: naa-1541

Terms, People, and Places

1. What do each of the key terms and people listed at the beginning of the section have in common? Explain.

Note Taking

2. **Reading Skill: Recognize Sequence** Use your completed flowchart to answer the Focus Question: How did the Atlantic slave trade shape the lives and economies of Africans and Europeans?

Comprehension and Critical Thinking

3. **Synthesize Information** What role did each of the following play in triangular trade: a New England merchant, an African slave, and a Southern plantation owner?

4. **Recognize Assumptions** What European assumptions about Africans does the Atlantic slave trade show?

5. **Predict Consequences** Would the growth of the American colonies have been different if there had been no Atlantic slave trade? Explain.

● Writing About History

Quick Write: Gather Evidence to Support a Thesis Statement Once you have written your thesis statement, gather specific evidence—facts and quotes—that support it. For example, assume for this section that your thesis statement concludes that the African slave trade was the most influential event of the age of exploration. Gather specific evidence from the section that supports this statement.

A trading post in the West Indies thrives in the mid-1500s; a powder horn is inscribed with North American fur trading routes.

WITNESS HISTORY 🔊 AUDIO

Uniting the World

❝The discovery of America, and that of a passage to the East Indies by the Cape of Good Hope, are the two greatest and most important events recorded in the history of mankind. By uniting, in some measure, the most distant parts of the world, by enabling them to relieve one another's wants, to increase one another's enjoyments, and to encourage one another's industry, their general tendency would seem to be beneficial.❞
—Adam Smith, *The Wealth of Nations,* 1776

Focus Question How did the voyages of European explorers lead to new economic systems in Europe and its colonies?

Effects of Global Contact

 Performance Standards

• **SSWH10b** Define the Columbian Exchange and its economic and cultural impact.

Terms, People, and Places

Columbian Exchange	entrepreneur
inflation	mercantilism
price revolution	tariff
capitalism	

Note Taking

Reading Skill: Recognize Sequence Create a flowchart like the one below to keep track of the events that resulted from global exchange in the 1500s and 1600s.

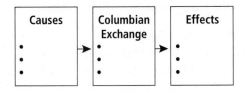

The voyages of exploration in the 1500s and 1600s marked the beginning of what would become European domination of the globe. By the 1700s, European exploration had brought major changes to the people of Europe, Asia, Africa, and the Americas.

The Columbian Exchange

When Columbus returned to Spain in March 1493, he brought with him plants and animals that he had found in the Americas. Later that year, Columbus returned to the Americas with some 1,200 settlers and a collection of European animals and plants. In this way, Columbus began a vast global exchange that would profoundly affect the world. Because this exchange began with Columbus, we call it the **Columbian Exchange.**

New Foods and Animals In the Americas, Europeans found a variety of foods that were new to them, including tomatoes, pumpkins, peppers. They eagerly transported these to Europe. Two of these new foods, corn and potatoes, became important foods in the Old World. Easy to grow and store, potatoes helped feed Europe's rapidly growing population. Corn spread all across Europe and to Africa and Asia, becoming one of the world's most important cereal crops.

Europeans also carried a wide variety of plants and animals to the Americas, including wheat and grapes from Europe and bananas and sugar cane from Africa and Asia. Cattle, pigs, goats, and chickens, unknown before the European encounter, joined the Native American diet. Horses and donkeys transported people and goods quickly. Horses also provided the nomadic peoples of western North America with a new, more effective way to hunt buffalo.

Horses Transform a Continent
The Spanish brought horses to the Americas by ship (below). A Spanish saying went "After God, we owe the victory to the horses." Horses also dramatically affected Native American life. An artist painted this scene of Plains Indians in 1830. *How does the artist show the importance of the horse to Native American life and culture?*

Vocabulary Builder
dispersal—(dih SPUR sul) *n.* scattering; spreading of

The Global Population Explodes The transfer of food crops from continent to continent took time. By the 1700s, however, corn, potatoes, manioc, beans, and tomatoes were contributing to population growth around the world. While other factors help account for the population explosion that began at this time, the dispersal of new food crops from the Americas was certainly a key cause.

The Columbian Exchange also sparked the migration of millions of people. Each year shiploads of European settlers sailed to the Americas, lured by the promise of a new life in a land of opportunities. Europeans also settled on the fringes of Africa and Asia, places made known to them because of exploration. In addition, as you have read, the Atlantic slave trade forcibly brought millions of Africans to the Americas.

In some parts of the world, populations declined as a result of increased global contact. The transfer of European diseases, such as smallpox and measles, decimated many Native American populations. Other populations were wiped out as a result of conflicts.

✓ **Checkpoint** Why did the global population explode?

A Commercial Revolution

The opening of direct links with Asia, Africa, and the Americas had far-reaching economic consequences for Europeans and their colonies.

The Price Revolution Strikes In the 1500s, prices began to rise in many parts of Europe. At the same time, there was much more money in circulation. A rise in prices that is linked to a sharp increase in the amount of money available is called **inflation.** The period in European history when inflation rose rapidly is known as the **price revolution.** Inflation was fueled by the enormous amount of silver and gold flowing into Europe from the Americas by the mid-1500s.

Capitalism Emerges

Expanded trade, an increased money supply, and the push for overseas empires spurred the growth of European **capitalism,** or an economic system in which most businesses are owned privately. **Entrepreneurs,** or people who take on financial risk to make profits, were key to the success of capitalism. Entrepreneurs organized, managed, and assumed the risks of doing business. They hired workers and paid for raw materials, transport, and other costs of production.

As trade increased, entrepreneurs sought to expand into overseas ventures. Capitalists, because of their resources, were more willing to take risks. Thus, the price revolution of the early modern age gave a boost to capitalism. Entrepreneurs and capitalists made up a new business class devoted to the goal of making profits. Together, they helped change local European economies into an international trading system.

Exploring New Business Methods

Early European capitalists discovered new ways to create wealth. From the Arabs, they adapted methods of bookkeeping to show profits and losses from their ventures. During the late Middle Ages, as you have read, banks increased in importance, allowing wealthy merchants to lend money at interest. Joint stock companies, also developed in late medieval times, grew in importance. They allowed people to pool large amounts of capital needed for overseas ventures. Individuals who invested in these companies could join in any profits that the company made. If the company lost money, individuals would only lose their initial investments.

Note Taking

Recognize Sequence Use a flowchart like this one to keep track of the sequence of events that led to new global economic systems.

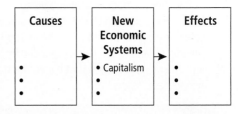

Causes	New Economic Systems	Effects
• • •	• Capitalism	• • •

TULIPMANIA
The Boom of the 1630s

In the 1630s, frenzy over a single good—the tulip—took hold in the Netherlands. People made and lost fortunes as the price of tulips rose from a handful of change to over a million dollars, only to abruptly crash. At the height of the mania, it was actually cheaper to purchase a painting of tulips by a Dutch master than to buy one tulip bulb.

Prices in Holland, 1630s

150 guilders	Average annual income
5,000 guilders	Price for a still-life painting of tulips by a Dutch master
10,000 guilders	Cost of a luxurious Amsterdam estate house

(Note: 100 guilders = approx. $12,500 in U.S. dollars today)

Joannes Busschaert painted *Still Life of Tulips, Roses, Fruit, and Shells* in the early 1600s. A tulip bulb with its flower is shown at right.

Price of a Single Tulip Bulb

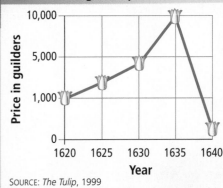

SOURCE: *The Tulip*, 1999

Who Loses in a Trade War?

In the 1990s, a trade war over bananas broke out between the United States and the European Union. The European Union wanted to buy bananas from small banana growers in its former colonies in Africa and the Caribbean. The United States, wanting to assist large South and Central American banana growers, responded by heavily taxing common European imports. In 2001, an agreement was reached that ended the trade war. **Critical Thinking** *In a trade war, who are the winners and losers?*

Everyone Wins

"The discrimination of the current illegal system is eliminated because all applicants will be treated equally and each applicant gains market access in the same proportion . . . . Dole believes that this system will benefit those banana exporters that invest in the jobs, people, countries and infrastructure that it takes to grow markets, open trade and compete. . . ."

—Dole Food Company press release, 2001

The Less Powerful Lose

"St. Lucia continues to be concerned that the thrust towards allowing market forces to totally determine the scope, structure and outcomes of economic activity, is not being counterbalanced by mechanisms to fairly distribute welfare gains and to protect the more vulnerable, small states like Saint Lucia, from the consequences of market failure. . . ."

—Earl Huntley, ambassador of Saint Lucia, in a statement to the UN, 2001

Bypassing the Guilds The growing demand for goods led merchants to find ways to increase production. Traditionally, guilds controlled the manufacture of goods. But guild masters often ran small-scale businesses without the capital to produce for large markets. They also had strict rules regulating quality, prices, and working conditions.

Enterprising capitalists devised a way to bypass the guilds called the "putting-out" system. It was first used to produce textiles but later spread to other industries. Under this system, for example, a merchant capitalist distributed raw wool to peasant cottages. Cottagers spun the wool into thread and then wove it into cloth. Merchants bought the wool cloth from the peasants and sent it to the city for finishing and dyeing. Finally, the merchants sold the finished product for a profit.

The "putting-out" system, also known by the term "cottage industry," separated capital and labor for the first time. In the 1700s, this system would lead to the capitalist-owned factories of the Industrial Revolution.

✓ **Checkpoint**   How did the "putting-out" system work?

Mercantilism Arises

European monarchs enjoyed the benefits of the commercial revolution. In the fierce competition for trade and empire, they adopted a new economic policy, known as **mercantilism,** aimed at strengthening their national economies. Mercantilists believed that a nation's real wealth was measured in its gold and silver treasure. To build its supply of gold and silver, they said, a nation must export more goods than it imported.

The Role of Colonies To mercantilists, overseas colonies existed for the benefit of the parent country. They provided resources and raw materials not available in Europe. In turn, they enriched a parent country by serving as a market for its manufactured goods. To achieve these goals, European powers passed strict laws regulating trade with their colonies. Colonists could not set up their own industries to manufacture goods. They were also forbidden to buy goods from a foreign country. In addition, only ships from the parent country or the colonies themselves could be used to send goods in or out of the colonies.

Increasing National Wealth Mercantilists urged rulers to adopt policies that they believed would increase national wealth and government revenues. To boost production, governments exploited mineral and timber resources, built roads, and backed new industries. They imposed national currencies and established standard weights and measures.

Governments also sold monopolies to large producers in certain industries as well as to big overseas trading companies. Finally, they imposed **tariffs,** or taxes on imported goods. Tariffs were designed to protect local industries from foreign competition by increasing the price of imported goods. All of these measures led to the rise of national economies, in which national governments had a lot of control over their economies. However, modern economists debate whether mercantilist measures actually made nations wealthier.

Impact on European Society By the 1700s, European societies were still divided into distinct social classes. Merchants who invested in overseas ventures acquired wealth, while the price revolution hurt nobles, whose wealth was in land. Economic changes took generations, even centuries, to be felt by the majority of Europeans, who were still peasants. The merchants and skilled workers of Europe's growing cities thrived. Middle-class families enjoyed a comfortable life. In contrast, hired laborers and those who served the middle and upper classes often lived in crowded quarters on the edge of poverty.

✔ **Checkpoint** How did economic changes affect different Europeans?

A Dutch Merchant Family
Dutch artist Adriaen van Ostade painted this scene of a Dutch family in the mid-1600s. With the Netherlands' trading wealth, even middle-class families could afford fine clothes, luxury goods, and paintings.

SECTION 5 Assessment

Progress Monitoring *Online*
For: Self-quiz with vocabulary practice
Web Code: naa-1551

Terms, People, and Places
1. For each term, person, or place listed at the beginning of the section, write a sentence explaining its significance.

Note Taking
2. **Reading Skill: Recognize Sequence** Use your completed flowcharts to answer the Focus Question: How did the voyages of European explorers lead to new economic systems in Europe and its colonies?

Comprehension and Critical Thinking
3. **Identify Point of View** How might a Native American assess the impact—both positive and negative—of the Columbian Exchange?
4. **Draw Inferences** What characteristics must a society have in order for capitalism to be possible?
5. **Identify Assumptions** What basic assumption did mercantilists hold about their colonies?
6. **Synthesize Information** Why did the economic changes of the time have little impact on many Europeans?

● **Writing About History**
Quick Write: Write the Body and Conclusion The body of a compare-and-contrast essay should include specific evidence to support your thesis. Suppose that you are comparing the effects of global contact on European merchants and European peasants. Find evidence in this section that you can use to make this comparison.

Transforming the World:
The Columbian Exchange

Christopher Columbus's landing in the Americas in 1492, and his later voyages, revolutionized the world. European ships—heading both to and from the Americas—carried animals, food plants, and diseases that transformed lives and ways of life around the world. Hundreds of years after the Columbian Exchange began, the patterns of people's lives still reflect the influence of those early European voyages of exploration.

NORTH AMERICA

Atlantic Ocean

SOUTH AMERICA

Barley, a grain cultivated by the ancient Egyptians, is widely used in the Americas to feed livestock. ▼

From the Western Hemisphere
Corn
Potatoes
Sweet potatoes
Beans
Peanuts
Squash
Pumpkins
Chili peppers
Turkeys
Pineapples
Tomatoes
Cocoa
Cassava/Manioc
Silver
Quinine
Sunflowers

Originally from India, chickens and their eggs shaped diets worldwide—adding nutrition that boosted population growth. ▼

A Cuban man plows a field with oxen, work animals brought to the Americas from Africa and Asia. ▼

GOAT

▲ Native to Asia, goats provide milk and wool to people throughout both hemispheres.

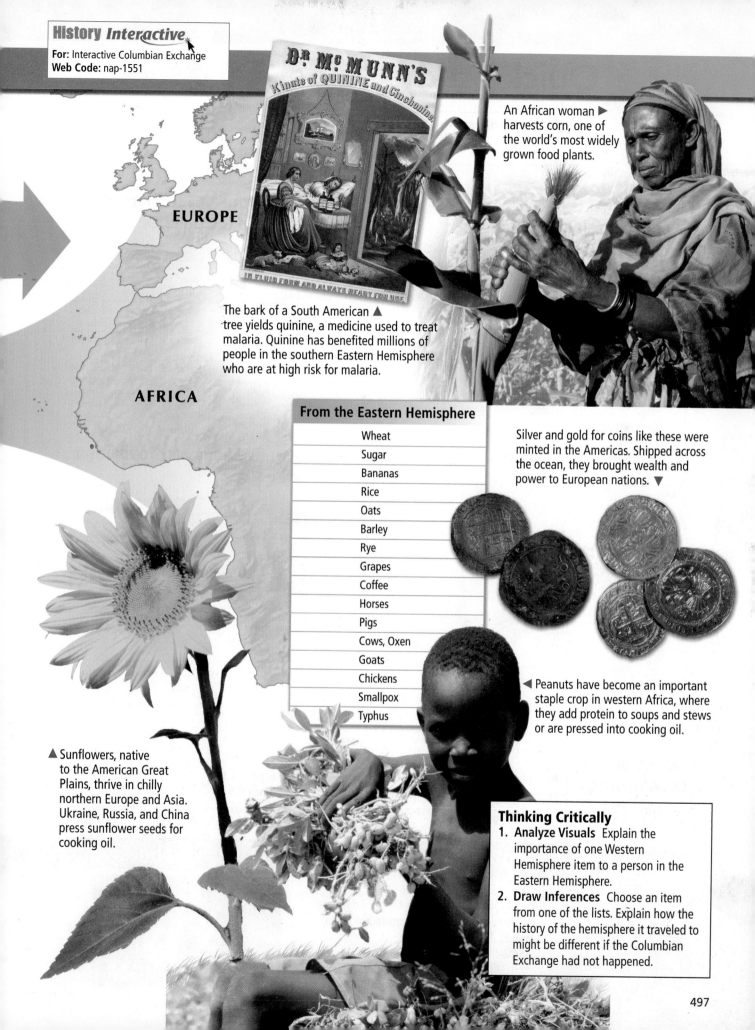

DR. McMUNN'S
Kinate of QUININE and Cinchonine.

IN FLUID FORM AND ALWAYS READY FOR USE.

EUROPE

AFRICA

An African woman ▶ harvests corn, one of the world's most widely grown food plants.

The bark of a South American ▲ tree yields quinine, a medicine used to treat malaria. Quinine has benefited millions of people in the southern Eastern Hemisphere who are at high risk for malaria.

From the Eastern Hemisphere

Wheat
Sugar
Bananas
Rice
Oats
Barley
Rye
Grapes
Coffee
Horses
Pigs
Cows, Oxen
Goats
Chickens
Smallpox
Typhus

Silver and gold for coins like these were minted in the Americas. Shipped across the ocean, they brought wealth and power to European nations. ▼

◀ Peanuts have become an important staple crop in western Africa, where they add protein to soups and stews or are pressed into cooking oil.

▲ Sunflowers, native to the American Great Plains, thrive in chilly northern Europe and Asia. Ukraine, Russia, and China press sunflower seeds for cooking oil.

Thinking Critically

1. **Analyze Visuals** Explain the importance of one Western Hemisphere item to a person in the Eastern Hemisphere.
2. **Draw Inferences** Choose an item from one of the lists. Explain how the history of the hemisphere it traveled to might be different if the Columbian Exchange had not happened.

Quick Study Guide

 SSWH10b

■ Key Elements of Europe's Commercial Revolution

- **Columbian Exchange** Foods, ideas, technologies, and diseases are exchanged between the hemispheres, resulting in population growth.
- **Inflation** Rising prices occur along with an increase in the money supply.
- **Price Revolution** Rising prices are coupled with inflation.
- **Capitalism** People invest money to make a profit.
- **Mercantilism** European countries adopt mercantilist policies—such as establishing colonies, increasing exports, and limiting imports—to compete for trade and empire.

■ Major European Settlements/ Colonies in the Americas

Date	Region Settled	Country	Purpose
1520s	Mexico	Spain	Find gold
1530s	Peru	Spain	Find gold
1530s	Brazil	Portugal	Establish settlements and plantations
Early 1500s	New France (eastern Canada)	France	Take part in fur trade and fishing
Early 1600s	13 colonies (present-day eastern United States)	England	Various reasons including establishing settlements and escaping religious persecution

■ Triangular Trade Routes

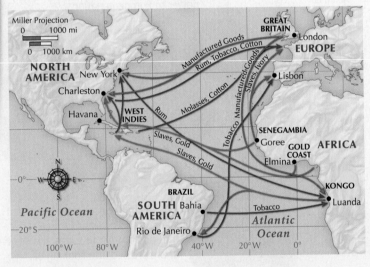

■ The Native American Population Declines

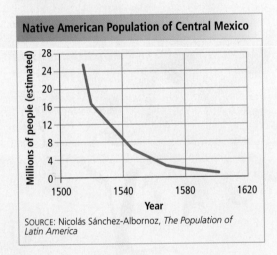

Native American Population of Central Mexico

SOURCE: Nicolás Sánchez-Albornoz, *The Population of Latin America*

■ Europe and the Americas, 1492–1750

1492 Columbus lands in the Americas.

1521 Cortés completes conquest of the Aztecs.

1530s Cartier explores the St. Lawrence River, claiming eastern Canada for France.

1607 British colonists found Jamestown, Virginia.

Chapter Events
Global Events

1500   **1550**   **1600**

1498 Portuguese explorer da Gama rounds Africa and reaches India.

1526 The Mughal dynasty is founded in India.

Concept Connector

? Essential Question Review

To connect prior knowledge with what you have learned in this chapter, answer the questions below in your Concept Connector journal. Use the journal in the Reading and Note Taking Study Guide to record your answers (or go to www.phschool.com **Web Code:** nad-1507). In addition, record information about the following concepts:

- Cooperation: Moctezuma welcomes Cortes and his men; Malinche helps the Spaniards
- Genocide: Native Americans

1. **Empire** Compare the establishment of the Spanish empire in the Americas with the establishment of the English empire in the Americas. Note similarities and differences in the following.
   - political systems
   - economic systems
   - religion
   - effects on the Native American population.

2. **Trade** The transatlantic slave trade expanded greatly between 1500 and 1800. Although some people reaped enormous profits from the slave trade, it resulted in disasters that went beyond the horrors of the Middle Passage. Who benefited most from slavery and why? What were some of the unintended consequences of the slave trade for African states and societies? How have the consequences of the slave trade influenced world history?

3. **Economic Systems** In the Middle Ages, wealth was based on the manorial system in which peasants worked on land owned by nobles. Following the Commercial Revolution, European nations adopted a policy of mercantilism to build their wealth and power. How did mercantilism change the source and distribution of wealth in European society?

■ Connections to Today

1. **Cultural Diffusion** During the Columbian Exchange, people were exposed to goods, ideas, and diseases that changed their lives forever. Many of these exchanges were positive, such as the introduction of the horse to the Americas. Some were negative, such as the introduction of European diseases to the Americas. Think about similar exchanges that have happened in recent times. Research and write about a positive exchange and a negative exchange. To direct your research, consider topics such as disease, new technology, the introduction of fish or animals into non-native regions, and the availability of new foods.

2. **Trade** Throughout history, people and governments have worked to establish profitable trade methods. Some very successful trade methods have had terrible consequences for other people. Consider how Europe's commercial revolution was achieved in large part because of the Atlantic slave trade. Then think about trade practices today that, though profitable, might hurt some people. Write two to three paragraphs describing the pros and cons of modern trade practices. Consider the following:
   - trade pacts like NAFTA
   - voluntary labeling of products such as Fair Trade
   - practices such as child labor

1619
First cargo of African slaves arrives in Virginia.

1750s
Olaudah Equiano writes a book about his experiences during the Atlantic slave trade.

1763
The Treaty of Paris is signed, ending the French and Indian War.

1650 **1700** **1750**

1630s
Japan bars foreign merchants from the country.

1687
Englishman Isaac Newton publishes his book explaining the laws of gravity.

1736
The reign of Chinese emperor Qianlong begins.

History *Interactive*
For: Interactive timeline
Web Code: nap-1561

499

Chapter Assessment

Terms, People, and Places

Match the following terms with the definitions listed below.

immunity	inflation
revenue	encomienda
privateer	mutiny

1. the right to demand labor from Native Americans
2. income from taxes
3. rise in prices linked to an increase in the money supply
4. pirate operating under government approval
5. resistance
6. revolt

Main Ideas

Section 1 (pp. 472–476)
7. How did the explorations of conquistadors such as Hernán Cortés and Francisco Pizarro contribute to the Spanish empire in the Americas?
8. What effect did European exploration have on Native American populations?

Section 2 (pp. 477–481)
9. How did Spain structure its American empire?
10. Write a sentence or two explaining the role of each of the following in Spanish colonial society: peon, peninsular, creole, mulatto, and mestizo.

Section 3 (pp. 482–486)
11. Why did the Pilgrims make a compact when they arrived in North America?
12. What was the result of the British and French struggle in North America?

Section 4 (pp. 487–490)
13. How did triangular trade affect Africans?
14. How did the slave trade benefit Europeans?

Section 5 (pp. 491–497)
15. What impact did American gold and silver have on European economies?
16. How did the policy of mercantilism affect global economies?

Chapter Focus Question
17. How did European colonization of the Americas shape global economies and societies?

Critical Thinking

18. **Compare Points of View** You read that many Native Americans saw the Spanish takeover as a sign that their gods were less powerful than those of the Spanish. How did the Spanish likely interpret their victory?
19. **Predict Consequences** How would society in the United States today be affected if mysterious diseases wiped out 90 percent or more of the population?
20. **Analyzing Visuals** The painting below, titled *First Landing of Columbus*, was painted in 1803. Consider what you have learned in this chapter. Do you think this painting accurately shows that event? Explain your answer.

● Writing About History

In this chapter's five Section Assessments, you developed skills for writing a compare-contrast essay.

Writing a Compare and Contrast Essay The European nations that settled the Americas all wanted wealth and empire—but went about getting them in different ways. Write a compare and contrast essay that discusses two of the European powers involved in settling the Americas. Consult page SH9 of the Writing Handbook for additional help.

Prewriting
• Choose a topic that lends itself to comparison and contrast. Possibilities include important leaders, economic goals, interactions with Native Americans, or religious goals.
• Create graphic organizers, such as tables or Venn diagrams, to help you see similarities and differences.

Drafting
• Write an introduction and a thesis statement. Your thesis statement should summarize the main points you want to make about the things you are comparing.
• Write the body text, introducing details and evidence that support your thesis statement. Organize your text by subject or by point. Then write a conclusion.

Revising
• Use the guidelines for revising your essay on page SH12 of the Writing Handbook.

Prepare for the GHSGT

The Impact of Piracy

In 1580, Admiral Francis Drake returned to England after circumnavigating the globe. A delighted Queen Elizabeth I knighted the commander when she visited his ship, the *Golden Hind*, in 1581. The British queen had good reason to be grateful. Drake's voyage brought huge revenues to the royal treasury and dealt a blow to her enemy, King Philip II of Spain. The documents below give different views of Drake's activities.

Document A

"Passing the Straits of Magellan, untraversed as yet by any Englishman, [Drake] swept the unguarded coast of [Chile] and Peru, loaded his bark with the gold-dust and silver-ingots of Potosí, and with the pearls, emeralds, and diamonds which formed the cargo of the great galleon that sailed once a year from Lima to Cadiz. With spoils of above half-a-million in value the daring adventurer steered undauntedly for the Moluccas, rounded the Cape of Good Hope, and after completing the circuit of the globe dropped anchor again in Plymouth harbour. . . . The welcome he received from Elizabeth on his return was accepted by Philip as an outrage which could only be expiated by war. . . . She met a request for Drake's surrender by knighting the freebooter, and by wearing in her crown the jewels he had offered her as a present."

—From ***A Short History of the English People*** by J.R. Green

Document B

"[The Ambassador urged his king] . . . that no foreign ship be spared, in . . . the . . . Indies, but that every one should be sent to the bottom, and not a soul on board of them allowed to live. This will be the only way to prevent the English and French from going to these parts to plunder, for at present there is hardly an Englishman who is not talking of undertaking the voyage, so encouraged are they by Drake's return."

—Don Bernardino de Mendoza, Philip II's ambassador to London, around 1580

Document C

"To Lima we came the 13th of February; and, being entered the haven, we found there about twelve sail of ships lying fast moored at an anchor, having all their sails carried on shore; for the masters and merchants were here most secure, having never been assaulted by enemies, and at this time feared the approach of none such as we were. Our general rifled these ships, and found in one of them a chest full of reals of plate, and good store of silks and linen cloth. . . . In which ship he had news of another ship called the *Cacafuego*, which was gone toward Payta, and that the same ship was laden with treasure. Whereupon we stayed no longer here, but cutting all the cables of the ships in the haven, we let them drive whither they would, either to sea or to the shore; and with all speed we followed the *Cacafuego* which was gone toward Payta. . . ."

—From ***Sir Francis Drake's Famous Voyage Round the World, 1580*** by Francis Pretty

Document D ▼

Analyzing Documents

Use your knowledge of American colonial history and Documents A, B, C, and D to answer questions 1–4.

1. According to Document A, Drake's exploits in Chile and Peru
   A were not commercially successful.
   B were done impulsively, without Queen Elizabeth's consent or approval.
   C gave King Philip II the excuse he'd been wanting to start a war against England.
   D met with outrage and anger from Queen Elizabeth and the English-speaking world.

2. According to Document B, what was Don Bernardino de Mendoza's main concern regarding Drake?
   A that Drake would return to the West Indies soon
   B that other seamen would copy Drake's exploits
   C that Spanish seamen would join future Drake expeditions
   D that other nations would join with England against Spain

3. Document D shows Queen Elizabeth I with Francis Drake. Which of the other documents does this one support?
   A Document A
   B Document B
   C Document C
   D Documents A, B, and C

4. **Writing Task** Write a news article about Drake's exploits that might have appeared in a Spanish newspaper around 1580. Use the documents along with information from the chapter to support your article.

16

The Age of Absolutism

1550–1800

A Child Becomes King

In 1643, the five-year-old heir to the French crown, Louis XIV, made his first public appearance. The tiny monarch climbed the throne and sat for hours as officials conducted the ceremony announcing the new reign. Louis XIV had been orphaned as a baby, and was a sickly, shy child. As a child, he would often bring a cat to government councils, stroking the fur as he sat in silence. Despite this quiet beginning, Louis XIV proved to be a strong, able ruler who came to symbolize the period of absolute monarchy we now call the "Age of Absolutism." Listen to the Witness History audio to hear more about this powerful king.

◄ Louis XIV receives foreign ambassadors at his Versailles court in 1678.

A French bishop's official seal

 Performance Standards

Chapter Focus Question What events led to the rise of absolute monarchies and the development of centralized nation-states in Europe?

Section 1
Spanish Power Grows
SSWH12a

Section 2
France Under Louis XIV
SSWH14a

Section 3
Parliament Triumphs in England
SSWH13b, SSWH14b

Section 4
Rise of Austria and Prussia
SSWH9d

Section 5
Absolute Monarchy in Russia
SSWH14a

Use the ☑ **Quick Study Timeline** at the end of this chapter to preview chapter events.

Oliver Cromwell's battle helmet

Spanish treasure from Mexico

 Concept Connector ONLINE

To explore Essential Questions related to this chapter, go to PHSchool.com
Web Code: nad-1607

Philip II wears royal dress. In the background, his Armada heads to England.

A late 1500s Spanish coin commemorates Philip's rule.

WITNESS HISTORY 🔊 AUDIO

A Working Monarch

"It is best to keep an eye on everything," Philip II of Spain often said—and he meant it. As king of the most powerful nation in Europe, he gave little time to pleasure. Instead, he plowed through a mountain of paperwork each day, making notes on even the most trivial matters. But Philip's determination to "keep an eye on everything" extended far beyond trivia. It helped him build Spain into a strong centralized state. By the late 1500s, he had concentrated all power in his own hands. Over the next 200 years, other European monarchs would pursue similar goals.

Focus Question How did Philip II extend Spain's power and help establish a golden age?

Spanish Power Grows

Performance Standards

- **SSWH12a** Describe the Ottoman Empire's borders when Suleyman the Magnificent ruled.

Terms, People, and Places

Hapsburg empire	divine right
Charles V	armada
Philip II	El Greco
absolute monarch	Miguel de Cervantes

Note Taking

Reading Skill: Identify Main Ideas and Supporting Details As you read about how Philip II extended Spanish power, create an outline to record details that support the main ideas in this section. This example will help you get started.

> I. Charles V Inherits Two Crowns
>   A. Ruling the Hapsburg Empire
>   1. Spain
>   2. Holy Roman Empire and Netherlands
>   B. Charles V abdicates

By the 1500s, Spain had shaken off its feudal past and emerged as the first modern European power. Queen Isabella and King Ferdinand had unified the country, enforced religious unity, and commanded the Spanish conquest of the Americas.

Charles V Inherits Two Crowns

In 1516, Ferdinand and Isabella's grandson, Charles I, became king of Spain, and thereby ruler of the Spanish colonies in the Americas as well.

Ruling the Hapsburg Empire When his other grandfather died in 1519, Charles I also became heir to the sprawling **Hapsburg empire,** which included the Holy Roman Empire and the Netherlands. As ruler of this empire, Charles took the name **Charles V.** Historians now usually refer to him by this title.

Ruling two empires involved Charles in constant warfare. As a devout Catholic, he fought to suppress Protestantism in the German states. After years of religious conflict, however, Charles was forced to allow the German princes to choose their own religion.

Charles also faced the Muslim Ottoman empire, which was based in Turkey but stretched across the Balkans. Under Suleiman, Ottoman forces advanced across central Europe to the walls surrounding Vienna, Austria. Although Austria held firm during the siege, the Ottomans occupied much of Hungary following their crushing victory at the Battle of Mohács. Ottoman naval forces also continued to challenge Spanish power in the Mediterranean.

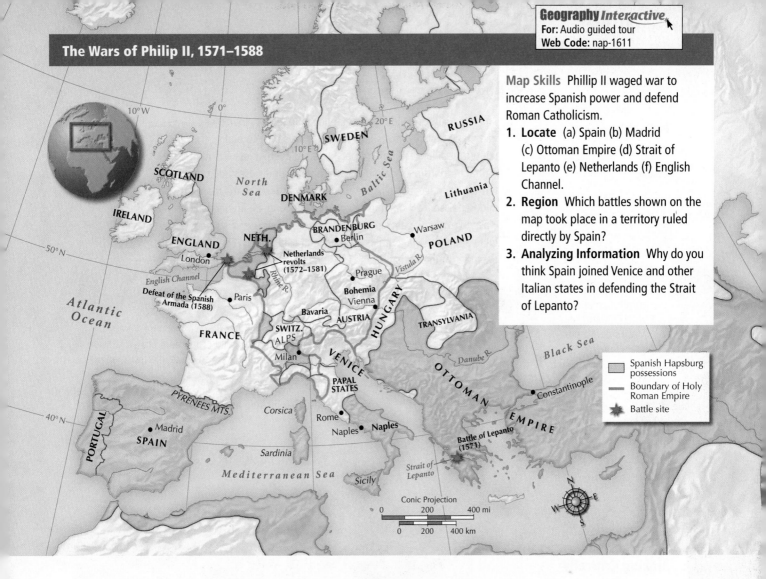

Geography *Interactive*

For: Audio guided tour
Web Code: nap-1611

Map Skills Phillip II waged war to increase Spanish power and defend Roman Catholicism.

1. **Locate** (a) Spain (b) Madrid (c) Ottoman Empire (d) Strait of Lepanto (e) Netherlands (f) English Channel.

2. **Region** Which battles shown on the map took place in a territory ruled directly by Spain?

3. **Analyzing Information** Why do you think Spain joined Venice and other Italian states in defending the Strait of Lepanto?

Spanish Hapsburg possessions
Boundary of Holy Roman Empire
Battle site

Charles V Abdicates

The Hapsburg empire proved to be too scattered and <u>cumbersome</u> for any one person to rule effectively. Exhausted and disillusioned, Charles V gave up his titles and entered a monastery in 1556. He divided his empire, leaving the Hapsburg lands in central Europe to his brother Ferdinand, who became Holy Roman emperor. He gave Spain, the Netherlands, some southern Italian states, and Spain's overseas empire to his 29-year-old son Philip, who became Philip II.

 Checkpoint Why did Charles V divide the Hapsburg Empire?

Vocabulary Builder

<u>cumbersome</u>—(KUM bur sum) *adj.* hard to handle because of size, weight, or many parts

Philip II Solidifies Power

During his 42-year reign, **Philip II** expanded Spanish influence, strengthened the Catholic Church, and made his own power absolute. Thanks in part to silver from Spanish colonies in the Americas, he made Spain the foremost power in Europe.

Centralizing Power Like his father, Philip II was hard working, devout, and ambitious. Unlike many other monarchs, Philip devoted most of his time to government work. He seldom hunted, never jousted, and lived as simply as a monk. The King's isolated, somber palace outside Madrid, known as the Escorial (es kohr YAHL), reflected his character. It served as a church, a residence, and a tomb for the royal family.

PHILIP II AND THE RISE OF SPAIN

Philip II's Marriages

Maria	Mary Tudor	Elizabeth Valois	Anna
Alliance: Portugal	Alliance: England	Allliance: France	Alliance: Austria

In his pursuit of building and extending Spanish power, Philip II had many tools in his arsenal. Marriage was one. To build important alliances—and to pacify potential enemies—he married a total of four times, gaining power and in some cases additional territory. Yet because alliances lasted only as long as the marriage, and Renaissance women often did not live long, Philip needed other ways to expand Spain's power. War was another useful strategy, it gained him the kingdom of Portugal and established him as the defender of the Roman Catholic Church. Wealth was perhaps his most important tool. Silver and gold from his colonies in the Americas fueled the Spanish economy and ensured Spanish power.

Philip's marriage to Mary Tudor in 1554 created an alliance with England until Mary's death four years later. ▼

The Spanish melted down Native American gold ornaments like this one to make Spanish coins like those above. ▲

Philip's victory against the Turks in the Battle of Lepanto assured his role as defender of the Catholic Church. ▼

Thinking Critically

1. **Apply Information** What various purposes could royal marriages serve during the age of absolutism?
2. **Understand Cause and Effect** How did Philip's colonies in the Americas affect his goals for Spain?

Philip surpassed Ferdinand and Isabella in making every part of the government responsible to him. He reigned as an **absolute monarch,** a ruler with complete authority over the government and the lives of the people. Like other European rulers, Philip asserted that he ruled by **divine right.** That is, he believed that his authority to rule came directly from God. Philip therefore saw himself as the guardian of the Roman Catholic Church. The great undertaking of his life was to defend the Catholic Reformation and turn back the rising Protestant tide in Europe. Within his empire, Philip enforced religious unity, turning the Inquisition against Protestants and other people thought to be heretics.

Battles in the Mediterranean and the Netherlands Philip fought many wars as he attempted to advance Spanish Catholic power. In the Mediterranean, the Ottoman empire continued to pose a threat to European control of the region. At the Battle of Lepanto in 1571, Spain and its Italian allies soundly defeated an Ottoman fleet off the coast of Greece. Although the Ottoman Empire would remain a major power in the Mediterranean region for three more centuries, Christians still hailed the battle as a great victory and a demonstration of Spain's power.

During the last half of his reign, Philip battled rebels in the Netherlands. At the time, the region included 17 provinces that are today Belgium, the Netherlands, and Luxembourg. It was the richest part of Philip's empire. Protestants in the region resisted Philip's efforts to crush their faith. Protestants and Catholics alike opposed high taxes and autocratic Spanish rule, which threatened local traditions of self-government.

In the 1560s, riots against the Inquisition sparked a general uprising in the Netherlands. Savage fighting raged for decades. In 1581, the northern, largely Protestant provinces declared their independence from Spain and became known as the Dutch Netherlands. They did not gain official recognition, however, until 1648. The southern, mostly Catholic provinces of the Netherlands remained part of the Spanish Empire.

The Armada Sails Against England By the 1580s, Philip saw England's Queen Elizabeth I as his chief Protestant enemy. First secretly, then openly, Elizabeth had supported the Dutch against Spain. She encouraged English captains such as Francis Drake, known as sea dogs, to plunder Spanish treasure ships and loot Spanish cities in the Americas. To Philip's dismay, Elizabeth made the pirate Drake a knight.

To end English attacks and subdue the Dutch, Philip prepared a huge **armada,** or fleet, to carry a Spanish invasion force to England. In 1588, the Spanish Armada sailed with more than 130 ships, 20,000 men, and 2,400 pieces of artillery. The Spanish were confident of victory. "When we meet the English," predicted one Spanish commander, "God will surely arrange matters so that we can grapple and board them, either by sending some strange freak of weather or, more likely, just by depriving the English of their wits."

This prediction did not come to pass. In the English Channel, lumbering Spanish ships were outmaneuvered by the lighter, faster English ships. Strong winds favored the English, scattering the Armada. After further disasters at sea, the tattered remnants limped home in defeat.

An Empire Declines The defeat of the Armada marked the beginning of the end of Spanish power. Throughout the 1600s, Spain's strength and prosperity decreased. One reason for this decline was that Philip II's successors ruled far less ably than he had.

Spain Loses Territory
The Treaty of Munster, signed in 1648, recognized the independence of the Netherlands' Protestant provinces.

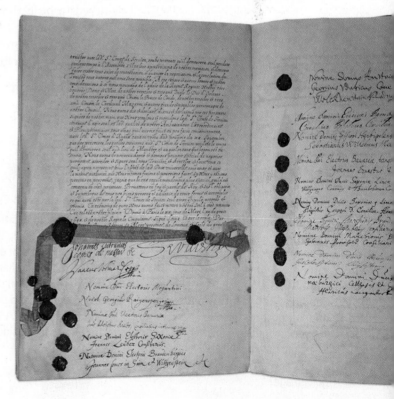

View of Toledo
El Greco's painting shows the Spanish city of Toledo, where he lived for 40 years. This is El Greco's only landscape painting. *How does El Greco express religious themes in this painting?*

Economic problems were also to blame. Costly overseas wars drained wealth out of Spain almost as fast as it came in. Treasure from the Americas led Spain to neglect farming and commerce. The government heavily taxed the small middle class, weakening a group that in other European nations supported royal power. The expulsion of Muslims and Jews from Spain deprived the economy of many skilled artisans and merchants. Finally, the influx of American gold and silver led to soaring inflation.

As Spain's power dwindled in the 1600s and 1700s, Dutch, English, and French fleets challenged—and eventually surpassed—Spanish power both in Europe and around the world.

✔ **Checkpoint** What were Philip II's motivations for waging war?

Spain's Golden Age

The century from 1550 to 1650 is often referred to as Spain's *Siglo de Oro* (SEEG loh day OHR oh), or "golden century," for the brilliance of its arts and literature. Philip II was an enthusiastic patron of the arts and also founded academies of science and mathematics.

Among the famous painters of this period was a man called **El Greco,** meaning "the Greek." Though not Spanish by birth, El Greco is considered to be a master of Spanish painting. Born on the Greek island of Crete, El Greco had studied in Italy before settling in Spain. He produced haunting religious pictures and striking portraits of Spanish nobles. El Greco's use of vibrant colors influenced the work of Diego Velázquez (vuh LAHS kes), court painter to King Philip IV. Velázquez is perhaps best known for his vivid portraits of Spanish royalty.

Spain's golden century produced several outstanding writers. Lope de Vega (LOH pay duh VAY guh), a peasant by birth, wrote more than 1,500 plays, including witty comedies and action-packed romances. **Miguel de Cervantes** (sur VAN teez) was the most important writer of Spain's golden age. His *Don Quixote*, which pokes fun at medieval tales of chivalry, is considered to be Europe's first modern novel. Although *Don Quixote* mocks the traditions of Spain's feudal past, Cervantes depicts with affection both the foolish but heroic idealism of Don Quixote and the unromantic, earthy realism of his sidekick, Sancho Panza.

✔ **Checkpoint** What was the *Siglo de Oro*?

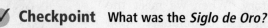

SECTION **1** Assessment

Progress Monitoring *Online*
For: Self-quiz with vocabulary practice
Web Code: naa-1611

Terms, People, and Places

1. For each term, person, or place listed at the beginning of the section, write a sentence explaining its significance.

Note Taking

2. **Reading Skill: Identify Main Ideas and Supporting Details** Use your completed outline to answer the Focus Question: How did Philip II extend Spain's power and help establish a golden age?

Comprehension and Critical Thinking

3. **Compare and Contrast** How were Charles V and Philip II alike and different in their goals of ensuring absolute power and strengthening Catholicism?

4. **Synthesize Information** Why did Spanish power and prosperity decline?

5. **Summarize** Why is the period from 1550 to 1650 considered Spain's golden age?

● **Writing About History**
Quick Write: Generate Arguments Choose a topic from this section that could be the subject of a persuasive essay—for example, whether England was really a threat to Spain. Then write two thesis statements, one arguing each side of your topic. Make sure that the arguments clearly explain opposite or differing opinions on the topic.

Don Quixote by Miguel de Cervantes

Although the age of chivalry had long passed, stories about knights-errant were still popular in the early 1600s. The heroes of these stories were brave knights who traveled far and wide performing noble deeds. Miguel de Cervantes's novel *Don Quixote* satirizes such romances. His hero, the elderly Don Quixote, has read too many tales of chivalry. Imagining himself a knight-errant, he sets out across the Spanish countryside with his practical servant, Sancho Panza. In this famous excerpt, Don Quixote's noble motives give dignity to his foolish battle with the windmills.

Just then they came in sight of thirty or forty windmills that rise from that plain, and no sooner did Don Quixote see them than he said to his squire: "Fortune is guiding our affairs better than we ourselves could have wished. Do you see over yonder, friend Sancho, thirty or forty hulking giants? I intend to do battle with them and slay them. With the spoils we shall begin to be rich, for this is a righteous war. . . ."

"What giants?" asked Sancho Panza.

"Those you see over there," replied his master, "with the long arms; some of them have them well-nigh[1] two leagues in length."

"Take care, sir," cried Sancho. "Those over there are not giants but windmills, and those things that seem to be armed are their sails, which when they are whirled around by the wind turn the millstone."

"It is clear," replied Don Quixote, "that you are not experienced in adventures. Those are giants, and if you are afraid, turn aside and pray whilst I enter into fierce and unequal battle with them."

Uttering these words, he clapped spurs to Rozinante, his steed, without heeding the cries of his squire, Sancho, who warned him that he was not going to attack giants, but windmills. But so convinced was he that they were giants that he neither heard his squire's shouts nor did he notice what they were, though he was very near them. Instead, he rushed on, shouting in a loud voice: "Fly not, cowards and vile caitliffs[2]; one knight alone attacks you!" At that moment a slight breeze arose and the great sails began to move. . . .

He ran his lance into the sail, but the wind twisted it with such violence that it shivered the lance in pieces and dragged both rider and horse after it, rolling them over and over on the ground, sorely damaged.

PORTRAIT DE MICHEL DE CERVANTES SAAVEDRA, PAR LUI MEME.

▲ Miguel de Cervantes

▼ An illustration from *Don Quixote* shows Sancho Panza shouting after his master, who is battling windmills.

Thinking Critically

1. **Synthesize Information** What values of chivalry motivate Don Quixote's attack on the windmills?
2. **Analyze Literature** How does Cervantes show both sides of Don Quixote—the noble and the foolish—in this excerpt?

1. **well-nigh** (wel ny) *adv.* nearly
2. **caitliff** (KAYT lif) *n.* cowardly person

Louis XIV rides a powerful horse, displaying his strength and abilities.

WITNESS HISTORY 🔊 AUDIO

Life at Versailles

At Versailles, the palace court of Louis XIV, life revolved around the king. Nobles waited days or weeks for the honor of attending the king while he dressed or bathed. Every evening the king was at the center of a lavish entertainment, followed by a supper of dozens of rich dishes. The elaborate and extravagant rituals that governed life at court masked a very serious purpose—they were a way for Louis XIV to control every aspect of court life and ensure his absolute authority.

Focus Question How did France become the leading power of Europe under the absolute rule of Louis XIV?

France Under Louis XIV

 Performance Standards

• **SSWH14a** Compare Louis XIV, Peter the Great and Tokugawa Ieyasu's absolutism.

Terms, People, and Places

Huguenots	intendant
Henry IV	Jean-Baptiste Colbert
Edict of Nantes	Versailles
Cardinal Richelieu	*levée*
Louis XIV	balance of power

N**ote Taking**

Reading Skill: Identify Supporting Details As you read about the rule of Louis XIV and how he strengthened the monarchy, use a concept web like the one below to record details that support the main ideas in this section. Add as many circles as you need.

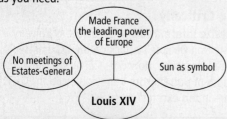

In the last half of the fifteenth century, France enjoyed a period of peace. After driving out the English, the French kings were able to solidify their power within their own realm. But in the 1500s, rivalry with Charles V of Spain and then religious conflict plunged the kingdom into turmoil.

Henry IV Restores Order

In the late 1500s France was torn apart by turbulent wars of religion. A century later, France was a strong, unified nation-state ruled by the most powerful monarch in Europe.

Religious Strife From the 1560s to the 1590s, religious wars between the Catholic majority and French Protestants, called **Huguenots** (HYOO guh nahts), tore France apart. Leaders on both sides used the strife to further their own ambitions.

The worst incident began on St. Bartholomew's Day (a Catholic holiday), August 24, 1572. While Huguenot and Catholic nobles were gathered for a royal wedding, a plot by Catholic royals led to the massacre of 3,000 Huguenots. In the next few days, thousands more were slaughtered. For many, the St. Bartholomew's Day Massacre symbolized the complete breakdown of order in France.

Bringing Peace to a Shattered Land In 1589, a Huguenot prince inherited the French throne as **Henry IV.** For four years Henry fought against fierce Catholic opposition to gain control of France. Finally, to end the conflict, he converted to Catholicism. "Paris is well worth a Mass," he is supposed to have said. To protect Protestants, however, in 1598 he issued the **Edict of Nantes** granting the Huguenots religious toleration and other freedoms.

Henry IV then set out to repair France. His goal, he said, was not the victory of one sect over another, but "a chicken in every pot"—a good Sunday dinner for every peasant. Under Henry, the government reached into every area of French life. Royal officials administered justice, improved roads, built bridges, and revived agriculture. By building the royal bureaucracy and reducing the influence of nobles, Henry IV laid the foundations on which future French monarchs would build absolute power.

Cardinal Richelieu Strengthens Royal Authority When Henry IV was killed by an assassin in 1610, his nine-year-old son, Louis XIII, inherited the throne. For a time, nobles reasserted their power. Then, in 1624, Louis appointed **Cardinal Richelieu** (ree shul YOO) as his chief minister. This cunning, capable leader devoted the next 18 years to strengthening the central government.

Richelieu sought to destroy the power of the Huguenots and nobles—two groups that did not bow to royal authority. Although he allowed the Huguenots to practice their religion, he smashed their walled cities and outlawed their armies. Likewise, he defeated the private armies of the nobles and destroyed their fortified castles. While reducing their independence, Richelieu tied the nobles to the king by giving them high posts at court or in the royal army.

Richelieu also handpicked his able successor, Cardinal Mazarin (ma za RAN). 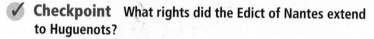 When five-year-old **Louis XIV** inherited the throne in 1643, the year after Richelieu's death, Mazarin was in place to serve as chief minister. Like Richelieu, Mazarin worked tirelessly to extend royal power.

✔ **Checkpoint** What rights did the Edict of Nantes extend to Huguenots?

An Absolute Monarch Rises

Soon after Louis XIV became king, disorder again swept France. In an uprising called the *Fronde*, nobles, merchants, peasants, and the urban poor each rebelled in order to protest royal power or preserve their own. On one occasion, rioters drove the boy king from his palace. It was an experience Louis would never forget. When Mazarin died in 1661, the 23-year-old Louis resolved to take complete control over the government himself. "I have been pleased to entrust the government of my affairs to the late Cardinal," he declared. "It is now time that I govern them myself."

"I Am the State" Like his great-grandfather Philip II of Spain, Louis XIV firmly believed in his divine right to rule. He took the sun as the symbol of his absolute power. Just as the sun stands at the center of the solar system, he argued, so the Sun King stands at the center of the nation. Louis is often quoted as saying, *"L'état, c'est moi"* (lay TAH seh MWAH), which in English translates as "I am the state."

During his reign, Louis did not once call a meeting of the Estates General, the medieval council made up of representatives of all French social classes. In fact, the Estates General did not meet between 1614 and 1789. Thus, the Estates General played no role in checking royal power.

BIOGRAPHY

Cardinal Richelieu
Armand Richelieu's (1585–1642) parents expected great things from him. They even invited the king of France to attend Armand's christening, promising that someday he would be a leader of France.

The young boy also aspired to greatness as he was growing up. At first, he received training to become a disciplined and authoritative military officer. Then, at his family's request, he switched direction. At age 17, he began training to become a bishop in the Catholic Church. The path was different but the purpose was the same: to become a leader and to serve the monarch.

Over the next 40 years, Armand Richelieu rose to the highest levels of authority in both religious and political circles. He became the true power behind the throne of King Louis XIII. **What characteristics of Richelieu does the artist portray in this painting?**

Louis XIV Strengthens Royal Power Louis spent many hours each day attending to government affairs. To strengthen the state, he followed the policies of Richelieu. He expanded the bureaucracy and appointed **intendants,** royal officials who collected taxes, recruited soldiers, and carried out his policies in the provinces. These and other government jobs often went to wealthy middle-class men. In this way Louis cemented his ties with the middle class, thus checking the power of the nobles and the Church. The king also built the French army into the strongest in Europe. The state paid, fed, trained, and supplied up to 300,000 soldiers. Louis used this highly disciplined army to enforce his policies at home and abroad.

Colbert Builds France's Finances Louis's brilliant finance minister, **Jean-Baptiste Colbert** (kohl behr), imposed mercantilist policies to bolster the economy. He had new lands cleared for farming, encouraged mining and other basic industries, and built up luxury trades such as lacemaking. To protect French manufacturers, Colbert put high tariffs on imported goods. He also fostered overseas colonies, such as New France in North America and several colonies in India, and regulated trade with the colonies to enrich the royal treasury. Colbert's policies helped make France the wealthiest state in Europe. Yet not even the financial genius of Colbert could produce enough income to support the huge costs of Louis's court and his many foreign wars.

✔ **Checkpoint** Why did Louis XIV choose the sun as his symbol?

Versailles: Symbol of Royal Power

In the countryside near Paris, Louis XIV turned a royal hunting lodge into the immense palace of **Versailles** (ver SY). He spared no expense to make it the most magnificent building in Europe. Its halls and salons displayed the finest paintings and statues, and they glittered with chandeliers and mirrors. In the royal gardens, millions of flowers, trees, and fountains were set out in precise geometric patterns. Versailles became the perfect symbol of the Sun King's wealth and power. As both the king's home and the seat of government, it housed nobles, officials, and servants.

Conducting Court Ceremonies Louis XIV perfected elaborate ceremonies that emphasized his own importance. Each day began in the king's bedroom with a major ritual known as the *levée* (luh VAY), or rising. High-ranking nobles competed for the honor of holding the royal washbasin or handing the king his diamond-buckled shoes. At night, the ceremony was repeated in reverse. Wives of nobles vied to attend upon women of the royal family.

Rituals such as the *levée* served a serious purpose. French nobles were descendants of the feudal lords who held power in medieval times. At liberty on their estates, these nobles were a threat to the power of the monarchy. By luring nobles to Versailles, Louis turned them into courtiers angling for privileges rather than rival warriors battling for power. His tactic worked because he carefully protected their prestige and left them exempt from paying taxes.

The Sun King developed his philosophy of absolutism with the help of a brilliant bishop named Jacques Bénigne Bossuet (1627–1704). In his writings, Bossuet argued that the Bible shows that a monarch rules by the will of God. Therefore, opposition to the monarch is a sin. Bossuet also believed that, although the monarch should rule absolutely, it was God's will that he or she act only in the best interest of the nation. **According to Bossuet, what is the role of a king?**

Primary Source

❝ The royal power is absolute. . . . The prince need render account of his acts to no one. . . . Without this absolute authority [he] could neither do good nor repress evil. It is necessary that his power be such that no one can hope to escape him. . . . The prince . . . is not regarded as a private person: he is a public personage, all the state is in him; the will of all the people is included in his. As all perfection and all strength are united in God, so all the power of individuals is united in the person of the prince.❞
—Bishop Jacques Bénigne Bossuet, "Politics Drawn from the Very Words of Scripture," 1679

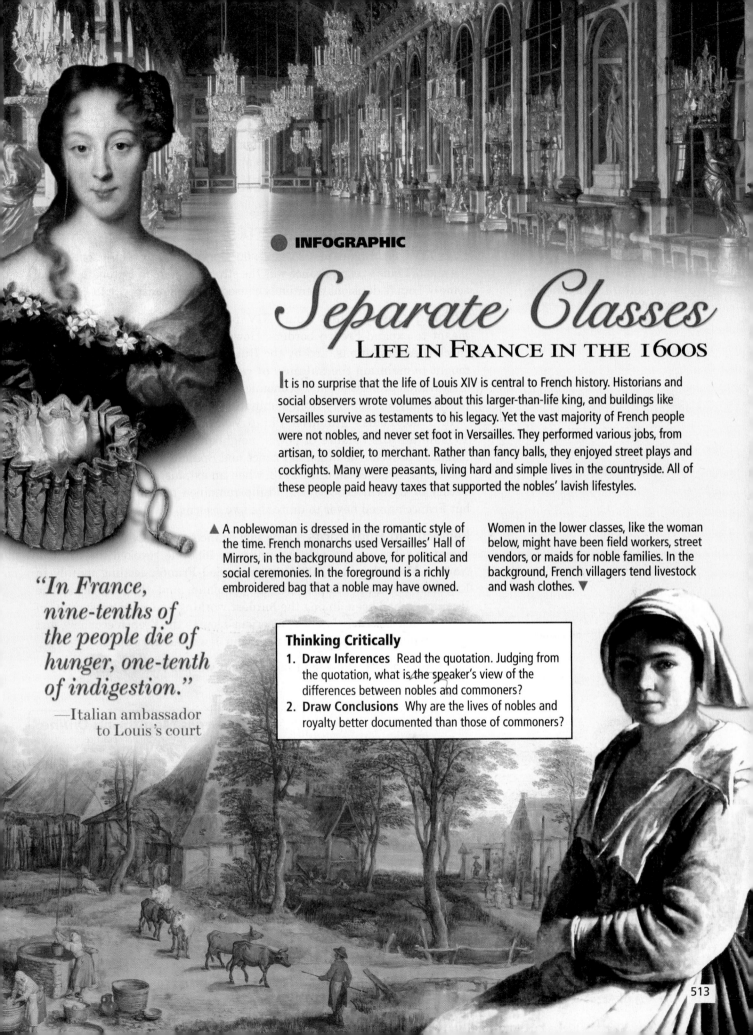

Separate Classes
LIFE IN FRANCE IN THE 1600S

It is no surprise that the life of Louis XIV is central to French history. Historians and social observers wrote volumes about this larger-than-life king, and buildings like Versailles survive as testaments to his legacy. Yet the vast majority of French people were not nobles, and never set foot in Versailles. They performed various jobs, from artisan, to soldier, to merchant. Rather than fancy balls, they enjoyed street plays and cockfights. Many were peasants, living hard and simple lives in the countryside. All of these people paid heavy taxes that supported the nobles' lavish lifestyles.

▲ A noblewoman is dressed in the romantic style of the time. French monarchs used Versailles' Hall of Mirrors, in the background above, for political and social ceremonies. In the foreground is a richly embroidered bag that a noble may have owned.

Women in the lower classes, like the woman below, might have been field workers, street vendors, or maids for noble families. In the background, French villagers tend livestock and wash clothes. ▼

"In France, nine-tenths of the people die of hunger, one-tenth of indigestion."

—Italian ambassador to Louis's court

Thinking Critically
1. **Draw Inferences** Read the quotation. Judging from the quotation, what is the speaker's view of the differences between nobles and commoners?
2. **Draw Conclusions** Why are the lives of nobles and royalty better documented than those of commoners?

Patronizing the Arts The king and his court supported a "splendid century" of the arts. The age of Louis XIV came to be known as the classical age of French drama. In painting, music, architecture, and decorative arts, French styles became the model for all Europe. A new form of dance drama, ballet, gained its first great popularity at the French court. As a leading patron of culture, Louis sponsored the French Academies, which set high standards for both the arts and the sciences.

✓ **Checkpoint** How did Louis XIV secure support from the nobility?

A Strong State Declines

Louis XIV ruled France for 72 years—far longer than any other monarch. At the end of Louis's reign, France was the strongest state in Europe. However, some of Louis's decisions eventually caused France's prosperity to erode.

Waging Costly Wars Louis XIV poured vast resources into wars meant to expand French borders. However, rival rulers joined forces to check these ambitions. Led by the Dutch or the English, these alliances fought to maintain the **balance of power.** The goal was to maintain a distribution of military and economic power among European nations to prevent any one country from dominating the region.

In 1700, Louis's grandson Philip V inherited the throne of Spain. To maintain the balance of power, neighboring nations led by England fought to prevent the union of France and Spain. The War of the Spanish Succession dragged on until 1713, when an exhausted France signed the Treaty of Utrecht (YOO trekt). Philip remained on the Spanish throne, but France agreed never to unite the two crowns.

Persecuting Huguenots Louis saw France's Protestant minority as a threat to religious and political unity. In 1685, he revoked the Edict of Nantes. More than 100,000 Huguenots fled France, settling mainly in England, the Netherlands, Germany, Poland, and the Americas. The Huguenots had been among the hardest working and most prosperous of Louis's subjects. Their loss was a serious blow to the French economy, just as the expulsion of Spanish Muslims and Jews had hurt Spain.

✓ **Checkpoint** How did Louis's actions weaken France's economy?

Vocabulary Builder

erode—(ee ROHD) *v.* wear away or disintegrate

SECTION 2 Assessment

Progress Monitoring *Online*
For: Self-quiz with vocabulary practice
Web Code: naa-1621

Terms, People, and Places

1. What do each of the key terms, people, and places listed at the beginning of the section have in common? Explain.

Note Taking

2. **Reading Skill: Identify Supporting Details** Use your completed concept web to answer the Focus Question: How did France become the leading power of Europe under the absolute rule of Louis XIV?

Comprehension and Critical Thinking

3. **Draw Inferences** How did Henry IV's conversion to Catholicism help France unite?

4. **Identify Central Issues** What was the purpose of Louis XIV's extravagant palace and daily rituals?

5. **Recognize Ideologies** Why did other European nations form alliances to oppose France's plans to expand?

● **Writing About History**

Quick Write: Support Opinions With Evidence Choose a topic from the section, such as whether or not you think Louis XIV's reign was good for France. Make a list of evidence from the text that supports your opinion.

THE ESSENTIAL

POLITICAL SYSTEMS

How do political systems rise, develop, and decline?

In This Chapter GA SSWH14a, SSWH19e

Every society has developed some political system by which either the one, the few, or the many rule over others. Some rulers, like King Louis XIV of France (right), have claimed to hold absolute power. Louis XIV's abuse of his power sowed the seeds for the later overthrow of the French monarchy.

Throughout History

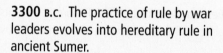

3300 B.C. The practice of rule by war leaders evolves into hereditary rule in ancient Sumer.

1766 B.C.–1911 A.D. In China, the idea of the Mandate of Heaven is used to explain why dynasties rise and fall.

321 B.C. Chandragupta Maurya forges an empire in India and maintains order with a well-organized bureaucracy.

900 A.D. Feudalism develops in Europe because individual monarchs are too weak to maintain law and order.

1556 Philip II of Spain asserts divine right, saying that his authority to rule comes directly from God.

1789 The United States Constitution creates the framework for the American federal system of government.

Continuing Today

With resistance to apartheid growing both in South Africa and in the international community, South Africa changed its constitution in 1996. Once a nation ruled by the minority population, South Africa became a nation with a democratic political system. Each election is another milestone in this transformation.

Ballot Box

21st Century Skills

? **TRANSFER Activities**

1. **Analyze** Throughout history, how have political systems developed?

2. **Evaluate** Why do you think political systems change over time?

3. **Transfer** Complete a Web Quest in which you research a particular political system; record your thoughts in the Concept Connector Journal; and learn to make a video. Web Code: nah-1608

A portrait of King James of England painted around 1619 gives no hint of the monarch's frequent clashes with Parliament.

WITNESS HISTORY 🔊 AUDIO

Charting a Collision Course

In 1603 James I, a monarch with strong ideas about his role, took the English throne. In 1610 the king made a speech to Parliament that would have quite the opposite effect of what he intended:

❝ The state of Monarchy is the supremest thing upon earth; for kings are not only God's lieutenants upon earth and sit upon God's throne, but even by God himself they are called gods. . . . Kings are justly called gods for that they exercise a manner or resemblance of Divine power upon earth. . . . And to the King is due both the affection of the soul and the service of the body of his subjects. . . . ❞
—James I

Focus Question How did the British Parliament assert its rights against royal claims to absolute power in the 1600s?

Parliament Triumphs in England

 Performance Standards

- **SSWH13b** Identify how Locke's ideas links politics and society.
- **SSWH14b** Identify the causes and results of the revolution in England.

Terms, People, and Places

James I	limited monarchy
dissenter	constitutional
Puritans	government
Charles I	cabinet
Oliver Cromwell	oligarchy
English Bill of Rights	

Note Taking

Reading Skill: Identify Supporting Details As you read the section, use a flowchart to record details about the evolution of the English Parliament. One has been started for you.

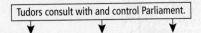

Tudors consult with and control Parliament.

In the 1600s, while Louis XIV perfected royal absolutism in France, political power in England took a different path. Despite attempts by English monarchs to increase royal authority, Parliament steadily expanded its own influence.

The Tudors Work With Parliament

From 1485 to 1603, England was ruled by Tudor monarchs. Although the Tudors believed in divine right, they shrewdly recognized the value of good relations with Parliament. As you have read, when Henry VIII broke with the Roman Catholic Church, he turned to Parliament to legalize his actions. Parliament approved the Act of Supremacy, making the monarch head of the Church of England.

A constant need for money also led Henry to consult Parliament frequently. Although he had inherited a bulging treasury, he quickly used up his funds fighting overseas wars. To levy new taxes, the king had to seek the approval of Parliament. Members of Parliament tended to vote as Henry's agents instructed. Still, they became accustomed to being consulted on important matters.

When Elizabeth I gained the throne, she too both consulted and controlled Parliament. Her advisors conveyed the queen's wishes to Parliament and forbade discussion of certain subjects, such as foreign policy or the queen's marriage. Her skill in handling Parliament helped make "Good Queen Bess" a popular and successful ruler.

✓ **Checkpoint** Why did Henry VIII work with Parliament?

A Century of Revolution Begins

Elizabeth died childless in 1603. Her heir was her relative James Stuart, the ruling king of Scotland. The Stuarts were neither as popular as the Tudors nor as skillful in dealing with Parliament. They also inherited problems that Henry and Elizabeth had long suppressed. The result was a "century of revolution" that pitted the Stuart monarchs against Parliament.

Vocabulary Builder

suppressed—(suh PRESD) *v.* kept from being revealed; put down by force

The Stuarts Issue a Challenge The first Stuart monarch, James I, had agreed to rule according to English laws and customs. Soon, however, he was lecturing Parliament about divine right. "I will not be content that my power be disputed upon," he declared. Leaders in the House of Commons fiercely resisted the king's claim to absolute power.

James repeatedly clashed with Parliament over money and foreign policy. He needed funds to finance his lavish court and wage wars. When members wanted to discuss foreign policy before voting funds, James dissolved Parliament and collected taxes on his own.

James also clashed with **dissenters,** Protestants who differed with the Church of England. One group, called **Puritans,** sought to "purify" the church of Catholic practices. Puritans called for simpler services and a more democratic church without bishops. James rejected their demands, vowing to "harry them out of this land or else do worse."

Parliament Responds In 1625, Charles I inherited the throne. Like his father, Charles behaved like an absolute monarch. He imprisoned his foes without trial and squeezed the nation for money. By 1628, however, his need to raise taxes forced Charles to summon Parliament. Before voting any funds, Parliament insisted that Charles sign the Petition of Right. This document prohibited the king from raising taxes without Parliament's consent or from jailing anyone without legal justification.

Charles did sign the Petition, but he then dissolved Parliament in 1629. For 11 years, he ignored the Petition and ruled the nation without Parliament. During that time, he created bitter enemies, especially among Puritans. His Archbishop of Canterbury, William Laud, tried to force all clergy to follow strict Anglican rules, dismissing or imprisoning dissenters. Many people felt that the archbishop was trying to revive Catholic practices.

In 1637, Charles and Laud tried to impose the Anglican prayer book on Scotland. The Calvinist Scots revolted. To get funds to suppress the Scottish rebellion, Charles once again had to summon Parliament in 1640. When it met, however, Parliament launched its own revolt.

The Long Parliament Begins The 1640 Parliament became known as the Long Parliament because it lasted on and off until 1653. Its actions triggered the greatest political revolution in English history. In a mounting struggle with Charles I, Parliament tried and executed his chief ministers, including Archbishop Laud. It called for the abolition of bishops and declared that the Parliament could not be dissolved without its own consent.

A Voice for Absolutism

In 1651, two years after the English Civil War ended, English political philosopher Thomas Hobbes published *Leviathan*. In this book, he explained why he favored an absolute monarchy. How might people who supported Parliament over the monarch have argued against Hobbes's view?

Primary Source

66 During the time men live without a common power to keep them all in awe, they are in that condition which is called war. . . . In such condition, there is no place for industry. . . . no arts; no letters; no society; and, which is worst of all, continual fear and danger of violent death. And the life of man [is] solitary, poor, nasty, brutish, and short. 99
—Thomas Hobbes, *Leviathan*

ENGLAND DIVIDED:
PARLIAMENT AND THE MONARCHY FIGHT FOR POWER

1485–1603
The Tudors rule England.
The Tudor monarchs, especially Henry VIII and Elizabeth I, ❶ control Parliament tactfully, recognizing and respecting its role in government.

1603–1625
Stuart king James I rules.
James I becomes king and immediately clashes with Parliament. In 1621, James scolds Parliament for usurping royal power, and Parliament responds with a declaration of its own rights. In the last Parliament of his reign, the aging James gives in to Parliament.

1625–1649
Stuart king Charles I rules.
Charles dissolves Parliament when it tries to expand powers to deal with an economic crisis. The Parliament of 1628 produces the Petition of Right, and later Parliaments ❷ clash with Charles over what they charge are violations of the document. Charles dissolves Parliament again.

1640–1653
The Long Parliament meets.
Faced with economic problems and invasions by Scotland, Charles is forced to call Parliament. The Long Parliament, as it became known, works to steadily expand its powers. Eventually Charles strikes back, adopting the motto "Give Caesar his Due."

Charles lashed back. In 1642, he led troops into the House of Commons to arrest its most radical leaders. They escaped through a back door and soon raised their own army. The clash now moved to the battlefield.

✔ **Checkpoint**   What was the Petition of Right?

Fighting a Civil War

The civil war that followed lasted from 1642 to 1651. Like the *Fronde* that occurred about the same time in France, the English Civil War posed a major challenge to absolutism. But while the forces of royal power won in France, in England the forces of revolution triumphed.

Cavaliers and Roundheads At first, the odds seemed to favor the supporters of Charles I, called Cavaliers. Many Cavaliers were wealthy nobles, proud of their plumed hats and fashionably long hair. Well trained in dueling and warfare, the Cavaliers expected a quick victory. But their foes proved to be tough fighters with the courage of their convictions. The forces of Parliament were composed of country gentry, town-dwelling manufacturers, and Puritan clergy. They were called Roundheads because their hair was cut close around their heads.

The Roundheads found a leader of genius in **Oliver Cromwell**. A Puritan member of the lesser gentry, Cromwell proved himself to be a skilled general. He organized a "New Model Army" for Parliament, made up of officers selected for skill rather than social class, into a disciplined fighting force.

Warrant to Execute King Charles the First. AD 1648.

1642–1649

The English Civil War rages.

War breaks out **3** between Parliament's Roundheads (right) and Charles I's Cavaliers (left). The parliamentary forces, led by Oliver Cromwell, eventually win. In 1649, Charles is executed. **4**

1649–1660

The English Commonwealth begins and ends.

Abolishing the monarchy and House of Lords, Parliament rules as a commonwealth with Cromwell as leader. **5** Problems plague the nation, and the Commonwealth falls apart upon Cromwell's death in 1658. Groups in favor of monarchy begin to gain power.

1660–1685

The monarchy is restored.

Charles II works with Parliament to repair the shattered nation, but clashes with Parliament when he works to restore Catholicism. In 1678, Charles dissolves Parliament and builds the monarchy's power. His successor, James II, continues to push for Catholic power, and incites a backlash. James II flees England in 1688.

1688

The Glorious Revolution assures Parliament's power.

William and Mary become England's monarchs **6** with Parliament's blessing— provided that they agree to very limited powers under Parliament's domination.

> **Thinking Critically**
> 1. **Recognize Point of View** What does Charles I's usage of the phrase "Give Caesar his Due" tell you about his view of royal power?
> 2. **Recognize Ideologies** How did the religious beliefs of key people on this timeline shape political outcomes?

XXVIII. WILLIAM *the* THIRD *and* MARY *the* SECOND, *from* 1688 *to* 1702.

WILLIAM the hero, with MARIA mild,
(He James's nephew, she his eldest child)
Fix'd freedom and the church, reform'd the coin;
Oppos'd the French, and settled Brunswick's line.

Cromwell's army defeated the Cavaliers in a series of decisive battles. By 1647, the king was in the hands of parliamentary forces.

A King Is Executed Eventually, Parliament set up a court to put the king on trial. It condemned him to death as "a tyrant, traitor, murderer, and public enemy." On a cold January day in 1649, Charles I stood on a scaffold surrounded by his foes. "I am a martyr of the people," he declared. Showing no fear, the king told the executioner that he himself would give the sign for him to strike. After a brief prayer, Charles knelt and placed his neck on the block. On the agreed signal, the executioner severed the king's neck with a single stroke.

The execution sent shock waves throughout Europe. In the past, a king had occasionally been assassinated or killed in battle. But for the first time, a ruling monarch had been tried and executed by his own people. The parliamentary forces had sent a clear message that, in England, no ruler could claim absolute power and ignore the rule of law.

✓ **Checkpoint** What was the result of the English Civil War?

Cromwell and the Commonwealth

After the execution of Charles I, the House of Commons abolished the monarchy, the House of Lords, and the established Church of England. It declared England a republic, known as the Commonwealth, under the leadership of Oliver Cromwell.

Cromwell's Armor
Oliver Cromwell wore this helmet and sword when he led the English forces into Ireland.

Vocabulary Builder
tolerate—(TAHL er ayt) v. to respect other's beliefs without sharing them

Challenging the Commonwealth The new government faced many threats. Supporters of Charles II, the uncrowned heir to the throne, attacked England by way of Ireland and Scotland. Cromwell led forces into Ireland and brutally crushed the uprising. He then took harsh measures against the Irish Catholic majority that are still vividly remembered in that nation today. In 1652, Parliament passed a law exiling most Catholics to barren land in the west of Ireland. Any Catholic found disobeying this order could be killed on sight.

Squabbles also splintered forces within the Commonwealth. One group, called Levellers, thought that poor men should have as much say in government as the gentry, lawyers, and other leading citizens. "The poorest he that is in England hath a life to live as the greatest he," wrote one Leveller. In addition, female Levellers asserted their right to petition Parliament. These ideas horrified the gentry, who dominated Parliament. Cromwell suppressed the Levellers, as well as more radical groups who threatened ownership of private property. In 1653, as the challenges to order grew, Cromwell took the title Lord Protector. From then on, he ruled as a virtual dictator through the army.

Puritans: A Sobering Influence Under the Commonwealth, Puritans—with their goal of rooting out godlessness—gained a new voice in society. The English Civil War thus ushered in a social revolution as well as a political one.

Parliament enacted a series of laws designed to make sure that Sunday was set aside for religious observance. Anyone over the age of 14 who was caught "profaning the Lord's Day" could be fined. To the Puritans, theaters were frivolous. So, like John Calvin in Geneva, Cromwell closed all theaters. Puritans also frowned on taverns, gambling, and dancing.

Puritans felt that every Christian, rich and poor, must be able to read the Bible. To spread religious knowledge, they encouraged education for all people. By mid-century, families from all classes were sending their children to school, girls as well as boys. Puritans also pushed for changes in marriage to ensure greater fidelity. In addition to marriages based on business interests, they encouraged marriages based on love. Still, as in the past, women were seen mainly as caretakers of the family, subordinate to men.

Although Cromwell did not <u>tolerate</u> open worship by Roman Catholics, he believed in religious freedom for other Protestant groups. He even welcomed Jews back to England after more than 350 years of exile.

The Commonwealth Ends Oliver Cromwell died in 1658. Soon after, the Puritans lost their grip on England. Many people were tired of military rule and strict Puritan ways. In 1660, a newly elected Parliament invited Charles II to return to England from exile.

England's "kingless decade" ended with the Restoration, or return of the monarchy. Yet Puritan ideas about morality, equality, government, and education endured. In the following century, these ideas would play an important role in shaping the future of Britain's colonies in the Americas.

✓ **Checkpoint** What was the Commonwealth?

From Restoration to Glorious Revolution

In late May 1660, cheering crowds welcomed Charles II back to London. John Evelyn, a supporter and diarist whose writings are an important source of information about English political and social history, wrote:

❝ This day came in his Majesties Charles the Second to London after a sad, and long Exile . . . with a Triumph of above 20,000 horse and [soldiers], brandishing their swords, and shouting with unexpressible joy; the [ways strewn] with flowers, the bells ringing, the streetes hung with [tapestry]. ❞
—John Evelyn, *Diary*

Charles II With his charm and flashing wit, young Charles II was a popular ruler. He reopened theaters and taverns and presided over a lively court in the manner of Louis XIV. Charles reestablished the Church of England but encouraged toleration of other Protestants such as Presbyterians, Quakers, and Baptists.

Although Charles accepted the Petition of Right, he shared his father's belief in absolute monarchy and secretly had Catholic sympathies. Still, he shrewdly avoided his father's mistakes in dealing with Parliament.

James II is Forced to Flee Charles's brother, James II, inherited the throne in 1685. Unlike Charles, James practiced his Catholic faith openly. He angered his subjects by suspending laws on a whim and appointing Catholics to high office. Many English Protestants feared that James would restore the Roman Catholic Church.

In 1688, • alarmed parliamentary leaders invited James's Protestant daughter, Mary, and her Dutch Protestant husband, William III of Orange, to become rulers of England. When William and Mary landed with their army late in 1688, James II fled to France. This bloodless overthrow of the king became known as the Glorious Revolution.

The English Bill of Rights Before they could be crowned, William and Mary had to accept several acts passed by Parliament in 1689 that became known as the **English Bill of Rights.** The Bill of Rights ensured the superiority of Parliament over the monarchy. It required the monarch to summon Parliament regularly and gave the House of Commons the "power of the purse," or control over spending. A king or queen could no longer interfere in parliamentary debates or suspend laws. The Bill of Rights also barred any Roman Catholic from sitting on the throne.

The Bill of Rights also restated the traditional rights of English citizens, such as trial by jury. It abolished excessive fines and cruel or unjust punishment. It affirmed the principle of *habeas corpus*. That is, no person could be held in prison without first being charged with a specific crime.

In addition, a separate Toleration Act, also of 1689, granted limited religious freedom to Puritans, Quakers, and other dissenters. Still, only members of the Church of England could hold public office. And Catholics were allowed no religious freedom.

Puritan girls spent hours working on embroidered samplers like this one. Such work was considered part of their education. ▼

Our Puritan Heritage

Decades before the Puritans gained power in England, Puritans living in the Massachusetts Bay colony worked to put into action their own ideas about religion and government. The Puritans knew that to assure survival of their beliefs and culture, they would have to educate their children to read and write. As soon as they were able, the Puritans began to set up schools, starting with the Boston Latin School in 1635 and then Harvard College (below) in 1636.

Eventually, the colonies became the United States. Over time, the rest of the country adopted the Puritan tradition of establishing public schools to help train children to become good citizens of their community. A literate, well-informed citizenry has continued to be a major aim of American schools to this day. **What other institutions help to train American children to be good citizens?**

A Limited Monarchy The Glorious Revolution created not a democracy, but a type of government called **limited monarchy,** in which a constitution or legislative body limits the monarch's powers. English rulers still had much power, but they had to obey the law and govern in partnership with Parliament. In the age of absolute monarchy elsewhere in Europe, the limited monarchy in England was quite radical.

The Glorious Revolution also greatly influenced important political thinkers of the time, such as John Locke. Locke's ideas were later used by leaders of the American Revolution as the basis for their struggle, and are found in documents such as the Declaration of Independence.

 Checkpoint What was the Glorious Revolution?

Constitutional Government Evolves

In the century following the Glorious Revolution, three new political institutions arose in Britain: political parties, the cabinet, and the office of prime minister. The appearance of these institutions was part of the evolution of Britain's **constitutional government**—that is, a government whose power is defined and limited by law.

Political Parties Emerge In the late 1600s, political parties emerged in England as a powerful force in politics. At first, there were just two political parties—Tories and Whigs. Tories were generally aristocrats who sought to preserve older traditions. They supported broad royal powers and a dominant Anglican Church. Whigs backed the policies of the Glorious Revolution. They were more likely to reflect urban business interests, support religious toleration, and favor Parliament over the crown.

The Cabinet System The cabinet, another new feature of government, evolved in the 1700s after the British throne passed to a German prince. George I spoke no English and relied on the leaders in Parliament to help him rule. Under George I and his German-born son George II, a handful of parliamentary advisors set policy. They came to be referred to as the **cabinet** because of the small room, or "cabinet," where they met. In time, the cabinet gained official status.

The Prime Minister Leads the Cabinet Over time, the head of the cabinet came to be known as the prime minister. This person was always the leader of the majority party in the House of Commons. Eventually, the prime minister became the chief official of the British government. From 1721 to 1742, the able Whig leader Robert Walpole molded the cabinet into a unified body by requiring all members to agree on major issues.

Influence of the Glorious Revolution

Outcome in England

English Bill of Rights	Writings of John Locke	Constitutional Government
• People elect representatives to Parliament, which is supreme over monarch. • All citizens have natural rights.	• People have natural rights such as life, liberty, and property. • There is a social contract between people and government.	• Government is limited and defined by law. • Political parties, the cabinet, and the office of prime minister arise.

Impact on the United States

Colonists believed that they too had rights, including the right to elect people to represent them.	Locke's ideas shaped the American Revolution and the writing of the Declaration of Independence and the Constitution.	The new American nation formed a constitutional government with two parties and a cabinet; the American system included even more provisions for the separation of powers.

Chart Skills A common protest during the American Revolution was "no taxation without representation." *Which English outcome of the Glorious Revolution influenced that idea?*

Although the title was not yet in use, Walpole is often called Britain's first prime minister. In time, the power of the prime minister would exceed that of the monarch. Other countries later adopted and adapted the cabinet system, including the United States.

✓ **Checkpoint** What three political institutions contributed to the evolution of Britain's constitutional government?

A Society Still Ruled by the Few

The decades that Walpole headed the cabinet were a time of peace and prosperity. But even as Parliament and the cabinet assumed new powers, British government was far from democratic. Rather, it was an **oligarchy**— a government in which the ruling power belongs to a few people.

In Britain, landowning aristocrats were believed to be the "natural" ruling class. The highest nobles held seats in the House of Lords. Other wealthy landowners and rich business leaders in the cities controlled elections to the House of Commons. The right to vote was limited to a relatively few male property owners.

Most Britons had neither the wealth nor the privileges of the upper class and lived very differently, making a meager living from the land. In the 1700s, even that poor existence was threatened. Wealthy landowners, attempting to increase agricultural production, bought up farms and took over common lands, evicting tenant farmers and small landowners. Because they controlled Parliament, they easily passed laws ensuring that their actions were legal. As a result many landless families drifted into towns, where they faced a harsh existence.

However, a relatively strong middle class—including merchants, craftspeople, and manufacturers—was growing. These prosperous and often wealthy people controlled affairs in the towns and cities. Some improved their social standing by marrying into the landed gentry. The middle class also produced talented inventors and entrepreneurs who would soon help usher in the Industrial Revolution.

✓ **Checkpoint** How did British society remain divided?

SECTION 3 Assessment

Progress Monitoring *Online*
For: Self-quiz with vocabulary practice
Web Code: naa-1631

Terms, People, and Places

1. Place each of the key terms at the beginning of the section into one of the following categories: politics, culture, or government. Write a sentence for each explaining your choice.

Note Taking

2. **Reading Skill: Identify Supporting Details** Use your completed flowchart to answer the Focus Question: How did the British Parliament assert its rights against royal claims to absolute power in the 1600s?

Comprehension and Critical Thinking

3. **Contrast** How did the Stuarts differ from the Tudors in their approach to Parliament?

4. **Identify Central Issues** In less than 100 years, England changed from a monarchy to a commonwealth and back to a monarchy. What central issue caused this political upheaval?

5. **Draw Conclusions** What were two results of the Glorious Revolution?

6. **Summarize** How did constitutional government evolve in England in the 1700s?

● **Writing About History**

Quick Write: Answer Opposing Arguments To write a strong persuasive essay you need to address arguments that could be raised to refute your own position. Choose a topic from this section—for example, whether Parliament had the right to replace James II—and list the arguments for and against your position.

The English Bill of Rights

When the Catholic James II was forced from the English throne in 1688, Parliament offered the crown to his Protestant daughter Mary and her husband, William of Orange. But Parliament insisted that William and Mary submit to a Bill of Rights. This document, reflecting the long-standing struggle between monarch and Parliament, sums up the powers that Parliament had been seeking since the Petition of Right in 1628. This document ensured the superiority of Parliament over the monarchy and spelled out basic rights.

An engraving made in 1689 shows the new English rulers, William and Mary.

The original English Bill of Rights, now more than 300 years old, is carefully preserved in a museum in London, England.

Whereas, the late King James II ... did endeavor to subvert[1] and extirpate[2] the Protestant religion and the laws and liberties of this kingdom ... and whereas the said late King James II having abdicated the government, and the throne being vacant ... the said lords [Parliament] ... being now assembled in a full and free representative [body] of this nation ... do in the first place ... declare:

1. That the pretended power of suspending of laws or the execution of laws by regal authority without consent of Parliament is illegal. ...

4. That levying money for or to the use of the crown by pretense of prerogative[3] without grant of Parliament ... is illegal;

5. That it is the right of the subjects to petition the king, and all commitments and prosecutions for such petitioning are illegal.

6. That ... raising or keeping a standing army within the kingdom in time of peace, unless it be with consent of Parliament, is against law. ...

8. That election of members of Parliament ought to be free. ...

9. That the freedom of speech and debates or proceedings in Parliament ought not to be challenged or questioned in any court or place out of Parliament. ...

10. That excessive bail ought not to be required, nor excessive fines imposed, nor cruel and unusual punishments inflicted. ...

13. And that, for redress of all grievances and for the amending, strengthening, and preserving of the laws, Parliaments ought to be held frequently. ...

---

1. subvert (sub VURT) *v.* to destroy, overthrow, or undermine

2. extirpate (EKS tur payt) *v.* to eliminate

3. prerogative (pree RAHG uh tiv) *n.* a right

Thinking Critically

1. **Synthesize Information** What is the meaning of item 6, and why do you think it was included in the Bill of Rights?
2. **Draw Inferences** Why do you think the members of Parliament included item 9? Why do you think this item might have been important?

Flemish artist Pieter Snayers painted several battles during the Thirty Years' War, including this one fought near Prague in 1620.

This silver flask held musket powder in the Thirty Years' War.

WITNESS HISTORY ◀)) AUDIO

War Rages in Germany

The conflict known as the Thirty Years' War ravaged the German states of central Europe for much of the first half of the seventeenth century. A German family Bible contained this entry describing the war's end:

66 They say that the terrible war is now over. But there is still no sign of a peace. Everywhere there is envy, hatred, and greed: that's what the war has taught us. . . . We live like animals, eating bark and grass. No one could have imagined that anything like this would happen to us. Many people say that there is no God. 99

Focus Question How did the two great empires of Austria and Prussia emerge from the Thirty Years' War and subsequent events?

Rise of Austria and Prussia

Performance Standards

• **SSWH9d** Analyze the impact of the Protestant Reformation.

Terms, People, and Places

elector	War of the Austrian
Ferdinand	Succession
mercenary	Prussia
depopulation	Frederick William I
Peace of Westphalia	Frederick II
Maria Theresa	

Note Taking

Reading Skill: Identify Supporting Details As you read this section, use a table like the one below to record details about the emergence of Austria and Prussia as European powers.

Rise of Austria	Rise of Prussia
• Austrian ruler keeps title of Holy Roman Emperor.	• Hohenzollern rulers take over German states.
•	•

The Thirty Years' War took a terrible toll on the people of the German states. Finally, two great German-speaking powers, Austria and Prussia, rose out of the ashes. Like Louis XIV in France, their rulers perfected skills as absolute monarchs.

The Thirty Years' War Ravages Europe

By early modern times, as the French philosopher Voltaire later observed, the Holy Roman Empire was neither holy, nor Roman, nor an empire. Instead, by the seventeenth century it had become a patchwork of several hundred small, separate states. In theory, these states were ruled by the Holy Roman emperor, who was chosen by seven leading German princes called **electors.** In practice, the emperor had little power over the many rival princes. This power vacuum contributed to the outbreak of the Thirty Years' War. Religion further divided the German states. The north had become largely Protestant, while the south remained Catholic.

A Brutal War Begins The Thirty Years' War was actually a series of wars. It began in Bohemia, the present-day Czech Republic. **Ferdinand,** the Catholic Hapsburg king of Bohemia, sought to suppress Protestants and to assert royal power over nobles. In May 1618, a few rebellious Protestant noblemen tossed two royal officials out of a castle window in Prague. This act, known as the Defenestration of Prague, sparked a general revolt, which Ferdinand moved to suppress. As both sides sought allies, what began as a local conflict widened into a general European war.

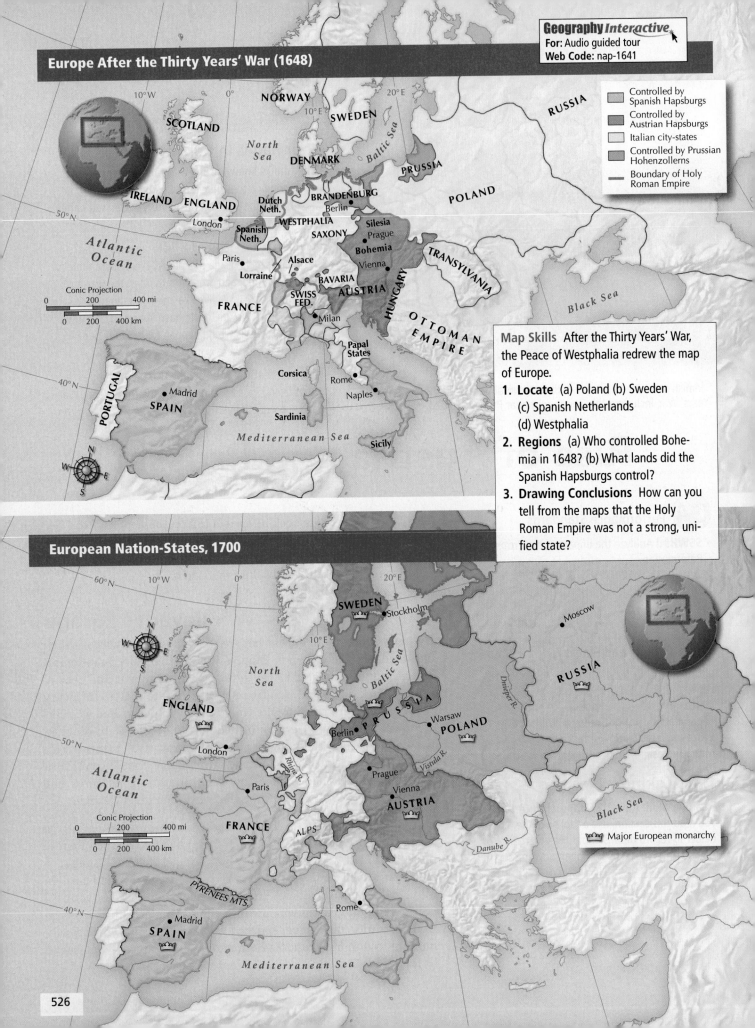

Geography *Interactive*

For: Audio guided tour
Web Code: nap-1641

Controlled by
Spanish Hapsburgs

Controlled by
Austrian Hapsburgs

Italian city-states

Controlled by Prussian
Hohenzollerns

Boundary of Holy
Roman Empire

NORWAY

SCOTLAND

SWEDEN

North
Sea

DENMARK

Baltic Sea

PRUSSIA

RUSSIA

IRELAND   ENGLAND

BRANDENBURG

POLAND

London

Dutch
Neth.

Berlin

50°N

Atlantic
Ocean

Spanish
Neth.

WESTPHALIA

SAXONY

Silesia

Prague

Bohemia

TRANSYLVANIA

Paris

Alsace

Vienna

Lorraine

BAVARIA

AUSTRIA

HUNGARY

Conic Projection

SWISS
FED.

0   200   400 mi

0   200   400 km

FRANCE

Milan

OTTOMAN

EMPIRE

Black Sea

Papal
States

40°N

Corsica

Rome

PORTUGAL

Madrid

Naples

SPAIN

Sardinia

Sicily

Mediterranean Sea

Map Skills After the Thirty Years' War,
the Peace of Westphalia redrew the map
of Europe.

1. **Locate** (a) Poland (b) Sweden
   (c) Spanish Netherlands
   (d) Westphalia
2. **Regions** (a) Who controlled Bohemia in 1648? (b) What lands did the
   Spanish Hapsburgs control?
3. **Drawing Conclusions** How can you
   tell from the maps that the Holy
   Roman Empire was not a strong, unified state?

60°N

SWEDEN

Stockholm

Moscow

10°W

0°

20°E

10°E

North
Sea

Baltic Sea

RUSSIA

ENGLAND

PRUSSIA

Warsaw

Dnieper R.

Berlin

POLAND

London

50°N

Vistula R.

Atlantic
Ocean

Paris

Prague

Rhine R.

Vienna

Black Sea

Conic Projection

AUSTRIA

0   200   400 mi

0   200   400 km

FRANCE

ALPS

Danube R.

Major European monarchy

PYRENEES MTS.

40°N

Rome

Madrid

SPAIN

Mediterranean Sea

The following year, Ferdinand was elected Holy Roman Emperor. With the support of Spain, Poland, and other Catholic states, he tried to roll back the Reformation by force. In the early stages of the war, he defeated the Bohemians (who had rebelled when he became emperor) and their Protestant allies. Alarmed, Protestant powers like the Netherlands and Sweden sent troops into Germany. Before long, political motives outweighed religious issues. Catholic and Protestant rulers shifted alliances to suit their own interests. At one point, Catholic France joined Lutheran Sweden against the Catholic Hapsburgs.

A Terrible Loss of Life The fighting took a terrible toll. Roving armies of **mercenaries,** or soldiers for hire, burned villages, destroyed crops, and killed without mercy. Murder and torture were followed by famine and disease. Wolves, not seen in settled areas since the Middle Ages, stalked the deserted streets of once-bustling villages. The war led to a severe **depopulation,** or reduction in population. Exact statistics do not exist, but historians estimate that as many as one third of the people in the German states may have died as a result of the war.

Peace at Last Finally, in 1648, the exhausted combatants accepted a series of treaties, known as the **Peace of Westphalia.** Because so many powers had been involved in the conflict, the treaties <u>aspired</u> both to bring about a general European peace and to settle other international problems. Among the combatants France emerged a clear winner, gaining territory on both its Spanish and German frontiers. The Hapsburgs were not so fortunate. They had to accept the almost total independence of all the princes of the Holy Roman Empire. In addition, the Netherlands and the Swiss Federation (present-day Switzerland) won recognition as independent states.

The Thirty Years' War left German lands divided into more than 360 separate states—"one for every day of the year." These states still acknowledged the rule of the Holy Roman emperor. Yet each state had its own government, currency, church, armed forces, and foreign policy. The German states, potentially the most powerful nation in Europe if they could be unified, thus remained fragmented for another 223 years.

 Checkpoint What were some effects of the Peace of Westphalia?

Hapsburg Austria Changes its Focus

Though weakened by war, the Hapsburgs still wanted to create a strong united state. They kept the title "Holy Roman emperor," but focused their attention on expanding their own lands. To Austria, they would soon add Bohemia, Hungary, and, later, parts of Poland and some Italian states.

Challenges to Unity Uniting these lands proved difficult. Not only were they divided by geography, they included a number of diverse peoples and cultures as well. By the 1700s, the Hapsburg Empire included Germans, Magyars, Slavs, and others. In many parts of the empire, people had their own languages, laws, political assemblies, and customs.

The Hapsburgs did exert some control over these diverse peoples. They sent German-speaking officials to Bohemia and Hungary and settled Austrians on lands they had seized in these provinces. They also put down revolts in Bohemia and Hungary. Still, the Hapsburgs never developed a centralized governmental system like that of France.

Vocabulary Builder

<u>aspired</u>—(uh SPY urd) *v.* aimed; sought

Maria Theresa

When Maria Theresa (1717–1780) became Hapsburg empress at the age of 23, her chances of remaining in power seemed very slim. She later said, "I found myself all at once without money, without troops, and without advice." A decade after her crowning she wrote, "I do not think anyone would deny that history hardly knows of a crowned head who started his rule under circumstances more grievous than those attending my accession."

But the determined empress survived. She appointed superb advisors and was able to maintain control of her empire. During her 40-year reign, Vienna became a center for music and the arts.

Maria Theresa had one thing in common with most women of her day—being a mother. She gave birth to a total of 16 children—11 girls and 5 boys. Among them were future emperors Joseph II and Leopold II and Queen Marie Antoinette of France. **What traits did Maria Theresa need to stay in power?**

A Woman Emperor Takes the Throne In the early 1700s, a new challenge threatened Hapsburg Austria. Emperor Charles VI had no male heir. His daughter, Maria Theresa, was intelligent and capable, but no woman had yet ruled Hapsburg lands in her own name. Charles persuaded other European rulers to recognize his daughter's right to succeed him. When he died, however, many ignored their pledge.

The War of the Austrian Succession Shortly after Charles's death in 1740, Frederick II of Prussia seized the rich Hapsburg province of Silesia. This action sparked the eight-year War of the Austrian Succession. Maria Theresa set off for Hungary to appeal for military help from her Hungarian subjects. The Hungarians were ordinarily unfriendly to the Hapsburgs. But she made a dramatic plea before an assembly of Hungarian nobles. According to one account, the nobles rose to their feet and shouted, "Our lives and blood for your Majesty!" She eventually got further help from Britain and Russia, who did not want Prussia to upset the balance of power by gaining new lands.

Maria Theresa never succeeded in forcing Frederick out of Silesia. Still, she did preserve her empire and win the support of most of her people. Equally important, she strengthened Hapsburg power by reorganizing the bureaucracy and improving tax collection. She even forced nobles and clergy to pay taxes and tried to ease the burden of taxes and labor services on peasants. As you will read, her son and successor, Joseph II, later extended many of her reforms.

✓ **Checkpoint**   What caused the War of the Austrian Succession?

Hohenzollern Prussia

While Austria was molding a strong Catholic state, a region called Prussia emerged as a new Protestant power. In the 1600s, the Hohenzollern (HOH un tsahl urn) family ruled scattered lands across north Germany. In the century following the Peace of Westphalia, ambitious Hohenzollern rulers united their holdings, creating Prussia.

Creating a Bureaucracy Hohenzollerns rulers set up an efficient central bureaucracy. Frederick William I was a Prussian ruler who came to power upon the death of his father in 1713. He cleverly gained the loyalty of the Prussian nobles, called *Junkers* (YOON kerz), by giving them positions in the army and government. His tactic reduced the nobles' independence and increased his own control. Frederick also placed great emphasis on military values and forged one of the best-trained armies in Europe. One Prussian military leader boasted, "Prussia is not a state which possesses an army, but an army which possesses a state." By 1740, Prussia was strong enough to challenge its rival Austria.

A Crown Prince Learns the Art of War Frederick William made sure that, from an early age, his son Frederick was trained in the art of war. He wrote,

Primary Source

 His tutor must take the greatest pains to imbue my son with a sincere love for the soldier's profession and to impress upon him that nothing else in the world can confer upon a prince such fame and honor as the sword. **"**

In fact, young **Frederick II** preferred playing the flute and writing poetry. His father despised these pursuits and treated the young prince so badly that he tried to flee the country. Discovering these plans, Frederick William put his son in solitary confinement. Then he forced the 18-year-old prince to watch as the friend who had helped him was beheaded.

Frederick's harsh military training had an effect. After becoming king in 1740, Frederick II lost no time in using his army. As you have read, he boldly seized Silesia from Austria, sparking the War of the Austrian Succession. In several later wars, Frederick continued to brilliantly use his disciplined army, forcing all to recognize Prussia as a great power. His exploits earned him the name Frederick the Great.

✔ **Checkpoint** How did Frederick William increase his power?

The Rivalry of Great Powers

By 1750, the great European powers included Austria, Prussia, France, Britain, and Russia. These nations formed various alliances to maintain the balance of power. Though nations sometimes switched partners, two basic rivalries persisted. Prussia battled Austria for control of the German states, while Britain and France competed to develop their overseas empires.

On occasion, these rivalries resulted in worldwide conflict. The Seven Years' War, which lasted from 1756 until 1763, was fought on four continents. Prussia, Austria, Russia, France, and Britain battled in Europe. Britain and France also fought in India and Africa. In North America, where the conflict is known as the French and Indian War, Native American groups took sides with the French or the British. The Treaty of Paris ending these wars gave Britain a huge empire, thus changing Europe's balance of power for the next hundred years.

✔ **Checkpoint** What were the two main rivalries after 1750?

Petitioning a King
Frederick the Great, strolling in his gardens, receives a petition from a common person. *What characteristics of Frederick does the artist hint at in the painting?*

SECTION **4** Assessment

Progress Monitoring *Online*
For: Self-quiz with vocabulary practice
Web Code: naa-1641

Terms, People, and Places
1. For each term, person, or place listed at the beginning of the section, write a sentence explaining its significance.

Note Taking
2. **Reading Skill: Identify Supporting Details** Use your completed table to answer the Focus Question: How did the two great empires of Austria and Prussia emerge from the Thirty Years' War and subsequent events?

Comprehension and Critical Thinking
3. **Recognize Cause and Effect** What impact did the Thirty Years' War have on the German states?
4. **Compare** What two major powers emerged in Europe at the end of the Thirty Years' War? How were the goals of these two nations similar?
5. **Make Generalizations** How did European nations maintain a balance of power?

● **Writing About History**
Quick Write: Write a Thesis Statement Select a topic from the section that you might use as the subject of a persuasive essay—for example, whether Austria or Prussia was more successful at developing a strong nation-state. Then write a thesis statement that summarizes your opinion on this topic.

The palace (left) of Catherine the Great (far left) reflects both European and traditional Russian architectural styles.

WITNESS HISTORY 🔊 AUDIO

A Foreign Princess Takes the Throne

For twenty years, the German princess Catherine lived at the Russian court, enduring an unhappy marriage to the Russian heir apparent, who was widely considered to be insane. She filled her time reading, studying French philosophy, building alliances behind the scenes, and biding her time. When her husband became emperor in 1762, she called on her allies to act. Within a few months he had been deposed and Catherine proclaimed empress of Russia. Like Peter the Great before her, Catherine would rule with intelligence, a firm hand, and a mind set on modernization.

Focus Question How did Peter the Great and Catherine the Great strengthen Russia and expand its territory?

Absolute Monarchy in Russia

 Performance Standards

- **SSWH14a** Compare Louis XIV, Peter the Great and Tokugawa Ieyasu's absolutism.

Terms, People, and Places

Peter the Great	warm-water port
westernization	St. Petersburg
autocratic	Catherine the Great
boyar	partition

N̲o̲te Taking

Reading Skill: Identify Main Ideas As you read this section, make a Venn diagram like the one below to compare events in the reigns of Peter the Great and Catherine the Great.

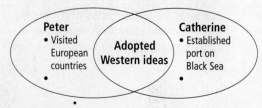

Peter
• Visited European countries
•

Adopted Western ideas

Catherine
• Established port on Black Sea
•

In the early 1600s, Russia was still a medieval state, untouched by the Renaissance or Reformation and largely isolated from Western Europe. As you have read, the "Time of Troubles" had plunged the country into a period of disorder and foreign invasions. The reign of the first Romanov tsar in 1613 restored a measure of order. Not until the end of the century, however, did a tsar emerge who was strong enough to regain the absolute power of earlier tsars. **Peter the Great,** as he came to be called, used his power to put Russia on the road to becoming a great modern power.

Peter the Great Modernizes Russia

Peter, just 10 years old when he took the throne in 1682, did not take control of the government until 1689. Although he was not well educated, the young tsar was immensely curious. He spent hours in the "German quarter," the Moscow neighborhood where many Dutch, Scottish, English, and other foreign artisans and soldiers lived. There, he heard of the new technology that was helping Western European monarchs forge powerful empires.

Journey to the West In 1697, Peter set out to learn about Western ways for himself. He spent hours walking the streets of European cities, noting the manners and homes of the people. He visited factories and art galleries, learned anatomy from a doctor, and even had a dentist teach him how to pull teeth. In England, Peter was impressed by Parliament. "It is good," he said, "to hear subjects speaking truthfully and openly to their king."

Peter brought to Russia a group of technical experts, teachers, and soldiers he had recruited in Europe. He then embarked on a policy of **westernization,** that is, the adoption of Western ideas, technology, and culture. But persuading fellow Russians to change their way of life proved difficult. To impose his will, Peter became the most **autocratic** of Europe's absolute monarchs, meaning that he ruled with unlimited authority.

Controlling the Church and the Nobles

Peter pursued several related goals. He wanted to strengthen the military, expand Russian borders, and centralize royal power. To achieve his ends, he brought all Russian institutions under his control, including the Russian Orthodox Church. He also forced the haughty **boyars,** or landowning nobles, to serve the state in civilian or military positions.

Some changes had a symbolic meaning. For example, after returning from the West, Peter <u>stipulated</u> that boyars shave their beards. He also forced them to replace their old-fashioned robes with Western-style clothes. To end the practice of secluding upper-class women in separate quarters, he held grand parties at which women and men were expected to dance together. Russian nobles opposed this radical mixing of the sexes in public, but they had to comply.

Peter knew that nobles would serve the state only if their own interests were protected. Therefore, he passed laws ensuring that nobles retained control over their lands, including the serfs on those lands. In doing so, Peter strengthened serfdom. Under his rule serfdom spread in Russia, long after it had died out in Western Europe. Further, he forced some serfs to become soldiers or to work as laborers on roads, canals, and other government projects.

Modernizing With Force

Using autocratic methods, Peter pushed through social and economic reforms. He imported Western technology, improved education, simplified the Russian alphabet, and set up academies for the study of mathematics, science, and engineering. To pay for his sweeping reforms, Peter adopted mercantilist policies, such as encouraging exports. He improved waterways and canals, developed mining and textile manufacturing, and backed new trading companies.

Peter had no mercy for any who resisted the new order. When elite palace guards revolted, he had more than 1,000 of the rebels tortured and executed. Then, as an example of his power, he left their rotting corpses outside the palace walls for months.

✔ **Checkpoint** What rewards and punishments did Peter use to solidify his control over the nobles?

Peter Expands Russia's Borders

From his earliest days as tsar, Peter worked to build Russia's military power. He created the largest standing army in Europe, built a world-class navy from scratch, and set out to extend Russian borders to the west and south.

Seeking a Warm-Water Port

Russian seaports, located along the Arctic Ocean, were frozen over during the winter. To increase Russia's ability to trade with the West, Peter desperately wanted a **warm-water port**—one that would be free of ice all year round.

Vocabulary Builder

<u>stipulated</u>—(STIP yuh layt ed) *v.* made a specific demand

A Russian cartoon shows Peter the Great personally cutting off the beard of a boyar.

The nearest warm-water coast was located along the Black Sea. To gain control of this territory, Peter had to push through the powerful Ottoman Empire. In the end, Peter was unable to defeat the Ottomans and gain his warm-water port, but the later Russian monarch Catherine the Great would achieve that goal before the century ended.

The Great Northern War In 1700, Peter began a long war against the kingdom of Sweden, which at the time, dominated the Baltic region. Early on, Russia suffered humiliating defeats. A Swedish force of only 8,000 men

Peter the Great and His Navy

As a sixteen-year-old boy, Peter found the hull of an old European sailing vessel in a storehouse. He restored the boat and taught himself to sail it on the lakes and rivers near Moscow. The find sparked a lifelong love for all things having to do with sailing. As tsar, Peter traveled to Europe to learn everything he could about shipbuilding. Armed with this knowledge, he created a European-style navy, thus turning Russia into a leading world power. In later years, Peter named the boat he had restored "the grandfather of the Russian navy." On his fifty-first birthday he sailed it into St. Petersburg harbor to meet its "grandchildren," Peter's navy.

A woodcut dating from the 1800s shows Peter, disguised as a ship's carpenter, learning from Dutch shipbuilders in the late 1600s. Peter's own drawing and notes are shown at bottom.

◄ A modern painter shows Peter as a common shipbuilder in the Netherlands.

A Russian artist who was a contemporary of Peter's shows St. Petersburg's harbor, filled with the ships that Peter had built. ▼

Russia's Navy Grows

Number of vessels (0, 400, 800, 1200) vs. Year (1705, 1714, 1725)

Thinking Critically
1. **Draw Inferences** Peter's motto was "I am a student and I seek teachers." How do you think this motto relates to his practice of passing himself off as a common man while studying in Europe?
2. **Make Comparisons** How did the absolute monarchies of Peter the Great and Louis XIV differ in terms of each monarch's dealings with common people?

defeated a Russian army five times its size. Undaunted, Peter rebuilt his army, modeling it after European armies. Finally, in 1709, he defeated the Swedes and won territory along the Baltic Sea.

Building St. Petersburg On this land won from Sweden, Peter built a magnificent new capital city, St. Petersburg. Seeking to open a "window on the West," he located the city on the Baltic coast along the swampy shores of the Neva River. He forced tens of thousands of serfs to drain the swamps. Many thousands died, but Peter's plan for the city succeeded. He then invited Italian architects and artisans to design great palaces in Western style. Peter even planned the city's parks and boulevards himself. Just as Versailles became a monument to French absolutism, St. Petersburg became a great symbol of Peter's effort to forge a modern Russia.

Blazing Trails to the Pacific Russian traders and raiders also crossed the plains and rivers of Siberia, expanding the Russian empire to the east. Under Peter, Russia signed a treaty with China that recognized Russia's claim to lands north of China and defined the empires' common border.

In the early 1700s, Peter hired the Danish navigator Vitus Bering to explore what became known as the Bering Strait between Siberia and Alaska (see map on the next page). After Peter's death, Russian traders built outposts in Alaska and northern California. Few Russians moved east of the Ural Mountains at this time, but the expansion made Russia the largest country in the world. It still is today, nearly 300 years later.

Peter the Great's Legacy When Peter died in 1725, he left a mixed legacy. He had expanded Russian territory, gained ports on the Baltic Sea, and created a mighty army. He had also ended Russia's long period of isolation. From the 1700s on, Russia would be increasingly involved in the affairs of Western Europe. Yet many of Peter's ambitious reforms died with him. Nobles, for example, soon ignored his policy of service to the state.

Like earlier tsars, Peter the Great had used terror to enforce his absolute power. His policies contributed to the growth of serfdom, which served only to widen the gap between Russia and the West that Peter had sought to narrow.

✔ **Checkpoint** What impact did Peter's defeat of Sweden have on Russia's expansion?

Catherine the Great Follows Peter's Lead

Peter died without an heir and without naming a successor. This set off a power struggle within the Romanov family, from whom all the tsars had come since the early 1600s. Under a series of ineffective rulers, Russian nobles reasserted their independence. Then, a new monarch took the reins of power firmly in hand. She became known to history as Catherine the Great.

A hundred years after Peter's reign, Russia's best-known poet, Alexander Pushkin, portrayed the tsar as a larger-than-life ruler, determined to tame nature no matter what the cost. How does Pushkin describe the tsar?

Primary Source

"There, by the billows desolate,
He stood, with mighty thoughts elate,
And gazed, but in the distance only
A sorry skiff on the broad spate
Of Neva drifted seaward, lonely. . . .
And thus He mused: 'From here, indeed
Shall we strike terror in the Swede?
And here a city by our labor
Founded, shall gall our haughty
    neighbor . . .'"
—Alexander Pushkin,
The Bronze Horseman ◀))) AUDIO

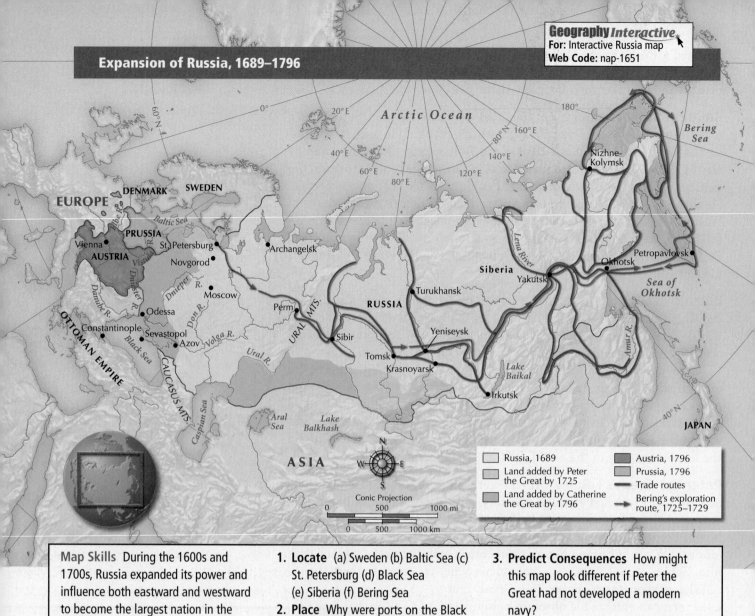

Geography *Interactive*
For: Interactive Russia map
Web Code: nap-1651

Legend:
- Russia, 1689
- Land added by Peter the Great by 1725
- Land added by Catherine the Great by 1796
- Austria, 1796
- Prussia, 1796
- Trade routes
- Bering's exploration route, 1725–1729

Conic Projection

Map Skills During the 1600s and 1700s, Russia expanded its power and influence both eastward and westward to become the largest nation in the world.	**1. Locate** (a) Sweden (b) Baltic Sea (c) St. Petersburg (d) Black Sea (e) Siberia (f) Bering Sea **2. Place** Why were ports on the Black Sea more appealing to Russia than those on the Baltic?	**3. Predict Consequences** How might this map look different if Peter the Great had not developed a modern navy?

Rise to Power A German princess by birth, Catherine came to Russia at the age of 15 to wed the heir to the Russian throne. She learned Russian, embraced the Russian Orthodox faith, and won the loyalty of the people. In 1762, a group of Russian army officers loyal to her deposed and murdered her mentally unstable husband, Tsar Peter III. Whether or not Catherine was involved in the assassination is uncertain. In any case, with the support of the military, she ascended the Russian throne.

An Enlightened Ruler Catherine proved to be an efficient, energetic empress. She reorganized the provincial government, codified laws, and began state-sponsored education for both boys and girls.

Like Peter the Great, Catherine embraced Western ideas and worked to bring Russia fully into European cultural and political life. At court, she encouraged French language and customs, wrote histories and plays, and organized performances. As you will read in the next chapter, she was also a serious student of the French thinkers who led the intellectual movement known as the Enlightenment.

A Ruthless Absolute Monarch Catherine was also an absolute monarch, like other European rulers of the time, and often she was among the most ruthless. She granted a charter to the boyars outlining important rights, such as exemption from taxes. She also allowed them to increase their stranglehold on the peasants. When peasants rebelled against the harsh burdens of serfdom, Catherine took firm action to repress them. As a result, conditions grew worse for Russian peasants. Under Catherine, even more peasants were forced into serfdom.

Like Peter the Great, Catherine was determined to expand Russia's borders. Waging the Russo-Turkish war against the Ottoman Empire gained her a warm-water port on the Black Sea in 1774. She also took steps to seize territory from neighboring Poland.

The Partitions of Poland In the 1770s, Catherine, King Frederick II of Prussia, and Emperor Joseph II of Austria hungrily eyed Poland. As you have read, the Polish-Lithuanian Commonwealth had once been a great European power. However, its rulers were unable to centralize their power or diminish the influence of the Polish nobility. The divided Polish government was ill-prepared to stand up to the increasing might of its neighbors, Russia, Prussia, and Austria.

To avoid fighting one another, the three monarchs agreed in 1772 to **partition,** or divide up, Poland. Catherine took part of eastern Poland, where many Russians and Ukrainians lived. Frederick and Joseph took control of Polish territory in the west. Poland was further partitioned in 1793. Then in 1795, Austria, Prussia, and Russia each took their final slices and the independent country of Poland vanished from the map. Not until 1919 would a free Polish state reappear.

✓ **Checkpoint** How were Catherine's goals similar to those of Peter?

Looking Ahead

By the mid-1700s, absolute monarchs ruled four of the five leading countries in Europe. Britain, with its strong Parliament, was the only exception. As these five nations competed with one another, they often ended up fighting to maintain a balance of power. At the same time, new ideas were in the air. Radical changes would soon shatter the French monarchy, upset the balance of power, and revolutionize European societies.

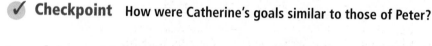

SECTION 5 Assessment

Progress Monitoring *Online*
For: Self-quiz with vocabulary practice
Web Code: naa-1651

Terms, People, and Places

1. For each term, person, or place listed in the beginning of the section, write a sentence explaining its significance.

Note Taking

2. **Reading Skill: Identify Main Ideas** Use your completed Venn diagram to answer the Focus Question: How did Peter the Great and Catherine the Great strengthen Russia and expand its territory?

Comprehension and Critical Thinking

3. **Identify Central Issues** What were three goals of Peter the Great and what was one step that he undertook to achieve each goal?

4. **Analyze Information** Why was obtaining a warm-water port a major priority for Peter?

5. **Compare Points of View** How did Peter and Catherine envision Russia's future?

● **Writing About History**

Quick Write: Write the Text Body
Choose a topic from the section on which you might write a persuasive essay—for example: Was Peter the Great really "great"? Write the body of your text, using a list of points you have made to guide you. Remember to open and close the body of the text with particularly strong arguments.

CHAPTER 16

Quick Study Guide

Progress Monitoring *Online*
For: Self-test with vocabulary practice
Web Code: naa-1652

■ Key Rulers

Spain: Charles V (Charles I of Spain); Philip II
France: Henry IV; Louis XIV
Britain: Henry VIII; Elizabeth I; James I; Charles I; Oliver Cromwell; Charles II; James II; William and Mary
Austria: Ferdinand; Charles VI; Maria Theresa
Prussia: Frederick William; Frederick the Great
Russia: Peter the Great; Catherine the Great

■ Key Events

- **Battle of Lepanto, 1571**—Spain and allies against Ottoman Empire
- **Netherlands rebellions, 1560s–1580s**—political and religious revolts against Spain
- **Spanish Armada attacks England, 1588**
- **St. Bartholomew's Day Massacre, 1572**—slaughter of French Huguenots
- **Thirty Years' War, 1618–1648**
- **English Civil War, 1642–1648**
- **The *Fronde*, 1648–1653**—uprising of various groups in France
- **Glorious Revolution, 1688**—bloodless change of monarchs in England
- **War of the Spanish Succession, 1700–1713**
- **Great Northern War, 1700–1721**—Russia and allies against Sweden
- **War of the Austrian Succession, 1740–1748**
- **Seven Years' War, 1756–1763**
- **Russo-Turkish War, 1768–1774**—Russia against the Ottoman Empire
- **Partitions of Poland, 1772, 1793, 1795**

■ Partitions of Poland, 1701–1795

1701

1772

1795

Conic Projection

0   200   400 mi

0   200   400 km

■ Key Events in the Age of Absolutism

1556
Philip II becomes king of Spain.

1618
The Thirty Years' War begins.

1642
The English Civil War begins.

Chapter Events
Global Events

| 1550 | 1600 | 1650 |

1556
Akbar the Great becomes emperor of Mughal India.

1607
British colonists found Jamestown.

Concept Connector

 Essential Question Review

To connect prior knowledge with what you have learned in this chapter, answer the questions below in your Concept Connector journal. Use the journal in the Reading and Note Taking Study Guide to record your answers (or go to www.phschool.com **Web Code**: nad-1607).

1. **Revolution** A revolution is a significant and widespread change in the social structure of a society or societies. Using this definition as a guide, discuss what makes the Glorious Revolution a revolution.

2. **Political Systems** Absolute monarchies were the dominant political system during the Age of Absolutism. Yet policies instituted by some monarchs weakened their empires and contributed to the decline of absolute monarchies as a political system. How did the use of absolute power by the following rulers weaken their empires?
   • Philip II
   • Louis XIV
   • Charles I
   • Peter the Great

3. **Democracy** The English Bill of Rights of 1688 granted basic rights to citizens, limited the power of the monarch, and gave Parliament the "power of the purse." These were critical steps in reducing the power of the monarchy and expanding the rights of the people. Write one or two paragraphs that summarize how these developments led to increased democracy in England.

■ **Connections to Today**

1. **Conflict** The Age of Absolutism was also an "age of religious conflicts." Many of these conflicts, primarily between Catholics and Protestants, were long lasting and extremely violent. Several caused major wars. Find and read a newspaper or Internet article about a country or region where religious conflict is still a concern today—for example, Bosnia, India, Iraq, Israel, or Northern Ireland. Write a two- or three-paragraph summary of what you learn.

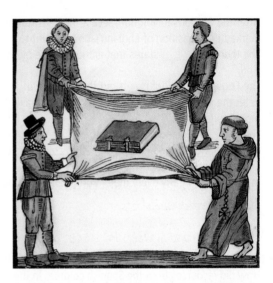

2. **Democracy** The English Bill of Rights is one of the source documents for ideas included in the American Declaration of Independence and the United States Constitution. Review the excerpt from the English Bill of Rights on page 524. Write a three-paragraph essay that summarizes how aspects of the English Bill of Rights are still present in American ideas of democracy today.

1697	1707	1715		1795
Peter	The Act of	King		Russia,
the Great	Union unites	Louis XIV of		Prussia,
of Russia	England and	France dies.		and Austria
tours	Scotland.			divide up
Europe.				Poland.

History Interactive
For: Interactive timeline
Web Code: nap-1652

1700   1750   1800

1680s	1736	1754	1793
The Asante	Qianlong begins	The French and	The emperor of
kingdom is	reign as emperor	Indian War erupts	China rejects
organized in	of China.	in North America.	British trade.
West Africa.			

Chapter Assessment

Terms, People, and Places

Complete each sentence by choosing the correct answer from the list of terms below. You will not use all the terms.

absolute monarch	constitutional monarchy
divine right	limited monarchy
balance of power	oligarchy
westernization	partition
habeas corpus	

1. After the Glorious Revolution, several new institutions marked the transition of England's government to a _____.
2. The theory of _____ states that monarchs rule by the will of God.
3. The English Bill of Rights sets out the principle of _____.
4. Peter the Great pursued a policy of _____ to make Russia more modern.
5. The _____ of Poland occurred in the 1700s when the rulers of Austria, Russia, and Prussia agreed to split that country among themselves.
6. In this period, nearly every major European nation was ruled by a(n) _____.

Main Ideas

Section 1 (pp. 504–509)
7. How did resources from the Spanish colonies in the Americas contribute to the decline of Spain?
8. What was the Spanish Armada?

Section 2 (pp. 510–515)
9. What were two symbols of the reign of Louis XIV and what was their significance?

Section 3 (pp. 516–524)
10. (a) What were the immediate causes of the English Civil War? (b) What were some important results?
11. How did the Glorious Revolution limit royal power in England?

Section 4 (pp. 525–529)
12. What events led to the start of the Thirty Years' War?

Section 5 (pp. 530–535)
13. What reforms did Peter the Great carry out?
14. What was one long-term goal of the Russian monarchs and how was it finally achieved?

Chapter Focus Question
15. What events led to the rise of absolute monarchies and the development of centralized nation-states in Europe?

Critical Thinking

16. **Draw Conclusions** Based on the material in the chapter, how effective do you think the policy of maintaining a balance of power was among European nations?
17. **Analyze Information** Explain what Louis XIV meant when he said, "I am the state."
18. **Test Conclusions** Based on what you have learned about the Glorious Revolution, do you think the name for that event is accurate? Why or why not?
19. **Compare** Compare the goals and policies of Peter the Great with those of one of the following monarchs: (a) Louis XIV (b) Frederick II (c) Maria Theresa.
20. **Synthesize Information** What was the historical significance of the execution of Charles I of England?
21. **Understand Effects** What was the general impact of the Thirty Years' War on Europe?

● Writing About History

In this chapter's five Section Assessments, you developed skills for writing a persuasive essay.

Writing a Persuasive Essay During the Age of Absolutism, strong monarchs created centralized nation-states whose governments they ruled with complete authority. Write a persuasive essay in which you argue a position on one aspect of this age. Consider topics such as: Was absolute monarchy an effective system? Was the divine right of kings a valid basis for rule? Consult page SH16 of the Writing Handbook for additional help.

Prewriting
• Choose a listed topic or another one that interests you, one that provokes an argument and has at least two sides. Then choose a side of the argument.

• Collect evidence, using a graphic organizer to list points on both sides of the issue.
• Research Internet or print sources to find materials that analyze your position from both sides. Take notes on relevant details, events, and people.

Drafting
• Clearly state the position that you will argue in a thesis statement. Use the rest of your introduction to provide readers necessary context about the issue.
• Make an outline to organize your argument and supporting details. Then choose information from your research that supports each part of your outline.

Revising
• Use the guidelines for revising your essay on page SH17 of the Writing Handbook.

Prepare for the GHSGT

The Rise of Parliament

The struggle between English monarchs and Parliament raged through the seventeenth century, and was fought on battlefields and legal fronts. The documents below illustrate the points of view of a monarch, Parliament, and a well-known philosopher.

Document A

"THE KINGS THEREAFTER in Scotland were before any estates or ranks of men within the same, before any Parliaments were holden or laws made; and by them was the land distributed (which at first was wholly theirs), states erected and decerned, and forms of government devised and established. And it follows of necessity that the Kings were the authors and makers of the laws and not the laws of the Kings."

—From **True Law of Free Monarchies,** 1598

Document B

"The Petition exhibited to his Majesty by the lords Spiritual and Temporal, and Commons, in this present Parliament assembled, concerning divers Rights and Liberties of the Subjects, with the King's Majesty's royal answer thereunto in full Parliament.
. . . Your subjects have inherited this freedom, that they should not be compelled to contribute to any tax, tallage, aid, or other like charge not set by common consent, in parliament.
. . . No man, of what estate or condition that he be, should be put out of his land or tenements, nor taken, nor imprisoned, nor disinherited nor put to death without being brought to answer by due process of law."

—From **The Petition of Right,** 1628

Document C

"Men, being, as has been said, by nature all free, equal, and independent, no one can be . . . subjected to the political power of another without his own consent. The only way whereby anyone divests himself of his natural liberty, and puts on the bonds of civil society is by agreeing with other men to join and unite into a community. . . .
It is evident, that *absolute monarchy*, which by some men is counted the only government in the world, is indeed *inconsistent with civil society*."

—From **Two Treatises on Government** by John Locke, 1690.

Document D

A mid-1600s engraving depicts Charles I as a political and religious martyr.

Analyzing Documents

Use your knowledge of the age of absolutism and Documents A, B, C, and D to answer questions 1–4.

1. What is the main point of Document A?
   A Kings are subject only to laws of parliament.
   B Kings make laws but are not subject to them.
   C Kings no longer have the power of life and death over subjects.
   D Parliament now has the power of life and death over subjects.

2. Document B is a declaration of whose rights?
   A the king's rights
   B Parliament's rights
   C subjects' rights
   D the landed aristocracy's rights

3. Document C
   A supports Document A.
   B supports Document B.
   C supports both Document A and Document B.
   D supports Document A and Document D.

4. **Writing Task** Would you describe the rise of Parliament in England as an evolution or a revolution? Use documents from this page along with information from the chapter in your response.

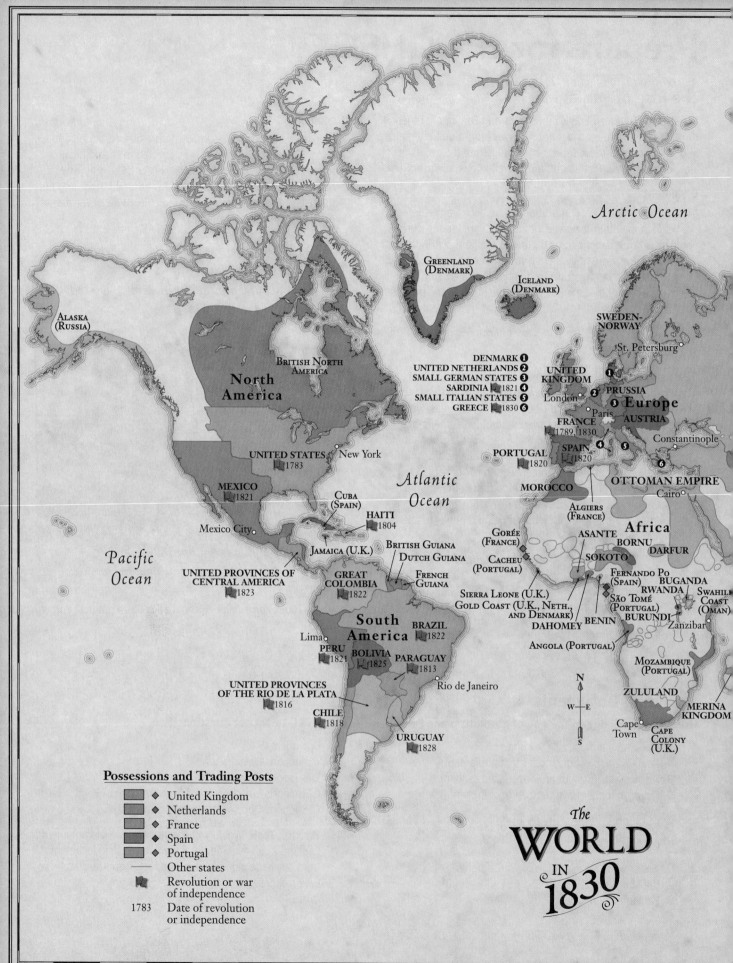

The WORLD IN 1830

Possessions and Trading Posts

- United Kingdom
- Netherlands
- France
- Spain
- Portugal
- Other states
- Revolution or war of independence
- 1783 Date of revolution or independence

Arctic Ocean

GREENLAND (DENMARK)

ICELAND (DENMARK)

ALASKA (RUSSIA)

BRITISH NORTH AMERICA

North America

DENMARK ❶
UNITED NETHERLANDS ❷
SMALL GERMAN STATES ❸
SARDINIA ❹ 1821
SMALL ITALIAN STATES ❺
GREECE ❻ 1830

SWEDEN-NORWAY

St. Petersburg

UNITED KINGDOM

London

PRUSSIA

Europe

FRANCE 1789, 1830

AUSTRIA

Paris

Constantinople

UNITED STATES 1783

New York

PORTUGAL 1820

SPAIN 1820

MEXICO 1821

Mexico City

Atlantic Ocean

CUBA (SPAIN)

HAITI 1804

MOROCCO

OTTOMAN EMPIRE

Cairo

ALGIERS (FRANCE)

JAMAICA (U.K.)

GORÉE (FRANCE)

ASANTE

Africa

BORNU

DARFUR

UNITED PROVINCES OF CENTRAL AMERICA 1823

CACHEU (PORTUGAL)

SOKOTO

Pacific Ocean

BRITISH GUIANA
DUTCH GUIANA

FERNANDO PO (SPAIN)

BUGANDA

GREAT COLOMBIA 1822

FRENCH GUIANA

SIERRA LEONE (U.K.)
GOLD COAST (U.K., NETH., AND DENMARK)

SÃO TOMÉ (PORTUGAL)

RWANDA

SWAHILI COAST (OMAN)

Lima

South America

BRAZIL 1822

DAHOMEY

BENIN

BURUNDI

Zanzibar

PERU 1821

BOLIVIA 1825

PARAGUAY 1813

Rio de Janeiro

ANGOLA (PORTUGAL)

MOZAMBIQUE (PORTUGAL)

UNITED PROVINCES OF THE RIO DE LA PLATA 1816

N
W—E
S

ZULULAND

CHILE 1818

URUGUAY 1828

Cape Town

CAPE COLONY (U.K.)

MERINA KINGDOM

RUSSIAN EMPIRE

Asia

CENTRAL
ASIAN
STATES
PERSIA
SIKH
KINGDOM
AFGHAN-
ISTAN
NEPAL
BHUTAN

CHINA   Beijing
KOREA
(CHINA)
JAPAN
Edo (Tokyo)
DESHIMA (NETHERLANDS)

Delhi

OMAN
Bombay
INDIA
(U.K.)
GOA
(PORTUGAL)
PONDICHERRY
(FRANCE)
CEYLON (U.K.)

BURMA
Calcutta
MACAO (PORTUGAL)
SOUTHEAST ASIAN STATES
SIAM
Bangkok
MALAY
STATES
PHILIPPINES
(SPAIN)

Pacific
Ocean

TENASSERIM (U.K.)
SINGAPORE (U.K.)

Indian
Ocean
Batavia
DUTCH EAST INDIES
PORTUGUESE TIMOR

MAURITIUS (U.K.)
RÉUNION (FRANCE)

Australia

WESTERN AUSTRALIA
(U.K.)
NEW SOUTH WALES
(U.K.)
Sydney

TASMANIA (U.K.)

MERCATOR PROJECTION
SCALE IN MILES
0   1000   2000   3000

0   1000   2000   3000
SCALE IN KILOMETERS
SCALE AT THE EQUATOR

Geography *Interactive*
For: Audio guided tour
Web Code: nap-4000

Enlightenment and Revolution 1700–1850

17 The Enlightenment and the American Revolution

1700–1800

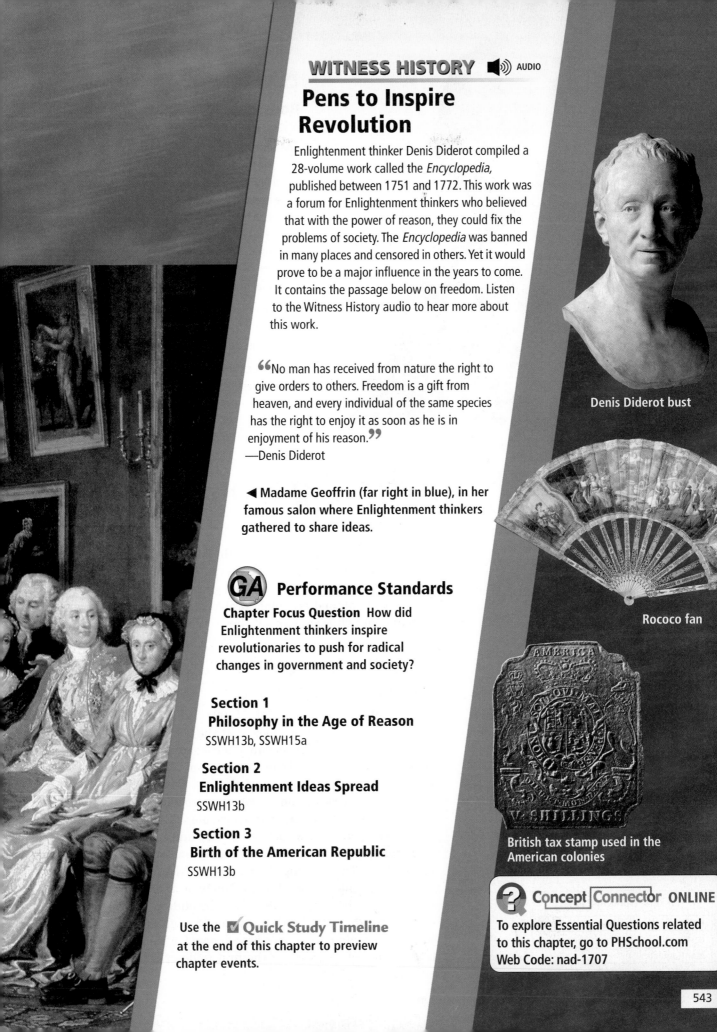

Pens to Inspire Revolution

Enlightenment thinker Denis Diderot compiled a 28-volume work called the *Encyclopedia,* published between 1751 and 1772. This work was a forum for Enlightenment thinkers who believed that with the power of reason, they could fix the problems of society. The *Encyclopedia* was banned in many places and censored in others. Yet it would prove to be a major influence in the years to come. It contains the passage below on freedom. Listen to the Witness History audio to hear more about this work.

❝No man has received from nature the right to give orders to others. Freedom is a gift from heaven, and every individual of the same species has the right to enjoy it as soon as he is in enjoyment of his reason.❞
—Denis Diderot

◀ **Madame Geoffrin (far right in blue), in her famous salon where Enlightenment thinkers gathered to share ideas.**

Denis Diderot bust

Rococo fan

GA Performance Standards

Chapter Focus Question How did Enlightenment thinkers inspire revolutionaries to push for radical changes in government and society?

Section 1
Philosophy in the Age of Reason
SSWH13b, SSWH15a

Section 2
Enlightenment Ideas Spread
SSWH13b

Section 3
Birth of the American Republic
SSWH13b

British tax stamp used in the American colonies

Use the ☑ **Quick Study Timeline** at the end of this chapter to preview chapter events.

? Concept Connector ONLINE

To explore Essential Questions related to this chapter, go to PHSchool.com
Web Code: nad-1707

Jean-Jacques Rousseau and quill pen

WITNESS HISTORY 🔊 AUDIO

Rousseau Stirs Things Up

In Jean-Jacques Rousseau's most important work, *The Social Contract,* he argued that in order to be free, people should do what is best for their community. Rousseau had many supporters who were inspired by his passionate writings. European monarchs, on the other hand, were angry that Rousseau was questioning authority. As a result, Rousseau worried about persecution for much of his life. The "chains" below represent the social institutions that confined society.

66 Man is born free, and everywhere he is in chains. 99
—Rousseau, *The Social Contract*

Focus Question What effects did Enlightenment philosophers have on government and society?

Philosophy in the Age of Reason

 Performance Standards

- **SSWH13b** Identify how Lock, Voltaire, and Rousseau's ideas link politics and society.
- **SSWH15a** Analyze the writings of Adam Smith and Karl Marx.

Terms, People, and Places

natural law	Montesquieu
Thomas Hobbes	Voltaire
John Locke	Diderot
social contract	Rousseau
natural right	laissez faire
philosophe	Adam Smith

N̲o̲te **Taking**

Reading Skill: Summarize Draw a table like the one shown here. As you read the section, summarize each thinker's works and ideas.

Thinkers' Works and Ideas	
Hobbes	*Leviathan*, social contract
Locke	
Montesquieu	

By the early 1700s, European thinkers felt that nothing was beyond the reach of the human mind. Through the use of reason, insisted these thinkers, people and governments could solve every social, political, and economic problem. In essence, these writers, scholars, and philosophers felt they could change the world.

Scientific Revolution Sparks the Enlightenment

The Scientific Revolution of the 1500s and 1600s had transformed the way people in Europe looked at the world. In the 1700s, other scientists expanded European knowledge. For example, Edward Jenner developed a vaccine against smallpox, a disease whose path of death spanned the centuries.

Scientific successes convinced educated Europeans of the power of human reason. **Natural law,** or rules discoverable by reason, govern scientific forces such as gravity and magnetism. Why not, then, use natural law to better understand social, economic, and political problems? Using the methods of the new science, reformers thus set out to study human behavior and solve the problems of society. In this way, the Scientific Revolution led to another revolution in thinking, known as the Enlightenment. Immanuel Kant, a German philosopher best known for his work *The Critique of Pure Reason,* was one of the first to describe this era with the word "Enlightenment." Despite Kant's skepticism about the power of reason, he was enthusiastic about the Enlightenment and believed, like many European philosophers, that natural law could help explain aspects of humanity.

✔ **Checkpoint** What convinced educated Europeans to accept the power of reason?

Hobbes and Locke Have Conflicting Views

Thomas Hobbes and **John Locke**, two seventeenth-century English thinkers, set forth ideas that were to become key to the Enlightenment. Both men lived through the upheavals of the English Civil War. Yet they came to very different conclusions about human nature and the role of government.

Hobbes Believes in Powerful Government

Thomas Hobbes outlined his ideas in a work titled *Leviathan*. In it, he argued that people were naturally cruel, greedy, and selfish. If not strictly controlled, they would fight, rob, and oppress one another. Life in the "state of nature"—without laws or other control—would be "solitary, poor, nasty, brutish, and short."

To escape that "brutish" life, said Hobbes, people entered into a **social contract,** an agreement by which they gave up their freedom for an organized society. Hobbes believed that only a powerful government could ensure an orderly society. For him, such a government was an absolute monarchy, which could impose order and compel obedience.

Locke Advocates Natural Rights

John Locke had a more optimistic view of human nature. He thought people were basically reasonable and moral. Further, they had certain **natural rights,** or rights that belonged to all humans from birth. These included the right to life, liberty, and property.

In *Two Treatises of Government,* Locke argued that people formed governments to protect their natural rights. The best kind of government, he said, had limited power and was accepted by all citizens. Thus, unlike Hobbes, Locke rejected absolute monarchy. England during this time experienced a shift in political power known as the Glorious Revolution. James II, an unpopular absolute monarch, left the throne and fled England in 1688. Locke later wrote that he thought James II deserved to be dethroned for violating the rights of the English.

Locke proposed a radical idea about this time. A government, he said, has an obligation to the people it governs. If a government fails its obligations or violates people's natural rights, the people have the right to overthrow that government. Locke's idea would one day influence leaders of the American Revolution, such as Benjamin Franklin, Thomas Jefferson, and James Madison. Locke's idea of the right of revolution would also echo across Europe and Latin America in the centuries that followed.

✔ **Checkpoint** How did Hobbes and Locke differ in their views on the role of government?

Hobbes Writes the *Leviathan*
The title page from *Leviathan* (1651) by Hobbes demonstrates his belief in a powerful ruler. The monarch here represents the Leviathan who rises above all of society.

Voltaire

François-Marie Arouet, known as Voltaire (1694–1778) was an impassioned poet, historian, essayist, and philosopher who wrote with cutting sarcasm and sharp wit. Voltaire was sent to the Bastille prison twice due to his criticism of French authorities and was eventually banned from Paris. When he was able to return to France, he wrote about political and religious freedom. Voltaire spent his life fighting enemies of freedom, such as ignorance, superstition, and intolerance. **What did Voltaire attack in his writings?**

Montesquieu

Born to wealth, Charles Louis de Secondat (1689–1755) inherited the title Baron de Montesquieu from his uncle. Like many other reformers, he did not let his privileged status keep him from becoming a voice for democracy. His first book titled *Persian Letters* ridiculed the French government and social classes. In his work published in 1748, *The Spirit of the Laws,* he advanced the idea of separation of powers—a foundation of modern democracy. **What did Montesquieu think was necessary to protect liberty?**

The *Philosophes*

In the 1700s, there was a flowering of Enlightenment thought. This was when a group of Enlightenment thinkers in France applied the methods of science to understand and improve society. They believed that the use of reason could lead to reforms of government, law, and society. These thinkers were called *philosophes* (fee loh ZOHFS), which means "philosophers." Their ideas soon spread beyond France and even beyond Europe.

Montesquieu Advances the Idea of Separation of Powers An early and influential thinker was Baron de **Montesquieu** (MAHN tus kyoo). Montesquieu studied the governments of Europe, from Italy to England. He read about ancient and medieval Europe, and learned about Chinese and Native American cultures. His sharp criticism of absolute monarchy would open doors for later debate.

In 1748, Montesquieu published *The Spirit of the Laws*, in which he discussed governments throughout history. Montesquieu felt that the best way to protect liberty was to divide the various functions and powers of government among three branches: the legislative, executive, and judicial. He also felt that each branch of government should be able to serve as a check on the other two, an idea that we call checks and balances. Montesquieu's beliefs would soon profoundly affect the Framers of the United States Constitution.

Voltaire Defends Freedom of Thought Probably the most famous of the *philosophes* was François-Marie Arouet, who took the name **Voltaire.** "My trade," said Voltaire, "is to say what I think," and he did so throughout his long, controversial life. Voltaire used biting wit as a weapon to expose the abuses of his day. He targeted corrupt officials and idle aristocrats. With his pen, he battled inequality, injustice, and superstition. He detested the slave trade and deplored religious prejudice.

Voltaire's outspoken attacks offended both the French government and the Catholic Church. He was imprisoned and forced into exile. Even as he saw his books outlawed and even burned, he continued to defend the principle of freedom of speech.

Diderot Edits the *Encyclopedia* Denis **Diderot** (DEE duh roh) worked for years to produce a 28-volume set of books called the *Encyclopedia*. As the editor, Diderot did more than just compile articles.

His purpose was "to change the general way of thinking" by explaining ideas on topics such as government, philosophy, and religion. Diderot's *Encyclopedia* included articles by leading thinkers of the day, including Montesquieu and Voltaire. In these articles, the *philosophes* denounced slavery, praised freedom of expression, and urged education for all. They attacked divine-right theory and traditional religions. Critics raised an outcry. The French government argued that the *Encyclopedia* was an attack on public morals, and the pope threatened to excommunicate Roman Catholics who bought or read the volumes.

Despite these and other efforts to ban the *Encyclopedia,* more than 4,000 copies were printed between 1751 and 1789. When translated into other languages, the *Encyclopedia* helped spread Enlightenment ideas throughout Europe and across the Atlantic Ocean to the Americas.

Rousseau Promotes *The Social Contract*

Jean-Jacques Rousseau (roo SOH), believed that people in their natural state were basically good. This natural innocence, he felt, was corrupted by the evils of society, especially the unequal distribution of property. Many reformers and revolutionaries later adopted this view. Among them were Thomas Paine and Marquis de Lafayette, who were leading figures of the American and French Revolutions.

In 1762, Rousseau set forth his ideas about government and society in *The Social Contract.* Rousseau felt that society placed too many limitations on people's behavior. He believed that some controls were necessary, but that they should be minimal. Additionally, only governments that had been freely elected should impose these controls.

Rousseau put his faith in the "general will," or the best conscience of the people. The good of the community as a whole, he said, should be placed above individual interests. Rousseau has influenced political and social thinkers for more than 200 years. Woven through his work is a hatred of all forms of political and economic oppression. His bold ideas would help fan the flames of revolt in years to come.

Women Challenge the *Philosophes*

The Enlightenment slogan "free and equal" did not apply to women. Though the *philosophes* said women had natural rights, their rights were limited to the areas of home and family.

By the mid- to late-1700s, a small but growing number of women protested this view. Germaine de Staël in France and Catharine Macaulay and Mary Wollstonecraft in Britain argued that women were being excluded from the social contract itself. Their arguments, however, were ridiculed and often sharply condemned.

Wollstonecraft was a well-known British social critic. She accepted that a woman's first duty was to be a good mother but felt that a woman should be able to decide what was in her own interest without depending on her husband. In 1792, Wollstonecraft published *A Vindication of the Rights of Woman.* In it, she called for equal education for girls and boys. Only education, she argued, could give women the tools they needed to participate equally with men in public life.

✓ **Checkpoint** What topics were addressed by the *philosophes* in their *Encyclopedia* articles?

Heated Debate
Rousseau (left) and Voltaire (right) are pictured here in the midst of an argument. Even though the *philosophes* were reform-minded, they disagreed about some issues. *Compare the beliefs of Rousseau and Voltaire.*

New Economic Thinking

French thinkers known as physiocrats focused on economic reforms. Like the *philosophes,* physiocrats based their thinking on natural laws. The physiocrats claimed that their rational economic system was based on the natural laws of economics.

Laissez Faire Replaces Mercantilism Physiocrats rejected mercantilism, which required government regulation of the economy to achieve a favorable balance of trade. Instead, they urged a policy of **laissez faire** (les ay FEHR), allowing business to operate with little or no government interference. Physiocrats also supported free trade and opposed tariffs.

Smith Argues for a Free Market Scottish economist **Adam Smith** greatly admired the physiocrats. In his influential work *The Wealth of Nations,* he argued that the free market should be allowed to regulate business activity. Smith tried to show how manufacturing, trade, wages, profits, and economic growth were all linked to the market forces of supply and demand. Wherever there was a demand for goods or services, he said, suppliers would seek to meet that demand in order to gain profits. Smith was a strong supporter of laissez faire. However, he felt that government had a duty to protect society, administer justice, and provide public works. Adam Smith's ideas would help to shape productive economies in the 1800s and 1900s.

✔ **Checkpoint** Why did Smith support laissez faire?

Investors in Paris, France, 1720

Progress Monitoring *Online*
For: Self-quiz with vocabulary practice
Web Code: naa-1711

SECTION 1
Assessment

Terms, People, and Places

1. For each term, person, or place listed at the beginning of the section, write a sentence explaining its significance.

Note Taking

2. **Reading Skill: Summarize** Use your completed tables to answer the Focus Question: What effects did Enlightenment philosophers have on government and society?

Comprehension and Critical Thinking

3. **Summarize** How did the achievements of the Scientific Revolution contribute to the Enlightenment?

4. **Recognize Cause and Effect** What did the *philosophes* do to better understand and improve society?

5. **Synthesize Information** Explain the connection between the policy of laissez faire and natural economic laws.

● **Writing About History**

Quick Write: Explore a Topic On some essay tests, you may have a choice of topic. You should choose one that you feel most knowledgeable about. Choose from the following, and draft a single sentence that identifies the main idea: (a) social contracts (b) freedom of speech (c) women in the mid-1700s

John Locke:
Two Treatises of Government

English philosopher John Locke (1632–1704) published *Two Treatises of Government* in 1690. Locke believed that all people had the same natural rights of life, liberty, and property. In this essay, Locke states that the primary purpose of government is to protect these natural rights. He also states that governments hold their power only with the consent of the people. Locke's ideas greatly influenced revolutions in America and France.

John Locke and a book of his writings

But though men, when they enter into society give up the equality, liberty, and executive power they had in the state of Nature into the hands of society . . . the power of the society or legislative constituted by them can never be supposed to extend farther than the common good. . . . Whoever has the legislative or supreme power of any commonwealth, is bound to govern by established standing laws, promulgated[1] and known to the people, and not by extemporary[2] decrees, by indifferent and upright judges, who are to decide controversies by those laws; and to employ the force of the community at home only in the execution of such laws, or abroad to prevent or redress foreign injuries and secure the community from inroads[3] and invasion. And all this to be directed to no other end but the peace, safety, and public good of the people. . . .

The reason why men enter into society is the preservation of their property; and the end while they choose and authorize a legislative is that there may be laws made, and rules set, as guards and fences to the properties of all the society, . . .

Whensoever, therefore, the legislative [power] shall transgress[4] this fundamental rule of society, and either by ambition, fear, folly, or corruption, endeavor to grasp themselves, or put into the hands of any other, an absolute power over the lives, liberties, and estates of the people, by this breach of trust they forfeit the power the people had put into their hands for quite contrary ends, and it devolves[5] to the people; who have a right to resume their original liberty, and by the establishment of a new legislative (such as they shall think fit), provide for their own safety and security. . . .

1. **promulgated** (PRAHM ul gayt id) *vt.* published or made known.
2. **extemporary** (ek STEM puh rehr ee) *adj.* without any preparation.
3. **inroads** (IN rohdz) *n.* advances at the expense of someone.
4. **transgress** (trans GRES) *vt.* go beyond; break.
5. **devolves** (dih VAHLVZ) *vt.* passes.

Thinking Critically

1. **Draw Inferences** According to Locke, how should a land be governed? Why do you think this is the case?

2. **Identify Central Issues** What does Locke say can happen if a government fails to protect the rights of its people?

Mozart and a sheet of his music

Mozart, the Musical Genius

As a young boy, Wolfgang Amadeus Mozart astonished royalty with his musical talent. Although his life was relatively short, he composed more than 600 pieces of music. Many pieces embraced the spirit of the Enlightenment.

❝ Few have captured the spirit of the Enlightenment, its intellectual and social agenda, as has Mozart in his opera, *The Magic Flute,* . . . [It] is a series of variations on the triumph of light over darkness, of sun over moon, of day over night, of reason, tolerance, and love over passion, hate, and revenge. ❞
—Isaac Kramnick, historian

Focus Question As Enlightenment ideas spread across Europe, what cultural and political changes took place?

Enlightenment Ideas Spread

 Performance Standards

- **SSWH13b** Identify how Voltaire's ideas link politics and society.

Terms, People, and Places

censorship	enlightened despot
salons	Frederick the Great
baroque	Catherine the Great
rococo	Joseph II

Note Taking

Reading Skill: Categorize On a sheet of paper, draw a concept web to help you record information from this section.

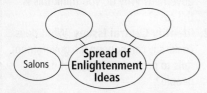

Paris, France, the heart of the Enlightenment, drew many intellectuals and others eager to debate new ideas. Reforms proposed one evening became the talk of the town the next day. Enlightenment ideas flowed from France, across Europe, and beyond. Everywhere, thinkers examined traditional beliefs and customs in the light of reason and found them flawed. Even some absolute monarchs experimented with Enlightenment ideas, although they drew back when changes threatened the established way of doing things.

New Ideas Challenge Society

Enlightenment ideas spread quickly through many levels of society. Educated people all over Europe eagerly read not only Diderot's *Encyclopedia* but also the small, inexpensive pamphlets that printers churned out on a broad range of issues. More and more, people saw that reform was necessary in order to achieve a just society.

During the Middle Ages, most Europeans had accepted without question a society based on divine-right rule, a strict class system, and a belief in heavenly reward for earthly suffering. In the Age of Reason, such ideas seemed unscientific and irrational. A just society, Enlightenment thinkers taught, should ensure social justice and happiness in this world. Not everyone agreed with this idea of replacing the values that existed, however.

Writers Face Censorship Most, but not all, government and church authorities felt they had a sacred duty to defend the old order. They believed that God had set up the old order. To protect against the attacks of the Enlightenment, they waged a war of **censorship,** or restricting access to ideas and information. They banned and burned books and imprisoned writers.

To avoid censorship, *philosophes* and writers like Montesquieu and Voltaire sometimes disguised their ideas in works of fiction. In the *Persian Letters,* Montesquieu used two fictional Persian travelers, named Usbek and Rica, to mock French society. The hero of Voltaire's satirical novel *Candide,* published in 1759, travels across Europe and even to the Americas and the Middle East in search of "the best of all possible worlds." Voltaire slyly uses the tale to expose the corruption and hypocrisy of European society.

Ideas Spread in Salons New literature, the arts, science, and philosophy were regular topics of discussion in **salons,** or informal social gatherings at which writers, artists, *philosophes,* and others exchanged ideas. The salon originated in the 1600s, when a group of noblewomen in Paris began inviting a few friends to their homes for poetry readings. By the 1700s, some middle-class women began holding salons. Here middle-class citizens could meet with the nobility on an equal footing to discuss and spread Enlightenment ideas.

Madame Geoffrin (zhoh FRAN) ran one of the most respected salons. In her home on the Rue St. Honoré (roo sant ahn ur AY), she brought together the brightest and most talented people of her day. The young musical genius Wolfgang Amadeus Mozart played for her guests, and Diderot was a regular at her weekly dinners for philosophers and poets.

✔️ **Checkpoint** What did those opposed to Enlightenment ideas do to stop the spread of information?

Arts and Literature Reflect New Ideas

In the 1600s and 1700s, the arts <u>evolved</u> to meet changing tastes. As in earlier periods, artists and composers had to please their patrons, the men and women who commissioned works from them or gave them jobs.

From Grandeur to Charm In the age of Louis XIV, courtly art and architecture were either in the Greek and Roman tradition or in a grand, ornate style known as **baroque.** Baroque paintings were huge, colorful, and full of excitement. They glorified historic battles or the lives of saints. Such works matched the grandeur of European courts at that time.

Louis XV and his court led a much less formal lifestyle than Louis XIV. Architects and designers reflected this change by developing the **rococo** style. Rococo art moved away from religion and, unlike the heavy splendor of the baroque, was lighter, elegant, and charming. Rococo art in salons was believed to encourage the imagination. Furniture and tapestries featured delicate shells and flowers, and more pastel colors were used. Portrait painters showed noble subjects in charming rural settings, surrounded by happy servants and pets. Although this style was criticized by the *philosophes* for its superficiality, it had a vast audience in the upper class and with the growing middle class as well.

Satire by Swift
Jonathan Swift published the satirical *Gulliver's Travels* in 1726. Here, an illustration from the book depicts a bound Gulliver and the Lilliputians, who are six-inch-tall, bloodthirsty characters. Although *Gulliver's Travels* satirizes political life in eighteenth-century England, it is still a classic today. *Why did writers hide their feelings about society?*

Vocabulary Builder

evolved—(ee VAHLVD) *v.* developed gradually over time

The Enlightenment Inspires Composers The new Enlightenment ideals led composers and musicians to develop new forms of music. There was a transition in music, as well as art, from the baroque style to rococo. An elegant style of music known as "classical" followed. Ballets and opera—plays set to music—were performed at royal courts, and opera houses sprang up from Italy to England. Before this era, only the social elite could afford to commission musicians to play for them. In the early to mid-1700s, however, the growing middle class could afford to pay for concerts to be performed publicly.

Among the towering musical figures of the era was Johann Sebastian Bach. A devout German Lutheran, Bach wrote beautiful religious works for organ and choirs. He also wrote sonatas for violin and harpsichord. Another German-born composer, George Frideric Handel, spent much of his life in England. There, he wrote *Water Music* and other pieces for King George I, as well as more than 30 operas. His most celebrated work, the *Messiah*, combines instruments and voices and is often performed at Christmas and Easter.

Composer Franz Joseph Haydn was one of the most important figures in the development of classical music. He helped develop forms for the string quartet and the symphony. Haydn had a close friendship with another famous composer, Wolfgang Amadeus Mozart. Mozart was a child prodigy who gained instant celebrity status as a composer and performer. His brilliant operas, graceful symphonies, and moving religious music helped define the new style of composition. Although he died in poverty at age 35, he produced an enormous amount of music during his lifetime. Mozart's musical legacy thrives today.

● **INFOGRAPHIC**

ROCOCO REACTION

In the eighteenth century, France experienced an aesthetic shift in art, clothing, music, and architecture. Curving lines, pastel colors, elegant music, and paintings depicting delightful love scenes replaced the formal lines and dark colors of the baroque style. The rise of this new style, referred to as rococo, reflected changes in French society that were brought about by the Enlightenment. As the French elite became more involved in the salons of the day (numbering about 800 in Paris), they competed with each other for the most fashionable home in which to host their intellectual discussions.

Composers adopted the graceful rococo style in their works of music. They wrote pieces for an instrument called the harpsichord (above) that reflected this new style. ◀)) AUDIO

The Novel Takes Shape By the 1700s, literature developed new forms and a wider audience. Middle-class readers, for example, liked stories about their own times told in straightforward prose. One result was an outpouring of novels, or long works of prose fiction. English novelists wrote many popular stories. Daniel Defoe wrote *Robinson Crusoe,* an exciting tale about a sailor shipwrecked on a tropical island. This novel is still well known today. In a novel called *Pamela,* Samuel Richardson used a series of letters to tell a story about a servant girl. This technique was adopted by other authors of the period.

✓ **Checkpoint** How did the arts and literature change as Enlightenment ideas spread?

Enlightened Despots Embrace New Ideas

The courts of Europe became enlivened as *philosophes* tried to persuade rulers to adopt their ideas. The *philosophes* hoped to convince the ruling classes that reform was necessary. Some monarchs did accept Enlightenment ideas. Others still practiced absolutism, a political doctrine in which a monarch had seemingly unlimited power. Those that did accept these new ideas became **enlightened despots,** or absolute rulers who used their power to bring about political and social change.

Frederick II Attempts Reform Frederick II, known as **Frederick the Great,** exerted extremely tight control over his subjects during his reign as king of Prussia from 1740 to 1786. Still, he saw himself as the "first servant of the state," with a duty to work for the common good.

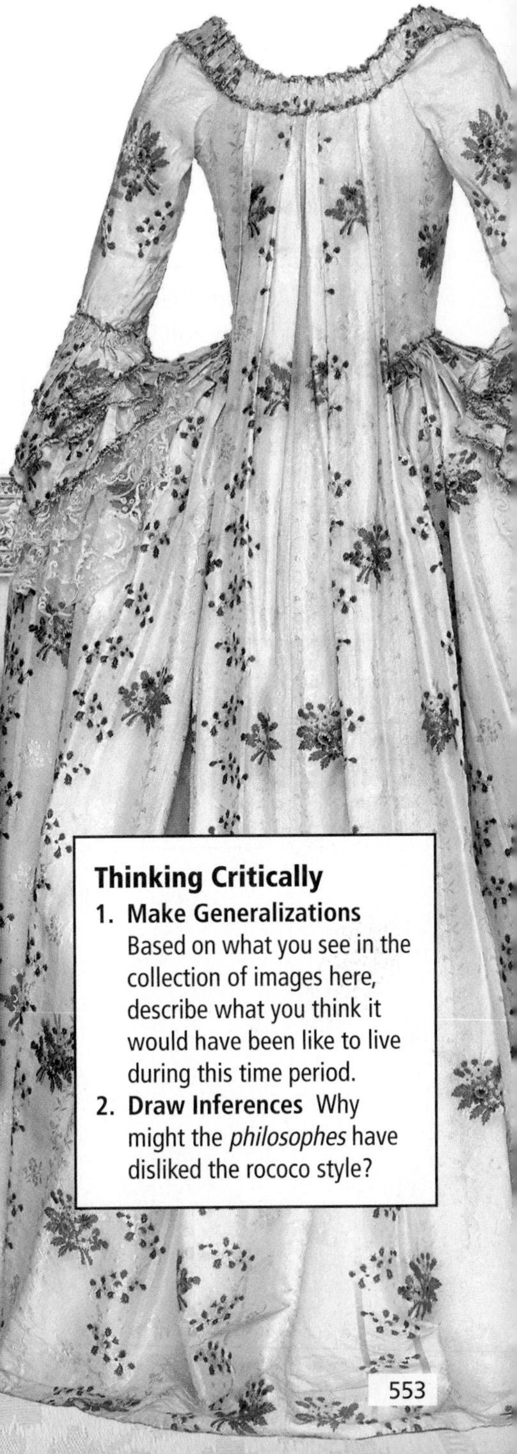

Ornate Artifacts
In the examples of the rococo style shown here, notice the elegance of the delicate lace and floral patterns, as well as the charming paintings depicting the pleasures of everyday life.

Thinking Critically
1. **Make Generalizations** Based on what you see in the collection of images here, describe what you think it would have been like to live during this time period.
2. **Draw Inferences** Why might the *philosophes* have disliked the rococo style?

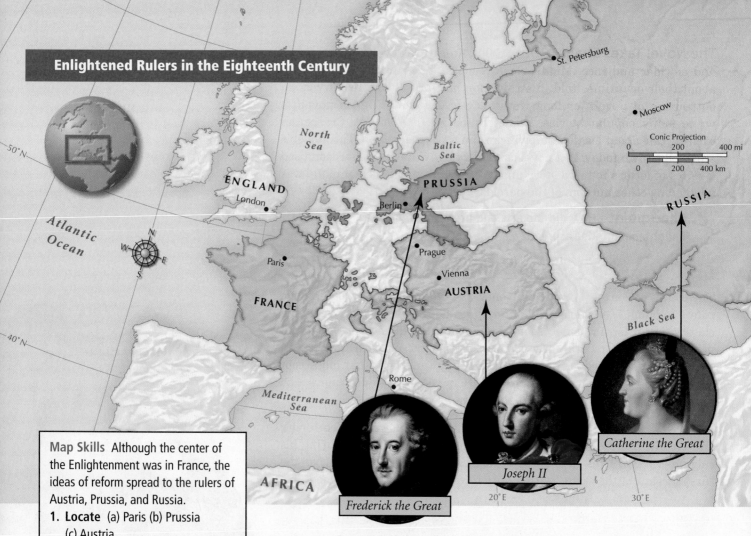

St. Petersburg

Moscow

North Sea

Baltic Sea

ENGLAND

London

PRUSSIA

Berlin

RUSSIA

Atlantic Ocean

50°N

Paris

Prague

Vienna

AUSTRIA

FRANCE

Black Sea

40°N

Rome

Mediterranean Sea

Catherine the Great

Joseph II

AFRICA

20° E

30° E

Frederick the Great

Conic Projection

0   200   400 mi

0   200   400 km

Map Skills Although the center of the Enlightenment was in France, the ideas of reform spread to the rulers of Austria, Prussia, and Russia.

1. **Locate** (a) Paris (b) Prussia (c) Austria
2. **Location** Which enlightened despot ruled farthest from Paris?
3. **Draw Conclusions** According to the map, what regions of Europe were affected by enlightened despots?

Geography *Interactive*
For: Audio guided tour
Web Code: nap-1721

Frederick openly praised Voltaire's work and invited several of the French intellectuals of the age to Prussia. Some of his first acts as king were to reduce the use of torture and allow a free press. Most of Frederick's reforms were directed at making the Prussian government more efficient. To do this, he reorganized the government's civil service and simplified laws. Frederick also tolerated religious differences, welcoming victims of religious persecution. "In my kingdom," he said, "everyone can go to heaven in his own fashion." His religious tolerance and also his disdain for torture showed Frederick's genuine belief in enlightened reform. In the end, however, Frederick desired a stronger monarchy and more power for himself.

Catherine the Great Studies *Philosophes'* Works Catherine II, or **Catherine the Great,** empress of Russia, read the works of the *philosophes* and exchanged letters with Voltaire and Diderot. She praised Voltaire as someone who had "fought the united enemies of humankind: superstition, fanaticism, ignorance, trickery." Catherine believed in the Enlightenment ideas of equality and liberty.

Catherine, who became empress in 1762, toyed with implementing Enlightenment ideas. Early in her reign, she made some limited reforms in law and government. Catherine abolished torture and established religious tolerance in her lands. She granted nobles a charter of rights and criticized the institution of serfdom. Still, like Frederick in Prussia, Catherine did not intend to give up power. In the end, her main political contribution to Russia proved to be an expanded empire.

Joseph II Continues Reform In Austria, Hapsburg empress Maria Theresa ruled as an absolute monarch. Although she did not push for reforms, she is considered to be an enlightened despot by some historians because she worked to improve peasants' way of life. The most radical of the enlightened despots was her son and successor, Joseph II. Joseph was an eager student of the Enlightenment, and he traveled in disguise among his subjects to learn of their problems.

Joseph continued the work of Maria Theresa, who had begun to modernize Austria's government. Despite opposition, Joseph supported religious equality for Protestants and Jews in his Catholic empire. He ended censorship by allowing a free press and attempted to bring the Catholic Church under royal control. He sold the property of many monasteries that were not involved in education or care of the sick and used the proceeds to support those that were. Joseph even abolished serfdom. Like many of his other reforms, however, this measure was canceled after his death.

 Checkpoint Why were the *philosophes* interested in sharing their beliefs with European rulers?

Lives of the Majority Change Slowly

Most Europeans were untouched by either courtly or middle-class culture. They remained what they had always been—peasants living in small rural villages. Echoes of serfdom still remained throughout Europe despite advances in Western Europe. Their culture, based on centuries-old traditions, changed slowly.

By the late 1700s, however, radical ideas about equality and social justice finally seeped into peasant villages. While some peasants eagerly sought to topple the old order, others resisted efforts to bring about change. In the 1800s, war and political upheaval, as well as changing economic conditions, would transform peasant life in Europe.

 Checkpoint During this time, why did change occur slowly for most Europeans?

Note Taking

Reading Skill: Summarize Fill in a concept web like the one below with information about the enlightened despots and their contributions.

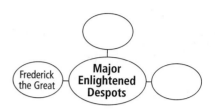

SECTION 2 Assessment

Progress Monitoring *Online*
For: Self-quiz with vocabulary practice
Web Code: naa-1721

Terms, People, and Places

1. For each term, person, or place listed at the beginning of the section, write a sentence explaining its significance.

Note Taking

2. **Reading Skill: Categorize** Use your completed concept webs to answer the Focus Question: As Enlightenment ideas spread across Europe, what cultural and political changes took place?

Comprehension and Critical Thinking

3. **Draw Conclusions** How did ideas of a "just society" change during the Age of Reason?

4. **Summarize** Explain the differences between baroque and rococo, and how these styles were reflected in art.

5. **Analyze Information** What did Frederick the Great mean when he said, "In my kingdom, everyone can go to heaven in his own fashion"?

6. **Predict Consequences** What actions might peasants take as they learn more about ideas such as equality?

● **Writing About History**

Quick Write: Narrowing Your Response In the essay prompt below, identify and list the key words. Then write a brief outline of the main ideas to help you form the best response. In your own words, explain what is being asked of you in the instructions.

• Think of the various effects of the Enlightenment. Identify which effect you think most contributed to society, both short-term and long-term. Explain your response.

View of La Scala in
Milan, mid-1800s ▼

Opera

Operas originated in Florence, Italy, in the seventeenth century. First called *drama per musica*, or drama through music, these musical performances typically involve large casts and elaborate sets and costumes. When Italian operas were performed in France, they emphasized glory and love, and included ballet and lavish stage settings to please the French court. Handel, Mozart, Verdi, Wagner, and Puccini composed some of the world's most famous operas. 🔊 AUDIO

◀ Empress Maria Theresa of Austria, whose country ruled Italy by the early 1700s, founded Milan's La Scala (background image), one of Europe's oldest and most celebrated opera houses. Built in 1776, this opera house still showcases the great operas of the nineteenth century, including composer Giuseppe Verdi's masterpieces, *Aida* and *La Traviata*. Verdi's first opera, *Oberto*, was performed at La Scala, and he was the beloved house composer for many years. After years of care and renovation, the interior of La Scala retains its elegance as operatic performances continue to entertain audiences today.

The "Three Tenors" (from left), Placido Domingo, José Carreras, and Luciano Pavarotti, are some of the best-known opera singers of the modern era. In the hierarchy of the opera stage, the tenor is the highest male voice and usually plays the part of the hero. The female lead is typically sung by a soprano, which is the highest female voice. Singers in the lower ranges (mezzo-soprano and alto for women, baritone and bass for men) generally play villainous or comic roles.

Thinking Critically

1. **Draw Inferences** How do you think composing an opera is different from composing a symphony?
2. **Determine Relevance** Why did operas appeal to composers and musicians during the Enlightenment?

Thomas Paine

British tax stamp

WITNESS HISTORY 🔊 AUDIO

Paine's *Common Sense*

Early in 1776, English colonists in North America eagerly read the newly published *Common Sense,* by Thomas Paine. This pamphlet called on them to declare their independence from Britain and echoed the themes of the Enlightenment.

❝ 'Tis repugnant to reason, to the universal order of things, to all examples from former ages, to suppose that this Continent can long remain subject to any external power.❞
—Thomas Paine, *Common Sense*

Focus Question How did ideas of the Enlightenment lead to the independence and founding of the United States of America?

Birth of the American Republic

 Performance Standards

- **SSWH13b** Identify how Lock, Voltaire, and Rousseau's ideas link politics and society.

Terms, People, and Places

George III	Yorktown, Virginia
Stamp Act	Treaty of Paris
George Washington	James Madison
Thomas Jefferson	Benjamin Franklin
popular sovereignty	federal republic

Note Taking

Reading Skill: Recognize Sequence As you read, complete a timeline like the one below with important dates that led up to the formation of the United States government.

French and Indian War ends.

1763

On the eve of the American Revolution, Britain was a formidable foe whose power stretched throughout the world. In addition, an ambitious new ruler sought to expand the powers of the monarchy.

Britain Becomes a Global Power

There are several key reasons for Britain's rise to global prominence:

- Location placed England in a position to control trade. In the 1500s and 1600s, English merchants sent ships across the world's oceans and planted outposts in the West Indies, North America, and India. From these tiny settlements, England would build a global empire.

- England offered a climate favorable to business and commerce and put fewer restrictions on trade than some of its neighbors.

- In the 1700s, Britain was generally on the winning side in European conflicts. With the Treaty of Utrecht, France gave Nova Scotia and Newfoundland to Britain. In 1763, the end of the French and Indian War and the Seven Years' War brought Britain all of French Canada. The British also monopolized the slave trade in Spanish America, which brought enormous wealth to British merchants.

- England's territory expanded closer to home as well. In 1707, England and Wales were united with Scotland to become the United Kingdom of Great Britain. Free trade with Scotland created a larger market for farmers and manufacturers. Ireland had come under English control during the 1600s. It was formally united with Great Britain in 1801.

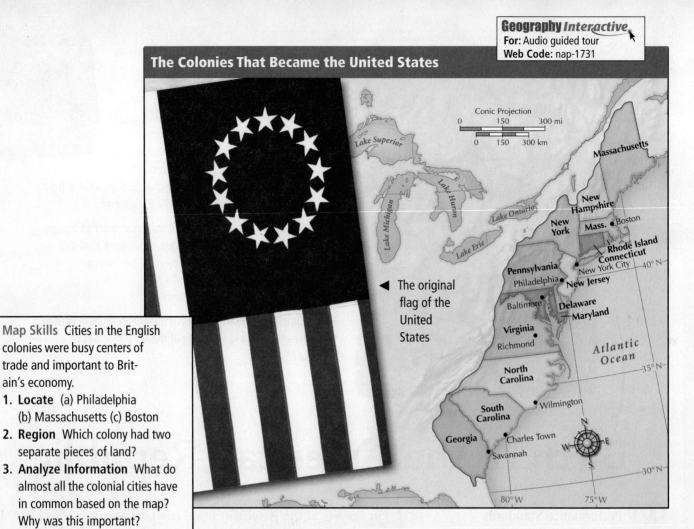

The Colonies That Became the United States

Geography *Interactive*
For: Audio guided tour
Web Code: nap-1731

◀ The original flag of the United States

Map Skills Cities in the English colonies were busy centers of trade and important to Britain's economy.

1. **Locate** (a) Philadelphia (b) Massachusetts (c) Boston
2. **Region** Which colony had two separate pieces of land?
3. **Analyze Information** What do almost all the colonial cities have in common based on the map? Why was this important?

Vocabulary Builder

assert—(uh SURT) *vt.* to insist on being recognized

In 1760, **George III** began a 60-year reign. Unlike his father and grandfather, the new king was born in England. He spoke English and loved Britain. But George was eager to recover the powers the crown had lost. Following his mother's advice, "George, be a king!" he set out to reassert royal power. He wanted to end Whig domination, choose his own ministers, dissolve the cabinet system, and make Parliament follow his will. Gradually, George found seats in Parliament for "the king's friends." Then, with their help, he began to <u>assert</u> his leadership. Many of his policies, however, would prove disastrous.

✓ **Checkpoint** What led to Britain's rise to global prominence in the mid-1700s?

The Colonies in the Mid-1700s

By 1750, a string of prosperous colonies stretched along the eastern coast of North America. They were part of Britain's growing empire. Colonial cities such as Boston, New York, and Philadelphia were busy commercial centers that linked North America to the West Indies, Africa, and Europe. Colonial shipyards produced many vessels for this trade.

Britain applied mercantilist policies to its colonies in an attempt to strengthen its own economy by exporting more than it imported. To this end, in the 1600s, Parliament had passed the Navigation Acts to regulate colonial trade and manufacturing. For the most part, however, these acts were not rigorously enforced. Therefore, activities like smuggling were common and not considered crimes by the colonists.

By the mid-1700s, the colonies were home to diverse religious and ethnic groups. Social distinctions were more blurred than in Europe, although wealthy landowners and merchants dominated government and society. In politics, as in much else, there was a good deal of free discussion. Colonists felt entitled to the rights of English citizens, and their colonial assemblies exercised much control over local affairs. Many also had an increasing sense of their own destiny separate from Britain.

✓ **Checkpoint** In what ways were the colonies already developing independence from Britain?

Colonists Express Discontent

The Seven Years' War and the French and Indian War in North America had drained the British treasury. King George III and his advisors thought that the colonists should help pay for these wars. To increase taxes paid by colonists, Parliament passed the Sugar Act in 1764, which imposed import taxes, and the **Stamp Act** in 1765, which imposed taxes on items such as newspapers and pamphlets. "No taxation without representation," the colonists protested. They believed that because they had no representatives in Parliament, they should not be taxed. Parliament repealed the Stamp Act in 1766, but then passed a Declaratory Act that said it had complete authority over the colonists.

Colonists Rebel Against Britain A series of violent clashes intensified the colonists' anger. In March 1770, British soldiers in Boston opened fire on a crowd that was pelting them with stones and snowballs. Colonists called the death of five protesters the Boston Massacre. Then in December 1773, a handful of colonists hurled a cargo of recently arrived British tea into the harbor to protest a tax on tea. The incident became known as the Boston Tea Party. When Parliament passed harsh laws to punish Massachusetts for the destruction of the tea, other colonies rallied to oppose the British response.

As tensions increased, fighting spread. Finally, representatives from each colony gathered in Philadelphia and met in a Continental Congress to decide what action to take. Among the participants were the radical yet fair-minded Massachusetts lawyer John Adams, who had defended the British soldiers involved in the Boston Massacre in their trial; Virginia planter and soldier **George Washington;** and political and social leaders from other colonies.

Colonists Declare Independence In April 1775, the ongoing tension between the colonists and the British exploded into war in Lexington and Concord, Massachusetts. This war is known as the Revolutionary War, or the American Revolution. The Congress met soon after and set up a Continental Army, with George Washington in command. Although many battles ended in British victories, the colonists were determined to fight at any cost. In 1776, the

Drafting the Declaration
Benjamin Franklin, John Adams, and Thomas Jefferson (from left to right)

The Declaration of Independence stands as one of the most important documents in all of history. It still serves as inspiration for people around the world. Where did some of the ideas of the Declaration originate?

Primary Source

66 We hold these truths to be self-evident, that all men are created equal, that they are endowed by their Creator with certain unalienable Rights, that among these are Life, Liberty and the pursuit of Happiness. That to secure these rights, Governments are instituted among Men, deriving their just powers from the consent of the governed; That whenever any Form of Government becomes destructive of these ends it is the Right of the People to alter or to abolish it, and to institute new Government, laying its foundation on such principles and organizing its powers in such form, as to them shall seem most likely to effect their Safety and Happiness. 99
—*Declaration of Independence,* July 4, 1776 AUDIO

George Washington

When George Washington (1732–1799) was chosen to lead the American army, the British thought he would be a failure. Washington indeed faced many challenges, including an army that did not have weapons, uniforms, or bedding. He struggled to incorporate order and discipline and to instill pride and loyalty in his soldiers. Washington persevered to American victory. His success as a leader continued when he became the nation's first President. **How did Washington hold the army together through difficult times?**

James Madison

James Madison (1751–1836) arrived at the Constitutional Convention in Philadelphia in May 1787 with his thick notebooks on history and government. Madison chose a seat in front of the president's chair and kept detailed notes of the debates. Madison was greatly respected and quickly became the Convention's floor leader. His notebooks remained unpublished for more than 50 years, but they are now our main source of information about the birth of the Constitution. **What did the Framers of the Constitution have in common?**

Benjamin Franklin

Benjamin Franklin (1706–1790) was a philosopher, scientist, publisher, legislator, and diplomat. Sent by Congress to France in 1776 to seek financial and military support for the war, he soon became popular in France because of his intellect and wit. Those who admired America's goal of attaining freedom also admired Franklin. When Franklin returned to America after nine years, he served as a delegate to the Constitutional Convention as the eldest of the delegates. **Why was Franklin admired in France?**

Second Continental Congress took a momentous step, voting to declare independence from Britain. **Thomas Jefferson** of Virginia was the principal author of the Declaration of Independence, a document that reflects John Locke's ideas of the government's obligation to protect the people's natural rights to "life, liberty, and property."

The Declaration included another of Locke's ideas: people had the right "to alter or to abolish" unjust governments—a right to revolt. The principle of **popular sovereignty,** which states that all government power comes from the people, is also an important point in the Declaration. Jefferson carefully detailed the colonists' grievances against Britain. Because the king had trampled colonists' natural rights, he argued, the colonists had the right to rebel and set up a new government that would protect them. Aware of the risks involved, on July 4, 1776, American leaders adopted the Declaration, pledging "our lives, our fortunes, and our sacred honor" to creating and protecting the new United States of America.

 Checkpoint What Enlightenment ideas are reflected in the Declaration of Independence?

The American Revolution Continues

At first, the American cause looked bleak. The British had a large number of trained soldiers, a huge fleet, and greater resources. About one third of the American colonists were Loyalists, or those who supported Britain. Many others refused to fight for either side. The Americans lacked military resources, had little money to pay soldiers, and did not have a strategic plan.

Still, colonists had some advantages. One was the geography of the diverse continent. Since colonists were fighting on their own soil, they were familiar with its thick woods and inadequate roads. Other advantages were their strong leader, George Washington, and their fierce determination to fight for their ideals of liberty.

To counteract these advantages, the British worked to create alliances within the colonies. A number of Native American groups sided with the British, while others saw potential advantages in supporting the colonists' cause. Additionally, the British offered freedom to any enslaved people who were willing to fight the colonists.

France Provides Support The first turning point in the war came in 1777, when the Americans triumphed over the British at the Battle of Saratoga. This victory persuaded France to join the Americans against its old rival, Britain. The alliance brought the Americans desperately needed supplies, trained soldiers, and French warships. Spurred by the French example, the Netherlands and Spain added their support.

Hard times continued, however. In the brutal winter of 1777–1778, Continental troops at Valley Forge suffered from cold, hunger, and disease. Throughout this crisis and others, Washington was patient, courageous, and determined. He held the ragged army together.

Fearless Leader
George Washington directs his troops on the battlefield. *What traits did Washington possess that helped lead Americans to victory?*

The Roots of American Democracy

The Framers of the United States Constitution were well educated and widely read. They were familiar with governments of ancient Greece and Rome and those of contemporary Great Britain and Europe. Political writings such as Montesquieu's *The Spirit of the Laws*, Rousseau's *Social Contract*, and Locke's *Two Treatises of Government* contained principles that greatly influenced the Framers in the development of the Constitution. Centuries later, these fundamental democratic principles of American government—popular sovereignty, limited government, separation of powers, and checks and balances—are still in place. The diagram here shows checks and balances, one of Montesquieu's ideas, which ensures that one branch does not accumulate too much power.

Judicial Branch

Legislative Branch

Executive Branch

Congress may impeach judges; Senate may reject appointment of judges.

Courts may declare acts of Congress unconstitutional.

Checks and Balances

Courts may declare executive actions unconstitutional.

President appoints judges.

President may veto legislation.

Congress may impeach the President and may override veto; Senate approves or rejects treaties and appointments.

History Interactive
For: Interactive diagram
Web Code: nap-1732

Thinking Critically

1. **Draw Conclusions** What additional ideas might the Framers have learned from the political writings of the Enlightenment thinkers?
2. **Summarize** Explain how the basic principle of checks and balances works.

Treaty of Paris Ends the War In 1781, the French fleet blockaded the Chesapeake Bay, which enabled Washington to force the surrender of a British army at **Yorktown, Virginia.** With that defeat, the British war effort crumbled. Two years later, American, British, and French diplomats signed the **Treaty of Paris,** ending the war. In that treaty, Britain recognized the independence of the United States of America. The Americans' victory can be attributed to their resilient dedication to attaining independence.

✓ **Checkpoint** What advantages did the colonists have in battling Britain for their independence?

A New Constitution

The Articles of Confederation was the nation's first constitution. It proved to be too weak to rule the new United States effectively. To address this problem, the nation's leaders gathered once more in Philadelphia. Among them were George Washington, **James Madison,** and **Benjamin Franklin.**

During the hot summer of 1787, they met in secret to redraft the articles of the new constitution. The result was a document that established a government run by the people, for the people.

Enlightenment Ideas Have Great Impact

The Framers of the Constitution had studied history and absorbed the ideas of Locke, Montesquieu, and Rousseau. They saw government in terms of a social contract into which "We the People of the United States" entered. They provided not only for an elective legislature but also for an elected president rather than a hereditary monarch. For the first President, voters would choose George Washington.

The Constitution created a **federal republic,** with power divided between the federal, or national, government and the states. A central feature of the new federal government was the separation of powers among the legislative, executive, and judicial branches, an idea borrowed directly from Montesquieu. Within that structure, each branch of government was provided with checks and balances on the other branches.

The Bill of Rights, the first ten amendments to the Constitution, was important to the passage of the Constitution. It recognized the idea that people had basic rights that the government must protect, such as freedom of religion, speech, and the press. The Bill of Rights, like the Constitution, put the *philosophes'* Enlightenment ideas into practice. In 1789, the Constitution became the supreme law of the land, which means it became the nation's fundamental law. This remarkable document has endured for more than 200 years.

Symbol of Freedom

The Constitution of the United States created the most progressive government of its day. From the start, the new republic was a symbol of freedom to European countries and reformers in Latin America. Its constitution would be copied or adapted by many lands throughout the world. The Enlightenment ideals that had inspired American colonists brought changes in Europe too. In 1789, a revolution in France toppled the monarchy in the name of liberty and equality. Before long, other Europeans would take up the cry for freedom as well.

✔ **Checkpoint** Explain the influence of Enlightenment ideas on the United States Constitution and Bill of Rights.

The U.S. Bill of Rights

1st: Guarantees freedom of religion, speech, press, assembly, and petition

2nd: Right to bear arms

3rd: Prohibits quartering of troops in private homes

4th: Protects from unreasonable searches and seizures

5th: No punishment without due process of law

6th: Right to a speedy and public trial in the state where the offense was committed

7th: Right to jury trial for civil cases if over $20

8th: Prohibits excessive bail and cruel and unusual punishments

9th: Civil rights are not restricted to those specified by these amendments.

10th: Powers not granted to the national government belong to the states and to the people.

Chart Skills The first ten amendments to the United States Constitution are known as the Bill of Rights. *What is the significance of the 10th Amendment?*

SECTION 3 Assessment

Progress Monitoring Online
For: Self-quiz with vocabulary practice
Web Code: naa-1731

Terms, People, and Places

1. For each term, person, or place listed at the beginning of the section, write a sentence explaining its significance.

Note Taking

2. **Reading Skill: Recognize Sequence** Use your completed timeline to answer the Focus Question: How did ideas of the Enlightenment lead to the independence and founding of the United States of America?

Comprehension and Critical Thinking

3. **Make Generalizations** Describe society and politics in the 13 English colonies during the mid-1700s.

4. **Express Problems Clearly** Explain why conflict between the colonists and Britain increased after 1763.

5. **Identify Point of View** What reasons might a Loyalist have for opposing the American Revolution?

6. **Determine Relevance** Give two examples of why the Bill of Rights is important to you.

● Writing About History

Quick Write: Providing Elaboration To prove that you fully understand a subject, you need to include specific details. You should use facts, dates, names, examples, explanations, or quotes to support your answer. Write a paragraph to describe the events that led to the American Revolution. Then read through your response and add specific details where you can.

SPREADING THE WORD OF REVOLUTION

While Enlightenment thinkers had a profound impact on the leaders of the American Revolution, newspapers made a great impact on the colonists. Colonists depended on newspapers for information about the war and the economy. News about the war was the first great news event to report in America. Would the colonists be free? Or would English control continue? As demand increased, newspapers began publishing several times a week instead of weekly. The number of newspapers increased from 29 to 48 from 1770 to 1775. During this time, the American newspaper changed from a weak form of communication to a propaganda machine that included controversial political cartoons and essays.

Trouble for newspapers came in 1765 when the British government passed the Stamp Act. Newspapers were forced to pay the tax imposed by the Stamp Act or face heavy penalties. Colonists already felt they had no representation so they became even more discontented. Many newspapers strongly opposed the Stamp Act and showed their resentment in their pages with cartoons, editorial content, and typographical devices. The *Maryland Gazette*, for example, set a skull and crossbones on its front page where the tax stamp belonged (facing page). Others ceased publication. The strength of the press was evident when the British government was forced to repeal the Stamp Act. Newspapers had voiced protest effectively and would continue to be a powerful medium of communication for years to come.

► Engraving by Paul Revere of the 1770 Boston Massacre. Revere exaggerated the event to incite anger among the colonists against the British.

▼ Engraving of the Battle of Lexington, the first battle of the American Revolution. Demand for exciting news of the war led to the creation of more newspapers.

The *Maryland Gazette*,
October 10, 1765

1789 French Revolution begins.

1775 American Revolution begins.

1821 Mexico gains independence from Spain.

1791 Haitian revolt against France begins.

1821 Peru declares independence from Spain.

1819 Colombia achieves independence from Spain.

1822 Brazil proclaims independence from Portugal.

1825 Bolivia achieves independence from Spain.

1811 Paraguay proclaims independence from Spain.

1818 Chile declares independence from Spain.

NORTH AMERICA

SOUTH AMERICA

EUROPE

AFRICA

The first political cartoon (left) in an American newspaper was created by Benjamin Franklin and appeared in 1754. The Sons of Liberty, an organization that loudly opposed the Stamp Act, used newspapers (above) to increase colonial participation.

An Era of Revolutions

As word of revolution spread throughout the colonies, the news also spread throughout the world. The American Revolution had a great impact on other parts of the world because it established the first government with all powers based on the consent of its people. Americans' attainment of freedom inspired revolts in France, in Hispaniola (present-day Haiti), and throughout Latin America as shown on this map.

History *Interactive*

For: Interactive map, audio, and more
Visit: PHSchool.com
Web Code: nap-1733

Thinking Critically
1. **Recognize Propaganda** Explain how the front page of the *Maryland Gazette* was used as a propaganda tool.
2. **Make Comparisons** How does the newspaper affect people's perceptions today?

CHAPTER 17

Quick Study Guide

 SSWH13b

Progress Monitoring *Online*
For: Self-test with vocabulary practice
Web Code: naa-1741

■ Enlightenment Thinkers

- **Thomas Hobbes:** social contract in which people give power to the government for an organized society
- **John Locke:** natural rights—life, liberty, and property
- **Baron de Montesquieu:** separation of powers; checks and balances
- **Voltaire:** battled corruption, injustice, and inequality; defended freedom of speech
- **Denis Diderot:** *Encyclopedia*
- **Jean-Jacques Rousseau:** social contract in which people follow the "general will" for true liberty
- **Adam Smith:** free market; laissez faire

■ Enlightenment Ideas Influence Democracy

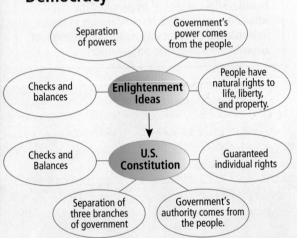

■ American Declaration of Independence: Main Ideas

Declaration of Independence: Main Ideas
• All men are created equal and have natural rights to life, liberty, and the pursuit of happiness.
• It is the government's obligation to protect these rights.
• If a government fails to protect these rights, the people can revolt and set up a new government.

■ The U.S. Bill of Rights

The U.S. Bill of Rights
1st: Guarantees freedom of religion, speech, press, assembly, and petition
2nd: Right to bear arms
3rd: Prohibits quartering of troops in private homes
4th: Protects from unreasonable searches and seizures
5th: No punishment without due process of law
6th: Right to a speedy and public trial in the state where the offense was committed
7th: Right to jury trial for civil cases if over $20
8th: Prohibits excessive bail and cruel and unusual punishments
9th: Civil rights are not restricted to those specified by these amendments.
10th: Powers not granted to the national government belong to the states and to the people.

■ Key Events From 1700–1789

1700s
France sees flowering of Enlightenment thought.

1721
Johann Sebastian Bach publishes his Brandenburg Concertos.

1740
Frederick II begins his reign in Prussia.

Chapter Events
Global Events

1720   **1730**   **1740**

1735
China's Emperor Qianlong begins his long reign.

Concept Connector

Essential Question Review

To connect prior knowledge with what you have learned in this chapter, answer the questions below in your Concept Connector journal. Use the journal in the Reading and Note Taking Study Guide to record your answers (or go to www.phschool.com **Web Code:** nad-1707). In addition, record information about the following concepts:

- Cultural Diffusion: Roots of American Democracy
- Political Systems: federal government
- Democracy: The American Declaration of Independence
- Impact of the Individual: John Locke

1. **Cooperation** During the American Revolution economic and military aid from France helped the American colonists defeat the British. Suggest at least one reason why France would have helped the American colonists. What role did Benjamin Franklin play in the alliance forged between the two nations? What French military tactic made the colonists' defeat of the British army possible?

2. **Conflict** Inspired by the American Revolution, colonists in Central and South America fought for freedom from their colonial rulers. In addition, many revolutionary leaders in Central and South America were influenced by the ideas of the Enlightenment. Review the concept web "Enlightenment Ideas Influence Democracy" in the Quick Study Guide in this chapter. Which Enlightenment ideas would be most likely to cause conflict between colonists and their rulers? Why?

3. **Impact of the Individual** Many individuals contributed to the success of the American Revolution. Review Section 4 in this chapter and choose one individual who you believe made the most significant impact. Describe this individual's contribution and explain its importance to winning the American Revolution.

■ Connections to Today

1. **Democracy: Still Strong Today** As you have read, the Framers of the United States Constitution were inspired by Montesquieu, Rousseau, and Locke. Democratic revolutions around the world were inspired by the same Enlightenment ideas that had inspired American colonists. Even today, nations seeking a model for democratic government often turn to the Constitution of the United States. Research and write a newspaper article about one of these nations.

2. **Culture: Modern Salons** Salons provided a way for people to gather and share ideas, especially during the Enlightenment. Today, we know that many people do this without ever meeting in person—through the Internet. People are able to join chat rooms and newsgroups to share their thoughts. Many discussions on the Internet lack the serious-minded tone of a salon conversation and the benefit of face-to-face conversation. The Internet does, however, provide a sense of community, where people can gather to discuss ideas, even if it is a "virtual" living room. Compare salons of the Enlightenment and Internet chat rooms. Explain which you think is the better forum for sharing ideas, and why.

| 1751 Diderot publishes *Encyclo-pedia*. | 1759 Voltaire publishes *Candide*. | 1762 Rousseau publishes *The Social Contract*. | 1776 American leaders sign the Declaration of Independence. | **History** *Interactive* **For:** Interactive timeline **Web Code:** nap-1701 |

1750   **1760**   **1770**   **1780**

| 1754 French and Indian War begins. | 1763 Treaty of Paris gives Britain control of Canada. | 1789 The French Revolution begins. |

Chapter Assessment

Terms, People, and Places

Complete each sentence by choosing the correct answer from the list of terms below. You will not use all of the terms.

natural rights	Montesquieu
John Locke	federal republic
laissez faire	Yorktown, Virginia
rococo	Frederick the Great
baroque	Treaty of Paris
Joseph II	Rousseau

1. In a _____, power is divided between the federal government and the states.
2. _____ advanced the idea of separation of powers.
3. The _____ style influenced by the Enlightenment was personal, elegant, and charming.
4. The enlightened despot who ended censorship was _____.
5. The American Revolution ended when George Washington forced the surrender of the British at _____.
6. _____ believed in _____, which are the rights to life, liberty, and property.

Main Ideas

Section 1 (pp. 544–549)
7. What idea did John Locke advocate for the role of a government?
8. Explain the economic policy of laissez faire.

Section 2 (pp. 550–556)
9. How did the Enlightenment affect some rulers in Europe, and what are these rulers known as?

Section 3 (pp. 557–565)
10. How did taxation create tensions between the American colonies and the British government?

11. How does the Bill of Rights reflect a key Enlightenment idea?

Chapter Focus Question
12. How did Enlightenment thinkers inspire revolutionaries to push for radical changes in government and society?

Critical Thinking

13. **Synthesize Information** Choose one *philosophe* from this chapter and describe how he or she might respond to a human rights issue that has been in the news recently.
14. **Predict Consequences** Given the impact the Enlightenment thinkers had on the American Revolution, what can you predict will happen in other areas of the world? Explain why you predicted what you did.
15. **Analyzing Visuals** Identify the style of this painting and describe its characteristics.

16. **Make Comparisons** Compare Britain and its North American colonies in the mid-1700s.
17. **Analyze Information** What ideas about government do you think English settlers brought with them to the Americas?

● Writing About History

In this chapter's three Section Assessments, you developed skills for writing for assessment.

Writing for Assessment Select either a philosopher from the Enlightenment or an important figure from the American Revolution. Explain how his or her actions, beliefs, and/or works contributed to improving society.

Prewriting
- Consider what you know about the people in this chapter and choose one who interests you.
- Develop a focus or main idea. Write a single sentence identifying the main idea you will develop.
- As you prepare to write your essay, make sure you understand the instructions. Circle verbs, nouns, or important phrases in the question.

Drafting
- Develop a thesis statement that identifies the focus of your essay.
- Make an outline for your essay and fill in facts and examples.
- Write an introduction to explain your thesis, a body to provide evidence for your thesis, and a conclusion.

Revising
- Even though time is limited on essay tests, you should still leave time to check your writing for accuracy and clarity.
- Use the guidelines for revising your essay on page SH22 of the Writing Handbook.

Prepare for the GHSGT

Enlightenment Thought

Enlightenment thinkers believed in the possibility of social, political, and economic change. Often critical of society during this time, they were driven by the power of human reason and progress.

Document A

"Common sense is not so common."

—From ***Philosophical Dictionary*** by Voltaire

Document B

"A prince ought not to deem it beneath his dignity to state that he considers it his duty not to dictate anything to his subjects in religious matters, but to leave them complete freedom."

—From ***What Is Enlightenment?*** by Immanuel Kant

Document C

"A strange consequence that necessarily follows from the use of torture is that the innocent person is placed in a condition worse than that of the guilty, for if both are tortured, the circumstances are all against the former. Either he confesses the crime and is condemned, or he is declared innocent and has suffered a punishment he did not deserve."

—From ***On Crimes and Punishments*** by Marchese di Beccaria

Document D

Diderot and Catherine the Great

Document E

Selected Enlightenment Thinkers			
Thinker	**Lifespan**	**Nationality**	**Key Work**
Jean D'Alembert	1717–1783	French	*Encyclopedia*
Jeremy Bentham	1748–1832	English	*The Principles of Morals and Legislation*
Cesare Beccaria	1738–1794	Italian	*Crimes and Punishment*
Denis Diderot	1713–1784	French	*Encyclopedia*
David Hume	1711–1776	Scottish	*Treatise of Human Nature*
Immanuel Kant	1724–1804	E. Prussian	*Critique of Pure Reason*
John Locke	1632–1704	English	*Essay Concerning Human Understanding*
Charles Montesquieu	1689–1755	French	*The Spirit of the Laws*
Jean-Jacques Rousseau	1712–1778	French	*The Social Contract*
Adam Smith	1723–1790	English	*The Wealth of Nations*
Voltaire	1694–1778	French	*Philosophical Dictionary*

Analyzing Documents

Use your knowledge of the Enlightenment and Documents A, B, C, D, and E to answer the questions below.

1. Kant believes in _____ based on Document B.
   A freedom of religion
   B freedom of speech
   C the government making a religious choice for its people
   D dignity

2. In Document C, the author condemned
   A capital punishment.
   B religion of any kind.
   C torture.
   D the Inquisition.

3. Catherine the Great and Diderot pictured in Document D are most likely
   A sharing war stories.
   B sharing Enlightenment ideas.
   C planning the American Revolution.
   D discussing population growth in France.

4. **Writing Task** Which of the above documents do you think best exemplifies the spirit of the Enlightenment? Why? Use your knowledge of the Enlightenment and specific information from the documents to support your opinion.

18 The French Revolution and Napoleon

1789–1815

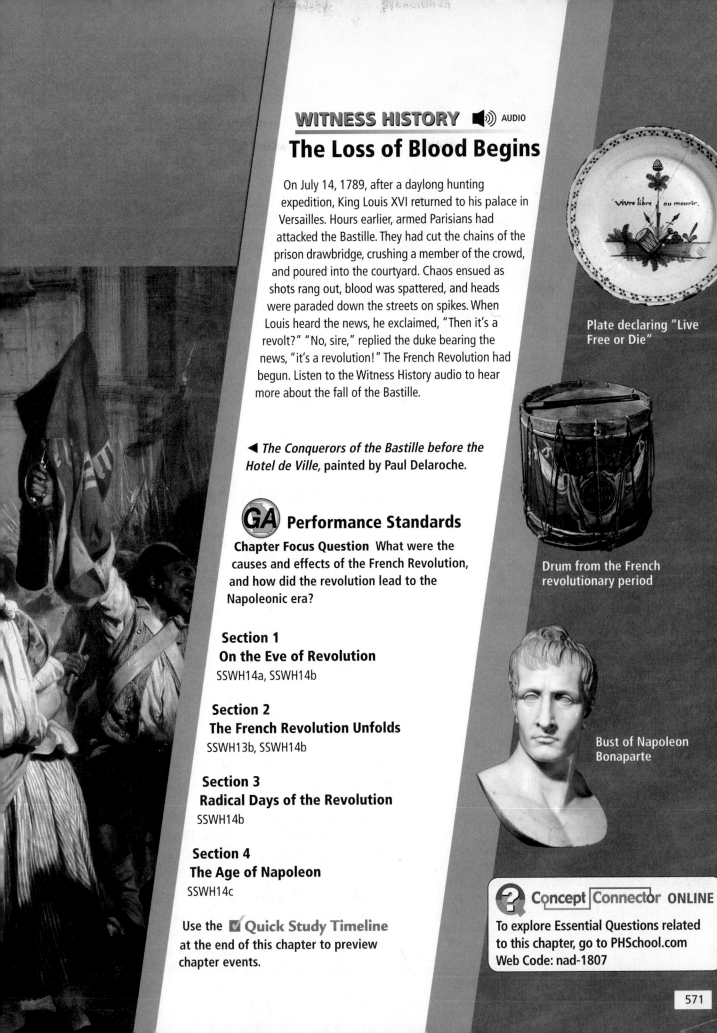

The Loss of Blood Begins

On July 14, 1789, after a daylong hunting expedition, King Louis XVI returned to his palace in Versailles. Hours earlier, armed Parisians had attacked the Bastille. They had cut the chains of the prison drawbridge, crushing a member of the crowd, and poured into the courtyard. Chaos ensued as shots rang out, blood was spattered, and heads were paraded down the streets on spikes. When Louis heard the news, he exclaimed, "Then it's a revolt?" "No, sire," replied the duke bearing the news, "it's a revolution!" The French Revolution had begun. Listen to the Witness History audio to hear more about the fall of the Bastille.

Plate declaring "Live Free or Die"

◀ *The Conquerors of the Bastille before the Hotel de Ville,* painted by Paul Delaroche.

Drum from the French revolutionary period

GA Performance Standards

Chapter Focus Question What were the causes and effects of the French Revolution, and how did the revolution lead to the Napoleonic era?

**Section 1
On the Eve of Revolution**
SSWH14a, SSWH14b

**Section 2
The French Revolution Unfolds**
SSWH13b, SSWH14b

**Section 3
Radical Days of the Revolution**
SSWH14b

**Section 4
The Age of Napoleon**
SSWH14c

Use the ☑ **Quick Study Timeline** at the end of this chapter to preview chapter events.

Bust of Napoleon Bonaparte

Concept Connector ONLINE

To explore Essential Questions related to this chapter, go to PHSchool.com
Web Code: nad-1807

Camille Desmoulins and
French Revolution banner

LIBERTÉ ÉGALITÉ

Inciting Revolution

Camille Desmoulins was a French revolutionary leader and journalist who wrote pamphlets and journals to express his views on the revolution. He also spoke to Parisian crowds and his stirring speeches in 1789 were a cause of the storming of the Bastille prison on July 14, 1789. This excerpt is from one of his speeches, "Better to Die than not Live Free":

> ❝In a democracy, tho the people may be deceived, yet they at least love virtue. It is merit which they believe they put in power as substitutes for the rascals who are the very essence of monarchies. The vices, concealments, and crimes which are the diseases of republics are the very health and existence of monarchies.❞

Focus Question What led to the storming of the Bastille, and therefore, to the start of the French Revolution?

On the Eve of Revolution

 Performance Standards

- **SSWH14a** Compare Louis XIV, Peter the Great and Tokugawa Ieyasu's absolutism.
- **SSWH14b** Identify the causes and results of revolution in France.

Terms, People, and Places

ancien régime
estate
bourgeoisie
deficit spending
Louis XVI

Jacques Necker
Estates-General
cahier
Tennis Court Oath
Bastille

Note Taking

Reading Skill: Recognize Multiple Causes
Create a chart to identify causes of the French Revolution. Add as many boxes as you need.

Causes of the French Revolution

Inequalities among classes

On April 28, 1789, unrest exploded at a Paris wallpaper factory. A rumor had spread that the factory owner was planning to cut wages even though bread prices were soaring. Enraged workers vandalized the owner's home.

Riots like these did not worry most nobles. They knew that France faced a severe economic crisis but thought financial reforms would ease the problem. The nobles were wrong. The crisis went deeper than government finances. Reform would not be enough. By July, the hungry, unemployed, and poorly paid people of Paris had taken up arms. Their actions would push events further and faster than anyone could have foreseen.

French Society Divided

In 1789, France, like the rest of Europe, still clung to an outdated social system that had emerged in the Middle Ages. Under this **ancien régime,** or old order, everyone in France was divided into one of three social classes, or **estates.** The First Estate was made up of the clergy; the Second Estate was made up of the nobility; and the Third Estate comprised the vast majority of the population.

The Clergy Enjoy Wealth During the Middle Ages, the Church had exerted great influence throughout Christian Europe. In 1789, the French clergy still enjoyed enormous wealth and privilege. The Church owned about 10 percent of the land, collected tithes, and paid no direct taxes to the state. High Church leaders such as bishops and abbots were usually nobles who lived very well. Parish priests, however, often came from humble origins and might be as poor as their peasant congregations.

The First Estate did provide some social services. Nuns, monks, and priests ran schools, hospitals, and orphanages. But during the Enlightenment, *philosophes* targeted the Church for reform. They criticized the idleness of some clergy, the Church's interference in politics, and its intolerance of dissent. In response, many clergy condemned the Enlightenment for undermining religion and moral order.

Nobles Hold Top Government Jobs The Second Estate was the titled nobility of French society. In the Middle Ages, noble knights had defended the land. In the 1600s, Richelieu and Louis XIV had crushed the nobles' military power but had given them other rights—under strict royal control. Those rights included top jobs in government, the army, the courts, and the Church.

At Versailles, ambitious nobles competed for royal appointments while idle courtiers enjoyed endless entertainments. Many nobles, however, lived far from the center of power. Though they owned land, they received little financial income. As a result, they felt the pinch of trying to maintain their status in a period of rising prices.

Many nobles hated absolutism and resented the royal bureaucracy that employed middle-class men in positions that once had been reserved for them. They feared losing their traditional privileges, especially their freedom from paying taxes.

Third Estate Is Vastly Diverse The Third Estate was the most diverse social class. At the top sat the **bourgeoisie** (boor zhwah ZEE), or middle class. The bourgeoisie included prosperous bankers, merchants, and manufacturers, as well as lawyers, doctors, journalists, and professors. The bulk of the Third Estate, however, consisted of rural peasants.

REVEIL DU TIERS ETAT

Analyzing Political Cartoons

The Old Regime This cartoon represents the social order in France before the French Revolution. While a member of the Third Estate is beginning to express anger and rise up, a nobleman representing the Second Estate and a priest, representing the First Estate, recoil in surprise and fear.

1. How does the cartoonist portray the Third Estate? Explain why.
2. What were the differences among the social classes in pre-revolutionary France?

Vocabulary Builder

urban—(UR bun) *adj.* of, relating to, or characteristic of a city

Some were prosperous landowners who hired laborers to work for them. Others were tenant farmers or day laborers.

Among the poorest members of the Third Estate were urban workers. They included apprentices, journeymen, and others who worked in industries such as printing or cloth making. Many women and men earned a meager living as servants, construction workers, or street sellers of everything from food to pots and pans. A large number of the urban poor were unemployed. To survive, some turned to begging or crime.

From rich to poor, members of the Third Estate resented the privileges enjoyed by their social "betters." Wealthy bourgeois families in the Third Estate could buy political office and even titles, but the best jobs were still reserved for nobles. Urban workers earned miserable wages. Even the smallest rise in the price of bread, their main food, brought the threat of greater hunger or even starvation.

Because of traditional privileges, the First and Second Estates paid almost no taxes. Peasants were burdened by taxes on everything from land to soap to salt. Though they were technically free, many owed fees and services that dated back to medieval times, such as the corvée (kawr VAY), which was unpaid labor to repair roads and bridges. Peasants were

● **INFOGRAPHIC**

What Is the Third Estate?

❝1. What is the Third Estate? *Everything.*
2. What has it been until now in the political order? *Nothing.*
3. What does it want to be? *Something.*❞
—Abbé Emmanuel Sieyès

Sieyès, a clergyman before the revolution, captured the spirit of the Third Estate with these words in a pamphlet published in January 1789. The vast Third Estate—peasants, dentists, laborers, and more—comprising more than 95 percent of France, was ready to fight for equality.

▲ Ceramic bottle depicting dentist and patient

▲ *Woman of the French Revolution*, painting of a peasant woman by Jacques-Louis David

▼ Eighteenth-century French street traders

Thinking Critically

1. **Identify Point of View** According to the quote by Sieyès, why was the Third Estate ready to revolt?
2. **Make Generalizations** Why did Sieyès say the Third Estate was "nothing"?

also incensed when nobles, hurt by rising prices, tried to reimpose old manor dues.

In towns and cities, Enlightenment ideas led people to question the inequalities of the old regime. Why, people demanded, should the first two estates have such great privileges at the expense of the majority? Throughout France, the Third Estate called for the privileged classes to pay their share.

✔ **Checkpoint** What was the social structure of the old regime in France?

Financial Troubles

Economic woes in France added to the social unrest and heightened tensions. One of the causes of the economic troubles was a mushrooming financial crisis that was due in part to years of **deficit spending.** This occurs when a government spends more money than it takes in.

National Debt Soars Louis XIV had left France deeply in debt. The Seven Years' War and the American Revolution strained the treasury even further. Costs generally had risen in the 1700s, and the lavish court soaked up millions. To bridge the gap between income and expenses, the government borrowed more and more money. By 1789, half of the government's income from taxes went to paying the interest on this enormous debt. Also, in the late 1780s, bad harvests sent food prices soaring and brought hunger to poorer peasants and city dwellers.

To solve the financial crisis, the government would have to increase taxes, reduce expenses, or both. However, the nobles and clergy fiercely resisted any attempt to end their exemption from taxes.

Economic Reform Fails The heirs of Louis XIV were not the right men to solve the economic crisis that afflicted France. Louis XV, who ruled from 1715 to 1774, pursued pleasure before serious business and ran up more debts. **Louis XVI** was well-meaning but weak and indecisive. He did, however, wisely choose **Jacques Necker,** a financial expert, as an advisor. Necker urged the king to reduce extravagant court spending, reform government, and abolish burdensome tariffs on internal trade. When Necker proposed taxing the First and Second Estates, however, the nobles and high clergy forced the king to dismiss him.

As the crisis deepened, the pressure for reform mounted. The wealthy and powerful classes demanded, however, that the king summon the **Estates-General,** the legislative body consisting of representatives of the three estates, before making any changes. A French king had not called the Estates-General for 175 years, fearing that nobles would use it to recover the feudal powers they had lost under absolute rule. To reform-minded nobles, the Estates-General seemed to offer a chance of carrying out changes like those that had come with the Glorious Revolution in England. They hoped that they could bring the absolute monarch under the control of the nobles and guarantee their own privileges.

✔ **Checkpoint** What economic troubles did France face in 1789, and how did they lead to further unrest?

Poorer peasants and city dwellers in France were faced with great hunger as bad harvests sent food prices soaring. People began to riot to demand bread. In the countryside, peasants began to attack the manor houses of the nobles. Arthur Young, an English visitor to France, witnessed these riots and disturbances. Why did the poor attack the nobles' homes?

Primary Source

❝ Everything conspires to render the present period in France critical: the [lack] of bread is terrible: accounts arrive every moment from the provinces of riots and disturbances, and calling in the military, to preserve the peace of the markets. ❞
—Arthur Young, *Travels in France During the Years 1787–1789*

Louis XVI Calls the Estates-General

As 1788 came to a close, France tottered on the verge of bankruptcy. Bread riots were spreading, and nobles, fearful of taxes, were denouncing royal tyranny. A baffled Louis XVI finally summoned the Estates-General to meet at Versailles the following year.

Estates Prepare Grievance Notebooks In preparation, Louis had all three estates prepare **cahiers** (kah YAYZ), or notebooks, listing their grievances. Many cahiers called for reforms such as fairer taxes, freedom of the press, or regular meetings of the Estates-General. In one town, shoemakers denounced regulations that made leather so expensive they could not afford to make shoes. Servant girls in the city of Toulouse demanded the right to leave service when they wanted and that "after a girl has served her master for many years, she receive some reward for her service."

The cahiers testified to boiling class resentments. One called tax collectors "bloodsuckers of the nation who drink the tears of the unfortunate from goblets of gold." Another one of the cahiers condemned the courts of nobles as "vampires pumping the last drop of blood" from the people. Another complained that "20 million must live on half the wealth of France while the clergy . . . devour the other half."

Delegates Take the Tennis Court Oath Delegates to the Estates-General from the Third Estate were elected, though only propertied men could vote. Thus, the delegates were mostly lawyers, middle-class officials, and writers. They were familiar with the writings of Voltaire, Rousseau, and other *philosophes*. They went to Versailles not only to solve the financial crisis but also to insist on reform.

The Estates-General convened in May 1789. From the start, the delegates were deadlocked over the issue of voting. Traditionally, each estate had met and voted separately. Each group had one vote. Under this system, the First and Second Estates always outvoted the Third Estate two to one. This time, the Third Estate wanted all three estates to meet in a single body, with votes counted "by head."

After weeks of stalemate, delegates of the Third Estate took a daring step. In June 1789, claiming to represent the people of France, they declared themselves to be the National Assembly. A few days later, the National Assembly found its meeting hall locked and guarded. Fearing that the king planned to dismiss them, the delegates moved to a nearby indoor tennis court. As curious spectators looked on, the delegates took their famous **Tennis Court Oath.** They swore "never to separate

The Oath Is Taken
Delegates of the Third Estate declare themselves to be the National Assembly, representing the people of France. They take the Tennis Court Oath (bottom), vowing to create a constitution. The National Assembly later issues the assignat (top) as currency to help pay the government's debts. *What was the significance of the Tennis Court Oath?*

and to meet wherever the circumstances might require until we have established a sound and just constitution."

When reform-minded clergy and nobles joined the Assembly, Louis XVI grudgingly accepted it. But royal troops gathered around Paris, and rumors spread that the king planned to dissolve the Assembly.

✔ **Checkpoint** What actions did delegates of the Third Estate take when the Estates-General met in 1789?

Parisians Storm the Bastille

On July 14, 1789, the city of Paris seized the spotlight from the National Assembly meeting in Versailles. The streets buzzed with rumors that royal troops were going to occupy the capital. More than 800 Parisians assembled outside the **Bastille,** a grim medieval fortress used as a prison for political and other prisoners. The crowd demanded weapons and gunpowder believed to be stored there.

The commander of the Bastille refused to open the gates and opened fire on the crowd. In the battle that followed, many people were killed. Finally, the enraged mob broke through the defenses. They killed the commander and five guards and released the handful of prisoners who were being held there, but found no weapons.

The Bastille was a symbol to the people of France representing years of abuse by the monarchy. The storming of and subsequent fall of the Bastille was a wake-up call to Louis XVI. Unlike any other riot or short-lived protest, this event posed a challenge to the sheer existence of the regime. Since 1880, the French have celebrated Bastille Day annually as their national independence day.

✔ **Checkpoint** What was the significance of the storming of the Bastille?

Parisians storm the Bastille on July 14, 1789.

Terms, People, and Places

1. What do many of the key terms, people, and places listed at the beginning of the section have in common? Explain.

Note Taking

2. **Reading Skill: Recognize Multiple Causes** Use your completed chart to answer the Focus Question: What led to the storming of the Bastille, and therefore, to the start of the French Revolution?

Comprehension and Critical Thinking

3. **Compare Point of View** How did the views of society differ between the nobles and peasants in 1789 France?

4. **Identify Point of View** Suppose that you are Jacques Necker. Write a paragraph that explains how your economic reform program will benefit France.

5. **Express Problems Clearly** What issues arose when Louis XVI called the Estates-General in 1789?

● **Writing About History**

Quick Write: Make a Cause-and-Effect Organizer Choose a specific event from this section and write it in the center of a piece of paper. List causes above it and effects below it. This will give you the details to include in your cause-and-effect essay. You may need to do additional research to gather more details.

Women march to the palace.

WITNESS HISTORY 🔊 AUDIO

Parisian Women Storm Versailles

On October 5, 1789, anger turned to action as thousands of women marched from Paris to Versailles. They wanted the king to stop ignoring their suffering. They also wanted the queen. French women were particularly angry with the Austrian-born queen, Marie Antoinette. They could not feed their children, yet she lived extravagantly. The women yelled as they looked for her in the palace:

66 Death to the Austrian! We'll wring her neck! We'll tear her heart out! 99
—mob of women at Versailles, October 6, 1789

Focus Question What political and social reforms did the National Assembly institute in the first stage of the French Revolution?

The French Revolution Unfolds

 Performance Standards

- **SSWH13b** Identify how Locke's ideas links politics and society.
- **SSWH14b** Identify the causes and results of revolution in France.

Terms, People, and Places

faction   émigré
Marquis de Lafayette   sans-culotte
Olympe de Gouges   republic
Marie Antoinette   Jacobins

Note Taking

Reading Skill: Identify Supporting Details As you read this section, prepare an outline like the one shown below. Remember to use numbers for supporting details.

    I. Political crisis leads to revolt
      A. The Great Fear
        1. Inflamed by famine and rumors
        2.
      B.

Excitement, wonder, and fear engulfed France as the revolution unfolded at home and spread abroad. Historians divide this revolutionary era into different phases. The moderate phase of the National Assembly (1789–1791) turned France into a constitutional monarchy. A radical phase (1792–1794) of escalating violence led to the end of the monarchy and a Reign of Terror. There followed a period of reaction against extremism, known as the Directory (1795–1799). Finally, the Age of Napoleon (1799–1815) consolidated many revolutionary changes. In this section, you will read about the moderate phase of the French Revolution.

Political Crisis Leads to Revolt

The political crisis of 1789 coincided with the worst famine in memory. Starving peasants roamed the countryside or flocked to towns, where they swelled the ranks of the unemployed. As grain prices soared, even people with jobs had to spend as much as 80 percent of their income on bread.

Rumors Create the "Great Fear" In such desperate times, rumors ran wild and set off what was later called the "Great Fear." Tales of attacks on villages and towns spread panic. Other rumors asserted that government troops were seizing peasant crops.

Inflamed by famine and fear, peasants unleashed their fury on nobles who were trying to reimpose medieval dues. Defiant peasants set fire to old manor records and stole grain from storehouses. The attacks died down after a period of time, but they clearly demonstrated peasant anger with an unjust regime.

Paris Commune Comes to Power Paris, too, was in turmoil. As the capital and chief city of France, it was the revolutionary center. A variety of **factions,** or dissenting groups of people, competed to gain power. Moderates looked to the **Marquis de Lafayette,** the aristocratic "hero of two worlds" who fought alongside George Washington in the American Revolution. Lafayette headed the National Guard, a largely middle-class militia organized in response to the arrival of royal troops in Paris. The Guard was the first group to don the tricolor—a red, white, and blue badge that was eventually adopted as the national flag of France.

A more radical group, the Paris Commune, replaced the royalist government of the city. It could mobilize whole neighborhoods for protests or violent action to further the revolution. Newspapers and political clubs—many even more radical than the Commune—blossomed everywhere. Some demanded an end to the monarchy and spread scandalous stories about the royal family and members of the court.

✔ **Checkpoint** What caused French peasants to revolt against nobles?

The National Assembly Acts

Peasant uprisings and the storming of the Bastille stampeded the National Assembly into action. On August 4, in a combative all-night meeting, nobles in the National Assembly voted to end their own privileges. They agreed to give up their old manorial dues, exclusive hunting rights, special legal status, and exemption from taxes.

Special Privilege Ends "Feudalism is abolished," announced the proud and weary delegates at 2 A.M. As the president of the Assembly later observed, "We may view this moment as the dawn of a new revolution, when all the burdens weighing on the people were abolished, and France was truly reborn."

Were nobles sacrificing much with their votes on the night of August 4? Both contemporary observers and modern historians note that the nobles gave up nothing that they had not already lost. Nevertheless, in the months ahead, the National Assembly turned the reforms of August 4 into law, meeting a key Enlightenment goal—the equality of all male citizens before the law.

Declaration of the Rights of Man In late August, as a first step toward writing a constitution, the Assembly issued the Declaration of the Rights of Man and the Citizen. The document was modeled in part on the American Declaration of Independence, written 13 years earlier. All men, the French declaration announced, were "born and remain free and equal in rights." They enjoyed natural rights to "liberty, property, security, and resistance to oppression." Like the writings of Locke and the *philosophes,* the constitution insisted that governments exist to protect the natural rights of citizens.

The declaration further <u>proclaimed</u> that all male citizens were equal before the law. Every Frenchman had an equal right to hold public office "with no distinction other than that of their virtues and talents." In addition, the declaration asserted freedom of religion and called for taxes to

French Reaction to the American Revolution

The Marquis de Lafayette (honored on ribbon at right) and Thomas Paine were leading figures in both the American and French revolutions. Lafayette, a French nobleman and military commander, helped the Americans defeat the British at Yorktown. He admired the American Declaration of Independence and American democratic ideals. With these in mind, Lafayette wrote the first draft of the French Declaration of the Rights of Man and the Citizen.

Thomas Paine was a famous American patriot and writer whose ideas in *Common Sense* had a great influence on the American Revolution. During the French Revolution, Paine moved to France. There, he defended the ideals of the revolution and was elected to serve in the revolutionary government.

Identify Central Issues How did the American Revolution influence the French Revolution?

Vocabulary Builder

<u>proclaimed</u>—(proh KLAYMD) *vt.* announced officially

be levied according to ability to pay. Its principles were captured in the enduring slogan of the French Revolution, "Liberty, Equality, Fraternity."

Many women were disappointed that the Declaration of the Rights of Man did not grant equal citizenship to them. In 1791, **Olympe de Gouges** (oh LAMP duh GOOZH), a journalist, demanded equal rights in her Declaration of the Rights of Woman and the Female Citizen. "Woman is born free," she proclaimed, "and her rights are the same as those of man." Therefore, Gouges reasoned, "all citizens, be they men or women, being equal in the state's eyes, must be equally eligible for all public offices, positions, and jobs." Later in the revolution, women met resistance for expressing their views in public, and many, including Gouges, were imprisoned and executed.

The Declaration of the Rights of Man met resistance as well. Uncertain and hesitant, Louis XVI did not want to accept the reforms of the National Assembly. Nobles continued to enjoy gala banquets while people were starving. By autumn, anger again turned to action.

Women March on Versailles On October 5, about six thousand women marched 13 miles in the pouring rain from Paris to Versailles. "Bread!" they shouted. They demanded to see the king.

Much of the crowd's anger was directed at the Austrian-born queen, **Marie Antoinette** (daughter of Maria Theresa and brother of Joseph II). The queen lived a life of great pleasure and extravagance, and this led to further public unrest. Although compassionate to the poor, her small acts went largely unnoticed because her lifestyle overshadowed them. She was against reforms and bored with the French court. She often retreated to the Petit Trianon, a small chateau on the palace grounds at Versailles where she lived her own life of amusement.

The women refused to leave Versailles until the king met their most important demand—to return to Paris. Not too happily, the king agreed. The next morning, the crowd, with the king and his family in tow, set out for the city. At the head of the procession rode women perched on the barrels of seized cannons. They told bewildered spectators that they were bringing Louis XVI, Marie Antoinette, and their son back to Paris. "Now

Playing Dress-Up
Marie Antoinette spent millions on her clothing and jewels and set fashion trends throughout France and Europe. This painting (top) was painted by her friend and portraitist, Elisabeth Vigée-Lebrun. Queens traditionally did not own property, but Marie Antoinette had her own small royal mansion and amusement village, or hamlet (bottom), where she played as milkmaid and shepherdess. *Why did the French common people resent Marie Antoinette?*

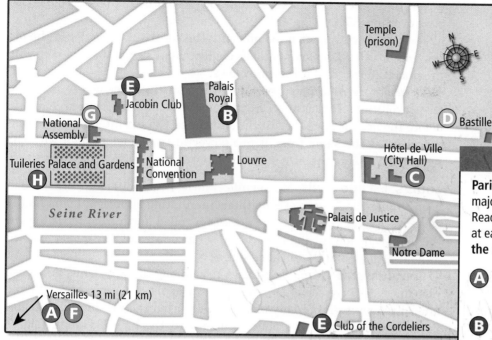

Temple (prison)

E Jacobin Club

Palais Royal

B

National Assembly

G

D Bastille

Tuileries Palace and Gardens

National Convention

Louvre

Hôtel de Ville (City Hall)

C

H

Seine River

Palais de Justice

Notre Dame

Versailles 13 mi (21 km)

A F

E Club of the Cordeliers

we won't have to go so far when we want to see our king," they sang. Crowds along the way cheered the king, who now wore the tricolor. In Paris, the royal family moved into the Tuileries (TWEE luh reez) palace. For the next three years, Louis was a virtual prisoner.

✓ **Checkpoint** How did the National Assembly react to peasant uprisings?

The National Assembly Presses Onward

The National Assembly soon followed the king to Paris. Its largely bourgeois members worked to draft a constitution and to solve the continuing financial crisis. To pay off the huge government debt—much of it owed to the bourgeoisie—the Assembly voted to take over and sell Church lands.

The Church Is Placed Under State Control In an even more radical move, the National Assembly put the French Catholic Church under state control. Under the Civil Constitution of the Clergy, issued in 1790, bishops and priests became elected, salaried officials. The Civil Constitution ended papal authority over the French Church and dissolved convents and monasteries.

Reaction was swift and angry. Many bishops and priests refused to accept the Civil Constitution. The pope condemned it. Large numbers of French peasants, who were conservative concerning religion, also rejected the changes. When the government punished clergy who refused to support the Civil Constitution, a huge gulf opened between revolutionaries in Paris and the peasantry in the provinces.

The Constitution of 1791 Establishes a New Government The National Assembly completed its main task by producing a constitution. The Constitution of 1791 set up a limited monarchy in place of the absolute monarchy that had ruled France for centuries. A new Legislative Assembly had the power to make laws, collect taxes, and decide on issues of war and peace. Lawmakers would be elected by tax-paying male citizens over age 25.

To make government more efficient, the constitution replaced the old provinces with 83 departments of roughly equal size. It abolished the old provincial courts, and it reformed laws.

To moderate reformers, the Constitution of 1791 seemed to complete the revolution. Reflecting Enlightenment goals, it ensured equality before the law for all male citizens and ended Church interference in government. At the same time, it put power in the hands of men with the means and leisure to serve in government.

Louis's Escape Fails Meanwhile, Marie Antoinette and others had been urging the king to escape their humiliating situation. Louis finally gave in. One night in June 1791, a coach rolled north from Paris toward the border. Inside sat the king disguised as a servant, the queen dressed as a governess, and the royal children.

The attempted escape failed. In a town along the way, Louis's disguise was uncovered by someone who held up a piece of currency with the king's face on it. A company of soldiers escorted the royal family back to Paris, as onlooking crowds hurled insults at the king. To many, Louis's dash to the border showed that he was a traitor to the revolution.

✓ **Checkpoint** What were the provisions of the Constitution of 1791?

Radicals Take Over

Events in France stirred debate all over Europe. Supporters of the Enlightenment applauded the reforms of the National Assembly. They saw the French experiment as the dawn of a new age for justice and equality. European rulers and nobles, however, denounced the French Revolution.

Rulers Fear Spread of Revolution European rulers increased border patrols to stop the spread of the "French plague." Fueling those fears were the horror stories that were told by **émigrés** (EM ih grayz)—nobles, clergy, and others who had fled France and its revolutionary forces. Émigrés reported attacks on their privileges, their property, their religion, and even their lives. Even "enlightened" rulers turned against France. Catherine the Great of Russia burned Voltaire's letters and locked up her critics.

Edmund Burke, a British writer and statesman who earlier had defended the American Revolution, bitterly condemned revolutionaries in Paris. He predicted all too accurately that the revolution would become more violent. "Plots and assassinations," he wrote, "will be anticipated by preventive murder and preventive confiscation." Burke warned: "When ancient opinions and rules of life are taken away ... we have no compass to govern us."

Threats Come From Abroad The failed escape of Louis XVI brought further hostile rumblings from abroad. In August 1791, the king of Prussia and the

emperor of Austria—who was Marie Antoinette's brother—issued the Declaration of Pilnitz. In this document, the two monarchs threatened to intervene to protect the French monarchy. The declaration may have been mostly a bluff, but revolutionaries in France took the threat seriously and prepared for war. The revolution was about to enter a new, more radical phase of change and conflict.

Radicals Fight for Power and Declare War In October 1791, the newly elected Legislative Assembly took office. Faced with crises at home and abroad, it survived for less than a year. Economic problems fed renewed turmoil. Assignats (AS ig nats), the revolutionary currency, dropped in value, causing prices to rise rapidly. Uncertainty about prices led to hoarding and caused additional food shortages.

In Paris and other cities, working-class men and women, called **sans-culottes** (sanz koo LAHTS), pushed the revolution into more radical action. They were called sans-culottes, which means "without breeches," because they wore long trousers instead of the fancy knee breeches that upper-class men wore. By 1791, many sans-culottes demanded a **republic**, or government ruled by elected representatives instead of a monarch.

Within the Legislative Assembly, several hostile factions competed for power. The sans-culottes found support among radicals in the Legislative Assembly, especially the Jacobins. A revolutionary political club, the **Jacobins** were mostly middle-class lawyers or intellectuals. They used pamphleteers and sympathetic newspaper editors to advance the republican cause. Opposing the radicals were moderate reformers and political officials who wanted no more reforms at all.

The National Assembly Declares War on Tyranny The radicals soon held the upper hand in the Legislative Assembly. In April 1792, the war of words between French revolutionaries and European monarchs moved onto the battlefield. Eager to spread the revolution and destroy tyranny abroad, the Legislative Assembly declared war first on Austria and then on Prussia, Britain, and other states. The great powers expected to win an easy victory against France, a land divided by revolution. In fact, however, the fighting that began in 1792 lasted on and off until 1815.

Sans-culotte, 1792

✔ **Checkpoint** How did the rest of Europe react to the French Revolution?

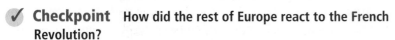

SECTION 2 Assessment

Progress Monitoring *Online*
For: Self-quiz with vocabulary practice
Web Code: naa-1821

Terms, People, and Places

1. For each term, person, or place listed at the beginning of the section, write a sentence explaining its significance.

Note Taking

2. **Reading Skill: Identify Supporting Details** Use your completed outline to answer the Focus Question: What political and social reforms did the National Assembly institute in the first stage of the French Revolution?

Comprehension and Critical Thinking

3. **Make Comparisons** How was the French Declaration of the Rights of Man and the Citizen similar to the American Declaration of Independence?

4. **Summarize** What did the Constitution of 1791 do, and how did it reflect Enlightenment ideas?

5. **Draw Inferences** Describe what happened to France's constitutional monarchy because of the French Revolution.

● **Writing About History**

Quick Write: Create a Flowchart As you prepare to write a cause-and-effect essay, you need to decide how to organize it. To do this, create a flowchart that shows the effects of the French Revolution on other countries. Do you want to write about the events in chronological order? By the importance of each event?

Declaration of the Rights of Man and the Citizen

Painting of the declaration

The National Assembly issued this document in 1789 after having overthrown the established government in the early stages of the French Revolution. The document was modeled in part on the English Bill of Rights and on the American Declaration of Independence. The basic principles of the French declaration were those that inspired the revolution, such as the freedom and equality of all male citizens before the law. The Articles below identify additional principles.

Therefore the National Assembly recognizes and proclaims, in the presence and under the auspices[1] of the Supreme Being, the following rights of man and of the citizen:

1. Men are born and remain free and equal in rights. Social distinctions may be founded only upon the general good.

2. The aim of all political association is the preservation of the natural and imprescriptible[2] rights of man. These rights are liberty, property, security, and resistance to oppression. . . .

4. Liberty consists in the freedom to do everything which injures no one else. . . .

5. Law can only prohibit such actions as are hurtful to society. . . .

6. Law is the expression of the general will. Every citizen has a right to participate personally, or through his representative, in its formation. It must be the same for all, whether it protects or punishes. All citizens, being equal in the eyes of the law, are equally eligible to all dignities and to all public positions and occupations, according to their abilities, and without distinction except that of their virtues and talents.

7. No person shall be accused, arrested, or imprisoned except in the cases and according to the forms prescribed by law. . . .

11. The free communication of ideas and opinions is one of the most precious of the rights of man. Every citizen may, accordingly, speak, write, and print with freedom. . . .

13. A common contribution is essential for the maintenance of the public [military] forces and for the cost of administration. This should be equitably distributed among all the citizens in proportion to their means.

Thinking Critically

1. **Summarize** Summarize article 6. Why is this article especially significant?

2. **Identify Central Issues** What central idea does this declaration share with the American Declaration of Independence?

1. **auspices** (AWS puh siz) *n.* approval and support
2. **imprescriptible** (im prih SKRIP tuh bul) *adj.* that which cannot be rightfully taken away

Marie Antoinette transported by cart to the guillotine

WITNESS HISTORY ◀ �)) AUDIO

The Engine of Terror

A new execution device called the guillotine was introduced during this phase of the revolution. With its large, diagonal blade that came crashing down from a great height, it cut off heads swiftly and accurately. Thousands of people were sent to the guillotine and executed without trial. In his novel *A Tale of Two Cities*, Charles Dickens describes daily life during the Reign of Terror:

❝ Along the Paris streets, the death-carts rumble, hollow and harsh. Six tumbrils [carts that carried condemned persons to the guillotine] carry the day's wine to La Guillotine. ❞

Focus Question What events occurred during the radical phase of the French Revolution?

Radical Days of the Revolution

 Performance Standards

- **SSWH14b** Identify the causes and results of revolution in France.

Terms, People, and Places

suffrage	Napoleon
Robespierre	nationalism
Reign of Terror	Marseilles
guillotine	

N**ote Taking**

Reading Skill: Recognize Sequence Make a timeline like the one shown here. Add dates and important events as you read this section.

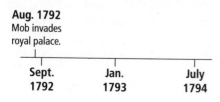

Aug. 1792
Mob invades
royal palace.

Sept.	Jan.	July
1792	1793	1794

In 1793, the revolution entered a radical phase. For a year, France experienced one of the bloodiest regimes in its long history as determined leaders sought to extend and preserve the revolution.

The Monarchy Is Abolished

As the revolution continued, dismal news about the war abroad heightened tensions. Well-trained Prussian forces were cutting down raw French recruits. In addition, royalist officers were deserting the French army, joining émigrés and others hoping to restore the king's power.

Tensions Lead to Violence Battle disasters quickly inflamed revolutionaries who thought the king was in league with the enemies. On August 10, 1792, a crowd of Parisians stormed the royal palace of the Tuileries and slaughtered the king's guards. The royal family fled to the Legislative Assembly, escaping before the mob arrived.

A month later, citizens attacked prisons that held nobles and priests accused of political offenses. About 1,200 prisoners were killed; among them were many ordinary criminals. Historians disagree about the people who carried out the "September massacres." Some call them bloodthirsty mobs. Others describe them as patriots defending France from its enemies. In fact, most were ordinary citizens fired to fury by real and imagined grievances.

Radicals Take Control and Execute the King Backed by Paris crowds, radicals then took control of the Assembly. Radicals

Chivas Vodka chon

Vocabulary Builder

radical—(RAD ih kul) *adj.* extreme; departure from the usual or traditional

called for the election of a new legislative body called the National Convention. **Suffrage,** the right to vote, was to be extended to all male citizens, not just to property owners.

The Convention that met in September 1792 was a more radical body than earlier assemblies. It voted to abolish the monarchy and establish a republic—the French Republic. Deputies then drew up a new constitution for France. The Jacobins, who controlled the Convention, set out to erase all traces of the old order. They seized lands of nobles and abolished titles of nobility.

During the early months of the Republic, the Convention also put Louis XVI on trial as a traitor to France. The king was convicted by a single vote and sentenced to death. On a foggy morning in January 1793, Louis mounted a scaffold in a public square in Paris. He started to speak, "Frenchmen, I die innocent. I pardon the authors of my death. I pray God that the blood about to be spilt will never fall upon the head of France. . . ." Then a roll of drums drowned out his words. Moments later, the king was beheaded. The executioner lifted the king's head by its hair and held it before the crowd.

In October, Marie Antoinette was also executed. The popular press celebrated her death. The queen, however, showed great dignity as she went to her death.

✔ **Checkpoint** What occurred after radicals took control of the Assembly?

■ **COMPARING VIEWPOINTS**

On the Execution of a King

On January 21, 1793, King Louis XVI of France was executed by order of the National Convention. Reaction to this event was both loud and varied throughout Europe. The excerpts below present two different views on this event. **Critical Thinking** *Which of the two viewpoints makes a better case for or against the execution of King Louis XVI? Cite examples from both statements to support your argument.*

For the Execution

The crimes of Louis XVI are unhappily all too real; they are consistent; they are notorious. Do we even have to ask the question of whether a nation has the right to judge, and execute, its highest ranking public official . . . when, to more securely plot against the nation, he concealed himself behind a mask of hypocrisy? Or when, instead of using the authority confided to him to protect his countrymen, he used it to oppress them? Or when he turned the laws into an instrument of violence to crush the supporters of the Revolution? Or when he robbed the citizens of their gold in order to subsidize their foes, and robbed them of their subsistence in order to feed the barbarian hordes who came to slaughter them? Or when he created monopolies in order to create famine by drying up the sources of abundance so that the people might die in misery and hunger? . . .

—Jean-Paul Marat

Against the Execution

The Republican tyrants of France have now carried their bloody purposes to the uttermost diabolical stretch of savage cruelty. They have murdered their King without even the shadow of justice, and of course they cannot expect friendship nor intercourse with any civilized part of the world. The vengeance of Europe will now rapidly fall on them; and, in process of time, make them the veriest wretches on the face of the earth. The name of Frenchman will be considered as the appellation of savage, and their presence shunned as a poison, deadly destructive to the peace and happiness of Mankind. It appears evident, that the majority of the National Convention, and the Executive Government of that truly despotic country, are comprised of the most execrable villains upon the face of the earth. . . .

—*London Times,* January 25, 1793

Terror and Danger Grip France

By early 1793, danger threatened France on all sides. The country was at war with much of Europe, including Britain, the Netherlands, Spain, and Prussia. In the Vendée (vahn DAY) region of France, royalists and priests led peasants in rebellion against the government. In Paris, the sans-culottes demanded relief from food shortages and inflation. The Convention itself was bitterly divided between Jacobins and a rival group, the Girondins.

The Convention Creates a New Committee To deal with the threats to France, the Convention created the Committee of Public Safety. The 12-member committee had almost absolute power as it battled to save the revolution. The Committee prepared France for all-out war, issuing a *levée en masse,* or mass levy (tax) that required all citizens to contribute to the war effort. In addition, the 12 members of the Committee were in charge of trials and executions.

Spurred by revolutionary fervor, French recruits marched off to defend the republic. Young officers developed effective new tactics to win battles with masses of ill-trained but patriotic forces. Soon, French armies overran the Netherlands. They later invaded Italy. At home, they crushed peasant revolts. European monarchs shuddered as the revolutionaries carried "freedom fever" into conquered lands.

Robespierre "the Incorruptible" At home, the government battled counterrevolutionaries under the guiding hand of Maximilien Robespierre (ROHBZ pyehr). Robespierre, a shrewd lawyer and politician, quickly rose to the leadership of the Committee of Public Safety. Among Jacobins, his selfless dedication to the revolution earned him the nickname "the incorruptible." The enemies of Robespierre called him a tyrant.

Robespierre had embraced Rousseau's idea of the general will as the source of all legitimate law. He promoted religious toleration and wanted to abolish slavery. Though cold and humorless, he was popular with the sans-culottes, who hated the old regime as much as he did. He believed that France could achieve a "republic of virtue" only through the use of terror, which he coolly defined as nothing more than "prompt, severe, inflexible justice." "Liberty cannot be secured," Robespierre cried, "unless criminals lose their heads."

The Guillotine Defines the Reign of Terror Robespierre was one of the chief architects of the **Reign of Terror**, which lasted from September 1793 to July 1794. Revolutionary courts conducted hasty trials. Spectators greeted death sentences with cries of "Hail the Republic!" or "Death to the traitors!"

In a speech given on February 5, 1794, Robespierre explained why the terror was necessary to achieve the goals of the revolution:

Primary Source

66 It is necessary to stifle the domestic and foreign enemies of the Republic or perish with them. . . . The first maxim of our politics ought to be to lead the people by means of reason and the enemies of the people by terror. . . . If the basis of popular government in time of peace is virtue, the basis of popular government in time of revolution is both virtue and terror. 99
—Maximilien Robespierre, quoted in *Pageant of Europe* (Stearns)

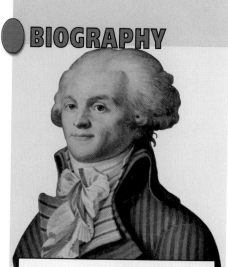

BIOGRAPHY

Robespierre

Maximilien Robespierre (1758–1794) did not have an easy childhood. His mother died when he was only 6 years old. Two years later, his father abandoned him and his three siblings. The children's aunts and grandfather then raised them. Because of this, Robespierre assumed responsibilities at an early age. Eventually, he went to study law at the University of Paris. His performance was so noteworthy that he was chosen to deliver a speech to Louis XVI on the occasion of the king's coronation. But young Robespierre was snubbed. After listening to the address in a pouring rainstorm, the king and queen left without acknowledging Robespierre in any way. Years later, in 1789, Robespierre was elected to the Estates-General, where his career as a revolutionary began. **How do you think Robespierre's early life might have influenced his political ideas?**

Suspect were those who resisted the revolution. About 300,000 were arrested during the Reign of Terror. Seventeen thousand were executed. Many were victims of mistaken identity or were falsely accused by their neighbors. Many more were packed into hideous prisons, where deaths from disease were common.

The engine of the Terror was the **guillotine** (GIL uh teen). Its fast-falling blade extinguished life instantly. A member of the legislature, Dr. Joseph Guillotin (gee oh TAN), had introduced it as a more humane method of beheading than the uncertain ax. But the guillotine quickly became a symbol of horror.

Within a year, the Terror consumed those who initiated it. Weary of bloodshed and fearing for their own lives, members of the Convention turned on the Committee of Public Safety. On the night of July 27, 1794, Robespierre was arrested. The next day he was executed. After the heads of Robespierre and other radicals fell, executions slowed dramatically.

✔ **Checkpoint** Why did Robespierre think the Terror was necessary to achieve the goals of the revolution?

The Revolution Enters Its Third Stage

In reaction to the Terror, the revolution entered a third stage. Moving away from the excesses of the Convention, moderates produced another constitution, the third since 1789. The Constitution of 1795 set up a five-

● **INFOGRAPHIC**

THE REIGN OF TERROR

From autumn 1793 to midsummer 1794, the revolution in France was overshadowed by a time of terror as the Committee of Public Safety rounded up "suspected persons" all over France. Only about 15 percent of those sentenced to death by guillotine (model at left) were of the nobility and clergy. Most were artisans and peasants of the Third Estate. Prisons in Paris—which included places such as former mansions and palaces, religious premises, and colleges—became more and more crowded as the number of suspects increased. Once sentenced to death, the condemned might travel an hour to the guillotine by cart as onlookers threw mud at them.

Thieves stole ▲ items such as silver as émigrés fled the country due to the Terror.

◄ Interrogation of aristocratic prisoners at L'Abbaye prison

man Directory and a two-house legislature elected by male citizens of property. The middle class and professional people of the bourgeoisie were the dominant force during this stage of the French Revolution. The Directory held power from 1795 to 1799.

Weak but dictatorial, the Directory faced growing discontent. Peace was made with Prussia and Spain, but war with Austria and Great Britain continued. Corrupt leaders lined their own pockets but failed to solve pressing problems. When rising bread prices stirred hungry sans-culottes to riot, the Directory quickly suppressed them. Another threat to the Directory was the revival of royalist feeling. Many émigrés were returning to France, and devout Catholics, who resented measures that had been taken against the Church, were welcoming them. In the election of 1797, supporters of a constitutional monarchy won the majority of seats in the legislature.

As chaos threatened, politicians turned to **Napoleon** Bonaparte, a popular military hero who had won a series of brilliant victories against the Austrians in Italy. The politicians planned to use him to advance their own goals. To their dismay, however, before long Napoleon would outwit them all to become ruler of France.

✔ **Checkpoint** What changes occurred after the Reign of Terror came to an end?

History Interactive

For: Interactive French Revolution
Web Code: nap-1821

◀ People never knew if friends or family might appear on a list of guillotine victims. There is some debate on the humanee-ness of death by guillotine. Some authorities claim that even after the head has been severed, the victim could remain conscious for up to 30 seconds.

Georges Danton, ▶ a Revolutionary leader, challenged the Terror and was guillotined.

◀ This engraving depicts Robespierre's execution by guillotine. His was not the last. "Twenty minutes later, [those condemned for the day] were in front of the scaffold.... Pale, tense, shivering... several of them lowered their heads or shut their eyes.... The third [victim] was...the Princess of Monaco.... On the platform, her youthful beauty shone in the dazzling July light." The executioners then tossed the bodies and heads into large baskets near the scaffold.

Thinking Critically
1. **Identify Point of View** What were the goals of the Committee of Public Safety?
2. **Predict Consequences** How do you think life in France changed after the Terror came to an end?

Revolution Brings Change

By 1799, the 10-year-old French Revolution had dramatically changed France. It had dislodged the old social order, overthrown the monarchy, and brought the Church under state control.

New symbols such as the red "liberty caps" and the tricolor confirmed the liberty and equality of all male citizens. The new title "citizen" applied to people of all social classes. All other titles were eliminated. Before he was executed, Louis XVI was called Citizen Capet, from the name of the dynasty that had ruled France in the Middle Ages. Elaborate fashions and powdered wigs gave way to the practical clothes and simple haircuts of the sans-culottes.

Nationalism Spreads Revolution and war gave the French people a strong sense of national identity. In earlier times, people had felt loyalty to local authorities. As monarchs centralized power, loyalty shifted to the king or queen. Now, the government rallied sons and daughters of the revolution to defend the nation itself. **Nationalism,** a strong feeling of pride in and devotion to one's country, spread throughout France. The French people attended civic festivals that celebrated the nation and the revolution. A variety of dances and songs on themes of the revolution became immensely popular.

By 1793, France was a nation in arms. From the port city of **Marseilles** (mahr say), troops marched to a rousing new song. It urged the "children of the fatherland" to march against the "bloody banner of tyranny." This song, "La Marseillaise" (mahr say ez), would later become the French national anthem.

Revolutionaries Push For Social Reform Revolutionaries pushed for social reform and religious toleration. They set up state schools to replace religious ones and organized systems to help the poor, old soldiers, and war widows. With a major slave revolt raging in the colony of St. Domingue (Haiti), the government also abolished slavery in France's Caribbean colonies.

French Nationalism
"La Marseillaise" (top) and a revolutionary-period drum (bottom) helped rally the French people.

 Checkpoint What changes occurred in France because of the French Revolution?

Progress Monitoring *Online*
For: Self-quiz with vocabulary practice
Web Code: naa-1831

SECTION 3 Assessment

Terms, People, and Places
1. Place each of the key terms at the beginning of the section into one of the following categories: politics, culture, geography, or technology. Write a sentence for each term explaining your choice.

Note Taking
2. **Reading Skill: Recognize Sequence** Use your completed timeline to answer the Focus Question: What events occurred during the radical phase of the French Revolution?

Comprehension and Critical Thinking
3. **Summarize** Summarize the goals and actions of the Jacobins.
4. **Identify Central Issues** Why was the Committee of Public Safety created?
5. **Recognize Cause and Effect** How did the Reign of Terror cause the National Convention to be replaced by the Directory?
6. **Predict Consequences** How do you think French nationalism affected the war between France and the powers of Europe?

● Writing About History
Quick Write: Provide Elaboration To illustrate each cause and effect of your essay, you should have supporting details, facts, and examples. Choose one of the events below and list as many specific details as possible. Then write a paragraph using the details you listed to explain what caused the event.
• Reign of Terror
• Execution of King Louis XVI
• Creation of the Committee of Public Safety

Art of Revolution

Revolutions have visual chronicles as well as written ones, and in the days before photography, these depictions were often rendered with paint. The French artist Jacques-Louis David (ZHAHK loo EE dah VEED) and the Spanish artist Francisco Goya both portrayed aspects of revolution on canvas, but they had differing viewpoints. David supported the early French Revolution and embraced the revolutionary spirit in his work. Goya, however, was a realist who showed human suffering and the horrors of war in his paintings.

▲ *Napoleon Crossing Mont Saint Bernard,* **Jacques-Louis David, 1801**
Imprisoned after moderates turned against the Reign of Terror, David barely escaped with his life. When Napoleon rose to power, David deftly switched his political allegiance to the new Emperor of France and became one of Bonaparte's chief portraitists. Notice the names carved into the rocks. David included these names of great past rulers to show Napoleon's level of greatness. David's depictions of Napoleon helped cement him as a strong and heroic leader.

▲ *The Third of May, 1808,* **Francisco José de Goya y Lucientes, 1814**
One of the consequences of the French Revolution and Napoleon's rise was that France soon found itself at war with the rest of Europe. Francisco Goya saw firsthand the impact of these wars. Born in northern Spain, he rose to become the official painter of the Spanish court. When Napoleon invaded Spain and deposed its king, Goya chronicled the horrors of the resulting guerrilla warfare.

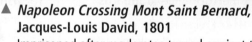

Thinking Critically
1. **Compare Points of View** What elements in each painting express the viewpoint of the artist? How are the elements different?
2. **Recognize Ideologies** How do you think the ideology of the French Revolution led to the scene Goya portrays here?

591

SECTION

4

Unfinished portrait of Napoleon by Jacques-Louis David and Napoleon's signature

Enter Napoleon Bonaparte

After the execution of King Louis XVI, France entered a state of confusion and chaos without a single leader. Meanwhile, Napoleon Bonaparte, a brilliant and ambitious captain in the French army, was rapidly rising in the military ranks. Soon enough, Napoleon would come to rule almost all of Europe. One of his earliest victories in Lodi, Italy, convinced him that he was only just beginning his successful rise to power:

> **❝** From that moment, I foresaw what I might be. Already I felt the earth flee from beneath me, as if I were being carried into the sky.**❞**
> —Napoleon Bonaparte

Focus Question Explain Napoleon's rise to power in Europe, his subsequent defeat, and how the outcome still affects Europe today.

The Age of Napoleon

GA **Performance Standards**

• **SSWH14c** Explain Napoleon's rise to power, the role of geography in Napoleon's defeat, and the consequences of France's defeat for Europe.

Terms, People, and Places

plebiscite	scorched-earth policy
Napoleonic Code	abdicate
annex	Congress of Vienna
Continental System	legitimacy
guerrilla warfare	Concert of Europe

N**o**te Taking

Reading Skill: Identify Main Ideas As you read the section, use a flowchart to list the important events that led from Napoleon's rise to power to his defeat. Add boxes as you need them.

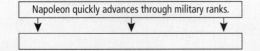

From 1799 to 1815, Napoleon Bonaparte would dominate France and Europe. A hero to some, an evil force to others, he gave his name to the final phase of the revolution—the Age of Napoleon.

Napoleon Rises to Power

Napoleon was born in Corsica, a French-ruled island in the Mediterranean. At age nine, he was sent to France to be trained for a military career. When the revolution broke out, he was an ambitious 20-year-old lieutenant, eager to make a name for himself.

Napoleon favored the Jacobins and republican rule. However, he found the conflicting ideas and personalities of the French Revolution confusing. He wrote to his brother in 1793: "Since one must take sides, one might as well choose the side that is victorious, the side which devastates, loots, and burns. Considering the alternative, it is better to eat than be eaten."

Victories Cloud Losses During the turmoil of the revolution, Napoleon rose quickly in the army. In December 1793, he drove British forces out of the French port of Toulon (too LOHN). He then went on to win several dazzling victories against the Austrians, capturing most of northern Italy and forcing the Hapsburg emperor to make peace. Hoping to disrupt British trade with India, he led an expedition to Egypt in 1798. The Egyptian campaign proved to be a disaster, but Napoleon managed to hide stories of the worst losses from his admirers in France. He did so by establishing a network of spies and censoring the press.

Success fueled Napoleon's ambition. By 1799, he moved from victorious general to political leader. That year, he helped overthrow the weak Directory and set up a three-man governing board known as the Consulate. Another constitution was drawn up, but Napoleon soon took the title First Consul. In 1800, he forced Spain to return Louisiana Territory to France. In 1802, Napoleon had himself named consul for life.

Napoleon Crowns Himself Emperor Two years later, Napoleon had acquired enough power to assume the title Emperor of the French. He invited the pope to preside over his coronation in Paris. During the ceremony, however, Napoleon took the crown from the pope's hands and placed it on his own head. By this action, Napoleon meant to show that he owed his throne to no one but himself.

At each step on his rise to power, Napoleon had held a **plebiscite** (PLEB uh syt), or popular vote by ballot. Each time, the French strongly supported him. As you will read, although the people theoretically had a say in government through their votes, Napoleon still held absolute power. This is sometimes called democratic despotism. To understand why people supported him, we must look at his policies.

 Checkpoint How did Napoleon rise to power so quickly in France?

Napoleon Reforms France

Napoleon consolidated his power by strengthening the central government. Order, security, and efficiency replaced liberty, equality, and fraternity as the slogans of the new regime.

To restore economic prosperity, Napoleon controlled prices, encouraged new industry, and built roads and canals. He set up a system of public schools under strict government control to ensure well-trained officials and military officers. At the same time, Napoleon backed off from some of the revolution's social reforms. He made peace with the Catholic Church in the Concordat of 1801. The Concordat kept the Church under state control but recognized religious freedom for Catholics. Revolutionaries who opposed the Church denounced the agreement, but Catholics welcomed it.

Napoleon won support across class lines. He encouraged émigrés to return, provided they take an oath of loyalty. Peasants were relieved when he recognized their right to lands they had bought from the Church and nobles during the revolution. The middle class, who had benefited most from the revolution, approved of Napoleon's economic reforms and the restoration of order after years of chaos. Napoleon also opened jobs to all, based on talent, a popular policy among those who remembered the old aristocratic monopoly of power.

Among Napoleon's most lasting reforms was a new code of laws, popularly called the **Napoleonic Code.** It embodied Enlightenment principles such as the equality of all citizens before the law, religious toleration, and the abolition of feudalism.

The Egyptian Campaign
The Battle of the Pyramids, July 21, 1798, painted by Louis-Francois Lejeune. *How did Napoleon hide the fact that the Egyptian campaign was a disaster?*

But the Napoleonic Code undid some reforms of the French Revolution. Women, for example, lost most of their newly gained rights and could not exercise the rights of citizenship. Male heads of households regained complete authority over their wives and children. Again, Napoleon valued order and authority over individual rights.

✓ **Checkpoint** What reforms did Napoleon introduce during his rise to power?

Napoleon Builds an Empire

From 1804 to 1812, Napoleon furthered his reputation on the battlefield. He successfully battled the combined forces of the greatest European powers. He took great risks and even suffered huge losses. "I grew up on the field of battle," he once said, "and a man such as I am cares little for the life of a million men." By 1812, his Grand Empire reached its greatest extent.

As a military leader, Napoleon valued rapid movements and made effective use of his large armies. He developed a new plan for each battle so opposing generals could never <u>anticipate</u> what he would do next. His enemies paid tribute to his leadership. Napoleon's presence on the battlefield, said one, was "worth 40,000 troops."

Vocabulary Builder

<u>anticipate</u>—(an TIS uh payt) *vt.* to foresee or expect

The Map of Europe Is Redrawn
As Napoleon created a vast French empire, he redrew the map of Europe. He **annexed,** or incorporated into his empire, the Netherlands, Belgium, and parts of Italy and Germany. He also abolished the tottering Holy Roman Empire and created a 38-member Confederation of the Rhine under French protection. He cut Prussian territory in half, turning part of old Poland into the Grand Duchy of Warsaw.

Napoleon controlled much of Europe through forceful diplomacy. One tactic was placing friends and relatives on the thrones of Europe. For example, after unseating the king of Spain, he placed his own brother, Joseph Bonaparte, on the throne. He also forced alliances on European powers from Madrid to Moscow. At various times, the rulers of Austria, Prussia, and Russia reluctantly signed treaties with the "Corsican ogre," as the monarchs he overthrew called him.

In France, Napoleon's successes boosted the spirit of nationalism. Great victory parades filled the streets of Paris with cheering crowds. The people celebrated the glory and grandeur that Napoleon had gained for France.

Napoleon Strikes Britain
Britain alone, of all the major European powers, remained outside Napoleon's European empire. With only a small army, Britain relied on its sea power to stop Napoleon's drive to rule the continent. In 1805, Napoleon prepared to invade England. But at the Battle of Trafalgar, fought off the southwest coast of Spain, British Admiral Horatio Nelson smashed the French fleet.

With an invasion ruled out, Napoleon struck at Britain's lifeblood, its commerce. He waged economic warfare through the **Continental System,** which closed European ports to British goods. Britain responded with its own blockade of European ports. A blockade involves shutting off ports to keep people or supplies from moving in or out. During their long struggle, both Britain and France seized neutral ships suspected of trading with the other side. British attacks on American ships sparked anger in the United States and eventually triggered the War of 1812.

Legend
- Empire of France
- States dependent on Napoleon
- States allied with Napoleon
- States against Napoleon
- ★ Battle sites, 1800–1815
- ➤ Route of Napoleon's invasion of Russia

Map labels (main map):

10° W · 0° · 20° E · 60° N · 50° N · 40° N · 30° N

SWEDEN
KINGDOM OF NORWAY AND DENMARK
North Sea
Baltic Sea
UNITED KINGDOM OF GREAT BRITAIN AND IRELAND
London
Smolensk · Borodino · Moscow
PRUSSIA · Friedland
Berlin · Warsaw
RUSSIAN EMPIRE
Atlantic Ocean
GRAND DUCHY OF WARSAW
Jena · Leipzig
Waterloo
Paris
CONFEDERATION OF THE RHINE
Austerlitz
Wagram
Versailles
Ulm · Vienna
FRENCH EMPIRE
SWITZ.
AUSTRIAN EMPIRE
Marengo
KINGDOM OF ITALY
Illyrian Provinces
Black Sea
PORTUGAL
Elba
MONTENEGRO
Madrid
Corsica
Adriatic Sea
SPAIN
Rome
KINGDOM OF NAPLES
OTTOMAN EMPIRE
SARDINIA
Balearic Islands
Mediterranean Sea
Cape Trafalgar
SICILY
AFRICA

Conic Projection
0   200   400 mi
0   200   400 km

Bust of Napoleon Bonaparte

Europe Today

Conic Projection
0   200   400 mi
0   200   400 km

Map labels (inset map):

FINLAND
NORWAY · SWEDEN
ESTONIA
RUSSIA
North Sea
LATVIA
Baltic Sea
LITH.
IRELAND
UNITED KINGDOM
DENMARK
RUSSIA
BELARUS
NETH.
GERMANY
POLAND
UKRAINE
BELG.
Atlantic Ocean
CZECH REP.
LUX.
SLOVAKIA
MOLDOVA
FRANCE
SWITZ.
AUSTRIA
HUNGARY
ROMANIA
Black Sea
SLOVENIA
SERB. & MONT.
CROATIA
BULGARIA
PORTUGAL
ITALY
BOS. & HERZ.
TURKEY
Corsica
SPAIN
Sardinia
ALBANIA
MACEDONIA
GREECE
Balearic Is.
Mediterranean Sea
Sicily
Crete
CYPRUS
MALTA

Map Skills Napoleon's empire reached its greatest extent in 1812. Most of the countries in Europe today have different names and borders.

1. **Locate:** (a) French empire, (b) Russian empire, (c) Germany
2. **Region** Locate the Confederation of the Rhine. What is this area called today?
3. **Make Comparisons** Compare Europe of Napoleon's empire to Europe of today on the maps above. How has Europe changed?

In the end, Napoleon's Continental System failed to bring Britain to its knees. Although British exports declined, Britain's powerful navy kept vital trade routes open to the Americas and India. Meanwhile, trade restrictions created a scarcity of goods in Europe, sent prices soaring, and intensified resentment against French power.

French armies under Napoleon spread ideas of the revolution across Europe. They backed liberal reforms in the lands they conquered. In some places, they helped install revolutionary governments that abolished titles of nobility, ended Church privileges, opened careers to men of talent, and ended serfdom and manorial dues. The Napoleonic Code, too, influenced countries in continental Europe and Latin America.

✔ **Checkpoint** How did Napoleon come to dominate most of Europe by 1812?

Napoleon's Empire Faces Challenges

In 1812, Napoleon continued his pursuit of world domination and invaded Russia. This campaign began a chain of events that eventually led to his downfall. Napoleon's final defeat brought an end to the era of the French Revolution.

Nationalism Works Against Napoleon Napoleon's successes contained seeds of defeat. Although nationalism spurred French armies to success, it worked against them too. Many Europeans who had welcomed the ideas of the French Revolution nevertheless saw Napoleon and his armies as foreign oppressors. They resented the Continental System and Napoleon's effort to impose French culture on them.

From Rome to Madrid to the Netherlands, nationalism unleashed revolts against France. In the German states, leaders encouraged national loyalty among German-speaking people to counter French influence.

Spain and Austria Battle the French Resistance to foreign rule bled French-occupying forces dry in Spain. Napoleon introduced reforms that sought to undermine the Spanish Catholic Church. But many Spaniards remained loyal to their former king and devoted to the Church. When the Spanish resisted the invaders, well-armed French forces responded with

As shown in this painting, the Russian winter took its toll on Napoleon's army. Philippe Paul de Ségur, an aide to Napoleon, describes the grim scene as the remnants of the Grand Army returned home. **What were the effects of this disaster in Russia?**

Primary Source

66 In Napoleon's wake [was] a mob of tattered ghosts draped in . . . odd pieces of carpet, or greatcoats burned full of holes, their feet wrapped in all sorts of rags. . . . [We] stared in horror as those skeletons of soldiers went by, their gaunt, gray faces covered with disfiguring beards, without weapons . . . with lowered heads, eyes on the ground, in absolute silence.99
—*Memoirs of Philippe Paul de Ségur*

brutal repression. Far from crushing resistance, however, the French response further inflamed Spanish nationalism. Efforts to drive out the French intensified.

Spanish patriots conducted a campaign of **guerrilla warfare,** or hit-and-run raids, against the French. (In Spanish, *guerrilla* means "little war.") Small bands of guerrillas ambushed French supply trains or troops before retreating into the countryside. These attacks kept large numbers of French soldiers tied down in Spain when Napoleon needed them elsewhere.

Spanish resistance encouraged Austria to resume hostilities against the French. In 1805, at the Battle of Austerlitz, Napoleon had won a crushing victory against an Austro-Russian army of superior numbers. Now, in 1809, the Austrians sought revenge. But once again, Napoleon triumphed—this time at the Battle of Wagram. By the peace agreement that followed, Austria surrendered lands populated by more than three million subjects.

Napoleon Falls From Power
A defeated Napoleon after his abdication on April 6, 1814, in a painting by Paul Delaroche

The Russian Winter Stops the Grand Army

Tsar Alexander I of Russia was once an ally of Napoleon. The tsar and Napoleon planned to divide Europe if Alexander helped Napoleon in his Continental System. Many countries objected to this system, and Russia became unhappy with the economic effects of the system as well. Yet another cause for concern was that Napoleon had enlarged the Grand Duchy of Warsaw that bordered Russia on the west. These and other issues led the tsar to withdraw his support from the Continental System. Napoleon responded to the tsar's action by assembling an army with soldiers from 20 nations, known as the Grand Army.

In 1812, with about 600,000 soldiers and 50,000 horses, Napoleon invaded Russia. To avoid battles with Napoleon, the Russians retreated eastward, burning crops and villages as they went. This **scorched-earth policy** left the French hungry and cold as winter came. Napoleon entered Moscow in September. He realized, though, that he would not be able to feed and supply his army through the long Russian winter. In October, he turned homeward.

The 1,000-mile retreat from Moscow turned into a desperate battle for survival. Russian attacks and the brutal Russian winter took a terrible toll. Fewer than 20,000 soldiers of the once-proud Grand Army survived. Many died. Others deserted. French general Michel Ney sadly concluded: "General Famine and General Winter, rather than Russian bullets, have conquered the Grand Army." Napoleon rushed to Paris to raise a new force to defend France. His reputation for success had been shattered.

✔ **Checkpoint** What challenges threatened Napoleon's empire and what led to the disaster in Russia?

Napoleon Falls From Power

The disaster in Russia brought a new alliance of Russia, Britain, Austria, and Prussia against a weakened France. In 1813, they defeated Napoleon in the Battle of the Nations at Leipzig.

Napoleon Abdicates Briefly The next year, Napoleon **abdicated,** or stepped down from power. The victors exiled him to Elba, an island in the Mediterranean. They then recognized Louis XVIII, brother of Louis XVI, as king of France.

The restoration of Louis XVIII did not go smoothly. He agreed to accept the Napoleonic Code and honor the land settlements made during the revolution. However, many émigrés rushed back to France bent on revenge. An economic depression and the fear of a return to the old regime helped rekindle loyalty to Napoleon.

As the victorious allies gathered in Vienna for a general peace conference, Napoleon escaped his island exile and returned to France. Soldiers flocked to his banner. As citizens cheered Napoleon's advance, Louis XVIII fled. In March 1815, Napoleon entered Paris in triumph.

Crushed at the Battle of Waterloo Napoleon's triumph was short-lived. His star soared for only 100 days, while the allies reassembled their forces. On June 18, 1815, the opposing armies met near the town of Waterloo in Belgium. British forces under the Duke of Wellington and a Prussian army commanded by General Blücher crushed the French in an agonizing day-long battle. Once again, Napoleon was forced to abdicate and to go into exile on St. Helena, a lonely island in the South Atlantic. This time, he would not return.

Napoleon's Legacy Napoleon died in 1821, but his legend lived on in France and around the world. His contemporaries as well as historians today have long debated his legacy. Was he "the revolution on horseback," as he claimed? Or was he a traitor to the revolution?

No one, however, questions Napoleon's impact on France and on Europe. The Napoleonic Code consolidated many changes of the revolution. The France of Napoleon was a centralized state with a constitution. Elections were held with expanded, though limited, suffrage. Many more citizens had rights to property and access to education than under the old regime. Still, French citizens lost many rights promised so fervently by republicans during the Convention.

On the world stage, Napoleon's conquests spread the ideas of the revolution. He failed to make Europe into a French empire. Instead, he sparked nationalist feelings across Europe. The abolition of the Holy Roman Empire would eventually help in creating a new Germany. Napoleon's impact also reached across the

BIOGRAPHY

Prince Clemens von Metternich
As Austria's foreign minister, Metternich (1773–1859) used a variety of means to achieve his goals. In 1809, when Napoleon seemed vulnerable, Metternich favored war against France. In 1810, after France had crushed Austria, he supported alliance with France. When the French army was in desperate retreat from Russia, Metternich became the "prime minister of the coalition" that defeated Napoleon. At the Congress of Vienna, Metternich helped create a new European order and made sure that Austria had a key role in it. He would skillfully defend that new order for more than 30 years. **Why did Metternich's policies toward France change?**

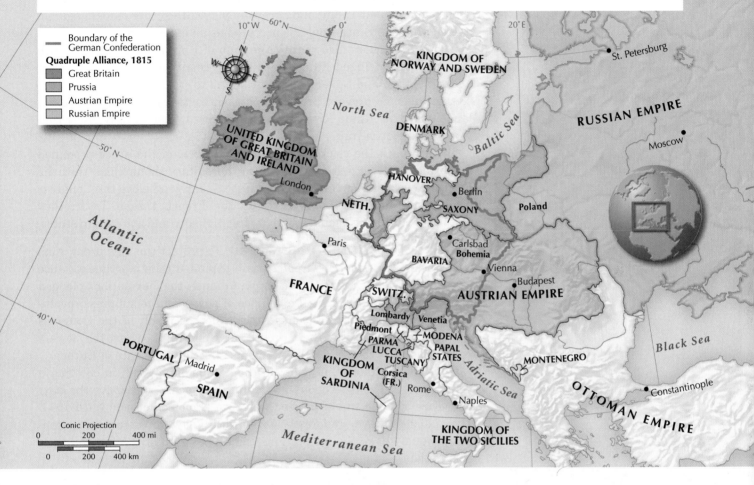

Europe After the Congress of Vienna, 1815

Map Skills At the Congress of Vienna, European leaders redrew the map of Europe in order to contain France and keep a balance of power.

1. **Locate** (a) German Confederation, (b) Netherlands, (c) Vienna
2. **Region** Name three states that were in the German Confederation.
3. **Recognize Cause and Effect** Why did the Congress enlarge some of the countries around France?

Geography *Interactive*
For: Audio guided tour
Web Code: nap-1842

Atlantic. In 1803, his decision to sell France's vast Louisiana Territory to the American government doubled the size of the United States and ushered in an age of American expansion.

✓ **Checkpoint** How did Napoleon impact Europe and the rest of the world?

Leaders Meet at the Congress of Vienna

After Waterloo, diplomats and heads of state again sat down at the **Congress of Vienna.** They faced the monumental task of restoring stability and order in Europe after years of war. The Congress met for 10 months, from September 1814 to June 1815. It was a brilliant gathering of European leaders. Diplomats and royalty dined and danced, attended concerts and ballets, and enjoyed parties arranged by their host, Emperor Francis I of Austria. The work fell to Prince Clemens von Metternich of Austria, Tsar Alexander I of Russia, and Lord Robert Castlereagh of Britain. Defeated France was represented by Prince Charles Maurice de Talleyrand.

Congress Strives For Peace The chief goal of the Vienna decision makers was to create a lasting peace by establishing a balance of power and protecting the system of monarchy. Each of the leaders also pursued his own goals. Metternich, the dominant figure at the Congress, wanted to restore things the way they were in 1792. Alexander I urged a "holy alliance" of Christian monarchs to suppress future revolutions. Lord Castlereagh was determined to prevent a revival of French military power. The aged diplomat Talleyrand shrewdly played the other leaders against one another so France would be accepted as an equal partner.

The peacemakers also redrew the map of Europe. To contain French ambitions, they ringed France with strong countries. In the north, they added Belgium and Luxembourg to Holland to create the kingdom of the Netherlands. To prevent French expansion eastward, they gave Prussia lands along the Rhine River. They also allowed Austria to reassert control over northern Italy.

To turn back the clock to 1792, the architects of the peace promoted the principle of **legitimacy,** restoring hereditary monarchies that the French Revolution or Napoleon had unseated. Even before the Congress began, they had put Louis XVIII on the French throne. Later, they restored "legitimate" monarchs in Portugal, Spain, and the Italian states.

Congress Fails to See Traps Ahead To protect the new order, Austria, Russia, Prussia, and Great Britain extended their wartime alliance into the postwar era. In the Quadruple Alliance, the four nations pledged to act together to maintain the balance of power and to suppress revolutionary uprisings, especially in France. Another result of the Congress was a system known as the **Concert of Europe,** in which the powers met periodically to discuss any problems affecting the peace of Europe.

The Vienna statesmen achieved their immediate goals in creating a lasting peace. Their decisions influenced European politics for the next 100 years. Europe would not see war on a Napoleonic scale until 1914. They failed, however, to foresee how powerful new forces such as nationalism would shake the foundations of Europe and Latin America in the next decades.

 Checkpoint Explain the chief goal and outcome of the Congress of Vienna.

Portrait of Louis XVIII

SECTION 4 **Assessment**

Progress Monitoring Online
For: Self-quiz with vocabulary practice
Web Code: naa-1841

Terms, People, and Places

1. For each term, person, or place listed at the beginning of the section, write a sentence explaining its significance.

Note Taking

2. **Reading Skill: Identify Main Ideas** Use your completed flowchart to answer the Focus Question: Explain Napoleon's rise to power in Europe, his subsequent defeat, and how the outcome still affects Europe today.

Comprehension and Critical Thinking

3. **Demonstrate Reasoned Judgment** If you were a French voter in 1803, how would you have voted on the plebiscite to make Napoleon emperor? Explain.

4. **Synthesize Information** Describe the resistance Napoleon encountered as countries grew to resent him.

5. **Make Comparisons** How does the peacekeeping solution adopted by the Congress of Vienna compare to today's peacekeeping missions?

● Writing About History

Quick Write: Clarify When you write a rough draft of a cause-and-effect essay, you should highlight the causes and effects. Use two highlighters, one to show causes, and the other to show effects. Eliminate causes or effects that do not support your main point, and add transitional phrases as needed. Write a paragraph about Napoleon's downfall. Highlight the causes and effects to evaluate the effectiveness of your paragraph.

THE ESSENTIAL ?

IMPACT OF THE INDIVIDUAL
How can an individual change the world?

In This Chapter GA SSWH14c

Some people have such an effect on history that historians name entire eras after them. During the Napoleonic Era, Napoleon Bonaparte's conquests changed the map of Europe. At the same time, his decision to sell the Louisiana Territory to the United States forever altered the course of American history.

The Louisiana Purchase

OREGON TERRITORY
(Claimed by Russia, the United States and Great Britain)

BRITISH TERRITORY

BRITISH TERRITORY

LOUISIANA PURCHASE
(Sold to the United States by Napoleon, 1803)

SPANISH TERRITORY

UNITED STATES
(in 1783)

ATLANTIC OCEAN

SPANISH TERRITORY

Gulf of Mexico

Throughout History

1700s B.C. Hammurabi sets up the first known code of laws.

500–400s B.C. The teachings of Confucius shape Chinese values.

1400s A.D. Brunelleschi revolutionizes art by finding a way to show perspective.

1517 Luther posts the 95 Theses and ignites the Protestant Reformation.

1558 Elizabeth I of England calms religious turmoil and expands international power.

1920s–1940s Gandhi urges nonviolent protest to win Indian independence from Britain.

Continuing Today

No one knows whose contributions will have the most impact in the years to come. Will it be a political leader? A person of great moral integrity? Or a brilliant scientist? Could it be you?

21st Century Skills

? TRANSFER Activities

1. **Analyze** How have individual people made lasting impacts on history?

2. **Evaluate** How could the small contributions of many individuals have as big an impact as the major contribution of one? Give an example.

3. **Transfer** Complete a Web quest in which you evaluate the impact of an individual; record your thoughts in the Concept Connector Journal; and learn to make a video. Web Code nah-1808

CHAPTER 18

Quick Study Guide

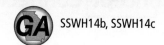

SSWH14b, SSWH14c

Progress Monitoring *Online*
For: Self-test with vocabulary practice
Web Code: naa-1851

■ What Inspired the French Revolution?

- **Social:** Enlightenment ideas such as equality and justice
- **Political:** Ideas from the American Revolution
- **Economic:** Inequalities among classes; unrest due to extravagant monarchy

■ Reforms of the National Assembly

Political
• Proclaimed all male citizens equal before the law.
• Limited the power of the monarchy.
• Established the Legislative Assembly to make laws.
• Granted all tax-paying male citizens the right to elect members of the Legislative Assembly.

Social and Economic
• Abolished special privileges of the nobility.
• Announced an end to feudalism.
• Called for taxes to be levied according to ability to pay.
• Abolished guilds and forbade labor unions.
• Compensated nobles for lands seized by peasants.

Religious
• Declared freedom of religion.
• Took over and sold Church lands.
• Placed the French Catholic Church under control of the state.
• Provided that bishops and priests be elected and receive government salaries.

■ Causes and Effects of the French Revolution

Cause and Effect	
Long-Term Causes	**Immediate Causes**
• Corrupt and inconsistent leadership • Prosperous members of Third Estate resent privileges of First and Second Estates. • Spread of Enlightenment ideas	• Huge government debt • Poor harvests and rising price of bread • Failure of Louis XVI to accept financial reforms • Formation of National Assembly • Storming of Bastille

The French Revolution

Immediate Effects	Long-Term Effects
• Declaration of the Rights of Man and the Citizen adopted. • France adopts its first written constitution. • Revolutionary France fights coalition of European powers. • Monarchy abolished; execution of king and queen. • Reign of Terror	• Napoleon gains power. • Napoleonic Code established. • French public schools set up. • French conquests spread nationalism. • Congress of Vienna convenes to restore stability to Europe. • Revolutions occur elsewhere in Europe and in Latin America.

Connections to Today
• French law reflects Napoleonic Code. • France eventually became a democratic republic.

■ Key Events From 1789–1815

Chapter Events

1789
Parisians storm the Bastille on July 14, starting the French Revolution.

1793
Radicals execute the king and queen, which leads to the Reign of Terror.

1799
Napoleon overthrows the Directory.

Global Events

1790   **1795**   **1800**

1789
The United States Constitution is ratified.

1793
China rejects British trade offer.

Concept Connector

Essential Question Review

To connect prior knowledge with what you have learned in this chapter, answer the questions below in your Concept Connector journal. Use the journal in the Reading and Note Taking Study Guide to record your answers (or go to www.phschool.com **Web Code: nad-1807**). In addition, record information about the following concept:

- Cooperation: Coalitions against Napoleon

1. **Nationalism** During the French Revolution, the people were inspired to rally to the cause of freedom. How did the leaders of the revolution motivate people? Consider the following.
   - songs
   - symbols
   - slogans

2. **Revolution** In 1524, German peasants rose up against the nobility in an effort to end serfdom. They hoped for but did not get the support of Martin Luther. The German nobility put down the rebellion and killed thousands of people. In the French Revolution, the Third Estate revolted against the Old Regime. Describe how the circumstances around the French Revolution were similar to and different from the Peasants' Revolt in Germany.

3. **Democracy** According to the text, "Napoleon's successes contained seeds of defeat." His conquests unleashed feelings of nationalism that led conquered countries to revolt against France. How did Napoleon strengthen democracy in France? How did he weaken democratic gains made during earlier phases of the Revolution? Focus on the following:
   - economic reforms
   - legal reforms
   - natural rights

■ Connections to Today

1. **Geography's Impact: Wars in the Middle East** Geography played an important role in Napoleon's defeat in Russia. Napoleon's Grand Army, once nearly 500,000 soldiers strong, shrank to about 20,000 due to the brutal Russian winter. Research newspaper and magazine articles to find how geography has impacted wars in the Middle East. Compile your research and write a script for your local newscast. Consider the following:
   - location
   - landforms
   - climate

Burning oil pipeline, September 14, 2004, caused by sabotage in the Middle East

2. **Cooperation: United Nations** Diplomats and heads of states from the powers that defeated Napoleon—Austria, Russia, Prussia, and Great Britain—gathered at the Congress of Vienna in 1814. Their main goal was to restore peace after the French Revolution and Napoleonic era. Today, U.N. peacekeeping operations take place around the globe with the same goal of keeping or restoring peace. Research to find more information on the Congress of Vienna and U.N. peacekeeping operations. Draw a table to write facts about each in individual columns. Think about the following:
   - history and purpose of the organizations
   - definitions of "peacekeeping"

1804
Napoleon crowns himself emperor of France.

1812
Napoleon invades Russia.

1814
Congress of Vienna meets.

1815
Napoleon is defeated at Waterloo.

1805   1810   1815

1804
Haiti declares independence from France.

1812
The United States declares war on Britain.

History Interactive
For: Interactive timeline
Web Code: nap-1801

Chapter Assessment

Terms, People, and Places

Match the following terms with the definitions below.

sans-culotte	Olympe de Gouges
bourgeoisie	plebiscite
Napoleonic Code	deficit spending
abdicate	Maximilien Robespierre
Estates-General	nationalism

1. a meeting of the representatives of the three estates
2. situation in which a government spends more money than it takes in
3. strong feeling of devotion to one's country
4. the middle class
5. journalist who demanded equal rights for women
6. leader of the Committee of Public Safety
7. ballot in which voters have a direct say on an issue
8. working-class men and women in France; means "without breeches"
9. law code that embodied Enlightenment principles such as equality
10. step down from power

Main Ideas

Section 1 (pp. 572–577)
11. What caused discontent in the old French regime?
12. When the Estates-General convened in May 1789, what actions did members of the Third Estate take and why?

Section 2 (pp. 578–584)
13. Describe one reform that the National Assembly enacted through each of the following documents: **(a)** the Declaration of the Rights of Man and the Citizen, **(b)** the Civil Constitution of the Clergy, **(c)** the Constitution of 1791.

Section 3 (pp. 585–591)
14. What was the Reign of Terror?

Section 4 (pp. 592–601)
15. List the reforms that Napoleon made as leader of France.
16. How did the Congress of Vienna try to restore the balance of power in Europe?

Chapter Focus Question
17. What were the causes and effects of the French Revolution, and how did the revolution lead to the Napoleonic era?

Critical Thinking

18. **Draw Conclusions** What impact did Enlightenment ideas have on the French Revolution?
19. **Recognize Cause and Effect** Explain the events that led to the end of the monarchy.
20. **Geography and History** How did the geography of the Russian empire work against Napoleon's Grand Army?
21. **Analyzing Cartoons** In the cartoon shown here, the figure on the left represents the British, and the other figure represents Napoleon. What are the figures carving, and why?

Writing About History

In this chapter's four Section Assessments, you developed skills for writing an expository essay.

Expository Essay: Cause and Effect There were many key events in the French Revolution and Napoleonic era that affected France and the rest of the world. Write an essay that explains the causes of one of the following events and discuss what resulted: Parisians storming the Bastille; Women marching on Versailles; Napoleon crowning himself emperor of the French. Consult page SH10 of the Writing Handbook for additional help.

Prewriting
• Consider what you know about these events and choose one that you think best shows cause and effect.

• Take time to research facts, descriptions, and examples, to clearly illustrate the causes and effects in your essay.

Drafting
• Choose one of the following to organize the causes and effects in your essay: show the chronological order of events, or order the events from the least important to the most important.
• As you draft your essay, illustrate each cause and effect with supporting facts and details.

Revising
• Review your entire draft to ensure you show a clear relationship between the causes and effects.
• Analyze each paragraph to check that you have provided a thorough set of facts and details.

Prepare for the GHSGT

Storming the Bastille

One of the most famous and dramatic moments of the French Revolution was the storming of the Bastille. This prison fortress with 90-foot-high walls symbolized the injustices of absolute monarchy. The following documents describe the event from different viewpoints.

Document A

"Shouts of 'Give us the Bastille' were heard, and nine hundred had pressed into the undefended outer courtyard, becoming angrier by the minute. . . . At about half past three in the afternoon the crowd was reinforced by companies of *gardes françaises* [French guards] and by defecting soldiers, including a number who were veterans of the American campaign. Two in particular, Second-Lieutenant Jacob Elie, the standard-bearer of the Infantry of the Queen, and Pierre-Augustin Hulin, the director of the Queen's laundry, were crucial in turning the incoherent assault into an organized siege."

—From ***Citizens: A Chronicle of the French Revolution,*** (1989) by Simon Schama

Document B

"How much the greatest event it is that ever happened in the world! and how much the best!"

—**Letter, July 30, 1789,** by Charles James Fox (1749–1806), British politician, on the fall of the Bastille

Document C

"The mob came closer and the governor declared his willingness to capitulate [give up]. . . The streets and houses, even the roofs were filled with people abusing and cursing me. Daggers, bayonets, pistols were constantly pointed at me. I did not know how I would be killed but was sure my last hour had come. Those who had no arms were throwing stones at me, the women wrenched their teeth and threatened me with their fists. Two soldiers behind me had already been killed by the furious mob and I am convinced I could not have reached City Hall had not one officer . . . escorted me."

—**"Reports of the Taking of the Bastille, July 14, 1789, by One of Its Defenders"** (1834) by Ludwig von der Fluhe (Swiss officer)

Document D

▼ *Demolition of the Bastille, 1789*

Analyzing Documents

Use your knowledge of the storming of the Bastille and Documents A, B, C, and D to answer questions 1–4.

1. In Document B, Charles James Fox was mostly likely enthusiastic about the fall of the Bastille because
   A he had a personal grudge against prison guards.
   B the people stood up to authority.
   C he supported King Louis XVI.
   D he was anxious to see what the people of France would do next.

2. Which document attempts to give an objective view of the storming of the Bastille?
   A Document B
   B Document A
   C Document C
   D Document D

3. In Document C, which words best indicate which side the author is on?
   A the governor declared his willingness to capitulate
   B daggers, bayonets, pistols
   C even the roofs were filled with people
   D furious mob

4. **Writing Task** Compare the four documents. Which lasting document best conveys the significance of the event? Use your knowledge of this event and specific evidence from the documents to support your opinion.

A Different Kind of Revolution

While the American Revolution and the French Revolution were being fought in the late 1700s, another kind of revolution took hold in Britain. Though not political, this revolution—known as the Industrial Revolution—brought about just as many changes to society. Paul Johnson, historian, describes this time period as "the age, above all in history, of matchless opportunities for penniless men with powerful brains and imaginations." Listen to the Witness History audio to hear more about the start of the Industrial Revolution.

Train ticket, 1830

◀ **On September 27, 1825, the Stockton and Darlington Railway in England became the world's first steam railway to offer passenger and freight service.**

James Watt

GA Performance Standards

Chapter Focus Question What technological, social, economic, and cultural changes occurred as the Industrial Revolution took hold?

Section 1
Dawn of the Industrial Age
SSWH15a

Section 2
Britain Leads the Way
SSWH15a

Section 3
Social Impact of the Industrial Revolution
SSWH15a

Socialist leaflet

Section 4
New Ways of Thinking
SSWH15a

Use the ☑ **Quick Study Timeline** at the end of this chapter to preview chapter events.

Concept Connector ONLINE

To explore Essential Questions related to this chapter, go to PHSchool.com
Web Code: nad-1907

Matthew
Boulton

WITNESS HISTORY 🔊 AUDIO

From Hand Power to Steam Power

For centuries, people used their own energy to provide the power for their work. While the idea of using steam power came about in the seventeenth century, it was not until engineer James Watt improved the steam engine that it could be applied to machinery. His financial partner Matthew Boulton, a successful manufacturer, proclaimed:

66 I have at my disposal what the whole world demands, something which will uplift civilization more than ever by relieving man of all undignified drudgery. I have *steam power.* 99

Focus Question What events helped bring about the Industrial Revolution?

Dawn of the Industrial Age

 Performance Standards

• **SSWH15a** Analyze industrialization in England, Germany, and Japan.

Terms, People, and Places

anesthetic
enclosure
James Watt
smelt

Note Taking

Reading Skill: Recognize Multiple Causes
Several key events led to the Industrial Revolution. As you read the section, create a flowchart of these causes. Add categories as needed.

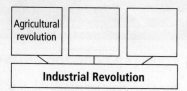

For thousands of years following the rise of civilization, most people lived and worked in small farming villages. However, a chain of events set in motion in the mid-1700s changed that way of life for all time. Today, we call this period of change the Industrial Revolution.

The Industrial Revolution started in Britain. The economic changes that Britain experienced affected people's lives as much as previous political changes and revolutions had. In contrast with most political revolutions, it was neither sudden nor swift. Instead, it was a long, slow, uneven process in which production shifted from simple hand tools to complex machines. From its beginnings in Britain, the Industrial Revolution has spread to the rest of Europe, North America, and around the globe.

Life Changes as Industry Spreads

In 1750, most people worked the land, using handmade tools. They lived in simple cottages lit by firelight and candles. They made their own clothing and grew their own food. In nearby towns, they might exchange goods at a weekly outdoor market.

Like their ancestors, these people knew little of the world that existed beyond their village. The few who left home traveled only as far as their feet or a horse-drawn cart could take them. Those bold adventurers who dared to cross the seas were at the mercy of the winds and tides.

With the onset of the Industrial Revolution, the rural way of life began to disappear. By the 1850s, many country villages had grown into industrial towns and cities. Those who lived there were able to buy clothing and food that someone else produced.

Industrial-age travelers moved rapidly between countries and continents by train or steamship. Urgent messages flew along telegraph wires. New inventions and scientific "firsts" poured out each year. Between 1830 and 1855, for example, an American dentist first used an **anesthetic,** or drug that prevents pain during surgery; an American inventor patented the first sewing machine; a French physicist measured the speed of light; and a Hungarian doctor introduced antiseptic methods to reduce the risk of women dying in childbirth.

Still more stunning changes occurred in the next century, which created our familiar world of skyscraper cities and carefully tended suburbs. How and why did these great changes occur? Historians point to a series of interrelated causes that helped trigger the industrialization of the West. The "West" referred originally to the industrialized countries in Europe but today includes many more.

✔ **Checkpoint** Why was the Industrial Revolution a turning point in world history?

Agriculture Spurs Industry

Oddly enough, the Industrial Revolution was made possible in part by a change in the farming fields of Western Europe. From the first agricultural revolution some 11,000 years ago, when people learned to farm and domesticate animals, until about 300 years ago, farming had remained pretty much the same. Then, a second agricultural revolution took place that greatly improved the quality and quantity of farm products.

Farming Methods Improve The Dutch led the way in this new agricultural revolution. They built earthen walls known as dikes to reclaim land from the sea. They also combined smaller fields into larger ones to make better use of the land and used fertilizer from livestock to renew the soil.

In the 1700s, British farmers expanded on Dutch agricultural experiments. Educated farmers exchanged news of experiments through farm journals. Some farmers mixed different kinds of soils to get higher crop yields. Others tried out new methods of crop rotation. Lord Charles Townshend urged farmers to grow turnips, which restored exhausted soil. Jethro Tull invented a new mechanical device, the seed drill, to aid farmers. It deposited seeds in rows rather than scattering them wastefully over the land.

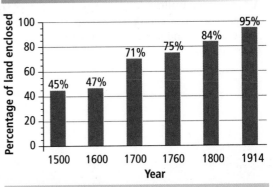

Land Enclosures in England, 1500–1914

Percentage of land enclosed

- 1500: 45%
- 1600: 47%
- 1700: 71%
- 1760: 75%
- 1800: 84%
- 1914: 95%

Year

Graph Skills According to the graph, between which years was the largest percentage of land enclosed? What was the result of these land enclosures?

SOURCE: *Oxford Atlas of World History,* 1999

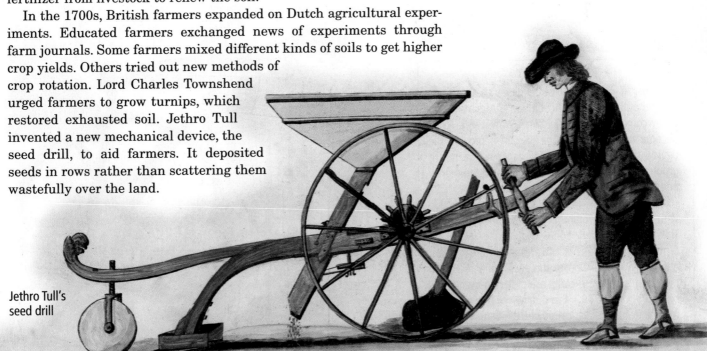

Jethro Tull's seed drill

Enclosure Increases Output but Causes Migration Meanwhile, rich landowners pushed ahead with **enclosure,** the process of taking over and consolidating land formerly shared by peasant farmers. In the 1500s, landowners had enclosed land to gain more pastures for sheep to increase wool output. By the 1700s, they wanted to create larger fields that could be cultivated more efficiently. The British Parliament facilitated enclosures through legislation.

As millions of acres were enclosed, farm output rose. Profits also rose because large fields needed fewer workers. But such progress had a large human cost. Many farm laborers were thrown out of work, and small farmers were forced off their land because they could not compete with large landholders. Villages shrank as cottagers left in search of work. In time, jobless farm workers migrated to towns and cities. There, they formed a growing labor force that would soon tend the machines of the Industrial Revolution.

Population Multiplies The agricultural revolution contributed to a rapid growth of population. Precise population statistics for the 1700s are rare, but those that do exist are striking. Britain's population, for example, soared from about 5 million in 1700 to almost 9 million in 1800. The population of Europe as a whole shot up from roughly 120 million to about 180 million during the same period. Such growth had never before been seen.

Why did this population increase occur? First, the agricultural revolution reduced the risk of death from famine because it created a surplus of food. Since people ate better, they were healthier. Also, better hygiene and sanitation, along with improved medical care, further slowed deaths from disease.

✓ **Checkpoint** How did an agricultural revolution contribute to population growth?

BIOGRAPHY

James Watt

How did a clever Scottish engineer become the "Father of the Industrial Revolution"? After repairing a Newcomen steam engine, James Watt (1736–1819) became fascinated with the idea of improving the device. Within a few months, he knew he had a product that would sell. Still, Watt lacked the money needed to produce and market it.

Fortunately, he was able to form a partnership with the shrewd manufacturer Matthew Boulton. They then founded Soho Engineering Works in Birmingham, England, to manufacture steam engines. Watt's version of the steam engine shown here had a separate condensing chamber and was patented in 1769. Eventually, a measure of mechanical and electrical power, the watt, would be named for James Watt. **How might the Industrial Revolution have been different if Watt had not found a business partner?**

New Technology Becomes Key

Another factor that helped trigger the Industrial Revolution was the development of new technology. Aided by new sources of energy and new materials, these new technologies enabled business owners to change the ways work was done.

An Energy Revolution During the 1700s, people began to harness new sources of energy. One vital power source was coal, used to develop the steam engine. In 1712, British inventor Thomas Newcomen had developed a steam engine powered by coal to pump water out of mines. Scottish engineer **James Watt** looked at Newcomen's invention in 1764 and set out to make improvements on the engine in order to make it more efficient. Watt's engine, after several years of work, would become a key power source of the Industrial Revolution. The steam engine opened the door not only to operating machinery but eventually to powering locomotives and steamships.

The Quality of Iron Improves Coal was also a vital source of fuel in the production of iron, a material needed for the construction of machines and steam engines. The Darby family of Coalbrookdale pioneered new methods of producing iron. In 1709, Abraham Darby used coal instead of charcoal to **smelt** iron, or separate iron from its ore.

Darby's experiments led him to produce less expensive and better-quality iron, which was used to produce parts for the steam engines. Both his son and grandson continued to improve on his methods. In fact, Abraham Darby III built the world's first iron bridge. In the decades that followed, high-quality iron was used more and more widely, especially after the world turned to building railroads.

Abraham Darby III completed the world's first iron bridge in 1779. The bridge still stands today.

 Checkpoint What new technologies helped trigger the Industrial Revolution?

SECTION 1 Assessment

Progress Monitoring Online
For: Self-quiz with vocabulary practice
Web Code: naa-1911

Terms, People, and Places

1. For each term, person, or place listed at the beginning of the section, write a sentence explaining its significance.

Note Taking

2. **Reading Skill: Recognize Multiple Causes** Use your completed flowchart to answer the Focus Question: What events helped bring about the Industrial Revolution?

Comprehension and Critical Thinking

3. **Recognize Cause and Effect** What were the immediate and long-term effects of the agricultural revolution that occurred in the 1700s?

4. **Predict Consequences** How do you think population growth contributed to the Industrial Revolution?

5. **Summarize** Explain how new sources of energy, specifically coal, contributed to the Industrial Revolution.

● Writing About History

Quick Write: Give Background To explain a historical process, you should first orient the reader to time and place. Ask yourself when and where the process occurred. Practice by explaining in one or two sentences how an agricultural revolution led to the Industrial Revolution.

Early train ticket

Train passengers in Britain

WITNESS HISTORY 🔊 AUDIO

Riding the Railway

One of the most important developments of the Industrial Revolution was the creation of a countrywide railway network. The world's first major rail line went from Liverpool to Manchester in England. Fanny Kemble, the most famous actress of the day, was one of the first passengers:

❝We were introduced to the little engine which was to drag us along the rails. . . This snorting little animal, . . . started at about ten miles an hour. . . . You can't imagine how strange it seemed to be journeying on thus, without any visible cause of progress other than the magical machine . . . ❞

Focus Question What key factors allowed Britain to lead the way in the Industrial Revolution?

Britain Leads the Way

 Performance Standards

• **SSWH15a** Analyze industrialization in England, Germany, and Japan.

Terms, People, and Places

capital	Eli Whitney
enterprise	turnpike
entrepreneur	Liverpool
putting-out system	Manchester

Note Taking

Reading Skill: Identify Causes and Effects Fill in the circles of a concept web like the one below with the key factors that helped Britain take an early lead in industrialization. In a separate concept web, fill in the effects of Britain's early lead.

When agricultural practices changed in the eighteenth century, more food was able to be produced, which in turn fueled population growth in Britain. The agricultural changes also left many farmers homeless and jobless. These two factors led to a population boom in the cities as people migrated from rural England into towns and cities. This population increase, in turn, created a ready supply of labor to mine the coal, build the factories, and run the machines. The start of the Industrial Revolution in Britain can be attributed to many factors. Population growth was just one of them.

Why Britain?

What characteristics of eighteenth-century Britain made it ripe for industrialization? Historians cite several reasons for Britain's lead.

Natural Resources Abound Britain had the advantage of plentiful natural resources such as natural ports and navigable rivers. Rivers supplied water power and allowed for the construction of canals. These canals increased accessibility for trade and were instrumental in bringing goods to market. In addition, Britain was able to establish communications and transport relatively cheaply due to its easy accessibility to the sea from all points. Britain's plentiful supply of coal was fundamental to its industrialization and was used to power steam engines. Vast supplies of iron were available to be used to build the new machines.

The Effects of Demand and Capital In the 1700s, Britain had plenty of skilled mechanics who were eager to meet the growing demand for new, practical inventions. This ready workforce, along with the population explosion, boosted demand for goods. In order to increase the production of goods to meet the demand, however, another key ingredient was needed. Money was necessary to start businesses.

From the mid-1600s to 1700s, trade from a growing overseas empire helped the British economy prosper. Beginning with the slave trade, the business class accumulated **capital,** or money used to invest in enterprises. An **enterprise** is a business organization in an area such as shipping, mining, railroads, or factories. Many businessmen were ready to risk their capital in new ventures due to the healthy economy.

In addition to the advantages already cited, Britain had a stable government that supported economic growth. While other countries in Europe faced river tolls and other barriers, Britain did not. The government built a strong navy that protected its empire, shipping, and overseas trade. Although the upper class tended to look down on business people, it did not reject the wealth produced by the new entrepreneurs. These **entrepreneurs** were those who managed and assumed the financial risks of starting new businesses.

✔ **Checkpoint** What conditions in Britain paved the way for the Industrial Revolution?

Shuttle used to speed up weaving process

Geography *Interactive*
For: Audio guided tour
Web Code: nap-1921

Resources and Industries in England, 1750

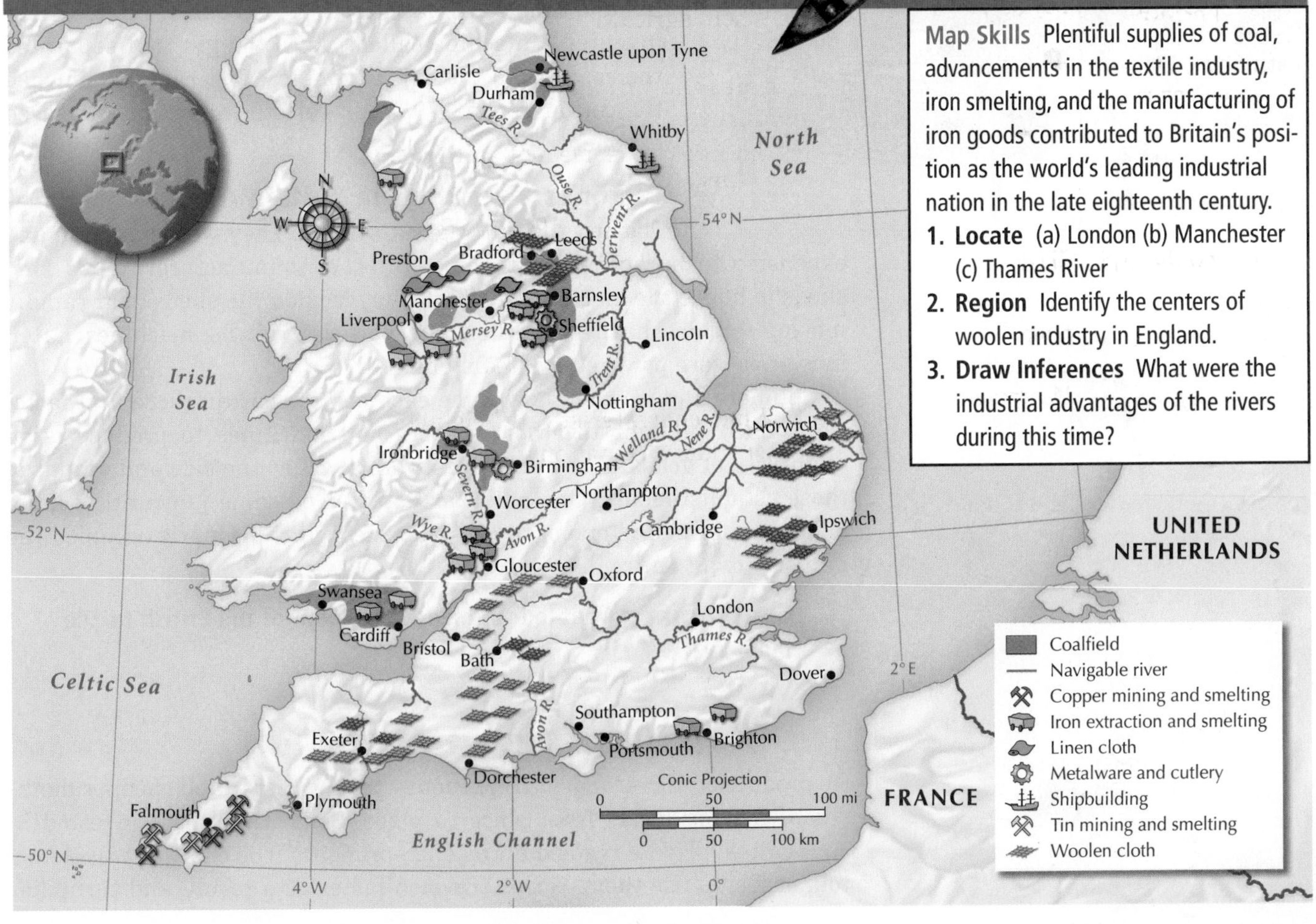

Map Skills Plentiful supplies of coal, advancements in the textile industry, iron smelting, and the manufacturing of iron goods contributed to Britain's position as the world's leading industrial nation in the late eighteenth century.

1. **Locate** (a) London (b) Manchester (c) Thames River
2. **Region** Identify the centers of woolen industry in England.
3. **Draw Inferences** What were the industrial advantages of the rivers during this time?

Legend:
- Coalfield
- Navigable river
- Copper mining and smelting
- Iron extraction and smelting
- Linen cloth
- Metalware and cutlery
- Shipbuilding
- Tin mining and smelting
- Woolen cloth

These textile machines were constructed to increase cotton production. The flying shuttle sped up weaving, while the spinning jenny and the water frame increased the speed of spinning thread. How did these inventions change the textile industry?

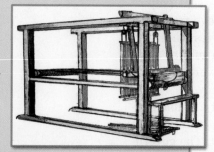

John Kay's flying shuttle, 1733 ▶

◀ James Hargreaves' spinning jenny, 1764

Richard Arkwright's water frame, 1769 ▶

The Textile Industry Advances

The Industrial Revolution first took hold in Britain's largest industry—textiles. In the 1600s, cotton cloth imported from India had become popular. British merchants tried to organize a cotton cloth industry at home. They developed the **putting-out system,** also known as cottage industry, in which raw cotton was distributed to peasant families who spun it into thread and then wove the thread into cloth in their own homes. Skilled artisans in the towns then finished and dyed the cloth.

Inventions Speed Production Under the putting-out system, production was slow. As the demand for cloth grew, inventors came up with a string of remarkable devices that revolutionized the British textile industry. For example, John Kay's flying shuttle enabled weavers to work so fast that they soon outpaced spinners. James Hargreaves solved that problem by producing the spinning jenny in 1764, which spun many threads at the same time. A few years later, in 1769, Richard Arkwright patented the water frame, which was a spinning machine that could be powered by water.

Meanwhile, in America, these faster spinning and weaving machines presented a challenge—how to produce enough cotton to keep up with England. Raw cotton grown in the South had to be cleaned of dirt and seeds by hand, a time-consuming task. To solve this, **Eli Whitney** invented a machine called the cotton gin that separated the seeds from the raw cotton at a fast rate. He finished the cotton gin in 1793, and cotton production increased exponentially.

Factories Are Born in Britain The new machines doomed the putting-out system. They were too large and expensive to be operated at home. Instead, manufacturers built long sheds to house the machines. At first, they located the sheds near rapidly moving streams, harnessing the water power to run the machines. Later, machines were powered by steam engines.

Spinners and weavers now came each day to work in these first factories, which brought together workers and machines to produce large quantities of goods. Early observers were awed at the size and output of these establishments. One onlooker noted: "The same [amount] of labor is now performed in one of these structures which formerly occupied the industry of an entire district."

 Checkpoint   What led to the advancement of the British textile industry?

The Transportation Revolution

As production increased, entrepreneurs needed faster and cheaper methods of moving goods from place to place. Some capitalists invested in **turnpikes,** private roads built by entrepreneurs who charged travelers a toll, or fee, to use them. Goods traveled faster as a result, and turnpikes soon linked every part of Britain. Other entrepreneurs had canals dug to connect rivers together or to connect inland towns with coastal ports. Engineers also built stronger bridges and upgraded harbors to help the expanding overseas trade.

Canals Boom During the late 1700s and early 1800s, factories needed an efficient, inexpensive way to receive coal and raw materials and then to ship finished goods to market. In 1763, when the Bridgewater canal opened, it not only made a profit from tolls, but it cut in half the price of coal in Manchester. The success of this canal set off a canal-building frenzy. Entrepreneurs formed companies to construct canals for profit. Not all the canals that were built had enough traffic to support them, however, and bankruptcy often resulted. Then, beginning in the 1830s, canals lost their importance as steam locomotives made railroads the new preferred form of transportation.

Welcome the Steam Locomotive It was the invention of the steam locomotive that made the growth of railroads possible. In the early 1800s, pioneers like George Stephenson developed steam-powered loco-motives to pull carriages along iron rails. The railroad did not have to fol-low the course of a river. This meant that tracks could go places where rivers did not, allowing factory owners and merchants to ship goods swiftly and cheaply over land. The world's first major rail line, from **Liverpool** to **Manchester,** opened in England in 1830. In the following decades, railroad travel became faster and railroad building boomed. By 1870, rail lines crisscrossed Britain, Europe, and North America.

Vocabulary Builder

decades—(DEK aydz) *n.* ten-year periods

One Thing Leads to Another As the Industrial Revolution got under way, it triggered a chain reaction. Once inventors developed machines that could produce large quantities of goods more efficiently, prices fell. Lower prices made goods more affordable and thus created more con-sumers who further fed the demand for goods. This new cycle caused a wave of economic and social changes that dramatically affected the way people lived.

✔ **Checkpoint** Why was the development of railroads important to industrialization?

Progress Monitoring Online
For: Self-quiz with vocabulary practice
Web Code: naa-1921

SECTION 2 Assessment

Terms, People, and Places

1. For each term, person, or place listed at the beginning of the section, write a sen-tence explaining its significance.

Note Taking

2. **Reading Skill: Identify Causes and Effects** Use your completed concept webs to answer the Focus Question: What key factors allowed Britain to lead the way in the Industrial Revolution?

Comprehension and Critical Thinking

3. **Analyze Information** Explain how each of the following helped contribute to demand for consumer goods in Britain: **(a)** population explosion, **(b)** general economic prosperity.

4. **Determine Relevance** What was the significance of new machines to the tex-tile industry?

5. **Summarize** Explain how advances in transportation contributed to Britain's global trade.

● **Writing About History**

Quick Write: Create a Flowchart Flowcharts are useful tools to help you write an explana-tory essay. Create a flowchart to show the changes that occurred in the textile industry. Be sure that the sequence of events is clear.

Monmouth
Street, London

WITNESS HISTORY 🔊 AUDIO

Stench and Sickness

As more and more people moved to the cities to work, they had little choice about where to live. There was no public water supply, waste lined the unpaved streets, and disease spread rapidly in these unsanitary conditions. Dr. Southwood-Smith worked in two districts of London and wrote:

❝Uncovered sewers, stagnant ditches and ponds, gutters always full of putrefying matter . . . It is not possible for any language to convey an adequate conception of the poisonous condition in which large portions of both these districts always remain, . . . from the masses of putrefying matter which are allowed to accumulate.❞

Focus Question What were the social effects of the Industrial Revolution?

Social Impact of the Industrial Revolution

 Performance Standards

• **SSWH15a** Analyze industrialization in England, Germany, and Japan, and urbanization and its effect on women.

Terms, People, and Places

urbanization
tenement
labor union

Note Taking

Reading Skill: Understand Effects As you read the section, complete a table that lists benefits and challenges of industrialization.

Industrialization	
Benefits	**Challenges**
• Created jobs	• Crowded cities
•	•

The Industrial Revolution brought great riches to most of the entrepreneurs who helped set it in motion. For the millions of workers who crowded into the new factories, however, the industrial age brought poverty and harsh living conditions.

In time, reforms would curb many of the worst abuses of the early industrial age in Europe and the Americas. As standards of living increased, people at all levels of society would benefit from industrialization. Until then, working people would suffer with dangerous working conditions; unsafe, unsanitary, and overcrowded housing; and unrelenting poverty.

People Move to New Industrial Cities

The Industrial Revolution brought rapid **urbanization,** or the movement of people to cities. Changes in farming, soaring population growth, and an ever-increasing demand for workers led masses of people to migrate from farms to cities. Almost overnight, small towns around coal or iron mines mushroomed into cities. Other cities grew up around the factories that entrepreneurs built in once-quiet market towns.

The British market town of Manchester numbered 17,000 people in the 1750s. Within a few years, it exploded into a center of the textile industry. Its population soared to 40,000 by 1780 and 70,000 by 1801. Visitors described the "cloud of coal vapor" that polluted

Population Growth in London, c. 1750–1900

Graph Skills Population increased dramatically as factories sprung up in cities such as London (pictured here). How many more people were in London in 1900 than in 1750 according to the line graph?

SOURCE: *International Historical Statistics, Europe 1750–1993, 1998*

the air, the pounding noise of steam engines, and the filthy stench of its river. This growth of industry and rapid population growth dramatically changed the location and distribution of two resources—labor and people.

✔ **Checkpoint** What led to the massive migration of people from farms to cities?

New Social Classes Emerge

The Industrial Revolution created a new middle class along with the working class. Those in the middle class owned and operated the new factories, mines, and railroads, among other industries. Their lifestyle was much more comfortable than that of the industrial working class.

When farm families moved to the new industrial cities, they became workers in mines or factories. Many felt lost and bewildered. They faced tough working conditions in uncomfortable environments. In time, though, factory and mine workers developed their own sense of community despite the terrible working conditions.

The Industrial Middle Class Those who benefited most from the Industrial Revolution were the entrepreneurs who set it in motion. The Industrial Revolution created this new middle class, or bourgeoisie (boor zhwah ZEE), whose members came from a variety of backgrounds. Some were merchants who invested their growing profits in factories. Others were inventors or skilled artisans who developed new technologies. Some rose from "rags to riches," a pattern that the age greatly admired.

Middle-class families lived in well-furnished, spacious homes on paved streets and had a ready supply of water. They wore fancy clothing and ate well. The new middle class took pride in their hard work and their determination to "get ahead." Only a few had sympathy for the poor. Women of the middle class did not leave the home to work but instead focused their energy on raising their children. This contrasted with the wealthy, who had maidservants to look after their children, and the working class, whose children were a part of the workforce.

The Industrial Working Class While the wealthy and the middle class lived in pleasant neighborhoods, vast numbers of poor struggled to survive in foul-smelling slums. They packed into tiny rooms in **tenements,** or multistory buildings divided into apartments. These tenements had no running water, only community pumps. There was no sewage or sanitation system, so wastes and garbage rotted in the streets. Sewage was also dumped into rivers, which created an overwhelming stench and <u>contaminated</u> drinking water. This led to the spread of diseases such as cholera.

Workers Stage Futile Protests Although **labor unions,** or workers' organizations, were illegal at this time, secret unions did exist among frustrated British workers. They wished to initiate worker reforms, such as increases in pay, but had no political power to effect change. Sometimes their frustration led to violence. The first instances of industrial riots occurred in England from 1811 to 1813. Groups of textile workers known as the Luddites (LUD yts) resisted the labor-saving machines that were costing them their jobs. Some of them smashed textile machines with sledgehammers and burned factories. They usually wore masks and operated at night. There was widespread support among the working class for these Luddite groups.

Workers Find Comfort in Religion Many working-class people found comfort in a religious movement called Methodism. This movement was influenced by the Industrial Revolution as people moved to cities and lost connections with their old churches. John Wesley had founded the Methodist movement in the mid-1700s. Wesley <u>stressed</u> the need for a personal sense of faith. He encouraged his followers to improve themselves by adopting sober, moral ways.

Methodist meetings featured hymns and sermons promising forgiveness of sin and a better life to come. Methodist preachers took this message of salvation into the slums. There, they tried to rekindle hope among the working poor. They set up Sunday schools where followers not only studied the Bible but also learned to read and write. Methodists helped channel workers' anger away from revolution and toward reform.

 Checkpoint How did members of the working class react to their new experiences in industrial cities?

Life in the Factories and Mines

The heart of the new industrial city was the factory. There, the technology of the machine age and the rapid pace of industrialization imposed a harsh new way of life on workers.

Factory Workers Face Harsh Conditions Working in a factory system differed greatly from working on a farm. In rural villages, people worked hard, but their work varied according to the season. Life was also hard for poor rural workers who were part of the putting-out system, but at least they worked at their own pace. In the grim factories of industrial towns, workers faced a rigid schedule set by the factory whistle.

Working hours were long, with shifts lasting from 12 to 16 hours, six or seven days a week. Workers could only take breaks when the factory owners gave permission. Exhausted workers suffered accidents from machines that had no safety devices. They might lose a finger, a limb, or even their lives. In textile mills, workers constantly breathed air filled with lint, which damaged their lungs. Those workers who became sick or injured lost their jobs.

The majority of early factory workers were women rather than men. Employers often preferred to hire women workers because they thought women could adapt more easily to machines and were easier to manage. In addition, employers generally paid women half what they paid men.

Factory work created a double burden for women. Their new jobs took them out of their homes for 12 hours or more a day. They then returned to their tenements, which might consist of one damp room with a single bed. They had to feed and clothe their families, clean, and cope with such problems as sickness and injury.

Miners Face Worse Conditions

The Industrial Revolution increased the demand for iron and coal, which in turn increased the need for miners. Although miners were paid more, working conditions in the mines were even worse than in the factories. They worked in darkness, and the coal dust destroyed their lungs. There were always the dangers of explosions, flooding, and collapsing tunnels. Women and children carted heavy loads of coal, sometimes on all fours in low passages. They also climbed ladders carrying heavy baskets of coal several times a day.

Children Have Dangerous Jobs

Factories and mines also hired many boys and girls. These children often started working at age seven or eight, a few as young as five. Nimble-fingered and quick-moving, they changed spools in the hot and humid textile mills where sometimes they could not see because of all the dust. They also crawled under machinery to repair broken threads in the mills. Conditions were even worse for children who worked in the mines. Some sat all day in the dark, opening

Even children as young as five years old worked in the mines. James Kay-Shuttleworth worked as a physician among the different classes of the Industrial Revolution in Manchester. His profession allowed him to see the working conditions of poor in the cities. How was work in factories and mines different from work on the farm?

Primary Source

66 Whilst the engine runs, people must work—men, women, and children are yoked together with iron and steam. The animal machine is chained fast to the iron machine, which knows no suffering and weariness. 99
—James Kay-Shuttleworth, 1832

and closing air vents. Others hauled coal carts in the extreme heat. Because children had helped with work on the farm, parents accepted the idea of child labor. The wages the children earned were needed to keep their families from starving.

Child labor reform laws called "factory acts" were passed in the early 1800s. These laws were passed to reduce a child's workday to twelve hours and also to remove children under the age of eight or nine from the cotton mills. Because the laws were generally not enforced, British lawmakers formed teams of inspectors to ensure that factories and mines obeyed the laws in the 1830s and 1840s. More laws were then passed to shorten the workday for women and require that child workers be educated.

 Checkpoint How did the Industrial Revolution affect the lives of men, women, and children?

Families could afford to take trips to such places as the zoo as wages increased.

The Results of Industrialization

Since the 1800s, people have debated whether the Industrial Revolution was a blessing or a curse. The early industrial age brought terrible hardships. In time, however, reformers pressed for laws to improve working conditions. Labor unions won the right to bargain with employers for better wages, hours, and working conditions. Eventually working-class men gained the right to vote, which gave them political power.

Despite the social problems created by the Industrial Revolution—low pay, dismal living conditions—the Industrial Age did have some positive effects. As demand for mass-produced goods grew, new factories opened, which in turn created more jobs. Wages rose so that workers had enough left after paying rent and buying food to buy a newspaper or visit a music hall. As the cost of railroad travel fell, people could visit family in other towns. Horizons widened and opportunities increased.

 Checkpoint Why was the Industrial Revolution seen as both a blessing and a curse?

SECTION **3** Assessment

Progress Monitoring Online
For: Self-quiz with vocabulary practice
Web Code: naa-1931

Terms, People, and Places

1. What do each of the key terms listed at the beginning of the section have in common? Explain.

Note Taking

2. **Reading Skill: Understand Effects** Use your completed table to answer the Focus Question: What were the social effects of the Industrial Revolution?

Comprehension and Critical Thinking

3. **Analyze Information** How did the Industrial Revolution affect (a) cities and (b) population distribution?

4. **Synthesize Information** Explain how the Industrial Revolution changed the living conditions for both the middle class and the working class.

5. **Demonstrate Reasoned Judgment** Do you think increases in wages justify harsh working conditions? Why or why not?

● Writing About History

Quick Write: Gather Details When writing an explanatory essay, you should include facts, examples, and descriptions that help explain your topic. Make a list of details to help explain what life was like when people moved from rural areas to the new industrial cities.

Friedrich Engels: *The Condition of the Working Class in England in 1844*

In *The Condition of the Working Class in England in 1844*, Friedrich Engels recorded his observations of the wretched living conditions in poor areas of nineteenth-century England. In this excerpt, Engels describes working-class districts in Manchester. He depicts the misery and filth typical of the living areas of industrial workers.

Friedrich Engels, 1845

The houses are packed very closely together and since the bank of the river is very steep it is possible to see a part of every house. All of them have been blackened by soot, all of them are crumbling with age and all have broken window-panes and window-frames. In the background there are old factory buildings which look like barracks. On the opposite, low-lying bank of the river, one sees a long row of houses and factories. The second house is a roofless ruin, filled with refuse, and the third is built in such a low situation that the ground floor is uninhabitable and has neither doors nor windows. In the background one sees the paupers'[1] cemetery, and the stations of the railways to Liverpool and Leeds. . . .

The recently constructed extension of the Leeds railway which crosses the Irk at this point has swept away some of these courts and alleys, but it has thrown open to public gaze some of the others. So it comes about that there is to be found immediately under the railway bridge a court which is even filthier and more revolting than all the others. This is simply because it was formerly so hidden and secluded that it could only be reached with considerable difficulty [but is now exposed to the human eye]. I thought I knew this district well, but even I would never have found it had not the railway viaduct [elevated roadway] made a breach[2] in the slums at this point. One walks along a very rough path on the river bank, in between clotheposts and washing lines, to reach a chaotic group of little, one-storied, one-roomed cabins. Most of them have earth floors, and working, living and sleeping all take place in the one room. In such a hole, barely six feet long and five feet wide, I saw two beds—and what beds and bedding!—which filled the room, except for the fireplace and the doorstep. Several of these huts, as far as I could see, were completely empty, although the door was open and the inhabitants were leaning against the door posts. In front of the doors filth and garbage abounded. I could not see the pavement, but from time to time I felt it was there because my feet scraped it. . . .

1. **pauper** (PAW pur) *n.* poor person
2. **breach** (breech) *n.* break

Thinking Critically

1. **Draw Inferences** **(a)** How did the development of the railways affect the working-class districts? **(b)** How does Engels feel about the living conditions he observes?
2. **Make Generalizations** What seems to be Engels' general attitude toward the Industrial Revolution?

Workers on
break, London

The Struggle of the Working Class

Karl Marx and Friedrich Engels give their view on how
the Industrial Revolution affected workers:

66Owing to the extensive use of machinery and to
division of labor, the work of the proletarians
has lost all individual character, and, consequently, all charm for the workman. He
becomes [a limb] of the machine, and it is
only the most simple, most monotonous,
and most easily acquired knack, that is
required of him. . . .99
—From *The Communist Manifesto*

Focus Question What new ideas about
economics and society were fostered as a result
of the Industrial Revolution?

New Ways of Thinking

Performance Standards

• **SSWH15a** Analyze the writings of Adam Smith
and Karl Marx.

Terms, People, and Places

Thomas Malthus	Robert Owen
Jeremy Bentham	Karl Marx
utilitarianism	communism
socialism	proletariat
means of production	social democracy

Note Taking

Reading Skill: Identify Main Ideas Write an
outline like the one here to show the new
economic and social theories.

> I. Laissez-faire economics
>   A. Adam Smith and free enterprise
>   1.
>   2.
> II. Malthus on population
>   A.

Everywhere in Britain, British economist **Thomas Malthus** saw
the effects of the population explosion—crowded slums, hungry families, unemployment, and widespread misery. After careful study, in
1798 he published *An Essay on the Principle of Population*. He concluded that poverty was unavoidable because the population was
increasing faster than the food supply. Malthus wrote: "The power of
population is [far] greater than the power of the Earth to produce
subsistence for man."

Malthus was one of many thinkers who tried to understand the
staggering changes taking place in the early Industrial Age. As
heirs to the Enlightenment, these thinkers looked for natural laws
that governed the world of business and economics.

Laissez-Faire Economics

During the Enlightenment, physiocrats argued that natural laws
should be allowed to operate without interference. As part of this philosophy, they believed that government should not interfere in the
free operation of the economy. In the early 1800s, middle-class
business leaders embraced this laissez-faire, or "hands-off," approach.

As you have learned, the main proponent of laissez-faire economics was Adam Smith, author of bestseller *The Wealth of
Nations*. Smith asserted that a free market—the unregulated
exchange of goods and services—would come to help everyone, not
just the rich. The free market, Smith said, would produce more
goods at lower prices, making them affordable to everyone. A
growing economy would also encourage capitalists to reinvest

profits in new ventures. Supporters of this free-enterprise capitalism pointed to the successes of the Industrial Age, in which government had played no part.

Malthus Holds Bleak View Also a laissez-faire economist, Thomas Malthus predicted that population would outpace the food supply. The only checks on population growth, he said, were nature's "natural" methods of war, disease, and famine. As long as population kept increasing, he went on, the poor would suffer. He thus urged families to have fewer children and discouraged charitable handouts and vaccinations.

During the early 1800s, many people accepted Malthus's bleak view as the factory system changed people's lifestyles for the worse. His view was proved wrong, however. Although the population boom did continue, the food supply grew even faster. As the century progressed, living conditions for the Western world slowly improved—and then people began having fewer children. By the 1900s, population growth was no longer a problem in the West, but it did continue to afflict many nations elsewhere.

Ricardo Shares View Another influential British laissez-faire economist, David Ricardo, dedicated himself to economic studies after reading Smith's *The Wealth of Nations*. Like Malthus, Ricardo did not hold out hope for the working class to escape poverty. Because of such gloomy predictions, economics became known as the "dismal science." In his "Iron Law of Wages," Ricardo pointed out that wage increases were futile because increases would only cover the cost of necessities. This was because when wages were high, families often had more children instead of raising the family's current standard of living.

Both Malthus and Ricardo opposed any government help for the poor. In their view, the best cure for poverty was not government relief but the unrestricted "laws of the free market." They felt that individuals should be left to improve their lot through thrift, hard work, and limiting the size of their families.

Population Theory
Thomas Malthus believed poor families should have fewer children to preserve the food supply. *What were the advantages of families with many children?*

✔ **Checkpoint** Explain the response to laissez-faire economics during the nineteenth century.

Utilitarians For Limited Government

Other thinkers sought to modify laissez-faire doctrines to justify some government intervention. By 1800, British philosopher and economist **Jeremy Bentham** was advocating **utilitarianism**, or the idea that the goal of society should be "the greatest happiness for the greatest number" of its citizens. To Bentham, all laws or actions should be judged by their "utility." In other words, did they provide more pleasure or happiness than pain? Bentham strongly supported individual freedom, which he believed guaranteed happiness. Still, he saw the need for government to become involved under certain circumstances.

Bentham's ideas influenced the British philosopher and economist John Stuart Mill. Although he believed strongly in individual freedom, Mill wanted the government to step in to improve the hard lives of the working class. "The only purpose for which power can be rightfully exercised over any member of a civilized community, against his will," Mill wrote, "is to prevent harm to others." Therefore, while middle-class business and factory owners were entitled to increase their own happiness, the government should prevent them from doing so in a manner that would harm workers.

Mill further called for giving the vote to workers and women. These groups could then use their political power to win reforms. Most middle-class people rejected Mill's ideas. Only in the later 1800s were his views

> *The population... is crowded into one dense mass of cottages. ...This is an atmosphere loaded with the exhalation of a large manufacturing city.*
> —J.P. Kay

Owen's Utopia

The poverty and filth of the Industrial Age did not sit well with Robert Owen, a British social reformer. Like other Utopians, he believed there was a way he could change society for the better. To prove his point, he set up his cotton mill in New Lanark, Scotland, as a model village. He insisted that the conditions in which people lived shaped their character. Owen reduced working hours, built homes for workers, started a school for children, and opened a company store where workers could buy food and clothes. He showed that an employer could offer decent living and working conditions and still run a profitable business. Between 1815 and 1825, about 20,000 people visited New Lanark to study Owen's reforms. The complex eventually fell into decline but visitors can still wander the village today.

▲ The Industrial Age brought harsh living conditions and poverty as people crowded into cities.

Thinking Critically
1. **Make Generalizations** Based on the images, how did life for children at New Lanark differ from those who lived in industrial cities?
2. **Recognize Ideologies** Do you think Utopianism was an effective solution for the challenges of the Industrial Age? Why or why not?

> *...[I have never seen] so much order, good government, tranquility, and rational happiness prevail.*
> —Visitor to New Lanark

History *Interactive*

For: Interactive Village
Web Code: nap-1941

▲ Children attended geography classes and dance lessons at the school in New Lanark.

slowly accepted. Today's democratic governments, however, have absorbed many ideas from Mill and the other utilitarians.

 Checkpoint What did John Stuart Mill see as the proper role of government?

Socialist Thought Emerges

While the champions of laissez-faire economics praised individual rights, other thinkers focused on the good of society in general. They condemned the evils of industrial capitalism, which they believed had created a gulf between rich and poor. To end poverty and injustice, they offered a radical solution—**socialism.** Under socialism, the people as a whole rather than private individuals would own and operate the **means of production—** the farms, factories, railways, and other large businesses that produced and distributed goods. Socialism grew out of the Enlightenment faith in progress and human nature and its concern for social justice.

Are Utopians Dreamers? A number of early socialists established communities in which all work was shared and all property was owned in common. When there was no difference between rich and poor, they said, fighting between people would disappear. These early socialists were called Utopians. The name implied that they were impractical dreamers. The Utopian **Robert Owen** set up a model community in New Lanark, Scotland, to put his own ideas into practice.

Owen Establishes a Utopia A poor Welsh boy, Owen became a successful mill owner. Unlike most industrialists at the time, he refused to use child labor. He campaigned vigorously for laws that limited child labor and encouraged the organization of labor unions.

 Checkpoint What did early socialists believe?

Karl Marx Calls for Worker Control

In the 1840s, **Karl Marx,** a German philosopher, condemned the ideas of the Utopians as unrealistic idealism. He <u>formulated</u> a new theory, "scientific socialism," which he claimed was based on a scientific study of history. He teamed up with another German socialist, Friedrich Engels, whose father owned a textile factory in England.

Marx and Engels wrote a pamphlet, *The Communist Manifesto*, which they published in 1848. "A spectre [ghost] is haunting Europe," it began, "the spectre of communism." Marx predicted a struggle between social classes that would lead to a classless society where all means of production would be owned by the community. In practice, however, **communism** later came to refer to a system in which governments led by a small elite controlled all economic and political life.

In *The Communist Manifesto*, Marx theorized that economics was the driving force in history. He argued that there was "the history of class struggles" between the "haves" and the "have-nots." The "haves" had always owned the means of production and thus controlled society and all its wealth. In industrialized Europe, Marx said, the "haves" were the bourgeoisie. The "have-nots" were the **proletariat,** or working class.

According to Marx, the modern class struggle pitted the bourgeoisie against the proletariat. In the end, he predicted, the proletariat would be

Vocabulary Builder

<u>formulated</u>—(FAWR myoo layt id) *vt.* devised or developed, as in a theory or plan

triumphant. Workers would then take control of the means of production and set up a classless, communist society. Such a society would mark the end of the struggles people had endured throughout history, because wealth and power would be equally shared. Marx despised capitalism. He believed it created prosperity for only a few and poverty for many. He called for an international struggle to bring about its downfall. "Workers of all countries," he urged, "unite!"

✓ **Checkpoint** What did Marx predict was the future of the proletariat?

Marxism in the Future

At first, Marxism gained popularity with many people around the world. Leaders of a number of reform movements adopted the idea that power should be held by workers rather than by business owners. Marx's ideas, however, would never be practiced exactly as he imagined.

Marxism Briefly Flourishes In the 1860s, German socialists adapted Marx's beliefs to form **social democracy,** a political ideology in which there is a gradual transition from capitalism to socialism instead of a sudden violent overthrow of the system. In the late 1800s, Russian socialists embraced Marxism, and the Russian Revolution of 1917 set up a communist-inspired government. For much of the 1900s, revolutionaries around the world would adapt Marxist ideas to their own situations and needs. Independence leaders in Asia, Latin America, and Africa would turn to Marxism.

Marxism Loses Appeal As time passed, however, the failures of Marxist governments would illustrate the flaws in Marx's arguments. He predicted that workers would unite across national borders to wage class warfare. Instead, nationalism won out over working-class loyalty. In general, people felt stronger ties to their own countries than to the international communist movement. By the end of the twentieth century, few nations remained with communist governments, while nearly every economy included elements of free-market capitalism.

✓ **Checkpoint** How accurate did Marx's predictions about social classes prove to be?

Workers of the World
An 1895 leaflet urges that "Workers of the World Unite," the slogan of the socialist movement of Marx (above) and Engels.

Progress Monitoring Online
For: Self-quiz with vocabulary practice
Web Code: naa-1941

Terms, People, and Places

1. For each term, person, or place listed at the beginning of the section, write a sentence explaining its significance.

Note Taking

2. **Reading Skill: Identify Main Ideas** Use your completed outline to answer the Focus Question: What new ideas about economics and society were fostered as a result of the Industrial Revolution?

Comprehension and Critical Thinking

3. **Identify Points of View** What were the views of laissez-faire economists (a) Adam Smith, (b) Thomas Malthus, and (c) David Ricardo?

4. **Compare Points of View** Contrast the approaches of utilitarians and socialists to solving economic problems.

5. **Synthesize Information** How might workplace reforms have altered Marxist predictions of world revolution?

● **Writing About History**

Quick Write: Write a Thesis Statement As in other types of essays, it is important to clearly state your thesis, or main idea, when writing an explanatory essay. Write a thesis statement followed by a short paragraph on one of the theories discussed in this section.

Concept Connector

 THE ESSENTIAL **?**

ECONOMIC SYSTEMS

How should resources and wealth be distributed?

In This Chapter   GA SSWH21b(D)

In the United States and Europe, industry began to replace traditional agriculture by the mid-1800s. New ways of thinking emerged about how to answer these three key economic questions: (1) What will be produced? (2) How will it be produced? (3) Who will get the product? In the illustration from Oliver Twist (right), a young orphan asks for more food.

"Please, sir, I want some more."

Throughout History

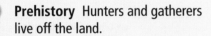

- **Prehistory** Hunters and gatherers live off the land.

- **900s A.D.** The self-sufficient manor is at the heart of the feudal economy.

- **1500s–1700s** Under mercantalism, colonies exist to enrich European powers.

- **1800s** In the free market system, individual businesses operate without government control.

- **1800s** Industrial workers struggle to gain better wages and living conditions.

- **1900s** Under communism, the Soviet government owns most businesses and property.

Continuing Today

The World Trade Organization (WTO) negotiates the rules of trade between nations. At an annual WTO meeting, protestors express their view that the rights of developing nations are insufficiently protected.

21st Century Skills

 TRANSFER Activities

1. **Analyze** Throughout history, how have answers to the key economic questions differed?

2. **Evaluate** Why does it matter who controls the economy?

3. **Transfer** Complete a Web quest in which you analyze how different economics systems allocate resources and wealth; record your thoughts in the Concept Connector Journal; and learn to make a video. Web Code nah-1908

Quick Study Guide

 SSWH15a

Progress Monitoring *Online*
For: Self-test with vocabulary practice
Web Code: naa-1951

■ New Inventions and Ideas

Inventors and Thinkers	Inventions and Ideas
Jethro Tull	Seed drill
Thomas Newcomen	Steam engine
James Watt	Improved steam engine
John Kay	Flying shuttle
James Hargreaves	Spinning jenny
Richard Arkwright	Water frame
Eli Whitney	Cotton gin
George Stephenson	Steam-powered locomotive
John Wesley	Methodism
Adam Smith	Laissez-faire economics
Thomas Malthus	Population growth could outpace food supply.
Jeremy Bentham	Utilitarianism
Robert Owen	Utopian communities
Karl Marx	Communism, Marxism

■ Effects of the Industrial Revolution

Industrial Revolution

↓

- Population growth
- Rural to urban migration
- Growth of cities

↓

- Poor working conditions in factories
- Low wages
- Overcrowding in cities

↓

- Laissez-faire economics
- Utilitarianism
- Socialism
- Marxism

■ Why Britain Industrialized First

Industrial Revolution in Britain
Plentiful natural resources
Ready workforce
Prosperous economy
Availability of capital and demand
Stable government

■ Responses to the Industrial Revolution

- Bentham/Mill: utilitarianism
- Socialism
- Owen: utopianism
- Marx/Engels: communism

■ Key Events From 1750–1850

Early Industrial Revolution Events
Global Events

1760s Watt improves the steam engine.

1764 The spinning jenny is invented.

1750

1775

1762 Catherine the Great comes to power in Russia.

1770 Cook claims Australia for Britain.

1788 Futa Toro outlaws slave trade.

Concept | Connector

Essential Question Review

To connect prior knowledge with what you have learned in this chapter, answer the questions below in your Concept Connector journal. Use the journal in the Reading and Note Taking Study Guide to record your answers (or go to www.phschool.com **Web Code:** nad-1907). In addition, record information about the following concepts:

- Economic Systems: market economy
- Economic Systems: centrally planned economy
- Economic Systems: mixed economy

1. **Economic Systems** The Commercial Revolution in the 1500s gave rise to capitalism and mercantalism. The Industrial Revolution gave rise to new economic theories: laissez-faire economics, utilitarianism, and socialism. Compare capitalism and socialism. Think about how wealth is gained and distributed in each economic system.

2. **Technology** Once James Watt made improvements to Thomas Newcomen's steam engine, it became a key power source of the Industrial Revolution. In a similar way, hundreds of years earlier, the printing press had dramatically changed how people communicated and shared information. Compare the impact of the two developments. Consider the following:
   - who benefited from the use of the invention
   - how the work was done before the invention
   - why the invention was important

■ Connections to Today

1. **Migration: Twentieth Century Global Migrations** During the Industrial Revolution, rural workers migrated to urban areas to live and work. Today, people still migrate in various parts of the world. Do online and library research to find information on rural-to-urban migration in a country located in Asia or Africa. Write a brief newspaper article in which you compare the experiences of those who migrated then and now.

Strawberry pickers at work, South Africa

2. **Geography's Impact** The population growth that occurred during the Industrial Revolution often created filth and unsanitary conditions as people crowded into tenements. The growth also caused an increase in the demand for products, which led to the opening of more factories. Do online and library research to find the history of population growth in the town or state in which you live. What are the patterns and results?

1800	1807	1830	1848
Owen begins social reforms at New Lanark.	Fulton develops the first successful steamboat, the *Clermont*.	The Liverpool-Manchester Railroad opens.	Marx and Engels publish *The Communist Manifesto*.

History *Interactive*
For: Interactive timeline
Web Code: nap-1901

1800   1825   1850

1804	1814	1819	1848
Napoleon becomes the emperor of France.	Congress of Vienna meets to restore stability in Europe.	Bolívar captures Bogotá.	Revolutions sweep Europe.

Chapter Assessment

Terms, People, and Places

Complete each sentence by choosing the correct answer from the list of terms below. You will not use all of the terms.

smelt	James Watt
urbanization	Manchester
Thomas Malthus	tenement
proletariat	socialism
enterprise	utilitarianism

1. _____ predicted that population would outpace the food supply.
2. A member of the _____ most likely lived in a small, crowded building called a _____.
3. Investors in Britain were ready to risk their capital to invest in _____.
4. Those who advocated _____ believed that the goal of society was to bring about the greatest happiness for the greatest number.
5. To _____ involves separating iron from its ore.
6. _____ improved the efficiency and design of Newcomen's steam engine.

Main Ideas

Section 1 (pp. 608–611)
7. How did the enclosure movement affect farmers?
8. Identify three causes of the population explosion that occurred in the 1700s.

Section 2 (pp. 612–615)
9. Describe four factors that helped bring about the Industrial Revolution in England.

10. How did the Industrial Revolution transform the textile industry?

Section 3 (pp. 616–621)
11. (a) What were the main characteristics of factory work? (b) What challenges did factory work create for women?

Section 4 (pp. 622–627)
12. List the government reforms sought by John Stuart Mill.
13. (a) Describe Karl Marx's view of history. (b) How have events challenged that view?

Chapter Focus Question
14. What technological, social, economic, and cultural changes occurred as the Industrial Revolution took hold?

Critical Thinking

15. **Synthesize Information** What were the impacts of each of the following technologies: (a) steam power, (b) improved methods for smelting iron, (c) railroad?
16. **Geography and History** Explain the link between Britain's natural resources and its rise as an industrial nation.
17. **Analyze Information** Describe how the Industrial Revolution affected each of the following: (a) size of population, (b) cities, (c) working and living conditions, (d) women and children.
18. **Predict Consequences** If more people had supported utilitarianism, how do you think it would have influenced society?
19. **Recognize Ideologies** Explain the major differences between Adam Smith's free market ideas and Karl Marx's socialist ideas.

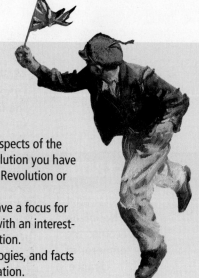

● Writing About History

In this chapter's four Section Assessments, you developed skills for writing an explanatory essay.

Expository: Explanatory Essay During the late 1700s, the Industrial Revolution began to transform Britain. An agricultural revolution triggered a chain of events, and Britain sped ahead of the rest of the world to become the first industrial nation. But why is the Industrial Revolution considered to be a "revolution"? Write an explanatory essay to answer this question.

Prewriting
• Ask yourself what you need to know in order to write an effective explanation. Think about what you already know about revolutions.

• Do research to gather facts, descriptions, examples, and other details to clearly illustrate your point.

Drafting
• Create a Venn diagram to compare aspects of the Industrial Revolution to another revolution you have learned about, such as the American Revolution or the French Revolution.
• Write a thesis statement once you have a focus for your essay. Begin your introduction with an interesting lead-in to get your reader's attention.
• Be sure to include comparisons, analogies, and facts in your essay to support your explanation.

Revising
• Use the guidelines for revising your essay on page SH12 of the Writing Handbook.

Prepare for the GHSGT

New Economic and Social Theories

Various thinkers of the day attempted to understand and interpret the dramatic changes brought about by the Industrial Revolution. They responded with a wide range of explanations and solutions, as the documents below illustrate.

Document A

"As every individual, therefore, endeavours as much as he can both to employ his capital in the support of domestic industry, and so to direct that industry that its produce may be of the greatest value; every individual necessarily labours to render the annual revenue of the society as great as he can. . . . By preferring the support of domestic to that of foreign industry, he intends only his own security; and by directing that industry in such a manner as its produce may be of the greatest value, he intends only his own gain, and he is in this, as in many other cases, led by an invisible hand to promote an end which was no part of his intention. . . . every individual it is evident, can, in his local situation, judge much better than any statesman or lawgiver can do for him."

—From ***The Wealth of Nations*** by Adam Smith, 1776

Document B

"In those characters which now exhibit crime, the fault is obviously not in the individual, but the defects proceed from the system in which the individual was trained. Withdraw those circumstances which tend to create crime in the human character, and crime will not be created. Replace them with such as are calculated to form habits of order, regularity, temperance, industry; and these qualities will be formed. . . . Proceed systematically on principles of undeviating persevering kindness, yet retaining and using, with the least possible severity, the means of restraining crime from immediately injuring society, and by degrees even the crimes now existing in adults will also gradually disappear. . . ."

—From ***A New View of Society*** by Robert Owen, 1816

Document C
New Lanark Mills, Scotland

Document D

". . . the power of population is indefinitely greater than the power in the earth to produce subsistence for man. Population, when unchecked, increased in a geometrical ratio. Subsistence increases only in an arithmetical ratio. A slight acquaintance with numbers will show the immensity of the first power in comparison of the second. . . . No fancied equality, no agrarian regulations in their utmost extent, could remove the pressure of it even for a single century. And it appears, therefore, to be decisive against the possible existence of a society, all the members of which should live in ease, happiness, and comparative leisure; and feel no anxiety about providing the means of subsistence for themselves and families. Consequently, if the premises are just, the argument is conclusive against the perfectibility of the mass of mankind."

—From ***An Essay on the Principle of Population 1798***
by Thomas Malthus

Analyzing Documents

Use your knowledge of the new economic and social theories and Documents A, B, C, and D to answer the questions below.

1. According to Adam Smith in Document A, individuals promote the good of society because of
   A high ideals.
   B self-interest.
   C government pressure.
   D religion.

2. How did Robert Owen explain the fact that some people become criminals?
   A the invisible hand of fate
   B struggles between the ruling class and the oppressed
   C the influence of problems in society
   D the power of population over production

3. Thomas Malthus argued that a society where all individuals enjoy happiness, comfort, and pleasure is
   A only possible with increased agricultural output.
   B impossible because of the base nature of human greed.
   C impossible because of the pressures of population.
   D possible when people are treated decently and fairly.

4. **Writing Task** Suppose you were working in Britain in the year 1840. Which of the above economic philosophies would you support? Remember to identify your occupation and social class. Use your knowledge of the Industrial Revolution and the documents above to support your opinion.

20 Revolutions in Europe and Latin America

1790–1848

Freedom From Tyranny

Several revolutions erupted in Europe between 1815 and 1829, and the spread of revolutionary ideals would ignite new uprisings in 1830 and 1848. Also occurring during this time were the wars of independence in Latin America. These revolts began in the late 1700s and early 1800s and were inspired by the success of the American Revolution and the ideals of the French Revolution. Simón Bolívar was one of the great heroes in the fight for independence in Spanish South America. He helped win independence for Bolivia, Colombia, Ecuador, Peru, and Venezuela. Listen to the Witness History audio to learn more about revolutions in Europe and Latin America.

❝A state too extensive in itself, or by virtue of its dependencies, ultimately falls into decay; its free government is transformed into a tyranny; it disregards the principles which it should preserve, and finally degenerates into despotism. The distinguishing characteristic of small republics is stability. . . .❞
—Simón Bolívar

◀ Bolívar fights Spanish troops in his endeavor to free South America.

 Performance Standards

Chapter Focus Question How did revolutionary ideals in Europe and Latin America ignite uprisings in the first half of the nineteenth century?

Section 1
An Age of Ideologies
SSWH14b, SSWH15a

Section 2
Revolutions of 1830 and 1848
SSWH14b

Section 3
Revolts in Latin America
SSWH14b

Use the ☑ **Quick Study Timeline** at the end of this chapter to preview chapter events.

Simón Bolívar's crown

French military hat

José de San Martín

 Concept Connector ONLINE

To explore Essential Questions related to this chapter, go to PHSchool.com
Web Code: nad-2007

Hungarian revolutionary
Lajos Kossuth

A "Revolutionary Seed"

Prince Clemens von Metternich warned that a seed had been planted in Europe that threatened Europe's monarchs and undermined its basic social values. This seed was nourished with the ideas spread by the French Revolution and Napoleon Bonaparte.

❝ Passions are let loose . . . to overthrow everything that society respects as the basis of its existence: religion, public morality, laws, customs, rights, and duties, all are attacked, confounded [defeated], overthrown, or called in question.**❞**

Focus Question What events proved that Metternich was correct in his fears?

An Age of Ideologies

 Performance Standards

- **SSWH14b** Identify the causes and results of revolutions.
- **SSWH15a** Analyze movements for political reform.

Terms, People, and Places

ideology
universal manhood suffrage
autonomy

Note Taking

Reading Skill: Identify Main Ideas As you read the section, fill in a table like the one below with main ideas about conservatism, liberalism, and nationalism.

Conservatism	Liberalism	Nationalism
•	•	•
•	•	•

At the Congress of Vienna, the powers of Europe tried to uproot the "revolutionary seed" and suppress nationalist fervor. Others, however, challenged the order imposed in 1815. The clash of people with opposing **ideologies,** or systems of thought and belief, plunged Europe into more than 30 years of turmoil.

Conservatives Prefer the Old Order

The Congress of Vienna was a victory for the conservative forces, which included monarchs and their officials, noble landowners, and church leaders. Conservatives agreed to work together—in an agreement called the Concert of Europe—to support the political and social order that had existed before Napoleon and the French Revolution. Conservative ideas also appealed to peasants, who wanted to preserve traditional ways.

Conservatives of the early 1800s wanted to return to the way things had been before 1789. After all, they had benefited under the old order. They wanted to restore royal families to the thrones they had lost when Napoleon swept across Europe. They supported a social hierarchy in which lower classes respected and obeyed their social superiors. Conservatives also backed an established church—Catholic in Austria and southern Europe, Protestant in northern Europe, and Eastern Orthodox in eastern Europe.

Conservatives believed that talk about natural rights and constitutional government could lead only to chaos, as in France in 1789. If change had to come, they argued, it must come slowly. Conservatives felt that they benefited all people by defending peace and stability. Conservative leaders like Metternich sought to suppress revolutionary ideas. Metternich urged monarchs to oppose freedom of the press, crush protests in their own countries, and send troops to douse the flames of rebellion in neighboring lands.

✔ **Checkpoint** What was the goal of the conservatives in the Concert of Europe?

Liberals and Nationalists Seek Change

Inspired by the Enlightenment and the French Revolution, liberals and nationalists challenged the conservatives at every turn. Liberalism and nationalism ignited a number of revolts against established rule.

Liberals Promise Freedom Because liberals spoke mostly for the bourgeoisie, or middle class, their ideas are sometimes called "bourgeois liberalism." Liberals included business owners, bankers, and lawyers, as well as politicians, newspaper editors, writers, and others who helped to shape public opinion.

Liberals wanted governments to be based on written constitutions and separation of powers. Liberals spoke out against divine-right monarchy, the old aristocracy, and established churches. They defended the natural rights of individuals to liberty, equality, and property. They called for rulers elected by the people and responsible to them. Thus, most liberals favored a republican form of government over a monarchy, or at least wanted the monarch to be limited by a constitution.

The liberals of the early 1800s saw the role of government as limited to protecting basic rights such as freedom of thought, speech, and religion. They believed that only male property owners or others with a financial stake in society should have the right to vote. Only later in the century did liberals support the principle of **universal manhood suffrage**, giving all adult men the right to vote.

Liberals also strongly supported the laissez-faire economics of Adam Smith and David Ricardo. They saw the free market as an opportunity for capitalist entrepreneurs to succeed. As capitalists (and often employers), liberals had different goals from those of workers laboring in factories, mines, and other enterprises of the early Industrial Revolution.

Nationalists Strive for Unity For centuries, European rulers had gained or lost lands through wars, marriages, and treaties. They exchanged territories and the people in them like pieces in a game. As a result, by 1815 Europe had several empires that included many nationalities. The Austrian, Russian, and Ottoman empires, for example, each included diverse peoples.

Analyzing Political Cartoons

Conflicting Ideologies This cartoon shows Prince Metternich standing resolute against the angry crowd behind him who are pushing for reform. Metternich represented the conservative order and opposed revolutionary ideals such as freedom and progress.
1. How does the cartoonist portray those in the crowd? What does the crowd support?
2. What did Metternich do to suppress revolutionary ideas?

In the 1800s, national groups who shared a common heritage set out to win their own states. Within the diverse Austrian empire, for example, various nationalist leaders tried to unite and win independence for each particular group. Nationalism gave people with a common heritage a sense of identity and the goal of creating their own homeland. At the same time, however, nationalism often bred intolerance and led to persecution of other ethnic or national groups.

✓ **Checkpoint** How did the liberalism of the early 1800s reflect Enlightenment ideals?

Central Europe Challenges the Old Order

Spurred by the ideas of liberalism and nationalism, revolutionaries fought against the old order. During the early 1800s, rebellions erupted in the Balkan Peninsula and elsewhere along the southern fringe of Europe. The Balkans, in southeastern Europe, were inhabited by people of various religions and ethnic groups. These peoples had lived under Ottoman rule for more than 300 years.

Serbia Seeks Independence The first Balkan people to revolt were the Serbs. From 1804 to 1813, the Serb leader Karageorge (ka rah JAWR juh) led a guerrilla war against the Ottomans. The intense struggle was unsuccessful, but it fostered a sense of Serbian identity. A revival of Serbian literature and culture added to the sense of nationhood.

In 1815, Milos Obrenovic (oh BRAY noh vich) led the Serbs in a second, more successful rebellion. One reason for the success was that Obrenovic turned to Russia for assistance. Like the Serbs, the Russian people were Slavic in language and Christian Orthodox in religion. By 1830, Russian support helped the Serbs win **autonomy,** or self-rule, within the

Serbs in Battle
Serb leader Karageorge (below left) led the Serbs in major battles against the Ottomans in the quest for independence. *(a) Why would this battle and others like it help lead to a sense of Serbian national identity? (b) Why was this sense of nationalism important for the Serbs?*

Ottoman empire. The Ottoman sultan later agreed to formal independence. In the future, Russia would continue to defend Serbian interests and affect events in the Balkans.

Greece Revolts to End Ottoman Rule

In 1821, the Greeks revolted, seeking to end centuries of Ottoman rule. At first, the Greeks were badly divided. But years of suffering in long, bloody wars of independence helped shape a national identity. Leaders of the rebellion justified their struggle as "a national war, a holy war, a war the object of which is to reconquer the rights of individual liberty." The Greeks had the support of romantic writers such as English poet Lord Byron, who went to Greece to aid the fight for independence.

Admirers of Greece in Europe backed the Greek rebels. In the late 1820s, Britain, France, and Russia forced the Ottomans to grant independence to some Greek provinces. By 1830, Greece was independent. The European powers, however, pressured the Greeks to accept a German king, a move meant to show that they did not support the nationalism that brought about the revolution.

More Challenges Erupt

Several other challenges to the Vienna peace settlement erupted in the 1820s. Revolts occurred along the southern fringe of Europe. In Spain, Portugal, and various states in the Italian peninsula, rebels struggled to gain constitutional governments.

Metternich urged conservative rulers to act decisively and crush the dangerous uprisings. In response, a French army marched over the Pyrenees to suppress a revolt in Spain. Austrian forces crossed the Alps to smash rebellious outbreaks in Italy.

Troops dampened the fires of liberalism and nationalism, but could not smother them. In the next decades, sparks would flare anew. Added to liberal and nationalist demands were the goals of the new industrial working class. By the mid-1800s, social reformers and <u>agitators</u> were urging workers to support socialism or other ways of reorganizing property ownership.

✔ Checkpoint Why would a monarch order his army to suppress an uprising in another country?

Note Taking

Reading Skill: Identify Supporting Details As you read, fill in a table like the one below with supporting details about revolts in Serbia, Greece, and other countries during the early 1800s.

Serbia	Greece	Other Revolts
•	•	•
•	•	•

Vocabulary Builder

agitator—(AJ ih tayt ur) *n.* someone who attempts to arouse feeling for or against something, especially a political cause

---

SECTION 1 Assessment

Progress Monitoring *Online*
For: Self-quiz with vocabulary practice
Web Code: naa-2011

Terms, People, and Places

1. For each term, person, or place listed at the beginning of the section, write a sentence explaining its significance.

Note Taking

2. **Reading Skill: Identify Main Ideas** Use your completed charts to answer the Focus Question: What events proved that Metternich was correct in his fears?

Comprehension and Critical Thinking

3. **Identify Point of View** What were the goals of conservative leaders?
4. **Compare Points of View** (a) How did the political goals of liberals differ from those of conservatives? (b) How did nationalists threaten the borders set up by European monarchs?
5. **Recognize Cause and Effect** (a) Why did the Serbs and Greeks revolt? (b) Why were there uprisings in Spain, Portugal, and the Italian states?

● Writing About History

Quick Write: Choose a Topic To write an effective persuasive essay, you should begin with a clearly stated opinion or argument on an issue that has more than one side. Look back over Section 1, jotting down issues that have two or more sides. Then choose an issue and write a well-constructed sentence that states your opinion or argument against it.

Alexis de Tocqueville

More Revolution in the Wind

Alexis de Tocqueville was a liberal French leader who closely observed the widespread support for revolutionary ideas. He knew that the revolutions of the 1820s were not over.

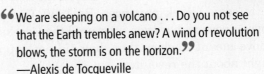

66 We are sleeping on a volcano . . . Do you not see that the Earth trembles anew? A wind of revolution blows, the storm is on the horizon. 99
—Alexis de Tocqueville

Focus Question What were the causes and effects of the revolutions in Europe in 1830 and 1848?

Revolutions of 1830 and 1848

Performance Standards

- **SSWH14b** Identify the causes and results of revolutions.

Terms, People, and Places

radicals	Napoleon III
Louis Philippe	Louis Kossuth
recession	

Note Taking

Reading Skill: Identify Main Ideas As you read the section, fill in a table like the one below with a country, date, and a main idea about the revolutions of 1830 and 1848. Add rows as needed.

Revolutions of 1830 and 1848		
France	1830	Radicals force king to abdicate.

The quick suppression of liberal and nationalist uprisings in the 1820s did not end Europe's age of revolutions. In 1830 and 1848, Europeans saw street protests explode into full-scale revolts. As in 1789, the upheavals began in Paris and radiated out across the continent.

French Rebels Win in 1830

When the Congress of Vienna restored Louis XVIII to the French throne, he wisely issued a constitution, the Charter of French Liberties. It created a two-house legislature and allowed limited freedom of the press. Still, the king retained much power.

Citizens Lead the July Revolution When Louis XVIII died in 1824, his younger brother, Charles X, inherited the throne. Charles, a strong believer in absolutism, rejected the very idea of the charter. In July 1830, he suspended the legislature, limited the right to vote, and restricted the press.

Liberals and **radicals**—those who favor extreme change—responded forcefully to the king's challenge. In Paris, angry citizens threw up barricades across the narrow streets. From behind them, they fired on the soldiers and pelted them with stones and roof tiles. Within days, rebels controlled Paris. The revolutionary tricolor flew from the towers of Notre Dame cathedral. A frightened Charles X abdicated and fled to England.

The "Citizen King" Rules France With the king gone, radicals wanted to set up a republic. Moderate liberals, however, insisted on a constitutional monarchy and chose **Louis Philippe** as king. Louis Philippe was a cousin of Charles X and in his youth had supported the revolution of 1789.

The French called Louis Philippe the "citizen king" because he owed his throne to the people. Louis got along well with the liberal bourgeoisie. He dressed like them in a frock coat and top hat. Sometimes he strolled the streets, shaking hands with well-wishers. Liberal politicians filled his government.

Under Louis Philippe, the upper bourgeoisie prospered. Louis extended suffrage, but only to France's wealthier citizens. The vast majority of the people still could not vote. The king's other policies also favored the middle class at the expense of the workers.

✔ **Checkpoint** What actions did Charles X take in 1830, and how did French rebels respond?

The Spirit of Reform Spreads

The revolts in Paris inspired the outbreak of uprisings elsewhere in Europe. As Metternich said, "When France sneezes, Europe catches cold." Most of the uprisings were suppressed by military force. But some rebels did win changes. Even when they failed, revolutions frightened rulers badly enough to encourage reform.

Belgium Wins Independence The one notable success in 1830 took place in Belgium. In 1815, the Congress of Vienna had united the Austrian Netherlands (present-day Belgium) and the Kingdom of Holland under the Dutch king. The Congress had wanted to create a strong barrier to help prevent French expansion in the future.

The French-speaking Belgian bourgeoisie resented the new arrangement. They and the Dutch had different languages. The Belgians were Catholic, while the Dutch king was Protestant. The Belgians relied on manufacturing; the Dutch, on trade.

In 1830, news of the Paris uprising ignited a revolutionary spark in Belgium. Citizens took up arms against the Dutch troops in Brussels, the

To the Barricades!
In 1830 and again in 1848, French rebels erected barricades in the streets using mattresses, wagons, furniture, and whatever else they could find that might offer protection during the fighting with government soldiers. *How does Hugo describe the barricades in his famous novel* Les Misérables?

Primary Source

❝You saw there, in a chaos full of despair, rafters from roofs, patches from garrets with their wall paper, window sashes with all their glass planted in the rubbish, awaiting artillery, chimneys torn down, wardrobes, tables, benches, a howling topsy-turvy, . . . which contain at once fury and nothingness.❞
—Victor Hugo

capital. Britain and France believed thay they would benefit from the separation of Belgium and Holland and supported Belgian demands for independence. As a result, in 1831, Belgium became an independent state with a liberal constitution.

Rebels Fail in Poland Nationalists in Poland also staged an uprising in 1830. But, unlike the Belgians, the Poles failed to win independence for their country.

In the late 1700s, Russia, Austria, and Prussia had divided up Poland. Poles had hoped that the Congress of Vienna would restore their homeland in 1815. Instead, the great powers handed most of Poland to Russia.

In 1830, Polish students, army officers, and landowners rose in revolt. The rebels failed to gain widespread support, however, and were brutally crushed by Russian forces. Some survivors fled to Western Europe and the United States, where they kept alive the dream of freedom.

✔ **Checkpoint** How did the Belgian and Polish revolutions in 1830 end differently?

The French Revolt Again in 1848

In the 1840s, discontent began to grow in France once again. Radicals formed secret societies to work for a French republic. Utopian socialists called for an end to private ownership of property. Even liberals <u>denounced</u> Louis Philippe's government for corruption and called for expanded suffrage.

Near the end of the decade, discontent was heightened by a **recession,** or period of reduced economic activity. Factories shut down and people lost their jobs. Poor harvests caused bread prices to rise. Newspapers blamed government officials for some of the problems. With conditions much like those in 1789, Paris was again ripe for revolution.

Vocabulary Builder

<u>denounce</u>—(dee NOWNS) *vt.* to express harsh criticism of something or somebody, usually in public

● **INFOGRAPHIC**

1848: The Year of Hope and Despair

Revolution in Europe spread like wildfire in the days and months of 1848. Although an outbreak in January occurred in Italy, France's successful February Revolution was the spark for other revolts throughout Europe. As shown on the map here, revolutions were not confined to one city or country. They engulfed the continent of Europe and numbered almost fifty in the first four months of the year alone. Despite the failures of the revolutions, Europe was transformed as governments and the rising middle class began to cooperate with one another.

Turmoil Spreads During "February Days" In February 1848, when the government took steps to silence critics and prevent public meetings, angry crowds took to the streets. During the "February Days," overturned carts, paving stones, and toppled trees again blocked the streets of Paris. Church bells rang alarms, while women and men on the barricades sang the revolutionary anthem "La Marseillaise." A number of demonstrators clashed with royal troops and were killed.

As the turmoil spread, Louis Philippe abdicated. A group of liberal, radical, and socialist leaders proclaimed the Second Republic. (The First Republic had lasted from 1792 until 1804, when Napoleon became emperor.)

From the start, deep differences divided the new government. Middle-class liberals wanted moderate political reforms. Socialists wanted far-reaching social and economic change and forced the government to set up national workshops to provide jobs for the unemployed.

The Working Class Loses Out During "June Days" By June, however, upper- and middle-class interests had won control of the government. They saw the national workshops as a waste of money and shut them down.

Furious, workers again took to the streets of Paris. This time, however, bourgeois liberals turned violently against the protesters. Peasants, who feared that socialists might take their land, also attacked the rioting workers. At least 1,500 people were killed before the government crushed the rebellion.

The fighting of the "June Days" left a bitter legacy. The middle class both feared and distrusted the socialists, while the working class harbored a deep hatred for the bourgeoisie.

A New Napoleon Comes to Power By the end of 1848, the National Assembly, now dominated by members who wanted to restore order,

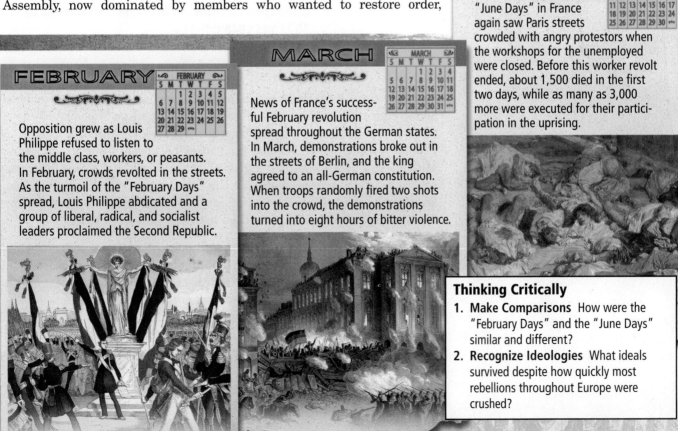

JUNE

		JUNE			
S	M	T	W	T	F	S
				1	2	3
4	5	6	7	8	9	10
11	12	13	14	15	16	17
18	19	20	21	22	23	24
25	26	27	28	29	30	

"June Days" in France again saw Paris streets crowded with angry protestors when the workshops for the unemployed were closed. Before this worker revolt ended, about 1,500 died in the first two days, while as many as 3,000 more were executed for their participation in the uprising.

FEBRUARY

		FEBRUARY			
S	M	T	W	T	F	S
						1
2	3	4	5	6	7	8
9	10	11	12	13	14	15
16	17	18	19	20	21	22
23	24	25	26	27	28	29

Opposition grew as Louis Philippe refused to listen to the middle class, workers, or peasants. In February, crowds revolted in the streets. As the turmoil of the "February Days" spread, Louis Philippe abdicated and a group of liberal, radical, and socialist leaders proclaimed the Second Republic.

MARCH

		MARCH			
S	M	T	W	T	F	S
				1	2	3	4
5	6	7	8	9	10	11
12	13	14	15	16	17	18
19	20	21	22	23	24	25
26	27	28	29	30	31	

News of France's successful February revolution spread throughout the German states. In March, demonstrations broke out in the streets of Berlin, and the king agreed to an all-German constitution. When troops randomly fired two shots into the crowd, the demonstrations turned into eight hours of bitter violence.

Thinking Critically
1. **Make Comparisons** How were the "February Days" and the "June Days" similar and different?
2. **Recognize Ideologies** What ideals survived despite how quickly most rebellions throughout Europe were crushed?

Cause and Effect

Long-Term Causes

- Spread of Enlightenment ideas
- Growth of nationalism and liberalism
- Poverty caused by the Industrial Revolution

Immediate Causes

- Uprisings in Paris
- Economic recession
- Poor harvests
- Corrupt governments

The Revolutions of 1848

Immediate Effects

- A new republic in France
- Fall of Metternich
- Promises of reform in Austria, Italy, and Prussia

Long-Term Effects

- A new empire in France
- Successes for liberalism, nationalism, and socialism
- Germany and Italy united
- Labor unions
- Increased voting rights for men

Connections to Today

- Ongoing efforts to ensure basic rights for all citizens
- Ongoing efforts to ensure limited government and popular sovereignty worldwide

Analyze Cause and Effect The revolutions of 1848 were the result of new ways of thinking and hard times for workers. *Could one of these factors by itself have caused such widespread rebellion? Why or Why not?*

Italian revolutionary flag

issued a constitution for the Second Republic. It created a strong president and a one-house legislature. But it also gave the vote to all adult men, the widest suffrage in the world at the time. Nine million Frenchmen now could vote, compared with only 200,000 who had that right before.

When elections for president were held, the overwhelming winner was Louis Napoleon, nephew of Napoleon Bonaparte. The "new" Napoleon attracted the working classes by presenting himself as a man who cared about social issues such as poverty. At the same time, his famous name, linked with order and past French glory, helped him with conservatives.

Once in office, Louis Napoleon used his position as a stepping-stone to greater power. By 1852, he had proclaimed himself emperor, taking the title **Napoleon III**. Thus ended the short-lived Second Republic.

Like his celebrated uncle, Napoleon III used a plebiscite to win public approval for his seizure of power. A stunning 90 percent of voters supported his move to set up the Second Empire. Many thought that a monarchy was more stable than a republic or hoped that Napoleon III would restore the glory days of Napoleon Bonaparte.

Napoleon III, like Louis Philippe, ruled at a time of rapid economic growth. For the bourgeoisie, the early days of the Second Empire brought prosperity and contentment. In time, however, Napoleon III would embark on foreign adventures that would bring down his empire and end French leadership in Europe.

✓ **Checkpoint** How did the French revolutions of 1830 and 1848 differ?

Revolution Surges Through Europe

In 1848, revolts in Paris again unleashed a tidal wave of revolution across Europe. For opponents of the old order, it was a time of such hope that they called it the "springtime of the peoples." Although events in France touched off the revolts, grievances had been piling up for years. Middle-class liberals wanted a greater share of political power for themselves, as well as protections for the basic rights of all male citizens. Workers demanded relief from the miseries of the Industrial Revolution. And nationalists of all classes ached to throw off foreign rule.

Change in the Austrian Empire In the Austrian empire, revolts broke out in the major cities. Even though Metternich censored the press, books were smuggled to universities throughout the empire. Students demanded change. When workers joined the students on the streets of Vienna, Metternich resigned and fled in disguise.

Revolution continued to spread. In Budapest, Hungarian nationalists led by journalist **Louis Kossuth** demanded an independent government, an end to serfdom, and a written constitution to protect basic rights. In Prague, the Czechs made similar demands. Overwhelmed by events, the Austrian government agreed to the reforms. The gains were temporary, however.

Austrian troops soon regained control of Vienna and Prague and smashed the rebels in Budapest.

Revolts in Italy Uprisings also erupted in the Italian states. Nationalists wanted to end Hapsburg domination and set up a constitutional government. From Venice in the north to Naples in the south, Italians set up independent republics. Revolutionaries even expelled the pope from Rome and installed a nationalist government. Before long, the forces of reaction surged back here, too. Austrian troops ousted the new governments in northern Italy. A French army restored the pope to power in Rome. In Naples, local rulers canceled the reforms they had reluctantly accepted.

Rebellion in the German States In the German states, university students demanded national unity and liberal reforms. Economic hard times and a potato famine brought peasants and workers into the struggle. In Prussia, liberals forced King Frederick William IV to agree to a constitution written by an elected assembly. Within a year, though, he dissolved the assembly.

Throughout 1848, delegates from German states met in the Frankfurt Assembly. Divisions soon <u>emerged</u> over whether Germany should be a republic or a monarchy and whether to include Austria in a united German state. Finally, the assembly offered Prussia's Frederick William IV the crown of a united Germany. To their dismay, the conservative king rejected the offer because it came not from the German princes but from the people—"from the gutter," as he described it.

By 1850, rebellion faded, ending the age of liberal revolution that had begun in 1789. Why did the uprisings fail? The rulers' use of military force was just one reason. Another was that revolutionaries did not have mass support, and in many instances, constitutions that represented their principles were withdrawn or replaced. In the decades ahead, liberalism, nationalism, and socialism would win successes not through revolution, but through political activity.

✔ **Checkpoint** What was the outcome of most of the revolutions outside France in 1848?

Analyzing Political Cartoons

A Year of Revolution This English cartoonist comments on the revolutions of 1848 and the reaction of European rulers. Based on the cartoon,
1. What ideal led to the revolutions of 1848?
2. How did the revolutions affect Europe's monarchs?

Vocabulary Builder

emerge—(ee MURJ) *v.* to arise, appear, or come out of

SECTION 2 Assessment

Progress Monitoring *Online*
For: Self-quiz with vocabulary practice
Web Code: naa-2021

Terms, People, and Places
1. For each term, person, or place listed at the beginning of the section, write a sentence explaining its significance.

Note Taking
2. **Reading Skill: Identify Causes and Effects** Use your completed chart to answer the Focus Question: What were the causes and effects of revolutions in Europe in 1830 and 1848?

Comprehension and Critical Thinking
3. **Draw Conclusions** What were the conditions under which the people of France lived that led to revolution rather than peace?
4. **Analyze Information** (a) Where did revolution spread in 1830? (b) Were these revolutions successful? Explain.
5. **Make Generalizations** Why did most of the revolutions of 1848 fail to achieve their goals?

● **Writing About History**

Quick Write: Gather and Organize Evidence In order to write a well-organized persuasive essay, you need to gather evidence to support your position. Gather evidence from the section to support an essay on whether workers were justified in taking to the streets in 1830 and 1848. Then create a chart that lists both sides of the issue.

Concept Connector

REVOLUTION
Why do political revolutions occur?

In This Chapter SSWH14b

The wave of revolution that swept Europe in the early 1800s mainly involved a clash between liberal and conservative political ideas. Conservatives wanted to keep the power in the hands of established institutions; liberals wanted to distribute power more widely, especially to the middle class. In Germany (right), the military clashed with revolutionaries.

Throughout History

200s A.D. Han empire is overthrown when it burdens peasants with heavy taxes.

1524 German peasants revolt against nobles to end serfdom.

1688 The Glorious Revolution replaces the Catholic King of England James II with his Protestant daughter Mary.

1789 Unequal distribution of wealth and power sparks the French Revolution.

1867 Social and economic unrest lead to the overthrow of the Japanese shogun.

1917 Bolsheviks seize power in Russia and overthrow the tsar.

Continuing Today

An election in Ukraine, seen by many to be fraudulent, sparked a series of nonviolent protests. The government was forced to call for a revote, which led to a change of leadership.

21st Century Skills

? TRANSFER Activities

1. **Analyze** Throughout history, why have people revolted?

2. **Draw Conclusions** Why do you think every age in history has witnessed revolution?

3. **Transfer** Complete a Web quest in which you analyze the influence of revolution on a specific country; record your thoughts in the Concept Connector Journal; and learn to make a video. Web Code nah-2008

Simón Bolívar

Crown awarded to Bolívar

WITNESS HISTORY ◄)) AUDIO

A Revolutionary Is Born

Like many wealthy Latin Americans, young Simón Bolívar was sent to Europe to complete his education. In Europe he became a strong admirer of the ideals of the Enlightenment and the French Revolution. One day while speaking with his Italian tutor about freedom and individual rights, he fell on his knees and swore an oath:

66 I swear before God and by my honor never to allow my hands to be idle nor my soul to rest until I have broken the chains that bind us to Spain. **99**

Focus Question Who were the key revolutionaries that led the movements for independence in Latin America, and what were their accomplishments?

Revolts in Latin America

 Performance Standards

• **SSWH14b** Identify the causes and results of revolution in France, Haiti, and Latin America.

Terms, People, and Places

peninsular	Toussaint L'Ouverture
creole	Father Miguel Hidalgo
mestizo	Father José Morelos
mulatto	José de San Martín
Simón Bolívar	Dom Pedro

Note Taking

Reading Skill: Identify Main Ideas As you read the section, fill in a table like the one below with a country, a date, and a main idea about revolts in Latin America. Add rows as needed.

Revolts in Latin America		
Haiti	1791	Toussaint L'Ouverture

Liberal ideas were spreading to Latin America with explosive results. From Mexico to the tip of South America, revolutionary movements arose to overthrow the reigning European powers. By 1825, most of Latin America was freed from colonial rule.

Discontent Fans the Fires

By the late 1700s, the revolutionary fever that gripped Western Europe had spread to Latin America. There, discontent was rooted in the social, racial, and political system that had emerged during 300 years of Spanish rule.

Social and Ethnic Structures Cause Resentment Spanish-born **peninsulares,** members of the highest social class, dominated Latin American political and social life. Only they could hold top jobs in government and the Church. Many **creoles**—the European-descended Latin Americans who owned the haciendas, ranches, and mines—bitterly resented their second-class status. Merchants fretted under mercantilist policies that tied the colonies to Spain.

Meanwhile, a growing population of **mestizos,** people of Native American and European descent, and **mulattoes,** people of African and European descent, were angry at being denied the status, wealth, and power that were available to whites. Native Americans suffered economic misery under the Spanish, who had conquered the lands of their ancestors. In the Caribbean region and parts of South America, masses of enslaved Africans who worked on plantations longed for freedom.

The Enlightenment Inspires Latin Americans In the 1700s, educated creoles read the works of Enlightenment thinkers. They watched colonists in North America throw off British rule. Translations of the Declaration of Independence and the Constitution of the United States circulated among the creole elite.

During the French Revolution, young creoles like **Simón Bolívar** (boh LEE vahr) traveled in Europe and were inspired by the ideals of "liberty, equality, and fraternity." Yet despite their admiration for Enlightenment ideas and revolutions in other lands, most creoles were reluctant to act.

Napoleon Invades Spain The spark that finally ignited widespread rebellion in Latin America was Napoleon's invasion of Spain in 1808. Napoleon ousted the Spanish king and placed his brother Joseph on the Spanish throne. In Latin America, leaders saw Spain's weakness as an opportunity to reject foreign domination and demand independence from colonial rule.

 Checkpoint Where did creoles get many of their revolutionary ideas?

Slaves Win Freedom for Haiti

Even before Spanish colonists hoisted the flag of freedom, revolution had erupted in a French-ruled colony on the island of Hispaniola. In Haiti, as the island is now called, French planters owned very profitable sugar plantations worked by nearly a half million enslaved Africans. Sugar plantations were labor-intensive. The slaves were overworked and underfed.

Toussaint L'Ouverture Leads a Slave Revolt Embittered by suffering and inspired by the talk of liberty and equality, the island's slaves rose up in revolt in 1791. The rebels were fortunate to find an intelligent and skillful leader in **Toussaint L'Ouverture** (too SAN loo vehr TOOR), a self-educated former slave. Although untrained, Toussaint was a brilliant general and inspiring commander.

Toussaint's army of former slaves faced many enemies. Some mulattoes joined French planters against the rebels. France, Spain, and Britain all sent armies against them. The fighting took more lives than any other revolution in the Americas. But by 1798, the rebels had achieved their goal: slavery was abolished, and Toussaint's forces controlled most of the island.

Haiti Wins Independence In 1802, Napoleon Bonaparte sent a large army to reconquer the former colony. Toussaint urged his countrymen to take up arms once again to resist the invaders. In April 1802 the French agreed to a truce, but then they captured Toussaint and carried him in chains to France. He died there in a cold mountain prison a year later.

The struggle for freedom continued, however, and late in 1803, with yellow fever destroying their army, the French surrendered. In January 1804, the island declared itself an independent country under the name Haiti. In the following years, rival Haitian leaders fought for power. Finally, in 1820, Haiti became a republic.

 Checkpoint How were slaves instrumental in achieving Haiti's independence?

Portrait of Joseph Bonaparte, King of Spain, 1808

Mexico and Central America Revolt

The slave revolt in Haiti frightened creoles in Spanish America. Although they wanted power themselves, most had no desire for economic or social changes that might threaten their way of life. In 1810, however, a creole priest in Mexico, **Father Miguel Hidalgo** (hee DAL goh), raised his voice for freedom.

Father Hidalgo Cries Out for Freedom Father Hidalgo presided over the poor rural parish of Dolores. On September 15, 1810, he rang the church bells summoning the people to prayer. When they gathered, he startled them with an urgent appeal, "My children, will you be free?" Father Hidalgo's speech became known as "el Grito de Dolores"—the cry of Dolores. It called Mexicans to fight for independence.

A ragged army of poor mestizos and Native Americans rallied to Father Hidalgo and marched to the outskirts of Mexico City. At first, some creoles supported the revolt. However, they soon rejected Hidalgo's call for an end to slavery and his plea for reforms to improve conditions for Native Americans. They felt that these policies would cost them power.

After some early successes, the rebels faced growing opposition. Less than a year after he issued the "Grito," Hidalgo was captured and executed, and his followers scattered.

José Morelos Continues the Fight Another priest picked up the banner of revolution. **Father José Morelos** was a mestizo who called for wide-ranging social and political reform. He wanted to improve

Liberty!
Toussaint L'Ouverture and his army of former slaves battle for independence from France and an end to slavery. Although Toussaint achieved his goal of ending slavery, Haiti (see inset) did not become independent until after his death. *Why do you think Toussaint and his army were willing to risk death to achieve their goals?*

conditions for the majority of Mexicans, abolish slavery, and give the vote to all men. For four years, Morelos led rebel forces before he, too, was captured and shot in 1815.

Spanish forces, backed by conservative creoles, hunted down the surviving guerrillas. They had almost succeeded in ending the rebel movement when events in Spain had unexpected effects.

Mexico Wins Independence In Spain in 1820, liberals forced the king to issue a constitution. This move alarmed Agustín de Iturbide (ee toor BEE day), a conservative creole in Mexico. He feared that the new Spanish government might impose liberal reforms on the colonies as well.

Iturbide had spent years fighting Mexican revolutionaries. Suddenly, in 1821, he reached out to them. Backed by creoles, mestizos, and Native Americans, he overthrew the Spanish viceroy. Mexico was independent at last. Iturbide took the title Emperor Agustín I. Soon, however, liberal Mexicans toppled the would-be monarch and set up the Republic of Mexico.

New Republics Emerge in Central America Spanish-ruled lands in Central America declared independence in the early 1820s. Iturbide tried to add these areas to his Mexican empire. After his overthrow, local leaders set up a republic called the United Provinces of Central America. The union soon fragmented into the separate republics of Guatemala, Nicaragua, Honduras, El Salvador, and Costa Rica.

 Checkpoint How did events in Spain affect the fight for Mexican independence?

Revolution Ignites South America

In South America, Native Americans had rebelled against Spanish rule as early as the 1700s, though with limited results. It was not until the 1800s that discontent among the creoles sparked a widespread drive for independence.

Bolívar Begins the Fight In the early 1800s, discontent spread across South America. Educated creoles like Simón Bolívar admired the French and American revolutions. They dreamed of winning their own independence from Spain.

In 1808, when Napoleon Bonaparte occupied Spain, Bolívar and his friends saw the occupation as a signal to act. In 1810, Bolívar led an uprising that established a republic in his native Venezuela. Bolívar's new republic was quickly toppled by conservative forces, however. For years, civil war raged in Venezuela. The revolutionaries suffered many setbacks. Twice Bolívar was forced into exile on the island of Haiti.

Then, Bolívar conceived a daring plan. He would march his army across the Andes and attack the Spanish at Bogotá, the capital of the viceroyalty of New Granada (present-day Colombia). First, he cemented an alliance with the hard-riding llañeros, or Venezuelan cowboys. Then, in a grueling campaign, he led an army through swampy lowlands and over the snowcapped Andes. Finally, in August 1819, he swooped down to take Bogotá from the surprised Spanish.

Other victories followed. By 1821, Bolívar had succeeded in freeing Caracas, Venezuela. "The Liberator," as he was now called, then moved south into Ecuador, Peru, and Bolivia. There, he joined forces with another great leader, **José de San Martín.**

LATIN AMERICAN INDEPENDENCE

LATIN AMERICA, 1844

Independent nations with dates of independence

*United Provinces of Central America had dissolved by 1844.

**Gran Colombia had dissolved by 1830.

UNITED STATES

Atlantic Ocean

MEXICO 1821

Gulf of Mexico

Because Father Miguel Hidalgo rang the church bells calling people to revolt against the Spanish, his name became the symbol of Mexican independence.

Mexico City ✪

Bahamas (Br.)

Cuba (Sp.)

DOMINICAN REPUBLIC 1844

Jamaica (Br.)

HAITI 1804

Puerto Rico (Sp.)

British Honduras (Br.)

Caribbean Sea

Once Toussaint L'Ouverture, who was born a slave, was legally freed, he devoted himself to freeing slaves in St-Domingue (now Haiti), which led to Haiti's independence.

UNITED PROVINCES OF CENTRAL AMERICA*

GUATEMALA 1838
EL SALVADOR 1838
HONDURAS 1838
NICARAGUA 1838
COSTA RICA 1838

Mosquito Coast (Br.)

Caracas ✪

Trinidad (Br.)

British Guiana (Br.)

Dutch Guiana (Neth.)

French Guiana (Fr.)

VENEZUELA 1830

COLOMBIA ✪ 1819

Bogotá

GRAN COLOMBIA**

Panama (PART OF COLOMBIA)

EQUAL AREA PROJECTION
SCALE IN MILES
0   500   1000
SCALE IN KILOMETERS
0   500   1000

Quito

ECUADOR 1822

Equator

N
W — E — 0°
S

Pacific Ocean

José de San Martín fought against Napoleon's army for years before helping Bolívar liberate Argentina, Chile, and Peru.

Lima ✪

PERU 1824

BRAZIL 1822

Atlantic Ocean

La Paz ✪

BOLIVIA 1825

PARAGUAY 1811

Rio de Janeiro

Asunción ✪

CHILE 1818

Santiago ✪

ARGENTINE CONFEDERATION 1816

URUGUAY 1828

Buenos Aires ✪

Montevideo

Simón Bolívar freed Venezuela, Colombia, Panama, Ecuador, Peru, and Bolivia from Spanish rule.

PATAGONIA

Falkland Islands (Br.) (ARGENTINE 1820–1833)

Geography *Interactive*

For: Interactive maps and biographies
Web Code: nap-2031

LATIN AMERICA ABOUT 1790

UNITED STATES

New Spain

Bahamas (Br.)

Mexico City ✪

Cuba   Hispaniola

West Indies

British Honduras (Br.)

Mosquito Coast (Br.)

New Granada

Guianas

Bogotá ✪

EQUAL AREA PROJECTION
SCALE IN MILES
0   2000
SCALE IN KILOMETERS
0   2000

Lima ✪

Brazil

Peru

La Plata

Rio de Janeiro

Buenos Aires ✪

British
Dutch
French
Portuguese
Spanish

Thinking Critically

1. **Synthesize Information** Why did so many Latin American nations gain independence by 1830?

2. **Recognize Cause and Effect** What influenced the leaders of Latin American independence?

Dom Pedro, Emperor of Brazil

San Martín Joins the Fight Like Bolívar, San Martín was a creole. He was born in Argentina but went to Europe for military training. In 1816, this gifted general helped Argentina win freedom from Spain. He then joined the independence struggle in other areas. He, too, led an army across the Andes, from Argentina into Chile. He defeated the Spanish in Chile before moving into Peru to strike further blows against colonial rule. San Martín turned his command over to Bolívar in 1822, allowing Bolívar's forces to win the final victories against Spain.

Freedom Leads to Power Struggles The wars of independence ended by 1824. Bolívar then worked tirelessly to unite the lands he had liberated into a single nation, called Gran Colombia. Bitter rivalries, however, made that dream impossible. Before long, Gran Colombia split into four independent countries: Colombia, Panama, Venezuela, and Ecuador.

Bolívar faced another disappointment as power struggles among rival leaders triggered destructive civil wars. Before his death in 1830, a discouraged Bolívar wrote, "We have achieved our independence at the expense of everything else." Contrary to his dreams, South America's common people had simply changed one set of masters for another.

Brazil Gains Independence When Napoleon's armies conquered Portugal, the Portuguese royal family fled to Brazil. When the king returned to Portugal, he left his son **Dom Pedro** to rule Brazil. "If Brazil demands independence," the king advised Pedro, "proclaim it yourself and put the crown on your own head."

In 1822, Pedro followed his father's advice. A revolution had brought new leaders to Portugal who planned to abolish reforms and demanded that Dom Pedro return. Dom Pedro refused to leave Brazil. Instead, he became emperor of an independent Brazil. He accepted a constitution that provided for freedom of the press, freedom of religion, and an elected legislature. Brazil remained a monarchy until 1889, when social and political turmoil led it to become a republic.

Vocabulary Builder
proclaim—(proh KLAYM) *vt.* to announce publicly or formally

 Checkpoint How were the goals of the South American revolutions different from their results?

Progress Monitoring *Online*
For: Self-quiz with vocabulary practice
Web Code: naa-2031

SECTION 3 Assessment

Terms, People, and Places

1. What do many of the key terms listed at the beginning of the section have in common? Explain.

Note Taking

2. **Reading Skill: Identify Supporting Details** Use your completed chart to answer the Focus Question: Who were the key revolutionaries that led the movements for independence in Latin America, and what were their accomplishments?

Comprehension and Critical Thinking

3. **Draw Conclusions** How did social structure contribute to discontent in Latin America?

4. **Analyze Information** (a) What was the first step on Haiti's road to independence? (b) Why did creoles refuse to support Hidalgo or Morelos?

5. **Identify Central Issues** Why did Bolívar admire the American and French revolutions?

● **Writing About History**

Quick Write: Use Effective Language Most effective persuasive essays contain memorable and convincing details and vivid, persuasive language. Suppose you were one of the revolutionary leaders mentioned in the section. Write notes for a speech in which you persuade others to join your cause. Include at least three compelling reasons why people should follow you.

Simón Bolívar: *Address to the Congress of Venezuela*

Encouraged by the revolutions in British North America and France, colonists in Spanish South America soon began to create a force for independence. Simón Bolívar was one of the leaders of this movement. The excerpt below is from Bolívar's Address to the Second National Congress of Venezuela, given in 1819. In this speech, Bolívar offers advice on what type of government to set up in Venezuela.

Subject to the threefold yoke of ignorance, tyranny, and vice, the American people have been unable to acquire knowledge, power, or [civic] virtue. The lessons we received and the models we studied, as pupils of such pernicious[1] teachers, were most destructive. . . .

If a people, perverted by their training, succeed in achieving their liberty, they will soon lose it, for it would be of no avail to endeavor to explain to them that happiness consists in the practice of virtue; that the rule of law is more powerful than the rule of tyrants, because, as the laws are more inflexible everyone should submit to their beneficent austerity; that proper morals, and not force, are the bases of law; and that to practice justice is to practice liberty.

Therefore, Legislators, your work is so much the more arduous[2], inasmuch as you have to reeducate men who have been corrupted by erroneous[3] illusions and false incentives[4]. Liberty, says Rousseau, is a succulent[5] morsel, but one difficult to digest. . . .

Legislators, meditate well before you choose. Forget not that you are to lay the political foundation for a newly born nation which can rise to the heights of greatness that Nature has marked out for it if you but proportion this foundation in keeping with the high plane that it aspires to attain. Unless your choice is based upon the peculiar . . . experience of Venezuelan people—a factor that should guide you in determining the nature and form of government you are about to adopt for the well-being of the people . . . the result of our reforms will again be slavery.

Statue of Bolívar as the Liberator, Mexico City

1. **pernicious** (pur NISH us) *adj.* harmful, injurious
2. **arduous** (AHR joo us) *adj.* difficult
3. **erroneous** (eh ROH nee us) *adj.* mistaken, wrong
4. **incentive** (in SEN tiv) *n.* reason for doing something
5. **succulent** (SUK yoo lunt) *adj.* juicy, tasty

Thinking Critically

1. **Analyze Literature** How did Bolívar feel the people of Latin America were prepared for new government?
2. **Draw Inferences** Do you think Bolívar was practical or idealistic? Use examples from the excerpt to defend your opinion.

651

Quick Study Guide

 SSWH14b

■ Revolutions in Europe

Successful	Unsuccessful
Serbia (autonomy 1830)	Poland (1830)
Greece (1830)	Austria (1848)
Belgium (1830)	Italy (1848)
	Germany (1848)

■ Events in France

July 1830	**1840**	**February 1848**
• Rebels take control of Paris. • Constitutional monarchy proclaimed. • Louis Philippe becomes king.	• Recession heightens discontent.	• Rebels take to the streets. • Second Republic is proclaimed. • Louis Philippe abdicates.

June 1848	**1850**	**1852**
• Bourgeois liberals crush workers' rebellion.	• Louis Napoleon is voted president of the Second Republic.	• Louis Napoleon becomes emperor of the Second Empire.

■ Independence Movements in Latin America

Cause and Effect	
Long-Term Causes	**Immediate Causes**
• European domination • Spread of Enlightenment ideas • American and French Revolutions • Growth of nationalism	• Social injustices • Revolutionary leaders emerge. • Napoleon invades Spain.

Independence Movements	
Immediate Effects	**Long-Term Effects**
• Toussaint L'Ouverture leads slave revolt in Haiti. • Bolívar, San Martin, and others lead successful revolts. • Colonial rule ends in much of Latin America.	• Numerous independent nations in Latin America • Continuing efforts to achieve stable democratic governments and to gain economic independence

■ Age of Revolution

Chapter Events	**1804** Haiti declares independence from France.	**1810** Father Miguel Hidalgo urges Mexicans to fight for independence from Spain.		**1819** Simón Bolívar seizes Bogotá from the Spanish.	**1821** Simón Bolívar liberates Caracas, Venezuela.
Global Events	**1800**	**1810**		**1820**	
	1803 United States buys Louisiana from France.	**1814** Napoleon is banished to Elba.		**1819** The United States acquires Spanish Florida.	**1823** U.S. President James Monroe issues the Monroe Doctrine.

Concept Connector

Essential Question Review

To connect prior knowledge with what you have learned in this chapter, answer the questions below in your Concept Connector journal. Use the journal in the Reading and Note Taking Study Guide to record your answers (or go to www.phschool.com **Web Code: nad-2007**). In addition, record information about the following concepts:

- Conflict: European revolutionaries in 1830 and 1848
- Revolution: Latin American revolutions against European rulers

1. **Conflict** The early 1800s saw a clash of opposing ideologies. Conservatives favored monarchies as a political system. Liberals supported a republican form of government. How did conservatives benefit from the status quo, or existing state of affairs? Why did liberals and nationalists oppose the status quo? What steps did Prince Clemens von Metternich urge monarchs to take to maintain their power?

2. **Democracy** Before his death in 1830, Simón Bolívar wrote, "We have achieved our independence at the expense of everything else." What did he mean? How were the outcomes of Latin American revolutions similar to, and different from, the American Revolution? Think about the following:
   - social classes
   - constitutions
   - cooperation between the colonies

Connections to Today

1. **Nationalism: Mexican Independence Day** Today, the people of Mexico remember Father Hidalgo's speech as "el Grito de Dolores." Every September 15, the anniversary of the speech, the president of Mexico rings a bell—suggestive of the church bell in Dolores. The president then honors the Grito de Dolores by repeating the speech. The next day, September 16, marks the anniversary of the beginning of the fight against the Spanish. It is celebrated as Mexican Independence Day, a national holiday. Schools and businesses shut down, and people throw huge parties. Fireworks light the night sky. Why is the ringing of bells an important custom of Mexican Independence Day?

2. **Conflict: Chechnya and Russia** There are many struggles for independence in the world today. Certain Basques in Spain, Tibetans in China, and Chechens in Russia are all seeking their independence. In some cases, such as in Chechnya, revolutionaries resort to terrorism to fight for their goals. Conduct research and write a one-page report about Chechnya and why its revolutionaries seek independence from Russia.

| 1830 French revolutionaries battle the king's troops in the streets of Paris. | | 1848 Revolutions break out across much of Europe. | **History Interactive** For: Interactive timeline Web Code: nap-2001 |

HISTOIRE DU GAMIN DE PARIS Par J. LERMINA.

1830   1840   1850

1839 China and Britain clash in the Opium War.

1850 Taiping Rebellion begins in China.

Chapter Assessment

Terms, People, and Places

Match the following terms with the definitions below.

creole	peninsular
autonomy	ideology
Louis Philippe	mestizo
recession	José de San Martín

1. system of thought and belief
2. self-rule
3. person in Spain's colonies in the Americas who was an American-born descendant of Spanish settlers
4. period of reduced economic activity
5. person in Spain's colonies in the Americas who was of Native American and European descent
6. known as the "citizen king"
7. fought for freedom in South America
8. member of the highest class in Spain's colonies in the Americas

Main Ideas

Section 1 (pp. 634–637)
9. In the early 1800s, what were the main goals of (a) conservatives, (b) liberals, and (c) nationalists?

Section 2 (pp. 638–644)
10. What were the causes of the French revolution of 1830?
11. Describe the outcomes of the 1848 rebellions in Europe.

Section 3 (pp. 645–651)
12. (a) How did Mexico gain independence from Spain? (b) How did Mexico's independence change the lives of its people?
13. Why is Simón Bolívar known as "The Liberator"?

Chapter Focus Question
14. How did revolutionary ideals in Europe and Latin America ignite uprisings in the first half of the nineteenth century?

Critical Thinking

15. **Recognize Cause and Effect** How did the clash of conservatism, liberalism, and nationalism contribute to unrest in Europe in the 1800s?
16. **Draw Conclusions** Why do you think liberals of the early 1800s supported limited voting rights?
17. **Synthesize Information** In the 1820s, Britain, France, and Russia supported the Greek struggle for independence. (a) Why did these European powers support the Greeks? (b) Did the European powers usually respond to revolution in this way? Explain.
18. **Analyze Information** You have read Metternich's comment: "When France sneezes, Europe catches cold." (a) What did he mean by these words? (b) Was Metternich correct?
19. **Geography and History** Review the map in Section 3. How does the map show that Bolívar failed to achieve one of his dreams?
20. **Analyzing Visuals** The scene below is part of a famous mural by José Clemente Orozco. How do you think Orozco feels about Father Hidalgo?

21. **Geography and History** (a) How did climatic conditions help Haitians defeat the French? (b) Do you think the distance between Europe and Latin America affected the Latin American wars for independence? Explain.

● Writing About History

In this Chapter's three Section Assessments, you developed skills for writing a persuasive essay.

Writing a Persuasive Essay The early 1800s were a time of revolution across Europe. Liberals and nationalists attempted to organize revolts that might overthrow Europe's colonial rule. Write a persuasive essay that a liberal or nationalist might have published in an attempt to persuade people to join a revolution.

Prewriting
• Take notes about the ideas that motivated revolutionaries in the early 1800s.

• Generate arguments that a liberal or nationalist might make.

Drafting
• Using a convincing thesis, or main argument, make an outline that organizes the essay.
• Write an attention-grabbing introduction, a body, and a conclusion.
• Open and close with your strongest argument.

Revising
• Use the guidelines for revising your essay on page SH17 of the Writing Handbook.

Prepare for the GHSGT

The Revolutions of 1848: The Aftermath

The revolutions of 1848 began spontaneously in February 1848 on the streets of Paris. Reformers won short-lived success with the abdication of Louis Philippe. Uprisings spread across Europe to Austria, Hungary, Germany, and Italy, among others. These rebellions were quelled in short order, as the documents below illustrate, but some reverberations were more lasting.

Document A

"[O]n June 23rd, 1848 . . . the proletarians of Paris were defeated, decimated [killed off so that a large part of the population was removed], crushed with such an effect that even now they have not yet recovered from the blow. And immediately, all over Europe, the new and old Conservatives and Counter-Revolutionists raised their heads with an effrontery [boldness] that showed how well they understood the importance of the event. The Press was everywhere attacked, the rights of meeting and association were interfered with, every little event in every small provincial town was taken profit of to disarm the people to declare a state of siege, to drill the troops in the new maneuvers and artifices [clever tricks] that Cavaignac [French general known for his harsh treatment of Parisian rebels] had taught them."

—From ***The Paris Rising—Frankfort Assembly***
by Frederich Engels (February, 1852)

Document B

"[German] factory workers failed to win any lasting class advantages in 1848–1849 . . . Many artisans exerted themselves for the revolution; in October 1849 the magazine of the cigar workers estimated that three hundred in this industry alone had been forced to flee to Switzerland. . . . For German democrats—whether workers or from the middle class—the revolution left little immediate consolation. In a few states democrats retained large representation in the parliaments, but reactionary changes in the suffrage systems soon ended that. . . . But the long-range results of the revolution were not altogether negative. To be sure, those who worked for democracy after 1849 knew better than to try to create a republic. They also knew the futility of resorting to revolutionary violence. But their effort did not cease."

—From ***The Democratic Movement in Germany, 1789–1914***
by John L. Snell

Document C

Metternich Flees Austria

Document D

"The rising of 1848 was a spontaneous expression of national feeling but completely uncoordinated and therefore defeated in detail. After it, once more patrolled by Austria, Italy sank back into inaction. . . . From the wreck of Italian political institutions in 1849 there was only one survival, the constitution granted by [King] Charles Albert in Piedmont [kingdom in northwestern Italy]. It provided for a Premier or President of the Council, who, like the Senate, was nominated by the King, and a Chamber of Deputies numbering two hundred and four, elected on a narrow franchise [vote]."

—From ***The Evolution of Modern Italy***
by Arthur James Whyte

Analyzing Documents

Use your knowledge of the revolutions of 1848 and Documents A, B, C, and D to answer questions 1–4.

1. Which words describe the attitude of the author of Document A toward the counter-revolutionaries?
   A admiration and pride
   B understanding and sympathy
   C hatred and disapproval
   D respect and sympathy

2. According to Document B, what strategies did the democrats of Germany follow after the revolution was put down?
   A revolutionary plots
   B voter-registration drives
   C underground efforts
   D parliamentary politics

3. In Document C, Prince Clemens von Metternich is
   A proud to resign.
   B continuing Austrian governance.
   C expressing nationalism.
   D unpopular and defeated.

4. **Writing Task** Describe the aftermath of the revolutions of 1848. If you had lived in 1849, would you have seen causes for optimism or pessimism? How would your answer be different from the viewpoint of the twenty-first century?

655

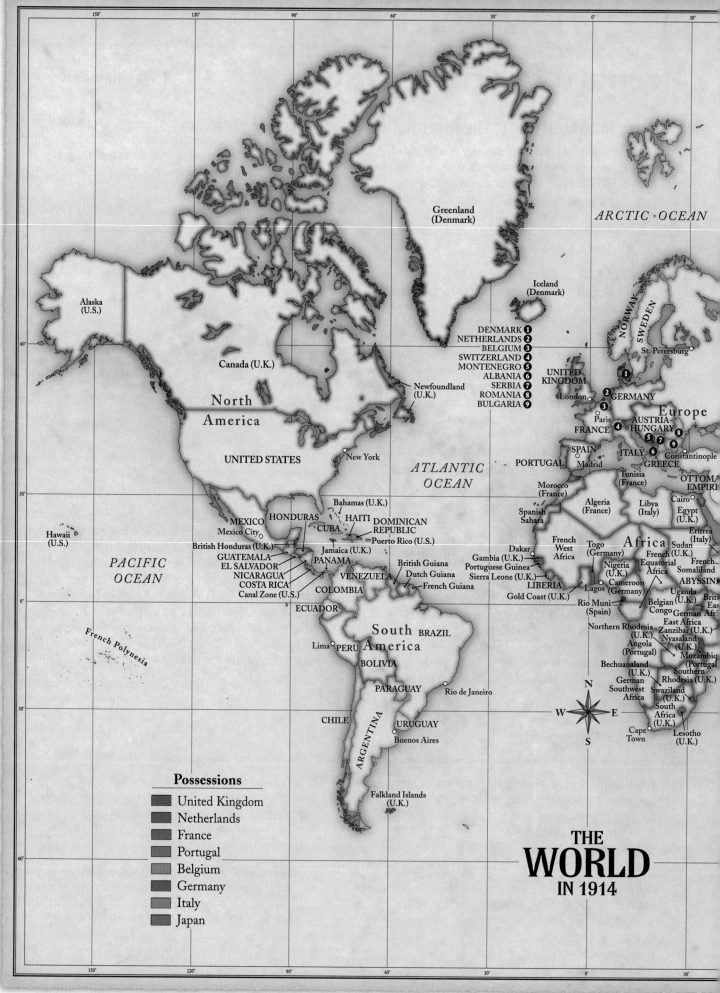

THE
WORD
IN 1914

Possessions

- United Kingdom
- Netherlands
- France
- Portugal
- Belgium
- Germany
- Italy
- Japan

ARCTIC · OCEAN

Greenland
(Denmark)

Iceland
(Denmark)

Alaska
(U.S.)

Canada (U.K.)

North
America

Newfoundland
(U.K.)

UNITED STATES

New York

ATLANTIC
OCEAN

Hawaii
(U.S.)

PACIFIC
OCEAN

MEXICO
Mexico City

HONDURAS
British Honduras (U.K.)
GUATEMALA
EL SALVADOR
NICARAGUA
COSTA RICA
Canal Zone (U.S.)

Bahamas (U.K.)
CUBA
HAITI
DOMINICAN
REPUBLIC
Puerto Rico (U.S.)
Jamaica (U.K.)
PANAMA

VENEZUELA
COLOMBIA
ECUADOR

British Guiana
Dutch Guiana
French Guiana

French Polynesia

South
America
BRAZIL

Lima PERU
BOLIVIA
PARAGUAY
Rio de Janeiro

CHILE
ARGENTINA
URUGUAY
Buenos Aires

Falkland Islands
(U.K.)

DENMARK ❶
NETHERLANDS ❷
BELGIUM ❸
SWITZERLAND ❹
MONTENEGRO ❺
ALBANIA ❻
SERBIA ❼
ROMANIA ❽
BULGARIA ❾

NORWAY
SWEDEN
St. Petersburg

UNITED
KINGDOM
London ❶ GERMANY
❷ Europe
❸
Paris ❹ AUSTRIA-
FRANCE HUNGARY ❽
❼ ❾
SPAIN ITALY ❺
PORTUGAL ❻ Constantinople
Madrid GREECE
Tunisia OTTOMAN
Morocco (France) EMPIRE
(France) Cairo
Spanish Algeria Libya Egypt
Sahara (France) (Italy) (U.K.)
Eritrea
(Italy)
Dakar French Africa Sudan
Gambia (U.K.) West French (U.K.) French
Portuguese Guinea Africa Togo Somaliland
Sierra Leone (U.K.) (Germany) Nigeria Equatorial ABYSSINI
LIBERIA (U.K.) Africa
Gold Coast (U.K.) Cameroon
Lagos (Germany) Uganda
Rio Muni (U.K.) Brit
(Spain) Belgian Eas
Congo German Afr
Northern Rhodesia East Africa
(U.K.) Zanzibar (U.K.)
Angola Nyasaland
(Portugal) (U.K.)
Bechuanaland Mozambi
(U.K.) (Portuga
German Southern
Southwest Rhodesia (U.K.)
Africa Swaziland
(U.K.)
South
Africa
Cape (U.K.) Lesotho
Town (U.K.)

N
W E
S

RUSSIAN EMPIRE

MONGOLIA

Asia

AFGHANISTAN
Tehran
PERSIA
Persian Gulf
Protectorates
(U.K.)
Oman
(U.K.)
Aden and South
Arabia (U.K.)

CHINA

TIBET   BHUTAN

Delhi   NEPAL

India
(U.K.)   Calcutta
Bombay

Beijing

Korea
(Japan)

JAPAN

Tokyo

PACIFIC
OCEAN

Macao
(Portugal)

Taiwan (Japan)

Hong Kong (U.K.)

SIAM   French
Indochina

Guam (U.S.)

German Pacific
Possessions

Marshall
Islands

British Somaliland
Italian
Somaliland

Bangkok
Malaya
(U.K.)   Saigon
Sarawak
(U.K.)
Ceylon   Singapore
(U.K.)

Brunei
(U.K.)

Philippines
(U.S.)

Caroline   Islands

British North Borneo

Kaiser
Wilhelm's
Land
(Germany)

Bismarck
Archipelago

Solomon
Islands
(U.K.)

INDIAN
OCEAN

Batavia

Dutch East Indies

Papua
(U.K.)

Portuguese Timor

Madagascar
(France)
Mauritius (U.K.)
Réunion (France)

Australia (U.K.)

New
Caledonia
(France)

Fiji (U.K.)

Sydney

New
Zealand
(U.K.)

Scale in Miles
0   1000   2000   3000

0   1000   2000   3000
Scale in Kilometers
Scale at the Equator
Mercator Projection

Geography *Interactive*
For: Audio guided tour
Web Code: nap-5000

21 Life in the Industrial Age
1800–1914

Factory Life

In 1888, Nell Cusack, a reporter for the Chicago *Times*, worked undercover to write a series of newspaper articles about the conditions under which factory girls worked:

❝ . . . The place was noisy with flying shuttles, clicking needles, and the whizzing wheels of the roaring machinery. . . . The clatter of the machines was deafening. . . . The room was low . . . and clouds of lint seemed floating about in space. Add to that poor light, bad ventilation, the exhalations of so many people, [and] the smell of dye from the cloth . . . and you have material for the make-up of [the] shop. All afternoon we sewed; sewed incessantly without uttering a syllable or resting a moment.**❞**

Listen to the Witness History audio to learn more about factory life.

German labor union poster

 ◀ **Spinner at a cotton mill in Whitnel, North Carolina, 1908**

Banner from the National Union of Women's Suffrage Societies

Performance Standards

Chapter Focus Question What were the technological, social, and economic effects of the Industrial Revolution?

Section 1
The Industrial Revolution Spreads
SSWH15a

Section 2
The Rise of the Cities
SSWH15a

Section 3
Changing Attitudes and Values
SSWH15a

Section 4
Arts in the Industrial Age
SSWHRC1c

Use the ✔ **Quick Study Timeline** at the end of this chapter to preview chapter events.

The first commercially successful typewriter, 1875

? Concept Connector ONLINE

To explore Essential Questions related to this chapter, go to PHSchool.com
Web Code: nad-2107

Painting of a nineteenth-century steel mill

The Steelmaking Process

By the 1880s, steel had replaced steam as the great symbol of the Industrial Revolution. In huge steel mills, visitors watched with awe as tons of molten metal were poured into giant mixers:

❝At night the scene is indescribably wild and beautiful. The flashing fireworks, the terrific gusts of heat, the gaping, glowing mouth of the giant chest, the quivering light from the liquid iron, the roar of a near-by converter . . . combine to produce an effect on the mind that no words can translate.❞
—J. H. Bridge, *The Inside History of the Carnegie Steel Company*

Focus Question How did science, technology, and big business promote industrial growth?

The Industrial Revolution Spreads

GA Performance Standards

- **SSWH15a** Analyze industrialization in England, Germany, and Japan.

Terms, People, and Places

Henry Bessemer	assembly line
Alfred Nobel	Orville and Wilbur Wright
Michael Faraday	Guglielmo Marconi
dynamo	stock
Thomas Edison	corporation
interchangeable parts	cartel

Note Taking

Reading Skill: Identify Main Ideas Fill in a chart like this one with the major developments of the Industrial Revolution.

The Second Industrial Revolution
- New Powers
- Industry/Business
- Transportation/Communication

The first phase of industrialization had largely been forged from iron, powered by steam engines, and driven by the British textile industry. By the mid-1800s, the Industrial Revolution entered a second phase. New industrial powers emerged. Factories powered by electricity used innovative processes to turn out new products. Changes in business organization contributed to the rise of giant companies. As the twentieth century dawned, this second Industrial Revolution transformed the economies of the Western world.

New Industrial Powers Emerge

During the early Industrial Revolution, Britain stood alone as the world's industrial giant. To protect its head start, Britain tried to enforce strict rules against exporting inventions.

For a while, the rules worked. Then, in 1807, British mechanic William Cockerill opened factories in Belgium to manufacture spinning and weaving machines. Belgium became the first European nation after Britain to industrialize. By the mid-1800s, other nations had joined the race, and several newcomers were challenging Britain's industrial supremacy.

Nations Race to Industrialize How were other nations able to catch up with Britain so quickly? First, nations such as Germany, France, and the United States had more abundant supplies of coal, iron, and other resources than did Britain. Also, they had the advantage of being able to follow Britain's lead. Like Belgium,

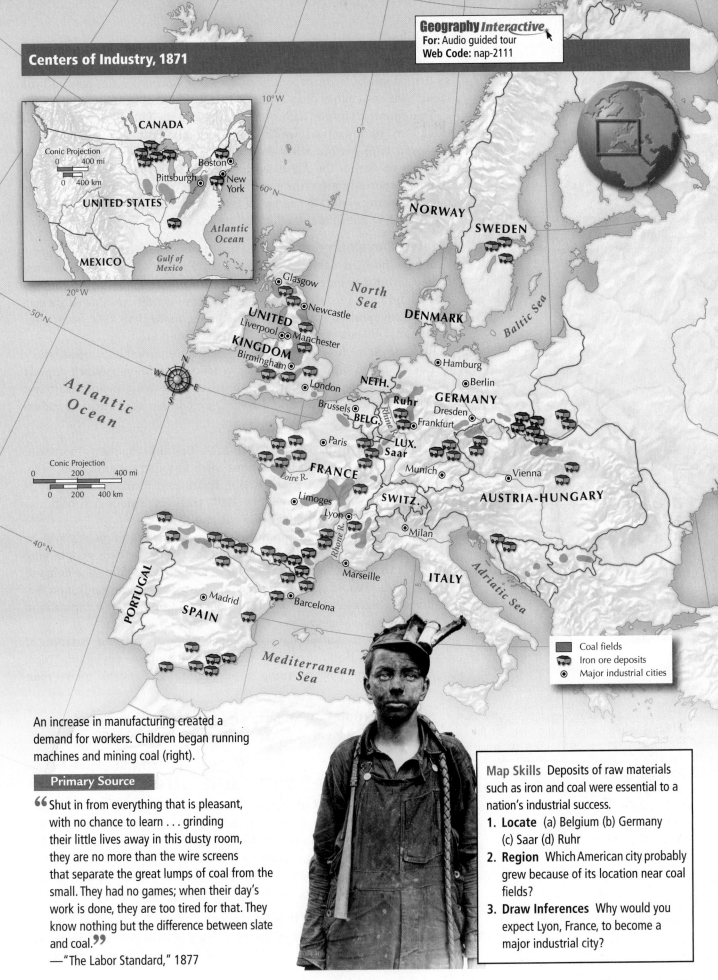

Centers of Industry, 1871

Geography *Interactive*
For: Audio guided tour
Web Code: nap-2111

Conic Projection
0   400 mi
0   400 km

CANADA

UNITED STATES

MEXICO

Boston
Pittsburgh
New York

Atlantic Ocean

Gulf of Mexico

NORWAY

SWEDEN

DENMARK

North Sea

Baltic Sea

Atlantic Ocean

Glasgow
Newcastle
UNITED KINGDOM
Liverpool Manchester
Birmingham
London

NETH.
Brussels
BELG.

Hamburg
Berlin

Ruhr   GERMANY
Dresden
Frankfurt

Paris
LUX.
Saar
FRANCE
Munich

Limoges

Lyon

SWITZ.

Milan

Vienna

AUSTRIA-HUNGARY

Conic Projection
0   200   400 mi
0   200   400 km

Loire R.
Rhône R.
Rhine R.

PORTUGAL
Madrid
SPAIN

Barcelona

Marseille

Mediterranean Sea

ITALY

Adriatic Sea

■ Coal fields
■ Iron ore deposits
⊙ Major industrial cities

An increase in manufacturing created a demand for workers. Children began running machines and mining coal (right).

Primary Source

❝Shut in from everything that is pleasant, with no chance to learn . . . grinding their little lives away in this dusty room, they are no more than the wire screens that separate the great lumps of coal from the small. They had no games; when their day's work is done, they are too tired for that. They know nothing but the difference between slate and coal.❞
—"The Labor Standard," 1877

Map Skills Deposits of raw materials such as iron and coal were essential to a nation's industrial success.
1. **Locate** (a) Belgium (b) Germany (c) Saar (d) Ruhr
2. **Region** Which American city probably grew because of its location near coal fields?
3. **Draw Inferences** Why would you expect Lyon, France, to become a major industrial city?

latecomers often borrowed British experts or technology. The first American textile factory was built in Pawtucket, Rhode Island, with plans smuggled out of Britain. American inventor Robert Fulton powered his steamboat with one of James Watt's steam engines.

Two countries in particular—Germany and the United States—thrust their way to industrial leadership. Germany united into a powerful nation in 1871. Within a few decades, it became Europe's leading industrial power. Across the Atlantic, the United States advanced even more rapidly, especially after the Civil War. By 1900, the United States was manufacturing about 30 percent of the world's industrial goods, surpassing Britain as the leading industrial nation.

Uneven Development Other nations industrialized more slowly, particularly those in eastern and southern Europe. These nations often lacked natural resources or the capital to invest in industry. Although Russia did have resources, social and political conditions slowed its economic development. Only in the late 1800s, more than 100 years after Britain, did Russia lumber toward industrialization.

In East Asia, however, Japan offered a remarkable success story. Although Japan lacked many basic resources, it industrialized rapidly after 1868 because of a political revolution that made modernization a priority. Canada, Australia, and New Zealand also built thriving industries during this time.

Effects of Industrialization Like Britain, the new industrial nations underwent social changes, such as rapid urbanization. Men, women, and children worked long hours in difficult and dangerous conditions. As you will read, by 1900, these conditions had begun to improve in many industrialized nations.

The factory system produced huge quantities of new goods at lower prices than ever before. In time, ordinary workers were buying goods that in earlier days only the wealthy could afford. The demand for goods created jobs, as did the building of cities, railroads, and factories. Politics changed, too, as leaders had to meet the demands of an industrial society.

Globally, industrial nations competed fiercely, altering patterns of world trade. Because of their technological and economic advantage, the Western powers came to <u>dominate</u> the world more than ever before.

✓ **Checkpoint** What factors led to the industrialization of other nations after Britain?

Technology Sparks Industrial Growth

During the early Industrial Revolution, inventions such as the steam engine were generally the work of gifted tinkerers. They experimented with simple machines to make them better. By the 1880s, the pace of change quickened as companies hired professional chemists and engineers to create new products and machinery. The union of science, technology, and industry spurred economic growth.

Steel Production and the Bessemer Process American inventor William Kelly and British engineer **Henry Bessemer** independently developed a new process for making steel from iron. In 1856, Bessemer

Vocabulary Builder

<u>dominate</u>—(DAHM uh nayt) *v.* to rule or control by power or influence

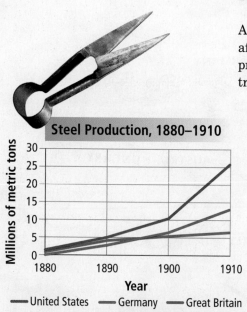

Steel Production, 1880–1910

United States — Germany — Great Britain

Graph Skills By the late 1800s, steel was the major material used in manufacturing tools, such as the sheep shears (above). The graph shows the amount of steel produced by the United States, Germany, and Great Britain. *Between 1890 and 1910, which nation had the greatest increase in steel production? The smallest?*

SOURCES: *European Historical Statistics, 1750–1970; Historical Statistics of the United States*

patented this process. Steel was lighter, harder, and more durable than iron, so it could be produced very cheaply. Steel quickly became the major material used in tools, bridges, and railroads.

As steel production soared, industrialized countries measured their success in steel output. In 1880, for example, the average German steel mill produced less than 5 million metric tons of steel a year. By 1910, that figure reached nearly 15 million metric tons.

Innovations in Chemistry Chemists created hundreds of new products, from medicines such as aspirin to perfumes and soaps. Newly developed chemical fertilizers played a key role in increasing food production.

In 1866, the Swedish chemist **Alfred Nobel** invented dynamite, an explosive much safer than others used at the time. It was widely used in construction and, to Nobel's dismay, in warfare. Dynamite earned Nobel a huge fortune, which he willed to fund the famous Nobel prizes that are still awarded today.

Electric Power Replaces Steam In the late 1800s, a new power source—electricity—replaced steam as the dominant source of industrial power. Scientists like Benjamin Franklin had tinkered with electricity a century earlier. The Italian scientist Alessandro Volta developed the first battery around 1800. Later, the English chemist **Michael Faraday** created the first simple electric motor and the first **dynamo,** a machine that generates electricity. Today, all electrical generators and transformers work on the principle of Faraday's dynamo.

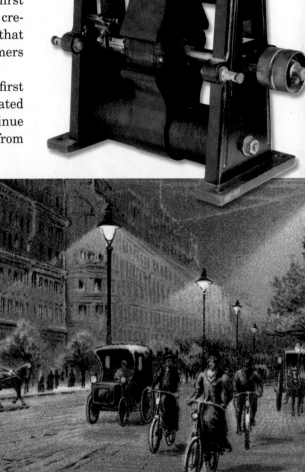

In the 1870s, the American inventor **Thomas Edison** made the first electric light bulb. Soon, Edison's "incandescent lamps" illuminated whole cities. The pace of city life quickened, and factories could continue to operate after dark. By the 1890s, cables carried electrical power from dynamos to factories.

New Methods of Production The basic features of the factory system remained the same during the 1800s. Factories still used large numbers of workers and power-driven machines to mass-produce goods. To improve efficiency, however, manufacturers designed products with **interchangeable parts,** identical components that could be used in place of one another. Interchangeable parts simplified both the assembly and repair of products.

By the early 1900s, manufacturers had introduced another new method of production, the **assembly line.** Workers on an assembly line add parts to a product that moves along a belt from one work station to the next. A different person performs each task along the assembly line. This division of labor in an assembly line, like interchangeable parts, made production faster and cheaper, lowering the price of goods. Although dividing labor into separate tasks proved to be more efficient, it took much of the joy out of the work itself.

Electricity Lights Up Cities
This early dynamo (above) generated enough electricity to power lights in factories. Electricity changed life outdoors as well. *Judging from this print, how did electricity make life easier for people in the city?*

✔ **Checkpoint** What was the dynamo's impact on the Industrial Revolution?

The Modern Office

The Bessemer process prepared the way for the use of steel in building construction. Before steel, frameworks consisted of heavy iron. Steel provided a much lighter framework and enabled the construction of taller buildings. The first skyscrapers were between 10 and 20 stories high. They were built in the United States in the 1880s to house large corporations.

Elevators made it practical for buildings to have more than five or six stories.

Offices could be illuminated with **electric lights** both night and day.

Telephones allowed workers to send and receive messages faster than the telegraph.

Typewriters enabled workers to type information faster than they could write it by hand.

Automobiles and subway systems permitted rapid transit to and from cities.

ILLUSTRATION NOT TO SCALE

Thinking Critically

1. **Draw Inferences** Why did industrialization create a need for skyscrapers?
2. **Synthesize Information** What invention do you think had the most impact on offices? Explain.

Transportation and Communication Advances

During the Industrial Revolution, transportation and communications were transformed by technology. Steamships replaced sailing ships, and railroad building took off. In Europe and North America, rail lines connected inland cities and seaports, mining regions and industrial centers. In the United States, a transcontinental railroad provided rail service from the Atlantic to the Pacific. In the same way, Russians built the Trans-Siberian Railroad, linking Moscow in European Russia to Vladivostok on the Pacific. Railroad tunnels and bridges crossed the Alps in Europe and the Andes in South America. Passengers and goods rode on rails in India, China, Egypt, and South Africa.

The Automobile Age Begins The transportation revolution took a new turn when a German engineer, Nikolaus Otto, invented a gasoline-powered internal combustion engine. In 1886, Karl Benz received a patent for the first automobile, which had three wheels. A year later, Gottlieb Daimler (DYM lur) introduced the first four-wheeled automobile. People laughed at the "horseless carriages," but they quickly transformed transportation.

The French nosed out the Germans as early automakers. Then the American Henry Ford started making models that reached the breathtaking speed of 25 miles per hour. In the early 1900s, Ford began using the assembly line to mass-produce cars, making the United States a leader in the automobile industry.

Airplanes Take Flight The internal combustion engine powered more than cars. Motorized threshers and reapers boosted farm production. Even more dramatically, the internal combustion engine made possible sustained, pilot-controlled flight. In 1903, American bicycle makers **Orville and Wilbur Wright** designed and flew a flimsy airplane at Kitty Hawk, North Carolina. Although their flying machine stayed aloft for only a few seconds, it ushered in the air age.

Soon, daredevil pilots were flying airplanes across the English Channel and over the Alps. Commercial passenger travel, however, would not begin until the 1920s.

Rapid Communication A revolution in communications also made the world smaller. An American inventor, Samuel F. B. Morse, developed

In 1901, Guglielmo Marconi (left) was in Newfoundland to receive the first overseas radio transmission from his assistant in England. Did Marconi's prediction come true? Explain.

Primary Source

❝ Shortly before mid-day I placed the single earphone to my ear and started listening. . . . I heard, faintly but distinctly, *pip-pip-pip*. . . . I now felt for the first time absolutely certain that the day would come when mankind would be able to send messages without wires not only across the Atlantic, but between the farthermost ends of the earth. ❞

the telegraph, which could send coded messages over wires by means of electricity. His first telegraph line went into service between Washington, D.C. and Baltimore, in 1844. By the 1860s, an undersea cable was relaying messages between Europe and North America. This trans-Atlantic cable was an amazing engineering accomplishment for its day.

Communication soon became even faster. In 1876, the Scottish-born American inventor Alexander Graham Bell patented the telephone. By the 1890s, Nikola Tesla had experimented with "wireless" transmissions and Italian pioneer **Guglielmo Marconi** had invented the radio. In 1901, Marconi received a radio message, using Morse code, sent from Britain to Canada. Radio would become a cornerstone of today's global communications network.

✔ **Checkpoint** How did technological advances in transportation and communications affect the Industrial Revolution?

Business Takes a New Direction

By the late 1800s, what we call "big business" came to dominate industry. Big business refers to an establishment that is run by entrepreneurs who finance, manufacture, and distribute goods. As time passed, some big businesses came to control entire industries.

Rise of Big Business New technologies required the investment of large amounts of money, or capital. To get the needed capital, owners sold **stock,** or shares in their companies, to investors. Each stockholder became owner of a tiny part of a company. Large-scale companies, such as steel foundries, needed so much capital that they sold hundreds of thousands of shares. These businesses formed giant **corporations,** businesses that are owned by many investors who buy shares of stock. With large amounts of capital, corporations could expand into many areas.

Move Toward Monopolies Powerful business leaders created monopolies and trusts, huge corporate structures that controlled entire industries or areas of the economy. In Germany, Alfred Krupp inherited a steelmaking business from his father. He bought up coal and iron mines as well as ore deposits—supply lines or raw materials that fed the steel business. Later, he and his son acquired plants that made tools, railroad cars, and weapons. In the United States, John D. Rockefeller built Standard Oil Company into an empire. By gaining control of oil wells, oil refineries, and oil pipelines, he dominated the American petroleum industry.

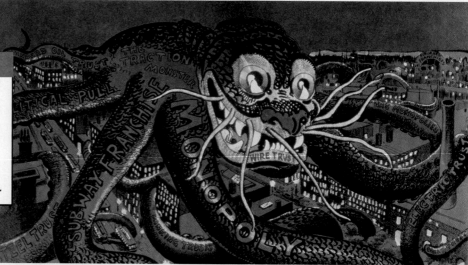

In their pursuit of profit, ruthless business leaders destroyed competing companies. With the competition gone, they were free to raise prices. Sometimes, a group of corporations would join forces and form a **cartel,** an association to fix prices, set production quotas, or control markets. In Germany, a single cartel fixed prices for 170 coal mines.

Move Toward Regulation The rise of big business and the creation of such great wealth sparked a stormy debate. Some people saw the Krupps and Rockefellers as "captains of industry" and praised their vision and skills. They pointed out that capitalists invested their wealth in worldwide ventures, such as railroad building, that employed thousands of workers and added to the general prosperity.

To others, the aggressive magnates were "robber barons." Destroying competition, critics argued, damaged the free-enterprise system, or the laissez-faire economy. Reformers called for laws to prevent monopolies and regulate large corporations. Despite questionable business practices, big business found support from many government leaders. By the early 1900s, some governments did move against monopolies. However, the political and economic power of business leaders often hindered efforts at regulation.

✔ **Checkpoint** Why were big business leaders "captains of industry" to some, but "robber barons" to others?

Assessment

Terms, People, and Places

1. For each term, person, or place listed at the beginning of the section, write a sentence explaining its significance.

Note Taking

2. **Reading Skill: Identify Main Ideas** Use your completed chart to answer the Focus Question: How did science, technology, and big business promote industrial growth?

Comprehension and Critical Thinking

3. **Summarize** How did the Industrial Revolution spread in the 1800s?
4. **Draw Conclusions** How did technology help industry expand?
5. **Recognize Cause and Effect** How did the need for capital lead to new business organizations and methods?
6. **Predict** How might government change as a result of industrialization?

● Writing About History

Quick Write: Define a Problem Choose one topic from this section that you could use to write a problem-and-solution essay. For example, you could write about the impact of powerful monopolies. Make a list of details, facts, and examples that define the problems that monopolies pose to a free market.

Charles Dickens with an illustration from one of his serialized novels

WITNESS HISTORY 🔊 AUDIO

London Fog

Between 1850 and 1900, London's population more than doubled, rising from about 2.6 million people to more than 6.5 million people. With the rapid population growth came increased pollution and health problems:

❝ It was a foggy day in London, and the fog was heavy and dark. Animate [living] London, with smarting eyes and irritated lungs, was blinking, wheezing, and choking; inanimate [nonliving] London was a sooty spectre, divided in purpose between being visible and invisible, and so being wholly neither. ❞
—Charles Dickens, *Our Mutual Friend*

Focus Question How did the Industrial Revolution change life in the cities?

The Rise of the Cities

 Performance Standards

- **SSWH15a** Analyze movements for political reform and urbanization and their effects on women.

Terms, People, and Places

germ theory	Joseph Lister
Louis Pasteur	urban renewal
Robert Koch	mutual-aid society
Florence Nightingale	standard of living

Note Taking

Reading Skill: Identify Supporting Details As you read, look for the main ideas and supporting details and how they relate to each other. Use the format below to create an outline of the section.

```
I. Medicine and the population explosion
   A. The fight against disease
      1.
      2.
   B.
II.
```

The population explosion that had begun during the 1700s continued through the 1800s. Cities grew as rural people streamed into urban areas. By the end of the century, European and American cities had begun to take on many of the features of cities today.

Medicine Contributes to the Population Explosion

Between 1800 and 1900, the population of Europe more than doubled. This rapid growth was not due to larger families. In fact, families in most industrializing countries had fewer children. Instead, populations soared because the death rate fell. Nutrition improved, thanks in part to improved methods of farming, food storage, and distribution. Medical advances and improvements in public sanitation also slowed death rates.

The Fight Against Disease Since the 1600s, scientists had known of microscopic organisms, or microbes. Some scientists speculated that certain microbes might cause specific infectious diseases. Yet most doctors scoffed at this **germ theory.** Not until 1870 did French chemist **Louis Pasteur** (pas TUR) clearly show the link between microbes and disease. Pasteur went on to make other major contributions to medicine, including the development of vaccines against rabies and anthrax. He also discovered a process called pasteurization that killed disease-carrying microbes in milk.

Florence Nightingale

When Florence Nightingale (1820–1910) arrived at a British military hospital in the Crimea in 1854, she was horrified by what she saw. The sick and wounded lay on bare ground. With no sanitation and a shortage of food, some 60 percent of all patients died. But Nightingale was a fighter. Bullying the military and medical staff, she soon had every available person cleaning barracks, digging latrines, doing laundry, and caring for the wounded. Six months later, the death rate had dropped to 2 percent.

Back in England, Nightingale was hailed as a saint. Ballads were even written about her. She took advantage of her popularity and connections to pressure the government for reforms.

How did Nightingale achieve reforms in British army hospitals?

In the 1880s, the German doctor **Robert Koch** identified the bacterium that caused tuberculosis, a respiratory disease that claimed about 30 million human lives in the 1800s. The search for a tuberculosis cure, however, took half a century. By 1914, yellow fever and malaria had been traced to microbes carried by mosquitoes.

As people understood how germs caused disease, they bathed and changed their clothes more often. In European cities, better hygiene helped decrease the rate of disease.

Hospital Care Improves In the early 1840s, anesthesia was first used to relieve pain during surgery. The use of anesthetics allowed doctors to experiment with operations that had never before been possible.

Yet, throughout the century, hospitals could be dangerous places. Surgery was performed with dirty instruments in dank rooms. Often, a patient would survive an operation, only to die days later of infection. For the poor, being admitted to a hospital was often a death sentence. Wealthy or middle-class patients insisted on treatment in their own homes.

"The very first requirement in a hospital," said British nurse **Florence Nightingale,** "is that it should do the sick no harm." As an army nurse during the Crimean War, Nightingale insisted on better hygiene in field hospitals. After the war, she worked to introduce sanitary measures in British hospitals. She also founded the world's first school of nursing.

The English surgeon **Joseph Lister** discovered how antiseptics prevented infection. He insisted that surgeons sterilize their instruments and wash their hands before operating. Eventually, the use of antiseptics drastically reduced deaths from infection.

✔ **Checkpoint** Which factors caused population rates to soar between 1800 and 1900?

City Life Changes

As industrialization progressed, cities came to dominate the West. City life, as old as civilization itself, underwent dramatic changes in Europe and the United States.

City Landscapes Change Growing wealth and industrialization altered the basic layout of European cities. City planners created spacious new squares and boulevards. They lined these avenues with government buildings, offices, department stores, and theaters.

The most extensive **urban renewal,** or rebuilding of the poor areas of a city, took place in Paris in the 1850s. Georges Haussmann, chief planner for Napoleon III, destroyed many tangled medieval streets full of tenement housing. In their place, he built wide boulevards and splendid public buildings. The project put many people to work, decreasing the threat of social unrest. The wide boulevards also made it harder for rebels to put up barricades and easier for troops to reach any part of the city.

Gradually, settlement patterns shifted. In most American cities, the rich lived in pleasant neighborhoods on the outskirts of the city. The poor crowded into slums near the city center, within reach of factories. Trolley lines made it possible to live in one part of the city and work in another.

Sidewalks, Sewers, and Skyscrapers

Sidewalks, Sewers, and Skyscrapers Paved streets made urban areas much more livable. First gas lamps, and then electric street lights <u>illuminated</u> the night, increasing safety. Cities organized police forces and expanded fire protection.

Beneath the streets, sewage systems made cities much healthier places to live. City planners knew that clean water supplies and better sanitation methods were needed to combat epidemics of cholera and tuberculosis. In Paris, sewer lines expanded from 87 miles (139 kilometers) in 1852 to more than 750 miles (1200 kilometers) by 1911. The massive new sewer systems of London and Paris were costly, but they cut death rates dramatically.

By 1900, architects were using steel to construct soaring buildings. American architects like Louis Sullivan pioneered a new structure, the skyscraper. In large cities, single-family middle-class homes gave way to multistory apartment buildings.

Slum Conditions

Slum Conditions Despite efforts to improve cities, urban life remained harsh for the poor. Some working-class families could afford better clothing, newspapers, or tickets to a music hall. But they went home to small, cramped row houses or tenements in overcrowded neighborhoods.

In the worst tenements, whole families were often crammed into a single room. Unemployment or illness meant lost wages that could ruin a family. High rates of crime and alcoholism were a constant curse. Conditions had improved somewhat from the early Industrial Revolution, but slums remained a fact of city life.

Vocabulary Builder

<u>illuminate</u>—(ih LOO muh nayt) *v.* to light up; to give light to

Jacob Riis, a police reporter, photographer, and social activist in New York City published *How the Other Half Lives* in 1890 in an effort to expose the horrible living conditions of the city slums and tenements. Conditions among the urban working class in Britain (right) were similar to those in New York described by Riis:

Primary Source

❝ Look into any of these houses, everywhere the same . . . . Here is a "flat" or "parlor" and two pitch-dark coops called bedrooms. . . . One, two, three beds are there, if the old boxes and heaps of foul straw can be called by that name; a broken stove with crazy pipe from which the smoke leaks at every joint, a table of rough boards propped up on boxes, piles of rubbish in the corner. The closeness and smell are appalling. How many people sleep here? The woman with the red bandanna shakes her head sullenly, but the bare-legged girl with the bright face counts on her fingers. . . "Six, sir!"❞

Cause and Effect

Causes

- Increased agricultural productivity
- Growing population
- New sources of energy, such as steam and coal
- Growing demand for mass-produced goods
- Improved technology
- Available natural resources, labor, and money
- Strong, stable governments

Industrial Revolution

Immediate Effects

- Rise of factories
- Changes in transportation and communication
- Urbanization
- New methods of production
- Rise of urban working class
- Growth of reform movements

Long-Term Effects

- Growth of labor unions
- Inexpensive new products
- Increased pollution
- Rise of big business
- Expansion of public education
- Expansion of middle class
- Competition for world trade
- Progress in medical care

Connections to Today

- Improvements in world health
- Growth in population
- Industrialization in developing nations
- New energy sources, such as oil and nuclear power
- Environmental pollution
- Efforts to regulate world trade

Analyze Cause and Effect The long-term effects of the Industrial Revolution touched nearly every aspect of life. *Identify two social and two economic effects of the Industrial Revolution.*

The Lure of the City Despite their drawbacks, cities attracted millions. New residents were drawn as much by the excitement as by the promise of work. For tourists, too, cities were centers of action.

Music halls, opera houses, and theaters provided entertainment for every taste. Museums and libraries offered educational opportunities. Sports, from tennis to bare-knuckle boxing, drew citizens of all classes. Few of these enjoyments were available in country villages.

 Checkpoint How did industrialization change the face of cities?

The Working Class Advances

Workers tried to improve the harsh conditions of industrial life. They protested low wages, long hours, unsafe conditions, and the constant threat of unemployment. At first, business owners and governments tried to silence protesters. By mid-century, however, workers began to make progress.

Labor Unions Begin to Grow Workers formed **mutual-aid societies,** self-help groups to aid sick or injured workers. Men and women joined socialist parties or organized unions. The revolutions of 1830 and 1848 left vivid images of worker discontent, which governments could not ignore.

By the late 1800s, most Western countries had granted all men the vote. Workers also won the right to organize unions to bargain on their behalf. Germany legalized labor unions in 1869. Britain, Austria, and France followed. By 1900, Britain had about three million union members, and Germany had about two million. In France, membership grew from 140,000 in 1890 to over a million in 1912.

The main tactic of unions was the strike, or work stoppage. Workers used strikes to demand better working conditions, wage increases, or other benefits from their employers. Violence was often a result of strikes, particularly if employers tried to continue operating their businesses without the striking workers. Employers often called in the police to stop strikes.

Pressured by unions, reformers, and working-class voters, governments passed laws to regulate working conditions. Early laws forbade employers to hire children under the age of ten. Later, laws were passed outlawing child labor entirely and banning the employment of women in mines. Other laws limited work hours and improved safety. By 1909, British coal miners had won an eight-hour day, setting a standard for workers in other countries. In Germany, and then elsewhere, Western governments established old-age pensions, as well as disability insurance for workers who were hurt or became ill. These programs protected workers from poverty once they were no longer able to work.

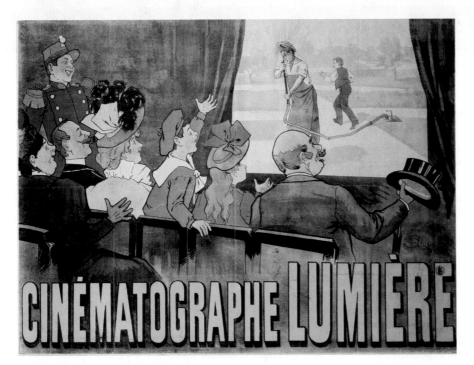

Family Life and Leisure
With standards of living rising, families could pursue activities such as going to the movies. This 1896 French poster (left) advertises the Cinématographe Lumière (loom YEHR), the most successful motion-picture camera and projector of its day. *What does the clothing of the people in the poster suggest about their social rank?*

Standards of Living Rise Wages varied throughout the industrialized world, with unskilled laborers earning less than skilled workers. Women received less than half the pay of men doing the same work. Farm laborers barely scraped by during the economic slump of the late 1800s. Periods of unemployment brought desperate hardships to industrial workers and helped boost union membership.

Overall, though, standards of living for workers did rise. The **standard of living** measures the quality and availability of necessities and comforts in a society. Families ate more varied diets, lived in better homes, and dressed in inexpensive, mass-produced clothing. Advances in medicine improved health. Some workers moved to the suburbs, traveling to work on subways and trolleys. Still, the gap between workers and the middle class widened.

✔ **Checkpoint** How did workers try to improve their living and working conditions?

SECTION 2 Assessment

Progress Monitoring *Online*
For: Self-quiz with vocabulary practice
Web Code: naa-2121

Terms, People, and Places
1. For each term, person, or place listed at the beginning of the section, write a sentence explaining its significance.

Note Taking
2. **Reading Skill: Identify Supporting Details** Use your completed outline to answer the Focus Question: How did the Industrial Revolution change life in the cities?

Comprehension and Critical Thinking
3. **Recognize Cause and Effect** Why did the rate of population growth increase in the late 1800s?
4. **Summarize** What are three ways that city life changed in the 1800s?
5. **Analyze Information** What laws helped workers in the late 1800s?
6. **Synthesize Information** How did the rise of the cities challenge the economic and social order of the time?

● **Writing About History**

Quick Write: Brainstorm Possible Solutions Choose one topic from this section, such as the hardships of city life, about which you could write a problem-solution essay. Use the text and your own knowledge to create a list of possible solutions to the problem that you've chosen to write about. Next, organize your list to rank the solutions from most effective to least effective.

Electricity's Impact on Daily Life

Few technologies have transformed daily life as dramatically as electrification. Electric power lit up city streets, helped to improve workplace productivity, revolutionized life at home, and modernized rural farms and businesses. Although electrification began in urban areas of Europe and the United States in the 1880s, it took several decades to spread to rural areas. Electrification remains an ongoing process in developing nations today.

Installing insulators on an electric pole in 1940

Electricity Customers in England and Wales	
Year	**Customers in Millions**
1920	0.9
1930	3.5
1940	9.6
1950	12.0
1960	15.5
1970	18.3
1980	20.3

SOURCE: Department of Trade and Industry, United Kingdom

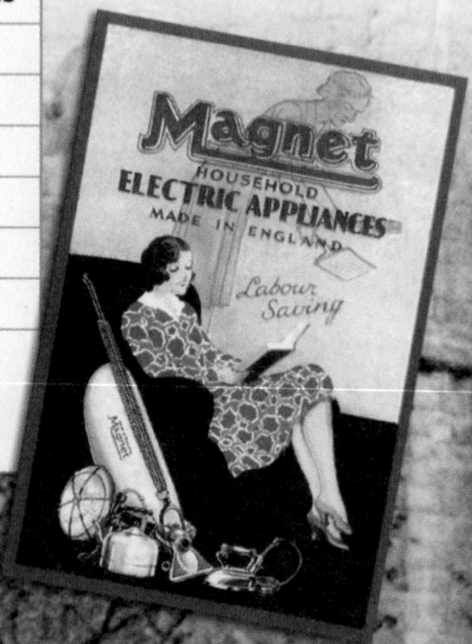

Advertisement for household electrical appliances

An electric streetcar in England, around 1900

Magnet HOUSEHOLD ELECTRIC APPLIANCES MADE IN ENGLAND *Labour Saving*

RESERVED

52

Poster celebrating the use of hydroelectric power in the former Soviet Union

Although only two percent of Japanese homes had electric power in 1907, nearly 90% had electric lighting by 1927. Above, the first electric streetlight in Tokyo's Ginza district draws a crowd.

Electric Generation Stations

Country	Year	Number of Stations
Russia	1913	220
Germany	1913	4,040
Great Britain	1912	568
Sweden	NA*	440
United States	1912	5,221

*NA Not available
SOURCE: *The Electrification of Russia, 1880–1926*

American electric mixer

The 1931 horror film *Frankenstein* exploited people's fear of electricity.

BORIS KARLOFF

Frankenstein

COLIN CLIVE
MAE CLARKE
JOHN BOLES

History Interactive

For: interactive map, audio, and more
Visit: PHSchool.com
Web Code: nap-2101

Thinking Critically

1. **Chart Skills** Which country had the fewest number of electric generation stations by 1913? Which country had the largest number? Why was there such a large difference between the two countries?
2. **Draw Conclusions** How did electricity change daily life?

National Union of Womens Suffrage Societies
LAW-ABIDING   NO PARTY

Women's suffrage banner

Suffragette arrested in London, 1914

WITNESS HISTORY ◀)) AUDIO

Votes for Women

After years of peacefully protesting the British government's refusal to allow women to vote, some activists turned to confrontation:

66 We have been driven to the conclusion that only through legislation can any improvement be effected, and that that legislation can never be effected until we have the same power as men have to bring pressure to bear upon our repre-sentatives and upon Governments to give us the necessary legislation. . . . We are here not because we are law-breakers; we are here in our efforts to become law-makers. 99
—Emmeline Pankhurst, October 21, 1908

Focus Question How did the Industrial Revolution change the old social order and long-held traditions in the Western world?

Changing Attitudes and Values

Performance Standards

• **SSWH15a** Analyze urbanization and its effect on women.

Terms, People, and Places

cult of domesticity	John Dalton
temperance movement	Charles Darwin
Elizabeth Cady Stanton	racism
women's suffrage	social gospel
Sojourner Truth	

Note Taking

Reading Skill: Identify Supporting Details As you read, create a table listing new attitudes and values in the left-hand column. List the supporting details in the right-hand column.

Changes in Social Order and Values	
Issue	**Change**
• New social order	•
• Rights for women	•
•	•

Demand for women's rights was one of many issues that chal-lenged the traditional social order in the late 1800s. By then, in many countries, the middle class—aspiring to upper-class wealth and privilege—increasingly came to dominate society.

A New Social Order Arises

The Industrial Revolution slowly changed the social order in the Western world. For centuries, the two main classes were nobles and peasants. Their roles were defined by their relationship to the land. While middle-class merchants, artisans, and lawyers played important roles, they still had a secondary position in society. With the spread of industry, a more complex social structure emerged.

Three Social Classes Emerge By the late 1800s, Western Europe's new upper class included very rich business families. Wealthy entrepreneurs married into aristocratic families, gaining the status of noble titles. Nobles needed the money brought by the industrial rich to support their lands and lifestyle.

Below this tiny elite, a growing middle class was pushing its way up the social ladder. Its highest rungs were filled with mid-level business people and professionals such as doctors and scien-tists. With comfortable incomes, they enjoyed a wide range of material goods. Next came the lower middle class, which included teachers and office workers. They struggled to keep up with their "betters."

Workers and peasants were at the base of the social ladder. In highly industrialized Britain, workers made up more than 30 percent of the population in 1900. In Western Europe and the United States, the number of farmworkers dropped, but many families still worked the land. The rural population was higher in eastern and southern Europe, where industrialization was more limited.

Middle-Class Tastes and Values By midcentury, the modern middle class had developed its own way of life. A strict code of etiquette governed social behavior. Rules dictated how to dress for every occasion, how to give a dinner party, how to pay a social call, when to write letters, and how long to mourn for dead relatives.

Parents strictly supervised their children, who were expected to be "seen but not heard." A child who misbehaved was considered to reflect badly on the entire family. Servants, too, were seen as a reflection of their employers. Even a small middle-class household was expected to have at least a cook and a housemaid.

The Ideal Home Within the family, the division of labor between wife and husband changed. Earlier, middle-class women had helped run family businesses out of the home. By the later 1800s, most middle-class husbands went to work in an office or shop. A successful husband was one who earned enough to keep his wife at home. Women spent their time raising children, directing servants, and doing religious or charitable service.

Books, magazines, and popular songs supported a **cult of domesticity** that idealized women and the home. Sayings like "home, sweet home" were stitched into needlework and hung on parlor walls. The ideal woman was seen as a tender, self-sacrificing caregiver who provided a nest for her children and a peaceful refuge for her husband to escape from the hardships of the working world.

This ideal rarely applied to the lower classes. Working-class women labored for low pay in garment factories or worked as domestic servants. Young women might leave domestic service after they married, but often had to seek other employment. Despite long days working for wages, they were still expected to take full responsibility for child care and homemaking.

✓ **Checkpoint** How had the social order changed by the late 1800s?

Tin toys (at right and below), about 1890

Domestic Life in the 1800s

During the Industrial Age, the middle-class nuclear family lived in a large house with a parlor like the one above, or perhaps in one of the new apartment houses. Rooms were crammed with large overstuffed furniture, and paintings and photographs lined the walls. Clothing reflected middle-class tastes for luxury and respectability. For the first time, women began spending more time buying household items than producing them. Women shopped at stores and through mail-order catalogs (below) that were geared toward attracting their business.

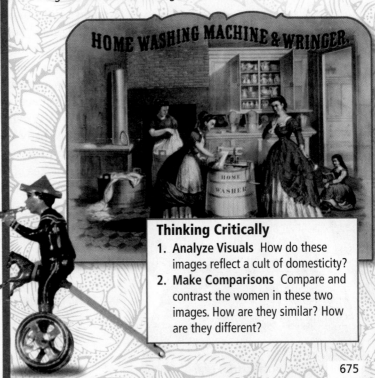

HOME WASHING MACHINE & WRINGER

Thinking Critically
1. **Analyze Visuals** How do these images reflect a cult of domesticity?
2. **Make Comparisons** Compare and contrast the women in these two images. How are they similar? How are they different?

675

Women Work for Rights

Some individual women and women's groups protested restrictions on women. They sought a broad range of rights. Across Europe and the United States, politically active women campaigned for fairness in marriage, divorce, and property laws. Women's groups also supported the **temperance movement,** a campaign to limit or ban the use of alcoholic beverages. Temperance leaders argued not only that drinking threatened family life, but that banning it was important for a productive and efficient workforce.

These reformers faced many obstacles. In Europe and the United States, women could not vote. They were barred from most schools and had little, if any, protection under the law. A woman's husband or father controlled all of her property.

Early Voices Before 1850, some women—mostly from the middle class—had campaigned for the abolition of slavery. In the process, they realized the severe restrictions on their own lives. In the United States, Lucretia Mott, **Elizabeth Cady Stanton,** and Susan B. Anthony crusaded against slavery before organizing a movement for women's rights.

Many women broke the barriers that kept them out of universities and professions. By the late 1800s, a few women trained as doctors or lawyers. Others became explorers, researchers, or inventors, often without recognition. For example, Julia Brainerd Hall worked with her brother to develop an aluminum-producing process. Their company became hugely successful, but Charles Hall received almost all of the credit.

The Suffrage Struggle By the late 1800s, married women in some countries had won the right to control their own property. The struggle for political rights proved far more difficult. In the United States, the Seneca Falls Convention of 1848 demanded that women be granted the right to vote. In Europe, groups dedicated to **women's suffrage,** or women's right to vote, emerged in the later 1800s.

Among men, some liberals and socialists supported women's suffrage. In general, though, suffragists faced intense opposition. Some critics claimed that women were too emotional to be allowed to vote. Others argued that women needed to be "protected" from grubby politics or that a woman's place was in the home, not in government. To such claims, **Sojourner Truth,** an African American suffragist, is believed to have replied, "Nobody ever helps me into carriages, or over mudpuddles, or gives me any best place! And ain't I a woman?"

On the edges of the Western world, women made faster strides. In New Zealand, Australia, and some western territories of the United States, women won the vote by the early 1900s. There, women who had "tamed the frontier" alongside men were not dismissed as weak and helpless. In the United States, Wyoming became the first state to grant women the right to vote. In Europe and most of the United States, however, the suffrage struggle succeeded only after World War I.

✔ **Checkpoint** What were the arguments against women's suffrage?

African American suffragist Sojourner Truth

Growth of Public Education

By the late 1800s, reformers persuaded many governments to set up public schools and require basic education for all children. Teaching "the three Rs"—reading, writing, and 'rithmetic—was thought to produce better citizens. In addition, industrialized societies recognized the need for a literate workforce. Schools taught punctuality, obedience to authority, disciplined work habits, and patriotism. In European schools, children also received basic religious education.

Public Education Improves At first, elementary schools were primitive. Many teachers had little schooling themselves. In rural areas, students attended class only during the times when they were not needed on the farm or in their parents' shops.

By the late 1800s, more and more children were in school, and the quality of elementary education improved. Teachers received training at Normal Schools, where the latest "norms and standards" of educational practices were taught. Beginning in 1879, schools to train teachers were established in France. In England, schooling girls and boys between the ages of five and ten became compulsory after 1881. Also, governments began to expand secondary schools, known as high schools in the United States. In secondary schools, students learned the "classical languages," Latin and Greek, along with history and mathematics.

In general, only middle-class families could afford to have their sons attend these schools, which trained students for more serious study or for government jobs. Middle-class girls were sent to school primarily in the hope that they might marry well and become better wives and mothers. Education for girls did not include subjects such as science, mathematics, or physical education because they were not seen as necessary subjects for girls to learn.

Higher Education Expands Colleges and universities expanded in this period, too. Most university students were the sons of middle- or upper-class families. The university curriculum emphasized ancient history and languages, philosophy, religion, and law. By the late 1800s, universities added courses in the sciences, especially in chemistry and physics. At the same time, engineering schools trained students who would have the knowledge and skills to build the new industrial society.

Some women sought greater educational opportunities. By the 1840s, a few small colleges for women opened, including Bedford College in England and Mount Holyoke in the United States. In 1863, the British reformer Emily Davies campaigned for female students to be allowed to take the entrance examinations for Cambridge University. She succeeded, but as late as 1897, male Cambridge students rioted against granting degrees to women.

✔ **Checkpoint** Why did more children attend school in the late 1800s than before?

Public Education
Before 1870, the only formal education available for British children was in religious schools or "ragged schools," which taught poor children basic skills, such as reading. The Industrial Revolution changed that as it created a growing need for people to be better educated. *How does this 1908 photo of a science class in London illustrate the changes that had taken place in the British educational system?*

Science Takes New Directions

Science in the service of industry brought great changes in the later 1800s. At the same time, researchers advanced startling theories about the natural world. Their new ideas challenged long-held beliefs.

Atomic Theory Develops A crucial breakthrough in chemistry came in the early 1800s when the English Quaker schoolteacher **John Dalton** developed modern atomic theory. The ancient Greeks had <u>speculated</u> that all matter was made of tiny particles called atoms. Dalton showed that each element has its own kind of atoms. Earlier theories put forth the idea that all atoms were basically alike. Dalton also showed how different kinds of atoms combine to make all chemical substances. In 1869, the Russian chemist Dmitri Mendeleyev (men duh LAY ef) drew up a table that grouped elements according to their atomic weights. His table became the basis for the periodic table of elements used today.

Debating the Earth's Age The new science of geology opened avenues of debate. In *Principles of Geology*, Charles Lyell offered evidence to

Vocabulary Builder

<u>speculate</u>—(SPEK yuh layt) *v.* to think about

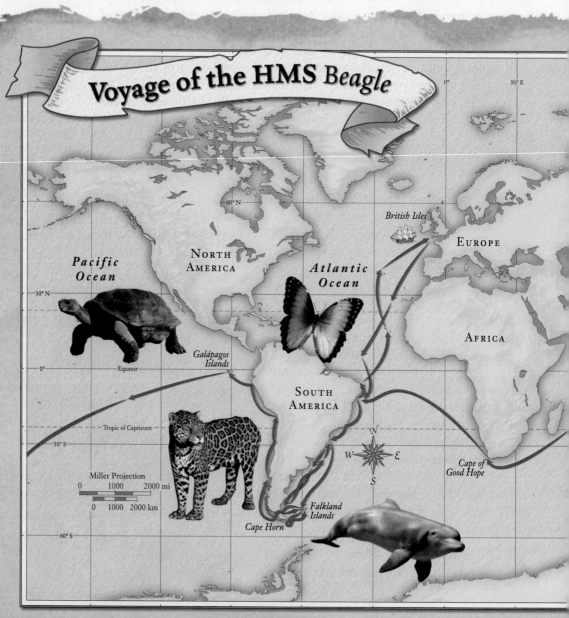

INFOGRAPHIC

In 1831, the HMS *Beagle* sailed from England on a five-year voyage around the world to survey and chart the oceans. Aboard was 22-year-old Charles Darwin, whose role was to observe, record, and collect samples of rocks, plants, animals, insects, and fossils. Some of the animals that he studied are pictured on the map. The specimens Darwin collected and studied helped him develop his theory of evolution. Controversy over Darwin's theory continues today.

▶ Clockwise from upper right: blue common Morpho butterfly, bottlenose dolphin, jaguar, Galápagos tortoise

Voyage of the HMS *Beagle*

Pacific Ocean

NORTH AMERICA

Atlantic Ocean

British Isles

EUROPE

AFRICA

Galápagos Islands

Equator

SOUTH AMERICA

Tropic of Capricorn

Miller Projection
0   1000   2000 mi
0   1000   2000 km

Falkland Islands

Cape of Good Hope

Cape Horn

show that Earth had formed over millions of years. His successors concluded that Earth was at least two billion years old and that life had not appeared until long after Earth was formed. These ideas did not seem to agree with biblical accounts of creation.

Archaeology added other pieces to an emerging debate about the origins of life on Earth. In 1856, workers in Germany accidentally uncovered fossilized Neanderthal bones. Later scholars found fossils of other early modern humans. These archaeologists had limited evidence and often drew mistaken conclusions. But as more discoveries were made, scholars developed new ideas about early humans and their ancestors.

Darwin's Theory of Natural Selection The most <u>controversial</u> new idea came from the British naturalist **Charles Darwin.** In 1859, after years of research, he published *On the Origin of Species.* Darwin argued that all forms of life, including human beings, had evolved into their present state over millions of years. To explain the long, slow process of evolution, he put forward his theory of natural selection.

Darwin adopted Thomas Malthus's idea that all plants and animals produced more offspring than the food supply could support. As a result,

Vocabulary Builder

<u>controversial</u>—(kahn truh VUR shul) *adj.* that is or can be argued about or debated

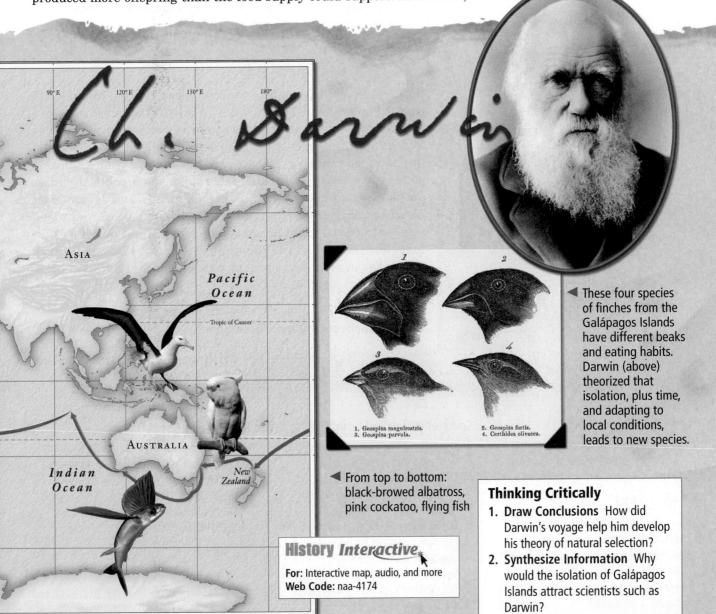

These four species of finches from the Galápagos Islands have different beaks and eating habits. Darwin (above) theorized that isolation, plus time, and adapting to local conditions, leads to new species.

1. Geospiza magnirostris.
2. Geospiza fortis.
3. Geospiza parvula.
4. Certhidea olivacea.

From top to bottom: black-browed albatross, pink cockatoo, flying fish

90° E   120° E   150° E   180°

ASIA

Pacific Ocean

Tropic of Cancer

AUSTRALIA

Indian Ocean

New Zealand

History *Interactive*

For: Interactive map, audio, and more
Web Code: naa-4174

Thinking Critically

1. **Draw Conclusions** How did Darwin's voyage help him develop his theory of natural selection?

2. **Synthesize Information** Why would the isolation of Galápagos Islands attract scientists such as Darwin?

he said, members of each species constantly competed to survive. Natural forces "selected" those with physical traits best adapted to their environment to survive and to pass the trait on to their offspring. This process of natural selection came to be known as "survival of the fittest."

Social Darwinism and Racism Although Darwin himself never promoted any social ideas, some thinkers used his theories to support their own beliefs about society. Applying the idea of survival of the fittest to war and economic competition came to be known as Social Darwinism. Industrial tycoons, argued Social Darwinists, were more "fit" than those they put out of business. War brought progress by weeding out weak nations. Victory was seen as proof of superiority.

Social Darwinism encouraged **racism,** the unscientific belief that one racial group is superior to another. By the late 1800s, many Europeans and Americans claimed that the success of Western civilization was due to the supremacy of the white race. As you will read, such powerful ideas would have a long-lasting impact on world history.

✓ **Checkpoint** How did science begin to challenge existing beliefs in the late 1800s?

Religion in an Urban Age

Despite the challenge of new scientific ideas, religion continued to be a major force in Western society. Christian churches and Jewish synagogues remained at the center of communities. Religious leaders influenced political, social, and educational developments.

The grim realities of industrial life stimulated feelings of compassion and charity. Christian labor unions and political parties pushed for reforms. Individuals, church groups, and Jewish organizations all tried to help the working poor. Catholic priests and nuns set up schools and hospitals in urban slums. Many Protestant churches backed the **social gospel,** a movement that urged Christians to social service. They campaigned for reforms in housing, healthcare, and education.

✓ **Checkpoint** How did religious groups respond to the challenges of industrialization?

The Salvation Army
By 1878, William and Catherine Booth had set up the Salvation Army in London to spread Christian teachings and provide social services. Their daughter, Evangeline (below), stands in front of one the kettles used to gather funds for the needy. *What services did religious organizations provide?*

Progress Monitoring Online
For: Self-quiz with vocabulary practice
Web Code: naa-2131

Terms, People, and Places

1. For each term, person, or place listed at the beginning of the section, write a sentence explaining its significance.

Note Taking

2. **Reading Skill: Identify Supporting Details** Use your completed table to answer the Focus Question: How did the Industrial Revolution change the old social order and long-held traditions in the Western world?

Comprehension and Critical Thinking

3. **Describe** What are three values associated with the middle class?

4. **Draw Conclusions** Why did the women's movement face strong opposition?

5. **Draw Inferences** Why do you think reformers pushed for free public education?

6. **Synthesize Information** Why did the ideas of Charles Darwin cause controversy?

● **Writing About History**

Quick Write: Write a Thesis Statement Imagine that you are writing a problem-solution essay on the unequal treatment of women in the 1800s. Based on what you have read in this section, write a thesis statement, or the main idea, for your problem-solution essay.

Albert Bierstadt, *Hetch Hetchy Canyon*, 1875

WITNESS HISTORY 🔊 AUDIO

Sunset

In the 1800s, many writers turned away from the harsh realities of industrial life to celebrate nature. The English poet William Wordsworth described the peace and beauty of sunset:

❝ It is a beauteous evening, calm and free,
The holy time is quiet as a Nun
Breathless with adoration; the broad sun
Is sinking down in its tranquillity.❞
—William Wordsworth,
Complete Poetical Works

Focus Question What artistic movements emerged in reaction to the Industrial Revolution?

Arts in the Industrial Age

 Performance Standards

- **SSWHRC1c** Demonstrate understanding of contextual vocabulary.

Terms, People, and Places

William Wordsworth	realism
William Blake	Charles Dickens
romanticism	Gustave Courbet
Lord Byron	Louis Daguerre
Victor Hugo	impressionism
Ludwig van Beethoven	Claude Monet
	Vincent van Gogh

Note Taking

Reading Skill: Identify Supporting Details Fill in a table like the one below with details about the artistic movements in the 1800s.

Major Artistic Movements of the 1800s		
Movement	**Goals/ Characteristics**	**Major Figures**
Romanticism	• Rebellion against reason	• Wordsworth
Realism	•	•
Impressionism	•	•

William Wordsworth, along with **William Blake,** Samuel Taylor Coleridge, and Percy Bysshe Shelley among others, was part of a cultural movement called romanticism. From about 1750 to 1850, romanticism shaped Western literature and arts.

The Romantic Revolt Against Reason

Romanticism does not refer to romance in the sense of an affectionate relationship, but rather to an artistic style emphasizing imagination, freedom, and emotion. Romanticism was a reaction to the neoclassical writers of the Enlightenment, who had turned to classical Greek and Roman literature and ideals that stressed order, harmony, reason, and emotional restraint. In contrast to Enlightenment literature, the works of romantic writers included simple, direct language, intense feelings, and a glorification of nature. Artists, composers, and architects were also followers of the movement.

The Romantic Hero Romantic writers created a new kind of hero—a mysterious, melancholy figure who felt out of step with society. "My joys, my grief, my passions, and my powers, / Made me a stranger," wrote Britain's George Gordon, **Lord Byron.** He himself was a larger-than-life figure equal to those he created. After a rebellious, wandering life, he joined Greek forces battling for freedom. When he died of a fever there, his legend bloomed. In fact, public interest in his poetry and adventures was so great that moody, isolated romantic heroes came to be described as "Byronic."

Ludwig van Beethoven

An accomplished musician by age 12, composer Ludwig van Beethoven (1770–1827) agonized over every note of every composition. The result was stunning music that expresses intense emotion. The famous opening of his Fifth Symphony conveys the sense of fate knocking at the door. His Sixth Symphony captures a joyful day in the countryside, interrupted by a violent thunderstorm.

Beethoven's career was haunted by perhaps the greatest tragedy a musician can face. In 1798, he began to lose his hearing. Still, he continued to compose music he could hear only in his mind. **How did Beethoven's music reflect romanticism?**

 AUDIO

The romantic hero often hid a guilty secret and faced a grim destiny. German writer Johann Wolfgang von Goethe (GUR tuh) wrote the dramatic poem *Faust.* The aging scholar Faust makes a pact with the devil, exchanging his soul for youth. After much agony, Faust wins salvation by accepting his duty to help others. In *Jane Eyre,* British novelist Charlotte Brontë weaves a tale about a quiet governess and her brooding, Byronic employer, whose large mansion conceals a terrifying secret.

Inspired by the Past Romantic writers combined history, legend, and folklore. Sir Walter Scott's novels and ballads evoked the turbulent history of Scottish clans or medieval knights. Alexandre Dumas (doo MAH) and **Victor Hugo** re-created France's past in novels like *The Three Musketeers* and *The Hunchback of Notre Dame.*

Architects, too, were inspired by old styles and forms. Churches and other buildings, including the British Parliament, were modeled on medieval Gothic styles. To people living in the 1800s, medieval towers and lacy stonework conjured up images of a glorious past.

Music Stirs Emotions Romantic composers also tried to stir deep emotions. Audiences were moved to laughter or tears at Hungarian Franz Liszt's piano playing. The passionate music of German composer **Ludwig van Beethoven** combined classical forms with a stirring range of sound. He was the first composer to take full advantage of the broad range of instruments in the modern orchestra. In all, Beethoven produced nine symphonies, five piano concertos, a violin concerto, an opera, two masses, and dozens of shorter pieces. To many, he is considered the greatest composer of his day.

Other romantic composers wove traditional folk melodies into their works to glorify their nations' pasts. In his piano works, Frederic Chopin (shoh PAN) used Polish peasant dances to convey the sorrows and joys of people living under foreign occupation.

Romanticism in Art Painters, too, broke free from the discipline and strict rules of the Enlightenment. Landscape painters like J.M.W. Turner sought to capture the beauty and power of nature. Using bold brush strokes and colors, Turner often showed tiny human figures struggling against sea and storm.

Romantics painted many subjects, from simple peasant life to medieval knights to current events. Bright colors conveyed violent energy and emotion. The French painter Eugène Delacroix (deh luh KRWAH) filled his canvases with dramatic action. In *Liberty Leading the People,* the Goddess of Liberty carries the revolutionary tricolor as French citizens rally to the cause.

✓ **Checkpoint** How did romantic writers, musicians, and artists respond to the Enlightenment?

The Call to Realism

By the mid-1800s, a new artistic movement, **realism,** took hold in the West. Realism was an attempt to represent the world as it was, without the sentiment associated with romanticism. Realists often focused their work on the harsh side of life in cities or villages. Many writers and artists were committed to improving the lot of the unfortunates whose lives they depicted.

Novels Depict Grim Reality The English novelist **Charles Dickens** vividly portrayed the lives of slum dwellers and factory workers, including children. In *Oliver Twist,* Dickens tells the story of a nine-year-old orphan raised in a grim poorhouse. In response to a request for more food, Oliver is smacked on the head and sent away to work. Later, he runs away to London. There he is taken in by Fagin, a villain who trains homeless children to become pickpockets. The book shocked many middle-class readers with its picture of poverty, mistreatment of children, and urban crime. Yet Dickens' humor and colorful characters made him one of the most popular novelists in the world.

French novelists also portrayed the ills of their time. Victor Hugo, who moved from romantic to realistic novels, revealed how hunger drove a good man to crime and how the law hounded him ever after in *Les Misérables* (lay miz ehr AHB). The novels of Émile Zola painted an even grimmer picture. In *Germinal,* Zola exposed class warfare in the French mining industry. To Zola's characters, neither the Enlightenment's faith in reason nor the romantic movement's feelings mattered at all.

Realism in Drama Norwegian dramatist Henrik Ibsen brought realism to the stage. His plays attacked the hypocrisy he observed around him. *A Doll's House* shows a woman caught in a straitjacket of social rules. In *An Enemy of the People,* a doctor discovers that the water in a local spa is polluted. Because the town's economy depends on its spa, the citizens denounce the doctor and suppress the truth. Ibsen's realistic dramas had a wide influence in Europe and the United States.

Arts Reject Romantic Ideas Painters also represented the realities of their time. Rejecting the romantic <u>emphasis</u> on imagination, they focused on ordinary subjects, especially working-class men and women. "I cannot paint an angel," said the French realist **Gustave Courbet** (koor BAY) "because I have never seen one." Instead, he painted works such as *The Stone Breakers,* which shows two rough laborers on a country road. Later in the century, *The Gross Clinic,* by American painter Thomas Eakins, shocked viewers with its realistic depiction of an autopsy conducted in a medical classroom.

✓ **Checkpoint** How did the realism movement differ from the romantic movement?

Realism in the Arts

A Thomas Eakins's 1875 painting *The Gross Clinic* depicts the realism of medical school where students learn by performing autopsies. The artist included many realistic elements such as the surgical tools in the foreground and the reaction of the spectator at the far left.

B Edvard Munch's 1898 painting shows an impression of Henrik Ibsen filled with psychological realism, similar to that found in Ibsen's plays.

C This 1896 portrait of Ibsen shows photographic realism in the playwright's appearance and expression.

D Victor Hugo's 1862 novel *Les Misérables* describes the reality of poverty, hunger, and corruption among the poor in Paris. This 1886 poster depicts the novel's main characters: the convict Jean Valjean at the center, and Cosette, the girl he adopts, at the right.

Vocabulary Builder

<u>emphasis</u>—(EM fuh sis) *n.* special attention given to something to make it stand out

Postimpressionism
This self-portrait of Dutch painter Vincent van Gogh shows his bandaged ear, which he cut off in a state of depression. *What postimpressionist features are demonstrated in Van Gogh's self-portrait?*

Vocabulary Builder
intense—(in TENS) *adj.* very strong or deep

The Visual Arts Take New Directions

By the 1840s, a new art form, photography, was emerging. **Louis Daguerre** (dah GEHR) in France and William Fox Talbot in England had improved on earlier technologies to produce successful photographs. At first, many photos were stiff, posed portraits of middle-class families or prominent people. Other photographs reflected the romantics' fascination with faraway places.

In time, photographers used the camera to present the grim realities of life. During the American Civil War, Mathew B. Brady preserved a vivid, realistic record of the corpse-strewn battlefields. Other photographers showed the harsh conditions in industrial factories or slums.

The Impressionists Photography posed a challenge to painters. Why try for realism, some artists asked, when a camera could do the same thing better? By the 1870s, a group of painters took art in a new direction, seeking to capture the first fleeting impression made by a scene or object on the viewer's eye. The new movement, known as **impressionism,** took root in Paris, capital of the Western art world.

Since the Renaissance, painters had carefully finished their paintings so that no brush strokes showed. But impressionists like **Claude Monet** (moh NAY) and Edgar Degas (day GAH) brushed strokes of color side by side without any blending. According to new scientific studies of optics, the human eye would mix these patches of color.

By concentrating on visual impressions rather than realism, artists achieved a fresh view of familiar subjects. Monet, for example, painted the cathedral at Rouen (roo AHN), France, dozens of times from the same angle, capturing how it looked in different lights at different times of day.

The Postimpressionists Later painters, called postimpressionists, developed a variety of styles. Georges Seurat (suh RAH) arranged small dots of color to define the shapes of objects. **Vincent van Gogh** experimented with sharp brush lines and bright colors. His unique brushwork lent a dreamlike quality to everyday subjects. Paul Gauguin (goh GAN) also developed a bold, personal style. In his paintings, people look flat, as in "primitive" folk art. But his brooding colors and black outlining of shapes convey <u>intense</u> feelings and images.

 Checkpoint How did photography influence the development of painting?

SECTION **4 Assessment**

Progress Monitoring *Online*
For: Self-quiz with vocabulary practice
Web Code: naa-2141

Terms, People, and Places

1. For each term, person, or place listed at the beginning of the section, write a sentence explaining its significance.

Note Taking

2. **Reading Skill: Identify Supporting Details** Use your completed table to answer the Focus Question: What artistic movements emerged in reaction to the Industrial Revolution?

Comprehension and Critical Thinking

3. **Summarize** What are three subjects romantics favored?

4. **Draw Conclusions** What did Courbet mean when he said, "I cannot paint an angel because I have never seen one"? Do you agree with his attitude? Explain.

5. **Recognize Cause and Effect** In what ways were the new artistic styles of the 1800s a reaction to changes in society?

● **Writing About History**

Quick Write: Support a Solution Based on what you've read, list supporting information, such as details, data, and facts, for the following thesis statement of a problem-solution essay: Artists in the 1800s portrayed subjects realistically to make the public more aware of some of the grim problems of life in industrialized nations.

Impressionism

Impressionism was one of the most important art movements of the 1800s. It marked a departure from tradition, both in subject matter and painting technique. Artists sought to depict the human eye's first perception of a scene. Characterized by the use of unmixed primary colors and small, visible brush strokes, impressionism attempted to show the effects of direct or reflected light. Impressionist artists often painted outdoors for maximum effect.

▲ **Claude Monet,** *Impression: Sunrise,* 1872
In the 1800s, "The Salon," an annual exhibition that accepted only traditional paintings, dominated the Parisian art scene. In 1874, a group of artists held their own exhibition at a local photographer's studio. Claude Monet's *Impression: Sunrise* was one of the works displayed. Monet's painting demonstrates several characteristics of impressionist work, including short, visible brush strokes and an idealized depiction of a landscape.

▲ **Edgar Degas,** *The Dancing Class,* *c.* 1873–1875
This painting by Edgar Degas shows the influence of the newly invented camera. Impressionists' paintings moved away from the traditional placement of subjects in favor of off-center compositions. Figures were also painted on the outermost parts of the canvas. Much like photographs, impressionist paintings were often snapshots of life rather than elaborate portraits.

▲ **Berthe Morisot,** *Eugène Manet and His Daughter at Bougival,* *c.* 1881
French impressionist painter Berthe Morisot also participated in the first impressionist exhibit in 1874. Morisot's delicate, subtle paintings often portrayed her family and friends—as this one of her husband and daughter.

Thinking Critically
1. **Summarize** How did impressionism depart from tradition?
2. **Draw Conclusions** What are the advantages and disadvantages of painting outdoors?

Quick Study Guide

GA SSWH15a

> **Progress Monitoring *Online***
> For: Self-test with vocabulary practice
> **Web Code:** naa-2151

■ Key People

Inventors/Developers

Henry Bessemer—steel processing
Michael Faraday—dynamo
Thomas Edison—electric light bulb
Gottlieb Daimler—automobile
Samuel F.B. Morse—telegraph
Alexander Graham Bell—telephone
Guglielmo Marconi—radio

Scientists

Louis Pasteur—vaccinations, pasteurization
Joseph Lister—antiseptics
John Dalton—modern atomic theory
Charles Darwin—theory of natural selection

Reformers

Florence Nightingale—sanitary measures in hospitals
Elizabeth Cady Stanton—womenís rights
Susan B. Anthony—women's rights
William and Catherine Booth—Salvation Army

Artists, Writers, and Composers

William Wordsworth—romantic writer
Lord Byron—romantic writer
Ludwig van Beethoven—romantic composer
Charles Dickens—realist writer
Émile Zola—realist writer
Gustave Courbet—realist painter
Claude Monet—impressionist painter
Edgar Degas—impressionist painter
Vincent van Gogh—postimpressionist painter

■ Life Expectancy in the Industrial Age

Average Life Expectancy in Selected Industrial Areas, 1850–1910		
Year	Male	Female
1850	40.3 years	42.8 years
1870	42.3 years	44.7 years
1890	45.8 years	48.5 years
1910	52.7 years	56.0 years

SOURCE: E.A. Wrigley, *Population and History* (based on data for parts of Western Europe and the United States)

■ Impact of the Industrial Revolution

Key Effects of the Industrial Revolution		
Industrialization	**Urbanization**	**Social Structure**
• Germany, France, and the U.S. join Great Britain as industrial powers. • Rise of factories; new production methods • Advances in transportation and communication • Rise of big business • Growth of labor unions	• Advances in medicine and science • Population growth due to falling death rates • Higher standard of living	• Three social classes emerge • Middle class expands • Rise of urban working class • Reform movements grow • Public education expands

■ Key Events of the Industrial Revolution

Early 1800s
Romanticism begins to shape Western art and literature.

1807
First factories open in Belgium, setting off the Industrial Revolution on the European continent.

1839
French inventor Louis Daguerre perfects an effective method of photography.

Chapter Events
Global Events

1800	1815	1830	1845

1819
Simón Bolívar establishes Gran Colombia.

1842
The Treaty of Nanjing gives Britain trading rights in China.

Concept Connector

? Essential Question Review

To connect prior knowledge with what you have learned in this chapter, answer the questions below in your Concept Connector journal. Use the journal in the Reading and Note Taking Study Guide to record your answers (or go to www.phschool.com **Web Code:** nad-2107).

1. **Science** Major shifts in how scientists thought about the world in the 1500s and 1600s led to a period called the Scientific Revolution. During this time, advances in mathematics, astronomy, medicine, chemistry, and other fields led to many new discoveries. In this chapter, you read about how scientific advances during the Industrial Revolution changed the way in which people lived and worked. Choose one scientific discovery or advance from the Scientific Revolution and one from the Industrial Revolution. In a few sentences, explain how these discoveries changed peoples' lives.

2. **Technology** During the High Middle Ages, an agricultural revolution brought about great change. Compare the technological changes that took place from about 1000 to 1300 to the changes that took place during the Industrial Revolution. Think about the following:
    *   how a new invention or method may have solved a problem
    *   how a new technology or method sparked economic growth
    *   how the invention or method changed people's lives

3. **Economic Systems** The revival of trade during the High Middle Ages resulted in a commercial revolution. Hundreds of years later, the Industrial Revolution brought about changes in business. In what ways were the changes during the two periods similar? Think about the following:
    *   new business practices
    *   role of guilds and labor unions

■ Connections to Today

1. **Technology: Power Outage** In August 2003, people in Canada and the northeastern part of the United States found out just how much their lives depend on electricity. When an energy plant unexpectedly shut down, it led to the largest power outage in North America's history—more than 50 million people were left in the dark.

    Lights and elevators stopped working in skyscrapers, and workers had to carefully make their way down darkened stairways. Others were trapped on trains or stuck in traffic jams caused by inoperable traffic lights. Airports experienced extended delays. Business slowed because Internet servers were not functioning properly, phone systems crashed, computerized cash registers could not ring up sales, and ATMs went down. With today's linked power grids, the possibility of more massive blackouts that disrupt the lives of millions of people across county, state, and international lines is very real. What economic effects might a power outage have?

2. **Belief Systems: Social Darwinism** British philosopher and Social Darwinist Herbert Spencer coined the phrase "survival of the fittest," meaning that the strong grow in power and influence over the weaker members of society. Social Darwinists promoted the beliefs that the group was more important than the individual, and that privileged, powerful people had the right to make decisions about those whom they believed were inferior.

    These ideas had horrific consequences for people throughout the world. For example, they led to unethical medical experimentation on people of color, abuse of the mentally ill, and countless acts of violence toward people of "different" religions, races, and ethnicities. To what degree do you think Social Darwinism is still a part of our culture today?

1859 Charles Darwin publishes *On the Origin of Species.* Many religious leaders denounce his theory of evolution.

1869 Germany legalizes labor unions.

1903 Wilbur and Orville Wright conduct tests of their airplane at Kitty Hawk, North Carolina.

History Interactive
For: Interactive timeline
Web Code: nap-2151

1860 **1875** **1890** **1905**

1861 Tsar Alexander II emancipates Russian serfs.

1884 European nations carve up Africa at the Berlin Conference.

1898 Spanish-American War is fought.

1914 The Panama Canal opens.

Chapter Assessment

Terms, People, and Places

Choose the italicized term in parentheses that best completes each sentence.

1. A *(dynamo/cartel)* is a machine that generates electricity.
2. Business owners sell *(corporations/stock),* or shares in their companies, to investors.
3. *(Racism/Germ theory)* is the belief that one racial group is superior to another.
4. The *(cult of domesticity/standard of living)* measures the quality and availability of necessities and comforts in a society.
5. A self-help group to aid sick or injured workers is called a *(social gospel/mutual-aid society).*
6. *(Impressionism/Realism)* attempted to represent the world as it was.

Main Ideas

Section 1 (pp. 660–666)
7. Describe the impact of new technology on industry, transportation, and communication.
8. Why did big businesses emerge during the Industrial Revolution?

Section 2 (pp. 667–673)
9. How did the Industrial Revolution improve city life? How did it make city life worse?

Section 3 (pp. 674–680)
10. How did the Industrial Revolution influence the class structure of Western Europe?
11. What existing beliefs did new scientific theories challenge?

Section 4 (pp. 681–685)
12. How did artists, composers, writers, and others respond to industrialization?

Chapter Focus Question
13. What were the technological, social, and economic effects of the Industrial Revolution?

Critical Thinking

14. **Geography and History** How did technology affect the movement of people and goods in the 1800s and in the early 1900s?
15. **Identify Point of View** How might each of the following have viewed the Industrial Revolution: (a) an inventor, (b) an entrepreneur, (c) a worker?
16. **Draw Conclusions** Do you think women's lives improved as a result of the Industrial Revolution? Why or why not?
17. **Draw Inferences** Referring to *Oliver Twist,* Dickens wrote that "to show [criminals] as they really are, for ever skulking uneasily through the dirtiest paths of life . . . would be a service to society." How does his claim reflect the goals of realism?
18. **Summarize** How would you describe Victorian middle-class values?
19. **Demonstrate Reasoned Judgment** Some historians have suggested that we are now in a third phase of the Industrial Revolution, characterized by information technology and computers. Do you agree or disagree? Explain the reasons for your answer.
20. **Analyzing Visuals** Which artistic movement of the 1800s does *Cathedral of Rouen, Afternoon* (right) by Claude Monet reflect: romanticism, realism, or impressionism? Explain your reasoning.

● Writing About History

In this chapter's four Section Assessments, you developed skills for writing a problem-solution essay.

Writing a Problem-Solution Essay The second Industrial Revolution ushered in a period of great change to the modern world. But it brought with it problems that people had not experienced before. Write a problem-solution essay about one of these topics or choose your own topic relating to the content in this chapter.

Prewriting
• Choose the topic that interests you most.

• Narrow your topic.
• Make a list of details, facts, and examples that proves there is a problem. Then, identify the specific parts of your solution.

Drafting
• Develop a working thesis and choose information to support it.
• Organize the paragraphs in a logical order so that readers can understand the solution you propose.

Revising
• Use the guidelines for revising your essay on page SH12 of the Writing Handbook.

Prepare for the GHSGT

Birth of the Modern City

The birth of the modern city helped to define the Industrial Age. The documents below show that the modern city represented progress, but not without costs.

Document A

"The first shock of a great earthquake had, just at that period, rent the whole neighborhood to its center. Traces of its course were visible on every side. Houses were knocked down; streets broken through and stopped; deep pits and trenches dug in the ground; enormous heaps of earth and clay thrown up; buildings that were undermined and shaking, propped by great beams of wood. . . . In short, the yet unfinished and unopened Railroad was in progress; and, from the very core of all this dire disorder, trailed smoothly away, upon its mighty course of civilization and improvement."

—from ***Dombey and Son*** by Charles Dickens

Document B

Selected Inventions, 1824–1911	
Cement	1824
Locomotive	1830
Dynamite	1866
Telephone	1876
Cash register	1879
Electric trolley car	1884–1887
Steel alloy	1891
Self-starting auto	1911

SOURCE: *The World Almanac, 2004*

Document C

Population of Major Cities		
City	1850	1900
Berlin, Germany	419,000	1,889,000
London, England	2,685,000	6,586,000
Moscow, Russia	365,000	989,000
New York, United States	696,000	3,437,000
Paris, France	1,053,000	2,714,000

SOURCE: *International Historical Statistics*

Document D

Brooklyn Bridge, 1883

Analyzing Documents

Use your knowledge of the industrial age and Documents A, B, C, and D to answer questions 1–4.

1. The cause of the earthquake described in Document A was
   A an underground fault in London.
   B poorly constructed tall buildings.
   C construction of a railroad.
   D deep pits and trenches in the ground.

2. Which inventions from Document B had the most impact on New York City at the time Document D was created?
   A trolley cars, steel alloy, cash registers
   B dynamite, telephones, cash registers
   C cement, locomotives, telephones
   D cement, locomotives, dynamite

3. Which trend does Document C illustrate?
   A the shift in population from Europe to the United States
   B the shift in population from East Coast to West Coast
   C the increase in population of cities
   D the decrease in rural population

4. **Writing Task** What were the most significant features of the modern city? Why? Use the information from Documents A through D, as well as what you've learned in this chapter, to support your opinion.

22 Nationalism Triumphs in Europe
1800–1914

The Price of Nationalism

The last half of the 1800s can be called the Age of Nationalism. By harnessing national feeling, European leaders fought ruthlessly to create strong, unified nations. Under Otto von Bismarck, Germany emerged as Europe's most powerful empire—but at a considerable cost. In his 1870 diary, Crown Prince Friedrich wrote:

66[Germany had once been admired as a] nation of thinkers and philosophers, poets and artists, idealists and enthusiasts . . . [but now the world saw Germany as] a nation of conquerors and destroyers, to which no pledged word, no treaty, is sacred. . . . We are neither loved nor respected, but only feared.99

Listen to the Witness History audio to learn more about nationalism.

Helmet from the Franco-Prussian war era

◀ Otto von Bismarck (center), chancellor of Germany, meets with European and Turkish leaders at the Congress of Berlin.

 Performance Standards

Chapter Focus Question What effects did nationalism and the demand for reform have in Europe?

Section 1
Building a German Nation
SSWH14c, SSWH15b

Section 2
Germany Strengthens
SSWH15b

Section 3
Unifying Italy
SSWH15a, SSWHRC1c

Section 4
Nationalism Threatens Old Empires
SSWH15b, SSWH16d

Section 5
Russia: Reform and Reaction
SSWH14c, SSWH16d

Use the ☑ **Quick Study Timeline** at the end of this chapter to preview chapter events.

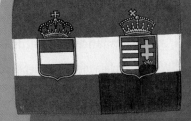

Austria-Hungary empire flag

Soviet stamp commemorating the Decembrist Revolt

 Concept Connector ONLINE

To explore Essential Questions related to this chapter, go to PHSchool.com
Web Code: nad-2207

Otto von Bismarck

Helmet from the Franco-Prussian war era

Blood and Iron

Prussian legislators waited restlessly for Otto von Bismarck to speak. He wanted them to vote for more money to build up the army. Liberal members opposed the move. Bismarck rose and dismissed their concerns:

❝ Germany does not look to Prussia's liberalism, but to her power. . . . The great questions of the day are not to be decided by speeches and majority resolutions—that was the mistake of 1848 and 1849—but by blood and iron!❞
—Otto von Bismarck, 1862

Focus Question How did Otto von Bismarck, the chancellor of Prussia, lead the drive for German unity?

Building a German Nation

 Performance Standards

- **SSWH14c** Explain the consequences of France's defeat for Europe.
- **SSWH15b** Compare and contrast the rise of Germany and Japan.

Terms, People, and Places

Otto von Bismarck   annex
chancellor   kaiser
Realpolitik   Reich

Note Taking

Reading Skill: Recognize Sequence Keep track of the sequence of events that led to German unification by completing a chart like the one below. Add more boxes as needed.

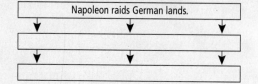

Otto von Bismarck delivered his "blood and iron" speech in 1862. It set the tone for his future policies. Bismarck was determined to build a strong, unified German state, with Prussia at its head.

Taking Initial Steps Toward Unity

In the early 1800s, German-speaking people lived in a number of small and medium-sized states as well as in Prussia and the Austrian Hapsburg empire. Napoleon's invasions unleashed new forces in these territories.

Napoleon Raids German Lands Between 1806 and 1812, Napoleon made important territorial changes in German-speaking lands. He annexed lands along the Rhine River for France. He dissolved the Holy Roman Empire by forcing the emperor of Austria to agree to the lesser title of king. He also organized a number of German states into the Rhine Confederation.

At first, some Germans welcomed the French emperor as a hero with enlightened, modern policies. He encouraged freeing the serfs, made trade easier, and abolished laws against Jews. However, not all Germans appreciated Napoleon and his changes. As people fought to free their lands from French rule, they began to demand a unified German state.

Napoleon's defeat did not resolve the issue. At the Congress of Vienna, Metternich pointed out that a united Germany would require dismantling the government of each German state. Instead, the peacemakers created the German Confederation, a weak alliance headed by Austria.

Economic Changes Promote Unity In the 1830s, Prussia created an economic union called the *Zollverein* (TSAWL fur yn). It dismantled tariff barriers between many German states. Still, Germany remained politically fragmented.

In 1848, liberals meeting in the Frankfurt Assembly again demanded German political unity. They offered the throne of a united German state to Frederick William IV of Prussia. The Prussian ruler, however, rejected the notion of a throne offered by "the people."

✓ **Checkpoint** What was the German Confederation?

Bismarck Unites Germany

Otto von Bismarck succeeded where others had failed. Bismarck came from Prussia's Junker (YOONG kur) class, made up of conservative landowning nobles. Bismarck first served Prussia as a diplomat in Russia and France. In 1862, King William I made him prime minister. Within a decade, the new prime minister had become **chancellor,** or the highest official of a monarch, and had used his policy of "blood and iron" to unite the German states under Prussian rule.

Geography *Interactive*
For: Audio guided tour
Web Code: nap-2211

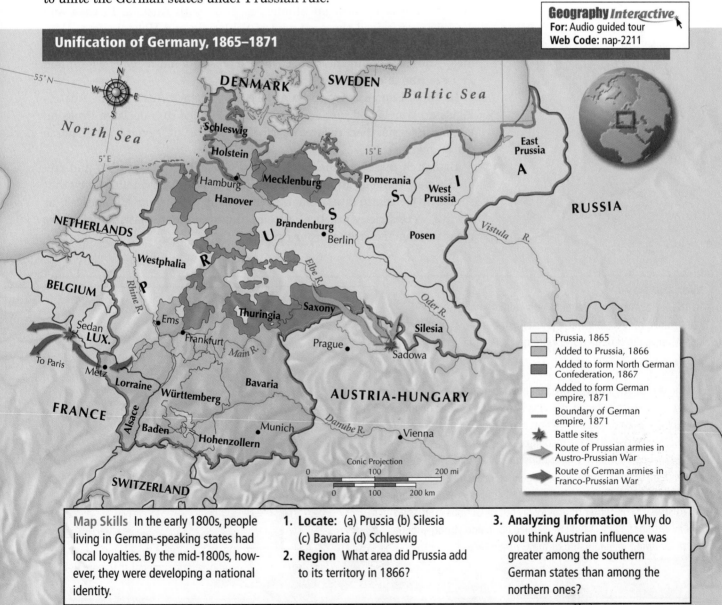

Unification of Germany, 1865–1871

Prussia, 1865
Added to Prussia, 1866
Added to form North German Confederation, 1867
Added to form German empire, 1871
Boundary of German empire, 1871
Battle sites
Route of Prussian armies in Austro-Prussian War
Route of German armies in Franco-Prussian War

Conic Projection
0   100   200 mi
0   100   200 km

Map Skills In the early 1800s, people living in German-speaking states had local loyalties. By the mid-1800s, however, they were developing a national identity.

1. **Locate:** (a) Prussia (b) Silesia (c) Bavaria (d) Schleswig

2. **Region** What area did Prussia add to its territory in 1866?

3. **Analyzing Information** Why do you think Austrian influence was greater among the southern German states than among the northern ones?

Master of Realpolitik Bismarck's success was due in part to his strong will. He was a master of **Realpolitik** (ray AHL poh lee teek), or realistic politics based on the needs of the state. In the case of Realpolitik, power was more important than principles.

Although Bismarck was the architect of German unity, he was not really a German nationalist. His primary loyalty was to the Hohenzollerns (hoh un TSAWL urnz), the ruling dynasty of Prussia, who represented a powerful, traditional monarchy. Through unification, he hoped to bring more power to the Hohenzollerns.

Strengthening the Army As Prussia's prime minister, Bismarck first moved to build up the Prussian army. Despite his "blood and iron" speech, the liberal legislature refused to vote for funds for the military. In response, Bismarck strengthened the army with money that had been collected for other purposes. With a powerful, well-equipped military, he was then ready to pursue an aggressive foreign policy. Over the next decade, Bismarck led Prussia into three wars. Each war increased Prussian prestige and power and paved the way for German unity.

Prussia Declares War With Denmark and Austria Bismarck's first maneuver was to form an alliance in 1864 with Austria. Prussia and Austria then seized the provinces of Schleswig and Holstein from Denmark. After a brief war, Prussia and Austria "liberated" the two provinces and divided up the spoils. Austria was to administer Holstein and Prussia was to administer Schleswig.

In 1866, Bismarck invented an excuse to attack Austria. The Austro-Prussian War lasted just seven weeks and ended in a decisive Prussian victory. Prussia then **annexed**, or took control of, several other north German states.

Bismarck dissolved the Austrian-led German Confederation and created a new confederation dominated by Prussia. Austria and four other southern German states remained independent. Bismarck's motives, as always, were strictly practical. Attempting to conquer Austria might have meant a long and risky war for Prussia.

War and Power

In 1866, Field Marshal Helmuth von Moltke analyzed the importance of Prussia's war against Austria. Why, according to von Moltke, did Prussia go to war against Austria?

Primary Source

66 The war of 1866 was entered on not because the existence of Prussia was threatened, nor was it caused by public opinion and the voice of the people; it was a struggle, long foreseen and calmly prepared for, recognized as a necessity by the Cabinet, not for territorial expansion, for an extension of our domain, or for material advantage, but for an ideal end—the establishment of power. Not a foot of land was exacted from Austria. . . . Its center of gravity lay out of Germany; Prussia's lay within it. Prussia felt itself called upon and strong enough to assume the leadership of the German races. 99

Austro-Prussian War painting (above) and a medal of victory (left)

France Declares War on Prussia In France, the Prussian victory over Austria angered Napoleon III. A growing rivalry between the two nations led to the Franco-Prussian War of 1870.

Germans recalled only too well the invasions of Napoleon I some 60 years earlier. Bismarck played up the image of the French menace to spur German nationalism. For his part, Napoleon III did little to avoid war, hoping to mask problems at home with military glory.

Bismarck furthered the crisis by rewriting and then releasing to the press a telegram that reported on a meeting between King William I and the French ambassador. Bismarck's editing of the "Ems dispatch" made it seem that William I had insulted the Frenchman. Furious, Napoleon III declared war on Prussia, as Bismarck had hoped.

A superior Prussian force, supported by troops from other German states, smashed the badly organized and poorly supplied French soldiers. Napoleon III, old and ill, surrendered within a few weeks. France had to accept a humiliating peace.

Vocabulary Builder

edit—(ED it) *v.* to make additions, deletions, or other changes to a piece of writing

✓ **Checkpoint** What techniques did Bismarck use to unify the German states?

Birth of the German Empire

Delighted by the victory over France, princes from the southern German states and the North German Confederation persuaded William I of Prussia to take the title **kaiser** (KY zur), or emperor. In January 1871, German nationalists celebrated the birth of the second **Reich,** or empire. They called it that because they considered it heir to the Holy Roman Empire.

A constitution drafted by Bismarck set up a two-house legislature. The Bundesrat (BOON dus raht), or upper house, was appointed by the rulers of the German states. The Reichstag (RYKS tahg), or lower house, was elected by universal male suffrage. Because the Bundesrat could veto any decisions of the Reichstag, real power remained in the hands of the emperor and his chancellor.

✓ **Checkpoint** How was the new German government, drafted by Bismarck, structured?

SECTION **1** Assessment

Progress Monitoring *Online*
For: Self-quiz with vocabulary practice
Web Code: naa-2211

Terms, People, and Places

1. For each term, person, or place listed at the beginning of the section, write a sentence explaining its significance.

Note Taking

2. **Reading Skill: Recognize Sequence** Use your completed chart to answer the Focus Question: How did Otto von Bismarck, the chancellor of Prussia, lead the drive for German unity?

Comprehension and Critical Thinking

3. **Summarize** What territorial and economic changes promoted German unity?

4. **Analyze Information** Identify three examples of Bismarck's use of Realpolitik.

5. **Draw Conclusions** How did the emperor and his chancellor retain power in the new German government?

● **Writing About History**

Quick Write: Generate Arguments Choose one topic from this section that you could use to write a persuasive essay. For example, you could write about whether Germany's war against Austria was justifiable. Make sure that the topic you choose to write about has at least two sides that could provoke an argument.

French bayonet

Prussian soldiers
at Versailles

 WITNESS HISTORY 🔊 AUDIO

The New German Empire

In 1870, German historian Heinrich von Treitschke (vawn TRYCH kuh) wrote a newspaper article demanding the annexation of Alsace and Lorraine from France. A year later, annexation became a condition of the peace settlement in the Franco-Prussian War:

❝ The sense of justice to Germany demands the lessening of France. . . . These territories are ours by the right of the sword, and . . . [by] virtue of a higher right—the right of the German nation, which will not permit its lost children to remain strangers to the German Empire. ❞

Focus Question How did Germany increase its power after unifying in 1871?

Germany Strengthens

GA **Performance Standards**

• **SSWH15b** Compare and contrast the rise of Germany and Japan.

Terms, People, and Places

Kulturkampf
William II
social welfare

Note Taking

Reading Skill: Recognize Sequence Keep track of the sequence of events described in this section by completing a chart like the one below. List the causes that led to a strong German nation.

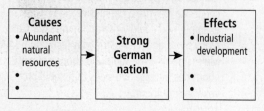

Causes	Strong German nation	Effects
• Abundant natural resources		• Industrial development
•		•
•		•

In January 1871, German princes gathered in the glittering Hall of Mirrors at the French palace of Versailles. They had just defeated Napoleon III in the Franco-Prussian War. Once home to French kings, the palace seemed the perfect place to proclaim the new German empire. To the winners as well as to the losers, the symbolism was clear: French domination of Europe had ended. Germany was now the dominant power in Europe.

Germany Becomes an Industrial Giant

In the aftermath of unification, the German empire emerged as the industrial giant of the European continent. By the late 1800s, German chemical and electrical industries were setting the standard worldwide. Among the European powers, German shipping was second only to Britain's.

Making Economic Progress Germany, like Great Britain, possessed several of the factors that made industrialization possible. Germany's spectacular growth was due in part to ample iron and coal resources, the basic ingredients for industrial development. A disciplined and educated workforce also helped the economy. The German middle class and educated professionals helped to create a productive and efficient society that prided itself on its sense of responsibility and deference to authority. Germany's rapidly growing population—from 41 million in 1871 to 67 million by 1914—also provided a huge home market along with a larger supply of industrial workers.

The new nation also benefited from earlier progress. During the 1850s and 1860s, Germans had founded large companies and built many railroads. The house of Krupp (kroop) boomed after 1871, becoming an enormous industrial complex that produced steel and weapons for a world market. Between 1871 and 1914, the business tycoon August Thyssen (TEES un) built a small steel factory of 70 workers into a giant empire with 50,000 employees. Optics was another important industry. German industrialist and inventor Carl Zeiss built a company that became known for its telescopes, microscopes, and other optical equipment.

Promoting Scientific and Economic Development German industrialists were the first to see the value of applied science in developing new products such as <u>synthetic</u> chemicals and dyes. Industrialists, as well as the government, supported research and development in the universities and hired trained scientists to solve technological problems in their factories.

The German government also promoted economic development. After 1871, it issued a single currency for Germany, reorganized the banking system, and <u>coordinated</u> railroads built by the various German states. When a worldwide depression hit in the late 1800s, Germany raised tariffs to protect home industries from foreign competition. The leaders of the new German empire were determined to maintain economic strength as well as military power.

Vocabulary Builder

<u>synthetic</u>—(sin THET ik) *adj.* prepared or made artificially

Vocabulary Builder

<u>coordinate</u>—(koh AWR dih nate) *v.* to design or adjust so as to have harmonious action

✔ **Checkpoint** What factors did Germany possess that made industrialization possible there?

The Iron Chancellor

As chancellor of the new German empire, Bismarck pursued several foreign-policy goals. He wanted to keep France weak and isolated while building strong links with Austria and Russia. He respected British naval power but did not seek to compete in that arena. "Water rats," he said, "do not fight with land rats." Later, however, he would take a more aggressive stand against Britain as the two nations competed for overseas colonies.

BIOGRAPHY

Otto von Bismarck

Otto von Bismarck (1815–1898) spent his early years on his father's country estate. He worked briefly as a civil servant, but found the work boring. At 24, Bismarck resigned his post as a bureaucrat. "My ambition strives more to command than to obey," the independent-minded young man explained.

The resignation did not end his career in government. While he was a delegate to a United Diet that was called by Prussian King Frederick William IV, Bismarck's conservative views and passionate speeches in defense of government policies won him the support of the king. He then served as a diplomat to the German Federation. He became chancellor of the German empire in 1871, a position he held for 19 years. **What path did Bismarck take to win political power?**

A Political Game of Chess This political cartoon shows Otto von Bismarck and Pope Pius IX trying to checkmate each other in a game of chess.

1. How does this cartoon reflect the relationship between Bismarck and the Catholic Church?
2. How did the conflict between church and state affect German politics in the 1870s?

On the domestic front, Bismarck applied the same ruthless methods he had used to achieve unification. The Iron Chancellor, as he was called, sought to erase local loyalties and crush all opposition to the imperial state. He targeted two groups—the Catholic Church and the Socialists. In his view, both posed a threat to the new German state.

Campaign Against the Church After unification, Catholics made up about a third of the German population. Bismarck, who was Lutheran, distrusted Catholics—especially the clergy—whose first loyalty, he believed, was to the pope instead of to Germany.

In response to what he saw as the Catholic threat, Bismarck launched the *Kulturkampf* (kool TOOR kahmpf), or "battle for civilization," which lasted from 1871 to 1878. His goal was to make Catholics put loyalty to the state above allegiance to the Church. The chancellor had laws passed that gave the state the right to supervise Catholic education and approve the appointment of priests. Other laws closed some religious orders, expelled the Jesuits from Prussia, and made it compulsory for couples to be married by civil authority.

Bismarck's moves against the Catholic Church backfired. The faithful rallied behind the Church, and the Catholic Center party gained strength in the Reichstag. A realist, Bismarck saw his mistake and worked to make peace with the Church.

Campaign Against the Socialists Bismarck also saw a threat to the new German empire in the growing power of socialism. By the late 1870s, German Marxists had organized the Social Democratic party, which called for parliamentary democracy and laws to improve conditions for the working class. Bismarck feared that socialists would undermine the loyalty of German workers and turn them toward revolution. Following a failed assassination plot against the kaiser, Bismarck had laws passed that dissolved socialist groups, shut down their newspapers, and banned their meetings. Once again, repression backfired. Workers were unified in support of the socialist cause.

Bismarck then changed course. He set out to woo workers away from socialism by sponsoring laws to protect them. By the 1890s, Germans had health and accident insurance as well as old-age insurance to provide retirement benefits. Thus, under Bismarck, Germany was a pioneer in social reform. Its system of economic safeguards became the model for other European nations.

Although workers benefited from Bismarck's plan, they did not abandon socialism. In fact, the Social Democratic party continued to grow in strength. By 1912, it held more seats in the Reichstag than any other party. Yet Bismarck's program showed that conditions for workers could be improved without the upheaval of a revolution. Later, Germany and other European nations would build on Bismarck's social policies, greatly increasing government's role in providing for the needs of its citizens.

✔ **Checkpoint** Why did Bismarck try to crush the Catholic Church and the Socialists?

Kaiser William II

In 1888, **William II** succeeded his grandfather as kaiser. The new emperor was supremely confident in his abilities and wished to put his own stamp on Germany. In 1890, he shocked Europe by asking the dominating Bismarck to resign. "There is only one master in the Reich," he said, "and that is I."

William II seriously believed that his right to rule came from God. He expressed this view when he said:

Primary Source

66 My grandfather considered that the office of king was a task that God had assigned to him. . . . That which he thought I also think. . . . Those who wish to aid me in that task . . . I welcome with all my heart; those who oppose me in this work I shall crush.99
—William II

Not surprisingly, William resisted efforts to introduce democratic reforms. At the same time, however, his government provided programs for social welfare, or programs to help certain groups of people. His government also provided services such as cheap transportation and electricity. An excellent system of public schools, which had flourished under Bismarck, taught students obedience to the emperor along with reading, writing, and mathematics.

Like his grandfather, William II lavished funds on the German military machine, already the most powerful in Europe. He also launched an ambitious campaign to expand the German navy and win an overseas empire to rival those of Britain and France. William's nationalism and aggressive military stance helped increase tensions on the eve of World War I.

✔ **Checkpoint** Why did William II ask Bismarck to resign in 1890?

Social Reform
Under Bismarck's leadership, Germany pioneered social reform. By 1884, Germans had health and accident insurance. By 1889, they had disability and old-age insurance. *Why did Bismarck introduce these social reforms?*

Progress Monitoring *Online*
For: Self-quiz with vocabulary practice
Web Code: naa-2222

Terms, People, and Places

1. For each term, person, or place listed at the beginning of the section, write a sentence explaining its significance.

Note Taking

2. **Reading Skill: Recognize Sequence** Use your completed chart to answer the Focus Question: How did Germany increase its power after unifying in 1871?

Comprehension and Critical Thinking

3. **Summarize** How did Germany become an industrial giant in the late 1800s?

4. **Demonstrate Reasoned Judgment** Do you think Bismarck's methods were justified by his social reforms? Explain.

5. **Draw Conclusions** Do you think the supporters of a democratic government in Germany in the late 1800s had hope of success? Explain.

● **Writing About History**

Quick Write: Answer Opposing Arguments To write a strong persuasive essay, you need to address arguments that can be used to contradict your position. Choose a topic from the section. For example, think about whether a government should guarantee that its citizens have adequate healthcare. List the arguments for and against your position on a piece of paper.

Giuseppe Mazzini, around 1865

Stirrings of Nationalism

After a failed revolution against Austrian rule in northern Italy, many rebels, fearing retribution, begged for funds to pay for safe passage to Spain. Giuseppe Mazzini (mat SEE nee), still a boy, described his reaction to the situation:

66 He (a rebel) held out a white handkerchief, merely saying, 'For the refugees of Italy.' My mother . . . dropped some money into the handkerchief. . . . That day was the first in which a confused idea presented itself to my mind . . . an idea that we Italians could and therefore ought to struggle for the liberty of our country. . . . 99
—Giuseppe Mazzini, *Life and Writings*

Focus Question How did influential leaders help to create a unified Italy?

Unifying Italy

 Performance Standards

- **SSWH15a** Analyze movements for political reform.
- **SSWHRC1c** Demonstrate understanding of contextual vocabulary.

Terms, People, and Places

Camillo Cavour
Giuseppe Garibaldi
anarchist
emigration

Note Taking

Reading Skill: Recognize Sequence As you read, create a timeline showing the sequence of events from 1831 to 1871 that led to Italian unification.

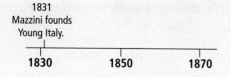

1831
Mazzini founds
Young Italy.

1830   1850   1870

Although the people of the Italian peninsula spoke the same language, they had not experienced political unity since Roman times. By the early 1800s, though, Italian patriots—including Mazzini, who would become a revolutionary—were determined to build a new, united Italy. As in Germany, unification was brought about by the efforts of a strong state and furthered by a shrewd, ruthless politician—Count **Camillo Cavour** (kah VOOR).

Obstacles to Italian Unity

For centuries, Italy had been a battleground for ambitious foreign and local princes. Frequent warfare and foreign rule had led people to identify with local regions. The people of Florence considered themselves Tuscans, those of Venice Venetians, those of Naples Neapolitans, and so on. But as in Germany, the invasions of Napoleon had sparked dreams of national unity.

The Congress of Vienna, however, ignored the nationalists who hoped to end centuries of foreign rule and achieve unity. To Prince Metternich of Austria, the idea of a unified Italy was laughable. At Vienna, Austria took control of much of northern Italy, while Hapsburg monarchs ruled various other Italian states. In the south, a French Bourbon ruler was put in charge of Naples and Sicily.

In response, nationalists organized secret patriotic societies and focused their efforts on expelling Austrian forces from northern Italy. Between 1820 and 1848, nationalist revolts exploded across the region. Each time, Austria sent in troops to crush the rebels.

Mazzini Establishes Young Italy In the 1830s, the nationalist leader Giuseppe Mazzini founded Young Italy. The goal of this secret society was "to <u>constitute</u> Italy, one, free, independent, republican nation." In 1849, Mazzini helped set up a revolutionary republic in Rome, but French forces soon toppled it. Like many other nationalists, Mazzini spent much of his life in exile, plotting and dreaming of a united Italy.

Nationalism Takes Root "Ideas grow quickly," Mazzini once said, "when watered by the blood of martyrs." Although revolution had failed, nationalist agitation had planted seeds for future harvests.

To nationalists like Mazzini, a united Italy made sense not only because of geography, but also because of a common language and history. Nationalists reminded Italians of the glories of ancient Rome and the medieval papacy. To others, unity made practical economic sense. It would end trade barriers among the Italian states and stimulate industry.

✔ **Checkpoint** What forces hindered Italian unity?

The Struggle for Italy

After 1848, leadership of the Risorgimento (ree sawr jee MEN toh), or Italian nationalist movement, passed to the kingdom of Sardinia, which included Piedmont, Nice, and Savoy as well as the island of Sardinia. Its constitutional monarch, Victor Emmanuel II, hoped to join other states to his own, thereby increasing his power.

Cavour Becomes Prime Minister In 1852, Victor Emmanuel made Count Camillo Cavour his prime minister. Cavour came from a noble family but favored liberal goals. He was a flexible, practical, crafty politician, willing to use almost any means to achieve his goals. Like Bismarck in Prussia, Cavour was a monarchist who believed in Realpolitik.

Once in office, Cavour moved first to reform Sardinia's economy. He improved agriculture, had railroads built, and encouraged commerce by supporting free trade. Cavour's long-term goal, however, was to end Austrian power in Italy and annex the provinces of Lombardy and Venetia.

Vocabulary Builder

<u>constitute</u>—(KAHN stuh toot) *v.* to set up; establish

Opposing Austrian Rule
In March 1848, nationalists in Venice took over the city's arsenal and declared the establishment of the Republic of Venice. Their success was short lived, however, as the republic was soon disbanded and Venice again fell under the rule of Austria in 1849.

Intrigue With France In 1855, Sardinia, led by Cavour, joined Britain and France against Russia in the Crimean War. Sardinia did not win territory, but it did have a voice at the peace conference. Sardinia also gained the attention of Napoleon III.

In 1858, Cavour negotiated a secret deal with Napoleon, who promised to aid Sardinia in case it faced a war with Austria. A year later, the shrewd Cavour provoked that war. With help from France, Sardinia defeated Austria and annexed Lombardy. Meanwhile, nationalist groups overthrew Austrian-backed rulers in several other northern Italian states. These states then joined with Sardinia.

Garibaldi's "Red Shirts" Next, attention shifted to the Kingdom of the Two Sicilies in southern Italy. There, **Giuseppe Garibaldi** (gah ree BAHL dee), a longtime nationalist and an ally of Mazzini, was ready for action. Like Mazzini, Garibaldi wanted to create an Italian republic. He did not hesitate, however, to accept aid from the monarchist Cavour. By 1860, Garibaldi had recruited a force of 1,000 red-shirted volunteers. Cavour provided weapons and allowed two ships to take Garibaldi and his "Red Shirts" south to Sicily. With surprising speed, Garibaldi's forces won control of Sicily, crossed to the mainland, and marched triumphantly north to Naples.

Unity at Last Garibaldi's success alarmed Cavour, who feared that the nationalist hero would set up his own republic in the south. To prevent this, Cavour urged Victor Emmanuel to send Sardinian troops to deal with Garibaldi. Instead, the Sardinians overran the Papal States and linked up with Garibaldi and his forces in Naples.

In a patriotic move, Garibaldi turned over Naples and Sicily to Victor Emmanuel. Shortly afterward, southern Italy voted to approve the move, and in 1861, Victor Emmanuel II was crowned king of Italy.

Two areas remained outside the new Italian nation: Rome and Venetia. Cavour died in 1861, but his <u>successors</u> completed his dream. Italy formed an alliance with Prussia in the Austro-Prussian War and won the province of Venetia. Then, during the Franco-Prussian War in 1870, France was forced to withdraw its troops from Rome. For the first time since the fall of the Roman empire, Italy was a united land.

✔ **Checkpoint** What steps did Camillo Cavour take to promote Italian unity?

Challenges Facing the New Nation

Italy faced a host of problems. Like the German empire that Bismarck cemented together out of many states, Italy had no tradition of unity. Few Italians felt ties to the new nation. Strong regional rivalries left Italy unable to solve critical national issues.

Divisions The greatest regional differences were between the north and the south. The north was richer and had more cities than the south. For centuries, northern Italian cities had flourished as centers of business and culture. The south, on the other hand, was rural and poor. Its population was booming, but illiterate peasants could extract only a meager existence from the exhausted farmland.

Hostility between Italy and the Roman Catholic Church further divided the nation. Popes bitterly resented the seizure of the Papal

Vocabulary Builder

<u>successor</u>—(suk SES ur) *n.* a person who succeeds another to an office or rank

Unifying Italy

The Italian peninsula had been divided into small independent states since the fall of the Roman empire in 476. Political unification seemed impossible. However, rebellion, nationalism, and unity slowly took hold with the help of four individuals: a revolutionary, a statesman, a soldier, and a king.

① Giuseppe Mazzini
Giuseppe Mazzini, founder of Young Italy, helps set up a revolutionary republic in Rome in 1849. French troops soon topple it.

② Camillo Cavour
In 1859, prime minister Camillo Cavour provokes a war with Austria after secret negotiations with Napoleon III, who promised aid to Sardinia.

③ Nationalist Revolts
Italian nationalists overthrow Austrian-backed rulers in several northern states.

④ Giuseppe Garibaldi
In 1860, Cavour provides weapons to Giuseppe Garibaldi, who invades Sicily with 1,000 Red Shirt volunteers (below). Garibaldi then captures Naples.

⑤ Victor Emmanuel II
In a patriotic move, Garibaldi turns over Naples and Sicily to Victor Emmanuel, who is crowned king. In 1870, Italians conquer Rome, which becomes the capital city of a unified Italy.

Map labels:
SWITZERLAND
AUSTRIA-HUNGARY
LOMBARDY
VENETIA
Venice
Trieste
SAVOY (To France)
Turin
Milan
PIEDMONT
Genoa
PARMA
MODENA
SAN MARINO
NICE (To France)
Florence
TUSCANY
PAPAL STATES
Adriatic Sea
CORSICA (France)
Rome
KINGDOM OF THE TWO SICILIES
Naples
SARDINIA
Tyrrhenian Sea
Mediterranean Sea
Palermo
SICILY

N W–E S

MILLER PROJECTION
SCALE IN MILES
0   100   200
SCALE IN KILOMETERS
0   100   200

Legend:
- Kingdom of Sardinia, 1858
- Added to Sardinia, 1859 and 1860
- Added to Italy, 1866
- Added to Italy, 1870
- → Route of Garibaldi's expedition, 1860

Thinking Critically
1. **Map Skills** What route did Garibaldi's expedition take?
2. **Draw Conclusions** Why was Italian unification difficult to achieve?

History Interactive
For: Interactive timeline
Web Code: nap-2232

States and of Rome. The government granted the papacy limited rights and control over church properties. Popes, however, saw themselves as "prisoners" and urged Italian Catholics—almost all Italians—not to cooperate with their new government.

Turmoil Under Victor Emmanuel, Italy was a constitutional monarchy with a two-house legislature. The king appointed members to the upper house, which could veto bills passed by the lower house. Although the lower house consisted of elected representatives, only a small number of men had the right to vote.

In the late 1800s, unrest increased as radicals on the left struggled against a conservative government. Socialists organized strikes while **anarchists,** people who want to abolish all government, turned to sabotage and violence. Slowly, the government extended suffrage to more men and passed laws to improve social conditions. Still, the turmoil continued. To distract attention from troubles at home, the government set out to win an overseas empire in Ethiopia.

Economic Progress Despite its problems, Italy did develop economically, especially after 1900. Although the nation lacked important natural resources such as coal, industries did sprout up in northern regions. Industrialization, of course, brought urbanization as peasants flocked to the cities to find jobs in factories. As in other countries, reformers campaigned to improve education and working conditions.

The population explosion of this period created tensions. One important safety valve for many people was **emigration,** or movement away from their homeland. Many Italians left for the United States, Canada, and Latin American nations. By 1914, the country was significantly better off than it had been in 1861. But, it was hardly prepared for the great war that broke out in that year.

Italian Emigration
Emigrants crowd the port of Naples (above). *Why did Italians immigrate to other countries in the early 1900s?*

✔ **Checkpoint** What problems did Italians experience after unification?

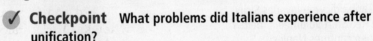

Progress Monitoring *Online*
For: Self-quiz with vocabulary practice
Web Code: naa-2233

SECTION 3 **Assessment**

Terms, People, and Places

1. For each term, person, or place listed at the beginning of the section, write a sentence explaining its significance.

Note Taking

2. **Reading Skill: Recognize Sequence** Use your completed timeline to answer the Focus Question: How did influential leaders help to create a unified Italy?

Comprehension and Critical Thinking

3. **Summarize** (a) What obstacles to unity did Italian nationalists face? (b) What conditions favored unity?

4. **Analyze Information** (a) What was the source of conflict between Garibaldi and Cavour? (b) How was the conflict resolved?

5. **Express Problems Clearly** What challenges did Italians face after unification?

● **Writing About History**

Quick Write: Decide on an Organizational Strategy Using clear organization to present a logical argument is a good way to keep the reader's attention in a persuasive essay. Choose an issue from the section about which you could make an argument. Then write an outline showing how you would organize a persuasive essay.

Hungarian parliament passes legislation funding an army to fight against the Hapsburg empire, 1848

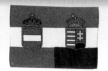

Austria-Hungarian empire flag

WITNESS HISTORY ◀)) AUDIO

Balkan Nationalism

66 How is it that they [European powers] cannot understand that less and less is it possible . . . to direct the destinies of the Balkans from the outside? We are growing up, gaining confidence, and becoming independent . . . 99
—Bulgarian statesman on the first Balkan War and the European powers

Focus Question How did the desire for national independence among ethnic groups weaken and ultimately destroy the Austrian and Ottoman empires?

Nationalism Threatens Old Empires

Performance Standards

- **SSWH15b** Identify the causes and results of the revolution in England.
- **SSWH16d** Analyze collapse of the Hapsburg dynasty.

Terms, People, and Places

Francis Joseph
Ferenc Deák
Dual Monarchy

Note Taking

Reading Skill: Recognize Sequence Complete a table like the one below to keep track of the sequence of events that led Austria into the Dual Monarchy. Look for dates and other clues to sequence in the text.

Events in Austrian History	
1840	
1848	
1859	
1866	
1867	

Napoleon had dissolved the Holy Roman Empire, which the Hapsburgs had led for nearly 400 years. Austria's center of power had shifted to Central Europe. Additional wars resulted in continued loss of territory to Germany and Italy. Why did nationalism bring new strength to some countries and weaken others?

In Eastern and Central Europe, the Austrian Hapsburgs and the Ottoman Turks ruled lands that included diverse ethnic groups. Nationalist feelings among these subject peoples contributed to tensions building across Europe.

The Hapsburg Empire Declines

In 1800, the Hapsburgs were the oldest ruling house in Europe. In addition to their homeland of Austria, over the centuries they had acquired the territories of Bohemia and Hungary, as well as parts of Romania, Poland, Ukraine, and northern Italy.

Austria Faces Change Since the Congress of Vienna, the Austrian emperor Francis I and his foreign minister Metternich had upheld conservative goals against liberal forces. "Rule and change nothing," the emperor told his son. Under Francis and Metternich, newspapers could not even use the word *constitution,* much less discuss this key demand of liberals. The government also tried to limit industrial development, which would threaten traditional ways of life.

Austria, however, could not hold back the changes that were engulfing the rest of Europe. By the 1840s, factories were springing up. Soon, the Hapsburgs found themselves facing the problems of industrial life that had long been familiar in Britain—the growth of cities, worker discontent, and the stirrings of socialism.

A Multinational Empire Equally disturbing to the old order were the urgent demands of nationalists. The Hapsburgs presided over a multinational empire. Of its 50 million people at mid-century, fewer than a quarter were German-speaking Austrians. Almost half belonged to different Slavic groups, including Czechs, Slovaks, Poles, Ukrainians, Serbs, Croats, and Slovenes. Often, rival groups shared the same region. The empire also included large numbers of Hungarians and Italians. The Hapsburgs ignored nationalist demands as long as they could. When nationalist revolts broke out in 1848, the government crushed them.

Francis Joseph Grants Limited Reforms Amid the turmoil, 18-year-old **Francis Joseph** inherited the Hapsburg throne. He would rule until 1916, presiding over the empire during its fading days into World War I.

An early challenge came when Austria suffered its humiliating defeat at the hands of France and Sardinia in 1859. Francis Joseph realized he needed to strengthen the empire at home. Accordingly, he made some limited reforms. He granted a new constitution that set up a legislature. This body, however, was dominated by German-speaking Austrians. The reforms thus satisfied none of the other national groups that populated the empire. The Hungarians, especially, were determined to settle for nothing less than total self-government.

✔ **Checkpoint** What actions did Francis Joseph take to maintain power?

Formation of the Dual Monarchy

Austria's disastrous defeat in the 1866 war with Prussia brought renewed pressure for change from Hungarians within the empire. One year later, **Ferenc Deák** (DEH ahk), a moderate Hungarian leader, helped work out a compromise that created a new political power known as the **Dual Monarchy** of Austria-Hungary.

The Austria-Hungary Government Under the agreement, Austria and Hungary were separate states. Each had its own constitution and parliament. Francis Joseph ruled both, as emperor of Austria and king of Hungary. The two states also shared ministries of finance, defense, and foreign affairs, but were independent of each other in all other areas.

Nationalist Unrest Increases Although Hungarians welcomed the compromise, other subject peoples resented it. Restlessness increased among various Slavic groups, especially the Czechs in Bohemia. Some nationalist leaders called on Slavs to unite, insisting that "only through liberty, equality, and <u>fraternal</u> solidarity" could Slavic peoples fulfill their "great mission in the history of mankind." By the early 1900s, nationalist unrest often left the government paralyzed in the face of pressing political and social problems.

✔ **Checkpoint** How did Hungarians and Slavic groups respond to the Dual Monarchy?

Vocabulary Builder
<u>fraternal</u>—(fruh TUR nul) *adj.* brotherly

Major Nationalities in Eastern Europe, 1800–1914

Geography *Interactive*
For: Audio guided tour
Web Code: nap-2243

GERMANY

POLES

WHITE RUSSIANS

GREAT RUSSIANS

CZECHS

POLES

UKRAINIANS

UKRAINIANS

FRANCE

SLOVAKS

SWITZ.

GERMANS

HUNGARIANS

ROMANIANS

ITALIANS

SLOVENES

ROMANIANS

GREAT RUSSIANS

ITALIANS

CROATS

ROMANIA
ROMANIANS

Black Sea

SERBIANS

BOSNIAKS

SERBIA

Adriatic Sea

ITALY

MONTENEGRINS

BULGARIANS

N

MONT.

ALBANIANS

Mediterranean Sea

MACEDONIANS

GREEKS

Aegean Sea

TURKS

30° E

40° N

10° E

Conic Projection

0   200   400 mi

0   200   400 km

GREECE

The Balkans, 1878

RUSSIA

AUSTRIA-HUNGARY

Bosnia-
Herzegovina
(occupied by
Austria)

ROMANIA

Danube R.

Black Sea

ITALY

SERBIA

Bulgaria
(autonomous)

Adriatic Sea

MONTENEGRO

Eastern Rumelia
(semi-autonomous)

✷ Constantinople

40° N

Aegean Sea

Conic Projection

0   300 mi

0   300 km

GREECE

Mediterranean Sea

20° E

30° E

Crete

Independent
Balkan states

Ottoman Empire

Colors reflect the major languages spoken
in Eastern Europe, 1800 to 1914.

Map Skills In the late 1800s, the Balkans had become a center of conflict, as various peoples and empires competed for power.

1. **Locate** (a) Black Sea (b) Ottoman empire (c) Serbia (d) Greece (e) Austria-Hungary
2. **Place** Which four large seas border the Balkan Peninsula?
3. **Identify Central Issues** Why do you think competing interests in the Balkans led the region to be called a powder keg?

The Ottoman Empire Collapses

Like the Hapsburgs, the Ottomans ruled a multinational empire. It stretched from Eastern Europe and the Balkans to North Africa and the Middle East. There, as in Austria, nationalist demands tore at the fabric of the empire.

Balkan Nationalism Erupts In the Balkans, Serbia won autonomy in 1830, and southern Greece won independence during the 1830s. But many Serbs and Greeks still lived in the Balkans under Ottoman rule. The Ottoman empire was also home to other national groups, such as Bulgarians and Romanians. During the 1800s, various subject peoples staged revolts against the Ottomans, hoping to set up their own independent states.

European Powers Divide Up the Ottoman Empire Such nationalist stirrings became mixed up with the ambitions of the great European powers. In the mid-1800s, Europeans came to see the Ottoman empire as "the sick man of Europe." Eagerly, they scrambled to divide up Ottoman lands. Russia pushed south toward the Black Sea and Istanbul, which Russians still called Constantinople. Austria-Hungary took control of the provinces of Bosnia and Herzegovina. This action angered the Serbs, who also had hoped to expand into that area. Meanwhile, Britain and France set their sights on other Ottoman lands in the Middle East and North Africa.

War in the Balkans In the end, a complex web of competing interests contributed to a series of crises and wars in the Balkans. Russia fought several wars against the Ottomans. France and Britain sometimes joined the Russians and sometimes the Ottomans. Germany supported Austrian authority over the discontented national groups. But Germany also encouraged the Ottomans because of their strategic location in the eastern Mediterranean. In between, the subject peoples revolted and then fought among themselves. By the early 1900s, observers were referring to the region as the "Balkan powder keg." The explosion that came in 1914 helped set off World War I.

 Checkpoint How did the European powers divide up Ottoman lands?

"The Sick Man of Europe"
Turkey's Abdul Hamid II (right) reacts to Bulgarian and Austrian rulers claiming parts of the Ottoman empire. *How does this cartoon show the Ottoman empire as "the sick man of Europe"?*

SECTION 4 Assessment

Progress Monitoring *Online*
For: Self-quiz with vocabulary practice
Web Code: naa-2244

Terms, People, and Places

1. For each term, person, or place listed at the beginning of the section, write a sentence explaining its significance.

Note Taking

2. **Reading Skill: Recognize Sequence** Use your completed table to answer the Focus Question: How did the desire for national independence among ethnic groups weaken and ultimately destroy the Austrian and Ottoman empires?

Comprehension and Critical Thinking

3. **Identify Alternatives** What alternatives did Francis Joseph have in responding to nationalist demands? How might Austrian history have been different if he had chosen a different course of action?

4. **Draw Conclusions** Why did the Dual Monarchy fail to end nationalist demands?

5. **Identify Central Issues** How did Balkan nationalism contribute to the decline of the Ottoman empire?

● Writing About History

Quick Write: Draft an Opening Paragraph In a persuasive essay, you want to grab the reader's attention by opening with a strong example, and then convincingly stating your views. Choose a topic from the section, such as whether the Hapsburgs or the Ottoman Turks could have built a modern, unified nation from their multinational empires. Then draft an opening paragraph.

NATIONALISM

How can nationalism be a unifying and a divisive force?

In This Chapter

Nationalism is a powerful force characterized by strong feelings of pride in and devotion to one's nation. In the 1800s, nationalism forged new nations and tore old empires apart. For example, nationalists who believed that all Italian-speaking people on the Italian peninsula should be united created the nation of Italy (right).

Throughout History

1776 Americans declare independence from Great Britain.

1800s Latin America colonies rise up in rebellion against Spain.

1800s The Ottoman Empire is weakened by nationalist movements.

1900s After World War II, African nations gain independence from colonial rulers.

1990s Nationalist feelings among diverse ethnic groups leads to war in Yugoslavia.

Continuing Today

People will fight to establish or preserve their national identity, defend their own land, or even aggressively grab the territory of others. In Canada, the English-speaking majority has sought to maintain national unity in the face of a movement by French Canadians to establish an independent Quebec.

21st Century Skills

TRANSFER Activities

1. **Analyze** How has nationalism changed the course of history?

2. **Evaluate** Why do people respond to nationalism?

3. **Transfer** Complete a Web quest in which you decide if you would or would not support a nationalist movement; record your thoughts in the Concept Connector Journal; and learn to make a video. Web Code nah-2208

SECTION

5

Russian peasant women clearing stones from a field

WITNESS HISTORY 🔊 AUDIO

Plight of the Serfs

Although serfdom had almost disappeared in Western Europe by the 1700s, it survived in Russia. Masters exercised almost total power over their serfs. A noble turned revolutionary described the treatment of the serfs:

❝ I heard . . . stories of men and women torn from their families and their villages, and sold, or lost in gambling, or exchanged for a couple of hunting dogs, and then transported to some remote part of Russia to create a [master's] new estate; of children taken from their parents and sold to cruel . . . masters. ❞
—Peter Kropotkin, *Memoirs of a Revolutionist*

Focus Question Why did industrialization and reform come more slowly to Russia than to Western Europe?

Russia: Reform and Reaction

 Performance Standards

- **SSWH15b** Compare and contrast the rise of Germany and Japan.
- **SSWH16d** Analyze collapse of the Romanov dynasty.

Terms, People, and Places

colossus	pogrom
Alexander II	refugees
Crimean War	Duma
emancipation	Peter Stolypin
zemstvo	

N̲o̲te Taking

Reading Skill: Recognize Sequence Create a timeline of Russian events like the one below to keep track of the sequence of events that led to the revolution of 1905. Look for dates and other clues to sequence in the text.

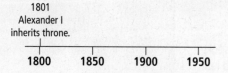

1801
Alexander I
inherits throne.

1800   1850   1900   1950

Reformers hoped to free Russia from autocratic rule, economic backwardness, and social injustice. But efforts to modernize Russia had little success, as tsars imprisoned critics or sent them into exile.

Conditions in Russia

By 1815, Russia was not only the largest, most populous nation in Europe but also a great world power. Since the 1600s, explorers, soldiers, and traders seeking furs had expanded Russia's empire eastward across Siberia to the Pacific. Seeking ports, Peter the Great and Catherine the Great had added lands on the Baltic and Black seas. Seeking to contain the Ottoman and British empires, tsars in the 1800s expanded into the Caucasus and Central Asia. Russia thus acquired a huge multinational empire, part European and part Asian.

Other European nations looked on the Russian **colossus**, or giant, anxiously. Russia had immense natural resources. Its vast size gave it global influence. But many Europeans disliked its autocratic government and feared its expansion. At the same time, Russia remained economically undeveloped. By the 1800s, tsars saw the need to modernize but resisted reforms that would undermine their absolute rule.

Russia's Social Structure A great obstacle to progress was the rigid social structure. Landowning nobles dominated society and rejected any change that would threaten their power. The middle class was small and weak. Most Russians were serfs, or laborers bound to the land and to the landowners who controlled them.

Most serfs were peasants. Others were servants, artisans, or soldiers forced into the tsar's army. As industry expanded, some masters sent serfs to work in factories but took much of their pay.

Many enlightened Russians knew that serfdom was inefficient. As long as most people had to serve the whim of their masters, Russia's economy would remain backward. However, landowning nobles had no reason to improve agriculture and took little interest in industry.

Ruling With Absolute Power For centuries, tsars had ruled with absolute power, imposing their will on their subjects. On occasion, the tsars made limited attempts at liberal reform, such as easing censorship or making legal and economic reforms to improve the lives of serfs. However, in each instance the tsars drew back from their reforms when they began to fear losing the support of nobles. In short, the liberal and nationalist changes brought about by the Enlightenment and the French Revolution had almost no effect on Russian autocracy.

✓ **Checkpoint** Describe the social structure that existed in Russia during the 1800s.

Emancipation and Stirrings of Revolution

Alexander II came to the throne in 1855 during the **Crimean War.** His reign represents the pattern of reform and repression used by his father and grandfather, Alexander I and Nicholas I. The Crimean War had broken out after Russia tried to seize Ottoman lands along the Danube River. Britain and France stepped in to help the Ottoman Turks, invading the Crimean peninsula that juts into the Black Sea. The war, which ended in a Russian defeat, revealed the country's backwardness. Russia had only a few miles of railroads, and the military bureaucracy was hopelessly inefficient. Many felt that dramatic changes were needed.

Freeing the Serfs A widespread popular reaction followed. Liberals demanded changes, and students demonstrated, seeking reform. Pressed from all sides, Alexander II finally agreed to reforms. In 1861, he issued a royal decree that required **emancipation,** or freeing of the serfs.

Freedom brought problems. Former serfs had to buy the land they had worked, but many were too poor to do so. Also, the lands allotted to peasants were often too small to farm efficiently or to support a family. Peasants remained poor, and discontent festered.

Still, emancipation was a turning point. Many peasants moved to the cities, taking jobs in factories and building Russian industries. Equally important, freeing the serfs boosted the drive for further reform.

Introducing Other Reforms Along with emancipation, Alexander II set up a system of local government. Elected assemblies, called **zemstvos,** were made responsible for matters such as road repair, schools, and agriculture. Through this system, Russians gained some experience of self-government at the local level.

The Decembrist Revolt
In 1825, army officers led an uprising known as the Decembrist Revolt (below). They had picked up liberal ideas while fighting in Western Europe and demanded reforms and a constitution. Tsar Nicholas I repressed the revolt. This stamp (inset) commemorates the 125th anniversary of the revolt. *How did the revolt symbolize Russia in the 1800s?*

The tsar also introduced legal reforms based on ideas like trial by jury, and he eased censorship. Military service terms were reduced, and brutal discipline was limited. Alexander also encouraged the growth of industry in Russia, which still relied heavily on agriculture.

Revolutionary Currents Alexander's reforms failed to satisfy many Russians. Peasants had freedom but not land. Liberals wanted a constitution and an elected legislature. Radicals, who had adopted socialist ideas from the West, demanded even more revolutionary changes. The tsar, meantime, moved away from reform and toward repression.

In the 1870s, some socialists went to live and work among peasants, preaching reform and rebellion. They had little success. The peasants scarcely understood them and sometimes turned them over to the police. The failure of this movement, combined with renewed government repression, sparked anger among radicals. Some turned to terrorism. On March 13, 1881, terrorists assassinated Alexander II.

Crackdown Alexander III responded to his father's assassination by reviving the harsh methods of Nicholas I. To wipe out liberals and revolutionaries, he increased the power of the secret police, restored strict censorship, and exiled critics to Siberia. The tsar also launched a program of Russification aimed at suppressing the cultures of non-Russian peoples within the empire. Alexander insisted on one language, Russian,

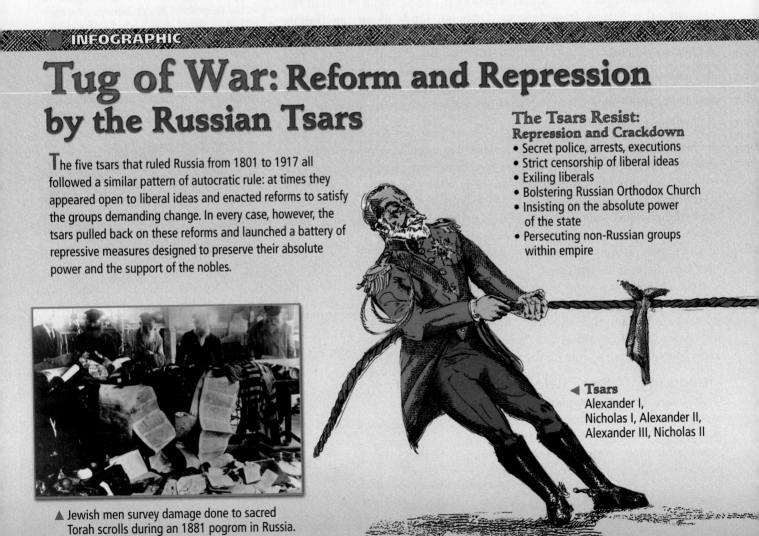

INFOGRAPHIC

Tug of War: Reform and Repression by the Russian Tsars

The five tsars that ruled Russia from 1801 to 1917 all followed a similar pattern of autocratic rule: at times they appeared open to liberal ideas and enacted reforms to satisfy the groups demanding change. In every case, however, the tsars pulled back on these reforms and launched a battery of repressive measures designed to preserve their absolute power and the support of the nobles.

The Tsars Resist:
Repression and Crackdown
- Secret police, arrests, executions
- Strict censorship of liberal ideas
- Exiling liberals
- Bolstering Russian Orthodox Church
- Insisting on the absolute power of the state
- Persecuting non-Russian groups within empire

◀ **Tsars**
Alexander I,
Nicholas I, Alexander II,
Alexander III, Nicholas II

▲ Jewish men survey damage done to sacred Torah scrolls during an 1881 pogrom in Russia.

712

and one church, the Russian Orthodox Church. Poles, Ukrainians, Finns, Armenians, Muslims, Jews, and many others suffered persecution.

Persecution and Pogroms Russia had acquired a large Jewish population when it carved up Poland and expanded into Ukraine. Under Alexander III, persecution of Jewish people in Russia increased. The tsar limited the number of Jewish people who were allowed to study in universities and practice certain professions. He also forced them to live in restricted areas.

Official persecution encouraged **pogroms,** or violent mob attacks on Jewish people. Gangs beat and killed Jewish people and looted and burned their homes and stores. Faced with savage persecution, many left Russia. They became **refugees,** or people who flee their homeland to seek safety elsewhere. Large numbers of Russian Jews went to the United States.

 Checkpoint How did Alexander III respond to the murder of his father?

The Drive to Industrialize

Russia finally entered the industrial age under Alexander III and his son Nicholas II. In the 1890s, Nicholas' government

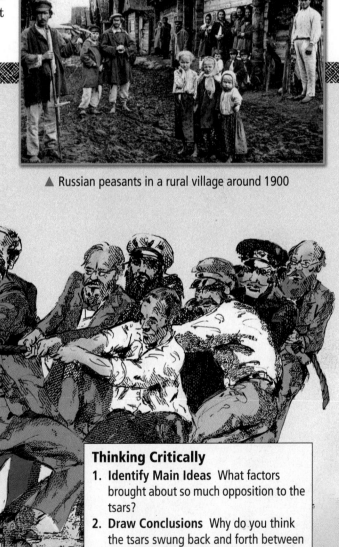

▲ Russian peasants in a rural village around 1900

The Tsars Give In:
Concessions and Reforms
- Easing censorship
- Revising law code
- Limiting the power of landowners
- Freeing serfs (1861)
- Creating local self-government, or zemstvos
- Creating national legislature, or Duma
- Land reforms

Opposing the Tsars ▶
Liberals, socialists, nationalists, army officers, workers

Thinking Critically
1. **Identify Main Ideas** What factors brought about so much opposition to the tsars?
2. **Draw Conclusions** Why do you think the tsars swung back and forth between repression and reform?

focused on economic development. It encouraged the building of railroads to connect iron and coal mines with factories and to transport goods across Russia. It also secured foreign capital to invest in industry and transportation systems, such as the Trans-Siberian Railroad, which linked European Russia to the Pacific Ocean.

Political and social problems increased as a result of industrialization. Government officials and business leaders applauded economic growth. Nobles and peasants opposed it, fearing the changes it brought. Industrialization also created new social ills as peasants flocked to cities to work in factories. Instead of a better life, they found long hours and low pay in dangerous conditions. In the slums around the factories, poverty, disease, and discontent multiplied. Radicals sought supporters among the new industrial workers. At factory gates, Socialists often handed out pamphlets that preached the revolutionary ideas of Karl Marx.

✔ **Checkpoint** How did Russia industrialize?

Turning Point: Crisis and Revolution

When war broke out between Russia and Japan in 1904, Nicholas II called on his people to fight for "the Faith, the Tsar, and the Fatherland." Despite all of their efforts, the Russians suffered one humiliating defeat after another.

Bloody Sunday News of the military disasters unleashed pent-up discontent created by years of oppression. Protesters poured into the streets. Workers went on strike, demanding shorter hours and better wages. Liberals called for a constitution and reforms to overhaul the government.

As the crisis deepened, a young Orthodox priest organized a peaceful march for Sunday, January 22, 1905. Marchers flowed through the streets of St. Petersburg toward the tsar's Winter Palace. Chanting prayers and singing hymns, workers carried holy icons and pictures of the tsar. They also brought a petition for justice and freedom.

Bloody Sunday
An artist's depiction shows the execution of workers in front of the Winter Palace in Saint Petersburg, January 9, 1905 (below). The magazine cover (inset) shows "Le Tzar Rouge," or "The Red Tsar." *Compare and contrast these images of Bloody Sunday.*

Fearing the marchers, the tsar had fled the palace and called in soldiers. As the people approached, they saw troops lined up across the square. Suddenly, gunfire rang out. Hundreds of men and women fell dead or wounded in the snow. One woman stumbling away from the scene moaned: "The tsar has deserted us! They shot away the orthodox faith." Indeed, the slaughter marked a turning point for Russians. "Bloody Sunday" killed the people's faith and trust in the tsar.

The Revolution of 1905 In the months that followed Bloody Sunday, discontent exploded across Russia. Strikes multiplied. In some cities, workers took over local government. In the countryside, peasants revolted and demanded land. Minority nationalities called for autonomy from Russia. Terrorists targeted officials, and some assassins were cheered as heroes by discontented Russians.

At last, the clamor grew so great that Nicholas was forced to announce sweeping reforms. In the October Manifesto, he promised "freedom of person, conscience, speech, assembly, and union." He agreed to summon a **Duma,** or elected national legislature. No law, he declared, would go into effect without approval by the Duma.

Results of the Revolution The manifesto won over moderates, leaving Socialists isolated. These divisions helped the tsar, who had no intention of letting strikers, revolutionaries, and rebellious peasants challenge him.

In 1906, the first Duma met, but the tsar quickly dissolved it when leaders criticized the government. Nicholas then appointed a new prime minister, **Peter Stolypin** (stuh LIP yin). Arrests, pogroms, and executions followed as the conservative Stolypin sought to restore order.

Stolypin soon realized that Russia needed reform, not just repression. To regain peasant support, he introduced moderate land reforms. He strengthened the zemstvos and improved education. Unfortunately, these reforms were too limited to meet the broad needs of most Russians, and dissatisfaction still simmered. Stolypin was assassinated in 1911. Several more Dumas met during this period, but new voting laws made sure they were conservative. By 1914, Russia was still an autocracy, but one simmering with unrest.

 Checkpoint Why was Bloody Sunday a turning point for the Russians?

Progress Monitoring Online
For: Self-quiz with vocabulary practice
Web Code: naa-2255

Terms, People, and Places

1. For each term, person, or place listed at the beginning of the section, write a sentence explaining its significance.

Note Taking

2. **Reading Skill: Recognize Sequence** Use your completed timeline to answer the Focus Question: Why did industrialization and reform come more slowly to Russia than to Western Europe?

Comprehension and Critical Thinking

3. **Summarize** What conditions in Russia challenged progress during the early 1800s?

4. **Draw Conclusions** How did Russian tsars typically react to change?

5. **Draw Inferences** What does Bloody Sunday suggest about the relationship between the tsar and the Russian people?

● **Writing About History**

Quick Write: Gather Evidence to Support Thesis Statement Choose a topic from the section, such as whether you think emancipation helped or hurt Russian serfs. Make a list of evidence from the section that supports your view.

CHAPTER 22

Quick Study Guide

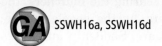 SSWH16a, SSWH16d

Progress Monitoring *Online*
For: Self-test with vocabulary practice
Web Code: naa-2266

■ Effects of Nationalism

Nationalism by Region				
Germany	**Italy**	**Austria**	**Balkans**	**Russia**
• German states unite under William I. • Empire takes leading role in Europe. • Bismarck becomes known as the Iron Chancellor.	• Mazzini founds Young Italy. • Garibaldi leads Red Shirts. • Victor Emmanuel II makes Cavour prime minister of Sardinia. • Italian states become unified by 1871.	• Francis I and Metternich uphold conservative goals. • Dual Monarchy with Hungary is set up. • Nationalist groups grow restless. • Empire becomes weakened.	• Serbians achieve autonomy in 1830. • Greeks achieve independence in the 1830s. • European nations divide up Ottoman lands. • "Balkan powder keg" helps set off World War I.	• Serfs are freed in 1861. • Alexander III encourages persecution and pogroms. • Russia enters the industrial age late. • Bloody Sunday leads to revolution in 1905. • Duma has limited power.

■ Unification in Europe, 1873

As the map below shows, nationalist movements led to the creation of several new nations across Europe.

■ Key Leaders

Germany
Otto von Bismarck, *chancellor*
William I, *Prussian king, German kaiser*
William II, *kaiser*

Italy
Giuseppe Mazzini, *founder of Young Italy*
Victor Emmanuel II, *king*
Count Camillo Cavour, *prime minister*
Giuseppe Garibaldi, *leader of Red Shirts*

Austria-Hungary
Ferenc Deák, *Hungarian politician*
Francis Joseph, *Austrian emperor, Hungarian king*

Russia
Alexander II, *tsar of Russia*
Alexander III, *tsar of Russia*
Nicholas II, *tsar of Russia*

■ Key Events of Nationalism

Early 1800s
Nationalism rises in Germany.

1814
The Congress of Vienna redraws the map of Europe after Napoleon's defeat.

1830s
Giuseppe Mazzini founds Young Italy to encourage Italian unification.

Chapter Events
Global Events

1800   **1825**   **1850**

1804
Haiti declares independence from France.

1848
Revolutions take place throughout Europe.

Concept Connector

Essential Question Review

To connect prior knowledge with what you have learned in this chapter, answer the questions below in your Concept Connector journal. Use the journal in the Reading and Note Taking Study Guide to record your answers (or go to www.phschool.com Web Code: nad-2207).

1. **Empire** In 1864, the Prussian prime minister, Otto von Bismarck, formed an alliance with Austria. Prussia and Austria then seized and "liberated" two provinces from Denmark. By 1871, German nationalists were celebrating the birth of the second Reich. Describe two actions that von Bismarck took between 1864 and 1871 that show why he was considered a master of Realpolitik. What was von Bismarck's ultimate goal? How did these events result in the formation of the second Reich?

2. **Nationalism** During the early1800s, nationalist rebellions erupted in the Balkans. Many of the ethnic groups in the region hoped to overthrow Austrian and Ottoman rule and set up independent states of their own. Re-read Section 4 in this chapter. Take notes on the situation in the Balkans between 1800 and the early 1900s. Using your notes, create a timeline of the events in the Balkans leading up to 1914.

3. **Revolution** Many revolutions involve a conflict between tradition and progress. How did the conditions in Russia leading to the Revolution of 1905 demonstrate this conflict? Consider the actions of the tsar, the liberals, and the peasants. How did industrialization intensify the struggle between opposing factions?

Connections to Today

1. **Nationalism: The State of Nationalism Today** You've read how nationalism was a strong enough force in the 1800s to help unify nations, such as Italy and Germany, but threatened to destroy the Austrian and Ottoman empires. Do you think that nationalism is still a force in the world today? Conduct research to learn more about current nationalist issues. You may want to focus your research on Kurdistan, Northern Ireland, the former Yugoslavia, or Russia. Write two paragraphs on nationalism today, citing examples from current events to support your answer.

2. **Economic Systems: Social Welfare Programs** Under Otto von Bismarck, Germany was a pioneer in social reform, providing several social welfare programs to its citizens. By the 1890s, Germans had health and accident insurance as well as retirement benefits. Social welfare programs soon spread to other European nations. Conduct research to learn more about social welfare programs today. Compare social welfare programs in one country in Europe with those in the United States. How are they similar? How are they different?

1861
Tsar Alexander II frees the serfs.

1870
Bismarck provokes Franco-Prussian War to create a unified German empire.

1905
Revolution breaks out in St. Petersburg after Bloody Sunday massacre.

1875

1900

1925

1861
The Civil War begins in the United States.

1898
The Philippines declares independence from Spain.

1914
World War I begins.

Chapter Assessment

Terms, People, and Places

Match the following definitions with the terms listed below.

chancellor	emigration
Realpolitik	emancipation
kaiser	pogrom
social welfare	Duma
anarchist	

1. someone who wants to abolish all government
2. elected national legislature in Russia
3. emperor of Germany
4. granting of freedom to serfs
5. the highest official of a monarch
6. violent attack on a Jewish community
7. movement away from one's homeland
8. realistic politics based on the needs of the state
9. programs to help people in need

Main Ideas

Section 1 (pp. 692–695)

10. What was Chancellor Otto von Bismarck's main goal? What policies did he follow to meet that goal?

Section 2 (pp. 696–699)

11. How did Germany increase its power in the late 1800s?

Section 3 (pp. 700–704)

12. Summarize the process by which Italy unified. Include information on the leaders who helped unify Italy.

Section 4 (pp. 705–709)

13. How did nationalism contribute to the decline of the Hapsburg and Ottoman empires?

Section 5 (pp. 710–715)

14. Why was Russia slow to industrialize?

Chapter Focus Question

15. What effects did nationalism and the demand for reform have in Europe?

Critical Thinking

16. **Make Comparisons** How did the nationalism represented by Bismarck differ from that embraced by liberals in the early 1800s?
17. **Make Comparisons** Compare and contrast the goals and methods of Cavour in Italy and Bismarck in Germany.
18. **Analyze Information** Tsar Alexander II declared that it is "better to abolish serfdom from above than to wait until it will be abolished by a movement from below." Explain his statement.
19. **Geography and History** How did regional differences contribute to continued divisions in Italy after unification?
20. **Analyzing Cartoons** How does this French cartoonist view Bismarck? Explain.
21. **Predict Consequences** Based on your reading of the chapter, predict the consequences of the following: (a) defeat of France in the Franco-Prussian War, (b) growth of German nationalism and militarism in the late 1800s, (c) failure to satisfy nationalist ambitions in Austria-Hungary, and (d) weakening of the Ottoman empire.

LE GRAND ÔCRE ALLEMAND.

● Writing About History

In this chapter's five Section Assessments, you developed skills to write a pursuasive essay.

Writing a Persuasive Essay Some people define nationalism as excessive, narrow, or jingoist patriotism. A nationalist might be described as someone who boasts of his patriotism and favors aggressive or warlike policies. The rise of nationalism in Europe led to both division and unification. For example, it unified Germany, but it led Russian tsars to suppress the cultures of national minorities within the country. Nationalism remains a powerful force to this day for unifying countries and for sparking rivalries, conflicts, and bloodshed. Write a persuasive essay in which you support or oppose the idea that nationalism is an excessive form of patriotism.

Prewriting
- Collect the examples and evidence that you need to support your position convincingly.
- Use a graphic organizer to list points on both sides of the issue.

Drafting
- Focus on a thesis statement. Clearly state the position that you will prove. Use the rest of your introduction to provide readers with the necessary context about the issue.
- Acknowledge the opposition by stating, and then refuting, opposing arguments.

Revising
- Use the guidelines for revising your essay on page SH17 of the Writing Handbook.

Prepare for the GHSGT

On the Crimean Front

In 1853, the British, the French, and their allies took on the vast Russian empire in the Crimean War. Called a "perfectly useless modern war," it was fought in the Black Sea region, although major campaigns took place well beyond that area. Like all wars, it was grim. More than 500,000 people died during the conflict.

Document A

"[The Crimean War] was one of the last times that the massed formations of cavalry and infantry were employed—the thin red line was to disappear forever. Henceforward, armies would rely on open, flexible formations and on trench warfare. For the British, it was the end of an era: never again would their soldiers fight in full-dress uniform. Never again would the colors be carried into the fray and the infantry would no longer march into battle to the stirring tunes of regimental bands. The Crimean War ushered in the age of the percussion cap rifle. The new Minie rifle was the decisive weapon, replacing the clumsy . . . musket. The weapon fired a cartridge, not a ball, with accuracy far superior to the old firelocks. . . ."

—From ***The Road to Balaklava,*** by Alexis S. Troubetzkoy

Document B

"I see men in hundreds rushing from the Mamelon [bastion] to the Malakoff [tower]. . . . with all its bristling guns. Under what a storm of fire they advance, supported by that impenetrable red line, which marks our own infantry! The fire from the Malakoff is tremendous—terrible. . . . Presently the twilight deepens, and the light of rocket, mortar, and shell falls over the town."

—From ***Journal kept during the Russian War: From the Departure of the Army from England in April 1854, to the Fall of Sebastopol,*** by Mrs. Henry Duberly, an army wife

Document C

"Men sent in there [French hospital] with fevers and other disorders were frequently attacked with the cholera in its worst form, and died with unusual rapidity, in spite of all that could be done to save them. I visited the hospital, and observed that a long train of . . . carts, filled with sick soldiers, were drawn up by the walls. . . . the quiet that prevailed was only broken now and then by the moans and cries of pain of the poor sufferers in the carts."

—From ***The British Expedition to the Crimea*** by W. H. Russell, ***Times*** correspondent

Document D

Treating Cholera

Analyzing Documents

Use your knowledge of the Crimean War and Documents A, B, C, and D to answer questions 1–4.

1. According to Document A, the Crimean War marked the end of
   A private soldiers in war.
   B most small wars in Europe.
   C old ways of fighting.
   D soldiers dying of diseases in military hospitals.

2. With what purpose did the author write Document B?
   A to help people understand the dangers of fighting with new weapons
   B to criticize inadequate technology
   C to describe the state of mind of the soldiers
   D to make the British public understand how quickly the war was progressing

3. With what purpose did the artist create Document D?
   A to help the British public understand the dangers of fighting with new weapons
   B to criticize the inadequate state of army hospitals
   C to describe the dangers of soldiering and soldiers' valor
   D to make the British public understand the toll that disease was taking on soldiers

4. **Writing Task** Suppose you are a surgeon working near the war front. Write a brief letter home describing your impressions. Use the four documents along with information from the chapter to write your letter.

23 Growth of Western Democracies

1815–1914

The People Demand Reform

A series of political reforms during the 1800s and early 1900s transformed Great Britain from a monarchy and aristocracy into a democracy. While some British politicians opposed the reforms, most sided in favor of reforming Parliament.

❝No doubt, at that very early period, the House of Commons did represent the people of England but. . . . the House of Commons, as it presently subsists, does not represent the people of England. . . . The people called loudly for reform, saying that whatever good existed in the constitution of this House—whatever confidence was placed in it by the people, was completely gone. ❞
—Lord John Russell, March 1, 1831

Listen to the Witness History audio to learn more about democratic developments in Britain.

◀ **Parliamentary Election of 1836**
Though most were unable to vote, many townspeople gathered in the marketplace to cheer or harass the candidates.

Queen Victoria of Great Britain and Ireland

A Liberal Party poster from 1911

 Performance Standards

Chapter Focus Question How did Britain, France, and the United States slowly extend democratic rights during the 1800s and early 1900s?

Section 1
Democratic Reform in Britain
SSWH15a

Section 2
Social and Economic Reform in Britain
SSWH15a

Section 3
Division and Democracy in France
SSWH16a

Section 4
Expansion of the United States
SSWHRC1c

Use the ☑ **Quick Study Timeline** at the end of this chapter to preview chapter events.

Advertisement for transportation to California during the Gold Rush

 Concept Connector ONLINE

To explore Essential Questions related to this chapter, go to PHSchool.com
Web Code: nad-2307

Fashions of the rich (above right), and poverty on the streets of London, circa 1877 (above)

Two Nations

One day a wealthy Englishman named Charles Egremont boasted to strangers that Victoria, the queen of England, "reigns over the greatest nation that ever existed."

"Which nation?" asks one of the strangers, "for she reigns over two. . . . Two nations; between whom there is no [communication] and no sympathy; who are as ignorant of each other's habits, thoughts, and feelings, as if they were . . . inhabitants of different planets."

What are these "two nations," Egremont asks. "THE RICH AND THE POOR," the stranger replies.
—Benjamin Disraeli, *Sybil*

Focus Question How did political reform gradually expand suffrage and make the British Parliament more democratic during the 1800s?

Democratic Reform in Britain

Performance Standards

- **SSWH15a** Analyze the writings of Adam Smith and Karl Marx.

Terms, People, and Places

rotten borough	Benjamin Disraeli
electorate	William Gladstone
secret ballot	parliamentary democracy
Queen Victoria	

Note Taking

Reading Skill: Identify Main Ideas As you read this section, complete an outline of the contents.

> I. Reforming Parliament
>   A. Reformers press for change
>   1.
>   2.

In the 1800s, Benjamin Disraeli and other political leaders slowly worked to bridge Britain's "two nations" and extend democratic rights. Unlike some of its neighbors in Europe, Britain generally achieved change through reform rather than revolution.

Reforming Parliament

In 1815, Britain was a constitutional monarchy with a parliament and two political parties. Still, it was far from democratic. Although members of the House of Commons were elected, less than five percent of the people had the right to vote. Wealthy nobles and squires, or country landowners, dominated politics and heavily influenced voters. In addition, the House of Lords—made up of hereditary nobles and high-ranking clergy—could veto any bill passed by the House of Commons.

Reformers Press for Change Long-standing laws kept many people from voting. Catholics and non-Anglican Protestants, for example, could not vote or serve in Parliament. In the 1820s, reformers pushed to end religious restrictions. After fierce debate, Parliament finally granted Catholics and non-Anglican Protestants equal political rights.

An even greater battle soon erupted over making Parliament more representative. During the Industrial Revolution, centers of population shifted. Some rural towns lost so many people that they had few or no voters. Yet local landowners in these **rotten boroughs** still sent members to Parliament. At the same time, populous new industrial cities like Manchester and Birmingham had no seats allocated in Parliament because they had not existed as population centers in earlier times.

Vocabulary Builder
allocate—(AL oh kayt) *vt.* to distribute according to a plan

Reform Act of 1832 By 1830, Whigs and Tories were battling over a bill to reform Parliament. The Whig Party largely represented middle-class and business interests. The Tory Party spoke for nobles, land-owners, and others whose interests and income were rooted in agriculture. In the streets, supporters of reform chanted, "The Bill, the whole Bill, and nothing but the Bill!" Their shouts seemed to echo the cries of revolutionaries on the continent.

Parliament finally passed the Great Reform Act in 1832. It redistributed seats in the House of Commons, giving representation to large towns and cities and eliminating rotten boroughs. It also enlarged the **electorate,** the body of people allowed to vote, by granting suffrage to more men. The Act did, however, keep a property requirement for voting.

The Reform Act of 1832 did not bring full democracy, but it did give a greater political voice to middle-class men. Landowning nobles, however, remained a powerful force in the government and in the economy.

The Chartist Movement The reform bill did not help rural or urban workers. Some of them demanded more radical change. In the 1830s, protesters known as Chartists drew up the People's Charter. This petition demanded universal male suffrage, annual parliamentary elections, and salaries for members of Parliament. Another key demand was for a **secret ballot,** which would allow people to cast their votes without announcing them publicly.

Meeting of the Unions on Newhall Hill, Birmingham
The Birmingham Political Union's enormous rallies (above) and calls for reform are credited with the final passage of the Great Reform Bill of 1832. As one politician said of the BPU, "To this body, more than to any other, is confessedly due the triumph (such as it was) of the Reform Bill. Its well-ordered proceedings, extended organisation, and immense assemblages of people, at critical periods of its progress, rendered the measure irresistible."

Twice the Chartists presented petitions with over a million signatures to Parliament. Both petitions were ignored. In 1848, as revolutions swept Europe, the Chartists prepared a third petition and organized a march on Parliament. Fearing violence, the government moved to suppress the march. Soon after, the unsuccessful Chartist movement declined. In time, however, Parliament would pass most of the major reforms proposed by the Chartists.

✔ **Checkpoint** How was the British Parliament reformed during the early 1800s?

The Victorian Age

From 1837 to 1901, the great symbol in British life was **Queen Victoria.** Her reign was the longest in British history. Although she exercised little real political power, she set the tone for what is now called the Victorian age.

Symbol of a Nation's Values As queen, Victoria came to embody the values of her age. These Victorian ideals included duty, thrift, honesty, hard work, and above all respectability. Victoria herself embraced a strict code of morals and manners. As a young woman, she married a German prince, Albert, and they raised a large family.

A Confident Age Under Victoria, the British middle class—and growing numbers of the working class—felt great confidence in the future. That confidence grew as Britain expanded its already huge empire.

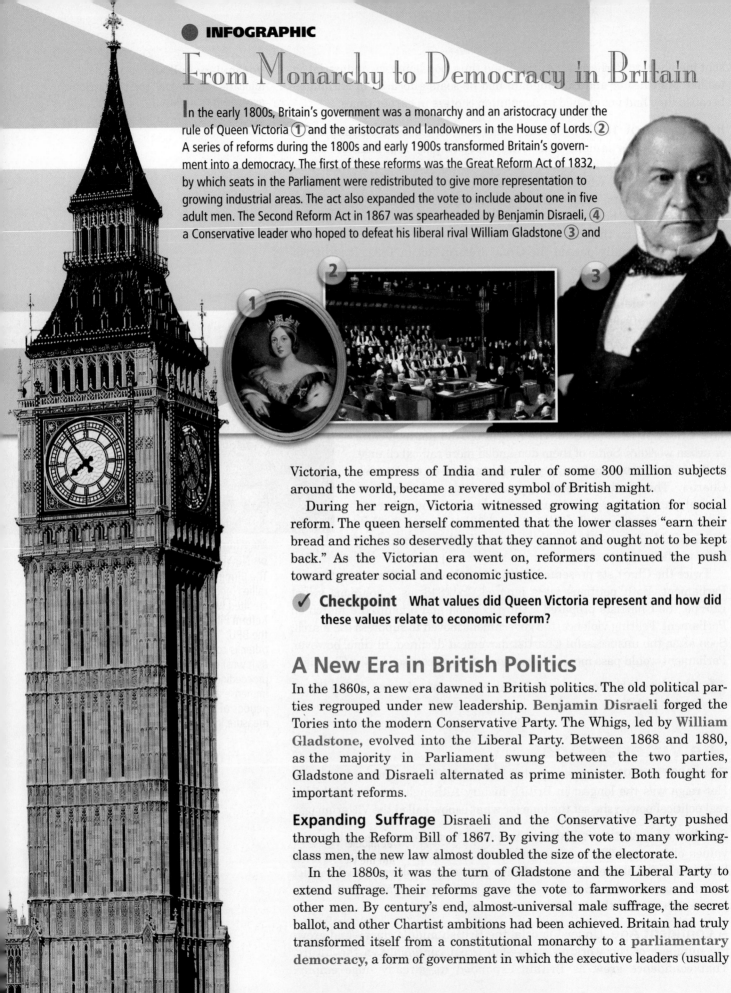

From Monarchy to Democracy in Britain

In the early 1800s, Britain's government was a monarchy and an aristocracy under the rule of Queen Victoria ① and the aristocrats and landowners in the House of Lords. ② A series of reforms during the 1800s and early 1900s transformed Britain's government into a democracy. The first of these reforms was the Great Reform Act of 1832, by which seats in the Parliament were redistributed to give more representation to growing industrial areas. The act also expanded the vote to include about one in five adult men. The Second Reform Act in 1867 was spearheaded by Benjamin Disraeli, ④ a Conservative leader who hoped to defeat his liberal rival William Gladstone ③ and

Victoria, the empress of India and ruler of some 300 million subjects around the world, became a revered symbol of British might.

During her reign, Victoria witnessed growing agitation for social reform. The queen herself commented that the lower classes "earn their bread and riches so deservedly that they cannot and ought not to be kept back." As the Victorian era went on, reformers continued the push toward greater social and economic justice.

✔ **Checkpoint** What values did Queen Victoria represent and how did these values relate to economic reform?

A New Era in British Politics

In the 1860s, a new era dawned in British politics. The old political parties regrouped under new leadership. **Benjamin Disraeli** forged the Tories into the modern Conservative Party. The Whigs, led by **William Gladstone,** evolved into the Liberal Party. Between 1868 and 1880, as the majority in Parliament swung between the two parties, Gladstone and Disraeli alternated as prime minister. Both fought for important reforms.

Expanding Suffrage Disraeli and the Conservative Party pushed through the Reform Bill of 1867. By giving the vote to many working-class men, the new law almost doubled the size of the electorate.

In the 1880s, it was the turn of Gladstone and the Liberal Party to extend suffrage. Their reforms gave the vote to farmworkers and most other men. By century's end, almost-universal male suffrage, the secret ballot, and other Chartist ambitions had been achieved. Britain had truly transformed itself from a constitutional monarchy to a **parliamentary democracy,** a form of government in which the executive leaders (usually

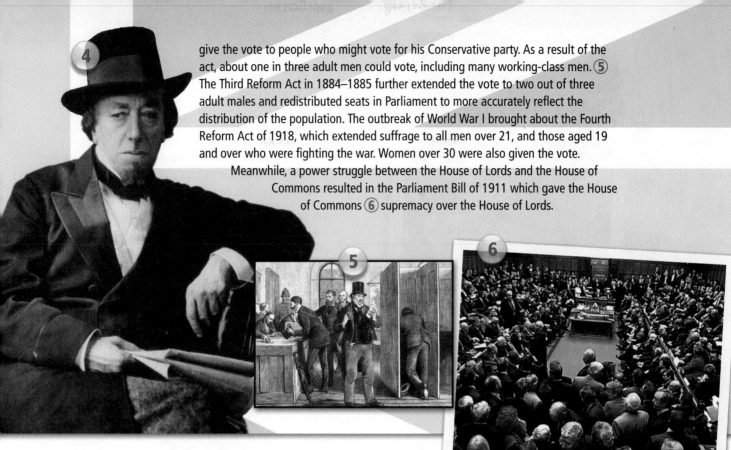

give the vote to people who might vote for his Conservative party. As a result of the act, about one in three adult men could vote, including many working-class men. ⑤ The Third Reform Act in 1884–1885 further extended the vote to two out of three adult males and redistributed seats in Parliament to more accurately reflect the distribution of the population. The outbreak of World War I brought about the Fourth Reform Act of 1918, which extended suffrage to all men over 21, and those aged 19 and over who were fighting the war. Women over 30 were also given the vote.

Meanwhile, a power struggle between the House of Lords and the House of Commons resulted in the Parliament Bill of 1911 which gave the House of Commons ⑥ supremacy over the House of Lords.

a prime minister and cabinet) are chosen by and responsible to the legislature (parliament), and are also members of it.

Limiting the Lords In the early 1900s, many bills passed by the House of Commons met defeat in the House of Lords. In 1911, a Liberal government passed measures to restrict the power of the Lords, including their power to veto tax bills. The Lords resisted. Finally, the government threatened to create enough new lords to approve the law, and the Lords backed down. People hailed the change as a victory for democracy. In time, the House of Lords would become a largely ceremonial body with little power. The elected House of Commons would reign supreme.

✓ **Checkpoint** How was Parliament reformed during the late 1800s and early 1900s?

Thinking Critically

1. **Recognize Ideologies** Which group in the early 1800s do you think most feared the "democratization" of Britain? Why?
2. **Identify Central Issues** How did the Parliament Bill in 1911 reflect the same trends occurring as a result of the reform acts?

Assessment

Progress Monitoring Online
For: Self-quiz with vocabulary practice
Web Code: naa-2312

Terms, People, and Places

1. What do each of the key terms listed at the beginning of the section have in common? Explain.

Note Taking

2. **Reading Skill: Identify Main Ideas** Use your completed outline to answer the Focus Question: How did political reform gradually expand suffrage and make the British Parliament more democratic during the 1800s?

Comprehension and Critical Thinking

3. **Summarize** How did the Reform Act of 1832 change Parliament?
4. **Categorize** What middle-class values are associated with the Victorian age?
5. **Identify Central Issues** What reforms did the Liberal and Conservative parties achieve?
6. **Draw Conclusions** Why do you think the Chartists demanded (a) a secret ballot, (b) salaries for members of Parliament?

● **Writing About History**

Quick Write: Gather Information If you were assigned to write a biographical essay on Queen Victoria, Benjamin Disraeli, or William Gladstone, what questions about these individuals would you want to answer in your essay? Choose one of these people and create a list of such questions about that person.

Forced feeding of English suffragist, 1912

WITNESS HISTORY ◀)) AUDIO

No Surrender

Lady Constance Lytton had been arrested for taking part in a women's suffrage protest. Once arrested, she refused to eat. Her hunger strike, she vowed, would go on until the British government granted the vote to women. Lytton later recalled:

❝ I was visited again by the Senior Medical Officer, who asked me how long I had been without food. I said I had eaten . . . on Friday at about midnight. He said, 'Oh, then, this is the fourth day; that is too long, I shall feed you, I must feed you at once.'❞
—Constance Lytton, *Prisons and Prisoners*

In the end, the doctor force-fed Lytton through a tube. Yet the painful ordeal failed to weaken her resolve. "No surrender," she whispered. "No surrender."

Focus Question What social and economic reforms were passed by the British Parliament during the 1800s and early 1900s?

Social and Economic Reform in Britain

Performance Standards

- **SSWH15a** Analyze movements for political reform and urbanization and its effect on women.

Terms, People, and Places

free trade	penal colony
repeal	absentee landlord
abolition movement	home rule
capital offense	

Note Taking

Reading Skill: Categorize Complete a chart like this one listing the reforms in Britain during the 1800s and early 1900s.

Lytton's 1910 hunger strike was part of the long struggle for women's suffrage in Britain. Suffragists were not the only people to fight for change. Between 1815 and 1914, Parliament responded to widespread discontent with a series of social and economic reforms. At the same time, the question of British control over Ireland was becoming a dominant and divisive political issue.

A Series of Reforms

During the early and mid-1800s, Parliament passed a wide variety of important new laws. One of the most controversial measures involved the issue of **free trade,** or trade between countries without quotas, tariffs, or other restrictions.

Free Trade and the Corn Laws In the early 1800s, Britain, like other European nations, taxed foreign imports in order to protect local economies. But supporters of free trade demanded an end to such protective tariffs. Free traders, usually middle-class business leaders, agreed with Adam Smith that a policy of laissez faire would increase prosperity for all. If tariffs were abolished, merchants everywhere would have larger markets in which to sell their goods, and consumers would benefit from open competition.

Some British tariffs were repealed in the 1820s. However, fierce debate erupted over the Corn Laws, which imposed high tariffs on imported grain. (In Britain, "corn" refers to all cereal grains, such as wheat, barley, and oats.) Farmers and wealthy landowners supported the Corn Laws because they kept the price of British grain high. Free traders, however, wanted Parliament to **repeal,** or cancel, the Corn Laws. They argued that repeal of these laws would lower the price of grain, make bread cheaper for workers, and open up trade in general.

Parliament finally repealed the Corn Laws in 1846, after widespread crop failures swept many parts of Europe. Liberals hailed the repeal as a victory for free trade and laissez-faire capitalism. However, in the late 1800s, economic hard times led Britain and other European countries to impose protective tariffs on many goods again.

Campaign Against Slavery During the 1700s, Enlightenment thinkers had turned the spotlight on the evils of the slave trade. At the time, British ships were carrying more Africans to the Americas than any other European country. Under pressure from middle-class reformers in Britain, France, and the United States, the **abolition movement,** or the campaign against slavery and the slave trade, slowly took off. In 1807, Britain became the first European power to abolish the slave trade.

Banning the slave trade did not end slavery. Although the Congress of Vienna had condemned slavery, it had taken no action. In Britain, liberals preached the immorality of slavery. Finally, in 1833, Parliament passed a law banning slavery in all British colonies.

Crime and Punishment Other reforms were aimed at the criminal justice system. In the early 1800s, more than 200 crimes were punishable by death. Such **capital offenses** included not only murder but also shoplifting, sheep stealing, and impersonating an army veteran. In practice, some juries refused to convict criminals, because the punishments were so harsh. Executions were public occasions, and the hanging of a well-known murderer might attract thousands of curious spectators. Afterward, instead of receiving a proper burial, the criminal's body might be given to a medical college for dissection.

Reformers began to reduce the number of capital offenses. By 1850, the death penalty was reserved for murder, piracy, treason, and arson. Many petty criminals were instead transported to **penal colonies,** or settlements for convicts, in the new British territory of Australia. In 1868, Parliament ended public hangings. Additional reforms improved prison conditions and outlawed imprisonment due to debt.

✔ **Checkpoint** How did abolition and criminal justice reform reflect Victorian values?

Victories for the Working Class

"Four [ghosts] haunt the Poor: Old Age, Accident, Sickness and Unemployment," declared Liberal politician David Lloyd George in 1905. "We are going to [expel] them." Parliament had begun passing laws aimed at improving social conditions as early as the 1840s. During the early 1900s, it passed a series of additional reforms designed to help the men, women, and children whose labor supported the new industrial society.

Improving Working Conditions As you have read, working conditions in the early industrial age were grim and often dangerous. Gradually, Parliament passed laws to regulate conditions in factories and mines. In 1842, for example, mineowners were forbidden to employ

Abolitionist Poster
Abolitionists hoped that ending the slave trade would also bring about the end of slavery. As this poster shows, even ending slavery did not end the economic mistreatment of people of African descent.

women or children under age 10. An 1847 law limited women and children to a 10-hour day. Later in the 1800s, the government regulated many safety conditions in factories and mines—and sent inspectors to see that the laws were enforced. Other laws set minimum wages and maximum hours of work.

The Growth of Labor Unions

Early in the Industrial Revolution, labor unions were outlawed. Under pressure, government and business leaders slowly accepted worker organizations. Trade unions were made legal in 1825 but it remained illegal to go on strike until later in the century.

Despite restrictions, unions spread, and gradually they won additional rights. Between 1890 and 1914, union membership soared. Besides winning higher wages and shorter hours for workers, unions pressed for other laws to improve the lives of the working class.

Later Reforms

During the late 1800s and early 1900s, both political parties enacted social reforms to benefit the working class. Disraeli sponsored laws to improve public health and housing for workers in cities. Under Gladstone, an education act called for free elementary education for all children. Gladstone also pushed to open up government jobs based on merit rather than on birth or wealth.

Another force for reform was the Fabian Society, a socialist organization founded in 1883. The Fabians promoted gradual change through legal means rather than by violence. Though small in number, the Fabians had a strong influence on British politics.

In 1900, socialists and union members backed the formation of a new political party, which became the Labour Party. ("Labour" is the British spelling of "labor.") The Labour Party would quickly grow in power and membership until, by the 1920s, it surpassed the Liberal Party and became one of Britain's two major parties.

▼ **Riots in Hyde Park, London**
An 1866 meeting of the Reform League in London dissolved into rioting. Riots such as these helped bring about the Second Reform Bill in 1867.

In the early 1900s, Britain began to pass social welfare laws to protect the well-being of the poor and disadvantaged. These laws were modeled on those Bismarck had introduced in Germany. They protected workers with accident, health, and unemployment insurance as well as old-age pensions. One result of such reforms was that Marxism gained only limited support among the British working class. The middle class hailed reforms as proof that democracy was working.

✔ **Checkpoint** Describe several social welfare reforms during the 1800s and early 1900s.

▲ A Liberal Party poster from 1911

The Struggle to Win Votes for Women

In Britain, as elsewhere, women struggled against strong opposition for the right to vote. Women themselves were divided on the issue. Some women opposed suffrage altogether. Queen Victoria, for example, called the suffrage struggle "mad, wicked folly." Even women in favor of suffrage disagreed about how best to achieve it.

Suffragists Revolt By the early 1900s, Emmeline Pankhurst, a leading suffragist, had become convinced that only aggressive tactics would bring victory. Pankhurst and other radical suffragists interrupted speakers in Parliament, shouting, "Votes for women!" until they were carried away. They collected petitions and organized huge public demonstrations. When mass meetings and other peaceful efforts brought no results, some women turned to more <u>drastic</u>, violent protest. They smashed windows or even burned buildings. Pankhurst justified such tactics as necessary to achieve victory. "There is something that governments care far more for than human life," she declared, "and that is the security of property, so it is through property that we shall strike the enemy." As you have read, some suffragists went on hunger strikes, risking their lives to achieve their goals.

Victory at Last Even middle-class women who disapproved of such radical and violent actions increasingly demanded votes for women. Still, Parliament refused to grant women's suffrage. Not until 1918 did Parliament finally grant suffrage to women over age 30. Younger women did not win the right to vote for another decade.

✔ **Checkpoint** Why do you think women disagreed about how best to gain suffrage?

Instability in Ireland

Throughout the 1800s, Britain faced the ever-present "Irish question." The English had begun conquering Ireland in the 1100s. In the 1600s, English and Scottish settlers colonized Ireland, taking possession of much of the best farmland.

The Irish never accepted English rule. They bitterly resented settlers, especially **absentee landlords** who owned large estates but did not live on them. Many Irish peasants lived in desperate poverty, while paying high rents to landlords living in England. In addition, the Irish, most of whom were Catholic, had to pay tithes to support the Church of England. Under these conditions, resistance and rebellion were common.

Vocabulary Builder

<u>drastic</u>—(DRAS tik) *adj.* severe, harsh, extreme

The Irish Potato Famine

Under British rule, three quarters of Irish farmland was used to grow crops that were exported. The potato was the main source of food for most of the Irish people. In 1845, disaster struck. A blight, or disease, destroyed the potato crop. Other crops, such as wheat and oats, were not affected. Yet British landowners continued to ship these crops outside Ireland, leaving little for the Irish except the blighted potatoes. The result was a terrible famine that the Irish called the "Great Hunger." In four years, about one million Irish men, women, and children died of starvation or disease. Many more emigrated to the United States and Canada. The Great Hunger left a legacy of Irish bitterness toward the English.

"Tumbled" Houses and Eviction ▶
Unable to grow potatoes to sell or eat, thousands of penniless tenants were evicted from their homes by landlords who needed the rent to pay their taxes. The roofs of the peasants' homes were "tumbled," or removed, to prevent the tenants from returning.

Number of Overseas Emigrants from Ireland, 1851–1921*	
1851–1860	1,216,219
1861–1870	818,582
1871–1880	542,703
1881–1890	734,475
1891–1900	461,282
1901–1910	485,461
1911–1921	355,295
Total 1851–1921	**4,614,017**

*Primarily to the United States, Canada, Australia, and New Zealand

SOURCE: Commission on Emigration and Other Population Problems, Dublin, 1954

Human Suffering ▼
One official told of entering what he thought was a deserted village. In one home, he saw "six famished and ghastly skeletons, to all appearances dead…" huddled in a corner on some filthy straw. "I approached with horror and found by a low moaning they were alive—they were in a fever, four children, a woman and what had once been a man…."

Limited Relief Measures ▲
Charles Trevelyan, the senior British official in charge of Irish relief efforts, held ruthless views of the Irish, insisting that they learn to "depend upon themselves…instead of…the assistance of the Government on every occasion."

Thinking Critically
1. **Graph Skills** Which decade saw the greatest number of emigrants from Ireland?
2. **Draw Conclusions** Do you think the Irish famine was more accurately described as a natural disaster or a human-made disaster? Why?

Irish Nationalism Like the national minorities in the Austrian empire, Irish nationalists campaigned vigorously for freedom and justice in the 1800s. Nationalist leader Daniel O'Connell, nicknamed "the Liberator," organized an Irish Catholic League and held mass meetings to demand repeal of unfair laws. "My first object," declared O'Connell, "is to get Ireland for the Irish."

Under pressure from O'Connell and other Irish nationalists, Britain slowly moved to improve conditions in Ireland. In 1829, Parliament passed the Catholic Emancipation Act, which allowed Irish Catholics to vote and hold political office. Yet many injustices remained. Absentee landlords could evict tenants almost at will. Other British laws forbade the teaching and speaking of the Irish language.

Struggle for Home Rule The famine in Ireland (see facing page) left the Irish with a legacy of bitterness and distrust toward Britain. In the 1850s, some Irish militants organized the Fenian Brotherhood. Its goal was to liberate Ireland from British rule by force. In the 1870s, moderate Irish nationalists found a rousing leader in Charles Stewart Parnell. He rallied Irish members of Parliament to press for **home rule,** or local self-government. The debate dragged on for decades.

The "Irish question" disrupted English politics. At times, political parties were so deeply split over the Irish question that they could not take care of other business. As prime minister, Gladstone pushed for reforms in Ireland. He ended the use of Irish tithe money to support the Anglican church and tried to ease the hardships of Irish tenant farmers. New laws prevented landlords from charging unfair rents and protected the rights of tenants to the land they worked.

Finally, in 1914, Parliament passed a home rule bill. But it delayed putting the new law into effect when World War I broke out that year. As you will read, the southern counties of Ireland finally became independent in 1921.

 Checkpoint How did English policies toward Ireland affect the cause of Irish Nationalism?

Progress Monitoring *Online*
For: Self-quiz with vocabulary practice
Web Code: naa-2323

Terms, People, and Places

1. Place each of the key terms at the beginning of the section into these two categories: economic or political. Write a sentence for each term explaining your choice.

Note Taking

2. **Reading Skill: Categorize** Use your chart to answer the Focus Question: What social and economic reforms were passed by the British Parliament during the 1800s and early 1900s?

Comprehension and Critical Thinking

3. **Summarize** Describe three reforms that helped the British working class.

4. **Compare Points of View** What actions did women suffragists take to achieve their goals? How did the views of women differ regarding tactics?

5. **Identify Central Issues** (a) Why did Irish nationalists oppose British rule? (b) Describe two reforms that improved conditions in Ireland.

● **Writing About History**

Quick Write: Write a Thesis Statement Write the thesis statement for an editorial written by an Irish nationalist of the late 1800s or early 1900s. First, decide whether your main goal is to win support for your cause from the Irish or to persuade members of the British Parliament.

MIGRATION

Under what circumstances do people migrate?

In This Chapter

 SSWH16a

In the 1800s, famine drove more than a million Irish to leave their homeland for distant shores (right). In later years, millions more Europeans would migrate to North and South America, mainly seeking economic opportunity. Like most emigrants, they left home for a future that was uncertain at best.

Throughout History

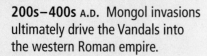

200s–400s A.D. Mongol invasions ultimately drive the Vandals into the western Roman empire.

900s Nomadic Magyars settle in what is now Hungary.

1500s–1800s In a forced migration, millions of enslaved Africans are transported to the Americas.

1930s Stalin forces millions of peasants and political opponents into labor camps in Siberia.

1947 Muslims flee to India and Hindus flee to Pakistan to escape religious persecution after the partition of India.

Continuing Today

While the circumstances surrounding migration change over time, the motives remain very constant. The migration to Europe of Muslims from the Middle East and North Africa began in the 1960s with Turkish guest workers. Many of these "guests" have become permanent residents.

21st Century Skills

? TRANSFER Activities

1. **Analyze** Throughout history, what has motivated people to move?

2. **Evaluate** How do the factors for voluntary migration differ from those for involuntary migration?

3. **Transfer** Complete a Web quest analyzing the paths and motives of migrants; record your thoughts in the Concept Connector Journal; and learn to make a video. Web Code nah-2308

Following Napoleon III's surrender (above), Georges Clemenceau (above right) rallied the people of Paris to defend their city.

WITNESS HISTORY 🔊 AUDIO

Vive la France!

The news sent shock waves through Paris. Napoleon III had surrendered to the Prussians and Prussian forces were now about to advance on Paris. Could the city survive? Georges Clemenceau (kleh mahn soh), a young French politician, rallied the people of Paris to defend their homeland:

66 Citizens, must France destroy herself and disappear, or shall she resume her old place in the vanguard of nations? . . . Each of us knows his duty. We are children of the Revolution. Let us seek inspiration in the example of our forefathers in 1792, and like them we shall conquer. *Vive la France!* (Long Live France!)99

Focus Question What democratic reforms were made in France during the Third Republic?

Division and Democracy in France

 Performance Standards

• **SSWH16a** Identify nationalism as a causes of WWI.

Terms, People, and Places

Napoleon III	coalition
Suez Canal	Dreyfus affair
provisional	libel
premier	Zionism

Note Taking

Reading Skill: Recognize Sequence Draw a timeline and label the main events described in this section.

For four months, Paris resisted the German onslaught. But finally, in January 1871, the French government at Versailles was forced to accept Prussian surrender terms.

The Franco-Prussian War ended a long period of French domination of Europe that had begun under Louis XIV. Yet a Third Republic rose from the ashes of the Second Empire of Napoleon III. Economic growth, democratic reforms, and the fierce nationalism expressed by Clemenceau all played a part in shaping modern France.

France Under Napoleon III

After the revolution of 1848, **Napoleon III,** nephew of Napoleon Bonaparte, rose to power and set up the Second Empire. His appeal cut across lines of class and ideology. The bourgeoisie saw him as a strong leader who would restore order. His promise to end poverty gave hope to the lower classes. People of all classes were attracted by his name, a reminder of the days when France had towered over Europe. Unlike his famous uncle, however, Napoleon III would bring France neither glory nor an empire.

Limits on Liberty On the surface, the Second Empire looked like a constitutional monarchy. In fact, Napoleon III ruled almost as a dictator, with the power to appoint his cabinet, the upper house of the legislature, and many officials. Although the assembly was elected by universal male suffrage, appointed officials "managed" elections so that supporters of the emperor would win. Debate was limited, and newspapers faced strict censorship.

In the 1860s, the emperor began to ease controls. He lifted some censorship and gave the legislature more power. On the eve of his disastrous war with Prussia, Napoleon III even issued a new constitution that extended democratic rights.

Promoting Economic Growth Like much of Europe, France prospered at mid-century. Napoleon III promoted investment in industry and large-scale ventures such as railroad building and the urban renewal of Paris. During this period, a French entrepreneur, Ferdinand de Lesseps (LAY seps), organized the building of the **Suez Canal** in Egypt to link the Mediterranean with the Red Sea and the Indian Ocean.

Workers enjoyed some benefits of economic growth. Napoleon legalized labor unions, extended public education to girls, and created a small public health program. Still, in France, as in other industrial nations, many people lived in great poverty.

Foreign Adventures Napoleon's worst failures were in foreign affairs. In the 1860s, he tried to place Maximilian, an Austrian Hapsburg prince, on the throne of Mexico. Through Maximilian, Napoleon hoped to turn Mexico into a French satellite. But after a large commitment of troops and money, the adventure failed. Mexican patriots resisted fiercely, and the United States protested. After four years, France withdrew its troops. Maximilian was overthrown and shot by Mexican patriots.

Napoleon's successes were almost as costly as his failures. He helped Italian nationalists defeat Austria, and in return, the regions of Nice (nees) and Savoy were ceded to France. But this victory soon backfired when a united Italy emerged as a rival on France's border. And, though

● **INFOGRAPHIC**

The Siege of Paris

For over four months beginning in September 1870, Prussian troops surrounded Paris. The city was almost completely cut off from the rest of the country except for messages that could be carried out on perilous balloon flights (far right top), by carrier pigeon, or by small capsules floated down the Seine River (far right bottom). Despite the large amounts of food that had been amassed prior to the siege, food was in short supply. Parisians searched for horses, rats (right), and even zoo and circus animals were consumed in the face of hunger. In the end, the French surrendered and agreed to disband their army and pay a war indemnity. Nearly 2,000 French troops were killed and thousands of Parisians died of diseases worsened by malnutrition and the cold weather.

Victorious Prussian troops pose in front of the ruins of the French Fort Issy near Paris.

France and Britain won the Crimean War, France had little to show for its terrible losses except a small foothold in the Middle East.

A Disastrous War With Prussia At this same time, France was growing increasingly concerned about the rise of a great rival, Prussia. The Prussian leader Otto von Bismarck shrewdly manipulated the French and lured Napoleon into war in 1870.

As you have read, the Franco-Prussian War was a disaster for France. Following the capture of Napoleon III, German forces advanced toward Paris and encircled the city. After four months of siege by Prussian troops, starving Parisians were reduced to catching rats and killing circus animals for food.

✓ **Checkpoint** What were some of the successes and failures of Napoleon III's Second Empire?

Challenges of the Third Republic

At the news of Napoleon's capture, republicans in Paris declared an end to the Second Empire. They set up a **provisional,** or temporary, government that shortly evolved into France's Third Republic. In 1871, the newly elected National Assembly accepted a harsh peace with Germany. France had to surrender the provinces of Alsace and Lorraine and pay a huge sum to Germany. The French were eager to avenge their loss.

The Paris Commune In 1871, an uprising broke out in Paris. Rebels set up the Paris Commune. Like the radical government during the French Revolution, its goal was to save the Republic from royalists. Communards,

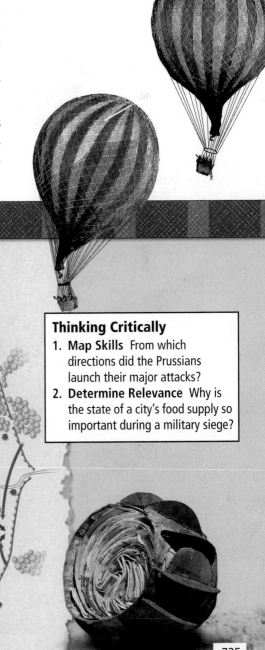

Paris Under Seige

- ⊢⊢ Prussian siege line
- ⫻ Prussian batteries
- → Prussian attacks
- ⊢╫⊣ French defensive line
- ⬠ French forts
- → French attacks
- ∿∿ City walls

Seine River

PARIS

VERSAILLES

Seine River

Marne River

Scale in Miles
0   1   2   3   4

Scale in Kilometers
0   1   2   3   4

Thinking Critically
1. **Map Skills** From which directions did the Prussians launch their major attacks?
2. **Determine Relevance** Why is the state of a city's food supply so important during a military siege?

as the rebels were called, included workers and socialists as well as bourgeois republicans. As patriots, they rejected the harsh peace that the National Assembly had signed with Germany. Radicals dreamed of creating a new socialist order.

The National Assembly ordered the Paris Commune to disband. When the Communards refused, the government sent troops to retake Paris. For weeks, civil war raged. As government troops advanced, the rebels set fire to several government buildings, toppled a monument commemorating Napoleon I, and slaughtered a number of hostages. Finally, government forces butchered some 20,000 Communards. The suppression of the Paris Commune left bitter memories that deepened social divisions within France.

The French Tricolor
The Third Republic eventually adopted the tricolor, a symbol of the French Revolution, as the official flag of France.

Government Structure Despite its shaky beginnings, the Third Republic remained in place for 70 years. The new republic had a two-house legislature. The powerful lower house, or Chamber of Deputies, was elected by universal male suffrage. Together with the Senate, it elected the president of the republic. However, he had little power and served mostly as a figurehead. Real power was in the hands of the **premier** (prih MIR), or prime minister.

Unlike Britain, with its two-party system, France had many parties, reflecting the wide splits within the country. Among them were royalists, constitutional monarchists, moderate republicans, and radicals. With so many parties, no single party could win a majority in the legislature. In order to govern, politicians had to form **coalitions,** or alliances of various parties. Once a coalition controlled enough votes, it could then name a premier and form a cabinet.

Multiparty systems and coalition governments are common in Europe. Such alliances allow citizens to vote for a party that most nearly matches their own beliefs. Coalition governments, however, are often unstable. If one party deserts a coalition, the government might lose its majority in the legislature. The government then falls, and new elections must be held. In the first 10 years of the Third Republic, 50 different coalition governments were formed and fell.

Political Scandals Despite frequent changes of governments, France made economic progress. It paid Germany the huge sum required by the peace treaty and expanded its overseas empire. But in the 1880s and 1890s, a series of political scandals shook public trust in the government.

One crisis erupted when a popular minister of war, General Georges Boulanger (boo lahn zhay), rallied royalists and ultranationalists eager for revenge on Germany. Accused of plotting to overthrow the republic, Boulanger fled to Belgium. In another scandal, a nephew of the president was caught selling nominations for the Legion of Honor, France's highest award. The president was forced to resign.

✓ **Checkpoint** What challenges did the Third Republic face during its 70 years in power?

Anti-Semitism and the Dreyfus Affair

The most serious and divisive scandal began in 1894. A high-ranking army officer, Alfred Dreyfus, was accused of spying for Germany. However, at his military trial, neither Dreyfus nor his lawyer was allowed to see the evidence against him. The injustice was rooted in anti-Semitism. The military elite detested Dreyfus, the first Jewish person to reach such a high position in the army. Although Dreyfus proclaimed his innocence, he was convicted and condemned to life imprisonment on Devil's Island, a desolate penal colony off the coast of South America. By 1896, new evidence pointed to another officer, Ferdinand Esterhazy, as the spy. Still, the army refused to grant Dreyfus a new trial.

Deep Divisions The **Dreyfus affair,** as it was called, scarred French politics and society for decades. Royalists, ultranationalists, and Church officials charged Dreyfus supporters, or "Dreyfusards," with undermining France. Paris echoed with cries of "Long live the army!" and "Death to traitors!" Dreyfusards, mostly liberals and republicans, upheld ideals of justice and equality in the face of massive public anger. In 1898, French novelist Émile Zola joined the battle. In an article headlined *J'Accuse!* (I Accuse!), he charged the army and government with suppressing the truth. As a result, Zola was convicted of **libel,** or the knowing publication of false and damaging statements. He fled into exile.

Slowly, though, the Dreyfusards made progress and eventually the evidence against Dreyfus was shown to be forged. In 1906, a French court finally cleared Dreyfus of all charges and restored his honors. That was a victory for justice, but the political scars of the Dreyfus affair took longer to heal.

Calls for a Jewish State The Dreyfus case reflected the rise of anti-Semitism in Europe. The Enlightenment and the French Revolution had spread ideas about religious toleration. In Western Europe, some Jews had gained jobs in government, universities, and other areas of life. Others had achieved success in banking and business, but most struggled to survive in the ghettos of Eastern Europe or the slums of Western Europe.

By the late 1800s, however, anti-Semitism was again on the rise. Anti-Semites were often members of the lower middle class who felt insecure in their social and economic position. Steeped in the new nationalist fervor, they adopted an aggressive intolerance for outsiders and a violent hatred of Jews.

The Dreyfus case and the pogroms in Russia stirred Theodor Herzl (HURT sul), a Hungarian Jewish journalist living in France. He called for Jews to form their own separate state, where they would have rights that were otherwise denied to them in European countries. Herzl helped launch **Zionism,** a movement devoted to rebuilding a Jewish state in the ancient homeland. Many Jews had kept this dream alive since the destruction of the temple in Jerusalem by the Romans. In 1897, Herzl organized the First Zionist Congress in Basel, Switzerland.

✔ **Checkpoint** In what ways was the Zionist movement a reaction to the Dreyfus case?

Reforms in France

Although shaken by the Dreyfus affair, France achieved serious reforms in the early 1900s. Like Britain, France passed laws regulating wages, hours, and safety conditions for workers. It set up a system of free public elementary schools. Creating public

Dreyfus Affair Caricature
This 1899 caricature, *The Traitor*, portrays Alfred Dreyfus as a lindworm, a mythical dragon with no wings in many German legends. In protest of Dreyfus's conviction, French novelist Émile Zola published a letter in 1898 in which he accused the army and government of suppressing the truth in the Dreyfus trial. "The truth is on the march, and nothing shall stop it," Zola wrote.

Penmanship Lesson
One of the many reforms of the early 1900s in France was the establishment of free public elementary schools.

Vocabulary Builder

repress—(ree PRES) *vt.* to put down, subdue

schools was also part of a campaign to reduce the power of the Roman Catholic Church, which controlled education.

Separating Church and State Like Germany, France tried to <u>repress</u> Church involvement in government. Republicans viewed the Church as a conservative force that opposed progressive policies. In the Dreyfus affair, it had backed the army and ultranationalists.

The government closed Church schools, along with many convents and monasteries. In 1905, it passed a law to separate church and state and stopped paying the salaries of the clergy. Catholics, Protestants, and Jews were all to enjoy freedom of worship, but none would have any special treatment from the government.

Women's Rights Under the Napoleonic Code, French women had few rights. By the 1890s, a growing women's rights movement sought legal reforms. It made some gains, such as an 1896 law giving married women the right to their own earnings. In 1909, Jeanne-Elizabeth Schmahl founded the French Union for Women's Suffrage. Rejecting the radical tactics used in Britain, Schmahl favored legal protests. Yet even liberal men were reluctant to grant women suffrage. They feared that women would vote for Church and conservative causes. In the end, French women did not win the vote until after World War II.

✔ **Checkpoint** Describe two social reforms during the late 1800s and early 1900s in France.

Looking Ahead

By 1914, France was the largest democratic country in Europe, with a constitution that protected basic rights. France's economy was generally prosperous, and its overseas empire was second only to that of Britain.

Yet the outlook was not all smooth. Coalition governments rose and fell at the slightest pressure. To the east loomed the industrial might of Germany. Many French citizens were itching for a chance to avenge the defeat in the Franco-Prussian War and liberate the "lost provinces" of Alsace and Lorraine. That chance came in 1914, when all of Europe exploded into World War I.

Progress Monitoring *Online*
For: Self quiz with vocabulary practice
Web Code: naa-2334

SECTION **3** Assessment

Terms, People, and Places

1. For each term, person, or place listed at the beginning of the section, write a sentence explaining its significance.

Note Taking

2. **Reading Skill: Recognize Sequence** Use your completed timeline to answer the Focus Question: What democratic reforms were made in France during the Third Republic?

Comprehension and Critical Thinking

3. **Summarize** Describe the government of France during the Second Empire.
4. **Draw Inferences** How did the Paris Commune and the Dreyfus affair heighten divisions in France?
5. **Summarize** Describe two reforms enacted in France in the early 1900s.
6. **Express Problems Clearly** (a) What solution did Zionists propose for the problem of widespread anti-Semitism? (b) Why do you think they felt it was the best solution?

● **Writing About History**

Quick Write: Write a Conclusion Do additional research to learn more about Ferdinand de Lesseps, the Frenchman who orchestrated the construction of the Suez Canal. Write a one-paragraph conclusion that could be used at the end of a biographical essay on de Lesseps.

The Statue of Liberty ▶

SECTION 4

WITNESS HISTORY 🔊 AUDIO

America!

For many Irish families fleeing hunger, Russian Jews escaping pogroms, or poor Italian farmers seeking economic opportunity, the answer was the same— America! A poem inscribed on the base of the Statue of Liberty expressed the welcome and promise of freedom that millions of immigrants dreamed of:

❝Give me your tired, your poor,
Your huddled masses yearning to breathe free,
The wretched refuse of your teeming shore.
Send these, the homeless, tempest-tossed to me.
I lift my lamp beside the golden door.❞
—Emma Lazarus, "The New Colossus"

Focus Question How did the United States develop during the 1800s?

Expansion of the United States

GA Performance Standards

- **SSWHRC1c** Explore understanding of new words in subject area texts.

Terms, People, and Places

expansionism
Louisiana Purchase
Manifest Destiny
secede
segregation

Note Taking

Reading Skill: Categorize Create a chart like the one below. As you read this section, list key events under the appropriate columns.

Civil War	
Before	**After**
• Western expansion	• Fifteenth Amendment
•	•
•	•

In the 1800s, the United States was a beacon of hope for many people. The American economy was growing rapidly, offering jobs to newcomers. The Constitution and Bill of Rights held out the hope of political and religious freedom. Not everyone shared in the prosperity or the ideals of democracy. Still, by the turn of the nineteenth century, important reforms were being made.

Territorial Expansion

From the earliest years of its history, the United States followed a policy of **expansionism,** or extending the nation's boundaries. At first, the United States stretched only from the Atlantic coast to the Mississippi River. In 1803, President Thomas Jefferson bought the Louisiana territory from France. In one stroke, the **Louisiana Purchase** virtually doubled the size of the nation.

By 1846, the United States had expanded to include Florida, Oregon, and the Republic of Texas. The Mexican War (1846–1848) added California and the Southwest. With growing pride and confidence, Americans claimed that their nation was destined to spread across the entire continent, from sea to sea. This idea became known as **Manifest Destiny.** Some expansionists even hoped to absorb Canada and Mexico. In fact, the United States did go far afield. In 1867, it bought Alaska from Russia and in 1898 annexed the Hawaiian Islands.

✓ **Checkpoint** Describe the United States' physical expansion during the 1800s.

Lewis and Clark Reach the Pacific Ocean

In 1803, Thomas Jefferson appointed Meriwether Lewis to lead an expedition from the Missouri River to the Pacific Ocean. Lewis invited William Clark to share the leadership. The expedition set out from St. Louis in May 1804 and returned in September 1806. Along the way, both Lewis and Clark kept extensive journals (background), which included detailed maps, drawings (below), and descriptions of the land, people, and animals they encountered. The entry here describes the events surrounding what he believed was the group's first view of the Pacific Ocean (above).

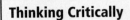

66 November 7th, 1805—A cloudy foggy morning some rain. …Two canoes of Indians met and returned with us to their village…. They gave us to eat some fish, and sold us, fish, wappato roots, three dogs, and 2 otter skins for which we gave fishhooks principally, of which they were very fond….

After delaying at this village one hour and a half we set out piloted by an Indian…. Rain continued moderately all day…our small canoe which got separated in the fog this morning joined us this evening….

Great joy in camp we are in view of the Ocean, …this great Pacific Ocean which we [have] been so long anxious to see. And the roaring or noise made by the waves breaking on the rocky shores (as I suppose) may be heard distinctly. 99

—*Captain William Clark,*
*from **The Journals of the Lewis and Clark Expedition***

Thinking Critically

1. **Summarize** According to Clark's entry, what was the land like in this area?
2. **Draw Conclusions** What conclusions can you draw about William Clark's character from this journal entry?

Expanding Democracy

In 1800, the United States had the most liberal suffrage in the world, but still only white men who owned property could vote. States slowly chipped away at requirements. By the 1830s, most white men had the right to vote. Democracy was still far from complete, however.

By mid-century, reformers were campaigning for many changes. Some demanded a ban on the sale of alcoholic beverages. Others called for better treatment of the mentally ill or pushed for free elementary schools. But two crusades stood out above all others because they highlighted the limits of American democracy—the abolition movement and the women's rights movement.

Calls for Abolition In the early 1800s, a few Americans began to call for an immediate and complete end to slavery. One of these abolitionists was William Lloyd Garrison, who pressed the antislavery cause through his newspaper, the *Liberator*. Another was Frederick Douglass. He had been born into slavery and escaped, and he spoke eloquently in the North about the evils of the system.

By the 1850s, the battle over slavery had intensified. As each new state entered the union, proslavery and antislavery forces met in violent confrontations to decide whether slavery would be legal in the new state. Harriet Beecher Stowe's novel *Uncle Tom's Cabin* helped convince many northerners that slavery was a great social evil.

Women's Rights Movement Women worked hard in the antislavery movement. Lucretia Mott and Elizabeth Cady Stanton traveled to London for the World Antislavery Convention—only to find they were forbidden to speak because they were women. Gradually, American women began to protest the laws and customs that limited their lives.

In 1848, in Seneca Falls, New York, Mott and Stanton organized the first women's rights convention. The convention passed a resolution, based on the Declaration of Independence. It began, "We hold these truths to be self evident: that all men and women are created equal." The women's rights movement set as its goal equality before the law, in the workplace, and in education. Some women also demanded the vote.

✔ **Checkpoint** How did the abolition movement and the women's rights movement highlight the limits of American democracy?

The Civil War and Its Aftermath

Economic differences, as well as the slavery issue, drove the Northern and Southern regions of the United States apart. The division reached a crisis in 1860 when Abraham Lincoln was elected president. Lincoln opposed extending slavery into new territories. Southerners feared that he would eventually abolish slavery altogether and that the federal government would infringe on their states' rights.

North Versus South Soon after Lincoln's election, most southern states **seceded,** or withdrew, from the Union and formed the Confederate States of America. This action sparked the Civil War, which lasted from 1861 to 1865.

The South had fewer resources, fewer people, and less industry than the North. Still, Southerners fought fiercely to defend their cause. The Confederacy finally surrendered in 1865. The struggle cost more than 600,000 lives—the largest casualty figures of any American war.

Challenges for African Americans During the war, Lincoln issued the Emancipation Proclamation, by which enslaved African Americans in the South were declared free. After the war, three amendments to the Constitution banned slavery throughout the country and granted political rights to African Americans. Under the Fifteenth Amendment, African American men won the right to vote.

Still, African Americans faced many restrictions. In the South, state laws imposed **segregation,** or legal separation of the races, in hospitals, schools, and other public places. Other state laws imposed conditions for voter eligibility that, despite the Fifteenth Amendment, prevented African Americans from voting.

✔ **Checkpoint** What changes did the Civil War bring about for African Americans?

The American Civil War, 1861–1865
During the American Civil War, Union forces from the North fought against the Confederate Army of the South. This scene shows the black 54th Massachusetts Regiment of the Union army attacking Fort Wagner in South Carolina.

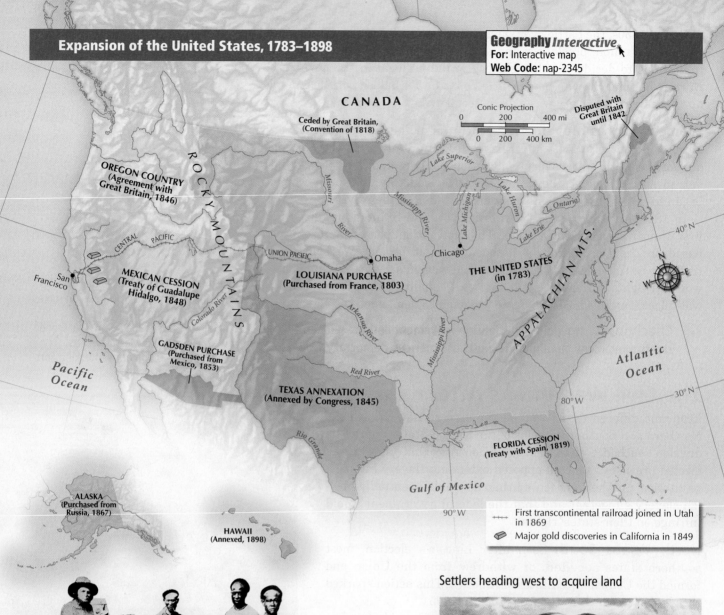

Expansion of the United States, 1783–1898

Geography *Interactive*
For: Interactive map
Web Code: nap-2345

CANADA

Conic Projection

Ceded by Great Britain, (Convention of 1818)

Disputed with Great Britain until 1842

OREGON COUNTRY (Agreement with Great Britain, 1846)

ROCKY MOUNTAINS

CENTRAL PACIFIC

UNION PACIFIC

Omaha

Chicago

Lake Superior

Lake Michigan

Lake Huron

L. Ontario

Lake Erie

San Francisco

MEXICAN CESSION (Treaty of Guadalupe Hidalgo, 1848)

Missouri River

LOUISIANA PURCHASE (Purchased from France, 1803)

THE UNITED STATES (in 1783)

Mississippi River

APPALACHIAN MTS.

40° N

Colorado River

Arkansas River

GADSDEN PURCHASE (Purchased from Mexico, 1853)

Pacific Ocean

Red River

Mississippi River

Atlantic Ocean

80° W

30° N

TEXAS ANNEXATION (Annexed by Congress, 1845)

Rio Grande

FLORIDA CESSION (Treaty with Spain, 1819)

ALASKA (Purchased from Russia, 1867)

90° W

Gulf of Mexico

HAWAII (Annexed, 1898)

First transcontinental railroad joined in Utah in 1869

Major gold discoveries in California in 1849

Settlers heading west to acquire land

Chinese laborers helped build the railroads.

Map Skills Through wars and treaties, the United States expanded its borders to its present size. During the 1800s, settlers flocked to newly acquired lands. The discovery of gold in California drew a flood of easterners. Other people, like the Mormons, sought a place to practice their religion freely. Still others headed west in the spirit of adventure. Some Native American nations resisted the invaders, but they were outgunned and outnumbered. By the 1890s, most surviving Native Americans had been driven onto reservations.

1. **Locate** (a) Louisiana Purchase (b) Florida (c) Texas (d) Alaska (e) Hawaii
2. **Place** Identify three countries that sold territories to the United States.
3. **Make Comparisons** Compare this map to a map of the present-day United States. How did the area where you live become part of the United States?

Economic Growth and Social Reform

After the Civil War, the United States grew to lead the world in industrial and agricultural production. A special combination of factors made this possible including political stability, private property rights, a free enterprise system, and an inexpensive supply of land and labor—supplied mostly by immigrants. Finally, a growing network of transportation and communications technologies aided businesses in transporting resources and finished products.

Business and Labor By 1900, giant monopolies controlled whole industries. Scottish-born Andrew Carnegie built the nation's largest steel company, while John D. Rockefeller's Standard Oil Company <u>dominated</u> the world's petroleum industry. Big business enjoyed tremendous profits.

But the growing prosperity was not shared by all. In factories, wages were low and conditions were often brutal. To defend their interests, American workers organized labor unions such as the American Federation of Labor. Unions sought better wages, hours, and working conditions. Struggles with management sometimes erupted into violent confrontations. Slowly, however, workers made gains.

Populists and Progressives In the economic hard times of the late 1800s, farmers also organized themselves to defend their interests. In the 1890s, they joined city workers to support the new Populist party. The Populists never became a major party, but their platform of reforms, such as an eight-hour workday, eventually became law.

By 1900, reformers known as Progressives also pressed for change. They sought laws to ban child labor, limit working hours, regulate monopolies, and give voters more power. Another major goal of the Progressives was obtaining voting rights for women. After a long struggle, American suffragists finally won the vote in 1920, when the Nineteenth Amendment went into effect.

✔ **Checkpoint** Describe the factors that helped the United States become an industrial and agricultural leader.

Vocabulary Builder

<u>dominate</u>—(DAHM un nayt) *vt.* to rule or control by superior power or influence

SECTION 4 Assessment

Progress Monitoring *Online*
For: Self-quiz with vocabulary practice
Web Code: naa-2346

Terms, People, and Places

1. Place each of the key terms at the beginning of the section into one of these two categories: geography or politics. Explain your choices.

Note Taking

2. **Reading Skill: Categorize** Use your completed chart to answer the Focus Question: How did the United States develop during the 1800s?

Comprehension and Critical Thinking

3. **Summarize** Describe how the United States grew in each of these areas in the 1800s: (a) territory, (b) population, (c) economy.
4. **Identify Central Issues** Describe two ways that democracy expanded.
5. **Draw Conclusions** (a) How did immigrants benefit from economic growth in the United States after the Civil War? (b) What problems did workers face?

● **Writing About History**

Quick Write: Write a Thesis Statement Conduct research to learn more about American entrepreneur, Andrew Carnegie. While some historians have portrayed Carnegie and others like him as philanthropists and captains of industry, others have portrayed him as a "robber baron." Write a thesis statement for a biographical essay on Carnegie in which you summarize your views of the man and his achievements.

CHAPTER 23

Quick Study Guide

 SSWH15a

Progress Monitoring *Online*
For: Self-test with vocabulary practice
Web Code: naa-2307

■ Democratic Reforms in Britain 1800s–Early 1900s

- Redistribution of seats in the House of Commons from rural towns to growing cities (1832)
- Expansion of suffrage for men with property (1832)
- Expansion of suffrage for many working-class men (1867)
- Expansion of suffrage to farm workers and most men
- Introduction of secret ballot
- Power of the House of Lords restricted (1911)

■ Social and Economic Reforms in Britain 1800s–Early 1900s

- Slave trade prohibited (1807)
- Slavery in all British colonies abolished (1833)
- Repeal of high tariffs on grains (1846)
- Women and children under ten forbidden to work in mines (1842)
- Women and children limited to 10-hour workday (1847)
- Improvements in public health and housing
- Free elementary education
- Accident, health, and unemployment insurance
- Old-age pensions
- Suffrage extended to women over 30 (1918)

■ Key Events in France, 1800s–Early 1900s

1852 Napoleon III sets up Second Empire.
1856 France and Britain defeat Russia in Crimean War.
1863 Napoleon III sends troops and Archduke Maximilian to Mexico.
1860 France gains Nice and Savoy by helping Italian nationalists defeat Austria.
1870 Napoleon III captured in Franco-Prussian war; Four-month siege of Paris by Prussians; France defeated and Alsace Lorraine ceded to Germany; Republicans in Paris establish the Third Republic.
1871 Paris Commune uprising
1894 Dreyfus affair
1905 Separation of church and state established by law.

■ Key Events in the United States 1800s–Early 1900s

1803	Louisiana Purchase
1846–1848	Mexican War
1849	California Gold Rush
1861–1865	Civil War
1867	Purchase of Alaska
1869	Completion of Transcontinental Railroad
1882	Formation of Standard Oil Trust
1898	Spanish-American War; Hawaiian islands annexed
1908	Development of Henry Ford's Model T

■ Key Events in the Growth of Western Democracies

Europe and North America World Events

1815	1835	1855

1832 Great Reform Act gives more British men suffrage and redistributes seats in House of Commons.

1845 Potato famine in Ireland begins.

1861–1865 American Civil War ends slavery in the United States.

1821 Mexico wins independence from Spain.

1858 Britain begins rule of India.

744

Concept Connector

Essential Question Review

To connect prior knowledge with what you have learned in this chapter, answer the questions below in your Concept Connector journal. Use the journal in the Reading and Note Taking Study Guide to record your answers (or go to www.phschool.com **Web Code: nad-2307**). In addition, record information about the following concept:

• **Migration:** Westward Movement in the United States

1. **Cooperation** During France's Third Republic, political parties had to form coalitions—alliances of various parties—in order to form a government. In other countries, different groups often formed coalitions or alliances to achieve common goals. Identify and explain the goals of alliances that were formed in
   • Britain in the 1830s
   • France during the Dreyfus affair
   • the United States in the 1860s and 1890s

2. **Migration** By the mid-1800s, the United States had expanded its borders through wars and treaties. Americans believed that their nation was destined to spread across the entire continent. How did American migration to the West in the late 1800s differ from Irish migration to the United States during the same period? How did migration to the West affect the Native American population?

3. **Democracy** Democratic reforms swept through Britain, France, and the United States during the 1800s. Identify specific reforms that each country achieved during this period. Focus on the following:
   • suffrage
   • natural rights
   • government
   • workers' rights

Connections to Today

1. **Trade: Free Trade and Tariffs** The British Corn laws imposed high, protective tariffs on imported grains and kept the price of British grown grain high. Do library research to learn more about a current protective tariff that is opposed by those who favor free trade. Which country has imposed this tariff on imports? What goods are affected? Which groups oppose the tariff and why?

2. **Conflict: Northern Ireland** The southern counties of Ireland gained independence from Britain in 1922, but Northern Ireland remained under British rule. Conflict ensued between minority Catholics in Northern Ireland, who demanded the reunification of Ireland, and majority Protestants, who favored a continued union with Britain. In 1998, the main political parties signed a peace accord that would eventually bring self-rule to Northern Ireland. Do research to learn more about the status of peace in Northern Ireland.

3. **Conflict: Native Americans** The expansion of the United States proved to be devastating for most Native American groups in North America. By the 1890s, most surviving Native Americans had been driven onto reservations. Conduct library research to learn more about the status of Native Americans living in the United States today. Write a paragraph summarizing the information you find.

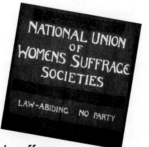

History Interactive
For: Interactive timeline
Web Code: nap-2308

1870	1897	1900s
France defeated in the Franco-Prussian War; Third Republic established.	Theodor Herzl organizes the First Zionist Congress for the purpose of founding a Jewish state.	The women's suffrage movement grows in Britain and the United States.

1875   1895   1915

1869	1889	1893	1910
The French-built Suez Canal opens in Egypt.	Brazil becomes a republic.	New Zealand is the first nation to give women the vote.	The Union of South Africa is formed.

Chapter Assessment

Terms, People, and Places

1. How did the Great Reform Act of 1832 correct the problem of **rotten boroughs?**
2. What group of people was added to the British **electorate** in 1918?
3. Why did members of the Chartist movement demand the use of **secret ballots?**
4. Why did the opponents of the Corn Laws in Britain favor **free trade?**
5. Why did French politicians need to form **coalitions?**
6. Where did Britain establish **penal colonies?**
7. What is **segregation?**
8. What is a **provisional** government?

Main Ideas

Section 1 (pp. 722–725)
9. What were the effects of the Great Reform Act of 1832?

Section 2 (pp. 726–732)
10. How did British policy toward slavery change in 1833?

Section 3 (pp. 733–738)
11. How did the party system in France's Third Republic differ from the British party system?
12. What was the main goal of the Zionist movement?

Section 4 (pp. 739–743)
13. List two goals of the Progressives in the United States in the early 1900s.

Chapter Focus Question

14. How did Britain, France, and the United States slowly extend democratic rights during the 1800s and early 1900s?

Critical Thinking

15. **Analyzing Cartoons** What views of suffrage does this cartoon reflect?

16. **Draw Conclusions** Britain and France faced many similar political and social problems in the 1800s. Why do you think Britain was able to avoid the upheavals that plagued France?

17. **Recognize Cause and Effect** (a) List two long-term causes and two immediate causes of the Great Hunger; (b) list two immediate effects. (c) Why do you think the famine sparked lasting feelings of bitterness against Britain?

18. **Synthesize Information** Describe how each of the following was related to nationalism: (a) the prestige of Queen Victoria, (b) the revolt of the Paris Commune, (c) the rise of Zionism.

19. **Geography and History** How did the geography of the United States encourage the American government to achieve its goal of Manifest Destiny?

● Writing About History

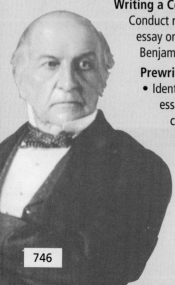

In this chapter's four Section Assessments, you developed skills for writing a compare and contrast essay.

Writing a Compare and Contrast Expository Essay
Conduct research and write a compare and contrast essay on the careers and accomplishments of Benjamin Disraeli and William Gladstone (left).

Prewriting
- Identify points of comparison and contrast for your essay. For example, you may want to compare and contrast the two men in terms of their background, political views, specific accomplishments, and impact on British politics. These categories will help you organize details in your essay.
- Create a Venn Diagram showing differences between the two men in the outside circles and similarities in the overlapping center.

- Collect the facts you need to write your essay.

Drafting
- Start with an engaging opening that defines the comparison/contrast and grabs readers' interest. This could be a quotation, surprising detail or statistic, or a question.
- Give details about each point of comparison to make it more accessible to readers. For example, you might give the years during which each man served as prime minister.
- Discuss the points about each man in the same order. You might even use similar sentence structure to emphasize this.

Revising
- Use the guidelines for revising your essay on page SH12 of the Writing Handbook.

Prepare for the GHSGT

The Dreyfus Affair

On December 22, 1894, a French military court convicted an innocent Jewish man, Captain Alfred Dreyfus, of selling state secrets to Germany. Dreyfus was imprisoned on Devil's Island off of South America and his conviction was reversed only after nearly twelve years. The Dreyfus affair caused a great division between conservatives, who still disliked the outcome of the French Revolution and held strong anti-Semitic beliefs, and liberals, who viewed the case as a gross abuse of individual rights.

Document A

". . . if my voice ceased to be heard, it would mean that it had been extinguished forever, for if I have survived, it has been in order to insist on my honor—my property and the patrimony of our children—and in order to do my duty, as I have done it everywhere and always, and as it must always be done, when right and justice are on one's side, without ever fearing anything or anyone."

—From a letter to his wife Lucie, by Alfred Dreyfus, September 1898, published in *Cinq Années*

Document B

"I accuse the offices of War of having conducted in the press, particularly in L'Eclair and in L'Echo de Paris, an abominable campaign designed to mislead public opinion and to conceal their wrongdoing."

"Finally, I accuse the first Court Martial of having violated the law in convicting a defendant on the basis of a document kept secret, and I accuse the second Court Martial of having covered up . . . [and] knowingly acquitting a guilty man."

—From **"J'Accuse"** a letter to the President of the Republic by Émile Zola

Document C

"Un Diner En Famille"
Translation: "It is agreed that there should be no talk of the affair! But they did talk about it . . ."

—From *Le Figaro* by Caran d'Ache, February, 1898

Analyzing Documents

Use your knowledge of the Dreyfus affair and Documents A, B, and C to answer questions 1–4.

1. In Document A, Dreyfus suggests that his wish to prove his innocence helped to
   A keep him close to his family.
   B keep him alive.
   C make the Army take illegal actions.
   D make anti-Semitic groups angry.

2. Which statement best summarizes Zola's letter in Document B?
   A Although the French military convicted the wrong man, they attempted to carry out a fair trial.
   B The French military was fooled by handwriting experts, who tried to convict the wrong man.
   C The French military knowingly and illegally convicted an innocent man.
   D The French military showed that the army was anti-Semitic at the highest levels.

3. Document C illustrates—
   A why many French families believed Dreyfus was guilty.
   B why Dreyfus was convicted unfairly of treason.
   C how the Dreyfus case divided France.
   D how anti-Semitism was a factor in the Dreyfus case.

4. **Writing Task** On July 21, 1906, a French general knighted Alfred Dreyfus a member of the Legion of Honor. Well wishers attended the ceremony in the courtyard of the École Militaire. Some shouted "Long live Dreyfus." Suppose you were reporting on the event for an American newspaper. Write a news story, using the documents on this page along with information from the chapter.

24 The New Imperialism
1800–1914

WITNESS HISTORY ◀)) AUDIO

Empire Builders

Lord Frederick Lugard, a British empire builder, tried to justify imperialism in Africa with these words:

66There are some who say we have no *right* to Africa at all, that 'it belongs to the natives.' I hold that our right is the necessity that is upon us to provide for our ever-growing population—either by opening new fields for emigration, or by providing work and employment . . . and to stimulate trade by finding new markets.99

Listen to the Witness History audio to learn more about imperialism.

◀ One of several journalists in South Africa, British writer Rudyard Kipling (bottom right) considered imperialism to be beneficial to Africans.

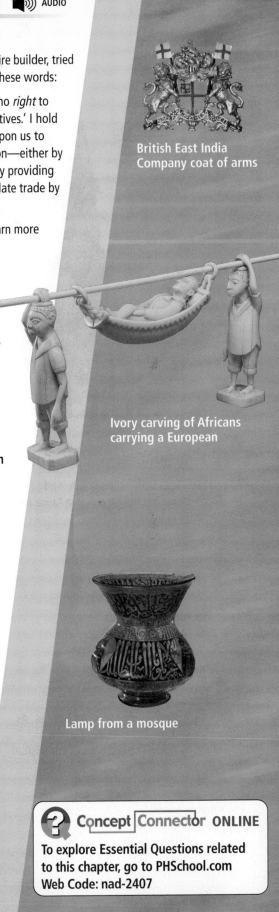

British East India Company coat of arms

Ivory carving of Africans carrying a European

Lamp from a mosque

GA Performance Standards

Chapter Focus Question How did Western industrial powers gain global empires?

Section 1
Building Overseas Empires
SSWH15d

Section 2
The Partition of Africa
SSWH15c, SSWH15d

Section 3
European Claims in Muslim Regions
SSWH15c

Section 4
The British Take Over India
SSWH15c

Section 5
China and the New Imperialism
SSWH14d

Use the ☑ **Quick Study Timeline** at the end of this chapter to preview chapter events.

② Concept Connector ONLINE

To explore Essential Questions related to this chapter, go to PHSchool.com
Web Code: nad-2407

English writer
Rudyard Kipling

Missionary prayer
book in Korean

The White Man's Burden

Born in India, English writer Rudyard Kipling witnessed British imperialism firsthand. His 1899 poem "The White Man's Burden" summarizes his view of the duties of imperial nations:

> 66 Take up the White Man's burden—
>   In patience to abide,
> To veil the threat of terror
>   And check the show of pride;
> By open speech and simple,
>   An hundred times made plain,
> To seek another's profit,
>   And work another's gain. 99

Focus Question How did Western nations come to dominate much of the world in the late 1800s?

Building Overseas Empires

 Performance Standards

- **SSWH15d** Describe how geography and resources influenced British policy in Africa and French policy in Indochina.

Terms, People, and Places

imperialism
protectorate
sphere of influence

Note Taking

Reading Skill: Recognize Multiple Causes As you read the section, make a chart like the one below showing the multiple causes of imperialism in the 1800s.

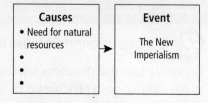

Causes	Event
• Need for natural resources • • •	The New Imperialism

Like Great Britain, other Western countries built overseas empires in the late 1800s. The Industrial Revolution had transformed the West. Advances in science and technology, industry, transportation, and communication provided Western nations with many advantages. Armed with new economic and political power, Western nations set out to dominate the world.

Motives Driving the New Imperialism

European imperialism did not begin in the 1800s. **Imperialism** is the domination by one country of the political, economic, or cultural life of another country or region. As you have learned, European states won empires in the Americas after 1492, established colonies in South Asia, and gained toeholds on the coasts of Africa and China. Despite these gains, between 1500 and 1800, Europe had little influence on the lives of the peoples of China, India, or Africa.

By the 1800s, however, Europe had gained considerable power. Strong, centrally governed nation-states had emerged, and the Industrial Revolution had greatly enriched European economies. Encouraged by their new economic and military strength, Europeans embarked on a path of aggressive expansion that today's historians call the "new imperialism." In just a few decades, beginning in the 1870s, Europeans brought much of the world under their influence and control. Like other key developments in world history, the new imperialism exploded out of a combination of causes.

Economic Interests Spur Expansion The Industrial Revolution created needs and desires that spurred overseas expansion. Manufacturers wanted access to natural resources such as rubber, petroleum, manganese for steel, and palm oil for machinery. They also hoped for new markets of consumers to whom they could sell their factory goods. Bankers sought ventures to invest their profits. In addition, colonies offered a valuable outlet for Europe's growing population.

Political and Military Motives Political and military issues were closely linked to economic motives. Steam-powered merchant ships and naval vessels needed bases around the world to take on coal and supplies. Industrial powers seized islands or harbors to satisfy these needs.

Nationalism played an important role, too. When France, for example, moved into West Africa, rival nations like Britain and Germany seized lands nearby to halt further French expansion. Western leaders claimed that colonies were needed for national security. They also felt that ruling a global empire increased a nation's <u>prestige</u> around the world.

Vocabulary Builder

<u>prestige</u>—(pres TEEZH) *n.* the power to impress or influence because of success or wealth

Humanitarian and Religious Goals Many Westerners felt a genuine concern for their "little brothers" beyond the seas. Missionaries, doctors, and colonial officials believed they had a duty to spread what they saw as the blessings of Western civilization, including its medicine, law, and Christian religion.

Applying Social Darwinism Behind the idea of the West's civilizing mission was a growing sense of racial superiority. Many Westerners had embraced the ideas of Social Darwinism. They applied Darwin's ideas about natural selection and survival of the fittest to human societies. European races, they argued, were superior to all others, and imperial domination of weaker races was simply nature's way of improving the human species. As a result, millions of non-Westerners were robbed of their cultural heritage.

✔ **Checkpoint** What factors contributed to European imperialism in the 1800s?

A Market for Goods
A driving force behind imperialism was the desire for access to new markets in which to sell goods. This British propaganda poster boasts that Africa would become a gold mine for British-made products. Britain's sense of national pride and aggressive foreign policy during this period came to be known as jingoism. *What does this poster show about the British attitude toward Africa?*

European Conquest of Africa

The excerpts below present two different views on the partition of Africa by European nations in the 1800s. **Critical Thinking** *What is Cecil Rhodes's argument for imperialism? What is Chief Kabongo's argument against it?*

Favoring Imperialism

"I contend that we are the first race in the world and that the more of the world we inhabit the better it is for the human race. I contend that every acre added to our territory provides for the birth of more of the English race, who otherwise would not be brought into existence . . . . I believe it to be my duty to God, my Queen and my country to paint the whole map of Africa red, red from the Cape to Cairo. That is my creed, my dream and my mission."

—*Cecil Rhodes*

Opposing Imperialism

"A Pink Cheek man came one day to our Council . . . and he told us of the King of the Pink Cheek who . . . lived in a land over the seas. 'This great king is now your king,' he said. This was strange news. For this land was ours. . . . We had no king, we elected our Councils and they made our laws. With patience, our leading Elders tried to tell this to the Pink Cheek. . . . But at the end he said, 'This we know, but in spite of this what I have told you is a fact. You have now a king . . . and his laws are your laws.'"

—*Chief Kabongo of the Kikuyu in Kenya*

The Rapid Spread of Western Imperialism

From about 1870 to 1914, imperialist nations gained control over much of the world. Leading the way were soldiers, merchants, settlers, missionaries, and explorers. In Europe, imperial expansion found favor with all classes, from bankers and manufacturers to workers. Western imperialism expanded rapidly for a number of reasons.

Weakness of Non-Western States While European nations had grown stronger in the 1800s, several older civilizations were in decline, especially the Ottoman Middle East, Mughal (MOO gul) India, and Qing (ching) China. In West Africa, wars among African peoples and the damaging effect of the slave trade had undermined established empires, kingdoms, and city-states. Newer African states were not strong enough to resist the Western onslaught.

Western Advantages European powers had the advantages of strong economies, well-organized governments, and powerful armies and navies. Superior technology, including riverboats and the telegraph, as well as improved medical knowledge also played a role. Quinine and other new medicines helped Europeans survive deadly tropical diseases. And, of course, advances such as Maxim machine guns, repeating rifles, and steam-driven warships were very strong arguments in persuading Africans and Asians to accept Western control.

Resisting Imperialism Africans and Asians strongly resisted Western expansion into their lands. Some people fought the invaders, even though they had no weapons to equal the Maxim gun. Ruling groups in certain areas tried to strengthen their societies against outsiders by reforming their own Muslim, Hindu, or Confucian traditions. Finally, many

The Maxim Gun
Sir Hiram Maxim with his invention, the Maxim machine gun. *Why were European armies often able to defeat African or Asian forces?*

Western-educated Africans and Asians organized nationalist movements to expel the imperialists from their lands.

Facing Criticism at Home In the West itself, a small group of anti-imperialists emerged. Some argued that colonialism was a tool of the rich. Others said it was immoral. Westerners, they pointed out, were moving toward greater democracy at home but were imposing undemocratic rule on other peoples.

✓ **Checkpoint** How did Western imperialism spread through Africa and Asia so quickly?

Forms of Imperial Rule

The leading imperial powers developed several kinds of colonial rule. The French practiced direct rule, sending officials and soldiers from France to administer their colonies. Their goal was to impose French culture on their colonies and turn them into French provinces.

The British, by contrast, often used a system of indirect rule. To govern their colonies, they used sultans, chiefs, or other local rulers. They then encouraged the children of the local ruling class to get an education in Britain. In that way, they groomed a new "Westernized" generation of leaders to continue indirect imperial rule and to spread British civilization. Like France and other imperialist nations, however, Britain could still resort to military force if its control over a colony was threatened.

In a **protectorate,** local rulers were left in place but were expected to follow the advice of European advisors on issues such as trade or missionary activity. A protectorate cost less to run than a colony did, and usually did not require a large commitment of military forces.

A third form of Western control was the **sphere of influence,** an area in which an outside power claimed exclusive investment or trading privileges. Europeans carved out these spheres in China and elsewhere to prevent conflicts among themselves.

Indian princes and British army officers play polo in 1880.

✓ **Checkpoint** Compare and contrast how Britain and France ruled their colonies.

SECTION 1 **Assessment**

Terms, People, and Places
1. What do each of the key terms listed at the beginning of the section have in common? Explain.

Note Taking
2. **Reading Skill: Recognize Multiple Causes** Use your completed chart to answer the Focus Question: How did Western nations come to dominate much of the world in the late 1800s?

Comprehension and Critical Thinking
3. **Explain** (a) What were three reasons for the rapid spread of Western imperialism? (b) How did people oppose it?
4. **Recognize Bias** Western colonial officials and missionaries thought that they had a duty to spread the "blessings of Western civilization" to their African and Asian "little brothers." How was this a biased viewpoint?

● **Writing About History**

Quick Write: Write a Thesis Statement
Suppose that you are writing a persuasive essay using the point of view of an anti-imperialist from a Western nation trying to persuade the public that imperialism is wrong. Based on what you have read in this section, write a thesis statement for your essay.

African soldiers in German uniforms

WITNESS HISTORY ◄)) AUDIO

Resisting Imperialism

In 1890, Chief Machemba (mah CHEM bah) of the Yao (YAH oh) people in East Africa wrote in Swahili to a German officer:

❝ If it be friendship that you desire, then I am ready for it . . . but to be your subject, that I cannot be. . . . I do not fall at your feet, for you are God's creature just as I am.❞
—Chief Machemba, Letter to Herman von Wissman

Focus Question How did imperialist European powers claim control over most of Africa by the end of the 1800s?

The Partition of Africa

 Performance Standards

- **SSWH15c** Describe reactions to foreign domination.
- **SSWH15d** Compare British, French and Japanese imperialism in Africa and Asia.

Terms, People, and Places

Usman dan Fodio	Boer War
Shaka	Samori Touré
paternalistic	Yaa Asantewaa
David Livingstone	Nehanda
Henry Stanley	Menelik II
King Leopold II	elite

Note Taking

Reading Skill: Identify Causes and Effects As you read the section, fill in the chart with information about the causes and effects of the partition of Africa by European nations.

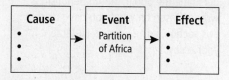

In the late 1800s, Britain, France, Germany, and other European powers began a scramble for African territories. Within about 20 years, the Europeans had carved up the continent and dominated millions of Africans. Although the Yao and others resisted, they could not prevent European conquest.

Africa in the Early 1800s

To understand the impact of European domination, we must look at Africa in the early 1800s, before the scramble for colonies began. Africa is a huge continent, nearly three times the size of Europe. Across its many regions, people spoke hundreds of languages and had developed varied governments. Some people lived in large centralized states, while others lived in village communities.

North Africa North Africa includes the enormous Sahara and the fertile land along the Mediterranean. Since long before 1800, the region was a part of the Muslim world. In the early 1800s, much of North Africa remained under the rule of the declining Ottoman empire.

Islamic Crusades in West Africa By the early 1800s, an Islamic revival spread across West Africa. It began among the Fulani people in northern Nigeria. The scholar and preacher **Usman dan Fodio** (oo SMAHN dahn foh DEE oh) denounced the corruption of the local Hausa rulers. He called for social and religious reforms based on the sharia, or Islamic law. Usman inspired Fulani herders and Hausa townspeople to rise up against their European rulers.

Usman and his successors set up a powerful Islamic state in northern Nigeria. Under their rule, literacy increased, local wars quieted, and trade improved. Their success inspired other Muslim reform movements in West Africa. Between about 1780 and 1880, more than a dozen Islamic leaders rose to power, replacing old rulers or founding new states in the western Sudan.

In the forest regions, strong states like the Asante (uh SAHN teh) kingdom had arisen. The Asante traded with Europeans and Muslims and controlled several smaller states. However, these tributary states were ready to turn to Europeans or others who might help them defeat their Asante rulers.

East Africa Islam had long influenced the east coast of Africa, where port cities like Mombasa (mahm BAH suh) and Kilwa (KEEL wah) carried on profitable trade. The cargoes were often slaves. Captives were marched from the interior to the coast to be shipped as slaves to the Middle East. Ivory and copper from Central Africa were also exchanged for goods such as cloth and firearms from India.

Southern Africa In the early 1800s, the Zulus emerged as a major force in southern Africa under a ruthless and brilliant leader, **Shaka.** Between 1818 and 1828, Shaka waged relentless war and conquered many nearby peoples. He absorbed their young men and women into Zulu regiments. By encouraging rival groups to forget their differences, he cemented a growing pride in the Zulu kingdom.

His conquests, however, set off mass migrations and wars, creating chaos across much of the region. Groups driven from their homelands by the Zulus then migrated north, conquering still other peoples and creating their own powerful states. By the 1830s, the Zulus faced a new threat, the arrival of well-armed, mounted Boers, descendants of Dutch farmers who were migrating north from the Cape Colony. In 1814, the Cape Colony had passed from the Dutch to the British. Many Boers resented British laws that abolished slavery and otherwise interfered with their way of life. To escape British rule, they loaded their goods into covered wagons and started north. Several thousand Boer families joined this "Great Trek."

As the migrating Boers came into contact with Zulus, fighting quickly broke out. At first, Zulu regiments held their own. But in the end, Zulu spears could not defeat Boer guns. The struggle for control of the land would rage until the end of the century.

Impact of the Slave Trade In the early 1800s, European nations began to outlaw the transatlantic slave trade, though it took years to end. Meanwhile, the East African slave trade continued to Asia.

Some people helped freed slaves resettle in Africa. In 1787, the British organized Sierra Leone in West Africa as a colony for former slaves. Later, some free blacks from the United States settled in nearby Liberia. By 1847, Liberia had become an independent republic.

✓ **Checkpoint** What factors shaped each of the main regions of Africa during the early 1800s?

Zulu King Cetshwayo
A nephew of Shaka, Cetshwayo (kech WY oh) was the last of the great Zulu kings. He ruled a disciplined army of about 40,000 men until the British defeated him in 1879. *Why was Cetshwayo considered a threat to British colonial interests?*

European Contact Increases

From the 1500s through the 1700s, Europeans traded along the African coast. Africans wanted trade with Europeans but did not want to "house them." Resistance by Africans, difficult geography, and diseases all kept Europeans from moving into the interior regions of the continent. Medical advances and river steamships changed all that in the 1800s.

Explorers Advance Into Africa's Interior In the early 1800s, European explorers began pushing into the interior of Africa. Explorers like Mungo Park and Richard Burton set out to map the course and sources of the great African rivers such as the Niger, the Nile, and the Congo. They were fascinated by African geography, but they had little understanding of the peoples they met. All, however, endured great hardships while exploring Africa.

Missionaries Follow Explorers Catholic and Protestant missionaries followed the explorers. All across Africa, they sought to win people to Christianity. The missionaries were sincere in their desire to help Africans. They built schools and medical clinics alongside churches. They also focused attention on the evils of the slave trade. Still, missionaries, like most Westerners, took a **paternalistic** view of Africans, meaning they saw them as children in need of guidance. To them, African cultures and religions were "degraded." They urged Africans to reject their own traditions in favor of Western civilization.

Missionaries at Work
Missionaries conduct a baptism ceremony in the Lower Congo in 1907. Others performed communion with chalices and patens, or ceremonial plates, like those above. *Why did missionaries seek to convert people to Christianity?*

Livingstone Blazes a Trail The best-known explorer and missionary was **Dr. David Livingstone.** For 30 years, he crisscrossed Africa. He wrote about the many peoples he met with more sympathy and less bias than did most Europeans. He relentlessly opposed the slave trade, which remained a profitable business for some African rulers and foreign traders. The only way to end this cruel traffic, he believed, was to open up the interior of Africa to Christianity and trade.

Livingstone blazed a trail that others soon followed. In 1869, the journalist **Henry Stanley** trekked into Central Africa to find Livingstone, who had not been heard from for years. He finally tracked him down in 1871 in what is today Tanzania, greeting him with the now-legendary phrase "Dr. Livingstone, I presume?"

 Checkpoint How did European contact with Africa increase in the late 1800s?

A Scramble for Colonies

Shortly afterward, **King Leopold II** of Belgium hired Stanley to explore the Congo River basin and arrange trade treaties with African leaders. Publicly, Leopold spoke of a civilizing mission to carry the light "that for millions of men still plunged in barbarism will be the dawn of a better era." Privately, he dreamed of conquest and profit. Leopold's activities in the Congo set off a scramble by other nations. Before long, Britain, France, and Germany were pressing rival claims to the region.

Berlin Conference To avoid bloodshed, European powers met at an international conference in 1884. It took place not in Africa but in Berlin, Germany. No Africans were invited to the conference.

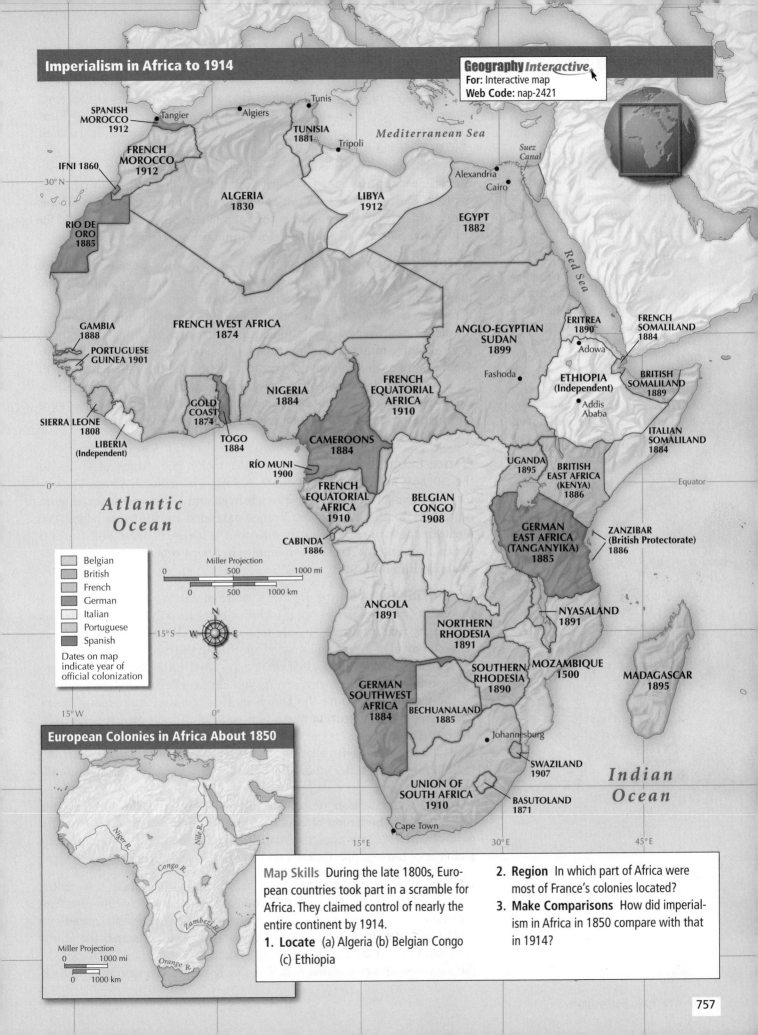

Imperialism in Africa to 1914

Geography *Interactive*
For: Interactive map
Web Code: nap-2421

SPANISH MOROCCO 1912
• Tangier

• Algiers

• Tunis
TUNISIA 1881

Mediterranean Sea

• Tripoli

Suez Canal

FRENCH MOROCCO 1912

IFNI 1860

30° N

ALGERIA 1830

LIBYA 1912

• Alexandria
• Cairo

Red Sea

EGYPT 1882

RIO DE ORO 1885

GAMBIA 1888

FRENCH WEST AFRICA 1874

ANGLO-EGYPTIAN SUDAN 1899

ERITREA 1890

FRENCH SOMALILAND 1884

PORTUGUESE GUINEA 1901

• Adowa

• Fashoda

SIERRA LEONE 1808

GOLD COAST 1874

NIGERIA 1884

FRENCH EQUATORIAL AFRICA 1910

ETHIOPIA (Independent)

BRITISH SOMALILAND 1889

LIBERIA (Independent)

TOGO 1884

CAMEROONS 1884

• Addis Ababa

RÍO MUNI 1900

FRENCH EQUATORIAL AFRICA 1910

UGANDA 1895

BRITISH EAST AFRICA (KENYA) 1886

ITALIAN SOMALILAND 1884

0°

BELGIAN CONGO 1908

Equator

Atlantic Ocean

CABINDA 1886

GERMAN EAST AFRICA (TANGANYIKA) 1885

ZANZIBAR (British Protectorate) 1886

Belgian
British
French
German
Italian
Portuguese
Spanish

Dates on map indicate year of official colonization

Miller Projection
0   500   1000 mi
0   500   1000 km

ANGOLA 1891

NYASALAND 1891

15° S

NORTHERN RHODESIA 1891

N
W   E
S

MOZAMBIQUE 1500

MADAGASCAR 1895

GERMAN SOUTHWEST AFRICA 1884

SOUTHERN RHODESIA 1890

15° W

0°

BECHUANALAND 1885

• Johannesburg

European Colonies in Africa About 1850

SWAZILAND 1907

Indian Ocean

UNION OF SOUTH AFRICA 1910

BASUTOLAND 1871

• Cape Town

Niger R.

Nile R.

Congo R.

15° E

30° E

45° E

Zambezi R.

Miller Projection
0   1000 mi
0   1000 km

Orange R.

Map Skills During the late 1800s, European countries took part in a scramble for Africa. They claimed control of nearly the entire continent by 1914.

1. **Locate** (a) Algeria (b) Belgian Congo (c) Ethiopia

2. **Region** In which part of Africa were most of France's colonies located?

3. **Make Comparisons** How did imperialism in Africa in 1850 compare with that in 1914?

757

Cecil Rhodes

Cecil Rhodes (1853–1902) arrived in South Africa at age 17, determined to make his fortune. He got off to a slow start. His first venture, a cotton-farming project, failed. Then, Rhodes turned to diamond and gold mining. By the age of 40, he had become one of the richest men in the world.

However, money was not his real interest. "For its own sake I do not care for money," he once wrote. "I want the power." Rhodes strongly supported British imperialism in Africa. He helped Britain extend its African empire by 1,000,000 square miles and had an entire British colony named after himself—Rhodesia (now Zimbabwe). Rhodes also helped promote the policy of the separation of races in southern Africa. **How was Cecil Rhodes' desire for power illustrated by his actions?**

At the Berlin Conference, European powers recognized Leopold's private claims to the Congo Free State but called for free trade on the Congo and Niger rivers. They further agreed that a European power could not claim any part of Africa unless it had set up a government office there. This principle led Europeans to send officials who would exert their power over local rulers and peoples.

The rush to colonize Africa was on. In the 20 years after the Berlin Conference, the European powers partitioned almost the entire continent. As Europeans carved out their claims, they established new borders and frontiers. They redrew the map of Africa with little regard for traditional patterns of settlement or ethnic boundaries.

Horrors in the Congo Leopold and other wealthy Belgians exploited the riches of the Congo, including its copper, rubber, and ivory. Soon, there were horrifying reports of Belgian overseers brutalizing villagers. Forced to work for almost nothing, laborers were savagely beaten or mutilated. The overall population declined drastically.

Eventually, international outrage forced Leopold to turn over his personal colony to the Belgian government. It became the Belgian Congo in 1908. Under Belgian rule, the worst abuses were ended. Still, the Belgians regarded the Congo as a possession to be exploited. Africans were given little or no role in the government, and the wealth of their mines went out of the country to Europe.

France Extends Its Influence France took a giant share of Africa. In the 1830s, it had invaded and conquered Algeria in North Africa. The victory cost tens of thousands of French lives and killed many times more Algerians. In the late 1800s, France extended its influence along the Mediterranean into Tunisia. It also won colonies in West and Central Africa. At its height, the French empire in Africa was as large as the continental United States.

Britain Takes Its Share Britain's share of Africa was more scattered than that of France. However, it included more heavily populated regions with many rich resources. Britain took chunks of West and East Africa. It gained control of Egypt and pushed south into the Sudan.

In southern Africa, Britain clashed with the Boers, who were descendants of Dutch settlers. As you have read, Britain had acquired the Cape Colony from the Dutch in 1814. At that time, many Boers fled British rule, migrating north and setting up their own republics. In the late 1800s, however, the discovery of gold and diamonds in the Boer lands led to conflict with Britain. The **Boer War,** which lasted from 1899 to 1902, involved bitter guerrilla fighting. The British won in the end, but at great cost.

In 1910, the British united the Cape Colony and the former Boer republics into the Union of South Africa. The new constitution set up a government run by whites and laid the foundation for a system of complete racial segregation that would remain in force until 1993.

Others Join the Scramble Other European powers joined the scramble for colonies, in part to bolster their national image, while also furthering their economic growth and influence. The Portuguese carved out large colonies in Angola and Mozambique. Italy reached across the Mediterranean to occupy Libya and then pushed into the "horn" of Africa, at the southern end of the Red Sea. The newly united German empire took lands in eastern and southwestern Africa, including Cameroons and Togo. A German politician, trying to ease the worries of European rivals, explained, "We do not want to put anyone in the shade, but we also demand our place in the sun."

✔ **Checkpoint** How did King Leopold II set off a scramble for colonies in Africa?

Africans Resist Imperialism

Europeans met armed resistance across the continent. The Algerians battled the French for years. **Samori Touré** (sah MAWR ee too RAY) fought French forces in West Africa, where he was building his own empire. The British battled the Zulus in southern Africa and the Asante in West Africa. When their king was exiled, the Asante put themselves under the command of their queen, **Yaa Asantewaa** (YA uh ah sahn TAY wuh). She led the fight against the British in the last Asante war. Another woman who became a military leader was **Nehanda** (neh HAHN duh), of the Shona in Zimbabwe. Although a clever tactician, Nehanda was captured and executed. However, the memory of her achievements inspired later generations to fight for freedom.

In East Africa, the Germans fought wars against the Yao and Herero (huh REHR oh). Fighting was especially fierce in the Maji-Maji Rebellion of 1905. The Germans triumphed only after burning acres and acres of farmland, leaving thousands of local people to die of starvation.

Ethiopia Survives One ancient Christian kingdom in East Africa, Ethiopia, managed to resist European colonization and maintain its independence. Like feudal Europe, Ethiopia had been divided up among a number of rival princes who ruled their own <u>domains</u>. In the late 1800s, however, a reforming ruler, **Menelik II,** began to modernize his country. He hired European experts to plan modern roads and bridges and set up a Western school system. He imported the latest weapons and European officers to help train his army. Thus, when Italy invaded Ethiopia in 1896, Menelik was prepared. At the battle of Adowa (AH duh wuh), the Ethiopians smashed the Italian invaders. Ethiopia was the only African nation, aside from Liberia, to preserve its independence.

Vocabulary Builder

<u>domain</u>—(doh MAYN) *n.* territory over which rule or control is exercised

BIOGRAPHY

Menelik II

Before becoming emperor of Ethiopia, Menelik II (1844–1913) ruled the Shoa region in central Ethiopia. He ensured that he would succeed John IV as emperor by marrying his daughter to John's son. After John died in 1889, Menelik took the throne.

Menelik used profits from ivory sales to buy modern weapons. He then hired European advisors to teach his soldiers how to use the new guns. Menelik's army conquered neighboring lands and won a stunning victory over the Italians at Adowa. European nations rushed to establish diplomatic ties with Ethiopia. Around the world, people of African descent hailed Menelik's victory over European imperialism. **How did Menelik preserve Ethiopian independence?**

An Asante King
A king of the Asante people in Ghana (center) sits surrounded by his people. *What do the clothes of the man to the left of the king suggest about his social rank?*

A New African Elite Emerges During the Age of Imperialism, a Western-educated African **elite,** or upper class, emerged. Some middle-class Africans admired Western ways and rejected their own culture. Others valued their African traditions and condemned Western societies that upheld liberty and equality for whites only. By the early 1900s, African leaders were forging nationalist movements to pursue self-determination and independence.

✔ **Checkpoint** How did Ethiopians resist imperialism?

 Assessment

Progress Monitoring *Online*
For: Self-quiz with vocabulary practice
Web Code: naa-2421

Terms, People, and Places

1. For each term, person, or place listed at the beginning of the section, write a sentence explaining its significance.

Note Taking

2. **Reading Skill: Identify Causes and Effects** Use your completed chart to answer the Focus Question: How did imperialist European powers claim control over most of Africa by the end of the 1800s?

Comprehension and Critical Thinking

3. **Describe** Name one development in each region of Africa in the early 1800s.
4. **Analyze Information** What impact did explorers and missionaries have on Africa?
5. **Draw Inferences** (a) Why do you think the Europeans did not invite Africans to the Berlin Conference? (b) What might be the effect of this exclusion upon later African leaders?
6. **Summarize** How did Africans resist European imperialism?

● **Writing About History**

Quick Write: Generate Arguments One way to approach a persuasive essay is to create a list of arguments that you can include to persuade your audience. For practice, create a list of three arguments that could be used in a persuasive essay either in favor of or opposed to the European colonization of Africa.

On Trial for My Country
by Stanlake Samkange

European imperialists gained control over much of Africa by signing treaties with local rulers. In most cases, the chiefs did not understand what rights they were signing away. Cecil Rhodes used this tactic with King Lobengula, who thought that he was allowing the British only to dig on his land. Rhodes, however, took control of the kingdom, eventually naming it Rhodesia. The novel *On Trial for My Country* is a fictional account of a conversation between King Lobengula and his father.

"Why did you not stand up to Rhodes and prevent him from taking your country by strength? Why did you not fight?"

"I thought that if I appealed to the white men's sense of justice and fair play, reminding them how good I had been to them since I had never killed or ill-treated a white man, they might hear my word and return to their homes. . . ."

"I . . . told them that I had not given them the road to Mashonaland."

"Yes, and they replied and told you that they had been given the road by their Queen and would only return on the orders of their Queen. What did you do then?"

"I mobilized[1] the army and told them to wait for my word."

"Did you give that word?"

"No."

"Were the soldiers keen to fight?"

"Yes, they were dying to fight."

"Why did you not let them fight?"

"I wanted to avoid bloodshed and war. . . ."

"And you allowed them to flout[2] your word as king of the Amandebele? You let them have their way. . . . Is that right?. . . . Why did you not . . . seek their protection and declare your country a British protectorate?"

". . . I knew that if I fought the white men I would be beaten. If I sought the white man's friendship and protection, there would be opposition to me or civil war. So I decided to pretend to the white men that if they came into the country I would fight, and hoped that they would be afraid and not come. . . . [T]hey called my bluff and came . . ."

"Was there no other way out of your dilemma?"

"I did consider marrying the Queen, but even though I hinted at this several times no one followed it up."

"I see!"

1. **mobilize** (MOH buh lyz) *v.* to assemble for war
2. **flout** (flowt) *v.* to mock

▲ King Lobengula of the Matabele nation in present-day Zimbabwe

Thinking Critically

1. **Synthesize Information** Why did King Lobengula want to avoid fighting the British?
2. **Analyze Literature** How does Samkange show that Lobengula's father disagreed with his son's decision?

NAPOLEON IN EGYPT

Poster of Napoleon in Egypt

WITNESS HISTORY 🔊 AUDIO

The Egyptian Campaign

By 1797, Napoleon Bonaparte felt that Europe offered too few chances for glory. Setting his sights toward Africa in 1798, he invaded Egypt, a province of the Ottoman empire.

❝ Europe is a molehill. . . . We must go to the East. . . . All great glory has been acquired there. ❞

Focus Question How did European nations extend their power into Muslim regions of the world?

Lamp from a mosque

European Claims in Muslim Regions

 Performance Standards

• **SSWH15c** Describe the Young Turks as a reaction to foreign control.

Terms, People, and Places

Muhammad Ahmad	genocide
Mahdi	Muhammad Ali
pasha	concession
sultan	

Note Taking

Reading Skill: Understand Effects As you read, fill in a concept web like the one below with the effects of European imperialism in Muslim regions of the world.

European Presence in Muslim Regions

Napoleon's Egyptian campaign highlighted Ottoman decline and opened a new era of European contact with Muslim regions of the world. European countries were just nibbling at the edges of Muslim countries. Before long, they would strike at their heartland.

Stresses in Muslim Regions

Muslim lands extended from western Africa to Southeast Asia. In the 1500s, three giant Muslim empires ruled much of this world—the Ottomans in the Middle East, the Safavids (sah FAH vidz) in Persia, and the Mughals in India.

Empires in Decline By the 1700s, all three Muslim empires were in decline. The decay had many causes. Central governments had lost control over powerful groups such as landowning nobles, military elites, and urban craft guilds. Corruption was widespread. In some places, Muslim scholars and religious leaders were allied with the state. In other areas, they helped to stir discontent against the government.

Rise of Muslim Reform Movements In the 1700s and 1800s, reform movements sprang up across various Muslim regions of Africa and Asia. Most stressed religious piety and strict rules of behavior. Usman dan Fodio led the struggle to reform Muslim practices in northern Africa. In the Sudan, **Muhammad Ahmad** (AHK mud) announced that he was the **Mahdi** (mahk DEE), the long-awaited savior of the faith. The Mahdi and his followers fiercely resisted British expansion into the region.

Another Islamic reform movement, the Wahhabi (wah HAHB ee) movement in Arabia, rejected the schools of theology and law that had emerged in the Ottoman empire. In their place, they wanted to recapture the purity and simplicity of Muhammad's original teachings. Although the revolt was put down, the Wahhabi movement survived. Its teachings remain influential in the kingdom of Saudi Arabia today.

European Imperialism In addition to internal decay and stress, the three Muslim empires faced powerful threats from Western imperialists. Through diplomacy and military threats, European powers won treaties giving them favorable trading terms. They then demanded special rights for Europeans residing in Muslim lands. At times, European powers protected those rights by intervening in local affairs.

✔ **Checkpoint** How was Western imperialism a source of stress in Muslim regions of the world?

Problems for the Ottoman Empire

At its height, the Ottoman empire had extended across North Africa, Southeastern Europe, and the Middle East. By the early 1800s, however, it faced serious challenges. Ambitious **pashas,** or provincial rulers, had increased their power. Economic problems and corruption added to Ottoman decay.

Nationalist Revolts Break Out As ideas of nationalism spread from Western Europe, internal revolts weakened the multiethnic Ottoman empire. Subject peoples in North Africa, Eastern Europe, and the Middle East threatened to break away. In the Balkans, Greeks, Serbs, Bulgarians, and Romanians gained their independence. Revolts against Ottoman rule also erupted in Arabia, Lebanon, and Armenia. The Ottomans suppressed these uprisings, but Egypt slipped out of their control.

European Pressure Increases European states sought to benefit from the slow crumbling of the Ottoman empire. After seizing Algeria in the 1830s, France hoped to gain more Ottoman territory. Russia schemed to gain control of the Bosporus (BAHS puh rus) and the Dardanelles. Control of these straits would give the Russians access to the Mediterranean Sea. Britain tried to thwart Russia's ambitions, which it saw as a threat to its own power in the Mediterranean and beyond to India. And in 1898, the new German empire hoped to increase its influence in the region by building a Berlin-to-Baghdad railway.

Efforts to Westernize Since the late 1700s, several Ottoman rulers had seen the need for reform and looked to the West for ideas. They reorganized the <u>bureaucracy</u> and system of tax collection. They built railroads, improved education, and hired Europeans to train a modern military. Young men were sent to the West to study science and technology. Many returned with Western political ideas about democracy and equality.

The reforms also brought improved medical care and revitalized farming. These improvements,

Vocabulary Builder

<u>bureaucracy</u> (bur OK re see) *n.* government staffed by administrators and officials who follow rigid rules.

General Ismail Pasha (center) fought for the British army in the Crimean War.

however, created a different set of problems. Better healthcare resulted in a population explosion that increased the already intense competition for the best land and led to unrest.

The adoption of Western ideas also increased tension. Many officials objected to changes that were inspired by a foreign culture. For their part, repressive **sultans,** rulers of the Ottoman Turkish empire, rejected reform and tried to rebuild the autocratic power enjoyed by earlier rulers.

Young Turks Demand Reform In the 1890s, a group of liberals formed a movement called the Young Turks. They insisted that reform was the only way to save the empire. In 1908, the Young Turks overthrew the sultan. Before they could achieve their planned reforms, however, the Ottoman empire was plunged into the world war that erupted in 1914.

Armenian Genocide Traditionally, the Ottomans had let minority nationalities live in their own communities and practice their own religions. By the 1890s, however, nationalism was igniting new tensions, especially between Turkish nationalists and minority peoples who sought their own states. These tensions triggered a brutal genocide of the Armenians, a Christian people concentrated in the eastern mountains of the empire. **Genocide** is a deliberate attempt to destroy a racial, political, or cultural group.

The Muslim Turks accused Christian Armenians of supporting Russian plans against the Ottoman empire. When Armenians protested repressive Ottoman policies, the sultan had tens of thousands of them slaughtered. Over the next 25 years, between 600,000 and 1.5 million Armenians were killed or died from disease and starvation.

 Checkpoint How were efforts to Westernize problematic for the Ottoman empire?

Egypt Seeks to Modernize

In the early 1800s, Egypt was a semi-independent province of the Ottoman empire, making great strides toward reform. Its success was due to **Muhammad Ali,** an ambitious soldier appointed governor of Egypt by the Ottomans. Ali used the opportunity created by Napoleon's invasion and the civil war that followed to seize power in 1805.

Muhammad Ali Introduces Reforms Muhammad Ali is sometimes called the "father of modern Egypt." He introduced a number of political and economic reforms, including improving tax collection, reorganizing the landholding system, and backing large irrigation projects to increase farm output. By expanding cotton production and encouraging the development of many local industries, Ali increased Egyptian participation in world trade.

Muhammad Ali also brought Western military experts to Egypt to help him build a well-trained, modern army. He conquered the neighboring lands of Arabia, Syria, and Sudan. Before he died in 1849, he had set Egypt on the road to becoming a major Middle Eastern power.

Building the Suez Canal Muhammad Ali's successors lacked his skills, and Egypt came increasingly under foreign control. In 1858, a French entrepreneur, Ferdinand de Lesseps (LAY seps), organized a company to build the Suez Canal. European nations gained power over the Ottomans by extending loans at high interest rates. In 1875, the ruler of

Suez Canal

The Suez Canal is a waterway in Egypt that stretches for more than 100 miles (160 kilometers). It connects the Mediterranean and Red seas, shortening the travel distance from Western Europe to ports in East Africa and Asia. After it opened in 1869, European ships no longer had to sail around the southern tip of Africa. The canal reduced the trip from London, England, to Bombay, India, by 5,150 miles (8,280 kilometers). The canal averaged between one and two ships per day (below) in its first year of operation and travel time averaged about 40 hours. Today, oil tankers and cargo ships make up most of the canal's traffic with a travel time of about 14 hours.

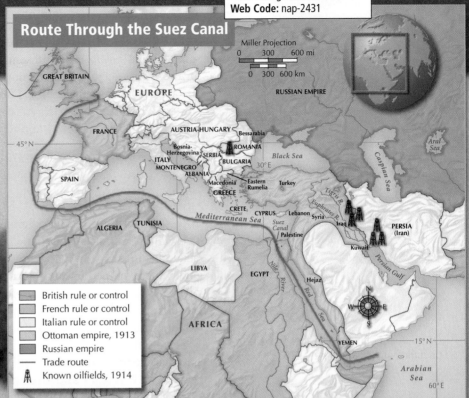

Geography *Interactive*
For: Audio guided tour
Web Code: nap-2431

Route Through the Suez Canal

Miller Projection

British rule or control
French rule or control
Italian rule or control
Ottoman empire, 1913
Russian empire
Trade route
Known oilfields, 1914

▲ Construction of the Suez Canal began in 1859 and took workers 10 years to complete. Although digging was first done by hand, laborers later used dredgers and steam shovels to remove sediment.

Thinking Critically

1. **Draw Conclusions** Why was the Suez Canal an important waterway?
2. **Map Skills** Which countries benefited the most from the Suez Canal? Explain.

Oil flows out of one of the first oil wells to be drilled in Persia, around 1910.

Egypt was unable to repay loans he had contracted for the canal and other projects. To pay his debts, he sold his shares in the canal. The British bought the shares, gaining a controlling interest in the canal.

Becoming a British Protectorate When Egyptian nationalists revolted against foreign influence in 1882, Britain made Egypt a protectorate. In theory, the governor of Egypt was still an official of the Ottoman government. In fact, he followed policies dictated by Britain. Under British influence, Egypt continued to modernize. However, nationalist discontent simmered and flared into protests and riots.

✔ **Checkpoint** How did Egypt fall under British control?

Persia and the European Powers

Like the Ottoman empire, Persia faced major challenges in the 1800s. The Qajar (kah JAHR) shahs, who ruled Persia from 1794 to 1925, exercised absolute power. Still, they did take steps to introduce reforms. The government helped build telegraph lines and railroads and experimented with a liberal constitution. Reform, however, did not save Persia from Western imperialism. Russia wanted to protect its southern frontier and expand into Central Asia. Britain wanted to protect its interests in India.

For a time, each nation set up its own sphere of influence in Persia. The discovery of oil in the early 1900s heightened foreign interest in the region. Both Russia and Britain plotted for control of Persian oil fields. They persuaded the Persian government to grant them **concessions,** or special rights given to foreign powers. To protect their interests, they sent troops into Persia. Persian nationalists were outraged. The nationalists included two very different groups. Some Persians wanted to move swiftly to adopt Western ways. Others, led by Muslim religious leaders, condemned the Persian government and Western influences.

✔ **Checkpoint** How did Persia attract foreign interest in the early 1900s?

Progress Monitoring *Online*
For: Self-quiz with vocabulary practice
Web Code: naa-2431

SECTION **3** Assessment

Terms, People, and Places

1. For each term, person, or place listed at the beginning of the section, write a sentence explaining its significance.

Note Taking

2. **Reading Skill: Understand Effects** Use your completed concept web to answer the Focus Question: How did European nations extend their power into Muslim regions of the world?

Comprehension and Critical Thinking

3. **Draw Conclusions** How did European nations take advantage of stresses in the Muslim world?

4. **Summarize** Describe two problems that contributed to Ottoman decline.

5. **Synthesize Information** How did Muhammad Ali modernize Egypt?

6. **Identify Central Issues** Why did Russia and Britain compete for power in Persia?

● **Writing About History**

Quick Write: Answer Opposing Arguments Suppose that you are writing a persuasive essay on whether the Suez Canal was a positive or negative development for Egypt. An effective way to make your arguments convincing is to address both sides of the topic. Create a chart noting facts and ideas that support your position on one side and arguments that might be used against your position on the other.

Critical of British Rule

In 1871, Indian nationalist Dadabhai Naoroji (DAH dah by now ROH jee) criticized British rule in India:

❝ [Indians] call the British system 'Sakar ki Churi' (SA kur kee CHOO ree), the knife of sugar. That is to say, there is no oppression, it is all smooth and sweet, but it is the knife notwithstanding. ❞

Focus Question How did Britain gradually extend its control over most of India, despite opposition?

Queen Victoria writes letters as her Indian servant waits for his orders.

British East India Company's coat of arms

The British Take Over India

 Performance Standards

• **SSWH15c** Describe reactions to foreign domination.

Terms, People, and Places

sati	deforestation
sepoy	Ram Mohun Roy
viceroy	purdah

Note Taking

Reading Skill: Identify Causes and Effects As you read this section, make a flowchart to show the causes and effects of British rule in India.

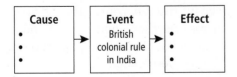

For more than 200 years, Mughal rulers governed a powerful empire in India. By the mid-1700s, however, the Mughal empire was collapsing from a lack of strong rulers. Britain then turned its commercial interests in the region into political ones.

East India Company and Rebellion

In the early 1600s, the British East India Company won trading rights on the fringe of the Mughal empire. As Mughal power declined, the company's influence grew. By the mid-1800s, it controlled three fifths of India.

Exploiting Indian Diversity The British were able to conquer India by exploiting its diversity. Even when Mughal power was at its height, India was home to many people and cultures. As Mughal power crumbled, India became fragmented. Indians with different traditions and dozens of different languages were not able to unite against the newcomers. The British took advantage of Indian divisions by encouraging competition and disunity among rival princes. Where diplomacy or intrigue did not work, the British used their superior weapons to overpower local rulers.

Implementing British Policies The East India Company's main goal in India was to make money, and leading officials often grew rich. At the same time, the company did work to improve roads, preserve peace, and reduce banditry.

THE SEPOY REBELLION

In 1857, the British issued new rifles to the sepoys. Troops were told to bite off the tips of cartridges before loading them into the rifles (right). Sepoys believed the cartridges (below) were greased with animal fat—from cows, which Hindus considered sacred, and from pigs, which were forbidden to Muslims. When sepoys (right) refused to load the guns, they were imprisoned. Angry sepoys rebelled against British officers, sparking a massacre of British troops, as well as women and children.

◄ A Sepoy rebels against British forces.

By the early 1800s, British officials introduced Western education and legal procedures. Missionaries tried to convert Indians to Christianity, which they felt was superior to Indian religions. The British also pressed for social change. They worked to end slavery and the caste system and to improve the position of women within the family. One law banned **sati** (SUH tee), a Hindu custom practiced mainly by the upper classes. It called for a widow to join her husband in death by throwing herself on his funeral fire.

Growing Discontent In the 1850s, the East India Company made several unpopular moves. First, it required **sepoys** (SEE poyz), or Indian soldiers in its service, to serve anywhere, either in India or overseas. For high-caste Hindus, however, overseas travel was an offense against their religion. Second, the East India Company passed a law that allowed Hindu widows to remarry. Hindus viewed both moves as a Christian conspiracy to undermine their beliefs.

Then, in 1857, the British issued new rifles to the sepoys. Troops were told to bite off the tips of cartridges before loading them into the rifles. The cartridges, however, were greased with animal fat—either from cows, which Hindus considered sacred, or from pigs, which were forbidden to Muslims. When the troops refused the order to "load rifles," they were imprisoned.

Rebellion and Aftermath Angry sepoys rose up against their British officers. The Sepoy Rebellion swept across northern and central India. Several sepoy regiments marched off to Delhi, the old Mughal capital. There, they hailed the last Mughal ruler as their leader.

In some places, the sepoys brutally massacred British men, women, and children. But the British soon rallied and crushed the revolt. They then took terrible revenge for their earlier losses, torching villages and slaughtering thousands of unarmed Indians.

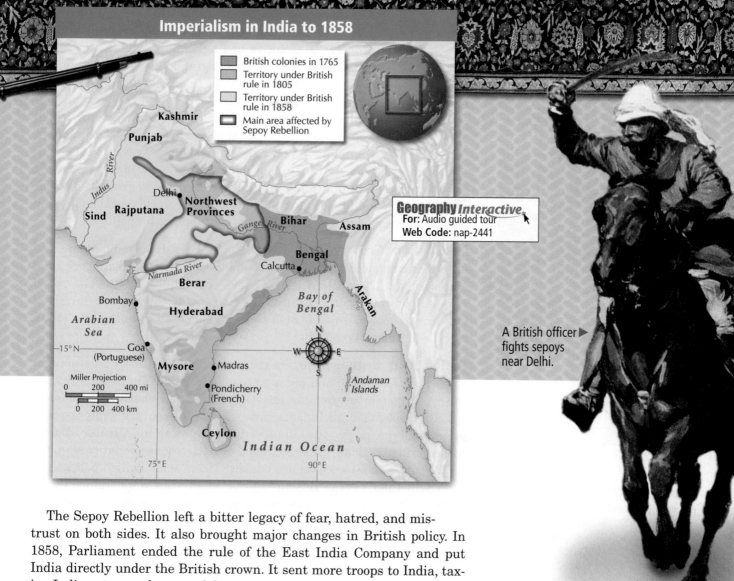

Imperialism in India to 1858

Legend:
- British colonies in 1765
- Territory under British rule in 1805
- Territory under British rule in 1858
- Main area affected by Sepoy Rebellion

Geography *Interactive*
For: Audio guided tour
Web Code: nap-2441

Map labels: Kashmir, Punjab, Indus River, Delhi, Northwest Provinces, Sind, Rajputana, Ganges River, Bihar, Assam, Bengal, Calcutta, Narmada River, Berar, Bombay, Hyderabad, Bay of Bengal, Arakan, Arabian Sea, Goa (Portuguese), Mysore, Madras, Pondicherry (French), Andaman Islands, Ceylon, Indian Ocean, 15° N, 75° E, 90° E, Miller Projection, 0 200 400 mi, 0 200 400 km

A British officer ▶ fights sepoys near Delhi.

The Sepoy Rebellion left a bitter legacy of fear, hatred, and mistrust on both sides. It also brought major changes in British policy. In 1858, Parliament ended the rule of the East India Company and put India directly under the British crown. It sent more troops to India, taxing Indians to pay the cost of these occupying forces. While it slowed the "reforms" that had angered Hindus and Muslims, it continued to develop India for Britain's own economic benefit.

 Checkpoint What were the causes of the Sepoy Rebellion in northern and central India?

Impact of British Colonial Rule

After 1858, Parliament set up a system of colonial rule in India called the British Raj. A British **viceroy** in India governed in the name of the queen, and British officials held the top positions in the civil service and army. Indians filled most other jobs. With their cooperation, the British made India the "brightest jewel" in the crown of their empire.

British policies were designed to incorporate India into the <u>overall</u> British economy. At the same time, British officials felt they were helping India to modernize. In their terms, modernizing meant adopting not only Western technology but also Western culture.

An Unequal Partnership Britain saw India both as a market and as a source of raw materials. To this end, the British built roads and an impressive railroad network. Improved transportation let the British sell

Thinking Critically
1. **Draw Conclusions** How was the Sepoy Rebellion a clash of cultures?
2. **Map Skills** Which regions were most affected by the Sepoy Rebellion?

Vocabulary Builder
<u>overall</u>—(OH vur awl) *adj.* total

their factory-made goods across the subcontinent and carry Indian cotton, jute, and coal to coastal ports for transport to factories in England. New methods of communication, such as the telegraph, also gave Britain better control of India. After the Suez Canal opened in 1869, British trade with India soared. But it remained an unequal partnership, favoring the British. The British flooded India with inexpensive, machine-made textiles, ruining India's once-prosperous hand-weaving industry.

Britain also transformed Indian agriculture. It encouraged nomadic herders to settle into farming and pushed farmers to grow cash crops, such as cotton and jute, that could be sold on the world market. Clearing new farmlands led to massive **deforestation,** or cutting of trees.

Population Growth and Famine The British introduced medical improvements and new farming methods. Better healthcare and increased food production led to rapid population growth. The rising numbers, however, put a strain on the food supply, especially as farmland was turned over to growing cash crops instead of food. In the late 1800s, terrible famines swept India.

Benefits of British Rule On the positive side, British rule brought some degree of peace and order to the countryside. The British revised the legal system to promote justice for Indians regardless of class or caste. Railroads helped Indians move around the country, while the telegraph and postal system improved communication. Greater contact helped bridge regional differences and develop a sense of national unity.

The upper classes, especially, benefited from some British policies. They sent their sons to British schools, where they were trained for posts in the civil service and military. Indian landowners and princes, who still ruled their own territories, grew rich from exporting cash crops.

Railroads and Trade
By building thousands of miles of railroads, the British opened up India's vast interior to trade. The British also encouraged Indians to grow tea (top photo) and jute (bottom photo). Today, tea is one of India's biggest crops. *What were some of the benefits of British rule?*

✔ **Checkpoint**   How did British colonial rule affect Indian agriculture?

Different Views on Culture

Some educated Indians were impressed by British power and technology and urged India to follow a Western model of progress. These mostly upper-class Indians learned English and adopted Western ways. Other Indians felt that the answer to change lay with their own Hindu or Muslim cultures.

Indian Attitudes In the early 1800s, **Ram Mohun Roy** combined both views. A great scholar, he knew Sanskrit, Persian, and Arabic classics, as well as English, Greek, and Latin works. Roy felt that India could learn from the West. He was a founder of Hindu College in Calcutta, which provided an English-style education to Indians. Many of its graduates went on to establish English schools all over the region. While Roy saw the value of Western education, he also wanted to reform traditional Indian culture.

Roy condemned some traditions, such as rigid caste distinctions, child marriage, sati, and **purdah** (PUR duh), the isolation of women in separate quarters. But he also set up educational societies that helped revive pride in Indian culture. Because of his influence on later leaders, he is often hailed today as the founder of Indian nationalism.

Western Attitudes The British disagreed among themselves about India. A few admired Indian theology and philosophy. As Western scholars translated Indian classics, they acquired respect for India's ancient heritage. Western writers and philosophers borrowed ideas from Hinduism and Buddhism.

However, most British people knew little about Indian achievements and dismissed Indian culture with contempt. In an essay on whether Indians should be taught in English or their own languages, British historian Thomas Macaulay arrogantly wrote that "a single shelf of a good European library is worth the whole native literature of India and Arabia."

✓ **Checkpoint** How did Indians and British view each other's culture in the 1800s?

Indian Nationalism Grows

During the years of British rule, a class of Western-educated Indians emerged. In the view of Macaulay and others, this elite class would bolster British power. As it turned out, exposure to European ideas had the opposite effect. By the late 1800s, Western-educated Indians were spearheading a nationalist movement. Schooled in Western ideals such as democracy and equality, they dreamed of ending imperial rule.

Indian National Congress In 1885, nationalist leaders organized the Indian National Congress, which became known as the Congress party. Its members believed in peaceful protest to gain their ends. They called for greater democracy, which they felt would bring more power to Indians like themselves. The Indian National Congress looked forward to eventual self-rule, but supported Western-style modernization.

Muslim League At first, Muslims and Hindus worked together for self-rule. In time, however, Muslims grew to resent Hindu domination of the Congress party. They also worried that a Hindu-run government would oppress Muslims. In 1906, Muslims formed the Muslim League to pursue their own goals. Soon, they were talking of a separate Muslim state.

✓ **Checkpoint** How are the origins of Indian nationalism linked to British rule?

SECTION 4 Assessment

Progress Monitoring *Online*
For: Self-quiz with vocabulary practice
Web Code: naa-2441

Terms, People, and Places
1. What do the key terms listed at the beginning of the section have in common?

Note Taking
2. **Reading Skill: Identify Causes and Effects** Use your completed flowchart to answer the Focus Question: How did Britain gradually extend its control over most of India, despite opposition?

Comprehension and Critical Thinking
3. **Recognize Cause and Effect** What were the causes and effects of the Sepoy Rebellion?
4. **Draw Conclusions** What were the positive and negative effects of British rule on Indians?
5. **Analyze Information** How did British rule lead to growing Indian nationalism?

● Writing About History
Quick Write: Draft an Opening Paragraph Write an opening paragraph for a persuasive essay on whether the British were right to pass laws that tried to reform the caste system. Remember that the first few sentences of your draft are your chance to build interest in your topic. Add details that will help grab the reader's attention.

In This Chapter SSWH19a

Britain brought much of the globe under its control in the 1800s because of its industrial strength and powerful navy. The "jewel in the crown" of the British Empire was India (right). India supplied British factories with raw materials and served as a huge market for British manufactured goods. But in the twentieth century, independence movements in India and elsewhere broke the British Empire apart.

Throughout History

522 B.C.–486 B.C. Darius I unifies the Persian empire by setting up a strong bureaucracy and building hundreds of miles of roads

31 B.C.–A.D. 14 Emperor Augustus encourages loyalty by allowing Roman provinces a large measure of self-government.

1500s Spain used wealth from its empire in the Americas to wage wars in Europe, neglecting its own economic development.

1800s The French Empire rises and falls with the rise and fall of Napoleon I.

1990s Economic weakness and involvement in a long war in Afghanistan leads to the breakup of the Soviet Union.

Continuing Today

Although the Soviet Union has broken apart, Russia maintains its interest in the affairs of former Soviet states. Russia will flex its military muscle to keep them in line. Here Russian tanks roll into neighboring Georgia to support South Ossetia.

21st Century Skills

TRANSFER Activities

1. **Analyze** Throughout history, how have different empires been strengthened or weakened?

2. **Evaluate** Why do you think no empire has even been able to maintain its influence forever?

3. **Transfer** Complete a Web quest, record your thoughts in the Concept Connector Journal, and learn to make a video. Web Code nah-2408

Lin Zexu,
Chinese official

WITNESS HISTORY 🔊 AUDIO

Trading Opium for Tea

By the 1830s, British merchant ships were arriving in China loaded with opium to trade with the Chinese for tea. In 1839, Chinese government official Lin Zexu (lin DZUH shoo) wrote a letter to Britain's Queen Victoria condemning the practice:

❝ We have heard that in your own country opium is prohibited with the utmost strictness and severity—this is strong proof that you know full well how hurtful it is. . . . Since . . . you do not permit it to injure your own country, you ought not to have the injurious drug transferred to another country.**❞**

Britain's Union Jack

Focus Question How did Western powers use diplomacy and war to gain power in Qing China?

China and the New Imperialism

 Performance Standards

- **SSWH14d** Examine the Opium War and the Taiping Rebellion.

Terms, People, and Places

balance of trade	Taiping Rebellion
trade surplus	Sino-Japanese War
trade deficit	Open Door Policy
Opium War	Guang Xu
indemnity	Boxer Uprising
extraterritoriality	Sun Yixian

Note Taking

Reading Skill: Recognize Multiple Causes As you read, create a flowchart like the one below in which you can record key events and developments that led to the decline of Qing China.

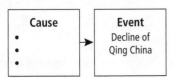

For centuries, Chinese regulations had ensured that China had a favorable **balance of trade** with other nations. A nation's balance of trade refers to the difference between how much a country imports and how much it exports. By the 1800s, however, Western nations were using their growing power to tilt the balance of trade with East Asia in their favor.

Trade Between Britain and China

Prior to the 1800s, Chinese rulers placed strict limits on foreign traders. European merchants were restricted to a small area in southern China. China sold them silk, porcelain, and tea in exchange for gold and silver. Under this arrangement, China enjoyed a **trade surplus,** or exported more than it imported. Westerners, on the other hand, had a **trade deficit** with China, buying more from the Chinese than they sold to them.

By the late 1700s, two developments were underway that would transform China's relations with the Western world. First, China entered a period of decline. Second, the Industrial Revolution created a need for expanded markets for European goods. At the same time, it gave the West superior military power.

The Opium War During the late 1700s, British merchants began making huge profits by trading opium grown in India for Chinese tea, which was popular in Britain. Soon, many Chinese had become addicted to the drug. Silver flowed out of China in payment for the drug, disrupting the economy.

The Chinese government outlawed opium and executed Chinese drug dealers. They called on Britain to stop the trade. The British refused, insisting on the right of free trade.

In 1839, Chinese warships clashed with British merchants, triggering the **Opium War.** British gunboats, equipped with the latest in firepower, bombarded Chinese coastal and river ports. With outdated weapons and fighting methods, the Chinese were easily defeated.

Unequal Treaties In 1842, Britain made China accept the Treaty of Nanjing (NAHN jing). Britain received a huge **indemnity,** or payment for losses in the war. The British also gained the island of Hong Kong. China had to open five ports to foreign trade and grant British citizens in China **extraterritoriality,** the right to live under their own laws and be tried in their own courts.

The treaty was the first of a series of "unequal treaties" that forced China to make concessions to Western powers. A second war, lasting from 1856 to 1858, ended with France, Russia, and the United States pressuring China to sign treaties <u>stipulating</u> the opening of more ports to foreign trade and letting Christian missionaries preach in China.

✔ **Checkpoint** How did British trade with China trigger the Opium Wars?

The Taiping Rebellion Weakens China

By the 1800s, the Qing dynasty was in decline. Irrigation systems and canals were poorly maintained, leading to massive flooding of the Huang valley. The population explosion that had begun a century earlier created hardship

Vocabulary Builder
<u>stipulate</u>—(STIP yuh layt) *v.* to specifically demand something in an agreement

● **INFOGRAPHIC**

Taiping Rebellion

Taiping Rebellion leader Hong Xiuquan (at right), was a village schoolteacher. Inspired by religious visions and Christian missionaries, he wanted to establish a "Heavenly Kingdom of Peace"—the Taiping. Hong endorsed ideas that Chinese leaders considered radical, including community ownership of property and the equality of women and men.

◀ Chinese coins *c.*1850

Imperialism in China

Spheres of Influence
- British
- French
- German
- Japanese
- Russian
- Occupied by Russia, 1897–1905
- Occupied by Japan by 1905
- Main area of Taiping Rebelliion

Miller Projection
0   500   1000 mi
0   500   1000 km

RUSSIA
Sakhalin
Outer Mongolia
Manchuria
Inner Mongolia
Lüshun (Port Arthur)   Vladivostok
Beijing   40°N
CHINA   Huang He   Qingdao (Tsingtao)   KOREA   JAPAN
Chongqing   Shanghai   Nagasaki
BHUTAN   Yangtze R.   Ningbo
NEPAL   Xiamen (Amoy)   Fuzhou
BRITISH INDIA   Guangzhou (Canton)   Taiwan
Burma   Macao (Portuguese)   Hong Kong (British)
20°N   Pacific Ocean
Bay of Bengal   SIAM   FRENCH INDOCHINA
120°E   140°E

for China's peasants. An extravagant imperial court, tax evasion by the rich, and widespread official corruption added to the peasants' burden. As poverty and misery increased, peasants rebelled. The **Taiping Rebellion** (TY ping), which lasted from 1850 to 1864, was probably the most devastating peasant revolt in history. The leader, Hong Xiuquan (hong shyoo CHWAHN), called for an end to the hated Qing dynasty. The Taiping rebels won control of large parts of China and held out for 14 years. However, with the help of loyal regional governors and generals, the government crushed the rebellion.

The Taiping Rebellion almost toppled the Qing dynasty. It is estimated to have caused the deaths of between 20 million and 30 million Chinese. The Qing government survived, but it had to share power with regional commanders. During the rebellion, Europeans kept up pressure on China, and Russia seized lands in the north.

✓ **Checkpoint** How did the Taiping Rebellion and other internal problems weaken the Qing dynasty?

Launching Reform Efforts

By the mid-1800s, educated Chinese were divided over the need to adopt Western ways. Most saw no reason for new industries because China's wealth and taxes came from land. Although Chinese merchants were allowed to do business, they were not seen as a source of prosperity.

Scholar-officials also disapproved of the ideas of Western missionaries, whose emphasis on individual choice challenged the Confucian order. They saw Western technology as dangerous, too, because it threatened Confucian ways that had served China successfully for so long.

Geography *Interactive*
For: Audio guided tour
Web Code: nap-2451

▼ Battle scene of the Taiping Rebellion

Thinking Critically
1. **Recognize Cause and Effect** How did conditions in China lead to the Taiping Rebellion?
2. **Map Skills** Which regions were most greatly affected by the Taiping Rebellion?

By the late 1800s, the empress Ci Xi (tsih shih) had gained power. A strong-willed ruler, she surrounded herself with advisors who were deeply committed to Confucian traditions.

Self-Strengthening Movement

In the 1860s, reformers launched the "self-strengthening movement." They imported Western technology, setting up factories to make modern weapons. They developed shipyards, railroads, mining, and light industry. The Chinese translated Western works on science, government, and the economy. However, the movement made limited progress because the government did not rally behind it.

War With Japan

Meanwhile, the Western powers and nearby Japan moved rapidly ahead. Japan began to modernize after 1868. It then joined the Western imperialists in the competition for a global empire.

In 1894, Japanese pressure on China led to the **Sino-Japanese War.** It ended in disaster for China, with Japan gaining the island of Taiwan.

Carving Spheres of Influence

The crushing defeat revealed China's weakness. Western powers moved swiftly to carve out spheres of influence along the Chinese coast. The British took the Chang River valley. The French acquired the territory near their colony of Indochina. Germany and Russia gained territory in northern China.

The United States, a longtime trader with the Chinese, did not take part in the carving up of China. It feared that European powers might shut out American merchants. A few years later, in 1899, it called for a policy to keep Chinese trade open to everyone on an equal basis. The imperial powers accepted the idea of an **Open Door Policy,** as it came to be called. No one, however, consulted the Chinese.

Hundred Days of Reform

Defeated by Japan and humiliated by Westerners, Chinese reformers blamed conservative officials for not modernizing China. They urged conservative leaders to stop looking back at China's past and to modernize as Japan had.

In 1898, a young emperor, **Guang Xu** (gwahng shoo), launched the Hundred Days of Reform. New laws set out to modernize the civil service exams, streamline government, and encourage new industries. Reforms affected schools, the military, and the bureaucracy. Conservatives soon rallied against the reform effort. The emperor was imprisoned, and the aging empress Ci Xi reasserted control. Reformers fled for their lives.

✔ **Checkpoint** How did reformers try to solve China's internal problems?

The Qing Dynasty Falls

As the century ended, China was in turmoil. Anger grew against Christian missionaries who threatened traditional Chinese Confucianism. The presence of foreign troops was another source of discontent. Protected by extraterritoriality, foreigners ignored Chinese laws and lived in their own communities.

Boxer Uprising Anti-foreign feeling finally exploded in the **Boxer Uprising.** In 1899, a group of Chinese had formed a secret society, the Righteous Harmonious Fists. Westerners watching them

The Boxer Rebellion
Suffering from the effects of floods and famine, poverty, and foreign aggression, Boxers (below) participated in an anti-foreign movement. In 1900, some 140,000 Boxers attempted to drive Westerners out of China. An international force eventually put down the uprising. *Why were Westerners and Western influences a source of discontent for the Boxers?*

train in the martial arts dubbed them Boxers. Their goal was to drive out the "foreign devils" who were polluting the land with their un-Chinese ways, strange buildings, machines, and telegraph lines.

In 1900, the Boxers attacked foreigners across China. In response, the Western powers and Japan organized a multinational force. This force crushed the Boxers and rescued foreigners besieged in Beijing. The empress Ci Xi had at first supported the Boxers but reversed her policy as they retreated.

Aftermath of the Uprising China once again had to make concessions to foreigners. The defeat, however, forced even Chinese conservatives to support Westernization. In a rush of reforms, China admitted women to schools and stressed science and mathematics in place of Confucian thought. More students were sent abroad to study.

China also expanded economically. Mining, shipping, railroads, banking, and exports of cash crops grew. Small-scale Chinese industry developed with the help of foreign capital. A Chinese business class emerged, and a new urban working class began to press for rights.

Three Principles of the People Although the Boxer Uprising failed, the flames of Chinese nationalism spread. Reformers wanted to strengthen China's government. By the early 1900s, they had introduced a constitutional monarchy. Some reformers called for a republic.

A passionate spokesman for a Chinese republic was **Sun Yixian** (soon yee SHYAHN), also known as Sun Yat-sen. In the early 1900s, he organized the Revolutionary Alliance to rebuild China on "Three Principles of the People." The first principle was nationalism, or freeing China from foreign domination. The second was democracy, or representative government. The third was livelihood, or economic security for all Chinese.

Birth of a Republic When Ci Xi died in 1908 and a two-year-old boy inherited the throne, China slipped into chaos. In 1911, uprisings in the provinces swiftly spread. Peasants, students, local warlords, and even court politicians helped topple the Qing dynasty.

In December 1911, Sun Yixian was named president of the new Chinese republic. The republic faced overwhelming problems and was almost constantly at war with itself or foreign invaders.

✔ **Checkpoint** What caused the Qing dynasty to fall?

BIOGRAPHY

Sun Yixian

Sun Yixian (1866–1925) was not born to power. His parents were poor farmers. Sun's preparation for leadership came from his travels, education, and personal ambitions. In his teen years, he lived with his brother in Hawaii and attended British and American schools. Later on, he earned a medical degree.

Sun left his career in medicine to struggle against the Qing government. After a failed uprising in 1895, he went into exile. Sun visited many nations, seeking support against the Qing dynasty. When revolution erupted in China, Sun was in Denver, Colorado. He returned to China to begin his leading role in the new republic. **How did Sun's background prepare him to lead?**

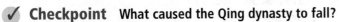

Progress Monitoring Online
For: Self-quiz with vocabulary practice
Web Code: naa-2451

5 Assessment

Terms, People, and Places

1. For each term, person, or place listed at the beginning of the section, write a sentence explaining its significance.

Note Taking

2. **Reading Skill: Recognize Multiple Causes** Use your completed flowchart to answer the Focus Question: How did Western powers use diplomacy and war to gain power in Qing China?

Comprehension and Critical Thinking

3. **Draw Conclusions** How did Western powers gain greater trading rights in China?

4. **Summarize** (a) What internal problems threatened the Qing dynasty? (b) What were the goals of Chinese reformers?

5. **Synthesize Information** How was the Qing dynasty replaced by a republic?

● **Writing About History**

Quick Write: Write a Conclusion Before writing a persuasive essay, make a list of your arguments. In organizing the essay, it's often a good idea to save your strongest argument for last. For practice, write a concluding paragraph for a persuasive essay that either supports or opposes internal reform efforts to Westernize China in the 1800s.

CHAPTER 24

Quick Study Guide

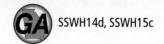 **GA** SSWH14d, SSWH15c

Progress Monitoring *Online*
For: Self-test with vocabulary practice
Web Code: naa-2461

■ Western Imperialism

Africa	Muslim Regions	India	China
• Berlin Conference • Raw materials exploited • Boer War • Racial segregation in South Africa • Western-educated African elite • Nationalism grows	• Islamic reform movements • Internal revolts • Armenian genocide • Egypt modernizes	• British East India Company • Changes to legal and caste systems • Sepoy Rebellion • Indians forced to raise cash crops • Population growth and famine • Indian National Congress • Muslim League	• Opium War • Unequal trade treaties • Self-strengthening movement • Sino-Japanese War • Boxer Uprising

■ Imports from Africa and Asia about 1870

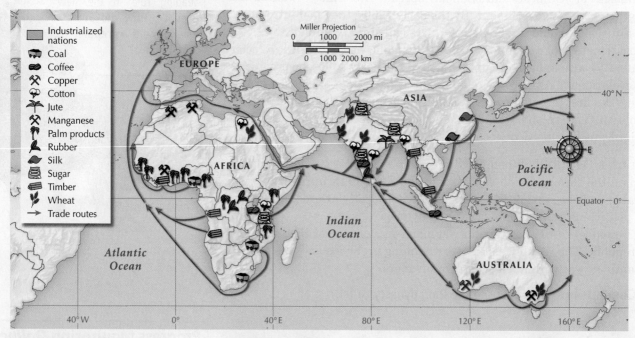

Legend:
Industrialized nations
Coal
Coffee
Copper
Cotton
Jute
Manganese
Palm products
Rubber
Silk
Sugar
Timber
Wheat
→ Trade routes

Miller Projection
0   1000   2000 mi
0   1000 2000 km

EUROPE
ASIA
AFRICA
Pacific Ocean
Indian Ocean
Atlantic Ocean
AUSTRALIA
40° N
Equator—0°
40° W   0°   40° E   80° E   120° E   160° E

■ Key Events of the New Imperialism

1805
Muhammad Ali is named governor of Egypt.

1830
France begins efforts to conquer Algeria in North Africa.

1857
The Sepoy Rebellion breaks out in India.

Chapter Events
Global Events

1800   **1825**   **1850**

1807
In the United States, Robert Fulton uses a steam engine to power a ship.

1848
Revolutions break out throughout much of Europe.

Concept Connector

Essential Question Review

To connect prior knowledge with what you have learned in this chapter, answer the questions below in your Concept Connector journal. Use the journal in the Reading and Note Taking Study Guide to record your answers (or go to www.phschool.com **Web Code:** nad-2407). In addition, record information about the following concepts:

• Nationalism: English nationalism
• Nationalism: American nationalism

1. **Belief Systems** Both foreign and Chinese belief systems influenced China during the 1800s. Some Chinese wanted to adopt Western ways, while others wanted to maintain Confucian ways. How did the choices China made influence its future relationship with Western nations? Do you think China's history would have been different if it had made the same choices as Japan? Why or why not?

2. **Genocide** In the 1890s, tensions between Muslim Turkish nationalists and Christian Armenians triggered a brutal genocide of the minority Armenians. It is estimated that more than one million Armenians were killed or died as a result. Review what you learned about Social Darwinism. How might a Social Darwinist explain the Armenian genocide?

3. **Empire** Powerful armies and navies, advanced weapons, and superior technologies were the tools of the "new imperialism." But the European powers also employed other strategies to gain and keep control over colonies. For example, in South Africa, the British set up a government run by whites and imposed a system of complete racial segregation. What were some of the other strategies Europeans used to control colonies or spheres of influence? Think about the following:
   • indirect rule
   • exploitation
   • trade
   • treaties

■ Connections to Today

1. **Economics: Trade and the Suez Canal** Reread the information in Section 3 on the Suez Canal. How did the opening of the Suez Canal in 1869 transform world trade? Then, find a recent newspaper or magazine article on the Suez Canal today. Do you think the canal is more or less important today than it was in 1869? Write two paragraphs on trade and the Suez Canal today, citing examples from current events to support your answer.

Suez Canal Traffic		
Year	Number of Ships	Net Tons
1975	5,579	50,441,000
1985	19,791	352,579,000
1995	15,051	360,372,000
2003	15,667	549,381,000

SOURCE: Leth Suez Transit Online, 2004

2. **Geography's Impact: Famine** You have read how disaster struck Ireland in October 1845 when a deadly plant disease ruined the potato crop. In the late 1800s, famines also swept through India. What were the major causes of these famines? What was the effect of growing cash crops instead of food? Conduct research to learn more about the causes of hunger and malnutrition in the world today.

1884
European officials meet at the Berlin Conference to settle rival land claims in Africa.

1899
Boer War erupts in South Africa.

1911
Sun Yixian becomes president of Chinese republic.

History *Interactive*
For: Interactive timeline
Web Code: nap-2462

1875   **1900**   **1925**

Mid-1880s
German engineers develop the first automobile.

1914
World War I begins in Europe.

Chapter Assessment

Terms, People, and Places

Match the following definitions with the terms listed below. You will not use all of the terms.

genocide	trade surplus
imperialism	trade deficit
indemnity	Menelik II
Sino-Japanese War	Muhammad Ali
pasha	Taiping Rebellion
viceroy	Boxer Uprising

1. the domination by one country of the political, economic, or cultural life of another country or region
2. war between China and Japan where Japan gained Taiwan
3. provincial ruler in the Ottoman empire
4. situation in which a country imports more than it exports
5. governor of Egypt, sometimes called the "father of modern Egypt"
6. peasant revolt in China from 1850–1864
7. a deliberate attempt to destroy an entire religious or ethnic group
8. payment for losses in war

Main Ideas

Section 1 (pp. 750–753)
9. Describe the four main motives of the new imperialists.
10. Why did Western imperialism spread so rapidly?

Section 2 (pp. 754–761)
11. How did European contact with Africa increase during the 1800s?
12. How did the scramble for African colonies begin?

Section 3 (pp. 762–766)
13. What problems faced the Ottoman empire in the 1800s?
14. How did the modernization of Egypt lead to British rule?

Section 4 (pp. 767–772)
15. Explain the impact of British colonial rule on India.
16. Describe the origins of Indian nationalism.

Section 5 (pp. 773–777)
17. How did westerners gain trading rights in China during the 1800s?
18. Why did the Qing dynasty come to an end?

Chapter Focus Question
19. How did Western industrial powers gain global empires?

Critical Thinking

20. **Geography and History** Why were the natural resources of Africa and Asia important to Europeans in the 1800s?
21. **Analyzing Cartoons** The political cartoon below shows a French soldier (left) and a British soldier (right) ripping apart a map. How do you think the situation depicted in the cartoon affected relations between Britain and France?

22. **Summarize** How did the Ottoman empire try to westernize?
23. **Predict Consequences** How do you think rivalries between religious groups affected anti-imperialism efforts in India? Explain your answer.
24. **Analyze Information** Why did Western industrial nations establish spheres of influence in China rather than colonies as they did in Africa and India?

● Writing About History

In this chapter's five Section Assessments, you developed skills for writing a persuasive essay.

Writing a Persuasive Essay During the 1800s, European powers embarked on a period of expansion known as the Age of Imperialism. Despite resistance, these powers brought much of the world under their control between 1870 and 1914. Write a persuasive essay from the point of view of a Chinese government official in which the official tries to persuade the British that the Treaty of Nanjing is too harsh and will lead to dangerous anti-foreign feelings. Consult page SH16 of the Writing Handbook for additional help.

Prewriting
- Make a list of what you believe to be the strongest arguments of the Chinese official.
- Organize the arguments from weakest to strongest.

Drafting
- Clearly state the position that you will prove in the thesis statement.
- Sequence your arguments so that you open or close with your strongest one.
- Write a conclusion that restates your thesis and closes with a strong argument.

Revising
- Review your arguments to make sure that you have explained them logically and clearly.

Prepare for the GHSGT

The Forgotten Genocide

The Armenian massacre has been called the "forgotten genocide." It refers to the destruction, between 1895 and 1923, of the Christian Armenians of Turkey under the Muslim Ottoman government. More than 2 million Armenians lived in Turkey before the genocide. Estimates of those killed vary from 600,000 to 1.5 million. The rest were driven from their ancestral home. Most perpetrators were freed, despite pledges by the Allies to punish them after World War I.

Document A

"As it got worse, all of us, and all the people, began gathering in our school. The word came around that the Turks were going on the streets and killing all the Armenians and leaving them on the streets. I, myself, was in school already, so I simply stayed there. Then orders came from the school that we, too, should run away. But where? All the buildings were on fire! The Turks were burning everything. There was a whole group of us running away from the school."

—Annalin, a survivor from Smyrna on events of 1922

Document B

"The massacre of Armenian subjects in the Ottoman Empire in 1896 . . . was amateur and ineffective compared with the largely successful attempt to exterminate [them] during the First World War in 1915. . . . [This] genocide was carried out under the cloak of legality by cold-blooded governmental action. These were not mass-murders committed spontaneously by mobs of private people. . . ."

—Arnold Toynbee, British historian, cited in *Experiences*

Document C

"The 1,000 Armenian houses are being emptied of furniture by the police one after the other. The furniture, bedding and everything of value is being stored in large buildings about the city. . . . The goods are piled in without any attempt at labeling or systematic storage. A crowd of Turkish women and children follow the police about like a lot of vultures and seize anything they can lay their hands on and when the more valuable things are carried out of the house by the police they rush in and take the balance. . . . I suppose it will take several weeks to empty all the houses and then the Armenian shops and stores will be cleared out."

—From a report to the American embassy by Oscar S. Heizer, American consul in Tebizond, July 1915

Document D

"The proportion of Armenians killed by the Turks in World War I out of the general number of Armenians in the Ottoman Empire was no less than that of the Jewish victims [during the Holocaust] out of the total Jewish population in Europe. Nor are the methods of killing unique. . . . The type of murder committed by the Germans in the USSR—mass machine-gunning—was the traditional method of mass murder in our century, and the death marches of Jews in the closing stages of the war had their precedent in the Armenian case as well. Nor is the fact that in the case of the Holocaust it was a state machine and a bureaucracy that was responsible for the murder unique, because there, too, the Young Turks had preceded the German Nazis in planning the execution of a population with such means as were modern at the time."

—From *Remembrance and Denial* by Richard G. Hovannisian

Analyzing Documents

Use your knowledge of the Armenian massacre and Documents A, B, C, and D to answer questions 1–4.

1. According to Document B, the 1915 massacre of Armenians
   A went unpunished.
   B was ineffective and unsuccessful.
   C was not as well documented as the 1896 massacre.
   D was committed with the knowledge of the Turkish government.

2. Document C shows that the Turkish police
   A tried to protect the property of Armenian citizens, despite their government's orders.
   B tried to help Armenian citizens as best they could.
   C took part in stealing the property of Armenian citizens.
   D protested to the American embassy to try to help their friends.

3. According to Document D, the Armenian Massacre and the Holocaust
   A were committed by the same people.
   B were carried out in a similar way.
   C had very few similarities, except for the large number of murders.
   D both took place in Germany.

4. **Writing Task** Ismayale Kemal Pasha, a governor in Marash, was described by one survivor as kind and justice-loving. He tried saving Armenian citizens, despite orders from his superiors to carry out the genocide without remorse. Suppose Ismayale Kemal Pasha explained his decision to help in a memoir. Write a brief explanation from his point of view. Use these documents along with information from the chapter in your writing.

Japanese women mingle with Europeans in Yokohama's trading compound in this woodcut print created by a Japanese artist in 1861.

A New Pattern

Japan's response to the threat of Western imperialism was different from that of many other countries. In 1871, a delegation of Japanese officials journeyed to the United States with the goal of learning as much as possible about Western culture and technology.

&&We expect and intend to reform and improve so as to stand upon a similar footing with the most enlightened nations. . . . It is our purpose to select from the various institutions prevailing among enlightened nations such as are the best suited to our present condition and adopt them, in gradual reforms and improvements of our policy and customs. . . .99

—Japanese emperor Meiji in a letter to the American president introducing the delegation

Listen to the Witness History audio to hear more about Japan's drive to modernize.

A New Zealand postage stamp featuring the British empire's Queen Victoria

An Australian Aborigine boomerang

GA Performance Standards

Chapter Focus Question How did political and economic imperialism influence nations around the world?

Section 1
Japan Modernizes SSWH14d, SSWH15a, SSWH15b, SSWH15c, SSWH15d

Section 2
Imperialism in Southeast Asia and the Pacific SSWH15d

Section 3
Self-Rule for Canada, Australia, and New Zealand SSWH10a

Section 4
Economic Imperialism in Latin America SSWH14b, SSWHRC1c

Use the ✓ **Quick Study Timeline** at the end of this chapter to preview chapter events.

A bottle of quinine, which was used to fight malaria in Panama

 Concept Connector ONLINE

To explore Essential Questions related to this chapter, go to PHSchool.com
Web Code: nad-2507

Emperor Meiji

A traditional Japanese fan

<...>

WITNESS HISTORY 🔊 AUDIO

Changes for Japan

The emperor Meiji wrote a poem to provide inspiration for Japan's efforts to become a modern country in the late 1800s:

❝ May our country,
Taking what is good,
and rejecting what is bad,
Be not inferior
To any other. ❞

Focus Question How did Japan become a modern industrial power, and what did it do with its new strength?

Japan Modernizes

 Performance Standards

- **SSWH14d** Examine Japan's interaction with Commodore Perry.
- **SSWH15a** Analyze industrialization in England, Germany, and Japan.
- **SSWH15b** Compare and contrast the rise of Germany and Japan.
- **SSWH15c** Describe the Russo-Japanese War as a reaction to foreign control.
- **SSWH15d** Describe how geography and resources influenced Japan's policies in Asia.

Terms, People, and Places

Matthew Perry	zaibatsu
Tokyo	homogeneous society
Meiji Restoration	First Sino-Japanese War
Diet	Russo-Japanese War

Note Taking

Reading Skill: Identify Causes and Effects
As you read this section, identify the causes and effects of the Meiji Restoration in a chart like the one below.

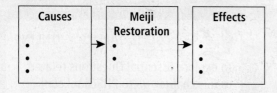

In 1853, the United States displayed its new military might, sending a naval force to make Japan open its ports to trade. Japanese leaders debated how to respond. While some resisted giving up their 215-year-old policy of seclusion, others felt that it would be wiser for Japan to learn from the foreigners.

In the end, Japan chose to abandon its centuries of isolation. The country swiftly transformed itself into a modern industrial power and then set out on its own imperialist path.

Discontent in Tokugawa Japan

In the early 1600s, Japan was still ruled by shoguns, or supreme military dictators. Although emperors still lived in the ceremonial capital of Kyoto, the shoguns held the real power in Edo. Daimyo, or landholding warrior lords, helped the shoguns control Japan. In 1603, a new family, the Tokugawas, seized power. The Tokugawa shoguns reimposed centralized feudalism, closed Japan to foreigners, and forbade Japanese people to travel overseas. The nation's only window on the world was through Nagasaki, where the Dutch were allowed very limited trade.

For more than 200 years, Japan developed in isolation. Internal commerce expanded, agricultural production grew, and bustling cities sprang up. However, these economic changes strained Japanese society. Many daimyo suffered financial hardship. They needed money in a commercial economy, but a daimyo's wealth was in land rather than cash. Lesser samurai were unhappy, too, because they lacked the money to live as well as urban merchants.

Merchants in turn resented their place at the bottom of the social ladder. No matter how rich they were, they had no political power. Peasants, meanwhile, suffered under heavy taxes.

The government responded by trying to revive old ways, <u>emphasizing</u> farming over commerce and praising traditional values. These efforts had scant success. By the 1800s, shoguns were no longer strong leaders, and corruption was common. Discontent simmered throughout Japan.

✓ **Checkpoint** By the mid-1800s, why did so many groups of people in Japan feel discontented?

Japan Opens Up

While the shoguns faced troubles at home, disturbing news of the British victory over China in the Opium War and the way in which imperialists had forced China to sign unequal treaties reached Japan. Surely, Japanese officials reasoned, it would not be long before Western powers turned towards Japan.

External Pressure and Internal Revolt The officials' fears were correct. In July 1853, a fleet of well-armed American ships commanded by Commodore **Matthew Perry** sailed into lower Tokyo Bay. Perry carried a letter from Millard Fillmore, the President of the United States. The letter demanded that Japan open its ports to diplomatic and commercial exchange.

The shogun's advisors debated what to do. Japan did not have the ability to defend itself against the powerful United States Navy. In the Treaty of Kanagawa in 1854, the shogun Iesada agreed to open two Japanese ports to American ships, though not for trade.

The United States soon won trading and other rights, including extraterritoriality and low taxes on American imports. European nations demanded and won similar rights. Like the Chinese, the Japanese felt humiliated by the terms of these unequal treaties. Some bitterly criticized the shogun for not taking a strong stand against the foreigners.

Vocabulary Builder

emphasizing—(EM fuh syz ing) *vt.* stressing

In the Japanese woodblock print below, Japanese boats go out to meet one of Commodore Matthew Perry's ships in Tokyo Bay. In response to Perry's expedition, the Japanese statesman Lord Ii considered Japan's strategy toward contact with foreign powers:

Primary Source

❝There is a saying that when one is besieged in a castle, to raise the drawbridge is to imprison oneself. . . . Even though the Shogun's ancestors set up seclusion laws, they left the Dutch and Chinese to act as a bridge. . . . Might this bridge not now be of advantage to us in handling foreign affairs, providing us with the means whereby we may for a time avert the outbreak of hostilities and then, after some time has elapsed, gain a complete victory?❞

Traveler's Tales
EYEWITNESS ACCOUNT

Japanese Diplomat
Fukuzawa Yukichi Visits America

In 1860, writer and educator Fukuzawa Yukichi (1835–1901) joined the first Japanese diplomatic mission to the United States. When he returned home, he wrote articles and books explaining Western customs and practices to the Japanese. In this selection from his autobiography, Fukuzawa recalls his early impressions of San Francisco and discusses some of the differences between American and Japanese cultures and attitudes.

Foreign pressure deepened the social and economic unrest. In 1867, discontented daimyo and samurai led a revolt that unseated the shogun and "restored" the 15-year-old emperor Mutsuhito to power. When he was crowned emperor, Mutsuhito took the name Meiji (MAY jee), which means "enlightened rule." He moved from the old imperial capital in Kyoto to the shogun's palace in Edo, which was renamed **Tokyo,** or "eastern capital."

The Meiji Restoration The young emperor began a long reign known as the **Meiji Restoration.** This period, which lasted from 1868 to 1912, was a major turning point in Japanese history. The Meiji reformers, who ruled in the emperor's name, were determined to strengthen Japan. Their goal was summarized in their motto, "A rich country, a strong military." The emperor supported and embodied the reforms.

The new leaders set out to study Western ways, adapt them to Japanese needs, and <u>thereby</u> keep Japan from having to give in to Western demands. In 1871, members of the government traveled overseas to learn about Western governments, economies, technology, and customs. The government brought experts from Western countries to Japan and sent young samurai to study abroad, furthering Japan's knowledge of Western industrial techniques.

Vocabulary Builder
<u>thereby</u>—(THEHR by) *adv.* by that means, because of that

✔ **Checkpoint**   How did Japan react when it was forced to accept unequal treaties?

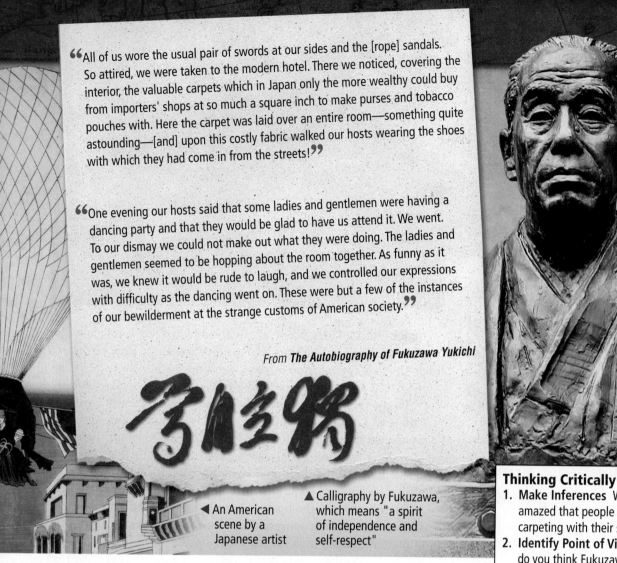

"All of us wore the usual pair of swords at our sides and the [rope] sandals. So attired, we were taken to the modern hotel. There we noticed, covering the interior, the valuable carpets which in Japan only the more wealthy could buy from importers' shops at so much a square inch to make purses and tobacco pouches with. Here the carpet was laid over an entire room—something quite astounding—[and] upon this costly fabric walked our hosts wearing the shoes with which they had come in from the streets!"

"One evening our hosts said that some ladies and gentlemen were having a dancing party and that they would be glad to have us attend it. We went. To our dismay we could not make out what they were doing. The ladies and gentlemen seemed to be hopping about the room together. As funny as it was, we knew it would be rude to laugh, and we controlled our expressions with difficulty as the dancing went on. These were but a few of the instances of our bewilderment at the strange customs of American society."

From *The Autobiography of Fukuzawa Yukichi*

◀ Fukuzawa Yukichi

◀ An American scene by a Japanese artist

▲ Calligraphy by Fukuzawa, which means "a spirit of independence and self-respect"

Thinking Critically
1. **Make Inferences** Why is Fukuzawa amazed that people in America walk on carpeting with their shoes on?
2. **Identify Point of View** What opinion do you think Fukuzawa has of American culture?

The Meiji Transformation

The Meiji reformers faced an enormous task. They were committed to replacing the rigid feudal order with a completely new political and social system and to building a modern industrial economy. Change did not come easily. In the end, however, Japan adapted foreign ideas with great speed and success.

A Modern Government The reformers wanted to create a strong central government, equal to those of Western powers. After studying various European governments, they adapted the German model. In 1889, the emperor issued the Meiji constitution. It set forth the principle that all citizens were equal before the law. Like the German system, however, it gave the emperor autocratic, or absolute, power. A legislature, or **Diet**, was formed, made up of one elected house and one house appointed by the emperor. Additionally, voting rights were sharply limited.

Japan then established a Western-style bureaucracy with separate departments to supervise finance, the army, the navy, and education. To strengthen the military, it turned to Western technology and ended the special privilege of samurai. In the past, samurai alone were warriors. In modern Japan, as in the West, all men were subject to military service.

Investment in Meiji Japan

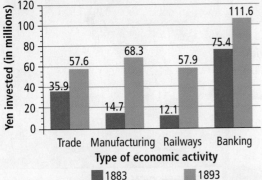

Yen invested (in millions)

Type of economic activity	1883	1893
Trade	35.9	57.6
Manufacturing	14.7	68.3
Railways	12.1	57.9
Banking	75.4	111.6

Chart Skills Japanese women (above) work in a silk manufacturing factory in the 1890s. *How does the graph reflect the Meiji reformers' drive to industrialize Japan?*

SOURCE: S. Uyehara, *The Industry and Trade of Japan*

Industrialization Meiji leaders made the economy a major priority. They encouraged Japan's businesses to adopt Western methods. They set up a modern banking system, built railroads, improved ports, and organized a telegraph and postal system.

To get industries started, the government typically built factories and then sold them to wealthy business families who developed them further. With such support, business dynasties like the Kawasaki family soon ruled over industrial empires. These powerful banking and industrial families were known as **zaibatsu** (zy baht soo).

By the 1890s, industry was booming. With modern machines, silk manufacturing soared. Shipyards, copper and coal mining, and steel making also helped make Japan an industrial powerhouse. As in other industrial countries, the population grew rapidly, and many peasants flocked to the growing cities for work.

Changes in Society The constitution ended legal distinctions between classes, thus allowing more people to become involved in nation building. The government set up schools and a university. It hired Westerners to teach the new generation how to use modern technology.

Despite the reforms, class distinctions survived in Japan as they did in the West. Also, although literacy increased and some women gained an education, women in general were still assigned a secondary role in society. The reform of the Japanese family system, and women's position in it, became the topic of major debates in the 1870s. Although the government agreed to some increases in education for women, it dealt harshly with other attempts at change. After 1898, Japanese women were forbidden any political participation and legally were lumped together with minors.

An Amazing Success Japan modernized with amazing speed during the Meiji period. Its success was due to a number of causes. Japan had a strong sense of identity, partly because it had a **homogeneous society**—that is, its people shared a common culture and language. Economic growth during Tokugawa times had set Japan on the road to development. Japan also had experience in learning and adapting ideas from foreign nations, such as China.

The Japanese were determined to resist foreign rule. By the 1890s, Japan was strong enough to force Western powers to revise the unequal treaties. By then, it was already acquiring its own overseas empire.

✔ **Checkpoint** What changes did the reforms of the Meiji Restoration bring about in Japan?

Japan's Growing Military Strength

As in Western industrial nations, Japan's economic needs fed its imperialist desires. As a small island nation, Japan lacked many basic resources that were essential for industrial growth. It depended on other countries to obtain raw materials. Spurred by this dependency and a strong ambition to equal the West, Japan sought to build an empire. With its modern army and navy, it maneuvered for power in East Asia.

Korea in the Middle Imperialist rivalries put the spotlight on Korea. Located at a crossroads of East Asia, the Korean peninsula was a focus of competition among Russia, China, and Japan. Korea had been a tributary state to China for many years. A tributary state is a state that is independent but acknowledges the supremacy of a stronger state. Although influenced by China, Korea had its own traditions and government. Korea had also shut its doors to foreigners. It did, however, maintain relations with China and sometimes with Japan.

By the 1800s, Korea faced pressure from outsiders. As Chinese power declined, Russia expanded into East Asia. Then, as Japan industrialized, it too eyed Korea. In 1876, Japan used its superior power to force Korea to open its ports to Japanese trade. Faced with similar demands from Western powers, Korea had to accept unequal treaties.

Japan Gains Power As Japan extended its influence in Korea, it came into conflict with China. In 1894, competition between Japan and China in Korea led to the **First Sino-Japanese War.** ("Sino" means "Chinese.") Although China had greater resources, Japan had benefited from modernization. To the surprise of China and the West, Japan won easily. It used its victory to gain treaty ports in China and control over the island of Taiwan, thus joining the West in the race for empire.

Japan Rising
In this political cartoon, Japan is depicted marching over Korea on its way to Russia. *Why would Russia feel threatened by Japan's aggression in Korea?*

■ COMPARING VIEWPOINTS

Colonization in Korea

The excerpts below present two different views of the effect of Japan's control of Korea in the early 1900s. **Critical Thinking** *How do the two views on the results of colonization in Korea differ?*

Positive Effects	**Negative Effects**
Mining, fishery, and manufacturing have advanced. The bald mountains have been covered with young trees. Trade has increased by leaps and bounds.... Study what we are doing in Korea.... Japan is a steward on whom devolves [falls] the gigantic task of uplifting the Far East. —*Japanese academic Nitobe Inazo*	The result of annexation, brought about without any conference with the Korean people, is that the Japanese ... by a false set of figures show a profit and loss account between us two peoples most untrue, digging a trench of everlasting resentment deeper and deeper.... —*From the Declaration of Korean Independence, 1919*

Ten years later, Japan successfully challenged Russia, its other rival for power in Korea and Manchuria. During the **Russo-Japanese War,** Japan's armies defeated Russian troops in Manchuria, and its navy destroyed almost an entire Russian fleet. For the first time in modern history, an Asian power humbled a European nation. In the 1905 Treaty of Portsmouth, Japan gained control of Korea as well as rights in parts of Manchuria.

Japan Rules Korea Japan made Korea a protectorate. In 1910, it annexed Korea outright, absorbing the kingdom into the Japanese empire. Japan ruled Korea for 35 years. Like Western imperialists, the Japanese set out to modernize their newly acquired territory. They built factories, railroads, and communications systems. Development, however, generally benefited Japan. Under Japanese rule, Koreans produced more rice than ever before, but most of it went to Japan.

The Japanese were as unpopular in Korea as Western imperialists were elsewhere. They imposed harsh rule on their colony and deliberately set out to erase the Korean language and identity. Repression bred resentment. And resentment, in turn, nourished a Korean nationalist movement.

Nine years after annexation, a nonviolent protest against the Japanese began on March 1, 1919, and soon spread throughout Korea. The Japanese crushed the uprising and massacred many Koreans. The violence did not discourage people who worked to end Japanese rule. Instead, the March First Movement became a rallying symbol for Korean nationalists.

The Koreans would have to wait many years for freedom. Japan continued to expand in East Asia during the years that followed, seeking natural resources and territory. By the early 1900s, Japan was the strongest power in Asia.

✓ **Checkpoint** How did industrialization help start Japan on an imperialist course?

The Japanese in Korea
In this illustration, Japanese soldiers march into Seoul, Korea's capital city. Japan controlled Korea from 1905 until 1945.

SECTION 1 Assessment

Progress Monitoring *Online*
For: Self-quiz with vocabulary practice
Web Code: naa-2511

Terms, People, and Places

1. Place each of the terms listed at the beginning of the section into one of the following categories: politics, culture, or economics. Write a sentence for each term explaining your choice.

Note Taking

2. **Reading Strategy: Identify Causes and Effects** Use your completed chart to answer the section Focus Question: How did Japan become a modern industrial power, and what did it do with its new strength?

Comprehension and Critical Thinking

3. **Identify Central Issues** What problems weakened shogun rule in Japan in the mid-1800s?

4. **Recognize Causes** What caused Japan to end over 200 years of seclusion?

5. **Draw Conclusions** List three ways in which Japan modernized. Explain how each of these actions helped strengthen Japan so it could resist Western pressure.

6. **Connect to Geography** Why was control of Korea desirable to both China and Japan?

● **Writing About History**

Quick Write: Choose a Topic When you write for assessment, you may occasionally be given a choice of topics. In that case, quickly jot down notes you could use to answer each prompt. Then, choose the prompt you know the most about. Practice this process using the two sample prompts below. Jot down notes about each prompt, choose one, and then write a sentence explaining why you chose that prompt.

• Explain how Japan modernized under the Meiji reformers.
• Summarize how and why Korea became a Japanese colony.

A European woman being transported in a rickshaw in French Indochina

Currency from a British colony in Malaya

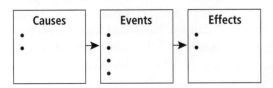

WITNESS HISTORY 🔊 AUDIO

A Patriot's Dilemma

In 1867, Phan Thanh Gian, a Vietnamese official, faced a dilemma. The French were threatening to invade. As a patriot, Phan Thanh Gian wanted to resist. But as a devoted follower of Confucius, he was obliged "to live in obedience to reason." And based on the power of the French military, he concluded that the only reasonable course was to surrender:

66 The French have immense warships, filled with soldiers and armed with huge cannons. No one can resist them. They go where they want, the strongest [walls] fall before them. 99

Focus Question How did industrialized powers divide up Southeast Asia and the Pacific, and how did the colonized peoples react?

Imperialism in Southeast Asia and the Pacific

GA **Performance Standards**

• **SSWH15d** Describe how geography and resources influenced French policy in Indochina.

Terms, People, and Places

French Indochina   Spanish-American War
Mongkut   Liliuokalani

Note Taking

Reading Skill: Identify Causes and Effects As you read, fill in a flowchart similar to the one below to record the causes, events, and effects of imperialism in Southeast Asia and the Pacific.

Causes	Events	Effects
• •	• • • •	• •

Leaders throughout Southeast Asia faced the same dilemma as Phan Thanh Gian did in 1867. As they had in Africa, Western industrial powers divided up the region in search of raw materials, new markets, and Christian converts.

Europeans Colonize Southeast Asia

Southeast Asia commands the sea lanes between India and China. The region had been influenced by both civilizations. From the 1500s through the 1700s, European merchants gained footholds in Southeast Asia, but most of the area remained independent. This changed in the 1800s. Westerners—notably the Dutch, British, and French—manipulated local rivalries and used modern armies and technology to colonize much of Southeast Asia.

The Dutch East Indies Established During the early 1600s, the Dutch East India Company established bases on the island of Java and in the Moluccas, or Spice Islands. From there, the Dutch slowly expanded to dominate the rest of the Dutch East Indies (now Indonesia). The Dutch expected their Southeast Asian colonies to produce profitable crops of coffee, indigo, and spices.

The British in Burma and Malaya In the early 1800s, rulers of Burma (present-day Myanmar) clashed with the British, who were expanding eastward from India. The Burmese suffered disastrous defeats in several wars. They continued to resist British rule, however, even after Britain annexed Burma in 1886.

At the same time, the British expanded their influence in Malaya. The busy port of Singapore grew up at the southern tip of the peninsula. Soon, natural resources and profits from Asian trade flowed through Singapore to enrich Britain.

French Indochina Seized The French, meanwhile, were building an empire on the Southeast Asian mainland. In the 1500s, Portuguese traders had set up a trading center in what today is Vietnam. Christian missionaries from France and other European countries moved into Vietnam and won some converts. Threatened by growing Western influence, Vietnamese officials tried to suppress Christianity by killing converts and missionary priests. Partly in response, France invaded Vietnam in 1858. The French also wanted more influence and markets in Southeast Asia.

The Vietnamese fought fiercely but could not withstand superior European firepower. By the early 1860s, France had seized a portion of southern Vietnam. Over the next decades, the French took over the rest of Vietnam and all of Laos and Cambodia. The French and other Westerners referred to these holdings as **French Indochina.** (Mainland Southeast Asia was known during this period as "Indochina.")

Siam Survives The kingdom of Siam (present-day Thailand) lay between British-ruled Burma and French Indochina. The king of Siam, **Mongkut** (mahng KOOT), who ruled from 1851 to 1868, did not underestimate Western power. He studied foreign languages and read widely on modern science and mathematics. He used this knowledge to negotiate with the Western powers and satisfy their goals in Siam by making agreements in unequal treaties. In this way, Siam escaped becoming a European colony.

Mongkut and his son, Chulalongkorn, (CHOO lah lawng kawrn) set Siam on the road to modernization. They reformed the government, modernized the army, and hired Western experts to teach Thais how to use the new technology. They abolished slavery and gave women some choice in marriage. As Siam modernized, Chulalongkorn bargained to remove the unequal treaties.

Colonial Southeast Asia During this period, many Chinese people migrated to Southeast Asia to take advantage of the economic opportunities there. They left China to escape hardship and turmoil. Despite local resentment, these communities formed vital networks in trade, banking, and other economic activities.

By the 1890s, Europeans controlled most of Southeast Asia. They introduced modern technology and expanded commerce and industry. Europeans directed the mining of tin, the harvesting of rubber, and the building of harbors and railroads. But these changes benefited the European colonizers far more than they did the Southeast Asians.

✔ **Checkpoint** How did the Burmese and the Vietnamese respond to attempts to colonize them?

Two Paths in Southeast Asia
King Mongkut of Siam managed to keep his kingdom out of European control. In other parts of Southeast Asia, colonized peoples labored to produce export crops for their colonial rulers. Below, workers process sugar cane in the Philippines in the early 1900s.

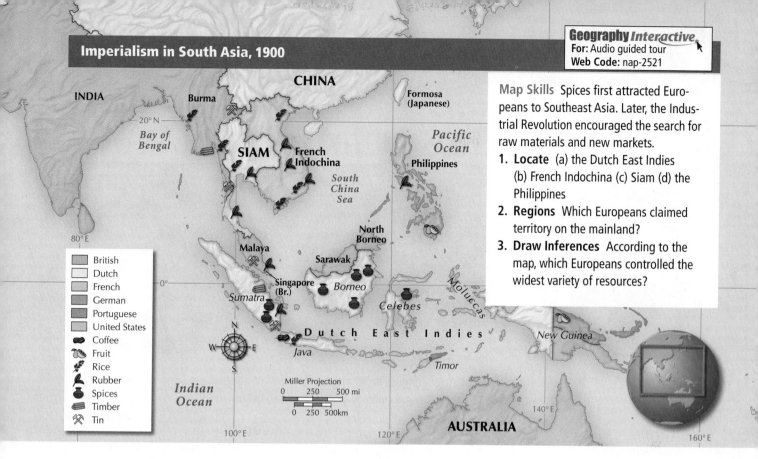

Geography *Interactive*
For: Audio guided tour
Web Code: nap-2521

CHINA

INDIA

Burma

20° N

Bay of Bengal

SIAM

French Indochina

Formosa (Japanese)

Pacific Ocean

Philippines

South China Sea

80° E

North Borneo

Malaya

Sarawak

Singapore (Br.)

Borneo

Sumatra

0°

Celebes

Moluccas

Java

D u t c h   E a s t   I n d i e s

New Guinea

Timor

Indian Ocean

Miller Projection

0   250   500 mi

0   250 500km

AUSTRALIA

100° E

120° E

140° E

160° E

British
Dutch
French
German
Portuguese
United States
Coffee
Fruit
Rice
Rubber
Spices
Timber
Tin

Map Skills Spices first attracted Europeans to Southeast Asia. Later, the Industrial Revolution encouraged the search for raw materials and new markets.

1. **Locate** (a) the Dutch East Indies (b) French Indochina (c) Siam (d) the Philippines
2. **Regions** Which Europeans claimed territory on the mainland?
3. **Draw Inferences** According to the map, which Europeans controlled the widest variety of resources?

The United States and the Philippines

In the 1500s, Spain had seized the Philippines. Catholic missionaries spread Christianity among the Filipinos. As the Catholic Church gained enormous power and wealth, many Filipinos accused the Church of abusing its position. By the late 1800s, their anger fueled strong resistance to Spanish rule.

The opening of the Suez Canal in 1860 helped the economy of the Philippines by making trade with European countries easier. Some upper class Filipinos gained access to better education. Leaders such as José Rizal inspired Filipinos to work to gain better treatment from Spain.

The **Spanish-American War** broke out in 1898 between Spain and the United States over Cuba's attempts to win independence from Spain. During the war, American battleships destroyed the Spanish fleet, which was stationed in the Philippines. Encouraged by American naval officers, Filipino rebel leaders declared independence from Spain. Rebel soldiers threw their support into the fight against Spanish troops.

In return for their help, the Filipino rebels expected the Americans to recognize their independence. Instead, in the treaty that ended the war with Spain, the United States agreed to give Spain $20 million in return for control of the Philippines. Within the United States, debate raged over the treaty's ratification. American imperialists wanted to join the European competition for territory. Anti-imperialists wanted the United States to steer clear of foreign entanglements. The United States Senate ratified the treaty by only one vote over the required two-thirds majority.

Bitterly disappointed, Filipino nationalists renewed their struggle. From 1899 to 1901, Filipinos led by Emilio Aguinaldo (ah gee NAHL doh) battled American forces. Thousands of Americans and hundreds of thousands of Filipinos died. In the end, the Americans crushed the rebellion.

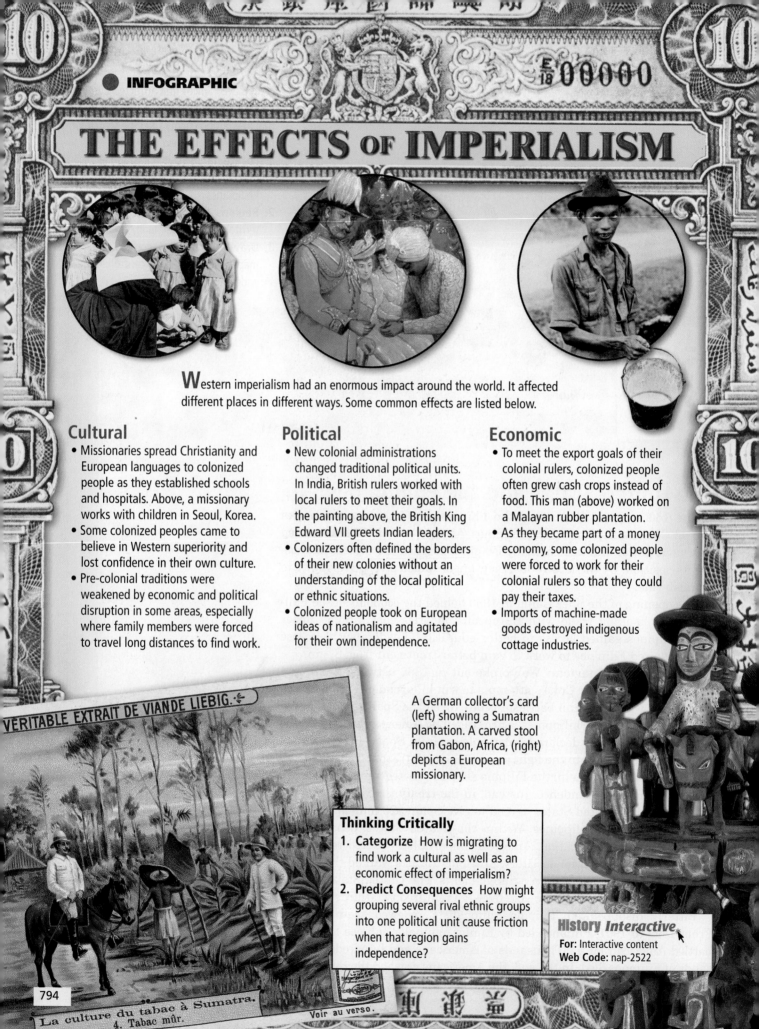

INFOGRAPHIC

THE EFFECTS OF IMPERIALISM

Western imperialism had an enormous impact around the world. It affected different places in different ways. Some common effects are listed below.

Cultural

- Missionaries spread Christianity and European languages to colonized people as they established schools and hospitals. Above, a missionary works with children in Seoul, Korea.
- Some colonized peoples came to believe in Western superiority and lost confidence in their own culture.
- Pre-colonial traditions were weakened by economic and political disruption in some areas, especially where family members were forced to travel long distances to find work.

Political

- New colonial administrations changed traditional political units. In India, British rulers worked with local rulers to meet their goals. In the painting above, the British King Edward VII greets Indian leaders.
- Colonizers often defined the borders of their new colonies without an understanding of the local political or ethnic situations.
- Colonized people took on European ideas of nationalism and agitated for their own independence.

Economic

- To meet the export goals of their colonial rulers, colonized people often grew cash crops instead of food. This man (above) worked on a Malayan rubber plantation.
- As they became part of a money economy, some colonized people were forced to work for their colonial rulers so that they could pay their taxes.
- Imports of machine-made goods destroyed indigenous cottage industries.

VERITABLE EXTRAIT DE VIANDE LIEBIG.

A German collector's card (left) showing a Sumatran plantation. A carved stool from Gabon, Africa, (right) depicts a European missionary.

La culture du tabac à Sumatra.
4. Tabac mûr.

Voir au verso.

Thinking Critically
1. **Categorize** How is migrating to find work a cultural as well as an economic effect of imperialism?
2. **Predict Consequences** How might grouping several rival ethnic groups into one political unit cause friction when that region gains independence?

History Interactive

For: Interactive content
Web Code: nap-2522

The United States set out to modernize the Philippines through education, improved health care, and economic reforms. The United States also built dams, roads, railways, and ports. In addition, the United States promised Filipinos a gradual <u>transition</u> to self-rule some time in the future.

✓ **Checkpoint** How did the United States gain control of the Philippines?

Vocabulary Builder

transition—(tran ZISH un) *n.* passage from one way to another

Western Powers Seize the Pacific Islands

In the 1800s, the industrialized powers also began to take an interest in the islands of the Pacific. The thousands of islands splashed across the Pacific include the three regions of Melanesia, Micronesia, and Polynesia.

At first, American, French, and British whaling and sealing ships looked for bases to take on supplies in the Pacific. Missionaries, too, moved into the region and opened the way for political involvement.

In 1878, the United States secured an unequal treaty from Samoa, a group of islands in the South Pacific. The United States gained rights such as extraterritoriality and a naval station. Other nations gained similar agreements. As their rivalry increased, the United States, Germany, and Britain agreed to a triple protectorate over Samoa.

Beginning in the mid-1800s, American sugar growers pressed for power in the Hawaiian Islands. When the Hawaiian queen **Liliuokalani** (lih lee uh oh kuh LAH nee) tried to reduce foreign influence, American planters overthrew her in 1893. They then asked the United States to annex Hawaii, which it finally did in 1898. Supporters of annexation argued that if the United States did not take Hawaii, Britain or Japan might do so. By 1900, the United States, Britain, France, and Germany had claimed nearly every island in the Pacific.

✓ **Checkpoint** Why did some Americans think the United States should control Hawaii?

SECTION 2 Assessment

Progress Monitoring Online
For: Self-quiz with vocabulary practice
Web Code: naa-2521

Terms, People, and Places

1. For each term, person, or place listed at the beginning of the section, write a sentence explaining its significance.

Note Taking

2. **Reading Strategy: Identify Causes and Effects** Use your completed chart to answer the Focus Question: How did industrialized powers divide up Southeast Asia and the Pacific, and how did the colonized peoples react?

Comprehension and Critical Thinking

3. **Summarize** What steps did Siam take to preserve its independence?
4. **Draw Conclusions** Why were Filipino rebels disappointed when the United States took control of the Philippines?
5. **Synthesize Information** How did Hawaii become part of the United States?
6. **Make Comparisons** Compare the partition of Southeast Asia to the partition of Africa. How was it similar? How was it different?

● **Writing About History**

Quick Write: Examine the Question To answer a short answer or extended-response question effectively, first examine the question. Look for key words like *explain, compare,* or *persuade,* which will tell you what type of answer to provide. Then look for words that signal the topic. Identifying key words will help you focus and organize your response. Copy the prompt below and underline its key words.

• Compare Siam's relationship with imperial powers to that of Vietnam.

Settler's Log House (above) was painted in 1856 by a Dutch immigrant to Canada, Cornelius Krieghoff. The maple leaf (above right) is an emblem of Canada.

WITNESS HISTORY 🔊 AUDIO

O Canada!

In the early 1860s, the separate colonies of British North America considered whether they should join together to create one powerful confederation—Canada. George Brown, an influential politician who helped bring about the confederation, shared his dream for Canada:

❝ Sir, it may be that some among us will live to see the day when, as the result of [the confederation], a great and powerful people may have grown up in these lands—when the boundless forests all around us shall have given way to smiling fields and thriving towns—and when one united government, under the British flag, shall extend from shore to shore. ❞

Focus Question How were the British colonies of Canada, Australia, and New Zealand settled, and how did they win self-rule?

Self-Rule for Canada, Australia, and New Zealand

 Performance Standards

• **SSWH10a** Explain the roles of Magellan and James Cook.

Terms, People, and Places

confederation
dominion
métis

indigenous
penal colony
Maori

Note Taking

Reading Skill: Identify Cause and Effects As you read, record the causes and effects of the events you read about in a chart like this one.

Cause	Event	Effect
Loyalist Americans flee to Canada.	Up to 30,000 loyalists settle in Canada.	Ethnic tensions arise between English- and French-speaking Canadians.

Canada, Australia, and New Zealand won independence faster and easier than other British colonies in Africa or Asia. The language and cultural roots they shared with Britain helped. Racial attitudes also played a part. Imperialists in nations like Britain felt that whites, unlike non-whites, were capable of governing themselves.

Canada Achieves Self-Rule

When France lost Canada to Britain in 1763, thousands of French-speaking Catholic settlers remained. After the American Revolution, about 30,000 British loyalists fled to Canada. They were English-speaking Protestants. In addition, in the 1790s, several groups of Native American peoples still lived in eastern Canada. Others, in the west and the north, had not yet come into contact with European settlers.

Unrest in the Two Canadas To ease ethnic tensions, Britain passed the Constitutional Act of 1791. The act created two provinces: English-speaking Upper Canada (now Ontario) and French-speaking Lower Canada (now Quebec). French traditions and the Catholic Church were protected in Lower Canada. English traditions and laws guided Upper Canada.

During the early 1800s, unrest grew in both colonies. The people of Upper Canada resented the power held by a small group of elites who controlled the government. Lower Canada had similar problems. In 1837, discontent flared into rebellion in both places. Louis Joseph Papineau, the head of the French Canadian Reform party, led the rebellion in Lower Canada. William Lyon Mackenzie led the revolt in Upper Canada, crying, "Put down the villains who oppress and enslave our country!"

Britain Responds The British had learned from the American Revolution. While they hurried to put down the disorder, they sent an able politician, Lord Durham, to <u>compile</u> a report on the causes of the unrest. In 1840, Parliament acted on some of Durham's recommendations by passing the Act of Union. The act joined the two Canadas into one province. It also gave them an elected legislature that determined some domestic policies. Britain still controlled foreign policy and trade.

Canada Becomes a Dominion In the mid-1800s, thousands of English, Scottish, and Irish people immigrated to Canada. As the country grew, two Canadians, John Macdonald and George Étienne Cartier, urged **confederation,** or unification, of Britain's North American colonies. These colonies included Nova Scotia, New Brunswick, Prince Edward Island, and British Columbia, as well as the united Upper and Lower Canadas. The two leaders felt that confederation would strengthen the new nation against American ambitions and help its economic development.

Britain finally agreed, passing the British North America Act of 1867. The act created the Dominion of Canada. A **dominion** is a self-governing nation. As a dominion, Canada had its own parliament, modeled on that

Vocabulary Builder

<u>compile</u>—(kum PYL) *vt.* to put together from several sources

Geography *Interactive*
For: Audio guided tour
Web Code: nap-2531

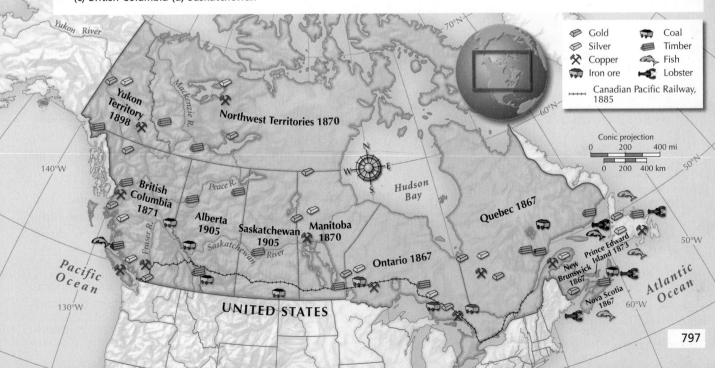

Canada, 1867–1914

Map Skills Canada grew throughout the latter half of the 1800s.
1. **Locate:** (a) Quebec (b) Ontario (c) British Columbia (d) Saskatchewan

2. **Movement** Why did British Columbia become a part of Canada before Alberta and Saskatchewan?

3. **Make Comparisons** Compare Nova Scotia's natural resources to those of Manitoba.

of Britain. By 1900, Canada also had some control over its own foreign policy. Still, Canada maintained close ties with Britain.

Canada Grows Like the United States, Canada expanded westward in the 1800s. In 1885, the Canadian Pacific Railway opened, linking eastern and western Canada. Wherever the railroad went, settlers followed. It moved people and products, such as timber and manufactured goods across the country. In the late 1800s and early 1900s, more immigrants flooded into Canada from Germany, Italy, Poland, Russia, Ukraine, China, and Japan. They enriched Canada's economy and culture.

As in the United States, westward expansion destroyed the way of life of Native Americans in Canada. Most were forced to sign treaties giving up their lands. Some resisted. In central Canada, Louis Riel led a revolt of the **métis,** people of mixed Native American and French Canadian descent, in 1869 and again in 1885. Many métis were French-speaking Catholics who believed that the government was trying to take their land and destroy their language and religion. Government troops put down both uprisings. Riel was executed in 1885.

By 1914, Canada was a flourishing nation. Still, French-speaking Canadians were determined to preserve their separate heritage, making it hard for Canadians to create a single national identity. Also, the cultural and economic influence of the United States threatened to dominate Canada. Both issues continue to affect Canada today.

✔ **Checkpoint** How did the British respond to the Canadians' desire for self-rule?

Europeans in Australia

The Dutch in the 1600s were the first Europeans to reach Australia. In 1770, Captain James Cook claimed Australia for Britain. For a time, however, Australia remained too distant to attract European settlers.

The First Settlers Like most regions claimed by imperialist powers, Australia had long been inhabited by other people. The first settlers had reached Australia perhaps 40,000 years earlier, probably from Southeast Asia, and spread across the continent. These **indigenous,** or original, people were called Aborigines, a word used by Europeans to denote the earliest people to live in a place. Today, many Australian Aborigines call themselves Kooris. Isolated from the larger world, the Aborigines lived in small hunting and food-gathering bands, much as their Stone Age ancestors had. Aboriginal groups spoke as many as 250 distinct languages. When white settlers arrived in Australia, the indigenous population suffered disastrously.

A Penal Colony During the 1700s, Britain had sent convicts to its North American colonies, especially to Georgia. The American Revolution closed that outlet. Prisons in London and other cities were jammed.

To fill the need for prisons, Britain made Australia into a **penal colony,** or a place where convicted

Life in Australia
Australian Aborigines used boomerangs, like this one decorated with traditional motifs, to hunt and in battles. The first British settlers in Australia were convicted criminals. The convicts in the illustration below are being forced to carry heavy loads of shingles as part of their hard labor. *What happened to Aborigines as British settlement spread?*

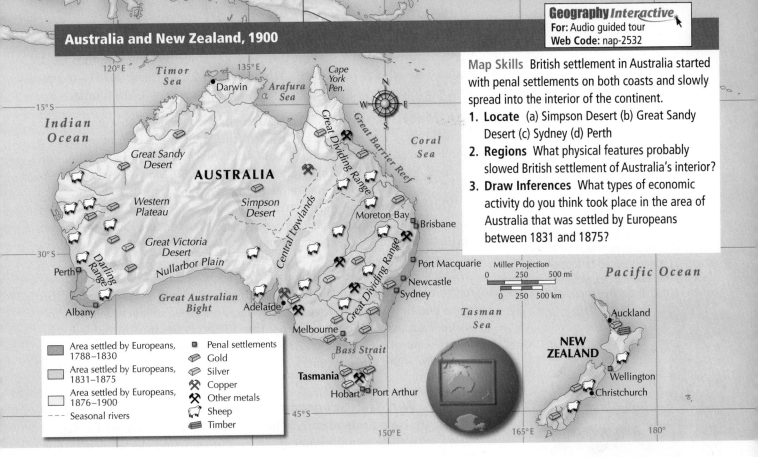

Geography *Interactive*
For: Audio guided tour
Web Code: nap-2532

Map Skills British settlement in Australia started with penal settlements on both coasts and slowly spread into the interior of the continent.

1. **Locate** (a) Simpson Desert (b) Great Sandy Desert (c) Sydney (d) Perth
2. **Regions** What physical features probably slowed British settlement of Australia's interior?
3. **Draw Inferences** What types of economic activity do you think took place in the area of Australia that was settled by Europeans between 1831 and 1875?

Map legend:
- Area settled by Europeans, 1788–1830
- Area settled by Europeans, 1831–1875
- Area settled by Europeans, 1876–1900
- Seasonal rivers
- Penal settlements
- Gold
- Silver
- Copper
- Other metals
- Sheep
- Timber

criminals are sent to be punished. The first British ships, carrying about 700 convicts, arrived in Botany Bay, Australia, in 1788. The people who survived the grueling eight-month voyage faced more hardships on shore. Many were city dwellers with no farming skills. Under the brutal discipline of soldiers, work gangs cleared land for settlement.

The Colonies Grow In the early 1800s, Britain encouraged free citizens to emigrate to Australia by offering them land and tools. A prosperous wool industry grew up as settlers found that the land and climate suited sheepherding. In 1851, a gold rush in eastern Australia brought a population boom. Many gold hunters stayed on to become ranchers and farmers. They pushed into the rugged interior known as the Outback, carving out huge sheep ranches and wheat farms. As the newcomers settled in, they thrust aside or killed the Aborigines.

Achieving Self-Government Like Canada, Australia was made up of separate colonies scattered around the continent. Britain worried about interference from other European powers. To counter this threat and to boost development, it responded to Australian demands for self-rule. In 1901, Britain helped the colonies unite into the independent Commonwealth of Australia. The new country kept its ties to Britain by recognizing the British monarch as its head of state.

The Australian constitution drew on both British and American models. Unlike Britain and the United States, Australia quickly granted women the right to vote. In 1856, it also became the first nation to introduce the secret ballot.

✔ **Checkpoint** What effect did colonization have on Australia's indigenous population?

New Zealand's Story

To the southeast of Australia lies New Zealand. In 1769, Captain Cook claimed its islands for Britain. Missionaries landed there in 1814 to convert the indigenous people, the **Maori** (MAH oh ree), to Christianity.

The Maori Struggle Unlike Australia, where the Aborigines were spread thinly across a large continent, the Maori were concentrated in a smaller area. They were descended from seafaring people who had reached New Zealand from Polynesia in the 1200s. The Maori were settled farmers. They were also determined to defend their land.

White settlers, who were attracted by New Zealand's mild climate and good soil, followed the missionaries. These settlers introduced sheep and cattle and were soon exporting wool, mutton, and beef. In 1840, Britain annexed New Zealand.

As colonists poured in, they took over more and more of the land, leading to fierce wars with the Maori. Many Maori died in the struggle. Still more perished from disease, alcoholism, and other misfortunes that followed European colonization. By the 1870s, resistance crumbled. The Maori population had fallen drastically, from about 200,000 to less than 45,000 in 1896. Only recently has the Maori population started to grow once more.

Settlers Win Self-Government Like settlers in Australia and Canada, white New Zealanders sought self-rule. In 1907, they won independence, with their own parliament, prime minister, and elected legislature. They, too, preserved close ties to the British empire.

✔ **Checkpoint** Compare and contrast the European settlement of Australia and New Zealand.

Maori Traditions

The portrait below shows a Maori leader in 1882. Many Maori men of high social standing commissioned tattoos on their faces. Maori war canoes, like the one below, often carried distinctive carving.

SECTION 3 Assessment

Terms, People, and Places

1. For each term, person, or place listed at the beginning of the section, write a sentence explaining its significance.

Note Taking

2. **Reading Skill: Identify Causes and Effects** Use your completed chart to answer the Focus Question: How were the British colonies of Canada, Australia, and New Zealand settled, and how did they win self-rule?

Comprehension and Critical Thinking

3. **Sequence** What steps led to Canadian self-rule?
4. **Compare** Compare the European settlement of Australia with that of Canada.
5. **Identify Causes** Why did the Maori fight colonists in New Zealand?
6. **Synthesize Information** What ethnic tensions did Australia, Canada, and New Zealand face?

● Writing About History

Quick Write: Focus Your Time To stay focused as you respond to a short answer or extended-response question on a test, plan to spend a quarter of the allotted time on prewriting, half on drafting, and the remaining quarter on revising. Write a short answer response to the following prompt using a 20-minute time limit. Time yourself to practice staying within the appropriate time limit during each stage.

• Compare how Canada and Australia gained self-rule.

Benito Juárez, Mexican president and national hero, stands firm against foreign intervention in this fresco by artist Gonzales Orozco.

Sugar cane, a Latin American cash crop

WITNESS HISTORY ◀)) AUDIO

La Reforma

The Mexican reformer Benito Juárez criticized the continuing inequality in Mexico:

❝ The constitution of 1824 was a compromise between progress and reaction, and [that compromise was a] seedbed of the incessant convulsions [disorders] that the Republic has suffered, and that it will still suffer while society does not recover its balance by making effective the equality of rights and duties of all citizens and of all persons who inhabit the national territory, without privileges, without exemptions [exceptions], without monopolies, and without odious distinctions . . . . ❞

Focus Question How did Latin American nations struggle for stability, and how did industrialized nations affect them?

Economic Imperialism in Latin America

 Performance Standards

- **SSWH14b** Identify the causes and results of revolutions in Latin America.
- **SSWHRC1c** Demonstrate understanding of contextual vocabulary.

Terms, People, and Places

regionalism   peonage
caudillo   Monroe Doctrine
Benito Juárez   Panama Canal
La Reforma

Note Taking

Reading Skill: Recognize Multiple Causes As you read, record the causes of instability in Latin America in a chart similar to this one. Then give an example of how each cause affected Mexico.

Instability in Latin America	
Causes	Mexican Example

Despite bright hopes, democracy failed to take root in most of the newly independent nations of Latin America in the 1800s. Instead, wealth and power remained in the hands of the few. At the same time, new technology such as refrigerated ships helped to intertwine the economies of nations that were thousands of miles apart. Latin American economies became increasingly dependent upon those of more developed countries. Britain, and later the United States, invested heavily in Latin America.

Lingering Political Problems

Simón Bolívar had hoped to create strong ties among the nations of Latin America. But feuds among leaders, geographic barriers, and local nationalism shattered that dream of unity. In the end, 20 separate nations emerged.

These new nations wrote constitutions modeled on that of the United States. They set up republics with elected legislatures. However, true democracy failed to take hold. During the 1800s, many succumbed to revolts, civil war, and dictatorships.

The Colonial Legacy Many of the problems in the new nations had their origins in colonial rule. The existing social and political hierarchy barely changed. Creoles simply replaced *peninsulares* as the ruling class. The Roman Catholic Church kept its privileged position and still controlled huge amounts of land.

For most people—mestizos, mulattoes, blacks, and Indians—life did not improve after independence. The new constitutions guaranteed equality before the law, but deep-rooted inequalities remained. Voting rights were limited. Many people felt the effects of racial prejudice. Small groups of people held most of the land. Owners of haciendas ruled their great estates, and the peasants who worked them, like medieval European lords.

The Search for Stability With few roads and no tradition of unity, **regionalism,** or loyalty to a local area, weakened the new nations. Local strongmen, called *caudillos* (kow THEE yohs), assembled private armies to resist the central government. At times, popular caudillos, occasionally former military leaders, gained national power. They looted the treasury and ruled as dictators. Power struggles led to frequent revolts that changed little except the name of the leader. In the long run, power remained in the hands of a privileged few who had no desire to share it.

As in Europe, the ruling elite in Latin America were divided between conservatives and liberals. Conservatives defended the traditional social order, favored press censorship, and strongly supported the Catholic Church. Liberals backed laissez-faire economics, religious toleration, greater access to education, and freedom of the press. Liberals saw themselves as <u>enlightened</u> supporters of progress but often showed little concern for the needs of the majority of the people.

✔ Checkpoint What factors undermined democracy in post-independence Latin America?

Mexico's Struggle for Stability

During the 1800s, each Latin American nation followed its own course. Mexico provides an example of the challenges facing many Latin American nations. Large landowners, army leaders, and the Catholic Church dominated Mexican politics. However, bitter battles between conservatives and liberals led to revolts and the rise of dictators. Deep social divisions separated wealthy creoles from mestizos and Indians who lived in poverty.

Santa Anna and War With the United States Between 1833 and 1855, an ambitious and cunning *caudillo,* Antonio López de Santa Anna, gained and lost power many times. At first, he posed as a liberal reformer.

Vocabulary Builder
<u>enlightened</u>—(en LYT und) *adj.* educated, informed

Life on a Hacienda
Peasant women process a crop grown on a hacienda in Mexico in the 1800s.

Soon, however, he reversed his stand and crushed efforts at reform.

In Mexico's northern territory of Texas, discontent grew. In 1835, settlers who had moved to Texas from the United States and other places revolted. After a brief struggle with Santa Anna's forces, the settlers gained independence from Mexico. They quickly set up an independent republic. Then in 1845 the United States annexed Texas. Mexicans saw this act as a declaration of war. In the fighting that followed, the United States invaded and defeated Mexico. In the Treaty of Guadalupe-Hidalgo, which ended the war, Mexico lost almost half its territory. The embarrassing defeat triggered new violence between conservatives and liberals.

La Reforma Changes Mexico In 1855, Benito Juárez (WAHR ez), a liberal reformer of Zapotec Indian heritage, and other liberals gained power and opened an era of reform known as La Reforma. Juárez offered hope to the oppressed people of Mexico. He and his fellow reformers revised the Mexican constitution to strip the military of power and end the special privileges of the Church. They ordered the Church to sell unused lands to peasants.

Conservatives resisted La Reforma and began a civil war. Still, Juárez was elected president in 1861 and expanded his reforms. His opponents turned to Europe for help. In 1863, Napoleon III sent troops to Mexico and set up Austrian archduke Maximilian as emperor.

For four years, Juárez's forces battled the combined conservative and French forces. When France withdrew its troops, Maximilian was captured and shot. In 1867, Juárez returned to power and tried to renew reform, but opponents resisted. Juárez died in office in 1872, never achieving all the reforms he envisioned. He did, however, help unite Mexico, bring mestizos into politics, and separate church and state.

Growth and Oppression Under Díaz After Juárez died, General Porfirio Díaz, a hero of the war against the French, staged a military coup and gained power. From 1876 to 1880 and 1884 to 1911, he ruled as a dictator. In the name of "Order and Progress," he strengthened the army, local police, and central government. He crushed opposition.

Under his harsh rule, Mexico made <u>tangible</u> economic advances. Railroads were built, foreign trade increased, some industry developed, and mining expanded. Growth, however, had a high cost. Capital for development came from foreign investors, to whom Díaz granted special rights. He also let wealthy landowners buy up Indian lands.

The rich prospered, but most Mexicans remained poor. Many Indians and mestizos fell into **peonage** to their employers. In the peonage system, hacienda owners would give workers advances on their wages and require them to stay on the hacienda until they had paid back what they owed. Wages remained low, and workers were rarely able to repay the hacienda owner. Many children died in infancy. Other children worked 12-hour days and never learned to read or write.

✔ **Checkpoint** What struggles did Mexico go through as it tried to find stability in the 1800s?

Remember the Alamo!
Mexican President Antonio López de Santa Anna (above) is well-known for his ruthless decision to give no quarter to the Texan defenders of the Alamo, a fort in San Antonio, Texas, during the Texas Revolution. The illustration above shows Texan defenders of the Alamo bravely fighting against overwhelming odds. *In what light does this illustration present the defenders of the Alamo?*

Vocabulary Builder
<u>tangible</u>—(TAN juh bul) *adj.* real or concrete

The Economics of Dependence

Under colonial rule, mercantilist policies made Latin America economically dependent on Spain and Portugal. Colonies sent raw materials such as cash crops or precious metals to the parent country and had to buy manufactured goods from them. Strict laws kept colonists from trading with other countries and possibly obtaining goods at a lower price. In addition, laws prohibited the building of local industries that would have competed with the parent country. In short, the policies prevented the colonies from developing their own economies.

The Cycle of Economic Dependence After independence, this pattern changed very little. The new Latin American republics did adopt free trade, welcoming all comers. Britain and the United States rushed into the new markets, replacing Spain as Latin America's chief trading partners. But the region remained as economically dependent as before.

Foreign Influence Mounts In the 1800s, foreign goods flooded Latin America, creating large profits for foreigners and for a handful of local business people. Foreign investment, which could yield enormous profits, was often accompanied by local interference. Investors from Britain, the United States, and other nations pressured their own governments to take action if political events or reform movements in a Latin American country seemed to threaten their interests.

Some Economic Growth After 1850, some Latin American economies did grow. With foreign capital, they were able to develop mining and agriculture. Chile exported copper and nitrates, and Argentina expanded

Note Taking

Reading Skill: Identify Effects Use a chart like the one below to record how foreign influence, including that of the United States, affected Latin America.

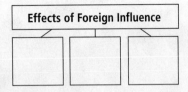

Effects of Foreign Influence

Geography *Interactive*
For: Audio guided tour
Web Code: nap-2541

Imperialism in Latin America, 1898–1917

Map Skills In the early 1900s, European powers held possessions in Latin America. The United States often intervened to protect business interests there.

1. **Locate** (a) Cuba (b) Canal Zone (c) British Guiana (d) Honduras
2. **Location** Why did the United States have a particularly strong interest in Latin American affairs?
3. **Identify Point of View** What natural resources did the Dutch exploit in Dutch Guiana?

its livestock and wheat production. Brazil exported the cash crops coffee and sugar, as well as rubber. By the early 1900s, both Venezuela and Mexico were developing important and lucrative oil industries.

Throughout the region, foreigners invested in modern ports and railroads to carry goods from the interior to coastal cities. European immigrants poured into Latin America. The newcomers helped to promote economic activity, and a small middle class emerged.

Thanks to trade, investment, technology, and migration, Latin American nations moved into the world economy. Yet internal development was limited. The tiny elite at the top benefited from the economic upturn, but very little trickled down to the masses of people at the bottom. The poor earned too little to buy consumer goods. Without a strong demand, many industries failed to develop.

✔ **Checkpoint** How did foreign influence and investment affect Latin America?

The Influence of the United States

As nations like Mexico tried to build stable governments, a neighboring republic, the United States, expanded across North America. Latin American nations began to feel threatened by the "Colossus of the North," the giant power that cast its shadow over the entire hemisphere.

The Monroe Doctrine In the 1820s, Spain plotted to recover its American colonies. Britain opposed any move that might close the door to trade with Latin America. British leaders asked American President James Monroe to join them in a statement opposing any new colonization of the Americas.

Monroe, however, wanted to avoid any "entangling alliance" with Britain. Acting alone, he issued the **Monroe Doctrine** in 1823. "The American continents," it declared, "are henceforth not to be considered as subjects for future colonization by any European powers." The United States lacked the military power to enforce the doctrine. But with the support of Britain's strong navy, the doctrine discouraged European interference. For more than a century, the Monroe Doctrine would be the key to United States policy in the Americas.

The United States Expands Into Latin America As a result of the war with Mexico, in 1848 the United States acquired the thinly populated regions of northern Mexico, gaining all or part of the present-day states of California, Arizona, New Mexico, Nevada, Utah, and Colorado. The victory fed dreams of future expansion. Before the century had ended, the United States controlled much of North America and was becoming involved in overseas conflicts.

For decades, Cuban patriots had battled to free their island from Spanish rule. As they began to make headway, the United States joined their cause, declaring war on Spain in 1898. The brief Spanish-American War ended in a crushing defeat for Spain. At the war's end, Cuba was granted independence. But in 1901, the United States forced Cubans to add the Platt Amendment to their constitution. The amendment gave the United States naval bases in Cuba and the right to intervene in Cuban affairs.

Analyzing Political Cartoons

Uncle Sam Takes Off This cartoon represents the entry of the United States into competition with European powers over new territory in the Eastern Hemisphere in the early 1900s.

(A) **Uncle Sam** represents the United States.

(B) **The horse** wears a saddle that reads "Monroe Doctrine."

(C) **European powers** watch in frustration.

1. What do the wheels on Uncle Sam's bicycle represent?
2. Why are the European powers shouting at Uncle Sam?

AN EPIC UNDERTAKING:
PANAMA CANAL

The Panama Canal was a massive undertaking. The sheer scale of the project astounded engineers, politicians, and tourists. Building the canal cost the American government $352 million (about $7 billion in today's money). Workers excavated about 232 million cubic yards of dirt, rocks, and debris from the Canal Zone—enough debris to create a pyramid seven times the height of the Washington Monument, as one newspaper writer noted. Nearly six thousand workers died from industrial accidents or disease in the ten years it took to build the canal.

Despite many challenges, the builders would not give up. They completed the canal in 1914. The beginning of World War I in the summer of 1914, however, overshadowed what was to be its grand opening.

Haut Obispo (Higher Obispo)—Showing one of the old French steam scoops now being used by Americans, and the height of bank it excavates.

Dump Train—Pedro Miguel. The greatest problem on the Isthmus is not to dig the Canal, but to get rid of the great mass of excavated dirt.

Steam Sho— pathway, lifting five scoops —utes and loading ten cars in thirty minutes.

▲ Playing cards featuring scenes from the canal's construction (above) helped to feed Americans' fascination with the canal.

◀ Two men (below) stand inside one of the canal lock's enormous gates. The gates allow water to flow in and out of the lock, raising or lowering ships to different levels.

▼ The tropical diseases malaria and yellow fever killed many workers. Quinine (below right) was used to treat some cases of malaria. The canal builders' massive efforts to kill disease-carrying mosquitoes, using methods, such as spraying swampy areas with oil (below left), were more effective.

Thinking Critically

1. **Draw Conclusions** Based on the map, why did Americans want to build a canal in Panama?
2. **Draw Inferences** Why was it important to control disease during the building of the canal?

The United States Interferes American investments in Latin America grew in the early 1900s. Citing the need to protect those investments, in 1904 the United States issued the Roosevelt Corollary to the Monroe Doctrine. Under this policy, the United States claimed "international police power" in the Western Hemisphere. When the Dominican Republic failed to pay its foreign debts, the United States sent in troops. Americans collected customs duties, paid off the debts, and remained for years.

Under the Roosevelt Corollary and then President William Howard Taft's policy of Dollar Diplomacy, American companies continued to invest in the countries of Latin America. To protect those investments, the United States sent troops to Cuba, Haiti, Mexico, Honduras, Nicaragua, and other countries in Central America and the Caribbean. As a result, like European powers in Africa and Asia, the United States became the target of increasing resentment and rebellion.

Building the Panama Canal From the late 1800s, the United States had wanted to build a canal across Central America. Panama was a proposed site. However, Panama belonged to Colombia, which refused to sell the United States land for the canal. In 1903, the United States backed a revolt by Panamanians against Colombia. The Panamanians quickly won independence and gave the United States control of the land to build the canal.

Construction began in 1904. Engineers solved many difficult problems in the course of building the canal. The **Panama Canal** opened in 1914. The canal cut the distance of a sea journey between such cities as New York and San Francisco by thousands of miles. It was an engineering marvel that boosted trade and shipping worldwide.

To people in Latin America, however, the canal was another example of "Yankee imperialism." Nationalist feeling in the hemisphere was often expressed as anti-Americanism. Panama did not gain complete control over the canal until 2000. It now forms a vital part of the Panamanian economy.

✔ **Checkpoint** How did the United States act as an imperialist power in Latin America?

SECTION **4** Assessment

Progress Monitoring Online
For: Self-quiz with vocabulary practice
Web Code: naa-2541

Terms, People, and Places

1. For each term, person, or place listed at the beginning of the section, write a sentence explaining its significance.

Note Taking

2. **Reading Skill: Recognize Multiple Causes** Use your completed charts to answer the Focus Question: How did Latin American nations struggle for stability, and how did industrialized nations affect them?

Critical Thinking and Comprehension

3. **Express Problems Clearly** What problems faced new nations in Latin America?
4. **Recognize Cause and Effect** How did the cycle of economic dependence continue after independence?
5. **Synthesize Information** Describe two ways the United States influenced Latin America.
6. **Draw Conclusions** Why might developing nations encourage foreign investment? Do you think foreign investors should have the right to intervene in another nation's affairs to protect their investments? Explain.

● **Writing About History**

Quick Write: Support Your Ideas As you respond to a short-answer or extended-response question on a test, keep in mind that each sentence or paragraph should support your main idea. Omit information, no matter how interesting, that is not central to your argument. To practice, write an outline of an argument responding to the following extended-response prompt.

• Explain how American interference led to the building of the Panama Canal.

Quick Study Guide

 SSWH15d

Progress Monitoring Online
For: Self-test with vocabulary practice
Web Code: naa-2551

■ Imperialism in Japan and Southeast Asia and the Pacific

Japan	Southeast Asia and the Pacific
• United States opens by show of force. • Meiji restoration begins modernization. • Japan becomes an imperialist power itself.	• European powers expand footholds. • Some countries resist, but succumb to European force. • Europeans gain resources and trade networks at expense of indigenous people.

■ Three British Colonies: Canada, Australia, and New Zealand

British Colony	Settled by	Impact on Indigenous People	Gained Self-Rule From Britain
Canada	First France, then Britain	Native Americans forced to give up lands	1867
Australia	Britain, as penal colony	Aborigines suffered disastrously	1901
New Zealand	Britain, attracted by climate	Maori fought against settlers, population reduced drastically	1907

■ The Cycle of Economic Dependence in Latin America

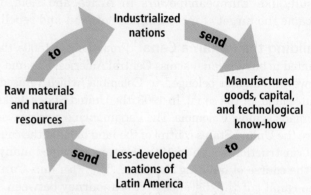

The relationship is unequal because the stronger, more developed nations control prices and terms of trade.

■ Key Events in Worldwide Imperialism

Southeast Asia, the Pacific, and Japan
British Colonies and Latin America

1835

1850

1865

1853
American ships commanded by Commodore Perry arrive in Japan.

1858
France invades Vietnam.

1868
Meiji Restoration begins in Japan.

1840
Britain annexes New Zealand.

1855
La Reforma begins in Mexico.

1867
Britain grants Canada self-rule.

Concept Connector

? Essential Question Review

To connect prior knowledge with what you have learned in this chapter, answer the questions below in your Concept Connector journal. Use the journal in the Reading and Note Taking Study Guide to record your answers (or go to www.phschool.com **Web Code: nad-2507**).

1. **Cooperation** In response to Commodore Perry's demands, Japanese statesman Lord Ii suggested a strategy for dealing with the Americans:

   "Even though the Shogun's ancestors set up seclusion laws, they left the Dutch and the Chinese to act as a bridge…. Might this bridge not now be of advantage to us in handling foreign affairs, providing us with the means whereby we may for a time avert the outbreak of hostilities and then, after some time has elapsed, gain a complete victory?"

   Why did Lord Ii want to cooperate with the Americans? What steps did the Japanese take to "gain a complete victory?" Did this prove to be a good strategy for Japan? Why or why not?

2. **Geography's Impact** Location links the fate of Latin America with that of the United States. In the 1800s, ideas about independence springing from the American Revolution inspired independence leaders in Latin America, such as Simón Bolívar. However, in the late 1800s, the United States began to interfere more aggressively in the affairs of Latin American countries. Create a timeline tracking the relationship between the United States and Latin America from 1800 through 1914. Include a brief description of the significance of each event on the timeline.

3. **Migration** Native Americans made up the original population of Canada, Kooris inhabited Australia, and Maoris lived in New Zealand. Today, along with descendents of these early people, more of the inhabitants of these countries are of British ancestry. Explain the role migration played in changing the population of these lands.

■ Connections to Today

1. **Conflict: Unrest in Quebec** Although French-Canadian leaders agreed to confederation with the rest of Canada in 1867, the French-English question was never truly put to rest. Many French-Canadians continued to feel that the English-speaking majority in Canada threatened their unique French culture. In the late 1900s, a movement for an independent Quebec arose. Research the path of this movement and create a bulleted list of significant events that occurred within the last fifty years.

Languages Spoken in Canada Today

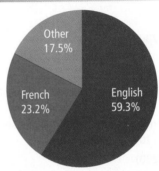

Other 17.5%

French 23.2%

English 59.3%

SOURCE: The World Factbook Online

2. **Cooperation: Japan as a World Power** After its rapid modernization in the late 1800s, Japan took its place among the leading powers of the world. It asserted that power throughout the 1900s, with varying results. Today, Japan's economy is second in size only to that of the United States. Conduct research on Japan and write a paragraph describing its role in international affairs today.

1886
Britain annexes Burma.

1898
The Philippines declares independence from Spain.

1910
Japan annexes Korea.

History Interactive
For: Interactive timeline
Web Code: nap-2551

| **1880** | **1895** | **1910** | **1925** |

1885
The Canadian Pacific Railway opens.

1904
The United States issues the Roosevelt Corollary.

1914
The Panama Canal opens.

Chapter Assessment

Terms, People, and Places

1. In what ways did **Matthew Perry's** opening of Japan lead to the **Meiji Restoration?**
2. How did the **Sino-Japanese** and **Russo-Japanese wars** spring out of Japan's new strength as a modernized nation?
3. What steps did **King Mongkut** take to help Siam avoid the fate of **French Indochina?**
4. How did Canada become a **dominion?**
5. Describe how the **Spanish-American War** affected both the Philippines and Cuba.
6. How did **regionalism** and *caudillos* weaken the stability of Latin American countries in the 1800s?

Main Ideas

Section 1 (pp. 784–790)
7. How did Japan change course in the late 1800s?

Section 2 (pp. 791–795)
8. Why were imperialist nations drawn to Southeast Asia and the Pacific?
9. How did the colonized peoples of Southeast Asia react to Western attempts to dominate the region?

Section 3 (pp. 796–800)
10. Describe settlement in Canada, Australia, and New Zealand.
11. How did these colonies gain independence?

Section 4 (pp. 801–807)
12. What factors caused instability in Latin America after independence?
13. How did the United States influence Latin America?

Chapter Focus question:
14. How did political and economic imperialism influence nations around the world?

Critical Thinking

15. **Compare** Compare Japan's response to Western imperialism to that of China. How were the two responses similar? How were they different?
16. **Identify Causes** In the image below, a Japanese woman wears Western clothing. What role did westernization play in helping both Japan and Siam avoid colonization by European nations?

17. **Connect to Geography** How did the creation of the Dominion of Canada encourage expansion?
18. **Synthesize Information** What principle did the United States express in the Monroe Doctrine? How did the Roosevelt Corollary alter the Monroe Doctrine?
19. **Draw Conclusions** List the benefits and disadvantages brought about by colonial rule. Do you think subject people were better or worse off as a result of the Age of Imperialism? Explain.

● Writing About History

In this chapter's four Section Assessments, you learned how to write for assessment.

Writing for Assessment Write an answer to one of the following extended response essay prompts. Spend only 40 minutes on the writing process. Consult page SH20 of the Writing Handbook for additional help.

- Analyze the effects of Japanese imperialism in Korea.
- Analyze the effects of American intervention in Latin America.

Prewriting
- Read both prompts and determine what you know about each. Choose the one whose topic you recall the most information about.

- Look for key words that will tell you what kind of answer to provide, such as *"explain."*

Drafting
- Focus your time by allowing 10 minutes for prewriting, 20 minutes for drafting, and 10 minutes for revising your response.
- Develop a thesis for your essay and make sure each piece of information supports it.

Revising
- Check that you open and close your response strongly, that each point supports your main idea, and that you've answered all aspects of the question.

Prepare for the GHSGT

The Imperialism Debate and the Philippines

After defeating Spain in Manila Bay in May 1898, American forces remained in the Philippines. In February 1899, the United States Senate voted to annex the Philippines. The Philippines were one aspect of the United States' efforts to compete with Europe in the scramble for new foreign markets, investment opportunities and raw materials. A great debate took place in the United States over the issue of imperialism, as the documents below show.

Document A

"I have been criticized a good deal about the Philippines, but don't deserve it. The truth is I didn't want the Philippines, and when they came to us, as a gift from the gods, I did not know what to do with them. . . . And one night late it came to me this way—I don't know how it was, but it came: (1) That we could not give them back to Spain—that would be cowardly and dishonorable; (2) that we could not turn them over to France and Germany—our commercial rivals in the Orient—that would be bad business and discreditable; (3) that we could not leave them to themselves—they were unfit for self-government—and they would soon have anarchy and misrule over there worse than Spain's was; and (4) that there was nothing left for us to do but to take them all, and to educate the Filipinos, and uplift and civilize and Christianize them . . ."

—From remarks to a visiting delegation of Methodist church leaders made by President William McKinley on November 21, 1899

Document B

"We hold that the policy known as imperialism is hostile to liberty and tends toward militarism, an evil from which it has been our glory to be free. . . . We maintain that governments derive their just powers from the consent of the governed. We insist that the subjugation of any people is "criminal aggression" and open disloyalty to the distinctive principles of our government.

We earnestly condemn the policy of the present National Administration in the Philippines. It seeks to extinguish the spirit of 1776 in those islands. . . . We denounce the slaughter of the Filipinos as a needless horror."

—From the Platform of the American Anti-Imperialist League, 1899

Document C

"Isn't Every American proud of the part that American soldiers bore in the relief of Pekin [i.e., Beijing, where some U.S. citizens were held hostage by the Boxers]? But that would have been impossible if our flag had not been in the Philippines.

Gen. Chaffee led two infantry regiments, the Ninth and the Fourteen, and one battery of the Fifth Artillery to Pekin. They did not come direct from the United States; there was not time. . . . But for these men and the marines from Manilla barracks, Minister Conger and his American comrades in the besieged legation would not have seen their country's flag, and would OWE THEIR RELIEF TO BRITISH, JAPANESE AND RUSSIANS.

When Mr. Bryan [Democratic candidate for president] tells you that the Philippines are worth nothing to America, you tell him to 'REMEMBER PEKIN!'"

—From a leaflet of the Republican Club of Massachusetts, 1900

Analyzing Documents

Use your knowledge of this chapter and Documents A, B, and C to answer questions 1–4.

1. In Document A, which of McKinley's four reasons for the takeover of the Philippines explained that important business interests were at stake?
   - A 1
   - B 2
   - C 3
   - D 4

2. In Document B, what is the meaning of "It seeks to extinguish the spirit of 1776 in those islands"?
   - A The U.S. vowed never to give the Philippines its freedom.
   - B The U.S. is undermining an independence movement that is like the American Revolution.
   - C Self-government in the Philippines is inevitable.
   - D The U.S. has the ability and the duty to educate Filipinos about self-government.

3. According to Document C, the Philippines are necessary to the United States as a(n)
   - A source for raw materials.
   - B outpost for Christian missionaries.
   - C base for military actions.
   - D market for U.S. goods.

4. William Jennings Bryan considered imperialism which he opposed, to be the top issue in the 1900 presidential campaign. Who would have received your vote, the Democratic candidate, Bryan, or the Republican, William McKinley? Give your reasons, using these documents and information from the chapter.

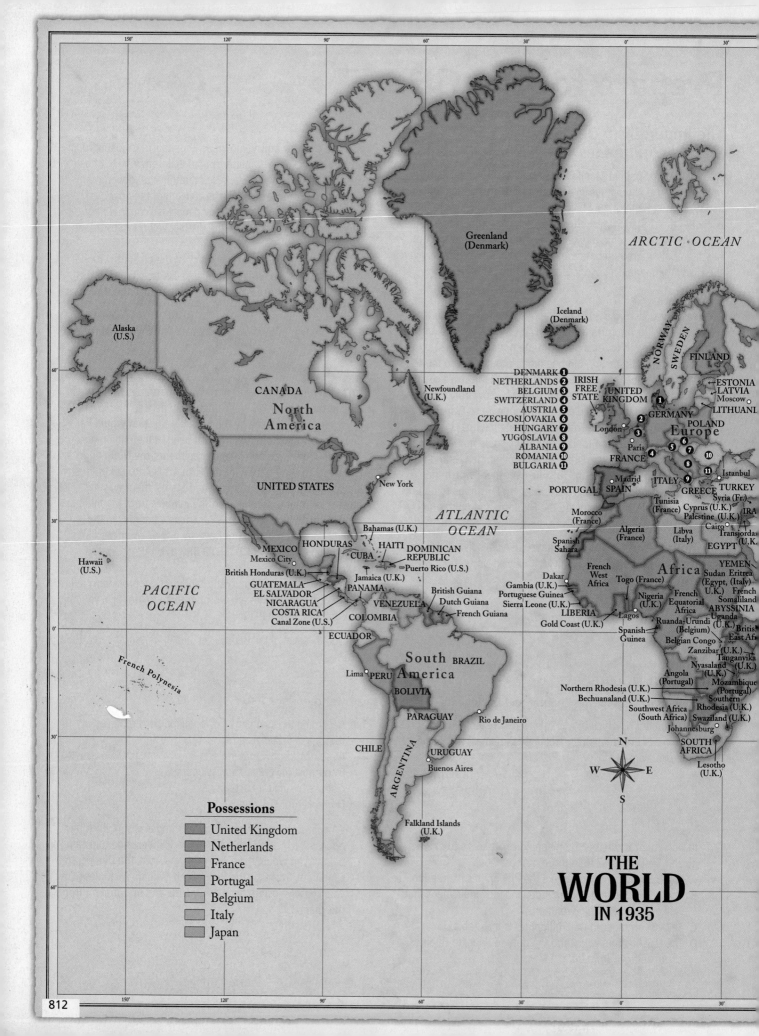

THE
WORLD
IN 1935

Possessions
- United Kingdom
- Netherlands
- France
- Portugal
- Belgium
- Italy
- Japan

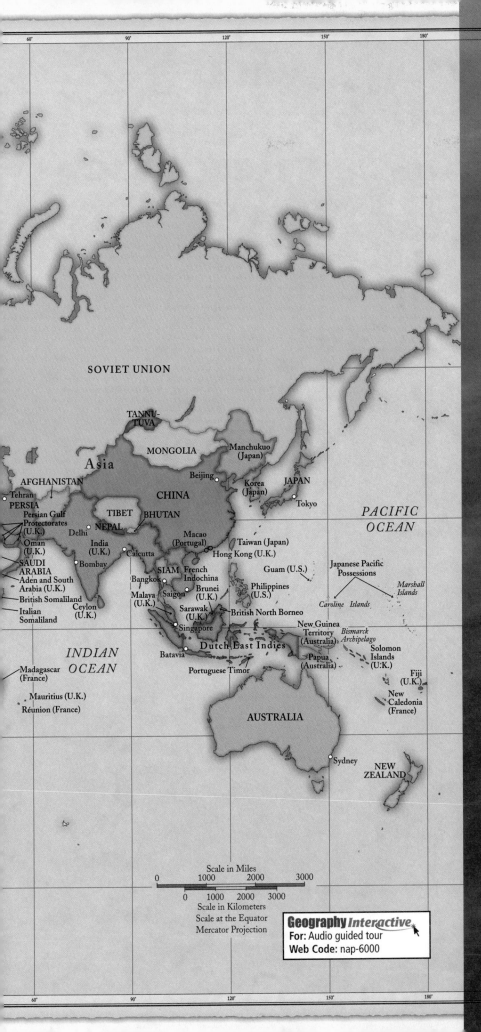

SOVIET UNION

TANNU-
TUVA

MONGOLIA

Manchukuo
(Japan)

Asia

AFGHANISTAN

Beijing

Korea
(Japan)

JAPAN

Tehran

PERSIA

CHINA

Tokyo

PACIFIC
OCEAN

Persian Gulf
Protectorates
(U.K.)

TIBET

BHUTAN

Oman
(U.K.)

Delhi

NEPAL

India
(U.K.)

Macao
(Portugal)

Taiwan (Japan)

SAUDI
ARABIA

Bombay

Calcutta

Hong Kong (U.K.)

Aden and South
Arabia (U.K.)

SIAM

French
Indochina

Guam (U.S.)

Japanese Pacific
Possessions

British Somaliland

Bangkok

Brunei
(U.K.)

Philippines
(U.S.)

Marshall
Islands

Italian
Somaliland

Ceylon
(U.K.)

Malaya
(U.K.)

Saigon

Sarawak
(U.K.)

British North Borneo

Caroline Islands

Singapore

New Guinea
Territory
(Australia)

Bismarck
Archipelago

INDIAN
OCEAN

Batavia

Dutch East Indies

Solomon
Islands
(U.K.)

Madagascar
(France)

Portuguese Timor

Papua
(Australia)

Fiji
(U.K.)

Mauritius (U.K.)

Réunion (France)

AUSTRALIA

New
Caledonia
(France)

Sydney

NEW
ZEALAND

Scale in Miles
0   1000   2000   3000
0   1000   2000   3000
Scale in Kilometers
Scale at the Equator
Mercator Projection

Geography Interactive
For: Audio guided tour
Web Code: nap-6000

26

World War I and the Russian Revolution

1914–1924

WITNESS HISTORY AUDIO

In Flanders Fields

Canadian John McCrae served as a military doctor on the Western Front in World War I. In 1915, McCrae wrote the following poem in the voice of those he had watched die.

66In Flanders fields the poppies blow
Between the crosses, row on row
That mark our place; and in the sky
The larks, still bravely singing, fly
Scarce heard amid the guns below.

We are the Dead. Short days ago
We lived, felt dawn, saw sunset glow,
Loved and were loved, and now we lie
In Flanders fields.99

—Dr. John McCrae, 1915

Listen to the Witness History audio to hear more about McCrae's experience during World War I.

◄ **American soldiers on a trench raid during World War I**

The poppy became a symbol of remembrance for veterans after World War I.

 Performance Standards

Chapter Focus Question What caused World War I and the Russian Revolution, and what effect did they have on world events?

Section 1
The Great War Begins
SSWH16a

Section 2
A New Kind of War
SSWH16b

Section 3
Winning the War
SSWH17b

Section 4
Making the Peace
SSWH16c

Section 5
Revolution and Civil War in Russia
SSWH16d, SSWH17b

Use the ☑ **Quick Study Timeline** at the end of this chapter to preview chapter events.

The sickle and hammer on this pin symbolize the Russian Revolution.

Poison gas was widely used for the first time during World War I.

? **Concept Connector ONLINE**

To explore Essential Questions related to this chapter, go to PHSchool.com
Web Code: nad-2607

▲ The assassin, Gavrilo Princip

◀ Austrian Archduke Francis Ferdinand and his wife Sophie

The Spark

On June 28, 1914, Gavrilo Princip, a member of a Serbian terrorist group, killed Austrian Archduke Francis Ferdinand and his wife Sophie.

❝ The first [bullet] struck the wife of the Archduke, the Archduchess Sofia, in the abdomen. . . . She died instantly.

The second bullet struck the Archduke close to the heart. He uttered only one word, 'Sofia'—a call to his stricken wife. Then his head fell back and he collapsed. He died almost instantly. ❞
—Borijove Jevtic, co-conspirator

The assassinations triggered World War I, called "The Great War" by people at the time.

Focus Question Why and how did World War I begin in 1914?

The Great War Begins

Performance Standards

• **SSWH16a** Identify Balkan nationalism, entangling alliances, and militarism as causes of WWI.

Terms, People, and Places

entente	ultimatum
militarism	mobilize
Alsace and Lorraine	neutrality

Note Taking

Reading Skill: Summarize As you read, use a chart to summarize the events that led up to the outbreak of World War I.

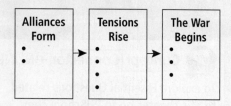

By 1914, Europe had enjoyed a century of relative peace. Idealists hoped for a permanent end to the scourge of war. International events, such as the first modern Olympic games in 1896 and the First Universal Peace Conference in 1899, were steps toward keeping the peace. "The future belongs to peace," said French economist Frédéric Passy (pa SEE).

Not everyone was so hopeful. "I shall not live to see the Great War," warned German Chancellor Otto von Bismarck, "but you will see it, and it will start in the east." It was Bismarck's prediction, rather than Passy's, that came true.

Alliances Draw Lines

While peace efforts were under way, powerful forces were pushing Europe towards war. Spurred by distrust of one another, the great powers of Europe—Germany, Austria-Hungary, Italy, Britain, France, and Russia—signed treaties pledging to defend one another. These alliances were intended to promote peace by creating powerful combinations that no one would dare attack. In the end, they had the opposite effect. Two huge alliances emerged.

The Triple Alliance The first of these alliances had its origins in Bismarck's day. He knew that France longed to avenge its defeat in the Franco-Prussian War. Sure that France would not attack Germany without help, Bismarck signed treaties with other powers. In 1882, he formed the Triple Alliance with Italy and Austria-Hungary. In 1914, when war did erupt, Germany and Austria-Hungary fought on the same side. They became known as the Central Powers.

European Alliances and Military Build-Up, 1914

Geography *Interactive*
For: Audio guided tour
Web Code: nap-2611

Legend:
- Central Powers
- Allies
- Neutral Nations
- Neutral nations that later joined the Allies
- Neutral nations that later joined the Central Powers
- The Balkans
- 100,000 soldiers

Map Skills By 1914, most of Europe was divided into two armed camps, the Allies and the Central Powers. Millions of troops stood ready for war.

1. **Locate** (a) Germany (b) Alsace-Lorraine (c) the Balkans (d) Serbia
2. **Regions** Why would Germans worry about the alliance between France and Russia?
3. **Synthesize Information** Based on the information on the map, which alliance do you think had the greater military advantage in 1914?

The Triple Entente A rival bloc took shape in 1893, when France and Russia formed an alliance. In 1904, France and Britain signed an **entente** (ahn TAHNT), a nonbinding agreement to follow common policies. Though not as formal as a treaty, the entente led to close military and diplomatic ties. Britain later signed a similar agreement with Russia. When war began, these powers became known as the Allies.

Other alliances also formed. Germany signed a treaty with the Ottoman empire. Britain drew close to Japan.

✔ **Checkpoint** What two large alliances took shape before the beginning of World War I?

Rivalries and Nationalism Increase Tension

The European powers jealously guarded their <u>status</u>. They competed for position in many areas. Two old empires, Austria-Hungary and Ottoman Turkey, struggled to survive in an age of nationalism.

Vocabulary Builder

<u>status</u>—(STAT us) *n.* high standing, rank, or prestige

Competition

Economic rivalries helped sour the international atmosphere. Germany, the newest of the great powers, was growing into an economic and military powerhouse. Britain felt threatened by its rapid economic growth. Germany, in turn, thought the other great powers did not give it enough respect. Germany also feared that when Russia caught up to other industrialized nations, its huge population and vast supply of natural resources would make it an unbeatable competitor.

<u>Overseas</u> rivalries also divided European nations. In 1905 and again in 1911, competition for colonies brought France and Germany to the brink of war in Morocco, then under France's influence. Although diplomats kept the peace, Germany did gain some territory in central Africa. As a result of the two Moroccan crises, Britain and France strengthened their ties against Germany.

With international tensions on the rise, the great powers began to build up their armies and navies. The fiercest competition was the naval rivalry between Britain and Germany. To protect its vast overseas empire, Britain had built the world's most respected navy. As Germany began acquiring overseas colonies, it began to build up its own navy. Suspicious of Germany's motives, Britain in turn increased naval spending. Sensational journalism dramatized the arms race and stirred national public opinion against rival countries.

The rise of **militarism,** or the glorification of the military, also helped to feed the arms race. The militarist tradition painted war in romantic colors. Young men dreamed of blaring trumpets and dashing cavalry charges—not at all the sort of conflict they would soon face.

Nationalism

Aggressive nationalism also caused tension. Nationalism was strong in both Germany and France. Germans were proud of their new empire's military power and industrial leadership. The French were bitter about their 1871 defeat in the Franco-Prussian War and yearned to recover the lost border province of **Alsace and Lorraine.**

In Eastern Europe, Russia sponsored a powerful form of nationalism called Pan-Slavism. It held that all Slavic peoples shared a common nationality. As the largest Slavic country, Russia felt that it had a duty to lead and defend all Slavs. By 1914, it stood ready to support Serbia, a proud young nation that dreamed of creating a South Slav state.

Germany's Glorious Military

Eager crowds watch a cavalry regiment, or group of troops serving on horseback, ride through Berlin in August 1914. Germany's army was known to be highly trained and well disciplined, making it a formidable fighting force. *How are the people pictured showing pride in their military?*

Two old multinational empires particularly feared rising nationalism. Austria-Hungary worried that nationalism might foster rebellion among the many minority populations within its empire. Ottoman Turkey felt threatened by nearby new nations, such as Serbia. If realized, Serbia's dream of a South Slav state could take territory away from both Austria-Hungary and Turkey.

In 1912, several Balkan states attacked Turkey and succeeded in taking a large area of land away from Turkish control. The next year, the Balkan states fought among themselves over the spoils of war. These brief but bloody Balkan wars raised tensions to a fever pitch. By 1914, the Balkans were called the "powder keg of Europe"—a barrel of gunpowder that a tiny spark might cause to explode.

✓ **Checkpoint** How did international competition and nationalism increase tensions in Europe?

The Powder Keg Ignites

As Bismarck had predicted, the Great War began in Eastern Europe. A regional conflict between tiny Serbia and the huge empire of Austria-Hungary grew rapidly into a general war.

Assassination in Sarajevo The crisis began when Archduke Francis Ferdinand of Austria-Hungary announced that he would visit Sarajevo (sa ruh YAY voh), the capital of Bosnia. Francis Ferdinand was the nephew and heir of the aging Austrian emperor, Francis Joseph. At the time of his visit, Bosnia was under the rule of Austria-Hungary. But it was also the home of many Serbs and other Slavs. News of the royal visit angered many Serbian nationalists. They viewed the Austrians as foreign oppressors. Some members of Unity or Death, a Serbian terrorist group commonly known as the Black Hand, vowed to take action.

The archduke ignored warnings of anti-Austrian unrest in Sarajevo. On June 28, 1914, he and his wife, Sophie, rode through Sarajevo in an open car. As the car passed by, a conspirator named Gavrilo Princip (GAV ree loh PREEN tseep) seized his chance and fired twice into the car. Moments later, the archduke and his wife were dead.

Austria Strikes Back The news of the assassination shocked Francis Joseph. Still, he was reluctant to go to war. The government in Vienna, however, saw the incident as an excuse to crush Serbia. In Berlin, Kaiser William II was horrified at the assassination of his ally's heir. He wrote to Francis Joseph, advising him to take a firm stand toward Serbia. Instead of urging restraint, Germany gave Austria a "blank check," or a promise of unconditional support no matter what the cost.

Austria sent Serbia a sweeping **ultimatum,** or final set of demands. To avoid war, said the ultimatum, Serbia must end all anti-Austrian agitation and punish any Serbian official involved in the murder plot. It must even let Austria join in the investigation. Serbia agreed to most, but not all, of the terms of Austria's ultimatum. This partial refusal gave Austria the opportunity it was seeking. On July 28, 1914, Austria declared war on Serbia.

✓ **Checkpoint** What happened because of the assassination of Francis Ferdinand and his wife?

BIOGRAPHY

Kaiser William II
"All the long years of my reign," William II (1859–1941) complained, "my colleagues, the monarchs of Europe, have paid no attention to what I have to say." As kaiser, he fought to win respect for himself and his empire.

William's rivalry with other rulers was in many ways a family feud. He and George V of Britain were cousins, grandchildren of Queen Victoria. Tsar Nicholas II was a cousin by marriage. When war broke out in 1914, the kaiser blamed "George and Nicky." "If my grandmother had been alive, she would never have allowed it!" **How did the kaiser's desire for respect influence his policies?**

Reasons for Entering the War, July–August 1914

Country	Allied With	Reasons for Entering War
Austria-Hungary	Germany	Wanted to punish Serbia for encouraging terrorism
Germany	Austria-Hungary	Stood by its one dependable ally, Austria-Hungary
Serbia	Russia	Attacked by Austria-Hungary after assassination of Archduke
Russia	Serbia, France, Britain	Wanted to defend Slavic peoples in Serbia
France	Russia and Britain	Wanted to avoid facing Germany alone at a later date
Belgium	Neutral	Invaded by Germany
Britain	France and Russia	Outraged by invasion of Belgium

Chart Skills Who started the war? During the war, each side blamed the other. Afterward, the victorious Allies placed all blame on Germany, because it invaded Belgium. Today, historians still debate who should bear the blame for a catastrophe nobody wanted. **Using information from the chart, describe why Russians might feel that Germany started the war.**

Alliances Kick In

The war between Austria and Serbia might have been another "summer war," like most European wars of the previous century. However, the carefully planned alliances soon drew the great powers deeper into conflict.

Russia and France Back Serbia After Austria's declaration of war, Serbia turned to its ally, Russia, the champion of Slavic nations. From St. Petersburg, Nicholas II telegraphed William II. The tsar asked the kaiser to urge Austria to soften its demands. When this plea failed, Russia began to **mobilize,** or prepare its military forces for war. On August 1, Germany responded by declaring war on Russia.

Russia, in turn, appealed to its ally France. In Paris, nationalists saw a chance to avenge France's defeat in the Franco-Prussian War. Though French leaders had some doubts, they gave Russia the same kind of backing Germany offered to Austria. When Germany demanded that France keep out of the conflict, France refused. Germany then declared war on France.

Germany Invades Belgium By early August, the battle lines were hardening. Italy and Britain still remained uncommitted. Italy chose to stay neutral for the time being. **Neutrality** is a policy of supporting neither side in a war. Britain had to decide quickly whether or not to support its ally France. Then, Germany's war plans suddenly made the decision for Britain.

A cornerstone of Germany's military policy was a plan developed years earlier by General Alfred von Schlieffen (SHLEE fun). Germany's location presented the possibility of a two-front war—against France in the west and Russia to the east. The Schlieffen Plan was designed to avoid this problem. Schlieffen reasoned that Germany should move against France first because Russia's lumbering military would be slow to mobilize.

However, Germany had to defeat France quickly so that its armies could then turn around and fight Russia.

To ensure a swift victory in the west, the Schlieffen Plan required German armies to march through neutral Belgium and then swing south behind French lines. The goal was to encircle and crush France's army. The Germans embarked on the plan by invading Belgium on August 3. However, Britain and other European powers had signed a treaty guaranteeing Belgian neutrality. Outraged by the invasion of Belgium, Britain declared war on Germany on August 4.

Once the machinery of war was set in motion, it seemed impossible to stop. Military leaders insisted that they must mobilize their forces immediately to accomplish their military goals. These military timetables made it impossible for political leaders to negotiate instead of fight.

✓ **Checkpoint** How did the alliance system deepen the original conflict between Austria-Hungary and Serbia into a general war?

War Enthusiasm
People cheered as soldiers marched off to war. In this photograph, a woman is giving a soldier an apple to eat on his journey.

Reaction to the War

Before the war, many countries were troubled by domestic problems. For example, Britain struggled with labor unrest and the issue of home rule in Ireland. Russia wrestled with problems stirred up by the Revolution of 1905. The outbreak of war brought a temporary relief from these internal divisions. A renewed sense of patriotism united countries. Governments on both sides emphasized that their countries were fighting for justice and a better world. Young men rushed to enlist, cheered on by women and their elders. Now that war had come at last, it seemed an exciting adventure.

British diplomat Edward Grey was less optimistic. As armies began to move, he predicted, "The lamps are going out all over Europe. We shall not see them lit again in our lifetime."

✓ **Checkpoint** Why were young men on both sides eager to fight when World War I started?

SECTION 1 **Assessment**

Progress Monitoring *Online*
For: Self-quiz with vocabulary practice
Web Code: naa-2611

Terms, People, and Places
1. For each term or place listed at the beginning of the section, write a sentence explaining its significance.

Note Taking
2. **Reading Skill: Summarize** Use your completed chart to answer the Focus Question: Why and how did World War I begin in 1914?

Comprehension and Critical Thinking
3. **Analyze Information** Why did European nations form alliances?
4. **Identify Central Issues** Why might the Balkans be called the "powder keg of Europe"?
5. **Recognize Causes** How did Austria's government react to the assassination of Archduke Francis Ferdinand?
6. **Determine Relevance** What role did geography play in the outbreak of World War I?

● **Writing About History**
Quick Write: Identify Causes and Effects Choose a specific event from the section and identify one cause and one effect of the event. Ask yourself the following questions:
• Why did this event happen? (cause)
• What happened as a result of this event? (effect)
Record your ideas in a chart that shows their cause-and-effect relationships.

▼ A wounded German soldier in 1915

WITNESS HISTORY 🔊 AUDIO

A Soldier on the Western Front

❝ The blue French cloth mingled with the German grey upon the ground, and in some places the bodies were piled so high that one could take cover from shell-fire behind them. The noise was so terrific that orders had to be shouted by each man into the ear of the next. And whenever there was a momentary lull in the tumult of battle and the groans of the wounded, one heard, high up in the blue sky, the joyful song of birds! Birds singing just as they do at home in spring-time! It was enough to tear the heart out of one's body! ❞
—German soldier Richard Schmieder, writing from the trenches in France

Focus Question How and where was World War I fought?

World War I artillery shell ▶

A New Kind of War

Performance Standards

• **SSWH16b** Describe conditions on the war front for soldiers and the Battle of Verdun.

The Great War was the largest conflict in history up to that time. The French mobilized almost 8.5 million men, the British nearly 9 million, the Russians 12 million, and the Germans 11 million. "One out of every four men who went out to the World War did not come back again," recalled a survivor, "and of those who came back, many are maimed and blind and some are mad."

Stalemate on the Western Front

As the war began, German forces fought their way through Belgium toward Paris. The Belgians resisted more than German generals had expected, but the German forces prevailed. However, Germany's plans for a quick defeat of France soon faltered.

The Germans' Schlieffen Plan failed for several reasons. First, Russia mobilized more quickly than expected. After a few small Russian victories, German generals hastily shifted some troops to the east, weakening their forces in the west. Then, in September 1914, British and French troops pushed back the German drive along the Marne River. The first battle of the Marne ended Germany's hopes for a quick victory on the Western Front.

Both sides then began to dig deep trenches to protect their armies from fierce enemy fire. They did not know that the conflict would turn into a long, deadly **stalemate,** a deadlock in which neither side is able to defeat the other. Battle lines in France would remain almost unchanged for four years.

Terms, People, and Places

stalemate   convoy
zeppelin   Dardanelles
U-boat   T. E. Lawrence

N̲o̲te Taking

Reading Skill: Identify Supporting Details
Record important details about the various battlefronts of World War I in a flowchart.

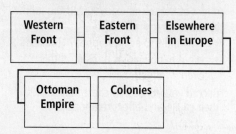

✔ **Checkpoint** How did the Allies stop the Germans from executing the Schlieffen Plan?

The Western Front and the Eastern Front, 1914–1918

Geography *Interactive*

For: Interactive map and timeline
Web Code: nap-2621

Legend:
- Allies, 1918
- Central Powers, 1918
- Neutral nations
- Front line 1914
- Front line 1915–1916
- Front line 1917
- Front line 1918
- ✦ Battle site

Map labels: 10°W, 60°N, 0°, 20°E, NORWAY, SWEDEN, 10°E, Riga, Moscow, DENMARK, Baltic Sea, North Sea, Masurian Lakes, Tannenberg, RUSSIA, UNITED KINGDOM, NETH., Elbe River, Berlin, Warsaw, Dnieper River, London, 50°N, Rhine, GERMANY, Brest-Litovsk, EASTERN FRONT, Ypres, Passchendaele, BELG., Somme, Paris, LUX., Verdun, Marne, WESTERN FRONT, Przemysl, FRANCE, Danube, Vienna, Budapest, Atlantic Ocean, SWITZ., AUSTRIA-HUNGARY, Caporetto, River, ROMANIA, Black Sea, SERBIA, BULGARIA, 30°E, ITALY, MONTENEGRO, SPAIN, Rome, OTTOMAN EMPIRE, Conic Projection, 0 300 mi, 0 300 km, 40°N, ALBANIA, Gallipoli, GREECE

Map Skills World War I was fought on several fronts in Europe. Despite huge loss of life and property, the two sides came to a stalemate on the Western and Eastern fronts in 1915 and 1916.

1. **Locate** (a) Paris (b) Battle of the Marne (c) Verdun (d) Tannenberg
2. **Movement** Using the scale, describe how the battle lines moved on the Western Front from 1914 to 1918.
3. **Draw Inferences** Based on this map, why do you think many Russians were demoralized by the progress of the war?

▲ Wounded soldiers on stretchers in Verdun in 1916

The Human Cost To break the stalemate on the Western Front, both the Allies and the Central Powers launched massive offensives in 1916. German forces tried to overwhelm the French at Verdun (vur DUN). The French defenders held firm, sending up the battle cry "They shall not pass." The 11-month struggle cost more than a half a million casualties, or soldiers killed, wounded, or missing, on both sides.

An Allied offensive at the Somme River (sum) was even more costly. In a single grisly day, nearly 60,000 British soldiers were killed or wounded. In the five-month battle, more than one million soldiers were killed, without either side winning an advantage.

Technology of Modern Warfare

The enormous casualties suffered on the Western Front proved the destructive power of modern weapons. Two significant new or improved weapons were the rapid-fire machine gun and the long-range artillery gun. Machine guns mowed down waves of soldiers. The shrapnel, or flying debris from artillery shells, killed or wounded even more soldiers than the guns. Artillery allowed troops to shell the enemy from more than 10 miles away.

Poison Gas In 1915, first Germany and then the Allies began using another new weapon—poison gas. Poison gas blinded or choked its victims or caused agonizing burns and blisters. It could be fatal. Though soldiers were eventually given gas masks, poison gas remained one of the most dreaded hazards of the war. One British soldier recalled the effects of being gassed:

> **Primary Source**
>
> 66 I suppose I resembled a kind of fish with my mouth open gasping for air. It seemed as if my lungs were gradually shutting up and my heart pounded away in my ears like the beat of a drum. . . . To get air into my lungs was real agony.99
> —William Pressey, quoted in *People at War 1914–1918*

Poison gas was an uncertain weapon. Shifting winds could blow the gas back on the soldiers who launched it.

● INFOGRAPHIC

Trench Warfare

From the end of 1914 through 1918, the warring armies on the Western Front faced each other from a vast system of deep trenches. There, millions of soldiers lived out in the open, sharing their food with rats and their beds with lice. Between the opposing trench lines lay "no man's land." In this tract of land pocked with shell holes, every house and tree had long since been destroyed. Sooner or later, soldiers would go "over the top," charging into this manmade desert. With luck, the attackers might overrun a few enemy trenches. In time, the enemy would launch a counterattack, with similar results. The struggle continued, back and forth, over a few hundred yards of territory.

Soldiers peered over the edges of their trenches, watching for the next attack.

▶ Soldiers ate, slept, and fought in trenches. Tea tins (above) supplied to British soldiers in World War I, contained 200 tablets of compressed tea.

Tanks, Airplanes, and Submarines During World War I, advances in technology, such as the gasoline-powered engine, led the opposing forces to use tanks, airplanes, and submarines against each other. In 1916, Britain introduced the first armored tank. Mounted with machine guns, the tanks were designed to move across no man's land. Still, the first tanks broke down often. They failed to break the stalemate.

Both sides also used aircraft. At first, planes were <u>utilized</u> simply to observe enemy troop movements. In 1915, Germany used **zeppelins** (ZEP uh linz), large gas-filled balloons, to bomb the English coast. Later, both sides equipped airplanes with machine guns. Pilots known as "flying aces" <u>confronted</u> each other in the skies. These "dogfights" were spectacular, but had little effect on the course of the war on the ground.

Submarines proved much more important. German **U-boats,** nicknamed from the German word for submarine, *Unterseeboot,* did tremendous damage to the Allied side, sinking merchant ships carrying vital supplies to Britain. To defend against the submarines, the Allies organized **convoys,** or groups of merchant ships protected by warships.

✔ **Checkpoint** What made World War I much more deadly than previous wars?

Battle on Other European Fronts

On Europe's Eastern Front, battle lines shifted back and forth, sometimes over large areas. Even though the armies were not mired in trench warfare, casualties rose even higher than on the Western Front. The results were just as indecisive.

Vocabulary Builder

<u>utilized</u>—(YOOT il yzd) *vt.* put to practical use

<u>confronted</u>—(kun FRUNT id) *vt.* faced in opposition

Messenger dogs, trained to leap over barbed wire, carried vital information to the front lines. ▼

◀ **Trench Design**

Front line trenches were dug in a zigzag pattern to prevent the enemy from firing down the line.

Communications trenches, perpendicular to the front line trenches, served as routes for mail, food, supplies, reinforcements, and the transport of wounded soldiers.

Tanks, developed during the ▶ war, rolled on sturdy tracks, which allowed them to navigate through barbed wire and over the rough terrain of no man's land.

Thinking Critically

1. **Determine Relevance** How did technological advances in machine guns and tanks affect soldiers in the trenches?
2. **Make Inferences** What effect do you think that trench warfare had on soldiers' morale?

Russian Losses on the Eastern Front In August 1914, Russian armies pushed into eastern Germany. Then, the Russians suffered a disastrous defeat at Tannenberg, causing them to retreat back into Russia. As the least industrialized of the great powers, Russia was poorly equipped to fight a modern war. Some troops even lacked rifles. Still, Russian commanders continued to send masses of soldiers into combat.

New Combatants in the Balkans and Southern Europe The Balkans were another battleground. In 1915, Bulgaria joined the Central Powers and helped defeat its old Balkan rival Serbia. Romania, hoping to gain some land in Hungary, joined the Allies in 1916, only to be crushed by the Central Powers.

Also in 1915, Italy declared war on Austria-Hungary and later on Germany. The Allies had agreed in a secret treaty to give Italy some Austrian-ruled lands inhabited by Italians. Over the next two years, the Italians and Austrians fought eleven battles along the Isonzo river, with few major breakthroughs. In October 1917, the Austrians and Germans launched a major offensive against the Italian position at Caporetto, also on the Isonzo. The Italians retreated in disarray. British and French forces later helped stop the Central Powers' advance into Italy. Still, Caporetto proved as disastrous for Italy as Tannenberg had been for Russia.

✓ **Checkpoint** In what way was the Eastern Front different from the Western Front?

War Around the World

Though most of the fighting took place in Europe, World War I was a global conflict. Japan, allied with Britain, used the war as an excuse to seize German outposts in China and islands in the Pacific.

The Ottoman Empire Joins the Central Powers

Because of its strategic location, the Ottoman empire was a desirable ally. If the Ottoman Turks had joined the Allies, the Central Powers would have been almost completely encircled. However, the Turks joined the Central Powers in late October 1914. The Turks then cut off crucial Allied supply lines to Russia through the **Dardanelles,** a vital strait connecting the Black Sea and the Mediterranean.

In 1915, the Allies sent a massive force of British, Indian, Australian, and New Zealander troops to attempt to open up the strait. At the battle of Gallipoli (guh LIP uh lee), Turkish troops trapped the Allies on the beaches of the Gallipoli peninsula. In January 1916, after 10 months and more than 200,000 casualties, the Allies finally withdrew from the Dardanelles.

Meanwhile, Turkey was fighting Russia in the Caucasus mountains on Turkey's northern border. This region was home to ethnic Armenians, some of whom lived under Ottoman rule and some of whom lived under Russian rule. As Christians, the Armenians were a minority in the Ottoman empire and did not have the same rights as Muslims. As the Russians advanced in 1914, some

Geography *Interactive*
For: Audio guided tour
Web Code: nap-2622

The Ottoman Empire, 1914–1918

Legend:
- Ottoman Empire, 1913
- Area of Arab Revolt, 1916–1918
- Allied forces under T.E. Lawrence
- Battle site

Map labels: RUSSIA, Black Sea, 30°E, Constantinople, Gallipoli, Tigris R., Euphrates R., Mediterranean Sea, Megiddo, Baghdad, Jerusalem, PERSIA, Miller Projection, 0 400 mi, 0 400 km, KUWAIT, Persian Gulf, EGYPT, NEJD, Red Sea, HEJAZ, ANGLO-EGYPTIAN SUDAN, BRITISH ARABIAN PROTECTORATES, 20°N, ERITREA, Arabian Sea, 50°E, ETHIOPIA, 60°E

Map Skills From 1914 to 1918, the Ottoman empire struggled against enemies on multiple fronts.

Location Given that Britain controlled Egypt at this time, describe how the Ottoman empire's location affected what happened to it during World War I.

Turkish Armenians joined or helped the Russian army against the Turks. The Ottoman government used this cooperation as a reason to deport the entire Armenian population south to Syria and Mesopotamia. During the deportation, between 600,000 and 1.5 million Armenians died. Many were killed by planned massacres; others starved as they were forced to march with no food. Many Armenians fled to other countries, including the United States, leaving almost no Armenians in the historic Armenian homeland in Turkey.

On a third front, the Turks were hard hit in the Middle East. The Ottoman empire included vast areas of Arab land. In 1916, Arab nationalists led by Husayn ibn Ali (HOO sayn IB un AH lee) declared a revolt against Ottoman rule. The British government sent Colonel **T. E. Lawrence**—later known as Lawrence of Arabia—to support the Arab revolt. Lawrence led guerrilla raids against the Turks, dynamiting bridges and supply trains. Eventually, the Ottoman empire lost a great deal of territory to the Arabs, including the key city of Baghdad.

War and the Colonies European colonies were also drawn into the struggle. The Allies overran scattered German colonies in Africa and Asia. They also turned to their own colonies and dominions for troops, laborers, and supplies. Colonial recruits from British India and French West Africa fought on European battlefields. Canada, Australia, and New Zealand sent troops to Britain's aid.

People in the colonies had mixed feelings about serving. Some were reluctant to serve rulers who did not treat them fairly. Other colonial troops volunteered eagerly. They expected that their service would be a step toward citizenship or independence. As you will read, such hopes would be dashed after the war.

Armenian Refugees
A group of Armenian refugees wait for their daily rations from Near East Relief, an American organization founded to help the surviving Turkish Armenians. Public opinion, especially in the United States, was sympathetic to the Armenians during and after World War I. However, the Allies' attempts to protect the Armenians through the treaty that ended the war with Turkey ultimately failed.

✓ **Checkpoint** How did World War I affect the Ottoman empire and European colonies and dominions?

SECTION

2 Assessment

Progress Monitoring Online
For: Self-quiz with vocabulary practice
Web Code: naa-2621

Terms, People, and Places
1. For each term, person, or place listed at the beginning of the section, write a sentence explaining its significance.

Note Taking
2. **Reading Skill: Identify Supporting Details** Use your chart and concept web to answer the Focus Question: How and where was World War I fought?

Comprehension and Critical Thinking
3. **Draw Conclusions** Why did a stalemate develop on the Western Front?

4. **Synthesize Information** Describe three ways in which technology affected the war.
5. **Predict Consequences** Governments on both sides of World War I tried to keep full casualty figures and other bad news from reaching the public. What effect do you think news about disastrous defeats such as Tannenberg and Caporetto would have had on the attitudes of people back home?
6. **Recognize Causes** How did nationalism within the Ottoman Empire come into play during the war?

● **Writing About History**
Quick Write: Write a Thesis Statement Suppose that you are writing an essay on the effects of Ottoman Turkey's decision to join the Central Powers during World War I. Answer the questions below. Use your answers to create a thesis statement for the essay.
• Why were the Dardanelles important to the Allies?
• Who won the Battle of Gallipoli?
• What impact do you think Gallipoli had on the Russian war effort?

Erich Maria Remarque: *All Quiet on the Western Front*

Erich Maria Remarque (1898–1970) was wounded five times while serving in the German army during World War I. In 1929, he published *All Quiet on the Western Front,* which is often considered the greatest novel about World War I.

It follows the narrator, Paul Baumer, from eager recruit to disillusioned veteran. In this passage, Paul is trapped for hours in a foxhole with a French soldier he has just killed.

In the afternoon, about three, he is dead.

I breathe freely again. But only for a short time. Soon the silence is more unbearable than the groans. I wish the gurgling were there again, gasping hoarse, now whistling softly and again hoarse and loud.

It is mad, what I do. But I must do something. I prop the dead man up again so that he lies comfortably, although he feels nothing any more. I close his eyes. They are brown, his hair is black and a bit curly at the sides. . . .

The silence spreads. I talk and must talk. So I speak to him and say to him: "Comrade, I did not want to kill you. If you jumped in here again, I would not do it, if you would be sensible too. But you were only an idea to me before, an abstraction[1] that lived in my mind and called forth its appropriate response. It was that abstraction I stabbed. But now, for the first time, I see you are a man like me. I thought of your hand-grenades, of your bayonet[2], of your rifle; now I see your wife and your face and our fellowship. Forgive me, comrade. We always see it too late. Why do they never tell us that you are poor devils like us, that your mothers are just as anxious as ours, and that we have the same fear of death, and the same dying and the

▲ This painting is titled *Notre-Dame de Lorette—A Soldier Walks Through the Flooded Trenches*. It was painted by François Flameng, a French artist who was given access to the front lines by the French government.

same agony—Forgive me, comrade; how could you be my enemy? If we threw away these rifles and this uniform you could be my brother just like Kat and Albert. Take twenty years of my life, comrade, and stand up—take more, for I do not know what I can even attempt to do with it now."

It is quiet, the front is still except for the crackle of rifle fire. The bullets rain over, they are not fired haphazard, but shrewdly aimed from all sides. I cannot get out.

---

1. **abstraction** (ab STRAK shun) *n.* an idea or term that is developed from a concrete reality
2. **bayonet** (bay oh NET) *n.* a blade attached to an end of a rifle for stabbing in hand-to-hand combat

---

Thinking Critically
1. **Recognize Point of View** Why does Paul speak to the dead French soldier?
2. **Synthesize Information** What does Paul mean by "We always see it too late"?

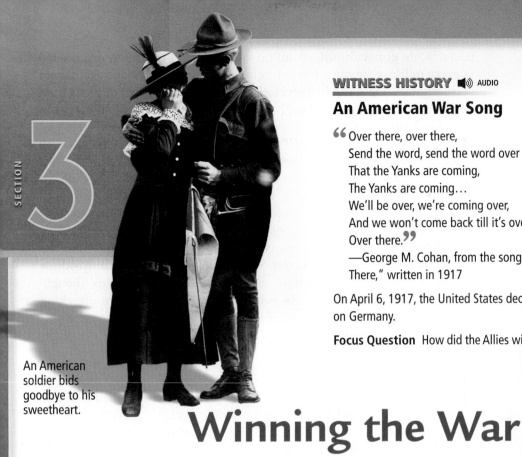

An American soldier bids goodbye to his sweetheart.

An American War Song

" Over there, over there,
Send the word, send the word over there,
That the Yanks are coming,
The Yanks are coming…
We'll be over, we're coming over,
And we won't come back till it's over
Over there. "
—George M. Cohan, from the song "Over There," written in 1917

On April 6, 1917, the United States declared war on Germany.

Focus Question How did the Allies win World War I?

Sheet music for the patriotic song "Over There"

Winning the War

GA **Performance Standards**

• **SSWH17b** Determine the causes and results of the Russian Revolution.

Terms, People, and Places

total war
conscription
contraband
Lusitania
propaganda

atrocity
Fourteen Points
self-determination
armistice

Note Taking

Reading Skill: Summarize As you read, use an outline to summarize the events in this section.

I. Waging total war
   A. Economies committed to war production
      1. Conscription
      2. Rationing
      3. Price controls
   B. Economic warfare

By 1917, European societies were cracking under the strain of war. Casualties on the fronts and shortages at home sapped morale. The stalemate dragged on, seemingly without end. Soon, however, the departure of one country from the war and the entry of another would tip the balance and end the stalemate.

Waging Total War

As the struggle wore on, nations realized that a modern, mechanized war required the channeling of a nation's entire resources into the war effort, or **total war.** To achieve total war, governments began to take a stronger role in directing the economic and cultural lives of their people.

Economies Committed to War Production Early on, both sides set up systems to recruit, arm, transport, and supply armies that numbered in the millions. All of the warring nations except Britain immediately imposed universal military **conscription,** or "the draft," which required all young men to be ready for military or other service. Britain, too, instituted conscription in 1916. Germany set up a system of forced civilian labor as well.

Governments raised taxes and borrowed huge amounts of money to pay the costs of war. They rationed food and other products, from boots to gasoline. In addition, they introduced other economic controls, such as setting prices and forbidding strikes.

Economic Warfare At the start of the war, Britain's navy formed a blockade in the North Sea to keep ships from carrying supplies in and out of Germany. International law allowed wartime blockades to confiscate **contraband,** or military supplies and raw materials needed to make military supplies, but not items such as food and clothing. In spite of international law, the British blockade stopped both types of goods from reaching Germany. As the war progressed, it became harder and harder to feed the German and Austrian people. In Germany, the winter of 1916 and 1917 was remembered as "the turnip winter," because the potato crop failed and people ate turnips instead.

To retaliate, Germany used U-boats to create its own blockade. In 1915, Germany declared that it would sink all ships carrying goods to Britain. In May 1915, a German submarine torpedoed the British liner *Lusitania* off the coast of Ireland. Almost 1,200 passengers were killed, including 128 Americans. Germany justified the attack, arguing that the *Lusitania* was carrying weapons. When American President Woodrow Wilson threatened to cut off diplomatic relations with Germany, though, Germany agreed to restrict its submarine campaign. Before attacking any ship, U-boats would surface and give warning, allowing neutral passengers to escape to lifeboats. Unrestricted submarine warfare stopped— for the moment.

Propaganda War Total war also meant controlling public opinion. Even in democratic countries, special boards censored the press. Their aim was to keep complete casualty figures and other discouraging news from reaching the public. Government censors also restricted popular literature, historical writings, motion pictures, and the arts.

Both sides waged a propaganda war. **Propaganda** is the spreading of ideas to promote a cause or to damage an opposing cause. Governments used propaganda to motivate military mobilization, especially in Britain before conscription started in 1916. In France and Germany, propaganda urged civilians to loan money to the government. Later in the war, Allied propaganda played up the brutality of Germany's invasion of Belgium. The British and French press circulated tales of **atrocities,** horrible acts

A German Submarine Sinks the *Lusitania*
The sinking of the British line *Lusitania* in 1915, illustrated below, was part of Germany's policy of unrestricted submarine warfare. The incident was featured in propaganda posters as evidence of German brutality. *How does the poster below use emotion to encourage men to enlist?*

committed against innocent people. Although some atrocities did occur, often the stories were distorted by exaggerations or completely made up.

Women Join the War Effort Women played a critical role in total war. As millions of men left to fight, women took over their jobs and kept national economies going. Many women worked in war industries, manufacturing weapons and supplies. Others joined women's branches of the armed forces. When food shortages threatened Britain, volunteers in the Women's Land Army went to the fields to grow their nation's food.

Nurses shared the dangers of the men whose wounds they tended. At aid stations close to the front lines, nurses often worked around the clock, especially after a big "push" brought a flood of casualties. In her diary, English nurse Vera Brittain describes sweating through 90-degree days in France, "stopping hemorrhages, replacing intestines, and draining and reinserting innumerable rubber tubes" with "gruesome human remnants heaped on the floor."

War work gave women a new sense of pride and confidence. After the war, most women had to give up their jobs to men returning home. Still, they had challenged the idea that women could not handle demanding and dangerous jobs. In many countries, including Britain, Germany, and the United States, women's support for the war effort helped them finally win the right to vote, after decades of struggle.

 Checkpoint Why was it important for both sides to keep civilian morale high during the war?

Morale Collapses

Despite inspiring propaganda, by 1917 the morale of troops and civilians had plunged. Germany was sending 15-year-old recruits to the front. Britain was on the brink of bankruptcy.

War Fatigue Long casualty lists, food shortages, and the failure of generals to win promised victories led to calls for peace. Instead of praising the glorious deeds of heroes, war poets began denouncing the leaders whose errors wasted so many lives. British poet and soldier Siegfried Sassoon captured the bitter mood:

> **Primary Source**
>
> 66 You smug-faced crowds with kindling eye
> Who cheer when soldier lads march by,
> Sneak home and pray you'll never know
> The hell where youth and laughter go. 99
> —Siegfried Sassoon, "Suicide in the Trenches"

As morale collapsed, troops in some French units mutinied. In Italy, many soldiers deserted during the retreat at Caporetto. In Russia, soldiers left the front to join in a full-scale revolution back home.

Revolution in Russia Three years of war had hit Russia especially hard. Stories of incompetent generals and corruption <u>eroded</u> public confidence. In March 1917, bread riots in St. Petersburg erupted into a revolution that brought down the Russian monarchy. (You'll read more about the causes and effects of the Russian Revolution in Section 5.)

At first, the Allies welcomed the overthrow of the tsar. They hoped Russia would institute a democratic government and become a stronger

BIOGRAPHY

Edith Cavell
Like most ordinary people caught up in war, Edith Cavell (1865–1915) did not plan on becoming a hero. An English nurse, she was in charge of a hospital in Belgium. After the German invasion, Cavell cared for wounded soldiers on both sides. She also helped Allied soldiers escape to the Netherlands.

In 1915, the Germans arrested Cavell for spying. As she faced a firing squad, her last reported words were, "Standing as I do in view of God and Eternity, I realize that patriotism is not enough. I must have no hatred or bitterness toward anyone." **Why do you think the British government spread the story of Edith Cavell?**

Vocabulary Builder
<u>eroded</u> (ee ROHD id)—*vt.* ate into or wore away

ally. But later that year V. I. Lenin came to power with a promise to pull Russian troops out of the war. Early in 1918, Lenin signed the Treaty of Brest-Litovsk (brest lih TAWFSK) with Germany. The treaty ended Russian participation in World War I.

Russia's withdrawal had an immediate impact on the war. With Russia out of the struggle, Germany could concentrate its forces on the Western Front. In the spring of 1918, the Central Powers stood ready to achieve the great breakthrough they had sought for so long.

✔ **Checkpoint** How did Russia's loss of morale affect the strategic position of the Allies in World War I?

American Troops "Over There"
The arrival of fresh American troops in Europe throughout 1918 helped turn the tide of the war in favor of the Allies. Recruitment posters, like the one above, inspired soldiers to enlist. *How was the experience of American soldiers different from that of other Allied soldiers?*

The United States Declares War

Soon after the Russian Revolution began, however, another event altered the balance of forces. The United States declared war on Germany. Many factors contributed to the decision of the United States to exchange neutrality for war in 1917.

Why Join the Allies? Many Americans supported the Allies because of cultural ties. The United States shared a cultural history and language with Britain and sympathized with France as another democracy. On the other hand, some German Americans favored the Central Powers. So did many Irish Americans, who resented British rule of Ireland, and Russian Jewish immigrants, who did not want to be allied with the tsar.

Germany had ceased submarine attacks in 1915 after pressure from President Wilson. However, in early 1917, Germany was desperate to break the stalemate. On February 1, the German government announced that it would resume unrestricted submarine warfare. Wilson angrily denounced Germany.

Also, in early 1917, the British intercepted a message from the German foreign minister, Arthur Zimmermann, to his ambassador in Mexico. In the note, Zimmermann authorized his ambassador to propose that Germany would help Mexico "to reconquer the lost territory in New Mexico, Texas, and Arizona" in return for Mexican support against the United States. Britain revealed the Zimmermann note to the American government. When the note became public, anti-German feeling intensified in the United States.

Declaring War In April 1917, Wilson asked Congress to declare war on Germany. "We have no selfish ends to serve," he stated. Instead, he painted the conflict idealistically as a war "to make the world safe for democracy" and later as a "war to end war."

The United States needed months to recruit, train, supply, and transport a modern army across the Atlantic. But by 1918, about two million American soldiers had joined the war-weary Allied troops fighting on the Western Front. Although relatively few American troops engaged in combat, their arrival gave Allied troops a much-needed morale boost. Just as important to the debt-ridden Allies was American financial aid.

The Fourteen Points Though he had failed to maintain American neutrality, Wilson still hoped to be a peacemaker. In January 1918, he issued the **Fourteen Points,** a list of his terms for resolving this and future wars. He called for freedom of the seas, free trade, large-scale reductions of arms, and an end to secret treaties. For Eastern Europe, Wilson favored **self-determination,** the right of people to choose their own form of government. Finally, Wilson urged the creation of a "general association of nations" to keep the peace in the future.

✓ **Checkpoint** What are three factors that led the United States to enter the war?

Victory at Last

A final showdown on the Western Front began in early 1918. The Germans badly wanted to achieve a major victory before eager American troops arrived in Europe. In March, the Germans launched a huge offensive that by July had pushed the Allies back 40 miles. These efforts exhausted the Germans, however, and by then American troops were arriving by the thousands. The Allies then launched a counterattack, slowly driving German forces back across France and Belgium. In September, German generals told the kaiser that the war could not be won.

Uprisings exploded among hungry city dwellers across Germany. German commanders advised the kaiser to step down. William II did so in early November, fleeing into exile in the Netherlands.

By autumn, Austria-Hungary was also reeling toward collapse. As the government in Vienna tottered, the subject nationalities revolted, splintering the empire of the Hapsburgs. Bulgaria and the Ottoman empire also asked for peace.

The new German government sought an **armistice,** or agreement to end fighting, with the Allies. At 11 A.M. on November 11, 1918, the Great War at last came to an end.

✓ **Checkpoint** Why did Germany ask the Allies for an armistice in November 1918?

Celebrating the Armistice
Around the globe, crowds celebrated the end of the war. Here, British and American soldiers and civilians wave the American and French flags in relief and jubilation.

Progress Monitoring Online
For: Self-quiz with vocabulary practice
Web Code: naa-2631

Terms, People, and Places

1. For each term, person, or place listed at the beginning of the section, write a sentence explaining its significance.

Note Taking

2. **Reading Skill: Summarize** Use your completed outline to answer the Focus Question: How did the Allies win World War I?

Comprehension and Critical Thinking

3. **Summarize** What measures did wartime governments take to control national economies and public opinion?

4. **Recognize Effects** What impact did wartime failures have on Russia?

5. **Draw Conclusions** Describe how the entry of United States into the war was a turning point.

6. **Analyze Information** Reread the poem by Siegfried Sassoon. What does it suggest about the effects of trench warfare?

● **Writing About History**

Quick Write: Gather Evidence to Support Thesis Statement Suppose you are writing an essay with the following thesis statement "Women played a critical role in World War I." Write three questions like the two below that would help you gather evidence to support this thesis.

• What types of things did women do during the war?

• Why was this work important?

Lloyd George,
Clemenceau, and
Wilson (left to right)
at the Paris Peace Conference.
Above right, a medal sold to raise
funds for wounded soldiers.

WITNESS HISTORY 🔊 AUDIO

Worth the Cost?

Vera Brittain, a British nurse, lost her
brother Edward and her fiancé Roland on
the battlefield.

❝ Although they would no doubt have welcomed
the idea of a League of Nations, Roland and
Edward certainly had not died in order that
Clemenceau should outwit Lloyd George, and
both of them bamboozle President Wilson, and
all three combine to make the beaten, blockaded enemy pay the cost of the War.❞
—Vera Brittain, *Testament of Youth*

Focus Question What factors influenced the
peace treaties that ended World War I, and how
did people react to the treaties?

Making the Peace

 Performance Standards

• **SSWH16c** Explain decisions on German
reparations and the mandate system in the
Versailles Treaty.

Terms, People, and Places

pandemic   radicals
reparations   collective security
                        mandate

Note Taking

Reading Skill: Summarize As you read,
summarize the main points of the text under
the heading "The Costs of War" in a
concept web like the one below.

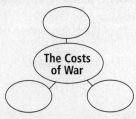

The Costs
of War

Just weeks after the war ended, President Wilson boarded a steamship bound for France. He had decided to go in person to Paris, where
Allied leaders would make the peace. Wilson was certain that he
could solve the problems of old Europe. "Tell me what is right," Wilson
urged his advisors, "and I'll fight for it." Sadly, it would not be that
easy. Europe was a shattered continent. Its problems, and those of the
world, would not be solved at the Paris Peace Conference, or for many
years afterward.

The Costs of War

The human and material costs of the war were staggering. Millions of
soldiers were dead, and even more wounded. The devastation was
made even worse in 1918 by a deadly **pandemic** of influenza. A pandemic is the spread of a disease across a large area—in this case, the
whole world. In just a few months, the flu killed more than 20 million
people worldwide.

The Financial Toll In battle zones from France to Russia, homes,
farms, factories, roads, and churches had been shelled into rubble.
People had fled these areas as refugees. Now they had to return and
start to rebuild. The costs of reconstruction and paying off huge war
debts would burden an already battered world.

Shaken and disillusioned, people everywhere felt bitter about the
war. The Allies blamed the conflict on their defeated foes and insisted
that the losers make **reparations**, or payments for war damage. The
stunned Central Powers, who had viewed the armistice as a cease-fire

rather than a surrender, looked for scapegoats on whom they could blame their defeat.

Political Turmoil Under the stress of war, governments had collapsed in Russia, Germany, Austria-Hungary, and the Ottoman empire. Political **radicals,** or people who wanted to make extreme changes, dreamed of building a new social order from the chaos. Conservatives warned against the spread of bolshevism, or communism, as it was soon called.

Unrest also swept through Europe's colonial empires. African and Asian soldiers had discovered that the imperial powers were not as invincible as they seemed. Colonial troops returned home with a more cynical view of Europeans and renewed hopes for independence.

✔ **Checkpoint** What were some of the human, economic, and political costs of the war?

● **INFOGRAPHIC**

The Costs of World War I

The war ended in 1918, but its effects would be felt for decades to come. More than 8.5 million men had died in battle. Twice that number had been wounded, many of them disabled for life. Historians estimate that from 6 to 13 million civilians also lost their lives as a result of the war. Many of the combatant nations had thrown all of their resources into the fight, leaving them little with which to rebuild. Below an American nurse tends to soldiers in France in 1918.

Financial Costs of the War*

British empire	$ $ $ $ $ $
France	$ $ $ $ $
Russia	$ $ $
United States	$ $ $ $
Germany	$ $ $ $ $ $
Austria-Hungary	$ $ $

$ Represents $10 billion

SOURCE: *The Harper Encyclopedia of Military History*, R. Ernest Dupuy and Trevor N. Dupuy
* Includes war expenditures, property losses, and shipping losses

Casualties of Mobilized Soldiers   ■ Died   ■ Taken prisoner   ■ Wounded and missing   ■ Unharmed

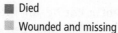

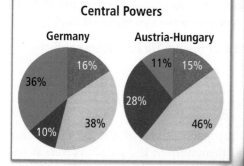

Central Powers

Germany: 16%, 36%, 10%, 38%
Austria-Hungary: 11%, 15%, 28%, 46%

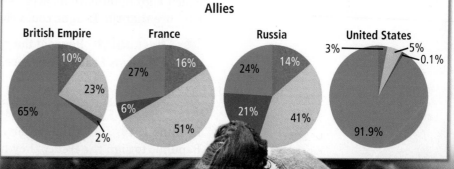

Allies

British Empire: 10%, 23%, 65%, 2%
France: 27%, 16%, 6%, 51%
Russia: 24%, 14%, 21%, 41%
United States: 3%, 5%, 0.1%, 91.9%

SOURCE: *Encyclopædia Britannica*, 2004

Thinking Critically

1. **Draw Conclusions** Which two nations suffered the highest proportion of soldier deaths? Why were American casualties relatively low?

2. **Predict Consequences** What long-term impact might the number of casualties have on a country like France?

Issue	Treaty Settlement	Problems
War Debt		
Fear of German Strength		
Nationalism		
Colonies and Other Non-European Territories		
League of Nations		

The Paris Peace Conference

The victorious Allies met at the Paris Peace Conference to discuss the fate of Europe, the former Ottoman empire, and various colonies around the world. The Central Powers and Russia were not allowed to take part in the negotiations.

Conflicting Goals Wilson was one of three strong leaders who dominated the Paris Peace Conference. He was a dedicated reformer and at times was so stubbornly convinced that he was right that he could be hard to work with. Wilson urged for "peace without victory" based on the Fourteen Points.

Two other Allied leaders at the peace conference had different aims. British prime minister David Lloyd George had promised to build a postwar Britain "fit for heroes"—a goal that would cost money. The chief goal of the French leader, Georges Clemenceau (KLEM un soh), was to weaken Germany so that it could never again threaten France. "Mr. Wilson bores me with his Fourteen Points," complained Clemenceau. "Why, God Almighty has only ten!"

Problems With the Peace Crowds of other representatives circled around the "Big Three" with their own demands and interests. The Italian prime minister, Vittorio Orlando (awr LAN doh), insisted that the Allies honor their secret agreement to give former Austro-Hungarian lands to Italy. Such secret agreements violated the principle of self-determination.

Self-determination posed other problems. Many people who had been ruled by Russia, Austria-Hungary, or the Ottoman empire now demanded national states of their own. The territories claimed by these peoples often overlapped, so it was impossible to satisfy them all. Some ethnic groups became unwanted minorities in newly created states.

Wilson had to compromise on his Fourteen Points. However, he stood firm on his goal of creating an international League of Nations. The League would be based on the idea of **collective security,** a system in which a group of nations acts as one to preserve the peace of all. Wilson felt sure that the League could correct any mistakes made in Paris.

 Checkpoint How did the goals of the Big Three leaders conflict at the Paris Peace Conference?

The Treaty of Versailles

In June 1919, the Allies ordered representatives of the new German Republic to sign the treaty they had drawn up at the palace of Versailles (vur SY) outside Paris. The German delegates were horrified. The treaty forced Germany to assume full blame for causing the war. It also imposed huge reparations that would burden an already damaged German economy. The reparations covered not only the destruction caused by the war, but also pensions for millions of Allied soldiers or their widows and families. The total cost of German reparations would later be calculated at $30 billion (the equivalent of about $2.7 trillion today).

Other parts of the treaty were aimed at weakening Germany. The treaty severely limited the size of the once-feared German military. It returned Alsace and Lorraine to France, removed hundreds of square miles of territory from western and eastern Germany, and stripped Germany of its overseas colonies. The treaty compelled many Germans to

Europe, 1914

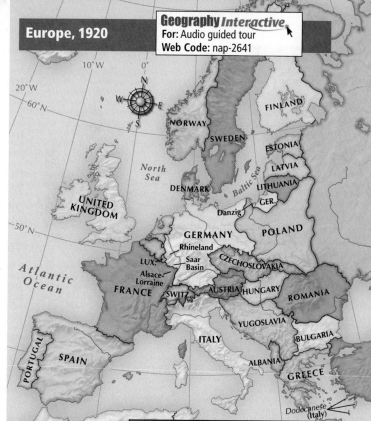

Europe, 1920

Geography *Interactive*
For: Audio guided tour
Web Code: nap-2641

leave the homes they had made in Russia, Poland, Alsace-Lorraine, and the German colonies to return to Germany or Austria.

The Germans signed because they had no choice. However, German resentment of the Treaty of Versailles would poison the international climate for 20 years. It would help spark an even deadlier world war in the years to come.

✔ **Checkpoint** Why were the German delegates surprised when they read the treaty?

Outcome of the Peace Settlements

The Allies drew up separate treaties with the other Central Powers. Like the Treaty of Versailles, these treaties left <u>widespread</u> dissatisfaction. Discontented nations waited for a chance to revise the peace settlements in their favor.

Self-Determination in Eastern Europe Where the German, Austrian, and Russian empires had once ruled, a band of new nations emerged. Poland became an independent nation after more than 100 years of foreign rule. The Baltic states of Latvia, Lithuania, and Estonia fought for and achieved independence.

Three new republics—Czechoslovakia, Austria, and Hungary—rose in the old Hapsburg heartland. In the Balkans, the peacemakers created a new South Slav state, Yugoslavia, dominated by Serbia.

The Mandate System European colonies in Africa, Asia, and the Pacific had looked to the Paris Peace Conference with high hopes. Colonial leaders expected that the peace would bring new respect and an end to imperial rule. However, the leaders at Paris applied self-determination only to parts of Europe. Outside Europe, the victorious Allies added to

Map Skills The peace treaties that ended World War I redrew the map of Europe.
1. **Locate** (a) Lithuania (b) Czechoslovakia (c) Yugoslavia (d) Poland (d) Danzig
2. **Regions** Which countries lost territory in Eastern Europe?
3. **Draw Conclusions** Why might the distribution of territory after World War I leave behind widespread dissatisfaction?

Vocabulary Builder

<u>widespread</u>—(wyd SPRED) *adj.* occurring in many places

COME ALONG, GENTS, DINNER'S READY.

Analyzing Political Cartoons

This cartoon portrays one view of the peace treaties that ended World War I.

(A) The turkey symbolizes Germany.

(B) Britain holds a carving knife and fork, ready to carve the turkey.

(C) Other Allies await the feast.

1. What does carving up the turkey symbolize?
2. What attitude do you think that the cartoonist has towards the treaties?

their overseas empires. The treaties created a system of **mandates,** territories administered by Western powers. Britain and France gained mandates over German colonies in Africa. Japan and Australia were given mandates over some Pacific islands. The treaties handled lands that used to be part of the Ottoman empire as if they were colonies, too.

In theory, mandates were to be held until they were able to stand alone. In practice, they became European colonies. From Africa to the Middle East and across Asia, people felt betrayed by the peacemakers.

The League of Nations Offers Hope The Paris Peace Conference did offer one beacon of hope with the establishment of the League of Nations. More than 40 nations joined the League. They agreed to negotiate disputes rather than resort to war and to take common action against any aggressor state.

Wilson's dream had become a reality, or so he thought. On his return from Paris, Wilson faced resistance from his own Senate. Some Republican senators, led by Henry Cabot Lodge, wanted to restrict the treaty so that the United States would not be obligated to fight in future wars. Lodge's reservations echoed the feelings of many Americans. Wilson would not accept Lodge's compromises. In the end, the Senate refused to ratify the treaty, and the United States never joined the League.

The loss of the United States weakened the League's power. In addition, the League had no power outside of its member states. As time soon revealed, the League could not prevent war. Still, it was a first step toward something genuinely new—an international organization dedicated to maintaining peace and advancing the interests of all peoples.

✓ **Checkpoint** Why did the League of Nations fail to accomplish Wilson's dreams?

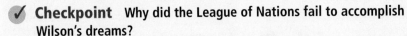

SECTION 4 **Assessment**

Terms, People, and Places

1. For each term, person, or place listed at the beginning of the section, write a sentence explaining its significance.

Note Taking

2. **Reading Skill: Summarize** Use your completed concept web and table to answer the Focus Question: What factors influenced the peace treaties that ended World War I, and how did people react to the treaties?

Comprehension and Critical Thinking

3. **Make Generalizations** Describe conditions in Europe after World War I.
4. **Draw Conclusions** How did the peace treaties both follow and violate the principle of self-determination?
5. **Draw Inferences** Wilson's closest advisor wrote of the Paris Peace Conference, "there is much to approve and much to regret." What do you think he might have approved? What might he have regretted?

● **Writing About History**

Quick Write: Choose an Organization Use an organizational strategy that suits the topic of your essay. For instance, if you are writing about one event with many causes, you might write one paragraph about each cause, followed by a paragraph that sums up the effects. If you are writing about a series of events, you might order your paragraphs chronologically.

Choose two topics from this section, one that suits the first type of organization and on that suits the second. Then write a brief outline for an essay about each.

66 Mr. War Minister!
We, soldiers from various regiments, . . . ask you to end the war and its bloodshed at any cost…. If this is not done, then believe us when we say that we will take our weapons and head out for our own hearths to save our fathers, mothers, wives, and children from death by starvation (which is nigh). And if we cannot save them, then we'd rather die with them in our native lands than be killed, poisoned, or frozen to death somewhere and cast into the earth like a dog.99
—Letter from the front, 1917

The voices from the front joined voices at home, calling for change in Russia.

Focus Question How did two revolutions and a civil war bring about Communist control of Russia?

A pin showing the Soviet hammer and sickle (left). A propaganda poster asks Russians to choose sides in the Russian Civil War (right).

SECTION 5

Revolution and Civil War in Russia

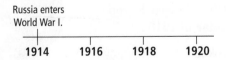 **Performance Standards**

• **SSWH16d** Analyze collapse of the Hapsburg dynasty.
• **SSWH17b** Determine the causes and results of the Russian Revolution.

Terms, People, and Places

proletariat   Cheka
soviet   commissar

N͟o͟te **Taking**

Reading Skill: Summarize Copy the timeline below and fill it in as you read this section. When you finish, write two sentences that summarize the information in your timeline.

Russia enters
World War I.

1914	1916	1918	1920

The year 1913 marked the 300th anniversary of the Romanov dynasty. Everywhere, Russians honored the tsar and his family. Tsarina Alexandra felt confident that the people loved Nicholas too much to ever threaten him. "They are constantly frightening the emperor with threats of revolution," she told a friend, "and here,—you see it yourself—we need merely to show ourselves and at once their hearts are ours."

Appearances were deceiving. In March 1917, the first of two revolutions would topple the Romanov dynasty and pave the way for even more radical changes.

The March Revolution Ends Tsarism

In 1914, the huge Russian empire stretched from Eastern Europe east to the Pacific Ocean. Unlike Western Europe, Russia was slow to industrialize despite its huge potential. Landowning nobles, priests, and an autocratic tsar controlled the government and economy. Much of the majority peasant population endured stark poverty. As Russia began to industrialize, a small middle class and an urban working class emerged.

Unrest Deepens After the Revolution of 1905, Nicholas had failed to solve Russia's basic political, economic, and social problems. The elected Duma set up after the revolution had no real power. Moderates pressed for a constitution and social change. But Nicholas II, a weak and ineffective leader, blocked attempts to limit his authority. Like past tsars, he relied on his secret police and other enforcers to impose his will. A corrupt bureaucracy and an overburdened court system added to the government's problems.

Revolutionaries hatched radical plots. Some hoped to lead discontented peasants to overthrow the tsarist regime. Marxists tried to ignite revolution among the **proletariat**—the growing class of factory and railroad workers, miners, and urban wage earners. A revolution, they believed, would occur when the time was ripe.

Impact of World War I The outbreak of war in 1914 fueled national pride and united Russians. Armies dashed to battle with enthusiasm. But like the Crimean and Russo-Japanese wars, World War I quickly strained Russian resources. Factories could not turn out enough supplies. The transportation system broke down, delivering only a trickle of <u>crucial</u> materials to the front. By 1915, many soldiers had no rifles and no ammunition. Badly equipped and poorly led, they died in staggering numbers. In 1915 alone, Russian casualties reached two million.

In a patriotic gesture, Nicholas II went to the front to take personal charge. The decision proved a disastrous blunder. The tsar was no more competent than many of his generals. Worse, he left domestic affairs to the tsarina, Alexandra. In Nicholas' absence, Alexandra relied on the advice of Gregory Rasputin, an illiterate peasant and self-proclaimed "holy man." The tsarina came to believe that Rasputin had miraculous powers after he helped her son, who suffered from hemophilia, a disorder in which any injury can result in uncontrollable bleeding.

By 1916, Rasputin's influence over Alexandra had reached new heights and weakened confidence in the government. Fearing for the monarchy, a group of Russian nobles killed Rasputin on December 29, 1916.

The Tsar Steps Down By March 1917, disasters on the battlefield, combined with food and fuel shortages on the home front, brought the monarchy to collapse. In St. Petersburg (renamed Petrograd during the war), workers were going on strike. Marchers, mostly women, surged through the streets, shouting, "Bread! Bread!" Troops refused to fire on the demonstrators, leaving the government helpless. Finally, on the advice of military and political leaders, the tsar abdicated.

Duma politicians then set up a provisional, or temporary, government. Middle-class liberals in the government began preparing a constitution for a new Russian republic. At the same time, they continued the war against Germany.

Outside the provisional government, revolutionary socialists plotted their own course. In Petrograd and other cities, they set up **soviets,** or councils of workers and soldiers. At first, the soviets worked democratically within the government. Before long, though, the Bolsheviks, a radical socialist group, took charge. The leader of the Bolsheviks was a determined revolutionary, V. I. Lenin.

The revolutions of March and November 1917 are known to Russians as the February and October revolutions. In 1917, Russia still used an old calendar, which was 13 days behind the one used in Western Europe. Russia adopted the Western calendar in 1918.

✔ **Checkpoint** What provoked the March Revolution?

Vocabulary Builder
<u>crucial</u>—(KROO shul) *adj.* of vital importance

The Tsar's Downfall
Tsarina Alexandra's reliance on the "mad monk" Gregory Rasputin (below left) to help her govern proved fatal for Rasputin, and ultimately for Alexandra. A lavish Fabergé egg (below right) details three centuries of Romanov tsars. *How do both images show the gulf between Russia's rulers and its people?*

Lenin and the Bolsheviks

Vladimir Ilyich Ulyanov (ool YAHN uf) was born in 1870 to a middle-class family. He adopted the name Lenin when he became a revolutionary. When he was 17, his older brother was arrested and hanged for plotting to kill the tsar. The execution branded his family as a threat to the state and made the young Vladimir hate the tsarist government.

A Brilliant Revolutionary As a young man, Lenin read the works of Karl Marx and participated in student demonstrations. He spread Marxist ideas among factory workers along with other socialists, including Nadezhda Krupskaya (nah DYEZ duh kroop SKY uh), the daughter of a poor noble family. In 1895, Lenin and Krupskaya were arrested and sent to Siberia. During their imprisonment, they were married. After their release, they went into exile in Switzerland. There they worked tirelessly to spread revolutionary ideas.

Lenin's View of Marx Lenin adapted Marxist ideas to fit Russian conditions. Marx had predicted that the industrial working class would rise spontaneously to overthrow capitalism. But Russia did not have a large urban proletariat. Instead, Lenin called for an elite group to lead the revolution and set up a "dictatorship of the proletariat." Though this elite revolutionary party represented a small percentage of socialists, Lenin gave them the name Bolsheviks, meaning "majority."

In Western Europe, many leading socialists had come to think that socialism could be achieved through gradual and moderate reforms such as higher wages, increased suffrage, and social welfare programs. A group of socialists in Russia, the Mensheviks, favored this approach. The Bolsheviks rejected it. To Lenin, reforms of this nature were merely capitalist tricks to repress the masses. Only revolution, he said, could bring about needed changes.

In March 1917, Lenin was still in exile. As Russia stumbled into revolution, Germany saw a chance to weaken its enemy by helping Lenin return home. Lenin rushed across Germany to the Russian frontier in a special train. He greeted a crowd of fellow exiles and activists with this cry: "Long live the world-wide Socialist revolution!"

☑ **Checkpoint** Why did Germany want Lenin to return to Russia in 1917?

The November Revolution Brings the Bolsheviks to Power

Lenin threw himself into the work of furthering the revolution. Another dynamic Marxist revolutionary, Leon Trotsky, helped lead the fight. To the hungry, war-weary Russian people, Lenin and the Bolsheviks promised "Peace, Land, and Bread."

The Provisional Government's Mistakes Meanwhile, the provisional government, led by Alexander Kerensky, continued the war effort and failed to deal with land reform. Those decisions proved fatal. Most Russians were tired of war. Troops at the front were deserting in droves. Peasants wanted land, while city workers demanded an end to the desperate shortages.

In July 1917, the government launched the disastrous Kerensky offensive against Germany. By November, according to one official report, the army was "a huge crowd of tired, poorly clad, poorly fed, embittered men." Growing numbers of troops mutinied. Peasants seized land and drove off fearful landlords.

The Bolshevik Takeover Conditions were ripe for the Bolsheviks to make their move. In November 1917, squads of Red Guards—armed factory workers—joined mutinous sailors from the Russian fleet in attacking the provisional government. In just a matter of days, Lenin's forces overthrew the provisional government without a struggle.

The Bolsheviks quickly seized power in other cities. In Moscow, it took a week of fighting to blast the local government out of the walled Kremlin, the former tsarist center of government. Moscow became the Bolsheviks' capital, and the Kremlin their headquarters.

"We shall now occupy ourselves in Russia in building up a proletarian socialist state," declared Lenin. The Bolsheviks ended private ownership of land and distributed land to peasants. Workers were given control of the factories and mines. A new red flag with an entwined hammer and sickle symbolized union between workers and peasants. Throughout the land, millions thought they had at last gained control over their own lives. In fact, the Bolsheviks—renamed Communists—would soon become their new masters.

✔ **Checkpoint**　How were the Bolsheviks able to seize power from the provisional government?

● **INFOGRAPHIC**

RUSSIA
WAR
1914 AND 1920
REVOLUTION

1914
July
Russia enters
World War I.

August
Germans defeat
Russians at the Battle
of Tannenberg.

1915
June–September
Russians retreat from
German-Austrian
offensive.

1917
March
The March Revolution forces Tsar
Nicholas to abdicate. The Duma
sets up a provisional government.

April
Lenin returns to Russia
to instigate revolution. ▶

November
The provisional government fails
to end the war and resolve internal
problems. The November Revolution
brings Bolsheviks to power.

Tsar Nicholas II (left), preoccupied by
war, neglected unrest at home. Revolts
erupted in March 1917 in response to
poor leadership and equipment on the
front and lack of food at home. ▶

Russia Plunges Into Civil War

After the Bolshevik Revolution, Lenin quickly sought peace with Germany. Russia signed the Treaty of Brest-Litovsk in March 1918, giving up a huge chunk of its territory and its population. The cost of peace was extremely high, but the Communist leaders knew that they needed all their energy to defeat a collection of enemies at home. Russia's <u>withdrawal</u> affected the hopes of both the Allies and the Central Powers, as you read in Section 3.

Opposing Forces For three years, civil war raged between the "Reds," as the Communists were known, and the counterrevolutionary "Whites." The "White" armies were made up of tsarist imperial officers, Mensheviks, democrats, and others, all of whom were united only by their desire to defeat the Bolsheviks. Nationalist groups from many of the former empire's non-Russian regions joined them in their fight. Poland, Estonia, Latvia, and Lithuania broke free, but nationalists in Ukraine, the Caucasus, and Central Asia were eventually subdued.

The Allies intervened in the civil war. They hoped that the Whites might overthrow the Communists and support the fight against Germany. Britain, France, and the United States sent forces to help the Whites. Japan seized land in East Asia that tsarist Russia had once claimed. The Allied presence, however, did little to help the Whites. The Reds appealed to nationalism and urged Russians to drive out the foreigners. In the long run, the Allied invasion fed Communist distrust of the West.

Vocabulary Builder

<u>withdrawal</u>—(with DRAW ul) *n.* the act of leaving

1918
March
Bolsheviks sign Treaty of Brest-Litovsk.

June–July
Civil war erupts between the Reds (Bolsheviks) and the Whites; the Reds execute the tsar and his family.

November
Allies sign armistice with Germany.

1920
November
Communist (Red) government wins civil war, after years of bloody fighting.

▲ The victorious Reds' symbol of worker and farmer unity—the hammer and sickle—comes to represent the new regime.

Thinking Critically
1. **Identify Central Issues** Describe Russia's performance in World War I.
2. **Draw Conclusions** How did involvement in World War I affect events within Russia?

Brutality was common in the civil war. Counterrevolutionary forces slaughtered captured Communists and tried to assassinate Lenin. The Communists shot the former tsar and tsarina and their five children in July 1918 to keep them from becoming a rallying symbol for counterrevolutionary forces.

War Under Communism The Communists used terror not only against the Whites, but also to control their own people. They organized the **Cheka,** a secret police force much like the tsar's. The Cheka executed ordinary citizens, even if they were only suspected of taking action against the revolution. The Communists also set up a network of forced-labor camps in 1919—which grew under Stalin into the dreaded Gulag.

The Communists adopted a policy known as "war communism." They took over banks, mines, factories, and railroads. Peasants in the countryside were forced to deliver almost all of their crops to feed the army and hungry people in the cities. Peasant laborers were drafted into the military or forced to work in factories.

Meanwhile, Trotsky turned the Red Army into an effective fighting force. He used former tsarist officers under the close watch of **commissars,** Communist party officials assigned to the army to teach party principles and ensure party loyalty. Trotsky's passionate speeches roused soldiers to fight. So did the order to shoot every tenth man if a unit performed poorly.

The Reds' position in the center of Russia gave them a strategic advantage. The White armies were forced to attack separately from all sides. They were never able to cooperate effectively with one another. By 1921, the Communists had managed to defeat their scattered foes.

 Checkpoint How did the Red army defeat the White army to end the civil war?

Building the Communist Soviet Union

Russia was in chaos. Millions of people had died since the beginning of World War I. Millions more perished from famine and disease. Lenin faced the enormous problem of rebuilding a shattered state and economy.

New Government, Same Problems In 1922, Lenin's Communist government united much of the old Russian empire into the Union of Soviet Socialist Republics (USSR), or Soviet Union. The Communists produced a constitution that seemed both democratic and socialist. It set up an elected legislature, later called the Supreme Soviet, and gave all citizens over 18 the right to vote. All political power, resources, and means of production would belong to workers and peasants. The Soviet Union was a multinational state made up of European and Asian peoples. In theory, all the member republics shared certain equal rights.

Reality, however, differed greatly from theory. The Communist party, not the people, reigned supreme. Just as the Russian tsars had, the party used the army and secret police to enforce its will. Russia, which was the largest republic, dominated the other republics.

Lenin's New Economic Policy On the economic front, Lenin retreated from his policy of "war communism," which had brought the economy to near collapse. Under party control, factory and mine output had fallen. Peasants stopped producing grain, knowing the government would only seize it.

In 1921, Lenin adopted the New Economic Policy, or NEP. It allowed some capitalist ventures. Although the state kept control of banks, foreign trade, and large industries, small businesses were allowed to reopen for private profit. The government also stopped squeezing peasants for grain. Under the NEP, peasants held on to small plots of land and freely sold their surplus crops.

Lenin's compromise with capitalism helped the Soviet economy recover and ended armed resistance to the new government. By 1928, food and industrial production climbed back to prewar levels. The standard of living improved, too. But Lenin always saw the NEP as just a temporary retreat from communism. His successor would soon return the Soviet Union to "pure" communism.

Stalin Takes Over Lenin died in 1924 at the age of 54. His death set off a power struggle among Communist leaders. The chief contenders were Trotsky and Joseph Stalin. Trotsky was a brilliant Marxist thinker, a skillful speaker, and an architect of the Bolshevik Revolution. Stalin, by contrast, was neither a scholar nor an orator. He was, however, a shrewd political operator and behind-the-scenes organizer. Trotsky and Stalin differed on the future of communism. Trotsky urged support for a worldwide revolution against capitalism. Stalin, more cautious, wanted to concentrate on building socialism at home first.

Eventually, Stalin isolated Trotsky within the party and stripped him of party membership. Trotsky fled the country in 1929, but continued to criticize Stalin. In 1940, a Stalinist agent murdered Trotsky in Mexico.

In 1922, Lenin had expressed grave doubts about Stalin's ambitious nature: "Comrade Stalin . . . has concentrated an enormous power in his hands; and I am not sure that he always knows how to use that power with sufficient caution." Just as Lenin had warned, in the years that followed, Stalin used ruthless measures to win dictatorial power.

Famine in Russia
Years of war took its toll on Russian people, like these starving families in the Volga region. An American journalist, accompanying an international relief team in Russia, described the horrible desolation. In village after village, he noted, "no one stirred from the little wooden house…where Russian families were hibernating and waiting for death."

✔ **Checkpoint** How did the government and the economy under Lenin differ from "pure" communism?

SECTION 5 Assessment

Progress Monitoring *Online*
For: Self-quiz with vocabulary practice
Web Code: naa-2651

Terms, People, and Places

1. For each term, person, or place listed at the beginning of the section, write a sentence explaining its significance.

Note Taking

2. **Reading Skill: Summarize** Use your completed timeline to answer the Focus Question: How did two revolutions and a civil war bring about Communist control of Russia?

Comprehension and Critical Thinking

3. **Draw Conclusions** What were the causes of the March Revolution?

4. **Recognize Ideologies** How did Lenin adapt Marxism to conditions in Russia?

5. **Recognize Cause and Effect** What were the causes and effects of the civil war in Russia?

6. **Recognize Effects** Why did Lenin compromise between the ideas of capitalism and communism in creating the NEP?

● **Writing About History**

Quick Write: Clarify Cause-and-Effect Transitions Writing clear transitions can help strengthen your points in a cause-and-effect essay. Connecting words like *since, as soon as, because* and *until* introduce causes. *Therefore, consequently, as a result,* and *then* introduce effects. Rewrite the sentence below to include a clear transition.

• Tsar Nicholas' government collapsed. He did not solve key problems.

Quick Study Guide

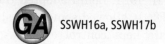

SSWH16a, SSWH17b

Progress Monitoring *Online*
For: Self-test with vocabulary practice
Web Code: naa-2611

■ Causes and Effects of World War I

Cause and Effect	
Long-Term Causes	**Immediate Causes**
• Rivalries among European powers • European alliance system • Militarism and arms race • Nationalist tensions in the Balkans	• Austria-Hungary's annexation of Bosnia and Herzegovina • Fighting in the Balkans • Assassination of Archduke Francis Ferdinand • Russian mobilization • German invasion of Belgium

↓

World War I	

↓

Immediate Effects	**Long-Term Effects**
• Enormous cost in lives and property • Revolution in Russia • Creation of new nations in Eastern Europe • German reparations • German loss of overseas colonies • Balfour Declaration • League of Nations	• Economic impact of war debts on Europe • Stronger central governments • Emergence of United States and Japan as important powers • Growth of nationalism in colonies • Rise of fascism • Increased anti-Semitism in Germany • World War II

■ The Allies Fight the Central Powers

- Allies
- Colonial possessions of Allies
- Central Powers
- Colonial possessions of Central Powers

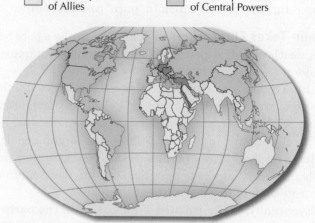

■ Key Events in the Russian Revolution

1914–1917 World War I pressures Russia.

March 1917 March Revolution causes tsar to abdicate; the provisional government takes power.

November 1917 Bolsheviks under Lenin topple provisional government (November Revolution).

■ Key Events of World War I

June 1914
Archduke Francis Ferdinand and his wife are assassinated in Sarajevo.

1916
More than two million soldiers are killed in the battle of Verdun and the battle of the Somme.

Chapter Events
Global Events

1914   **1915**   **1916**

August 1914
The Panama Canal opens.

January 1915
Japan tries to establish a protectorate over China with the Twenty-One Demands.

Concept Connector

Essential Question Review

To connect prior knowledge with what you have learned in this chapter, answer the questions below in your Concept Connector journal. Use the journal in the Reading and Note Taking Study Guide to record your answers (or go to www.phschool.com **Web Code:** nad-2607).

1. **Conflict** By 1914, the Balkans were known as the "powder keg of Europe." That same year, a Serbian terrorist assassinated Austrian Archduke Francis Ferdinand and his wife. Write a paragraph explaining why, in addition to avenging the assassination, Austria-Hungary and Germany went to war against Serbia. Think about the following:
   - nationalism
   - international rivalries
   - militarism

2. **Revolution** Compare the Russian Revolution and the French Revolution. How were they similar and different? Create a chart comparing the two revolutions in the following categories:
   - causes
   - duration/phases
   - leaders
   - world reaction
   - results

3. **Cooperation** In his farewell address, President George Washington warned against "entangling alliances." Prewar treaties between European powers were intended to promote peace by creating alliances that no country would dare attack. Identify other reasons for the formation of these prewar European alliances. Do you think the true cause of World War I was entangling alliances? Why or why not?

■ Connections To Today

1. **Conflict: The Balkan Powder Keg** The formation of Yugoslavia after World War I fulfilled the dream of a South Slav state in the Balkans. Yet unrest continued, erupting as recently as 2008. Conduct research and create a timeline of major events in the Balkans from 1918 to the present.

2. **Genocide: Memory and the Armenian Genocide** The Republic of Turkey still maintains that the deportation of the Turkish Armenian population during World War I was a result of civil unrest, not a genocide. Armenian advocacy groups disagree and wage an ongoing campaign for recognition of the Armenians' experience as a planned genocide. Find out where the campaign stands now. Summarize your findings in an essay.

Armenian Genocide in the Ottoman Empire

● Centers of deportation and massacre
→ Principal routes of deportation

| April 1917 The United States joins the Allies. | | November 1918 Armistice with Germany ends the war. | | April–May 1919 Delegates to the Paris Peace Conference draft the Treaty of Versailles. |

1917   1918   1919

1918–1919 A deadly influenza pandemic sweeps across the world, killing more than 20 million people.

February 1919 The first Pan-African Congress meets in Paris.

History *Interactive*
For: Interactive timeline
Web Code: nap-2662

Chapter Assessment

Terms, People, and Places

Choose the italicized term in parentheses that best completes each sentence.

1. The Allies tried to regain access to (*Alsace and Lorraine/the Dardanelles*) in the Battle of Gallipoli.
2. After the first battle of the Marne, the war on the Western Front turned into a/an (*entente/stalemate*) until 1918.
3. The British blockade kept both (*contraband/conscription*) and goods like food and clothing from reaching Germany.
4. Both sides used (*reparations/propaganda*) to influence public opinion as a part of total war.
5. After World War I, parts of the Middle East became (*soviets/mandates*) of Britain and France.
6. Lenin wanted to set up a "dictatorship of the (*Fourteen Points/proletariat*)" in Russia.

Main Ideas

Section 1 (pp. 816–821)
7. How did the alliance system that developed in the early 1900s help cause World War I?

Section 2 (pp. 822–828)
8. Describe trench warfare.
9. How did technology affect the way the war was fought?

Section 3 (pp. 829–833)
10. What nation joined the Allied war effort in 1917? What nation dropped out of the war in 1918? How did these two changes affect the war?

Section 4 (pp. 834–838)
11. How did the Treaty of Versailles punish Germany?

Section 5 (pp. 839–845)
12. How did World War I contribute to the collapse of the Russian monarchy?
13. How did the Bolsheviks take power in Russia?

Chapter Focus Question
14. What caused World War I and the Russian Revolution, and what effect did they have on world events?

Critical Thinking

15. **Geography and History** What role did geography play in Germany's war plans?
16. **Synthesize Information** Describe how World War I was a global war.

17. **Analyze Visuals** How did the poster above appeal to the emotions of its intended audience?
18. **Draw Inferences** What do you think Woodrow Wilson meant by "peace without victory"? Why do you think the European Allies were unwilling to accept this idea?
19. **Make Comparisons** In what ways did Soviet communism conform to the teachings of Marx? In what ways did it differ?

● Writing About History

In this chapter's five Section Assessments, you developed skills for writing a Cause-and-Effect Essay.

Writing a Cause-and-Effect Essay World War I was a definitive event of the 1900s. Write an essay in which you analyze the causes and effects of an event that took place during the World War I era. Consider using one of the following topics: Archduke Francis Ferdinand's assassination or Russia's March Revolution.

Prewriting
- Choose the topic listed above that interests you most, or choose another topic that appeals to you.
- Consider multiple causes and immediate and long-term effects of the event you've chosen. Create a cause-and-effect chart to identify your essay's most important points.

Drafting
- Develop a thesis and find information to support it.
- Choose an organizational structure for your essay.
- Write an introduction, several body paragraphs, and a conclusion. State the cause-and-effect relationship you are focusing on clearly in your introduction, and follow up your points in the conclusion.

Revising
- As you review your essay, make sure that each body paragraph supports or develops the cause-and-effect relationship you laid out in your thesis statement.
- Use the guidelines for revising your essay on page SH12 of the Writing Handbook.

Prepare for the GHSGT

The United States Enters the War

The entry of the United States into the war in April 1917 was a turning point in World War I. The documents below describe different ways that the United States affected the war.

Document A

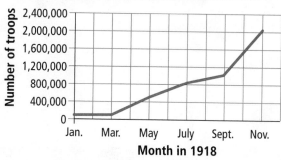

American Soldiers Arrive in Europe, 1918

Number of troops (y-axis): 0, 400,000, 800,000, 1,200,000, 1,600,000, 2,000,000, 2,400,000

Month in 1918 (x-axis): Jan., Mar., May, July, Sept., Nov.

SOURCE: *The First World War: An Eyewitness History*, Joe H. Kirchberger

Document B

"British shipping losses, especially since the declaration of unrestricted submarine warfare, had risen dangerously. . . . But the entry of the United States into the war made the German submarine warfare an evident failure, because thereafter the number of ships convoyed and the number of ships protecting the convoys was increased steadily. Convoys of ships transporting food, war materials, and troops arrived safely in Britain, and the rate of shipping construction soon exceeded the rate of loss."

—From **The End of the European Era, 1890 to the Present,**
by Felix Gilbert and David Clay Large

Document C

Winston Churchill, who served in Britain's navy and army during World War I, wrote about the effect American troops had on their tired Allies.

"The impression made upon the hard-pressed French by this seemingly inexhaustible flood of gleaming youth in its first maturity of health and vigour was prodigious [amazing]. None were under twenty, and few were over thirty . . . the French Headquarters were thrilled with the impulse of new life. . . . Half trained, half organized, with only their courage, their numbers and their magnificent youth behind their weapons, they were to buy their experience at a bitter price. But this they were quite ready to do."

Document D

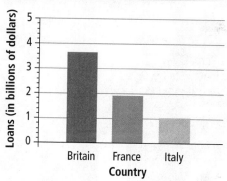

Loans From the United States to Allies

Loans (in billions of dollars) (y-axis): 0, 1, 2, 3, 4, 5

Country (x-axis): Britain, France, Italy

SOURCE: *The End of the European Era, 1890 to the Present*, Felix Gilbert and David Clay Large

Analyzing Documents

Use your knowledge of World War I and Documents A, B, C, and D to answer questions 1–4.

1. How would you describe the arrival of American troops in Europe in 1918?
   A slow at first, but rapid after March
   B steady throughout the year
   C rapid at first, but slow after March
   D No American troops arrived in Europe in 1918.

2. How did the United States navy help break Germany's submarine blockade of Britain?
   A by completely destroying the German submarine fleet
   B by finding new routes around the German submarine fleet
   C by strengthening the convoys
   D by sending supplies to France rather than Britain

3. Based on Document C, how did Churchill feel about American soldiers?
   A They were experienced, but had a poor attitude towards the war.
   B They were energetic and willing to fight, although not experienced.
   C They were well-trained and energetic.
   D They were neither energetic nor experienced.

4. **Writing Task** How did the United States help bring about the Allied victory in 1918? Use your knowledge of World War I and specific evidence from the documents to support your points.

27 Nationalism and Revolution Around the World
1910–1939

Revolution in Mexico

This Mexican peasants' song from the early 1900s reflected many Mexican's desire for change under the rule of the dictator Porfirio Díaz:

❝Our homes and humble dwellings
always full of sadness
living like animals
in the midst of riches.
On the other hand, the haciendados,
owners of lives and lands,
appear disinterested
and don't listen to our complaints.**❞**

Listen to the Witness History audio to learn more about the Mexican Revolution.

◀ **General Carranza with some of his rebel forces during the Mexican Revolution**

Mexico's Coat of Arms

Beaded elephant mask from Africa

 Performance Standards

Chapter Focus Question How did nationalism and the desire for change shape world events in the early 1900s?

Section 1
Struggle in Latin America
SSWH14b, SSWHRC1c

Section 2
Nationalism in Africa and the Middle East SSWH17d, SSWH20a

Section 3
India Seeks Self-Rule SSWH17d

Section 4
Upheavals in China SSWH17d, SSWH17f, SSWH19a

Section 5
Conflicting Forces in Japan SSWH17d, SSWH17f

Use the ☑ **Quick Study Timeline** at the end of this chapter to preview chapter events.

Japan's naval flag

 Concept Connector ONLINE

To explore Essential Questions related to this chapter, go to PHSchool.com
Web Code: nad-2707

851

Mexican peasant revolutionaries

Coffee beans, one of Latin America's major export crops

WITNESS HISTORY 🔊 AUDIO

Fighting for an Ideal

Zeferino Diego Ferreira, a peasant soldier at the time of the Mexican Revolution, describes his feelings on fighting with the rebel leaders Pancho Villa and Emiliano Zapata:

66 I am glad to have fought in the same cause with Zapata . . . and so many of my dear revolutionary friends who were left behind in the hills, their bones eaten by animals. I wasn't afraid. Just the opposite, I was *glad*. It's a *beautiful* thing to fight to realize an ideal. 99

Mexico's revolution was a dramatic fight for reform, with mixed results.

Focus Question How did Latin Americans struggle for change in the early 1900s?

Struggle in Latin America

GA Performance Standards

- **SSWH14b** Identify the causes and results of revolutions in Latin America.
- **SSWHRC1c** Explore understanding of new words in subject area texts.

Terms, People, and Places

haciendas
nationalization
economic nationalism
cultural nationalism
Good Neighbor Policy

Note Taking

Reading Skill: Identify Causes and Effects As you read, note the causes and effects of the Mexican Revolution in a chart like the one below.

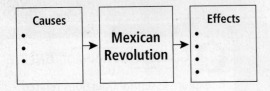

In the early 1900s, Latin America's economy was booming because of exports. Latin Americans sold their plentiful natural resources and cash crops to industrialized countries. In return, they bought products made in those countries. Meanwhile, foreign investors controlled many of Latin America's natural resources.

Stable governments helped to keep the region's economy on a good footing. Some Latin American nations, such as Argentina and Uruguay, had democratic constitutions. However, military dictators or small groups of wealthy landowners held the real power. The tiny ruling class kept the economic benefits of the booming economy for themselves. The growing middle class and the lower classes—workers and peasants—had no say in their own government. These inequalities troubled many Latin American countries, but in Mexico the situation led to an explosive revolution.

The Mexican Revolution

By 1910, the dictator Porfirio Díaz had ruled Mexico for almost 35 years, winning reelection as president again and again. On the surface, Mexico enjoyed peace and economic growth. Díaz welcomed foreign investors who developed mines, built railroads, and drilled for oil. However, underneath the surface, discontent rippled through Mexico. The country's prosperity benefited only a small group. Most Mexicans were mestizos or Indian peasants who lived in desperate poverty. Most of these peasants worked on **haciendas**, or large plantations, controlled by the landowning elite. Some peasants earned meager wages in factories and mines in Mexico's cities. Meanwhile, the growing urban middle class wanted democracy and the elite resented the power of foreign companies. All of these groups opposed the Diáz dictatorship.

The unrest boiled over in 1910 when Francisco Madero, a liberal reformer from an elite family, demanded free elections. Faced with rebellion in several parts of the country, Díaz resigned in 1911. Soon a bloody, complex struggle engulfed Mexico. (See below.)

✓ **Checkpoint** What political and economic factors helped to cause the Mexican Revolution?

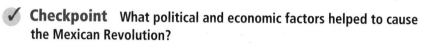

THE MEXICAN REVOLUTION

Fighting raged across Mexico for over a decade. Peasants, small farmers, ranchers, and urban workers were drawn into the violent struggle. Women soldiers called *soldaderas* cooked, tended the wounded, and fought alongside the men. The struggle took a terrible toll. When it ended, the Mexican economy was in shambles and more than one million people were dead.

1 Faced with rebellion, Díaz resigned after holding power for almost 30 years.

◄ Porfirio Díaz

2 Madero, a liberal reformer, was democratically elected in 1911. But within two years he was assassinated by one of his generals, Victoriano Huerta.

Francisco Madero ►

Victoriano Huerta

3 Huerta lost no time setting up his own dictatorship.

Emiliano Zapata ▼

Francisco "Pancho" Villa ▼

4 Villa, Zapata, and Carranza formed an uneasy coalition against Huerta. Villa and Zapata, peasants themselves, wanted to make broad changes to improve peasants' lives. Carranza, a rich landowner, disagreed. After defeating Huerta, Carranza turned on Villa and Zapata and defeated them.

◄ Venustiano Carranza

Venustiano ► Carranza

5 Carranza became president of Mexico in 1917. A new constitution passed, but reforms were slow to materialize.

Thinking Critically

1. **Sequence** Describe the events of the Mexican Revolution.
2. **Draw Inferences** Why might Carranza feel that it was in his best interests to eliminate Zapata and Villa?

Revolution Leads to Change

In 1917, voters elected Venustiano Carranza president of Mexico. That year, Carranza reluctantly approved a new constitution that included land and labor reform. With amendments, it is still in force today.

The Constitution of 1917 The Constitution of 1917 addressed three major issues: land, religion, and labor. The constitution strengthened government control over the economy. It permitted the breakup of large estates, placed restrictions on foreigners owning land, and allowed **nationalization,** or government takeover, of natural resources. Church land was made "the property of the nation." The constitution set a minimum wage and protected workers' right to strike.

Although the constitution gave suffrage only to men, it did give women some rights. Women doing the same job as men were entitled to the same pay. In response to women activists, Carranza also passed laws allowing married women to draw up contracts, take part in legal suits, and have equal authority with men in spending family funds.

The PRI Controls Mexico Fighting continued on a smaller scale throughout the 1920s, including Carranza's overthrow in 1920. In 1929, the government organized what later became the Institutional Revolutionary Party (PRI). The PRI managed to accommodate many groups in Mexican society, including business and military leaders, peasants, and workers. The PRI did this by adopting some of the goals of these groups, while keeping real power in its own hands. It suppressed opposition and dissent. Using all of these tactics, the PRI brought stability to Mexico and over time carried out many desired reforms. The PRI dominated Mexican politics from the 1930s until the free election of 2000.

Reforms Materialize At first, the Constitution of 1917 was just a set of goals to be achieved in the future. But in the 1920s and 1930s, as the government finally restored order, it began to carry out reforms.

In the 1920s, the government helped some Indian communities regain lands that had been taken from them. In the 1930s, under President Lázaro Cárdenas, millions of acres of land were redistributed to peasants

A President of the People

Mexican President Lázaro Cárdenas greets people at a train station in the 1930s (below). Between 1915 and 1940, nearly 75 million acres of land was distributed to Mexico's people, fulfilling one of the goals of the Mexican Revolution. *Which president distributed the most land?*

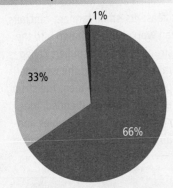

Land Distribution in Mexico by President, 1915–1940

1%
33%
66%

- ■ Lázaro Cárdenas, 1934–1940
- ■ Five presidents, 1920–1934
- ■ Venustiano Carranza, 1915–1920

SOURCE: Michael C. Meyer and William L. Sherman, *The Course of Mexican History*

under a communal land program. The government supported labor unions and launched a massive effort to combat illiteracy. Schools and libraries were set up. Dedicated teachers, often young women, worked for low pay. While they taught basic skills, they spread ideas of nationalism that began to bridge the gulf between the regions and the central government. As the revolutionary era ended, Mexico became the first Latin American nation to pursue real social and economic reforms for the majority of its people.

The government also took a strong role in directing the economy. In 1938, labor disputes broke out between Mexican workers and the management of some foreign-owned petroleum companies. In response, President Cárdenas decreed that the Mexican government would nationalize Mexico's oil resources. American and British oil companies resisted Cárdenas's decision, but eventually accepted compensation for their losses. Mexicans felt that they had at last gained economic independence from foreign influence.

 Checkpoint How did the Constitution of 1917 try to resolve some of the problems that started the revolution?

Nationalism at Work in Latin America

Mexico's move to reclaim its oil fields from foreign investors reflected a growing spirit of nationalism throughout Latin America. This spirit focused in part on ending economic dependence on the industrial powers, especially the United States, but it echoed throughout political and cultural life as well.

Economic Nationalism During the 1920s and 1930s, world events affected Latin American economies. After World War I, trade with Europe fell off. The Great Depression that struck the United States in 1929 spread around the world in the 1930s. Prices for Latin American exports plunged as demand dried up. At the same time, the cost of imported consumer goods rose. Latin America's economies, dependent on export trade, declined rapidly.

A tide of economic nationalism, or emphasis on home control of the economy, swept Latin American countries. They were determined to develop their own industries so they would not have to buy so many products from other countries. Local entrepreneurs set up factories to produce goods. Governments raised tariffs, or taxes on imports, to protect the new industries. Governments also invested directly in new businesses. Following Mexico's lead, some nations took over foreign-owned assets. The drive to create domestic industries was not wholly successful. Unequal distribution of wealth held back economic development.

Political Nationalism The Great Depression also triggered political changes in Latin America. The economic crisis caused people to lose faith in the ruling oligarchies and the ideas of liberal government. Liberalism, a belief in the individual and in limited government, was a European theory. People began to feel that it did not work in Latin America. However, ideas about what form a new type of government should take varied.

In the midst of economic crisis, stronger, authoritarian governments of different types rose in Latin American countries. People hoped that these governments could control, direct, and protect each country's economy more effectively.

Analyzing Political Cartoons

Nationalizing Oil In 1938, Mexican President Cárdenas nationalized foreign-owned oil companies. In response, some nations boycotted Mexican oil.
1. Why is Cárdenas shown standing on a pile of oil barrels?
2. Do you think the cartoonist is Mexican? Why or why not?

Vocabulary Builder

assets—(AS ets) *n.* things of value

Note Taking

Identify Effects As you read, identify the effects of nationalism in Latin America and record them a chart like the one below.

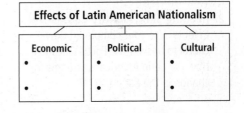

Effects of Latin American Nationalism		
Economic	Political	Cultural
•	•	•
•	•	•

Mexico's Heritage
This stained glass image shows one variation of the Mexican coat of arms that appears on Mexico's flag today. An ancient prophecy dictated that the Aztec capital should be founded where scouts saw an eagle perched on a cactus growing out of a rock surrounded by water, holding a snake in its beak. Accordingly, the founders of Tenochtitlán were believed to have seen this sign in 1325 at the site of present-day Mexico City. The symbol is an emblem of Mexican nationalism. *Why do you think that an Aztec symbol is included on the Mexican flag?*

Vocabulary Builder

intervening—(in tur VEEN ing) *vi.* coming between two arguing factions

Cultural Nationalism By the 1920s, Latin American writers, artists, and thinkers began to reject European influences in culture as well. Instead, they took pride in their own culture, with its blend of Western and native traditions.

In Mexico, **cultural nationalism,** or pride in one's own culture, was reflected in the revival of mural painting, a major art form of the Aztecs and Maya. In the 1920s and 1930s, Diego Rivera, José Clemente Orozco (oh ROHS koh), David Alfaro Siqueiros (see KEH rohs), and other muralists created magnificent works. On the walls of public buildings, they portrayed the struggles of the Mexican people for liberty. The murals have been a great source of national pride ever since.

The Good Neighbor Policy During and after World War I, investments by the United States in the nations of Latin America soared. British influence declined. The United States continued to play the role of international policeman, intervening to restore order when it felt its interests were threatened.

During the Mexican Revolution, the United States stepped in to support the leaders who favored American interests. In 1914, the United States attacked the port of Veracruz to punish Mexico for imprisoning several American sailors. In 1916, the U.S. army invaded Mexico after Pancho Villa killed more than a dozen Americans in New Mexico. This interference stirred up anti-American feelings, which increased throughout Latin America during the 1920s. For example, in Nicaragua, Augusto César Sandino led a guerrilla movement against United States forces occupying his country.

In the 1930s, President Franklin Roosevelt took a new approach to Latin America and pledged to follow "the policy of the good neighbor." Under the **Good Neighbor Policy,** the United States pledged to lessen its interference in the affairs of Latin American nations. The United States withdrew troops stationed in Haiti and Nicaragua. It lifted the Platt Amendment, which had limited Cuban independence. Roosevelt also supported Mexico's nationalization of its oil companies. The Good Neighbor policy strengthened Latin American nationalism and improved relations between Latin America and the United States.

 Checkpoint Describe how economic and political nationalism in Latin America were related.

SECTION **1** Assessment

Progress Monitoring *Online*
For: Self-quiz with vocabulary practice
Web Code: naa-2711

Terms, People, and Places
1. What do each of the key terms listed at the beginning of the section, except "haciendas," have in common? Explain.

Note Taking
2. **Reading Skill: Identify Causes and Effects** Use your completed flowcharts to answer the Focus Question: How did Latin Americans struggle for change in the early 1900s?

Comprehension and Critical Thinking
3. **Recognize Causes** Describe three causes of the Mexican Revolution.
4. **Analyze Credibility** How did the PRI fulfill some goals of the revolution but not others?
5. **Identify Central Issues** How did nationalism affect Latin America?
6. **Summarize** How did Franklin Roosevelt change the policy of the United States toward Latin America?

● **Writing About History**

Quick Write: Write a Thesis Statement A persuasive essay seeks to convince its reader to accept the writer's position on a topic. To be effective, the thesis statement must state a position that provokes valid arguments. Write an effective thesis statement on the topic of economic nationalism in Latin America.

Mexican Murals

Diego Rivera ▶

During the 1920s and 1930s, the Mexican government commissioned artists to paint beautiful murals about revolutionary themes on the walls of public buildings. The murals were meant to help all Mexicans, even those who couldn't read, learn about the ideals of the Revolution.

The most famous Mexican muralist was Diego Rivera. The panel to the right is part of a huge work on Mexican history that Rivera painted on the stairway of the National Palace in Mexico City.

Zapata, Villa, and other revolutionaries appear at the top of the panel, holding a banner that reads "Tierra y Libertad" ("Land and Liberty")—Zapata's slogan.

The center of the composition shows an eagle sitting on a cactus. The eagle is part of a national symbol of Mexico. A variation of it appears on the current Mexican flag. However, here, the eagle holds the Aztec war symbol in its beak rather than the traditional serpent.

The bottom segment shows the conquest of Mexico by Hernán Cortés. Cortés's armies battle the native Aztecs.

Thinking Critically

1. **Make Inferences** Why do you think Diego Rivera has the Mexican eagle holding the Aztec war symbol rather than the serpent?
2. **Draw Conclusions** What do Rivera's murals reveal about how he viewed Mexican history?

AIR AFRIQUE
VISITEZ L'AFRIQUE EN AVION

A French poster urges Europeans to visit Africa.

WITNESS HISTORY 🔊 AUDIO

An African Protests Colonialism

❝If you woke up one morning and found that somebody had come to your house, and had declared that house belonged to him, you would naturally be surprised, and you would like to know by what arrangement. Many Africans at that time found that, on land that had been in the possession of their ancestors from time immemorial, they were now working as squatters or as laborers.❞
—Jomo Kenyatta, Kenyan independence leader

Focus Question How did nationalism contribute to changes in Africa and the Middle East following World War I?

Nationalism in Africa and the Middle East

 Performance Standards

- **SSWH17d** Analyze nationalism as seen in the ideas of Ataturk.
- **SSWH20a** Identify pan-Africanism and pan-Arabism.

Terms, People, and Places

apartheid	Asia Minor
Pan-Africanism	Pan-Arabism
négritude movement	Balfour Declaration

Note Taking

Reading Skill: Identify Causes and Effects Record reasons for the rise of nationalism in Africa and the Middle East and its effects in a chart like the one below.

Rise of Nationalism		
Region	**Reasons for Rise**	**Effects**
Africa		
Turkey and Persia		
Middle East		

Jomo Kenyatta, quoted above, was a leader in Kenya's struggle for independence from British rule. During the 1920s and 1930s, a new generation of leaders, proud of their unique heritage, struggled to stop imperialism and restore Africa for Africans.

Africans Resist Colonial Rule

During the early 1900s, almost every part of Africa was a European colony. Agricultural improvements in some areas caused a boom in export crops. However, the colonizers exploited the boom solely for their own benefit.

Some Africans were forced to work on plantations or in mines run by Europeans. The money they earned went to pay taxes to the colonial government. In Kenya and Rhodesia, white settlers forced Africans off the best land. The few who kept their land were forbidden to grow the most profitable crops. Only Europeans could grow these. Also in Kenya, the British made all Africans carry identification cards, imposed a tax, and restricted where they could live or travel. In other parts of Africa, farmers kept their land but had to grow cash crops, like cotton, instead of food. This led to famines in some regions.

During World War I, more than one million Africans had fought on behalf of their colonial rulers. Many had hoped that their service would lead to more rights and opportunities. Instead, the situation remained mostly the same or even worsened.

Opposing Imperialism Many Western-educated Africans criticized the injustice of imperial rule. Although they had trained for professional careers, the best jobs went to Europeans. Inspired by President Woodrow Wilson's call for self-determination, Africans condemned the colonial system. In Africa, as in other regions around the world, socialism found a growing audience. Protests and opposition to imperialism multiplied.

Racial Segregation and Nationalism in South Africa Between 1910 and 1940, whites strengthened their grip on South Africa. They imposed a system of racial segregation. Their goal was to ensure white economic, political, and social supremacy. New laws, for example, restricted better-paying jobs in mines to whites only. Blacks were pushed into low-paid, less-skilled work. As in Kenya, South African blacks had to carry passes at all times. They were evicted from the best land, which was set aside for whites, and forced to live on crowded "reserves," which were located in dry, infertile areas.

Other laws chipped away at the rights of blacks. In one South African province, educated blacks who owned property had been allowed to vote in local elections. In 1936, the government abolished that right. The system of segregation set up at this time would become even stricter after 1948, when **apartheid** (uh PAHR tayt), a policy of rigid segregation, became law.

Yet South Africa was also home to a vital nationalist movement. African Christian churches and African-run newspapers demanded rights for black South Africans. They formed a political party, later known as the African National Congress (ANC), to protest unfair laws. Their efforts, however, had no effect on South Africa's white government. Still, the ANC did build a framework for political action in later years.

✔ **Checkpoint** In what ways did colonial powers try to control African life?

Nationalism and an "Africa for Africans"

In the 1920s, a movement known as **Pan-Africanism** began to nourish the nationalist spirit and strengthen resistance. Pan-Africanism emphasized the unity of Africans and people of African descent worldwide. Among its most inspiring leaders was Jamaica-born Marcus Garvey. He preached a forceful, appealing message of "Africa for Africans" and

Segregation in South Africa
In the early 1900s, white people in South Africa began to force urban Africans to move to camps outside of the larger cities, such as this settlement outside of Cape Town. *Why do you think that the white people have forced the African people behind a barbed wire fence?*

INFOGRAPHIC

African Resistance

Opposition to imperialism grew among Africans in the 1920s and 1930s. Resistance took many forms. Those who had lost their lands to Europeans sometimes squatted, or settled illegally, on European-owned plantations. In cities, workers began to form labor unions, even though they were illegal under colonial law codes. Africans formed associations and political parties to express their opposition to the colonial system. Although large-scale revolts were rare, protests were common.

Nigeria

In 1929, Ibo market women in Nigeria denounced British policies. They demanded a voice in decisions that affected their markets (below). The "Women's War," as it was called, soon became a full-fledged revolt.

South Africa

In 1912, Pixley Ka Isaka Seme organized a political party that later became the African National Congress (ANC). Its members worked through legal means, protesting laws that restricted the freedom of black Africans.

Africa, 1925

demanded an end to colonial rule. Garvey's ideas influenced a new generation of African leaders.

Pan-African Congress Forges Ties African American scholar and activist W.E.B. DuBois (doo BOYS) organized the first Pan-African Congress in 1919. It met in Paris, where the Allies were holding their peace conference. Delegates from African colonies, the West Indies, and the United States called on the Paris peacemakers to approve a charter of rights for Africans. Although the Western powers ignored their demands, the Pan-African Congress established cooperation among African and African American leaders.

The Négritude Movement Shows Pride French-speaking writers in West Africa and the Caribbean further awakened self-confidence among Africans through the **négritude movement.** In the négritude movement, writers expressed pride in their African roots and protested colonial rule. Best known among them was the Senegalese poet Léopold Senghor, who celebrated Africa's rich cultural heritage. He fostered African pride by rejecting the negative views of Africa spread by colonial rulers. Later, Senghor would take an active role in Senegal's drive to independence, and he would serve as its first president.

Egypt Gains Independence African nationalism brought little political change, except to Egypt. Egyptians had suffered during World War I. After the war, protests, strikes, and riots forced Britain to grant Egypt independence in 1922. However, Britain still controlled Egypt's monarchy.

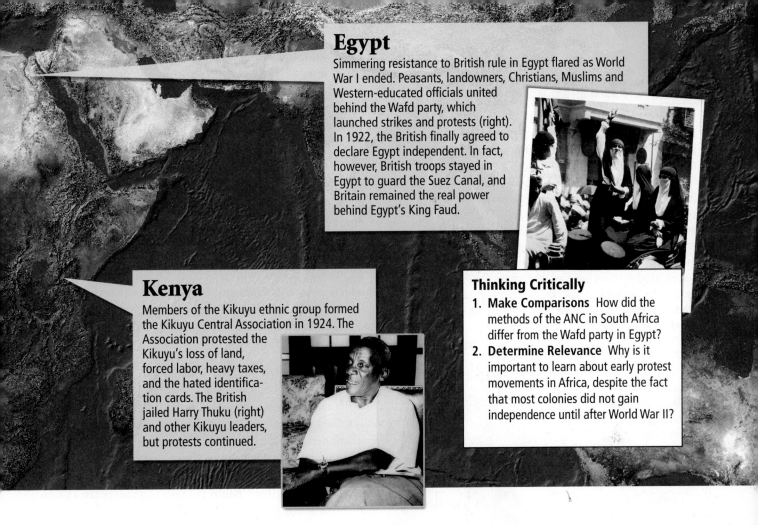

Egypt

Simmering resistance to British rule in Egypt flared as World War I ended. Peasants, landowners, Christians, Muslims and Western-educated officials united behind the Wafd party, which launched strikes and protests (right). In 1922, the British finally agreed to declare Egypt independent. In fact, however, British troops stayed in Egypt to guard the Suez Canal, and Britain remained the real power behind Egypt's King Faud.

Kenya

Members of the Kikuyu ethnic group formed the Kikuyu Central Association in 1924. The Association protested the Kikuyu's loss of land, forced labor, heavy taxes, and the hated identification cards. The British jailed Harry Thuku (right) and other Kikuyu leaders, but protests continued.

Thinking Critically

1. **Make Comparisons** How did the methods of the ANC in South Africa differ from the Wafd party in Egypt?
2. **Determine Relevance** Why is it important to learn about early protest movements in Africa, despite the fact that most colonies did not gain independence until after World War II?

Displeased with this state of affairs, during the 1930s many young Egyptians joined an organization called the Muslim Brotherhood. This group fostered a broad Islamic nationalism that rejected Western culture and denounced corruption in the Egyptian government.

✓ **Checkpoint** What significance does the phrase "Africa for Africans" have?

Turkey and Persia Modernize

Nationalist movements brought immense changes to the Middle East in the aftermath of World War I. The defeated Ottoman empire was near collapse in 1918. Its Arab lands, as you have read, were divided between Britain and France. However, in **Asia Minor,** the Turkish peninsula between the Black Sea and the Mediterranean Sea, Turks resisted Western control and fought to build a modern nation.

Atatürk Sets Goals In 1920, the Ottoman sultan reluctantly signed the Treaty of Sèvres, in which the empire lost its Arab and North African lands. The sultan also had to give up some land in Asia Minor to a number of Allied countries, including Greece. A Greek force landed in the city of Smyrna (now Izmir) to <u>assert</u> Greece's claims. Turkish nationalists, led by the determined and energetic Mustafa Kemal, overthrew the sultan, defeated the Greeks, and declared Turkey a republic. Kemal negotiated a new treaty. Among other provisions, the treaty called for about 1.3 million Greeks to leave Turkey, while some 400,000 Turks left Greece.

Vocabulary Builder
<u>assert</u>—(uh SURT) *vt.* maintain or defend

BIOGRAPHY

Atatürk (1881–1938)

"Atatürk" is the name that Mustafa Kemal gave himself when he ordered all Turkish people to take on surnames, or last names. It means "Father of the Turks." In 1920, he led Turkish nationalists in the fight against Greek forces trying to enforce the Treaty of Sèvres, establishing the borders of the modern Republic of Turkey. Once in power, he passed many reforms to modernize, Westernize, and secularize Turkey. Atatürk is still honored throughout Turkey today—his portrait appears on postage and all currency. **Why is Atatürk considered the "Father of the Turks"?**

Atatürk's Reforms in Turkey

- Replaced Islamic law with European model
- Replaced Muslim calendar with Western (Christian) calendar
- Moved day of rest from Friday to Sunday
- Closed religious schools and opened state schools
- Forced people to wear Western-style clothes
- Replaced Arabic alphabet with Latin alphabet
- Gave women the right to vote and to work outside the home.

Kemal later took the name Atatürk (ah tah TURK), meaning "father of the Turks." Between 1923 and his death in 1938, Atatürk forced through an ambitious program of radical reforms. His goals were to modernize Turkey along Western lines and to separate religion from government. To achieve these goals, Atatürk mandated that Islamic traditions in several fields be replaced with Western alternatives (see Biography).

Westernization Transforms Turkey Atatürk's government encouraged industrial expansion. The government built railroads, set up factories, and hired westerners to advise on how to make Turkey economically independent.

To achieve his reforms, Atatürk ruled with an iron hand. To many Turks, he was a hero who was transforming Turkey into a strong, modern power. Others questioned Atatürk's dictatorial powers and complete rejection of religion in laws and government. They believed that Islam could play a constructive role in a modern, civil state.

Nationalism and Reform at Work in Persia The success of Atatürk's reforms inspired nationalists in neighboring Persia (present-day Iran). Persian nationalists greatly resented the British and Russians, who had won spheres of influence over Persia in 1907. In 1925, an ambitious army officer, Reza Khan, overthrew the shah. He set up his own dynasty, with himself as shah.

Like Atatürk, Reza Khan rushed to modernize Persia and make it fully independent. He built factories, roads, and railroads and strengthened the army. He forced Persians to wear Western clothing and set up modern, secular schools. In addition, he moved to replace Islamic law with secular law and encouraged women to take part in public life. Muslim religious leaders fiercely condemned Reza Khan's efforts to introduce Western ways to the nation.

Reza Khan also persuaded the British company that controlled Persia's oil industry to give Persia a larger share of the profits and insisted that Persian workers be hired at all levels of the company. In the decades ahead, oil would become a major factor in Persia's economy and foreign policy.

 Checkpoint What did the reforms of Atatürk and Reza Khan have in common?

Arab Nationalism in the Middle East

Oil became a major factor throughout the Middle East during this period. The use of gasoline-powered engines in various vehicles during World War I showed that oil was the fuel of the future. Foreign companies began to move into the Middle East to exploit its large oil reserves.

Pan-Arabism Grows Partly in response to foreign influence, Arab nationalism grew after World War I and gave rise to **Pan-Arabism.** This nationalist movement was built on the shared heritage of Arabs who lived in lands from the Arabian Peninsula to North Africa. Today, this

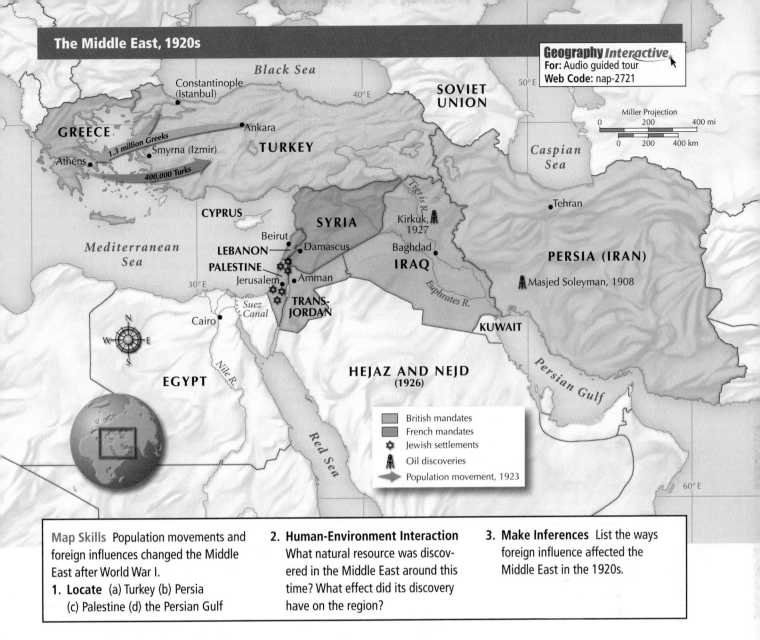

The Middle East, 1920s

Black Sea

Constantinople (Istanbul)

SOVIET UNION

50°E

GREECE

Ankara

1.3 million Greeks

Smyrna (Izmir)

TURKEY

Athens

400,000 Turks

Miller Projection

0   200   400 mi

0   200   400 km

CYPRUS

Caspian Sea

Mediterranean Sea

SYRIA

Beirut

LEBANON   Damascus

PALESTINE

Jerusalem   Amman

30°E

Kirkuk, 1927

Baghdad

IRAQ

Tigris R.

Euphrates R.

Tehran

PERSIA (IRAN)

Masjed Soleyman, 1908

Suez Canal

TRANS-JORDAN

Cairo

KUWAIT

Persian Gulf

Nile R.

EGYPT

HEJAZ AND NEJD (1926)

60°E

Red Sea

British mandates
French mandates
Jewish settlements
Oil discoveries
Population movement, 1923

Map Skills Population movements and foreign influences changed the Middle East after World War I.

1. Locate (a) Turkey (b) Persia (c) Palestine (d) the Persian Gulf

2. Human-Environment Interaction What natural resource was discovered in the Middle East around this time? What effect did its discovery have on the region?

3. Make Inferences List the ways foreign influence affected the Middle East in the 1920s.

area includes Syria, Jordan, Iraq, Egypt, Algeria, and Morocco. Pan-Arabism emphasized the common history and language of Arabs and recalled the golden age of Arab civilization. The movement sought to free Arabs from foreign domination and unite them in their own state.

Betrayal at the Peace Conference Arabs were outraged by the European-controlled mandates set up at the Paris Peace Conference. During World War I, Arabs had helped the Allies against the Central Powers, especially the Ottoman empire. In return for their help, the Allies led the Arabs to believe that they would gain independence after the war. Instead, the Allies carved up the Ottoman lands, giving France mandates in Syria and Lebanon and Britain mandates in Palestine and Iraq. Later, Britain gave a large part of the Palestinian mandate, Trans-Jordan, to Abdullah for a kingdom.

Arabs felt betrayed by the West—a feeling that has endured to this day. During the 1920s and 1930s, their anger erupted in frequent protests and revolts against Western imperialism. A major center of turmoil was the British mandate of Palestine. There, Arab nationalists and Jewish nationalists, known as Zionists, increasingly clashed.

Two Views of One Place
Posters encouraged visitors and settlers to go to Palestine. At the same time, Palestinian Arabs tried to limit Jewish settlement in the area.

Promises in Palestine Since Roman times, Jews had dreamed of returning to the land of Judea, or Israel. In 1897, Theodor Herzl (HURT sul) responded to growing anti-Semitism, or prejudice against Jewish people, in Europe by founding the modern Zionist movement. His goal was to rebuild a Jewish state in Palestine. Among other things, violent pogroms against Jews in Russia prompted thousands of them to migrate to Palestine. They joined the small Jewish community that had lived there since biblical times.

During World War I, the Allies made two conflicting sets of promises. First, they promised Arabs their own kingdoms in former Ottoman lands, including Palestine. Then, in 1917, the British attempted to win the support of European Jews by issuing the **Balfour Declaration.** In it, the British <u>advocated</u> the idea of setting up "a national home for the Jewish people" in Palestine. The declaration noted, however, that "nothing shall be done which may prejudice the civil and religious rights of existing non-Jewish communities in Palestine." Those communities were Arab. The stage was thus set for conflict between Arab and Jewish nationalists.

A Bitter Struggle Begins From 1919 to 1940, tens of thousands of Jews immigrated to Palestine due to the Zionist movement and the effects of anti-Semitism in Europe. Despite great hardships, Jewish settlers set up factories, built new towns, and established farming communities. At the same time, the Arab population almost doubled. Some were immigrants from nearby lands. As a result, Palestine's population included a changing mix of newcomers. The Jewish population, which was less than 60,000 in 1919, grew to about 400,000 in 1936, while the Muslim population increased from about 568,000 in 1919 to about 1 million in 1940.

At first, some Arabs welcomed the money and modern technical skills that the newcomers brought with them. But as more Jews moved to Palestine, tensions between the two groups developed. Jewish organizations tried to purchase as much land as they could, while Arabs sought to slow down or stop Jewish immigration. Arabs attacked Jewish settlements, hoping to discourage settlers. The Jewish settlers established their own military defense force. For the rest of the century, Arabs and Jews fought over the land that Arabs called Palestine and Jews called Israel.

 Checkpoint Why did Palestine become a center of conflict after World War I?

Progress Monitoring *Online*
For: Self-quiz with vocabulary practice
Web Code: naa-2721

Terms, People, and Places
1. For each term, person, or place listed at the beginning of the section, write a sentence explaining its significance.

N<u>ote</u> Taking
2. **Reading Skill: Identify Causes and Effects** Use your completed chart to answer the Focus Question: How did nationalism contribute to changes in Africa and the Middle East following World War I?

Comprehension and Critical Thinking
3. **Identify Central Issues** How did Africans resist colonial rule?
4. **Summarize** What are three examples of the rise of nationalism in Africa?
5. **Identify Central Issues** Why might Muslim religious leaders object to reforms in Turkey and Persia?
6. **Draw Conclusions** How did the Balfour Declaration affect the Middle East?

● Writing About History
Quick Write: Generate Arguments
When you write a persuasive essay, you want to support your thesis statement with valid, convincing arguments. You'll need to read about your topic in order to formulate your list of arguments. Write down ideas for three arguments supporting the following thesis: The ANC was a valuable political party even though it did not affect the white-run government of South Africa for many years.

Indian Frustration

In the early 1900s, many Indians were dissatisfied with British rule. An early leader of the Indian National Congress party expressed his frustration with an unpopular policy to divide the province of Bengal into smaller sections:

A Hindu servant serves tea to his mistress in colonial India.

❝ The scheme [to divide Bengal] . . . will always stand as a complete illustration of the worst features of the present system of bureaucratic rule—its utter contempt for public opinion, its arrogant pretensions to superior wisdom, its reckless disregard of the most cherished feelings of the people, the mockery of an appeal to its sense of justice, [and] its cool preference of [British civil service workers'] interests to those of the governed.❞
—Gopal Krishna Gokhale, 1905

Focus Question How did Gandhi and the Congress party work for independence in India?

India Seeks Self-Rule

 Performance Standards

- **SSWH17d** Analyze nationalism as seen in the ideas of Gandhi.

Terms, People, and Places

Amritsar massacre   untouchables
ahimsa   boycott
civil disobedience

N̲o̲te Taking

Reading Skill: Identify Causes and Effects
Recognizing causes and effects can help you understand the significance of certain events. In a chart like the one below, record the causes and effects of Gandhi's leadership of India's independence movement.

Tensions were running high in Amritsar, a city in northern India. Protests against British rule had sparked riots and attacks on British residents. On April 13, 1919, a large but peaceful crowd of Indians jammed into an enclosed field. The British commander, General Reginald Dyer, had banned public meetings, but the crowd either ignored or had not heard the order. As Indian leaders spoke, Dyer and 50 soldiers opened fire on the unarmed crowd, killing nearly 400 people and wounding more than 1,100. The **Amritsar massacre** was a turning point for many Indians. It convinced them that India needed to govern itself.

Calls for Independence

The tragedy at Amritsar was linked to broader Indian frustrations after World War I. During the war, more than a million Indians had served overseas. Under pressure from Indian nationalists, the British promised Indians greater self-government. But when the fighting ended, Britain proposed only a few minor reforms.

Since 1885, the Indian National Congress party, called the Congress party, had pressed for self-rule within the British empire. After Amritsar, it began to call for full independence. But party members were mostly middle-class, Western-educated elite who had little in common with the masses of Indian peasants. In the 1920s, a new leader named Mohandas Gandhi emerged and united Indians across class lines.

Gandhi came from a middle-class Hindu family. At age 19, he went to England to study law. Then, like many Indians, Gandhi

The Salt March

Gandhi's march to the sea to collect forbidden salt started out with Gandhi and 78 followers, but gathered strength as it progressed. As he picked up the first lump of salt, he declared, "With this, I am shaking the foundations of the British empire." *How do you think people in other countries would have reacted to British authorities using violence against this group?*

Vocabulary Builder

discriminated—(dih SKRIM ih nayt ed) *vi.* treated differently because of a prejudice

went to South Africa. For 20 years, Gandhi fought laws that <u>discriminated</u> against Indians in South Africa. In 1914, Gandhi returned to India. Soon, he became the leader of the Congress party.

✔ **Checkpoint** Why did Indians call for independence after World War I?

The Power of Nonviolence

Gandhi's ideas inspired Indians of all religious and ethnic backgrounds. His nonviolent protests caught the attention of the British government and the world.

Gandhi's Ideas Gandhi's theories embraced Hindu traditions. He preached the ancient doctrine of **ahimsa** (uh HIM sah), or nonviolence and reverence for all life. By using the power of love, he believed, people could convert even the worst wrongdoer to the right course of action. To fight against injustice, he advocated the use of nonviolent resistance.

Gandhi's philosophy reflected Western as well as Indian influences. He admired Christian teachings about love. He believed in the American philosopher Henry David Thoreau's ideas about **civil disobedience,** the refusal to obey unjust laws. Gandhi was also influenced by Western ideas of democracy and nationalism. He urged equal rights for all Indians, women as well as men. He fought hard to end the harsh treatment of **untouchables,** who were members of the lowest caste, or class.

Gandhi Sets an Example During the 1920s and 1930s, Gandhi launched a series of nonviolent actions against British rule. He called for Indians to **boycott,** or refuse to buy, British goods, especially cotton textiles. He worked to restore pride in India's traditional industries, making the spinning wheel a symbol of the nationalist movement. Gandhi's campaigns of civil disobedience attracted wide support.

✔ **Checkpoint** What methods did Indians under Gandhi use to resist British rule?

Gandhi Takes a Stand: The Salt March

To mobilize mass support, Gandhi decided to take a stand against the British salt monopoly, which he saw as a symbol of British oppression. Natural salt was available in the sea, but the British government required Indians to buy only salt sold by the monopoly.

Breaking the Law On March 12, 1930, Gandhi set out with 78 followers on a 240-mile march to the sea. As the tiny band passed through villages, crowds responded to Gandhi's message. By the time they reached the sea, the marchers numbered in the thousands. On April 6, Gandhi waded into the surf and picked up a lump of sea salt. He was soon arrested and jailed. Still, Indians followed his lead. Coastal villages started collecting salt. Indians sold salt on city streets. As Gandhi's campaign gained force, tens of thousands of Indians were imprisoned.

Steps Toward Freedom All around the world, newspapers criticized Britain's harsh reaction to the protests. Stories revealed how police brutally clubbed peaceful marchers who tried to occupy a government saltworks. Slowly, Gandhi's campaign forced Britain to hand over some power to Indians. Britain also agreed to meet other demands of the Congress party.

 Checkpoint What did the Salt March symbolize?

Looking Ahead

In 1939, a new world war exploded. Britain outraged Indian leaders by postponing independence and bringing Indians into the war without consulting them. Angry nationalists launched a campaign of noncooperation and were jailed. Millions of Indians, however, did help Britain during World War II.

When the war ended in 1945, India's independence could no longer be delayed. As it neared, Muslim fears of the Hindu majority increased. Conflict between Hindus and Muslims would trouble the new nation in the years to come.

SECTION 3 Assessment

Progress Monitoring *Online*
For: Self-quiz with vocabulary practice
Web Code: naa-2731

Terms, People, and Places

1. Place each of the key terms listed at the beginning of the section into one of the following categories: politics, culture, or economy. Write a sentence for each term explaining your choice.

Note Taking

2. **Reading Skill: Identify Causes and Effects** Use your completed chart to answer the Focus Question: How did Gandhi and the Congress party work for independence in India?

Comprehension and Critical Thinking

3. **Identify Point of View** How did the Amritsar massacre affect the movement for Indian independence?

4. **Recognize Cause and Effect** Why do you think Gandhi was able to unite Indians when earlier attempts had not succeeded?

5. **Analyze Information** How did the Salt March force Britain to respond to Indian demands?

● Writing About History

Quick Write: Use Valid Logic In a persuasive essay, you must back up your conclusions with valid logic. One common pattern of weak logic is circular reasoning, where a writer simply restates ideas instead of defending them. Bring in an example of weak logic from recent editorials in your local paper. Include a paragraph explaining the problems with the author's logic.

Mohandas Gandhi:
Hind Swaraj

Mohandas Gandhi led a successful, peaceful revolution in India against British rule. In the following excerpt from his book *Hind Swaraj (Indian Home Rule),* Gandhi explains the ideas behind his nonviolent method of passive resistance in the form of an imaginary conversation between an editor and a reader. *Hind Swaraj* was first published in 1909 in South Africa, but was banned in India.

Mohandas Gandhi ▶

Editor: Passive resistance is a method of securing rights by personal suffering; it is the reverse of resistance by arms. When I refuse to do a thing that is repugnant [offensive] to my conscience, I use soul-force. For instance, the government of the day has passed a law which is applicable to me. I do not like it. If by using violence, I force the government to repeal the law, I am employing what may be termed body-force. If I do not obey the law, and accept the penalty for its breach, I use soul-force. It involves sacrifice of self.

Everybody admits that sacrifice of self is infinitely superior to sacrifice of others. Moreover, if this kind of force is used in a cause that is unjust, only the person using it suffers. He does not make others suffer for his mistakes. Men have before now done many things which were subsequently found to have been wrong. No man can claim that he is absolutely in the right, or that a particular thing is wrong, because he thinks so, but it is wrong for him so long as that is his deliberate judgment. It is therefore meet [proper] that he should not do that which he knows to be wrong, and suffer the consequence whatever it may be. This is the key to the use of soul-force.

Reader: You would then disregard laws—this is rank disloyalty. We have always been considered a law-abiding nation. You seem to be going even beyond the extremists. They say that we must obey the laws that have been passed, but that, if the laws be bad, we must drive out the lawgivers even by force.

Editor: Whether I go beyond them or whether I do not is a matter of no consequence to either of us. We simply want to find out what is right, and to act accordingly. The real meaning of the statement that we are a law-abiding nation is that we are passive resisters. When we do not like certain laws, we do not break the heads of law-givers, but we suffer and do not submit to the laws.

Thinking Critically
1. **Identify Central Issues** What is the goal of passive resistance?
2. **Draw Conclusions** According to Gandhi, could soul-force ever be used to support an unjust cause? What does Gandhi mean when he says that a person using soul-force "does not make others suffer for his mistakes"?

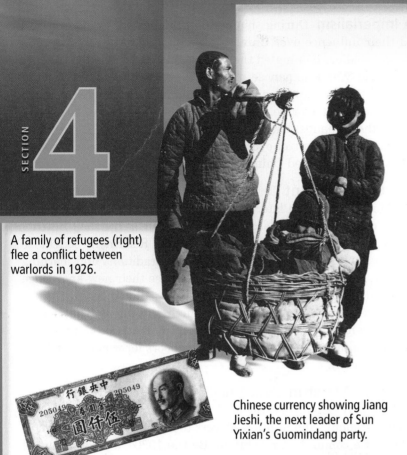

A family of refugees (right) flee a conflict between warlords in 1926.

Chinese currency showing Jiang Jieshi, the next leader of Sun Yixian's Guomindang party.

WITNESS HISTORY ◀)) AUDIO

Change in China

Sun Yixian, "father" of modern China, painted a grim picture of China after the end of the Qing dynasty.

❝ But the Chinese people have only family and clan solidarity; they do not have national spirit. Therefore, even though we have four hundred million people gathered together in one China, in reality they are just a heap of loose sand. Today we are the poorest and weakest nation in the world and occupy the lowest position in international affairs. Other men are the carving knife and serving dish, we are the fish and the meat. ❞

As Sun emphasized, China needed to change, but how and in what direction?

Focus Question How did China cope with internal division and foreign invasion in the early 1900s?

Upheavals in China

Performance Standards

- **SSWH17d** Analyze nationalism as seen in the ideas of Sun Yat Sen.
- **SSWH17f** Explain the Rape of Nanjing in China.
- **SSWH19a** Analyze Mao Zedong, Chang Kai-shek and the revolutionary movement in China.

Terms, People, and Places

Twenty-One Demands   Guomindang
May Fourth Movement   Long March
vanguard

Note Taking

Reading Skill: Recognize Multiple Causes
Use a chart like the one below to record the causes of upheaval in the Chinese Republic.

Causes of Upheaval

As the new Chinese republic took shape, nationalists like Sun Yixian (soon yee SHYAHN) set the goal of "catching up and surpassing the powers, east and west." But that goal would remain a distant dream as China suffered the turmoil of civil war and foreign invasion.

The Chinese Republic in Trouble

As you have read, China's Qing dynasty collapsed in 1911. The president of China's new republic, Sun Yixian (also called Sun Yat-sen) hoped to rebuild China on the Three Principles of the People—nationalism, democracy, and economic security for everyone. But he made little progress. China quickly fell into chaos in the face of the "twin evils" of warlord uprisings and foreign imperialism.

The Warlord Problem In 1912, Sun Yixian stepped down as president in favor of Yuan Shikai (yoo AHN shih KY), a powerful general. Sun hoped that Yuan would create a strong central government, but instead, the ambitious general tried to set up a new dynasty. The military, however, did not support Yuan, and opposition divided the nation. When Yuan died in 1916, China plunged into still greater disorder.

In the provinces, local warlords seized power. As rival armies battled for control, the economy collapsed and millions of peasants suffered terrible hardships. Famine and attacks by bandits added to their misery.

Note Taking

Reading Skill: Sequence Use a chart like the one below to sequence the fighting that went on among the Guomindang, the warlords, the Chinese Communists, and the Japanese from 1921 through 1937.

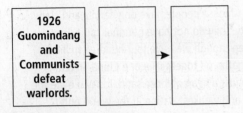

| 1926 Guomindang and Communists defeat warlords. | → | | → | |

Vocabulary Builder

intellectual—(in teh LEK choo ul) *adj.* involving the ability to reason or think clearly

Foreign Imperialism During this period of upheaval, foreign powers increased their influence over Chinese affairs. Foreign merchants, missionaries, and soldiers dominated the ports China had opened to trade.

During World War I, Japanese officials presented Yuan Shikai with the **Twenty-One Demands,** a list of demands that sought to make China a Japanese protectorate. With China too weak to resist, Yuan gave in to some of the demands. Then, in 1919, at the Paris Peace Conference, the Allies gave Japan control over some former German possessions in China. That news infuriated Chinese Nationalists.

May Fourth Movement In response, student protests erupted in Beijing on May 4, 1919, and later spread to cities across China. The protests set off a cultural and <u>intellectual</u> ferment known as the **May Fourth Movement.** Its goal was to strengthen China. Reformers sought to improve China's position by rejecting Confucian traditions and learning from the West. As in Meiji Japan, they hoped to use their new knowledge to end foreign domination.

Women played a key role in the May Fourth Movement. They joined marches and campaigned to end a number of traditional practices, including footbinding. Their work helped open doors for women in education and the economy.

The Appeal of Marxism Some Chinese turned to the revolutionary ideas of Marx and Lenin. The Soviet Union was more than willing to train Chinese students and military officers to become the **vanguard,** or elite leaders, of a communist revolution. By the 1920s, a small group of Chinese Communists had formed their own political party.

✔ **Checkpoint** How did warlord uprisings and foreign imperialism lead to the May Fourth movement?

Struggle for a New China

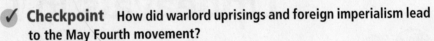

In 1921, Sun Yixian and his **Guomindang** (gwoh meen DAWNG) or Nationalist party, established a government in south China. Sun planned to raise an army, defeat the warlords, and spread his government's rule over all of China. When Western democracies refused to help, Sun accepted aid from the Soviet Union and joined forces with the small group of Chinese Communists. However, he still believed that China's future should be based on his Three Principles of the People.

Jiang Jieshi Leads the Nationalists After Sun's death in 1925, an energetic young army officer, Jiang Jieshi (jahng jeh shur), took over the Guomindang. Jiang Jieshi (also called Chiang Kai-Shek) was determined to smash the power of the warlords and reunite China, but he had little interest in either democracy or communism.

In 1926, Jiang Jieshi began the Northern Expedition in cooperation with the Chinese Communists. In the Northern Expedition, Jiang led the combined forces into northern China, crushing or winning over local warlords as he advanced and capturing Beijing. Jiang would go on to take control of a new government led by the Guomindang—but without the Communists.

Jiang Jieshi, Leader of the Guomindang
Jiang Jieshi headed the Guomindang (Nationalist) government in China from the late 1920s until 1949.

Who Should Lead the New China?

The excerpts below present the views of China's two most influential leaders on who should direct the future of China. **Critical Thinking** *Who does each person think should lead China?*

One Strong Leader	Peasant Masses
The most important point of fascism is absolute trust in a sagely able leader. Aside from complete trust in one person, there is no other leader or ism. Therefore, with the organization, although there are cadre, council members, and executives, there is no conflict among them, there is only the trust in the one leader. The leader has final decision in all matters. —Jiang Jieshi, 1933	The broad peasant masses have risen to fulfill their historic mission … the democratic forces in the rural areas have risen to overthrow the rural feudal power.… To overthrow this feudal power is the real objective of the national revolution. What Dr. Sun Yat-sen [Yixian] wanted to do … but failed to accomplish, the peasants have accomplished in a few months. —Mao Zedong, 1927

In mid-campaign, Jiang seized the chance to strike at the Chinese Communist Party, which he saw as a threat to his power. The Communists were winning converts among the small proletariat in cities like Shanghai. Early in 1927, on orders from Jiang, Guomindang troops slaughtered Communist Party members and the workers who supported them. In Shanghai and elsewhere, thousands of people were killed. This massacre marked the beginning of a bitter civil war between the Communists and the Guomindang that lasted for 22 years.

Mao Zedong and the Communists Among the Communists who escaped Jiang's attack was a young revolutionary of peasant origins, Mao Zedong (mow dzuh doong) (also called Mao Tse-tung). Unlike earlier Chinese Communists, Mao believed that the Communists should seek support not among the small urban working class but among the large peasant masses.

Although the Communists were pursued at every turn by Guomindang forces, Mao was optimistic about eventual success. In southeastern China, Mao and the Communists redistributed land to peasants and promised other reforms.

The Long March Jiang Jieshi, however, was determined to destroy the "Red bandits," as he called the Communists. He led the Guomindang in a series of "extermination campaigns" against them. The Guomindang harassed Mao's retreating army throughout the **Long March** from 1934 to 1935. Mao's forces used guerrilla, or irregular hit-and-run, tactics to fight back. At the end of the Long March, the Communists set up a new base in a remote region of northern China. There, Mao rebuilt his forces and plotted new strategies for fighting the Guomindang.

During the march, the Communists enforced strict discipline. Soldiers were told to treat peasants politely, pay for goods they wanted, and avoid damaging crops. Such behavior made Mao's forces welcome among peasants, many of whom had suffered greatly at the hands of the Guomindang.

✔ **Checkpoint** How did the Communists manage to survive Jiang's "extermination campaigns"?

Mao Zedong, Leader of the Communists
Mao Zedong led the Chinese Communists through some of their darkest times, including the Long March.

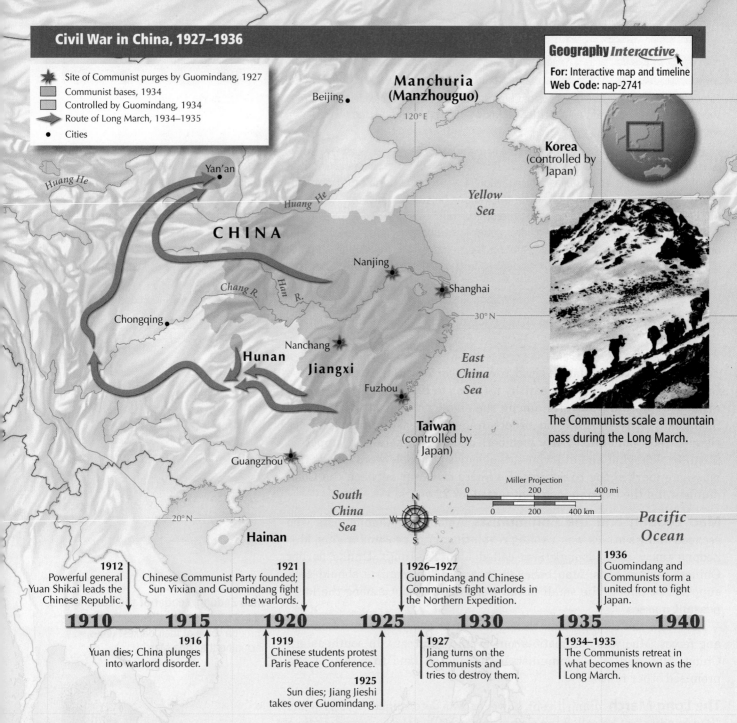

Civil War in China, 1927–1936

- ✦ Site of Communist purges by Guomindang, 1927
- ▢ Communist bases, 1934
- ▢ Controlled by Guomindang, 1934
- ➤ Route of Long March, 1934–1935
- • Cities

Geography *Interactive*

For: Interactive map and timeline
Web Code: nap-2741

Manchuria
(Manzhouguo)

Beijing •

120° E

Korea
(controlled by
Japan)

Huang He

Yan'an

Huang He

Yellow
Sea

CHINA

Nanjing

Shanghai

Chang R.   *Han R.*

30° N

Chongqing

Hunan

Nanchang

Jiangxi

*East
China
Sea*

Fuzhou

Taiwan
(controlled by
Japan)

Guangzhou

*South
China
Sea*

Miller Projection

0   200   400 mi

0   200   400 km

20° N

Hainan

*Pacific
Ocean*

The Communists scale a mountain
pass during the Long March.

1912
Powerful general
Yuan Shikai leads the
Chinese Republic.

1921
Chinese Communist Party founded;
Sun Yixian and Guomindang fight
the warlords.

1926–1927
Guomindang and Chinese
Communists fight warlords in
the Northern Expedition.

1936
Guomindang and
Communists form a
united front to fight
Japan.

1910   1915   1920   1925   1930   1935   1940

1916
Yuan dies; China plunges
into warlord disorder.

1919
Chinese students protest
Paris Peace Conference.

1925
Sun dies; Jiang Jieshi
takes over Guomindang.

1927
Jiang turns on the
Communists and
tries to destroy them.

1934–1935
The Communists retreat in
what becomes known as the
Long March.

Map Skills The Guomindang and the Communists waged a long and bitter war for control of China.

1. **Locate:** (a) Beijing (b) Shanghai (c) Jiangxi (d) Yan'an
2. **Movement** What natural features made the Long March difficult?
3. **Synthesize Information** Based on the map and timeline, describe the relationship between the Guomindang and the Communists.

One of the most dramatic events in the conflict between the Guomindang and the Communists was the epic retreat known as the Long March. During the Long March, Mao and about 100,000 of his followers fled the Guomindang. In the next year, they trekked more than 6,000 miles, facing daily attacks as they crossed rugged mountains and mighty rivers. Only about 8,000 marchers survived the ordeal. For decades, the Long March stood as a symbol of communist heroism and inspired new recruits to follow Mao. He claimed the great retreat as a victory. As he observed:

Primary Source

❝The Long March is also a seeding-machine. It has sown many seeds in eleven provinces, which will sprout, grow leaves, blossom into flowers, bear fruit, and yield a crop.❞
—Mao Zedong, "On the Tactics of Fighting Japanese Imperialism"

Japanese Invasion

While Jiang was pursuing the Communists across China, the country faced another danger. In 1931, Japan invaded Manchuria in northeastern China, adding it to the growing Japanese empire. As Japanese aggression increased, a <u>faction</u> within the Guomindang forced Jiang to form a united front with the Communists against Japan.

In 1937, the Japanese struck again, starting what became the Second Sino-Japanese War. Airplanes bombed Chinese cities, and Japanese troops overran eastern China, including Beijing and Guangzhou. Jiang Jieshi and his government retreated to the interior and set up a new capital at Chongqing (chawng CHING).

After a lengthy siege, Japanese troops marched into the city of Nanjing (nahn jing) on December 13. Nanjing was an important cultural center and had been the Guomindang capital before Chongqing. After the city's surrender, the Japanese killed hundreds of thousands of soldiers and civilians and brutalized still more. The cruelty and destruction became known around the world as the "rape of Nanjing."

The united Chinese fought back against the Japanese. The Soviet Union sent advisors and equipment to help. Great Britain, France, and the United States gave economic aid. The Guomindang and the Communists still clashed occasionally, but the united front stayed intact until the end of the war with Japan.

✔ **Checkpoint** How did the Japanese invasion help unify the Chinese temporarily?

Vocabulary Builder

faction—(FAK shun) *n.* a group within a larger group

Looking Ahead

The bombing of Pearl Harbor in 1941 brought the United States into the war against Japan and into an alliance with the Chinese. By the end of World War II, Jiang and the Guomindang controlled China's central government, but Mao's Communist Party controlled much of northern and central China. The Communists had organized hundreds of thousands of Chinese peasants at the village level, spreading their political ideas. Meanwhile, corruption grew in Jiang's government. Soon, the Communists would triumph, and Mao would impose revolutionary change on China.

SECTION 4 Assessment

Progress Monitoring *Online*
For: Self-quiz with vocabulary practice
Web Code: naa-2741

Terms, People, and Places
1. What do many of the key terms listed at the beginning of the section have in common? Explain.

Note Taking
2. **Reading Skill: Recognize Multiple Causes** Use your completed charts to answer the Focus Question: How did China cope with internal division and foreign invasion in the early 1900s?

Comprehension and Critical Thinking
3. **Identify Central Issues** Why did the new republic of China fall into chaos after 1912?
4. **Identify Point of View** Do you think that the retreating Communists' policy to pay for goods they wanted during the Long March was a good idea? Why or why not?
5. **Predict Consequences** How do you think the "rape of Nanjing" affected Japan's reputation around the world?

● **Writing About History**
Quick Write: Answer Opposing Arguments Every persuasive essay should present arguments that support the thesis *and* refute arguments that oppose the thesis. Your thesis for a persuasive essay is "The Long March ultimately helped the Chinese Communists' cause." Think of the strongest argument against this thesis, and then write a paragraph to refute that argument.

Japanese soldiers occupying a Chinese city

Japan in the Midst of Change

Groups with conflicting ideologies fought for control of Japan in the 1930s.

66 Look straight at the present state of your father-land, Japan! Where, we dare ask, can you find the genuine manifestation of the godliness of the Imperial Country of Japan? Political parties are blind in their pursuit of power and egoistic gains. Large enterprises are firmly in collusion with politicians as they suck the sweat and blood of the common people . . . Diplomacy is weak-kneed. Education is rotten to the core. Now is the time to carry out drastic, revolutionary change. Rise, and take action now! 99
—A Japanese ultranationalist criticizing the government, 1932

Focus Question How did Japan change in the 1920s and 1930s?

Conflicting Forces in Japan

 Performance Standards

- **SSWH17d** Analyze the rise of nationalism.
- **SSWH17f** Explain the conflicts that led to WWI in Europe and Asia.

Terms, People, and Places

Hirohito
ultranationalist
Manchuria

Note Taking

Reading Skill: Understand Effects As you read this section, fill in the effects of two opposing outlooks in Japan in the 1920s and 1930s in a table like the one below.

Conflicting Forces in Japan	
Liberalism in the 1920s	Militarism in the 1930s
•	•
•	•
•	•

Solemn ceremonies marked the start of Emperor Hirohito's reign. In the Secret Purple Hall, the new emperor sat on the ancient throne of Japan. Beside him was his wife, the empress Nagako. Calling on the spirits of his ancestors, he pledged "to preserve world peace and benefit the welfare of the human race."

In fact, **Hirohito** reigned from 1926 to 1989—an astonishing 63 years. During those decades, Japan experienced remarkable successes and appalling tragedies. In this section, we will focus on the 1920s and 1930s, when the pressures of extreme nationalism and economic upheaval set Japan on a militaristic and expansionist path that would engulf all of Asia.

Japan on the Rise in the 1920s

In the 1920s, Japan moved toward greater prosperity and democracy. To strengthen its relationship with other countries, Japan drew back from some of its imperial goals in the 1920s. The country grew in international prestige. However, conflicts lurked beneath the surface. The economic crisis of the Great Depression in the 1930s would bring them to light.

Growth and Expansion After World War I During World War I, the Japanese economy enjoyed remarkable growth. Its exports to Allied nations soared. Heavy industrial production grew, making Japan a true industrial power.

While Western powers battled in Europe, Japan expanded its influence throughout East Asia. Japan had already annexed Korea as a colony in 1910. During the war, Japan also sought further rights in China with the Twenty-One Demands. After the war, Japan took over former German possessions in East Asia, including the Shandong province in China.

Liberal Changes in the 1920s During the 1920s, Japan moved toward more widespread democracy. Political parties grew stronger. Elected members of the Diet—the Japanese parliament—exercised their power. In 1925, all adult men, regardless of class, won the right to vote. In addition, Western ideas about women's rights brought some changes. Overall, however, the status of Japanese women remained below that of men. They would not win suffrage, or the right to vote, until 1945.

Despite leaning toward greater democracy, political parties were <u>manipulated</u> by the zaibatsu (zy baht soo), Japan's powerful business leaders. The zaibatsu influenced the government through donations to political parties. They pushed for policies that favored international trade and their own interests.

Japan's aggressive expansion began to affect its economic relationship with the Western powers. To protect relations, moderate Japanese politicians decided to slow down foreign expansion. In 1922, Japan signed an agreement to limit the size of its navy with the United States, Britain, and France. It also agreed to leave Shandong. The government reduced military spending.

Problems Below the Surface Behind this well-being, Japan faced some grave problems. Rural peasants did not share in the nation's prosperity. They were still very poor. In the cities, factory workers earned low wages. Their poverty drew them to the socialist ideas of Marx and Lenin.

In the cities, members of the younger generation were also in revolt against tradition. They adopted Western fads and fashions. Also, they rejected family authority for the Western ideal of individual freedom, shocking their elders.

During the 1920s, tensions between the government and the military simmered not far below the surface. Conservatives, especially military officers, blasted government corruption, including payoffs by powerful zaibatsu. They also condemned Western influences for undermining basic Japanese values of obedience and respect for authority.

Although the economy grew throughout the 1920s, it experienced many highs and lows. One low point occurred when a devastating earthquake, one of the most destructive quakes in history, struck the Tokyo area in 1923. The earthquake and the widespread fires it caused resulted in the deaths of over 100,000 people and damaged more than 650,000 buildings. As many as 45 percent of surviving workers lost their jobs because so many businesses were destroyed. With help from the government, the Tokyo area gradually recovered—just as Japan faced a worldwide economic crisis.

✓ **Checkpoint** How did democratic participation in Japan both grow and stagnate in the 1920s?

Vocabulary Builder

<u>manipulated</u>—(muh NIP yoo layt id) *vt.* influenced skillfully, often unfairly

A Combination of the Old and the New In this lithograph (above), Japanese people in traditional clothing walk with others in Western clothing in one of Tokyo's parks. A woman protests low wages at a Japanese factory in 1920 (left).

Geography *Interactive*
For: Audio guided tour
Web Code: nap-2751

SOVIET UNION

Miller Projection
0   200   400 mi
0   200   400 km

Sakhalin

MONGOLIA

Manchuria
(Manzhouguo)

Vladivostok

Beijing

Port
Arthur

Korea

Yellow
Sea

*Sea of
Japan
(East Sea)*

50° N

40° N

CHINA

Shanghai

Tokyo

Osaka

JAPAN

N
W   E
S

30° N

*East
China
Sea*

Taiwan

Hong Kong
(Britain)

*Pacific
Ocean*

20° N

140° E

*South
China
Sea*

PHILIPPINES

10° N

120° E   130° E

Japan, 1890
Territory added by 1918
Territory added by 1934
Main manufacturing areas
Bauxite
Coal
Copper
Gold
Iron ore
Petroleum

Map Skills Japan expanded its territory in Asia between 1918 and 1934. From their conquered lands, the Japanese acquired natural resources to fuel their industries.

1. **Locate:** (a) Japan (b) Korea (c) Manchuria (d) Taiwan
2. **Region** Where were Japan's main manufacturing areas located?
3. **Draw Conclusions** What natural resource does Korea lack but Manchuria have?

The Nationalist Reaction

In 1929, the Great Depression rippled across the Pacific, striking Japan with devastating force. Trade suffered as foreign buyers could no longer afford to purchase Japanese silks and other exports. Unemployment in the cities soared, while rural peasants were only a mouthful from starvation.

Unrest Grows Economic disaster fed the discontent of the leading military officials and extreme nationalists, or **ultranationalists.** They condemned politicians for agreeing to Western demands to stop overseas expansion. Western industrial powers, they pointed out, had long ago grabbed huge empires. By comparison, Japan's empire was tiny.

Japanese nationalists were further outraged by racial policies in the United States, Canada, and Australia that shut out Japanese immigrants. The Japanese took great pride in their industrial achievements. They bitterly resented being treated as second-class citizens in other parts of the world.

As the economic crisis worsened, nationalists demanded renewed expansion. An empire in Asia, they argued, would provide much-needed raw materials as well as an outlet for Japan's rapidly growing population. They set their sights on the northern Chinese province of **Manchuria.** This region was rich in natural resources, and Japanese businesses had already invested heavily there.

The Manchurian Incident In 1931, a group of Japanese army officers provoked an incident that provided an excuse to seize Manchuria. They set explosives and blew up tracks on a Japanese-owned railroad line. Then, they claimed that the Chinese had committed the act. Claiming self-defense, the army attacked Chinese forces. Without consulting their own government, the Japanese military forces conquered all of Manchuria and set up a puppet state there that they called Manzhouguo (man choo KWOO). They brought in Puyi, the last Chinese emperor, to head the puppet state. When politicians in Tokyo objected to the army's highhanded actions, public opinion sided with the military.

When the League of Nations condemned Japanese aggression against China, Japan simply withdrew itself from the League. Soon, the Japanese government nullified the agreements limiting naval armament that it had signed with the Western democracies in the 1920s. The League's member states failed to take military action against Japanese aggression.

✔ **Checkpoint** How did the Great Depression lead to calls for renewed expansion?

Militarists in Power

In the early 1930s, ultranationalists were winning support from the people for foreign conquests and a tough stand against the Western powers. Members of extreme nationalist societies assassinated a number of politicians and business leaders who opposed expansion. Military leaders plotted to overthrow the government and, in 1936, briefly occupied the center of Tokyo.

Traditional Values Revived Civilian government survived, but the unrest forced the government to accept military domination in 1937. To please the ultranationalists, the government cracked down on socialists and suppressed most democratic freedoms. It revived ancient warrior values and built a cult around Emperor Hirohito, whom many believed was descended from the sun goddess. To spread its nationalist message, the government used schools to teach students absolute obedience to the emperor and service to the state.

More Expansion in China During the 1930s, Japan took advantage of China's civil war to increase its influence there. Japan expected to complete its conquest of China within a few years. But in 1939, while the two nations were locked in deadly combat, World War II broke out in Europe. That conflict swiftly spread to Asia.

In 1936, Japan allied with two aggressive European powers, Germany and Italy. These three powers signed the Tripartite Pact in September 1940, cementing the alliance known as the Axis Powers. That alliance, combined with renewed Japanese conquests, would turn World War II into a brutal, wide-ranging conflict waged not only across the continent of Europe but across Asia and the islands of the Pacific as well.

✔ **Checkpoint** What changes did militarists make when they came to power?

SECTION 5 Assessment

Terms, People, and Places

1. For each term, person, or place listed at the beginning of the section, write a sentence explaining its significance.

Note Taking

2. **Reading Skill: Understand Effects** Use your completed chart to answer the Focus Question: How did Japan change in the 1920s and 1930s?

Comprehension and Critical Thinking

3. **Summarize** What changes occurred in Japan in the 1920s?

4. **Recognize Effects** How did nationalists respond to the Great Depression?

5. **Geography and History** What role did geography play in Japan's desire to expand its empire?

6. **Predict Consequences** Why might a nation turn to military leaders and extreme nationalists during a crisis?

⬤ **Writing About History**

Quick Write: Decide on an Organizational Strategy Most persuasive essays follow this organization:

  I. Introduction, including thesis statement
 II. Second-strongest argument
III. Answer to opposing arguments
IV. Strongest argument
 V. Conclusion

Write a thesis statement based on the content of this section, and write an outline showing how you would organize your arguments.

CHAPTER 27

Quick Study Guide

SSWH17d,
SSWH19a

Progress Monitoring *Online*
For: Self-test with vocabulary practice
Web Code: naa-2761

■ Nationalism Around the World 1910–1939

Location	Goals	Expression
Mexico	To reject foreign influence	Nationalizing foreign companies; emphasizing Latin American culture
Africa	To fight for rights under colonial system	Organizing resistance, including protests, boycotts, strikes, squatting; founding of associations and political parties
Turkey and Persia	To strengthen countries by modernizing and westernizing	Secularizing daily life; adopting Western ways; building industry
The Middle East	To create a Pan-Arab state	Resisting mandate system; ongoing friction between Jewish settlers and Palestinians
India	To gain independence from British	Protesting British rule using nonviolent methods, under Gandhi's leadership
China	To lessen foreign domination of China	Resisting Japanese encroachment; attempting to strengthen China
Japan	To build an empire	Issuing the Twenty-One Demands; invading China multiple times

■ Key Leaders

Emiliano Zapata—Mexican land reformer
Venustiano Carranza—conservative Mexican president
Atatürk—father of modern Turkey
Reza Khan—modernizing Shah of Persia
Gandhi—Congress Party leader (led self-rule protest movement)
Jiang Jieshi—leader of Guomindang (Chinese Nationalists)
Mao Zedong—leader of Chinese Communist Party

■ Effects of World War I on World Events

Effects of World War I				
Trade fell off in Latin America after war.	Resistance to colonial rule grew when war service failed to improve treatment of African and Indian colonies.	Atatürk united Turkey and fought to renegotiate the Treaty of Sévres.	The Allies broke promises in the Middle East, fostering bitterness.	Japan expanded its influence in China.

■ Key Events in Latin America, Africa, and Asia

Latin America and Africa
Asia

1910
Mexican Revolution begins.

1912
Black South Africans form a political party, which later becomes the African National Congress (ANC).

1917
A new Mexican constitution is passed, but fighting continues.

1910

1915

1920

1911
Sun Yixian and the Guomindang establish the Republic of China.

1923
Atatürk founds modern Turkey.

Concept Connector

 Essential Question Review

To connect prior knowledge with what you have learned in this chapter, answer the questions below in your Concept Connector journal. Use the journal in the Reading and Note Taking Study Guide to record your answers (or go to www.phschool.com **Web Code:** nad-2707).

1. **Democracy** Mohandas Gandhi used the power of nonviolence to protest British rule and achieve democratic reforms in India. Create a flowchart to describe how Gandhi's protests launched a democratic movement in India. Focus on the following:
   - the class system
   - civil disobedience
   - boycotts
   - the Salt March

2. **Impact of the Individual** In this chapter, you read about the influence of Jiang Jieshi and Mao Zedong in China. How were the goals of Jiang and Mao similar? How were their goals different? How did each of these leaders influence events in China?

3. **Nationalism** As you have read, During the 1920s and the 1930s, economic, political, and cultural nationalism in Latin American nations were triggered by world events. Do you think nationalism unified or divided the nations of Latin America? Write a paragraph that explains your point of view. Focus on the following:
   - the world economy
   - influence of the United States on Latin America
   - the types of governments that developed in Latin America

■ Connections to Today

1. **Conflict: The Zapatista Army of National Liberation** Although Emiliano Zapata was assassinated in 1919, the spirit of his movement has lived on. In the early 1990s, poverty-stricken Indian peasants in the southern state of Chiapas formed a revolutionary group named the Zapatista Army of National Liberation, after Zapata. Conduct research on the issues behind the Zapatista movement, and then create a chart comparing issues from the Mexican Revolution era to those of the Zapatistas today.

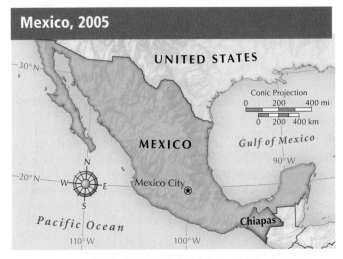

Mexico, 2005

2. **Conflict: Soweto, Then and Now** Soweto, a poor suburb of Johannesburg, South Africa, was a harsh symbol of apartheid. Soweto has changed since apartheid began to end in 1990, but poverty is still widespread. Conduct research and write two paragraphs about life in Soweto today.

1929
Ibo women protest British policies in Nigeria.

1938
Mexico nationalizes foreign-owned oil companies.

History Interactive
For: Interactive timeline
Web Code: nap-2762

1925

1930

1935

1940

1925
Jiang Jieshi becomes the leader of the Guomindang in China.

1930
Thousands of Indians join Gandhi in the Salt March.

1937
The Japanese army captures Nanjing.

Chapter Assessment

Terms, People, and Places

1. Define **economic nationalism**. How did this movement bring change to Latin America in the early 1900s?
2. What was the **Balfour Declaration**? Did it further or hinder the aims of **Pan-Arabism**? Explain.
3. Define **ahimsa** and **civil disobedience**. How did Gandhi use both in his campaign for self-rule in India?
4. What were the **Twenty-One Demands**? How were they an example of foreign imperialism in China?
5. Define **Manchuria** and **ultranationalist**. Describe how what happened in Manchuria was a result of ultranationalist aims in Japan.

Main Ideas

Section 1 (pp. 852–857)
6. What caused the Mexican Revolution?
7. How did nationalism affect Latin America in the early 1900s?

Section 2 (pp. 858–864)
8. How did African nationalism grow in the early 1900s?
9. What changes took place in the Middle East?

Section 3 (pp. 865–868)
10. How did Mohandas Gandhi help Indians work to gain self-rule?

Section 4 (pp. 869–873)
11. Describe the two phases of civil war in China.
12. How did Japan interfere in China in the 1930s?

Section 5 (pp. 874–877)
13. Describe how ultranationalists in Japan sought to solve Japan's economic problems during the Great Depression.

Chapter Focus Question
14. How did nationalism and the desire for change shape world events in the early 1900s?

Critical Thinking

15. **Draw Conclusions** How did the Good Neighbor Policy change the relationship between the United States and Latin America?
16. **Draw Inferences** How did Pan-Africanism affect people around the world?
17. **Recognize Cause and Effect** How did World War I affect relations between India and Britain?

18. **Analyzing Visuals** In the photo above, Mexican *soldaderas* stand with some male soldiers. How does this image embody some of the goals of the Mexican Revolution?
19. **Identify Central Issues** What three-sided struggle took place in China from 1937 to 1945?
20. **Predict Consequences** How were liberal changes in 1920s Japan reversed by ultranationalists in the 1930s?

● Writing About History

In this chapter's five Section Assessments, you developed skills for writing a persuasive essay.

Writing a Persuasive Essay In this chapter, you learned about how people in many different regions of the world struggled to change their lives in the early 1900s. Pick a major issue from one of these regions, choose a stance on it, and then write an essay that persuades the reader to believe in your point of view.

Prewriting
• Choose a topic that provokes a valid argument, not a topic on which most people would agree or disagree.
• Gather information about your topic to help you generate arguments.

Drafting
• Develop a thesis and arguments that support your position.
• Use an organizational structure to help build your argument.
• Write an introduction outlining your position and arguments on the topic, a body, and a conclusion.

Revising
• As you review your essay, look for and eliminate weak logic.
• Use the guidelines for revising your essay on page SH17 of the Writing Handbook.

Prepare for the GHSGT

A Fistful of Salt

Mohandas Gandhi's campaign of nonviolent resistance was a potent weapon in the Indian struggle for independence from Britain. The documents below describe one hard-fought battle: the Salt March of 1930.

Document A

"Wherever possible, civil disobedience of the salt laws should be started. These laws can be violated in three ways. It is an offense to manufacture salt wherever there are facilities for doing so. The possession and sale of contraband salt, which includes natural salt or salt earth, [is] also an offense. The purchasers of such salt will be equally guilty. To carry away the natural salt deposits on the seashore is likewise violation of the law. So is the hawking of such salt. In short, you may choose any one or all of these devices to break the salt monopoly."

—Gandhi on the Salt March

Document B

"The Salt Satyagraha started with a dramatic long march by Gandhi and a group of picked companions from Sabarmati to the coast at Dandi, 240 miles away, where he proceeded to make salt illegally by boiling sea water. The march was a publicity enterprise of great power as the press followed the party's progress . . . As he journeyed . . ., deliberately challenging established authority, village headmen began to resign in large numbers . . . in April, [India's Viceroy, Lord] Irwin reported to London that in Gujarat 'the personal influence of Gandhi threatens to create a position of real embarrassment to the administration . . . as in some areas he has already achieved a considerable measure of success in undermining the authority of Government.'"

—From ***Modern India: The Origins of Asian Democracy***
by Judith M. Brown

Document C

"Suddenly, at a word of command, scores of native policemen rushed upon the advancing marchers and rained blows on their heads with their steel-shod *lathis.* Not one of the marchers even raised an arm to fend off the blows. They went down like tenpins. . . . The survivors, without breaking ranks, silently and doggedly marched on until struck down."

—Webb Miller, a British journalist reporting on a march to the salt deposits at Dharsana

Document D

Gandhi picking up salt at the coastal village of Dandi in India, April 6, 1930

Analyzing Documents

Use your knowledge of India's struggle for self-rule and Documents A, B, C, and D to answer questions 1–4.

1. In Document A, Gandhi was mainly addressing
   A British authorities.
   B journalists around the world.
   C the British people.
   D the Indian people.

2. In Document B, the historian describes the effect of the Salt March on
   A the supply of salt.
   B the authority of the British government.
   C protesters in other countries.
   D Gandhi's health.

3. Which words from Document C reflect the attitude of the reporter toward the marchers?
   A suddenly, command
   B steel-shod *lathis,* ten-pins
   C fend, blows
   D silently, doggedly

4. **Writing Task** How was the Salt March a turning point in India's struggle for independence? Use what you have learned from these documents and the chapter in your response.

STURMABTEILUNG

WITNESS HISTORY AUDIO

Nazi Germany

Martin Niemöller, a Lutheran minister, preached against ruthless Nazi policies and was ultimately jailed. He later observed:

66 [The Nazis] came first for the Communists, and I didn't speak up because I wasn't a Communist. Then they came for the Jews, and I didn't speak up because I wasn't a Jew. Then they came for the Catholics, and I didn't speak up because I was a Protestant. Then they came for me, and by that time there was no one left to speak up. 99
—Martin Niemöller, quoted in *Time* magazine

Listen to the Witness History audio to learn more about totalitarian states in Europe.

◄ Adolf Hitler surrounded by supporters at a Nazi party rally in 1934

 Performance Standards

Chapter Focus Question What political and economic challenges did the Western world face in the 1920s and 1930s, and how did various countries react to these challenges?

Section 1
Postwar Social Changes
SSWH17a

Section 2
The Western Democracies Stumble
SSWH16c

Section 3
Fascism in Italy
SSWH17c, SSWH17e, SSWH17f

Section 4
The Soviet Union Under Stalin
SSWH17b, SSWH17e

Section 5
Hitler and the Rise of Nazi Germany
SSWH17c, SSWH17e, SSWH17f

Use the ☑ **Quick Study Timeline** at the end of this chapter to preview chapter events.

A toy replica of a Nazi storm trooper

A magazine cover showing a Jazz Age flapper

A mug shot from a Soviet secret police file

 Concept Connector ONLINE

To explore Essential Questions related to this chapter, go to PHSchool.com Web Code: nad-2807

Jazz musician
Louis Armstrong

WITNESS HISTORY 🔊 AUDIO

The Jazz Age

Many young people reacted to the trauma of World War I by rejecting the values of their parents. During the Jazz Age, this rebellion was exemplified by a new type of young woman—the flapper.

66 The Flapper awoke from her lethargy [tiredness] . . . bobbed her hair, put on her choicest pair of earrings and a great deal of audacity [boldness] and rouge, and went into the battle. She flirted because it was fun to flirt and . . . refused to be bored chiefly because she wasn't boring. . . . Mothers disapproved of their sons taking the Flapper to dances, to teas, to swim, and most of all to heart. 99
—Zelda Fitzgerald, flapper and wife of author F. Scott Fitzgerald

Focus Question What changes did Western society and culture experience after World War I?

Postwar Social Changes

 Performance Standards

- **SSWH17a** Examine the influence of Albert Einstein on science, Sigmund Freud on social thinking, and Pablo Picasso on art.

Terms, People, and Places

flapper
Prohibition
speakeasies
Harlem Renaissance

psychoanalysis
abstract
dada
surrealism

Note Taking

Reading Skill: Identify Supporting Details Use a concept web like the one below to record details related to the main ideas of this section.

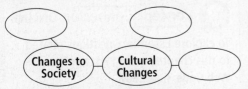

The catastrophe of World War I shattered the sense of optimism that had grown in the West since the Enlightenment. Despair gripped survivors on both sides as they added up the staggering costs of the war. It seemed as though a whole generation of young men had been lost on the battlefields. In reaction, the society and culture of Europe, the United States, and many other parts of the world experienced rapid changes.

Changes in Society After World War I

During the 1920s, new technologies helped create a mass culture shared by millions in the world's developed countries. Affordable cars, improved telephones, and new forms of media such as motion pictures and radio brought people around the world closer together than ever before.

The Roaring Twenties In the 1920s, many radios tuned into the new sounds of jazz. In fact, the 1920s are often called the Jazz Age. African American musicians combined Western harmonies with African rhythms to create jazz. Jazz musicians, like trumpeter Louis Armstrong and pianist Duke Ellington, took simple melodies and improvised endless subtle variations in rhythm and beat. They produced original music, and people loved it. Much of today's popular music has been influenced by jazz.

While Europe recovered from the war, the United States experienced a boom time. Europeans embraced American popular culture, with its greater freedom and willingness to experiment. The nightclub and the sounds of jazz were symbols of that freedom.

After the war, rebellious young people, disillusioned by the war, rejected the moral values and rules of the Victorian Age and chased after excitement. One symbol of rebellious Jazz Age youth was the liberated young woman called the **flapper**. The first flappers were American, but their European sisters soon adopted the fashion. Flappers rejected old ways in favor of new, exciting freedom.

Women's Lives Flappers were highly visible, but they were a small minority. Most women saw limited progress in the postwar period. During the war, women had held a wide range of jobs. Although most women left those jobs when the war ended, their war work helped them win the vote in many Western countries. A few women were elected to public office, such as Texas governor Miriam Ferguson or Lady Nancy Astor, the first woman to serve in the British Parliament.

By the 1920s, labor-saving devices had become common in middle-class homes. Washing machines, vacuum cleaners, and canned foods lightened the burden of household chores. Some women then sought work outside the home or did volunteer work to help the less fortunate.

In the new atmosphere of <u>emancipation</u>, women pursued careers in many areas—from sports to the arts. Women golfers, tennis players, swimmers, and pilots set new records. Women worked as newspaper reporters, published bestselling novels, and won recognition as artists. Most professions, though, were still dominated by men.

Reactions to the Jazz Age Not everyone approved of the freewheeling lifestyle of the Jazz Age. For example, many Americans supported **Prohibition,** a ban on the manufacture and sale of alcoholic beverages. For almost 90 years, social activists had waged an intense campaign against the abuse of alcohol. Finally, they gained enough support to get the Eighteenth, or Prohibition, Amendment ratified in 1919. Prohibition was meant to keep people from the negative effects of drinking. Instead, it caused an explosion of organized crime and **speakeasies,** or illegal bars. The Amendment was repealed in 1933.

In the United States in the early 1900s, a Christian fundamentalist movement swept rural areas. Fundamentalists support traditional Christian ideas about Jesus and believe that all of the events described in the Bible are literally true. Popular fundamentalist preachers traveled around the country holding inspirational revival meetings. Some used the new technology of radio to spread their message.

In 1925, a biology teacher in Tennessee named John T. Scopes was tried for teaching evolution in his classroom. His action broke a law that barred any teaching that went against the Bible's version of creation. The teacher was found guilty in the well-publicized Scopes trial, but many fundamentalists believed that the proceedings had hurt their cause.

✔ **Checkpoint** Describe the Jazz Age and some of the reactions to it.

Life Under Prohibition
A well-dressed couple waits to enter an illicit speakeasy (below right). Members of the United States Prohibition Service wore badges (below left) when they raided speakeasies and breweries and fought bootleggers such as Al Capone. *What does the clothing the couple is wearing tell you about who could afford to go to speakeasies?*

Popular Culture in the JAZZ AGE

During the Jazz Age, new ideas and new technology transformed the daily lives of many Americans and Europeans. New, reasonably priced cars allowed the middle-class population to travel with greater ease. People used better telephones to communicate across great distances in an instant. Silent movie stars had fans on every continent. Radios brought news, music, and sports into homes throughout the Western world.

▲ An image of a flapper dancing to jazz music on the cover of *McClure's* magazine

Daily Life in the United States, 1920s		
	1922	**1929**
Households with radios	60,000	10.25 million
Daily local telephone calls	55,160	79,141
Motion picture attendance per week	40 million	80 million
Dwellings with electricity	40%	68%

SOURCE: *Historical Statistics of the United States, Colonial Times to 1970*

More and more ▶ families were able to afford cars.

▲ Jazz Age flappers shocked their elders by bobbing, or cutting short, their hair and wearing skirts far shorter than those of prewar fashions. They went out on dates unchaperoned, enjoyed wild new dance fads such as the Charleston, smoked cigarettes, and drank in nightclubs.

The New Literature

In the 1920s, war novels, poetry, plays, and memoirs flowed off the presses. *All Quiet on the Western Front* by German novelist Erich Remarque, and other works like it, exposed the grim horrors of modern warfare. These works reflected a powerful disgust with war.

A Loss of Faith To many postwar writers, the war symbolized the moral breakdown of Western civilization. In 1922, the English poet T. S. Eliot published *The Waste Land*. This long poem portrays the modern world as spiritually empty and barren. In *The Sun Also Rises*, the American novelist Ernest Hemingway shows the rootless wanderings of young people who lack deep convictions. "I did not care what it was all about," says the narrator. "All I wanted to know was how to live in it." Many of these authors, including Hemingway and F. Scott Fitzgerald, left the United States and moved to Paris. Gertrude Stein, an American writer living in Paris, called them the "lost generation." Her label caught on. It referred to Stein's literary friends, and their generation as a whole.

Literature of the Inner Mind Some writers experimented with stream of consciousness. In this technique, a writer appears to present a character's random thoughts and feelings without imposing any logic or order. In the novel *Mrs. Dalloway*, British novelist Virginia Woolf used stream of consciousness to explore the thoughts of people going through the

In 1921, the Irish poet William Butler Yeats summed up the mood of many in postwar Europe and the United States:

Primary Source

❝ Things fall apart; the centre cannot hold;
Mere anarchy is loosed upon the world,
The blood-dimmed tide is loosed, and everywhere
The ceremony of innocence is drowned. ❞
—William Butler Yeats, "The Second Coming"

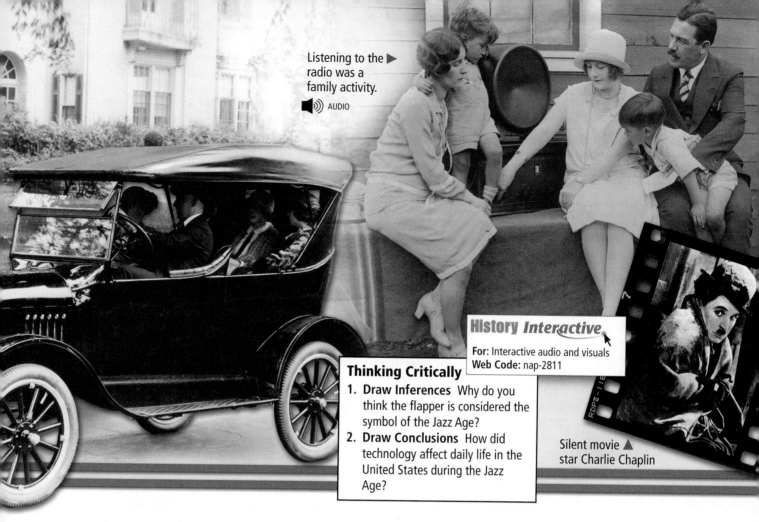

◀ Listening to the radio was a family activity.

🔊 AUDIO

History *Interactive*

For: Interactive audio and visuals
Web Code: nap-2811

Silent movie ▲ star Charlie Chaplin

Thinking Critically
1. **Draw Inferences** Why do you think the flapper is considered the symbol of the Jazz Age?
2. **Draw Conclusions** How did technology affect daily life in the United States during the Jazz Age?

ordinary actions of their everyday lives. In *Finnegans Wake,* the Irish novelist James Joyce explored the inner mind of a hero who remains sound asleep throughout the novel.

The Harlem Renaissance Also during the 1920s, an African American cultural awakening called the **Harlem Renaissance** began in Harlem, a neighborhood in New York City that was home to many African Americans. African American writers and artists expressed their pride in their unique culture. James Weldon Johnson, Jean Toomer, and Zora Neale Hurston explored the African American experience in their novels and essays. The poets Claude McKay and Langston Hughes experimented with new styles, while Countee Cullen adapted traditional poetic forms to new content.

✓ **Checkpoint** How did postwar authors show disillusionment with prewar institutions?

New Scientific Theories

It was not only the war that fostered a sense of uncertainty. New scientific discoveries challenged long-held ideas about the nature of the world. Discoveries made in the late 1800s and early 1900s showed that the atom was more complex than anyone suspected.

Marie Curie and Radioactivity In the early 1900s, the Polish-born French scientist Marie Curie and others found that the atoms of certain elements, such as radium and uranium, <u>spontaneously</u> release charged particles. As scientists studied radioactivity further, they discovered that

Vocabulary Builder

<u>spontaneously</u>—(spahn TAY nee us lee) *adv.* caused by inner forces, self-generated

Marie Curie

Marie Curie (1867–1934) won two Nobel prizes, one in physics and one in chemistry. Still, like many other women, she struggled to balance her work with home duties. "I have a great deal of work," she said, "what with the housekeeping, the children, the teaching, and the laboratory, and I don't know how I shall manage it all."

Curie won worldwide fame for her groundbreaking research on radioactivity. But she paid a high price for knowledge. Although she shrugged off the health dangers, she died from radiation poisoning. **Why do you think Marie Curie's achievements were unique for her time?**

it can change atoms of one element into atoms of another. Such findings proved that atoms are not solid and indivisible.

Einstein's Theory of Relativity In 1905 and 1916, the German-born physicist Albert Einstein introduced his theories of relativity. Einstein argued that measurements of space and time are not absolute but are determined by the relative position of the observer. Einstein's ideas raised questions about Newtonian science, which compared the universe to a machine operating according to absolute laws.

In 1934, building on Curie's and Einstein's theories, Italian physicist Enrico Fermi and other scientists around the world discovered atomic fission, or the splitting of the nuclei of atoms in two. This splitting produces a huge burst of energy. In the 1940s, Fermi (now an American), along with fellow American physicists J. Robert Oppenheimer and Edward Teller, would use this discovery to create the devastating atomic bomb.

In the postwar years, many scientists came to accept the theories of relativity. To the general public, however, Einstein's ideas were difficult to understand. They seemed to further reinforce the unsettling sense of a universe whirling beyond the understanding of human reason.

Fleming Discovers Penicillin In 1928, the Scottish scientist Alexander Fleming made a different type of scientific discovery. He accidentally discovered a type of nontoxic mold that kills bacteria, which he called "penicillin." Later, other scientists used Fleming's work to develop antibiotics, which are now used all over the world to treat infections.

Freud Probes the Mind The Austrian physician Sigmund Freud (froyd) also challenged faith in reason. He suggested that the subconscious mind drives much of human behavior. Freud said that learned social values such as morality and reason help people to repress, or check, powerful urges. But an individual feels constant tension between repressed drives and social training. This tension, argued Freud, may cause psychological or physical illness. Freud pioneered **psychoanalysis,** a method of studying how the mind works and treating mental disorders. Although many of his theories have been discredited, Freud's ideas have had an extraordinary impact far beyond medicine.

 Checkpoint How did scientific discoveries in the 1920s change people's views of the world?

Modern Art and Architecture

In the early 1900s, many Western artists rejected traditional styles. Instead of trying to reproduce the real world, they explored other dimensions of color, line, and shape. Painters like Henri Matisse (ma TEES) utilized bold, wild strokes of color and odd distortions to produce works of strong emotion. He and fellow artists outraged the public and were dubbed *fauves* (fohv), or wild beasts, by critics.

New Directions in Painting While Matisse continued in the fauvist style, other artists explored styles based on new ideas. Before World War I, the Spanish artist Pablo Picasso and the French artist Georges Braque (brak) created a revolutionary new style called cubism. Cubists painted three-dimensional objects as complex patterns of angles and planes, as if they were composed of fragmented parts.

Later, the Russian Vasily Kandinsky and the Swiss Paul Klee moved even further away from representing reality. Their artwork was **abstract,** composed only of lines, colors, and shapes, sometimes with no recognizable subject matter at all.

During and after the war, the **dada** movement burst onto the art world. Dadaists rejected all traditional conventions and believed that there was no sense or truth in the world. Paintings and sculptures by Jean Arp and Max Ernst were intended to shock and disturb viewers. Other dadaist artists created collages, photomontages, or sculptures made of objects they found abandoned or thrown away.

Cubism and dada both helped to inspire **surrealism,** a movement that attempted to portray the workings of the unconscious mind. Surrealism rejected rational thought, which had produced the horrors of World War I, in favor of irrational or unconscious ideas. The Spanish surrealist Salvador Dali used images of melting clocks and burning giraffes to suggest the chaotic dream state described by Freud.

New Styles of Architecture Architects, too, rejected classical traditions and developed new styles to match a new world. The famous Bauhaus school in Germany influenced architecture by blending science and technology with design. Bauhaus buildings feature glass, steel, and concrete but have little ornamentation. The American architect Frank Lloyd Wright held that the function of a building should determine its form. He used materials and forms that fit a building's environment.

 Checkpoint What effect did World War I have on art movements in the 1920s?

Abstract Art
Vasily Kandinsky painted *Swinging* (above) in 1925. He used geometrical shapes to convey the feeling of movement that the title suggests. **Analyzing Art** *How does* Swinging *show the abstract style of art that Kandinsky pioneered?*

Looking Ahead

Stunned by the trauma of World War I, many people sought to change the way they thought and acted during the turbulent 1920s. As nations recovered from the war, people began to feel hope rising out of their disillusionment. But soon, the "lost generation" would face a new crisis—this one economic—that would revive many old problems and spark new conflicts.

Progress Monitoring *Online*
For: Self-quiz with vocabulary practice
Web Code: naa-2811

SECTION **1** Assessment

Terms, People, and Places

1. What do many of the key terms listed at the beginning of the section have in common? Explain.

Note Taking

2. **Reading Skill: Identify Supporting Details** Use your completed concept web to answer the Focus Question: What changes did Western society and culture experience after World War I?

Comprehension and Critical Thinking

3. **Determine Relevance** How did flappers symbolize changes in Western society during the 1920s?

4. **Identify Point of View** How did the ideas of Einstein and Freud contribute to a sense of uncertainty?

5. **Synthesize Information** Choose one postwar writer and one postwar artist. Explain how the work of each reflected a new view of the world.

● Writing About History

Quick Write: Choose a Topic The topic of a compare-and-contrast essay must involve two things that are neither nearly identical nor extremely different. Think of a topic from this section that would be a good candidate for a compare-and-contrast essay. Show why it would be a good topic by listing categories in which the two items could be compared and contrasted.

Pablo Picasso

The painter Pablo Picasso was one of the most important artists of the last century. Picasso and his friend Georges Braque together developed the art movement known as Cubism. The movement began around 1907 and continued through the First World War into the 1920s. Picasso's work continued to develop until his death in 1973 at the age of 91. Here are some of his best known artworks.

Picasso in his studio working on a sculpture

Still Life With Violin, 1912. In this Cubist still life, the objects, which include a violin, are fragmented into so many views that they are barely distinguishable.

Mother and Child, 1901. The years 1901 to 1904 are known as Picasso's Blue Period. Following the death of a close friend, Picasso used the color blue in many paintings to express his sadness.

Hands With Flowers, 1958. This lithograph, done after Picasso's Cubist period, is a simple image of a hand holding flowers.

Thinking Critically

1. **Compare** Describe the differences between *Mother and Child* and *Still Life With Violin*.
2. **Synthesize Information** Describe how Picasso's style changed over time, based on the artworks shown here.

Tin cup

Men eating at a soup kitchen during the Great Depression

Brother, Can You Spare a Dime?

In the early 1930s, a worldwide economic depression threw thousands out of work and into lives of poverty. The song below summed up the mood of the time:

❝ They used to tell me I was building a dream
With peace and glory ahead—
Why should I be standing in line,
Just waiting for bread?

Once I built a railroad, I made it run,
Made it race against time.
Once I built a railroad, now it's done—
Brother, can you spare a dime? ❞

— from the song "Brother, Can You Spare a Dime?," lyrics by E.Y. "Yip" Harburg & Jay Gorney. Published by Glocca Morra Music (ASCAP) & Gorney Music (ASCAP). Administered by Next Decade Entertainment, Inc. All rights reserved. Used by permission.

Focus Question What political and economic challenges did the leading democracies face in the 1920s and 1930s?

The Western Democracies Stumble

Performance Standards

• **SSWH16c** Explain decisions on German reparations in the Versailles Treaty.

Terms, People, and Places

Maginot Line	finance
Kellogg-Briand Pact	Federal Reserve
disarmament	Great Depression
general strike	Franklin D. Roosevelt
overproduction	New Deal

Note Taking

Reading Skill: Identify Main Ideas Record main ideas from the first part of this section in a table like the one below.

Postwar Issues			
Country	Politics	Foreign Policy	Economics

In 1919, the three Western democracies—Britain, France, and the United States—appeared powerful. They had ruled the Paris Peace Conference and boosted hopes for democracy among the new nations of Eastern Europe. Beneath the surface, however, postwar Europe faced grave problems. To make matters worse, many members of the younger generation who might have become the next great leaders had been killed in the war.

Politics in the Postwar World

At first, the most pressing issues were finding jobs for returning veterans and rebuilding war-ravaged lands. Economic problems fed social unrest and made radical ideas more popular.

Party Struggles in Britain In Britain during the 1920s, the Labour party surpassed the Liberal party in strength. The Labour party gained support among workers by promoting a gradual move toward socialism. The Liberal party passed some social legislation, but it traditionally represented middle-class business interests. As the Liberal party faltered, the middle class began to back the Conservative party, joining the upper class, professionals, and farmers. With this support, the Conservative party held power during much of 1920s. After a massive strike of over three million workers in 1926, Conservatives passed legislation limiting the power of workers to strike.

The Irish Resist
Members of the Irish Republican Army prepare to resist the British occupation of Dublin in 1921 by erecting a barbed wire barricade. The Irish Free State, established in 1922, was a compromise between the opposing sides, but peace was short-lived.

Vocabulary Builder
suppressed—(suh PRESD) *vt.* put down by force, subdued

Irish Independence at Last Britain still faced the "Irish question." In 1914, Parliament passed a home-rule bill that was shelved when the war began. On Easter 1916, a small group of militant Irish nationalists launched a revolt against British rule. Although the Easter Rising was quickly <u>suppressed</u>, it stirred wider support for the Irish cause. When Parliament again failed to grant home rule in 1919, members of the Irish Republican Army (IRA) began a guerrilla war against British forces and their supporters. In 1922, moderates in Ireland and Britain reached an agreement. Most of Ireland became the self-governing Irish Free State. The largely Protestant northern counties remained under British rule. However, the IRA and others fought for decades against the division.

France's Troubled Peace Like Britain, France emerged from World War I both a victor and a loser. Political divisions and financial scandals plagued the government of the Third Republic. Several parties—from conservatives to communists—competed for power. The parties differed on many issues, including how to get reparations payments from Germany. A series of quickly changing coalition governments ruled France.

"The Red Scare" and Isolationism in the United States In contrast, the United States emerged from World War I in good shape. A late entrant into the war, it had suffered relatively few casualties and little loss of property. However, the United States did experience some domestic unrest. Fear of radicals and the Bolshevik Revolution in Russia set off a "Red Scare" in 1919 and 1920. Police rounded up suspected foreign-born radicals, and a number were expelled from the United States.

The "Red Scare" fed growing demands to limit immigration. Millions of immigrants from southern and eastern Europe had poured into the United States between 1890 and 1914. Some native-born Americans sought to exclude these newcomers, whose cultures differed from those of earlier settlers from northern Europe. In response, Congress passed laws limiting immigration from Europe. Earlier laws had already excluded or limited Chinese and Japanese immigration.

✓ **Checkpoint** What political issues did each of the three democracies face after World War I?

Postwar Foreign Policy

In addition to problems at home, the three democracies faced a difficult international situation. The peace settlements caused friction, especially in Germany and among some ethnic groups in Eastern Europe.

Arguing Allies France's chief concern after the war was securing its borders against Germany. The French remembered the German invasions of 1870 and 1914. To prevent a third invasion, France built massive fortifications called the **Maginot Line** (ma zhee NOH) along its border with Germany. However, the line would not be enough to stop another German invasion in 1940.

In its quest for security, France also strengthened its military and sought alliances with other countries, including the Soviet Union. It insisted on strict enforcement of the Versailles treaty and complete payment of reparations. France's goal was to keep the German economy weak.

Britain disagreed with this aim. Almost from the signing of the Treaty of Versailles, British leaders wanted to relax the treaty's harsh treatment of Germany. They feared that if Germany became too weak, the Soviet Union and France would become too powerful.

The Search for Peace Despite disagreements, many people worked for peace in the 1920s. Hopes soared in 1925 when representatives from seven European nations signed a series of treaties at Locarno, Switzerland. These treaties settled Germany's disputed borders with France, Belgium, Czechoslovakia, and Poland. The Locarno treaties became the symbol of a new era of peace.

The **Kellogg-Briand Pact,** which was sponsored by the United States in 1928, echoed the hopeful "spirit of Locarno." Almost every independent nation signed this agreement, promising to "renounce war as an instrument of national policy." In this optimistic spirit, the great powers pursued **disarmament,** the reduction of armed forces and weapons. The United States, Britain, France, Japan, and other nations signed treaties to reduce the size of their navies. However, they failed to agree on limiting the size of their armies.

From its headquarters in Geneva, Switzerland, the League of Nations encouraged cooperation and tried to get members to make a commitment to stop aggression. In 1926, after signing the Locarno agreements, Germany joined the League. Later, the Soviet Union was also admitted.

The League's Weakness The peace was fragile. Although the Kellogg-Briand Pact outlawed war, it provided no way of enforcing the ban. The League of Nations, too, was powerless to stop aggression. In 1931, the League vigorously condemned Japan's invasion of Manchuria, but did not take military action to stop it. Ambitious dictators in Europe noted the League's weakness and began to pursue aggressive foreign policies.

✔ **Checkpoint** How did the Treaty of Versailles affect the relationship between France and Britain?

Analyzing Political Cartoons

An End to War? The Kellogg-Briand Pact raised hopes for an end to war. But not everyone was so optimistic, as this 1929 American cartoon shows.

A Kellogg-Briand Pact framed as a fire insurance policy

B Adequate navy as a fire extinguisher

C Uncle Sam looking at both

1. Do you think that the cartoonist feels that a fire insurance policy is enough to prevent a fire?
2. What point do you think the cartoonist is making about the Kellogg-Briand Pact?

HAVING AN INSURANCE POLICY DOESN'T MEAN YOU CAN DO WITHOUT FIRE PREVENTION

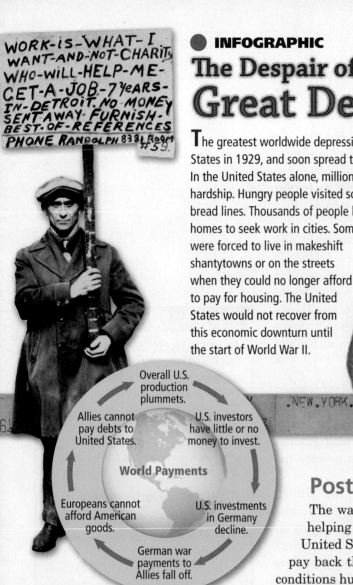

The Despair of the
Great Depression

The greatest worldwide depression in history began in the United States in 1929, and soon spread to touch most parts of the world. In the United States alone, millions lost their jobs and endured great hardship. Hungry people visited soup kitchens or waited in long bread lines. Thousands of people left their homes to seek work in cities. Some were forced to live in makeshift shantytowns or on the streets when they could no longer afford to pay for housing. The United States would not recover from this economic downturn until the start of World War II.

Unemployment led people to visit soup kitchens like the one below in Berlin. In New York and other cities, bread lines spanned multiple city blocks (below right), and many people became homeless (far right).

World Payments

Overall U.S. production plummets.

U.S. investors have little or no money to invest.

U.S. investments in Germany decline.

German war payments to Allies fall off.

Europeans cannot afford American goods.

Allies cannot pay debts to United States.

WORK-IS-WHAT-I WANT-AND-NOT-CHARITY WHO-WILL-HELP-ME-GET-A-JOB-7 YEARS- IN-DETROIT. NO MONEY SENT AWAY FURNISH BEST-OF-REFERENCES PHONE RANDOLPH 8338 Room #59.

NEW YORK STOCK EXCHANGE OCT 29.1929... 5000 .10. 3.107. 3.1 SHO NKPPR NSC

▲ A man tries to find work (above). The cycle of war payments helped spread the Great Depression to Europe.

Postwar Economics

The war affected economies all over the world, hurting some and helping others. Britain and France both owed huge war debts to the United States. Both relied on reparation payments from Germany to pay back their loans. Meanwhile, the crushing reparations and other conditions hurt Germany's economy.

Britain and France Recover Britain faced serious economic problems in the 1920s. It was deeply in debt, and its factories were out of date. Unemployment was severe. Wages remained low, leading to worker unrest and frequent strikes. In 1926, a **general strike,** or strike by workers in many different industries at the same time, lasted nine days and involved some three million workers.

In comparison, the French economy recovered fairly rapidly. Financial reparations and territories gained from Germany helped. Still, economic swings did occur, adding to an unstable political scene.

Despite these problems, Europe made a shaky recovery during the 1920s. Economies returned to peacetime manufacturing and trade. Veterans gradually found jobs, although unemployment never ceased to be a problem. Middle-class families enjoyed a rising standard of living.

Vocabulary Builder

affluent—(AF loo unt) *adj.* rich, wealthy

The United States Booms In contrast, the United States emerged from the war as the world's leading economic power. In the affluent 1920s, middle-class Americans enjoyed the benefits of capitalism. American loans and investments backed the recovery in Europe. As long as the American economy prospered, the global economy remained stable.

✓ **Checkpoint** How did the war and its peace treaties affect the international economy?

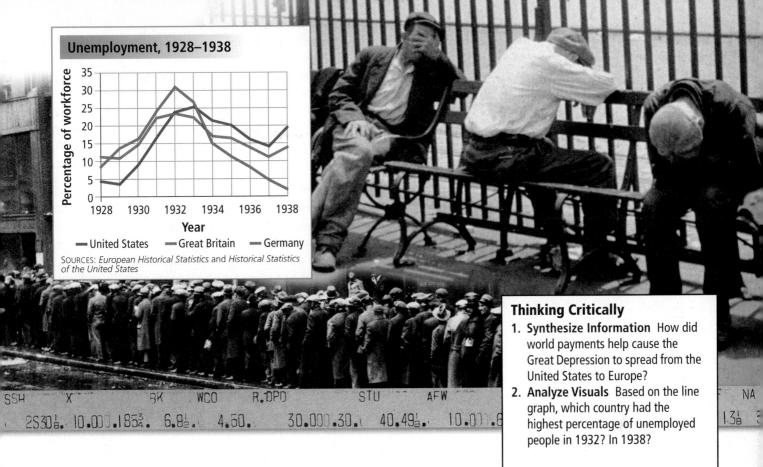

Unemployment, 1928–1938

Percentage of workforce (y-axis: 0, 5, 10, 15, 20, 25, 30, 35)

Year (x-axis: 1928, 1930, 1932, 1934, 1936, 1938)

— United States — Great Britain — Germany

SOURCES: *European Historical Statistics* and *Historical Statistics of the United States*

Thinking Critically

1. **Synthesize Information** How did world payments help cause the Great Depression to spread from the United States to Europe?
2. **Analyze Visuals** Based on the line graph, which country had the highest percentage of unemployed people in 1932? In 1938?

The Great Depression

This prosperity did not last. At the end of the 1920s, an economic crisis began in the United States and spread to the rest of the world, leaving almost no corner untouched.

Falling Demand and Overproduction The wealth created during the 1920s in the United States was not shared evenly. Farmers and unskilled workers were on the losing end. Though demand for raw materials and agricultural products had skyrocketed during the war, demand dwindled and prices fell after the war. Farmers, miners and other suppliers of raw materials suffered. Because they earned less, they bought less. At the same time, better technology allowed factories to make more products faster. This led to **overproduction,** a condition in which the production of goods exceeds the demand for them. As demand slowed, factories cut back on production and workers lost their jobs.

Crash and Collapse Meanwhile, a crisis in finance—the management of money matters, including the circulation of money, loans, investments, and banking—was brewing. Few saw the danger. Prices on the New York Stock Exchange were at an all-time high. Eager investors acquired stocks through risky methods. To slow the run on the stock market, the **Federal Reserve,** the central banking system of the United States, which regulates banks, raised interest rates in 1928 and again 1929. It didn't work. Instead, the higher interest rates made people nervous about borrowing money and investing, thereby hurting demand.

In the autumn of 1929, jitters about the economy caused many people to sell their stocks at once. Financial panic set in. Stock prices crashed, wiping out the fortunes of many investors. The **Great Depression,** a painful time of global economic collapse, had begun quietly in the

Note Taking

Reading Skill: Identify Main Ideas To help you to remember what you've read, use a chart like the one below to record the main ideas of the next two subsections.

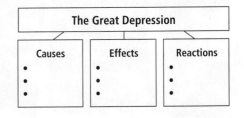

The Great Depression		
Causes	Effects	Reactions
•	•	•
•	•	•
•	•	•

summer of 1929 with decreasing production. The October stock market crash aggravated the economic decline.

In 1931, the Federal Reserve again increased the interest rate, with an even more disastrous effect. As people bought and invested less, businesses closed and banks failed, throwing millions out of work. The cycle spiraled steadily downward. The jobless could not afford to buy goods, so more factories had to close, which in turn increased unemployment. People slept on park benches and lined up to eat in soup kitchens.

The Depression Spreads The economic problems quickly spread around the world. American banks stopped making loans abroad and demanded repayment of foreign loans. Without support from the United States, Germany suffered. It could not make its reparations payments. France and Britain were not able to make their loan payments.

Desperate governments tried to protect their economies from foreign competition. The United States imposed the highest tariffs in its history. The policy backfired when other nations retaliated by raising their tariffs. In 1932 and 1933, global world trade sank to its 1900 level. As you have read, the Great Depression spread misery from the industrial world to Latin America, Africa, and Asia.

✔ **Checkpoint** How did the Federal Reserve's policies affect the Great Depression?

The Democracies React to the Depression

The governments of Britain, France, and the United States, like others around the world, tried to find ways to lift the Depression. None of their methods provided a quick fix, but they did alleviate some of the suffering.

Britain and France Search for Solutions In response to the Depression, Britain set up a coalition government made up of leaders from all three of its major political parties. The government provided some unemployment benefits but failed to take decisive action to improve the economy. By 1931, one in every four workers was unemployed.

The Great Depression took longer to hurt France than some other countries. However, by the mid-1930s, France was feeling the pinch of decreased production and unemployment. In response, several leftist parties united behind the socialist leader Leon Blum. His Popular Front government tried to solve labor problems and passed some social legislation. But it could not satisfy more radical leftists. Strikes soon brought down Blum's government. Democracy survived, but the country lacked strong leadership able to respond to the clamor for change.

The Dust Bowl
In Dorothea Lange's famous 1936 photo *Migrant Mother, Nipomo, California,* a mother looks into the future with despair. She migrated to escape scenes like the one below, where huge dust storms buried farm equipment in Dallas, Texas. *How did geography help aggravate the depression in the United States?*

Roosevelt Offers the United States a New Deal Meanwhile, in the United States, President Herbert Hoover firmly believed that the government should not intervene in private business matters. Even so, he did try a variety of limited measures to solve the crisis. Nothing seemed to work. In 1932, Americans elected a new President, **Franklin D. Roosevelt.** "FDR" argued that the government had to take an active role in combating the Great Depression. He introduced the **New Deal,** a massive package of economic and social programs.

Under the New Deal, the federal government became more directly involved in people's everyday lives than ever before. New laws regulated the stock market and protected bank deposits. Government programs created jobs and gave aid to farmers. A new Social Security system provided pensions for the elderly and other benefits.

As the New Deal programs were being put into effect, a natural disaster in 1934 hit several central states. After years of drought and over-farming, huge winds blew across the plains. The winds picked up and carried away the topsoil exposed by erosion, creating the Dust Bowl. The storms destroyed crops, land, and equipment. Thousands of farmers lost their land. Many migrated to the cities of the West Coast in search of work and a new life.

The New Deal failed to end the Great Depression, although it did ease the suffering for many. Still, some critics fiercely condemned FDR's expansion of the role of government. The debate about the size and role of the federal government continues to this day.

Loss of Faith in Democracy As the Depression wore on, many people lost faith in the ability of democratic governments to solve the problems of the modern world. Postwar disillusionment, soothed by the few good years of the 1920s, turned into despair in Europe. Misery and hopelessness created fertile ground for extremists who promised radical solutions.

✔ **Checkpoint** How did the government of the United States react to the Depression?

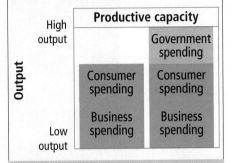

Economic Theories and the Great Depression

According to classical economists, free market economies naturally regulate their own highs and lows. The government should interfere as little as possible. The economist John Maynard Keynes argued that during a depression, the government should step in and spend more to bring the economy back up to its full productive capacity.

Diagram Skills *What role did Keynes envision for government in the economy?*

SECTION 2 **Assessment**

Progress Monitoring Online
For: Self-quiz with vocabulary practice
Web Code: naa-2821

Terms, People, and Places

1. For each term, person, or place listed at the beginning of the section, write a sentence explaining its significance.

Note Taking

2. **Reading Skill: Identify Main Ideas** Use your completed table and chart to answer the Focus Question: What political and economic challenges did the leading democracies face in the 1920s and 1930s?

Comprehension and Critical Thinking

3. **Synthesize Information** How did Britain and France emerge from World War I as both victors and losers?

4. **Predict Consequences** What steps did the major powers take to protect the peace? Why did these moves have limited effects?

5. **Recognize Cause and Effect** Explain how each of the following contributed to the outbreak or spread of the Great Depression: (a) falling demand, (b) Federal Reserve Board, and (c) financial crisis.

6. **Identify Central Issues** How did the Great Depression affect political developments in the United States?

● **Writing About History**

Quick Write: Make a Venn Diagram A useful way to gather details for a compare-and-contrast essay is to use a Venn diagram. Place similarities between two ideas in the overlapping part of the circles; place differences in the parts that don't overlap. Create a Venn diagram for an essay on the following thesis statement: The United States was in better shape than Britain and France after World War I.

An image from a magazine of Benito Mussolini leading his nation to war ▶

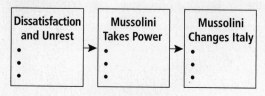

◀ Italian national flag during Mussolini's rule

SECTION 3

A New Leader: Mussolini

In the early 1920s, a new leader named Benito Mussolini arose in Italy. The Italian people were inspired by Mussolini's promises to bring stability and glory to Italy.

❝ [Only joy at finding such a leader] can explain the enthusiasm [Mussolini] evoked at gathering after gathering, where his mere presence drew the people from all sides to greet him with frenzied acclamations. Even the men who at first came out of mere curiosity and with indifferent or even hostile feelings gradually felt themselves fired by his personal magnetic influence. . . . ❞

—Margherita G. Sarfatti, *The Life of Benito Mussolini* (tr. Frederic Whyte)

Focus Question How and why did fascism rise in Italy?

Fascism in Italy

 Performance Standards

- **SSWH17c** Describe the fascist policies of Mussolini.
- **SSWH17e** Describe the nature of totalitarianism, and the police state that existed in Italy.
- **SSWH17f** Explain the conflicts that led to WWII in Europe and Asia.

Terms, People, and Places

Benito Mussolini	totalitarian state
Black Shirts	fascism
March on Rome	

Note Taking

Reading Skill: Identify Main Ideas Find the main points of the text under the first two headings and record them in a flowchart like the one below.

Dissatisfaction and Unrest	→	Mussolini Takes Power	→	Mussolini Changes Italy
• • •		• • •		• • •

"I hated politics and politicians," said Italo Balbo. Like many Italian veterans of World War I, he had come home to a land of economic chaos and political corruption. Italy's constitutional government, he felt, "had betrayed the hopes of soldiers, reducing Italy to a shameful peace." Disgusted and angry, Balbo rallied behind a fiercely nationalist leader, Benito Mussolini. Mussolini's rise to power in the 1920s served as a model for ambitious strongmen elsewhere in Europe.

Mussolini's Rise to Power

When Italy agreed to join the Allies in 1915, France and Britain secretly promised to give Italy certain Austro-Hungarian territories. When the Allies won, Italy received some of the promised territories, but others became part of the new Yugoslavia. The broken promises outraged Italian nationalists.

Disorders within Italy multiplied. Inspired in part by the revolution in Russia, peasants seized land, and workers went on strike or seized factories. Amid the chaos, returning veterans faced unemployment. Trade declined and taxes rose. The government, split into feuding factions, seemed powerless to end the crisis.

A Leader Emerges Into this turmoil stepped **Benito Mussolini.** The son of a socialist blacksmith and a teacher, Mussolini had been a socialist in his youth. During the war, however, he rejected socialism for intense nationalism. In 1919, he organized veterans and other discontented Italians into the Fascist party. They took the name from the Latin *fasces*, a bundle of sticks wrapped around an ax. In ancient Rome, the fasces symbolized unity and authority.

Mussolini was a fiery and charismatic speaker. He promised to end corruption and replace turmoil with order. He also spoke of reviving Roman greatness, pledging to turn the Mediterranean into a "Roman lake" once again.

Mussolini Gains Control Mussolini organized his supporters into "combat squads." The squads wore black shirts to emulate an earlier nationalist revolt. These **Black Shirts,** or party militants, rejected the democratic process in favor of violent action. They broke up socialist rallies, smashed leftist presses, and attacked farmers' cooperatives. Fascist gangs used intimidation and terror to oust elected officials in northern Italy. Many Italians accepted these actions because they, too, had lost faith in constitutional government.

In 1922, the Fascists made a bid for power. At a rally in Naples, they announced their intention to go to Rome to demand that the government make changes. In the **March on Rome,** tens of thousands of Fascists swarmed towards the capital. Fearing civil war, King Victor Emmanuel III asked Mussolini to form a government as prime minister. Mussolini entered the city triumphantly on October 30, 1922. He thus obtained a nominally legal, constitutional appointment from the king to lead Italy.

✓ **Checkpoint** How did postwar disillusionment contribute to Mussolini's rise?

Mussolini's Rule

At first, Fascists held only a few cabinet posts in the new government. By 1925, though, Mussolini had assumed more power and taken the title Il Duce (eel DOO chay), "The Leader." He suppressed rival parties, muzzled the press, rigged elections, and replaced elected officials with Fascist supporters. In 1929, Mussolini received support from Pope Pius XI in return for recognizing Vatican City as an independent state, although the pope continued to disagree with some of Mussolini's goals. In theory, Italy remained a parliamentary monarchy. In fact, it was a dictatorship upheld by terror. Critics were thrown into prison, forced into exile, or murdered. Secret police and propaganda bolstered the regime.

State Control of the Economy To spur economic growth and end conflicts between owners and workers, Mussolini brought the economy under state control. However, he preserved capitalism. Under Mussolini's corporate state, representatives of business, labor, government, and the Fascist

Mussolini and the People
An excited crowd of women and children greets the Italian leader in 1940.

party controlled industry, agriculture, and trade. Mussolini's system favored the upper classes and industrial leaders. Although production increased, success came at the expense of workers. They were forbidden to strike, and their wages were kept low.

The Individual and the State In Mussolini's new system, loyalty to the state replaced conflicting individual goals. To Fascists, the glorious state was all-important, and the individual was unimportant except as a member of the state. Men, women, and children were bombarded with slogans glorifying the state and Mussolini. "Believe! Obey! Fight!" loudspeakers blared and posters <u>proclaimed</u>. Men were urged to be ruthless, selfless warriors fighting for the glory of Italy. Women were pushed out of paying jobs. Instead, Mussolini called on women to "win the battle of motherhood." Those who bore more than 14 children were given a medal by Il Duce himself.

Shaping the young was a major Fascist goal. Fascist youth groups toughened children and taught them to obey strict military discipline. Boys and girls learned about the glories of ancient Rome. Young Fascists marched in torchlight parades, singing patriotic hymns and chanting, "Mussolini is always right." By the 1930s, a generation of young soldiers stood ready to back Il Duce's drive to expand Italian power.

✔ **Checkpoint** How did the Fascist party transform Italy's government and economy?

Vocabulary Builder
<u>proclaimed</u>—(proh KLAYMD) *vt.* announced officially

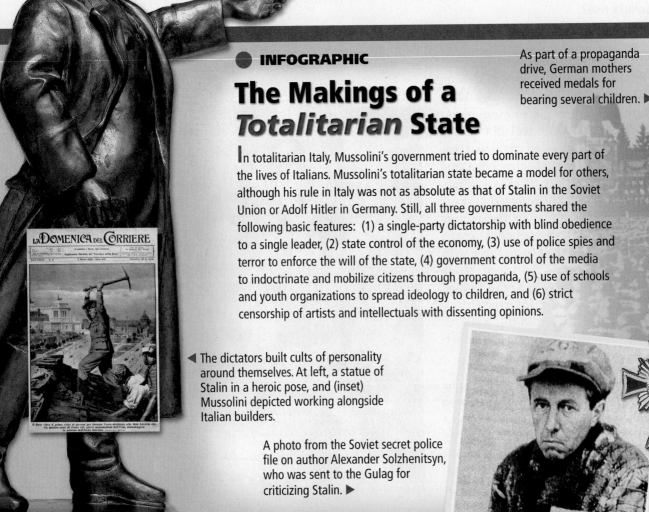

● **INFOGRAPHIC**

The Makings of a *Totalitarian* State

In totalitarian Italy, Mussolini's government tried to dominate every part of the lives of Italians. Mussolini's totalitarian state became a model for others, although his rule in Italy was not as absolute as that of Stalin in the Soviet Union or Adolf Hitler in Germany. Still, all three governments shared the following basic features: (1) a single-party dictatorship with blind obedience to a single leader, (2) state control of the economy, (3) use of police spies and terror to enforce the will of the state, (4) government control of the media to indoctrinate and mobilize citizens through propaganda, (5) use of schools and youth organizations to spread ideology to children, and (6) strict censorship of artists and intellectuals with dissenting opinions.

As part of a propaganda drive, German mothers received medals for bearing several children. ▶

◀ The dictators built cults of personality around themselves. At left, a statue of Stalin in a heroic pose, and (inset) Mussolini depicted working alongside Italian builders.

A photo from the Soviet secret police file on author Alexander Solzhenitsyn, who was sent to the Gulag for criticizing Stalin. ▶

900

The Nature of Fascism

Mussolini built the first **totalitarian state.** In this form of government, a one-party dictatorship attempts to regulate every aspect of the lives of its citizens. Other dictators, notably Stalin and Hitler, followed Mussolini's lead. Mussolini's rule was fascist in nature, as was Hitler's, but totalitarian governments rise under other kinds of ideology as well, such as communism in Stalin's Soviet Union.

What Is Fascism? Historians still debate the real nature of Mussolini's fascist <u>ideology</u>. Mussolini coined the term, but fascists had no unifying theory as Marxists did. Today, we generally use the term **fascism** to describe any centralized, authoritarian government that is not communist whose policies glorify the state over the individual and are destructive to basic human rights. In the 1920s and 1930s, though, fascism meant different things in different countries.

All forms of fascism, however, shared some basic features. They were rooted in extreme nationalism. Fascists glorified action, violence, discipline, and, above all, blind loyalty to the state. Fascists also pursued aggressive foreign expansion. Echoing the idea of "survival of the fittest," Fascist leaders glorified warfare as a noble struggle for survival.

Fascists were also antidemocratic. They rejected faith in reason and the concepts of equality and liberty. To them, democracy led to corruption and weakness and put individual or class interests above national goals. Instead, fascists emphasized emotion and the supremacy of the state.

▼ Huge numbers of people turned out for Nazi Party rallies.

▼ Mussolini spread his ideal of Italian military supremacy to Italian children through the Young Fascists.

Thinking Critically
1. **Draw Inferences** Why did totalitarian governments try to win the loyalty of their nations' young people?
2. **Recognize Ideologies** Why did leaders honor women for having many children?

A Fascist Childhood
Children were required to use notebooks that featured fascist drawings and quotes from Mussolini.

The Appeal of Fascism Given its restrictions on individual freedom, why did fascism appeal to many Italians? First, it promised a strong, stable government and an end to the political feuding that had paralyzed democracy in Italy. Mussolini projected a sense of power and confidence at a time of disorder and despair. Mussolini's intense nationalism also revived national pride.

At first, newspapers in Britain, France, and North America applauded the discipline and order of Mussolini's government. "He got the trains running on time," admirers said. Only later, when Mussolini embarked on a course of foreign conquest, did Western democracies protest.

Fascism Compared to Communism Fascists were the sworn enemies of socialists and communists. While communists worked for international change, fascists pursued nationalist goals. Fascists supported a society with defined classes. They found allies among business leaders, wealthy landowners, and the lower middle class. Communists touted a classless society. They won support among both urban and agricultural workers.

Despite such differences, the products of these two ideologies had much in common. Both drew their power by inspiring a blind devotion to the state, or a charismatic leader as the embodiment of the state. Both used terror to guard their power. Both flourished during economic hard times by promoting extreme programs of social change. In both, a party elite claimed to rule in the name of the national interest.

✔ **Checkpoint** Describe the similarities between fascism and communism.

Looking Ahead

Three systems of government competed for influence in postwar Europe. Democracy endured in Britain and France but faced an uphill struggle in hard times. Communism emerged in Russia and won support elsewhere. In Italy, fascism offered a different option. As the Great Depression spread, other nations—most notably Germany—looked to fascist leaders.

SECTION **3** Assessment

Progress Monitoring Online
For: Self-quiz with vocabulary practice
Web Code: naa-2831

Terms, People, and Places

1. For each term listed at the beginning of the section, write a sentence explaining its significance.

Note Taking

2. **Reading Skill: Identify Main Ideas** Use your completed flowchart and table to answer the section Focus Question: How and why did fascism rise in Italy?

Comprehension and Critical Thinking

3. **Recognize Cause and Effect** What problems did Italy face after World War I? How did these problems help Mussolini win power?

4. **Summarize** Describe one of Mussolini's economic or social goals, and explain the actions he took to achieve it.

5. **Compare and Contrast** List two similarities and two differences between fascism and communism.

6. **Identify Point of View** Mussolini said, "Machines and women are the two main causes of unemployment." (a) What do you think he meant? (b) How did Mussolini's policies reflect his attitude toward women?

● **Writing About History**

Quick Write: Write a Thesis Statement A compare-and-contrast thesis statement should introduce the items you are comparing and the point you intend to make. Which of the following thesis statements would work best for a compare-and-contrast essay?

• Fascism and communism are very different ideologies, but they both led to the imposition of totalitarian governments.
• Fascism led to a totalitarian government in Italy.

Concept Connector

DICTATORSHIP

Why do people sometimes support dictators?

In This Chapter SSWH17c

Following World War I, European countries experienced economic and political turmoil. In Germany, money was worth so little that people used it as fuel for cooking (right). As society seemed to unravel, desperate people looked to strong leaders to create stability. In some countries, people were willing to give up individual freedoms to gain security and order.

Throughout History

- **48 B.C.– 44 B.C.** Julius Caesar forces the Roman Senate to grant him absolute power and initiates reforms.

- **1547–1580 A.D.** Ivan the Terrible, the Russian tsar, organizes agents of terror to enforce his will.

- **1920s** Mussolini promises to restore order to Italy and revive its Roman greatness.

- **1930s** Stalin uses terror and censorship to strengthen his power over the Soviet people.

- **1934** Hitler's extreme nationalism, racism, and economic goals appeal to many German people.

- **1950s–1970s** Military leaders in Brazil, Argentina, and Chile use force to seize and maintain power.

Continuing Today

To maintain power, dictators like Kim Jong-Il of North Korea (below) create a cult of personality. They present themselves as heroic figures and people are encouraged to view them as an objects of worship.

21st Century Skills

❓ *TRANSFER Activities*

1. **Analyze** Throughout history, how have dictators maintained control?

2. **Evaluate** What are the dangers of giving up rights in order to gain stability and order?

3. **Transfer** Complete a Web quest in which you speak out against a modern dictator; record your thoughts in the Concept Connector Journal; and learn to make a video. Web Code nah-2808

In this propaganda image, people offer Stalin flowers.

WITNESS HISTORY 🔊 AUDIO

The Heart of the Party

On the occasion of Stalin's sixtieth birthday, the Communist party newspaper, *Pravda*, or "Truth," printed this praise of Stalin:

❝ There is no similar name on the planet like the name of Stalin. It shines like a bright torch of freedom, it flies like a battle standard for millions of laborers around the world. . . . Stalin is today's Lenin! Stalin is the brain and heart of the party! Stalin is the banner of millions of people in their fight for a better life. ❞

Far from helping people fight for a better life, Stalin's ruthless policies brought suffering and death to millions of Soviets.

Focus Question How did Stalin transform the Soviet Union into a totalitarian state?

The Soviet Union Under Stalin

 Performance Standards

- **SSWH17b** Determine the causes and results of the Russian Revolution.
- **SSWH17e** Describe the police state that existed in Russia.

Terms, People, and Places

command economy	russification
collectives	atheism
kulaks	Comintern
Gulag	
socialist realism	

N̲ote **Taking**

Reading Strategy: Identify Main Ideas
Summarize the main points of the section in a chart like the one below.

The Soviet Union Under Stalin		
Five-Year Plans	Methods of Control	Daily Life

In January 1924, tens of thousands of people lined up in Moscow's historic Red Square. They had come to view the body of Lenin, who had died a few days earlier. Lenin's widow, Nadezhda Krupskaya, wanted to bury him simply next to his mother. Communist party officials—including Joseph Stalin—wanted to preserve Lenin's body and put it on permanent display. In the end, Lenin's body was displayed in Red Square for more than 65 years. By preserving Lenin's body, Stalin wanted to show that he would carry on the goals of the revolution. However, in the years that followed, he used ruthless measures to control the Soviet Union and its people.

A Totalitarian State

Karl Marx had predicted that under communism the state would eventually wither away. Under Stalin, the opposite occurred. He turned the Soviet Union into a totalitarian state controlled by a powerful and complex bureaucracy.

Stalin's Five-Year Plans Once in power, Stalin imposed government control over the Soviet Union's economy. In the past, said Stalin, Russia had suffered because of its economic backwardness. In 1928, he proposed the first of several "five-year plans" aimed at building heavy industry, improving transportation, and increasing farm output. He brought all economic activity under government control. The government owned all businesses and distributed all resources. The Soviet Union developed a **command economy,** in which government officials made all basic economic decisions. By contrast, in a capitalist system, the free market determine most economic decisions. Privately owned businesses compete to win the consumer's choice. This competition regulates the price and quality of goods.

Mixed Results in Industry

Stalin's five-year plans set high production goals, especially for heavy industry and transportation. The government pushed workers and managers to meet these goals by giving bonuses to those who succeeded—and by punishing those who did not. Between 1928 and 1939, large factories, hydroelectric power stations, and huge industrial complexes rose across the Soviet Union. Oil, coal, and steel production grew. Mining expanded, and new railroads were built.

Despite the impressive progress in some areas, Soviet workers had little to show for their efforts. Some former peasants did become skilled factory workers or managers. Overall, though, the standard of living remained low. Central planning was often inefficient, causing shortages in some areas and surpluses in others. Many managers, concerned only with meeting production quotas, turned out large quantities of low-quality goods. Consumer products such as clothing, cars, and refrigerators were scarce. Wages were low and workers were forbidden to strike. The party restricted workers' movements.

Forced Collectivization in Agriculture

Stalin also brought agriculture under government control, but at a horrendous cost. The government wanted farmers to produce more grain to feed workers in the cities. It also hoped to sell grain abroad to earn money.

As you have read, under Lenin's New Economic Plan (NEP), peasants had held on to small plots of land. Many had prospered. Stalin saw that system as being inefficient and a threat to state power. Stalin wanted all peasants to farm on either state-owned farms or **collectives,** large farms owned and operated by peasants as a group. On collectives, the government would provide tractors, fertilizers, and better seed, and peasants would learn modern farm methods. Peasants would be permitted to keep their houses and personal belongings, but all farm animals and implements were to be turned over to the collective. The state set all prices and controlled access to farm supplies.

Some peasants did not want to give up their land and sell their crops at the state's low prices. They resisted collectivization by killing farm animals, destroying tools, and burning crops. Stalin was furious. He believed that **kulaks,** or wealthy farmers, were behind the resistance. He responded with brutal force. In 1929, Stalin declared his intention to "liquidate the kulaks as a class." To this end, the government confiscated kulaks' land and sent them to labor camps. Thousands were killed or died from overwork.

Even after the "de-kulakization," angry peasants resisted by growing just enough to feed themselves. In response, the government seized all of their grain to meet industrial goals, purposely leaving the peasants to starve. In 1932, this ruthless policy, combined with poor harvests, led to a terrible

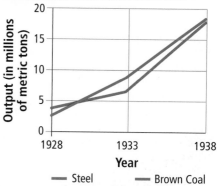

Effects of the Five-Year Plans on Soviet Industry

SOURCE: B.R. Mitchell, *European Historical Statistics, 1750–1970*

This 1931 propaganda poster supports the Five Year Plan for industry. Stalin's government saw rapid industrialization as the key to the success of the Soviet Union. *Using the line graph, describe the effect of the Five-Year Plans on steel and brown coal output.*

famine. Later called the Terror Famine, it caused between five and eight million people to die of starvation in the Ukraine alone.

Although collectivization increased Stalin's control of the peasantry, it did not improve farm output. During the 1930s, grain production inched upward, but meat, vegetables, and fruits remained in short supply. Feeding the population would remain a major problem in the Soviet Union.

✔ **Checkpoint** How did Stalin take control of the Soviet Union's economic life?

Stalin's Terror Tactics

In addition to tactics like the Terror Famine, Stalin's Communist party used secret police, torture, and violent purges to ensure obedience. Stalin tightened his grasp on every aspect of Soviet life, even stamping out any signs of dissent within the Communist elites.

Terror as a Weapon Stalin ruthlessly used terror as a weapon against his own people. He perpetrated crimes against humanity and systematically violated his people's individual rights. Police spies did not hesitate to open private letters or plant listening devices. Nothing appeared in print without official approval. There was no free press, and no safe method of voicing protest. Grumblers or critics were rounded up and sent to the **Gulag,** a system of brutal labor camps, where many died.

The Great Purge Even though Stalin's power was absolute, he still feared that rival party leaders were plotting against him. In 1934, he launched the Great Purge. During this reign of terror, Stalin and his secret police cracked down especially on Old Bolsheviks, or party activists from the early days of the revolution. His net soon widened to target army heroes, industrial managers, writers, and ordinary citizens. They were charged with a wide range of crimes, from counterrevolutionary plots to failure to meet production quotas.

Between 1936 and 1938, Stalin staged a series of spectacular public "show trials" in Moscow. Former Communist leaders confessed to all kinds of crimes after officials tortured them or threatened their families or friends. Many of the purged party members were never tried but were sent straight to the Gulag. Secret police files reveal that at least four million people were purged during the Stalin years. Some historians estimate the toll to be much greater.

Results of the Purge The purges increased Stalin's power. All Soviet citizens were now well aware of the consequences of disloyalty. However, Stalin's government also paid a price. Among the purged were experts in industry, economics, and engineering, and many of the Soviet Union's most talented

Food as a Weapon

In 1932, when peasants failed to meet unrealistic crop quotas, Stalin retaliated by seizing all of their grain to sell on the market, leaving millions to starve. Below, a woman and her son search for food during the famine. *Describe the effect of Stalin's ruthless policies on the production of oats, wheat, and potatoes.*

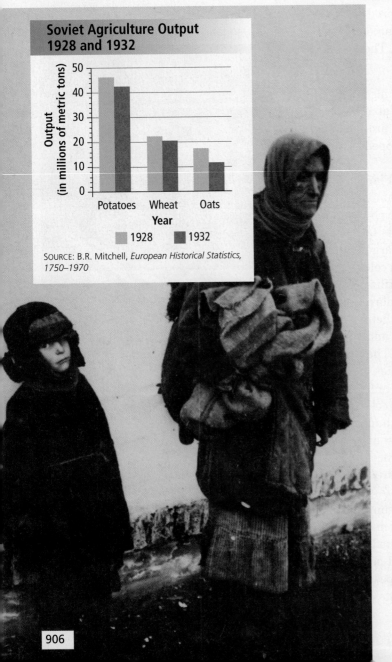

Soviet Agriculture Output 1928 and 1932

(bar graph, Output in millions of metric tons vs. Year, showing Potatoes, Wheat, Oats for 1928 and 1932)

SOURCE: B.R. Mitchell, *European Historical Statistics, 1750–1970*

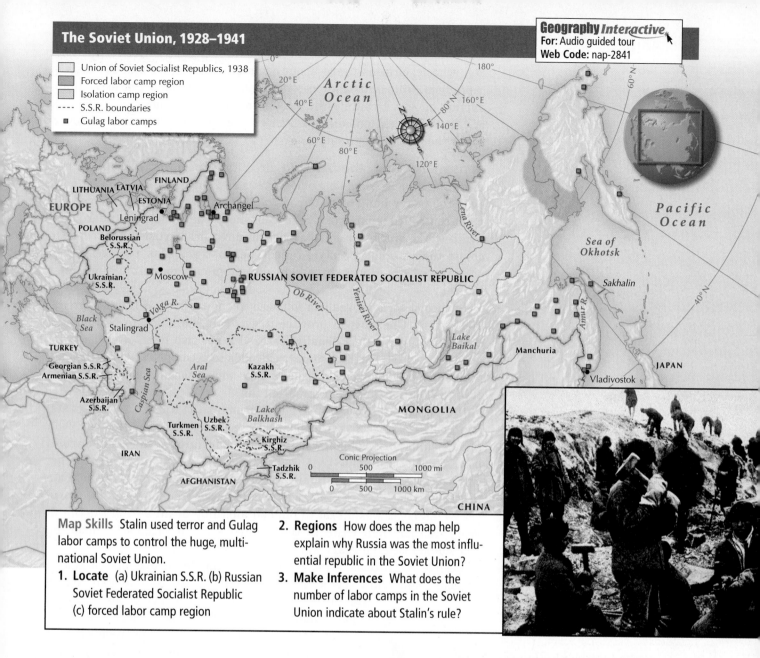

The Soviet Union, 1928–1941

Legend:
- Union of Soviet Socialist Republics, 1938
- Forced labor camp region
- Isolation camp region
- ----- S.S.R. boundaries
- ■ Gulag labor camps

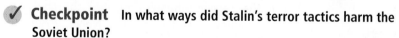

Map Skills Stalin used terror and Gulag labor camps to control the huge, multi-national Soviet Union.

1. **Locate** (a) Ukrainian S.S.R. (b) Russian Soviet Federated Socialist Republic (c) forced labor camp region

2. **Regions** How does the map help explain why Russia was the most influential republic in the Soviet Union?

3. **Make Inferences** What does the number of labor camps in the Soviet Union indicate about Stalin's rule?

A Gulag labor camp in 1934

writers and thinkers. The victims included most of the nation's military leaders and about half of its military officers, a loss that would weigh heavily on Stalin in 1941, when Germany invaded the Soviet Union.

✔ **Checkpoint** In what ways did Stalin's terror tactics harm the Soviet Union?

Communist Attempts to Control Thought

At the same time that he was purging any elements of resistance in Soviet society, Stalin also sought to control the hearts and minds of Soviet citizens. He tried to do this by tirelessly distributing propaganda, censoring opposing ideas, imposing Russian culture on minorities, and replacing religion with communist ideology.

Propaganda Stalin tried to boost morale and faith in the communist system by making himself a godlike figure. He used propaganda as a tool to build up a "cult of personality" around himself. Using modern technology, the party bombarded the public with relentless propaganda. Radios and loudspeakers blared into factories and villages. In movies, theaters, and schools, citizens heard about communist successes and the evils of capitalism. Billboards and posters urged workers to meet or exceed production quotas. Headlines in the Communist party newspaper *Pravda*, or "Truth," linked enemies at home to foreign agents seeking to overthrow the Communist regime.

Censorship and the Arts At first, the Bolshevik Revolution had meant greater freedom for Soviet artists and writers. Under Stalin, however, the heavy hand of state control also gripped the arts. The government controlled what books were published, what music was heard, and which works of art were displayed. Stalin required artists and writers to create their works in a style called **socialist realism.** Its goal was to show Soviet life in a positive light and promote hope in the communist future.

In theory, socialist realism followed in the footstep of Russian greats Tolstoy and Chekhov; in practice it was rarely allowed to be realistic. Socialist realist novels usually featured a positive hero, often an engineer or scientist, battling against the odds to accomplish a goal. Popular themes for socialist-realist visual artists were peasants, workers, heroes of the revolution, and—of course—Stalin.

If they refused to <u>conform</u> to government expectations, writers, artists, and composers faced government persecution. The Jewish poet Osip Mandelstam, for example, was imprisoned, tortured, and exiled for composing a satirical verse that was critical of Stalin. Out of fear for his wife's safety, Mandelstam finally submitted to threats and wrote an "Ode to Stalin." Boris Pasternak, who would later win fame for his novel *Doctor Zhivago*, was afraid to publish anything at all during the Stalin years. Rather than write in the favored style of socialist realism, he translated foreign literary works instead.

Despite restrictions, some Soviet writers produced magnificent works. Yevgeny Zamyatin's classic anti-Utopian novel *We* became well known outside of the Soviet Union, but was not published in his home country until 1989. The novel depicts a nightmare future in which people go by numbers, not names, and the "One State" controls people's thoughts. *And Quiet Flows the Don*, by Mikhail Sholokhov, passed the censor. The novel tells the story of a man who spends years fighting in World War I, the Russian Revolution, and the civil war. Sholokhov later won the Nobel Prize for literature.

Russification Yet another way Stalin controlled the cultural life of the Soviet Union was by promoting a policy of **russification,** or making a nationality's culture more Russian. By 1936, the U.S.S.R. was made up of 11 Soviet Socialist Republics. The Russian Soviet Federated Socialist Republic consisted of the old Russian heartland and was the largest and dominant republic. The other

Vocabulary Builder

<u>conform</u>—(kun FAWRM) *vi.* to obey a set of standards

Soviet Art

In this Socialist Realist sculpture, a factory worker and a collective farmer raise the hammer and sickle together.

Anna Akhmatova (ahk MAH tuh vuh), one of Russia's greatest poets, could not publish her works because she had violated state guidelines. Still, she wrote secretly. In this passage from "Requiem," she describes the ordeal of trying to visit her 20-year-old son, imprisoned during the Stalinist terrors:

Primary Source

66 For seventeen long months my pleas,
My cries have called you home.
I've begged the hangman on my knees,
My son, my dread, my own.
My mind's mixed up for good, and I'm
No longer even clear
Who's man, who's beast, nor how much time
Before the end draws near. 99
—Anna Akhmatova, "Requiem"
(tr. Robin Kemball)

 AUDIO

SSRs, such as Uzbek and the Ukraine, were the homelands of other nationalities and had their own languages, historical traditions, and cultures. At first, Stalin encouraged the autonomy, or independence, of these cultures. However, in the late 1920s, Stalin turned this policy on its head and systematically tried to make the cultures of the non-Russian SSRs more Russian. He appointed Russians to high-ranking positions in non-Russian SSRs and required the Russian language to be used in schools and businesses.

War on Religion The Communist party also tried to strengthen its hold on the minds of the people by destroying their religious faith. In accordance with the ideas of Marx, **atheism,** or the belief that there is no god, became an official state policy. Early on, the Communists targeted the Russian Orthodox Church, which had strongly supported the tsars. Many priests and other religious leaders were among those killed in the purges or sent to die in prison camps. Other religions were persecuted as well. At one show trial, 15 Roman Catholic priests were charged with teaching religion to the young, a counterrevolutionary activity. The state seized Jewish synagogues and banned the use of Hebrew. Islam was also officially discouraged.

The Communists tried to replace religion with their own ideology. Like a religion, communist ideology had its own "sacred" texts—the writings of Marx and Lenin—and its own shrines, such as the tomb of Lenin. Portraits of Stalin replaced religious icons in Russian homes. However, millions of Soviets continued to worship, in private and sometimes in public, in defiance of the government's prohibitions.

 Checkpoint How did Stalin use censorship and propaganda to support his rule?

The Party Versus the Church
To weaken the power of the Russian Orthodox Church, the party seized church property and converted churches into offices and museums. Here, Red Army soldiers carry off religious relics from a Russian church. *How might the policy of destroying churches in such a public way have backfired on the party?*

Soviet Society Under Stalin

The terror and cultural coercion of Stalin's rule made a mockery of the original theories and promises of communism. The lives of most Russians did change. But, while the changes had some benefits, they were often outweighed by continuous shortages and restricted freedoms.

The New Elite Takes Control The Communists destroyed the old social order of landowning nobles at the top and peasants at the bottom. But instead of creating a society of equals as they promised, they created a society where a few elite groups emerged as a new ruling class. At the head of society were members of the Communist party. Only a small fraction of Soviet citizens could join the party. Many who did so were motivated by a desire to get ahead, rather than a belief in communism.

The Soviet elite also included industrial managers, military leaders, scientists, and some artists and writers. The elite enjoyed benefits denied to most people. They lived in the best apartments in the cities and rested at the best vacation homes in the country. They could shop at special stores for scarce consumer goods. On the other hand, Stalin's purges often fell on the elite.

Benefits and Drawbacks

Although excluded from party membership, most people did enjoy several new benefits. The party required all children to attend free Communist-built schools. The state supported technical schools and universities as well. Schools served many important goals. Educated workers were needed to build a modern industrial state. The Communist party also set up programs for students outside school. These programs included sports, cultural activities, and political classes to train teenagers for party membership. However, in addition to important basic skills, schools also taught communist values, such as atheism, the glory of collective farming, and love of Stalin.

The state also provided free medical care, day care for children, inexpensive housing, and public recreation. While these benefits were real, many people still lacked vital necessities. Although the state built massive apartment complexes, housing was scarce. Entire families might be packed into a single room. Bread was plentiful, but meat, fresh fruit, and other foods remained in short supply.

Women in the Soviet Union

Long before 1917, women such as Nadezhda Krupskaya and Alexandra Kollontai worked for the revolution, spreading radical ideas among peasants and workers. Under the Communists, women won equality under the law. They gained <u>access</u> to education and a wide range of jobs. By the 1930s, many Soviet women were working in medicine, engineering, or the sciences. By their labor, women contributed to Soviet economic growth. They worked in factories, in construction, and on collectives. Within the family, their wages were needed because men and women earned the same low salaries.

✔ **Checkpoint** How did Communist schools benefit the state and the Communist party?

Vocabulary Builder

<u>access</u>—(AK ses) *n.* the ability to get and use

Women at Work
Soviet women, such as these concrete workers, were able to take jobs alongside men as equals, doing the same work and earning the same party. *What role did women play in the Soviet Union?*

Soviet Foreign Policy

Between 1917 and 1939, the Soviet Union pursued two very different goals in foreign policy. As Communists, both Lenin and Stalin wanted to bring about the worldwide revolution that Marx had predicted. But as Soviets, they wanted to guarantee their nation's security by winning the support of other countries. The result of pursuing these two different goals was a contradictory and generally unsuccessful foreign policy.

In 1919, Lenin formed the Communist International, or **Comintern.** The purpose of the Comintern was to encourage world-wide revolution. To this end, it aided revolutionary groups around the world and urged colonial peoples to rise up against imperialist powers.

The Comintern's support of revolutionary groups outside the Soviet Union and its propaganda against capitalism made Western powers highly suspicious of the Soviet Union. In the United States, fear of Bolshevik plots led to the "Red Scare" in the early 1920s. Britain broke off relations with the Soviet Union when evidence revealed Soviet schemes to turn a 1926 strike into a revolution. Even so, the Soviet Union slowly won recognition from Western powers and increased trade with capitalist countries. It also joined the League of Nations. However, mistrust still poisoned relations, especially after the Great Purge.

 Checkpoint How did the Soviet Union's foreign policy goals contradict one another?

Looking Ahead

By the time Stalin died in 1953, the Soviet Union had become a military superpower and a world leader in heavy industry. Yet Stalin's efforts exacted a brutal toll. The Soviet people were dominated by a totalitarian system based on terror. The reality of communism fell far short of Lenin's promises. Most people in the Soviet Union lived meager lives compared with people in the West.

SECTION 4 Assessment

Progress Monitoring *Online*
For: Self-quiz with vocabulary practice
Web Code: naa-2841

Terms, People, and Places
1. What do many of the key terms listed at the beginning of the section have in common? Explain.

Note Taking
2. **Reading Skill: Identify Main Ideas** Use your completed chart to answer the section Focus Question: How did Stalin transform the Soviet Union into a totalitarian state?

Comprehension and Critical Thinking
3. **Identify Effects** What were the goals and results of Stalin's five-year plans? How did the effects differ between industry and agriculture?

4. **Contrast** How did the command economy under Stalin differ from a capitalist economy?
5. **Synthesize Information** What methods did Stalin use to create a totalitarian state?
6. **Synthesize Information** One historian has said that socialist realism was "communism with a smiling face." What do you think he meant?
7. **Compare** Compare life under Stalin's rule with life under the Russian tsars.

● **Writing About History**
Quick Write: Choose an Organization Compare-and-contrast essays are often organized either point by point or by block. The first organization involves a discussion of one idea first, followed by the discussion of another, and emphasizes the two ideas. The second discusses all of the similarities, followed by all the differences, and emphasizes the comparison or contrast itself. Write an outline for each type for an essay comparing and contrasting the results of the Five-Year Plans in industry and agriculture.

Adolf Hitler with a member of a
Nazi youth organization

WITNESS HISTORY 🔊 AUDIO

The Nazis in Control of Germany

In the 1930s, Adolf Hitler and the Nazi party brought hope to Germans suffering from the Great Depression. On the dark side of Hitler's promises was a message of hate, aimed particularly at Jews. A German Jewish woman recalls an attack on her family during *Kristallnacht,* a night in early November 1938 when Nazi mobs attacked Jewish homes and businesses.

66 They broke our windowpanes, and the house became very cold. . . . We were standing there, outside in the cold, still in our night clothes, with only a coat thrown over. . . . Then they made everyone lie face down on the ground . . . 'Now, they will shoot us,' we thought. We were very afraid. 99

Focus Question How did Hitler and the Nazi party establish and maintain a totalitarian government in Germany?

Hitler and the Rise of Nazi Germany

 Performance Standards

- **SSWH17c** Describe the fascist policies of Hitler.
- **SSWH17e** Describe the police state that existed in Germany.
- **SSWH17f** Explain the German annexation of the Sudetenland.

Terms, People, and Places

chancellor   Gestapo
Ruhr Valley   Nuremberg Laws
Third Reich

Note Taking

Reading Skill: Identify Main Ideas As you read, summarize the section's main ideas in a flowchart like the one below.

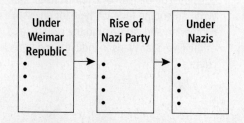

In November 1923, a German army veteran and leader of an extremist party, Adolf Hitler, tried to follow Mussolini's example by staging a small-scale coup in Munich. The coup failed, and Hitler was soon behind bars. But Hitler proved to be a force that could not be ignored. Within a decade, he made a new bid for power. This time, he succeeded by legal means.

Hitler's rise to power raises disturbing questions that we still debate today. Why did Germany, which had a democratic government in the 1920s, become a totalitarian state in the 1930s? How could a ruthless, hate-filled dictator gain the enthusiastic support of many Germans?

The Weimar Republic's Rise and Fall

As World War I drew to a close, Germany tottered on the brink of chaos. Under the threat of a socialist revolution, the kaiser abdicated. Moderate leaders signed the armistice and later, under protest, the Versailles treaty.

In 1919, German leaders drafted a constitution in the city of Weimar (VY mahr). It created a democratic government known as the Weimar Republic. The constitution set up a parliamentary system led by a **chancellor,** or prime minister. It gave women the vote and included a bill of rights.

Political Struggles The republic faced severe problems from the start. Politically, it was weak because Germany, like France, had many small parties. The chancellor had to form coalitions that easily fell apart.

The government, led by moderate democratic socialists, came under constant fire from both the left and right. Communists demanded radical changes like those Lenin had brought to Russia. Conservatives—including the old Junker nobility, military officers, and wealthy bourgeoisie—attacked the government as too liberal and weak. They longed for another strong leader like Bismarck. Germans of all classes blamed the Weimar Republic for the hated Versailles treaty. Bitter, they looked for scapegoats. Many blamed German Jews for economic and political problems.

Runaway Inflation Economic disaster fed unrest. In 1923, when Germany fell behind in reparations payments, France occupied the coal-rich **Ruhr Valley** (roor). Germans workers in the Ruhr protested using <u>passive</u> resistance and refused to work. To support the workers, the government continued to pay them, and printed huge quantities of paper money to do so. Inflation soon spiraled out of control, spreading misery and despair. The German mark became almost worthless. An item that cost 100 marks in July 1922 cost 944,000 marks by August 1923. Salaries rose by billions of marks, but they still could not keep up with skyrocketing prices. Many middle-class families saw their savings wiped out.

Recovery and Collapse With help from the Western powers, the government did bring inflation under control. In 1924, the United States gained British and French approval for a plan to reduce German reparations payments. Under the Dawes Plan, France withdrew its forces from the Ruhr, and American loans helped the German economy recover. Germany began to prosper. Then, the Great Depression hit, reviving memories of the miseries of 1923. Germans turned to an energetic leader, Adolf Hitler, who promised to solve the economic crisis and restore Germany's former greatness.

Weimar Culture Culture flourished in the Weimar Republic even as the government struggled through crisis after crisis. The tumultuous times helped to stimulate new cultural movements, such as dadaist art and Bauhaus architecture. Berlin attracted writers and artists from around the world, just as Paris did. The German playwright Bertolt Brecht sharply criticized middle-class values with *The Three-Penny Opera*. The artist George Grosz, through scathing drawings and paintings, blasted the failings of the Weimar Republic. However, many believed that this modern culture and the Weimar Republic itself were not in keeping with Germany's illustrious past.

✓ **Checkpoint** What political and economic problems did the Weimar Republic face?

The Nazi Party's Rise to Power

Adolf Hitler was born in Austria in 1889. When he was 18, he went to Vienna, then the capital of the multinational Hapsburg empire. German Austrians

Vocabulary Builder

<u>passive</u>—(PAS iv) *adj.* not active, nonviolent

Inflation Rocks Germany
A man uses German marks to paper his wall because it costs less than buying wallpaper. At the height of the inflation, it would have taken 84,000 fifty-million mark notes like the one below, to equal a single American dollar. *Why would inflation hit middle class people with modest savings hard?*

Adolf Hitler

As a boy, Adolf Hitler (1889–1945) became obsessed with Germany's 1871 victory in the Franco–Prussian War. "The great historic struggle would become my greatest spiritual experience," he later wrote. "I became more and more enthusiastic about everything . . . connected with war."

In school, young Hitler was known as a ringleader. One of his teachers recalled, "He demanded of his fellow pupils their unqualified obedience." He failed to finish high school and was later crushed when he was rejected by art school.

After Hitler came to power, he used his elite guard of storm troopers to terrorize his opponents. But when he felt his power threatened, Hitler had leaders of the storm troopers murdered during the "Night of the Long Knives" on June 30, 1934. **Why do you think historians study Hitler's upbringing?**

made up just one of many ethnic groups in Vienna. Yet they felt superior to Jews, Serbs, Poles, and other groups. While living in Vienna, Hitler developed the fanatical anti-Semitism, or prejudice against Jewish people, that would later play a major role in his rise to power.

Hitler went to Germany and fought in the German army during World War I. In 1919, he joined a small group of right-wing extremists. Like many ex-soldiers, he despised the Weimar government, which he saw as weak. Within a year, he was the unquestioned leader of the National Socialist German Workers, or Nazi, party. Like Mussolini, Hitler organized his supporters into fighting squads. Nazi "storm troopers" fought in the streets against their political enemies.

Hitler's Manifesto In 1923, as you have read, Hitler made a failed attempt to seize power in Munich. He was arrested and found guilty of treason. While in prison, Hitler wrote *Mein Kampf ("My Struggle")*. It would later become the basic book of Nazi goals and ideology.

Mein Kampf reflected Hitler's obsessions—extreme nationalism, racism, and anti-Semitism. Germans, he said, belonged to a superior "master race" of Aryans, or light-skinned Europeans, whose greatest enemies were the Jews. Hitler's ideas were rooted in a long tradition of anti-Semitism. In the Middle Ages, Christians persecuted Jews because of their different beliefs. The rise of nationalism in the 1800s caused people to identify Jews as ethnic outsiders. Hitler viewed Jews not as members of a religion but as a separate race. (He defined a Jew as anyone with one Jewish grandparent.) Echoing a familiar right-wing theme, he blamed Germany's defeat in World War I on a conspiracy of Marxists, Jews, corrupt politicians, and business leaders.

In his recipe for revival, Hitler urged Germans everywhere to unite into one great nation. Germany must expand, he said, to gain *Lebensraum* (LAY buns rowm), or living space, for its people. Slavs and other inferior races must bow to Aryan needs. To achieve its greatness, Germany needed a strong leader, or Führer (FYOO rur). Hitler was determined to become that leader.

Hitler Comes to Power After less than a year, Hitler was released from prison. He soon renewed his table-thumping speeches. The Great Depression played into Hitler's hands. As unemployment rose, Nazi membership grew to almost a million. Hitler's program appealed to veterans, workers, the lower middle classes, small-town Germans, and business people alike. He promised to end reparations, create jobs, and defy the Versailles treaty by rearming Germany.

With the government paralyzed by divisions, both Nazis and Communists won more seats in the Reichstag, or lower house of the legislature. Fearing the growth of communist political power, conservative politicians turned to Hitler. Although they despised him, they believed they could control him. Thus, with conservative support, Hitler was appointed chancellor in 1933 through legal means under the Weimar constitution.

Within a year, Hitler was dictator of Germany. He and his supporters suspended civil rights, destroyed the socialists and Communists, and disbanded other political parties. Germany became a one-party state. Like Stalin in Russia, Hitler purged his own party, brutally executing Nazis he felt were disloyal. Nazis learned that Hitler demanded unquestioning obedience.

 Checkpoint Describe the Nazi party's ideology and Hitler's plans for ruling Germany.

The Third Reich Controls Germany

Once in power, Hitler and the Nazis moved to build a new Germany. Like Mussolini, Hitler appealed to nationalism by recalling past glories. Germany's First Reich, or empire, was the medieval Holy Roman Empire. The Second Reich was the empire forged by Bismarck in 1871. Under Hitler's new **Third Reich,** he boasted, the German master race would dominate Europe for a thousand years.

To combat the Great Depression, Hitler launched large public works programs (as did Britain and the United States). Tens of thousands of people were put to work building highways and housing or replanting forests. Hitler also began a crash program to rearm Germany and schemed to unite Germany and Austria. Both measures were a strong repudiation, or rejection, of the hated Versailles treaty.

Germany Becomes a Totalitarian State To achieve his goals, Hitler organized an efficient but brutal system of totalitarian rule. Nazis controlled all areas of German life—from government to religion to education. Elite, black-uniformed troops, called the SS, enforced the Führer's will. His secret police, the **Gestapo** (guh STAH poh), rooted out opposition. The masses, relieved by belief in the Nazis' promises, cheered Hitler's accomplishments in ending unemployment and reviving German power. Those who worried about Hitler's terror apparatus quickly became its victims or were cowed into silence in fear for their own safety.

The Campaign Against the Jews Begins In his fanatical anti-Semitism, Hitler set out to drive Jews from Germany. In 1935, the Nazis passed the **Nuremberg Laws,** which deprived Jews of German citizenship and placed severe restrictions on them. They were prohibited from marrying non-Jews, attending or teaching at German schools or universities, holding government jobs, practicing law or medicine, or publishing

"Night of Broken Glass"
On the night of November 9, 1938, and into the next day, German mobs smashed the windows of Jewish homes and businesses, looted Jewish shops, and burned synagogues. Many Jewish people were dragged from their homes and beaten in the streets. Not only did the Nazi government authorize these attacks, it made the Jewish victims pay for the damage.

books. Nazis beat and robbed Jews and roused mobs to do the same. Many German Jews fled, seeking refuge in other countries.

Night of Broken Glass On November 7, 1938, a young Jew whose parents had been mistreated in Germany shot and wounded a German diplomat in Paris. Hitler used the incident as an excuse to stage an attack on all Jews. *Kristallnacht* (krih STAHL nahkt), or the "Night of Broken Glass," took place on November 9 and 10. Nazi-led mobs attacked Jewish communities all over Germany, Austria, and the annexed portions of Czechoslovakia. Before long, Hitler and his henchmen were making even more sinister plans for what they called the "Final Solution"—the extermination of all Jews.

Nazi Youth To build for the future, the Nazis indoctrinated young people with their ideology. In passionate speeches, the Führer spewed his message of racism. He urged young Germans to destroy their so-called enemies without mercy. On hikes and in camps, the "Hitler Youth" pledged absolute loyalty to Germany and undertook physical fitness programs to prepare for war. School courses and textbooks were rewritten to reflect Nazi racial views.

Like Fascists in Italy, Nazis sought to limit women's roles. Women were dismissed from upper-level jobs and turned away from universities. To raise the birthrate, Nazis offered "pure-blooded Aryan" women rewards for having more children. Still, Hitler's goal to keep women in the home and out of the workforce applied mainly to the privileged. As German industry expanded, women factory workers were needed.

Purging German Culture The Nazis also sought to purge, or purify, German culture. They denounced modern art, saying that it was corrupted by Jewish influences. They condemned jazz because of its African roots. Instead, the Nazis glorified old German myths such as those re-created in the operas of Richard Wagner (VAHG nur).

Hitler despised Christianity as "weak" and "flabby." He sought to replace religion with his racial creed. To control the churches, the Nazis combined all Protestant sects into a single state church. They closed Catholic schools and muzzled the Catholic clergy. Although many clergy either supported the new regime or remained silent, some courageously spoke out against Hitler.

✔ **Checkpoint** How did the Nazi party maintain its control of Germany?

Authoritarian Rule in Eastern Europe

Like Germany, most new nations in Eastern Europe slid from democratic to authoritarian rule in the postwar era. In 1919, a dozen countries were carved out of the old Russian, Austro-Hungarian, Ottoman and German empires. Although they differed from one another in important ways, they faced some common problems. They were small countries whose rural agricultural economies lacked capital to develop industry. Social and economic inequalities separated

poor peasants from wealthy landlords. None had much experience with the democratic process. Further complicating the situation, tensions leftover from World War I hindered economic cooperation between countries. Each country in the region tried to be independent of its neighbors, which hurt all of them. The region was hit hard by the Great Depression.

Ethnic Conflict Old rivalries between ethnic and religious groups created severe tensions. In Czechoslovakia, Czechs and Slovaks were unwilling partners. Serbs dominated the new state of Yugoslavia, but restless Slovenes and Croats living there pressed for independence. In Poland, Hungary, and Romania, conflict flared among various ethnic groups.

Democracy Retreats Economic problems and ethnic tensions contributed to instability, which in turn helped fascist rulers gain power. In Hungary, military strongman Nicholas Horthy (HAWR tay) overthrew a Communist-led government in 1919. By 1926, the military hero Joseph Pilsudski (peel SOOT skee) had taken control over Poland. Eventually, right-wing dictators emerged in every Eastern European country except Czechoslovakia and Finland. Like Hitler, these dictators promised order and won the backing of the military and wealthy. They also turned to anti-Semitism, using Jewish people as scapegoats for many national problems. Meanwhile, strong, aggressive neighbors eyed these small, weak states of Eastern Europe as tempting targets.

✔ **Checkpoint** Why did authoritarian states rise in Eastern Europe after World War I?

Notable Jewish Figures of Europe, Early 1900s

Person	Achievements
Marc Chagall	Forerunner of Surrealism
Gustav Mahler	Composed symphonies and conducted many major orchestras
Arnold Schoenberg	Pioneered new styles of music
Franz Kafka	Influential style of surrealist writing
Albert Einstein	Important scientist
Sigmund Freud	Founder of psychoanalysis
Edmund Husserl	Founder of phenomenology movement
Rudolph Lipschitz	Worked on number theory and potential theory

The table above lists a few of the notable Jewish people whose exceptional talents flew in the face of Hitler's claims of Aryan superiority. Some of these people fled Europe in the face of the Nazi regime. **Chart Skills** *Describe how losing some of its leading thinkers might have hurt Nazi Germany.*

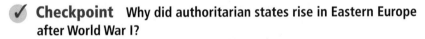

SECTION 5 Assessment

Progress Monitoring *Online*
For: Self-quiz with vocabulary practice
Web Code: naa-2851

Terms, People, and Places

1. Place each of the terms listed at the beginning of the section into one of the following categories: politics, culture, or economy. Write a sentence explaining your choice.

Note Taking

2. **Reading Skill: Identify Main Ideas** Use your completed flowchart to answer the section Focus Question: How did Hitler and the Nazi Party establish and maintain a totalitarian government in Germany?

Comprehension and Critical Thinking

3. **Express Problems Clearly** List three problems faced by the Weimar Republic.

4. **Recognize Ideologies** What racial and nationalistic ideas did Nazis promote?

5. **Summarize** What were some of the restrictions that Hitler placed on German Jews?

6. **Demonstrate Reasoned Judgment** Do you think that there are any reasons why a government would be justified in banning books or censoring ideas? Explain.

7. **Identify Effects** Why did dictators gain power in much of Eastern Europe?

8. **Draw Conclusions** Both Stalin and Hitler instituted ruthless campaigns against supposed enemies of the state. Why do you think dictators need to find scapegoats for their nation's ills?

● **Writing About History**

Quick Write: Use Compare-and-Contrast Transitions Use strong transitions to help readers navigate your compare-and-contrast essays. Words such as *however, but, nevertheless, yet, likewise, similarly,* and *instead* signal comparison-and-contrast relationships. Add one of these words to the statements below to clarify their meanings.

- Hitler's rise was based on hate. He was a popular leader.
- Germany became a fascist state. Many of the countries of Eastern Europe became fascist states.

Quick Study Guide

 SSWH17e

Progress Monitoring *Online*
For: Self-test with vocabulary practice
Web Code: naa-2861

Causes and Effects of the Great Depression

Cause and Effect	
Long-Term Causes	**Immediate Causes**
• Worldwide interrelationship of governments and economies • Gold standard • Overproduction of goods • Agricultural slump • Uneven distribution of wealth	• Falling demand • Financial crisis kicked off by New York stock market crash • Banks demand repayment of loans • American loans to other countries dry up • Without capital, businesses and factories fail

↓

Worldwide Economic Depression	

↓

Immediate Effects	**Long-Term Effects**
• Vast unemployment and misery • Protective tariffs imposed • Countries abandon gold standard • Loss of faith in capitalism and democracy • Authoritarian leaders emerge	• Rise of fascism and Nazism • Governments experiment with social programs • People blame scapegoats • World War II begins

Three Totalitarian States: Italy, the Soviet Union, and Germany

Country	Dictator in Power	Ideology	Example of Terror Tactics
Italy	Benito Mussolini in power in 1922	Fascist; Fanatic nationalism	Black Shirts suppressed dissent.
Soviet Union	Joseph Stalin in power in 1924	Communist	Stalin sent millions to Gulag labor camps.
Germany	Adolf Hitler in power in 1933	Fascist; Racial policies of hatred, aimed particularly at Jews	Nazis began to restrict and terrorize German Jews.

Some Cultural Figures of the Post World War I Era

Literature
Ernest Hemingway
Virginia Woolf
Langston Hughes
Mikhail Sholokhov

Music and Theater
Louis Armstrong
Bertolt Brecht

Visual Arts
Pablo Picasso
Jean Arp
Salvador Dali
Frank Lloyd Wright
George Grosz
Vasily Kandinsky

Key Events in Europe and the United States, 1919–1939

Britain, France, and the United States
Germany, Italy, and the Soviet Union

1919–1920
Red Scare sweeps the United States.

1925
Seven European nations sign the Locarno treaties, raising hopes for world peace.

1926
More than three million workers in several different industries strike in Britain.

1920

1925

1919
The Weimar Republic is established in Germany.

1922
Benito Mussolini comes to power after the March on Rome.

Concept Connector

Essential Question Review

To connect prior knowledge with what you have learned in this chapter, answer the questions below in your Concept Connector journal. Use the journal in the Reading and Note Taking Study Guide to record your answers (or go to www.phschool.com **Web Code:** nad-2807). In addition, record information about the following concept:

- Dictatorship: Mussolini and Hitler

1. **Dictatorship** As the Western democracies stumbled after World War I, totalitarian governments gained power in Italy, Germany, and the Soviet Union. Summarize social, political, and economic conditions in postwar Europe. Then create a list of reasons that explain why an average citizen living in postwar Europe in the 1920s or early 1930s might support a dictator.

2. **Human Rights** Mussolini, Hitler, and Stalin were brutal dictators. In disregard for human rights, political opponents were murdered, imprisoned, or exiled. But terror was not the dictator's only weapon. Give examples of other methods they used to maintain power, strengthen their totalitarian states, and strip people of their human rights. Focus on the following:
   - culture
   - education
   - propaganda

3. **Science and Technology** In the 1940s, scientists built on Marie Curie's research on radioactivity and Albert Einstein's theories of relativity to develop atomic energy. How do these discoveries demonstrate the benefits and costs of technology?

■ Connections To Today

1. **Dictatorship: North Korea's Kim Jong Il** Dictatorship as a form of government still exists today. Kim Jong Il (below), head of a communist totalitarian regime in North Korea, is considered among the most dangerous of the present-day dictators. In fact, Kim has been described as "Stalinist." Kim took over as dictator from his father, Kim Il-Sung, in 1994. Since then, he has violated the civil liberties of his own people, and he has destabilized international relations in the region with claims that North Korea possesses nuclear weapons. Research Kim Jong Il's record in North Korea and write two paragraphs comparing his regime to Stalin's in Russia.

2. **Political Systems: The Former Soviet Union** The Soviet Union came to an end in 1991. Its collapse produced 14 new republics, besides the Russian Federation, as each of the former SSRs became independent. The transition was not easy. Choose one of the following countries and then research and write a brief report on its transition from SSR to independent republic: Armenia, Azerbaijan, Belarus, Estonia, Georgia, Kazakhstan, Kyrgyzstan, Latvia, Lithuania, Moldova, Tajikistan, Turkmenistan, Ukraine, Uzbekistan.

1929
The Great Depression begins in the United States.

1930
Construction on the Maginot Line begins on the border of France and Germany.

1933
Prohibition is repealed in the United States.

History Interactive
For: Interactive timeline
Web Code: nap-2862

1930   1935

1928
Joseph Stalin launches the first of his Five-Year Plans in the Soviet Union.

1932
Stalin's ruthless policies, combined with failed crops, cause mass starvation in the Soviet Union.

1933
Adolf Hitler becomes chancellor of Germany.

1935
The Nazi Party in Germany passes the Nuremberg Laws, limiting the rights of Jews.

Chapter Assessment

Terms, People, and Places

Match the following terms with the definitions below.

flapper	Benito Mussolini
Harlem Renaissance	command economy
Franklin Delano Roosevelt	Gulag
disarmament	Ruhr Valley
totalitarian state	Third Reich

1. rebellious young woman of the 1920s
2. leader of the first modern fascist state
3. reduction of armed forces and weapons
4. government in which a one-party dictatorship regulates every aspect of citizens' lives
5. president of the United States who established the New Deal to help Americans during the Great Depression
6. African American cultural movement in the 1920s and 1930s
7. coal-rich industrial region of Germany

Main Ideas

Section 1 (pp. 884–890)

8. How did Western culture and society change in reaction to World War I?

Section 2 (pp. 891–897)

9. Describe the search for peace in the 1920s and its results.
10. What were the effects of the Great Depression?

Section 3 (pp. 898–903)

11. What is fascism?
12. How did Mussolini's fascist regime rule Italy?

Section 4 (pp. 904–911)

13. Summarize conditions in the Soviet Union under Stalin.

Section 5 (pp. 912–917)

14. How did Hitler establish a totalitarian state in Germany?

Chapter Focus Question

15. What political and economic challenges did the Western world face in the 1920s and 1930s, and how did various countries react to these challenges?

Critical Thinking

16. **Synthesize Information** How did the literature and art of the 1920s reflect the influence of World War I?
17. **Identify Causes** What imbalances helped cause the Great Depression of the 1930s?
18. **Recognize Ideologies** Why did the ideology of fascism appeal to many Italians?
19. **Compare Points of View** Describe the similarities and differences between fascism and communism.
20. **Recognize Propaganda** Why was propaganda an important tool of totalitarian dictators?
21. **Make Comparisons** Both Germany under Hitler and the Nazis and the Soviet Union under Stalin and the Communists were totalitarian states. How was totalitarian rule similar in these two countries? How did Nazi totalitarianism differ from that of the Communist Soviet Union?

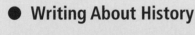

● Writing About History

In this chapter's five Section Assessments, you developed skills for writing a compare-and-contrast essay.

Writing a Compare-and-Contrast Essay The period between World War I and World War II was a time of rapid change with some serious crises of its own. Write a compare-and-contrast essay on one of the following pairs of ideas: society before and after World War I, solutions to alleviate the Great Depression in the United States and in Germany, fascism compared to democracy in the 1920s and 1930s, or a topic of your own choosing.

Prewriting

• Choose a valid topic for your essay by choosing two things that are neither too similar nor wildly different.

• Choose categories in which the two items could be compared and contrasted.
• Use a Venn diagram to gather and record details for your essay.

Drafting

• Develop a thesis that introduces the items you are comparing and the point you intend to make by the comparison.
• Outline how you will organize your arguments and the details that will support them.
• Write an introduction explaining what you are comparing and contrasting, a body, and a conclusion that restates your main points.

Revising

• Use the guidelines for revising your essay on page SH12 of the Writing Handbook.

Prepare for the GHSGT

Hitler's Rise to Power

In 1919, Hitler joined the National Socialist German Workers Party, later known as the Nazi party. It was a marginal party that only received one million votes in 1924. By 1932, however, the Nazi party, with Hitler at its helm, was Germany's largest party. Many factors contributed to Hitler's surprising rise to power, as the documents below illustrate.

Document A

This poster, displayed in Berlin in 1932, tells voters: "We want work and bread! Elect Hitler!"

Document B

"The National Socialist movement must strive to eliminate the disproportion between our population and our area—viewing this latter as a source of food as well as a basis for power politics. . . . We must hold unflinchingly to our aim . . . to secure for the German people the land and soil to which they are entitled. . . ."

—From ***Mein Kampf*** by Adolf Hitler

Document C

". . . [T]hough the Fuehrer's anti-Semitic programme furnished the National Socialist party in the first instance with a nucleus and a rallying-cry, it was swept into office by two things with which the "Jewish Problem" did not have the slightest connexion. On the one side was economic distress and the revulsion against Versailles; on the other, chicanery and intrigue. . . . Hitler and his party had promised the unhappy Germans a new heaven and a new earth, coupled with the persecution of the Jews. Unfortunately, a new heaven and earth cannot be manufactured to order. But a persecution of the Jews can. . . ."

—From ***The Jewish Problem*** by Louis Golding, 1939

Document D

"The Versailles settlement was seen as a means by which Germany's enemies aimed to keep the Reich prostrate forever and had to be overturned not merely to restore the status quo ante, but to allow Germany to expand and seize the "living space" that it allegedly needed in the east. And violence was viewed as the means by which to achieve a Third Reich and a German-dominated Europe—by smashing the democratic Weimar "system," destroying Marxism, solving the "Jewish question," breaking the "chains of Versailles," and building up the armed forces so that Germany again could go to war."

—From ***Nazism and War*** by historian Richard Bessel

Analyzing Documents

Use your knowledge of the rise of Nazism in Germany and Documents A, B, C, and D to answer questions 1–4.

1. Document A focuses on which factor that aided Hitler's rise to power?
   A anger over World War I
   B social considerations
   C the economy
   D racial and religious prejudice

2. According to Document C, the Nazis persecuted the Jews, because
   A most Germans hated them.
   B they wanted to keep attention from other problems.
   C they had already achieved their other goals.
   D their opponents were all Jews.

3. According to Document D, the Nazi's main goal was to
   A dominate Europe.
   B get revenge for the Treaty of Versailles.
   C stop communism.
   D end democracy.

4. Explain why Germany was fertile soil for the Nazis following World War I. Give your reasons, using these documents and information from the chapter.

29

World War II and Its Aftermath

1931–1955

A City Lies in Ruins

March 6, 1944—The Allies' mission to bomb Berlin, Germany, includes 810 bombers plus 800 fighter escorts. The stream of aircraft stretches a mile wide and a half-mile deep and takes more than half an hour to pass over any given point. Approaching the city, the bombers press on through flak—anti-aircraft fire from the ground—"so thick you can walk on it." Then, bomb bay doors open, and their payloads rain down on the city.

Listen to the Witness History audio to hear more about the Allied bombing efforts.

◄ Cologne, Germany, in ruins, 1944

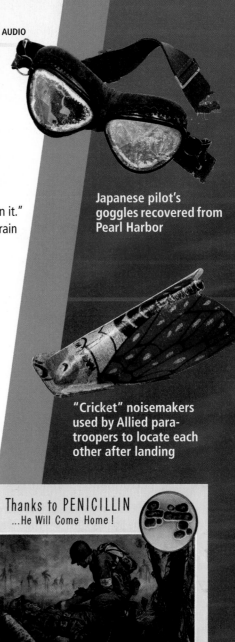

Japanese pilot's goggles recovered from Pearl Harbor

"Cricket" noisemakers used by Allied paratroopers to locate each other after landing

GA Performance Standards

Chapter Focus Question How did aggressive world powers emerge, and what did it take to defeat them during World War II?

Use the ☑ **Quick Study Timeline** at the end of this chapter to preview chapter events.

Thanks to PENICILLIN
...He Will Come Home!

FROM ORDINARY MOLD—
the Greatest Healing Agent of this War!

SCHENLEY LABORATORIES, INC.
Producers of PENICILLIN-Schenley

An advertisement praising the benefits of penicillin

❓ Concept Connector ONLINE

To explore Essential Questions related to this chapter, go to PHSchool.com
Web Code: nad-2907

WITNESS HISTORY ◀)) AUDIO

A Desperate Peace

British Prime Minister Neville Chamberlain spoke to a jubilant crowd upon returning to London from a conference with Adolf Hitler in Munich, Germany, in September 1938:

❝ For the second time in our history, a British Prime Minister has returned from Germany bringing peace with honor. I believe it is peace for our time . . . Go home and get a nice quiet sleep. ❞

Focus Question What events unfolded between Chamberlain's declaration of "peace for our time" and the outbreak of a world war?

Neville Chamberlain and headlines announcing the Munich Pact

From Appeasement to War

 Performance Standards

- **SSWH17f** Explain the Italian invasion of Ethiopia, the Spanish Civil War, and the German annexation of the Sudetenland.
- **SSWH18a** Describe the major conflicts and outcomes of WWII.

Terms, People, and Places

appeasement	Francisco Franco
pacifism	Anschluss
Neutrality Acts	Sudetenland
Axis powers	Nazi-Soviet Pact

Note Taking

Reading Skill: Recognize Sequence As you read, keep track of the sequence of events that led to the outbreak of World War II by completing a table like the one below.

Acts of Aggression	
Japan	
Italy	
Germany	
Spain	

After the horrors of World War I, Western democracies desperately tried to preserve peace during the 1930s while ignoring signs that the rulers of Germany, Italy, and Japan were preparing to build new empires. Despite the best efforts of Neville Chamberlain and other Western leaders, the world was headed to war again.

Aggression Goes Unchecked

Throughout the 1930s, challenges to peace followed a pattern. Dictators took aggressive action but met only verbal protests and pleas for peace from the democracies. Mussolini, Hitler, and the leaders of Japan viewed that desire for peace as weakness and responded with new acts of aggression. With hindsight, we can see the shortcomings of the democracies' policies. These policies, however, were the product of long and careful deliberation. At the time, some people believed they would work.

Japan Overruns Manchuria and Eastern China One of the earliest tests had been posed by Japan. Japanese military leaders and ultranationalists thought that Japan should have an empire equal to those of the Western powers. In pursuit of this goal, Japan seized Manchuria in 1931. When the League of Nations condemned the aggression, Japan simply withdrew from the organization. Japan's easy success strengthened the militarist faction in Japan. In 1937, Japanese armies overran much of eastern China, starting the Second Sino-Japanese War. Once again, Western protests did not stop Japan.

Hitler Remilitarizes Germany
Hitler rebuilt the German military during the 1930s in defiance of the Treaty of Versailles. The government's investment in armaments also helped pull Germany out of the Great Depression. Here, German police march in goose step as Hitler salutes in the background. *How did rearmament affect the rest of Germany?*

Italy Invades Ethiopia In Italy, Mussolini decided to act on his own imperialist ambitions. Italy's defeat by the Ethiopians at the battle of Adowa in 1896 still rankled. In 1935, Italy invaded Ethiopia, located in northeastern Africa. Although the Ethiopians resisted bravely, their outdated weapons were no match for Mussolini's tanks, machine guns, poison gas, and airplanes. The Ethiopian king Haile Selassie (HY luh suh lah SEE) appealed to the League of Nations for help. The League voted <u>sanctions</u> against Italy for violating international law. But the League had no power to enforce the sanctions, and by early 1936, Italy had conquered Ethiopia.

Vocabulary Builder
<u>sanctions</u>—(SANGK shunz) *n.* penalties

Hitler Goes Against the Treaty of Versailles By then, Hitler, too, had tested the will of the Western democracies and found it weak. First, he built up the German military in defiance of the treaty that had ended World War I. Then, in 1936, he sent troops into the "demilitarized" Rhineland bordering France—another treaty violation.

Germans hated the Versailles treaty, and Hitler's successful challenge made him more popular at home. The Western democracies denounced his moves but took no real action. Instead, they adopted a policy of **appeasement,** or giving in to the demands of an aggressor in order to keep the peace.

Keeping the Peace The Western policy of appeasement developed for a number of reasons. France was demoralized, suffering from political divisions at home. It could not take on Hitler without British support. The British, however, had no desire to confront the German dictator. Some even thought that Hitler's actions constituted a justifiable response to the terms of the Treaty of Versailles, which they believed had been too harsh on Germany.

In both Britain and France, many saw Hitler and fascism as a defense against a worse evil—the spread of Soviet communism. Additionally, the Great Depression sapped the energies of the Western democracies. Finally, widespread **pacifism,** or opposition to all war, and disgust with the destruction from the previous war pushed many governments to seek peace at any price.

Three leaders in Europe and one in Japan launched ambitious plans to increase their power.

● Benito Mussolini—Italy

● Adolf Hitler—Germany

● Tojo Hideki—Japan

● Francisco Franco—Spain

As war clouds gathered in Europe in the mid-1930s, the United States Congress passed a series of **Neutrality Acts.** One law forbade the sale of arms to any nation at war. Others outlawed loans to warring nations and prohibited Americans from traveling on ships of warring powers. The fundamental goal of American policy, however, was to avoid involvement in a European war, not to prevent such a conflict.

Rome-Berlin-Tokyo Axis In the face of the apparent weakness of Britain, France, and the United States, Germany, Italy, and Japan formed what became known as the Rome-Berlin-Tokyo Axis. Known as the **Axis powers,** the three nations agreed to fight Soviet communism. They also agreed not to interfere with one another's plans for territorial expansion. The agreement cleared the way for these anti-democratic, aggressor powers to take even bolder steps.

✔ **Checkpoint** Describe the German, Italian, and Japanese drives for empire.

Spain Collapses Into Civil War

In 1936, a local struggle in Spain polarized public opinion throughout Europe. Trouble in Spain started in 1931, when popular unrest against the old order forced the king to leave Spain. A republic was set up with a new, more liberal constitution. The government passed a series of controversial reforms, taking land and privileges away from the Church and old ruling classes. Still, leftists demanded more radical reforms. Conservatives, backed by the military, rejected change.

In 1936, a conservative general named **Francisco Franco** led a revolt that touched off a bloody civil war. Fascists and supporters of right-wing policies, called Nationalists, rallied to back Franco. Supporters of the republic, known as Loyalists, included Communists, Socialists, and those who wanted democracy.

People from other nations soon jumped in to support both sides. Hitler and Mussolini sent arms and forces to help Franco. The Soviet Union sent soldiers to fight against fascism alongside the Spanish Loyalists. Although the governments of Britain, France, and the United States remained neutral, individuals from those countries, as well as other countries, also fought with the Loyalists. Anti-Nazi Germans and anti-Fascist Italians joined the Loyalist cause as well.

Both sides committed horrible atrocities. The ruinous struggle took more than 500,000 lives. One of the worst horrors was a German air raid on Guernica, a small Spanish market town, in April 1937. German planes dropped their load of bombs, and then swooped low to machine-gun anyone who had survived the bombs. Nearly 1,000 innocent civilians were killed. To Nazi leaders, the attack on Guernica was an experiment to identify what their new planes could do. To the rest of the world, it was a grim warning of the destructive power of modern warfare.

By 1939, Franco had triumphed. Once in power, he created a fascist dictatorship similar to the dictatorships of Hitler and Mussolini. He rolled back earlier reforms, killed or jailed enemies, and used terror to promote order.

✔ **Checkpoint** How did the Spanish Civil War involve combatants from other countries?

German Aggression Continues

In the meantime, Hitler pursued his goal of bringing all German-speaking people into the Third Reich. He also took steps to gain "living space" for Germans in Eastern Europe. Hitler, who believed in the superiority of the German people, thought that Germany had a right to conquer the Slavs to the east. Hitler claimed, "I have the right to remove millions of an inferior race that breeds like vermin."

Hitler's aggressive plans also served economic purposes. Production of military equipment would benefit German industry, which would also gain new raw materials and markets in the east.

Austria Annexed By March, 1938, Hitler was ready to engineer the **Anschluss** (AHN shloos), or union of Austria and Germany. When Austria's chancellor refused to agree to Hitler's demands, Hitler sent in the German army to "preserve order." To indicate his new role as ruler of Austria, Hitler made a speech from the Hofburg Palace, the former residence of the Hapsburg emperors.

The Anschluss violated the Versailles treaty and created a brief war scare. Some Austrians favored annexation. Hitler quickly silenced any Austrians who opposed it. And since the Western democracies took no action, Hitler easily had his way.

The Czech Crisis Germany turned next to Czechoslovakia. At first, Hitler insisted that the three million Germans in the **Sudetenland** (soo DAY tun land)—a region of western Czechoslovakia—be given autonomy. Czechoslovakia was one of only two remaining democracies in Eastern Europe. (Finland was the other.) Still, Britain and France were not willing to go to war to save it. As British and French leaders searched for a peaceful solution, Hitler increased his demands. The Sudetenland, he said, must be annexed to Germany.

Note Taking

Reading Skill: Recognize Sequence
Complete this timetable of German aggression as you read.

German Aggression	
March 1938	
September 1938	
March 1939	
September 1939	

Germany in Czechoslovakia
A Sudeten woman grieves while dutifully saluting Hitler's troops (below). German tanks roll through Wenceslas Square in Prague (left).

927

At the Munich Conference in September 1938, British and French leaders again chose appeasement. They caved in to Hitler's demands and then persuaded the Czechs to surrender the Sudetenland without a fight. In exchange, Hitler assured Britain and France that he had no further plans to expand his territory.

"Peace for Our Time" Returning from Munich, British Prime Minister Neville Chamberlain told cheering crowds that he had achieved "peace for our time." He told Parliament that the Munich Pact had "saved Czechoslovakia from destruction and Europe from Armageddon." French leader Edouard Daladier (dah lahd yay) reacted differently to the joyous crowds that greeted him in Paris. "The fools, why are they cheering?" he asked. British politician Winston Churchill, who had long warned of the Nazi threat, judged the diplomats harshly: "They had to choose between war and dishonor. They chose dishonor; they will have war."

✔ **Checkpoint** Why did Hitler feel justified in taking over Austria and the Sudetenland?

Geography *Interactive*
For: Audio guided tour
Web Code: nap-2911

Aggression in Europe and Africa to September, 1939

Map Skills Between 1936 and 1939, Germany and Italy repeatedly threatened peace in Europe.

1. Locate (a) Austria (b) Rhineland (c) Poland

2. Regions The strip of land between East Prussia and the rest of Germany is called the Polish Corridor. Why is that an appropriate name for the region?

3. Predict Consequences Which countries in 1939 were probably the most likely targets for future acts of German or Italian aggression? Explain.

Germany, 1935
Occupied by Germany, 1936
Occupied by Germany, 1938–1939
Italy and Italian territories, 1935
Occupied by Italy, 1935–1939

Europe Plunges Toward War

Just as Churchill predicted, Europe plunged rapidly toward war. In March 1939, Hitler broke his promises and gobbled up the rest of Czechoslovakia. The democracies finally accepted the fact that appeasement had failed. At last thoroughly alarmed, they promised to protect Poland, most likely the next target of Hitler's expansion.

Nazi-Soviet Pact In August 1939, Hitler stunned the world by announcing a nonaggression pact with his great enemy—Joseph Stalin, the Soviet dictator. Publicly, the Nazi-Soviet Pact bound Hitler and Stalin to peaceful relations. Secretly, the two agreed not to fight if the other went to war and to divide up Poland and other parts of Eastern Europe between them.

The pact was based not on friendship or respect but on mutual need. Hitler feared communism as Stalin feared fascism. But Hitler wanted a free hand in Poland. Also, he did not want to fight a war with the Western democracies and the Soviet Union at the same time. For his part, Stalin had sought allies among the Western democracies against the Nazi menace. Mutual suspicions, however, kept them apart. By joining with Hitler, Stalin tried to protect the Soviet Union from the threat of war with Germany and grabbed a chance to gain land in Eastern Europe.

Invasion of Poland On September 1, 1939, a week after the Nazi-Soviet Pact, German forces invaded Poland. Two days later, Britain and France declared war on Germany. World War II had begun.

The devastation of World War I and the awareness of the destructive power of modern technology made the idea of more fighting unbearable. Unfortunately, the war proved to be even more horrendous than anyone had imagined.

✓ **Checkpoint** What convinced Britain and France to end their policy of appeasement? Why?

Why the West Appeased Hitler

- Fear of the destructive power of modern technology
- Widespread pacifism following World War I
- Hitler's actions seen as a justifiable response to the harsh Treaty of Versailles
- Widespread economic depression
- Hitler's fascism seen as a defense against Soviet communism
- Faith in diplomacy and compromise
- Misreading of Hitler's intentions

Chart Skills Agree or disagree with the following statement: "World War II was in large part a continuation of World War I." Provide evidence from the chart and your knowledge of history to support your view.

Vocabulary Builder

technology—(tek NAHL uh jee) *n.* scientific advances applied to practical purposes

---

SECTION **1 Assessment**

Progress Monitoring Online
For: Self-quiz with vocabulary practice
Web Code: naa-2911

Terms, People, and Places

1. For each term, person, or place listed at the beginning of the section, write a sentence explaining its significance.

Note Taking

2. **Reading Skill: Recognize Sequence** Use your completed tables to answer the Focus Question: What events unfolded between Chamberlain's declaration of "peace for our time" and the outbreak of a world war?

Comprehension and Critical Thinking

3. **Identify Central Issues** How did the Western democracies respond to the aggression of the Axis powers during the 1930s?

4. **Synthesize Information** Why did Germany and Italy become involved in the Spanish Civil War?

5. **Recognize Cause and Effect** How was the Munich Conference a turning point in the road toward world war?

6. **Analyze Information** Why do you think some historians call the period between 1919 and 1939 the 20-year truce?

● Writing About History

Quick Write: Explore a Topic Choose one specific event from this section and write a series of questions that you could use to direct research on the topic. For example, on the formation of the Rome-Berlin-Tokyo Axis you could ask

- How did the Axis benefit each of the member countries?
- How did the Axis clear the way for the members to take even bolder aggressive actions?

► Janina Sulkowska in the early 1930s

► German fighter plane

WITNESS HISTORY ◀)) AUDIO

Janina's War Story

❝It was 10:30 in the morning and I was helping my mother and a servant girl with bags and baskets as they set out for the market. . . . Suddenly the high-pitch scream of diving planes caused everyone to freeze. . . . Countless explosions shook our house followed by the *rat-tat-tat* of strafing machine guns. We could only stare at each other in horror. Later reports would confirm that several German Stukas had screamed out of a blue sky and . . . dropped several bombs along the main street— and then returned to strafe the market. The carnage was terrible.❞

—Janina Sulkowska, Krzemieniec, Poland, September 12, 1939

Focus Question Which regions were attacked and occupied by the Axis powers, and what was life like under their occupation?

The Axis Advances

 Performance Standards

- **SSWH17e** Describe the police state that existed in Germany.
- **SSWH18a** Describe Pearl Harbor.
- **SSWH18b** Identify Nazi ideology, policies, and consequences that led to the Holocaust.

Terms, People, and Places

blitzkrieg	General Erwin Rommel
Luftwaffe	concentration camps
Dunkirk	Holocaust
Vichy	Lend-Lease Act

Note Taking

Reading Skill: Recognize Sequence Sequence events as you read in a flowchart.

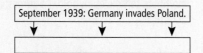

September 1939: Germany invades Poland.

Diplomacy and compromise had not satisfied the Axis powers' hunger for empire. Western democracies had hoped that appeasement would help establish a peaceful world order. But Nazi Germany, Fascist Italy, and imperial Japan plunged ahead with their plans for conquest.

The Axis Attacks

On September 1, 1939, Nazi forces stormed into Poland, revealing the enormous power of Hitler's **blitzkrieg,** or "lightning war." The blitzkrieg utilized improved tank and airpower technology to strike a devastating blow against the enemy. First, the **Luftwaffe,** or German air force, bombed airfields, factories, towns, and cities, and screaming dive bombers fired on troops and civilians. Then, fast-moving tanks and troop transports pushed their way into the defending Polish army, encircling whole divisions of troops and forcing them to surrender.

While Germany attacked from the west, Stalin's forces invaded from the east, grabbing lands promised to them under the Nazi-Soviet Pact. Within a month, Poland ceased to exist. Because of Poland's location and the speed of the attacks, Britain and France could do nothing to help beyond declaring war on Germany.

Hitler passed the winter without much further action. Stalin's armies, however, forced the Baltic states of Estonia, Latvia, and

Lithuania to agree to host bases for the Soviet military. Soviet forces also seized part of Finland, which put up stiff but unsuccessful resistance.

The Miracle of Dunkirk During that first winter, the French hunkered down behind the Maginot Line. Britain sent troops to wait with them. Some reporters referred to this quiet time as the "phony war." Then, in April 1940, Hitler launched a blitzkrieg against Norway and Denmark, both of which soon fell. Next, his forces slammed into the Netherlands and Belgium.

In May, German forces surprised the French and British by attacking through the Ardennes Forest in Belgium, an area that was considered invasion proof. Bypassing the Maginot Line, German troops poured into France. Retreating British forces were soon trapped between the Nazi army and the English Channel. In a desperate gamble, the British sent all available naval vessels, merchant ships, and even fishing and pleasure boats across the channel to pluck stranded troops off the beach of **Dunkirk.** Despite German air attacks, the improvised armada ferried more than 300,000 troops to safety in Britain. This heroic rescue raised British morale.

France Falls Meanwhile, German forces headed south toward Paris. Italy declared war on France and attacked from the south. Overrun and demoralized, France surrendered. On June 22, 1940, Hitler forced the French to sign the surrender documents in the same railroad car in which Germany had signed the armistice ending World War I. Following the surrender, Germany occupied northern France. In the south, the Germans set up a "puppet state," with its capital at **Vichy** (VEE shee).

Some French officers escaped to England and set up a government-in-exile. Led by Charles de Gaulle, these "free French" worked to liberate their homeland. Within France, resistance fighters used guerrilla tactics against German forces.

Operation Sea Lion With the fall of France, Britain stood alone in Western Europe. Hitler was sure that the British would sue for peace. But Winston Churchill, who had replaced Neville Chamberlain as prime minister, had other plans. Faced with this defiance, Hitler made plans for Operation Sea Lion—the invasion of Britain. In preparation for the invasion, he launched massive air strikes against the island nation.

Beginning in August 1940, German bombers began a daily bombardment of England's southern coast. For a month, Britain's Royal Air Force valiantly battled the Luftwaffe. Then, the Germans changed their tactics. Instead of bombing military targets in the south, they began to bomb London and other cities.

Winston Churchill's defiance gave voice to the determination of the British. *How did Churchill give weight to his speech?*

Primary Source

66 We shall defend our island, whatever the cost may be, we shall fight on the beaches, we shall fight on the landing grounds, we shall fight in the fields and in the streets, we shall fight in the hills; we shall never surrender. 99
—*Winston Churchill, June 4, 1940*   AUDIO

Germany Launches the Blitz German bombers first appeared over London late on September 7, 1940. All through the night, relays of aircraft showered high explosives and firebombs on the sprawling capital. The bombing continued for 57 nights in a row and then sporadically until the next May. These bombing attacks are known as "the blitz." Much of London was destroyed, and thousands of people lost their lives.

SURVIVING THE BLITZ

From 1940 to 1941, Germany tried to pummel Britain into submission during a months-long bombing campaign known as "the blitz." From September through May, German pilots targeted London with night after night of bombing, but other cities such as Liverpool, Glasgow, and Belfast became targets, too. These nighttime raids sent ordinary civilians scrambling for safety—in crowded public shelters, in homemade shelters, or even in the London Underground. During the blitz, German bombers killed more than 40,000 British civilians and damaged millions of homes. AUDIO 🔊

◄ Fearing poisonous gas attacks, the British government issued gas masks to its citizens. However, gas was never used against British civilians.

Small gestures of kindness helped Londoners deal with the effects of bombing raids. ▼

MOTHERS
Send them
out of
London

▲ Nearly three million people were evacuated from Britain's cities to the safer countryside.

London did not break under the blitz. Defiantly, Parliament continued to meet. Citizens carried on their daily lives, seeking protection in shelters and then emerging to resume their routines when the all-clear sounded. Even the British king and queen chose to support Londoners by joining them in bomb shelters rather than fleeing to the countryside.

Hitler Fails to Take Britain German planes continued to bomb London and other cities off and on until May 1941. But contrary to Hitler's hopes, the Luftwaffe could not gain air superiority over Britain, and British morale was not destroyed. In fact, the bombing only made the British more determined to turn back the enemy. Operation Sea Lion was a failure.

Africa and the Balkans Axis armies also pushed into North Africa and the Balkans. In September 1940, Mussolini ordered forces from Italy's North African colony of Libya into Egypt. When the British army repulsed these invaders, Hitler sent one of his most brilliant commanders, **General Erwin Rommel,** to North Africa. The "Desert Fox," as he was called, chalked up a string of successes in 1941 and 1942. He pushed the British back across the desert toward Cairo, Egypt.

In October 1940, Italian forces invaded Greece. They encountered stiff resistance, and in 1941 German troops once again provided reinforcements. Both Greece and Yugoslavia were added to the growing Axis empire. Even after the Axis triumph, however, Greek and Yugoslav

Thinking Critically
1. **Draw Conclusions** What lessons might the British have learned from their experience of the blitz?
2. **Make Inferences** Why do you think that the blitz failed to break the morale of the British people?

During air raids, some 60,000 Londoners sought shelter in the Underground, or subway, each night. Thousands of others slept in church crypts, basements, and other underground shelters.

guerrillas plagued the occupying forces. Meanwhile, both Bulgaria and Hungary had joined the Axis alliance. By 1941, the Axis powers or their allies controlled most of Europe.

✓ **Checkpoint** Which regions fell under Axis rule between 1939 and 1941?

Germany Invades the Soviet Union

After the failure in Britain, Hitler turned his military might to a new target—the Soviet Union. The decision to invade the Soviet Union helped relieve Britain. It also proved to be one of Hitler's costliest mistakes.

An Unstoppable German Army Stalls In June 1941, Hitler <u>nullified</u> the Nazi-Soviet Pact by invading the Soviet Union in Operation Barbarossa, a plan which took its name from the medieval Germanic leader, Frederick Barbarossa. Hitler made his motives clear. "If I had the Ural Mountains with their incalculable store of treasures in raw materials," he declared, "Siberia with its vast forests, and the Ukraine with its tremendous wheat fields, Germany under National Socialist leadership would swim in plenty." He also wanted to crush communism in Europe and defeat his powerful rival, Stalin.

Hitler unleashed a new blitzkrieg in the Soviet Union. About three million German soldiers invaded. The Germans caught Stalin unprepared.

Vocabulary Builder
<u>nullified</u>—(NUL uh fyd) *vt.* made invalid

The Holocaust

When Hitler's forces invaded the Soviet Union in 1941, Hilter began implementing what he called the "Final Solution"—the organized murder of all European Jews under his control. At first, Nazi troops began rounding up Jews, executing them and burying them in mass graves. Other Jews were sent to forced labor camps, where many were worked to death. But the Nazis were not satisfied with the pace of these ruthless murders. Beginning in 1942, they began to force Jews from Nazi-occupied Europe into specially designed death camps. By 1945, the Nazis had mercilessly killed some six million Jews—nearly two thirds of all European Jews.

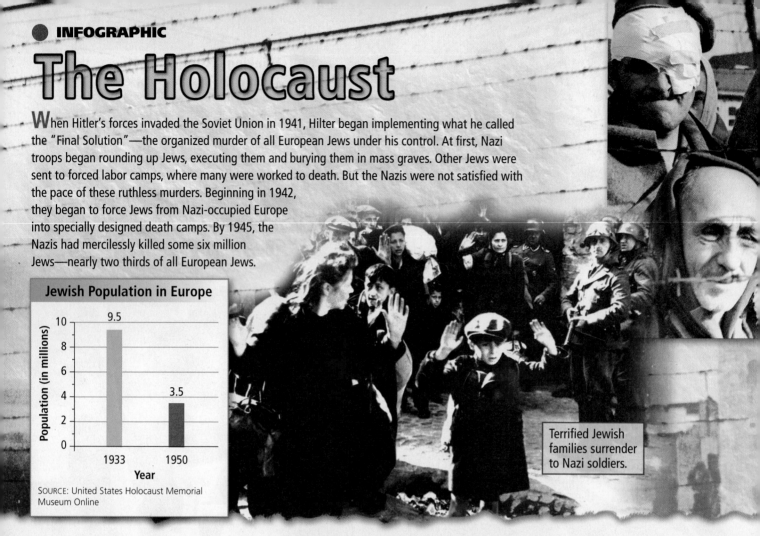

Jewish Population in Europe

Population (in millions)

1933: 9.5
1950: 3.5

Year

SOURCE: United States Holocaust Memorial Museum Online

Terrified Jewish families surrender to Nazi soldiers.

His army was still suffering from the purges that had wiped out many of its top officers.

The Soviets lost two and a half million soldiers trying to fend off the invaders. As they were forced back, Soviet troops destroyed factories and farm equipment and burned crops to keep them out of enemy hands. But they could not stop the German war machine. By autumn, the Nazis had smashed deep into the Soviet Union and were poised to take Moscow and Leningrad (present-day St. Petersburg).

There, however, the German advance stalled. Like Napoleon's Grand Army in 1812, Hitler's forces were not prepared for the fury of "General Winter." By early December, temperatures plunged to –40°F (–4°C). Thousands of German soldiers froze to death.

Germany's Siege of Leningrad The Soviets, meanwhile, suffered appalling hardships. In September 1941, the two-and-a-half-year siege of Leningrad began. Food was rationed to two pieces of bread a day. Desperate Leningraders ate almost anything. For example, they boiled wallpaper scraped off walls because its paste was said to contain potato flour.

Although more than a million Leningraders died during the siege, the city did not fall to the Germans. Hoping to gain some relief for his exhausted people, Stalin urged Britain to open a second front in Western Europe. Although Churchill could not offer much real help, the two powers did agree to work together.

✓ **Checkpoint** What caused Hitler's invasion of the Soviet Union to stall?

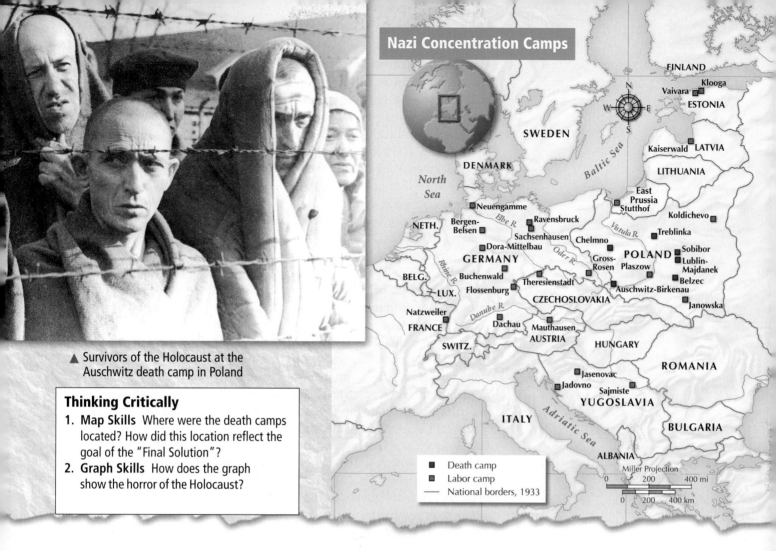

Nazi Concentration Camps

▲ Survivors of the Holocaust at the Auschwitz death camp in Poland

Thinking Critically

1. **Map Skills** Where were the death camps located? How did this location reflect the goal of the "Final Solution"?
2. **Graph Skills** How does the graph show the horror of the Holocaust?

Death camp
Labor camp
— National borders, 1933

Life Under Nazi and Japanese Occupation

While Nazi forces rampaged across Europe, the Japanese military conquered an empire in Asia and the Pacific. Each set out to build a "new order" in the occupied lands.

Hitler's "New Order" Hitler's new order grew out of his racial obsessions. As his forces conquered most of Europe, Hitler set up puppet governments in Western European countries that were peopled by Aryans, or light-skinned Europeans, whom Hitler and his followers believed to be a "master race." The Slavs of Eastern Europe were considered to be an inferior "race." They were shoved aside to provide more "living space" for Germans, the strongest of the Aryans.

To the Nazis, occupied lands were an economic resource to be plundered and looted. The Nazis systematically stripped conquered nations of their works of art, factories, and other resources. To counter resistance movements that emerged in occupied countries, the Nazis took savage revenge, shooting hostages and torturing prisoners.

But the Nazis' most sinister plans centered on the people of the occupied countries. During the 1930s, the Nazis had sent thousands of Jewish people and political opponents to **concentration camps,** detention centers for civilians considered enemies of the state. Over the course of the war, the Nazis forced these people, along with millions of Polish and Soviet Slavs and people from other parts of Europe, to work as slave laborers. Prisoners were poorly fed and often worked to death.

Note Taking

Reading Skill: Identify Supporting Details In a concept web like the one below, fill in details about how the Nazis and Japanese military treated people under their power during World War II. Add circles as necessary.

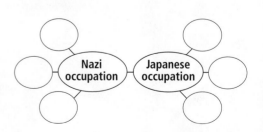

The Nazis Commit Genocide At the same time, Hitler pursued a vicious program to kill all people he judged "racially inferior," particularly Europe's Jews. The Nazis also targeted other groups who did not meet the Aryan racial ideal, including Slavs, Romas (Gypsies), homosexuals, and the disabled. Political and religious leaders who spoke out against Nazism also suffered abuse. Starting in 1939, the Nazis forced Jews in Poland and other countries to live in ghettos, or sections of cities where Jewish people were confined. Many died from starvation, disease, overwork, and the harsh elements. By 1941, however, German leaders had devised plans for the "Final Solution of the Jewish problem"—the genocide of all European Jews.

To accomplish this goal, Hitler had six special "death camps" built in Poland. The Nazis shipped "undesirables" from all over occupied Europe to the camps. There, Nazi engineers designed the most efficient means of killing millions of men, women, and children.

As the prisoners reached the camps, they were stripped of their clothes and valuables. Their heads were shaved. Guards separated men from women and children from their parents. The young, elderly, and sick were targeted for immediate killing. Within a few days, they were herded into "shower rooms" and gassed. The Nazis worked others to death or used them for perverse "medical" experiments. By 1945, the Nazis had massacred some six million Jews in what became known as the **Holocaust.** Nearly six million other people were killed as well.

Jewish people resisted the Nazis even though they knew their efforts could not succeed. In July 1942, the Nazis began sending Polish Jews from the Warsaw ghetto to the Treblinka death camp at a rate of about 5,000 per day. In the spring of 1943, knowing that their situation was hopeless, the Jews took over the ghetto and used a small collection of guns and homemade bombs to damage the Nazi forces as much as possible. On May 16, the Nazis regained control of the ghetto and eliminated the remaining Warsaw Jews. Still, their courage has inspired many over the years.

In some cases, friends, neighbors, or strangers protected Jews. Italian peasants hid Jews in their villages. Denmark and Bulgaria saved almost

The Japanese in China
Since 1937, the Japanese had been trying to expand into Asia by taking over China. Although the Japanese occupied much of Eastern China, the Chinese refused to surrender. The occupying Japanese treated the Chinese brutally. Below, Japanese soldiers load Chinese civilians onto trucks to take them to an execution ground during the sacking of Nanjing in 1937.

all their Jewish populations. Many people, however, pretended not to notice what was happening. Some even became collaborators and cooperated with the Nazis. In France, the Vichy government helped ship thousands of Jewish people to their deaths. Strict immigration policies in many Western countries as well as conscious efforts to block Jewish immigration prevented many Jews from gaining refuge elsewhere.

The scale and savagery of the Holocaust are unequaled in history. The Nazis deliberately set out to destroy the Jews for no reason other than their religious and ethnic heritage. Today, the record of that slaughter is a vivid reminder of the monstrous results of racism and intolerance.

Japan's Brutal Conquest Japanese forces took control across Asia and the Pacific. Their self-proclaimed mission was to help Asians escape Western colonial rule. In fact, the real goal was a Japanese empire in Asia. The Japanese invaders treated the Chinese, Filipinos, Malaysians, and other conquered people with great brutality, killing and torturing civilians throughout East and Southeast Asia. The occupiers seized food crops, destroyed cities and towns, and made local people into slave laborers. Whatever welcome the Japanese had first met as "liberators" was soon turned to hatred. In the Philippines, Indochina, and elsewhere, nationalist groups waged guerrilla warfare against the Japanese invaders.

✔ **Checkpoint** How did Hitler's views about race lead to the murder of six million Jewish people and millions of Slavs, Gypsies, and others?

Japan Attacks the United States

When the war began in 1939, the United States declared its neutrality. Still, although isolationist feeling remained strong, many Americans sympathized with those who battled the Axis powers. As one of those sympathizers, President Franklin Delano Roosevelt (FDR) looked for ways around the Neutrality Acts to provide warships and other aid to Britain as it stood alone against Hitler.

American Involvement Grows In March 1941, FDR persuaded Congress to pass the **Lend-Lease Act.** It allowed him to sell or lend war materials to "any country whose defense the President deems vital to the defense of the United States." The United States, said Roosevelt, would not be drawn into the war, but it would become "the arsenal of democracy," supplying arms to those who were fighting for freedom.

To show further support, Roosevelt met secretly with Churchill on a warship in the Atlantic in August 1941. The two leaders issued the Atlantic Charter, which set goals for the war—"the final destruction of the Nazi tyranny"—and for the postwar world. They pledged to support "the right of all peoples to choose the form of government under which they will live" and called for a "permanent system of general security."

Japan and the United States Face Off When war broke out in Europe in 1939, the Japanese saw a chance to grab European possessions in Southeast Asia. The rich resources of the region, including oil, rubber, and tin, would be of immense value in fighting its war against the Chinese.

In 1940, Japan advanced into French Indochina and the Dutch East Indies. In response, the United States banned the sale of war materials, such as iron, steel, and oil, to Japan. Japanese leaders saw this move as a threat to Japan's economy and its Asian sphere of influence.

Meeting at Sea
President Roosevelt and Prime Minister Churchill issued the Atlantic Charter in August 1941.

Damage at Pearl Harbor	
U.S. ships sunk or damaged	19
U.S. aircraft destroyed	188
Americans killed	2,348
Americans injured	1,109

SOURCE: *Columbia Encyclopedia, Sixth Edition*

December 7, 1941

On the sleepy Sunday morning of December 7, 1941, the military complex at Pearl Harbor was suddenly jolted awake by a surprise attack. Planes screamed down from the sky, dropping bombs and torpedoes. Americans were shocked and horrified by the attacks. *How did Pearl Harbor change the isolationist policies of the United States?*

Japan and the United States held talks to ease the growing tension. But extreme militarists, such as General Tojo Hideki, hoped to expand Japan's empire, and the United States was interfering with their plans.

Attack on Pearl Harbor With talks at a standstill, General Tojo ordered a surprise attack. Early on December 7, 1941, Japanese airplanes bombed the American fleet at Pearl Harbor in Hawaii. The attack took the lives of about 2,400 people and destroyed battleships and aircraft. The next day, a grim-faced President Roosevelt told the nation that December 7 was "a date which will live in infamy." He asked Congress to declare war on Japan. On December 11, Germany and Italy, as Japan's allies, declared war on the United States.

Japanese Victories In the long run, the Japanese attack on Pearl Harbor would be as serious a mistake as Hitler's invasion of the Soviet Union. But in the months after Pearl Harbor, possessions in the Pacific fell to the Japanese one by one. The Japanese captured the Philippines and other islands held by the United States. They overran the British colonies of Hong Kong, Burma, and Malaya, and advanced deeper into the Dutch East Indies and French Indochina. By 1942, the Japanese empire stretched from Southeast Asia to the western Pacific Ocean.

 Checkpoint Why did Japanese leaders view the United States as an enemy?

SECTION 2 **Assessment**

Progress Monitoring *Online*
For: Self-quiz with vocabulary practice
Web Code: naa-2921

Terms, People, and Places

1. For each term, person, or place listed at the beginning of the section, write a sentence explaining its significance.

Note Taking

2. **Reading Skill: Recognize Sequence** Use your completed flowchart and concept web to answer the Focus Question: Which regions were attacked and occupied by the Axis powers, and what was life like under their occupation?

Comprehension and Critical Thinking

3. **Summarize** Describe Hitler's blitzkrieg tactics.
4. **Recognize Effects** Referring to the Battle of Britain in 1940, Winston Churchill said "Never in the field of human conflict was so much owed by so many to so few." What did he mean?
5. **Recognize Ideologies** Hitler translated his hatred into a program of genocide. How do ethnic, racial, and religious hatreds weaken society?

● Writing About History

Quick Write: Gather Information Use the library and reliable Internet sources to find information about Pearl Harbor. Create a source card for each book or Web site you use. Then create note cards to record and organize at least three pieces of information.

American medal awarded
for supporting the war

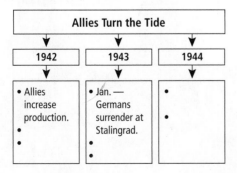

British poster
encouraging
women to work
in factories to
increase
production

SECTION 3

Support the War!

For the Allies to succeed against the relentless Axis war machine, everyone—on the home front as well as on the battlefield—had to work tirelessly. Ships needed to be built in a matter of days, not months. Airplanes, tanks, and ammunition had to be mass-produced. As factories converted to war production, the production of consumer goods such as automobiles ceased. All efforts were focused on the massive production of the materials of war.

Focus Question How did the Allies begin to push back the Axis powers?

The Allies Turn the Tide

 Performance Standards

- **SSWH18a** Describe the major conflicts and outcomes of WWII, El-Alamein, Stalingrad, and D-Day.
- **SSWH18c** Explain the negotiations at Teheran and Yalta.

Terms, People, and Places

Rosie the Riveter	Stalingrad
aircraft carrier	D-Day
Dwight Eisenhower	Yalta Conference

Note Taking

Recognize Sequence In a flowchart like the one below, sequence the events that turned the tide of the war towards the Allies.

Allies Turn the Tide		
↓	↓	↓
1942	1943	1944
↓	↓	↓
• Allies increase production.	• Jan. — Germans surrender at Stalingrad.	•
•	•	•
	•	

As 1942 began, the Allies were in trouble. German bombers flew unrelenting raids over Britain, and the German army advanced deep into the Soviet Union. In the Pacific, the Japanese onslaught seemed unstoppable. But helped by extraordinary efforts on the home front and a series of military victories, the tide was about to turn.

All-Out War

To defeat the Axis war machine, the Allies had to commit themselves to total war. Total war means nations devote all of their resources to the war effort.

Governments Increase Power To achieve maximum war production, democratic governments in the United States and Great Britain increased their political power. They directed economic resources into the war effort, ordering factories to stop making cars or refrigerators and to turn out airplanes or tanks instead. Governments implemented programs to ration or control the amount of food and other vital goods consumers could buy. They raised money by holding war bond drives, in which citizens lent their government certain sums of money that would be returned with interest later. Prices and wages were also regulated. While the war brought some shortages and hardships, the increase in production ended the unemployment of the depression era.

Under the pressures of war, even democratic governments limited the rights of citizens, censored the press, and used propaganda to win public support for the war. In the United States and Canada, many citizens of Japanese descent lost their jobs, property, and civil rights. Many Japanese Americans and Japanese Canadians were even interned in camps after their governments decided that they were a security risk. The British took similar action against German refugees. Some 40 years later, both the United States and Canada provided former internees with reparations, or payment for damages, but for many the compensation came too late.

Women Help Win the War As men joined the military, millions of women around the world replaced them in essential war industry jobs. Women, symbolized by the character **"Rosie the Riveter"** in the United States, built ships and planes and produced munitions.

British and American women served in the armed forces in many auxiliary roles—driving ambulances, delivering airplanes, and decoding messages. In occupied Europe, women fought in the resistance. Marie Fourcade, a French woman, helped downed Allied pilots escape to safety. Soviet women served in combat roles. Soviet pilot Lily Litvak, for example, shot down 12 German planes before she herself was killed.

✓ **Checkpoint** How did the Allies mobilize all of their resources for the war effort?

The Allies Forge Ahead

The years 1942–1943 marked the turning point of the war. The Allies won victories on four fronts—the Pacific, North Africa and Italy, the Soviet Union, and France—to push back the Axis tide.

Japanese Navy Battered In the Pacific, the Japanese suffered their first serious setback at the Battle of the Coral Sea. The battle lasted for five days in May 1942. For the first time in naval history, the enemy ships never even saw each other. Attacks were carried out by planes launched from **aircraft carriers,** or ships that transport aircraft and accommodate the take-off and landing of airplanes. The Japanese were prevented from seizing several important islands. More importantly, the Americans sank one Japanese aircraft carrier and several cruisers and destroyers.

This Allied victory was followed by an even more impressive win at the Battle of Midway in June 1942, which was also fought entirely from the air. The Americans destroyed four Japanese carriers and more than 250 planes. The battle was a devastating blow to the Japanese. After Midway, Japan was unable to launch any more offensive operations.

The Big Three Plot Their Strategy After the United States entered the war, the Allied leaders met periodically to hammer out their strategy.

Air War in the Pacific
Allied forces won decisive victories in the Coral Sea and at Midway Island. The Japanese pilots below may have taken part in these battles, which were fought from planes launched from aircraft carriers. *How do you think aircraft carriers changed naval warfare?*

Technology That Helped Win the War

Deadlier bombs, machines that broke secret codes, dive-bombers—all of these technologies gave those who used them a military advantage. Scientists and engineers on both sides of World War II created and improved technologies at a fast and furious pace in a desperate effort to win the war.

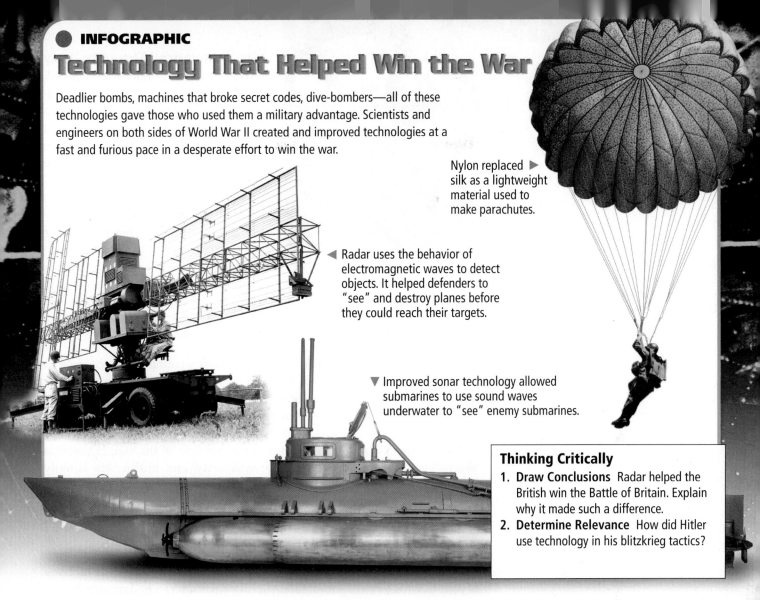

Nylon replaced ▶ silk as a lightweight material used to make parachutes.

◀ Radar uses the behavior of electromagnetic waves to detect objects. It helped defenders to "see" and destroy planes before they could reach their targets.

▼ Improved sonar technology allowed submarines to use sound waves underwater to "see" enemy submarines.

Thinking Critically

1. **Draw Conclusions** Radar helped the British win the Battle of Britain. Explain why it made such a difference.
2. **Determine Relevance** How did Hitler use technology in his blitzkrieg tactics?

In 1942, the "Big Three"—Roosevelt, Churchill, and Stalin—agreed to focus on finishing the war in Europe before trying to end the war in Asia.

From the outset, the Allies distrusted one another. Churchill and Roosevelt feared that Stalin wanted to dominate Europe. Stalin believed the West wanted to destroy communism. None of the new Allies wanted to risk a breakdown in their alliance, however. At a conference in Tehran, Iran, in late 1943, Churchill and Roosevelt yielded to Stalin by agreeing to let the borders outlined in the Nazi-Soviet Pact stand, against the wishes of Poland's government-in-exile. However, Stalin also wanted Roosevelt and Churchill to open a second front against Germany in Western Europe to relieve the pressure on the Soviet Union. Roosevelt and Churchill replied that they did not yet have the resources. Stalin saw the delay as a deliberate policy to weaken the Soviet Union.

Allied Victory in North Africa In North Africa, the British led by General Bernard Montgomery fought Rommel. After the fierce Battle of El Alamein in November 1942, the Allies finally halted the Desert Fox's advance. Allied tanks drove the Axis back across Libya into Tunisia.

Later in 1942, American General **Dwight Eisenhower** took command of a joint British and American force in Morocco and Algeria. Advancing on Tunisia from the west, the Allies trapped Rommel's army, which surrendered in May 1943.

The Pain of Defeat
German prisoners are marched through the snowy streets of Stalingrad after their defeat by the Soviet army.

Allies Advance Through Italy

With North Africa under their control, the Allies were able to cross the Mediterranean into Italy. In July 1943, a combined British and American army landed first in Sicily and then in southern Italy. They defeated the Italian forces there in about a month.

After the defeats, the Italians overthrew Mussolini and signed an armistice, but fighting did not end. Hitler sent German troops to rescue Mussolini and stiffen the will of Italians fighting in the north. For the next 18 months, the Allies pushed slowly up the Italian peninsula, suffering heavy losses against strong German resistance. Still, the Italian invasion was a decisive event for the Allies because it weakened Hitler by forcing him to fight on another front.

Germans Defeated at Stalingrad A major turning point occurred in the Soviet Union. After their lightning advance in 1941, the Germans were stalled outside Moscow and Leningrad. In 1942, Hitler launched a new offensive. This time, he aimed for the rich oil fields of the south. His troops, however, got only as far as **Stalingrad.**

The Battle of Stalingrad was one of the costliest of the war. Hitler was determined to capture Stalin's namesake city, and Stalin was equally determined to defend it. The battle began when the Germans surrounded the city. As winter closed in, a bitter street-by-street, house-by-house struggle raged. A German officer wrote that soldiers fought for two weeks for a single building. Corpses "are strewn in the cellars, on the landings and the staircases," he said. In November, the Soviets encircled their attackers. Trapped, without food or ammunition and with no hope of rescue, the German commander finally surrendered in January 1943.

After the Battle of Stalingrad, the Red Army took the offensive and drove the invaders out of the Soviet Union entirely. Hitler's forces suffered irreplaceable losses of both troops and equipment. By early 1944, Soviet troops were advancing into Eastern Europe.

✔ **Checkpoint** How did the Allies push back the Axis powers on four fronts?

The Allies Push Toward Germany

By 1944, the Western Allies were at last ready to open a second front in Europe by invading France. Allied leaders under Eisenhower faced the enormous task of planning the operation and assembling troops and supplies. To prepare the way for the invasion, Allied bombers flew constant missions over Germany. They targeted factories and destroyed aircraft that might be used against the invasion force. They also bombed railroads and bridges in France.

The D-Day Assault The Allies chose June 6, 1944—known as **D-Day**—for the invasion of France. Just before midnight on June 5, Allied planes dropped paratroopers behind enemy lines. Then, at dawn, thousands of ships ferried 156,000 Allied troops across the English Channel. The troops

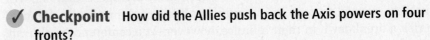

World War II in Europe and North Africa, 1942–1945

Geography *Interactive*
For: Interactive map and timeline
Web Code: nap-2931

Map Skills Axis power reached its height in Europe in 1942. Then the tide began to turn.

1. **Locate** (a) Vichy France (b) Soviet Union (c) El Alamein (d) Normandy (e) Berlin

2. **Place** Describe the extent of Axis control in 1942.

3. **Make Inferences** How did geography both help and hinder Allied advances?

Legend:
- Europe Axis powers, 1942
- Maximum Axis control, 1942
- Neutral nations, 1942
- Allied territory, 1942
- Allied advances
- Major battles

Timeline:
- **Jan 1943** Germans surrender at Stalingrad
- **Jul 1943** Allied forces land in Sicily
- **Jan 1945** Soviets enter Warsaw
- **May 7, 1945** Germany surrenders

1942 — **1943** — **1944** — **1945** — **1946**

- **Nov 1942** British defeat Germans at El Alamein
- **Sep 1943** Italians surrender to Allies
- **Jun 6, 1944** D-Day invasion at Normandy
- **Mar 1945** British and American forces cross Rhine

Churchill

Winston Churchill (1874–1965) was a staunch antisocialist and defender of the British Empire. As a member of Parliament, he loudly warned the British of the threat posed by Nazi Germany. After Neville Chamberlain's government failed to defend Norway from Hitler, Churchill replaced him as prime minister on May 10, 1940. Within seven weeks, France had surrendered, and Nazi forces threatened Britain. Churchill's courage and defiance steeled British resolve in the darkest days of the war when Britain stood alone against the Nazis. **How did Churchill inspire the British people?**

Roosevelt

In 1933, Franklin Delano Roosevelt (1882–1945) started his first term as president, promising to bring the United States out of the Great Depression. During his second term, FDR lent, and then gave, millions of dollars in war supplies to the struggling British. Japan's attack on Pearl Harbor quickly brought the United States into the war. From the start of American involvement, Roosevelt took the lead in establishing alliances among all countries fighting the Axis powers—including the Soviet Union. **How did Roosevelt influence World War II before Pearl Harbor?**

Stalin

Joseph Stalin (1879–1953) was born Joseph Dzhugashvili (joo gush VYEE lyee). He changed his name to Stalin, meaning "man of steel," after he joined the Bolshevik underground in the early 1900s. Stalin emerged as the sole ruler of the Soviet Union in the 1920s, and he maintained an iron grasp on the nation until his death in 1953. When Hitler's army invaded the Soviet Union and threatened Moscow in 1941, Stalin refused to leave the capital city. He eventually forced the Germans into retreat. **Why would Churchill and Roosevelt have distrusted Stalin?**

fought their way to shore amid underwater mines and raking machine-gun fire. As one soldier who landed in the first wave of D-Day assault recalled,

> **Primary Source**
>
> 66 It all seemed unreal, a sort of dreaming while awake, men were screaming and dying all around me. . . I honestly could have walked the full length of the beach without touching the ground, they were that thickly strewn about. 99
> —Melvin B. Farrell, *War Memories*

Still, the Allied troops clawed their way inland through the tangled hedges of Normandy. In early August, a massive armored division under American General George S. Patton helped the joint British and American forces break through German defenses and advance toward Paris. Meanwhile, other Allied forces sailed from Italy to land in southern France. In Paris, French resistance forces rose up against the occupying Germans. Under pressure from all sides, the Germans retreated. On August 25, the Allies entered Paris. Within a month, all of France was free.

Allies Continue to Advance By this time, Germany was reeling under <u>incessant</u>, round-the-clock bombing. For two years, Allied bombers had hammered military bases, factories, railroads, oil depots, and cities.

Vocabulary Builder
<u>incessant</u>—(in SES unt) *adj.* uninterrupted, ceaseless

The goal of this kind of bombing was to cripple Germany's industries and destroy the morale of its civilians. In one 10-day period, bombing almost erased the huge industrial city of Hamburg, killing 40,000 civilians and forcing one million to flee their homes. In February 1945, Allied raids on Dresden, not an industrial target, but considered one of the most beautiful cities in Europe, killed as many as 135,000 people.

After freeing France, Allied forces battled toward Germany. As their armies advanced into Belgium in December, Germany launched a massive counterattack. At the bloody Battle of the Bulge, which lasted more than a month, both sides took terrible losses. The Germans were unable to break through. The battle delayed the Allied advance from the west, but only for six weeks. Meanwhile, the Soviet army battled through Germany and advanced on Berlin from the east. Hitler's support within Germany was declining, and he had already survived one assassination attempt by senior officers in the German military. By early 1945, the defeat of Germany seemed <u>inevitable</u>.

Uneasy Agreement at Yalta In February 1945, Roosevelt, Churchill, and Stalin met again at Yalta, in the southern Soviet Union. Once again, the Big Three planned strategy in an atmosphere of distrust. Stalin insisted that the Soviet Union needed to maintain control of Eastern Europe to be able to protect itself from future aggression. Churchill and Roosevelt favored self-determination for Eastern Europe, which would give people the right to choose their own form of government. However, Churchill and Roosevelt needed Stalin's help to win the war.

At the **Yalta Conference,** the three leaders agreed that the Soviet Union would enter the war against Japan within three months of Germany's surrender. In return, Churchill and Roosevelt promised Stalin that the Soviets would take possession of southern Sakhalin Island, the Kuril Islands, and an occupation zone in Korea. They also agreed that Germany would be temporarily divided into four zones, to be governed by American, French, British, and Soviet forces. Stalin agreed to hold free elections in Eastern Europe. However, as you will read later, growing mistrust would later cause a split between the Allies.

✔ **Checkpoint** What agreements did Churchill, Roosevelt, and Stalin come to at Yalta?

Vocabulary Builder

<u>inevitable</u>—(in EV ih tuh bul) *adj.* unavoidable, inescapable

---

SECTION **3** Assessment

Progress Monitoring *Online*
For: Self-quiz with vocabulary practice
Web Code: naa-2931

Terms, People, and Places

1. For each term, person, or place listed at the beginning of the section, write a sentence explaining its significance.

Note Taking

2. **Reading Skill: Recognize Sequence** Use your completed timeline to answer the Focus Question: How did the Allies begin to push back the Axis powers?

Comprehension and Critical Thinking

3. **Analyze Information** How did democratic governments mobilize their economies for war?
4. **Determine Relevance** Explain why the battles of Midway, El Alamein, and Stalingrad were important turning points in the war.
5. **Predict Consequences** Why didn't the Yalta Conference lead to lasting unity among the Big Three leaders?

● **Writing About History**

Quick Write: Develop a Thesis A thesis statement summarizes the main idea of your research paper. The thesis statement should express an idea that can be defended or refuted. It should also be narrow enough to be addressed clearly in your writing.

Based on what you have read, write a thesis statement for an essay explaining the importance of the Battle of Stalingrad.

D-DAY

In the earliest hours of June 6, 1944, the Allies launched a surprise invasion of Normandy in France—the largest amphibious, or land and water, invasion in history. More than 156,000 Allied troops crossed the English Channel. Thousands of these troops landed on the beaches, fighting and clawing their way up the steep cliffs under heavy German fire. Paratroopers dropped from the sky. By the end of the day, about 2,500 men had given their lives. But by August, the Allies had made their way to Paris and freed it from German control.

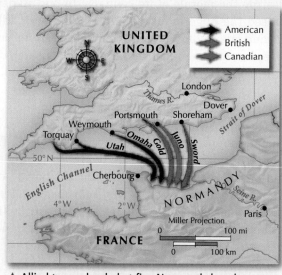

▲ Allied troops landed at five Normandy beaches, code-named Utah, Omaha, Gold, Juno, and Sword.

Overcoming Hitler's Defenses at Normandy

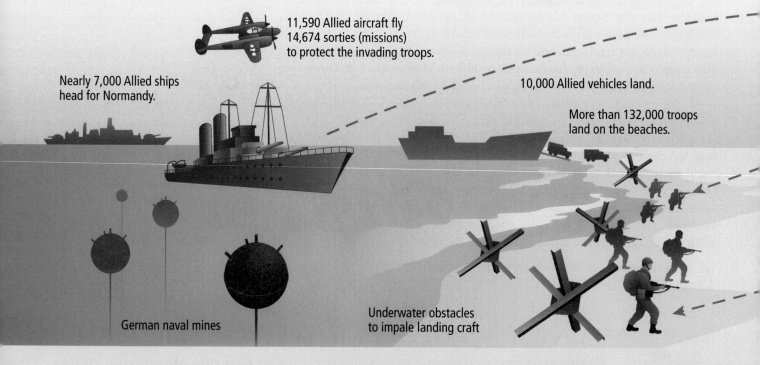

11,590 Allied aircraft fly 14,674 sorties (missions) to protect the invading troops.

Nearly 7,000 Allied ships head for Normandy.

10,000 Allied vehicles land.

More than 132,000 troops land on the beaches.

German naval mines

Underwater obstacles to impale landing craft

Allied troops faced daunting obstacles on D-Day. Naval mines threatened ships trying to land. Steel obstacles on the beaches could rip the bottoms out of landing craft at high tide. The Germans waited atop the steep cliffs.

▼ British special forces storm the beach.

Allied Troop Strengths and Casualties on D-Day		
Country	Troops	Estimated Casualties*
United States	73,000	6,603
Britain	61,715	2,700
Canada	21,400	946
Allied Total	**156,115**	**10,249**

*includes those killed, wounded, missing, and captured
SOURCE: The D-Day Museum Online

▲ Wounded Allied soldiers after the battle

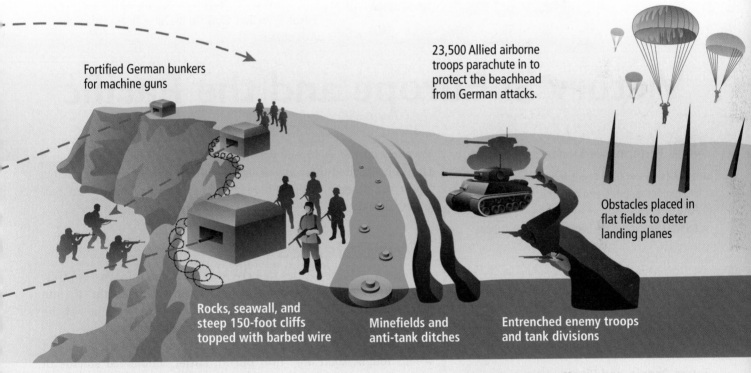

Fortified German bunkers for machine guns

23,500 Allied airborne troops parachute in to protect the beachhead from German attacks.

Obstacles placed in flat fields to deter landing planes

Rocks, seawall, and steep 150-foot cliffs topped with barbed wire

Minefields and anti-tank ditches

Entrenched enemy troops and tank divisions

▼ Omaha Beach at the end of D-Day

Thinking Critically

1. **Chart Skills** Which of the Allies suffered the greatest losses on D-Day?
2. **Draw Conclusions** Why do you think the D-Day landings were made on beaches instead of at established harbors?
3. **Diagram Skills** What do you think was the greatest obstacle the Allies had to overcome on D-Day? Explain.

History *Interactive*

For: interactive map, audio, and more
Visit: PHSchool.com
Web Code: nap-2932

1st Marine Division patch from Guadalcanal

Allied soldier in the Pacific

A Soldier Remembers

A defeated General Douglas MacArthur left the Philippines in 1942. As he departed, he pledged his determination to free the islands with the words "I shall return." In October 1944, that pledge became a reality when MacArthur landed on the Philippine island of Leyte. As one soldier recalled,

66 When I heard that he had returned, I finally had the feeling that I might have a chance of living through the war. . . . [O]nce they landed in Leyte, I knew it was only a question of hanging on for a few more months and I would be able to live through it.99
—Edwin Ramsey

Focus Question How did the Allies finally defeat the Axis powers?

Victory in Europe and the Pacific

 Performance Standards

- **SSWH18a** Describe Guadalcanal, the Philippines, and the end of war in Europe and Asia.
- **SSWH18c** Explain the negotiations of Potsdam.

By early spring 1945, the war in Europe was nearing its end, and the Allies turned their attention to winning the war in the Pacific. There remained a series of bloody battles ahead, as well as an agonizing decision for American President Harry Truman.

Nazis Defeated

By March 1945, the Allies had crossed the Rhine into western Germany. From the east, Soviet troops closed in on Berlin. In late April, American and Russian soldiers met and shook hands at the Elbe River. All over Europe, Axis armies began to surrender.

In Italy, guerrillas captured and executed Mussolini. As Soviet troops fought their way into Berlin, Hitler committed suicide in his underground bunker. On May 7, Germany surrendered. Officially, the war in Europe ended the next day, May 8, 1945, which was proclaimed **V-E Day** (Victory in Europe). After just 12 years, Hitler's "thousand-year Reich" was bomb-ravaged and in ruins.

The Allies were able to defeat the Axis powers in Europe for a number of reasons. Because of the location of Germany and its allies, they had to fight on several fronts simultaneously. Hitler, who took almost complete control over military decisions, made some poor ones. He underestimated the ability of the Soviet Union to fight his armies.

The enormous productive capacity of the United States was another factor. By 1944, the United States was producing twice as much as all of the Axis powers combined. Meanwhile, Allied bombing hindered German production. Oil became so scarce because of

Terms, People, and Places

V-E Day	kamikaze
Bataan Death March	Manhattan Project
Douglas MacArthur	Hiroshima
island-hopping	Nagasaki

Note Taking

Reading Skill: Recognize Sequence Use a timeline like the one below to sequence the events that led to the defeat of the Axis powers.

Oct.	Feb.	June	Oct.
1944	1945	1945	1945

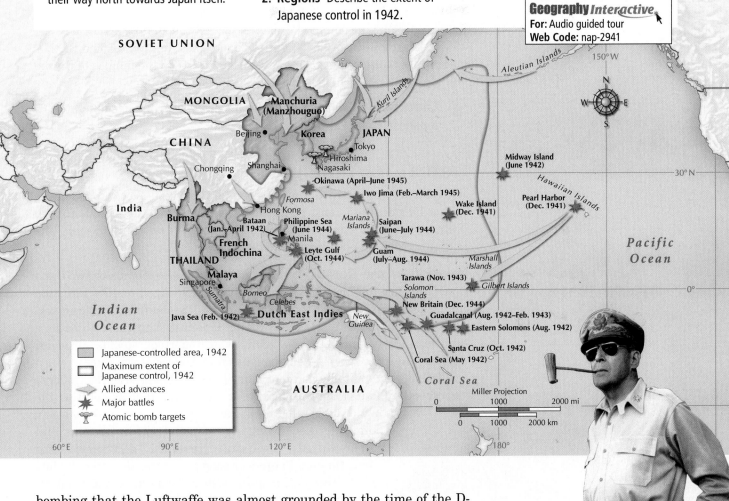

World War II in the Pacific, 1941–1945

Map Skills After the Battle of Midway, the Allies took the offensive in the Pacific. They gradually worked their way north towards Japan itself.

1. **Locate** (a) Japan (b) Pearl Harbor (c) Iwo Jima (d) Okinawa (e) Hiroshima (f) Manila

2. **Regions** Describe the extent of Japanese control in 1942.

3. **Draw Conclusions** How did geography make it difficult for Japan to maintain control of its empire?

Geography *Interactive*
For: Audio guided tour
Web Code: nap-2941

General Douglas MacArthur

bombing that the Luftwaffe was almost grounded by the time of the D-Day invasion. With victory in Europe achieved, the Allies now had to triumph over Japan in the Pacific.

✔ **Checkpoint** How did the Allied forces finally defeat the Germans?

Struggle for the Pacific

Until mid-1942, the Japanese had won an uninterrupted series of victories. They controlled much of Southeast Asia and many Pacific islands. By May 1942, the Japanese had gained control of the Philippines, killing several hundred American soldiers and as many as 10,000 Filipino soldiers during the 65-mile **Bataan Death March.** One survivor described the ordeal as "a macabre litany of heat, dust, starvation, thirst, flies, filth, stench, murder, torture, corpses, and wholesale brutality that numbs the memory." Many Filipino civilians risked—and sometimes lost—their lives to give food and water to captives on the march.

After the battles of Midway and the Coral Sea, however, the United States took the offensive. That summer, United States Marines landed at Guadalcanal in the Solomon Islands. Victory at Guadalcanal marked the beginning of an "island-hopping" campaign. The goal of the campaign was to recapture some Japanese-held islands while bypassing others. The captured islands served as steppingstones to the next objective. In this way, American forces, led by General **Douglas MacArthur,** gradually moved north towards Japan. By 1944, the United States Navy, commanded by Admiral Chester Nimitz, was blockading Japan, and American bombers pounded Japanese cities and industries. In October 1944, MacArthur began the fight to retake the Philippines. The British, meanwhile, were pushing Japanese forces back into the jungles of Burma and Malaya.

✅ **Checkpoint**   What strategy did General MacArthur use to fight the Japanese in the Pacific?

Defeat for Japan

With war won in Europe, the Allies poured their resources into defeating Japan. By mid-1945, most of the Japanese navy and air force had been destroyed. Yet the Japanese still had an army of two million men. The road to victory, it appeared, would be long and costly.

Invasion or the Bomb? In bloody battles on the islands of Iwo Jima from February to March 1945 and Okinawa from April to July 1945, the Japanese had shown that they would fight to the death rather than surrender. Beginning in 1944, some young Japanese men chose to become **kamikaze** (kah muh KAH zee) pilots who undertook suicide missions, crashing their explosive-laden airplanes into American warships.

While Allied military leaders planned for invasion, scientists offered another way to end the war. Scientists understood that by splitting the atom, they could create an explosion far more powerful than any yet known. Allied scientists, some of them German and Italian refugees, conducted research, code-named the **Manhattan Project,** racing to harness the atom. In July 1945, they successfully tested the first atomic bomb at Alamogordo, New Mexico.

News of this test was brought to the new American president, Harry Truman. Truman had taken office after Franklin Roosevelt died unexpectedly on April 12. He realized that the atomic bomb was a terrible new force for destruction. Still, after consulting with his advisors, and

Nuclear Blast
The world's first nuclear explosion instantly vaporized the tower from which it was launched. Seconds later an enormous blast sent searing heat across the desert and knocked observers to the ground. Shown here is an atomic bomb's characteristic mushroom cloud. *Why might the scientists who created the bomb have counseled leaders not to use it?*

determining that it would save American lives, he decided to use the new weapon against Japan.

At the time, Truman was meeting with other Allied leaders in the city of Potsdam, Germany. They issued a warning to Japan to surrender or face "complete destruction" and "utter devastation." When the Japanese ignored the warning, the United States took action.

Utter Devastation On August 6, 1945, an American plane dropped an atomic bomb over the city of **Hiroshima.** The bomb flattened four square miles and instantly killed more than 70,000 people. In the months that followed, many more would die from radiation sickness, a deadly after-effect of exposure to radioactive materials.

On August 8, the Soviet Union declared war on Japan and invaded Manchuria. Again, Japanese leaders did not respond. The next day, the United States dropped a second atomic bomb, this time on the city of **Nagasaki.** More than 40,000 people were killed in this second explosion.

Finally, on August 10, Emperor Hirohito intervened, an action unheard of for a Japanese emperor, and forced the government to surrender. On September 2, 1945, the formal peace treaty was signed on board the American battleship *Missouri,* anchored in Tokyo Bay.

✓ **Checkpoint** What strategies did the Allies use to end the war with Japan?

Hiroshima in Ruins
The atomic bomb reduced the center of Hiroshima to smoldering ruins (top left), but the full effect of the bomb would take years to materialize. A woman (above) pays respects to the victims of the atomic bomb at the Memorial Cenotaph in Peace Memorial Park in Hiroshima. A cenotaph is a monument that honors people who are buried elsewhere.

The Potsdam Conference was a meeting where the Allied leaders continued to plan for after the war. They debated which type of government would be best for Eastern Europe; established four occupied zones for a post-war Germany, and called for Japan's unconditional surrender.

Progress Monitoring *Online*
For: Self-quiz with vocabulary practice
Web Code: naa-2941

Terms, People, and Places

1. For each term, person, or place listed at the beginning of the section, write a sentence explaining its significance.

Note Taking

2. **Reading Skill: Recognize Sequence** Use your completed flowchart to answer the Focus Question: How did the Allies finally defeat the Axis powers?

Comprehension and Critical Thinking

3. **Determine Relevance** How did the location of the Axis powers in Europe contribute to their defeat?

4. **Draw Inferences** What factors besides ending the war in the Pacific might have contributed to President Harry Truman's decision to drop the atomic bomb?

● **Writing About History**

Quick Write: Make an Outline Once you have a thesis and have gathered research on your topics, you must choose an organization. Some choices are compare and contrast, order of importance, chronological, and cause and effect. Using one of these organizations, create an outline for the following thesis statement: The atomic bomb was a decisive weapon in World War II.

▲ Newspaper headline on the day Japan surrendered

▶ A sailor embraces a nurse when the end of the war is announced.

WITNESS HISTORY ◀))) AUDIO

The War Is Over!

American President Harry Truman made these remarks on the day the Japanese surrendered:

66 Our first thoughts, of course—thoughts of gratefulness and deep obligation—go out to those of our loved ones who have been killed or maimed in this terrible war. On land and sea and in the air, American men and women have given their lives so that this day of ultimate victory might come and assure the survival of a civilized world . . . 99

Focus Question What issues arose in the aftermath of World War II and how did new tensions develop?

The End of World War II

Performance Standards

• **SSWH18d** Explain allied Post-World War II policies, the formation of the United Nations, and the Marshall Plan.

Terms, People, and Places

Nuremberg	Marshall Plan
United Nations (UN)	North Atlantic Treaty
Cold War	Organization (NATO)
Truman Doctrine	Warsaw Pact

Note Taking

Reading Skill: Recognize Sequence Sequence the events following World War II by creating an outline of this section. Use the outline below as a starting point.

> I. The War's Aftermath
>   A. Devastation
>   1. As many as 50 million dead
>   2.

Even as the Allies celebrated victory, the appalling costs of the war began to emerge. The war had killed as many as 50 million people around the world. In Europe alone, over 30 million people had lost their lives, more than half of them civilians. The Soviet Union suffered the worst casualties, with over 20 million dead. As they had after World War I, the Allies faced difficult decisions about the future.

The War's Aftermath

"Give me ten years and you will not be able to recognize Germany," said Hitler in 1933. Indeed, Germany in 1945 was an unrecognizable ruin. Parts of Poland, the Soviet Union, Japan, China, and other countries also lay in ruins. Total war had gutted cities, factories, harbors, bridges, railroads, farms, and homes. Over twenty million refugees wandered Europe. Amid the devastation, hunger, disease, and mental illness took their toll for years after the fighting ended. As they had after World War I, the Allies faced difficult decisions about the future.

Horrors of the Holocaust Numbers alone did not tell the story of the Nazi nightmare in Europe or the Japanese brutality in Asia. During the war, the Allies were aware of the existence of Nazi concentration camps and death camps. But only at war's end did they learn the full extent of the inhumanity of the Holocaust. American General Dwight Eisenhower, who visited the camps, was stunned to come "face to face with indisputable evidence of Nazi brutality and ruthless disregard of every sense of decency."

War Crimes Trials At wartime meetings, the Allies had agreed that Axis leaders should be tried for "crimes against humanity." In Germany, the Allies held war crimes trials in **Nuremberg,** where Hitler had staged mass rallies in the 1930s. Nearly 200 Germans and Austrians were tried, and most were found guilty. A handful of top Nazis received death sentences. Others were imprisoned. Similar war crimes trials were held in Japan. Many of those accused of war crimes were never captured or brought to trial. However, the trials showed that political and military leaders could be held accountable for actions in wartime.

Occupying Allies The war crimes trials further discredited the totalitarian ideologies that had led to the war. Yet disturbing questions remained. Why had ordinary people in Germany, Poland, France, and elsewhere accepted—and even collaborated in—Hitler's "Final Solution"?

The United States felt that strengthening democracy would ensure tolerance and peace. The Western Allies built new governments in occupied Germany and Japan with democratic constitutions to protect the rights of all citizens. In Japan, the occupying forces under General MacArthur helped Japanese politicians to create a new constitution that gave power to the Japanese people, rather than the emperor.

✔ **Checkpoint** Why did the Allies hold war crimes trials for Axis leaders?

Establishing the United Nations

In April 1945, delegates from 50 nations <u>convened</u> in San Francisco to draft a charter for the **United Nations (UN).** The UN would play a greater role in world affairs than did its predecessor, the League of Nations.

Under the UN Charter, each of the member nations has one vote in the General Assembly. A much smaller body called the Security Council has greater power. Each of its five permanent members—the United States, the Soviet Union (today Russia), Britain, France, and China—has the right to veto any council decision. The goal was to give these great powers the authority to ensure the peace. The Security Council has the power to apply economic sanctions or send a peace-keeping military force to try to resolve disputes. Differences among the nations on the Security Council, most notably the United States and the Soviet Union, have often kept the UN from taking action. Since the fall of the Soviet Union in 1991, more peacekeeping delegations have been approved.

The UN's work would go far beyond peacekeeping. The organization would take on many world problems—from preventing the outbreak of disease and improving education to protecting refugees and helping nations to develop economically. UN agencies like the World Health Organization and the Food and Agricultural Organization have provided aid for millions of people around the world.

✔ **Checkpoint** Compare and contrast the United Nations and the League of Nations.

Casualties of World War II

	Military Dead*	Military Wounded*	Civilian Dead*
Allies			
Britain	264,000	277,000	93,000
France	213,000	400,000	350,000
China	1,310,000	1,753,000	1,000,000
Soviet Union	7,500,000	14,012,000	15,000,000
United States	292,000	672,000	6,000
Axis Powers			
Germany	3,500,000	5,000,000	780,000
Italy	242,000	66,000	153,000
Japan	1,300,000	4,000,000	672,000

World War II resulted in enormous casualties and disruption. Afterwards, millions of displaced Europeans, like the Germans above, searched for relatives they had been separated from during the war. **Chart Skills** *Which nation suffered the greatest number of both civilian and military casualties?*

* All figures are estimates.
SOURCE: *Encyclopædia Britannica; The Harper Encyclopedia of Military History,* R. Ernest Dupuy and Trevor N. Dupuy

Vocabulary Builder
<u>convened</u>—(kun VEEND) *vi.* met; assembled

The Alliance Breaks Apart

Amid the rubble of war, a new power structure emerged. In Europe, Germany was defeated. France and Britain were exhausted. Two other powers, the United States and the Soviet Union, emerged as the new world leaders. The United States abandoned its traditional policy of isolationism to counter what President Truman saw as the communist threat.

Differences Grow Between the Allies During the war, the Soviet Union and the nations of the West had cooperated to defeat Nazi Germany. After the war's end, the Allies set up councils made up of foreign ministers from Britain, France, China, the United States, and the Soviet Union to iron out the peace agreements discussed at various conferences during the war. The councils concluded peace agreements with several Axis nations in 1947. However, reparations in Germany and the nature of the governments of Eastern Europe caused divisions to deepen between the former Allies. Conflicting ideologies and mutual distrust soon led to the conflict known as the Cold War. The **Cold War** was a state of tension and hostility between nations aligned with the United States on one side and the Soviet Union on the other, without armed conflict between the major rivals.

The Cold War Begins Stalin had two goals in Eastern Europe. First, he wanted to spread communism in the area. Second, he wanted to create a buffer zone of friendly governments as a defense against Germany, which had invaded Russia during World War I and again in 1941.

As the Red Army had pushed German forces out of Eastern Europe, it had left behind occupying forces. At wartime conferences, Stalin tried to persuade the West to accept Soviet influence in Eastern Europe. The Soviet dictator pointed out that the United States was not consulting the Soviet Union about peace terms for Italy or Japan, both of which were defeated and occupied by American and British troops. In the same way, the Soviet Union would determine the fate of the Eastern European lands that it occupied.

Roosevelt and Churchill rejected Stalin's view, making him promise "free elections" in Eastern Europe. Stalin ignored that pledge. Most Eastern European countries had existing Communist parties, many of which had actively resisted the Nazis during the war. Backed by the Red Army, these local Communists in Poland, Czechoslovakia, and elsewhere destroyed rival political parties and even assassinated democratic leaders. By 1948, pro-Soviet communist governments were in place throughout Eastern Europe.

A Widening Gulf
Although Stalin and Truman were friendly at the Potsdam Conference (above), this Soviet propaganda poster from 1949 shows that relations between the two nations were becoming strained. The poster urges support "For a stable peace! Against those who would ignite a new war." The small caricatures of Churchill and Uncle Sam in the lower corner indicate who "those" people are.

✓ **Checkpoint** What post-war issues caused the Western Allies and the Soviet Union to disagree?

New Conflicts Develop

Stalin soon showed his aggressive intentions outside of Eastern Europe. In Greece, Stalin backed communist rebels who were fighting to overturn a right-wing monarchy supported by Britain. By 1947, however, Britain could no longer afford to defend Greece. Stalin was also menacing Turkey in the Dardanelles.

The Truman Doctrine Truman took action. On March 12, 1947, Truman outlined a new policy to Congress: "I believe that it must be the policy of the United States to support free peoples who are resisting attempted subjugation by armed minorities or by outside pressures." This policy, known as the **Truman Doctrine,** was rooted in the idea of containment, limiting communism to the areas already under Soviet control.

The Truman Doctrine would guide the United States for decades. It made clear that Americans would resist Soviet expansion in Europe or elsewhere in the world. Truman soon sent military and economic aid and advisors to Greece and Turkey so that they could withstand the communist threat.

The Marshall Plan Postwar hunger and poverty made Western European lands fertile ground for communist ideas. To strengthen democratic governments, the United States offered a massive aid package, called the **Marshall Plan.** Under it, the United States funneled food and economic assistance to Europe to help countries rebuild. Billions of dollars in American aid helped war-shattered Europe recover rapidly.

President Truman also offered aid to the Soviet Union and its satellites, or dependent states, in Eastern Europe. However, Stalin declined and forbade Eastern European countries to accept American aid. Instead, he promised help from the Soviet Union in its place.

Germany Stays Divided Defeated Germany became another focus of the Cold War. The Soviet Union took reparations for its massive war losses by dismantling and moving factories and other resources in its occupation zone to help rebuild the Soviet Union. France, Britain, and the United States also took some reparations out of their portions of Germany. However, Western leaders wanted the German economy to recover in order to restore political stability to the region. The Western Allies decided to unite their zones of occupation. Then, they extended the Marshall Plan to western Germany. The Soviets were furious at Western moves to rebuild the German economy and deny them further reparations. They strengthened their hold on eastern Germany.

The Berlin Airlift
After World War II, Germany, and Berlin within it, was divided into communist and noncommunist zones. In the photo below, children in West Berlin greet a plane delivering supplies during the Berlin Airlift.

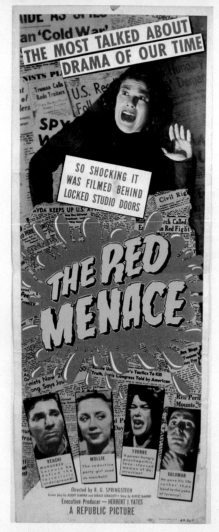

The Red Menace
Films like *The Red Menace* (1949) dramatized the threat of communism in the United States and formed a vital part of the propaganda war.

Vocabulary Builder

invoked—(in VOKED) *vt.* resorted to; called upon

Germany thus became a divided nation. In West Germany, the democratic nations allowed the people to write their own constitution and regain self-government. In East Germany, the Soviet Union installed a socialist dictatorship under Stalin's control.

The Berlin Airlift Stalin's resentment at Western moves to rebuild Germany triggered a crisis over Berlin. Even though it lay deep within the Soviet zone, the former German capital was occupied by all four victorious Allies. In June 1948, Stalin tried to force the Western Allies out of Berlin by sealing off every railroad and highway into the Western sectors of the city. The Western powers responded to the blockade by mounting a round-the-clock airlift. For more than a year, cargo planes supplied West Berliners with food and fuel. Their success forced the Soviets to end the blockade. Although the West had won, the crisis deepened.

Opposing Alliances Tensions continued to grow. In 1949, the United States, Canada, and ten other countries formed a new military alliance called the **North Atlantic Treaty Organization (NATO).** Members pledged to help one another if any one of them were attacked.

In 1955, the Soviet Union responded by forming its own military alliance, the **Warsaw Pact.** It included the Soviet Union and seven satellites in Eastern Europe. Unlike NATO, however, the Warsaw Pact was often <u>invoked</u> by the Soviets to keep its satellites in order. The Warsaw Pact cemented the division of Europe into "eastern" and "western" blocs. In the East were the Soviet-dominated countries of Eastern Europe. These countries were communist in name but dictatorships in practice, like the Soviet Union itself. In the West were the Western democracies, led by the United States.

The Propaganda War Both sides participated in a propaganda war. The United States spoke of defending capitalism and democracy against communism and totalitarianism. The Soviet Union claimed the moral high ground in the struggle against Western imperialism. Yet linked to those stands, both sides sought world power.

 Checkpoint What foreign policy pattern did the United States establish with the Truman Doctrine?

SECTION 5 Assessment

Progress Monitoring *Online*
For: Self-quiz with vocabulary practice
Web Code: naa-2951

Terms, People, and Places

1. What do many of the key terms listed at the beginning of the section have in common? Explain.

Note Taking

2. **Reading Skill: Recognize Sequence** Use your completed outline to answer the Focus Question: What issues arose in the aftermath of World War II and how did new tensions develop?

Comprehension and Critical Thinking

3. **Compare and Contrast** How did the peace made after World War II differ from that made after World War I?

4. **Identify Central Issues** What was the main purpose of the UN when it was founded?

5. **Recognize Causes** List two causes of the Cold War.

6. **Draw Conclusions** Why is it important to remember the inhumanity of the Holocaust?

● **Writing About History**

Quick Write: Credit Sources When you use quotes or ideas from your sources in your paper, you must give proper credit. One way to do this is to list the author and page number of the material you have used in parentheses following the statement. Then, include a bibliography at the end of your paper. Research a topic from this section and write a paragraph using two sources. Credit the sources where appropriate and list them at the end.

GENOCIDE

Why do people sometimes commit the crime of genocide?

In This Chapter SSWH18b

Hitler's Final Solution involved rounding up all the Jews in German-held territory (right). Millions were then brutally killed in death camps. British Prime Minister Winston Churchill called this well-organized plan of mass murder "a crime that has no name." After the war, the United Nations gave the crime a name: genocide. Genocide is any act committed with the intention of destroying an entire national, ethnic, racial or religious group.

Throughout History

1500s European guns and disease kill millions of Native Americans in the Americas.

1915–1916 Muslim Turks slaughter members of the Armenian Christian minority in the Ottoman Empire.

1938 Nazis urge mobs to attack and rob German Jews during Kristallnacht.

1994 Ethnic conflict in Rwanda leads to the murder of 800,000 Tutsis and moderate Hutus.

2004 Arab militias in Sudan unleash violence against non-Arab Muslim villagers in Darfur.

Continuing Today

In recent times, countries on the Balkan peninsula and in Africa have witnessed widespread violence against ethnic or religious minorities. The struggle in Darfur has driven thousands of refugees into refugee camps (below), where they depend on international relief agencies for food and medical help.

21st Century Skills

TRANSFER Activities

1. **Analyze** Throughout history, what motives have led people to commit genocide?

2. **Infer** Under what conditions is genocide more likely to occur?

3. **Transfer** Complete a Web quest in which you document the motives for genocide; record your thoughts in the Concept Connector Journal; and learn to make a video. Web Code nah-2908

CHAPTER 29

Quick Study Guide

GA SSWH16c, SSWH17c, SSWH17e

Progress Monitoring Online
For: Self-test with vocabulary practice
Web Code: naa-2961

Key Causes of World War II

- Failure of World War I peace settlement, Treaty of Versailles
- Global economic depression
- Fascism, militarism, and imperialism in Germany, Italy, and Japan
- Weakness of the League of Nations
- British and French appeasement

The Allies vs. the Axis

As the map below shows, most of the world was divided into areas controlled by the Allies or the Axis powers during the war.

Allies or under Allied control, July 1943
Axis or under Axis control, July 1943
Neutral, July 1943

Key Political Leaders

Allies
Franklin Delano Roosevelt, *U.S. president*
Harry S Truman, *U.S. president*
Neville Chamberlain, *British prime minister*
Winston Churchill, *British prime minister*
Joseph Stalin, *Soviet dictator*
Charles de Gaulle, *leader of Free French*

Axis Powers
Adolf Hitler, *German dictator*
Benito Mussolini, *Italian dictator*
Hirohito, *Japanese emperor*
Tojo Hideki, *Japanese prime minister*

Reasons for Allied Victory

Location of Germany—surrounded by enemies
Location of Japan—dependent on imported goods
Poor military decisions by Axis leaders
Huge productive capability of the United States
Better technology developed and used by Allies

Key Events of World War II

Sept. 1939
Germany invades Poland. France and Britain declare war on Germany.

June–July 1940
France falls to Germany. Germany begins Battle of Britain.

June 1941
Germany invades the Soviet Union.

Europe and Africa
The Pacific

1939   **1940**   **1941**

Sept. 1940
Japan signs Tripartite Pact with Germany and Italy.

Dec. 1941
Japan attacks Pearl Harbor.

Concept Connector

Essential Question Review

To connect prior knowledge with what you have learned in this chapter, answer the questions below in your Concept Connector journal. Use the journal in the Reading and Note Taking Study Guide to record your answers (or go to www.phschool.com **Web Code:** nad-2907). In addition, record information about the following concepts:

• Cooperation: United Nations
• Conflict: World War II
• Technology: Nuclear Power

1. **Democracy** During World War II, the United States government interned Japanese Americans in camps, citing security concerns. This was a curtailment of American citizens' individual rights. Do you think such actions are ever justified by a democratic government? Why or why not?

2. **Genocide** In *Mein Kampf,* Hitler said that Germans were a "master race" whose greatest enemies were the Jews. In 1935, the Nazis passed the Nuremberg Laws, which deprived Jews of German citizenship. The Nazis massacred six million Jews in the Holocaust. Read the Witness History at the beginning of Chapter 28. Then suggest reasons why ordinary Germans and other Europeans accepted, or even collaborated in, Hitler's "Final Solution." Focus on the following:
   • conditions in Depression-era Europe
   • anti-Semitism
   • propaganda
   • Nazi occupation

■ Connections to Today

1. **Conflict: The Arab-Israeli Conflict** Partly in response to the horrors of the Holocaust, the United Nations created a plan to divide Palestine into two states—one Arab and one Jewish. Jews accepted the plan, but Arabs rejected it. When the Jewish state of Israel was born in 1948, the surrounding Arab countries invaded Israel. Between 1956 and 1973, three more wars erupted between Israel and Arab states. Conflict between Arabs and Israelis continued into the 2000s despite many attempts at peace. What historical reasons did the United Nations have for creating a Jewish state in Palestine?

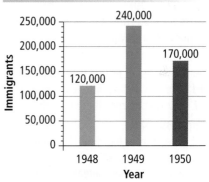

Jewish Migration to Israel

SOURCE: United States Holocaust Memorial Museum Online

2. **Cooperation: The United Nations Is Established** Fifty nations met in April 1945 to draft a charter for the United Nations. Today, the UN's work goes far beyond peacekeeping to include economic development, disease prevention, and refugee protection. Conduct research and write two paragraphs about a program sponsored by the UN in the last five years.

History *Interactive*
For: Interactive timeline
Web Code: nap-2962

Nov. 1942	Jan. 1943	June 1944	May 1945
The Allies push Rommel back in North Africa.	Germans surrender at Stalingrad.	D-Day invasion of Normandy	Germany surrenders.

1942   **1943**   **1944**   **1945**

June 1942	Feb. 1943	Oct. 1944	Aug–Sept. 1945
Japan defeated at Battle of Midway.	Japan defeated at Guadalcanal.	Japan defeated at Battle of Leyte Gulf.	U.S. drops atomic bombs on Hiroshima and Nagasaki, Japan. Japan surrenders.

Chapter Assessment

Terms, People, and Places

1. Define **appeasement** and **Anschluss**. How was Hitler's Anschluss an example of British and French appeasement?
2. Define **blitzkrieg**. What were the advantages of this war tactic?
3. Where did the **D-Day** invasion take place? What was its significance?
4. What happened at the **Yalta Conference**? How did it foreshadow later events?
5. What technological advantage did the **Manhattan Project** give the Allies? How was it used?
6. Describe how the **Marshall Plan** was part of the **Truman Doctrine**.

Main Ideas

Section 1 (pp. 924–929)

7. Summarize the steps that Axis powers took to achieve world power prior to World War II.

Section 2 (pp. 930–938)

8. How did the people of Britain fend off a German invasion?
9. How did Germany and Japan rule the people they conquered? How did this contribute to their hold on power?

Section 3 (pp. 939–947)

10. How did government control of economic production help defeat Germany and Japan?
11. Summarize how the Allies defeated Germany.

Section 4 (pp. 948–951)

12. What strategy did the Allies use to defeat Japan?

Section 5 (pp. 952–957)

13. What conflicts emerged between the former Allies after the end of World War II?

Chapter Focus Question

14. How did aggressive world powers emerge, and what did it take to defeat them during World War II?

Critical Thinking

15. **Recognize Cause and Effect** How did the World War I peace settlement help cause World War II?
16. **Analyze Information** What lessons does the Holocaust have for people today?

17. **Analyzing Cartoons** How does this cartoon reflect the cause of Hitler's defeat?
18. **Predict Consequences** The Atlantic Charter called for the establishment of a "permanent system of general security." What form did this "system" take when it was established following the war?
19. **Synthesize Information** Was participation by the United States crucial to winning the war? Explain.
20. **Draw Conclusions** Which battle was most important in the war in Europe? In the war in the Pacific? Explain.

● Writing About History

In this chapter's five Section Assessments, you developed skills to write a research report.

Writing a Research Report The history of World War II includes many stories of great courage and personal sacrifice. Write a research report on one of the following topics in which you describe the actions of the person or group: the Kindertransport, Oskar Schindler, Miep Gies, Raoul Wallenberg, Dietrich Bonhoeffer. Consult pages SH13–SH15 of the Writing Handbook for additional help.

Prewriting

• Do some preliminary research on each of the topics listed above.

• Choose the topic that interests you most and take notes about the people involved and the personal risks they took.
• Create a set of questions about the topic and gather additional resources.

Drafting

• Develop a working thesis and choose information to support the thesis.
• Make an outline organizing the report.
• Write an introduction in which you explain why the topic is interesting, a body, and a conclusion.

Revising

• Use the guidelines for revising your report on page SH15 of the Writing Handbook.

Prepare for the GHSGT

The Decision to Use the Atomic Bomb

Perhaps no decision in American history has been more hotly debated than Harry S. Truman's decision to drop atomic bombs on Hiroshima and Nagasaki, Japan, in August 1945. Documents A and B are two historians' views on Truman's decision.

Document A

"It was believed with deep apprehension that many thousands, probably tens of thousands, of lives of Allied combatants would have been spent in the continuation of our air and sea bombardment and blockade. . . . But the people who would have suffered most, had the war gone on much longer and their country invaded, were the Japanese. One American incendiary air raid on the Tokyo area in March 1945 did more damage and killed and injured more Japanese than the bomb on Hiroshima."

—From ***The Atomic Bomb and the End of World War II*** by Herbert Feis

Document B

"Even without the use of the atomic bombs, the war would probably have ended before an American invasion of Kyushu [one of the four main islands of Japan] became necessary. Conditions in Japan were steadily deteriorating . . . The destruction of cities from B-29 raids, diminishing food supplies, [and] decreased public morale fostered enough discontent to worry the emperor and his advisors. . . . Even without the atomic attacks, it seems likely that the emperor at some point would have acted in the same way that he did in the aftermath of Hiroshima to end the war."

—From ***Prompt and Utter Destruction: Truman and the Use of Atomic Bombs Against Japan*** by J. Samuel Walker

Document C

In the spring of 1945, the Allies' island-hopping campaign in the Pacific brought them closer to the heart of Japan. When American troops invaded first the island of Iwo Jima, then the island of Okinawa, the Japanese fought fiercely, but unsuccessfully, to keep them from gaining control. They knew that the Allies planned to use the islands as a base for an invasion of Japan itself.

Troops Killed at Iwo Jima and Okinawa, 1945		
Battle	Japanese troops killed	American troops killed
Iwo Jima	21,000	6,800
Okinawa	100,000	12,000

SOURCE: Encyclopaedia Brittannica

Document D

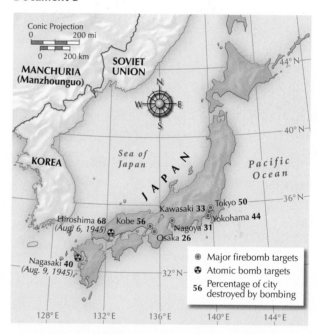

Analyzing Documents

Use your knowledge of World War II and Documents A, B, C, and D to answer questions 1–4.

1. Which of the following cities experienced the most damage from the American bombing raids?
   A Tokyo
   B Yokohama
   C Hiroshima
   D Osaka

2. Which of the following statements BEST summarizes Herbert Feis's explanation for Truman's use of the atomic bomb?
   A Use of the atomic bombs would cause more destruction.
   B Use of the atomic bombs would save lives.
   C Use of the atomic bombs would ensure surrender.
   D Use of the atomic bombs would make it more difficult for Japan to rebuild its military.

3. J. Samuel Walker's main argument against the use of atomic bombs is that
   A atomic bombs were more destructive than conventional bombs.
   B an American invasion would not have been as destructive as the bombs.
   C the war would have ended anyway.
   D the Japanese emperor opposed the use of atomic bombs.

4. **Writing Task** Which of the historians quoted in Documents A and B do you agree with most strongly? Why? Use your knowledge of World War II and specific evidence from the documents to support your opinion.

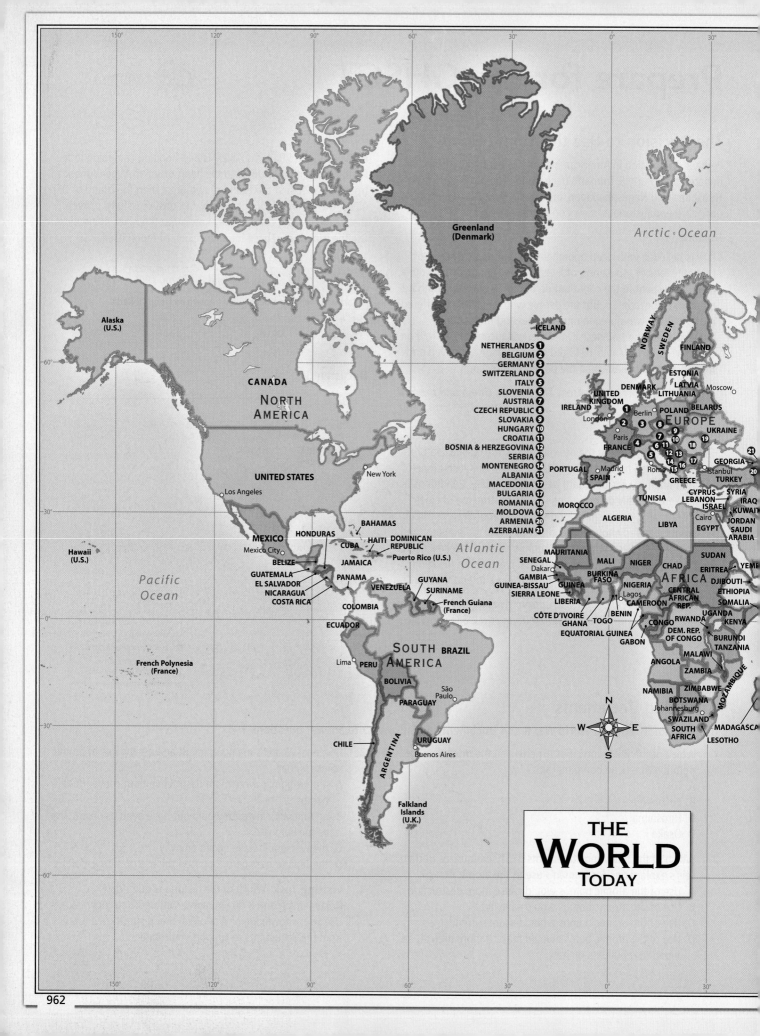

THE **WORLD** Today

Geography *Interactive*
For: Audio guided tour
Web Code: nap-7000

30

The Cold War
1945–1991

Berlin Is Walled In

On August 13, 1961, the first morning after the Berlin Wall was built, thousands of East Berliners arrived at the main border crossing hoping to travel to West Berlin. Transportation Police, or Trapos, blocked the way. Robert Lochner recalls, "A timid old woman . . . asked one of the Trapos when the next train would go to West Berlin. Sneeringly he answered: 'None of that anymore, grandma. You are all now caught in a mousetrap.'" Listen to the Witness History audio to hear more about the Berlin Wall.

**U.S. President
Ronald Reagan**

◄ **East German guards watch the newly built Berlin Wall.**

GA Performance Standards

Chapter Focus Question How did the Cold War develop, how did it shape political and economic life in individual nations, and how did it end?

**Section 1
The Cold War Unfolds**
SSWH19c

**Section 2
The Industrialized Democracies**
SSWH18d, SSWH19e, SSWH20d, SSWH21a

**Section 3
Communism Spreads in East Asia**
SSWH19a

**Section 4
War in Southeast Asia**
SSWHRC1c

**Section 5
The End of the Cold War**
SSWH19d, SSWH20b

Use the ✓ **Quick Study Timeline** at the end of this chapter to preview chapter events.

Pin promoting the Soviet reforms that helped to end the Cold War

U.S. military helicopter over Vietnam

 Concept Connector ONLINE

**To explore Essential Questions related to this chapter, go to PHSchool.com
Web Code: nad-3007**

Winston Churchill

WITNESS HISTORY 🔊 AUDIO

An Iron Curtain

In 1946, Winston Churchill, former prime minister of Britain, spoke of an "iron curtain" sealing off the countries in Eastern Europe that the Soviet Union had occupied at the end of World War II:

❝ [A]n iron curtain has descended [fallen] across the Continent. Behind that line lie all the capitals of the ancient states of Central and Eastern Europe. . . . [A]ll these famous cities . . . lie in what I must call the Soviet sphere, and are all subject . . . to a very high . . . measure of control from Moscow. ❞

Focus Question What were the military and political consequences of the Cold War in the Soviet Union, Europe, and the United States?

The Cold War Unfolds

 Performance Standards

- **SSWH19c** Explain the arms race, the development of the hydrogen bomb, and the Strategic Arms Limitation Treaty (SALT).

Terms, People, and Places

superpowers	John F. Kennedy
anti-ballistic missiles (ABMs)	ideology
Ronald Reagan	Nikita Khrushchev
détente	Leonid Brezhnev
Fidel Castro	containment

N**o**te **Taking**

Reading Skill: Summarize Sum up the consequences of the Cold War in the United States, Europe, and the Soviet Union in a chart like the one below.

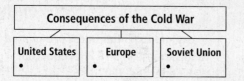

Consequences of the Cold War

United States	Europe	Soviet Union
•	•	•

After World War II devastated Europe and Japan, two great powers remained: the United States and the Soviet Union. These two nations were known as **superpowers,** or nations stronger than other powerful nations. The Cold War between these superpowers cast a shadow over the world for more than 40 years.

Two Sides Face Off in Europe

Cold War confrontation began in Europe, where the two superpowers' armies confronted each other after World War II. Each superpower formed a European military alliance made up of the nations that it occupied or protected. The United States led the North Atlantic Treaty Organization, or NATO, in Western Europe. The Soviet Union led the Warsaw Pact in Eastern Europe. The two alliances in Europe faced each other along the Iron Curtain, the tense line between the democratic West and the communist East.

A Wall Divides Berlin Berlin was a key focus of Cold War tensions. The city was split into democratic West Berlin and communist East Berlin. In the 1950s, West Berlin became a showcase for West German prosperity. A massive exodus of low-paid East Germans, unhappy with communism, fled into West Berlin. To stop the flight, East Germany built a wall in 1961 that sealed off West Berlin. When completed, the Berlin Wall was a massive concrete barrier, topped with barbed wire and patrolled by guards. The wall showed that workers, far from enjoying a communist paradise, had to be forcibly kept from fleeing.

Eastern Europe Resists Other explosions of Cold War tension included revolts against Soviet domination in East Germany, Poland, Hungary, and Czechoslovakia. One of the earliest revolts occurred in East Berlin. In 1953, some 50,000 workers confronted the Soviet army in the streets of the German capital. The uprising spread to other East German cities, but the demonstrators could not stand up to Russian tanks.

In 1956, Eastern Europeans challenged Soviet authority in the name of economic reform in both Poland and Hungary. Poles were responding in part to Soviet-backed mass arrests of noncommunist leaders and government seizures of private lands and industry. Hungarian leader Imre Nagy (nahj) went furthest, ending one-party rule and seeking to pull his country out of the Warsaw Pact. In response, Soviet troops launched a massive assault that overwhelmed resistance. Nagy was later executed.

In early 1968, Czechoslovak leader Alexander Dubček introduced greater freedom of expression and limited democracy. This blossoming of freedom came to be known as the "Prague Spring." Soviet leaders feared that democracy would threaten communist power and Soviet domination. Warsaw Pact troops launched a massive invasion of Czechoslovakia in August of that year to put an end to these freedoms.

✓ **Checkpoint** How was Europe divided, and what were three consequences of its division?

Nuclear Weapons Threaten the World

One of the most terrifying aspects of the Cold War was the arms race that began right after World War II. At first, the United States was the only nuclear power. By 1949, however, the Soviet Union had also developed nuclear weapons. By 1953, both sides had developed hydrogen bombs, which are much more destructive than atomic bombs.

Critics argued that a nuclear war would destroy both sides. Yet each superpower wanted to be able to deter the other from launching its nuclear weapons. Both sides engaged in a race to match each other's new weapons. The result was a "balance of terror." Mutually assured destruction—in which each side knew that the other side would itself be

Soviet Nuclear Missiles
Every year on May 1, the Soviet Union demonstrated its military and nuclear strength in a parade through Moscow's Red Square. *Why might the Soviet Union have wanted to show off its nuclear might?*

Arms Control Agreements

Date	Agreement	Effect
1963	Nuclear Test Ban Treaty	Banned testing of nuclear weapons in the atmosphere
1972	SALT I Interim Agreement	Froze existing number of weapons held by each side
1972	SALT I Anti-Ballistic Missile Treaty	Set strict limits on missiles that could shoot down missiles from the other side
1979	SALT II Treaty	Set absolute limit on number of weapons each side could hold
1991	START Treaty	Required both sides to reduce the number of weapons each held

Chart Skills Compare the Nuclear Test Ban Treaty, the SALT II Treaty, and the START Treaty. *How did each of the later treaties advance beyond the treaty that came before it?*

SOURCE: *Encyclopaedia Britannica*

destroyed if it launched its weapons—discouraged nuclear war. Still, the world's people lived in constant fear of nuclear doom.

Limiting Nuclear Weapons To reduce the threat of nuclear war, the two sides met at disarmament talks. Although mutual distrust slowed progress, the rival powers did reach some agreements. In 1969, the United States and the Soviet Union began Strategic Arms Limitation Talks (SALT) to limit the number of nuclear weapons held by each side. In 1972 and 1979, both sides signed agreements setting these limits.

One of these agreements limited **anti-ballistic missiles (ABMs),** or missiles that could shoot down other missiles from hostile countries. ABMs were seen as a particular threat to the balance of terror because, by giving one side some protection against the other, they might encourage the protected side to attack. They were also seen as a technology that could provoke a renewed arms race. During the 1980s, U.S. President **Ronald Reagan** launched a program to build a "Star Wars" missile defense against nuclear attack. Critics objected that this program would violate the ABM treaty. Nonetheless, the two sides signed the Strategic Arms Reduction Treaty (START) in 1991.

Building Détente American and Soviet arms control agreements led to an era of **détente** (day TAHNT), or relaxation of tensions, during the 1970s. The American strategy under détente was to restrain the Soviet Union through diplomatic agreements rather than by military means. The era of détente ended in 1979, when the Soviet Union invaded Afghanistan.

Stopping the Spread of Nuclear Weapons By the late 1960s, Britain, France, and China had developed their own nuclear weapons. However, many world leaders worked to keep the arms race from spreading any further. In 1968, many nations signed the Nuclear Non-Proliferation Treaty (NPT). These nations agreed not to develop nuclear weapons or to stop the proliferation, or spread, of nuclear weapons.

✔ **Checkpoint** What factors discouraged the use of nuclear weapons during the Cold War?

The Cold War Goes Global

Although the Cold War began in Central Europe, it quickly spread around the world. When World War II ended, the Soviets were assisting communist forces in China and Korea. American leaders saw that the United States faced a conflict as global as the two world wars that had preceded it. They therefore developed policies to respond to challenges anywhere in the world.

Building Alliances and Bases As part of its strategy to contain Soviet power, the United States reached out to the rest of the world both diplomatically and militarily. The NATO alliance with Europe's democracies was only one of several regional alliances.

SOVIET UNION

UNITED
STATES

Area of
inset map

TURKEY

AFGHANISTAN

LEBANON

IRAN

KOREA

ISRAEL

IRAQ

VIETNAM

CUBA

CAMBODIA

Atlantic
Ocean

MALAYSIA

Pacific
Ocean

EL SALVADOR

NICARAGUA

Pacific
Ocean

CONGO

ANGOLA

Indian
Ocean

N

W   E

S

CHILE

Robinson Projection

0   2000   4000 mi

0   2000   4000 km

Soviet Union and allies
Other communist countries
United States and allies
Other noncommunist countries
Cold War conflicts

ICELAND

Atlantic
Ocean

NORWAY

FINLAND

SWEDEN

Conic Projection

0   300   600 mi

0   300   600 km

North
Sea   DENMARK

Baltic Sea

IRELAND   UNITED

SOVIET UNION

KINGDOM   NETH.

BELGIUM

EAST
GER.

POLAND

LUX.

WEST
GERMANY

CZECH.

FRANCE

SWITZ.

AUST.   HUNG.

ITALY

ROMANIA

PORTUGAL

SPAIN

YUGOSLAVIA

Black Sea

BULGARIA

ALB.

N

W   E

S

GREECE

TURKEY

Mediterranean Sea

Map Skills During the Cold War, much of the world was divided into two powerful alliances, led by the United States and the communist Soviet Union. Communism reached its maximum extent around 1977, the date of this map. The inset shows details in Europe.

1. **Locate** (a) the Soviet Union (b) the United States (c) Poland
2. **Location** Where were most Cold War conflicts located in relation to the two alliances shown on the map?
3. **Draw Inferences** Why might Cold War conflicts be concentrated as they are?

Soviet troops in Afghanistan ▶

In 1955, the United States and its allies formed another alliance, the Southeast-Asia Treaty Organization (SEATO). SEATO included the United States, Britain, France, Australia, Pakistan, Thailand, New Zealand, and the Philippines. The Central Treaty Organization (CENTO) comprised Britain, Turkey, Iran, and Pakistan. The United States also formed military alliances with individual nations, such as Japan and South Korea.

Meanwhile, the Soviet Union formed its own alliances. In addition to the Warsaw Pact in Europe, the Soviet Union formed alliances with governments in Africa and Asia. A Soviet alliance with the government of Communist China lasted from 1949 to 1960. The Soviet Union and its allies were often known as the Soviet bloc.

Unlike the Soviets, the Americans established army, navy, and air force bases around the globe. By the end of the Cold War, the Soviets faced the military nightmare of encirclement by an enemy. American army camps, naval stations, and air bases spread across Europe, Asia, North America, and the Pacific islands, while American fleets patrolled the world's oceans.

Where the Cold War Got Hot Because both superpowers had a global reach, local conflicts in many places played into the Cold War. Often, the United States and its allies supported one side, and the Soviet bloc supported the other. Through such struggles, the superpowers could confront each other indirectly rather than head to head. Political shifts around the world added to Cold War tensions. When communist forces won control of mainland China in 1949, the United States feared that a tide of communism would sweep around the world. During this period, European colonies in Africa and Asia demanded independence. As colonies battled for independence, liberation leaders and guerrillas frequently sought help from one or the other Cold War power.

On occasion, the Cold War erupted into "shooting wars," especially in Asia. Both Korea and Vietnam were torn by brutal conflicts in which the United States, the Soviet Union, and China played crucial roles. More commonly, however, the superpowers provided weapons, training, or other aid to opposing forces in Asia, Africa, or Latin America.

Cuba Goes Communist The most serious Cold War conflict in the Western Hemisphere involved the Latin American island nation of Cuba, just 90 miles off the coast of Florida. In the 1950s, Fidel Castro organized an armed rebellion against the corrupt dictator who then ruled Cuba. By 1959, Castro had led his guerrilla army to victory and set about transforming the country. This transformation is known as the Cuban Revolution. Castro sought the support of the Soviet Union. He nationalized businesses and put most land under government control. In addition, Castro severely restricted Cubans' political freedom. Critics of the new regime were jailed or silenced, and hundreds of thousands fled to Florida.

The United States attempted to bring down the communist regime next door. In 1961, President John F. Kennedy supported an invasion attempt by U.S.-trained Cuban exiles. The Bay of Pigs Invasion, known for the bay where the invaders came ashore in Cuba, quickly ended in failure when Castro's forces captured the invaders. The United States imposed a trade embargo on Cuba that remains in effect today.

Cuban Missiles Spark a Crisis In 1962, the Soviet Union sent nuclear missiles to Cuba. President Kennedy responded by imposing a naval blockade that prevented further Soviet shipments. Kennedy demanded that the Soviet Union remove its nuclear missiles from Cuba, and for a few tense days, the world faced a risk of nuclear war over the issue. Finally, however, Soviet Premier Nikita Khrushchev agreed to remove the Soviet missiles, and war was averted.

✔ **Checkpoint** How did the U.S. and the Soviet Union confront each other around the world during the Cold War?

● **INFOGRAPHIC**

THE CUBAN MISSILE *CRISIS*

In the summer of 1962, the United States learned that the Soviet Union was shipping nuclear missiles to Cuba, less than 100 miles off the coast of Florida. President John F. Kennedy demanded that the Soviet Union remove the missiles from Cuba. In October 1962, the United States imposed a naval blockade on Cuba. For one week, a tense confrontation brought the world to the brink of nuclear war. Finally, on October 28, Khrushchev agreed to remove the Soviet missiles.

▲ Soviet Premier Nikita Khrushchev

◀ U.S. President John F. Kennedy

During the U.S. naval blockade, the U.S. Navy surrounded Cuba with ships. (See the map below). In this photo, the USS *Barry* inspects the cargo of a Soviet freighter returning from Cuba.

This aerial photo shows Soviet missiles being unloaded at a Cuban port.

Thinking Critically

1. **Map Skills** Considering Cuba's location on the map, why did Soviet nuclear missiles on the island pose a threat to the United States?
2. **Draw Conclusions** Why might Khrushchev have agreed to withdraw the missiles from Cuba?

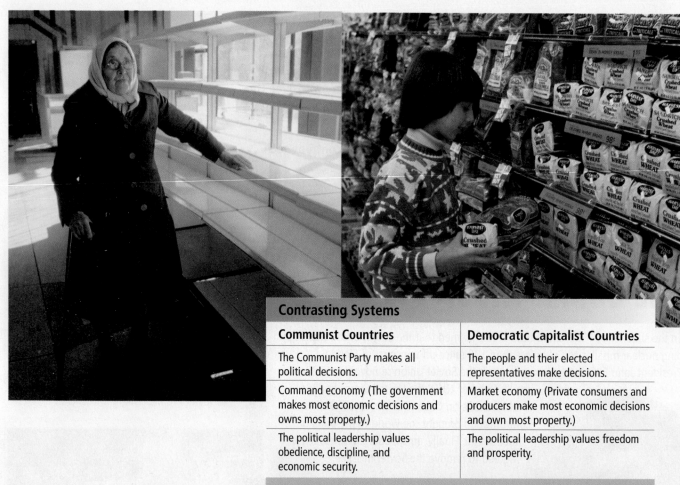

Contrasting Systems

Communist Countries	Democratic Capitalist Countries
The Communist Party makes all political decisions.	The people and their elected representatives make decisions.
Command economy (The government makes most economic decisions and owns most property.)	Market economy (Private consumers and producers make most economic decisions and own most property.)
The political leadership values obedience, discipline, and economic security.	The political leadership values freedom and prosperity.

Chart Skills The communist system often offered few choices for consumers, such as for the Russian woman above. By contrast, capitalist societies provided a wealth of choices for consumers, such as for the American girl at the right. *What facts in the chart above help to explain the different experiences of consumers under these contrasting systems?*

The Soviet Union in the Cold War

Victory in World War II brought few rewards to the Soviet people. Stalin continued his ruthless policies. He filled labor camps with "enemies of the state" and seemed ready to launch new purges when he died in 1953.

Soviet Communism In the Soviet Union, the government controlled most aspects of public life. Communists valued obedience, discipline, and economic security. They sought to spread their communist **ideology,** or value system and beliefs, around the globe. The Soviet Union also aimed to spread its communist command economy to other countries. In command economies, government bureaus make most economic decisions. They often make decisions for political reasons that do not make much economic sense. The government owns most property.

Stalin's Successors Hold the Line After Stalin's death in 1953, **Nikita Khrushchev** (KROOSH chawf) emerged as the new Soviet leader. In 1956, he shocked top Communist Party members when he publicly denounced Stalin's abuse of power. Khrushchev maintained the Communist Party's political control, but he closed prison camps and eased censorship. He called for a "peaceful coexistence" with the West.

Khrushchev's successor, **Leonid Brezhnev** (BREZH nef) held power from the mid-1960s until he died in 1982. Under Brezhnev, critics faced arrest and imprisonment.

Some Soviets Bravely Resist Despite the risk of punishment, some courageous people dared to criticize the government. Andrey Sakharov (SAH kuh rawf), a distinguished Soviet scientist, spoke out for civil liberties. Brezhnev's government silenced him. As a Soviet soldier during World War II, Aleksandr Solzhenitsyn (sohl zhuh NEET sin) wrote a letter to a friend criticizing Stalin. He was sent to a prison camp. Under Khrushchev, he was released and wrote fiction that drew on his experience as a prisoner. His writing was banned in the Soviet Union, and in 1974 he was exiled. Despite the government's actions, Sakharov and Solzhenitsyn inspired others to resist communist policies.

✔ **Checkpoint** How did the Soviet government handle critics of its policies?

The United States in the Cold War

The Cold War was not just a military rivalry. It was also a competition between two contrasting economic and political value systems. Unlike the communist countries, the democratic, capitalist countries, led by the United States, gave citizens the freedom to make economic and political choices. These nations valued freedom and prosperity.

Free Markets While communist countries had command economies, capitalist countries had market economies. In market economies, producers and consumers make economic decisions. Prices are based on supply and demand in a free market. Property is privately owned. Producers compete to offer the best products for the lowest prices. By deciding what to buy, consumers ultimately decide which products are produced. Producers who win consumers' business make profits and grow.

The United States economy is basically a market economy. However, the United States and Western Europe have what can be called mixed economies, because their governments have an economic role.

Containing the Soviet Union America's basic policy toward communist countries was known as **containment.** This was a strategy of containing communism, or keeping it within its existing boundaries and preventing further expansion. This strategy meant supporting any government facing invasion or internal rebellion by communists.

Living With Nuclear Dangers The nuclear threat led many people in the United States and other countries to build fallout shelters. Fallout shelters

Preparing for a Nuclear Attack
"Duck and cover" air-raid drills were common during the Cold War, even though it is doubtful that ducking and covering would offer much protection in an actual nuclear attack. *What does this photo suggest about Americans' fears during the Cold War?*

were structures, often underground, designed to protect people from fallout, or radioactive particles from a nuclear explosion. In 1961, the U.S. government launched a community fallout shelter program to create fallout shelters in public and commercial buildings, stocked with a two-week supply of food for the surrounding population. The fear of nuclear attack reached a peak in the United States during the Cuban missile crisis of 1962. Thousands of Americans built private fallout shelters underneath their backyards.

From the 1950s into the 1970s, American schools conducted air-raid drills in anticipation of a nuclear attack. These drills were nearly as common as fire drills. Children were trained to duck underneath desks and crouch with their hands over their heads. Although this would not have protected them from an actual nuclear explosion, the drills reflected the widespread fear of nuclear war.

Red Scare Culture
Pop culture during the "red scare" of the 1940s and 1950s reflected the fears of the times. "I Was a Communist for the FBI" thrilled movie-goers in 1951.

Seeking Enemies Within Cold War fears led to a "red scare" within the United States. During the late 1940s and early 1950s, many Americans feared that communists inside the United States might try to undermine the U.S. government. Around 1950, Senator Joseph McCarthy led a hunt for suspected American communists. McCarthy became notorious for unproven charges. Accusing innocent people of communism, and the fear that this created, became known as McCarthyism. McCarthy's influence, however, faded after he attacked the patriotism of the United States Army.

During the same period, the House Un-American Activities Committee (HUAC) led a similar campaign to identify supposed communist sympathizers. HUAC was made up of members of the U.S. House of Representatives. In 1947, the Committee sought to expose communist sympathizers in Hollywood's movie industry. People who had flirted with communist ideas in their youth and later rejected them were labeled as communists. Many who were labeled in this way were no longer able to get decent jobs.

✔ **Checkpoint** How did America respond to the threat of communism at home and overseas?

SECTION 1 **Assessment**

Progress Monitoring *Online*
For: Self-quiz with vocabulary practice
Web Code: naa-3011

Terms, People, and Places

1. For each term, person, or place listed at the beginning of the section, write a sentence explaining its significance.

Note Taking

2. **Reading Skill: Summarize** Use your completed chart to answer the Focus Question: What were the military and political consequences of the Cold War in the Soviet Union, Europe, and the United States?

Comprehension and Critical Thinking

3. **Make Generalizations** What kinds of conflicts resulted from the global confrontation between the two superpowers?

4. **Draw Inferences** How did the buildup of nuclear weapons discourage their use?

5. **Make Comparisons** Identify similarities and differences between the Soviet Union and the United States during the Cold War.

● **Writing About History**

Quick Write: Understand the Purpose
To write a problem-solution essay, you first need to understand the purpose of this type of essay. In this section, you learned that the superpowers' possession of nuclear weapons posed a risk of nuclear war. Write sentences answering each of the following questions: What makes this issue a problem? What benefit comes from solving this problem?

COOPERATION

With whom should we cooperate and why?

In This Chapter SSWH19c

Cooperation between the United States and the Soviet Union broke down as soon as Germany was defeated. Each superpower developed its own network of allies, NATO and the Warsaw Pact, and built large nuclear arsenals. Faced with the possibility of devastating war, American and Soviet leaders (right) negotiated treaties that gradually reduced the number of nuclear weapons.

"LET'S GET A LOCK FOR THIS THING"

NUCLEAR WAR

FALLOUT SHELTER

CAPACITY 1730

Throughout History

- **400s B.C.** Greek city-states unite to defeat the Persians.

- **1200s A.D.** Hanseatic League promotes trade in northern Europe.

- **Late 1500s** Five Iroquois groups form the Iroquois League to keep peace among themselves.

- **Late 1800s** European and American workers form unions to improve pay and working conditions.

- **2000s** The Kyoto Protocol to reduce greenhouse gas emissions is signed by 140 countries.

Continuing Today

Despite political differences, many nations come together every four years to take part in the Olympic Games. Athletes compete in individual and team events.

21st Century Skills

TRANSFER Activities

1. **Analyze** What goals have motivated people to cooperate throughout history?

2. **Evaluate** Why is it sometimes necessary to cooperate with an enemy?

3. **Transfer** Complete a Web quest in which you, as an advisor to the President, consider whether or not to cooperate with a new regime; record your thoughts in the Concept Connector Journal; and learn to make a video. Web Code nah-3008

Marshall Plan poster

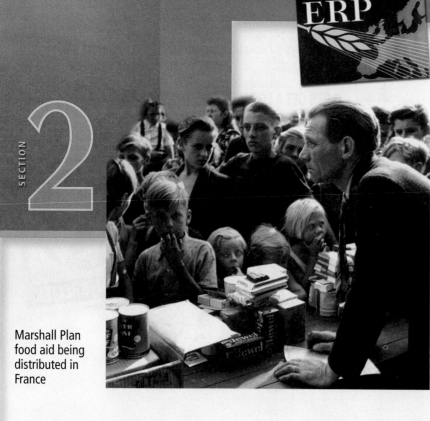
Marshall Plan food aid being distributed in France

WITNESS HISTORY 🔊 AUDIO

The Marshall Plan

In a speech at Harvard University in June 1947, U.S. Secretary of State George Marshall made the case for the Marshall Plan, a United States assistance program for Western Europe.

66 Our policy is directed not against any country or doctrine but against hunger, poverty, desperation, and chaos. Its purpose should be the revival of a working economy in the world so as to permit the emergence of . . . conditions in which free institutions can exist.99

Focus Question How did the United States, Western Europe, and Japan achieve economic prosperity and strengthen democracy during the Cold War years?

The Industrialized Democracies

 Performance Standards

- **SSWH18d** Explain MacArthur's Post-World War II plan for Japan.
- **SSWH19e** Analyze efforts in pursuit of freedom.
- **SSWH20d** Examine the rise of Margaret Thatcher as a major world leader.
- **SSWH21a** Describe how television integrated countries into a world economy.

Terms, People, and Places

recession	Konrad Adenauer
suburbanization	welfare state
segregation	European Community
discrimination	gross domestic product
Dr. Martin Luther King, Jr.	(GDP)

Note Taking

Reading Skill: Categorize Keep track of changes in the industrialized democracies with a chart like the one below.

Economic and Political Changes in the Industrialized Democracies		
United States	Western Europe	Japan
•	•	•
•	•	•
•	•	•

The industrialized democracies of North America, Western Europe, and Japan grew in prosperity and went through social change during the Cold War. Throughout this period, the United States was the world's wealthiest and most powerful country. By the end of the Cold War, however, Western Europe and Japan rivaled the United States economically.

America Prospers and Changes

In the postwar decades, American businesses expanded into markets around the globe. The dollar was the world's strongest currency. Foreigners flocked to invest in American industry and to buy U.S. government bonds. America's wealth was a model for other democracies and a challenge to the stagnant economies of the communist world.

America Plays a Central Role During the Cold War, the United States was a global political leader. The headquarters of the League of Nations had been symbolically located in neutral Switzerland. The headquarters of the newly formed United Nations was built in New York City.

The United States also played a leading economic role. America had emerged untouched from the horrendous destruction of the Second World War. Other nations needed American goods and services, and foreign trade helped the United States achieve a long postwar boom. The long postwar peace among democratic nations helped to spread this boom worldwide. The World Bank, an international agency that finances world economic development, was headquartered in Washington, D.C. The International Monetary Fund (IMF), which oversees the finances of the world's nations, was based there as well.

The Postwar American Boom America's economic strength transformed life in the United States itself. During the 1950s and 1960s, boom times prevailed. **Recessions,** or periods when the economy shrinks, were brief and mild. Although segments of the population were left behind, many Americans prospered in the world's wealthiest economy. As Americans grew more affluent, many moved from the cities to the suburbs. The movement to communities outside an urban core is known as **suburbanization.** Suburbanites typically lived in single-family houses with lawns and access to good schools. Suburban highways allowed residents to commute to work by car.

During the postwar decades, many Americans also moved to the Sunbelt, or the states in the South and Southwest of the United States. Jobs in these states were becoming more plentiful than in the industrialized North, and the warmer climate was an added bonus. The growing availability of air conditioning and water for irrigation in states such as Arizona helped make the movement to the Sunbelt possible.

The wide popularity of American culture abroad vividly illustrated the global influence of the United States. The world embraced twentieth-century art forms such as American movies, television, and rock-and-roll music. American originals such as Elvis Presley, musical comedies, Hollywood romances, and action movies had a worldwide following.

The federal government contributed to the economic boom. Under President Truman, Congress created programs that helped veterans, the elderly, and the poor. Truman's successor, Dwight Eisenhower, approved government funding to build a vast interstate highway system. Government programs also made it easier for people to buy homes.

Moving to the Suburbs
This image shows a family watching the progress as their new, suburban home is built. The photo below shows a suburb in New York in 1954. *Why might suburbs such as this attract families from cities?*

The Oil Shock of the 1970s
In 1973 and 1974, a reduction in the supply of oil led to shortages and higher prices for gasoline. In the photos above, motorists wait on line to fill up with scarce gasoline.

An Oil Shock Brings Recession However, America's growing dependence on the world economy brought problems. In the early 1970s, a political crisis in the Middle East led to decreased oil exports. Oil prices soared worldwide. Waiting in long lines for scarce and expensive gasoline, Americans became aware of their dependence on imported oil and on global economic forces.

In America and in the other industrialized democracies, which were even more dependent on imported oil, higher prices for oil left businesses and consumers with less to spend on other products. The decades of postwar prosperity ended with a serious recession in 1974. During the 1970s and 1980s, the world's economies suffered a series of recessions alternating with years of renewed prosperity.

 Checkpoint How was the U.S. economy linked to the broader global economy during the Cold War?

Democracy Expands Opportunities

Although America <u>prospered</u> after World War II, the American promise of equality and opportunity had not yet been fulfilled for ethnic minorities and women. In the postwar decades, these groups demanded equality. In American politics, liberals and conservatives offered contrasting programs to increase opportunities for the American people.

Segregation and Discrimination The prosperity of the postwar years failed to benefit all Americans equally. Although slavery had been abolished a century before, many states denied equality to African Americans and other minority groups. These groups faced legal **segregation,** or forced separation, in education and housing. Minorities also suffered **discrimination**—unequal treatment or barriers—in jobs and voting. After World War II, President Harry Truman desegregated the armed forces. Then, in 1954, the U.S. Supreme Court made a landmark ruling, *Brown* v. *Board of Education of Topeka,* declaring that segregated schools were unconstitutional.

Americans Demand Civil Rights By 1956, a gifted preacher, Dr. Martin Luther King, Jr., had emerged as a leader of the civil rights movement. This movement aimed to extend equal rights to all Americans, and particularly African Americans. King organized boycotts and led peaceful marches to end segregation in the United States. In 1963, King made a stirring speech. "I have a dream," he proclaimed, "that one day this nation will rise up and live out the true meaning of its creed: 'We hold these truths to be self-evident, that all men are created equal.'"

Americans of all races joined the civil rights movement. Their courage in the face of sometimes brutal attacks stirred the nation's conscience. Asians, Latinos, Native Americans, and other groups joined African Americans in demanding equality. The U.S. Congress outlawed public segregation, protected voting rights, and required equal access to housing and jobs. Poverty, unemployment, and discrimination still plagued many African Americans. However, some were elected to political office or gained top jobs in business and the military.

Women Demand Equality Women too faced discrimination in employment and other areas. Inspired by the civil rights movement, women fought gender-based discrimination during the 1960s and 1970s. The women's rights movement won laws banning discrimination against women. More women also gained higher salaries and positions in politics and business.

The Government's Role Grows During the 1960s, the government further expanded social programs to help the poor and disadvantaged. Under Presidents John F. Kennedy and Lyndon Johnson, both Democrats,

BIOGRAPHY

MARTIN LUTHER KING, Jr.

Dr. Martin Luther King, Jr. (1929–1968) was born in Atlanta, Georgia, and grew up in the segregated American South. He earned a doctorate in divinity in 1955 and became a minister at a church in Montgomery, Alabama. Beginning that year, King helped lead the Montgomery Bus Boycott to protest segregation on the city's buses. In the years that followed, King emerged as the most respected leader of the American civil rights movement. He was repeatedly attacked and jailed for his beliefs. He helped organize the massive March on Washington, D.C., for civil rights in 1963. He gave his famous "I Have a Dream" speech at this event. King lived to see the passage of the Civil Rights Act of 1965 that outlawed segregation. However, he was killed in 1968 by an assassin. **How did King's actions show courage?**

Congress funded Medicare, providing health care for the elderly. Other programs offered housing for the poor.

Republicans Respond In the 1980s, President Reagan and the Republican Party called for cutbacks in taxes and government spending. They argued that cutting taxes was the best way to improve opportunities for Americans. Congress ended some social programs, reduced government regulation of the economy, and cut taxes. At the same time, however, military spending increased.

The combination of increased spending and tax cuts greatly increased the national budget deficit, or the shortfall between what the government spends and what it receives in taxes and other income. To deal with the deficit, Republicans pushed for deeper cuts in social and economic programs, including education, welfare, and environmental protection.

✔ **Checkpoint** Over time, how did the U.S. government expand opportunities for Americans?

Western Europe Rebuilds

Americans arriving in Europe as liberators or occupiers in 1945 were astonished at the damage that the war had inflicted. Germany in particular lay in ruins. Many Europeans had suffered grievously. However, Western Europe recovered economically more rapidly than anyone had expected—and then moved on to even higher standards of living.

Germany Divided and Reunited At the end of World War II, the United States, Britain, and France—all democracies—occupied the western portion of Germany. The Soviet Union occupied eastern Germany. The goal had been to hold elections throughout Germany for a single German government, but disputes between the Soviet Union and the Western powers led to Germany's division into two separate countries by 1949. West Germany became a member of NATO, while East Germany became a member of the Warsaw Pact. For 40 years, differences between the two Germanys widened.

Primary Source

❝ There are no homes, no shops, no transportation, no government buildings. Only a few walls. . . . Berlin can now be regarded only as a geographical location heaped with mountainous mounds of debris.❞
—*New York Herald Tribune,* May 3, 1945

Wartime Destruction in Germany
Many German cities suffered serious wartime damage. In this photo, civilians walk through the rubble left by wartime bombing in Nuremberg, Germany, in 1945. *What challenges would residents of a city face after such heavy destruction?*

The Iron Curtain Divides Germany
While the Berlin Wall divided the city of Berlin, a much longer series of concrete walls, barbed wire, and watchtowers ran along the border between East and West Germany, forming part of the Iron Curtain. *Why might East Germany have built a fortified border such as this?*

While West Germany had a democratic government, East Germany was a communist state. While West Germany enjoyed an economic boom, East Germany's command economy stagnated. Before the Berlin Wall was built, millions of East Germans fled to the freedom and prosperity of West Germany. After the wall was built, some East Germans still managed to escape, but others were shot as they tried to cross the border.

In 1989, as Soviet communism declined, Germany moved toward reunification. Without Soviet backing, East German communist leaders were unable to maintain control. They were forced to reopen their western borders. Quickly, East Germans demanded reunification with the West. In 1990, German voters approved reunification.

West Germany's "Economic Miracle" Early in the Cold War, the United States rushed aid to its former enemy through the Marshall Plan and other programs. It wanted to strengthen West Germany against communist Eastern Europe. From 1949 to 1963, **Konrad Adenauer** (AHD uh now ur) was West Germany's chancellor, or prime minister. He guided the rebuilding of cities, factories, and trade. Because many of its old factories had been destroyed, Germany built a modern and highly productive industrial base. Despite high taxes to pay for the recovery, West Germans created a booming industrial economy.

Britain's Narrowed Horizons Britain's economy was slow to recover after the war. Despite U.S. assistance through the Marshall Plan, Britain could no longer afford a large military presence overseas. Therefore, Britain abandoned its colonial empire in the face of demands for independence. After several years of economic hardship, however, Britain's economy recovered during the 1950s and 1960s. Although Britain did not enjoy a boom like Germany's, its living standard did improve.

Other European Nations Prosper Most European nations emerged from World War II greatly weakened. Like Britain, European colonial powers such as Belgium and the Netherlands gave in to demands for independence from former colonies. France was forced to abandon its empire after bloody colonial wars in Vietnam and Algeria drained and demoralized the country.

Most Western European countries had suffered serious wartime damage. Like West Germany, they received U.S. assistance through the Marshall Plan. As in West Germany, this helped them to build more modern and productive facilities. During the 1950s and 1960s, most of Europe enjoyed an economic boom. Living standards improved greatly for most Dutch, Belgians, French, and Italians. Poorer European countries, such as Spain and Ireland, were able to attract outside investment that led to economic growth.

Building the Welfare State In the postwar decades, Europeans worked to secure their economic prosperity. From the 1950s through the 1970s, European nations expanded social benefits to their citizens. During this time, many European nations also moved toward greater economic cooperation.

Many European political parties, and particularly those representing workers, wanted to extend the **welfare state.** A welfare state is a country with a market economy but with increased government responsibility for the social and economic needs of its people. The welfare state had its roots in the late 1800s. During that period, Germany, Britain, and other nations had set up basic old-age pensions and unemployment insurance.

After 1945, European governments expanded these social programs. Both the middle class and the poor enjoyed increased benefits from national healthcare, unemployment insurance, and old-age pensions. Other programs gave aid to the poor and created an economic cushion to help people get through difficult times.

However, the welfare state brought high taxes and greater government regulation of private enterprise. In Britain, France, and elsewhere, governments took over basic industries such as railroads, airlines, and steel. Conservatives, or people who favor free markets and a limited role for government, condemned this drift from the free enterprise system toward socialism.

Limiting the Welfare State In 1979, British voters turned to the Conservative Party, which denounced the welfare state as costly and inefficient. The Conservatives were led by Margaret Thatcher. Thatcher's government reduced social welfare programs and returned government-owned industries to private control. Faced with soaring costs, other European nations also moved to limit social welfare benefits and to privatize state-owned businesses during the 1980s and 1990s.

Toward European Unity Greater economic cooperation helped fuel Europe's economic boom during the 1950s and 1960s. In 1952, six nations—West Germany, the Netherlands, Belgium, Luxembourg, France, and Italy—set up the European Coal and Steel Community. This agency established free trade in coal and steel among member states by eliminating tariffs, or fees, and other barriers that limited trade. This small start spurred economic growth across Western Europe and led to further regional cooperation.

In 1957, the same six European nations signed a treaty to form the European Economic Community, later known simply as the **European Community.** This was an organization dedicated to establishing free trade among member nations for all products. The European Community

Building Britain's Welfare State
Britain's Labour Party won support after World War II by expanding social programs and the government's role in the economy.

gradually ended tariffs and allowed workers and capital to move freely across national borders. In later years, the European Community expanded to include Britain and other European countries.

✓ **Checkpoint** What were some advantages and disadvantages of the welfare state in Europe?

Japan Is Transformed

In 1945, Japan, like Germany, lay in ruins. It had suffered perhaps the most devastating damage of any nation involved in World War II. Tens of thousands of Japanese were homeless and hungry.

American Occupiers Bring Changes Under General Douglas MacArthur, the Japanese emperor lost all political power. Japan's new constitution established a parliamentary democracy. Occupation forces also introduced social reforms. They opened the education system to all people, with legal equality for women. A land-reform program bought out large landowners and gave land to landless farmers. The United States also provided funds to rebuild Japan's cities and economy.

In 1952, the United States ended the occupation and signed a peace treaty with Japan. Still, the two nations kept close ties. American military forces maintained bases in Japan, which in turn was protected by American nuclear weapons. The two countries were also trading partners, eventually competing with each other in the global economy.

Japan Develops a Democracy Over the years, democracy took root in Japan. The Liberal Democratic Party (LDP) dominated the government from the 1950s to the 1990s. The LDP, however, differs from political parties in the United States. The LDP is a coalition, or alliance, of factions that compete for government positions.

Peace Comes to Japan
A 1945 poster printed by a Japanese bank encourages people to "make a bright future for Japan."

Land Reform Benefits Japanese Farmers
Japan's postwar land reform redistributed land from wealthy landlords to small farmers such as the ones in this photo. *How would ownership of land benefit farmers?*

Japan's Economic Miracle
By the 1970s and 1980s, Japan prospered by manufacturing products to be sold overseas, such as the televisions being assembled in this photo.

An Economic Miracle Relies on Exports Like Western Europe, Japan achieved an economic miracle between 1950 and 1970. Its **gross domestic product (GDP)** soared year after year. GDP is the total value of all goods and services produced in a nation within a particular year.

Japan's success was built on producing goods for export. At first, Japan sold textiles. Later, it shifted to selling steel and machinery. By the 1970s, Japanese cars, cameras, and televisions found eager buyers on the world market. Soon, a wide range of Japanese electronic goods were competing with Western, and especially American, products.

How did Japan enjoy such success? After World War II, Japan, like Germany, had to rebuild from scratch. Also like Germany, it had successfully industrialized in the past, so it quickly built efficient, modern factories that outproduced older industries in the West. With American military protection, Japan spent little money on its own military and could invest more in its economy. In addition, Japan benefited from an educated and skilled workforce. Finally, the government protected home industries by imposing tariffs and regulations that limited imports.

These policies, along with the high quality of Japanese exports, resulted in a trade surplus for Japan. That is, Japan sold more goods overseas than it bought from other countries. By the 1980s, United States manufacturers were angered by what they saw as unfair competition, and the United States pushed Japan to open its economy to more imports. However, Japan's trade surplus persisted.

 Checkpoint What factors explain Japan's economic success in the decades after World War II?

Progress Monitoring *Online*
For: Self-quiz with vocabulary practice
Web Code: naa-3021

SECTION 2 Assessment

Terms, People, and Places

1. Place each of the key terms at the beginning of the section into one of the following categories: politics, culture, or the economy. Write a sentence for each term explaining your choice.

Note Taking

2. **Reading Skill: Categorize** Use your completed chart to answer the Focus Question: How did the United States, Western Europe, and Japan achieve economic prosperity and strengthen democracy during the Cold War years?

Comprehension and Critical Thinking

3. **Compare Points of View** How did Democrats and Republicans differ on the best ways to improve opportunity for Americans?

4. **Make Comparisons** How was the economic development of Western Europe during the Cold War years similar to or different from that of Japan?

5. **Make Generalizations** How was trade important to the economic development of Western Europe, the United States, and Japan during the postwar decades?

● **Writing About History**

Quick Write: Brainstorm Possible Solutions To write a problem-solution essay, you first need to brainstorm possible solutions to a problem you have defined. In this section, you learned that European welfare states offered social benefits but that these benefits were very costly. List possible solutions to this problem, and explain the advantages and disadvantages of each.

Chinese communist soldier marching into Beijing, 1949

The "little red book" of quotations from Mao Zedong

WITNESS HISTORY 🔊 AUDIO

Communist Victory in China

On September 21, 1949, at a rally in the Chinese capital, Beijing, the victorious communist leader Mao Zedong said:

66 We have closed our ranks and defeated both domestic and foreign oppressors through the People's War of Liberation and the great people's revolution, and now we are proclaiming the founding of the People's Republic of China. 99

Focus Question What did the communist victory mean for China and the rest of East Asia?

Communism Spreads in East Asia

 Performance Standards

• **SSWH19a** Analyze Mao Zedong, Chang Kai-shek and the revolutionary movement in China.

Terms, People, and Places

collectivization	Kim Il Sung
Great Leap Forward	Syngman Rhee
Cultural Revolution	Pusan Perimeter
38th parallel	demilitarized zone

Note Taking

Reading Skill: Summarize Complete this chart to summarize the effects of the Communist Revolution on China and the impact of the Cold War on China and Korea.

```
        Impact of Communism and
         the Cold War in East Asia

  Chinese        China in the      Korea in the
  Communist       Cold War          Cold War
  Revolution

    •                •                 •

    •                •                 •

    •                •                 •
```

In the late 1940s, communism made advances in East Asia. With their victory in China in 1949, the Communists gained control of one fifth of the world's people.

China's Communist Revolution

By the end of World War II, the Chinese Communists had gained control of much of northern China. After Japan's defeat, Communist forces led by Mao Zedong (Mao Tse-tung) fought a civil war against Nationalists headed by Jiang Jieshi (jahng jeh shur). Battles raged until Mao's forces swept to victory and set up the People's Republic of China. The defeated Nationalists fled to the island of Taiwan, off the Chinese coast. After decades of struggle, China was finally under Communist control.

How the Communists Won Mao's Communists triumphed for several reasons. Mao had won the support of China's huge peasant population. Peasants had long suffered from brutal landlords and crushing taxes. The Communists redistributed land to poor peasants and ended oppression by landlords.

While support for the Communists grew, the Nationalists lost popularity. Nationalist policies had led to widespread economic hardship. Many Chinese people also resented corruption in Jiang's government and the government's reliance on support from Western "imperialist" powers. They hoped that the Communists would build a new China and end foreign domination.

Widespread support for the Communists in the countryside helped them to capture rail lines and surround Nationalist-held cities. One after another, these cities fell, and Mao's People's Liberation Army

Mao Zedong

During the mid-1950s, divisions arose within the Communist Party in China. In response, Mao Zedong (1893–1976) launched a campaign under the slogan "Let a hundred flowers bloom, let a hundred thoughts contend." Mao hoped that by offering people the opportunity to openly express their views he would gain more support. When people began to criticize the Communist Party, however, Mao ended the campaign. Of the nearly 550,000 Chinese who had spoken out, thousands were executed and hundreds of thousands were exiled to the countryside to "rectify their thinking through labor." **What methods did Mao use to keep power for himself?**

Vocabulary Builder

communes—(KAHM yoonz) *n.* commonly owned and operated farms or communities

emerged victorious. After their victory against the Nationalists, the Communists conquered Tibet in 1950. In 1959, Tibet's most revered religious leader, the Dalai Lama, was forced to flee the country.

Changing Chinese Society

Mao Zedong built a Communist one-party totalitarian state in the People's Republic of China. Communist ideology guided the government's efforts to reshape the economy and society that China had inherited from the dynastic period. The Communist government discouraged the practice of Buddhism, Confucianism, and other traditional Chinese beliefs. Meanwhile, the government seized the property of rural landlords and urban business owners throughout China.

Opponents of the Communists were put down as "counterrevolutionaries." Many thousands of people who had belonged to the propertied middle class, or "bourgeoisie," were accused of counterrevolutionary beliefs. They were then beaten, sent to labor camps, or killed.

With Soviet help, the Chinese built dams and factories. To boost agriculture, Mao at first distributed land to peasants. Soon, however, he called for **collectivization,** or the forced pooling of peasant land and labor, in an attempt to increase productivity.

The Great Leap Forward Fails

From 1958 to 1960, Mao led a program known as the **Great Leap Forward.** He urged people to make a superhuman effort to increase farm and industrial output. In an attempt to make agriculture more efficient, he created communes. A typical commune brought together several villages, thousands of acres of land, and up to 25,000 people. Rural communes set up small-scale "backyard" industries to produce steel and other products.

The Great Leap Forward, however, proved to be a dismal failure. Backyard industries turned out low-quality, useless goods. The commune system cut food output partly by removing incentives for individual farmers and families, leading to neglect of farmland and food shortages. Bad weather added to the problems and led to a terrible famine. Between 1959 and 1961, as many as 55 million Chinese are thought to have starved to death.

The Cultural Revolution Disrupts Life

China slowly recovered from the Great Leap Forward by reducing the size of communes and taking a more practical approach to the economy. However, in 1966, Mao launched the Great Proletarian **Cultural Revolution.** Its goal was to purge China of "bourgeois" tendencies. He urged young Chinese to experience revolution firsthand, as his generation had.

In response, teenagers formed bands of Red Guards. Waving copies of the "little red book," *Quotations From Chairman Mao Tse-tung* [Zedong], Red Guards attacked those they considered bourgeois. The accused were publicly humiliated or beaten, and sometimes even killed. Skilled workers and managers were forced to leave their jobs and do manual labor on rural farms or in forced labor camps. Schools and factories closed. The economy slowed, and civil war threatened. Finally, Mao had the army restore order.

✓ **Checkpoint** What were the main successes and failures of the Chinese Communist Revolution?

China, the Cold War's "Wild Card"

In 1949, the triumph of the Communists in China had seemed like a gain for the Soviet Union and a loss for the United States and its democratic allies. The number of people under communist rule had more than tripled. China's role in the Cold War, however, proved to be more complex than a simple expansion of communist power.

Split With the Soviet Union The People's Republic of China and the Soviet Union were uneasy allies in the 1950s. Stalin sent economic aid and technical experts to help China modernize, but distrust between the two countries created tensions. Some of these tensions dated back to territorial disputes between tsarist Russia and dynastic China. By 1960, border clashes and disputes over ideology led the Soviets to withdraw all aid and advisors from China. Western fears of a strong alliance between the Soviet Union and China had proved unfounded.

Promoting the Cultural Revolution
The Cultural Revolution poster above shows soldiers holding "little red books" and urges them to "destroy all enemies." The photo to the left shows Chinese soldiers waving their "little red books" during this same period. *What do these images suggest about freedom of speech and freedom of thought during the Cultural Revolution in China?*

Washington Plays the China Card Relations between China and the United States were even more complex. After Jiang Jieshi (Chiang Kai-shek) fled to Taiwan, the United States supported his Nationalist government as the rightful representative of China. Washington refused diplomatic recognition of the mainland People's Republic of China, which American leaders saw as a communist threat to all of Asia.

As the Cold War dragged on, however, the United States took a second look at the People's Republic. From the American point of view, there were strategic advantages to improving relations with Communist China after its split with the Soviet Union. By "playing the China card," as this strategy was sometimes called, the United States might isolate the Soviets between NATO in the west and a hostile China in the east.

The United States allowed the People's Republic to replace Taiwan in the United Nations in 1971. A year later, U.S. President Richard Nixon visited Mao in Beijing. Finally, in 1979, the United States set up formal diplomatic relations with China.

Taiwan and the Nationalists Jiang Jieshi's government continued to rule Taiwan under martial law as a one-party dictatorship. Not until the late 1980s did Taiwan's government end martial law and allow opposition

The Korean War

North Korean control
Communist attack
South Korean control
UN attack
Line of control
Conic Projection
0   100 mi
0   100 km

▼ U.S. soldiers advance to fight North Koreans as South Korean civilians retreat from the front.

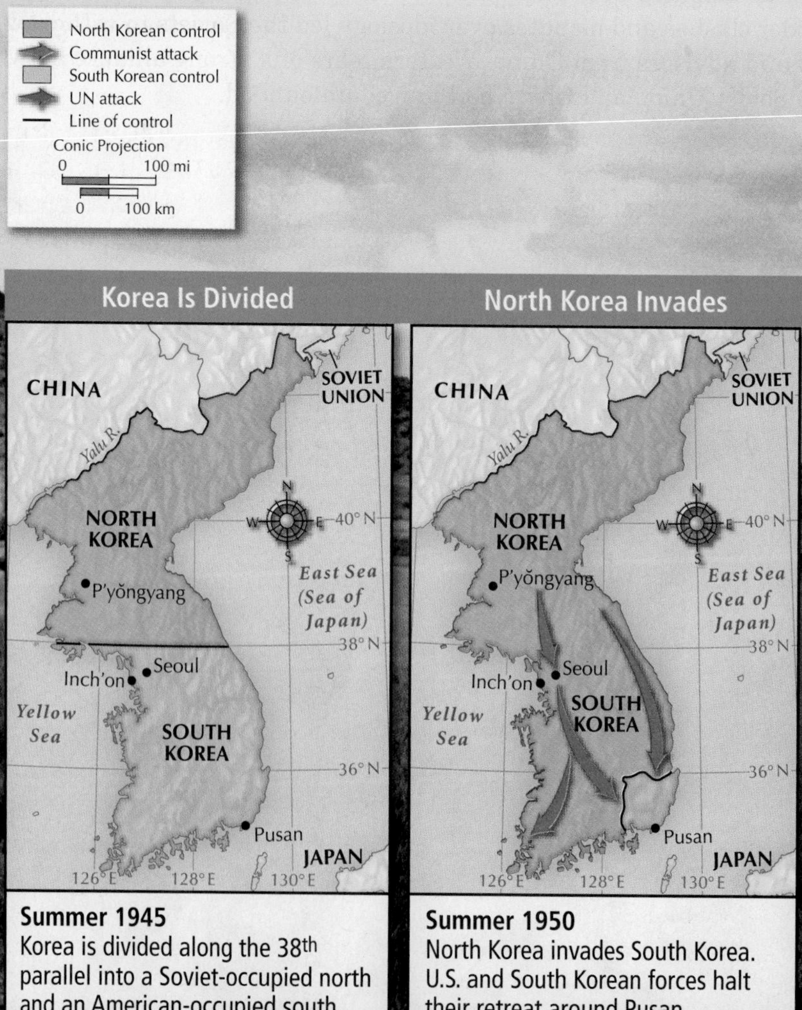

Korea Is Divided

CHINA
SOVIET UNION
Yalu R.
NORTH KOREA
•P'yŏngyang
East Sea (Sea of Japan)
40° N
Inch'on •Seoul
38° N
Yellow Sea
SOUTH KOREA
36° N
•Pusan
JAPAN
126° E   128° E   130° E

Summer 1945
Korea is divided along the 38th parallel into a Soviet-occupied north and an American-occupied south.

North Korea Invades

CHINA
SOVIET UNION
Yalu R.
NORTH KOREA
•P'yŏngyang
East Sea (Sea of Japan)
40° N
Inch'on •Seoul
SOUTH KOREA
38° N
Yellow Sea
36° N
•Pusan
JAPAN
126° E   128° E   130° E

Summer 1950
North Korea invades South Korea. U.S. and South Korean forces halt their retreat around Pusan.

parties. Mainland China saw Taiwan as a breakaway province and threatened military action when Taiwanese politicians proposed declaring the island's formal independence. In the long term, the mainland government insisted that Taiwan be rejoined with China. Taiwan's government resisted such pressure.

✔ **Checkpoint** How did China's relationships with the Soviet Union and the United States change during the Cold War?

War Comes to Korea

The nation of Korea occupies a peninsula on China's northeastern border. Like East and West Germany, Korea was split in two by rival forces after World War II. And like other divided lands, the two Koreas found themselves on opposite sides in the Cold War.

A Divided Nation Korea was an independent kingdom until Japan conquered it in the early twentieth century. After Japan's defeat in World War II, Soviet and American forces agreed to divide Korea temporarily along the 38th **parallel** of latitude. However, North Korea, ruled by the

Map Skills In June 1950, North Korea invaded South Korea. U.S. troops made up the bulk of the UN force that aided South Korea. When UN troops neared the Chinese border, communist China sent troops to aid North Korea.

1. **Locate** (a) the 38th parallel (b) Pusan (c) Inch'on (d) Yalu River
2. **Movement** Which nation gained new territory by the end of the war?
3. **Draw Conclusions** How might UN forces have avoided war with China?

Geography *Interactive*
For: Audio guided tour
Web Code: nap-3031

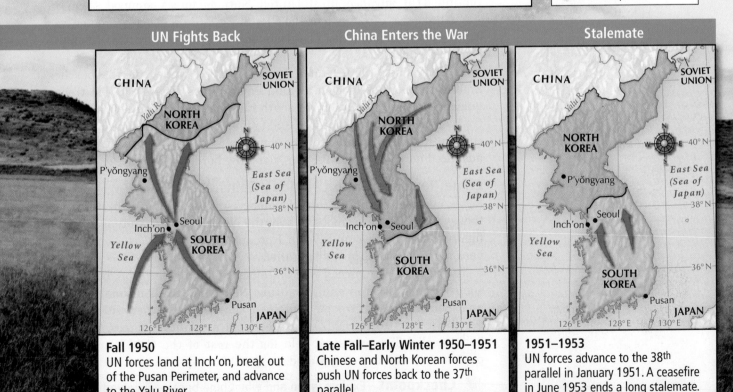

UN Fights Back

Fall 1950
UN forces land at Inch'on, break out of the Pusan Perimeter, and advance to the Yalu River.

China Enters the War

Late Fall–Early Winter 1950–1951
Chinese and North Korean forces push UN forces back to the 37th parallel.

Stalemate

1951–1953
UN forces advance to the 38th parallel in January 1951. A ceasefire in June 1953 ends a long stalemate.

Winter Battle Scene in Korea
U.S. soldiers rest after winning a battle for a snowy hill in Korea, February 1951. *Based on the photograph, what advantage did these soldiers gain by winning control of this hill?*

dictator **Kim Il Sung,** became a communist ally of the Soviet Union. In South Korea, the United States backed the dictatorial—but noncommunist—leader, **Syngman Rhee.**

North Korean Attack Brings a United Nations Response
Both leaders wanted to rule the entire country. In early 1950, Kim Il Sung called for a "heroic struggle" to reunite Korea. North Korean troops attacked in June of that year and soon overran most of the south. The United Nations Security Council condemned the invasion. The United States then organized a United Nations force to help South Korea.

United Nations forces were made up mostly of Americans and South Koreans. Although U.S. troops arrived in early July, North Korean troops continued to advance until United Nations forces stopped them in August along a line known as the **Pusan Perimeter.** This perimeter was centered on the port city of Pusan, in the southeastern corner of the Korean peninsula.

In September 1950, United Nations troops landed on the beaches around the port of Inch'on, behind enemy lines. These U.S.-led troops quickly captured Korea's north-south rail lines and cut off North Korean troops from their supply of food and ammunition. North Korean forces in the south soon surrendered. By November, United Nations forces had advanced north to the Yalu River, along the border of China.

China Reverses United Nations Gains
The success of the U.S.-led forces alarmed China. In late November, Mao Zedong sent hundreds of thousands of Chinese troops to help the North Koreans. In tough winter fighting, the Chinese and North Koreans forced United Nations troops back to the south of the 38th parallel.

The Korean War turned into a stalemate. Finally, in 1953, both sides signed an armistice, or end to fighting. Nearly two million North Korean and South Korean troops remained dug in on either side of the **demilitarized zone** (DMZ), an area with no military forces, near the 38th parallel. The armistice held for the rest of the Cold War, but no peace treaty was ever negotiated.

✔ **Checkpoint** Explain when and why China became involved in the Korean War.

Two Koreas

Like the two Germanys, North and South Korea developed separately after the armistice—North Korea as a communist command economy, South Korea as a capitalist market economy. As in Germany, the capitalist portion of the country had an economic boom and rising standards of living, while the communist zone went through economic stagnation and decline. Also as in Germany, the United States gave economic and military aid to capitalist South Korea, while the Soviets helped the communist north.

Unlike democratic West Germany, however, South Korea was governed by a series of dictators and military rulers during much of the Cold War. Unlike East Germany, where a series of officials led the communist government, a single dictator controlled North Korea throughout the Cold War. Whereas Germany was reunited at the end of the Cold War, Korea remained divided.

South Korea Recovers After the war, South Korea slowly rebuilt its economy. By the mid-1960s, South Korea's economy had leapt ahead. After decades of dictatorship and military rule, a prosperous middle class and fierce student protests pushed the government to hold direct elections in 1987. These elections began a successful transition to democracy. Despite the bloody Korean War, most South Koreans during the Cold War years wanted to see their ancient nation reunited, as did many North Koreans. All Koreans shared the same history, language, and traditions. For many, this meant more than Cold War differences.

North Korea Digs In Under Kim Il Sung, the command economy increased output for a time in North Korea. However, in the late 1960s, economic growth slowed. Kim's emphasis on self-reliance kept North Korea isolated and poor. The government built a personality cult around Kim, who was constantly glorified as the "Great Leader" in propaganda. Even after its Soviet and Chinese allies undertook economic reforms in the 1980s, North Korea clung to hard-line communism.

 Checkpoint How did North Korea's economic performance compare to South Korea's?

SECTION 3 Assessment

Progress Monitoring *Online*
For: Self-quiz with vocabulary practice
Web Code: naa-3031

Terms, People, and Places

1. For each term, person, or place listed at the beginning of the section, write a sentence explaining its significance.

Note Taking

2. **Reading Skill: Summarize** Use your completed chart to answer the Focus Question: What did the communist victory mean for China and the rest of East Asia?

Comprehension and Critical Thinking

3. **Recognize Ideologies** What ideologies did Mao's programs to transform China reflect?

4. **Draw Inferences** How did the United States use the changing relationship between China and the Soviet Union to its own advantage?

5. **Predict Consequences** How might the history of Korea have been different if United Nations forces had not stepped in to oppose the North Korean invasion in 1950?

● Writing About History

Quick Write: Write a Thesis Statement
To write a problem-solution essay, you need to choose the best solution to a problem. In this section, you learned that both North and South Koreans wanted to reunify their country, but that Cold War differences got in the way. List possible solutions to Korea's Cold War division and write a thesis statement arguing for the best solution.

U.S. military helicopter in Vietnam

A family watches President Kennedy speak on television.

America's Role in Vietnam

In a television interview on September 2, 1963, U.S. President John F. Kennedy referred to U.S. support for the noncommunist government of South Vietnam. He did not foresee that five years later, more than 500,000 Americans would be fighting a bloody and divisive war there.

❝ I don't think that unless a greater effort is made by the Government to win popular support that the war can be won out there. . . . We can help them, we can give them equipment, we can send our men out there as advisors, but they have to win it, the people of Viet-nam, against the Communists.**❞**

Focus Question What were the causes and effects of war in Southeast Asia, and what was the American role in this region?

War in Southeast Asia

Performance Standards

• **SSWHRC1c** Demonstrate understanding of contextual vocabulary.

Terms, People, and Places

guerrillas
Ho Chi Minh
Dienbienphu
domino theory

Viet Cong
Tet Offensive
Khmer Rouge
Pol Pot

Note Taking

Reading Skill: Summarize Complete a chart like the one below to summarize the events connected to the wars in Southeast Asia.

War in Southeast Asia		
Indochina After World War II	Vietnam War	Aftereffects of War
•	•	•

Southeast Asia's wars were, for many local participants, nationalist struggles against foreign domination. Like Korea, however, Southeast Asia eventually played a part in the global Cold War.

Indochina After World War II

In mainland Southeast Asia after World War II, an agonizing liberation struggle tore apart the region once known as French Indochina. The nearly 30-year conflict had two major phases. First was the war against the French, dating from 1946 to 1954. Second was the Cold War conflict that involved the United States and raged from 1955 to 1975.

Indochina Under Foreign Rule The eastern part of mainland Southeast Asia, or Indochina, was conquered by the French during the 1800s. The Japanese overran Indochina during World War II, but faced fierce resistance, especially in Vietnam, from local **guerrillas** (guh RIL uz), or small groups of loosely organized soldiers making surprise raids. The guerrillas, determined to be free of all foreign rule, turned their guns on the European colonialists who returned after the war. The guerrillas were strongly influenced by communist opposition to European colonial powers.

Ho Chi Minh Fights the French After the Japanese were defeated, the French set out in 1946 to re-establish their authority in Indochina. In Vietnam, they faced guerrilla forces led by

Ho Chi Minh (hoh chee min). Ho was a nationalist and communist who had fought the Japanese. He then fought the French in what is known as the First Indochina War. An unexpected Vietnamese victory at the bloody battle of **Dienbienphu** (dyen byen foo) in 1954 convinced the French to leave Vietnam. Cambodia and Laos had meanwhile gained their independence separately.

Vietnam Is Divided After 1954, however, the struggle for Vietnam became part of the Cold War. At an international conference that year, Western and communist powers agreed to a temporary division of Vietnam. Ho's communists controlled North Vietnam. A noncommunist government led by Ngo Dinh Diem (ngoh din dee EM), supported by the United States, ruled South Vietnam. The agreement called for elections to reunite the two Vietnams. These elections were never held, largely because the Americans and Ngo Dinh Diem feared that the Communists would win.

Some South Vietnamese preferred Ho Chi Minh, a national hero, to the South Vietnamese government backed by the United States, a foreign power. But Ho's communist rule in the North alienated some Vietnamese. Many Catholic and pro-French Vietnamese fled to the south.

The United States supported Ngo Dinh Diem's regime against what American leaders saw as the communist threat from North Vietnam. Meanwhile, Ngo Dinh Diem's dictatorial regime alienated many Vietnamese with its corruption and brutal tactics against political opponents.

By the early 1960s, communist guerrilla fighters had appeared in the jungles of South Vietnam. Many of them were South Vietnamese, but they received strong support from the north. Many saw their fight as a nationalist struggle to liberate Vietnam from foreign domination.

✓ **Checkpoint** Why did Vietnamese guerrillas fight the French in Indochina?

BIOGRAPHY

Ho Chi Minh

Ho Chi Minh (1890–1969) was born in central Vietnam at a time when Vietnam was under French colonial control. Ho discovered communism while working abroad and quickly adapted it to his struggle against French rule back in Vietnam. While Soviet communism gave a leading role to urban workers, Ho saw rural peasants as the driving force behind a successful revolution. Ho was more interested in national liberation than following a Soviet communist model. As president of North Vietnam, he led his people first against French control and later against the U.S-backed South Vietnamese government. **How did Ho Chi Minh's approach to communism differ from the Soviet model?**

America Enters the Vietnam War

American foreign policy planners saw the situation in Vietnam as part of the global Cold War. They developed the **domino theory**—the view that a communist victory in South Vietnam would cause noncommunist governments across Southeast Asia to fall to communism, like a row of dominoes. America's leaders wanted to prevent this from happening.

The War Intensifies Ho Chi Minh remained determined to unite Vietnam under communist rule. He continued to aid the National Liberation Front, or **Viet Cong,** the communist rebels trying to overthrow South Vietnam's government. At first, the United States sent only supplies and military advisors to South Vietnam. Later, it sent thousands of troops, turning a local struggle into a major Cold War conflict.

THE VIETNAM WAR

The Vietnam War thrust American soldiers into an alien and dangerous environment of jungles and swamps. The Viet Cong guerrillas were often local villagers, so it was hard for American soldiers to tell friend from foe. Local guerrillas' knowledge of the land allowed them to hide behind vegetation or behind the earthen banks of canals before a surprise ambush. The map at the right shows how North Vietnam delivered supplies to the Viet Cong in South Vietnam along the Ho Chi Minh Trail. These supply lines and the Viet Cong's knowledge of the land made the Viet Cong a deadly foe, even against the better-equipped American forces.

 AUDIO

Viet Cong guerrillas train in a ditch for combat against American soldiers.

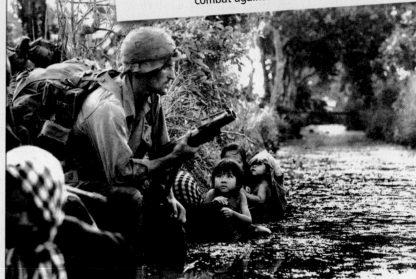
An American soldier sits on the bank of a canal during a skirmish with Viet Cong snipers. Vietnamese children are clinging to their mothers nearby, trying to stay low to avoid gunfire.

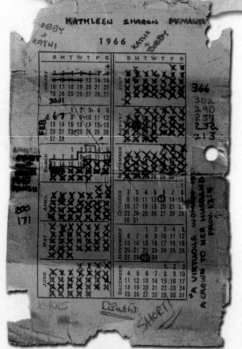
▲ This 1966 calendar may have belonged to one of the 58,000 American soldiers killed in the Vietnam War. It was left at the Vietnam Veterans Memorial in Washington, D.C., by a visitor.

On August 1, 1964, South Vietnamese commandos conducted raids on North Vietnamese islands in the Gulf of Tonkin. The following day, the North Vietnamese attacked a nearby U.S. Navy destroyer, the *Maddox,* which they mistakenly believed had assisted the South Vietnamese raids. Three days later, sailors on the *Maddox* thought that they had been attacked a second time, although it seems likely that their sonar and radar equipment were malfunctioning due to heavy seas.

U.S. President Johnson reported the attacks to Congress without mentioning the South Vietnamese raids or the doubts about the second attack. Believing that the attacks had been unprovoked, Congress passed the Gulf of Tonkin Resolution on August 7, 1964. The resolution authorized the President to take all necessary measures to prevent further aggression in Southeast Asia.

After the resolution passed, the United States began bombing targets in North Vietnam. Eventually, more than 500,000 American troops were committed to the war. At the same time, both the Soviet Union and China sent aid—but no troops—to help North Vietnam.

The Vietnam War, 1968–1975

Legend:
- Tet Offensive, 1968
- North Vietnam's final offensive, 1975
- Ho Chi Minh Trail
- American bases

Miller Projection

▲ This American soldier is patrolling a swamp in the Mekong Delta in the summer of 1969.

Thinking Critically

1. **Map Skills** Based on the map and the accompanying text, why might the United States have wanted to attack targets in Cambodia?
2. **Draw Conclusions** How did Vietnam's geography and landscape create disadvantages for U.S. forces?

During the Vietnam era, young American men were required to register for the military draft. Men were then selected for the draft in a random lottery. Many saw fighting for their country as their patriotic duty. However, to avoid being drafted, some military-age American men left the country and sought refuge in other nations not involved in the war.

Guerrilla War Like the French in Vietnam, America faced a guerrilla war. The rebels in South Vietnam tended to be local peasants. They thus knew the countryside much better than their American enemies. They also knew the local people. Villagers frequently offered them safe haven against foreign troops. The close connections between guerrilla fighters and the villagers turned the Vietnamese villages themselves into military targets. Supplies for the guerrillas came from the north, following trails that wound through the jungles of neighboring Cambodia and Laos. In response, American aircraft and ground troops crossed the borders of these nations, drawing them into the war.

The Tet Offensive Despite massive American support, South Vietnam failed to defeat the communist guerrillas and their North Vietnamese allies. In 1968, guerrilla forces came out of the jungles and attacked American and South Vietnamese forces in cities all across the south. The assault was unexpected because it took place during Tet, the Vietnamese New Year. The communists lost many of their best troops and did not hold any cities against American counterattacks. Nevertheless, the bloody **Tet Offensive** marked a turning point in public opinion in the United States.

✔ **Checkpoint** How did the domino theory lead the United States to send troops to Vietnam?

The Vietnam War Ends

As the fighting continued, civilian deaths caused by the bombing of North Vietnam and growing American casualties inflamed antiwar opinion in the United States. Growing numbers of American troops were prisoners of war (POWs) or missing in action (MIAs). Some Americans began to think that the Vietnam War was a quagmire, or swamp, in which the United States was becoming more and more bogged down.

More Americans Oppose the War As the war continued, the nation became deeply and bitterly divided over the ongoing struggle. Many Americans of all ages continued to support the war effort in Vietnam. Others wanted to end the loss of lives. More and more young people turned out for massive street demonstrations, all part of a growing anti-war movement. It was clear that an increasing number of Americans wanted no more "body bags" coming back or television footage of burned Vietnamese villages. At the same time, many agreed with a housewife who said, "I want to get out, but I don't want to give up."

America Withdraws In the end, American leaders decided that they had to get out of Vietnam. Faced with conflict at home and abroad, President Lyndon Johnson, who had presided over the massive expansion of the war in the 1960s, decided not to run for a second term. Johnson also opened peace talks with North Vietnam in Paris.

Although American troops had seldom lost a battle in the long struggle, they had not destroyed the Vietnamese Communists' determination to keep fighting. Johnson's successor, President Nixon, came under increasing pressure to <u>terminate</u> American involvement. Nixon finally negotiated the Paris Peace Accord in January 1973. This agreement established a cease-fire, or a halt in fighting. The United States agreed to withdraw its troops, and North Vietnam agreed not to send any more troops into the South. The accord left South Vietnam to determine its own future and set a goal of peaceful reunification with the North.

North Vietnam Wins the War Two years after American troops had withdrawn from the country, the North Vietnamese conquered South Vietnam. The South Vietnamese capital, Saigon, was renamed Ho Chi Minh City in 1976 in honor of the late leader. The North Vietnamese capital, Hanoi, became the capital of the reunited nation.

✔ **Checkpoint** Why did the United States withdraw its troops from Vietnam?

Southeast Asia After the War

After the American withdrawal from Vietnam, some dominos did fall. Both Cambodia and Laos ended up with governments dominated by Communist Vietnam. However, the falling dominos stopped at the

Peace Necklace
The peace sign on this necklace was a popular symbol of protest against the Vietnam War.

Vocabulary Builder
<u>terminate</u>—(TUR mih nayt) *vt.* finish, bring to an end

former borders of French Indochina. Other parts of Southeast Asia remained thoroughly capitalist, if less than democratic.

Tragedy in Cambodia During the Vietnam War, fighting had spilled over into neighboring Cambodia. In 1970, the United States bombed North Vietnamese supply routes in Cambodia and then briefly invaded the country. Afterwards, the **Khmer Rouge** (kuh MEHR roozh), a force of Cambodian communist guerrillas, gained ground in Cambodia. Finally, in 1975, the Khmer Rouge overthrew the Cambodian government.

Led by the brutal dictator **Pol Pot,** the Khmer Rouge unleashed a reign of terror. To destroy all Western influences, they drove people from the cities and forced them to work in the fields. They slaughtered, starved, or worked to death more than a million Cambodians, about a third of the population.

In the end, it took a Vietnamese invasion to drive Pol Pot and his Khmer Rouge back into the jungle. Vietnam imposed an authoritarian government on Cambodia, but they at least ended the genocide.

Vietnam Under the Communists In the newly reunited Vietnam, the communist victors imposed a harsh rule of their own on the south. Hundreds of thousands of Vietnamese fled their country, most in small boats. Many of these "boat people" drowned. Survivors landed in refugee camps in neighboring countries. Eventually, some settled in the United States. Meanwhile, Vietnam had to rebuild a land destroyed by war. Recovery was slow due to a lack of resources and an American-led embargo, or blockage of trade. For years, the country remained mired in poverty.

✔ **Checkpoint** How did communist Vietnam dominate parts of Southeast Asia after the Vietnam War?

Fleeing Communist Control
These South Vietnamese refugees are fleeing their country after communist forces took control in April 1975. Refugees who fled in small boats like this one were known as "boat people." *Why might people choose to flee across the open ocean in a small boat like this one?*

SECTION 4 **Assessment**

Progress Monitoring Online
For: Self-quiz with vocabulary practice
Web Code: naa-3041

Terms, People, and Places

1. For each term, person, or place listed at the beginning of the section, write a sentence explaining its significance.

Note Taking

2. **Reading Skill: Summarize** Use your completed chart to answer the Focus Question: What were the causes and effects of war in Southeast Asia, and what was the American role in this region?

Comprehension and Critical Thinking

3. **Draw Conclusions** Why did the French withdraw from Indochina in the 1950s?

4. **Summarize** How did a local struggle in Vietnam become a major Cold War conflict?

5. **Compare Points of View** What different opinions did Americans have about U.S. involvement in the Vietnam War?

6. **Synthesize Information** When the text states that "dominos fell" after the Vietnam War, what does this mean?

● **Writing About History**

Quick Write: Write a Supporting Paragraph To write a problem-solution essay, you need to provide arguments to support a proposed solution to a problem. In this section, an American was quoted as wanting to "get out" of South Vietnam without giving up on it. Write a thesis statement proposing a way to do this. Based on the text or your own ideas, write a paragraph with arguments supporting your thesis statement.

THE FALL OF THE SOVIET UNION

Soviet president Mikhail Gorbachev was due to sign a treaty that would reduce the power of the Soviet government. On August 18, 1991, two days before the signing, a committee of Communist hardliners detained Gorbachev at his summer home. The next day, the committee announced to the nation that Gorbachev had resigned and that they were taking control of the government. The committee sent columns of tanks and troops to take control of the capital, Moscow. (See photo at the right.) However, Boris Yeltsin, the president of Russia, the largest Soviet republic, defied the hardliners. Yeltsin called on thousands of Russians to resist the unlawful takeover. Finally, on August 21, the hardliners gave up their takeover and ordered Soviet troops to retreat from Moscow. Yeltsin's defeat of the hardliners led a few months later to the breakup of the Soviet Union.

◀ Soviet president Mikhail Gorbachev

Soviet Union, 1991

998

History *Interactive*

For: Interactive timeline, audio, and more
Visit: www.PHSchool.com
Web Code: nap-3041

▲ Russian president Boris Yeltsin, holding a sheet of paper at left, stands atop a Soviet tank on August 19, 1991, and calls on Russians to resist the attempted takeover of the Soviet Union by hardliners. Behind him, a supporter holds a Russian flag. Yeltsin's success in defying the takeover broke the power of the central Soviet government and led to the independence of Russia and the other Soviet republics.

◄ Stanislav Shushkevich (left), president of Belarus; Boris Yeltsin (center), president of Russia; and Leonid Kravchuk (right), president of Ukraine, agreed on December 8, 1991, to dissolve the Soviet Union, effective at the end of 1991.

Thinking Critically
1. **Analyze Images** Why is it significant that Russian President Yeltsin is standing on top of a Soviet tank in the photo at the top of the page?
2. **Synthesize Information** How did the events of August 1991 cause the Soviet government to lose power to Russia?
3. **Map Skills** Based on the maps, why would Russia's wish for independence lead to the Soviet Union's breakup?

Independent Republics, 1992

Arctic Ocean

Baltic Sea

EUROPE
LITHUANIA
ESTONIA
LATVIA
BELARUS
MOLDOVA
UKRAINE
GEORGIA
Black Sea
ARMENIA
Caspian Sea
KAZAKHSTAN
AZERBAIJAN
TURKMENISTAN
UZBEKISTAN
KYRGYZSTAN
TAJIKISTAN

RUSSIA

ASIA

Pacific Ocean

Conic Projection
0   500   1000 mi
0 500 1000 km

Demonstrators
in East Berlin,
November 4, 1989

Soviet pin promoting
"openness, democracy,
and restructuring"

WITNESS HISTORY 🔊 AUDIO

A Democratic Transformation

On November 4, 1989, hundreds of thousands of people demonstrated for democracy in the streets of East Berlin. Never before had so many dared to speak out. Speaking to the crowd, author Stefan Heym captured the mood:

66 Dear friends, fellow citizens, it is as if someone had thrown open the window after all the years of stagnation. . . . What a transformation! 99

Ultimately, the transformation in Eastern Europe led to the end of the Cold War.

Focus Question What were the causes and effects of the end of the Cold War?

The End of the Cold War

 Performance Standards

- **SSWH19d** Compare and contrast the reforms of Khrushchev and Gorbachev.
- **SSWH20b** Describe the breakup of the USSR that made Ukraine, Kazakhstan, and the Baltic States independent.

Terms, People, and Places

mujahedin	Lech Walesa
Mikhail Gorbachev	Solidarity
glasnost	Václav Havel
perestroika	Nicolae Ceausescu

Note Taking

Reading Skill: Categorize Complete a flowchart like the one below to categorize each event connected to the end of the Cold War.

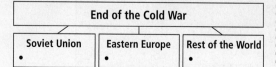

End of the Cold War		
Soviet Union	Eastern Europe	Rest of the World
•	•	•

The global Cold War between two armed camps led by the United States and the Soviet Union lasted almost half a century. In the years around 1990, however, the struggle finally ended. The much-feared nuclear confrontation between the two superpowers never came about, but the end was as clear as any military victory.

The Soviet Union Declines

Western fears of growing Soviet power did not come true. In fact, Soviet communism was doomed. Signs of the weakness of the Soviet system had in fact been visible from the beginning.

A Hollow Victory Stalin's Soviet Union emerged from World War II as a superpower with an Eastern European sphere of influence stretching from the Baltic to the Balkans. Victory, however, brought few rewards to the Soviet people. Stalin continued to fill forced labor camps with "enemies of the state."

Reforms Give Way to Repression Under Stalin's successor, Nikita Khrushchev, Soviets enjoyed greater freedom of speech. Some government critics were freed from prisons and labor camps. Khrushchev oversaw a shift in economic priorities away from heavy industry and toward the production of consumer goods. But Khrushchev remained firmly committed to a command economy.

The thaw in Moscow inspired some East Europeans to move toward greater independence. However, Khrushchev himself remained a determined cold warrior. When Hungarians tried to break free of Soviet control in 1956, Khrushchev sent tanks in to enforce obedience, and his successor, Leonid Brezhnev, did the same thing when Czechs challenged the Soviets in the "Prague spring" of 1968.

The Command Economy Stagnates

The Soviet Union rebuilt its shattered industries after World War II, using equipment stripped from Germany. The government poured resources into science and technology, launching *Sputnik I,* the first artificial satellite, in 1957.

Yet the Soviet economy faced severe problems. Collectivized agriculture remained so unproductive that Russia, a grain exporter in tsarist times, had to import grain to feed its people. The Soviet command economy could not match Western market economies in producing consumer goods. Soviet shoes and television sets were far inferior, while such luxuries as clothes washers or automobiles remained rare.

Central economic planning led to inefficiency and waste. A huge bureaucracy decided what and how much to produce. Government planners in Moscow, however, knew little about local needs. They chose to produce many unneeded goods. Consumers' needs often were not met. Although workers were paid low wages, lifetime job security gave them little <u>incentive</u> to produce better-quality goods.

Unlike the economies of Western Europe and the United States, which experienced booms during the Cold War, the economies of Eastern Europe and the Soviet Union stagnated. People saw little improvement in their standards of living and envied the prosperity of the West. Soviet economic inferiority made it impossible for the Soviet Union to keep up with the United States in the arms race and in military preparedness.

Cracking Under the Burden of Military Commitments

As you have read, Soviet-American relations swung between confrontation and détente during the Cold War. Meanwhile, both sides maintained large military budgets and built expensive nuclear weapons.

Vocabulary Builder

<u>incentive</u>—(in SEN tiv) *n.* something that encourages a person to take action or work harder

Soviet Tanks Bring Repression

A boy watches Soviet tanks in the Hungarian capital, Budapest, in 1956. The Soviet Union sent tanks to stop Hungary's attempt to take an independent course. *What does this suggest about the independence of Eastern European countries such as Hungary during the Cold War?*

The arms race put a particular strain on the inefficient Soviet command economy. And when U.S. President Ronald Reagan launched a new round of missile development, it was clear that the Soviet economy could not afford to match it.

Soviets Have Their Own "Vietnam" in Afghanistan In 1979, the Soviet Union became involved in a long war in Afghanistan, an Islamic country just south of the Soviet Union. A Soviet-supported Afghan government had tried to modernize the nation. Its policies included social reforms and land redistribution that would reduce the power of regional landlords. Afghan landlords—who commanded armed men as warlords—and Muslim conservatives charged that both policies threatened Islamic tradition. When these warlords took up arms against the government, Soviet troops moved in.

Battling **mujahedin** (moo jah heh DEEN), or Muslim religious warriors, in the mountains of Afghanistan, however, proved as difficult as fighting guerrillas in the jungles of Vietnam had been for Americans. By the mid-1980s, the American government began to smuggle modern weaponry to the mujahedin. The Soviets had years of heavy casualties, high costs, and few successes. Like America's Vietnam War, the struggle in Afghanistan provoked a crisis in morale for the Soviets at home.

Gorbachev Tries Reform In 1985, an energetic new leader, **Mikhail Gorbachev** (GAWR buh chawf), came to power in the Soviet Union. With the economy in bad shape and the war dragging on in Afghanistan, Gorbachev was eager to bring about reforms. The changes he urged, however, soon spiraled out of control.

Gorbachev sought to avoid Cold-War confrontations. He signed arms control treaties with the United States and pulled Soviet troops out of Afghanistan.

At home, he called for **glasnost,** or openness. He ended censorship and encouraged people to discuss the country's problems openly. He also urged **perestroika** (pehr uh STROY kuh), or restructuring, of the government and economy. To improve efficiency, he reduced the size of the bureaucracy and backed limited private enterprise. His reforms made factory managers rather than central planners responsible for decisions. They also allowed farmers to sell produce on the free market.

Analyzing Political Cartoons

The Crumbling Soviet Union This cartoon shows Soviet leader Mikhail Gorbachev with an egg-shaped head sitting on a wall marked with the national symbol of the Soviet Union. The cartoon draws on the nursery rhyme *Humpty Dumpty.*

1. What does the cartoon suggest about the state of the Soviet Union under Gorbachev?
2. What does it imply about Gorbachev's future?
3. How does this cartoon communicate ideas without using any words?

An Empire Crumbles Gorbachev's reforms, however, brought economic turmoil. Shortages grew worse and prices soared. Factories that could not survive without government help closed, leading to high unemployment. Those whose jobs were threatened denounced the reforms. Other critics demanded even more radical changes.

Gorbachev's policies also fed unrest across the Soviet empire. Eastern European countries from Poland to Bulgaria broke out of the Soviet orbit beginning in 1989. The Baltic States—Estonia, Latvia, and Lithuania—which the Soviet Union had seized in 1940, regained full independence in 1991. Russia's postwar empire seemed to many to be collapsing. Soviet hard-liners tried to overthrow Gorbachev that year and restore the old order. Their attempted coup failed, but it further weakened Gorbachev, who soon resigned as president.

At the end of 1991, the remaining Soviet republics separated to form 12 independent nations, in addition to the three Baltic States. The largest of these was Russia, which had most of the population and territory of the former Soviet Union. The next largest were Kazakhstan and Ukraine. Maps of Europe and Asia had to be redrawn to reflect the new political boundaries. After 69 years, the Soviet Union had ceased to exist.

✔ **Checkpoint** How did Gorbachev's policies lead to a new map of Europe and Asia?

Defending Lithuania's Independence
This woman, holding a Lithuanian flag, is guarding Lithuania's parliament building and TV tower from Soviet troops that tried and failed to regain control after Lithuania declared independence in January 1991.

Changes Transform Eastern Europe

The Soviet Union had maintained control over its Eastern European satellites by force. When Gorbachev introduced glasnost and perestroika in the Soviet Union, Eastern Europeans began to seek greater freedom in their own countries. As the Soviet Union crumbled, Eastern Europeans demanded an end to Soviet domination. This time they got it.

Demands for Freedom Increase As you have read, unrest had long simmered across the Soviet bloc. Many Eastern Europeans opposed communist rule. Nationalists resented Russian domination. Revolts had erupted in Poland, Hungary, Czechoslovakia, and elsewhere in the 1950s and 1960s. In the 1980s, demands for change mounted once again.

Hungary Quietly Reforms In 1968, when Czechoslovakia's defiance of Soviet control led to a Soviet invasion, Hungary quietly introduced modest economic reforms. Because Hungary remained loyal to the Warsaw Pact and maintained communist political control, it was allowed to go ahead with these reforms, which included elements of a market economy. During the 1970s, Hungary expanded its market economy. During the late 1980s, under the spirit of glasnost, Hungarians began to criticize the communist government more openly. Economic troubles led to greater discontent. Finally, in 1988 and 1989, under public pressure, the communist government allowed greater freedoms. New political parties were allowed to form, and the western border with Austria was opened.

Poland Embraces Solidarity Poland led the way in the new surge of resistance that shattered the Soviet satellite empire. In 1980, economic hardships ignited strikes by shipyard workers. Led by **Lech Walesa** (lek vah WEN suh), they organized **Solidarity,** an independent labor union. It won millions of members and demanded political as well as economic change.

Lech Walesa and Solidarity
Lech Walesa, at the left, speaks at a shipyard workers' strike in August 1980. The following month, he helped found the Polish national union known as Solidarity (Solidarnosc in Polish). At the right, Poles defy the government by holding a banner for the outlawed Solidarity union in 1983. *Why would a communist government ban a labor union?*

Under pressure from the Soviet Union, the Polish government outlawed the union and arrested its leaders, including Walesa. Still, unrest continued. Walesa became a national hero, and the Polish government eventually released him from prison. Pope John Paul II visited Poland, met with Solidarity leaders, and criticized communist policies. The pope was the former Karol Wojtyla, archbishop of the Polish city of Cracow.

East Germans Demand Change Unlike Poland or Hungary, East Germany resisted Gorbachev's calls for change. In 1988, the rigidly communist East German government banned Soviet publications, because it considered glasnost subversive. East Germany's communists blocked moves toward a market economy or greater political freedom. However, East Germans could watch television broadcasts from West Germany. They were thus intensely aware how much more prosperity and political freedom existed on the other side of the Berlin Wall. When Hungary opened its border with Austria in 1989, thousands of East Germans fled through Hungary and Austria to West Germany. Thousands more held demonstrations across East Germany demanding change.

Communist Governments Fall In the late 1980s, Gorbachev declared that he would not interfere with Eastern European reforms. Poland legalized Solidarity and, in 1989, held the first free elections in 50 years. A year later, Lech Walesa was elected president of Poland. The new government began a difficult, but peaceful, transition from a command economy to a market economy.

A flowering of opposition and reform movements spread across the Eastern European countries. By late 1989, a powerful democracy movement was sweeping throughout the region. Everywhere, people took to the streets, demanding reform. One by one, communist governments fell. In Czechoslovakia, **Václav Havel** (VAHTS lahv HAH vul), a dissident writer and human rights activist, was elected president. In East Germany, the gates of the Berlin Wall were opened, and the country started down the road to reunification with West Germany. Most changes came peacefully, but when **Nicolae Ceausescu** (chow SHES koo), Romania's longtime dictator, refused to step down, he was overthrown and executed.

For the first time since 1939, Eastern European countries were free. They dissolved the Warsaw Pact in 1991 and requested that Russian troops leave. By then, the Soviet Union itself had crumbled.

Czechoslovakia Splits Czechoslovakia was a relatively new nation, formed in 1918 at the breakup of the Austro-Hungarian Empire. Before 1918, the country's Czech and Slovak ethnic groups—each with its own language and traditions—had lived separately. After Czechoslovakia's founding, Czechs dominated the country's government. During World War II, Czechoslovakia was conquered and partitioned, or divided, by Nazi Germany. Czechoslovakia was reunified under communist control after the war. When the communists lost power in 1989, some Slovaks began to call for independence. In 1992, the Slovaks and Czechs peacefully agreed to divide Czechoslovakia into the new nations of Slovakia and the Czech Republic.

✔ **Checkpoint** How did glasnost in the Soviet Union lead to the end of communism in Eastern Europe?

Communism Declines Around the World

The collapse of communism in the Soviet bloc affected communist countries from China to Castro's Cuba. Many were already suffering economic decline by the 1980s as their command economies stagnated. Although political dictatorships still prevailed, rigid, government-run economies sometimes gave way to freer, more productive economic systems.

China Builds on Deng's Reforms Gorbachev had urged the leaders of other communist states to consider both political and economic changes. China's leaders, building on Deng Xiaoping's 1980s economic reforms, generated an amazing economic boom in the 1990s. China became a major producer of consumer goods and achieved double-digit growth rates.

China's government undertook no major political reforms. However, as the global economic crisis that began in 2008 led to factory closings, protests by unemployed workers increased. China's government responded with a $600 billion stimulus package to retrain workers and improve productivity.

Vietnam and North Korea Differ Communist Vietnam established diplomatic relations with the United States in the 1990s. Vietnam also began to change economically, encouraging tourism and becoming a leading exporter of coffee.

North Korea, on the other hand, hunkered down in grim isolation, rejecting all reforms. Its rigidly totalitarian regime often proved unable to feed its own

Capitalism Comes to China
Chinese consumers shop for mobile phones in this recent photo. *Do the activities in this photo reflect a command economy or a market economy? Explain why.*

people, leading to hundreds of thousands of deaths. A 2007 agreement to dismantle its nuclear weapons program in exchange for U.S. aid seemed to founder as the decade drew to a close.

Cuba Declines Cuba's economy, deprived of Soviet support and still crippled by American sanctions, deteriorated. Many felt that communism in Cuba would not outlive its leader, Fidel Castro. In 2006, the ailing Castro surrendered control of the government to his younger brother Raúl, who allowed some market reforms.

 Checkpoint How did communist countries react differently to the collapse of the Soviet bloc?

The United States as Sole Superpower

With the collapse of its great rival, the United States was widely recognized as the only remaining superpower. After years of thin budgets, Russia's armed forces seemed weak and ineffective. Only the United States could project its power around the world.

The United States thus emerged as the world's leading military power. From time to time, the United States exercised this power. Beginning in the 1990s, the United States staged several military missions around the world. You will learn more about these in upcoming chapters.

Americans seemed unsure of their proper role in the world. Some objected to the risk and expense of being "the world's policeman." Others, however, believed that the United States should play an even more aggressive part in world affairs.

America's unrivaled power produced mixed reactions around the world. When the Soviet threat had loomed, American power had been seen as a valuable counterweight. Some continued to see the United States as a protector of freedom. With no rival threat in sight, however, people in many parts of the world were less pleased to see any single nation as powerful as the United States had become.

 Checkpoint Why did America's position as the sole superpower produce mixed reactions?

Progress Monitoring *Online*
For: Self-quiz with vocabulary practice
Web Code: naa-3051

SECTION 5 Assessment

Terms, People, and Places

1. For each term, person, or place listed at the beginning of the section, write a sentence explaining its significance.

Note Taking

2. **Reading Skill: Categorize** Use your completed chart to answer the Focus Question: What were the causes and effects of the end of the Cold War?

Comprehension and Critical Thinking

3. **Draw Conclusions** Why was the Soviet Union unable to keep up with the market economies of the West?

4. **Summarize** How did Gorbachev's reforms lead to the breakup of the Soviet empire?

5. **Recognize Cause and Effect** Why were Eastern Europeans able to break free of communist governments and Soviet domination in the late 1980s?

6. **Draw Inferences** How did the collapse of the Soviet Union affect the power of other countries around the world?

● **Writing About History**

Quick Write: Gather Evidence To write a problem-solution essay, you need to gather evidence to support a proposed solution to a problem. In this section, you learned that rigidly communist countries faced isolation and economic decline after the fall of the Soviet Union. Identify a solution to this problem and gather evidence to support your solution. Then write a paragraph with a thesis statement proposing a solution. Include the evidence you have gathered in support of your thesis statement.

Václav Havel: *New Year's Address*

Václav Havel was a leading dissident and human rights activist in communist Czechoslovakia. When the "democracy movement" swept through Eastern Europe in 1989, Havel was elected president. In the following speech delivered on January 1, 1990, Havel asks the citizens of Czechoslovakia to accept responsibility for their past and to move forward in building a democracy. Havel calls on Czechs and Slovaks to be active participants in their new democracy.

Václav Havel

Our country is not flourishing. The enormous creative and spiritual potential of our nations is not being used sensibly. Entire branches of industry are producing goods that are of no interest to anyone.... [W]e have today the most contaminated environment in Europe....

But all this is still not the main problem. The worst thing is that we live in a contaminated moral environment. We fell morally ill because we became used to saying something different from what we thought. We learned not to believe in anything, to ignore each other, to care only about ourselves. Concepts such as love, friendship, compassion, humility, or forgiveness lost their depth and dimensions.... Only a few of us were able to cry out loud that the powers that be should not be all-powerful....

We had all become used to the totalitarian system and accepted it as an unchangeable fact and thus helped to perpetuate it. In other words, we are all ... responsible for the operation of the totalitarian machinery....

Why do I say this? It would be very unreasonable to understand the sad legacy of the last forty years as something alien, which some distant relative bequeathed to us. On the contrary, we have to accept this legacy as a sin we committed against ourselves. If we accept it as such, we will understand that it is up to us all, and up to us only, to do something about it. We cannot blame the previous rulers for everything, not only because it would be untrue but also because it could blunt the duty that each of us faces today, namely, the obligation to act independently, freely, reasonably, and quickly. Let us not be mistaken: the best government in the world, the best parliament and the best president, cannot achieve much on their own. And it would also be wrong to expect a general remedy from them only. Freedom and democracy include participation and therefore responsibility from us all.

Czechoslovak democracy demonstrators

Thinking Critically

1. **Identify Point of View** Who does Havel hold responsible for Czechoslovakia's totalitarian past?
2. **Draw Conclusions** What does Havel see as the solution to his country's problems?

CHAPTER 30

Quick Study Guide

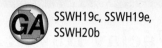

SSWH19c, SSWH19e, SSWH20b

Progress Monitoring *Online*
For: Self-test with vocabulary practice
Web Code: naa-3061

■ Cold War Contrasts

Communist Countries	Industrialized Democracies
Compete in arms race to maintain "balance of terror."	Compete in arms race to maintain "balance of terror."
Form Warsaw Pact. China follows separate path.	Form NATO and SEATO.
Seek to spread communism.	Seek to contain communism.
Command economies	Market economies
Economic stagnation, low standards of living	Economic "miracles," prosperity with scattered recessions
Repression of dissent, labor camps	Free expression, but fears lead to an episode of McCarthyism
Power is closely held by communist parties.	Democracy is established in Japan, civil rights movement extends democracy in the United States.
Lost arms race.	Won arms race.

■ Cold War Hot Spots

Korea	Vietnam
Divided into communist north and noncommunist, U.S.-supported south.	Divided into communist north and noncommunist, U.S.-supported south.
China provided troops to support North Korea.	China and the Soviet Union provided economic and military aid, but not troops, to North Vietnam.
The United States led United Nations troops supporting South Korea.	The United States and some allies provided troops to support South Vietnam.
Warfare mainly involved regular troops.	Viet Cong fighting in the south were mainly guerrillas.
United States troops remained in South Korea after war.	United States troops withdrew before the war ended.
Korean War ended in a stalemate between the two sides and a ceasefire.	Vietnam War ended when North Vietnam defeated South Vietnam and reunited the country.

■ Steps in the Collapse of the Soviet Empire

- The command economy could not create wealth or raise living standards as quickly as market economies.
- The Soviet Union could not afford the expense of maintaining a "balance of terror" in the arms race.
- East Europeans resisted communism and Soviet control.
- Soviet military failure in Afghanistan led to calls for change.
- Reforms in Russia included glasnost, or freedom of expression, and perestroika, or market reforms.

- East Germans forced their government to open the Berlin Wall.
- Eastern European nations rejected Soviet control and adopted market economies and democracy.
- Glasnost led to drive for independence by Soviet ethnic minorities and the breakup of the Soviet Union.
- Soviet Union was divided into 15 independent nations.
- The Warsaw Pact was dissolved.

■ Key Events of the Cold War

Americas, Europe, and Soviet Union

East and Southeast Asia

1945
World War II ends in Europe.

1949
Germany is divided.

1959
Fidel Castro leads communist revolution in Cuba.

1945

1955

1945
World War II ends in Asia.

1949
Mao Zedong leads communists to victory in China.

1950–1953
Korean War

毛主席语录
QUOTATIONS FROM CHAIRMAN MAO TSE-TUNG

Concept Connector

Essential Question Review

To connect prior knowledge with what you have learned in this chapter, answer the questions below in your Concept Connector journal. Use the journal in the Reading and Note Taking Study Guide to record your answers (or go to www.phschool.com **Web Code:** nad-3007). In addition, record information about the following concepts:

• Cooperation: European Community

1. **Empire** During the 1950s and 1960s, Soviet military forces crushed democratic reforms in East Germany, Poland, Hungary, and Czechoslovakia. By the mid-1980s, the weakness of the Soviet system was becoming apparent. Compare the decline of the Soviet empire to the decline of the Ottoman empire. Identify any similarities. Then identify the single most important reason for the fall of communist governments in Eastern Europe.

2. **Dictatorship** Mao Zedong built a one-party totalitarian state in China. Critics and opponents were labeled "counter-revolutionaries" and beaten, exiled, or killed. How do you think adult Chinese might have viewed the Cultural Revolution? Did the Cultural Revolution strengthen Mao's hold on China? Focus on:
    • Red Guards
    • propaganda
    • forced labor camps
    • civil war

3. **Human Rights** After World War II, the American promise of equality and opportunity had not yet been fulfilled for minorities and women. African Americans and other minority groups faced segregation and discrimination. What tactics did these groups use to gain their civil rights? What were the results? Think about:
    • protests
    • spending power
    • legislation

Connections to Today

1. **Conflict: India and Pakistan** The Cold War was a tense standoff between the United States and the Soviet Union, with only brief outbreaks of actual fighting. Since India and Pakistan gained independence in 1947, the two countries have engaged in a similar conflict. This conflict involves occasional fighting, often involving guerrillas in the disputed Kashmir region. Since 1998, both India and Pakistan have had nuclear weapons. Using recent news articles and the Internet, research the current state of this conflict. How is it similar to the Cold War? How is it different?

Kashmir Sweater

2. **Democracy: The Global Spread of Democracy** This chapter describes the spread of democracy to West Germany and Japan and later to Eastern Europe. Using an encyclopedia, research the move to democracy in an Eastern European country. Then research a move to democracy in a country in Latin America, East Asia, or Africa. How was the transition to democracy similar or different in these two countries?

| 1961 Berlin Wall is built. | 1989 Eastern Europeans overthrow communist rulers. | 1991 The Soviet Union breaks up and the Cold War ends. |

1965   **1975**   **1985**   **1995**

| 1964 U.S. enters the Vietnam War. | 1975 Vietnam War ends with North Vietnamese victory. | 1976 Mao Zedong dies. |

History *Interactive*

For: Interactive timeline
Web Code: nap-3061

Chapter Assessment

Terms, People, and Places

Choose the italicized term in parentheses that best completes each sentence.

1. The United States aimed to prevent the spread of communism through a policy of (*containment/glasnost*).
2. (*Ngo Dinh Diem/Ho Chi Minh*) was the leader of North Vietnam.
3. European nations eliminated barriers to trade by establishing the (*welfare state/European Community*).
4. At the end of the Korean War, a cease-fire line was established near the (*38th parallel/Pusan Perimeter*).
5. A period of economic decline is a (*budget deficit/recession*).
6. During the 1970s, the United States and the Soviet Union had a period of reduced Cold War tensions known as (*collectivization/détente*).

Main Ideas

Section 1 (pp. 966–975)

7. How did the Cold War develop in the Soviet Union, Europe, and the United States?
8. What were the main features of the nuclear arms race?

Section 2 (pp. 976–984)

9. How did political and economic life change during the Cold War years in the United States?
10. What was the relationship between economic growth and trade in Western Europe and Japan?

Section 3 (pp. 985–991)

11. How did the Korean War influence U.S. relations with Communist China? How did those relations change as a result of hostility between China and the Soviet Union?

Section 4 (pp. 992–999)

12. Why did the United States enter the Vietnam War?

Section 5 (pp. 1000–1007)

13. How did Gorbachev's reforms lead to the breakup of the Soviet Union?
14. What events marked the end of the Cold War?

Chapter Focus Question

15. How did the Cold War develop, how did it shape political and economic life in individual nations, and how did it end?

Critical Thinking

16. **Analyze Visuals** Turn to the photo of the Berlin Wall on the first page of this chapter. How do you think that the Berliners in this photo felt about the wall that had been built through their city?
17. **Make Comparisons** What factors contributed to economic booms after World War II in Western Europe, the United States and Japan? Why was the economic performance of Eastern Europe and the Soviet Union different?
18. **Draw Inferences** You have read that the leaders of the Soviet Union retained power in Poland and elsewhere in Eastern Europe for over forty years. How were they able to do so despite lacking the consent of the governed?
19. **Predict Consequences** During the Cold War, many nations formed alliances with one superpower for protection against the other. After the Cold War, the United States emerged as the sole superpower. How might this change the nature of alliances?
20. **Recognize Cause and Effect** Which factors allowed North Vietnam to achieve victory over South Vietnam? What were some consequences of North Vietnam's victory in Vietnam and other parts of Southeast Asia?

● Writing About History

In this chapter's five Section Assessments, you developed skills to write a problem-solving essay.

Writing a Problem-Solution Essay Write a problem-solution essay on one of the Cold War problems listed below. Problems to address include the military standoff on the Iron Curtain, the arms race, and the division of Germany, Korea, or Vietnam. Consult page SH10 of the Writing Handbook for additional help.

Prewriting

- Go online or do library research to find evidence on each of the problems listed above.
- Choose the problem that interests you most and take notes about the evidence you find.

- Decide on the best solution to this problem and gather the evidence that supports your solution.

Drafting

- Write a first paragraph stating the problem and explaining why it is important.
- Write a thesis statement arguing for your solution to the problem.
- Write a second paragraph beginning with your thesis statement, followed by supporting sentences.

Revising

- Use the guidelines for revising your report on page SH12 of the Writing Handbook.

Prepare for the GHSGT

Cold War Chills

The United States and the Soviet Union confronted each other in the Cold War—a global conflict that included a nuclear arms race. In Document A, Nikita Khrushchev discusses the border fortifications that prevented East Germans from entering West Germany. In Document B, U.S. Vice President Richard Nixon warns Khrushchev about restricting western access to Berlin.

Document A

"Seeing that their government had reasserted control over its own frontiers, the East Germans were heartened by the solidification and fortification of their state. . . . I know there are people who claim that the East Germans are imprisoned in paradise and that the gates of the Socialist paradise are guarded by armed troops. I'm aware that a defect exists, but I believe it's a necessary and only temporary defect."

—From ***Khrushchev Remembers*** by Nikita Khrushchev

Document B

". . . I hope the Prime Minister has understood all the implications of what I said," Nixon went on, with an oblique [indirect] reference to Berlin. "What I mean is that the moment we place either one of these powerful nations, through an ultimatum, in a position where it has no choice but to accept dictation or fight, then you are playing with the most destructive force in the world."

Khrushchev: (flushed, wagging a finger near Nixon's face): We too are giants. If you want to threaten, we will answer threat with threat.

Nixon: We never engage in threats.

Khrushchev: You wanted indirectly to threaten me. But we have means at our disposal that can have very bad consequences.

Nixon: We have too.

—From ***Time***, August 3, 1959

Document C

Divided Germany and Berlin, 1949–1990

Document D

Fortifications that kept East Germans from crossing into West Germany

Analyzing Documents

Use your knowledge of the Cold War and Documents A, B, C, and D to answer questions 1–4.

1. The author's purpose in Document A was to
   A explain East German discipline.
   B offer a balanced perspective on the Cold War.
   C argue for a fortified barrier between East and West Germany.
   D explain the role of the Soviet Union in East Germany.

2. The tone of the exchange in Document B is
   A friendly and joking.
   B tense and hostile.
   C cautious.
   D businesslike.

3. Document C shows that
   A West Berlin was located inside West Germany.
   B the border between East and West Germany passed through Berlin.
   C East Germany surrounded West Germany.
   D two East German borders separated West Berlin from West Germany.

4. **Writing Task** How was the Cold War fought? Use what you have read in the chapter, along with these documents, to write a response.

WE FOUGHT
FOR PEACE
AND
WE LIVE IN PEACE

Independence in Eritrea

To escape the dangers of the war for independence in the African nation of Eritrea, Almaz Isaac fled to America as a refugee when she was a teenager. When Eritrea won its independence ten years later and peace returned, Almaz returned to Eritrea. She said, "This is the first time I've been able to come back, to see my family. We waited, our people fought, and now this is it. We have our freedom." As in Eritrea, independence brought a new sense of hope to many countries in Africa and elsewhere in recent decades. Listen to the Witness History audio to hear more about independence in Africa.

◄ Eritreans celebrate independence in 1993 at the end of their long war for freedom.

Monument showing the sandals worn by soldiers in Eritrea's war for independence

GA Performance Standards

Chapter Focus Question How did former European colonies gain independence, and what challenges did they face after independence?

Section 1
Independent Nations of South Asia
SSWH19a, SSWH20d

Section 2
New Nations of Southeast Asia
SSWH20a, SSWH20d

Section 3
African Nations Gain Independence
SSWH19a

Section 4
The Modern Middle East
SSWH19b, SSWH21b

Use the ☑ **Quick Study Timeline** at the end of this chapter to preview chapter events.

Flag of the Southeast Asian nation of Malaysia

Hat worn by border guards in India

 Concept Connector ONLINE

To explore Essential Questions related to this chapter, go to PHSchool.com
Web Code: nad-3107

A family of refugees flees the religious violence that broke out during the partition of India.

WITNESS HISTORY 🔊 AUDIO

Fleeing Religious Violence

At independence, India was partitioned, or divided, into India and Pakistan, a new, largely Muslim country. Damyanti Sahgal, a Hindu, describes fleeing from Hindu-Muslim violence during the partition.

> 66 When we came close to Amritsar, we found that they had started stopping trains, killing people in them, but we were lucky. Everyone said put your windows up, they are cutting down people. 99

While people in India and Pakistan welcomed independence, they had to live with the violence of partition and its legacy of distrust.

Focus Question How did nationalist demands for independence affect South Asia and the world?

Independent Nations of South Asia

 Performance Standards

- **SSWH19a** Analyze Gandhi, Nehru, and the revolutionary movement in India.
- **SSWH20d** Examine the rise of Indira Gandhi as a major world leader.

Terms, People, and Places

partition	Indira Gandhi
Sikhs	Punjab
Kashmir	Golden Temple
Jawaharlal Nehru	Bangladesh
dalits	nonalignment

Note Taking

Reading Skill: Identify Causes and Effects Fill in a concept web like this one to keep track of causes and effects of events in South Asia. Add ovals as needed for additional concepts.

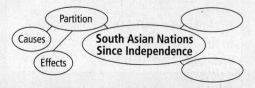

At the same time that the Cold War was unfolding, a global independence movement was reshaping the world. Among the first new nations to win independence were the former British colonies of South Asia.

Independence Brings Partition

Nationalists in British-ruled India had demanded self-rule since the late 1800s. As independence neared, however, a long-simmering issue surfaced. What would happen to the Muslim minority in a Hindu-dominated India?

Two New Nations Emerge Like Mohandas Gandhi, most of the leaders and members of the Congress Party were Hindus. However, the party wanted a unified India that would include both Muslims and Hindus. The Muslim League, led by Muhammad Ali Jinnah, had a different view of liberation. The Muslim League feared discrimination against the Muslim minority in a unified India. Therefore, the Muslim League demanded the creation of a separate nation, called Pakistan, that would include the parts of British India where Muslims formed a majority. In the 1940s, tensions between Muslims and the Hindu majority in British India led to increasing violence.

After World War II, the British government decided that it could no longer afford to resist Indian demands for independence.

As independence approached, violence between Hindus and Muslims accelerated. In response, Britain decided to accept the idea of **partition,** or dividing the subcontinent into two nations. Hindu-dominated India, and Pakistan, which had a Muslim majority, both won independence on August 13, 1947.

Refugees Flee Amid Violence However, Hindus and Muslims still lived side by side in many cities and rural areas. As soon as the new borders became known, millions of Hindus on the Pakistani side of the borders packed up their belongings and fled to the new India. At the same time, millions of Muslims fled into newly created Pakistan. An estimated 10 million people fled their homes, most of them on foot.

Muslims fleeing along the crowded roads into Pakistan were slaughtered by Hindus and **Sikhs** (seeks), members of an Indian religious minority. Muslims massacred Hindu and Sikh neighbors. Around one million people died in these massacres. Others died of starvation and exposure on the road.

Struggles Over Kashmir Since independence, India and Pakistan have fought a series of wars over **Kashmir,** a state in the Himalayas. In 1947, Kashmir's Hindu ruler tried to join India. However, Kashmir's Muslim majority wanted to be part of Pakistan. For decades, Kashmiri separatists, often supported by Pakistani militants, have fought Indian troops. Indian and Pakistani forces have also battled along Kashmir's mountainous border. Today, Kashmir remains a flashpoint in the tense relations between India and Pakistan.

Map Skills The former British colony of India had become the independent nations of Pakistan, India, and Bangladesh by 1971. The region's other nations had also achieved independence by that date. The status of Kashmir, however, remained in dispute.

1. **Locate** (a) Bangladesh (b) Pakistani Kashmir (c) Indian Kashmir

2. **Regions** Which other nation also has a stake in the Kashmir conflict?

3. **Make Inferences** Bangladesh was once part of Pakistan. How might its location have contributed to its people's desire for independence?

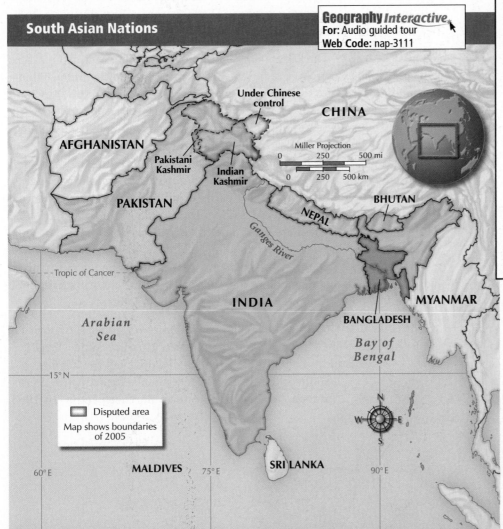

South Asian Nations

Geography *Interactive*
For: Audio guided tour
Web Code: nap-3111

Under Chinese control

CHINA

AFGHANISTAN

Pakistani Kashmir

Indian Kashmir

Miller Projection
0   250   500 mi
0   250   500 km

PAKISTAN

BHUTAN

NEPAL

Ganges River

- - Tropic of Cancer - -

Arabian Sea

INDIA

MYANMAR

BANGLADESH

Bay of Bengal

15° N

Disputed area
Map shows boundaries of 2005

MALDIVES   75° E   SRI LANKA   90° E

60° E

A Nuclear Arms Race In the 1970s, first India and then Pakistan developed nuclear weapons programs. By 1998, both nations had successfully tested nuclear weapons. The emergence of these two nuclear powers alarmed neighbors in South Asia and the world, in part because of the ongoing hostility between India and Pakistan. Another concern was the danger that extremists might get access to nuclear technology or even nuclear weapons.

Conflict Divides Sri Lanka The island of Ceylon won freedom from Britain in 1948. Later, it took the name Sri (sree) Lanka. Most Sri Lankans are Buddhists who speak Sinhalese. However, a large Tamil-speaking Hindu minority lives in the north and east. The Sri Lankan government favored the Sinhalese majority, which angered many Tamils. In the late 1970s, Tamil rebels battled to set up their own separate nation. For three decades, terrorism and brutality fed a deadly conflict between government forces and Tamil rebels. By 2009, the government had regained control of Tamil-held towns, but peace was by no means assured.

✔ **Checkpoint** Why was Kashmir a source of conflict between India and Pakistan?

Building a Modern Nation

At independence, India established a parliamentary democracy. Although India remains the world's largest democracy, it has faced many challenges. Ethnic and religious tensions threatened its unity. Its people speak over 100 languages and many dialects. Hundreds of millions of Indians lived in desperate poverty. Despite unrest and diversity, India has emerged as a major world power.

Strong Leaders During its early decades, India benefited from strong leadership. The Congress Party, which had spearheaded the independence movement, worked to turn India into a modern nation. From 1947 to 1964, **Jawaharlal Nehru,** leader of the Congress Party, was India's prime minister. He promoted economic growth and social change. Under Nehru, food output rose, but so did India's population. The government encouraged family planning to reduce the birthrate, but with limited success.

Although India's 1947 constitution banned discrimination against **dalits,** or people in the lowest castes, discrimination based on caste continued. Nehru's government set aside jobs and places in universities for dalits and other lower-caste Indians. Still, higher-caste Hindus generally got better schooling and jobs.

Later, Nehru's daughter, **Indira Gandhi,** served as prime minister for most of the years between 1966 and 1984. She led India with a firm hand and challenged traditional discrimination against women.

Religious Conflicts India was a land of many religions. A majority of Indians were Hindu, but millions were Muslim, Sikh, Christian, or Buddhist. At times, religious divisions led to violence.

Some Sikhs wanted independence for **Punjab,** a prosperous, largely Sikh state in northern India. In 1984,

Indira Gandhi
Prime Minister Indira Gandhi led India from 1966 to 1977 and again from 1980 to 1984.

armed Sikh separatists took dramatic action. They occupied the **Golden Temple,** the holiest Sikh shrine. When Indira Gandhi sent troops to oust them, bloody fighting erupted. Soon after, Gandhi was assassinated by her Sikh bodyguards, igniting terrible violence.

In the late 1980s, the Hindu nationalist party, Bharatiya Janata Party (BJP) challenged the secular, or nonreligious, Congress Party. The BJP wanted a government based on Hindu traditions and sometimes encouraged violence against Muslims.

✔ **Checkpoint** How did the Indian government try to improve conditions for lower castes?

Pakistan and Bangladesh Separate

Pakistan gained independence in 1947, at the same time as India. Geographically, it was a divided country, with West Pakistan and East Pakistan located on either side of India. A thousand miles of Indian territory separated the two regions, and India made trade and travel between the two Pakistans difficult.

Religions of India

Religion	Population (millions)	Percentage	Regional Concentration
Hinduism	828	80.5	Throughout India
Islam	138	13.4	Kashmir, Northern India, Southwest Coast
Christianity	24	2.3	Northeastern India, Southwest Coast
Sikhism	19	1.9	Northwestern India
Buddhism	8	0.8	Northeastern India, West Coast
Others	11	1.0	Throughout India

Chart Skills What is India's largest minority religion? Where do most of its followers live?

SOURCE: Census of India 2001

Bangladesh Breaks Away From the start, West Pakistan dominated the government even though East Pakistan had a larger population. The government concentrated most economic development programs in West Pakistan, while East Pakistan remained deep in poverty. Most people in East Pakistan were Bengalis, while West Pakistan was home to other ethnic groups. Many Bengalis resented governmental neglect of East Pakistan.

In 1971, Bengalis in East Pakistan declared independence. They named their country **Bangladesh,** or "Bengali nation." When the Pakistani army tried to crush the rebellion, India sent forces to help Bangladesh. Pakistan was then <u>compelled</u> to recognize the new country.

Pakistan's Shaky Government After independence, Pakistan struggled to build a stable government. Power shifted back and forth between elected civilian leaders and military rulers. Tensions among the country's diverse ethnic groups posed problems. The fiercely independent people in the northwestern "tribal areas" were left largely on their own and resisted government control. The activities of Islamic fundamentalists created tension. The fundamentalists wanted a government that followed strict Islamic principles, while other Pakistanis wanted greater separation between religion and state.

Ongoing Challenges In 2008, after nine years in power, General Pervez Musharraf allowed elections. Before the election, Islamic extremists assassinated one of the candidates, Benazir Bhutto, a popular former prime minister. Pakistan's new civilian government faced tough challenges, including the global economic recession.

Vocabulary Builder

compelled—(kum PELD) *v.* made to or forced

Meanwhile, support for Islamic fundamentalist groups based in Pakistan grew, especially in the northwest. In November 2008, Islamic militants from Pakistan launched terror attacks on hotels and tourists in Mumbai, India, fueling tensions between the hostile neighbors.

Islamic traditions were strong in the rugged border area between Pakistan and Afghanistan. When the Soviet Union invaded Afghanistan in 1979, one million Afghan refugees fled into Pakistan. There, many joined Islamic fundamentalist groups to battle the invaders.

After Russia withdrew from Afghanistan, the Taliban, an extreme Islamist group, seized power with the support of Pakistan. The Taliban backed Al Qaeda, which launched terrorist attacks on the United States in 2001. When U.S. forces invaded Afghanistan and overthrew the Taliban, its supporters fled into Pakistan. They set up strongholds in northwestern Pakistan, where their influence spread. Pakistan's government had limited success fighting the terrorists. However, it was angered by American missile attacks on suspected terrorists within its borders.

Bangladesh Struggles Bangladesh ranks among the world's poorest, most crowded countries. Its population, more than half as large as that of the United States, lives in an area the size of Alabama. The flat Ganges Delta, just a few feet above sea level, covers much of the country. Bangladesh has suffered repeatedly from devastating tropical storms and floods.

Floods Ravage Bangladesh
Summer rains often flood much of low-lying Bangladesh. Here, aid workers bring supplies to a family trapped on the roof of their home. *How might frequent floods hurt efforts to improve conditions in Bangladesh?*

Geographic conditions made it hard for the government to ease the desperate poverty that most people endure. One hopeful program, however, came from the Grameen Bank, founded by Bangladeshi economist Muhammad Yunus. It gave tiny loans, or "microcredit" to poor people so they could open small businesses. Although microcredit helped only a few, it offered a model to poor nations around the world. In 2006, Yunus was awarded the Nobel Peace Prize for his efforts.

✓ **Checkpoint** How did geography pose challenges for Bangladesh?

Finding an Independent Path

India and Pakistan were among the first of more than 90 new nations to emerge after World War II. By the 1930s, nationalist movements had taken root in European colonies across Africa, Asia, and the Middle East. After World War II, nationalist leaders such as Ghandi and Nehru insisted on independence. After India and Pakistan gained independence, nationalist leaders in Africa and other regions demanded the same for their countries.

India, Pakistan, and other new nations condemned colonialism and rejected Cold War expansion and the divisions between the West and the Soviet Union. In response, they sought **nonalignment,** or political and diplomatic independence from the Cold War superpowers. In 1955, India and Pakistan helped organize a conference of newly independent nations in Bandung, Indonesia, which marked the birth of the nonaligned movement.

The nonaligned movement had its first formal meeting in 1961 in Yugoslavia. India was a leader of the nonaligned movement, which came to include more than 100 nations, mainly in Asia, Africa, and Latin America. Because they rejected both the Western allies, or the First World, and the Soviet alliance, or the Second World, the Nonaligned Movement was seen as the voice of a "Third World" of countries.

✓ **Checkpoint** What global role did India and Pakistan play after independence?

SECTION **1** Assessment

Progress Monitoring *Online*
For: Self-quiz with vocabulary practice
Web Code: naa-3111

Terms, People, and Places

1. For each term, person, or place in the beginning of the section, write a sentence explaining its significance.

Note Taking

2. **Reading Skill: Identify Causes and Effects** Use your completed concept web to answer the Focus Question: What were the consequences of independence in South Asia for the region and for the world?

Comprehension and Critical Thinking

3. **Recognize Cause and Effect** Why did the partition of British India cause refugees to flee?

4. **Express Problems Clearly** What problems did India's religious diversity pose?

5. **Summarize** Why did Bangladesh separate from Pakistan?

6. **Draw Conclusions** How did a policy of nonalignment influence the relations of India and Pakistan with the Cold War superpowers?

● **Writing About History**

Quick Write: Outline Your Topic To write a compare-and-contrast essay, you need to consider two subjects and find similarities and differences between them. In this section, you learned that India and Pakistan share a common history but were separated at independence. Write features of each country's history in three lists: a list of features specific to India, a list of features specific to Pakistan, and a list of features shared by both countries.

Indonesia's flag

Sukarno, Indonesia's first president

WITNESS HISTORY 🔊 AUDIO

All for All

Most Southeast Asian nations are home to diverse people speaking many languages and practicing different religions. Indonesia's independence leader, Sukarno, stressed the importance of unity for his nation:

66 [W]e are establishing an Indonesian state which all of us must support. All for all. Not the Christians for Indonesia, not the Islamic group for Indonesia . . . but the Indonesians for Indonesia—all for all! 99

Achieving unity was one of many challenges that Indonesia faced after independence.

Focus Question What challenges did Southeast Asian nations face after winning independence?

New Nations of Southeast Asia

 Performance Standards

- **SSWH20a** Identify ethnic conflicts and new nationalisms since the 1960s.
- **SSWH20d** Examine the rise of women as world leaders.

Terms, People, and Places

autocratic	East Timor
Aung San Suu Kyi	Ferdinand Marcos
Sukarno	Benigno Aquino
Suharto	Corazon Aquino

Note Taking

Reading Skills: Understand Effects Fill in a concept web like the one below to keep track of the effects of recent historical processes in Southeast Asia. Add to it as needed for additional concepts in the section.

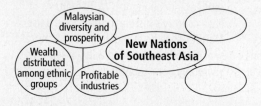

Southeast Asia includes part of the Asian mainland and thousands of islands that stretch from the Indian Ocean to the South China Sea. In 1939, most of the region was under colonial rule by European nations or the United States. During World War II, Japan seized the region. After the war, nationalist groups demanded independence and resisted reoccupation by European nations.

Mainland Contrasts

Mainland Southeast Asia is a region of contrasts. Thailand and Malaysia have mostly prospered as market economies, although they have been affected by global financial crises. However, nearby Myanmar has suffered under a brutal **autocratic,** or repressive, government with unlimited power.

Malaysia Prospers British colonies on the Malay Peninsula and the island of Borneo gained independence in the 1950s and joined to form the nation of Malaysia. The oil-rich monarchy of Brunei, on Borneo, and the prosperous city-state of Singapore gained independence as separate nations.

Malaysia has a very diverse population. People of Chinese and Indian descent have long dominated business. They have made the nation a Southeast Asian leader in profitable industries such as rubber and electronics. The government, however, has tried to include the Malay majority in the country's prosperity. The result has been a more equal distribution of wealth in Malaysia than in most countries in the region.

Myanmar Suffers Burma won independence from Britain in 1948 and took the name Myanmar in 1989. Ethnic tensions and a repressive government have plagued the country. The Burmese majority dominated other ethnic groups. The harsh military government limited foreign trade, and living standards remained low.

Under mounting pressure, the military held elections in1990. When an opposition party won the election, the military rejected the results. It put the opposition leader, **Aung San Suu Kyi,** (awn sahn soo chee) under house arrest, and jailed, killed, or exiled many opponents. In 1991, Suu Kyi won the Nobel Peace Prize for her "nonviolent struggle for democracy and human rights." For twenty years, the military has silenced demands for new elections and crushed peaceful demonstrations by Buddhist monks. It even prevented humanitarian aid from reaching areas of Myanmar that were devastated by a cyclone in 2008.

 Checkpoint How did Malaysia's approach to ethnic diversity differ from Myanmar's?

Indonesia's Size Poses Challenges

After World War II, the Netherlands attempted to regain power in Indonesia, formerly the Dutch East Indies. The Dutch, however, were forced to give up their possessions when the Indonesian government declared independence in 1949 after the Japanese defeat.

Geography and diversity posed an obstacle to unity in Indonesia. Indonesia includes more than 13,000 islands, many very small but some as large as European nations. Javanese make up almost half of the population, but there are hundreds of other ethnic groups. About 90 percent of Indonesians are Muslims, but the population includes substantial Christian, Buddhist, and Hindu minorities.

Seeking Stability At independence, Indonesia formed a parliamentary government under its first president, **Sukarno.** But Sukarno shifted from democracy to authoritarian rule. In 1967, an army general, **Suharto,** seized power. Suharto claimed that communists were responsible for an earlier attempt by military officers to overthrow the government and ordered the slaughter of hundreds of thousands of communists and suspected communists. For decades, Suharto imposed his will on Indonesia. A financial crisis finally forced Suharto to resign from power in 1998.

Since then, elected governments have worked to build democracy, strengthen the economy, and fight corruption. Indonesia is home to the world's largest Muslim population. But Islamic extremists have challenged Indonesia's long tradition of religious tolerance. Islamic terrorist groups in Indonesia have targeted foreigners and non-Muslims and threatened the stability of the government.

East Timor Fights for Freedom Indonesia seized **East Timor** in 1975, just after it had been granted independence by Portugal. However, most East Timorese wanted independence. For years, the government battled the mostly Catholic East Timorese. East Timor finally won independence from Indonesia in 2002. This very poor new nation struggled to meet its people's need for jobs and decent living standards.

Brunei's Oil Wealth
A few Southeast Asian nations such as Indonesia have oil and gas reserves. This oil well produces revenues for Brunei (broo NY), a tiny kingdom located on the island of Borneo.

RELIGIOUS DIVERSITY IN SOUTHEAST ASIA

Southeast Asia is one of the world's most religiously diverse regions. This diversity is a result of its history as a crossroads between South and East Asia. In some countries, such as Indonesia and the Philippines, religious differences have played a part in civil conflicts. In others, such as Malaysia and Singapore, people of different religions live together in peace.

Islam links many Southeast Asians to other parts of the Muslim world. The Indonesian Muslim woman to the left is attending a prayer service.

Religions of Southeast Asia

Legend:
- Roman Catholic Christianity
- Protestant Christianity
- Sunni Islam
- Hinduism
- Buddhism
- Traditional religions

Religious Composition of Major Southeast Asian Nations

SOURCE: Encyclopaedia Britannica

Legend: Muslim Buddhist Christian Hindu Other

Buddhism plays an important role in the lives of many mainland Southeast Asians. In Thailand, all young Buddhist men are expected to live for at least a short time as monks, such as the ones in this photo.

Thinking Critically

1. **Graph Skills** Based on the graph, are the people in the two photos members of their country's majority or minority religion?
2. **Map Skills** Notice that some religious groups shown on the graph for Malaysia do not have distinct areas on the map. What might explain this?

Ethnic Conflicts and Natural Disasters Religious and ethnic conflicts fueled violence in parts of Indonesia. In the Moluccas, a group of eastern islands, fighting between Muslims and Christians killed thousands. Discrimination against Chinese people led to vicious attacks. Rebels in Papua, on the island of New Guinea, sought independence, as did Muslim separatists in Aceh (AH chay) in the northwest.

Natural disasters have added to Indonesia's troubles. In 2004, a tsunami (tsoo NAH mee), or giant wave, devastated the coast of Aceh and killed more than 100,000 people. The tsunami also ravaged Thailand, Sri Lanka, and other lands around the Indian Ocean. Following the disaster, rebels in Aceh and the Indonesian government signed a peace accord. Helped by international aid donors, they worked together to rebuild Aceh.

✓ **Checkpoint** How has diversity posed challenges to Indonesia?

The Philippines Seeks Democracy

Like Indonesia, the Philippines include thousands of islands with diverse ethnic and religious groups. Catholics are <u>predominant</u>, but many Muslims live in the south. In 1946, the Philippines gained independence after almost 50 years of American rule. American influence remained strong through military and economic aid.

Marcos Becomes a Dictator
Although the Filipino constitution set up a democratic government, a wealthy elite controlled politics and the economy. The peasant majority was poor. For years, the government battled Huks (hooks), local communists with strong peasant support. **Ferdinand Marcos,** elected president in 1965, abandoned democracy. He became a dictator and cracked down on basic freedoms. He even had **Benigno Aquino** (beh NEE nyoh ah KEE noh), a popular rival, murdered.

Filipinos Demand Democracy
When Marcos finally held elections in 1986, voters chose **Corazon Aquino** (kawr ah SOHN), the widow of the slain Benigno. Marcos tried to deny the results, but massive protests forced him to resign during the "people power" revolution. Under Aquino and her successors, this fragile democracy survived, despite many political scandals. Economic growth was limited, and poverty remained widespread. With the highest birth rate in Asia, the population continues to rise rapidly, straining already limited resources.

Clashes With Rebels Continue
For decades, various rebel groups have waged guerrilla wars across the Philippines. Some rebels were communists. Others were Muslim separatists. Some Muslim rebels have links to international terrorist groups such as Al Qaeda. In the early 2000s, the Filipino government accepted aid from its ally, the United States, to fight rebels and pursue President George W. Bush's "war on terror."

✔️ **Checkpoint** Why has the Philippines had trouble preserving its democracy?

Vocabulary Builder

<u>predominant</u>—(pree DAHM uh nunt) *adj.* most common or numerous

---

SECTION 2 Assessment

Progress Monitoring *Online*
For: Self-quiz with vocabulary practice
Web Code: naa-3121

Terms, People, and Places
1. For each term, person, or place listed at the beginning of the section, write a sentence explaining its significance.

Note Taking
2. **Reading Skill: Understand Effects** Use your completed concept web to answer the Focus Question: What challenges did Southeast Asian nations face after winning independence?

Comprehension and Critical Thinking
3. **Make Comparisons** Why did policies toward ethnic diversity lead to prosperity in Malaysia but to conflict in other parts of Southeast Asia?
4. **Synthesize Information** How have religious and ethnic diversity affected the recent history of Indonesia?
5. **Draw Inferences** What conclusions might separatist movements in Indonesia draw from East Timor's successful independence struggle?
6. **Recognize Cause and Effect** What causes explain the overthrow of Ferdinand Marcos?

● Writing About History
Quick Write: Evaluate Your Topic To write a compare-and-contrast essay, you can organize your ideas in a point-by-point comparison. In this section, you learned that Malaysia and Indonesia are both ethnically diverse. Draft two sentences for an essay. In each sentence, compare or contrast an aspect of ethnic diversity in one of these countries with a related aspect of ethnic diversity in the other.

The Union Jack, the flag of the United Kingdom, flew over many African countries before independence.

Britain's Prince Philip and Queen Elizabeth II congratulate Jomo Kenyatta as his nation, Kenya, gains independence in 1963.

WITNESS HISTORY 🔊 AUDIO

Kenya Achieves Independence

A scene from a novel by Ngugi wa Thiong'o describes the moment of independence in Nairobi, Kenya's capital:

❝A minute before midnight, lights were put out. . . . In the dark, the Union Jack [British flag] was quickly lowered. When next the lights came on the new Kenya flag was . . . waving in the air.❞
—Ngugi wa Thiong'o, *A Grain of Wheat*

Kenya was one of more than 40 African nations that gained independence from European colonial powers in the decades after World War II.

Focus Question What challenges did new African nations face?

African Nations Gain Independence

 Performance Standards

• **SSWH19a** Analyze Kwame Nkrumah and the revolutionary movement in Ghana.

Terms, People, and Places

savannas	Mobutu Sese Seko
Kwame Nkrumah	Islamist
Jomo Kenyatta	Katanga
coup d'état	Biafra

Note Taking

Reading Skill: Identify Causes and Effects Fill in a concept web like this one to keep track of the causes and effects of independence in Africa.

Colonists demand rights → Independent African Nations

In new nations all across Africa, crowds celebrated their freedom, while bands played each country's new national anthem. However, even as independence celebrations took place, the new nations of Africa faced tough challenges.

New Nations Emerge in Africa

After World War II, European colonial powers could no longer afford to hold onto their colonies. As nationalist demands forced Britain to withdraw from India, African leaders, too, pressed for independence.

A Geographically Diverse Continent Africa is the world's second-largest continent, more than three times the size of the United States. Tropical rain forests cover central Africa's Congo Basin and coastal West Africa. Vast **savannas,** or grasslands with scattered trees, make up interior West Africa, East Africa, and much of central and southern Africa. Africa has the world's largest desert—the Sahara—in the north and the smaller Kalahari Desert in the south, as well as fertile coastal strips in North and South Africa.

Africa's people are concentrated in the most fertile areas, such as the savanna and forest regions of Nigeria and the moist highlands of East Africa. These regions produce enough food to support large populations. Like people in other parts of the world, however, millions of Africans were migrating, or moving, from rural areas to cities.

Africa has rich deposits of minerals such as gold ore, copper ore, and diamonds. Some African nations produce valuable cash crops, including coffee and cacao—used to make chocolate. Some regions also have large oil reserves. European powers had established colonies in Africa to tap into these natural resources.

Nationalist Leaders Demand Freedom By the 1950s, nationalist movements in Africa had grown stronger. Skilled organizers such as **Kwame Nkrumah** (KWAH may un KROO muh) in Gold Coast (later Ghana), **Jomo Kenyatta** in Kenya, and Léopold Senghor (sahn GAWR) in Senegal led independence movements in their own countries.

Most African nations won independence through largely peaceful means. Drained by World War II, European powers had few resources to resist the pressure to give up their colonial empires. The struggle for freedom turned violent, however, in a few colonies where large numbers of Europeans had settled, such as Kenya and Algeria.

✔ **Checkpoint**   Why did some African countries have to fight for independence?

New Nations Build Governments

Some new nations enjoyed peace and had democratic governments. Others were plunged into crisis by civil war, military rule, or corrupt dictators. In recent decades, a number of African nations have taken steps toward democracy.

Challenges to Unity The new nations of Africa faced many difficulties, including the need to unify their people. European colonial powers had drawn boundaries around their colonies without regard to the many rival ethnic groups living in a particular region. At independence, most African nations included a patchwork of peoples with different languages, religions, and traditions. Within these new nations, people often felt their first loyalty was to their own ethnic group, not to a distant national government. As a result, conflict between different ethnic groups plagued many new nations..

Dictators Gain Power Many leaders of the new nations were heroes of the liberation struggle. Some chose to build one-party states. These leaders claimed that multiparty systems encouraged disunity. In time, these one-party governments became repressive, and some liberation leaders became dictators. Dictators often used their positions to enrich themselves and their supporters at the expense of the nation.

When bad or corrupt governments led to civil unrest, the military seized power in many countries. More than half of all African nations suffered military coups (kooz). A coup, or **coup d'état** (koo day TAH) is the forcible overthrow of a government. Some military rulers were brutal tyrants. Others tried to end corruption and improve conditions. Military leaders usually promised to restore civilian rule. But in many cases, they only surrendered power when they were toppled by another coup.

Moves Toward Democracy By the 1990s, some African nations were moving away from strongman rule. Western

Mineral Resources
A miner in the West African nation of Sierra Leone sifts gravel to find rough diamonds. Minerals are important to the economy of many African nations.

governments and lenders, such as the World Bank, demanded political reforms before granting loans. In response, some governments allowed opposition parties to emerge and expanded freedom of expression. In nations such as Nigeria, Tanzania, and Benin, multiparty elections were held, removing long-ruling leaders from office.

The Superpowers Compete for Influence Even after African nations won independence, colonial powers and foreign companies often retained control of businesses and resources in these former colonies. Many new nations remained dependent on their former colonial rulers for aid, trade, and investment.

The new nations were also buffeted by the Cold War. Both the United States and the Soviet Union competed for military and strategic advantage through alliances with several African countries. The United States, for example, backed **Mobutu Seso Seko,** the dictator of Zaire (now called the Democratic Republic of Congo). It wanted to counter Soviet influence in nearby Angola. During the 1970s, the United States backed Somalia, while the Soviet Union supported neighboring Ethiopia. Both African countries were important because they controlled access to the Red Sea, a vital world-shipping route.

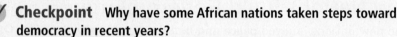 **Checkpoint** Why have some African nations taken steps toward democracy in recent years?

The Stories of Five African Nations

While the new nations of Africa faced many of the same challenges, each nation had a unique history. To gain a better understanding of the process of nation-building in Africa, we will examine the recent histories of five important nations.

Ghana In 1957, Ghana was the first African nation south of the Sahara to win independence. Britain had called this colony Gold Coast, for its rich mineral resources. Under independence leader Kwame Nkrumah, it took the name Ghana, after the ancient West African kingdom.

As president, Nkrumah supported socialism and government ownership of major industries. He backed the building of a huge dam to provide electric power, but the project left Ghana with massive debts. Nkrumah's government became increasingly corrupt and dictatorial. In 1966, Nkrumah was toppled by the first of several military coups.

This pattern repeated itself in many new African nations. Large costly projects, often poorly planned, left many countries in debt to foreign lenders. Coups and dictators became common.

Market Women in Ghana
In West African countries such as Ghana, women have traditionally sold goods in the markets. These women wait for customers with a display of food and other goods. *Why might political candidates in Ghana and elsewhere seek support from local market women?*

Independence in Africa

Map Skills From the late 1800s until the 1950s and 1960s, most African countries were colonies of European powers, which drew their borders. Most African nations gained independence during the 1950s and 1960s.

1. Locate (a) Kenya (b) Democratic Republic of the Congo (c) Angola (d) Ghana

2. Regions Which was the last of the Democratic Republic of the Congo's neighbors to gain independence?

3. Draw Conclusions When must the Cold War conflict involving independent Angola have taken place?

Geography *Interactive*
For: Interactive map
Web Code: nap-3131

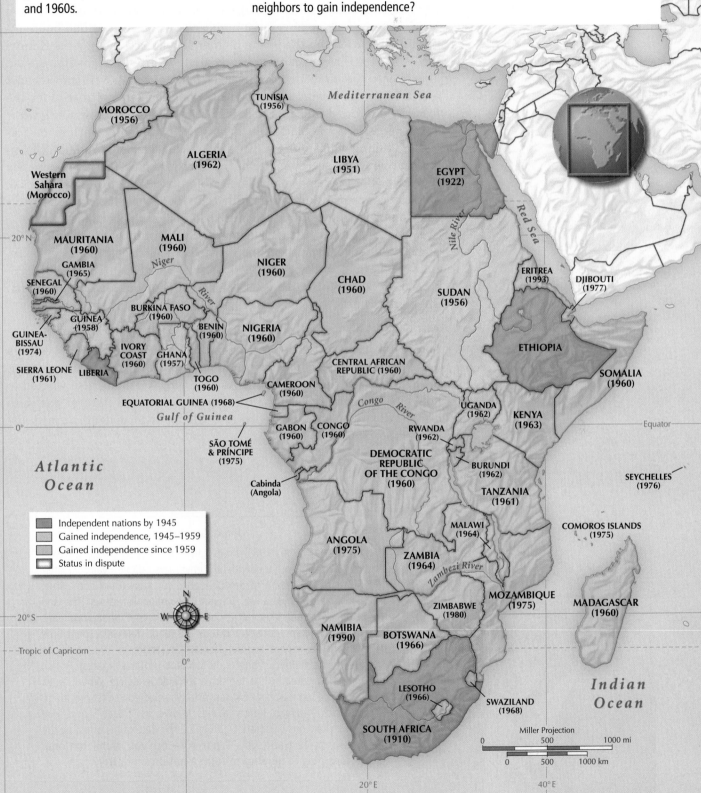

Map legend:
- Independent nations by 1945
- Gained independence, 1945–1959
- Gained independence since 1959
- Status in dispute

MOROCCO (1956)
Western Sahara (Morocco)
TUNISIA (1956)
ALGERIA (1962)
LIBYA (1951)
EGYPT (1922)
MAURITANIA (1960)
MALI (1960)
GAMBIA (1965)
SENEGAL (1960)
GUINEA (1958)
GUINEA-BISSAU (1974)
SIERRA LEONE (1961)
LIBERIA
IVORY COAST (1960)
BURKINA FASO (1960)
GHANA (1957)
TOGO (1960)
BENIN (1960)
NIGER (1960)
NIGERIA (1960)
CHAD (1960)
SUDAN (1956)
ERITREA (1993)
DJIBOUTI (1977)
ETHIOPIA
SOMALIA (1960)
CENTRAL AFRICAN REPUBLIC (1960)
CAMEROON (1960)
EQUATORIAL GUINEA (1968)
SÃO TOMÉ & PRÍNCIPE (1975)
GABON (1960)
CONGO (1960)
Cabinda (Angola)
UGANDA (1962)
RWANDA (1962)
KENYA (1963)
DEMOCRATIC REPUBLIC OF THE CONGO (1960)
BURUNDI (1962)
TANZANIA (1961)
SEYCHELLES (1976)
ANGOLA (1975)
ZAMBIA (1964)
MALAWI (1964)
COMOROS ISLANDS (1975)
MOZAMBIQUE (1975)
MADAGASCAR (1960)
ZIMBABWE (1980)
NAMIBIA (1990)
BOTSWANA (1966)
LESOTHO (1966)
SWAZILAND (1968)
SOUTH AFRICA (1910)

Mediterranean Sea
Nile River
Red Sea
Niger River
Gulf of Guinea
Congo River
Atlantic Ocean
Zambezi River
Indian Ocean
Tropic of Capricorn
Equator

Miller Projection
0 500 1000 mi
0 500 1000 km

In the 1980s, Jerry Rawlings, a military officer, took power in a coup. He strengthened the economy and moved Ghana toward democracy. In 1992, Rawlings allowed multiparty elections and was chosen president. Other elections followed. Although the economy suffered from falling prices for cocoa and gold, its main exports, Ghana made progress toward improving life for its people. The recent discovery of offshore oil raised hopes for more economic growth.

Kenya While Ghana made a peaceful transition to freedom, Kenya faced an armed struggle. A large number of white settlers had built successful plantations on the fertile highlands once occupied by the Kikuyu (kee KOO yoo), Kenya's largest ethnic group. White Kenyans had passed laws to <u>ensure</u> their domination over the black majority. Nationalist leader and Kikuyu spokesman Jomo Kenyatta had long sought justice for the black majority and called for nonviolent means to end oppressive laws.

In the 1950s, some black Kenyans turned to guerrilla warfare, attacking and killing white settlers. The British called them Mau Mau. Claiming that he was a secret leader of the Mau Mau, the British imprisoned Kenyatta. Both sides committed terrible atrocities during this period, and thousands of Kikuyu were killed. In 1963, the British finally withdrew, and Kenyatta became the first leader of an independent Kenya.

Kenyatta and his successor dominated the country for decades. They limited freedom of expression and resisted free elections. Since the 1990s, Kenya has held multiparty elections, but corruption remained widespread. In 2007, a disputed election sparked violence and ethnic unrest. The conflict hurt tourism—one of Kenya's largest industries.

Algeria Like Kenya, the French colony of Algeria had a large population of European settlers. Over one million French people called Algeria home and were determined to remain part of France. The French government, which had recently lost its Asian colony, Vietnam, also wanted to hold onto Algeria, especially after deposits of oil and natural gas were discovered there. As a result, the struggle for independence turned violent in the 1950s.

Vocabulary Builder

<u>ensure</u>—(en SHOOR) *v.* make sure or certain, guarantee

BIOGRAPHY

Jomo Kenyatta

On December 12, 1963, Jomo Kenyatta (c. 1894–1978) watched the flag of an independent Kenya rise above Nairobi. After 50 years, his dream of independence for Kenya had come true. Early in life, Kenyatta was drawn to the nationalist cause. "The land is ours," declared Kenyatta, who was a Kikuyu. "When Europeans came, they kept us back and took our land." Kenyatta spent time in England, where he met Mahatma Gandhi in 1932. Back in Kenya, he helped organize nonviolent protests against British injustices. Later, he led the drive for independence. When Kenya became a republic in 1964, Kenyatta was elected its first president. To black Kenyans, Kenyatta was known as "Mzee," or "Wise Elder." Kenyans celebrate October 20, the date of his arrest by the British, as Kenyatta Day. **What role do you think national heroes play in helping to form a nation's identity?**

An Election Celebration
Citizens of Mauritania, in West Africa, celebrate the reelection of the country's president in 2003. *Why did many nations have difficulty building democratic governments?*

Algerian nationalists set up the National Liberation Front, which turned to guerrilla warfare to win freedom. From 1954 to 1962, more than one million Algerians were killed in this bloody conflict. When public opinion in France finally turned against the war, Algeria won independence.

Algeria's oil and gas resources have helped it economically. Politically, it has suffered through periods of military rule and internal conflict. During the 1970s, the government nationalized, or took over, foreign-owned companies and created a command economy. Since the 1980s, Algeria has been moving toward a market economy.

By the 1990s, a growing struggle had erupted between the military and **Islamists,** people who want a government based on Islamic law and beliefs. In 1992, the Algerian government allowed free elections. When an Islamist party won, the military rejected the results. For seven years, civil war raged between Islamist militants and the military, leaving as many as 150,000 dead. The violence slowed after 1999, but tensions remained.

Democratic Republic of Congo The Democratic Republic of Congo (or Congo) covers a vast region of central Africa. It includes a million square miles of rain forest and savanna centered on the Congo River basin. Congo was a Belgian colony, and the Belgians were eager to keep control of Congo's rich resources, such as copper and diamonds.

When Congo gained independence in 1960, it was not prepared for self-government. The new nation included 14 million people from more than 200 separate groups. Competing economic interests and rival political leaders soon plunged Congo into civil war when the copper-rich **Katanga** province broke away. Belgian mining companies supported Katanga, hoping to control its mineral resources. The Cold War superpowers backed rival leaders, further complicating the fighting. The United Nations ended the Katanga rebellion in 1963.

In 1965, Colonel Joseph Mobutu, later known as Mobutu Sese Seko, seized power. For 32 years, Mobutu's harsh, corrupt rule brought poverty and unrest to Congo. Rebels finally forced Mobutu from power in 1997. But civil war again raged as rival military leaders battled to control Congo's mineral riches.

The country's first free elections in 41 years brought Joseph Kabila to power in 2006. As on and off violence continued in the eastern region, Kabila had to reduce corruption, calm ethnic tensions, protect Congo's mineral resources, and heal the scars caused by decades of war.

Nigeria Nigeria, on the coast of West Africa, includes diverse people and climates. Nigeria's huge population is the largest in Africa. Its people belong to more than 250 ethnic groups, speak many languages, and practice different religions. The dominant groups are the mainly Christian Ibo (EE boh) and Yoruba (YOH roo buh) in the south, and the Muslim Hausa (HOW suh) in the north.

Nigeria won independence peacefully from Britain in 1960. The next year, oil was discovered, raising hopes for the country's economic future. Instead, the country faced military coups, corruption, and economic crises. In 1966, the Ibo people in the oil-rich south rebelled and set up the independent Republic of Biafra. A brutal civil war led to famine, the death of an estimated half million people, and the end of Biafra's independence.

Between 1996 and 1999, the military was in and out of power in Nigeria. Military leaders ruled with an iron hand but failed to improve Nigeria's government or its economy. In 1999, Nigeria again held elections. A new civilian government introduced reforms to strengthen the economy and restore political freedom.

Because Nigeria relied heavily on oil exports, it was affected by the rise and fall of oil prices. Nigeria also faced ethnic and religious violence. In the north, Islamists wanted strict Sharia law. In the oil-producing Niger Delta region, local people were bitter about the environmental damage caused by oil drilling and the huge profits going to foreign companies. Armed groups attacked pipelines and held foreign oil workers for ransom.

Nigeria's Oil Industry
This oil worker is drilling for oil in southeastern Nigeria. Nigeria's vital oil industry is threatened by conflict in this oil-producing region.

✓ **Checkpoint** How did Katanga and Biafra reflect the challenges that new African nations faced after independence?

Progress Monitoring *Online*
For: Self-quiz with vocabulary practice
Web Code: naa-3131

SECTION 3 **Assessment**

Terms, People, and Places

1. Place each of the key terms at the beginning of the section into one of the following categories: politics, economy, or geography. Write a sentence for each term explaining your choice.

Note Taking

2. **Reading Skill: Identify Causes and Effects** Use your completed concept web to answer the Focus Question: What challenges did new African nations face?

Comprehension and Critical Thinking

3. **Make Comparisons** Why did some countries gain independence peacefully, while others faced violent struggles?

4. **Identify Central Issues** Why did the Cold War superpowers seek alliances with African nations?

5. **Express Problems Clearly** Based on what you have read about Algeria, what problems caused the civil war in Algeria?

6. **Draw Conclusions** How have religious and ethnic divisions affected Nigeria's history?

● **Writing About History**

Quick Write: Provide Elaboration To write a compare-and-contrast essay, you need to provide examples that support the main point of the essay. Suppose that the point of your essay is to compare and contrast challenges faced by Algeria and Nigeria since independence. Draft two sentences for an essay. In each sentence, give examples that compare or contrast a challenge faced by these countries.

Kwame Nkrumah: *Autobiography*

Kwame Nkrumah led the people of Gold Coast in their quest for independence from Britain. After succeeding in 1957, Nkrumah became the first prime minister and renamed the country Ghana. In this excerpt from his *Autobiography,* Nkrumah speaks of the need to establish economic independence as a means of maintaining political independence. Nkrumah describes the difficult work of building an independent economy.

▲ Prime Minister Kwame Nkrumah of Ghana

Independence for the Gold Coast was my aim. It was a colony, and I have always regarded colonialism as the policy by which a foreign power binds territories to herself by political ties with the primary object of promoting her own economic advantage. No one need be surprised if this system has led to disturbances and political tension in many territories. There are few people who would not rid themselves of such domination if they could. . . .

I saw that the whole solution to [our] problem lay in political freedom for our people, for it is only when a people are politically free that other races can give them the respect that is due to them. It is impossible to talk of equality of races in any other terms. No people without a government of their own can expect to be treated on the same level as peoples of independent sovereign[1] states. It is far better to be free to govern or misgovern yourself than to be governed by anybody else. . . .

Once this freedom is gained, a greater task comes into view. All dependent[2] territories are backward in education, in science, in agriculture, and in industry. The economic independence that should follow and maintain political independence demands every effort from the people, a total mobilization of brain and manpower resources. What other countries have taken three hundred years or more to achieve, a once dependent territory must try to accomplish in a generation if it is to survive. . . .

▲ Ghana's leaders—including Kwame Nkrumah, at center—celebrate Ghana's independence in 1957.

Thinking Critically

1. **Identify Point of View** What does Nkrumah think the people of a dependent territory must do before they can achieve economic independence?
2. **Draw Inferences** Based on Nkrumah's remarks, what makes economic independence difficult for newly independent nations to achieve?

1. **sovereign** (SAHV run) *adj.* not subject to any other power
2. **dependent** (dee PEN dunt) *adj.* subject to the power of another

Egypt's leader, Gamal Abdel Nasser, greets children in 1956.

Islamic ornamental writing from a mosque in Iran

WITNESS HISTORY 🔊 AUDIO

Remembering Nasser

As a young boy in Syria, Nasser Rabbat recalls seeing the Arab leader, Gamal Abdel Nasser.

❝One of my earliest memories dates back to the winter of 1960 when I was almost four years old. I remember . . . screaming with the crowd around us 'Nasser, Nasser.' . . . I had been taught . . . to be proud of . . . Nasser, 'the unifier of the Arabs' and 'the leader of our new renaissance.'❞
—Nasser Rabbat, "On being named Nasser"

In the decades after World War II, nationalism was a major force shaping Middle Eastern nations from Egypt and Israel to Turkey and Iran.

Focus Question What were some similarities and differences in the nations of the Middle East?

The Modern Middle East

 Performance Standards

- **SSWH19b** Describe the formation of Israel, and the importance of its geography in its development.
- **SSWH21b** Analyze OPEC.

Terms, People, and Places

kibbutz	Anwar Sadat
secular	Mohammad Mosaddeq
hejab	Ruhollah Khomeini
Suez Canal	theocracy
Gamal Abdel Nasser	

Note Taking

Reading Skill: Identify Causes and Effects Fill in a concept web like this one to keep track of events in the Middle East since 1945.

In the 1950s, leaders like Egypt's Gamal Abdel Nasser set out to build strong nations across the Middle East. Most Middle Eastern countries were poor—only a few had rich oil reserves. Autocratic governments and internal divisions hindered progress throughout the region.

Diversity Brings Challenges

The Middle East, as we use the term in this chapter, is the region stretching from Egypt in the west to Iran in the east and from Turkey in the north to the Arabian Peninsula in the south. Though most people in the region today are Muslims, there are also Christian communities and the predominantly Jewish nation of Israel. Most countries have large ethnic or religious minorities.

Mandates Gain Independence After World War I, Britain and France were given mandates over parts of the Middle East. During the 1930s and 1940s, nationalists demanded an end to European control, and the mandates became the independent states of Iraq, Syria, Lebanon, Jordan, and Israel.

Kurds Seek Rights In the Middle East, as elsewhere, new nations faced challenges from ethnic minorities that demanded self rule, or even independence. The Kurds are an ethnic group with their own language and culture, and are an important minority in Turkey, Iran, and Iraq.

Kurds faced discrimination and harsh treatment, especially in Iraq and Turkey. In Turkey, Kurdish rebels resisted government efforts to suppress their culture. Thousands died fighting the government. In Iraq, a Kurdish rebellion after the 1991 Gulf War was brutally suppressed. As you will read, Kurds form one of the three main groups sharing power in Iraq. However, some Kurds still want their own state.

Israel Is Founded As you have learned, Britain supported a Jewish national homeland in part of its Palestine Mandate. The horrific experience of Jews in the Holocaust added to worldwide support for a Jewish homeland. Jews, including many Holocaust survivors, sought to migrate there after World War II. In 1947, the UN drew up a plan to divide the Palestine Mandate into an Arab and a Jewish state. Jews accepted the plan, but Arabs rejected it. They felt that all of Palestine should belong to them.

After Britain withdrew from Palestine in 1948, Jews proclaimed the independent State of Israel. Arab states launched the first of several wars against Israel but were defeated. Israel developed rapidly. A skilled workforce built businesses. Kibbutzim produced crops for export. A **kibbutz** (kih BOOTS) is a collective farm. Israel attracted Jews from around the world, including Jews expelled from other Middle Eastern lands.

The conflicts of 1948 created enormous refugee problems. As a result of the war, hundreds of thousands of Palestinian Arabs fled their homes

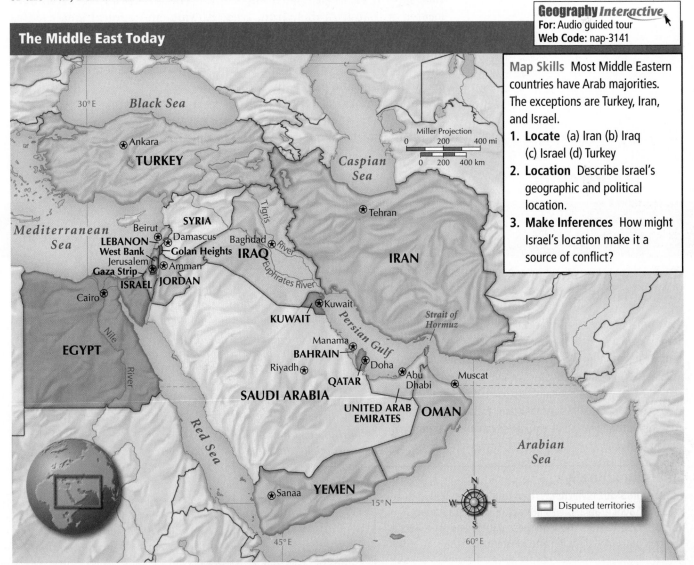

Geography *Interactive*
For: Audio guided tour
Web Code: nap-3141

The Middle East Today

Map Skills Most Middle Eastern countries have Arab majorities. The exceptions are Turkey, Iran, and Israel.
1. **Locate** (a) Iran (b) Iraq (c) Israel (d) Turkey
2. **Location** Describe Israel's geographic and political location.
3. **Make Inferences** How might Israel's location make it a source of conflict?

in Israeli territory. The UN set up camps in neighboring areas to house them. Hundreds of thousands of Jews from Arab lands were also driven from their homes. Both sides feel embittered by the displacements.

Political Systems Limit Freedom Most Middle Eastern nations have had autocratic governments. In some countries, nationalist military leaders seized power. In other countries, such as Jordan and Saudi Arabia, hereditary monarchs remained in power. Only Israel and Turkey had stable multiparty democratic systems by 2005.

✔ **Checkpoint** Why did many people around the world support a Jewish homeland in Palestine?

Sources of Conflict

Some Middle Eastern nations sit atop vast oil and gas reserves. These oil-rich nations have prospered. Although these countries have helped their less fortunate neighbors, many Middle Eastern nations struggled economically. Meanwhile, Muslims have disagreed over the role of Islam in a modern society.

Supplying the World With Oil The huge oil resources of the Middle East gave it strategic, global importance. The largest oil resources were located in Saudi Arabia, Iran, Iraq, Kuwait, and several small states along the Persian Gulf. In 1960, these nations, along with Venezuela, set up the Organization of Petroleum Exporting Countries (OPEC). OPEC wanted to end the power of Western oil companies and determine oil production quotas and prices. In 1973, Middle Eastern members of OPEC used oil as a weapon. They stopped oil shipments to countries that had supported Israel in the

● **INFOGRAPHIC**

Islam and the Modern World

Like other religions, Islam faces the challenge of adapting its traditions to a changing modern world. While religious traditions remain important to Muslims, Western culture has gained influence. Traditionally, in Islamic countries, women were not expected to read or write. Today, Muslim women are pursuing educations and new career opportunities. While Islamists call for a return to tradition, many Muslims embrace a mixture of traditional and modern ways.

The Iraqi artist ▲ Hassan Massoudy combines the Islamic tradition of calligraphy, or ornamental writing, with abstract Western styles.

◀ The basic principles of Islam, such as pilgrimage and prayer, remain important to modern Muslims, such as the Iraqi pilgrim to the left.

Thinking Critically
1. **Graph Skills** Which has risen faster since 1990 in Turkey and Saudi Arabia, men's literacy or women's literacy?
2. **Analyze Visuals** How do these photos and art reflect a mix of Islamic tradition and Western styles?

Yom Kippur War. This oil embargo triggered a worldwide recession. Since then, OPEC has focused on setting production quotas.

Islam in the Modern World After independence, some Middle Eastern countries adopted Western-style **secular,** or nonreligious, governments. At the same time, Western cultural influences grew. In cities, people bought imported goods from the West, wore Western fashions, and watched American television shows and movies.

Some Muslims claimed that secular Western culture was undermining Islamic society. They called for a return to Sharia, or Islamic law based on the Quran. These conservative reformers, known as Islamists, blamed social and economic ills on the West. Only a renewed commitment to Islamic <u>doctrine</u>, they declared, could improve conditions in the Muslim world. Many Muslims welcomed the Islamist movement as a way to cope with rapid social and economic changes. Although some people advocated violence to achieve their goals, most Muslims opposed Islamic extremists.

Vocabulary Builder
<u>doctrine</u>—(DAHK trin) *n.* teachings, principles, or beliefs

Changes Affect Women's Lives Conditions for women vary greatly across the Middle East. In most countries, women won equality before the law. Educated women entered professions such as law and medicine. In Turkey, Egypt, and Syria, many urban women gave up the **hejab,** or traditional Muslim headscarf, or wearing loose, ankle-length garments meant to conceal. Some women, however, embraced these traditions as a symbol of their Islamic faith.

In religiously conservative countries like Saudi Arabia and Iran, women must follow Islamic traditions, such as wearing the hejab. In many Middle Eastern countries, girls are less likely to attend school than boys, because of a traditional belief that girls do not need a formal education for their expected roles as wives and mothers. Women's rights movements, however, have challenged these traditions.

✓ **Checkpoint** Why did Islamists oppose secular government and culture in the Muslim world?

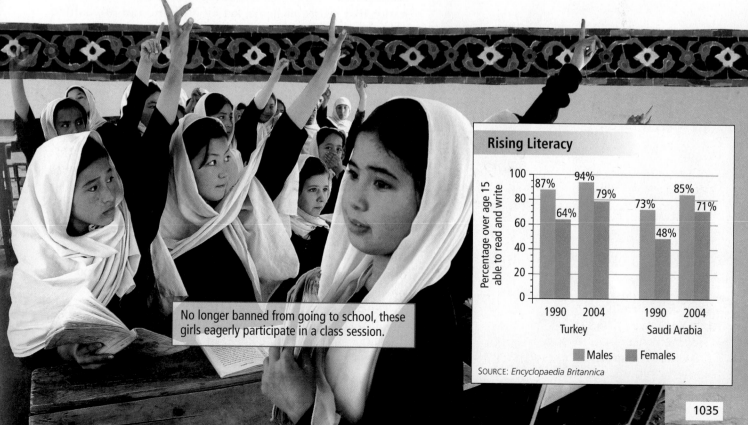

No longer banned from going to school, these girls eagerly participate in a class session.

Rising Literacy

Percentage over age 15 able to read and write

Turkey: 1990 — 87% (Males), 64% (Females); 2004 — 94% (Males), 79% (Females)

Saudi Arabia: 1990 — 73% (Males), 48% (Females); 2004 — 85% (Males), 71% (Females)

■ Males ■ Females

SOURCE: *Encyclopaedia Britannica*

Building Nations in the Middle East

Across the Middle East, leaders sought to build strong and prosperous nations. However, in the years since World War II, each nation has faced different challenges.

Egypt, a Leader in the Arab World Egypt has the largest population of the Arab nations. While most of Egypt is desert, its large population is crammed into the narrow Nile River valley. Egypt's location is strategically important, because it shares a long border with Israel and controls the **Suez Canal,** which links Europe with Asia and East Africa.

In 1952, **Gamal Abdel Nasser** seized power in Egypt. Determined to modernize Egypt and stop Western domination, Nasser nationalized the Suez Canal in 1956, ending British and French control. Although Britain and France responded militarily, the United States and the Soviet Union forced them to withdraw. Nasser's Arab nationalism made him popular throughout the Arab world. Nasser led two unsuccessful wars against Israel. To counter U.S. support for Israel, Egypt relied on Soviet aid. Egypt's foreign relations thus took on Cold War significance.

In 1979, Nasser's successor, **Anwar Sadat,** became the first Arab leader to make peace with Israel. Sadat also weakened ties with the Soviet Union and sought U.S. aid. However, Islamists denounced the undemocratic government's failure to end corruption and poverty. In 1981, Muslim fundamentalists assassinated Sadat. Under Sadat's appointed successor, Hosni Mubarak, extremists turned to terrorist attacks, and harsh government crackdowns tended to increase support for Islamists.

Iran's Islamic Revolution Because of its vast oil fields, Iran was a focus of Cold War interest. Iran's ruler, Shah Mohammad Reza Pahlavi, favored the West but faced nationalist critics at home, led by **Mohammad Mosaddeq** (MAW sah dek). When Mosaddeq was elected prime minister in 1951, he nationalized the foreign-owned oil industry. With American help, the shah ousted Mosaddeq and returned Iran's oil industry to Western control. This move outraged many Iranians.

Over the next decades, the shah used oil wealth to build industries and redistribute land to peasants. He also gave new rights to women. Opposition to the shah grew, especially among the Islamic clergy. In response, the shah's secret police terrorized critics.

The shah's foes rallied behind Ayatollah **Ruhollah Khomeini** (ROO hoh lah koh MAY nee). The ayatollah, a religious leader, condemned Western influences and accused the shah of violating Islamic law. In 1979, massive protests drove the shah from power. Khomeini and his supporters proclaimed an Islamic republic.

The new government was a **theocracy,** or government by religious leaders. They ran the country based on Islamic law. Like the shah, they silenced critics. In 1979, Islamists seized the American embassy in the capital and held 52 hostages for more than a year. The new Islamic republic soon

An Islamist Government
Iran's political leaders, who are Muslim clergymen, gather in 2003 to commemorate the death of Ayatollah Khomeini, a religious leader and the founder of Iran's Islamist government. The leaders are seated beneath a giant portrait of Khomeini. *How does promoting the memory of Khomeini help to justify rule by religious leaders?*

faced a long, bloody war with its neighbor, Iraq, and tense relations with the West. The United States imposed economic sanctions and accused Iran of backing terrorists. After the 2003 U.S. occupation of Iraq, American officials accused Iran of providing weapons to Iraqi fighters for use against U.S. forces. Iran was also accused of using nuclear research as a cover for developing nuclear weapons.

Oil, Religion, and Threats to Stability Saudi Arabia, a vast desert land, has the world's largest oil reserves. It also includes Islam's holy land. Since the 1920s, kings from the Sa'ud (sah OOD) family have ruled Saudi Arabia. They justify their rule by their commitment to the strict Wahhabi sect of Sunni Islam.

However, Saudi Arabia's economic development after World War II depended on massive oil exports to the Western world. In return, Saudi leaders relied on the military support of the United States. Although Saudi Arabia joined the OPEC oil embargo in 1973, the nation's rulers quickly returned to their cooperative relationship with the West.

To build support within the country, the royal family backed fundamentalist religious leaders. However, some of these leaders and their followers criticized the kingdom's close ties to the West. They also charged that Western influence in the kingdom violated Islamic principles.

Increasingly, opponents of the kingdom's Western ties adopted violent or terrorist tactics. Attacks on western targets included an attack on a U.S. military compound in 1996 and another on a U.S. consulate in 2004. These attacks threatened to disrupt the Saudi oil industry, which depends on Western expertise. Some feared that growing unrest could threaten the country's ability to supply oil vital to the world's economy.

Other oil-rich monarchies along the Persian Gulf, such as Kuwait, Bahrain, Qatar, and the United Arab Emirates, face similar threats. In Kuwait, Qatar, and the U.A.E., foreign citizens are a majority of the population. In Bahrain, there has been growing opposition among the majority of the people, who follow Shiite Islam, toward Bahrain's royal family, who follow the Sunni branch of Islam.

 Checkpoint What were Ayatollah Khomeini's reasons for opposing the shah?

SECTION 4 Assessment

Progress Monitoring *Online*
For: Self-quiz with vocabulary practice
Web Code: naa-3141

Terms, People, and Places

1. For each term, person, or place listed in the beginning of the section, write a sentence explaining its significance.

Note Taking

2. **Reading Skill: Identify Causes and Effects** Use your completed concept web to answer the Focus Question: What were some main similarities and differences in the nations of the Middle East?

Comprehension and Critical Thinking

3. **Summarize** How was the Holocaust connected to the birth of Israel?

4. **Identify Central Issues** What changes in government policies did the Islamists seek?

5. **Draw Conclusions** Why did Egypt attract the interest of the superpowers during the Cold War?

6. **Synthesize Information** How has the Saudi royal family's support for fundamentalism made their kingdom more unstable in recent years?

● **Writing About History**

Quick Write: Revise Your Writing When you write a compare-and-contrast essay, combining short sentences can improve your writing. Write a short sentence that states a fact about a Middle Eastern country. Write a second sentence stating a similar or different fact about another Middle Eastern country. Revise your sentences by joining them into a single sentence that compares or contrasts these facts, using conjunctions such as *while, whereas, yet, both, and,* or *also.*

Quick Study Guide

SSWH19a, SSWH20a, SSWH20d

■ Common Themes in New Nations

- Borders drawn by European colonial powers left nations with diverse religions and ethnic groups.
- Ethnic and religious diversity has brought conflict.
- Military coups, one-party systems, and dictatorships kept some countries from achieving democracy.
- Citizens and foreign lenders have forced former dictatorships to hold elections and transition to democracy.
- Natural resources such as oil have been a source of wealth for some nations but have fueled conflicts in others.
- During the Cold War, the United States and Soviet Union competed for influence, particularly in regions with natural resources such as oil, or locations near strategic waterways.

■ Leaders of New Nations

- Jawaharlal Nehru, *first prime minister of India*
- Indira Gandhi, *first female prime minister of India*
- Aung San Suu Kyi, *leader of Myanmar democracy movement*
- Sukarno, *founder and first president of Indonesia*
- Suharto, *military dictator of Indonesia*
- Corazon Aquino, *democratic president of the Philippines*
- Kwame Nkrumah, *founder and first president of Ghana*
- Jomo Kenyatta, *founder and first president of Kenya*
- David Ben-Gurion, *first prime minister of Israel*
- Gamal Abdel Nasser, *an Arab nationalist and first president of Egypt*
- Mohammad Reza Pahlavi, *shah of Iran*
- Ruhollah Khomeini, *leader of the religious government of Iran*

■ New Nations Emerge

Decade country gained independence
- Before 1940
- 1940s
- 1950s
- 1960s
- 1970s
- Since 1980

■ Key Events in the Emergence of New Nations

Africa and the Middle East
South and Southeast Asia

1946 Syria and Jordan gain independence.

1948 Israel is founded.

1956–1966 More than 30 African nations win independence.

1940 **1950** **1960** **1970**

1947 India and Pakistan win independence after partition.

1966 Suharto establishes military dictatorship in Indonesia.

Concept Connector

Essential Question Review

To connect prior knowledge with what you have learned in this chapter, answer the questions below in your Concept Connector journal. Use the journal in the Reading and Note Taking Study Guide to record your answers (or go to www.phschool.com **Web Code**: nad-3107).

1. **Revolution** Between 1946 and 1970, European colonies around the world won independence. Choose one of these colonies and compare its struggle for independence with the American Revolution, which brought independence to the United States in the late 1700s. Consider the following:
   - the presence or the absence of military conflict
   - the challenge of forming stable governments after independence

2. **Nationalism** Although India has large religious minorities, the Bharatiya Janata Party (BJP) promoted Hindu nationalism, or the idea that India should favor the Hindu majority and the Hindu religion. How do you think the BJP's stand affected peace and stability in India?

3. **Dictatorship** In many African nations that gained independence after World War II, dictators seized power and established one-party political systems. These leaders claimed that multiparty systems encouraged disunity. Do you think the dictators' concerns were genuine? What appeal might the disunity argument have for citizens of a newly independent nation?

4. **Geography's Impact** The world's largest reserves of oil are located in the Middle East. What impact has the location of this valuable resource had on global politics and the economy?

Connections to Today

1. **Conflict: Struggles for Independence** Former European colonies such as Algeria had to fight deadly wars to win their independence. Today, in different parts of the world, people continue to fight for independence. Examples include Darfur, where rebels have fought against Sudan, and Papua, where rebels seek independence from Indonesia. Research one of these regions. Explain why this region is fighting for independence.

2. **Belief Systems: World Religions** In this chapter, you have seen that religions remain an important force in today's world. Turn to the Concept Connector Handbook on Culture at the back of your textbook. There you will find a list of world religions and their key beliefs. List the beliefs, traditions, customs, and sacred writings of Judaism, Christianity, Islam, Buddhism, and Hinduism. Then, using reliable sources from the Internet or a library, research and list the present-day geographic distribution of each of these religions.

1973
OPEC oil embargo

1979
Iranian revolution

1990–2002
African nations move toward democracy.

Mid-2000s
Tensions grow between Iran and the West.

1980   **1990**   **2000**   **2010**

1971
Bangladesh wins independence.

1986
"People power" revolution in the Philippines

1998
Indonesia returns to democracy.

History Interactive
For: Interactive timeline
Web Code: nap-3151

Chapter Assessment

Terms, People, and Places

Match the following definitions with the terms listed below.

Indira Gandhi	coup d'état
nonalignment	theocracy
Corazon Aquino	kibbutz

1. rule by religious leaders
2. a political leader in the Philippines
3. the first female prime minister of India
4. a collective farm
5. political and diplomatic independence
6. the forcible overthrow of a government

Main Ideas

Section 1 (pp. 1014–1019)

7. Why was British India divided into India and Pakistan?
8. How did religious and ethnic diversity pose challenges for South Asian nations after independence?

Section 2 (pp. 1020–1023)

9. Compare the nations of Southeast Asia in the progress that they have made toward democracy.

Section 3 (pp. 1024–1031)

10. How did African nations win their independence? How did this differ among nations?
11. What obstacles slowed progress toward democracy for some African nations?

Section 4 (pp. 1032–1037)

12. How has the Islamist movement affected politics in the Middle East?

Chapter Focus Question

13. How did former European colonies gain independence, and what challenges did they face after independence?

Critical Thinking

14. **Draw Conclusions** How did the Philippines and Indonesia achieve democracy?
15. **Synthesize Information** How has religion influenced the recent history of the Middle East?
16. **Analyzing Visuals** The photograph below shows refugees from the partition of India and Pakistan. What does it suggest about conditions for these refugees?

17. **Make Comparisons** Compare the impact of ethnic and religious diversity on the histories of India and Pakistan.
18. **Analyze Information** How have the natural resources of the Middle East affected its recent history?
19. **Draw Conclusions** How were African nations affected by military rule and dictatorships? Support your conclusions with examples.
20. **Recognize Cause and Effect** What have been some lasting effects of colonial rule on African nations?

● Writing About History

In this chapter's four Section Assessments, you learned how to write a compare-contrast essay.

Writing a Compare-Contrast Essay Write a compare-contrast essay on the post-independence histories of two countries covered in different sections of this chapter. Discuss similarities and differences in the histories of the two countries. Consult page SH10 of the Writing Handbook for additional help.

Prewriting

• Go online or do library research to find information about the post-independence histories of countries covered in this chapter.

• Choose two countries that interest you and take notes about the challenges these countries faced.
• Gather evidence that supports comparisons and contrasts between these countries.

Drafting

• Write a first paragraph with a thesis statement and details about similarities between the two countries.
• Write a second paragraph with a topic sentence and details about differences between the two countries.

Revising

• Use the guidelines for revising your report on page SH12 of the Writing Handbook.

Prepare for the GHSGT

The Kashmir Question

In 1947, British India was partitioned into Hindu-majority India and Muslim-majority Pakistan. Kashmir is claimed by both India and Pakistan and has been a battleground between the two countries. The documents below help to show why the "Kashmir problem" remains worrisome today.

Document A

Hum kya chahtey? Azaadi! (What do we want? Freedom!)

—Slogan in Kashmir Valley

Document B

"Mr. Jinnah and his colleagues in the Muslim League, the creators of Pakistan, had always considered that the Vale of Kashmir at least would form part of the new Islamic State . . . When in 1933 Choudhri Rahmat Ali coined the word Pakistan as a suitable name for the State, he intended the letter K in 'Pak' to stand for Kashmir. The geographical and historical links between the Panjab and the Vale of Kashmir were so close that it was inevitable that the two regions should find themselves combined in the thoughts of the protagonists of a separate Islamic State."

—From ***Crisis in Kashmir, 1947–1966*** by Alastair Lamb

Document C

Document D

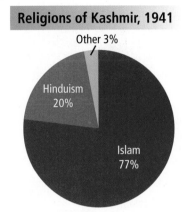

Religions of Kashmir, 1941

Other 3%
Hinduism 20%
Islam 77%

SOURCE: *Census of India, 1941*

Document E

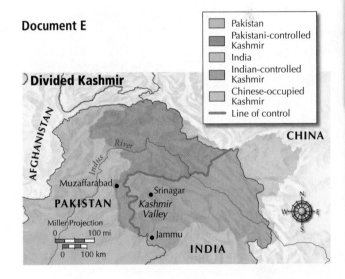

Pakistan
Pakistani-controlled Kashmir
India
Indian-controlled Kashmir
Chinese-occupied Kashmir
Line of control

Divided Kashmir

Analyzing Documents

Use your knowledge of World War II and Documents A, B, C, D, and E to answer questions 1–4.

1. According to Document B, Kashmir and Pakistan share
   A the same heroes and poets.
   B a similar history and geography.
   C the same language and literature.
   D similar architecture and art.

2. What argument does the billboard in Document C support?
   A India is a diverse country, and the region of Kashmir is an important part of it.
   B India will never let go of Kashmir.
   C Kashmir is more beautiful than other parts of India.
   D Indians are tired of dealing with Kashmir and its thorny problems.

3. According to Document D, Kashmir's population
   A is evenly balanced among its different religions.
   B is about one-half Hindu and "Other."
   C only has two religious affiliations.
   D is more than three-quarters Muslim.

4. **Writing Task** Why has Kashmir continued to be a volatile spot for so long? What are the main causes of the conflict there? Use information from these documents along with information from the chapter to write your response.

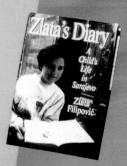

Zlata's Diary, a teenage girl's account of the conflict in Bosnia

Life in a War Zone

For more than a year, hostile troops surrounded the city of Sarajevo in Bosnia and fired down on it from the hills above. Zlatko Dizdarević, a journalist in Sarajevo, wrote this journal entry during the conflict:

66 It's been a relentless morning. Shells are falling close by us, perhaps closer than ever before. The official alert remains in force; so does our private and personal alert. We evaluate our chances, run risks, and keep hoping. 99

Listen to the Witness History audio to hear more about the war in Bosnia.

◄ **A boy dodging sniper fire to get water, Sarajevo, Bosnia, 1993**

 Performance Standards

Chapter Focus Question Why have deadly conflicts plagued some regions of the world?

Section 1
Conflicts Divide Nations
SSWH20a

Section 2
Struggles in Africa
SSWH19e, SSWH20a

Section 3
Conflicts in the Middle East
SSWH19b, SSWH20a, SSWH20c, SSWH20d

Nelson Mandela, who led a struggle against racial discrimination and became president of South Africa

A fallen statue of Saddam Hussein, the dictator of Iraq, who was overthrown by American troops

Use the ☑ **Quick Study Timeline** at the end of this chapter to preview chapter events.

 Concept Connector ONLINE

To explore Essential Questions related to this chapter, go to PHSchool.com
Web Code: nad-3207

Zlata Filipovic in 1994

WITNESS HISTORY ◀)) AUDIO

A Young Girl in Wartime

Zlata Filipovic (fee LEEP uh vich) was 11 years old in 1992 when she began a diary about her life in war-torn Sarajevo, the capital of Bosnia. Here is an excerpt:

“Today a shell fell on the park in front of my house, the park where I used to play and sit with my girl-friends. A lot of people were hurt . . . AND NINA IS DEAD . . . She was such a sweet, nice little girl.”
—Zlata Filipovic, *Zlata's Diary*

Bosnia is just one of the nations that have faced ethnic, religious, or national conflicts in recent decades.

Focus Question Why have ethnic and religious conflicts divided some nations?

Conflicts Divide Nations

 Performance Standards

- **SSWH20a** Identify conflict in Bosnia-Herzegovina, other ethnic conflicts, and new nationalisms since the 1960s.

Terms, People, and Places

Northern Ireland	Slobodan Milosevic
Good Friday Agreement	ethnic cleansing
Chechnya	Kosovo
multiethnic	

N̲o̲te Taking

Reading Skill: Recognize Sequence Fill in a flowchart like the one below to keep track of the sequence of events in the conflicts in Northern Ireland, Chechnya, and Yugoslavia.

Sequence of Conflicts		
Northern Ireland	**Chechnya**	**Yugoslavia**
• 1922: Six Irish counties vote to remain in the United Kingdom. •	• •	• •

In recent decades, wars have raged in many parts of the world. These conflicts had complex causes. But rivalries between different ethnic, religious, and nationalist groups have often led to civil wars and regional conflicts.

Sources of Conflict

Nationalism led to the creation of many new nations after World War II. Many of these nations were former colonies or mandates. Their borders had been drawn by European powers with little concern for ethnic, religious, or regional differences. As a result, these new nations had culturally diverse populations. In some cases, minorities controlled the government and imposed their will on the majority. Often, the majority ethnic or religious group dominated the government and the economy and oppressed other groups.

War in Sri Lanka Discrimination, or unfair treatment, based on language, ethnicity, and culture has frequently set one group against another. In the island nation of Sri Lanka, discrimination and violence by majority Sinhalese Buddhists against Tamil-speaking Hindus led to rebellion. Since 1983, Tamil rebels, known as the Tamil Tigers, have fought to establish a separate Tamil homeland. The Tamil Tigers used terrorist tactics and guerrilla warfare. Peace talks held in 2002 led to a truce that slowed, but did not end the violence. However, by early 2009, government troops had toppled several Tamil rebel strongholds in a final push to end the 25-year-old civil war.

Divisions in Canada Some countries, such as Canada, have found peaceful ways to resolve internal conflicts. Although Canada is mostly English-speaking, the province of Quebec is mainly French-speaking. At times, many people in Quebec wanted to separate from Canada. While a few separatists turned to violence, most worked within Canada's democratic system to protect their language and culture.

Troubles in Northern Ireland Religious and economic discrimination fueled a long struggle in Northern Ireland. When Ireland won independence in 1922, Britain kept control of **Northern Ireland,** the six northern counties that had a Protestant majority. Faced with discrimination, minority Catholics demanded civil rights and unification with the rest of Ireland. Protestants wanted Northern Ireland to remain part of Britain.

In the 1960s, extremists on both sides turned to violence and terrorism. The mostly Catholic Irish Republican Army (IRA) attacked Protestants, while armed Protestant groups targeted Catholics. The violence, known as "the Troubles," raged for three decades. Finally, in 1998, both sides signed a peace accord, known as the **Good Friday Agreement.** Protestants and Catholics set up a power-sharing government in 2007. Although there have been isolated acts of violence, most people hoped that peace would last after years of conflict.

✔ **Checkpoint** Why did conflict break out in Northern Ireland?

Contrasting Ethnic Relations

Nation	Political System	Ethnic Conflict
Sri Lanka	Limits rights of minority groups	Has led to violence
Canada	Protects minority groups	Resolved democratically

Chart Skills Based on the chart and the information in this section, explain why the response of the ethnic minority to discrimination in Sri Lanka differed from that in Canada.

Russia and Its Neighbors

Ethnic and religious tensions in Russia and in several former Soviet republics fueled conflicts within Russia. In 1994, separatists in **Chechnya** tried to break away from Russian rule. Chechnya was home to diverse ethnic and religious groups, including Muslim Chechens.

Russia crushed the Chechen revolt, killing many civilians. During two wars and nearly ten years of fighting, both sides committed atrocities. In the early 2000s, Chechen rebels launched terrorist attacks on Moscow, and killed school children in the city of Beslan. By 2009, a Russian-backed leader was rebuilding Chechnya, despite occasional violence.

In the oil-rich former Soviet republic of Azerbaijan, Azeris are the majority. In the region of Nagorno-Karabakh, however, ethnic Armenians outnumbered Azeris. When Armenians declared independence, fierce fighting raged. The Armenians gained control of the region, creating one million Azeri refugees.

In Georgia, another former Soviet republic, two provinces, South Ossetia and Abkhazia, wanted to break away. Russia backed the separatists. In 2008, after Georgia attacked separatists in South Ossetia, fighting erupted between Russian and Georgian troops. International pressure soon ended the conflict, but tensions remained high.

Grozny in Ruins
Russian forces destroyed Grozny, the capital of Chechnya, during the fighting in 2000. The city was later rebuilt.

✔ **Checkpoint** What were the causes of the conflicts that erupted in the former Soviet Union?

Yugoslavia Breaks Apart

Ethnic, nationalist, and religious tensions tore Yugoslavia apart during the 1990s. Before 1991, Yugoslavia was **multiethnic,** or made up of several ethnic groups. These groups included Serbs, Montenegrins, and Macedonians, who were Orthodox Christians; Croats and Slovenes, who were Roman Catholics; and the mostly Muslim Bosniaks and Albanians. A majority of Yugoslavians—including the Serbs, Montenegrins, Croats, and Bosniaks—all spoke the same language, Serbo-Croatian, but these groups had different religions. Albanians, Slovenes, and Macedonians spoke minority languages.

Yugoslavia was made up of six republics, similar to states in the United States. These were Slovenia, Croatia, Serbia, Bosnia and Herzegovina (often known as Bosnia for short), Montenegro, and Macedonia. Each republic had a dominant ethnic group but also was home to ethnic minorities. Serbs formed the majority in Serbia but were an important ethnic minority in several of the other republics. Serbs <u>dominated</u> Yugoslavia, which was held together and controlled by its Communist Party.

Vocabulary Builder

<u>dominate</u>—(DAHM uh nayt) *v.* to control or have power over

Republics Break Away

The fall of communism fed nationalist unrest throughout Yugoslavia. The Serbian-dominated government tried to preserve the country. In 1991, however, Slovenia and Croatia declared independence. This move triggered fighting between Croats and the Serbian minority within Croatia. Macedonia and Bosnia soon broke away from Yugoslavia as well, leaving only Serbia and Montenegro. In 2006, Montenegro also went its own way, separate from Serbia.

Civil War Devastates Bosnia

When Bosnia declared independence in 1992, civil war erupted among Bosniaks, Serbs, and Croats. Bosnian Serbs wanted to set up their own government. They received money and arms from Serbian president **Slobodan Milosevic** (mih LOH shuh vich), an extreme Serb nationalist. The largest group in Bosnia, the Muslim Bosniaks, lived scattered across Bosnia. They did not want the country divided into ethnic regions.

During the war, all sides committed atrocities. Bosnian Serbs conducted a vicious campaign of **ethnic cleansing.** This meant killing people from other ethnic groups or forcibly removing them from their homes to create ethnically "pure" areas, in this case for Serbs. Tens of thousands of Bosniaks and Croats were brutalized or killed, sometimes in mass executions. Croat and Bosnian fighters took revenge. Croats launched an ethnic cleansing campaign to drive ethnic Serbs from parts of Croatia.

Finally, NATO air strikes against the Bosnian Serb military forced the warring parties to the peace table. Guided by the United States, the rival groups signed the Dayton Accords, ending the war in 1995. An international force helped maintain a fragile peace in Bosnia.

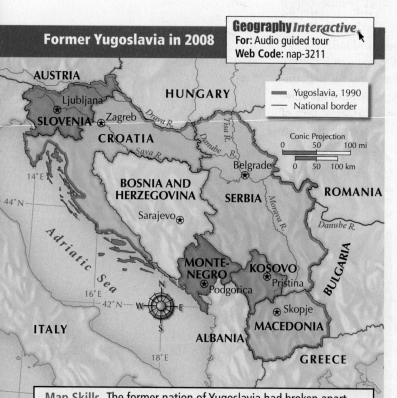

Former Yugoslavia in 2008

Geography *Interactive.*
For: Audio guided tour
Web Code: nap-3211

Yugoslavia, 1990
National border

Conic Projection
0   50   100 mi
0   50   100 km

Map Skills The former nation of Yugoslavia had broken apart into six new nations by 2006. In 2008, Kosovo declared its independence from Serbia.

1. **Locate** (a) Sarajevo (b) Serbia (c) Kosovo
2. **Location** Which new nation does not share a border with Serbia on any side?
3. **Make Inferences** How did the location of Bosnia and Herzegovina put it at risk of becoming involved in conflicts between Serbians and Croatians?

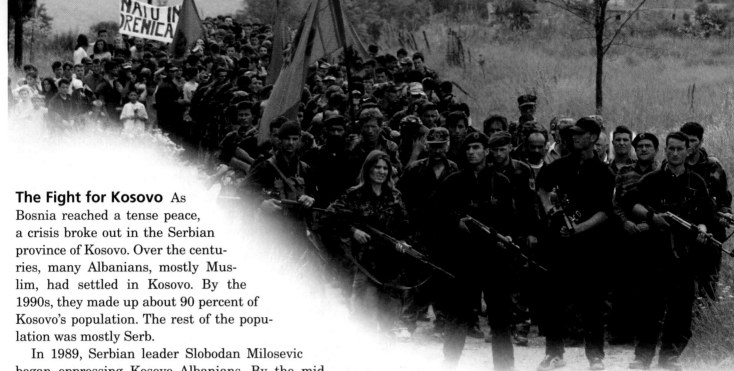

The Fight for Kosovo As Bosnia reached a tense peace, a crisis broke out in the Serbian province of Kosovo. Over the centuries, many Albanians, mostly Muslim, had settled in Kosovo. By the 1990s, they made up about 90 percent of Kosovo's population. The rest of the population was mostly Serb.

In 1989, Serbian leader Slobodan Milosevic began oppressing Kosovo Albanians. By the mid-1990s, a small guerrilla force of Kosovo Albanians had emerged. It attacked Serbian targets. Milosevic rejected international peace efforts and stepped up a campaign of ethnic cleansing against Kosovo Albanians. In response, NATO launched air attacks against Serbia in 1999.

The air strikes forced Milosevic to withdraw Serbian forces from **Kosovo.** UN and NATO forces then supervised a tense peace. After years of negotiation, Kosovo declared independence in 2008. While Kosovo Albanians celebrated, Serbs angrily protested. For them, Kosovo was a historic part of Serbia. A small NATO force remained in Kosovo to keep the peace between the majority Albanians and the minority Serbs.

Fighters in Kosovo
Kosovo Albanians claim an area after Serbian forces withdrew in 1999. *What does this photograph suggest about relations between Albanians and Serbs in Kosovo?*

✓ **Checkpoint** How did the breakup of Yugoslavia lead to ethnic cleansing in Bosnia and Herzegovina?

Progress Monitoring *Online*
For: Self-quiz with vocabulary practice
Web Code: naa-3211

SECTION 1 **Assessment**

Terms, People, and Places

1. What do many of the terms, people, and places listed at the beginning of the section have in common? Explain.

Note Taking

2. **Reading Skill: Recognize Sequence** Use your completed flowchart to answer the Focus Question: Why have ethnic and religious conflicts divided some nations?

Comprehension and Critical Thinking

3. **Synthesize Information** How might Malaysia and Singapore serve as examples of how to resolve ethnic conflict in the nations that make up the former Yugoslavia?

4. **Predict Consequences** Do you think Kosovo will be able to maintain its independence and resolve the conflict between Albanians and Serbs?

5. **Draw Conclusions** Why do you think Russia intervened in Georgia's conflict with its provinces?

● **Writing About History**

Quick Write: Explore a Topic To write a research report, you first need to frame questions that will help you to explore your topic. Choose one of the conflicts in this section and write a series of questions that you could try to answer through research. For example, if you choose the Northern Ireland conflict, you might ask why the IRA has been reluctant to turn over weapons, or who has been responsible for recent attacks in Northern Ireland.

Since 1994, peace has returned to Rwanda. This recent photo shows Rwandan boys running home after school.

WITNESS HISTORY ◀)) AUDIO

Recovering From Genocide

Although other African nations suffered brutal ethnic conflicts and civil wars, Rwanda's 1994 genocide was one of the most deadly. However, as UN Secretary General Kofi Annan points out, Rwanda's recovery in the years since offers hope that the continent's conflicts can be resolved.

❝ Rwanda has much to show the world about confronting the legacy of the past and is demonstrating that it is possible to reach beyond tragedy and rekindle hope.❞
— Tribute by Kofi Annan on the tenth anniversary of genocide in Rwanda

This section explores the problems that have led to conflicts in Rwanda and in other African countries.

Focus Question Why have conflicts plagued some African countries?

Struggles in Africa

 Performance Standards

- **SSWH19e** Analyze the anti-apartheid movement.
- **SSWH20a** Identify pan-Africanism.

Terms, People, and Places

apartheid	Desmond Tutu
African National	F.W. de Klerk
Congress (ANC)	Hutus
Sharpeville	Tutsis
Nelson Mandela	Darfur

Note Taking

Reading Skill: Recognize Sequence Keep track of the sequence of events in the conflicts in South Africa and its neighbors. Add boxes as needed.

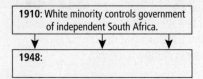

In the 1950s and 1960s, many new nations won independence in Africa. National unity, however, was hard to achieve. Most African nations were home to diverse ethnic groups. Often, people did not even share a common language. They spoke dozens of local languages. Religious differences and longstanding rivalries further divided people within a nation.

After independence, a single ethnic group often dominated a nation's government and economy at the expense of other groups. The Cold War further complicated matters, as you have read. As a result, several African nations suffered internal conflicts and civil war.

South Africa Struggles for Freedom

In South Africa, the struggle for freedom was different from that elsewhere in Africa. In 1910, South Africa achieved self-rule from Britain. Freedom, however, was limited to white settlers. The black majority was denied the right to vote. Whites made up less than 20 percent of the population but controlled the government and the economy. The white-minority government passed racial laws that severely restricted the black majority.

Apartheid Divides South Africa After 1948, the government expanded the existing system of racial segregation, creating what was known as **apartheid,** or the separation of the races. Under apartheid, all South Africans were registered by race: Black,

White, Colored (people of mixed ancestry), Asian. Supporters of apartheid claimed it would allow each race to protect its culture. In fact, the policy was designed to keep white control over South Africa.

Under apartheid, nonwhites faced many restrictions. Blacks were treated like foreigners in their own land. Under the pass laws, they had to get permission to travel. Other laws banned marriages between the races and <u>stipulated</u> segregated restaurants, beaches, and schools. Black workers were paid less than whites for the same job. Blacks could not own land in most areas. Low wages and inferior schooling condemned most blacks to poverty.

Vocabulary Builder

<u>stipulated</u>—(STIP yuh layt ed)
v. required, specified

The Struggle for Majority Black Rule
Black South Africans resisted apartheid. The **African National Congress (ANC)** emerged as the main party opposed to apartheid and led the struggle for majority rule. In the 1950s, the government imposed strict new rules to separate the races. The ANC organized marches, boycotts, and strikes. In 1960, police gunned down 69 men, women, and children during a peaceful protest in **Sharpeville**, a black township. The government then outlawed the ANC and cracked down on other groups that opposed apartheid.

The Sharpeville massacre led some ANC activists to shift from nonviolent protest to armed struggle. Some leaders, like **Nelson Mandela**, went underground. As an ANC leader, Mandela had first mobilized young South Africans to peacefully resist apartheid laws. As government oppression grew, Mandela joined ANC militants who called for armed struggle against the white-minority government. In the early 1960s, Mandela was arrested, tried, and condemned to life in prison for treason. Even in prison, he remained a powerful symbol of the struggle for freedom.

In the 1980s, demands for an end to apartheid and for Mandela's release increased. Many countries, including the United States, imposed economic sanctions on South Africa. In 1984, black South African bishop **Desmond Tutu** won the Nobel Peace Prize for his nonviolent opposition to apartheid.

Ending Apartheid
Outside pressure and protests at home finally convinced South African president **F. W. de Klerk** to end apartheid. In 1990, he lifted the ban on the ANC and freed Mandela. In 1994, South Africans of every race were allowed to vote for the first time.

The Sharpeville Massacre
When South African police opened fire on peaceful demonstrators at Sharpeville in 1960, many demonstrators ran for their lives. *How might this police action lead anti-apartheid activists to give up on peaceful methods?*

Apartheid's Impact

For more than 40 years, apartheid shaped the lives of the black majority and of whites and other minorities in South Africa. Whites made up less than one fifth of South Africa's population, as you can see in the graph at the right. However, apartheid gave whites not only political power, but also control of South Africa's best lands and economic resources. This hurt blacks, Asians, and people of mixed backgrounds economically and socially. *Based on the information in the graph and elsewhere in this section, about what percentage of South Africa's population suffered from apartheid?*

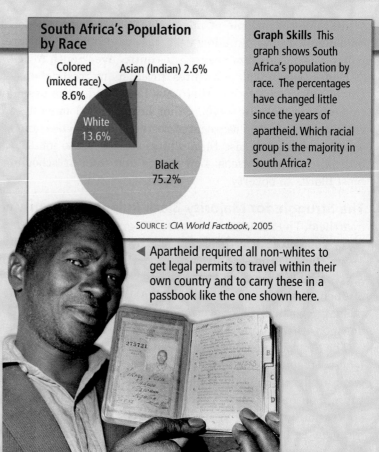

South Africa's Population by Race

Colored (mixed race) 8.6%
Asian (Indian) 2.6%
White 13.6%
Black 75.2%

SOURCE: *CIA World Factbook*, 2005

Graph Skills This graph shows South Africa's population by race. The percentages have changed little since the years of apartheid. Which racial group is the majority in South Africa?

◀ Apartheid required all non-whites to get legal permits to travel within their own country and to carry these in a passbook like the one shown here.

▲ Apartheid gave many white South Africans a life of privilege.

Deprived of opportunities, many black South Africans lived in poverty.

Voters chose Nelson Mandela as president in South Africa's first multiracial election. Mandela worked to heal the country's wounds. "Let us build together," he declared. He welcomed old foes into his government, including whites who had supported apartheid.

Since 1994, South Africa has faced huge challenges. With majority rule, black South Africans expected a better life. Although South Africa was a rich, industrial country, it had limited resources to spend on housing, education, and other programs. The income and education gap between blacks and whites remained large. Poverty and unemployment were high among blacks. The AIDS epidemic hit South Africa severely. As South Africa's government struggled with these problems, the global economic slowdown created new challenges.

 Checkpoint What factors finally brought an end to apartheid in South Africa?

Struggles in Southern Africa

Most African nations achieved independence through peaceful means during the 1950s and 1960s. In southern Africa, however, the road to freedom was marked by some long, violent struggles. For many years, the apartheid government of South Africa supported white minority rule in neighboring nations.

Zimbabwe As African nations won independence, whites in Southern Rhodesia refused to share power with the black majority. Conservative whites, led by Ian Smith, declared independence in 1965. For years, black guerrilla groups fought for majority rule. In 1980, after a ceasefire and elections, the country gained independence and was renamed Zimbabwe.

Robert Mugabe, a liberation leader, was elected president. Although popular at first, Mugabe grew increasingly dictatorial. He cracked down on opponents and was accused of electoral fraud. Despite international pressure and an economic crisis, the aging Mugabe held onto power.

Angola and Mozambique While Britain and France gave up their African possessions, Portugal clung fiercely to its colonies of Angola and Mozambique. In response, nationalist groups waged a long guerrilla war. In 1975, after Portugal finally agreed to withdraw, Angola and Mozambique celebrated independence.

Both countries then faced brutal civil wars fueled by Cold War rivalries. Because some liberation leaders had ties to the Soviet Union or the ANC, the United States and South Africa aided a rebel group in Angola. South Africa also supported a rebel group in Mozambique. The fighting continued until 1992 in Mozambique, and 2002 in Angola. Decades of war had ravaged both countries, which slowly began to rebuild.

 Checkpoint Why did fighting continue after Angola and Mozambique achieved independence?

Ethnic Conflicts Fuel Power Struggles

After independence, ethnic conflicts plagued several African nations. The causes were complex. Historic resentments divided ethnically diverse nations. Unjust governments and regional rivalries fed ethnic violence.

Rwanda and Burundi Power struggles between ethnic groups led to a deadly genocide in Rwanda, a small central African nation. The country was home to two main ethnic groups. **Hutus** were the majority group, but **Tutsis** had long dominated Rwanda. Both groups spoke the same language, but they had different traditions. After independence, Hutu violence against Tutsis increased.

Tensions worsened in early 1994, after the presidents of Rwanda and neighboring Burundi were killed in a suspicious plane crash. Extremist Hutu officials urged civilians to turn on their Tutsi neighbors. At least 800,000 Tutsis and moderate Hutus were slaughtered. Millions of Rwandans lost their homes to destructive mobs. Even as the death toll rose, the world community was slow to act to stop the genocide.

In July 1994, a Tutsi exile army conquered Rwanda and set up a unity government. Those accused of genocide faced trials in an international court.

Nearby Burundi faced similar ethnic tensions between Hutus and Tutsis. In 1993, Tutsi military officers killed Burundi's Hutu president in a failed coup attempt. Violence erupted, but did not lead to genocide as in Rwanda. In 2005, voters approved a new constitution that guaranteed both groups participation in the government and military.

Strife in Sudan Genocide also took place in oil-rich Sudan. Since independence, Sudan's Arab Muslim north has dominated the non-Muslim, non-Arab south. Sudan's Muslim government even tried to impose

Note Taking

Reading Skill: Identify Causes and Effects Fill in a concept web like the one below to keep track of the causes and effects of the conflicts in Rwanda and Sudan.

Terror in Darfur
Arab militias, known as *janjaweed* or "bandits," spread terror across the Darfur region of Sudan. Above is all that is left of the village of Tontobay after a Janjaweed attack killed 80 and forced 3,000 other residents to flee to nearby Chad. *How might an attack by the janjaweed affect unarmed villagers?*

Islamic law in non-Muslim areas. For decades, rebel groups in the south battled northern political domination. The fighting also spilled into neighboring Chad. Sudan's north-south conflict killed millions and displaced many more.

In 2005, the Sudanese government and rebels in the south agreed to a peace accord. However, in 2004, fighting worsened in the western region of **Darfur.** With government backing, Arab militias conducted widespread killings of civilians. They burned homes and drove farmers off the land.

The United States and other countries sent humanitarian aid to the refugees. Sudan allowed UN peacekeepers into the region, but they were unable to end the violence. In 2009, the International Criminal Court charged Sudan's president with crimes against humanity.

✓ **Checkpoint** How was the conflict in Rwanda similar to the conflict in Darfur?

Progress Monitoring *Online*
For: Self-quiz with vocabulary practice
Web Code: naa-3221

SECTION **2** Assessment

Terms, People, and Places

1. For each term, person, or place listed at the beginning of the section, write a sentence explaining its significance.

Note Taking

2. **Reading Skill: Recognize Sequence** Use your completed flowchart to answer the Focus Question: Why have conflicts plagued some African countries?

Comprehension and Critical Thinking

3. **Analyze Information** Was apartheid a product of a democratic system of government? Explain.

4. **Summarize** What was South Africa's role in the conflicts that plagued its neighbors from the 1960s to the 1990s?

5. **Make Comparisons** How was the ethnic conflict in Burundi similar to or different from the conflict in Rwanda?

6. **Synthesize Information** A newspaper headline read, "Looking at Darfur, Seeing Rwanda." Explain what that headline meant. How did the world community respond to genocide after the events in Rwanda?

● **Writing About History**

Quick Write: Gather Information To write a research report, you need to gather information about your topic. Choose one of the conflicts in this section and gather facts about the topic from the library or reliable sources online. Make a list of facts about your topic.

Nelson Mandela: *Glory and Hope*

Nelson Mandela delivered this speech after having been elected president in South Africa's first multiracial election in 1994. Knowing that the injustices of apartheid would be hard to overcome, Mandela asked the people to work together for peace and justice.

Today, all of us do, by our presence here, and by our celebrations . . . confer glory and hope to newborn liberty.

Out of the experience of an extraordinary human disaster that lasted too long must be born a society of which all humanity will be proud.

Our daily deeds as ordinary South Africans must produce an actual South African reality that will reinforce humanity's belief in justice, strengthen its confidence in the nobility of the human soul and sustain all our hopes for a glorious life for all. . . .

The time for the healing of the wounds has come. . . .

The time to build is upon us.

We have, at last, achieved our political emancipation.[1] We pledge ourselves to liberate all our people from the continuing bondage of poverty, deprivation, suffering, gender and other discrimination. . . .

We have triumphed in the effort to implant hope in the breasts of the millions of our people. We enter into a covenant[2] that we shall build the society in which all South Africans, both black and white, will be able to walk tall, without any fear in their hearts, assured of their inalienable right to human dignity—a rainbow nation at peace with itself and the world. . . .

We understand it still that there is no easy road to freedom.

We know it well that none of us acting alone can achieve success.

We must therefore act together as a united people, for national reconciliation,[3] for nation building, for the birth of a new world.

Let there be justice for all. Let there be peace for all. Let there be work, bread, water, and salt for all. . . . The sun shall never set on so glorious a human achievement!

Students in South Africa after the end of apartheid

Thinking Critically

1. **Identify Alternatives** When apartheid ended, there was a danger of a backlash by blacks against whites who supported apartheid. How does Mandela's speech respond to that danger?
2. **Draw Inferences** In addition to political freedom, what further freedoms does Mandela call for in his speech?

Nelson Mandela with supporters in 1994

---

1. emancipation (ee man suh PAY shun) *n.* the gaining of freedom from bondage or control by others

2. covenant (KUV uh nunt) *n.* a binding and solemn pledge to do something

3. reconciliation (rek un sil ee AY shun) *n.* a settling of differences that results in harmony

An Israeli soldier and a Palestinian Arab pass each other in the street.

WITNESS HISTORY ◀)) AUDIO

Two Peoples Claim the Same Land

Many Jewish Israelis believe that the quotation from the Bible, below, promises Israel to the Jewish people as descendants of Abraham (Abram). Many Muslims also believe that they are the spiritual heirs to Abraham, as stated in the Quran. They too feel entitled to the land as part of Abraham's legacy. Representatives of both peoples have lived in the land for centuries.

❝ On that day the LORD made a covenant with Abram, saying, 'To your descendants I give this land. . . .'❞

—Genesis 15:18

❝ He [Allah] has chosen you and has placed no hardship on you in practicing your religion—the religion of your father Abraham. ❞

—Quran 22:78

Focus Question What are the causes of conflict in the Middle East?

Conflicts in the Middle East

 Performance Standards

- **SSWH19b** Describe importance of Israel's geography in its development.
- **SSWH20a** Identify ethnic conflicts ad new nationalisms since 1960s.
- **SSWH20c** Analyze the terrorism of Hamas.
- **SSWH20d** Examine the rise of Golda Meir as a major world leader.

Terms, People, and Places

occupied territories	Saddam Hussein
Yasir Arafat	no-fly zone
intifada	weapons of mass
Yitzhak Rabin	destruction (WMDs)
Jerusalem	insurgent
militia	

Note Taking

Reading Skill: Recognize Sequence Keep track of the sequence of events in the conflicts in the Middle East with a flowchart like the one below.

Middle Eastern Conflicts		
Arab-Israeli Conflict	Lebanon	Iraq
• 1948: Israel is founded •	• •	• •

For decades, the Middle East has been the focus of conflicts that have had a global impact. The Middle East commands vast oil resources and key waterways such as the Persian Gulf. During the Cold War, both the United States and the Soviet Union wanted access to the oil and the waterways. Since the end of the Cold War, Western nations have acted to prevent regional powers from interfering with the region's oil supply. Meanwhile, the persistent dispute between Israelis and Palestinian Arabs has added to tensions.

Arabs and Israelis Fight Over Land

Modern Israel was established in 1948 in accordance with the United Nations Partition Plan. The Palestinian Arabs regarded the UN action as illegitimate and rejected the state offered to them. Conflicting claims to this land led to repeated violence. After the 1948 war that followed Israel's founding, Israel and its Arab neighbors fought three more wars, in 1956, 1967, and 1973. In these wars, Israel defeated Arab forces and gained more land. Between the wars, Israel faced guerrilla and terrorist attacks. Repeatedly, the United States tried to bring about peace.

Israel Controls the Occupied Territories In the 1967 war, in response to hostility by its neighbors, Israeli forces took control of territories occupied by Jordan and Egypt since 1948, including the West Bank, East Jerusalem, and the Gaza Strip. They also took control of the Sinai Peninsula from Egypt and the Golan Heights from Syria. In 1973, these nations attacked Israel on Yom Kippur, one of the holiest days of the Jewish year.

In the 1973 war, Arabs failed to regain the regions they had lost to Israel, known today as the **occupied territories.** Israel's government later helped Jewish settlers build homes in settlements in these territories, causing more bitterness among the Palestinians.

Palestinian Attacks Bring Israeli Response For decades, the Palestinian Liberation Organization (PLO) led the struggle against Israel. Headed by **Yasir Arafat,** the PLO had deep support among Palestinians. The PLO called for the destruction of Israel. It attacked Israelis at home and abroad. The PLO gained world attention with airplane hijackings and the killing of Israeli athletes at the 1972 Olympic games.

In 1987, Palestinians in the occupied territories started to resist Israel with **intifadas,** or uprisings. Demanding an end to Israeli occupation, young Palestinians stoned and fired on Israeli troops. Suicide bombers blew up buses, stores, and clubs in Israel, killing many civilians. Israel responded by sealing off and raiding Palestinian towns and targeting terrorist leaders. Many Palestinian civilians lost their lives in these raids.

Seeking Peace Despite the violence, the United States, the UN, and other nations pushed for peace. Golda Meir, Israel's first woman prime minister, was planning peace talks when Arab nations attacked in 1973. As you have read, Israel and Egypt signed a peace accord in 1979. Israel then returned the Sinai Peninsula to Egypt. In 1994, Jordan's King Hussein made peace with Israel. However, talks between Syria and Israel failed over various issues, including control of the Golan Heights.

In 1993, Yasir Arafat and Israeli Prime Minister **Yitzhak Rabin** (rah BEEN) signed the Oslo Accords. This plan gave Palestinians in Gaza and the West Bank limited self-rule under a Palestinian Authority. The PLO recognized Israel's right to exist and pledged to stop terrorist attacks on Israel. Arafat led the Palestinian Authority until his death in 2004.

A City Sacred to Many
Jerusalem is dotted with many places that are sacred to the Jewish people, Christians, and Muslims. This photograph shows the Western Wall, a Jewish holy place. In the background is the Dome of the Rock, an important Islamic shrine. *How might Jerusalem's sacred status make it harder to resolve competing Israeli and Palestinian Arab claims to the city?*

The Israeli-Palestinian Conflict

Conflict has dragged on for years in the region. Palestinian Arabs resent the Israeli occupation. Some have responded with suicide bombings targeting Israeli civilians. Israeli forces have responded with attacks on Palestinian militants that have also killed some civilians. Hopes for peace in the region center on ending this cycle of violence and retaliation.

- Israel, 1949
- Occupied by Israel after 1967, some areas under Palestinian administration after 1994
- * Israeli troops withdrawn, 2005

LEBANON
SYRIA
Golan Heights
Haifa
Sea of Galilee
Mediterranean Sea
Tel Aviv
West Bank
Jordan River
Ramallah
Jericho
Jerusalem
Bethlehem
Hebron
Dead Sea
Gaza
Gaza Strip*
ISRAEL
JORDAN
EGYPT
Elat

◄ Palestinian suicide bombers have set off deadly explosions in public places that have killed Israeli civilians. The bus in this photo was torn apart by a bomb carried by a Palestinian terrorist.

Ongoing Violence Although Arafat's successor, Mahmoud Abbas (ah BAHS), pledged to stop Palestinian attacks on Israel, violence continued. Fierce divisions split the Palestinian Authority between Fatah, the party of Arafat and his successors, and Hamas, a radical Islamist group. Hamas was funded by Iran and rejected Israel's right to exist. After its impressive victory in the 2006 Palestinian parliamentary election, Hamas seized control of Gaza in 2007, ousting Fatah supporters.

In response, Israel imposed an economic blockade on Gaza, allowing only humanitarian aid to enter. Hamas used Gaza as a launching ground for rocket attacks on Israel. In early 2009, Israeli forces invaded the densely populated Gaza Strip to stop the attacks. A short destructive war resulted in high civilian casualties and ended in a shaky ceasefire.

Obstacles to Peace Decades of conflict and mistrust make peace hard to achieve. Many issues pose obstacles. One issue is land claims. Palestinians who were forced off their lands in earlier wars want the "right of return," or the right to resettle on their lands in Israel. Israelis oppose this right, which could overwhelm the Jewish state with large numbers of Palestinians.

A second obstacle to peace is the issue of Jewish settlements in the West Bank, an area claimed by Palestinians. In the early 2000s, the Israeli government forced Jewish settlers to leave Gaza. Palestinians also insist that Jewish settlers must leave the West Bank.

A third stumbling block is **Jerusalem,** a city sacred to Jews, Christians, and Muslims. Israel occupied Arab East Jerusalem in 1967. Later, it added East Jerusalem to Israel and made the city the capital of Israel. The government allowed Muslims and Christians to control their holy sites within the city. Palestinians, however, insist that East Jerusalem must be the capital of any Palestinian state.

Israeli counterattacks in the occupied territories have killed Palestinians, including some civilians. Some 20,000 people attended this funeral for Palestinians killed in an Israeli attack.

History *Interactive*

For: Interactive map
Web Code: nap-3231

Some Israelis and Palestinians, such as the men in this photograph, have chosen peaceful dialogue rather than violence as a way to bridge their differences. Dialogue between the two sides offers the best hope for ending this regional conflict. ▼

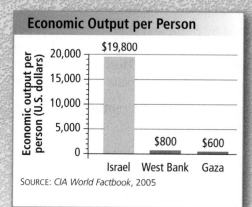

Economic Output per Person

Economic output per person (U.S. dollars)

- Israel: $19,800
- West Bank: $800
- Gaza: $600

SOURCE: *CIA World Factbook*, 2005

◀ Lack of development, years of conflict, and corruption have crippled the economy of the West Bank and Gaza. Meanwhile, Palestinian attacks have forced Israel to limit Palestinians' access to jobs in Israel. Poverty in the West Bank and Gaza Strip has led to desperation among Palestinians.

Over time, the Israeli-Palestinian conflict has fueled the anger of radical Islamist groups around the world. The growing popularity of Hamas and Hezbollah, a radical Islamist group based in Lebanon, created more conflict. These groups reject Israel's right to exist and condemn its ally, the United States, as well as moderate Arab governments involved in the peace process.

By the early 2000s, the United States, the European Union, Russia, and the UN supported a plan known as the "road map" to peace in the Middle East. It supports a two-state solution, with peaceful coexistence between Israel and a stable, democratic Palestinian state. To achieve this, it called for an end to violence and terrorism. Some Israeli and Palestinian leaders accepted the plan, while Iran and radical Islamist groups rejected it.

✔️ **Checkpoint** What obstacles have prevented peace between Israel and the Palestinians?

Thinking Critically
1. **Graph Skills** How does economic output in the West Bank and Gaza Strip compare with that in Israel?
2. **Draw Conclusions** How might violence by both sides tend to prolong the Palestinian-Israeli conflict?

Civil War Ravages Lebanon

Historically, Lebanon was a thriving center of commerce. Its population included <u>diverse</u> ethnic and religious groups. After Lebanon won independence, the government depended on a delicate balance among Arab Christian sects, Sunni and Shiite Muslims, and Druze, people with a religion related to Islam. Arab Christians held the most power, but local strongmen controlled their own districts with private armies.

Growing Tensions By the 1970s, the Arab-Israeli conflict was contributing to problems in nearby Lebanon. As Palestinian refugees fled into Lebanon after each new conflict with Israel, Lebanon's Muslim population grew to outnumber Christians. Tensions rose as PLO guerrillas disguised as refugees then crossed the border to attack Israel.

Vocabulary Builder

diverse—(dih VURS) *adj.* multiple, varied, different

Civil War and Conflict With Israel In 1975, Lebanon was plunged into civil war. Christian and Muslim **militias,** or armed groups of citizen soldiers, battled each other. In 1982, Israel invaded southern Lebanon to stop cross-border attacks. Syria occupied eastern Lebanon. UN peacekeepers tried to end the fighting but withdrew after hundreds were killed by suicide bombers. After 16 years, Lebanese leaders finally restored order. Beirut, the ruined capital, was slowly rebuilt.

Deep divisions remained in Lebanon. Rival militias controlled different regions. In 2006, Hezbollah attacked Israel from southern Lebanon, sparking a war that lasted just over a month. The war killed civilians in both Israel and Lebanon and caused widespread damage across Lebanon. Despite the costs, Hezbollah, backed by Syria and Iran, remained popular among Lebanon's Shiite Muslims. In 2008, a new power-sharing agreement was reached in Lebanon. The agreement increased Hezbollah's power, but contained a pledge that no faction would use its weapons within Lebanon.

✔ **Checkpoint** How did an influx of Palestinians contribute to conflict in Lebanon?

Iraq's History of Conflict

Since the 1950s, ethnic and religious divisions, oil resources, and border disputes have led to conflict in Iraq. During the Cold War, the United States and the Soviet Union competed for influence in Iraq, which had vast oil reserves and was strategically located on the Persian Gulf.

Iraq was carved out of the Ottoman Empire after World War I. Its population included Sunni and Shiite Arabs as well as Kurds. Although Shiites formed a majority in Iraq, Sunni Arabs controlled the government. Kurds, who lived in the north, distrusted the government and wanted self-rule. Divisions among these groups fed tensions in Iraq.

The Iran-Iraq War In 1980, Iraqi dictator, **Saddam Hussein,** took advantage of turmoil in neighboring Iran following its Islamic revolution by seizing a disputed border region. His action sparked a long, costly war.

Iraq used superior weapons and poison gas to stop waves of Iranian soldiers. After both sides attacked foreign oil tankers and oil fields in the Persian Gulf, the United States sent naval forces to protect shipping lanes. The war ended in a stalemate in 1988. For both Iran and Iraq, the human and economic toll was enormous.

During the war, Saddam Hussein brutally repressed a Kurdish revolt in the north. He also used chemical weapons on Kurdish civilians. His actions sparked outrage and charges of genocide.

The 1991 Gulf War In 1990, Iraq invaded its oil-rich neighbor, Kuwait. Saddam Hussein claimed that Kuwait was historically part of Iraq. In fact, he wanted control of Kuwait's vast oil fields and greater access to the Persian Gulf.

The United States saw Saddam's move not only as illegal, but also as a threat to its ally, Saudi Arabia, and to the oil resources of the region. It formed an international coalition to drive Iraq out of Kuwait. In the 1991 Gulf War, the U.S.-led coalition operated under the UN banner. It quickly crushed Iraqi forces and freed Kuwait.

Despite defeat, Saddam Hussein remained in power. He brutally crushed revolts by Shiite Muslims and the minority Kurds. He used torture and terror to impose his will.

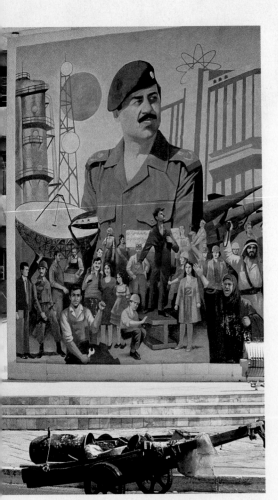

Saddam Hussein's Dictatorship
Saddam Hussein, shown here in a propaganda poster in 1988, turned Iraq into a brutal police state, in which critics were tortured and killed.

Saddam Defies the UN To protect the Shiites and Kurds, the UN set up **no-fly zones,** or areas where Iraqi aircraft were banned. The UN also tried to discover if Saddam Hussein was building **weapons of mass destruction (WMDs),** or nuclear, biological, and chemical weapons. It imposed economic sanctions on Iraq to limit its oil sales and its use of oil profits. For years, Saddam Hussein defied the UN.

U.S. Forces Invade After the 2001 terrorist attacks, the United States claimed that Saddam Hussein had weapons of mass destruction and was supporting terrorists. It formed a coalition that invaded Iraq in 2003. Coalition forces toppled Saddam, who was later tried and executed for war crimes by a new Iraqi government.

Backed by U.S. and coalition forces, Shiite, Kurdish, and Sunni leaders wrote a constitution and held national elections in 2005. Efforts to rebuild Iraq were hampered by guerrilla attacks and suicide bombings. **Insurgents,** or rebels, from rival Shiite and Sunni groups targeted civilians and government workers.

Civil War Threatens Iraq By 2005, ethnic and religious divisions had pushed the country to the brink of civil war. The United States and Britain worked to train the Iraqi military and police. In 2007, the United States increased troop levels in a "surge" to end the fighting. The violence and death tolls declined.

Urban Warfare in Iraq
Iraqi foot soldiers accompany a U.S. military vehicle. They are patrolling a war-torn neighborhood of Baghdad, Iraq's capital, in 2007. U.S. and Iraqi forces worked together to try to stop violence between Sunni and Shiite forces.

Iraq's Shiite-led government faced many obstacles. It needed to promote reconciliation among bitterly divided factions. Sunnis claimed that the new government failed to represent their interests. Kurds in the north still sought autonomy. Much of the country's oil industry had been destroyed. An estimated 2 million Iraqi refugees remained outside the country.

Despite the troubles, Iraqi leaders grew more confident. They expanded their security forces and agreed to a withdrawal of all U.S. troops by 2011.

✔ **Checkpoint** Why has conflict persisted in Iraq since the defeat of Saddam Hussein?

SECTION **3** Assessment

Progress Monitoring _Online_
For: Self-quiz with vocabulary practice
Web Code: naa-3231

Terms, People, and Places
1. What do each of the terms, people, and places listed at the beginning of the section have in common? Explain.

Note Taking
2. **Reading Skill: Recognize Sequence** Use your finished flowchart to answer the Focus Question: What are the causes of conflict in the Middle East?

Comprehension and Critical Thinking
3. **Draw Conclusions** Why has the Arab-Israeli conflict been difficult to resolve?
4. **Identify Central Issues** What were the causes of Lebanon's civil war?
5. **Synthesize Information** Why did the UN impose economic sanctions in Iraq after the 1991 Gulf War?

● **Writing About History**

Quick Write: Make an Outline To write a research report, you need to make an outline that organizes information that you have gathered. Suppose that you are writing a research report on the Arab-Israeli conflict. Make an outline that organizes the information in this section about that conflict.

Quick Study Guide

 SSWH20a

■ Conflicts in Iraq

Conflict	Duration	Main Events
Iran-Iraq War	1980–1988	Saddam Hussein tried to seize an Iranian border region. Saddam used chemical weapons against Kurds.
Gulf War	1990–1991	Saddam Hussein invaded Kuwait. Coalition led by United States defeated Saddam's army and freed Kuwait.
Iraq War	2003–	Coalition led by the United States defeated Saddam Hussein's forces and occupied Iraq. Fighting with insurgents continued after Saddam's defeat in 2003.

■ Conflicts in Former Yugoslavia

Area of Conflict	Duration	Main Events
Croatia	1991–1995	Croatian forces fought with ethnic Serbs and the Yugoslav army over ethnic Serb areas. Serbs faced ethnic cleansing.
Bosnia	1992–1995	Ethnic Serbs, Croats, and Muslim Bosniaks fought each other. Muslims faced ethnic cleansing by Serbs.
Kosovo	1996–1999	Ethnic Albanians clashed with the Yugoslav army. Yugoslav forces attempted ethnic cleansing of Albanians.

■ Locations of Regional Conflicts

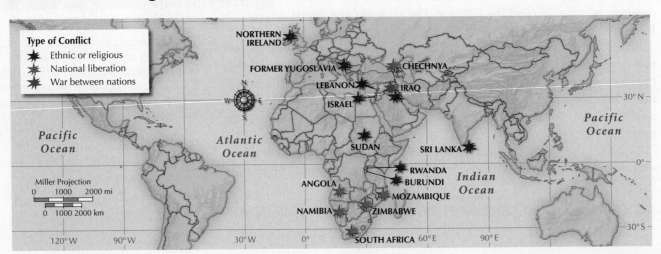

■ Key Events of Regional Conflicts

1948
South Africa expands apartheid system.

1960
Sharpeville massacre marks violent turn in anti-apartheid struggle.

Late 1960s
Conflict in Northern Ireland turns violent.

Africa and Europe
Middle East

1940   **1950**   **1960**   **1970**

1948
Israel's founding brings attack by Arab neighbors.

1967
Israel gains territory in the 1967 war, and Palestinians increase attacks on Israel.

Concept Connector

Essential Question Review

To connect prior knowledge with what you have learned in this chapter, answer the questions below in your Concept Connector journal. Use the journal in the Reading and Note Taking Study Guide to record your answers (or go to www.phschool.com **Web Code: nad-3207**). In addition, record information about the following concepts:

- Impact of the Individual: Nelson Mandela

1. **Dictatorship** Iraq was carved out of the old Ottoman empire after World War I, without regard for the ethnic and religious divisions of the population. Differences between Sunni Arabs, Shiite Arabs, and Kurds often led to conflicts. Given these differences, why might Iraqis support a dictator like Saddam Hussein? Identify at least one other reason for Iraqi support of Saddam Hussein.

2. **Genocide** During Bosnia's civil war, Bosnian Serbs conducted a campaign of ethnic cleansing—killing people from other ethnic groups or forcibly removing them from their homes to create ethnically "pure" areas. Croat and Bosnian fighters responded by launching ethnic cleansing campaigns against Serbs in Croatia. Suggest other possible motives for ethnic cleansing.

3. **Human Rights** After 1948, South Africa's government created apartheid, or the separation of the races. Because apartheid was designed to protect white control over South Africa, blacks were treated like foreigners in their own land. What restrictions did black South Africans face under apartheid? How did the ANC respond to apartheid? What factors caused South African president F.W. de Klerk to end apartheid?

■ Connections to Today

1. **Democracy** In this chapter, you read that Canada's democracy has allowed ethnic differences to be resolved peacefully, rather than through violent conflict. Through democratic means, the French-speaking majority in Quebec has secured rights for their language in Canada, even though French speakers are a minority in Canada (see the graphs below). Use the library and online research to identify another country where a democratic system has recently helped bring a peaceful resolution to ethnic differences. Compare your country's ethnic politics to those in Canada.

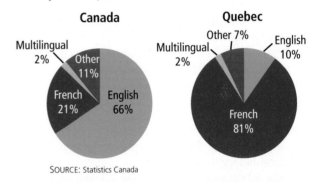

SOURCE: Statistics Canada

2. **Cooperation** In this chapter, you learned that members of the NATO military alliance cooperated to end ethnic cleansing and warfare in Kosovo in 1999. Use the library and online research to identify a more recent case in which cooperation among concerned nations has helped to bring peace to a country involved in a violent conflict. How does this recent case compare to what you learned about Kosovo?

History *Interactive*
For: Interactive timeline
Web Code: nap-3241

	1992 Ethnic conflict erupts in Bosnia.	1994 Open elections bring end of apartheid in South Africa.	1999 Brutal ethnic conflict in Kosovo brings NATO intervention.	
1980	**1990**		**2000**	**2010**
1975 Lebanon plunges into civil war.		1991 U.S.-led coalition defeats Iraq in Gulf War.		2003– U.S.-led coalition occupies Iraq and faces ongoing resistance.

Chapter Assessment

Terms, People, and Places

Choose the italicized term in parentheses that best completes each sentence.

1. Muslim nationalists in (*Kosovo/Chechnya*) have fought to free their homeland from Russian control.
2. There were hopes that (*the Good Friday Agreement/ethnic cleansing*) would provide for a peaceful resolution of the conflict in Northern Ireland.
3. (*Desmond Tutu/Nelson Mandela*) led the struggle against apartheid even when he was imprisoned for his role in the African National Congress.
4. In Rwanda, extremist (*Hutus/Tutsis*), the country's ethnic majority, slaughtered members of the country's ethnic minority in 1994.
5. Both Israel and the Palestinians claim (*Mecca / Jerusalem*) as their capital.
6. The Palestine Liberation Organization was headed by (*Yasir Arafat/Yitzhak Rabin*).
7. Efforts to rebuild Iraq after Saddam Hussein's overthrow were slowed by (*intifada/insurgent*) attacks.

Main Ideas

Section 1 (pp. 1044–1047)

8. Why does ethnic diversity lead to violent conflicts in some places but not in others?
9. How did Yugoslavia's breakup lead to ethnic conflicts?

Section 2 (pp. 1048–1053)

10. How did South Africa overcome apartheid?
11. What factors contributed to Africa's deadly ethnic conflicts?

Section 3 (pp. 1054–1059)

12. Explain the basic causes of the Israeli-Palestinian conflict.
13. Why did the removal of Saddam Hussein's regime fail to bring peace to Iraq?

Chapter Focus Question

14. Why have deadly conflicts plagued some regions of the world?

Critical Thinking

15. **Predict Consequences** Identify possible solutions to the ethnic conflicts in Bosnia and Kosovo and predict the consequences of these solutions.
16. **Draw Conclusions** Why was the idea of majority rule important to people in South Africa and in neighboring African countries?
17. **Express Problems Clearly** What are the main problems that have stood in the way of a peace settlement between Palestinians and Israelis?
18. **Recognize Cause and Effect** How did Saddam Hussein's policies cause suffering for Iraqis?
19. **Analyzing Visuals** What is the main message of the cartoon below? How might violence have been prevented in these countries?

Writing About History

In this chapter's three Section Assessments, you developed skills for writing a research report.

Writing a Research Report This chapter discusses several ethnic and regional conflicts. Choose one of the conflicts covered or find another conflict that interests you. Write a research report on the causes of the conflict, how the conflict unfolded, and how it was resolved or might be resolved. Consult page SH13 of the Writing Handbook for additional help.

Prewriting

- Do online or library research to read background materials about your conflict.
- Take notes on relevant details, events, and the people involved in the conflict.
- Create a set of questions about your conflict and gather additional resources.

Drafting

- Develop a working thesis about the cause of this conflict—for example, is the main issue control of land, government policies, or some other issue?
- Make an outline to organize a report that supports your thesis. Find information from your research that supports each part of your outline.
- Write an introduction explaining your thesis, a body, and a conclusion.

Revising

- Use the guidelines for revising your report on page SH15 of the Writing Handbook.

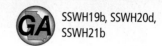
The Palestinian Question

In 1947, the United Nations drew up a plan dividing the Palestine Mandate into two states, Jewish and Arab, which the Arabs rejected. The next year, Israel was established as an independent nation according to the United Nations guidelines. As a result of the 1967 war, Israel gained control of the West Bank and Gaza. Israeli troops and civilians withdrew from Gaza in 2005. Palestinians still do not have an independent state of their own. Despite ongoing conflict between Israelis and Palestinians, many on both sides still hope for peace.

Document A

UN Partition Plan, 1947

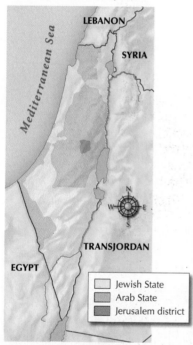

Document B

Israel and Occupied Territories, 2005

Document C

"As I have said, we came to Palestine to do away with the helplessness of the Jewish people through our own endeavors. Therefore, you will realize what it meant for us to watch from here millions of Jews being slaughtered during these years of war. . . . We Jews only want that which is given naturally to all peoples of the world to be masters of our own fate . . . . We are certain that given an opportunity of bringing in large masses of Jews into this country, of opening the doors of Palestine to all Jews who wish to come here, we can . . . create a free Jewish society built on the basis of cooperation, equality, and mutual aid."

—From **"The Zionist Case"** by Golda Meir (speech given March 25, 1946)

Document D

"Late at night when everything is quiet I think about how I will ever forgive the Israelis for what they did to me. I don't mean stealing my homeland, killing my people, turning me into a refugee, or depriving me from having a Palestinian state. I'm talking about myself—what they did to my personality.

I wish I had a normal life: no tension, no rage, no hatred, no hard feelings toward anybody. Even if they leave my country and give me back my rights, how will I overcome these feelings inside me?"

—From **"Children of a Tenth-Class God?"** by Nihaya Qawasmi (1998)

Analyzing Documents

Use your knowledge of the Palestinian-Israeli conflict and Documents A, B, C, and D to answer questions 1–4.

1. According to Documents A and B, what is the present status of the area outlined in the UN Partition Plan?
   A It is divided between Israel and neighboring countries.
   B Palestine is now an independent nation.
   C Part of it is the State of Israel, part is occupied by Israel, and part is ruled by the Palestinians.
   D It is divided among three independent nations.

2. In Document C, "helplessness" refers to
   A Israel's inability to help the Palestinians.
   B the inability of Jews in Palestine to help Jews in Nazi territory.
   C the inability of Palestinians to change their attitude toward Israel.
   D the inability of the Allies to do anything about Nazi atrocities.

3. Which words best describe the feelings of the author of Document D toward Israel?
   A acceptance and understanding
   B discouragement and fear
   C anger and resentment
   D trust and hope

4. **Writing Task** What are the prospects for a peaceful settlement of the Palestinian question? Use the documents on this page along with information from the chapter to write a short essay on this topic.

WITNESS HISTORY 🔊)) AUDIO

A Sleeping Giant Awakes

In the past few decades, many nations in the developing world have experienced rapid social and economic change. One such nation is China. Fifty years ago, China was recovering from civil war and just starting to modernize. Today, China is an economic powerhouse. Robert Broadfoot, managing director of Hong Kong's Political and Economic Risk Consultancy, said,

❝ . . . I have never seen so much hope in China. The Chinese will produce much cheaper items and export them. I think that will shape the course of commerce in the coming century.**❞**

Listen to the Witness History audio to hear more about China's economic development.

◀ China's rapid development is reflected in the city of Shenzhen, where modern glass buildings tower above old, shabby houses.

Exports like toys have fueled China's economy.

The flag of Brazil's Landless Peasants' Movement.

GA Performance Standards

Chapter Focus Question What challenges have nations of the developing world faced, and what steps have they taken to meet those challenges?

Section 1
The Challenges of Development
SSWH21b

Section 2
Africa Seeks a Better Future
SSWH21c, SSWHRC1c

Section 3
China and India: Two Giants of Asia
SSWH19e, SSWH21a

Section 4
Latin America Builds Democracy
SSWH21b

Use the ☑ **Quick Study Timeline** at the end of this chapter to preview chapter events.

Bananas are an important cash crop in many Latin American nations.

? Concept Connector ONLINE

To explore Essential Questions related to this chapter, go to PHSchool.com
Web Code: nad-3307

A loan recipient poses with the cows she bought to help generate income.

Bangladesh's currency, the taka

WITNESS HISTORY 🔊 AUDIO

Building a Better Life

Bangladeshi Laily Begum used to sleep in a cow shed and spend her days begging. Then she got a loan for $119 from Grameen Bank, a Bangladesh-based organization that lends money to the poor. She bought a cow and began to build her own business selling milk. Today she and her husband own several shops and a restaurant.

❝ People now come to me for help . . . I can feed myself and my family, and now other people look at me and they treat me with respect.❞
—Laily Begum, February 12, 1998

Focus Question How have the nations of the developing world tried to build better lives for their people?

The Challenges of Development

 Performance Standards

- **SSWH21b** Analyze global economic and political connections.

Many new nations emerged in Africa and Asia in the decades after World War II. These new nations, along with countries in Latin America, focused on development. **Development** means building stable governments, improving agriculture and industry, and raising standards of living. The nations working toward development in Africa, Asia, and Latin America are known collectively as the **developing world.** From the beginning, nations in the developing world faced many challenges.

Terms, People, and Places

development
developing world
literacy
traditional economies

Green Revolution
fundamentalists
shantytowns

Note Taking

Reading Skill: Identify Supporting Details
Expand this chart to record details about development as you read.

Development		
Economic Change	Obstacles	Changes in Patterns of Life
•	•	•
•	•	•

Goals of Development

At independence, new nations wrote constitutions that set up representative governments and protected the rights of citizens. Their leaders also pushed to build strong modern economies. Since a modern economy needs well-trained workers, developing nations built schools to increase **literacy,** or the ability to read and write.

The Global South The developing world is sometimes called the global South because it is located mostly south of the Tropic of Cancer. The global South holds 75 percent of the world's people and much of its natural resources. It was poor, however, compared to the global North, the rich industrial nations located mostly north of the Tropic of Cancer.

Transforming Economies Leaders of new nations in the developing world set ambitious economic goals. They wanted to increase food output, develop industry, construct roads, airports, and railroads, and build power plants.

Despite these goals, much of the developing world still lived and worked in traditional economies. **Traditional economies** are undeveloped economic systems that rely on custom and tradition, using simple tools and methods of production passed down from earlier generations. In traditional economies, most people are farmers or craftspeople who make or grow enough to meet their own needs. They trade any surplus, or extra, for goods they cannot make themselves.

Economic Policies Developing nations needed vast amounts of capital to finance projects to modernize their economies. After independence, some political leaders tried to speed development by replacing traditional and market economies with government-led command economies. This meant that governments owned most businesses and controlled farming.

To pay for development, many countries <u>procured</u> large loans from banks and governments in the global North. When poor economic conditions made it difficult for these countries to repay their loans, lenders insisted that developing countries sell government businesses, hold free elections, and establish market economies. Lenders required these changes so developing countries could pay off debts and be eligible for new loans.

Vocabulary Builder

<u>procure</u>—(proh KYOOR) *v.* obtain, make an effort to get

Geography *Interactive*
For: Audio guided tour
Web Code: nap-3311

The Global North and Global South

Map Skills The developed countries are also known as the global North, while the developing countries are known as the global South.

1. **Locate** (a) Brazil (b) India (c) Japan
2. **Regions** Which continents lie partly within both the global North and the global South?

3. **Make Comparisons** Based on the graph, how does the standard of living of nations in the global North compare with that in the global South?

Economic Output per Person

Nation	Dollars
Congo (Dem. Rep.)	$300
India	$2,700
Brazil	$9,700
Japan	$33,000
United States	$45,800

SOURCE: *CIA World Factbook*

Global North (Developed countries)

Global South (Developing countries)

After developing countries shifted to market economies, companies and individuals from the global North invested in industries in these countries. Investors put money into businesses that produced income for them, but were not always best for the developing nation's economy.

The Green Revolution During the 1950s and 1960s, new high-yield seeds, fertilizers, and pesticides, along with mechanical equipment such as tractors, were introduced in many parts of the developing world. These new products, along with new methods of farming, are known as the **Green Revolution.** The Green Revolution raised farm output in developing countries. But it had unforeseen consequences. Only big land-owners could afford these new tools and methods. Because they farmed more land, they could grow crops more cheaply than farmers with small plots. As a result, prices for crops dropped below what smaller farmers needed to make to earn a living. Many were forced to sell their farms to big landowners. They became farm workers or moved to cities.

 Checkpoint How did the Green Revolution affect traditional economies?

Obstacles to Development

Despite ambitious goals, many new nations made little progress toward development. The reasons varied, but many countries shared similar problems. Poverty, rapidly rising populations, economic dependence, and unstable governments all posed challenges to development.

Rising Populations Strain Resources In developing countries, improved healthcare and greater food supplies lowered death rates and led to explosive population growth. All of these people need food, housing, education, jobs, and healthcare. Meeting these needs puts a huge burden on governments already strapped for funding.

Although the governments of many developing nations have tried to slow population growth, their efforts have met with limited success. In many cultures with traditional economies, children are valued as a source of labor and a support for parents in old age. Religious traditions also encourage large families.

Across the developing world, millions are trapped in a cycle of poverty. Many people, especially children, die each year from starvation, disease, and other effects of poverty. Without education and jobs, people cannot earn living wages and are unable to escape this tragic cycle.

Economic Dependence Despite their efforts to build industry, many developing nations remain economically dependent on their former colonial rulers. Western nations had used their colonies as sources of raw materials. They used the raw materials to produce manufactured goods that they sold to their colonies.

This pattern continued after colonies won their independence. Industrialized countries purchase agricultural goods and raw materials from the developing world. In turn, the industrial nations provide technology, investment, and manufactured goods to developing countries. However, in recent years, lower labor costs have led Western companies to relocate their manufacturing operations to the global South.

Some developing nations produce only a single export crop or commodity, such as sugar or cocoa. Their economies depend on global demand for the cash crop or commodity. If demand weakens and prices drop, their economies suffer.

Unstable Governments Civil wars and other conflicts hinder development in some countries. Poor leadership and corrupt governments also prevent growth. Dictators spend resources on weapons instead of on education or healthcare. Corrupt leaders loot their nations' treasuries and allow a culture of bribery to thrive.

✔ **Checkpoint** How did population growth affect developing nations?

Different Kinds of Labor
A mechanical harvester cuts rice in South America, while women in West Africa prepare fields for planting. *How do traditional economies affect economic development?*

Patterns of Life Change

Economic development has unleashed great changes across the developing world. Just as the Industrial Revolution disrupted traditional ways of life in Europe and North America, economic development is now transforming life in the global South.

Women's Lives Change In the developing world, the move away from traditional ways of life has brought new opportunities for women. New constitutions granted equality to women, at least on paper. In some countries, such as India, Argentina, and Liberia, women have served as heads of state. Although women still have less access to education than men, the gap has narrowed. Women are joining the work force in growing numbers and contributing their skills to their nations' wealth.

Child Labor In traditional economies, children worked alongside parents, farming or herding to meet the family's needs. When development forces people off their farms, they often move to cities and take low-paying manufacturing jobs. Because these jobs do not pay enough to cover basic needs, parents depend on the low wages that children earn in factory jobs to survive. In India, around 44 million children work for pay. In Pakistan, children make up 10 percent of the workforce.

Religious Revivals In recent decades, religious revivals have swept many developing nations. Some religious leaders are called **fundamentalists,** because they call for a return to what they see as the fundamental, or basic values of their faiths. Many seek political power to oppose changes that undermine their valued religious traditions.

Rapid Growth of Cities Across the developing world, people have flooded into cities to escape rural poverty and find jobs. Besides economic opportunities, cities offer attractions such as entertainment and sports. With no money and few jobs, most newcomers settle in **shantytowns,** crowded, dangerous slums on the edges of cities. These crime-ridden slums lack basic services such as running water, electricity, or sewer systems.

✔ **Checkpoint**   How did development change life for women?

Mumbai: A Divided City
In Mumbai, India, the poverty of slums stands in stark contrast to the comfortable high-rise apartments of wealthier city dwellers. *How did rapid population growth create problems for cities?*

Progress Monitoring *Online*
For: Self-quiz with vocabulary practice
Web Code: naa-3311

SECTION 1
Assessment

Terms, People, and Places

1. For each term, person, or place listed at the beginning of the section, write a sentence explaining its significance.

Note Taking

2. **Reading Skill: Identify Supporting Details** Use your completed chart to answer the Focus Question: How have the nations of the developing world tried to build better lives for their people?

Comprehension and Critical Thinking

3. **Summarize** In general, what are the economic goals of developing nations?
4. **Categorize** What are the differences between the global North and the global South?
5. **Identify Central Issues** Why do developing countries remain dependent on former colonial powers or other industrialized countries?
6. **Predict Consequences** How might modern products and technologies weaken traditional cultures?

● **Writing About History**

Quick Write: Explore a Topic Choose one challenge facing developing nations and write a series of questions you could use to direct research on the topic. For example, on the topic of industrialization in developing nations you could ask:
- Which five developing nations have the highest level of industrialization today?
- What industries do these nations engage in?

Concept Connector

THE ESSENTIAL ?

DEMOCRACY

Under what conditions is democracy most likely to succeed?

In This Chapter

Developing countries have had to overcome many obstacles in order to establish democratic governments. Poverty, illiteracy, political corruption, and inequality among ethnic groups are among the factors that have stood in their way. The education of children like these (right) will be critical to the future of democratic government everywhere.

Throughout History

400s B.C. The Athenian leader, Pericles, believes all citizens should take part in government.

400s B.C. Plebeians in ancient Rome demand and get the right to elect their own officials.

1215 A.D. English nobles force King John to sign the Magna Carta, limiting the power of the king.

1776 The American colonies wage a war to gain independence and the right to rule themselves.

1930s Germany, facing economic and social problems, turns away from democracy.

Continuing Today

Zimbabwe went from being a model of development to one of the poorest nations in the world under the leadership of Robert Mugabe. Mugabe has ruthlessly held on to power, threatening anyone who has challenged him.

21st Century Skills

? TRANSFER Activities

1. **Analyze** Throughout history, how have people gained the right to a say in government?

2. **Explain** How can democratic government be undermined?

3. **Transfer** Complete a Web quest in which you compare democratic countries; record your thoughts in the Concept Connector Journal; and learn to make a video. Web Code nah-3308

A Nigerian child stands in front of the massive trunk of a felled ironwood tree.

Plundering Forests

Civil wars, economic development, and the demand for valuable woods have led to the destruction of ancient African forests. In Ivory Coast, also known as Côte d'Ivoire (koht dee VWAHR), rebels cut trees to sell for money to buy weapons. Illegal logging is devastating local economies. A village chief, Kouadio Yao (KWAH dyoh yow), told a UN worker of watching helplessly as valuable teak trees were chopped down:

❝ If someone came with a gun, would you be able to stop them and demand that they pay for the trees? What I do know is that because of the conflict, we have lost everything. ❞
—Integrated Regional Information Networks (IRIN), December 23, 2004

Focus Question What challenges have African nations faced in their effort to develop their economies?

Africa Seeks a Better Future

 Performance Standards

- **SSWH21c** Explain how governments cooperate to protect the environment.
- **SSWHRC1c** Demonstrate understanding of contextual vocabulary.

Terms, People, and Places

socialism
desertification
urbanization

endangered species
Wangari Maathai
sustainable development

Note Taking

Reading Skill: Identify Main Ideas As you read, use a concept web to record the main ideas in this section and to note details that support those main ideas.

More than fifty new nations emerged in Africa in the decades after World War II. African nations are a large part of the developing world. As they set out to build stable governments and modern economies, they faced serious challenges.

Making Economic Choices

In Africa, as elsewhere, development meant building productive economies and raising standards of living. To achieve these goals, African nations had to establish industries, build transportation systems, increase literacy, and reduce poverty. Many countries had little capital to invest in such projects. Each nation had to make difficult choices about how to achieve their goals.

Socialism or Capitalism Many newly independent nations were attracted to **socialism,** a system in which the people as a whole own all property and operate all businesses. Through socialism, the new nations hoped to reduce dependence on their former colonial rulers and end the inequalities between rich and poor. To regulate the economy, socialism relied on large, generally inefficient bureaucracies.

Some nations chose capitalism, or market economies with private ownership of property, as a path to development. To get the huge sums needed for development, they turned to foreign lenders to invest capital in new industries. These countries often had more efficient economies, but foreign lenders took more profits out of the country.

Cash Crops or Food Governments tried to raise development funds by producing raising cash crops for export, such as coffee or cotton. Some nations or exporting a commodity, such as copper or oil. However, dependence on a single crop or commodity is risky, because it puts economies at the mercy of sudden price changes in the market.

Because land used for cash crops could not be used to produce food, some countries had to buy costly imported food. To prevent unrest among the urban poor, many governments kept food prices artificially low. However, low prices discouraged local farmers from growing food crops. Governments then had to <u>subsidize</u> part of the cost of importing food.

✓ **Checkpoint** Why did governments promote cash crops?

Vocabulary Builder

<u>subsidize</u>—(SUB suh dyz) *v.* support with government spending

Obstacles to Progress

Developing African nations faced numerous problems. The challenges included deadly civil wars, rapid population growth, epidemics, and damage to the environment and wildlife.

Drought Brings Starvation From time to time, droughts struck parts of Africa, killing livestock and crops. The Sahel, a semi-desert region just south of the Sahara, was especially hard hit in the late 1960s. The drought, which lasted for decades, led to famine. Overgrazing and farming in this fragile area removed topsoil and led to **desertification,** or a change of semi-dry land into desert. International relief efforts eased the famine, but wars that raged in several countries in the Sahel added to the suffering.

The AIDS Epidemic Since the 1980s, the deadly disease AIDS (Acquired Immune Deficiency Syndrome), has spread across Africa. AIDS is caused by HIV, a virus that damages the body's ability to fight infections. In South Africa and Botswana, up to one third of adults were infected with HIV. More than 11 million children in Africa have been orphaned by the AIDS epidemic.

The loss of so many skilled and productive workers hurt the economies of African countries. A global effort to combat AIDS led to the development of drugs to treat people infected with HIV. African nations set up treatment programs and worked hard to stop the spread of AIDS.

People Move to Cities African nations experienced rapid **urbanization,** or the movement of people from rural areas to cities. The newcomers hoped to find a better life. Instead, millions faced unemployment, terrible living conditions, and crime. However, in much of West Africa, the growth of cities has provided increased opportunities for women, who have historically dominated urban markets as traders.

Urbanization also brought people from different ethnic groups together and helped replace ethnic loyalties with a larger national identity. But modern urban lifestyles weakened traditional cultures and undermined ethnic and kinship ties. Despite rapid urbanization, most people in Africa still lived in villages.

Displaced by Drought
A Sudanese mother and children escape famine caused by years of drought. *How can geography affect migration patterns?*

ENDANGERED SPECIES

The threats to Africa's endangered species include a loss of habitats and poaching, or illegal hunting. The map below shows that most of Africa's forests have been disturbed or cut down. However, Africans have taken steps to save their rich wildlife. Earnings from tourism have given local people a stake in saving these animals' lives.

▲ Foreign demand for leopard skins has encouraged illegal killing of leopards.

Elephants have been killed ▶ for their valuable tusks.

▲ Africa's wildlife draw foreign tourists, who provide a steady income to local guides and tour operators. This gives Africans a stake in preventing poaching.

◀ African nations have set aside preserves to protect endangered species such as these mountain gorillas in Rwanda.

Undisturbed forest
Disturbed forest
Formerly forested land

Miller Projection
0   1000 mi
0   1000 km

Thinking Critically

1. **Draw Conclusions** Based on the map at the right, how have changes in Africa's forest cover affected its forest species?
2. **Synthesize Information** How might wildlife tourism discourage poaching in Africa?

Development Hurts the Environment In Africa, as elsewhere, urbanization, population growth, farming, and logging led to the destruction of Africa's animal habitats. As habitats were destroyed, some animals became **endangered species,** or species threatened with extinction. Foreign demand for elephant tusks to make ivory, or for rare pelts or furs, has encouraged impoverished Africans to kill endangered animals, even when it is illegal.

In Kenya, **Wangari Maathai** (mah THY), an environmental activist, started the Green Belt Movement. She was inspired to plant trees with women to help them meet basic needs, such as energy, clean drinking water, and nutritious food. Maathai wanted to heal the land, empower women, and promote **sustainable development,** or development that meets the needs of the present without compromising the ability of future generations to meet their own needs.

✔ **Checkpoint** What are some advantages and disadvantages of urbanization in Africa?

Tanzania: A Closer Look

Tanganyika, a large country in East Africa, gained independence in the early 1960s and later merged with the island state of Zanzibar to form the republic of Tanzania. Julius Nyerere, the country's first president, wanted to raise the standard of living for Tanzania's impoverished, population.

African Socialism Tanzania had little capital or technology. Most people were farmers. The country's main exports were coffee, cotton, tea, and tobacco. To improve life for Tanzanians, Nyerere's government embraced what he called "African socialism." This was based on village traditions of cooperation and shared responsibility.

The government took over banks, businesses, and factories. In a program of rural development called *ujamaa* (pulling together), farmers were encouraged to move to large villages and work on collective farms. The goal was to increase output and produce surplus crops for export.

Nyerere's experiment failed, partly because farmers did not want to leave their own land for collective farms. Agricultural output did not rise. However, Tanzania did make important advances in education and healthcare during this period.

Debt Leads to Reforms The experiment created a huge and inefficient government bureaucracy. The expense of this huge bureaucracy, along with high oil prices, plunged Tanzania into debt. In 1985, President Nyerere resigned. Tanzania's new leaders introduced economic reforms, cutting the size of government and promoting a market economy. By 2003, Tanzania's debt was being reduced through participation in an IMF/World Bank program.

Outlook Today, Tanzania still has an overwhelmingly agricultural economy. Although Tanzania remains poor, its economy received a boost in the early 2000s from the opening of a huge new gold mine. The government planned to use gold mine profits along with foreign aid to reduce poverty and improve basic services.

✔ **Checkpoint** What was the result of Tanzania's experiment with socialism?

BIOGRAPHY

Wangari Maathai

While working with a women's rights group, Kenyan activist Wangari Maathai (born in 1940) came up with the idea of getting ordinary women involved in tree-planting projects. In 1977, she launched the Green Belt Movement (GBM). This grassroots organization promotes reforestation and controlled wood cutting to ensure a sustainable supply of wood fuel. The group also sought jobs for women in Kenya, Tanzania, and other East African countries. In 2004, Maathai became the first African woman to be awarded the Nobel Peace Prize. Today, Maathai continues to work with the GBM. She is also a member of Kenya's government. **In what ways might planting trees help improve women's lives?**

Progress Monitoring *Online*
For: Self-quiz with vocabulary practice
Web Code: naa-3321

SECTION

2 Assessment

Terms, People, and Places

1. For each term or person listed at the beginning of the section, write a sentence explaining its significance.

Note Taking

2. **Reading Skill: Identify Main Ideas**
Use your completed concept web to answer the Focus Question: What challenges have African nations faced in their effort to develop their economies?

Comprehension and Critical Thinking

3. **Summarize** What obstacles kept many African nations from developing strong economies?

4. **Synthesize Information** Why have African nations had trouble feeding their people?

5. **Draw Inferences** Urbanization is a problem for many developing nations. Why do you think this is?

6. **Summarize** Why did socialism in Tanzania fail?

● **Writing About History**

Quick Write: Gather Information
Review the material in this section on social issues in Africa. For each problem, list the causes, the effects, and any actions that have been taken to solve that problem.

A man tries to stop a line of tanks heading into the crowd of protesters in Tiananmen Square (top). Protesters erect a statue of the goddess of democracy in front of a poster of Mao (right).

WITNESS HISTORY 🔊 AUDIO

A Violent Crackdown

When students and other Chinese citizens protested to demand more political freedom in the 1980s, the government cracked down. Cheng Zhen, a student, describes what she saw in Beijing's Tiananmen (TYEN ahn mun) Square on the night of June 4, 1989.

66 [A]t about 2 A.M. we . . . could see that the troops were already in the square, and we quickly ran to the other side. . . . While I was running, I noticed a young man ahead of me. He picked up a bottle on the ground, and was about to throw it at the troops, angry because they were holding up their guns and firing. Suddenly, he fell to the ground. . . . He was shot. . . . 99
—BBC News Online, June 2, 2004

Focus Question What are the similarities and differences between the economies and governments of China and India?

China and India: Two Giants of Asia

Performance Standards

- **SSWH19e** Analyze Tiananmen Square.
- **SSWH21a** Describe how computers integrated countries into a world economy.

Terms, People, and Places

Deng Xiaoping	Mumbai
Tiananmen Square	Mother Teresa
one-child policy	dalits
Kolkata	

Note Taking

Reading Skill: Identify Main Ideas As you read, make a table like this one to record the main ideas.

Reform and Change in China and India		
Type	**China**	**India**
Economic	• Free market •	
Political		

China and India dominate much of Asia. Together, they are home to about two-fifths of the world's population. China is a major industrial nation. Although India's economy is smaller, like China, it is a leading Asian and global power. Over the last 60 years, China and India have taken different paths toward development.

China Mixes Reform and Repression

Mao Zedong, China's communist revolutionary leader, died in 1976. After Mao's death, more moderate leaders took control of China. By 1981, **Deng Xiaoping** (dung show ping), had taken a new approach to China's economy. Deng was a practical reformer, more interested in improving economic output than in political purity. "I don't care if a cat is black or white," he declared, "as long as it catches mice."

Modernizing the Economy Deng's program, the Four Modernizations, emphasized agriculture, industry, science, and defense. The plan allowed some features of a free market, such as some private ownership of property. Communes, or collectively owned farms, were dismantled, and peasant families were allotted plots of farmland in what was called the "responsibility system." Farmers still did not own the land, and the government took a share of their crops. However, farmers could sell any surplus produce and keep their profits. Chinese entrepreneurs were allowed to set up businesses. Managers of state-run factories were given more freedom, but they had to make their plants more efficient. Deng also welcomed foreign capital and technology. Investors from Japan, Hong Kong, Taiwan, and Western nations invested heavily in Chinese firms.

Economic reforms brought a surge of growth. In coastal cities, foreign investment created an economic boom. Some Chinese enjoyed an improved standard of living. They bought refrigerators, televisions, and cars. On the other hand, crime and corruption increased and a growing economic and regional gap developed between poor rural farmers and wealthy city dwellers.

Vocabulary Builder

disperse—(dih SPURS) *v.* break up and scatter

The Government Crushes Protests Economic reforms and increased contact with the West led some Chinese to demand greater political freedom. In the late 1980s, students, workers, and others created a democracy movement similar to those sweeping across Eastern Europe. However, Deng and other Chinese leaders refused to allow democratic reforms.

In 1989, thousands of protesters, many of them students, occupied **Tiananmen** (TYEN ahn mun) **Square,** a huge public plaza in Beijing. They raised banners calling for democracy. The government ordered the protesters to disperse. When they refused, the government sent in troops and tanks. Thousands of demonstrators were killed or wounded in the Tiananmen Square Massacre. Many others were imprisoned and tortured. The crackdown showed that the communist government was determined to keep control.

China Limits Population Growth China's population, at more than 1.3 billion, is the largest in the world. In the 1980s, the government imposed a **one-child policy,** which limited urban families to a single child, and rural families to two children. The goal was to keep population growth from hurting economic development. The government enforced the policy with fines and other penalties. Although the one-child policy was harshly condemned, it did slow population growth.

✔ **Checkpoint** How did economic reforms benefit China?

China Faces Ongoing Challenges

Economic reforms had more than quadrupled China's economic output by the early 2000s. China's industrial power made it a growing rival of the United States. China's achievements—symbolized by the newly built Beijing National Stadium—were displayed to the world when it hosted the 2008 summer Olympic games. But the country still faced serious internal challenges.

Growth Brings Problems Boom times led to rapid urbanization as millions of rural workers flooded into China's cities. Urban newcomers worked for low wages in manufacturing jobs. Although these workers lived in poverty, their needs strained local resources. Rapid development brought

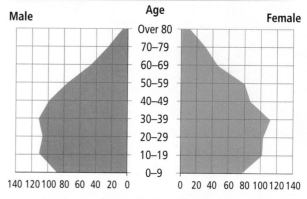

China, Estimated Population by Age and Gender, 2008

Male — Age — Female

Over 80
70–79
60–69
50–59
40–49
30–39
20–29
10–19
0–9

140 120 100 80 60 40 20 0   0 20 40 60 80 100 120 140

Population (in millions)

Graph Skills China's population growth has slowed in recent years due to government efforts like the one-child policy, encouraged in the billboard below. *According to the graph, in what age groups is most of China's population concentrated? What might this mean for China's future?*

SOURCE: U.S. Census Bureau, International Data Base

India and China: The Economic Rise of Two Asian Giants

India and China are both huge Asian nations with rapidly growing populations. They have very different governments: India is a democracy, while China is communist. However, they have taken similar economic paths in recent years. Study the chart (right) and graph (left) below. *Which country has achieved a higher economic output in recent years? How might policies adopted by that nation help explain this success?*

Economic Growth in India and China, 1960–2007

[Graph showing Economic output (billions of dollars) on the y-axis from 0 to 3500, and Year on the x-axis from 1960 to 2010. Two lines labeled China and India show growth over time.]

SOURCE: The World Bank

Comparing India and China

China	India
Shift to free market economy in 1980s	Shift to free market economy in 1980s
Government policies limit population growth	Population growth remains a serious issue
Autocratic communist government	Democratic government

A man casts a vote in an election in Kashmir, India. Religious and political conflict has limited economic growth in that region. ▶

◀ A pedestrian in Shanghai, China, walks past the construction of a new high-rise apartment building.

other problems. Industrial production led to dangerously polluted air and water. In 2007, China's Ministry of Health said that pollution caused hundreds of thousands of premature deaths each year. Increased travel and trade helped spread AIDS and other diseases across China.

The global economic recession that began in 2008 took its toll. Chinese factories closed as overseas orders fell. As the economy slowed and unemployment rose, many workers returned to family homes in rural areas. Protests by unemployed urban workers increased. To prevent social unrest, the government announced an economic stimulus package to improve productivity and retrain workers.

Human Rights Abuses Despite the global outcry after the Tiananmen Square massacre, China continued to jail critics and limit freedom. Human rights activists inside and outside China protested abuses such as the use of prison labor to produce cheap goods for export and the suppression of Tibetan culture and rights. China's trading partners called for an end to human rights abuses. Party leaders said that outsiders had no right to try to impose "Western-style" ideas of human rights on China. However, China's cabinet issued the country's first human rights action plan in 2009. It included the right to question government policies.

✓ **Checkpoint** How did the global economic recession affect China?

India Builds a Modern Economy

Like China, India is a big country with a large, diverse population and widespread poverty. After gaining independence in 1947, India set up a democratic government and planned to develop a modern economy.

Agriculture and Industry Expand Like other developing nations, India was determined to use modern technology to expand agriculture and industry. The government followed a socialist model, using five-year plans to set economic goals and manage resources. Development, however, was uneven. India built some industries, but it lacked oil and natural gas, key resources for economic growth. Instead, it had to rely on costly imported oil.

India benefited from the Green Revolution. High-yield crops, chemical fertilizers, and better irrigation systems increased output. Still, most farmers used traditional methods and relied on seasonal rains for water. They produced enough to survive, but little surplus.

By the 1980s, an economic slowdown and outside pressure pushed India toward a market economy. Some industries were privatized and limits on foreign investment were eased. During the 1990s, Indian textiles, technology, and other industries saw rapid expansion. By 2000, India was a leader in information technology, providing computer software services to the world. Although India's booming economy slowed after 2008 as a result of the global recession, it stood ready to move ahead when economic conditions improved.

Population Growth and Poverty In India, as in China, rapid population growth hurt efforts to improve living conditions. As food output rose, so did demand. More than one-third of Indians lived in poverty, unable to meet basic needs for food, clothing, and shelter. The growing population put added pressure on India's healthcare system, which faced additional challenges after 1990 from the spread of AIDS.

The population boom and the labor-saving methods of the Green Revolution led millions of rural families to migrate to cities. But overcrowded cities like **Kolkata** (or Calcutta) and **Mumbai** (or Bombay) could not provide jobs

Bangalore: A Customer Support Center
Workers in Bangalore, India, serve as customer service operators for American and European companies. To make callers feel more comfortable, the operators are trained in English and American slang. *How do you expect the customer service industry to change as more countries develop?*

Combating Poverty
Mother Teresa, shown with children in Calcutta, inspired others to help people living in poverty.

for everyone or even basic services, such as water or sewage systems. To help the urban poor, **Mother Teresa,** a Roman Catholic nun, founded the Missionaries of Charity in Calcutta. This group provided food and medical care to thousands. Still, millions more remained in desperate need.

The Indian government supported family planning but did not adopt the harsh policies that were used in China. Efforts to slow population growth had limited success. Poor families, especially in rural areas, saw children as an economic resource to work the land and care for parents in old age.

 Checkpoint   How did market reforms affect India's economy during the 1990s?

Reforming Indian Society

In India, as elsewhere, urbanization, education, and the growth of a modern economy undermined traditional ways of life. These changes benefited India's lowest social castes and women. In the cities, many people adopted western-style clothing and bought modern consumer goods. Yet most Indians still lived in villages and followed traditional ways.

Caste Discrimination Persists   India's constitution banned discrimination against **dalits,** or people of the lowest caste. To improve conditions, the government set aside jobs and places in universities for members of these groups. However, discrimination based on caste continued.

Women Make Progress   India's constitution granted equal rights to women. In the cities, girls from well-to-do families were educated. Women entered many professions. Some, like Indira Gandhi, won political office. Girls from poor families, however, received little or no education. Although women in rural areas worked the land or contributed to household industries, few received wages. Across India, women organized self-help groups to start small businesses and improve their lives.

 Checkpoint   How did the Indian government try to improve the status of dalits?

SECTION **3** Assessment

Progress Monitoring *Online*
For: Self-quiz with vocabulary practice
Web Code: naa-3331

Terms, People, and Places
1. For each term, person, or place listed at the beginning of the section, write a sentence explaining its significance.

Note Taking
2. **Reading Skill: Identify Main Ideas**
Use your completed table to answer the Focus Question: What are the similarities and differences between the economies and governments of China and India?

Comprehension and Critical Thinking
3. **Identify Central Issues**   What obstacles to economic development does China still face?
4. **Draw Inferences**   How did the Green Revolution contribute to urbanization in India?
5. **Summarize**   What economic goals has the Indian government pursued and how has it met these goals?
6. **Predict Consequences**   Do you think that China can continue to develop economically without making political reforms? Explain.

● **Writing About History**
Quick Write: Write a Conclusion
Choose one subheading from this section—for example "Reforming Indian Society." After rereading the text under that subheading, write a conclusion that summarizes the information.

SSWHRC1b

Brotherhood by Octavio Paz

▲ Octavio Paz

Mexican poet, essayist, and critic Octavio Paz (1914–1998) was one of Latin America's great modern writers. Besides enjoying enormous success as an author, he was also a diplomat. Paz held diplomatic positions in France and India, where he was exposed to different schools of literature. In France, he explored surrealism. This literary movement encouraged the expression of the irrational and freed Paz to write beyond the limits of literal meaning. In India, Paz studied Buddhism, which also influenced his work. However, even as he contributed to the global culture, Paz maintained his national identity. He thought and wrote much about Mexico, its past, and its place in the modern world. In 1990, Paz became the first Mexican writer to receive the Nobel Prize for Literature. The poem below is dedicated to the Greek scientist and geographer Ptolemy (TAHL uh mee), who wrote one of the most influential astronomy texts of the ancient world.

Brotherhood
Homage to Claudius Ptolemy

I am a man: little do I last
and the night is enormous.
But I look up:
the stars write.
Unknowing I understand:
I too am written,
and at this very moment
someone spells me out.

Hermandad
Homenaje a Claudio Ptolomeo

Soy hombre: duro poco
y es enorme la noche.
Pero miro hacia arriba:
las estrellas escriben.
Sin entender comprendo:
también soy escritura
y en este mismo instante
alguien me deletrea.

Thinking Critically

1. **Analyze Literature** What do you think is the meaning of the lines "I am a man: little do I last / and the night is enormous"?
2. **Draw Conclusions** Why do you think Paz chose the title "Brotherhood" for this poem?

A woman at a municipal dump in Mexico collects garbage to sell.

SECTION 4

WITNESS HISTORY 🔊 AUDIO

A Daily Struggle

Carolina Maria de Jesus (day zhay ZOOS) faced a life of hardship in the slums of São Paulo (sow POW loh), Brazil. Like millions of other poor, rural people, she came to the city hoping to improve her life. Instead, to buy food, she spent her days combing through garbage for paper, cans, and other scraps to sell. In her diary, de Jesus described her daily struggle against poverty:

❝ July 16 . . . I went to Senhor Manuel, carrying some cans to sell. . . . He gave me 13 [coins]. I kept thinking that I had to buy bread, soap, and milk. . . . The 13 [coins] wouldn't make it. I returned . . . to my shack, nervous and exhausted. I thought of the worrisome life that I led. Carrying paper, washing clothes for children, staying in the street all day long. ❞
—Carolina Maria de Jesus, *Child of the Dark*

Focus Question What challenges have Latin American nations faced in recent decades in their struggle for democracy and prosperity?

Latin America Builds Democracy

GA **Performance Standards**

• **SSWH21b** Analyze multinational corporations.

Terms, People, and Places

import substitution
agribusiness
liberation theology
Organization of
    American States
    (OAS)
Sandinista
contra
indigenous
Juan Perón
Mothers of the
    Plaza de Mayo

Note Taking

Reading Skill: Identify Main Ideas and Supporting Details As you read this section, make an outline like the one below.

> I. Economic and Social Forces
>   A. Society
>   1.
>   2.

Latin America comprises Mexico, Central America, the Caribbean, and South America. It includes 33 independent nations, ranging from small islands, such as Grenada, to giant Brazil.

For decades, Latin American nations have faced political, economic, and social challenges similar to those of other developing nations—rapid population growth, poverty, illiteracy, political instability, and authoritarian governments.

Latin America Grapples With Poverty

From the 1950s to the 1980s, economic development failed to change deep-rooted inequalities in many Latin American countries. Due to inequality and growing populations, most countries saw little improvement in living standards.

Promoting Industry and Agriculture In Latin America, as in other developing regions, nations often relied heavily on a single cash crop or commodity to earn money for needed imports. If harvests failed or if world demand fell, their economies were hard hit.

To reduce their dependence on imported goods, many Latin American governments adopted a policy of **import substitution,** or manufacturing goods locally to replace imports. This policy, pursued mainly in the 1950s and 1960s, was a mixed success. Many of the new industries needed government help or foreign capital to survive.

Latin America: Economic Activity

Geography *Interactive*

For: Interactive map
Web Code: nap-3341

Map Skills Latin American nations have been diversifying their economies in recent decades.

1. **Locate** (a) Venezuela (b) Nicaragua (c) Brazil (d) Haiti

2. **Region** Which region is the least diversified? What factors might explain this?

3. **Synthesize Information** Locate the areas on the map with manufacturing and trade. Are those areas likely to be near cities or countryside? Explain.

▲ Mexican men harvest tangerines, carrying baskets weighing up to 200 pounds.

UNITED STATES

Atlantic Ocean

Gulf of Mexico

MEXICO

BAHAMAS

DOMINICAN REPUBLIC

CUBA

U.S. Virgin Islands (U.S.)

British Virgin Islands (U.K.)

ST. KITTS AND NEVIS

ANTIGUA AND BARBUDA

HAITI

JAMAICA

Puerto Rico (U.S.)

Guadeloupe (Fr.)

BELIZE

Martinique (Fr.)

DOMINICA

GUATEMALA HONDURAS

Caribbean Sea

BARBADOS

EL SALVADOR

NICARAGUA

ST. LUCIA

ST. VINCENT & THE GRENADINES

GRENADA

COSTA RICA PANAMA

TRINIDAD AND TOBAGO

VENEZUELA

GUYANA SURINAME

COLOMBIA

French Guiana (Fr.)

ECUADOR

Equator

▲ A man works at an off-shore oil rig in Venezuela. Like many oil companies in Venezuela, the company he works for is foreign-owned.

PERU

BRAZIL

Pacific Ocean

BOLIVIA

PARAGUAY

CHILE

Forestry
Livestock raising
Mainly commercial farming
Mainly subsistence farming
Manufacturing and trade
Little or no activity
Petroleum (oil)

ARGENTINA

URUGUAY

Atlantic Ocean

Equal Area Projection

| 0 | 500 | 1000 mi |

| 0 | 500 | 1000 km |

Falkland Islands (U.K.)

Tropic of Cancer

Tropic of Capricorn

20° N

20° S

40° S

60° W

120° W   100° W   80° W   40° W   20° W

FIGHTING POVERTY IN BRAZIL

More than a quarter of Brazil's population lives on less than two dollars a day. A minority controls most of the country's wealth and income. In recent years, though, better jobs and education have provided more opportunities for many Brazilians. The country's steady economic growth, shown in the graph at right, has helped make these improvements possible.

◀ In Brazil's countryside, most land is owned by a wealthy few. In this photo, members of the Landless Peasants' Movement occupy a large privately owned ranch.

To escape rural poverty, many ▶ Brazilians seek better-paying urban employment, such as the factory job shown here.

In time, Latin American governments moved away from import substitution because of its high cost. Instead, they have tried to generate income by promoting exports. Specifically, they have focused on developing a variety of cash crops and encouraging industries that they hope will produce goods for export.

Governments also backed efforts to open more land to farming through irrigation and the clearing of forests. Much of the best farmland belongs to **agribusinesses,** or giant commercial farms owned by multinational corporations. In Central America and Brazil, developers continue to clear tropical rain forests for use as farmland. This practice has had environmental costs, as you will read in the next chapter.

A Growing Gap One major obstacle to progress in Latin America is the uneven distribution of wealth. In many countries, a tiny elite controls the land, businesses, and factories. These powerful groups oppose changes that might undermine their position. As a result, the gap between the rich and the poor has widened, fueling discontent.

Poverty Latin American nations, like the rest of the developing world, experienced a population explosion that contributed to poverty. Although population growth rates slowed somewhat in the 1990s, economies were hard-pressed to keep pace with growing populations. Overall, the population of Latin America was 570 million in 2008.

In rural areas, population pressures made life more difficult for peasant farmers. Even though a family might own a small plot to grow their own food, most farmers worked on the estates of large landowners for low wages. Their wages pay for needed essentials like clothing, tools, and the food they cannot grow themselves.

Harsh conditions and limited land drove millions of peasants to the cities. Today, more than half of all people in Latin America live in cities. Some newcomers found jobs in factories, offices, and stores. Many more, like Carolina de Jesus, survive by working odd jobs. They fill the shantytowns on the edges of Latin American cities such as Mexico City and Sao Paulo. The shantytowns in these cities are among the largest in the world.

Brazilians have also escaped from poverty through education, such as this adult literacy class. ▼

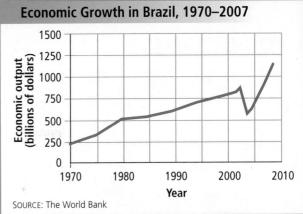

Economic Growth in Brazil, 1970–2007

SOURCE: The World Bank

Thinking Critically
1. **Make Generalizations** How did Brazil's economic output change from 1970 to 2002?
2. **Synthesize Information** How did this change help Brazilians to move out of poverty?

Churches Help the Poor The Catholic Church remained a powerful force across Latin America. Although it was often tied to the ruling class, some church leaders spoke up for the poor. During the 1960s and 1970s, many priests, nuns, and church workers crusaded for social justice and an end to poverty. This movement, known as **liberation theology,** urged the church to become a force for reform. Meanwhile, evangelical Protestant groups won converts among the poor in many countries.

✔ **Checkpoint** How did the gulf between the rich and the poor cause problems in Latin America?

Dictatorships and Democracy

Democracy was difficult to achieve in Latin American nations plagued by poverty and inequality. From the 1950s on, many groups pressed for reforms. They included liberals, socialists, urban workers, peasants, and Catholic priests and nuns. Although they differed over how to achieve their goals, all wanted to improve conditions for the poor. Conservatives, however, resisted reforms. Conflict between conservatives and reformers contributed to political unrest in many nations.

Military Leaders Seize Power Between the 1950s and 1970s, as social unrest grew, military leaders in Argentina, Brazil, Chile, and other nations seized power. Claiming the need for order, they imposed harsh, autocratic regimes. These military rulers outlawed political parties, censored the press, and closed universities. They also imprisoned and executed thousands. "Death squads" linked to the government murdered many more. Latin American writers, such as Pablo Neruda of Chile and Gabriel García Márquez of Colombia, went into exile after speaking out against repressive governments or social inequality.

Threats of Revolution Beginning in the 1950s, leftist guerrillas battled repressive governments across much of Latin America. They believed that only socialism could end inequalities. Others were nationalists who opposed economic and cultural domination by the United States.

Lula da Silva

As a child, Luíz Inácio Lula da Silva sold peanuts and shined shoes on the streets of Sao Paulo, Brazil. The son of poor peasants with eight children, the boy did not learn to read and write until he was 10 years old. From this humble background, Lula, as he is called, rose to become president of Brazil. Lula left school at age 14 to become a metal worker in a factory. Ambitious and bright, he worked his way up and took courses to improve his skills. Lula also became active in workers rights issues. A fierce union leader, he helped start the Workers' Party, which became a major political force in Brazil. Even though he vigorously supported workers' rights, Lula gradually moved the party platform from revolutionary idealism to practical goals. Lula ran three times for president before finally winning the office in 2002 on his fourth try. As president, he expanded social programs and tried to narrow the huge gap between rich and poor in Brazil. When he won a second term in 2006, Lula declared, "The foundation is in place and now we have to get to work." **How does Lula's life illustrate both the problems and successes of development in Brazil?**

Cold War fears about the spread of Marxism complicated moderate reform efforts. Many Latin American conservatives saw any call for reform as a communist threat. These groups were often supported by the United States.

Civil Wars Shake Central America Several Central American nations were torn by civil wars as revolutionaries battled authoritarian governments. In 1954, the United States helped the Guatemalan military overthrow an elected, leftist government. Leftists and others fought the military regime, which responded savagely. The military targeted Guatemala's **indigenous,** or native people, slaughtering tens of thousands. The fighting ended in the 1990s, after the government finally held elections and signed a peace accord with leftist guerillas.

In the 1970s and 1980s, reformers and revolutionaries challenged El Salvador's landowning and military elite. One reformer, Archbishop Oscar Romero, preached liberation theology until he was assassinated while celebrating mass in 1980. A brutal civil war shook El Salvador until the rebels and the military agreed to a UN-backed peace plan in 1991.

In 1979, the **Sandinistas,** socialist rebels in Nicaragua, toppled the ruling Somoza family. The Sandinistas introduced land reform and tried to redistribute wealth to the country's poor. Claiming that Nicaragua could become "another Cuba," United States President Ronald Reagan financed the **contras,** guerrillas who fought the Sandinistas. Fighting raged until a 1990 compromise brought peace and multiparty elections.

Progress Toward Democracy By the 1990s, pressure from democracy activists and foreign lenders led military rulers to restore civilian rule. Argentina, Brazil, Chile, and other countries held elections. In some countries, such as Brazil, Venezuela, and Bolivia, leftist leaders won office. These new leaders challenged U.S. economic and political dominance over the region.

In Mexico, which had escaped military rule, demands for reform grew. There, a single party–the Institutional Revolutionary Party (PRI)–had controlled the government for 70 years. It claimed to represent all groups in Mexican society. But in reality, PRI bosses moved forcefully against any serious opposition.

Under pressure, the PRI made some reforms in the1990s. In 2000, Vicente Fox became the first candidate from an opposition party to be elected president. Fox and his successor, conservative Felipe Calderón, faced tough challenges, ranging from desperate rural poverty, to crime, corruption, and violent drug gangs.

 Checkpoint What conditions led to civil wars in many Latin American countries?

Latin America and the United States

Politically, a fact of life for Latin Americans has been the looming presence of the United States. An economic and military giant, the United

States has dominated the **Organization of American States (OAS),** a group formed in 1948 to promote democracy, economic cooperation, and peace in the Americas. Today, Latin America and the United States are still closely linked. The United States is the region's most important investor and trading partner.

Despite these links, the United States and Latin American nations view each other very differently. The United States sees itself as the defender of democracy and capitalism in the region. It also provides much-needed aid. While many Latin Americans admire the wealth of the United States, they resent what they see as its political, economic, and cultural domination. However, in 2000, when the United States honored its 1977 treaty and turned control of the Panama Canal over to Panama, many Latin American nations welcomed it as a sign of respect for Panama's independence.

The United States Intervenes During the Cold War, the United States backed anti-communist dictators in Latin America. On several occasions, it intervened militarily to stop the spread of communism. As you have read, in 1954, the United States helped overthrow Guatemala's leftist government. In 1961, President John F. Kennedy supported the Bay of Pigs invasion of Castro's Cuba. Since that failed invasion, the United States has imposed economic sanctions on Cuba. In 1973, the United States secretly backed the military coup that toppled Chile's democratically elected socialist president, Salvador Allende (ah YEN day), putting military dictator, Augusto Pinochet (pee noh SHAY), in power.

In 1994, a UN force led by the United States stepped into Haiti to restore its elected leader three years after a military coup. In 2004, the U.S. withdrew, leaving UN peacekeepers the job of restoring democracy to poverty-stricken, hurricane-ravaged Haiti.

The War on Drugs In the 1980s, illegal drug use grew in the United States, leading the U.S. government to declare a "war on drugs." The United States tried to stop illegal drugs from being smuggled into the country from Colombia, Peru, Bolivia, and elsewhere. It pressed Latin American governments to destroy drug crops and crush the drug cartels, or criminal gangs that ran the drug trade.

Governments cooperated, but critics in Latin America <u>alleged</u> that the main problem was growing demand for illegal drugs in the United States. Efforts to stop the drug trade led drug gangs to bribe government officials and hire assassins to kill judges, journalists, and others who worked against them. In 1989, U.S. forces invaded Panama and arrested its president, Manuel Noriega (noh ree AY guh), for drug trafficking. He was later tried and convicted.

Migration Poverty and unrest led many people to flee their homes in Latin America for the United States. Many entered the country legally. A large number were illegal immigrants. Their remittances, or the earnings they sent home, helped raise the standard of living for their families in Latin America. As the economic slowdown worsened after 2008, many newcomers lost their jobs and returned to their homelands.

✔ **Checkpoint** Why do people in Latin America have mixed reactions to the United States?

Vocabulary Builder
<u>allege</u>—(uh LEJ) *v.* assert, charge, claim

Democracy in Mexico
Mexican president Felipe Calderón waves after being sworn in on December 1, 2006. Although his opponent claimed that he was elected unfairly, international observers and Mexico's courts rejected these claims. *What does the free election of two presidents in a row suggest about the stability of Mexico's democracy?*

Argentina Survives Upheavals

Once the most prosperous country in Latin America, Argentina enjoyed a robust economy based on exports of beef and grain. It attracted millions of immigrants. But since the Great Depression of the 1930s, Argentina has experienced more than 60 years of political and economic upheavals.

Remembering the Disappeared
The Mothers of the Plaza de Mayo demanded to know the fate of family members who had disappeared under military rule.

Military Rule From 1946 to 1955, nationalist president **Juan Perón** enjoyed great support from workers. He increased the government's economic role, boosted wages, and backed labor unions. He also suppressed opposition.

When Perón's policies led to an economic crisis, he was ousted in a 1955 military coup. Although Perón was reelected in 1973, the military was in and out of power for two decades. In 1976, as a wave of political unrest swept Argentina, the military again seized control. As the military battled leftist guerrillas, it waged a "dirty war" of torture and murder against its own citizens. As many as 20,000 people were kidnapped by the government and disappeared. Every week, women, known as the **Mothers of the Plaza de Mayo,** marched in Buenos Aires, the capital of Argentina. They demanded to know what had happened to their missing sons and daughters.

Democracy Is Restored By 1983, failed policies and a lost war with Britain over the Falkland Islands forced the military to restore civilian rule and allow elections. A financial crisis in 2001 devastated Argentina's economy and brought widespread poverty. Argentina's democracy survived the economic crisis and its economy recovered after 2003. However, like other Latin American nations, Argentina's economic progress was undermined by the 2008 global recession.

✓ **Checkpoint** Why did the military restore civilian rule in Argentina?

SECTION 4 Assessment

Progress Monitoring *Online*
For: Self-quiz with vocabulary practice
Web Code: naa-3341

Terms, People, and Places

1. For each term or person listed at the beginning of the section, write a sentence explaining its significance.

Note Taking

2. **Reading Skill: Identify Main Ideas and Supporting Details** Use your completed outline to answer the Focus Question: What challenges have Latin American nations faced in recent decades in their struggle for democracy and prosperity?

Comprehension and Critical Thinking

3. **Draw Conclusions** How has U.S. involvement in Latin America affected the region?

4. **Analyze Information** Explain the impact of social inequality on politics in Argentina.

5. **Make Inferences** What do you think was the appeal of liberation theology to people in Latin American nations?

● **Writing About History**

Quick Write: Develop a Working Thesis and Choose Supporting Information Reread the information in this section or review your outline. Then develop a thesis statement that expresses what you think is the main idea of this section. Locate details within the text that support your thesis statement. Evaluate your thesis to be sure that the details support it, and if not, revise it accordingly.

Mario Vargas Llosa:
Latin America—The Democratic Option

In this speech delivered in 1987, Peruvian novelist, playwright, and journalist Mario Vargas Llosa (BAHR gahs YOH sah) (born 1936) discussed the state of democracy in Latin America. He also described the changes that he believed were needed to maintain and extend that democracy.

The democratization of Latin America, even though it has today an unprecedented[1] popular base, is very fragile. To maintain and extend this popular base, governments will have to prove to their citizens that democracy means not only the end of political brutality but progress—concrete benefits in areas such as labor, health, and education, where so much remains to be done. But, given Latin America's current economic crisis, when the prices of its exports are hitting record lows and the weight of its foreign debt is crushing, those governments have virtually no alternative but to demand that their citizens—especially the poor—make even greater sacrifices than they've already made. . . .

A realistic and ethically sound approach that our creditors could take would be to demand that each debtor nation pay what it can without placing its stability in jeopardy. . . .

If we want democracy to take hold in our countries, our most urgent task is to broaden it, give it substance and truth. Democracy is fragile in so many countries because it is superficial[2], a mere framework within which institutions and political parties go about their business in their traditionally arbitrary, bullying way. . . .

Perhaps the hardest struggle we Latin Americans will have will be against ourselves. Centuries of intolerance, of absolute truths, of despotic governments, weigh us down—and it won't be easy to shake that burden off. The tradition of absolute power that began with our pre-Columbian empires, and the tradition that might makes right that the Spanish and Portuguese explorers practiced, were perpetuated in the nineteenth century, after our independence, by our *caudillos*[3] and our oligarchies[4], often with the blessing or direct intervention of foreign powers.

▲ Mario Vargas Llosa in 1997

1. **unprecedented** (un PRES uh den tid) *adj.* new; never having happened before
2. **superficial** (SOO pur FISH ul) *adj.* shallow; on the surface
3. *caudillos* (kow THEE yohs) *n. pl.* military dictators
4. **oligarchies** (AHL ih gahr keez) *n. pl.* governments run by a few powerful individuals or families

Thinking Critically
1. **Synthesize Information** According to Vargas Llosa, what currently threatens democracy in Latin America?
2. **Recognize Cause and Effect** How has Latin America's past led to the region's difficulty in maintaining democracy?

Quick Study Guide

 SSWH21b

Progress Monitoring *Online*
For: Self-test with vocabulary practice
Web Code: naa-3351

■ Key Problems Facing Developing Nations

- rapid population growth
- urbanization
- widespread poverty
- food shortages
- economic dependence on foreign lenders and on exports
- repressive, authoritarian governments
- diseases
- environmental damage
- poor education

■ Global North and Global South

■ Economic Output for Selected Developing Nations

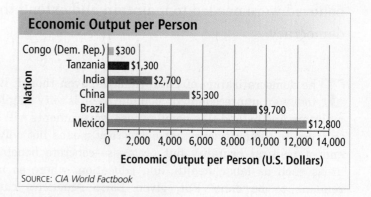

Economic Output per Person

Nation	Economic Output per Person (U.S. Dollars)
Congo (Dem. Rep.)	$300
Tanzania	$1,300
India	$2,700
China	$5,300
Brazil	$9,700
Mexico	$12,800

SOURCE: *CIA World Factbook*

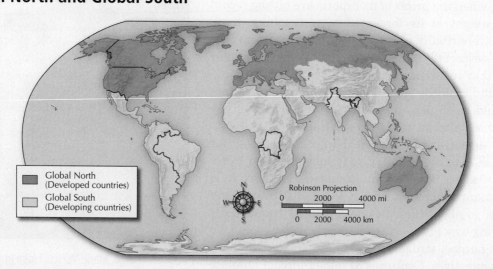

Global North (Developed countries)
Global South (Developing countries)

Robinson Projection

0   2000   4000 mi
0   2000   4000 km

■ Key Events in the Developing World

**1950s–1960s
Green Revolution
transforms agriculture.**

**Africa and Asia
Latin America**

1940   1950   1960   1970

**1946
Juan Perón is
elected president
of Argentina.**

**1950s–1960s
Latin American countries pursue
policy of import substitution.**

Concept Connector

Essential Question Review

To connect prior knowledge with what you have learned in this chapter, answer the questions below in your Concept Connector journal. Use the journal in the Reading and Note Taking Study Guide to record your answers (or go to www.phschool.com **Web Code:** nad-3307).

1. **Economic Systems** Developing countries face economic challenges as they industrialize and urbanize. Choose one of the nations described in this chapter. Discuss how that nation's economic development created challenges for its people. Consider some of the following in your response:
   - poverty and the gap between the rich and poor
   - lack of resources for healthcare, education, and food
   - human rights

2. **Dictatorship** The United States sees itself as the defender of democracy and free markets in Latin America. However, from the 1950s to the 1980s, the United States helped overthrow democratically elected governments and install dictators in some Latin American countries. Provide a list of reasons that explain why the United States government would support dictators or repressive governments in Latin America. Think about the following:
   - Cold War
   - policy of containment
   - economy

3. **Revolution** During the French Revolution, the poor and the middle classes rebelled against privileged monarchs and aristocrats. During the Russian Revolution, the Communists mobilized working people to overthrow the privileged rulers of Russia. How do recent rebellions in Latin America, for example in Guatemala or Nicaragua, compare with earlier revolutions? Consider social and economic inequalities and ideologies or belief systems.

■ Connections to Today

1. **Cooperation** In this chapter, you read about cooperation between the United States and the nations of Latin America. In recent years, cooperation among Latin American nations and between the United States and Latin America has spread to include economic development. Mercosur is a trade alliance among South American nations. Meanwhile, the United States has proposed trade alliances with Chile and Central American nations. Refer to online news services or other sources to learn about Latin American trade alliances today. Investigate whether cooperation in the area of trade has spread in recent years within Latin America and between Latin America and the United States.

2. **Nationalism** In this chapter, you learned that during the 1950s and 1960s many developing nations tried to decrease their economic dependence on foreign investors by developing their own industries. Then, in the 1980s and 1990s, many of these nations put more emphasis on foreign trade and investment, often under pressure from foreign lenders. However, the pendulum has begun to swing back toward economic independence. After 2000, China, Argentina, and other nations put the economic concerns of their own people ahead of those of foreign investors. Why might a nation choose a course of economic independence? Consult news sources to find out how countries that resisted foreign economic pressure have fared in recent years.

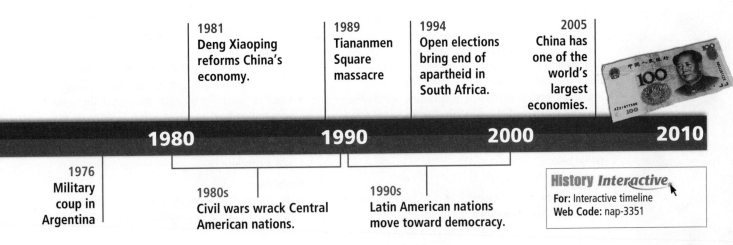

1981
Deng Xiaoping reforms China's economy.

1989
Tiananmen Square massacre

1994
Open elections bring end of apartheid in South Africa.

2005
China has one of the world's largest economies.

1980 **1990** **2000** **2010**

1976
Military coup in Argentina

1980s
Civil wars wrack Central American nations.

1990s
Latin American nations move toward democracy.

History Interactive
For: Interactive timeline
Web Code: nap-3351

Chapter Assessment

Terms, People, and Places

Complete each sentence by choosing the correct answer from the list of terms below. You will not use all the terms.

desertification	sustainable development
developing world	Tiananmen Square
Green Revolution	urbanization
liberation theology	Mumbai

1. In parts of Africa, drought and over-farming have brought about the _____ of land that was previously farmable.
2. Many Catholic clergy were part of a movement known as _____ that called for social justice and an end to poverty.
3. New nations attempting to improve their economies and achieve higher living standards are known as the _____.
4. Many poorer nations have seen rapid _____, or the movement of rural people to the cities.
5. In 1989, troops had a deadly encounter with protesters in _____.
6. The use of new technologies in the mid-1900s for improving crop production was known as the _____.

Main Ideas

Section 1 (pp. 1066–1071)
7. Summarize the challenges faced by most developing nations.
8. Compare and contrast the global North with the global South.

Section 2 (pp. 1072–1075)
9. How successful were new African nations that tried to develop by creating command economies?
10. Who is Wangari Maathai and what was her role in sustainable development efforts in Africa?

Section 3 (pp. 1076–1081)
11. After Mao's death, what reforms did China's government make and what reforms did they block?
12. What were the main challenges to economic growth in India?

Section 4 (pp. 1082–1089)
13. What role did the military play in the governments of Latin America?
14. Describe the democratic progress that was made in Mexico in 2000.

Chapter Focus Question
15. What challenges have nations of the developing world faced and what steps have they taken to meet those challenges?

Critical Thinking

16. **Synthesize Information** How has rapid population growth affected developing nations?
17. **Draw Conclusions** Which problem facing developing nations do you think is the most important one to solve? Explain your answer.
18. **Analyze Images** How does the photo of Mumbai at the end of Section 1 reflect some of the challenges facing developing nations? Explain your answer.
19. **Make Inferences** Many developing nations are ruled by dictators or by one party, as in China. Does autocratic rule help or hurt economic progress? Explain.
20. **Cause and Effect** How did the Cold War affect the United States' relations with Latin American nations?

● Writing About History

In this chapter's four Section Assessments, you developed skills to write a research report.

Writing a Research Report As governments in the developing world struggle to grow their economies and improve the well being of their citizens, they may set policies that cause damage to the environment and threaten local plant and animal species. Write a research report in which you discuss how one developing nation you read about in this chapter is balancing economic development with environmental concerns. Consult page SH13 of the Writing Handbook for additional help.

Prewriting
• Do online or library research to read background materials about developing nations.

• Choose a developing nation and take notes on relevant details, events, and the people.
• Create a set of questions about your developing nation and gather additional resources.

Drafting
• Develop a thesis about this nation's economic status—for example, is it succeeding or failing?
• Make an outline to organize the report. Then choose information from your research that supports each part of your outline.
• Write an introduction explaining your thesis, a body, and a conclusion.

Revising
• Use the guidelines for revising your report on page SH15 of the Writing Handbook.

Prepare for the GHSGT

China's Economy

China has one of the fastest-growing economies in the world. Many who once thought of China as backward now see the country as a lively economic giant. Though China's economic gains are impressive, China's critics see a dark underside, as Documents C and D illustrate.

Document A

"China's annual GDP [gross domestic product, or economic output] growth has averaged more than 8 percent in the past 25 years, and in 2003, its GDP grew by a record-breaking 9.1 percent. . . . Noting these economic achievements as well as the complete success of China's first manned space flight in 2003, Premier Wen Jiabao in his annual address to the NPC [National People's Congress] in March 2004 pointed to a national strength that has reached new heights. . . ."

—From **China Internet Information Center**, May 4, 2005

Document B

Chinese workers assemble electronic parts.

Document C

". . . China has not changed in non-economic matters . . . [T]he leadership remains deaf to democracy and human rights. Religion is on a tight leash. . . . Basic legal safeguards are non-existent in the judicial system, and prison conditions are harsh. Privacy rights are routinely violated, and the government maintains tight restrictions on freedom of speech and the press. Increased control and monitoring of the Internet has led to arrest of dissidents, and most "Netizens" practice self-censorship, or face the long arm of the law. Freedom of association and assembly are virtually non-existent. . . ."

—From **"Only China's Economy Has Changed"** in *Taipei Times*, April 29, 2005, by Robert Bedeski

Document D

"China's grim 19th century style mines—many of them little more than holes in the ground—claimed yet more lives this week. A gas explosion ripped through the Sunjiawan coal mine in the northeastern province of Liaoning on Monday, killing at least 210. . . . They were just the latest casualties in a familiar story of mining accidents, which routinely claim the lives of dozens of young miners every month. . . . Many of those who die belong to China's growing underclass. They are desperately impoverished boys and men from rural villages."

—From **The Wall Street Journal**, February 18, 2005, by Sara Davis and Mickey Spiegel

Analyzing Documents

Use your knowledge of China's economic reforms and Documents A, B, C, and D to answer questions 1–4.

1. The author of Document A is best described as a
   A harsh critic of China's economic inequality.
   B strong supporter of China's economic policies.
   C shrewd observer of China's social system.
   D half-hearted supporter of the socialist market economy.

2. What is the main point of Document C?
   A China's social progress is equal to the country's economic gains.
   B China's human rights record is poor, despite economic progress.
   C China's economic progress outweighs any human rights problems.
   D China's economic success had led a commitment to human rights.

3. Some critics of China say that China's new wealth has not been evenly shared. According to Document D, one of the groups that has been left out is
   A people from the large cities.
   B young people.
   C women.
   D males from rural villages.

4. Do the current leaders of China deserve praise or criticism? Give your opinions based on the documents on this page and information from the chapter.

WITNESS HISTORY AUDIO

A Changing World

In 2001, Mongolia's prime minister declared that "in order to survive we have to stop being nomads." His words—and his plans to settle 90% of Mongolia's people in cities by the year 2030—came as a shock to a people who have been nomadic herders for centuries. At the same time, his idea seemed inevitable. Listen to the Witness History audio to hear more about how Mongolians are struggling to modernize without losing their traditions.

◀ This nomadic family in Mongolia lives in a yurt, or tent, with a solar-powered satellite dish that picks up television broadcasts.

Logo for the international aid organization CARE

 Performance Standards

Chapter Focus Question What are the major issues facing the world today?

Section 1
Industrialized Nations After the Cold War SSWH21b

Section 2
Globalization
SSWH21b

Section 3
Social and Environmental Challenges
SSWH21b, SSWH21c

Section 4
Security in a Dangerous World
SSWH20c

Section 5
Advances in Science and Technology
SSWH21a

Euro coin

NASA seal

Use the ☑ **Quick Study Timeline** at the end of this chapter to preview chapter events.

 Concept Connector ONLINE

To explore Essential Questions related to this chapter, go to PHSchool.com
Web Code: nad-3407

A euro coin

Turks celebrate their country's efforts to join the European Union (EU).

WITNESS HISTORY 🔊 AUDIO

The Nations of Europe Unite

❝Resolved to mark a new stage in the process of European integration . . . Recalling the historic importance of the ending of the division of the European continent and the need to create firm bases for the construction of the future Europe . . . Desiring to deepen the solidarity between their peoples while respecting their history, their culture, and their traditions . . . [We] have decided to establish a European Union . . .❞
—The Maastricht Treaty on the European Union, 1992

Focus Question How did the end of the Cold War affect industrialized nations and regions around the world?

Industrialized Nations After the Cold War

 Performance Standards

- **SSWH21b** Analyze global economic and political connections.

Terms, People, and Places

European Union	Vladimir Putin
euro	surplus
default	deficit
Barack Obama	Pacific Rim

Note Taking

Reading Skill: Compare and Contrast Create a chart to compare and contrast developments in industrialized nations after the Cold War.

Europe	Russia/ United States	Asia
• 1991 Germany reunified	•	•
•	•	•

The end of the Cold War created favorable conditions for the spread of democracy. It also marked the beginning of a new global economy. Growing economic ties and increased international trade would become a driving force shaping the world in the new millennium.

The New Face of Europe

The collapse of communism ended decades of division between communist Eastern Europe and democratic Western Europe. Trade, business, travel, and communications across the continent became easier. Yet, many European nations faced common problems such as large-scale immigration from the developing world, growing discrimination against foreigners, and rising unemployment.

Germany Reunifies After more than 45 years of division, East and West Germany were reunited in 1990. Germans welcomed reunification, but they paid a high price. East Germany's economy and infrastructure were weak and had to be modernized. Unemployment rose in the former East Germany when inefficient communist-era factories were closed. West Germans paid higher taxes to finance the rebuilding of the eastern part of the country.

Reunification brought social problems. Racist groups, such as neo-Nazis, a hate group modeled on the Nazi party, blamed immigrants for the country's problems and viciously attacked foreign workers. The vast majority of Germans condemned such actions. Twenty years after reunification, Germany remained an economic giant and a strong European leader.

NATO Evolves The collapse of the Soviet Union ended the Warsaw Pact. Many of the nations of Eastern Europe wanted to join NATO. Poland, Hungary, and the Czech Republic joined in 1999, soon followed by other countries. Russia disliked NATO's eastward expansion, but agreed to a NATO-Russia Council to consult on issues of common interest.

Europe was changing and NATO had to reassess its purpose. Many NATO officials believed that NATO's primary goal should be that of peace-keeper and protector of human rights. Following terrorist attacks in the United States, Europe, and elsewhere, the fight against terrorism has become a priority for the alliance.

The European Union Expands Like NATO, the European Economic Community expanded over the years to add nations from Eastern Europe. In 1993, the European Economic Community became the **European Union (EU),** a group of European nations that work together to promote a freer flow of capital, labor, services, and goods. Members also cooperate on security matters.

In 2002, the **euro** became the common currency for most of Western Europe. By then, EU passports had replaced national passports. Today, the expanded EU has the world's largest economy and competes with economic superpowers like the United States and Japan.

Some European leaders supported even greater economic and political unity for the region. However, many ordinary citizens felt greater loyalty to their own nations than to the EU. Also the economies of Eastern Europe were weaker than those in the West, causing worries about the EU's overall economic outlook.

Turkey, long a member of NATO, wants full membership in the EU. But Turkey's application faced opposition because of its poor record on human rights and other issues. Also, some Europeans are concerned about admitting countries with large Muslim populations into the EU. They worry that if the EU changes too quickly, it will be less stable.

✔ **Checkpoint** What challenges did Germany face after reunification?

The European Union

Geography *Interactive*
For: Audio guided tour
Web Code: nap-3411

Map Skills By 2007, 27 countries had joined the EU.
1. **Locate** (a) The Netherlands (b) Turkey (c) Germany (d) Croatia
2. **Identify** Which nations are applicant nations?
3. **Draw Inferences** How does geography help explain why these nations applied for EU membership later than many other nations?

Member of EU
Applicant nation
Non-EU nations

Global Power Shifts

After the Soviet Union collapsed and the Cold War ended, the balance of global power shifted. The United States became the world's sole superpower. Recently, though, Russia has reemerged as a powerful force.

Vocabulary Builder

inflation—(in FLAY shun) *n.* a rise in prices linked to an increase in the amount of money available

Russia Rebuilds Russia faced hard times after the breakup of the Soviet Union. In an effort to shift to a market economy, Russia's president, Boris Yeltsin, privatized many state-run industries and collective farms. This change brought great hardships to many Russians as unemployment and prices soared.

In 1998, Russia barely avoided financial collapse. It **defaulted,** or failed to make payments, on much of its foreign debt. High <u>inflation</u> and the collapse of the ruble, Russia's currency, forced many banks and businesses to close. People lost their savings and jobs, although some Russians did prosper in the new economy.

In 2000, **Vladimir Putin** was elected president in Russia's second free election. Putin, who served two terms, helped rebuild Russia's economy. However, his government was plagued by corruption and Putin came under fire for increasing the power of the central government at the expense of peoples' civil liberties. Putin's handpicked successor, Dmitri Medvedev, was sworn in as president in May 2008. The next day, Putin was appointed prime minister by Russia's Parliament. While Russia benefited from rising prices for its oil and gas exports, the 2008 global economic slowdown posed challenges for Russia, as it did for other nations.

As Russia rebounded, it defended its interests, which sometimes caused tensions with the West. Despite UN sanctions against Iran, Russia assisted Iran with its nuclear energy program. In 2008, Russia sent troops into neighboring Georgia to help two breakaway regions gain independence.

The United States Faces New Challenges As the world's only superpower, the United States had a great deal of military and political influence. After the terrorist attacks on the United States in September 2001, President George W. Bush declared a "war on terror." In 2002, the United States sent forces to Afghanistan, where the terrorist plot had been hatched. The next year, U.S. forces invaded Iraq and toppled its dictator Saddam Hussein. When **Barack Obama,** the nation's first African American President, took office in January 2009, U.S. forces still occupied Afghanistan and Iraq. Obama had to decide the future course of U.S. policy toward both countries.

Meeting Economic Challenges
World leaders, including U.S. President Barack Obama, met at the G20 Summit in 2009, to discuss solutions to global economic problems. *Why might economic problems in one country affect the economy of other nations?*

The United States weathered economic ups and downs. An economic boom in the 1990s produced a budget **surplus,** or money left over after expenditures. During George W. Bush's presidency, slower growth, massive military spending, and tax cuts led to a huge budget **deficit,** or gap between what the government spends and what it takes in through taxes and other measures.

In 2008, a financial crisis shook the American economy, sparking a global recession. Millions of Americans lost their jobs as businesses cut back or closed. President Obama responded with a multi-billion dollar economic stimulus package that called for increased federal spending and tax cuts to revive the economy and create millions of new jobs.

✔ **Checkpoint** What troubles did Russia face after the collapse of the Soviet Union?

Changes in Asia

As the Cold War ended, Asia experienced the successes and downturns of being part of the global economy.

The Pacific Rim A major force in the global economy is the **Pacific Rim,** the many Asian nations that border the Pacific Ocean. The Pacific Ocean first became a highway for world trade in the 1500s. By the mid-1900s, links across the Pacific had grown dramatically. By the 1990s, the volume of trade across the Pacific was greater than that across the Atlantic. Some analysts predict that the 2000s will be the "Pacific century" because of this region's potential for further growth.

Japan and China For decades, Japan dominated the Asian Pacific Rim. But in the 1990s, as Japan suffered a long economic downturn, China's economy boomed. However, the global recession that began in 2008 hurt China's export-based economy.

The Asian Tigers Among the powerhouses of the Pacific Rim were Taiwan, Hong Kong, Singapore, and South Korea. Although they differed in important ways, all had quickly modernized and industrialized by the 1980s. All four were influenced to some degree by China, and Confucian traditions of loyalty, hard work, and consensus. Each stressed education as a way to increase worker productivity.

Because of their economic success, these countries were nicknamed the "Asian tigers" or "four tigers." The Asian tigers first focused on light industries, such as textiles. As their economies grew, they shifted to higher-priced exports, such as electronics. Their stunning growth was due in part to low wages, long hours, and other worker sacrifices. Like other export-driven economies, the Asian tigers were hurt by the 2008 global economic slowdown.

✔ **Checkpoint** Why did the Asian Tigers enjoy strong economic growth?

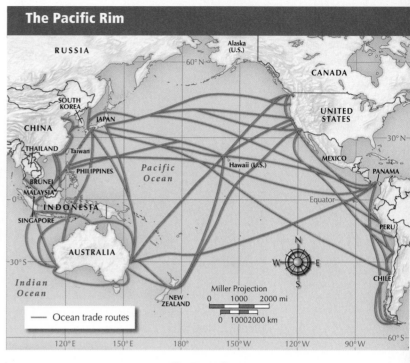

The Pacific Rim

Pacific Powerhouse
The countries of the Pacific Rim have geographic, cultural, and economic ties. The region is a major center of ocean trade routes, shown on the map above.

SECTION 1 Assessment

Progress Monitoring *Online*
For: Self-quiz with vocabulary practice
Web Code: naa-3411

Terms, People, and Places
1. For each term, person, or place listed at the beginning of the section, write a sentence explaining its significance.

Note Taking
2. **Reading Skill: Compare and Contrast** Use your completed chart to answer the Focus Question: How did the end of the Cold War affect industrialized nations and regions around the world?

Comprehension and Critical Thinking
3. **Determine Relevance** How did the collapse of the Soviet Union affect organizations such as NATO and the EU?
4. **Draw Conclusions** Do you think an American investor would choose to invest large sums of money in Russia? Why or why not?
5. **Analyze Information** Why is the Pacific Rim seen as an important link in the global economy?

● **Writing About History**

Quick Write: Write a Thesis Statement
To persuade someone in an essay, you must have a strong opinion on a subject and express it clearly in a thesis statement. Write a single sentence that expresses the main point you want to make about developments in the industrialized world after the Cold War.

Russian immigrants sell caviar at a kiosk in Brooklyn, New York.

WITNESS HISTORY 🔊 AUDIO

A Connected World

❝Few topics are as controversial as globalization. That is hardly surprising. It is the defining feature of our time. Bringing distant markets and people across the world together is a huge change that affects everyone, whether they are peasants in India, students in London, or bankers in New York.❞
—Mike Moore, director-general of the WTO, 2000

Focus Question How is globalization affecting economies and societies around the world?

Globalization

 Performance Standards

• **SSWH21b** Analyze multinational corporations, the United Nations, OPEC, and the World Trade Organization.

Terms, People, and Places

globalization	World Trade Organization
interdependence	(WTO)
outsourcing	protectionism
multinational	bloc
corporation	sustainability

No̲te Taking

Reading Skill: Compare and Contrast As you read, use the Venn diagram to track how globalization has affected developed and developing nations.

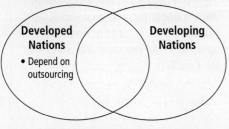

Globalization defines the world of the post-Cold War. **Globalization** refers to the process by which national economies, politics, cultures, and societies become integrated with those of other nations around the world. Globalization began on a small scale 500 years ago, with the European Age of Exploration. By the 2000s, globalization was occurring at a dramatic, unprecedented pace.

An Interdependent World

One major effect of globalization is economic interdependence. **Interdependence** is the dependence of countries on each other for goods, resources, knowledge, and labor from other parts of the world. Improvements in transportation and communication, the spread of democratic systems, and the rise of free trade—the buying and selling of goods by private individuals and corporations in a free market—have made the world increasingly interdependent. The spread of goods and ideas has even led to the development of a global culture. All of these links, from economic to cultural, have created both challenges and opportunities.

Doing the World's Work The world's rich and poor nations are linked. The nations of the developed world control much of the world's capital, trade, and technology. Yet they increasingly depend on largely low-paid workers in developing countries to produce manufactured goods cheaply. Companies in industrial nations also choose to outsource jobs. **Outsourcing** is the practice of sending work to the developing world in order to save money or increase efficiency. Many technological jobs have been outsourced to India, Russia, China, and the Philippines.

Multinational Corporations Grow Globalization has led to the growth of huge, powerful, multinational corporations. **Multinational corporations** have <u>assets</u> in many countries and sell their goods and services worldwide. These corporations have invested heavily in the developing world. They brought new technology to industries, built factories, improved transportation networks, and provided jobs. Critics, however, have blasted multinational corporations for taking large profits out of developing countries, causing environmental damage, and paying low wages.

Global Economic Crises Globalization led to financial interdependence in the world's markets. As a result, an economic crisis in one country or region can have a global impact. In 1997, a financial crisis struck Thailand and quickly spread across Asia. A 2008 banking crisis in the United States and Europe set off global shockwaves as world stock markets plunged. Wealthy nations shored up their economies with economic stimulus packages and costly bailout plans for banks and other troubled industries. Developing countries felt the impact as prices for their goods fell and international aid decreased.

Oil Prices Rise and Fall Energy resources play a huge role in the global economy. All nations, for example, need oil for transportation and to manufacture products ranging from plastics to fertilizers. Any change in the global oil supply can have a huge impact worldwide.

In 1973, OPEC limited oil exports and raised prices, creating shortages and hurting economies throughout the world. Since then, whenever oil prices have risen sharply, people have faced economic uncertainties. In 2008, oil prices shot up, partly because the growing economy in China, India, and elsewhere led to increased demand. When the global economic crisis slowed demand, prices fell. This sudden, rapid change in oil prices has led to renewed calls to develop alternative energy sources. Still, the world has remained largely dependent on oil.

Vocabulary Builder

<u>asset</u>—(AS et) *n.* any property that has exchange value

Geography *Interactive*
For: Audio guided tour
Web Code: nap-3421

World Oil Resources and Consumption

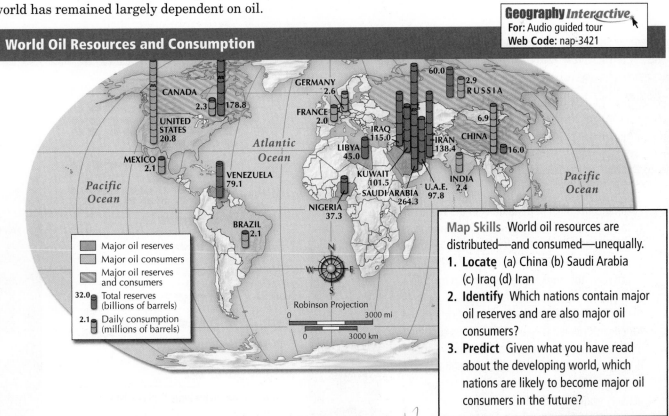

Major oil reserves
Major oil consumers
Major oil reserves and consumers
32.0 Total reserves (billions of barrels)
2.1 Daily consumption (millions of barrels)

CANADA 2.3 / 178.8
UNITED STATES 20.8
MEXICO 2.1
VENEZUELA 79.1
BRAZIL 2.1
GERMANY 2.6
FRANCE 2.0
LIBYA 45.0
NIGERIA 37.3
IRAQ 115.0
KUWAIT 101.5
SAUDI ARABIA 264.3
U.A.E. 97.8
IRAN 138.4
60.0 / 2.9 RUSSIA
6.9
CHINA 16.0
INDIA 2.4

Atlantic Ocean
Pacific Ocean
Pacific Ocean

Robinson Projection
0 — 3000 mi
0 — 3000 km

Map Skills World oil resources are distributed—and consumed—unequally.
1. **Locate** (a) China (b) Saudi Arabia (c) Iraq (d) Iran
2. **Identify** Which nations contain major oil reserves and are also major oil consumers?
3. **Predict** Given what you have read about the developing world, which nations are likely to become major oil consumers in the future?

Debt Hurts the Developing World Developing nations borrowed heavily in order to modernize. In the 1980s, bank interest rates rose as the world economy slowed. As demand for their goods fell, poor nations could not repay their debts or even interest on their loans. Their economies stalled as they spent much of their export incomes on payments to foreign creditors.

The debt crisis hurt rich nations, too. Banks were stuck with billions of dollars of bad debts. To ease the crisis, lenders made agreements with debtor nations to lower interest rates or allow more time to repay their loans. Some debts were canceled. In return, debtor nations had to accept market reforms to help improve their economies. Debt has remained a major issue throughout the developing world.

✔ **Checkpoint** How do changes in the supply of oil affect economies around the world?

Global Trade Organizations and Treaties

Many international organizations and treaties connect people and nations around the world. These organizations have various goals, such as supporting development, settling economic issues, and promoting free trade.

International Organizations Expand The United Nations is an international organization whose membership has grown from 50 nations in 1945 to 192 in 2009. As a result, its global role has expanded. The UN has sent peacekeepers to many trouble spots, including Cambodia, Congo, and the Balkans. In addition, the UN deals with economic and social development, human rights, humanitarian aid, and international law.

INFOGRAPHIC

COFFEE: From Shrub to Cup

Coffee is the most popular drink in the world today, other than water. Each year, people consume over 500 billion cups of coffee. Coffee is believed to have originated in the Kaffa region of Ethiopia, which gave the drink its name. Demand for coffee slowly spread from Africa to the Middle East and then to Europe. Eventually it reached Asia and the Americas. Coffee has had a tremendous cultural impact, shaping diets and social customs. Coffee has also dramatically influenced the global economy. After crude oil, it is the world's most actively traded commodity.

Top Ten Coffee Producers, 2007

Brazil	
Colombia	
Vietnam	
Indonesia	
India	
Mexico	
Guatemala	
Honduras	
Ethiopia	
Peru	

🫘 Represents 1 million bags of coffee

SOURCE: International Coffee Organization

Other organizations deal with economic issues. The World Bank, for example, offers loans and technical advice to developing nations. The International Monetary Fund (IMF) encourages global economic growth, promotes international monetary cooperation, and helps developing nations solve economic problems. It also lends to countries in crisis.

Organizations not affiliated with governments also provide aid. These non-governmental organizations (NGOs) perform a variety of functions, such as monitoring human rights, supplying disaster relief, and providing medical care. The International Red Cross is an example of an NGO.

Treaties Promote Global Trade A variety of international treaties help regulate world trade. The General Agreement on Tariffs and Trade (GATT) was signed in 1947 to expand world trade and reduce tariffs, or taxes on imported goods. In 1995, more than 100 nations joined to form the **World Trade Organization (WTO)** to strengthen GATT. Its goal was to set global rules to ensure that trade flows as smoothly and as freely as possible. The WTO opposes **protectionism,** or the use of tariffs and other restrictions that protect a country's home industries against international competition. The Group of Eight (G-8) is an organization of industrialized nations that meets annually to discuss a wide range of economic and other issues. The G-8 consists of Canada, France, Germany, Great Britain, Italy, Japan, Russia, and the United States.

Regional Trade Many nations have formed regional **blocs,** or groups, to boost trade and meet common needs. Among the largest is the EU (European Union.) In 1994, NAFTA (North American Free Trade Association) set out to ease restrictions and promote trade among the United States, Canada, and Mexico. APEC (Asia-Pacific Economic Cooperation) was formed to further trade among Pacific Rim nations. OPEC, representing oil-producing countries, regulates the production of oil to stabilize the market. Regional trade groups like these work to lower trade barriers

Growing Coffee
A worker in Thailand picks raw coffee beans from a shrub. Less than 10 percent of the money made from coffee actually goes to the grower.

The Fair Trade Movement ▶
The fair trade movement seeks to ensure that coffee growers receive fair prices for their crops and have decent living and working conditions. Coffee that has met these conditions is stamped with the fair trade logo.

Drinking Coffee
By the time coffee beans are turned into cups of coffee in the developed world, they have passed through the hands of many middlemen and have been re-sold a number of times. The coffee crop that a small farmer earned $8,000 for growing is worth nearly a million dollars to the people who sell it.

Thinking Critically
1. **Chart Skills** What regions are the top 5 coffee producers located in?
2. **Draw Inferences** Why does a crop of coffee become more expensive each time it is sold by middlemen?

and encourage the free exchange of goods and services. Often, regional organizations like the African Union (AU), deal with both economic and political issues.

> ✓ **Checkpoint** How does the IMF help developing nations?

Costs and Benefits of Globalization

With advanced communications and increased economic ties, globalization is expected to increase in the years ahead. Yet the debate about the impact of globalization on people and nations around the world continues.

Benefits Global trade provides consumers with a greater variety of goods and services. And because many people compete to provide these goods and services, prices are generally lower. People in the industrial world, especially, benefited from these changes.

Millions of people worldwide moved from rural areas to cities. There, they often had better access to education and health care. Globalization introduced people to new ideas, technologies, and communications. The money that developing nations earn from trade can be used to improve infrastructure, raise standards of living, and provide better services. Nations that practice free trade often become more democratic.

The Anti-Globalization Movement Critics point to the costs of free trade and globalization. Generally, anti-globalizers focus on poverty. They claim that rich nations exploit, or take advantage of poor countries by raising their debt and lowering their standard of living. Some anti-globalizers target the World Bank and the IMF. Although these organizations provide aid to ease economic problems, they also require developing nations to make tough reforms and cut costly social programs. Anti-globalizers also oppose the United States, which is seen as the force behind policies they oppose.

Environmentalists claim that industries eager for profits encourage too-rapid development, endangering **sustainability**, or development that balances people's needs today while preserving the environment for future generations.

> ✓ **Checkpoint** How has globalization improved the lives of people around the world?

Anti-Globalization in Action
In 1999, an anti-globalization demonstration led to rioting when thousands of protesters disrupted WTO meetings in Seattle, Washington.

Terms, People, and Places

1. What do each of the key terms listed at the beginning of the section have in common? Explain.

Note Taking

2. **Reading Skill: Compare and Contrast** Use your completed Venn diagram to answer the Focus Question: How is globalization affecting economies and societies around the world?

Comprehension and Critical Thinking

3. **Make Comparisons** Which countries benefit more from economic interdependence—developed or developing countries? Explain.

4. **Draw Inferences** Given what you have read in this section, do you think developing nations would support or oppose globalization?

5. **Demonstrate Reasoned Judgment** Do you think that increased globalization is inevitable? Explain.

● Writing About History

Quick Write: Generate Arguments One of the most effective ways to persuade is to address both sides of the topic you are covering. Create a chart to record facts about globalization. In one column, record the facts that support your position on globalization. In the second column, note arguments that could be used to attack your position.

Concept Connector

HUMAN RIGHTS

How are human rights won or lost?

In This Chapter SSWH21b

What rights are basic to all human beings? The Declaration of Independence lists "life, liberty, and the pursuit of happiness." In 1948, the United Nations Declaration of Human Rights added more, including the rights to own property and to enjoy a basic standard of living. The Grameen Bank has granted loans to many poor women (right) to help them start businesses and provide for their families.

Throughout History

- **100s B.C.** Romans enslave captives taken in war.

- **1100s A.D.** Under King Henry II, England develops an early jury system.

- **1300s** Smaller medieval African societies reach decisions by general agreement.

- **1800s** Women actively seek social and political equality in Britain and the United States.

- **1980s** Trade embargos are used to pressure South Africa to end apartheid.

Continuing Today

Limitation of human rights continues to be an issue in China. Members of the Chinese community in Australia protest severe abuses of freedom of belief and freedom of speech in their homeland.

21st Century Skills

TRANSFER Activities

1. **Analyze** Throughout history, how have people's rights been limited?

2. **Evaluate** What role does economic power play in gaining or maintaining human rights?

3. **Transfer** Complete a Web quest in which you act as a human rights "watch dog"; record your thoughts in the Concept Connector Journal; and learn to make a video. Web Code nah-3408.

A family in Indonesia tries to make their way to shelter after tsunamis destroyed their village in 2004. Aid organizations like CARE (logo above) worked to bring relief to the devastated region.

WITNESS HISTORY ◀》 AUDIO

Giant Waves Arrive

On December 26, 2004, an Indonesian man named Harmi went to the beach with hundreds of other people. An earthquake had hit his village, and people gathered to watch the sea recede from the beach.

66 Suddenly . . . oh my God . . . there was a thundering sound from the sea. I saw the rolls of the waves ten meters (33 feet) high . . . the waves came three times. The worst was the second one, which swallowed thousands of houses in our village. 99

Harmi's village was completely destroyed.

Focus Question How do poverty, disease, and environmental challenges affect people around the world today?

Social and Environmental Challenges

 Performance Standards

- **SSWH21b** Analyze the multinational corporations, the United Nations, OPEC, and the World Trade Organization.
- **SSWH21c** Explain how governments cooperate to protect the environment.

Terms, People, and Places

tsunami	acid rain
epidemic	deforestation
famine	erosion
refugee	global warming

Note Taking

Reading Skill: Compare Use a chart like this one to compare aspects of globalization.

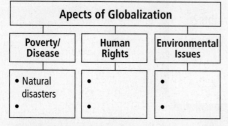

Globalization involves much more than economic links and the spread of technology. It has brought all kinds of social and environmental issues to the world's attention. Poverty, disease, environmental threats, and human rights may originate in countries or regions. But they have global dimensions that often require global solutions.

Global Poverty, Disasters, and Disease

Half of the world's population, or almost 3 billion people, live on less than $2 a day. Almost 1 billion people cannot read or write. About 790 million people in the developing world suffer from hunger— many from extreme hunger. Millions suffer from life-threatening diseases. Although these are problems mainly of the developing world, they affect the nations of the developed world as well.

Causes of Poverty Experts cannot agree on the exact number of people living in poverty worldwide, in part because there are many ways to measure poverty. Experts do agree about some trends, however. First, the gap between rich and poor nations is huge and growing. Second, some progress has been made toward reducing poverty, but it has been uneven. India and China, for example, have enjoyed economic growth, which has meant fewer people overall living in poverty there, but extreme poverty still persists.

Poverty is a complex issue with many causes. Many poor nations owe billions in debt and have no extra money to spend to improve living conditions. Political upheavals, civil war, corruption, and poor planning also <u>inhibit</u> efforts to reduce poverty worldwide. Rapid population growth—especially in India, China, and the nations of Africa and Latin America—has made it harder for countries to provide basic services.

Organizations like the World Bank believe that erasing poverty is essential to global security and peace. In this spirit, they call on poor nations to limit population growth. They also encourage rich nations to forgive the debt of poor nations, making more funds available for education, healthcare, and other services.

Natural Disasters Affect Millions In 2004, a huge underwater earthquake in the Indian Ocean triggered a massive tidal wave, or **tsunami** (tsoo NAH mee). It swept over islands and the coasts of 11 countries ringing the Indian Ocean. More than 160,000 people were killed, mainly in Indonesia, Thailand, Sri Lanka, and India. Millions were left homeless or lost their livelihood.

Natural disasters range from earthquakes, floods, and avalanches to droughts, fires, hurricanes, and volcanic eruptions. They strike all over the world all the time. They cause death, destruction, and unsanitary conditions that often lead to disease. Even a local disaster can disrupt

Vocabulary Builder

<u>inhibit</u>—(in HIB it) *v.* to hold back or keep from some action

MALARIA: WHEN A MOSQUITO STRIKES

Malaria is a disease that kills more than a million people a year worldwide, mostly children. Malaria is a parasite that is usually found in unsanitary conditions, especially stagnant water, in warm climates. Mosquitoes who breed on water pick up the parasite and then pass it to humans when they bite them. Forty percent of the world's population is at risk for contracting malaria, especially in developing countries. *Why do you think malaria is a risk mainly in developing countries?*

Global Malaria Risk
- Significant
- Low
- None

An African child receives a malaria vaccination.

Workers plan a new sewage project in Pakistan.

the economy of an entire country and have a ripple effect on the global economy. For example, a recent typhoon destroyed Myanmar's rice-producing region, leading to the threat of famine in that country. One benefit of globalization is that news of natural disasters spreads instantly and triggers a quick aid response.

Global Diseases With millions of people on the move daily, diseases can spread rapidly. Still, health experts, working together, can often identify and limit outbreaks of many diseases. In the early 2000s, air travelers spread SARS (severe acute respiratory syndrome), a respiratory disease, from China to more than two dozen countries. Health officials took quick action to stop the SARS outbreak. Other diseases, including the avian flu (bird flu), mad cow disease, West Nile virus, swine flu (H1N1), and influenza have raised concerns about the global spread of disease. Diseases often spread before health officials know they exist. Globalization has meant that health experts around the world cooperate to quickly identify and contain outbreaks of disease.

Some diseases have proved hard to contain. When a disease spreads rapidly, it is called an **epidemic.** HIV/AIDS is an epidemic that began in the 1980s. HIV/AIDS has taken a staggering human and economic toll worldwide, especially in southern Africa and Southeast Asia. An estimated 25 million people have died from HIV/AIDS and as many as 40 million are infected with HIV. By 2010, the treatment and prevention of AIDS had been a global priority for a decade. In some nations, education about how to prevent the transmission of AIDS had lowered infection rates. Despite progress, HIV/AIDS continues to spread, especially in Asia and Eastern Europe.

Ending Hunger and Famine For tens of millions of people, hunger poses a daily threat. A major problem is that food does not get distributed to the people who need it most—especially in countries racked by poverty and civil strife. Hunger escalates into **famine** when large numbers of people in a region or country face death by starvation.

Natural disasters can cause famine. Human activity can also cause famine. War disrupts food distribution. During the 1970s and 1980s, civil wars raging in Ethiopia and Sudan intensified the effects of drought, leading to famine. Each side in the conflict tried to keep relief supplies from reaching the other. In many instances, only the efforts of international aid groups have saved millions of people from starvation.

Global Migration Globalization has led to a vast movement of people around the world. Although some people choose to migrate to find jobs or reunite with their families, millions more are **refugees,** people who are forced to move because of poverty, war, persecution, natural disasters, or other crises.

Many migrants find jobs and homes and create better lives in their new countries. But others face hostility and discrimination. Many people in developed countries resent immigrants, who they claim take away jobs and services from natural-born citizens. Millions of migrants, both legal and illegal, head to Europe, Asia, and North America. Each year, the United States alone receives

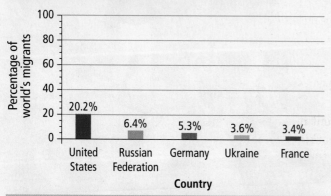

Top Five Destination Countries for International Migrants

Percentage of world's migrants

United States 20.2%
Russian Federation 6.4%
Germany 5.3%
Ukraine 3.6%
France 3.4%

Country

Chart Skills In 2005, ten nations received over 50 percent of the world's total migrants. *What characteristics of the top five destination nations might attract migrants?*

SOURCE: *United Nations, Trends in Total Migrant Stock, 2005*

about one million legal immigrants and 300,000 or more illegal immigrants. Since World War II, Germany has welcomed large numbers of Turkish, Italian, and Russian immigrants to make up for the part of the labor force that was lost in two world wars.

As migration has grown, so has the smuggling of human beings across borders. Many illegal immigrants pay smugglers large sums to help them reach their destinations. In 2006, the United Nations estimated that human smuggling was a $10 billion-a-year global industry.

✔ **Checkpoint** What are some of the causes of famine and migration?

Human Rights

In 1948, UN members approved the Universal Declaration of Human Rights. It stated that all people are entitled to basic rights "... without distinction of any kind, such as race, colour, sex, language, religion, political or other opinion, national or social origin, property, birth or other status." In 1975, nations signing the Helsinki Accords guaranteed such basic rights as freedom of speech, religion, and the press as well as the rights to a fair trial, to earn a living, and to live in safety. Despite such agreements, human rights abuses—ranging from arbitrary arrest to torture and slavery—occur daily around the world.

The Role of the World Community Human rights abuses are not new, but globalization has brought them to the attention of the world in a new way. And the spread of democracy has forced people to question how human rights abuses can still happen in a modern world. In response, the world community has pressed countries to end abuses. In the 1980s, for example, economic pressure was used against South Africa to end apartheid, its system of legalized segregation.

Sometimes there is no stable government to pressure, or direct pressure does not work. Still, the UN, the United States, and human rights groups monitor and report on human rights violations, from Afghanistan, to Bosnia, to Congo. They even monitor human rights in nations that are part of the developed world, such as Russia.

Women Work for Rights For decades, a global women's movement has focused attention on the needs of women worldwide. The UN Charter supported "equal rights for men and women." By 1950, women had won the right to vote in most European nations, as well as in Japan, China, Brazil, and other countries. In most African nations, both women and men won the vote when their countries gained independence. Women have headed governments in Britain, Israel, India, Pakistan, the Philippines, and elsewhere.

Still, a report to the UN noted that while women represent half of the world's people, "they perform nearly two thirds of all working hours, receive only one tenth of the world's income, and own less than one percent of world property." The UN and other groups thus carefully monitor the human rights of women. They also condemn violence and discrimination against women. More than 165 countries have ratified a new women's human rights treaty.

Women in the Developed and Developing Worlds In the developed world, more and more women now work outside their homes.

An Illegal Crossing
Each year tens of thousands of illegal immigrants, like this family, risk their lives to cross the border between Mexico and the United States. *What factors lead people to risk their lives in illegal border crossings?*

They have gained high-profile jobs as business owners and executives, scientists, and technicians. Yet women often receive less pay for the same job that men do, and many must balance demanding jobs with child-rearing and housework. Still, many women do not have the option of not working, because many families need two incomes just to maintain a decent standard of living. Poor families need two incomes just to survive.

The education gap has been narrowing in developing nations, and women from the middle and elite classes have entered the workforce in growing numbers. Still, women often shoulder a heavy burden of work. In rural areas, especially in Africa where many men have migrated to cities to work, women do much of the farm work in addition to household tasks. In other regions, such as Southeast Asia, young women often leave home in search of work to support the family or to pay for their brothers' education. In many places, cultural traditions still confine women to the home or segregate men and women in the workplace.

Protecting Children Worldwide, children suffer terrible abuses. A 2005 UN report showed that half of the world's children suffer the effects of extreme poverty, armed conflict, and AIDS. Children are also the targets of human rights violations. In some nations, children are forced to serve as soldiers or even slaves. The resulting abuses not only damage children but also hurt a country's hope for the future. In 1989, the UN General Assembly approved the Convention on the Rights of the Child. This human rights treaty sets standards for basic rights for children, including the right to life, liberty, education, and healthcare. But ensuring these rights has proved difficult or even impossible.

In developing countries, tens of millions of children between the ages of 5 and 14 do not attend school. Instead, they work full time. Often, these child laborers work long hours in dangerous, unhealthy conditions for little pay. Many are physically abused by their employers and live in conditions of near slavery. Still, their families need the income the children earn. In some cases, children must work to pay off a family's debt. Human rights groups, the UN, and developed nations have focused a spotlight on child labor in order to end such practices.

Indigenous Peoples Face Challenges Indigenous peoples—including Native Americans, Aborigines in Australia, and Maoris in New Zealand—face discrimination and other abuses. Often, their lands have been forcibly taken. In South America, for example, developers have pushed into once-isolated areas, threatening the ways of life of indigenous peoples. Many Indians have died of diseases carried by the newcomers. During Guatemala's long civil war, the government targeted Mayan villagers, killing tens of thousands. The UN has worked to set standards to protect the rights of indigenous peoples.

✔ **Checkpoint** How are the human rights of children around the world violated?

Development and the Environment

Since earliest times, people have taken what they wanted from the environment. In the past, damage was limited because the world's population was small and technology was simple. Industrialization and the world population explosion have increased the damage done to the environment.

Ending Child Labor
RUGMARK, an organization that works to end child labor, sponsors the education of South Asian students like this girl. The RUGMARK label shown below appears on carpets and rugs that were made without child labor. *What effect might labels like this one have on people's buying habits?*

Health of the World Today

In the year 2000, the world population stood at just over 6 billion people. In 2050, it is projected to reach over 9 billion. The world's population in 2000 was sharply divided in terms of health and access to resources. Despite improvements in agriculture, medicine, and technology, huge numbers of people around the world lacked adequate food and access to safe water. Disease threatened some regions more than others. And in certain areas, poverty-stricken people made up the majority of the population.

Global HIV/AIDS Mortality

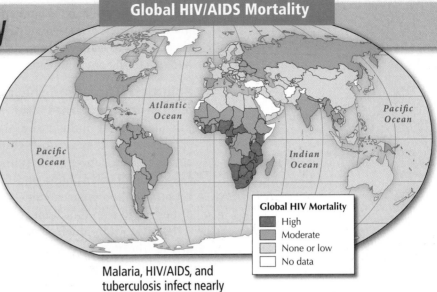

Global HIV Mortality
- High
- Moderate
- None or low
- No data

Malaria, HIV/AIDS, and tuberculosis infect nearly 50% of the world's population.

Access to Safe Water

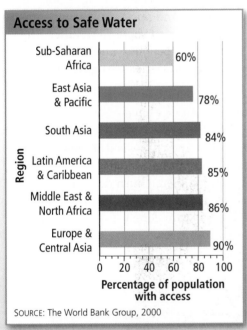

Region:
- Sub-Saharan Africa — 60%
- East Asia & Pacific — 78%
- South Asia — 84%
- Latin America & Caribbean — 85%
- Middle East & North Africa — 86%
- Europe & Central Asia — 90%

Percentage of population with access: 0, 20, 40, 60, 80, 100

SOURCE: The World Bank Group, 2000

Many people around the world have no access to safe water. Drinking and using unsafe water spreads unsanitary conditions and disease.

World Per Capita GDP

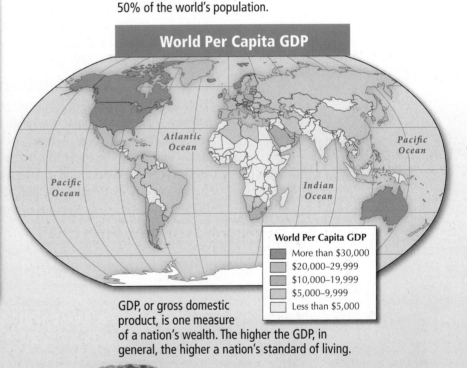

World Per Capita GDP
- More than $30,000
- $20,000–29,999
- $10,000–19,999
- $5,000–9,999
- Less than $5,000

GDP, or gross domestic product, is one measure of a nation's wealth. The higher the GDP, in general, the higher a nation's standard of living.

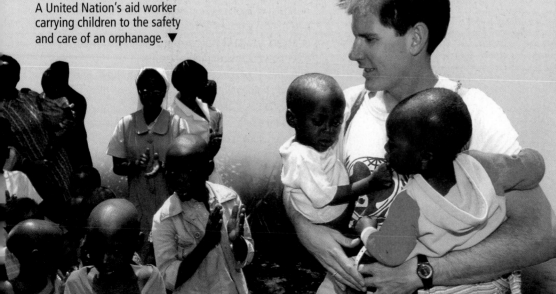

A United Nation's aid worker carrying children to the safety and care of an orphanage. ▼

History Interactive

For: Interactive world health statistics
Web Code: nap-3431

Thinking Critically

1. **Map Skills** Which regions have high rates of disease and low percentages of their population with access to safe water?
2. **Compare** Compare the HIV/AIDS map and the chart with the map of global GDP. What can a nation's GDP suggest about the health of its people?

As you have read, development improves lives and strengthens economies—but at a price. One of the great challenges of the twenty-first century is how to achieve necessary development without causing permanent damage to the environment.

Pollution Threatens the Environment Since the 1970s, environmentalists have warned about threats to the environment. Strip mining provides ores for industry but destroys land. Chemical pesticides and fertilizers produce larger food crops but harm the soil and water and may cause certain cancers. Oil spills pollute waterways and kill marine life. Gases from power plants and factories produce **acid rain,** a form of pollution in which toxic chemicals in the air fall back to Earth as rain, snow, or hail. Acid rain has damaged forests, lakes, and farmland.

Pollution from nuclear plants is another concern. In 1986, an accident at the Chernobyl nuclear power plant in the Soviet Union exposed people, crops, and animals to deadly radiation over a wide area. A similar accident occurred in 1978 at the Three Mile Island nuclear plant in Pennsylvania. Although the fallout was limited and no people were killed, the accident sparked a great debate about the benefits and hazards of nuclear power. Such accidents have caused industries and governments to develop better safety measures.

Growing Deserts, Shrinking Forests As you have read, desertification is a major problem, especially in the Sahel region of Africa. Another threat—especially in Africa, Latin America, and Asia—is **deforestation,** or the cutting of trees without replacing them. People cut trees for firewood or shelter, or to sell in markets abroad. Some burn down forests to make way for farms and cattle ranches, or for industry. In the Amazon basin region of Brazil, the world's largest rain forest, forests are also cleared in order to tap into rich mineral resources.

BIOGRAPHY

Edward O. Wilson

As a child in Alabama, Edward O. Wilson (1929–) developed a love for nature. His poor eyesight and limited physical strength encouraged him to focus on ants—small creatures that he could hold and look at closely. Wilson never grew out of his "bug period," becoming a renowned professor of biology at Harvard. In recent years, Wilson has increasingly focused his attention on environmental issues. In his 2002 book *The Future of Life,* he writes about how Earth's growing human population is affecting the planet and its resources. Calling the 2000s the "Century of the Environment," he appeals to "science and technology, combined with foresight and moral courage," to meet modern environmental challenges. *Why does Wilson believe that "foresight and moral courage" are needed to preserve the environment?*

Once forests are cleared, rains wash nutrients from the soil, destroying its fertility. Deforestation also causes **erosion,** or the wearing away of land, which encourages flooding. The deforestation of rain forests is particularly worrisome. Rain forests like the Amazon play a key role in absorbing poisonous carbon dioxide from the air and releasing essential oxygen. They are also home to millions of animal and plant species, many of which have become extinct because of deforestation.

Global Warming Another environmental challenge—one that is hotly debated—is **global warming.** Global warming refers to the rise of Earth's surface temperature over time. A rise in Earth's temperature could bring about changes such as the following: a rise in sea level, changes in weather patterns, increased desertification in some areas, and an increase in precipitation in others. Because climates in some areas could become colder, many scientists prefer to call the trend "climate change."

Scientists agree that Earth's temperature has risen slightly over the past century. Many scientists think that this warming comes from gases released into the atmosphere by human activity such as the burning of fossil fuels. These "greenhouse" gases trap warmth in Earth's atmosphere. Some scientists, however, and many policymakers, argue that global warming is due to natural <u>fluctuations</u> in Earth's climate.

The debate over a treaty called the Kyoto Protocol points to a central challenge facing world leaders: Does economic development have to conflict with protecting the environment? The treaty, signed by 140 countries, with the major exceptions of the United States and Australia, went into effect in 2005. Its purpose is to lower the emissions of carbon dioxide and other "greenhouse" gases that contribute to global warming. Many developing nations refuse to sign because they say they must exploit their resources in order to develop fully. The United States has not signed the Kyoto Protocol because it believes the treaty could strain economic growth. Nations that have signed the treaty, however, argue that developed nations must lead the way in slowing emissions.

Vocabulary Builder

<u>fluctuation</u>—(fluk choo AY shun) *n.* swing; rising and falling of something

✓ **Checkpoint** What kinds of environmental issues do people face today?

Assessment

SECTION 3

Progress Monitoring *Online*
For: Self-quiz with vocabulary practice
Web Code: naa-3431

Terms, People, and Places

1. Place each of the key terms at the beginning of the section into one of the following categories: politics, culture, government, economy, or environment. Write a sentence for each term explaining your choice.

Note Taking

2. **Reading Skill: Compare** Use your completed chart to answer the Focus Question: How do poverty, disease, and environmental challenges affect people around the world today?

Comprehension and Critical Thinking

3. **Synthesize Information** How are global poverty, disease, disasters, and migration linked to each other? How might they be linked to globalization?

4. **Identify Central Issues** Why is protecting human rights not a central issue for many developing countries?

5. **Identify Assumptions** What assumptions can you make about the lack of participation on the part of some nations in the Kyoto Protocol?

● **Writing About History**

Quick Write: Decide on an Organizational Strategy Make a draft of a persuasive essay about social and environmental challenges. Your draft should include a thesis statement, begin with your second-strongest argument, and conclude with your strongest argument. To organize most efficiently, rank your remaining arguments from weakest to strongest.

Aung San Suu Kyi: *Freedom From Fear*

Aung San Suu Kyi, leader of Myanmar's National League for Democracy and winner of the Nobel Peace Prize, has worked courageously for human rights and democracy in her country. Because of her opposition to Myanmar's ruling military junta, she was held under house arrest from 1989 to 1995 and severely restricted thereafter. In this essay, Aung San Suu Kyi describes the need for courage when living under an oppressive government.

▲ Aung San Suu Kyi

Fearlessness may be a gift but perhaps more precious is the courage acquired through endeavor, courage that comes from cultivating the habit of refusing to let fear dictate one's actions, courage that could be described as 'grace under pressure'—grace which is renewed repeatedly in the face of harsh, unremitting[1] pressure.

Within a system which denies the existence of basic human rights, fear tends to be the order of the day. Fear of imprisonment, fear of torture, fear of death, fear of losing friends, family, property or means of livelihood, fear of poverty, fear of isolation, fear of failure. A most insidious[2] form of fear is that which masquerades as common sense or even wisdom, condemning as foolish, reckless, insignificant or futile the small, daily acts of courage which help to preserve man's self-respect and inherent[3] human dignity. It is not easy for a people conditioned by fear under the iron rule of the principle that might is right to free themselves from the enervating[4] miasma[5] of fear. Yet even under the most crushing state machinery courage rises up again and again, for fear is not the natural state of civilized man.

The wellspring[6] of courage and endurance in the face of unbridled power is generally a firm belief in the sanctity of ethical principles combined with a historical sense that despite all setbacks the condition of man is set on an ultimate course for both spiritual and material advancement.... It is man's vision of a world fit for rational, civilized humanity which leads him to dare and to suffer to build societies free from want and fear. Concepts such as truth, justice and compassion cannot be dismissed as trite[7] when these are often the only bulwarks[8] which stand against ruthless power.

▲ Burmese children living in Bangladesh protested for the release of Aung San Suu Kyi on the occasion of the Burmese foreign minister's visit to Bangladesh.

1. **unremitting** (un rih MIT ing) *adj.* not letting up
2. **insidious** (in SID ee us) *adj.* meant to harm
3. **inherent** (in HIHR unt) *adj.* part of one's basic nature
4. **enervating** (EN ur vayt ing) *adj.* weakening or destroying
5. **miasma** (my AZ muh) *n.* harmful atmosphere or influence
6. **wellspring** (WEL spring) *n.* source
7. **trite** (tryt) *adj.* overused; uninteresting
8. **bulwark** (BOOL wurk) *n.* serving as a defense

Thinking Critically

1. **Identify Main Ideas** Why does the author believe that even in harsh, cruel societies courage will rise up again and again?

2. **Apply Information** Give one example of a person refusing to let fear dictate his or her actions.

SECTION 4

Taking a Stand

In the fall of 2002, United States President George W. Bush delivered a speech on international security before the United Nations in New York:

❝We must choose between a world of fear and a world of progress. We cannot stand by and do nothing while dangers gather. We must stand up for our security and for the permanent rights and for the hopes of mankind.❞
—George W. Bush, Remarks at the United Nations General Assembly, September 12, 2002

Focus Question What kinds of threats to national and global security do nations face today?

President Bush emphasizes the importance of national security in a speech to U.S. Coast Guard members in 2003.

Security in a Dangerous World

 Performance Standards

- **SSWH20c** Analyze terrorism as a form of 20th century warfare, the terrorism of the Red Brigade, Hamas, and Al Qaeda and terrorism's impact on daily life, travel, energy and markets.

Terms, People, and Places

proliferate
terrorism
al Qaeda

Afghanistan
Taliban

Note Taking

Reading Skill: Compare and Contrast Use the chart to compare threats to global security.

Threats to Security	
Nuclear Weapons	Nuclear weapons unsecured in former Soviet Union

The end of the Cold War seemed to promise an end to global conflict and the threat of nuclear war. However, since the fall of the Iron Curtain, new and unpredictable threats continue to haunt the world.

The Threat of Modern Weapons

During the Cold War, the United States and the Soviet Union built huge arsenals of nuclear weapons. When the Cold War ended, those weapons still existed. Since then, keeping nuclear, chemical, and biological weapons out of the hands of dangerous groups has become an important issue.

The Nuclear Nonproliferation Treaty In 1968, during a thaw in the Cold War, the United States, the Soviet Union, and 60 other nations signed the Nuclear Nonproliferation Treaty (NPT). The purpose of the treaty was to ensure that nuclear weapons did not **proliferate,** or rapidly spread to nations that had no nuclear weapons. Since then, the treaty has been renewed, with 189 nations agreeing not to develop or possess nuclear weapons.

The International Atomic Energy Agency (IAEA) monitors nations regularly to check that they comply with the treaty. Three nations have not signed the NPT: India, Israel, and Pakistan. All three have nuclear weapons. India and Pakistan's testing of nuclear weapons in 1998 raised fears of a nuclear arms race in Asia. A few signers of the NPT, such as Iran, have tried to sidestep the treaty by acquiring nuclear technology that they claim is being used to develop nuclear power as an energy source.

Russia's Nuclear Weapons During the 1990s, the United States and Russia agreed to reduce their nuclear arsenals. However, after the collapse of the Soviet Union, Russia's nuclear weapons were scattered across a vast territory. With aid from the United States and Europe, Russia dismantled, or took apart, some nuclear weapons. Despite the agreements, however, both the United States and Russia held on to their nuclear stockpiles.

Weapons of Mass Destruction As you have read, weapons of mass destruction (WMDs) include nuclear, biological, and chemical weapons. Nuclear weapons include the atomic bomb. Biological weapons refer mainly to germs that can be released into the air or into water supplies. Chemical weapons are toxins, such as nerve gas and mustard gas.

Recently, however, the danger from WMDs has grown, as terrorist groups and "rogue states"—nations that ignore international law and threaten other nations—try to acquire them. One concern is that terrorists will seize nuclear weapons during transport. Another fear is that terrorists, or those who sympathize with their causes, will gain access to nuclear weapons programs in countries with unstable governments, such as Pakistan.

A Risky Situation
Vials of the bacteria that cause plague were left improperly secured in Kazakhstan by Soviet scientists.

✓ **Checkpoint** What was the purpose of the NPT?

Terrorism Threatens Global Security

Since the 1990s, the world has witnessed a growing threat from terrorism. **Terrorism** is the use of violence by groups of extremists to achieve political goals. Terrorists' goals range from getting political prisoners released to gaining territory or autonomy for a particular ethnic group. Terrorists have bombed buildings, slaughtered civilians, police, and soldiers, and assassinated political leaders. Although terrorists have seldom achieved their larger goals, they have inflicted terrible damage and generated widespread fear.

Terrorists use headline-grabbing tactics to draw attention to their demands. They might attack hotels and tourists in Mumbai, bomb commuter trains in Madrid, or blow themselves up as "suicide bombers" to kill Israeli or Iraqi civilians. Terrorism has led to greater international cooperation between governments in an effort to prevent further attacks.

Regional Terrorist Groups Regional terrorist groups have operated in the developed world for decades. For 30 years, the Irish Republican Army (IRA) used terrorist tactics to force Britain out of Northern Ireland. Protestant paramilitary groups loyal to Great Britain responded with the same tactics. During the Cold War, the communist Red Brigade in Italy used violence in an attempt to gain power. The ETA, a Basque terrorist group, wants the Spanish government to grant independence to the Basque region in northern Spain.

In South America, leftist groups like the Shining Path in Peru and FARC in Colombia use kidnappings, murder, and bombings to overthrow national governments. They finance their operations with the sale of illegal drugs. In Asia, terrorist activities were linked to the long conflict between India and Pakistan over Kashmir.

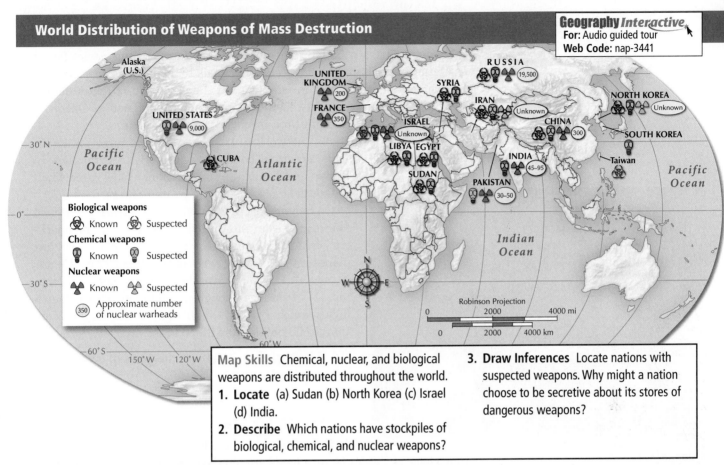

World Distribution of Weapons of Mass Destruction

Biological weapons
Known   Suspected

Chemical weapons
Known   Suspected

Nuclear weapons
Known   Suspected

(350) Approximate number of nuclear warheads

Map Skills Chemical, nuclear, and biological weapons are distributed throughout the world.
1. **Locate** (a) Sudan (b) North Korea (c) Israel (d) India.
2. **Describe** Which nations have stockpiles of biological, chemical, and nuclear weapons?

3. **Draw Inferences** Locate nations with suspected weapons. Why might a nation choose to be secretive about its stores of dangerous weapons?

Conflicts in the Middle East Decades of conflict between Israel and its neighbors have fueled terrorism. In 1964, a group of Arabs founded the Palestine Liberation Organization (PLO), with the goal of creating an independent Palestinian state. In its early years, the PLO used terrorist methods.

The PLO renounced terrorism in 1988. Meanwhile, other terrorist groups have emerged and continue their calls for the establishment of a Palestinian state and the destruction of Israel. The Al-Aqsa Martyrs Brigade, Hamas, Hezbollah, and Islamic Jihad are among the groups that practice terror to achieve their goals. They found support in poverty-stricken Palestinian refugee camps in Gaza and trained suicide bombers to attack Israeli targets.

Islamic Fundamentalism By the 1980s, Islamic fundamentalism was on the rise. This conservative reform movement wanted to revive Islamic values and install governments that strictly followed Islamic law, or Sharia. The Islamist movement was partly a response to the rise of secular governments in many Muslim nations and the impact of Western culture. It was also a backlash against foreign support for Israel and the presence of foreign powers in the Middle East. Islamic fundamentalists made Israel or Western nations scapegoats for their problems.

The 1979 Iranian revolution brought an Islamist government to power. Later, an Islamist group called the Taliban gained power in Afghanistan. Fundamentalist movements have also emerged in countries from Algeria to Indonesia. Iran and Saudi Arabia have both provided financial support for terrorist organizations.

Al Qaeda Attacks Some Islamic fundamentalists turned to terrorism. The most widely known Islamic terrorist organization is **al Qaeda** (ahl KY duh), which means "the Base" in Arabic. The founder and leader of al Qaeda is Osama bin Laden, a wealthy Saudi businessman.

In the 1980s, bin Laden joined Muslim fighters battling Soviet forces in Afghanistan. Later, he broadened his goals to include the overthrow of governments considered "un-Islamic" and the expulsion of non-Muslims from Muslim countries. In the 1990s, bin Laden mobilized al Qaeda to expel U.S. interests and military power from Saudi Arabia.

Al Qaeda built a global network to train and finance terrorist activities. In 1998, al Qaeda terrorists bombed the American embassies in Kenya and Tanzania. But the major blow came when al Qaeda struck inside the United States.

On September 11, 2001, al Qaeda terrorists hijacked four airplanes in the United States. Most of the hijackers were from Saudi Arabia. They slammed two airplanes into the twin towers of the World Trade Center in New York and one into the Pentagon near Washington, D.C. Passengers fought the hijackers on the fourth flight, which crashed on the way to its target. More than 2,500 people were killed in the attacks.

✔ **Checkpoint** What are the goals of Islamic fundamentalists?

A Dangerous Leader
New York City police stand near a "Wanted" poster in 2001. *How does bin Laden threaten the United States' security?*

Response to Terrorism

Al Qaeda's attack on the United States triggered a startling global shake-up. Governments around the world questioned their ability to keep their citizens safe. U.S. President George W. Bush declared a "war on terror" in general, and against al Qaeda in particular.

New Security Measures After the 2001 attacks, the United States made national security a top priority. To this end, the government strengthened and reorganized its intelligence services and passed new counter terrorism laws. In the United States and elsewhere, there were more rigorous security measures at airports and public buildings. A long-term effort was launched to find out how terrorist groups were funded, with the goal of cutting off terrorists' money supply and limiting their activities. The United States worked with other countries to coordinate intelligence about terrorist groups.

These measures were costly. In addition, some believed the federal government was using the threat of terrorism to increase its power and violate the constitutional rights and freedoms of its citizens. But many felt that the threat was serious enough to justify extreme measures.

Vocabulary Builder
priority—(pry AWR uh tee) *n.* something deemed of greater importance than other things

The Wars in Afghanistan As part of its "war on terror," the United States made it a priority to find and punish the organizers of the 2001 attacks. Osama bin Laden was based in **Afghanistan.** The government of Afghanistan, an extreme Islamic fundamentalist group called the **Taliban,** refused U.S. demands to surrender the terrorists. The United States then formed a coalition of nations to invade Afghanistan. In 2002, with the help of Afghan warlords, American and allied forces overthrew the Taliban and drove al Qaeda into hiding or flight. Bin Laden and many Taliban leaders escaped capture.

Coalition forces helped Afghanistan hold elections for a new government. The new government lifted many harsh Taliban laws, such as those that forbid girls and women from getting an education. From hideouts along the Pakistan border, Taliban fighters resisted the new government and its Western allies. The war soon spilled into neighboring Pakistan, where Taliban and al Qaeda fighters took refuge.

War in Iraq In 2003, President Bush urged Congress to agree to an invasion of Iraq, citing intelligence reports that said Iraq was secretly producing WMDs. The Bush administration also suggested that Iraq was involved in the 2001 terrorist attacks against the United States. The war was bitterly debated among Americans and around the world, because no WMDs were found after the U.S. invasion.

A 2008 report by the Senate Intelligence Committee said that prior to the invasion, the Bush administration had repeatedly exaggerated the threat posed by Iraq. The report also revealed that there had been no credible intelligence to support the Bush administration's claims that Iraq was developing nuclear weapons, or that Iraq had longstanding ties to terrorist groups.

Threats From Iran and North Korea When Iran announced a plan to develop nuclear power plants in the early 2000s, the United States and other nations feared that Iran truly intended to develop nuclear weapons. Although Iran insisted its nuclear energy program was for peaceful purposes, the UN Security Council imposed some sanctions on Iran.

For years, North Korea violated its agreement under the Nuclear Nonproliferation Treaty and worked on developing nuclear weapons. Tensions grew as the United States tried to pressure North Korea to stop its nuclear weapons program. In 2003, North Korea withdrew from the NPT. In 2006, it tested a small nuclear bomb.

Many people feared that if Iran or North Korea developed nuclear weapons, that nuclear technology could be passed on to terrorist groups. A nuclear-armed Iran or North Korea also posed threats to their regions and to world peace.

Iran's Nuclear Plans
Iranians form a chain around a nuclear research facility to show their support for their country's nuclear program. *Why do Western nations object to the program?*

✔ **Checkpoint** Why did the United States invade Iraq?

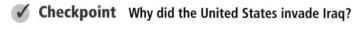

SECTION **4** Assessment

Progress Monitoring *Online*
For: Self-quiz with vocabulary practice
Web Code: naa-3441

Terms, People, and Places

1. For each term, person, or place listed at the beginning of the section, write a sentence explaining its significance.

Note Taking

2. **Reading Skill: Compare and Contrast** Use your completed chart to answer the Focus Question: What kinds of threats to national and global security do nations face today?

Comprehension and Critical Thinking

3. **Draw Inferences** Why might the United States and Russia be reluctant to fully commit to nuclear disarmament?

4. **Predict Consequences** How might nations around the world react should Middle Eastern nations democratically elect Islamic fundamentalist governments?

5. **Demonstrate Reasoned Judgment** Do you think that "preemptive" wars, or wars waged to prevent other wars or attacks, are sometimes necessary? Explain your answer.

● **Writing About History**

Quick Write: Draft the Opening Paragraph The paragraph that opens your essay is the place to grab the reader's interest. Remember that if the reader loses interest after reading the first paragraph, he or she is unlikely to continue reading. Draft an opening paragraph about threats to global security, using specific details to grab the reader's interest. An opening such as "There are many threats to global security" is much less compelling than a description of a specific threat.

Buzz Aldrin walks on the moon in 1969. The space capsule that he traveled in is reflected on his visor.

A logo of the National Aeronautic and Space Administration (NASA)

WITNESS HISTORY 🔊 AUDIO

A Giant Leap for Mankind

On July 20, 1969, American astronauts Neil Armstrong and Edwin Aldrin landed on the moon after a four-day trip in the spacecraft *Apollo 11*. Stepping out onto the powdery surface, Armstrong—the first person ever to have walked on the moon—said, "That's one small step for man, one giant leap for mankind." Those words electrified a nation and defined a new era of world history.

Focus Question How have advances in science and technology shaped the modern world?

Advances in Science and Technology

 Performance Standards

- **SSWH21a** Describe how satellites and computers integrated countries into a world economy.

Terms, People, and Places

artificial satellite
International Space Station (ISS)
personal computer (PC)
Internet

biotechnology
laser
genetics
genetic engineering

Note Taking

Reading Skill: Compare Use the chart to compare the impacts of modern science and technology.

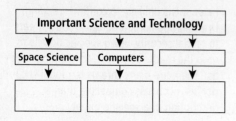

People in the past half century have used various terms to describe the age they live in, including "the atomic age," the "electronic age," and the "automobile age." All of these labels have one thing in common: their connection to modern science and technology. Since 1945, scientific research and technological development have had a transforming effect on human history. Startling new inventions, the computer revolution, and advances in the life sciences have redefined the world we live in and the lives we lead.

Exploring and Making Use of Space

By the second half of the twentieth century, there were few places on Earth that people had not begun to explore. Space was seen as the "final frontier"—an unknown world filled with opportunity. Within a few short decades, people had traveled to this frontier and had used its resources to help develop practical applications that transformed their lives.

The Space Race Begins Rockets are projectiles or vehicles propelled by the ejection of burning gasses from the rear of the rocket. In the early twentieth century, pioneers in rocketry like the American physicist Robert Goddard probed the potential of liquid-fueled rockets. From the beginning, Goddard believed that a rocket could carry people to the moon. At first people met his ideas with disbelief. Increasingly, German scientists took interest in Goddard's work, prompting him to work with great secrecy.

Nevertheless, during World War II German scientists, led by Wernher von Braun, developed Germany's "secret weapon," the V-2 rockets that flew across the English Channel to rain down on London.

During the Cold War, the United States and the Soviet Union competed with each other to build both rocket-propelled weapons and rocketry for the purpose of space exploration. Von Braun, who moved to the United States after World War II, became a leader in the American missiles and space program. In 1957, the space age began when the Soviet Union launched into orbit *Sputnik*, the first **artificial satellite,** or manmade object that orbits a larger body. In 1969, the United States Apollo program landed the first man on the moon. Both superpowers also explored the military uses of space and sent spy satellites to orbit Earth. Since the end of the Cold War, the United States and Russia have cooperated in joint space ventures.

Space Science Develops In the decades since *Sputnik* and *Apollo*, rockets have been launched to other planets and beyond. Robotic space vehicles have penetrated the mists of Venus and the rings of Saturn, landed on Mars, and circled the moons of Jupiter. Rocket missions have various goals. They can take scientific measurements, release permanent satellites or telescopes, and if they are manned, conduct medical or biological experiments. They can also provide information about the composition and formation of the universe itself.

Increasingly, nations have worked together to explore space. For example, Russia, the United States, Canada, Japan, and several countries in Europe are developing the **International Space Station (ISS).**

Traveler's Tales
EYEWITNESS ACCOUNT

An Astronaut Views Earth From Space

Alan Bean is an American astronaut who participated in the United States' Apollo 12 moon-landing project. In 1969, Bean became the fourth person to walk on the moon. Deeply moved by his experience, he began taking art lessons upon his return to Earth to express visually what he had seen. He resigned from NASA in 1981 to devote himself to painting. The excerpt below, taken from a book about the Apollo mission that he wrote and illustrated, describes the view from the moon.

❝It was incredible to stand on the moon… and take a moment to reflect on all the dedicated people it took to get us there for America. We were the lucky ones. The stars were not visible because the sunlight reflecting from the bright lunar surface caused the irises of our eyes to contract, just as they do on earth at night when standing on a brightly lit patio. As we looked up, the sky was a deep, shiny black. I guessed that deep, shiny black was the color one sees looking into infinity . . . . I thought: Can all the people we know, all the people we love, who we've seen on TV, or read about in the newspapers, all be up there on that tiny blue-and-white marble? Earth—small but so lovely—was easily the most beautiful object we could see from the moon. It was a wondrous moment.❞

—*Alan Bean,*
from ***Apollo, 1998***

Thinking Critically
1. **Draw Inferences** Why does Bean call the astronauts the "lucky ones"?
2. **Analyze Information** How does Bean contrast his view of Earth with that of the lunar sky? What point does he make by contrasting these two views?

Construction on the ISS began in 1998. When it is completed in 2010, it will serve as a space laboratory, allowing scientists from many different countries to observe space, conduct research, and develop new space-related technologies.

The Impact of Artificial Satellites The thousands of artificial satellites that orbit Earth have a number of very specific applications. These applications can be divided into three groups—communications, observation, and navigation. Communications satellites relay information that is used in advanced communications, including television, telephone, and high-speed data transmission. Observation satellites observe Earth, providing data to scientists, weather forecasters, and military planners. Navigation satellites beam precise locations to ship captains and others who need to navigate Earth's surface.

By 2000, artificial satellites had revolutionized global communications. Maintaining stationary orbits over specific points on Earth's surface, artificial satellites can transmit phone messages or television pictures anywhere on Earth. Linked to cell phones or computers, they allow people separated by thousands of miles to communicate instantly.

✓ **Checkpoint** What is the International Space Station and what is its significance?

The Computer Revolution

The invention of the computer in the twentieth century caused an unprecedented information revolution. Very few aspects of modern life remain untouched by computers. Computers run businesses and power plants, help scientists conduct advanced research, and when connected to satellites, make global communications possible. The development of computer technology has given rise to the term "Information Age."

⬤ INFOGRAPHIC

Twentieth Century Scientific Milestones

Developing Nuclear Energy

During World War II, the United States was determined to create an atomic bomb that could be used against the Axis Powers. Scientists including Albert Einstein, J. Robert Oppenheimer, Enrico Fermi, and Edward Teller participated in the Manhattan Project, as it was called. The project achieved success in 1945 with the explosion of a test bomb in New Mexico.

◀ Einstein and Oppenheimer in 1947

Early Computers A computer is a device for making mathematical calculations and for storing, processing, and rapidly manipulating data. Computers have made it possible to preserve vast amounts of data. And when linked up in a vast network, they have brought written communication over enormous distances instantaneously.

The first electronic computers, built in the 1940s, were huge, slow machines. Later, thanks to inventions like the silicon chip, the computer was reduced in size. **Personal computers,** or **PCs,** became widely available in the 1970s for individual users, both at work and at home. By inserting basic programs into the machine, the user could perform complex and difficult tasks quickly and easily.

Over the next few decades, PCs replaced typewriters and account books in homes and businesses worldwide. At the same time, computer technology spread into many different fields. Computerized robots operate in factories. Computers remotely control satellites and probes in space and students use them in school classrooms. And computers increasingly aid scientists and architects in developing models to predict disasters, understand environmental changes, and plan urban development.

The Internet In the 1970s, various branches of the U.S. government along with groups in several American universities led efforts to link computer systems together via cables and satellites. By the 1990s, the "Internet" or "World Wide Web" was well established, again revolutionizing information technology. Using the **Internet,** a person can instantly communicate with other users around the world. The same person can also instantly access vast storehouses of information of all sorts.

By 2000, the Internet had grown to a gigantic network, linking individuals, governments, and businesses around the world. E-commerce, or buying and selling on the Internet, contributed to economic growth. The Internet also began to shape life in developing nations.

Breakthroughs in Medicine

Twentieth-century discoveries in medicine had a major impact on people around the world. For example, in 1952 researcher Jonas Salk (left) developed a vaccine for polio. Polio is a virus that spreads rapidly among people, especially children, causing paralysis. Before Salk's discovery, around 20,000 people in the United States contracted polio each year. Because of Salk's vaccine, the disease is extremely rare in the world today.

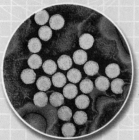

◀ the polio virus

DNA ▶ sequencer

Expanding the Science of Genetics

The study of genes was not new to the twentieth century. The work of James Watson and Francis Crick, (right) however, dramatically transformed the science of genetics. In 1953, the two men discovered the basic structure of DNA—the material in the chromosomes of all cells that determines how every organism functions. This discovery revolutionized the study of heredity and paved the way for genetic engineering.

Thinking Critically
1. **Draw Inferences** Why did Albert Einstein later regret his work on the Manhattan Project?
2. **Cause and Effect** How did the discovery of DNA affect the field of genetics?

◀)) AUDIO

A GLOBAL FOOD EVOLVES

What we now know as corn originally grew as a wild grass in the Americas. Thousands of years ago, ancient peoples began experimenting with this grass, carefully selecting good seeds and nurturing plants. About 7,000 years ago, Native Americans near present-day Mexico City developed small ears of corn, calling them *maize*. Indians throughout the Americas, and then European settlers, constantly experimented with corn to produce bigger and better ears. The experimentation still continues today.

▲ Eventually, Native Americans produced maize, a plant with ears of plump, soft kernels like today's corn. Maize became a staple crop for many Native American groups. They also developed multi-colored ears of corn, like those above, using them for food and in religious activities.

◄ Ancient wild corn was called *teosinte* (tee oh *SIN* tee). Teosinte kernels, hard and nut-like, grew on thick grassy stalks. Over thousands of years Native Americans domesticated teosinte, carefully preserving the seeds of the plants that produced the best ears.

▲ A biotechnology worker cuts into an ear of corn to extract a section of DNA, or genetic material, that will be used to improve the next corn crop. By selecting only specific DNA, scientists can transfer only the genes that will result in desirable crop traits, such as hardiness or resistance to insects.

At the beginning of the twenty-first century, about 6 percent of the world's population could access the Internet. By 2010, it is estimated that about one third of the world's population will have access to the Internet—connecting them to a new world of ideas and information.

✓ **Checkpoint** What impact have personal computers had on people's lives?

Advances in Medicine and Biotechnology

Science and technology have revolutionized our understanding and our control of both human life and other forms of life on this planet. Developments in medicine and **biotechnology,** the application of biological research to industry, engineering, and technology, have resulted in new ways to combat and prevent disease.

Breakthroughs Transform Medicine In the postwar era, pioneers in the life sciences such as Dr. Jonas Salk became household names. Before the Salk vaccine, the paralyzing disease polio had crippled thousands of children and adults—including President Franklin D. Roosevelt. Other medical researchers developed vaccines to help prevent the spread of smallpox and other diseases.

Breakthroughs in surgery also transformed the field of medicine. In the 1970s, surgeons learned to transplant organs, including the human heart, to save lives. **Lasers** made many types of surgery safer and more precise. Lasers are high-energy light beams that surgeons use to cut or repair tissues and organs. Scientists have also had success in treating some cancers, a disease that affects the global population. In recent decades, computers and other technologies have become partners with doctors in diagnosing and treating disease. They have also made it easier for people to share information, thus making diseases easier to treat.

Biotechnology and Genetic Engineering In the past couple of decades, the field of biotechnology has exploded. Biotechnology companies make products including vaccinations, medicines, and industrial bacteria that can be used to treat waste or clean up toxic spills.

Biotechnology is closely related to the fields of genetics and genetic engineering, which have also made dramatic advances in recent years. **Genetics** is the study of genes and heredity, while **genetic engineering** is the manipulation of genetic material to produce specific results. Beginning in the 1950s, genetic researchers, spearheaded by Rosalind Franklin, J. D. Watson, and F.H.C. Crick, examined the chemical code carried by all living things. Their research established the central role of DNA—deoxyribonucleic acid—in the chromosomes that determine human heredity. Their work revealed the "double helix," spiral-shaped DNA that carries hereditary traits from parents to children.

Ongoing genetic research has produced new drug therapies to fight human diseases. Research has also created new strains of fruits and vegetables that are intended to resist disease or thrive in conditions that usually inhibit growth. Genetic cloning, or the process of creating identical organisms from the cell of a host organism, has many practical applications in raising livestock and in biological research.

Biotechnology and genetic engineering have brought benefits, but also debate. Some people believe that genetically modified foods are unnatural and potentially dangerous. The possibility of cloning genetically identical mammals—including human beings—has also raised ethical questions about the role of science in creating and changing life.

Standards of Living Rise As you have read, science and technology have often had a direct and powerful impact on human life. Advances in diagnosing and treating disease and increased agricultural output have raised life expectancies worldwide, as well as standards of living. Yet great challenges still remain, from overpopulation to disasters to corrupt governments. In the decades ahead, people will continue to look for ways to solve global problems, using whatever tools they have.

✓ **Checkpoint** How have scientific advances affected people's standard of living?

Vocabulary Builder

manipulation—(muh nip yoo LAY shun) *n.* the skillful handling of something with the purpose of achieving a specific result

---

SECTION 5 Assessment

Progress Monitoring *Online*
For: Self-quiz with vocabulary practice
Web Code: naa-3451

Terms, People, and Places

1. What do each of the key terms listed at the beginning of the section have in common? Explain.

Note Taking

2. **Reading Skill: Compare** Use your completed chart to answer the Focus Question: How have advances in science and technology shaped the modern world?

Comprehension and Critical Thinking

3. **Synthesize Information** Considering the history of the Cold War, explain why the United States and Russia competed against each other to achieve dominance in the space race.

4. **Recognize Cause and Effect** What impact has the computer revolution had on globalization?

5. **Express Problems Clearly** Biotechnology has provided many benefits, but many people worry about its long-term effects. Explain why this is so.

● **Writing About History**

Quick Write: Write a Conclusion Write a conclusion that restates your thesis, sums up the supporting details, and leaves readers with a final impression. This final impression can be a memorable statement or even a call to action. As you write a conclusion about science and technology in the modern world, consider what basic impression you want the reader to remember about the topic, even if he or she takes nothing else away from the essay.

Quick Study Guide

GA SSWH21a,
SSWH21c

■ Key Components of Globalization

- Interdependence: dependence of countries on goods, resources, knowledge, and labor from other parts of the world
- Advances in communications and transportation
- Rise of huge multinational corporations
- Far-reaching effects of financial crisis, shortages of natural resources, and debt
- Rise of global economy with many global organizations and treaties

■ Influential Technology of the Twentieth Century

Technology	Description	Uses
Artificial satellite	Man-made object that orbits a larger body	Space exploration; spying and other military purposes; scientific research; navigation; communications
Computer	Device for storing, processing, and rapidly manipulating data	Creating and preserving data; making businesses and homes run more efficiently; controlling satellites and factories
Internet	Network of world computer systems linked by cables and satellites	Instant communication with users around world; instant data retrieval; means of commerce
Biotechnology	Application of biological research to industry	Vaccinations and medicines; industrial bacteria; genetic engineering

■ Major Challenges to Society Today

- Global poverty, disasters, and disease
- Ensuring human rights for all, including women, children, and indigenous peoples
- Environmental problems including pollution, deforestation, desertification, and climate change
- Threat of misuse of nuclear technology and weapons of mass destruction
- Terrorism

■ Important Industrialized Regions

Region	Description	Role in Global Economy
The United States	World's only superpower	Important world leader; largest trading country in world
The European Union	Union of 25 European nations with distinct governments but common economic, political, and cultural institutions	Currently includes over half of European nations and is growing; world's largest trading region
The Pacific Rim	Geographical region that includes the countries that border the Pacific Ocean	With many countries and huge populations, potential to be major player in global economy

■ Recent World Events

1986
Nuclear accident occurs in Chernobyl.

1990
Germany is reunited.

1995
The WTO forms.

1985

1990

1995

1988
Osama bin Laden forms al Qaeda.

1994
NAFTA is created.

Concept Connector

 Essential Question Review

To connect prior knowledge with what you have learned in this chapter, answer the questions below in your Concept Connector journal. Use the journal in the Reading and Note Taking Study Guide to record your answers (or go to www.phschool.com **Web Code**: nad-3407). In addition, record information about the following concepts:

- Trade: United States trade in the twentieth century
- Economic systems: Globalization

1. **Technology** Since their introduction, personal computers have become more common around the world. If everyone in the world could have access to a computer and the Internet, how might society, culture, and the economy change?

2. **Trade** The formation of the European Union improved the economy of many nations in Europe and created a sense of unity. But not all people and all member nations were equally happy with the many changes. What were some of the unintended consequences of the formation of the EU?

3. **Cooperation** Is the work of NGOs essential in the 21st century? Think about the work that organizations like the International Red Cross do. Are there situations in which an NGO would be better suited to provide relief than a government or an organization like the United Nations? Why might groups of people in some situations be more likely to welcome aid from an NGO than from a government?

4. **Democracy** Look at the image at the start of this chapter. Artificial satellites can transmit phone messages or television pictures anywhere on earth. Do you think better communication will lead to the spread of democracy? Explain.

Connections to Today

1. **Advances in Science: Medical Procedures** In 1954, American doctor Joseph Murray performed the first organ transplant, successfully transplanting a kidney from a man into his twin brother. In 2004, nearly 30,000 organ transplants were performed. Think about the issues that people grappled with decades ago as they considered the ethics of organ transplantation. Then choose a medical procedure that is being debated today. (Possibilities might include stem cell research, genetic cloning, or the use of surrogate mothers.) Research your topic and then write two paragraphs: one that supports the procedure and one that opposes it.

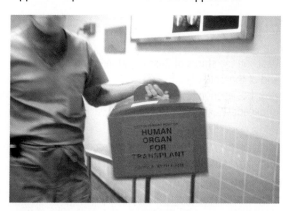

2. **Cultural Diffusion: Spread of Popular Culture** During the 20th century, American popular culture—especially American movies, music, and clothing—influenced people around the world. Consider the factors necessary for cultural diffusion. Why is popular culture from the United States widely influential? Predict which countries' popular culture will become widely influential in the early 21st century.

History Interactive
For: Interactive timeline
Web Code: nap-3461

1997 The Asian financial crisis hits.	Sept. 11, 2001 Al Qaeda attacks the United States.		
2000		**2005**	**2010**
2000 Vladimir Putin is elected president of Russia.	October 2001 The United States begins war on the Taliban in Afghanistan.	Dec. 26, 2004 Tsunami devastates Southeast Asia.	2007 The United States commits more troops to Iraq and Afghanistan.

Chapter Assessment

Terms, People, and Places

Choose the italicized term in parentheses that best completes each sentence.

1. A *(deficit/default)* is the gap between what a government spends and what it takes in through taxes and other resources.
2. One of the WTO's basic policies is its opposition to *(outsourcing/protectionism)*.
3. *(Famine/Acid rain)* is a particular concern in areas where there has been a natural disaster.
4. The belief that society should be governed by Islamic law is known as *(Islamic fundamentalism/terrorism)*.
5. *(Genetics/Artificial satellites)* have revolutionized communications.

Main Ideas

Section 1 (pp. 1096–1099)
6. Describe the status of Russia and the United States after the end of the Cold War.
7. How has economic power in Asia shifted over the past couple of decades?

Section 2 (pp. 1100–1105)
8. What are the main characteristics of economic interdependence?
9. Summarize the benefits and costs of globalization.

Section 3 (pp. 1106–1114)
10. What are the main causes of poverty?
11. Describe some of the environmental challenges of the 21st century.

Section 4 (pp. 1115–1119)
12. Why are nuclear weapons a particular problem in Russia?
13. What is al Qaeda, and why is it such a threat?

Section 5 (pp. 1120–1125)
14. Summarize the impact of science and technology on modern life.

Chapter Focus Question
15. What are the major issues facing the world today?

Critical Thinking

16. **Analyze Information** Which region do you think will be the most important economically during the next half-century: the EU, the Pacific Rim, or the United States? Explain your answer.
17. **Predict Consequences** What might be the global impact if terrorists cut off supplies of natural gas or another important resource to a large American city?
18. **Geography and History** Consider the space race of the late 1900s. Why have nations throughout history found it important to explore frontiers?
19. **Recognize Cause and Effect** In this chapter you have read about how economic and technological changes have had an impact on people around the world. How might these changes also affect people's values and beliefs?

"Nothing's labeled. How are we supposed to know which fruit has been genetically engineered?"

20. **Analyze Visuals** What point is the cartoonist making about genetically modified foods in the cartoon above?
21. **Recognize Cause and Effect** How does outsourcing jobs affect both the home country and the country where the jobs are outsourced?
22. **Draw Inferences** How can globalization bring about a stronger commitment to human rights? How can it encourage human rights abuses, such as child labor?

● Writing About History

In this chapter's five Section Assessments, you developed the skills to write a persuasive essay.

Write a Persuasive Essay People strongly debate many of the issues that face the world today. Choose a topic that interests you—and that you have a strong opinion about—and then write a persuasive essay. You may choose your own topic or select from the following: free trade, global warming, the war on terrorism, WMDs, or HIV/AIDS. Consult page SH16 of the Writing Handbook for additional help.

Prewriting
- Do library or Internet research to read about each of the topics listed above.
- Choose a topic that interests you.
- List questions about the topic and gather sources.

Drafting
- Develop your thesis and select persuasive arguments that support it.
- Organize and write the essay, using your second best argument in the introduction and your best argument in the conclusion.
- Be sure to include a personal appeal or an example that many people can relate to.

Revising
- Use the guidelines for revising your report on page SH17 of the Writing Handbook.

The Use of Alternative Energy

For many scientists, politicians, and citizens, energy consumption is a troubling issue. Most people agree that the world is too dependent on fossil fuels, which are not renewable. However, intense debate surrounds the questions of which alternate energy sources we should focus on and how quickly we need to have them developed.

Document A

U. S. Energy Consumption by Energy Source, 2007

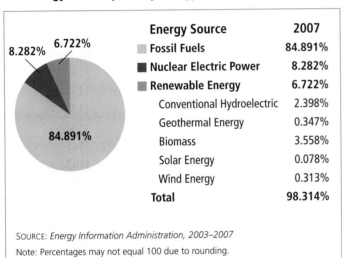

Energy Source	2007
Fossil Fuels	84.891%
Nuclear Electric Power	8.282%
Renewable Energy	6.722%
Conventional Hydroelectric	2.398%
Geothermal Energy	0.347%
Biomass	3.558%
Solar Energy	0.078%
Wind Energy	0.313%
Total	98.314%

8.282%   6.722%

84.891%

SOURCE: *Energy Information Administration, 2003–2007*
Note: Percentages may not equal 100 due to rounding.

Document B

"As we approach the end of the twentieth century there is no single thing we can do that will have as large an impact on the people of the world during the new century than the development of solar power satellites. They will bring prosperity, an opportunity for the poor nations of the earth to achieve true freedom from want, healing of our environment, and open the vast new frontier of space to all of us.

. . . With the development of solar power satellites we will tap directly into the power of the sun and save the world from impending chaos. There will be hope for the future as we enter the twenty-first century."

—From **Sun Power** by Ralph Nansen

Document C

"Renewables are not without their drawbacks. Solar and wind farms cannot generate much electricity on cloudy or still days. As intermittent energy sources, they require vast systems to store the energy they produce, or must rely on the rest of the electrical system for backup. And despite federal subsidies to spur technological innovation, renewable sources have not become economical enough to seriously challenge fossil fuels in an open market."

—From **CQ Researcher**, November 7, 1997

Analyzing Documents

Use your knowledge of global issues and Documents A, B, and C to answer questions 1–4.

1. Which document is supported by the actual U.S. energy consumption data shown in Document A?
   A Document B
   B Document C
   C both Documents B and C
   D neither Document B nor C

2. Which statement best describes the viewpoint of the author of Document B?
   A Biomass generators are a better alternative to fossil fuel than solar powered satellites.
   B Solar powered satellites are the most promising alternative to fossil fuel.
   C Solar powered satellites are not realistic or cost effective as an alternative to fossil fuel.
   D More research must be carried out to determine whether solar powered satellites are a realistic alternative to fossil fuel.

3. According to Document C, all are drawbacks of renewables except which of the following?
   A They are intermittent energy sources.
   B They are not cost-efficient.
   C They rely on traditional electricity sources.
   D They are worse for the environment.

4. **Writing Task** What does our energy future hold? Make some predictions for 50 years in the future. Use information from these documents along with information from the chapter to support your predictions.

Concept Connector Handbooks

Spanish doubloons

Lithuanian woman, 1991

Contents

The Concept Connector Handbooks provide you with reference information that will make it easier for you to compare key concepts and events across time and place.

Ancient Egypt

Great Wall of China

Detail of the Bayeux Tapestry

What Is Geography?

Geography is the study of Earth's features, including its people, their surroundings, and the resources available to them. By describing the human environment in different times and places, geographers have added to our knowledge of world history. Often geographers must draw conclusions from limited evidence. For example, studies might turn up common artistic styles or religious rituals in two widely separated groups of people. A geographer might conclude that the groups traded with each other and, in the process, developed shared cultural traits. Geographers use their favorite tool, the map, to show the results of their observations.

Landforms and Water Bodies

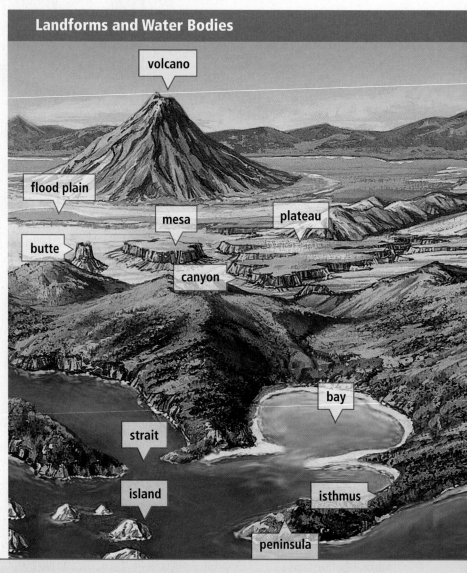

Glossary of Geographic Terms

basin
an area that is lower than surrounding land areas; some basins are filled with water

bay
a part of a larger body of water that extends into the land

butte
a small, high, flat-topped landform with cliff-like sides

canyon
a deep, narrow valley with steep sides; often has a stream flowing through it

cataract
a large waterfall or steep rapids

delta
a plain at the mouth of a river, often triangular in shape, formed when sediment is deposited by flowing water

flood plain
a broad plain on either side of a river, formed when sediment settles during floods

glacier
a huge, slow-moving mass of snow and ice

hill
an area that rises above surrounding land and has a rounded top; lower and usually less steep than a mountain

island
an area of land completely surrounded by water

isthmus
a narrow strip of land that connects two larger areas of land

mesa
a high, flat-topped landform with cliff-like sides; larger than a butte

mountain
a landform that rises steeply at least 2,000 feet (610 m) above surrounding land; usually wide at the bottom and rising to a narrow peak or ridge

mountain pass
a gap between mountains

peninsula
an area of land almost completely surrounded by water and connected to the mainland by an isthmus

plain
a large area of flat or gently rolling land

plateau
a large, flat area that rises above the surrounding land; at least one side has a steep slope

river mouth
the point where a river enters a lake or sea

strait
a narrow stretch of water that connects two larger bodies of water

tributary
a river or stream that flows into a larger river

valley
a low stretch of land between mountains or hills; land that is drained by a river

volcano
an opening in the Earth's surface through which molten rock, ashes, and gases from the Earth's interior escape

Atlas and Geography

The World: Political

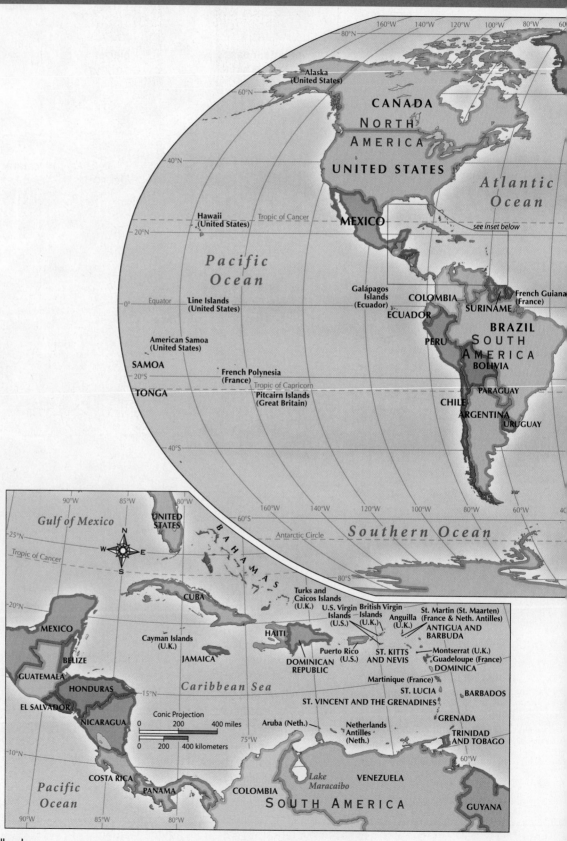

Robinson Projection

0 1000 2000 miles
0 1000 2000 kilometers

Azimuthal Equidistant Projection

0 200 400 miles
0 200 400 kilometers

Conic Projection

0 200 400 miles
0 200 400 kilometers

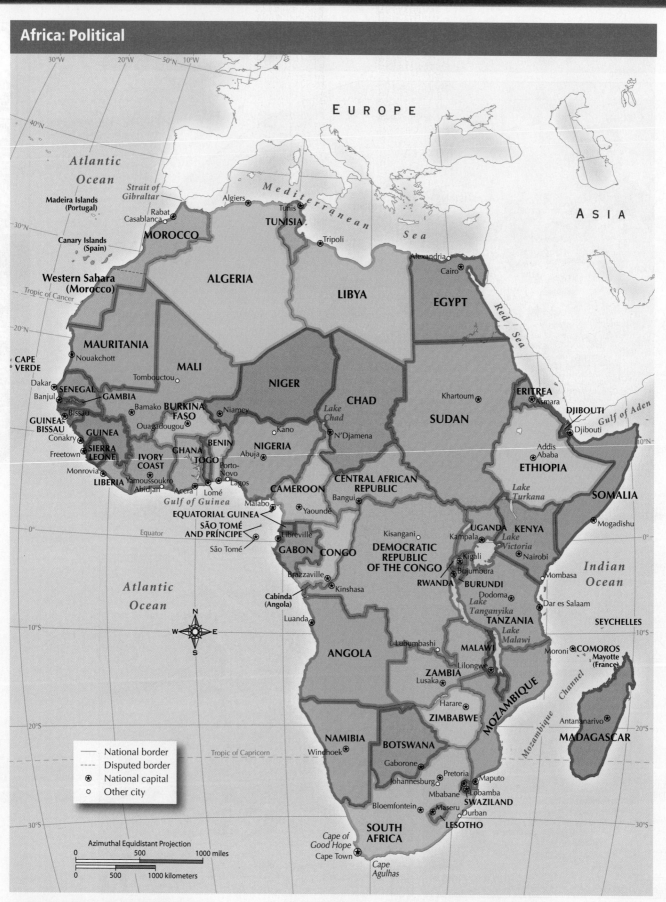

National border
Disputed border
⊛ National capital
○ Other city

Azimuthal Equidistant Projection

0   500   1000 miles
0   500   1000 kilometers

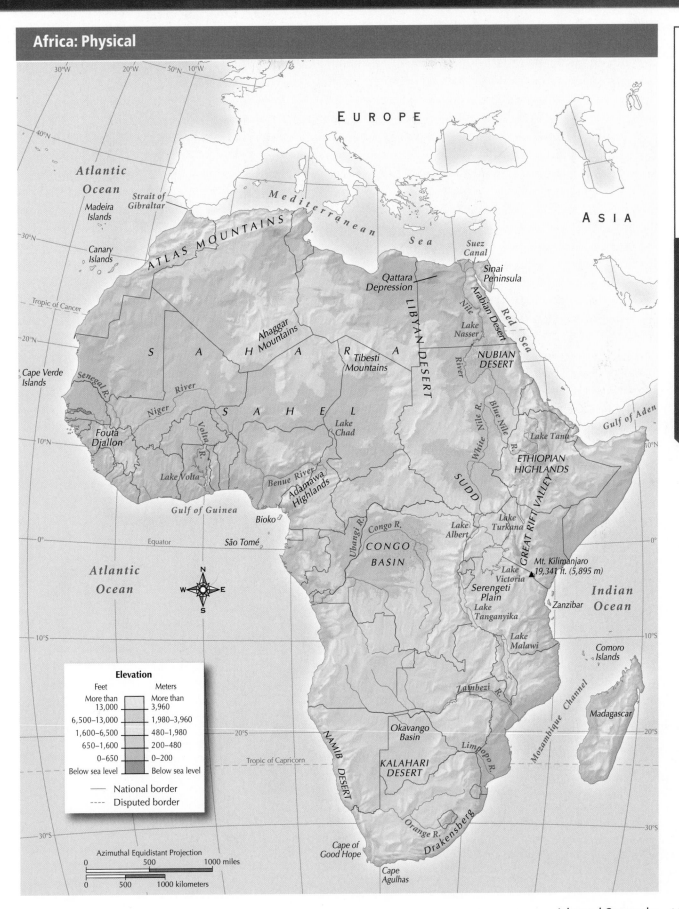

Africa: Physical

EUROPE

Atlantic Ocean

Madeira Islands

Strait of Gibraltar

Canary Islands

Mediterranean Sea

Suez Canal

Sinai Peninsula

ASIA

Qattara Depression

ATLAS MOUNTAINS

Cape Verde Islands

Senegal R.

Niger River

Fouta Djallon

S   A   H   A   R   A

Ahaggar Mountains

Tibesti Mountains

LIBYAN DESERT

Nile

Arabian Desert

Red Sea

Lake Nasser

NUBIAN DESERT

Gulf of Aden

S   A   H   E   L

Volta R.

Lake Chad

River

White Nile R.

Blue Nile R.

Lake Tana

ETHIOPIAN HIGHLANDS

Lake Volta

Benue River

Adamawa Highlands

SUDD

Gulf of Guinea

Bioko

Ubangi R.

Congo R.

Lake Albert

Lake Turkana

GREAT RIFT VALLEY

Mt. Kilimanjaro 19,341 ft. (5,895 m)

São Tomé

Equator

Atlantic Ocean

CONGO BASIN

Lake Victoria

Serengeti Plain

Zanzibar

Indian Ocean

Lake Tanganyika

Lake Malawi

Comoro Islands

Zambezi R.

Mozambique Channel

Madagascar

NAMIB DESERT

Okavango Basin

KALAHARI DESERT

Limpopo R.

Tropic of Capricorn

Elevation

Feet	Meters
More than 13,000	More than 3,960
6,500–13,000	1,980–3,960
1,600–6,500	480–1,980
650–1,600	200–480
0–650	0–200
Below sea level	Below sea level

—— National border
---- Disputed border

Orange R.

Drakensberg

Cape of Good Hope

Cape Agulhas

Azimuthal Equidistant Projection

0   500   1000 miles

0   500   1000 kilometers

Asia: Political

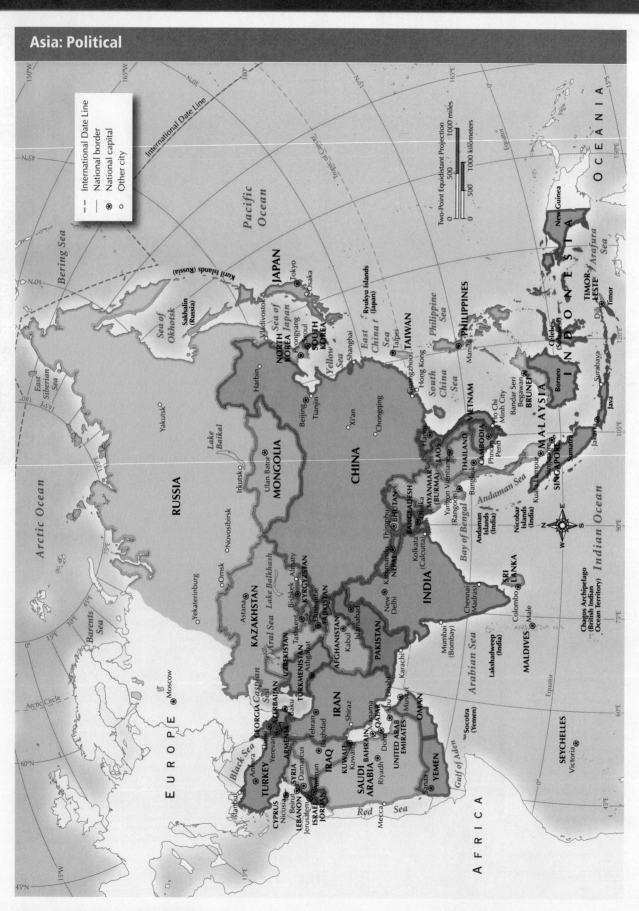

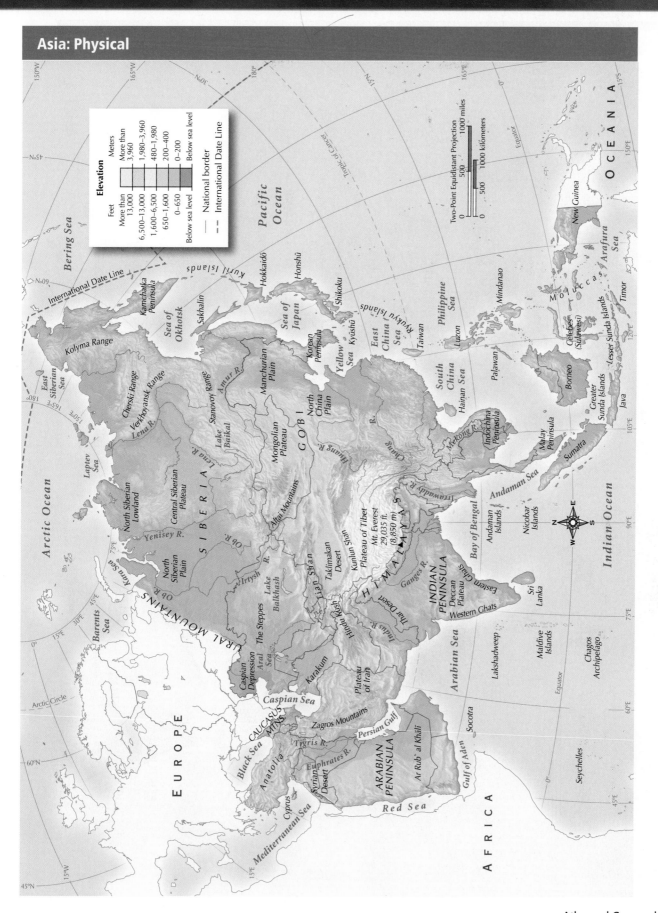

Asia: Physical

Elevation

Feet	Meters
More than 13,000	More than 3,960
6,500–13,000	1,980–3,960
1,600–6,500	480–1,980
650–1,600	200–400
0–650	0–200
Below sea level	Below sea level

— National border
- - - International Date Line

Two-Point Equidistant Projection

1000 miles
1000 kilometers

Pacific Ocean

Arctic Ocean

Bering Sea

International Date Line

Kamchatka Peninsula

Sea of Okhotsk

Kolyma Range

Kuril Islands

Sakhalin

Hokkaidō

Honshū

Sea of Japan

Shikoku

Kyūshū

Korean Peninsula

Yellow Sea

Ryūkyū Islands

Taiwan

East China Sea

Philippine Sea

Luzon

Mindanao

OCEANIA

New Guinea

Arafura Sea

Timor

Moluccas

Celebes (Sulawesi)

Lesser Sunda Islands

Borneo

Greater Sunda Islands

Java

Sumatra

Malay Peninsula

Indochina Peninsula

South China Sea

Hainan Sea

Palawan

Mekong R.

Chang Jiang R.

Irrawaddy R.

Andaman Sea

Andaman Islands

Nicobar Islands

Bay of Bengal

Indian Ocean

Cherski Range

Verkhoyansk Range

Stanovoy Range

Amur R.

Manchurian Plain

Lake Baikal

Mongolian Plateau

GOBI

North China Plain

Huang R.

Lena R.

SIBERIA

East Siberian Sea

Laptev Sea

North Siberian Lowland

Central Siberian Plateau

Yenisey R.

Ob R.

North Siberian Plain

Irtysh

Lake Balkhash

Altai Mountains

Tian Shan

Taklimakan Desert

Kunlun Shan

Plateau of Tibet

Mt. Everest 29,035 ft. (8,850 m)

HIMALAYAS

Ganges R.

INDIAN PENINSULA

Deccan Plateau

Eastern Ghats

Western Ghats

Sri Lanka

Thar Desert

Indus R.

Hindu Kush

Karakum

Aral Sea

The Steppes

Ob R.

URAL MOUNTAINS

Barents Sea

Kara Sea

Arctic Circle

EUROPE

Black Sea

Caspian Sea

Caspian Depression

Cyprus

Anatolia

Mediterranean Sea

CAUCASUS MTS.

Zagros Mountains

Tigris R.

Euphrates R.

Persian Gulf

ARABIAN PENINSULA

Ar Rub' al Khālī

Syrian Desert

Red Sea

Gulf of Aden

Socotra

Arabian Sea

Lakshadweep

Maldive Islands

Chagos Archipelago

Seychelles

AFRICA

Plateau of Iran

Tropic of Cancer

Equator

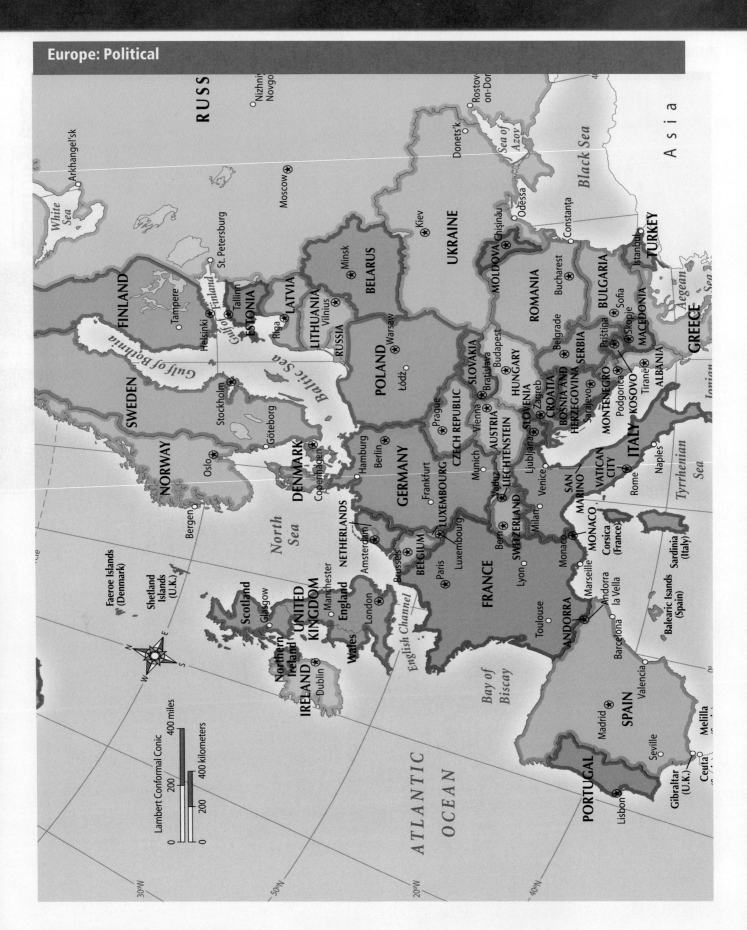

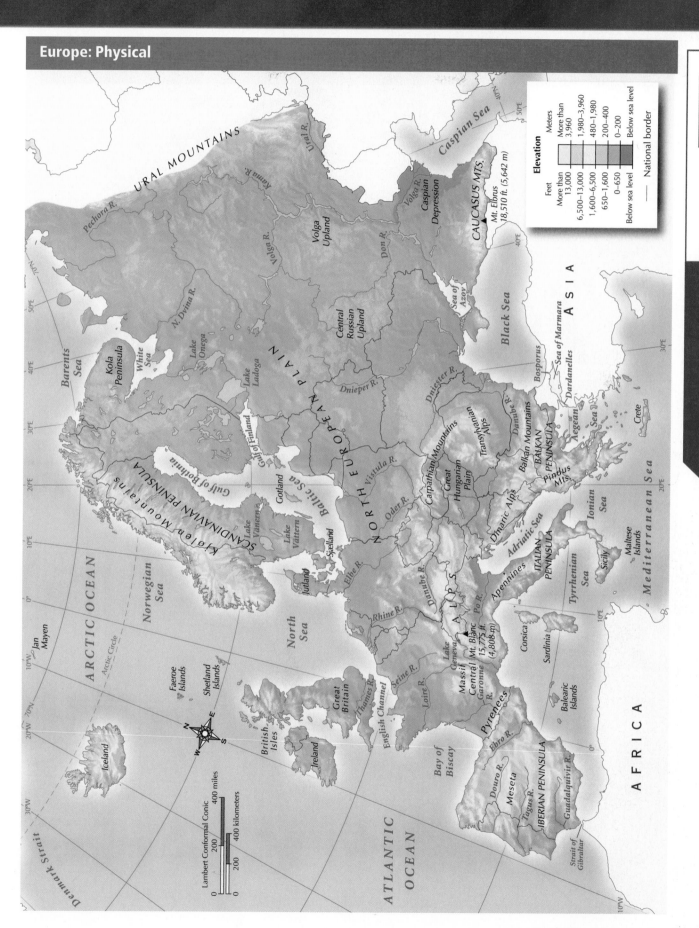

Elevation

Feet	Meters
More than 13,000	More than 3,960
6,500–13,000	1,980–3,960
1,600–6,500	480–1,980
650–1,600	200–400
0–650	0–200
Below sea level	Below sea level

— National border

URAL MOUNTAINS

Pechora R.

Kama R.

Ural R.

40°E

50°E

60°N

Caspian Sea

Caspian Depression

Volga R.

Volga Upland

Don R.

CAUCASUS MTS.

Mt. Elbrus 18,510 ft. (5,642 m)

40°E

50°E

Barents Sea

Kola Peninsula

White Sea

Lake Onega

Lake Ladoga

N. Dvina R.

Central Russian Upland

Dnieper R.

Sea of Azov

Black Sea

Sea of Marmara

Bosporus

Dardanelles

A S I A

30°E

N O R T H E U R O P E A N P L A I N

SCANDINAVIAN PENINSULA

Kjølen Mountains

Gulf of Finland

Gulf of Bothnia

Baltic Sea

Gotland

Lake Vänern

Lake Vättern

Sjælland

Jutland

Dniester R.

Vistula R.

Oder R.

Elbe R.

Carpathian Mountains

Great Hungarian Plain

Transylvanian Alps

Danube R.

Balkan Mountains

BALKAN PENINSULA

Pindus Mts.

Dinaric Alps

Adriatic Sea

Aegean Sea

Crete

Ionian Sea

Mediterranean Sea

30°E

20°E

Barents Sea

ARCTIC OCEAN

Arctic Circle

Norwegian Sea

Jan Mayen

Faeroe Islands

Shetland Islands

North Sea

Great Britain

English Channel

Thames R.

British Isles

Ireland

Iceland

Denmark Strait

70°W

60°W

50°W

40°W

30°W

20°W

10°W

ATLANTIC OCEAN

Bay of Biscay

Seine R.

Loire R.

Garonne R.

Massif Central

Lake Geneva

Mt. Blanc 15,775 ft. (4,808 m)

A L P S

Rhine R.

Danube R.

Po R.

Apennines

ITALIAN PENINSULA

Corsica

Sardinia

Tyrrhenian Sea

Sicily

Maltese Islands

Balearic Islands

10°E

0°

Pyrenees

Ebro R.

Douro R.

Meseta

Tagus R.

IBERIAN PENINSULA

Guadalquivir R.

Strait of Gibraltar

A F R I C A

Lambert Conformal Conic

400 miles

200

0

400 kilometers

200

0

N E S W

North and South America: Political

National border

International Date Line

⊛ National capital

○ Other city

Lambert Azimuthal Equal-Area Projection

0   1000   2000 miles

0   1000   2000 kilometers

North and South America: Physical

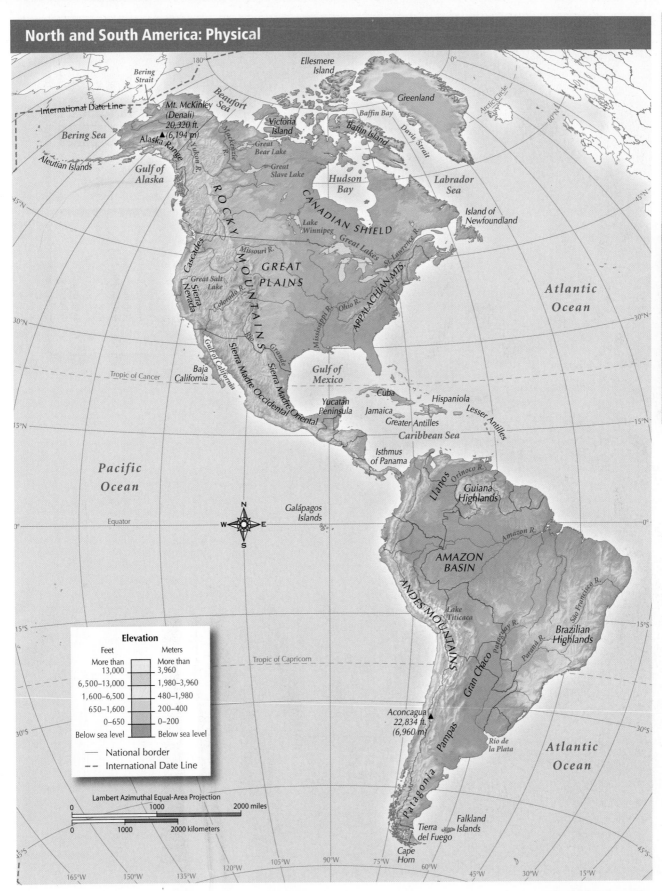

Elevation

Feet	Meters
More than 13,000	More than 3,960
6,500–13,000	1,980–3,960
1,600–6,500	480–1,980
650–1,600	200–400
0–650	0–200
Below sea level	Below sea level

— National border
-- International Date Line

Lambert Azimuthal Equal-Area Projection

0   1000   2000 miles

0   1000   2000 kilometers

Australia, New Zealand, and Oceania: Political-Physical

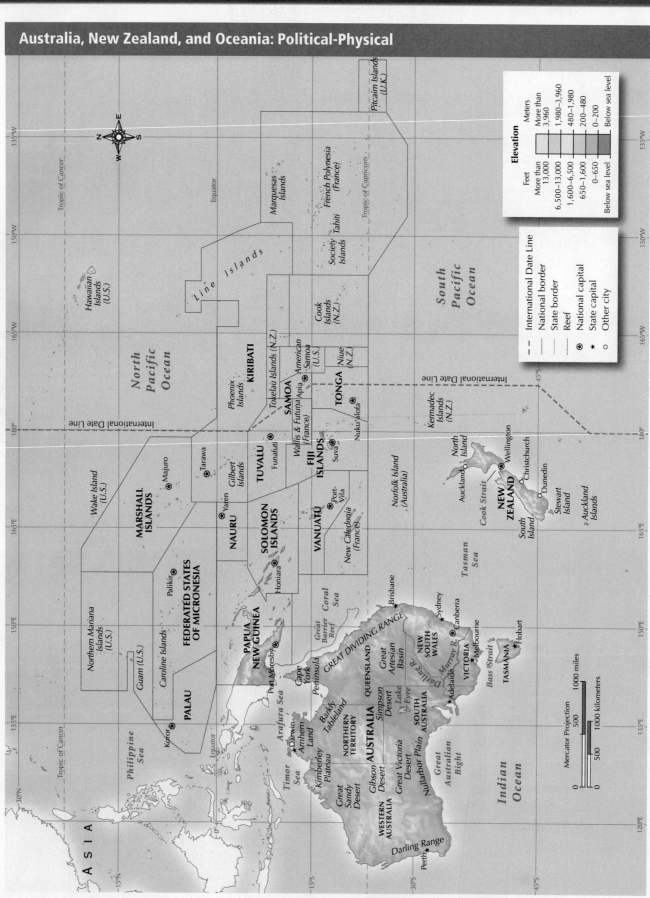

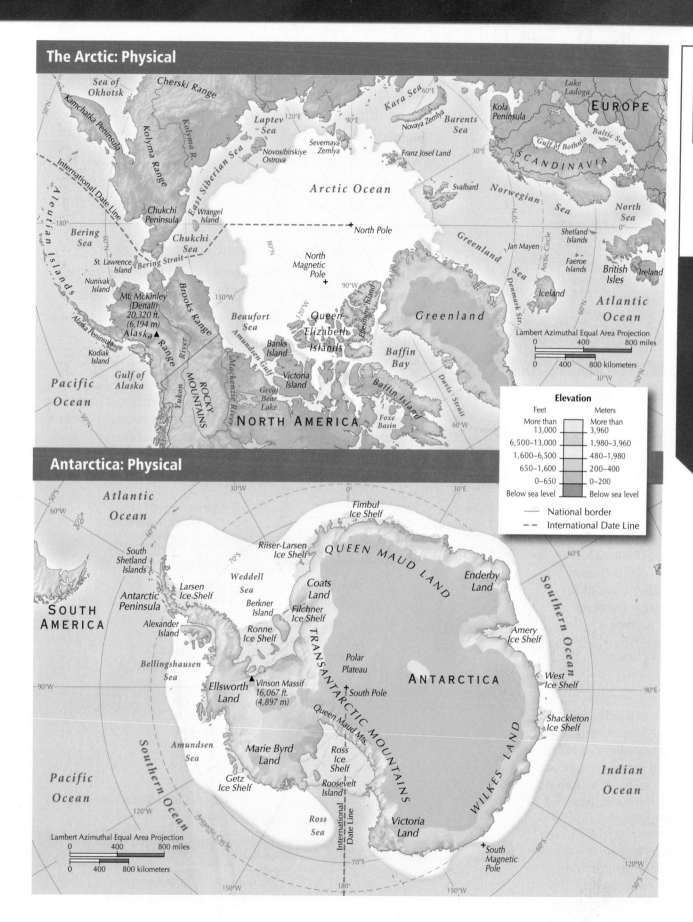

The Arctic: Physical

Sea of Okhotsk
Cherski Range
Kamchatka Peninsula
Kolyma Range
Kolyma R.
Laptev Sea
120°E
Kara Sea
60°E
Kola Peninsula
Lake Ladoga
EUROPE
Novaya Zemlya
Barents Sea
90°E
Severnaya Zemlya
Franz Josef Land
30°E
SCANDINAVIA
Gulf of Bothnia
Baltic Sea
Novosibirskiye Ostrova
East Siberian Sea
Arctic Ocean
Svalbard
Norwegian Sea
North Sea
International Date Line
Aleutian Islands
Chukchi Peninsula
Wrangel Island
North Pole
70°N
0°
Greenland Sea
Jan Mayen
Arctic Circle
Shetland Islands
Bering Sea
Chukchi Sea
North Magnetic Pole
Faeroe Islands
British Isles
Ireland
St. Lawrence Island
Bering Strait
90°W
Iceland
Denmark Str.
60°N
Atlantic Ocean
Nunivak Island
150°W
Ellesmere Island
Mt. McKinley (Denali) 20,320 ft. (6,194 m)
Brooks Range
Beaufort Sea
120°W
Queen Elizabeth Islands
Greenland
Baffin Bay
30°W
Alaska Peninsula
Alaska Range
Yukon River
Banks Island
Amundsen Gulf
Davis Strait
Kodiak Island
ROCKY MOUNTAINS
Mackenzie River
Victoria Island
Baffin Island
Pacific Ocean
Gulf of Alaska
Great Bear Lake
Foxe Basin
60°W
NORTH AMERICA

Lambert Azimuthal Equal Area Projection
0   400   800 miles
0   400   800 kilometers

Elevation

Feet	Meters
More than 13,000	More than 3,960
6,500–13,000	1,980–3,960
1,600–6,500	480–1,980
650–1,600	200–400
0–650	0–200
Below sea level	Below sea level

——— National border
– – – International Date Line

Antarctica: Physical

Atlantic Ocean
50°S
60°W
30°W
Fimbul Ice Shelf
30°E
South Shetland Islands
60°S
70°S
Riiser-Larsen Ice Shelf
QUEEN MAUD LAND
Enderby Land
60°E
Weddell Sea
Coats Land
Larsen Ice Shelf
Antarctic Peninsula
Berkner Island
Filchner Ice Shelf
Amery Ice Shelf
Alexander Island
Ronne Ice Shelf
Southern Ocean
Bellingshausen Sea
TRANSANTARCTIC MOUNTAINS
Polar Plateau
ANTARCTICA
West Ice Shelf
90°W
Ellsworth Land
Vinson Massif 16,067 ft. (4,897 m)
South Pole
90°E
Queen Maud Mts.
Shackleton Ice Shelf
Amundsen Sea
Marie Byrd Land
Ross Ice Shelf
WILKES LAND
Indian Ocean
Pacific Ocean
Getz Ice Shelf
Roosevelt Island
International Date Line
120°W
Victoria Land
Southern Ocean
Antarctic Circle
Ross Sea
South Magnetic Pole
60°S
SOUTH AMERICA

Lambert Azimuthal Equal Area Projection
0   400   800 miles
0   400   800 kilometers

120°W
150°W
180°
150°E
70°S

History

History and Prehistory

You might think of history as everything that has ever happened. For historians, however, history began around 5,000 years ago with the appearance of writing in two civilizations—Sumer and Egypt. Everything before that is prehistory.

Prehistory   **3000 B.C.**   **History**

Writing systems appear in Sumer (above) and in Egypt c. 3000 B.C.*

* The c. before the date is Latin for *circa*, meaning ìaround " or "approximately."

Historians study how people lived in the past. They might examine their tools, weapons, jewelry, and building sites, but they rely mainly on written records. For this reason, we say that history began when writing began.

History is a changing story. A historian living at the time of an event may write what seems like a valid description, but a historian writing 100 years later may describe the same event another way entirely. This is because different generations have different perspectives on, or ways of looking at, history. In addition, as time passes, new evidence may appear to alter the interpretation of an event.

Major Eras in World History

Historians attempt to make sense of vast stretches of history by dividing them into periods. This periodization makes it easier to discuss a group of events by relating them to a broader theme.

Technology Periodization
This model of periodization divides history according to the technology that drove economic progress.

Western Periodization
This model of periodization reflects a European perspective. Classical generally refers to the Greek and Roman civilizations. Middle Ages refers to Europe between the fall of Rome and the Renaissance.

Global Periodization
This model of periodization reflects a more global perspective.

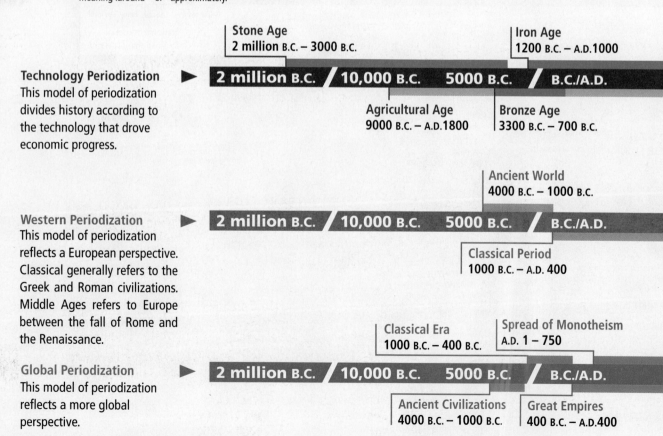

Stone Age
2 million B.C. – 3000 B.C.

Iron Age
1200 B.C. – A.D.1000

Agricultural Age
9000 B.C. – A.D.1800

Bronze Age
3300 B.C. – 700 B.C.

Ancient World
4000 B.C. – 1000 B.C.

Classical Period
1000 B.C. – A.D. 400

Classical Era
1000 B.C. – 400 B.C.

Spread of Monotheism
A.D. 1 – 750

Ancient Civilizations
4000 B.C. – 1000 B.C.

Great Empires
400 B.C. – A.D.400

Your textbook is divided this way, into units. Each unit deals with a period, or era, in world history. There are endless ways to categorize the past, depending on one's point of view. The time-lines below show three different examples of periodization.

Decades, Centuries, and Millenniums

Most nations today use a standard calendar that dates events from the believed birth of Jesus. For dates preceding his birth, this calendar uses the abbreviation B.C. ("before Christ"). For dates after his birth, it uses A.D. (anno Domini, Latin for "in the year of our Lord"). An alternative version of this calendar uses the abbreviations B.C.E. and C.E., meaning "Before the Common Era" and "Common Era."

| B.C. | 1 B.C./A.D. 1 | A.D. 100 | A.D. 200 | A.D. 300 | A.D. 400 |

Decade = 10 Years

Century = 100 Years
10 Centuries = 1000 years = 1 millennium
What we call the "Third Century" is the 200s, just as the "Twentieth Century" is the 1900s.

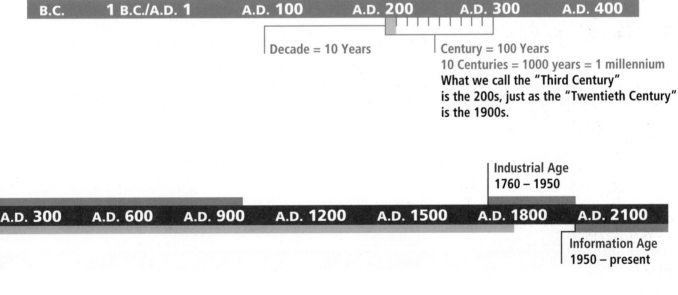

Industrial Age 1760 – 1950

| A.D. 300 | A.D. 600 | A.D. 900 | A.D. 1200 | A.D. 1500 | A.D. 1800 | A.D. 2100 |

Information Age 1950 – present

Middle Ages A.D. 400 – A.D. 1300

| A.D. 300 | A.D. 600 | A.D. 900 | A.D. 1200 | A.D. 1500 | A.D. 1800 | A.D. 2100 |

Modern Era A.D. 1300 – present

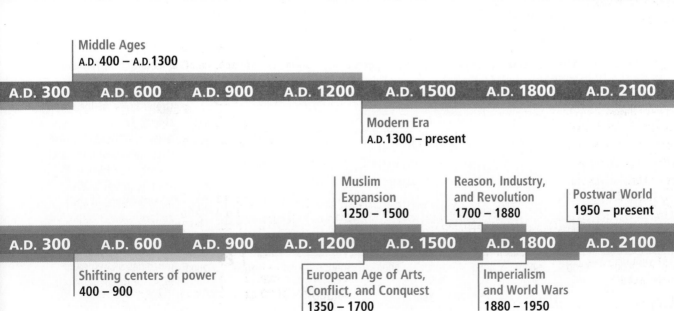

Muslim Expansion 1250 – 1500

Reason, Industry, and Revolution 1700 – 1880

Postwar World 1950 – present

| A.D. 300 | A.D. 600 | A.D. 900 | A.D. 1200 | A.D. 1500 | A.D. 1800 | A.D. 2100 |

Shifting centers of power 400 – 900

European Age of Arts, Conflict, and Conquest 1350 – 1700

Imperialism and World Wars 1880 – 1950

History

World Regional Timelines

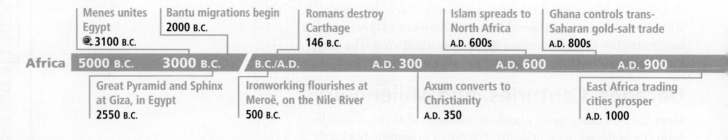

Africa

Menes unites Egypt
🔍 3100 B.C.

Bantu migrations begin
2000 B.C.

Romans destroy Carthage
146 B.C.

Islam spreads to North Africa
A.D. 600s

Ghana controls trans-Saharan gold-salt trade
A.D. 800s

Great Pyramid and Sphinx at Giza, in Egypt
2550 B.C.

Ironworking flourishes at Meroë, on the Nile River
500 B.C.

Axum converts to Christianity
A.D. 350

East Africa trading cities prosper
A.D. 1000

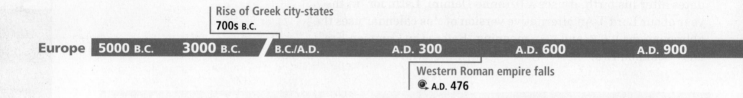

Europe

Rise of Greek city-states
700s B.C.

Western Roman empire falls
🔍 A.D. 476

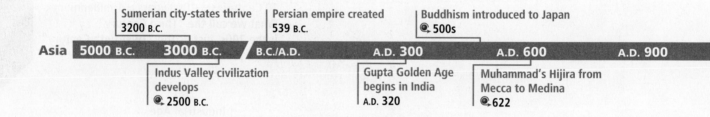

Asia

Sumerian city-states thrive
3200 B.C.

Persian empire created
539 B.C.

Buddhism introduced to Japan
🔍 500s

Indus Valley civilization develops
🔍 2500 B.C.

Gupta Golden Age begins in India
A.D. 320

Muhammad's Hijira from Mecca to Medina
🔍 622

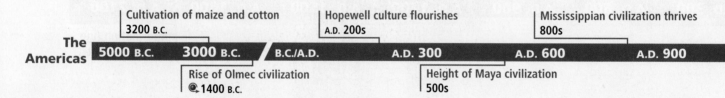

The Americas

Cultivation of maize and cotton
3200 B.C.

Hopewell culture flourishes
A.D. 200s

Mississippian civilization thrives
800s

Rise of Olmec civilization
🔍 1400 B.C.

Height of Maya civilization
500s

🔍 Turning point: a decisive moment in world history that triggers a major social, political, economic, or cultural transformation.

World Population Growth

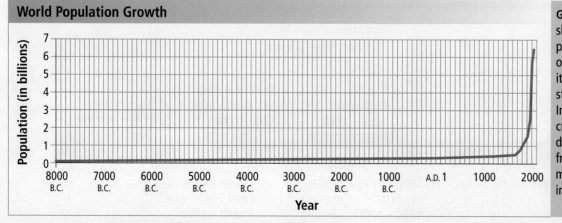

Graph Skills As the graph shows, the world's population gradually rose over many centuries, until it shot up suddenly, starting in the 1700s. Improvements in agriculture, greater control of disease, and the shift from manual labor to machines all helped to increase the population.

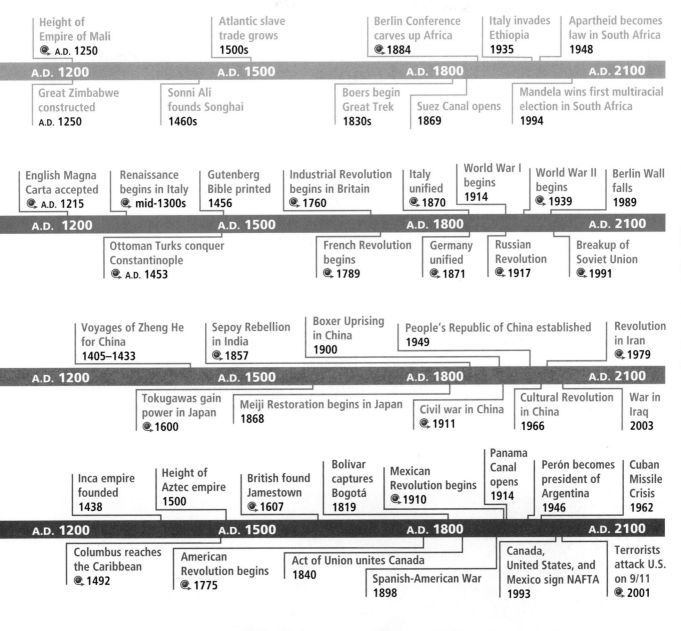

Height of Empire of Mali
A.D. **1250**

Atlantic slave trade grows
1500s

Berlin Conference carves up Africa
1884

Italy invades Ethiopia
1935

Apartheid becomes law in South Africa
1948

A.D. **1200**　　A.D. **1500**　　A.D. **1800**　　A.D. **2100**

Great Zimbabwe constructed
A.D. **1250**

Sonni Ali founds Songhai
1460s

Boers begin Great Trek
1830s

Suez Canal opens
1869

Mandela wins first multiracial election in South Africa
1994

English Magna Carta accepted
A.D. **1215**

Renaissance begins in Italy
mid-1300s

Gutenberg Bible printed
1456

Industrial Revolution begins in Britain
1760

Italy unified
1870

World War I begins
1914

World War II begins
1939

Berlin Wall falls
1989

A.D. **1200**　　A.D. **1500**　　A.D. **1800**　　A.D. **2100**

Ottoman Turks conquer Constantinople
A.D. **1453**

French Revolution begins
1789

Germany unified
1871

Russian Revolution
1917

Breakup of Soviet Union
1991

Voyages of Zheng He for China
1405–1433

Sepoy Rebellion in India
1857

Boxer Uprising in China
1900

People's Republic of China established
1949

Revolution in Iran
1979

A.D. **1200**　　A.D. **1500**　　A.D. **1800**　　A.D. **2100**

Tokugawas gain power in Japan
1600

Meiji Restoration begins in Japan
1868

Civil war in China
1911

Cultural Revolution in China
1966

War in Iraq
2003

Inca empire founded
1438

Height of Aztec empire
1500

British found Jamestown
1607

Bolívar captures Bogotá
1819

Mexican Revolution begins
1910

Panama Canal opens
1914

Perón becomes president of Argentina
1946

Cuban Missile Crisis
1962

A.D. **1200**　　A.D. **1500**　　A.D. **1800**　　A.D. **2100**

Columbus reaches the Caribbean
1492

American Revolution begins
1775

Act of Union unites Canada
1840

Spanish-American War
1898

Canada, United States, and Mexico sign NAFTA
1993

Terrorists attack U.S. on 9/11
2001

The Parthenon, Athens, Greece

History

Flag of Giovine
Italia, 1833

Imperialism, Colonialism, Nationalism, and Revolution

Imperialism
A policy of pursuing, often through conquest, the economic and political domination of another state.

Colonialism
A policy of politically dominating a dependent territory or people.

↓   ↓

Nationalism
A strong feeling of pride in, or devotion to, one's nation.

↓

Revolution
The overthrow of a government from within.

Conquest and Empire

An empire is a group of states or territories controlled by one ruler. Empires often form in a haphazard way. For example, a small state with a strong army successfully defends itself against one neighboring state after another and incorporates their lands. Or at some point, an able ruler aggressively seeks more territory. Over time, the state expands into an empire. A strong military and able leadership are two factors that go into creating an empire. However, successful empires also must develop a government system that can maintain control of conquered peoples.

First Landing of Columbus by Frederick Kemmelmeyer

Selected Empires in World History

Conquests	Time Span	Location
Roman	509 B.C.–A.D. 180	Mediterranean region, Western Europe, Britain
Arab Muslim	A.D. 624–750	Southwest Asia, North Africa, Spain
Mongol	1206–1294	China, Central Asia, Eastern Europe
Ottoman	1299–1566	Southwest Asia, North Africa, Balkans, Eastern Europe
Spanish	1492–1560	Mexico, Central America, South America, Cuba, Florida

Major Conflicts in World History

This table shows selected major wars and conquests. Hundreds of other conflicts, large and small, have occurred throughout history. The cause of a conflict may be as simple as "I want what you have." For example, the basic need for food—and the land to grow it on—has been a prime cause of war. But most of the time, the reasons for wars are more complex. They can involve intertwining economic, political, religious, and cultural forces.

A sans-culotte figure from the French Revolutionary period

Selected Conflicts in World History

Conflict	Time Span	Location	Combatants
Persian Wars	499–448 B.C.	Greece	Greeks vs. Persians
Peloponnesian War	431–404 B.C.	Greece	Athens vs. Sparta
Punic Wars	264–146 B.C.	Mediterranean region	Rome vs. Carthage
Crusades	A.D. 1096–1291	Southwest Asia	Christians vs. Muslims
Hundred Years' War	1337–1443	France	England vs. France
Wars of King Philip II	1571–1588	Europe	Spain vs. Dutch Netherlands; Spain vs. England
Thirty Years' War	1618–1648	Central Europe (German states)	Holy Roman Empire, Spain, Poland, and others vs. Netherlands, Sweden, France, and others
English Civil War	1642–1649	England	Parliament (Roundheads) vs. Charles I and supporters (Cavaliers)
Seven Years' War (includes French and Indian War)	1756–1763	Europe; North America; India	Austria, Russia, and France vs. Prussia and Britain; Britain and its American colonies vs. France and its Native American allies; Britain vs. France
American Revolution	1775–1783	North America	Britain vs. its American colonies
French Revolution	1789–1799	France	Reformers (mainly middle class and peasants) vs. Louis XVI and supporters (mainly nobles and clergy)
Napoleonic Wars (end of the French Revolution)	1799–1815	Europe	France vs. combined European powers
Latin American Wars of Independence	1802–1824	Latin America	Colonies in Latin America vs. France and Spain
American Civil War	1860–1865	United States	North (Unionists) vs. South (Secessionists)
World War I	1914–1918	Europe (mainly France and Russia)	Allied powers vs. Central powers
World War II	1939–1945	North Africa, Europe, East Asia, Pacific Islands	Allies vs. Axis powers
Korean War	1950–1953	Korea	North Korea and China vs. South Korea and United States
Vietnam War	1959–1975	Vietnam	North Vietnam vs. South Vietnam and the United States

Regional Organizations

Through treaties, nations with common regional interests often work together to improve themselves politically, economically, and socially.

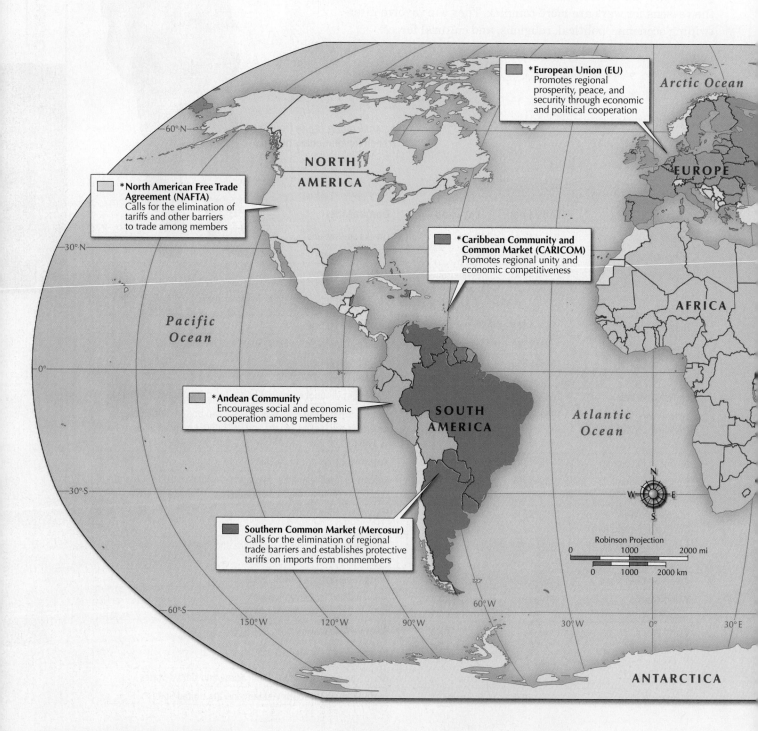

*European Union (EU)
Promotes regional prosperity, peace, and security through economic and political cooperation

*North American Free Trade Agreement (NAFTA)
Calls for the elimination of tariffs and other barriers to trade among members

*Caribbean Community and Common Market (CARICOM)
Promotes regional unity and economic competitiveness

*Andean Community
Encourages social and economic cooperation among members

Southern Common Market (Mercosur)
Calls for the elimination of regional trade barriers and establishes protective tariffs on imports from nonmembers

Robinson Projection

0   1000   2000 mi

0   1000   2000 km

NORTH AMERICA

SOUTH AMERICA

EUROPE

AFRICA

Arctic Ocean

Pacific Ocean

Atlantic Ocean

ANTARCTICA

International Organizations

These organizations promote cooperation across regions:

- Arab League
- International Monetary Fund (IMF)
- North Atlantic Treaty Organization (NATO)
- Organization for Economic Cooperation and Development (OECD)
- Organization of American States (OAS)
- Organization of Petroleum Exporting Countries (OPEC)
- United Nations (UN)
- World Trade Organization (WTO)

The United Nations

Of all the organizations in the world, the UN stands out as the main coordinator of international activities. With the support of its 191 member nations, the UN plays a vital, ongoing role in keeping the peace, fighting disease, promoting economic development, and providing humanitarian aid.

International aid poured into Indonesia following the December 2004 tsunami. Here an American navy pilot delivers supplies from the United States Agency for International Development (USAID), an independent federal agency.

Commonwealth of Independent States (CIS)
Encourages regional economic cooperation and the coordination of foreign and immigration policies

ASIA

*South Asian Association for Regional Cooperation (SAARC)
Provides a platform for working together to accelerate economic and social development

Pacific Ocean

Gulf Cooperation Council (GCC)
Promotes regional unity through coordination of economic and defense policies

Indian Ocean

AUSTRALIA

African Union (formerly Organization of African Unity)
Promotes unity, democracy, and economic development among member states

*Association of Southeast Asian Nations (ASEAN)
Seeks to advance economic cooperation, trade, and joint research and to promote peace and security in the region

°E   90°E   120°E   150°E

*Free trade zone

Economics

Three Key Economic Questions		
What goods and services should be produced?	How should goods and services be produced?	Who consumes the goods and services?
How much of our resources should we devote to national defense, education, public health, or consumer goods? Which consumer goods should we produce?	Should we produce food on large corporate farms or on small family farms? Should we produce electricity with oil, nuclear power, coal, or solar power?	How do goods and services get distributed? The question of who gets to consume which goods and services lies at the very heart of the differences between economic systems. Each society answers the question of distribution based on its combination of social values and goals.

In 1923, due to the collapse of German currency, it was cheaper to paper a wall with Deutsche marks than it was to buy wallpaper.

In every society throughout history, people have had access to resources, such as water, fertile land, and human labor. Yet everywhere in the world, people's resources are limited. Economics is the study of how people choose to use their limited resources to meet their wants and needs.

Until modern times, people focused largely on resources related to agriculture. They farmed the land to produce food, mainly for their own consumption. This traditional way of meeting basic needs still defines some economies today. However, modern societies have also developed other economic systems to deal with the complexities of expanding trade and industrialization. An economic system is the method used by a society to produce and distribute goods and services.

Basic Economic Questions

Through its economic system, society answers three key questions. How a society answers these questions depends on how much it values different economic goals. Four different economic systems have developed in response to these three questions.

Economic Goals	
Economic efficiency	Making the most of resources
Economic freedom	Freedom from government intervention in the production and distribution of goods and services
Economic security and predictability	Assurance that goods and services will be available, payments will be made on time, and a safety net will protect individuals in times of economic disaster
Economic equity	Fair distribution of wealth
Economic growth and innovation	Innovation leads to economic growth, and economic growth leads to a higher standard of living.
Other goals	Societies pursue additional goals, such as environmental protection.

Modern Economic Systems

A society's economic system reflects how that society answers the three key economic questions. Different systems produce different results in terms of productivity, the welfare of workers, and consumer choice. This table provides information about the main economic systems in the world today.

A Grameen Bank officer meets with loan recipients in India.

Modern Economic Systems

	Description	Origin	Location Today
Traditional	People make economic decisions based on custom or habit. They produce what they have always produced and just as much as they need, using long-established methods.	Accompanied the rise of agriculture and home crafts	Mainly in rural areas within developing nations
Market (Capitalist, Free-Enterprise)	Economic decisions are made in the marketplace through interactions between buyers and sellers according to the laws of supply and demand. Individual capitalists own the means of production. Government regulates some economic activities and provides such "public goods" as education.	Capitalism has existed since the earliest buying and selling of goods in a market. The market economic system developed in response to Adam Smith's ideas and the shift from agriculture to industry in the 1800s.	Canada, Germany, Japan, United States, and a handful of other nations
Centrally Planned (Command, Socialist, Communist)	Central government planners make most economic decisions for the people. In theory, the workers own the means of production. In practice, the government does. Some private enterprise, but government dominates.	In the 1800s, criticism of capitalism by Karl Marx and others led to calls for distributing wealth according to need. After the 1917 Russian Revolution, the Soviet Union developed the first command economy.	Communist countries, including China, Cuba, North Korea, and Vietnam
Mixed (Social Democratic, Liberal Socialist)	A mix of socialism and free enterprise in which the government plays a significant role in making economic decisions.	The Great Depression of the 1930s ended laissez-faire capitalism in most countries. People insisted that government take a stronger role in fixing economic problems. The fall of communism in Eastern Europe in the 1990s ended central planning in most countries. People insisted on freer markets.	Most nations, including Brazil, France, India, Italy, Poland, Russia, Sweden, and the United Kingdom

Economics

Major Trade Organizations

This map shows the major regional trade associations in the world today. In addition, 147 countries belong to the World Trade Organization (WTO). The WTO works to encourage trade by reducing tariffs, promoting international agreements, and mediating trade disputes among member nations.

This illustration represents the cooperation among nations involved in NAFTA.

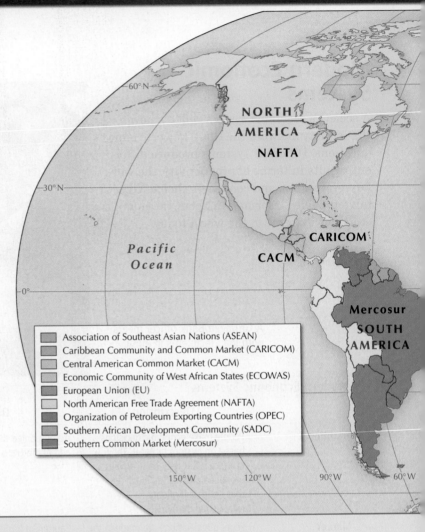

- Association of Southeast Asian Nations (ASEAN)
- Caribbean Community and Common Market (CARICOM)
- Central American Common Market (CACM)
- Economic Community of West African States (ECOWAS)
- European Union (EU)
- North American Free Trade Agreement (NAFTA)
- Organization of Petroleum Exporting Countries (OPEC)
- Southern African Development Community (SADC)
- Southern Common Market (Mercosur)

Glossary of Economic Terms

barter
the direct exchange of one set of goods or services for another

budget
a plan for income and spending

capital
any human-made resource that is used to create other goods or services

communism
a political system characterized by a centrally planned economy with all economic and political power resting in the hands of the central government

currency
coins and paper bills used as money

depression
a recession that is especially long and severe

developed nation
industrialized country with a higher average level of material well-being

developing nation
country with limited industrialization and a lower average level of material well-being

economic system
the method used by a society to produce and distribute goods and services

entrepreneur
ambitious leader who combines land, labor, and capital to create and market new goods or services

export
a good that is sent to another country for sale

free enterprise
an economic system that permits the conduct of business with minimal government intervention

goods
physical objects such as clothes or shoes

import
a good that is brought in from another country for sale

industrialization
the extensive organization of an economy for the purpose of manufacturing

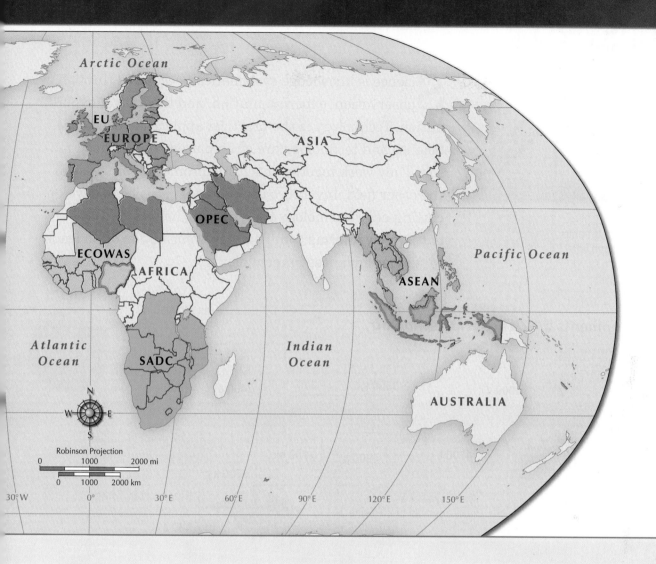

inflation
a general increase in prices

law of demand
economic law that states that consumers buy more of a good when its price decreases and less when its price increases

law of supply
tendency of suppliers to offer more of a good at a higher price

market
an arrangement that allows buyers and sellers to exchange things

market economy
economic system in which decisions on production and consumption of goods and services are based on voluntary exchange in markets

mixed economy
economic system that combines tradition and the free market with limited government involvement

opportunity cost
the most desirable alternative given up as the result of a decision

recession
a prolonged economic contraction

scarcity
limited quantities of resources to meet unlimited wants

socialism
a social and political philosophy based on the belief that democratic means should be used to evenly distribute wealth throughout a society.

tariff
a tax on imported goods

tax
a required payment to a government

traditional economy
economic system that relies on habit, custom, or ritual to decide questions of production and consumption of goods and services

welfare
government aid to the poor

Science and Technology

Science is knowledge systematically acquired through observation, experimentation, and theoretical explanation. Technology is the practical application of science. Science and technology are often paired, and for good reason. They work together, each one promoting progress in the other field. Inventors use the latest science to develop cutting-edge technology that, in turn, helps scientists gather new information. That new information often leads to further advances in technology.

▲ Egyptian A-frame
and plumb line

Coin showing
Alexander the Great ▶

■ Key Developments in Science and Technology

Science and Technology

Copper tools and ornaments	Light wooden plow	Kiln-fired bricks, pots	Irrigation	Iron weapons
10,000 B.C.	4000 B.C.	3500 B.C.	2400 B.C.	1400 B.C.

10,000 B.C. — **5000 B.C.** — **B.C. / A.D.**

Widespread domestication of plants and animals	Bronze objects	Dam	Pyramids	Plumbing, water pipes, sewer drains	Coins
9000–6000 B.C.	4500 B.C.	4000 B.C.	2800 B.C.	2700 B.C.	600 B.C.

Medicine

Greek symbol of peace, now a symbol of medicine ▶

Hippocrates, father of medicine, born
460 B.C.

10,000 B.C. — **5000 B.C.** — **B.C. / A.D.**

Greek physician Galen born
A.D. **130**

Egyptian cursive writing on papyrus ▼

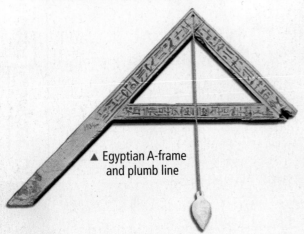

Communication

Pictographs	Writing	Alphabet	Paper
3500 B.C.	3200 B.C.	1700 B.C.	A.D. 105

10,000 B.C. — **5000 B.C.** — **B.C. / A.D.**

Papyrus
2800 B.C.

Transportation

Ancient dugout canoe	Wheeled cart from Sumer	Roman chariot
c. 6000 B.C.	c. 3500 B.C.	c. A.D. 1

10,000 B.C. — **5000 B.C.** — **B.C. / A.D.**

Portuguese square-sailed ship ▶

Square-sailed ships
3000 B.C.

◄ Italian compass

▼ Seed drill

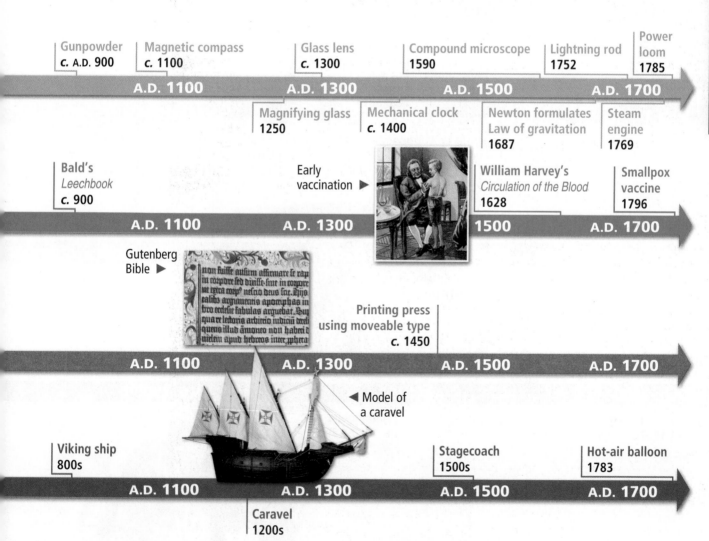

Gunpowder	Magnetic compass		Glass lens		Compound microscope	Lightning rod	Power loom
c. A.D. 900	*c.* 1100		*c.* 1300		1590	1752	1785

A.D. 1100 — **A.D. 1300** — **A.D. 1500** — **A.D. 1700**

		Magnifying glass	Mechanical clock	Newton formulates Law of gravitation	Steam engine
		1250	*c.* 1400	1687	1769

Bald's *Leechbook*		Early vaccination ►		William Harvey's *Circulation of the Blood*	Smallpox vaccine
c. 900				1628	1796

A.D. 1100 — **A.D. 1300** — **1500** — **A.D. 1700**

Gutenberg Bible ►

Printing press using moveable type
c. 1450

A.D. 1100 — **A.D. 1300** — **A.D. 1500** — **A.D. 1700**

◄ Model of a caravel

Viking ship			Stagecoach	Hot-air balloon
800s			1500s	1783

A.D. 1100 — **A.D. 1300** — **A.D. 1500** — **A.D. 1700**

Caravel
1200s

Science and Technology

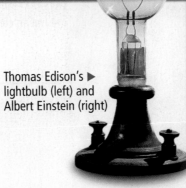

Thomas Edison's ▶
lightbulb (left) and
Albert Einstein (right)

Science and Technology

| | Electric motor **1821** | | Theory of evolution **1849** | | Incandescent lamp **1879** | | Quantum theory **1900** | Frozen food **1924** |

A.D. 1800 — **A.D. 1850** — **A.D. 1900**

Canning of food **1809** | Mechanical reaper **1843** | Special Theory of Relativity **1905** | Plastics **1909** | Liquid fuel rocket **1926**

Medicine

| | Anesthesia **1842** | Pasteurization of milk **1865** | Antiseptic surgery **1867** | Diphtheria antitoxin **1891** | Typhus vaccine **1909** |

A.D. 1800 — **A.D. 1850** — **A.D. 1900**

Government focus on improving hygiene and public sanitation **1850–1950** | Genetics; laws of heredity **1866** | Rabies vaccine **1885** | X-ray **1895** | Penicillin, first antibiotic **1928**

Communication

| | Telegraph **1837** | | Radio **1895** |

A.D. 1800 — **A.D. 1850** — **A.D. 1900**

Telephone **1846** | ◄ Early telephone | Electronic television **1927**

Transportation

| | Steam locomotive **1825** | | Biplane **1903** |

A.D. 1800 — **A.D.1850** — **A.D. 1900**

Steamboat **1807** | Automobile *c.* 1860–1890

Daimler motor car ▶

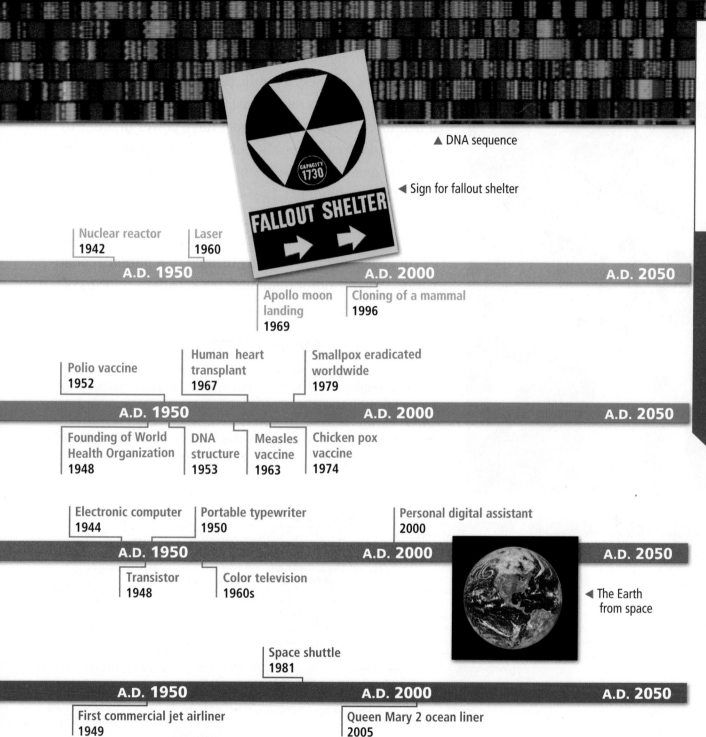

▲ DNA sequence

◀ Sign for fallout shelter

FALLOUT SHELTER CAPACITY 1730

Nuclear reactor
1942

Laser
1960

A.D. **1950**   A.D. **2000**   A.D. **2050**

Apollo moon landing
1969

Cloning of a mammal
1996

Polio vaccine
1952

Human heart transplant
1967

Smallpox eradicated worldwide
1979

A.D. **1950**   A.D. **2000**   A.D. **2050**

Founding of World Health Organization
1948

DNA structure
1953

Measles vaccine
1963

Chicken pox vaccine
1974

Electronic computer
1944

Portable typewriter
1950

Personal digital assistant
2000

A.D. **1950**   A.D. **2000**   A.D. **2050**

Transistor
1948

Color television
1960s

◀ The Earth from space

Space shuttle
1981

A.D. **1950**   A.D. **2000**   A.D. **2050**

First commercial jet airliner
1949

Queen Mary 2 ocean liner
2005

Government and Civics

The main purpose of government is to create and enforce a society's public policies. Public policies cover such matters as defense, crime, taxation, and much more. Governments must have power in order to make and carry out public policies. Every government has and exercises three basic kinds of power: legislative, executive, and judicial. Legislative refers to the power to make laws. Executive refers to the power to enforce laws. Judicial refers to the power to interpret laws. These powers of government are often outlined in a nation's constitution, or body of fundamental laws. Different forms of government exercise their powers in different ways.

Forms of Government

Political scientists classify governments in order to help them describe, compare, and analyze different forms. Three particularly helpful classifications involve determining (1) the geographic distribution of governmental power within the state, (2) the relationship between the legislative and executive branches of the government, and (3) who can participate in the government. As the chart shows, modern forms of government vary widely.

Forms of Government

Country	Where is the power?		What is the relationship between the legislative and executive branches?		Who can participate?	
	Unitary: All powers held by the government belong to a single, central agency.	**Federal**: The powers of government are divided between a central government and several regional governments.	**Parliamentary**: The executive branch is made up of the prime minister, or premier, and that official's cabinet. The prime minister and cabinet are members of the legislative branch, or parliament.	**Presidential**: The executive and legislative branches of government are separate, independent of each other, and coequal.	**Democracy**: Supreme political authority rests with the people, who choose a small group of individuals to act as their representatives to carry out the day-to-day conduct of government.	**Dictatorship**: The government is not accountable to the people for its policies or for how they are carried out. Those who rule do not represent or consider the will of the people.
Botswana	✓		✓		✓	
Brazil		✓		✓	✓	
Costa Rica	✓		✓		✓	
Cuba	✓		✓			✓
France	✓			✓	✓	
India		✓	✓		✓	
Syria	✓			✓		✓
United States		✓		✓	✓	

Federal vs. Unitary Government

Today, about two dozen nations, including the United States, have a federal system of government. In this kind of system, two levels of government—central and state—divide power between them. In the unitary system, which is more common by far, all powers belong to the central government. One disadvantage of a federal system is its inefficiency. People must obey two sets of laws, which may overlap or even conflict. In a unitary system, one government governs all the people directly, even though it may yield certain powers to the states. On the other hand, a federal system allows for checks on the power of the central government and for some diversity of laws in regions with a distinctive culture, history, or language.

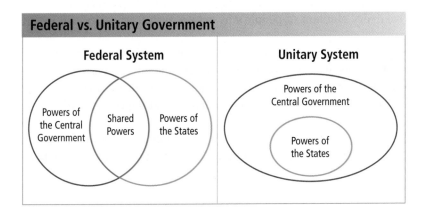

Federal vs. Unitary Government

Federal System

Powers of the Central Government | Shared Powers | Powers of the States

Unitary System

Powers of the Central Government

Powers of the States

Presidential and Parliamentary Governments

The Presidential Relationship Voters elect the legislature and the chief executive, who is part of the executive branch. The legislative and executive branches are independent and coequal.

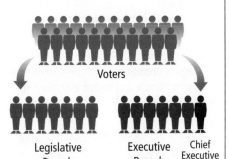

Voters

Legislative Branch

Executive Branch

Chief Executive

The Parliamentary Relationship Voters elect the legislature. The chief executive is drawn from the legislature.

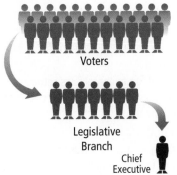

Voters

Legislative Branch

Chief Executive

Basic Concepts of Democracy

1. A recognition of the fundamental worth and dignity of every person. At various times, the welfare of one or a few individuals is subordinate to the interests of the many in a democracy. For example, a democratic society may force people to pay a tax or obey traffic signals.

2. A respect for the equality of all persons. The democratic concept of equality insists that all people are entitled to equality of opportunity and equality before the law—not necessarily equal distribution of wealth.

3. A faith in the majority rule and an insistence upon minority rights. In a democracy, the will of the people and not the dictate of the ruling few determine public policy. Unchecked, however, a majority could destroy its opposition and, in the process, destroy democracy. Thus, democracy insists upon majority rule restrained by minority rights.

4. An acceptance of the necessity of compromise. In a democracy, public decision making must be largely a matter of give-and-take among the various competing interests. People must compromise to find the position most acceptable to the largest number. Compromise is the process of blending and adjusting competing views and interests.

5. An insistence upon the widest possible degree of individual freedom. In a democracy, each individual must be as free to do as he or she pleases as far as the freedom of all will allow. Oliver Wendell Holmes once had this to say about the relative nature of each individuals rights: "The right to swing my fist ends where the other man's nose begins."

Louis XIV of France

Catherine the Great of Russia

Forms of Dictatorship

Typically militaristic in character, an authoritarian or dictatorial regime usually acquires political power by force and may turn to foreign aggression to enhance its military strength and prestige. Authoritarianism has taken several related forms throughout history.

Absolutism   A system in which the ruler holds complete authority over the government and the lives of the people. Some absolute monarchs ruled according to the principle of divine right. Modern forms of absolutism include military dictatorships that try to control every element of people's lives (see Totalitarianism).

Despotism   Absolute rule with no constitutional restraints. The term *despot* was an honorable title in ancient times. Later, absolute monarchs who favored reforms became known as enlightened despots. Today, despot refers to a brutal and oppressive ruler.

Autocracy   The concentration of power in one individual or group that uses force to maintain absolute control and smother any political opposition.

Mehmed II of the Ottoman Empire

Glossary of Political Terms

bureaucracy
a large, complex administrative structure that handles the everyday business of government

citizen
a member of a state or nation who is entitled to full civil rights

civil service
those civilian employees who perform the administrative work of government

compromise
an adjustment of opposing principles or systems by modifying some aspect of each

constitution
the body of fundamental laws setting out the principles, structures, and processes of a government

foreign policy
everything a nation's government says and does in world affairs

immigrant
a person legally admitted as a permanent resident of a country

jury
a legally chosen group of persons who hear evidence and decide questions of fact in a court case

nation
a group of people who share the same way of life and live in the same area and under the same central government

Totalitarianism A form of absolutism in which the government sweeps away existing political institutions and exerts complete control over nearly every aspect of the society. In this system, a supreme leader often becomes the sole source of society's rules.

Communism An ideology that, in theory, calls for ownership of all land and other productive property by the workers. In practice, a system of repressive, single-party government that completely controls its citizens' lives and stifles all opposition.

Fascism A form of government that seeks to renew society by demanding citizens' complete devotion to the state. Often led by a dictator who strictly controls industry and labor, denies freedom and individual rights, and uses police and the military to silence opposition.

Adolf Hitler of Germany

Mural of Saddam Hussein

Mao Zedong's
Little Red Book

politics
the activities of those who run or seek to run a government

rule of law
idea that all citizens, including government officials, are subject to the law

sovereign
having supreme power within its own territory

state
a group of people living in a defined territory who have a government with the power to make and enforce law without the consent of any higher authority

suffrage
the right to vote

tax
a charge levied by government on persons or property to meet public needs

treaty
a formal agreement between two or more sovereign states

Culture

Culture is a way of life, or a set of values and behaviors, that people in a society learn, share, and pass on from generation to generation. Culture mainly involves what people think, what they do, and what they create. It consists of such elements as language, religion, art, social organization, and technology. Cultures can change over time. Some elements are forgotten, and others are improved or replaced. Still others are picked up from outside cultures. This spread of ideas, customs, and technologies from one culture to another is known as cultural diffusion. Historically, cultures have spread mainly through trade, migration, and conquest.

World Languages

Language is a part of culture. Yet it is also the main tool by which people transmit their culture. Many thousands of languages have arisen since humans first began to communicate. Some 6,800 of those languages still survive. Related languages can be grouped into language families.

Principal Languages of the World

Language	Speakers* (in millions)
Mandarin (Chinese)	873
Spanish	322
English	309
Hindi	180
Portuguese	177
Bengali	171
Russian	145
Japanese	122
German	95
Wu (Chinese)	77

* estimated number for whom this is their first language

Sign in a Native American language and English (above); fragment of a Dead Sea scroll, written in ancient Hebrew (below)

Major Belief Systems

Most of the world's major belief systems have existed for more than 2,000 years. Today, if the world included only 1,000 people, 330 of them would be Christian, 215 would be Muslim, 149 would be Hindu, 140 would follow no religion, 59 would be Buddhist, 37 would follow Chinese traditional religions, and 41 would hold primal-indigenous beliefs.

Major World Religions/Belief Systems

	Leading Figures; Dates	Key Beliefs	Writings	Number of Followers
Buddhism	Siddhartha Gautama (the Buddha); late sixth to fourth century B.C.	No gods, but buddhas, or "enlightened ones" exist; reincarnation (cycle of birth, death, and rebirth); the Four Noble Truths: (1) suffering is a part of life; (2) selfish desire leads to suffering; (3) desire can be overcome; (4) the Eightfold Path leads away from desire, toward release from the cycle of birth, death, and rebirth	*Tripitaka (The Three Baskets)*; the sutras; the tantras	373 million
Chinese Traditional Religions (blend of Buddhism, Confucianism, and Daoism)	Blending began in the A.D. 900s	Reincarnation (from Buddhism); virtuous way of life (from Confucianism); acting in harmony with nature and avoiding aggressive action (from Daoism)	*Dao de Jing (The Way of Power)*; *Zhuangzi* (named after the greatest interpreter of Daoism); (see also Buddhism and Confucianism)	398 million
Christianity	Jesus of Nazareth; early first century A.D.	One God; to save humans, God sent Jesus, who suffered, died, and rose from the dead; the Trinity: three figures (God the Father, God the Son, and God the Holy Spirit) united as one; love God above all else	The Bible: the Old Testament (Hebrew Bible) and the New Testament; various creeds and statements of faith	2.07 billion
Confucianism	Confucius; around 500 B.C.	No gods; not an organized religion, but a system of moral conduct based on the teachings of Confucius; kindness, love, and respect lead to a virtuous way of life	The *Lun yü (Analects)*; the *Wu-ching (Five Classics)*; the *Ssu Shu (Four Books)*	6.43 million (mainly in Korea)
Hinduism	No founder or central institution; around 1500 B.C.	Brahman, the ultimate God, is the source of all existence; many lesser gods, the main ones being Vishnu and Siva; reincarnation; law of karma (actions in one life affect next life); ahimsa (principle of noninjury or nonviolence)	The Vedas, sutras, epics, and puranas	837 million
Islam	Muhammad; early A.D. 600s	One God, Allah; Five Pillars, or duties: (1) profession of faith; (2) prayer; (3) charity; (4) fasting; (5) pilgrimage to Mecca in Saudi Arabia	Quran	1.25 billion
Judaism	Abraham; around 2000 B.C.	One God; God made a covenant, with Abraham and the Jewish people that if they obey God's commands, God will make Israel a great nation; moral actions are more important than beliefs	Hebrew Bible: The Torah (the "Law"), the Nevi'im (the "Prophets"), and the Ketuvim (the "Writings"); oral tradition, written as the Talmud	14.6 million
primal-indigenous (includes tribal religions, animism, shamanism, and paganism)	Such religions have existed since prehistoric times	May be a high god; nature spirits (powerful life forces inhabiting the elements of nature); communication with spirits through prayers and offerings ensures the support of the spirits	none	238 million
Shinto	No founder; well established by the A.D. 500s	Many gods; Kami (superior, mystical, or divine powers) are the sources of human life; main deity is sun goddess Amaterasu O-mikami; each person is worthy of respect; truthfulness and purification (physical and spiritual) bring the blessings of the kami	No central sacred scripture; chief books: *Kojiki (Records of Ancient Matters)* and *Nihon shoki (Chronicles of Japan)*	2.68 million
Sikhism (combines elements of Hinduism and Islam)	Nanak; around A.D. 1500	One God; reincarnation; meditation can release one from the cycle of reincarnation; law of karma; all humans are equal	*Adi Granth (First Book)*	24.3 million

Culture

The Arts

The arts tell much about a culture. Ancient civilizations produced artists only after they were capable of generating an agricultural surplus. Some people could then be spared from the fields to devote themselves to other pursuits, including the arts. Works of art, from paintings and sculptures to music, dance, and writing, reflect the culture in which the artist lived. Notice the variations among the arts presented in these pictures. Think about what each picture says about the culture that produced it.

Romantic poet, writer, and artist William Blake's *Songs of Innocence*, 1789 ▼

▲ Neoclassical bust of Napoleon by Antonio Canova, *c.* 1802

Major Art Movements

classicism
Greek and Roman art; emphasis on harmony, proportion, balance, and simplicity

byzantine
500s–1400s, Europe, Russia

Romanesque
late eleventh century, Europe

Gothic
1100s–1400s, Europe; cathedral architecture and religious art

Renaissance
c. 1400–1600, Europe; Leonardo, Michelangelo, Raphael

mannerism
c. 1520–1600, Europe; Parmigianino

baroque
seventeenth and early eighteenth centuries, Europe; Bernini, Caravaggio, Rubens

rococo
eighteenth century, Europe; Fragonard

neoclassicism
late eighteenth and early nineteenth centuries, Europe; revival of ancient Greek and Roman art; David, Canova

romanticism
late eighteenth to mid-nineteenth century, Europe, United States; Delacroix, Géricault, Turner, Blake, Hudson River school

Barbizon School
c. 1840–1870, France; landscapes; Rousseau, Corot, Millet

realism
nineteenth century, Europe and United States; Daumier, Courbet, Eakins

impressionism
late nineteenth century, France and United States; Monet, Renoir, Cassatt

pointillism
1880s, France; Seurat, Signac

Costume from Georg Friedrich Handel's baroque opera *Agrippina*, 1709 (right) ▶

Pointillist painting by Georges Seurat, *Porte-en-Bessin*, 1888 (far right) ▶

Poster for ►
Émile Zola's
realist novel
La Terre, 1887

▲ Self-portrait by
German expressionist
Käthe Kollwitz, 1920

◄ Bronze sculpture by Italian
futurist Umberto Boccioni,
*Unique Forms of Continuity
in Space*, 1913

postimpressionism
late nineteenth century, France;
Cézanne, Van Gogh, Gauguin

art nouveau
late nineteenth century, Europe;
decorative arts

cubism
early twentieth century, Europe;
Picasso, Braque

fauvism
c. 1905–1908, France; pure, bold
colors applied in a spontaneous
manner; Matisse

expressionism
c. 1905–1925, northern Europe;
Rouault, Kokoschka, Schiele

futurism
c. 1909–1919, Italy; Boccioni

constructivism
c. 1915, Russia; abstract style using
non-traditional materials;
Rodchenko, Tatlin, Gabo, Pevsner

dadaism
c. 1915–1923, France; rejected
accepted aesthetic standards;
Duchamp

surrealism
1920s–1930s, Europe; Magritte, Dalí,
Miró, Ernst, de Chirico

art deco
1920s–1930s; decorative arts characterized by sleek lines and slender
forms

abstract expressionism
1940s, New York City; Pollock,
de Kooning, Motherwell, Kline

minimalism
late 1950s, United States; Judd,
Martin, Kelly

color field painting
1950s, United States; Newman,
Rothko, Frankenthaler

pop art
1950s, United States; Warhol,
Lichtenstein, Oldenburg

conceptual art
1960s and 1970s, interna-
tional; questioned the definition of "art"

Sculpture for a park in Minneapolis
by pop artist Claes Oldenburg,
Spoonbridge and Cherry, 1988 ▼

A

Abbasids dynasty that ruled in Bagdad from 750–1258 (p. 314)

Abbasids dinastía que gobernó Bagdad durante los años 750–1258

abdicate to give up or step down from power (p. 598)

abdicar renunciar de un puesto de poder

abolition movement the campaign against slavery and the slave trade (p. 727)

movimiento por la abolición campaña contra la esclavitud y contra el tráfico de esclavos

absentee landlord one who owns a large estate but does not live there (p. 729)

dueño ausente dueño de una gran propiedad que no vive en ella

absolute monarch ruler with complete authority over the government and lives of the people he or she governs (p. 506)

monarca absoluto gobernante que tiene autoridad absoluta sobre la administración y la vida de los que están bajo su mando

abstract style of art composed of lines, colors, and shapes, sometimes with no recognizable subject matter at all (p. 889)

abstracto estilo de arte compuesto de líneas, colores y formas, y que a veces no tiene un tema reconocible

acculturation the blending of two or more cultures (p. 72)

aculturación mezcla de dos o más culturas

acid rain a form of pollution in which toxic chemicals in the air come back to Earth in the form of rain, snow, or hail (p. 1112)

lluvia ácida forma de polución en la que los productos químicos tóxicos que se encuentran en el aire vuelven a la tierra en la lluvia, nieve o granizo

acropolis highest and most fortified point within a Greek city-state (p. 119)

acrópolis el punto más alto y fortificado de una ciudad-estado griega

acupuncture medical treatment, originated in ancient China, in which needles are inserted into the skin at specific points to relieve pain or treat various illnesses (p. 106)

acupuntura tratamiento médico, originario de China, por el que se introducen agujas en la piel en puntos específicos para aliviar el dolor o como tratamiento de diversas enfermedades

adobe a mixture of clay and plant fibers that becomes hard as it dries in the sun and that can be used for building (p. 196)

adobe mezcla de arcilla y fibras vegetales que se endurece al secarse al sol y se puede usar en la construcción

Adulis strategic trading port of the kingdom of Axum (p. 352)

Adulis puerto comercial estratégico del reino de Axum

Afghanistan an Islamic country in Central Asia; invaded by the Soviet Union in 1979; later home to the radical Islamist Taliban and the terrorist al Qaeda (p. 1119)

Afganistán país islámico en Asia Central; invadido por la Unión Soviética en 1979; más tarde hogar de los radicales islamistas Talibán y de los terroristas de al Qaeda

African National Congress (ANC) the main organization that opposed apartheid and pushed for majority rule in South Africa; later a political party (p. 1049)

Congreso Nacional Africano (ANC, por sus siglas en inglés) principal organización que se opuso al apartheid y que abogó por el gobierno de la mayoría de Sudáfrica; posteriormente, partido político

agribusinesses giant commercial farms, often owned by multinational corporations (p. 1084)

industria agropecuaria inmensas granjas comerciales, generalmente administradas por corporaciones multinacionales

ahimsa Hindu belief in nonviolence and reverence for all life (pp. 77, 866)

ahimsa creencia hindú en la no violencia y en el respeto a todas las formas de vida

aircraft carriers ships that accommodate the taking off and landing of airplanes, and transport aircraft (p. 940)

portaaviones buque dotado de las instalaciones necesarias para el transporte, despegue y aterrizaje de aparatos de aviación

al Qaeda a fundamentalist Islamic terrorist organization led by Saudi Arabian Osama bin Laden (p. 1118)

al Qaeda organización fundamentalista islámica terrorista liderada por el saudí Osama bin Laden

Alexandria an ancient Hellenistic city in Egypt (p. 140)

Alejandría antigua ciudad helenista en Egipto

alliance formal agreement between two or more nations or powers to cooperate and come to one another's defense (pp. 126, 473)

alianza acuerdo formal de cooperación y defensa mutua entre dos o más naciones o potencias

alphabet writing system in which each symbol represents a single basic sound (p. 43)

alfabeto sistema de escritura en el que cada símbolo representa un único sonido

Alsace and Lorraine provinces on the border of Germany and France, lost by France to Germany in 1871; regained by France after WWI (p. 818)

Alsacia y Lorena provincias en la frontera entre Alemania y Francia, que Alemania arrebató a Francia en 1871, y que Francia recuperó después de la Primera Guerra Mundial

Amritsar massacre an incident in 1919 in which British troops fired on an unarmed crowd of Indians (p. 865)

masacre de Amritsar incidente en 1919 en el que las tropas británicas dispararon contra un grupo de indios indefensos

anarchist someone who wants to abolish all government (p. 704)

anarquista persona que quiere abolir toda forma de gobierno

ancien régime old order; system of government in pre-revolution France (p. 572)

ancien regime antiguo orden; sistema de gobierno en la Francia prerevolucionaria

anesthetic drug that prevents pain during surgery (p. 609)

anestesia fármaco que suprime el dolor durante la cirugía

animism the belief that spirits and forces live within animals, objects, or dreams (p. 13)

animismo creencia de que los espíritus y fuerzas pueden vivir en animales, objetos o sueños

annex add a territory to an existing state or country (pp. 594, 694)

anexar agregar un territorio a un estado o país existente

Anschluss union of Austria and Germany (p. 927)

Anschluss unión de Austria y Alemania

anthropology the study of the origins and development of people and their societies (p. 5)

antropología estudio del origen y desarrollo de los pueblos y sus sociedades

anti-ballistic missiles (ABMs) missiles that can shoot down other missiles (p. 968)

misiles anti-balísticos (ABM, por sus siglas) misiles que pueden derribar otros misiles

anti-Semitism prejudice against Jews (p. 230)

antisemitismo prejuicio contra los judíos

apartheid a policy of rigid segregation of non-white people in the Republic of South Africa (pp. 859, 1048)

apartheid política de estricta separación racial en Sudáfrica que fue abolida en 1989

apostle leader or teacher of a new faith or movement (p. 168)

apóstol líder o maestro de una nueva fe o movimiento

appeasement policy of giving in to an aggressor's demands in order to keep the peace (p. 925)

contemporización política de aceptación de las exigencias de un agresor para mantener la paz

apprentice a young person learning a trade from a master (p. 235)

aprendiz persona joven que aprendía un oficio de un maestro

aqueduct in ancient Rome, underground or bridgelike stone structure that carried water from the hills into the cities (p. 164)

acueducto en la antigua Roma, estructura parecida a un puente que llevaba agua desde las colinas hasta las ciudades

archaeology the study of people and cultures through their material remains (p. 5)

arqueología estudio de pueblos y culturas antiguas por medio de sus restos materiales

archipelago chain of islands (p. 387)

archipiélago cadena de islas

aristocracy government headed by a privileged minority or upper class (p. 120)

aristocracia gobierno encabezado por una minoría privilegiada o de clase alta

armada fleet of ships (p. 507)

armada flota de barcos

armistice agreement to end fighting in a war (p. 833)

armisticio acuerdo para dejar de luchar en una guerra

artifact an object made by human beings (p. 4)

artefacto objeto hecho por seres humanos

artificial satellite man-made object that orbits a larger body in space (p. 1121)

satélite artificial objeto artificial que gira en el espacio alrededor de un cuerpo más grande

artisan a skilled craftsperson (p. 20)

artesano trabajador cualificado que hace objetos a mano

Asante kingdom kingdom that emerged in the 1700s in present-day Ghana and was active in the slave trade (p. 454)

reino Asante reino que surgió en el siglo XVIII en el actual Ghana y que tenía comercio de esclavos

Asia Minor the Turkish peninsula between the Black Sea and the Mediterranean Sea (p. 861)

Asia Menor la península turca entre el Mar Negro y el Mar Mediterráneo

assassination murder of a public figure, usually for political reasons (p. 139)

asesinato acto de dar muerte a una figura pública, generalmente por razones políticas

assembly line production method that breaks down a complex job into a series of smaller tasks (p. 663)

cadena de montaje método de producción que divide un trabajo complejo en una serie de tareas menores

assimilate absorb or adopt another culture (p. 139)

asimilar absorber o adoptar otra cultura

atheism belief that there is no god (p. 909)

ateísmo creencia de que no existen dioses

Athens a city-state in ancient Greece (p. 121)

Atenas ciudad-estado en la antigua Grecia

atman in Hindu belief, a person's essential self (p. 77)

atman según la creencia hindú, el ser esencial de una persona

atrocity horrible act committed against innocent people (p. 830)

atrocidad acto brutal cometido en contra de inocentes

autocrat ruler who has complete authority (p. 285)

autócrata gobernante que tiene autoridad total

autocratic having unlimited power (pp. 531, 1020)

autocrático que tiene poder ilimitado

autonomy self-rule (p. 636)

autonomía autogobierno

Axis powers group of countries led by Germany, Italy, and Japan that fought the Allies in World War II (p. 926)

Potencias del Eje grupo de países liderado por Alemania, Italia y Japón que luchó contra los Aliados durante la Segunda Guerra Mundial

Axum trading center, and powerful ancient kingdom in northern present-day Ethiopia (p. 352)

Axum ciudad capital, centro de comercio y poderoso antiguo reino del norte de la presente Etiopía

ayllu in the Inca empire, a close-knit village (p. 198)

ayllu en el imperio Inca, aldea muy unida

B

Baghdad capital city of present-day Iraq; capital of the Muslim empire during Islam's golden age (p. 314)

Baghdad capital del actual Iraq; capital del imperio musulmán durante la época dorada del islam

balance of power distribution of military and economic power that prevents any one nation from becoming too strong (p. 514)

equilibrio de poder distribución del poder military y económico que evita que una nación se vuelva demasiado fuerte

balance of trade difference between how much a country imports and how much it exports (p. 773)

balance commercial diferencia entre lo que importa y exporta un país

Balfour Declaration statement issued by the British government in 1917 supporting the establishment of a homeland for Jews in Palestine (p. 864)

Declaración Balfour declaración hecha por el gobierno británico en 1917 en la que apoyaba la constitución de un estado judío en Palestina

Balkan Peninsula triangular arm of land that juts from southeastern Europe into the Mediterranean (p. 294)

Península Balcánica extensión triangular de tierra que sobresale del sudeste de Europa hasta el Mediterráneo

Bangladesh nation east of India that was formerly part of Pakistan (p. 1017)

Bangladesh país al este de India que antiguamente formaba parte de Pakistán

Bantu root language of West Africa on which some early African migration patterns are based (p. 341)

Bantú lengua madre del África occidental en la que están basados algunos patrones migratorios africanos

baroque ornate style of art and architecture popular in the 1600s and 1700s (p. 551)

barroco estilo artístico y arquitectónico elaborado que se dio en los siglos XVII y XVIII

barter economy economic system in which one set of goods or services is exchanged for another (p. 42)

economía de trueque sistema económico en el que se utiliza el intercambio de mercancías o servicios

Bastille fortress in Paris used as a prison; French Revolution began when Parisians stormed it in 1789 (p. 577)

Bastilla fortificación en París usada como prisión; la Revolución Francesa empezó cuando los parisinos la asaltaron en 1789

Bataan Death March during World War II, the forced march of Filipino and American prisoners of war under brutal conditions by the Japanese military (p. 949)

Jornada de la Muerte desde Baatan episodio acaecido durante la Segunda Guerra Mundial, en el que prisioneros de guerra filipinos y estadounidenses fueron obligado a marchar bajo condiciones brutales por parte de militares japoneses

Battle of Tours battle in 732 in which the Christian Franks led by Charles Martel defeated Muslim armies and stopped the Muslim advance into Europe (pp. 215, 312)

Batalla de Tours batalla en 732 en la que los francos cristianos liderados por Charles Martel derrotaron al ejército musulmán y detuvieron el avance árabe en Europa

Bedouin a desert-dwelling Arab nomad (p. 304)

Beduino nómada árabe que vive en el desierto

Benedictine Rule rules drawn up in 530 by Benedict, a monk, regulating monastic life. The Rule emphasizes obedience, poverty, and chastity and divides the day into periods of worship, work, and study. (p. 227)

Regla Benedictina en 530, reglas establecidas por Benedicto, un monje, para regular la vida monástica. La Regla enfatizaba la obediencia, pobreza y castidad, y divide el día en períodos de adoración, trabajo y estudio.

Biafra region of southeastern Nigeria that launched a failed bid for independence from Nigeria in 1966, launching a bloody war (p. 1030)

Biafra región del sudeste de Nigeria que lanzó un fallido intento de independizarse de Nigeria en 1966, y por el que se desató una cruenta guerra

biotechnology the application of biological research to industry, engineering, and technology (p. 1124)

biotecnología la aplicación de investigaciones biológicas en la industria, la ingeniería y la tecnología

bishop high-ranking Church official with authority over a local area, or diocese (p. 171)

Obispo funcionario eclesiástico de alto nivel con autoridad sobre un área local o diócesis

Black Death an epidemic of the bubonic plague that ravaged Europe in the 1300s (p. 269)

Peste Negra epidemia de la peste bubónica que arrasó Europa en el siglo XIV

Black Shirt any member of the militant combat squads of Italian Fascists set up under Mussolini (p. 899)

Camisa Negra cualquier miembro de las escuadras militantes de combate de los fascistas italianos que estableció Mussolini

blitzkrieg lightning war (p. 930)

blitzkrieg guerra relámpago o guerra intensa y muy breve

bloc a group of nations acting together in support of one another (p. 1103)

bloque grupo de naciones que actúan conjuntamente en apoyo mutuo

Boer War (1899–1902) a war in which Great Britain defeated the Boers of South Africa (p. 758)

Guerra Boer (1899–1902) guerra en la que Gran Bretaña venció a los Boer de Sudáfrica

Boers Dutch people who settled in Cape Town, Africa, and eventually migrated inland (p. 455)

Boers holandeses establecidos en Ciudad del Cabo, África, que con el tiempo emigraron hacia el interior

bourgeoisie the middle class (p. 573)

burguesía clase media

Boxer Uprising anti-foreign movement in China from 1898–1900 (p. 776)

Rebelión Bóxer movimiento en contra de los extranjeros ocurrido en China de 1898 a 1900

boyar landowning noble in Russia under the tsars (p. 531)

boyar noble ruso que poseía tierras en la época de los zares (p. 531)

boycott refuse to buy (p. 866)

boicot negarse a comprar

brahman in the belief system established in Aryan India, the single spiritual power that resides in all things (p. 73)

brahman en el sistema de creencias establecido en la India aria, el único poder espiritual que reside en todas las cosas

bureaucracy system of government that includes different job functions and levels of authority (p. 45)

burocracia sistema de gobierno que incluye diferentes trabajos y niveles de autoridad

bushido code of conduct for samurai during the feudal period in Japan (p. 391)

bushido código de conducta de los samuráis durante el período feudal japonés

C

cabinet parliamentary advisors to the king who originally met in a small room, or "cabinet" (p. 522)
gabinete miembros del parlamento consejeros del rey que originalmente se reunían en un pequeño cuarto o "gabinete"

cahier notebook used during the French Revolution to record grievances (p. 576)
memorándum cuaderno usado durante la Revolución Francesa para anotar los agravios

Cahokia in Illinois, the largest earthwork of the Mississippian culture, c. A.D. 700 (p. 204)
Cahokia en Illinois, el mayor terraplén de la cultura de los mississippianos, construido alrededor del 700 D.C.

calculus a branch of mathematics in which calculations are made using special symbolic notations; developed by Isaac Newton (p. 438)
cálculo rama de las matemáticas en la que los cálculos se hacen con notaciones simbólicas especiales; fue desarrollado por Isaac Newton

caliph successor to Muhammad as political and religious leader of the Muslims (p. 310)
califa sucesor de Mahoma como líder religioso y político de los musulmanes

calligraphy the art of producing beautiful handwriting (pp. 100, 320)
caligrafía arte de producir una bella escritura a mano

canon law body of laws of a church (p. 229)
ley canónica serie de leyes de una iglesia

canonize recognize a person as a saint (p. 429)
canonizar reconocer a una persona como santo

Cape Town seaport city and legislative capital of South Africa; first Dutch colony in Africa (p. 455)
Ciudad del Cabo ciudad portuaria y capital legislativa de Sudáfrica; fue la primera colonia holandesa en África

capital money or wealth used to invest in business or enterprise (pp. 234, 613)
capital dinero o bienes que se usan para invertir en negocios o empresas

capital offense crime punishable by death (p. 727)
ofensa capital crimen que puede castigarse con la muerte

capitalism economic system in which the means of production are privately owned and operated for profit (p. 493)
capitalismo sistema económico por el que los medios de producción son propiedad privada y se administran para obtener beneficios

cartel a group of companies that join together to control the production and price of a product (p. 666)
cartel asociación de grandes corporaciones formada para controlar la producción y el precio de un producto

cartographer mapmaker (p. 447)
cartógrafo persona que hace mapas

caste in traditional Indian society, an unchangeable social group into which a person is born (p. 78)
casta grupo social en la sociedad tradicional de India, en el que una persona nace y del que no se puede cambiar

Çatalhüyük one of the world's first villages, established in modern-day Turkey around 7000 B.C. (p. 14)
Çatalhüyük una de las primeras aldeas del mundo establecida en la Turquía actual alrededor del 7000 A.C.

cataract waterfall (pp. 45, 340)
catarata cascada, caída de agua

caudillo military dictator in Latin America (p. 802)
caudillo dictador militar en América Latina

celadon porcelain made in Korea with an unusual blue-green glaze (p. 385)
celadon porcelana hecha en Korea con brillo azulverdoso poco común

censorship restriction on access to ideas and information (p. 551)
censura restricción en el acceso a ideas o información

census population count (p. 159)
censo recuento de la población

chancellor the highest official of a monarch, prime minister (pp. 693, 912)
canciller oficial con más rango dentro de una monarquía, primer ministro

character written symbol in writing systems such as that of the Chinese (p. 100)
carácter símbolo escrito en los sistemas de escritura como en el chino

charter in the Middle Ages, a written document that set out the rights and privileges of a town (p. 233)
fuero en la Edad Media, documento escrito que establecía los derechos y privilegios de un pueblo

Chavín a culture that thrived in the Andean region from about 900 B.C. to 200 B.C. (p. 195)
chavín cultura que tuvo su apogeo en la región andina, desde alrededor de 900 A.C. a 200 A.C.

Chechnya a republic within Russia where rebels have fought for independence (p. 1045)
Chechenia república dentro del territorio ruso en la que grupos rebeldes luchan por su independencia

Cheka early Soviet secret police force (p. 844)
 Cheka una de las primeras fuerzas policiales secretas soviética

chinampas in the Aztec empire, artificial islands used to cultivate crops and made of mud piled atop reed mats that were anchored to the lakebed with willow trees (p. 192)
 chinampas en el imperio azteca, islas artificiales que se usaban para la agricultura y que estaban hechas de barro apilado sobre esteras de junco ancladas al fondo del lago con ramas de sauce

chivalry code of conduct for knights during the Middle Ages (p. 222)
 caballería código de conducta para los caballeros durante la Edad Media

Choson dynasty Korean dynasty that ruled from 1392 to 1910, the longest-lived of Korea's three dynasties (p. 386)
 dinastía Choson dinastía coreana que gobernó desde 1392 a 1910, la que más duró de las tres dinastías coreanas

circumnavigate to travel completely around the world (p. 451)
 circunnavegar viajar alrededor del mundo

citizen a native or resident of a town or city (p. 119)
 ciudadano nativo o residente de un pueblo o ciudad

city-state a political unit that includes a city and its surrounding lands and villages (p. 23)
 ciudad estado unidad polítca compuesta por una diudad y las tierras que la rodean

civil disobedience the refusal to obey unjust laws (p. 866)
 desobediencia civil negarse a obedecer leyes injustas

civil law branch of law that deals with private rights and matters (p. 37)
 derecho civil cuerpo legal que trata de los derechos y asuntos privados de los individuos

civil servant government official (p. 104)
 funcionario público oficial del gobierno

civil war war fought between two groups of people in the same nation (p. 475)
 guerra civil guerra en la que luchan dos grupos de personas de una misma nación

civilization a complex, highly organized social order (p. 19)
 civilización orden social complejo y altamente organizado

clan group of families with a common ancestor (p. 94)

clan grupo de familias con un antepasado en común

clergy the body of people who conduct Christian services (p. 171)
 clero grupo de gente que oficia en los servicios religiosos cristianos

coalition temporary alliance of various political parties (p. 736)
 coalición alianza temporal de varios partidos políticos

codify to arrange or set down in writing (p. 37)
 codificar organizar o establecer por escrito

Cold War state of tension and hostility between nations aligned with the United States on one side and the Soviet Union on the other that rarely led to direct armed conflict (p. 954)
 Guerra Fría estado de tensión y hostilidad entre las naciones alineadas con Estados Unidos, por una parte, y con la Unión Soviética, por la otra, que salvo raras excepciones desembocó en un conflicto armado

collective large farm owned and operated by peasants as a group (p. 905)
 granja colectiva granja grande que pertenece a campesinos que la administran en grupo

collective security system in which a group of nations acts as one to preserve the peace of all (p. 836)
 seguridad colectiva sistema por el que un grupo de naciones actúa como una para preservar la paz común

collectivization the forced joining together of workers and property into collectives, such as rural collectives that absorb peasants and their land (p. 986)
 colectivización unión forzada de trabajadores y propiedad en colectivos, como colectivos rurales que absorben a campesinos y sus tierras

colony territory settled and ruled by people from another land (p. 43)
 colonia territorio poblado y gobernado por personas de otro lugar

colossus giant (p. 710)
 coloso gigante

Columbian Exchange the global exchange of goods, ideas, plants and animals, and disease that began with Columbus' exploration of the Americas (p. 491)
 Intercambio colombino intercambio global de bienes, ideas, plantas, animales y enfermedades que comenzaron con la exploración de las Américas por parte de Colón

comedy in ancient Greece, play that mocked people or social customs (p. 135)

comedia en la antigua Grecia, obra de teatro donde se hacía burla de personas o costumbres

Comintern Communist International, international association of communist parties led by the Soviet Union for the purpose of encouraging worldwide communist revolution (p. 911)

Comintern Internacional Comunista, asociación internacional de partidos comunistas liderada por la Unión Soviética con el propósito de extender por el mundo una revolución comunista

command economy system in which government officials make all basic economic decisions (p. 905)

economía controlada sistema en el que los funcionarios del gobierno toman todas las decisiones económicas básicas

commissar Communist party officials assigned to the army to teach party principles and ensure party loyalty during the Russian Revolution (p. 844)

comisario funcionario del partido comunista asignado al ejército para enseñar los principios del partido y para asegurar la lealtad al mismo durante la revolución rusa

commodity valuable product (p. 347)

mercancía producto valioso

common law a legal system based on custom and court rulings (p. 245)

derecho consuetudinario sistema legal basado en la costumbre y en las sentencias de los tribunales

communism form of socialism advocated by Karl Marx; according to Marx, class struggle was inevitable and would lead to the creation of a classless society in which all wealth and property would be owned by the community as a whole (p. 625)

comunismo forma de socialismo defendido por Karl Marx; según Marx, la lucha de clases era inevitable y llevaría a la creación de una sociedad sin clases en la que toda la riqueza y la propiedad pertenecería a la comunidad como un todo

compact an agreement among people (p. 484)

pacto acuerdo

compromise an agreement in which each side makes concessions; an acceptable middle ground (p. 430)

compromiso acuerdo en el que cada parte hace concesiones; un término medio aceptable

concentration camp detention center for civilians considered enemies of the state (p. 935)

campo de concentración centro de detención de los civiles que se considera enemigos del estado

Concert of Europe a system in which Austria, Russia, Prussia, and Great Britain met periodically to discuss any problems affecting the peace in Europe; resulted from the post-Napoleon era Quadruple Alliance (p. 600)

Concierto de Europa sistema por el cual Austria, Rusia, Prusia y Gran Bretaña se reunían periódicamente para discutir cualquier problema que afectara a la paz en Europa; resultado de la Cuádruple Alianza de la era postnapoleónica

concession special economic rights given to a foreign power (p. 766)

concesión derechos económicos especiales que se dan a un poder extranjero

confederation unification (p. 797)

confederación unificación

Congress of Vienna assembly of European leaders that met after the Napoleonic era to piece Europe back together; met from September 1814 to June 1815 (p. 599)

Congreso de Viena asamblea de líderes europeos que se reunió después de la era napoleónica para reconstruir Europa; se reunieron desde septiembre de 1814 a junio de 1815

conquistador Spanish explorers who claimed lands in the Americas for Spain in the 1500s and 1600s (p. 472)

conquistador los exploradores españoles que apropiaron tierras en América para España en los siglos XVI y XVII

conscription "the draft," which required all young men to be ready for military or other service (p. 829)

conscripción llamado a filas que exigía que todos los hombres jóvenes estuvieran listos para el servicio militar u otro servicio

consensus general agreement (p. 359)

consenso acuerdo general

Constantinople the capital of the eastern Roman empire; capital of the Byzantine and Ottoman empires, now called Istanbul (pp. 174, 282)

Constantinopla capital del Imperio Romano Oriental; capital de los imperios bizantino y otomano, en la actualidad llamada Estambul

constitutional government government whose power is defined and limited by law (p. 522)

gobierno constitucional gobierno cuyo poder está definido y limitado por las leyes

consul in ancient Rome, official from the patrician class who supervised the government and commanded the armies (p. 152)

cónsul funcionario de la clase patricia que en la Roma antigua supervisaba el gobierno y dirigía los ejércitos

containment the U.S. strategy of keeping communism within its existing boundaries and preventing its further expansion (p. 973)

contención estrategia de Estados Unidos de mantener el comunismo dentro de sus fronteras existentes y de prevenir su expansión

Continental System blockade designed by Napoleon to hurt Britain economically by closing European ports to British goods; ultimately unsuccessful (p. 594)

sistema continental bloqueo diseñado por Napoleón para dañar a Gran Bretaña económicamente que consistía en cerrar los puertos europeos a los productos británicos; con el tiempo no tuvo éxito

contraband during wartime, military supplies and raw materials needed to make military supplies that may legally be confiscated by any belligerent (p. 830)

contrabando durante el tiempo de guerra, provisiones militares y materias primas necesarios para fabricar artículos militares, y que pueden ser confiscados legalmente por cualquiera de las partes beligerantes

contras guerrillas who fought the Sandinistas in Nicaragua (p. 1086)

contras grupo guerrillero que luchó contra los sandinistas en Nicaragua

convoy group of merchant ships protected by warships (p. 825)

convoy grupo de barcos mercantes protegidos por barcos de guerra

corporation business owned by many investors who buy shares of stock and risk only the amount of their investment (p. 665)

corporación empresa propiedad de muchos inversores que compran acciones y que sólo arriesgan el monto de su inversión

Council of Trent a group of Catholic leaders that met between 1545 and 1563 to respond to Protestant challenges and direct the future of the Catholic Church (p. 431)

Concilio de Trento grupo de líderes católicos que se reunieron entre 1545 y 1563 para tratar los retos protestantes y liderar el futuro de la Iglesia Católica

coup d'état the forcible overthrow of a government (p. 1025)

golpe de estado derrocamiento por la fuerza de un gobierno

covenant a binding agreement; specifically, in the Jewish tradition, the binding agreement God made with Abraham (p. 58)

convenio acuerdo vinculante; específicamente, en la tradición judía, el acuerdo vinculante hecho entre Dios y Abraham

creole person in Spain's colonies in the Americas who was an American-born descendent of Spanish settlers (pp. 480, 645)

criollo descendiente de colonos españolas nacido en las colonias españolas de América

Crimean War war fought mainly on the Crimean Peninsula between the Russians and the British, French, and Turks from 1853–1856 (p. 711)

Guerra de Crimea guerra librada principalmente en la península de Crimea entre los rusos y los británicos, franceses y turcos entre 1853 y 1856

criminal law branch of law that deals with offenses against others (p. 37)

derecho penal rama de la ley que se ocupa de los delitos contra otros

Crusades a series of wars from the 1000s through 1200s in which European Christians tried to win control of the Holy Land from Muslims (p. 255)

Cruzadas serie de guerras entre el siglo XI y el siglo XIII en las que los cristianos europeos intentaron ganar el control sobre los musulmanes de la Tierra Santa

cult of domesticity idealization of women and the home (p. 675)

culto a lo doméstico idealización de las mujeres y del hogar

cultural diffusion the spread of ideas, customs, and technologies from one people to another (p. 23)

difusión cultural divulgación de ideas, costumbres y tecnología de un pueblo a otro

cultural nationalism pride in the culture of one's country (p. 856)

nacionalismo cultural orgullo de la cultura del país propio

Cultural Revolution a Chinese Communist program in the late 1960s to purge China of nonrevolutionary tendencies that caused economic and social damage (p. 986)

Revolución Cultural programa de la China comunista a finales de la década de 1960 que pretendía eliminar de China todas las tendencias no revolucionarias y que causó daños económicos y sociales

culture the way of life of a society, which is handed down from one generation to the next by learning and experience (p. 5)

cultura forma de vida de una sociedad que se pasa de una generación a la siguiente mediante el aprendizaje y la experiencia

cuneiform in the ancient Middle East, a system of writing that used wedge-shaped marks (p. 33)
cuneiforme en el antiguo Oriente Medio, sistema de escritura cuyos caracteres tenían forma de cuña

Cuzco capital city of the Inca empire (p. 197)
Cuzco capital del imperio Inca

Cyrillic relating to the Slavic alphabet derived from the Greek and traditionally attributed to St. Cyril; in modified form still used in modern Slavic languages (p. 290)
cirílico relativo al alfabeto eslavo, derivado del griego y tradicionalmente atribuido a San Cirilo; todavía en uso, de forma modificada, en las lenguas eslavas modernas

D

dada artistic movement in which artists rejected tradition and produced works that often shocked their viewers (p. 889)
dadaísmo movimiento artístico en el que los artistas rechazaban la tradición y producían obras que a menudo sorprendían a su público

dalits outcastes or members of India's lowest caste (pp. 72, 1016, 1080)
dalits (o intocables) los marginados o miembros de las castas más bajas de India

Dardanelles vital strait connecting the Black Sea and the Mediterranean Sea in present-day Turkey (p. 826)
Dardanelos estrecho de vital importancia que conecta el Mar Negro y el Mar Mediterráneo en la actual Turquía

Darfur a region in western Sudan where ethnic conflict threatened to lead to genocide (p. 1052)
Darfur región occidental de Sudán donde un conflicto étnico amenaza con provocar un genocidio

D-Day code name for June 6, 1944, the day that Allied forces invaded France during WWII (p. 944)
Día D nombre en clave del día en que las fuerzas aliadas invadieron Francia durante la Segunda Guerra Mundial (6 de junio de 1944)

decimal system system of numbers based on 10 (p. 88)
sistema de decimal sistema numérico basado en el número 10

decipher to figure out the meaning of (p. 55)
descrifrar descubrir el significado de algo

default fail to make payments (p. 1098)
cese de pagos imposibilidad de realizar pagos

deficit gap between what a government spends and what it takes in through taxes and other sources (p. 1098)
déficit diferencia entre los gastos de un gobierno y las recaudaciones por impuestos y otras fuentes de ingresos

deficit spending situation in which a government spends more money than it takes in (p. 575)
gasto deficitario situación en la que un gobierno gasta más de lo que recauda

deforestation the destruction of forest land (pp. 770, 1112)
deforestación destrucción de tierras forestales

Delhi the third-largest city in India; capital of medieval India (p. 324)
Delhi tercera ciudad más grande de India; capital de la India medieval

delta triangular area of marshland formed by deposits of silt at the mouth of some rivers (p. 45)
delta área triangular de tierra pantanosa que se forma con los depósitos de limo en la desembocadura de algunos ríos

demilitarized zone a thin band of territory across the Korean peninsula separating North Korean forces from South Korean forces; established by the armistice of 1953 (p. 990)
zona desmilitarizada estrecha franja de tierra que cruza la península de Corea y que separa las fuerzas de Corea del Norte y las fuerzas de Corea del Sur; establecida por el armisticio de 1953

democracy government in which the people hold ruling power (p. 121)
democracia forma de gobierno en el que la soberanía reside en el pueblo

depopulation reduction in the number of people in an area (p. 527)
despoblación reducción del número de la población en una zona

desertification process by which fertile or semi-desert land becomes desert (pp. 341, 1073)
desertización proceso por el que la tierra fértil o semifértil se convierte en desierto

détente the relaxation of Cold War tensions during the 1970s (p. 968)
distensión relajamiento de las tensiones de la Guerra Fría en los años 70

developing world nations working toward development in Africa, Asia, and Latin America (p. 1066)

mundo en desarrollo países en vías de desarrollo de á frica, Asia y Latinoamérica

development the process of building stable governments, improving agriculture and industry, and raising the standard of living (p. 1066)

desarrollo proceso de establecer gobiernos estables, mejorar la agricultura, la industria y las condiciones de vida

dharma in Hindu belief, a person's religious and moral duties (p. 77)

dharma según la creencia hindú, las obligaciones morales y religiosas de un individuo

Diaspora the spreading of the Jews beyond their historic homeland (p. 60)

Diáspora diseminación de los judíos más allá de su patria histórica

dictator ruler who has complete control over a government; in ancient Rome, a leader appointed to rule for six months in times of emergency (p. 152)

dictador dirigente con control absoluto sobre el gobierno; en la antigua Roma, líder designado para gobernar durante seis meses en casos de emergencia

Dienbienphu small town and former French army base in northern Vietnam; site of the battle that ended in a Vietnamese victory, the French withdrawal from Vietnam, and the securing of North Vietnam's independence (p. 993)

Dienbienphu pequeño pueblo y antigua base del ejército francés en el norte de Vietnam; lugar de la batalla que terminó con la victoria vietnamita, la expulsión de los franceses de Vietnam y la obtención de la independencia de Vietnam del Norte

diet assembly or legislature (pp. 296, 425, 787)

dieta asamblea o cuerpo legislativo

direct democracy system of government in which citizens participate directly in the day-to-day affairs of government rather than through elected representatives (p. 126)

democracia directa sistema de gobierno en el que los ciudadanos participan directamente en lugar de hacerlo a través de representantes electos en los asuntos diarios del gobierno

disarmament reduction of armed forces and weapons (p. 893)

desarme reducción del ejército y del armamento

discrimination unequal treatment or barriers (p. 978)

discriminación tratamiento desigual o barreras

dissent ideas that oppose those of the government (p. 84)

disentir ideas que se oponen a las del gobierno

dissenter Protestant whose views and opinions differed from those of the Church of England (p. 517)

disidente protestante cuyos puntos de vista y opiniones diferían de los de la Iglesia de Inglaterra

divine right belief that a ruler's authority comes directly from God (p. 506)

derecho divino creencia de que la autoridad de un gobernante proviene directamente de Dios

domesticate to tame animals and adapt crops so they are best suited to use by humans (p. 13)

domesticar domar animales y adaptar plantas con el propósito de adecuarlos para el uso humano

dominion self-governing nation (p. 797)

dominio nación que se gobierna a sí misma

domino theory the belief that a communist victory in South Vietnam would cause noncommunist governments across Southeast Asia to fall to communism, like a row of dominoes (p. 993)

teoría del dominó creencia de que una victoria comunista en Vietnam del Sur podría causar que los gobiernos no comunistas del sudeste de Asia cayeran bajo dominio del comunismo, como una fila de fichas de dominó

dowry in some societies, payment a bride's family makes to the bridegroom and his family; payment a woman brings to a marriage (pp. 89, 372)

dote en algunas sociedades, pago de la familia de la novia al novio y a su familia; pago que una mujer proporciona a sumatrimonio

Dreyfus affair a political scandal that caused deep divisions in France between Royalists and liberals and republicans; centered on the 1894 wrongful conviction of Alfred Dreyfus, a Jewish officer in the French army (p. 737)

Caso Dreyfus escándalo político que causó divisiones profundas en Francia entre los realistas, liberales y republicanos; basado en la in justa condena en 1894 de Alfred Dreyfus, un oficial judío del ejérci to francés

Dual Monarchy the monarchy of Austria-Hungary (p. 706)

monarquía dual monarquía de Austria-Hungría

due process of law the requirement that the government act fairly and in accordance with established rules in all that it does (p. 246)

garantías procesales debidas requisito para que el gobierno actúe justamente y en concordancia con las normas establecidas en todo lo que hace

Duma elected national legislature in Russia (p. 715)
Duma en Rusia, asamblea legislative nacional electa

Dunkirk port in France from which 300,000 Allied troops were evacuated when their retreat by land was cut off by the German advance in 1940 (p. 931)
Dunkirk puerto de Francia desde donde fueron evacuadas 300,000 tropas aliadas en 1940 al ser bloqueada su retirada terrestre por el avance del ejército alemán

Dutch East India Company a trading company established by the Netherlands in 1602 to protect and expand its trade in Asia (p. 458)
Compañía Holandesa de las Indias Orientales compañía de comercio establecida por Holanda en 1602 para proteger y aumentar su comercio con Asia

dynamo a machine used to generate electricity (p. 663)
dínamo máquina que se usa para generar electricidad

dynastic cycle rise and fall of Chinese dynasties according to the Mandate of Heaven (p. 95)
ciclo dínastico florecimiento y caída de las dinastías chinas de acuerdo con el Mandato del Cielo

dynasty ruling family (p. 45)
dinastía familia gobernante

E

earthwork an embankment or other construction made of earth (p. 203)
terraplén muro de contención u otra construcción hecha de tierra

East Timor a former Portuguese colony, seized by Indonesia, that gained independence in 2002 (p. 1021)
Timor Oriental antigua colonia portuguesa, ocupada por Indonesia, que obtuvo su independencia en 2002

economic nationalism an emphasis on domestic control and protection of the economy (p. 855)
nacionalismo económico énfasis en el control nacional y en la protección de la economía

Edict of Nantes law issued by French king Henry IV in 1598 giving more religious freedom to French Protestants (p. 510)
Edicto de Nantes ley promulgada por el rey francés Enrique IV en 1598 por la que se con-

cedía mayor libertad religiosa a los protestantes frances (p. 510)

Eightfold Path as taught by the Buddha, the path one must follow to achieve nirvana (p. 80)
Óctuple Sendero como enseñó Buda, el camino que debe seguir todo individuo para conseguir el nirvana

elector one of seven German princes who would choose the Holy Roman emperor (p. 525)
elector uno de los siete príncipes germanos que elegían al emperador del Sacro Romano

electorate body of people allowed to vote (p. 723)
electorado conjunto de personas a quienes se permite votar

elite upper class (p. 760)
élite clase alta

emancipation granting of freedom to serfs or slaves (p. 711)
emancipación concesión de libertad a esclavos o siervos

emigration movement away from one's homeland (p. 704)
emigración trasladarse de su propio país a otro

émigré person who flees his or her country for political reasons (p. 582)
exiliado persona que deja su país por razones políticas

empire a group of states or territories controlled by one ruler (p. 23)
imperio grupo de estados o territorios controlados por un gobernante

enclosure the process of taking over and consolidating land formerly shared by peasant farmers (p. 610)
cercamiento proceso de consolidar y apropiarse de una tierra que anteriormente compartían campesinos

encomienda right the Spanish government granted to its American colonists to demand labor or tribute from Native Americans (p. 478)
encomienda derecho a exigir tributo o trabajo a los natives americanos, que el gobierno español otorgó a sus colonos en América

endangered species species threatened with extinction (p. 1074)
especies en vías de extinción especies amenazadas de extinción, es decir, de desaparición

engineering application of science and mathematics to develop useful structures and machines (p. 164)
ingeniería aplicación de las ciencias y matemáticas al desarrollo do máquinas y estructuras útiles

English Bill of Rights series of acts passed by the English Parliament in 1689 that limited the rights of the monarchy and ensured the superiority of Parliament (p. 521)

Declaración de derechos de los ingleses serie de leyes aprobadas por el parlamento inglés en 1689 que limitaba los derechos de la monarquía y establecía la primacía del parlamento

engraving art form in which an artist etches a design on a metal plate with acid and then uses the plate to make multiple prints (p. 419)

grabado forma de arte en la que un artista graba un diseño con ácido en una placa de metal y después la usa para producir múltiples impresiones

enlightened despot absolute ruler who used his or her power to bring about political and social change (p. 553)

déspota ilustrado gobernante absoluto que usa su poder para precipitar cambios políticos y sociales

entente nonbinding agreement to follow common policies (p. 817)

entendimiento acuerdo no vinculante de seguir normas comunes

enterprise a business organization in such areas as shipping, mining, railroads, or factories (p. 613)

empresa entidad empresarial en áreas como transportes, minería, ferrocariles o fábricas

entrepreneur person who assumes financial risk in the hope of making a profit (pp. 493, 613)

empresario persona que asume riesgos financieros con la esperanza de obtener beneficios

Epic of Gilgamesh Mesopotamian narrative poem that was first told in Sumer (p. 30)

El poema de Gilgamesh poema narrativo de Mesopotamia que se contó por primera vez en Sumeria

epidemic outbreak of a rapidly spreading disease (pp. 269, 1108)

epidemia brote de una enfermedad que se extiende rápidamente

erosion the wearing away of land (p. 1113)

erosión el desgaste paulatino de la tierra

estate social class (p. 572)

estado clase social

Estates-General legislative body made up of representatives of the three estates in pre-revolutionary France (p. 575)

Estados Generales cuerpo legislativo formado por representantes de los tres estados en la Francia prerevolucionaria

ethics moral standards of behavior (p. 60)

ética estándar moral de conducta

Ethiopia ancient Greek term for Axumite kingdom; present-day country in East Africa (p. 353)

Etiopía antiguo término griego para el reino de Axumite; también es un país actual del este de África

ethnic cleansing the killing or forcible removal of people of different ethnicities from an area by aggressors so that only the ethnic group of the aggressors remains (p. 1046)

limpieza étnica la matanza o expulsión forzosa de personas de diferentes grupos étnicos de una zona, llevadas a cabo por agresores para que su grupo étnico tenga permanencia exclusiva

ethnic group large group of people who share the same language and cultural heritage (p. 295)

étnico grupo grande de personas que comparten el idioma y la herencia cultural

Etruscans a people who inhabited early Italy (p. 151)

estrucos pueblo que habitaba principalmente al norte the Roma

euro common currency used by member nations of the European Union (p. 1097)

euro moneda común usada por las naciones que pertenecen a la Unión Europea

European Community an international organization dedicated to establishing free trade among its European member nations (p. 982)

Comunidad Europea organización internacional dedicada a establecer un comercio libre entre sus naciones europeas miembros de todos los productos

European Union an international organization made up of over two dozen European nations, with a common currency and common policies and laws (p. 1097)

Unión Europea organización internacional compuesta por más de dos docenas de países, con una misma moneda, y políticas y leyes en común

excommunication exclusion from the Roman Catholic Church as a penalty for refusing to obey Church law (p. 229)

excomunión exclusión de la Iglesia Católica Romana como castigo por rehusar obedecer la ley de la Iglesia

expansionism policy of increasing the amount of territory a government holds (pp. 104, 739)

expansionismo política de aumentar el territorio que posee un gobierno

extraterritoriality right of foreigners to be protected by the laws of their own nation (p. 774)

extraterritorialidad derecho de los extranjeros a recibir protección de las leyes de su propio país

F

faction dissenting group of people (p. 579)

facción grupo de disidentes

famine a severe shortage of food in which large numbers of people starve (p. 1108)

hambruna escasez severa de alimentos por la que perece gran número de personas

fascism any centralized, authoritarian government system that is not communist whose policies glorify the state over the individual and are destructive to basic human rights (p. 901)

fascismo cualquier sistema de gobierno autoritario centralizado no comunista cuya política glorifica al estado o encima del individuo y que destruye los derecho humanos fundamentales

federal republic government in which power is divided between the national, or federal, government and the states (p. 563)

república federal gobierno en el que el poder se divide entre el gobierno nacional o federal y los estados

Federal Reserve central banking system of the United States, which regulates banks (p. 895)

Reserva Federal sistema central de banca de Estados Unidos que regula los bancos

Fertile Crescent region of the Middle East in which civilizations first arose (p. 30)

Medialuna Fértil región de Oriente Medio en la cual surgieron las primeras civilizaciones

feudal contract exchange of pledges between lords and vassals (p. 219)

contrato feudal intercambio de garantías entre los señores y los vasallos

feudalism loosely organized system of government in which local lords governed their own lands but owed military service and other support to a greater lord (pp. 95, 219)

feudalismo sistema de gobierno poco organizado en el que los señores goberna ban sus propias tierras, pero debían servicio militar y otras formas de apoyo a un superior

fief in medieval Europe, an estate granted by a lord to a vassal in exchange for service and loyalty (p. 219)

estado feudal durante la Edad Media, terreno que un señor cedía a un vasallo a cambio de servicio y lealtad

filial piety respect for parents (p. 97)

piedad filial respeto hacia los padres

finance the management of money matters including the circulation of money, loans, investments, and banking (p. 895)

finanzas o gestión de los asuntos monetarios incluyendo la circulación de dinero, préstamos, inversiones y banca

First Sino-Japanese War conflict between China and Japan in 1894–1895 over control of Korea (p. 789)

Primera guerra sino-japonesa conflicto entre China y Japón de 1894 a 1895 por el control de Corea

Flanders a region that included parts of present-day northern France, Belgium, and the Netherlands; was an important industrial and financial center of northern Europe during the Middle Ages and Renaissance (p. 419)

Flandes región que incluye partes de los actuales norte de Francia, Bélgica y Holanda; fue un importante centro industrial y financiero del norte de Europa durante la Edad Media y el Renacimiento

flapper in the United States and Europe in the 1920s, a rebellious young woman (p. 885)

flapper mujer joven y rebelde en los años 20 en Estados Unidos y Europa

Florence a city in the Tuscany region of northern Italy that was the center of the Italian Renaissance (p. 412)

Florencia ciudad de la región de Toscana en el norte de Italia que fue el centro del Renacimiento italiano

flying buttresses stone supports on the outside of a building that allowed builders to construct higher, thinner walls that contained large stained-glass windows (p. 266)

contrafuertes flotantes soportes de piedra en la parte exterior de un edificio que permitía a los constructores construir paredes más finas y más altas que contenían ventanas con vidrieras

Four Noble Truths as taught by the Buddha, the four basic beliefs that form the foundation of Buddhism (p. 80)

Cuatro Verdades Nobles como enseñó Buda, las cuatro creencias básicas que forman la base del budismo

Fourteen Points list of terms for resolving WWI and future wars outlined by American President Woodrow Wilson in January 1918 (p. 833)

Catorce puntos lista de condiciones para resolver la Primera Guerra Mundial y futuras guerras, esbozada por el presidente estadounidense Woodrow Wilson en enero de 1918

Franks a Germanic tribe that conquered present-day France and neighboring lands in the 400s (p. 215)

francos tribu germánica que conquistó la actual Francia y las tierras colindantes en el siglo V

free trade trade between countries without quotas, tariffs, or other restrictions (p. 726)

libre comercio comercio entre países, sin cuotas, tasas u otras restricciones

French and Indian War war between Britain and France in the Americas that happened from 1754 to 1763; it was part of a global war called the Seven Years' War (p. 486)

Guerra franco-india guerra entre Gran Bretaña y Francia en América, que duró desde 1754 a 1763; fue parte de una guerra global que se conoció como la Guerra de los Siete Años

French Indochina Western name for the colonial holdings of France on mainland Southeast Asia; present-day Vietnam, Laos, and Cambodia (p. 792)

Indochina francesa nombre occidental para las colonias de Francia en el sudeste asiático continental

fresco colorful painting completed on wet plaster (p. 115)

fresco pintura colorida realizada sobre una pared de yeso húmedo

friar a medieval European monk who traveled from place to place preaching to the poor (p. 229)

fraile monje de la Europa medieval que viajaba de un lugar a otro predicando a los pobres

fundamentalists religious leaders who call for a return to what they see as the fundamental, or basic, values of their faiths (p. 1070)

fundamentalistas líderes religiosos que abogan por el retorno de lo que consideran ser los valores fundamentales, o básicos, de sus creencias

G

general strike strike by workers in many different industries at the same time (p. 894)

huelga general huelga de trabajadores de muchas industrias diferentes al mismo tiempo

genetic engineering manipulation of living organisms' chemical code in order to produce specific results (p. 1125)

ingeniería genética alteración del código genético que portan todas las formas de vida con el fin de producir resultados específicos

genetics a branch of biology dealing with heredity and variations among plants and animals (p. 1125)

genética rama de la biología que trata sobre la herencia y las variaciones entre sí de los animales y las plantas

Geneva Swiss city-state which became a Calvinist theocracy in the 1500s; today a major city in Switzerland (p. 427)

Ginebra ciudad estado suiza que se convirtió en una teocracia calvinista en el siglo XVI; en la actualidad es una de las principales ciudades de Suiza

genocide deliberate attempt to destroy an entire religious or ethnic group (p. 764)

genocidio intento deliberado de destruir la totalidad de un grupo religioso o étnico

gentry wealthy, landowning class (p. 371)

alta burguesía clase social rica, dueña de tierras

germ theory the theory that infectious diseases are caused by certain microbes (p. 667)

teoría de los gérmenes teoría de que las enfermedades infecciosas son causadas por ciertos microbios

Gestapo secret police in Nazi Germany (p. 915)

Gestapo policía secreta de la Alemania nazi

Ghana early West African trading kingdom located in parts of present-day Mauritania and Mali (p. 347)

Ghana antiguo reino comerciante de África occidental ubicado en partes de la actual Mauritania y Mali

ghetto separate section of a city where members of a minority group are forced to live (p. 433)

gueto área separada de una ciudad donde se fuerza a vivir a los miembros de una minoría

glasnost "openness" in Russian; a Soviet policy of greater freedom of expression introduced by Mikhail Gorbachev in the late 1980s (p. 1002)

glasnost "apertura" en ruso; política soviética de mayor libertad de expresión introducida por Mikhail Gorbachev a finales de la década de 1980

global warming the rise of Earth's surface temperature over time (p. 1113)

calentamiento global el aumento de la temperatura de la superficie terrestre a través del tiempo

globalization the process by which national economies, politics, cultures, and societies become integrated with those of other nations around the world (p. 1100)

globalización proceso mediante el cual las economías nacionales, la política, la cultura y la sociedades se integran con las de otros países del mundo

Goa a state in western India; formerly a coastal city that was made the base of Portugal's Indian trade (p. 457)

Goa estado en el oeste de India; antiguamente una ciudad costera que se convirtió en la base del comercio en la India de Portugal

golden age period of great cultural achievement (p. 86)

edad de oro período de grandes logros culturales

Golden Bull of 1222 charter that strictly limited royal power in Hungary (p. 297)

Bula de Oro de 1222 carta constitucional que limitaba rigurosamente el poder de la realeza en Hungría

Golden Horde the Mongol armies that invaded Europe in 1237 and ruled Russia for over two centuries (p. 291)

Horda Dorada los ejércitos mongoles que invadieron Europa en 1237 y que gobernaron Rusia durante más de dos siglos

Golden Temple the Sikh religion's holiest shrine (p. 1017)

Templo Dorado santuario de mayor peso sagrado de la religión sikh

Good Friday Agreement an agreement to end the conflict in Northern Ireland signed in 1998 by Protestants and Catholics (p. 1045)

Acuerdo del Viernes Santo acuerdo firmado por protestantes y católicos en 1998 para poner fin al conflicto en Irlanda del Norte

Good Neighbor Policy policy in which American President Franklin Roosevelt promised that the United States would interfere less in Latin American affairs (p. 856)

Política del Buen Vecino politica con la que el presidente estadounidense Franklin Roosevelt prometio que Estados Unidos interferiria menos en los asuntos de America Latina

Gothic style type of European architecture that developed in the Middle Ages, characterized by flying buttresses, ribbed vaulting, thin walls, and high roofs (p. 266)

estilo gótico tipo de arquitectura europea que se desarrolló en la Edad Media caracterizada por contrafuertes flotantes, bóvedas estriadas, paredes finas y techos altos

gravity force that pulls objects in Earth's sphere to the center of Earth (p. 438)

gravedad fuerza que atrae los objetos dentro de la esfera terrestre al centro de la Tierra

Great Depression a painful time of global economic collapse, starting in 1929 and lasting until about 1939 (p. 895)

Gran Depresión período nefasto de colapso de la economía mundial que empezó en 1929 y duró hasta 1939

Great Leap Forward a Chinese Communist program from 1958 to 1960 to boost farm and industrial output that failed miserably (p. 986)

Gran Salto hacia Adelante programa de la China comunista de 1958 a 1960 para aumentar la producción agrícola e industrial que fracasó miserablemente

Great Schism the official split between the Roman Catholic and Byzantine churches that occurred in 1054 (p. 286)

Gran Cisma división oficial entre las iglesias católica romana y bizantina ocurrida en 1054

Great Zimbabwe powerful East African medieval trade center and city-state located in southeastern present-day Zimbabwe (p. 356)

Gran Zimbabwe poderoso centro de comercio medieval de África oriental y ciudad estado ubicada en el sureste del actual Zimbabwe

Green Revolution the improved seeds, pesticides, mechanical equipment, and farming methods introduced in the developing world beginning in the 1950s (p. 1068)

revolución verde la introducción, en los países en vías de desarrollo durante la década de 1950, de semillas, pesticidas, equipo mecánico y métodos de agricultura perfeccionados

griot professional storyteller in early West Africa (p. 361)

griot antiguo narrador de historias profesional en África occidental

gross domestic product (GDP) the total value of all goods and services produced in a nation within a particular year (p. 984)

producto interior bruto (PIB) valor total de todos los productos y servicios producidos en una nación en un determinado año

Guangzhou a coastal city in southeastern China, also known as Canton (p. 461)

Guangzhou ciudad costera del sudeste de China, también conocida como Cantón

guerrilla a soldier in a loosely organized force making surprise raids (p. 992)

guerrilla pequeños grupos de soldados pertenecientes a una fuerza poco organizada que despliega ataques por sorpresa

guerrilla warfare fighting carried on through hit-and-run raids (p. 597)

guerra de guerrillas lucha que se caracteriza por rápidos ataques y retiradas

guild in the Middle Ages, an association of merchants or artisans who cooperated to uphold standards of their trade and to protect their economic interests (p. 235)

gremio en la Edad Media, asociación de mercaderes o artesanos que cooperaban para mantener los valores de sus oficios y para proteger sus intereses económicos

guillotine device used during the Reign of Terror to execute thousands by beheading (p. 588)

guillotina aparato usado durante el Reinado del Terror para decapitar a miles de personas

Gulag in the Soviet Union, a system of forced labor camps in which millions of criminals and political prisoners were held under Stalin (p. 906)

Gulag en la Unión Soviética, un sistema de campos de trabajo forzado donde millones de criminales y prisioneros políticos fueron detenidos durante el gobierno de Stalin

Guomindang Nationalist party; active in China 1912 to 1949 (p. 870)

Guomindang partido nacionalista, activo en China entre 1912 y 1949

H

habeas corpus principle that a person cannot be held in prison without first being charged with a specific crime (p. 247)

habeus corpus principio por el que no puede encarcelarse a una persona sin haber sido antes acusada formalmente de un delito específico

hacienda a large plantation (p. 852)

hacienda plantación grande

hajj one of the Five Pillars of Islam, the pilgrimage to Mecca that all Muslims are expected to make at least once in their lifetime (p. 306)

hayyi uno de los Cinco Pilares del Islam, la peregrinación a la Meca que se espera hagan todos los musulmanes por lo menos una vez en la vida

hangul alphabet that uses symbols to represent the sounds of spoken Korean (p. 386)

hangul alfabeto que usa símbolos para representar gráficamente los sonidos del idioma coreano

Hapsburg empire Central European empire that lasted from the 1400s to the 1900s and at its height included the lands of the Holy Roman Empire and the Netherlands (p. 504)

Imperio Habsburgo imperio centroeuropeo que duró desde el siglo XV hasta el siglo XX, y que en su plenitud abarcó los territorios del Sacro Imperio Romano y Holanda

Harappa large ancient city of the Indus civilization, located in present-day Pakistan (p. 70)

Harappa antigua gran ciudad de la civilización del Indo, ubicada en el presente Pakistán

Harlem Renaissance an African American cultural movement in the 1920s and 1930s, centered in Harlem (p. 887)

Renacimiento de Harlem movimiento cultural afroamericano durante las décadas de 1920 y 1930, que estaba centrado en Harlem

hejab headscarves and loose-fitting, ankle-length garments meant to conceal the body (p. 1035)

hejab velos, pañuelos y prendas de vestir amplias y hasta los tobillos cuya finalidad es ocultar el cuerpo

heliocentric based on the belief that the sun is the center of the universe (pp. 142, 434)

heliocéntrico sistema basado en la creencia de que el Sol es el centro del universo

heresy religious belief that is contrary to the official teachings of a church (p. 171)

herejía creencia religiosa contraria a las enseñanzas oficiales de la iglesia

hierarchy system of ranking groups (p. 32)

jerarquía sistema que clasifica a las personas de una sociedad

hieroglyphics system of writing in which pictures called hieroglyphs represent objects, concepts, or sounds (p. 54)

jeroglíficos sistema de escritura cuyos dibujos, llamados jeroglíficos, representan objetos, conceptos o sonidos

hijra Muhammad's journey from Mecca to Medina in 622 (p. 305)

héjira trayecto de Mahoma de la Meca a Medina en el año 622

Hiroshima city in Japan where the first atomic bomb was dropped in August 1945 (p. 951)

Hiroshima ciudad de Japón donde fue lanzada la primera bomba atómica en agosto de 1945

historian a person who studies how people lived in the past (p. 4)

historiador persona que estudia el modo de vida de la gente en el pasado

Holocaust the systematic genocide of about six million European Jews by the Nazis during World War II (p. 936)

Holocausto el genocidio sistemático por parte de los nazis de alrededor de seis millones de judíos europeos durante la Segunda Guerra Mundial

Holy Land Jerusalem and other places in Palestine where Christians believe Jesus had lived and preached (p. 256)

Tierra Santa Jerusalem y otros lugares en Palestina donde los cristianos creen que Jesús vivió y predicó

Holy Roman Empire empire of west central Europe from 962 to 1806, comprising present-day Germany and neighboring lands (p. 251)

Sacro Imperio Romano imperio de la Europa central occidental desde 962 a 1806, que comprendía la actual Alemania y las tierras aledañas

home rule local self-government (p. 731)

autogobierno autogobierno local

homogeneous society society that has a common culture and language (p. 788)

sociedad homogénea sociedad que tiene un lenguaje y una cultura común

Huari a culture that thrived in the Andean region from about A.D. 600–A.D. 1000 (p. 196)

huari cultura que tuvo su apogeo en la región andina desde alrededor de 600 D.C. a 1000 D.C.

Huguenots French Protestants of the 1500s and 1600s (p. 510)

Hugonotes protestantes franceses de los siglos XVI y XVII

humanism an intellectual movement at the heart of the Renaissance that focused on education and the classics (p. 411)

humanismo movimiento intelectual durante el auge del Renacimiento que se centraba en la educación y los clásicos

humanities study of subjects such as grammar, rhetoric, poetry, and history, that were taught in ancient Greece and Rome (p. 411)

humanidades estudio de asignaturas como la gramática, la retórica, poesía e historia que se enseñaban en las antiguas Grecia y Roma

Huns a nomadic people of central Asia (p. 175)

hunos pueblo nómada del centro de Asia

Hutus the group that forms the majority in Rwanda and Burundi (p. 1051)

Hutus grupo mayoritario de Ruanda y Burundi

hypothesis an unproved theory accepted for the purposes of explaining certain facts or to provide a basis for further investigation (p. 436)

hipótesis teoría sin probar aceptada con el propósito de explicar determinados hechos o de proveer una base para una investigación posterior más profunda

I

icon holy image of Christ, the Virgin Mary, or a saint venerated in the Eastern Orthodox Church (p. 286)

ícono imagen sagrada de Cristo, la Vírgen María o de un santo venerado por la iglesia ortodoxa oriental

ideology system of thought and belief (pp. 634, 972)

ideología sistema de pensamiento y creencias

illumination the artistic decoration of books and manuscripts (p. 267)

iluminación decoración artística de libros y manuscritos

immunity natural protection, resistance (p. 473)

inmunidad protección natural, resistencia

imperialism domination by one country of the political, economic, or cultural life of another country or region (pp. 156, 750)

imperialismo dominio por parte de un país de la vida política, económica o cultural de otro país o región

import substitution manufacturing goods locally to replace imports (p. 1082)

sustitución de importaciones la producción local de bienes para reemplazar su importación

impressionism school of painting of the late 1800s and early 1900s that tried to capture fleeting visual impressions (p. 684)

impresionismo escuela de pintura de finales del siglo XIX y principios del siglo XX que trataba de captar impresiones visuales fugaces

indemnity payment for losses in war (p. 774)

indemnización compensación como pago por pérdidas de guerra

indigenous original or native to a country or region (pp. 798, 1087)

indígena originario o nativo de un país o región

indulgence in the Roman Catholic Church, pardon for sins committed during a person's lifetime (p. 424)

indulgencia perdón por los pecados cometidos en vida concedido por la Iglesia Católica Romana

inflation economic cycle that involves a rapid rise in prices linked to a sharp increase in the amount of money available (pp. 174, 270, 492)

inflación ciclo económico caracterizado por un rápida subida de los precios ligada a un aumento rápido del dinero disponible

Inquisition a Church court set up to try people accused of heresy (p. 260)

Inquisición tribunal de la Iglesia establecido para juzgar a la gente acusada de herejía

insurgents rebel forces (p. 1059)

insurgentes fuerzas rebeldes

intendant official appointed by French king Louis XIV to govern the provinces, collect taxes, and recruit soldiers (p. 512)

intendente oficial publico nombrado por el rey francés Luis XIV para gobernar las provincias, recaudar impuestos y reclutar soldados

interchangeable parts identical components that can be used in place of one another in manufacturing (p. 663)

repuestos intercambiables componentes idénticos que pueden usarse unos en lugar de otros en el proceso de producción

interdependence mutual dependence of countries on goods, resources, labor, and knowledge from other parts of the world (p. 1100)

interdependencia dependencia mutua de los países con los de otras partes del mundo en cuanto a productos, recursos, mano de obra y conocimientos

interdict in the Roman Catholic Church, excommunication of an entire region, town, or kingdom (p. 229)

interdicto en la Iglesia Católica Romana, excomunión de una región, pueblo o reino

International Space Station (ISS) an artificial structure built and maintained by a coalition of nations with the purpose of research (p. 1121)

Estación Espacial Internacional (ISS, por sus siglas en inglés) estructura artificial construida y mantenida por una coalición de naciones con el fin de llevar a cabo investigaciones

Internet a huge international computer network linking millions of users around the world (p. 1123)

Internet inmensa red internacional de computadoras que une a millones de ususarios en todo el mundo

Inti the Inca sun god (p. 199)

Inti dios sol inca

intifada Palestinian Arab uprisings against the Israeli occupation (p. 1055)

intifadas levantamientos de árabes palestinos en contra de la ocupación israelí

Iroquois League political alliance of five Iroquois groups, known as the Five Nations, in the late 1500s (p. 205)

Liga de los iroqueses alianza política de cinco grupos iroqueses, conocida como las Cinco Naciones, de finales del siglo XVI

Isfahan capital of Safavid empire during the 1600s; located in present-day Iran (p. 333)

Isfahan capital del imperio safavid durante el siglo XVII, situada en actual Irán

Islamist a person who wants government policies to be based on the teachings of Islam (p. 1029)

islamista persona que desea que las políticas del gobierno tengan su fundamento en las enseñanzas del Islam

island-hopping during World War II, Allied strategy of recapturing some Japanese-held islands while bypassing others (p. 950)

salto entre islas estrategia aliada durante la Segunda Guerra Mundial de retomar algunas de las islas ocupadas por los japoneses e ignorar y pasar de largo de otras

Istanbul capital of the Ottoman empire; located in the northwest of present-day Turkey; formerly Constantinople (p. 329)

Estambul capital del imperio otomano; situada en el noroeste de la actual Turquía; anteriormente llamada Constantinopla

J

Jacobin member of a radical political club during the French Revolution (p. 583)

jacobino miembro de un club político radical durante la Revolución Francesa

janizary elite force of the Ottoman army (p. 331)

jenízaro fuerza de élitedel ejército otomano

Jericho the world's first village, established in the modern-day West Bank between 10,000 and 9000 B.C. (p. 14)

Jericó la primera aldea del mundo establecidas en la actual Cisjordania entre alrededor del año 10,000 y 9000 A.C.

Jerusalem capital of the Jewish state of Judea in ancient times and capital of the modern State of Israel; city sacred to Jews, Muslims, and Christians (p. 1056)

Jerusalén capital del estado judío de Judea en la antigüedad, y capital del actual estado de Israel; ciudad sagrada para los judíos, musulmanes y cristianos

jihad in Islam, an effort in God's service (p. 306)

yihad en el Islam, un esfuerzo al servicio de Dios

joint family family organization in which several generations share a common dwelling (p. 89)

familia extendida organización familiar en la que varias generaciones comparten una vivienda

journeyman a salaried worker employed by a guild master (p. 235)
   oficial trabajador asalariado empleado por el maestro del gremio

jury legal group of people sworn to make a decision in a legal case (pp. 126, 245)
   jurado grupo de personas que han prestado juramento para tomar una decisión en un caso legal

Justinian's Code collection of Roman laws organized by the Byzantine emperor Justinian and later serving as a model for the Catholic Church and medieval monarchs (p. 283)
   Código Justiniano recopilación de leyes romanas organizada por el emperador bizantino Justiniano y que luego sirvió como modelo para la iglesia católica y los monarcas medievales

K

Kaaba the most sacred temple of Islam, located at Mecca (p. 305)
   Kaaba el templo más sagrado del islam, ubicado en La Meca

kaiser emperor of Germany (p. 695)
   kaiser emperador de Alemania

kamikaze Japanese pilot who undertook a suicide mission (p. 950)
   kamikaze piloto japonés que emprendía una misión suicida

kana in the Japanese writing system, phonetic symbols representing syllables (p. 390)
   kana en el sistema japonés de escritura, símbolos fonéticos que representan sílabas

karma in Hindu belief, all the actions that affect a person's fate in the next life (p. 77)
   karma según la creencia hindú, todas las acciones que afectan el destino de una persona en su próxima vida

Kashmir a former princely state in the Himalayas, claimed by both India and Pakistan, which have fought wars over its control (p. 1015)
   Cachemira antiguo estado principesco de los Himalayas, reclamado tanto por India como Pakistán, y por cuyo control han librado varias guerras

Katanga a province of the Democratic Republic of the Congo with rich copper and diamond deposits that tried to gain independence from Congo in 1960 (p. 1029)
   Katanga provincia de la República Democrática del Congo con ricos depósitos de cobre y diamantes, que intentó independizarse del Congo en 1960

Kellogg-Briand Pact an international agreement, signed by almost every nation in 1928, to stop using war as a method of national policy (p. 893)
   Pacto de Kellogg-Briand acuerdo internacional firmado por casi todas las naciones en 1928 para erradicar el uso de la guerra como un metodo de politica nacional

Khmer Rouge a political movement and a force of Cambodian communist guerrillas that gained power in Cambodia in 1975 (p. 997)
   Khmer Rouge movimiento político y fuerza guerrillera comunista de Camboya que llegó al poder en ese país en 1975

kibbutz a collective farm in Israel (p. 1033)
   kibbutz en Israel, granja comunitaria

Kiev capital of medieval Russia and of present-day Ukraine (p. 290)
   Kiev capital de la Rusia medieval y de la actual Ucrania

kiva large underground chamber that the Anasazi used for religious ceremonies and political meetings (p. 203)
   kiva gran sala subterránea que usaban los anazasi para ceremonias religiosas y reuniones políticas

knight a European noble who served as a mounted warrior (p. 220)
   caballero noble europeo que servía como guerrero montado

Knossos an ancient Minoan city on the island of Crete (p. 114)
   Cnosos antigua ciudad minoica en la isla de Creta

Kolkata a large city in India, also known as Calcutta (p. 1080)
   Kolkata ciudad grande de India, conocida también como Calcuta

Koryo dynasty Korean dynasty that ruled from 935 to 1392 (p. 385)
   dinastía Koryo dinastía coreana que gobernó desde 935 a 1392

Kosovo a province of Serbia with an Albanian ethnic majority that was the site of an ethnic conflict during the 1990s (p. 1047)
   Kosovo provincia de Serbia de mayoría étnica albanesa que sufrió un conflicto étnico durante la década de 1990

kulak wealthy peasant in the Soviet Union in the 1930s (p. 905)
   campesino adinerado de la Unión Soviética en la década de 1930

Kulturkampf Bismarck's "battle for civilization," intended to make Catholics put loyalty to the state above their allegiance to the Church (p. 698)

Kulturkampf "batalla por civilización" de Bismarck, cuyo objetivo era que los católicos pusieran la lealtod al estado por encima de la lealtad a la Iglesia

L

La Reforma an era of liberal reform in Mexico from 1855 to 1876 (p. 803)

La Reforma era de reforma liberal en México desde 1855 a 1876

labor union workers' organization (p. 618)

sindicato organización de trabajadores

laissez faire policy allowing business to operate with little or no government interference (p. 548)

laissez faire política que permite a los negocios y empresas operar con poca o ninguna interferencia del gobierno

land reform breakup of large agricultural holdings for redistribution among peasants (p. 369)

reforma agraria división de grandes propiedades dedicadas a la agricultura para distribuirlas entre los campesinos

laser a high-energy light beam that can be used for many purposes including surgery, engineering, and scientific research (p. 1124)

láser haz luminoso de alta energía que puede ser usado para muchos fines, entre ellos la cirugía, la ingeniería y la investigación científica

latifundia huge estates bought up by newly wealthy Roman citizens (p. 157)

latifundios grandes propiedades adquiridas por los ciudadanos romanos que se habían vuelto ricos recientemente

lay investiture appointment of bishops by anyone who is not a member of the clergy (p. 252)

investidura nombramiento de obispos por cualquiera que no sea miembro del clero

legion basic unit of the ancient Roman army, made up of about 5,000 soldiers (p. 154)

legión unidad básica del ejército de la antigua Roma, que consistía de unos 5,000 soldados

legislature lawmaking body (p. 122)

asamblea legislativa cuerpo encargado de promover y promulgar las leyes

legitimacy principle by which monarchies that had been unseated by the French Revolution or Napoleon were restored (p. 600)

legitimidad principio por el que las monarquías que habían sido derrocadas por la Revolución Francesa o por Napoleón fueron restituidas

Lend-Lease Act act passed by the U. S. Congress in 1941 that allowed the president (FDR) to sell or lend war supplies to any country whose defense was considered vital to the United States (p. 937)

Ley de Préstamo y Arriendo decreto aprobado por el Congreso de Estados Unidos en 1941 que permitió al presidente (FDR) vender o arrendar materiales de guerra a cualquier país cuya defensa fuese considerada de vital importancia para Estados Unidos

levée morning ritual during which nobles would wait upon French king Louis XIV (p. 512)

recepción matutina ritual de la mañana en el que los nobles atendían al rey Luis XIV

libel knowing publication of false and damaging statements (p. 737)

libelo publicación intencional de declaraciones falsas que perjudican a alguien

liberation theology movement within the Catholic Church that urged the church to become a force for reform, social justice, and put an end to poverty (p. 1085)

teología de la liberación movimiento dentro de la Iglesia Católica que urgía a la iglesia a liderar un llamamiento por la reforma, la justicia social el fin de la pobreza

limited monarchy government in which a constitution or legislative body limits the monarch's powers (p. 522)

monarquía limitada gobierno en el que la constitución o el cuerpo legislativo limitan los poderes de la monarquía

Line of Demarcation line set by the Treaty of Tordesillas dividing the non-European world into two zones, one controlled by Spain and the other by Portugal (p. 450)

Línea de demarcación línea establecida por el Tratado de Tordesillas que dividía el mundo fuera de Europa en dos zonas: una controlada por España y otra por Portugal

lineage group claiming a common ancestor (p. 358)

linaje grupo que reivindica un antepasado en común

literacy the ability to read and write (p. 1066)

alfabetismo capacidad de leer y escribir

literacy rate percentage of people who can read and write (p. 386)

tasa de alfabetización porcentaje de personas que pueden leer y escribir

ENGLISH/SPANISH GLOSSARY

Liverpool city and one of the largest ports in England; first major rail line linked Liverpool to Manchester in 1830 (p. 615)

Liverpool ciudad y uno de los puertos más grandes de Inglaterra; línea importante de ferrocarril unió Liverpool con Manchester en 1830

loess fine windblown yellow soil (p. 93)

loes tierra fina y amarilla que se llava el viento

logic rational thinking (p. 130)

lógica pensamiento racional

Long March epic march in which a group of Chinese Communists retreated from Guomindang forces by marching over 6,000 miles (p. 871)

Gran Marcha marcha épica en la que un grupo de comunistas chinos marcharon en retirada de las fuerzas del Guomindang por más de 6,000 millas

longbow six-foot-long bow that could rapidly fire arrows with enough force to pierce most armor (p. 272)

arco largo arco de seis pies de largo que podía disparar rápidamente flechas con suficiente fuerza como para agujerear una armadura

Louisiana Purchase territory purchased by Thomas Jefferson from France in 1803 (p. 739)

Compra de Luisiana territorio que Thomas Jefferson compró a Francia en 1803

Luftwaffe German air force (p. 930)

Luftwaffe fuerza aérea alemana

Lusitania British liner torpedoed by a German submarine in May 1915 (p. 830)

Lusitania crucero británico torpedeado por un submarino alemán en mayo de 1915

M

Macao region of southeastern China made up of a peninsula and two islands, a Portuguese territory from the mid-1800s to 1999 (p. 461)

Macao región al sudeste de China formada por una península y dos islas; fue territorio portugués desde mediados del siglo XIX a 1999

Maginot Line massive fortifications built by the French along their border with Germany in the 1930s to protect against invasion (p. 893)

Línea Maginot fortificaciones masivas construídas por los franceses a lo largo de la frontera france sa con Alemania en la década de 1930 para protegerse contra invasiones futuras

Magna Carta the Great Charter approved by King John of England in 1215; it limited royal power and established certain rights of English freemen (p. 246)

Carta Magna carta constitucional aprobada por el Rey Juan de Inglaterra en 1215; limitaba el poder real y establecía ciertos derechos de los ingleses libres

Magyars an ethnic group centered in present-day Hungary (p. 218)

magiar grupo étnico establecido en la actual Hungría

Mahdi a Muslim savior of the faith (p. 762)

Mahdi salvador musulmán de la fe

maize corn (p. 187)

maíz elote

Malacca a state and coastal city in SW Malaysia, was an early center of the spice trade (p. 457)

Malacca estado y ciudad costera en el sudoeste de Malasia; fue uno de los primeros centros del comercio de especias

Mali medieval West African trading empire located in present-day Mali (p. 348)

Mali imperio comerciante de África occidental medieval ubicado en el actual Mali

Malindi a coastal town in SE Kenya (p. 452)

Malindi pueblo costero al sudeste de Kenia

Manchester city in England; one of the leading industrial areas; example of an Industrial Revolution city; first major rail line linked Manchester to Liverpool in 1830 (p. 615)

Manchester ciudad de Inglaterra; una de las principales áreas industriales; ejemplo de ciudad de la Revolución Industrial; la primera línea importante de ferrocarril unió Manchester con Liverpool en 1830

Manchuria historic province in northeastern China; rich in natural resources (p. 876)

Manchuria provincia histórica en el noreste de China; rica en recursos naturales

Manchus people originally from Manchuria, north of China, who conquered the Ming dynasty and ruled China as the Qing dynasty from the mid-1600s to the early 1900s (p. 462)

manchus personas originalmente de Manchuria, al norte de China, que derrotaron a la dinastía Ming y gobernaron como la dinastía Chin desde mediados del siglo XVII a principios del siglo XX

mandate after World War I, a territory administered by a Western power (p. 838)

mandato territorio administrado por un poder occidental después de la Primera Guerra Mundial

Manhattan Project code name for the project to build the first atomic bomb during WWII (p. 950)

Proyecto Manhattan nombre en clave del proyecto para la fabricación de la primera bomba atómica durante la Segunda Guerra Mundial

Manifest Destiny American idea that the United States should stretch across the entire North American continent (p. 739)

Destino Manifiesto idea estadounidense de que Estados Unidos debería extenderse hasta ocupar todo el continente norteamericano

manor during the Middle Ages in Europe, a lord's estate which included one or more villages and the surrounding lands (p. 222)

señorío durante la Edad Media en Europa, propiedad de un señor que incluía uno o más pueblos y sus terrenos adyacentes

Maori indigenous people of New Zealand (p. 800)

maoríe pueblo indígena de Nueva Zelanda

March on Rome planned march of thousands of Fascist supporters to take control of Rome; in response Mussolini was given the legal right to control Italy (p. 899)

Marcha sobre Roma marcha planeada de miles de simpatizantes fascistas sobre Roma para tomar su control; en respuesta a ella a Mussolini se le concedió el derecho legal del control de Italia

Marseilles French port city; troops marched to a patriotic song as they marched from this city, the song eventually became the French national anthem (p. 590)

Marsella ciudad portuaria francesa; las tropas que marcharon al ritmo de una canción patriótica desde esta ciudad inspiraron el himno nacional francés

Marshall Plan massive aid package offered by the U. S. to Europe to help countries rebuild after WWII (p. 955)

Plan Marshall paquete de ayuda a gran escala ofrecido por Estados Unidos a Europa para apoyar la reconstrucción de los países después de la Segunda Guerra Mundial

martyr person who suffers or dies for his or her beliefs (p. 170)

mártir persona que sufre o muere por sus creencias

matrilineal term for a family organization in which kinship ties are traced through the mother (pp. 358, 399)

matrilineal organización familiar en la que los lazos de parentesco se siguen a través de la madre

May Fourth Movement cultural movement in China that sought to reform China and make it stronger (p. 870)

Movimiento del Cuatro de Mayo movimiento cultural de China que se centró en reformar China y hacerla más fuerte

means of production farms, factories, railways, and other large businesses that produce and distribute goods (p. 625)

medios de producción granjas, fábricas, ferrocarriles y otros grandes negocios que producen y distribuyen mercancías

Mecca a city in western Saudi Arabia; birthplace of the prophet Muhammad and most holy city for Islamic people (p. 304)

Meca ciudad en el oeste de Arabia Saudita; lugar de nacimiento del profeta Mahoma y ciudad sagrada para los creyentes islámicos

medieval referring to the Middle Ages in Europe or the period of history between ancient and modern times (p. 214)

medieval se refiere a la Edad Media en Europa, es decir, el período de la historia entre la edad antigua y la edad moderna

Medina a city in western Saudi Arabia; a city where Muhammad preached (p. 305)

Medina ciudad en el oeste de Arabia Saudita; ciudad donde predicó Mahoma

Meiji Restoration in Japan, the reign of emperor Meiji from 1868 to 1912 which was marked by rapid modernization and industrialization (p. 786)

restauración de Meiji en Japón, reino del emperador Meiji desde 1868 a 1912 que fue marcado por la rápida modernización e industrialización

mercantilism policy by which a nation sought to export more than it imported in order to build its supply of gold and silver (p. 494)

mercantilismo política por la que una nación trataba de exportar más de lo que importaba para aumentar sus reservas de o ro y plata

mercenary soldier serving in a foreign army for pay (pp. 177, 527)

mercenario soldado que sirve en un ejército extranjero a cambio de dinero

Meroë capital of the ancient kingdom of Nubia (p. 343)

Meroë capital del antiguo reino de Nubia

Mesa Verde the largest complex of Anasazi cliff-dwellings in the United States Southwest, built between about A.D. 1150 and A.D. 1300 (p. 203)

Mesa Verde el mayor complejo de viviendas anazasi construidas en acantilados en el sudoeste de Estados Unidos, entre alrededor de 1150 D.C. y 1300 D.C.

Mesoamerica region of North America, including Mexico and Central America, in which civilizations with common cultural features developed before Europeans entered the continent (p. 186)

Mesoamérica región de América del Norte, que incluye a México y América Central, en la cual se desarrollaron, antes de la llegada de los europeos al continente, civilizaciones con características culturales similares

Mesopotamia region within the Fertile Crescent that lies between the Tigris and Euphrates rivers (p. 30)

Mesopotamia región del Creciente Fértil que se encuentra entre los ríos Tigris y Éufrates

messiah savior sent by God (p. 167)

mésias salvador enviado por Dios

mestizo person in Spain's colonies in the Americas who was of Native American and European descent (pp. 480, 645)

mestizo persona de las colonias españolas de América descendiente de nativos y europeos

métis people of mixed Native American and French Canadian descent (p. 798)

métis pueblo de descendientes con mezcla de indígenas americanos y franceses canadienses

middle class a group of people, including merchants, traders, and artisans, whose rank was between nobles and peasants (p. 235)

clase media grupo de personas, incluyendo mercaderes, comerciantes y artesanos, cuyo rango estaba entre los nobles y los campesinos

Middle Passage the leg of the triangular trade route on which slaves were transported from Africa to the Americas (p. 487)

Travesía Intermedia parte de la ruta del comercio triangular en la que los esclavos eran transportados desde África a las Américas

militarism glorification of the military (p. 818)

militarismo glorificación de las fuerzas armadas

militias armed groups of citizen soldiers (p. 1058)

milicias grupos armados de soldados-ciudadanos

minaret slender tower of a mosque, from which Muslims are called to prayer (p. 314)

minarete torre esbelta de una mezquita desde la que se convoca a los musulmanes a la oración

Ming dynasty Chinese dynasty in which Chinese rule was restored; held power from 1368 to 1644 (p. 379)

dinastía Ming dinastía china en la que se restauro el gobierno chino; se mantuvo en el poder desde a 1644

missionary someone sent to do religious work in a territory or foreign country (pp. 85, 453)

misioneros personas enviadas para hacer trabajos religiosos en un territorio u otro país

mobilize prepare military forces for war (p. 820)

mobilizar preparar las fuerzas militares para la guerra

Moche a culture that thrived in the Andean region from about 400 B.C. to A.D. 600 (p. 196)

moche cultura preincaica que tuvo su apogeo en la región andina, desde alrededor de 400 A.C. a 600 D.C.

Mohenjo-Daro ancient city of the Indus civilization, located in present-day Pakistan (p. 70)

Mohenjo-Daro antigua ciudad de la civilización del Indo, ubicada en el presente Pakistán

moksha in Hindu belief, the ultimate goal of existence, which is to achieve union with brahman (p. 77)

moksha según la creencia hindú, el objetivo final de la existencia, que es llegar a la unión con el brahman

Moluccas a group of islands in eastern Indonesia; was the center of the spice trade in the 1500s and 1600s (p. 446)

Molucas grupo de islas en el este de Indonesia; fue el centro del comercio de especias en los siglos XVI y XVII

Mombasa a city in southeastern Kenya, located on a small coastal island (p. 452)

Mombasa ciudad al sudeste de Kenia, localizada en una pequeña isla costera

monarchy government in which a king or queen exercises central power (p. 120)

monarquía gobierno en el que el poder reside en el rey o la reina

money economy economic system in which goods or services are paid for through the exchange of a token of an agreed value (p. 42)

economía de dinero sistema económico en el que las mercancías y los servicios se pagan mediante el intercambio de una moneda con un valor establecido

monopoly complete control of a product or business by one person or group (pp. 103, 454)

monopolio control total de un producto o negocio por una persona o grupo

monotheistic believing in one God (p. 57)

monoteísta creencia en un solo Dios

Monroe Doctrine American policy of discouraging European intervention in the Western Hemisphere (p. 805)

Doctrina Monroe política estadounidense de rechazo a la intervención europea en el hemisferio occidental

monsoon seasonal wind that regularly blows from a certain direction for part of the year (p. 69)

monzón viento estacional que regularmente sopla desde una dirección específica durante una parte del año

mosaic picture made from chips of colored stone or glass (p. 162)

mosaico imagen hecha con pedazos de piedras o vidrios de colores

mosque Muslim house of worship; (p. 306)

mezquita templo musulmán

Mothers of the Plaza de Mayo a movement of women who protested weekly in a central plaza in the capital of Argentina against the disappearance or killing of relatives (p. 1088)

Madres de la Plaza de Mayo asociación de mujeres que se reunían semanalmente en una céntrica plaza de la capital de Argentina para protest por la desaparición o asesinato de sus familiares

Mughal Muslim dynasty that ruled much of present-day India from 1526 to 1857 (p. 327)

Mughal dinastía musulmana que gobernó gran parte de la India actual de 1526 a 1857

Mughal empire Muslim empire that ruled most of northern India from the mid-1500s to the mid-1700s; also known as the Mogul or Mongol empire (p. 457)

imperio Mughal imperio musulmán que gobernó la mayor parte del norte de India desde mediados del siglo XVI a mediados del siglo XVIII; también se conoce como imperio Mogul o Mongol

mujahedin Muslim religious warriors (p. 1002)

mujaedin guerreros religiosos musulmanes

mulatto in Spain's colonies in the Americas, person who was of African and European descent (pp. 480, 645)

mulato en las colonias españolas de América descendiente de africanos y europeos

multiethnic made up of several ethnic groups (p. 1046)

multiétnico compuesto de varios grupos étnicos

multinational corporation company with branches in many countries (p. 1101)

corporación multinacional empresa con sucursales en muchos países

Mumbai a large city in India, also known as Bombay (p. 1080)

Mumbai ciudad grande de India, conocida también como Bombay

mummification the preservation of dead bodies by embalming and wrapping them in cloth (p. 53)

momificación práctica de preservar los cuerpos de los muertos embalsamándolos y envolviéndolos en vendas

mutiny revolt, especially of soldiers or sailors against their officers (p. 490)

motín revuelta, especialmente de soldados y marineros contra sus oficiales

mutual-aid societies self-help groups to aid sick or injured workers (p. 670)

sociedades de ayuda mutua grupos de apoyo establecidos para ayudar a los trabajadores enfermos o heridos en accidentes laborales

mystic person who devotes his or her life to seeking direct communion with divine forces (p. 73)

místico persona que dedica su vida a buscar la comunión directa con las fuerzas divinas

N

Nagasaki a coastal city in southern Japan on the island of Kyushu; city in Japan where the second atomic bomb was dropped in August, 1945 (pp. 465, 951)

Nagasaki ciudad costera en el sur de Japón en la isla de Kyushu; ciudad de Japón donde fue lanzada la segunda bomba atómica en agosto de 1945

Napoleonic Code body of French civil laws introduced in 1804; served as model for many nations' civil codes (p. 593)

Código Napoleónico cuerpo de las leyes civiles francesas presentadas en 1804, que sirvieron como modelo para los códigos civiles de muchos países

nationalism a strong feeling of pride in and devotion to one's country (p. 590)

nacionalismo fuerte sentimiento de orgullo y devoción hacia el país propio

nationalization takeover of property or resources by the government (p. 854)

nacionalización apropiación de propiedades o recursos por parte del gobierno

natural law rules of conduct discoverable by reason (p. 544)

leyes naturales normas de conducta que se pueden descubrir mediante la razón

natural right right that belongs to all humans from birth, such as life, liberty, and property (p. 545)

derecho natural derecho que pertenece a todos los humanos desde el nacimiento: vida, libertad y propiedad

Nazca a culture that thrived in the Andean region from about 200 B.C. to A.D. 600 (p. 196)

Nazca cultura que tuvo su apogeo en la región andina desde alrededor de 200 A.C. a 600 D.C.

Nazi-Soviet Pact agreement between Germany and the Soviet Union in 1939 in which the two nations promised not to fight each other and to divide up land in Eastern Europe (p. 929)

Pacto nazi-soviético acuerdo en 1939 entre Alemania y la Unión Soviética mediante el cual las dos naciones prometen no atacarse mutuamente y dividirse entre sí territorio de Europa del Este

négritude movement movement in which writers and artists of African descent expressed pride in their African heritage (p. 860)

movimiento de la negritud movimiento en el que los escritores y artistas descendientes de africanos expresabansu orgullo por la herencia africana

Neolithic Period the final era of prehistory, which began about 9000 B.C.; also called the New Stone Age (p. 11)

período Neolítico era final de la prehistoria que empezó hacia el 9000 A.C.; también llamado Nueva Edad de Piedra

Neolithic Revolution the period of time during which the introduction of agriculture led people to transition from nomadic to settled life (p. 13)

revolución neolítica período durante el cual el comienzo de la agricultura llevó a la gente a la transición de la vida nómada a la vida sedentaria

neutrality policy of supporting neither side in a war (p. 820)

neutralidad política de mantenerse al margen en una guerra

Neutrality Acts a series of acts passed by the U.S. Congress from 1935 to 1939 that aimed to keep the U. S. from becoming involved in WWII (p. 926)

Leyes de Neutralidad serie de decretos aprobados por el Congreso de Estados Unidos de 1935 a 1939 con el fin de evitar la implicación del país en la Segunda Guerra Mundial

New Deal a massive package of economic and social programs established by FDR to help Americans during the Great Depression (p. 897)

Nuevo Tratado paquete masivo de programas económicos y sociales establecidos por FDR para ayudar a los estadounidenses durante la Gran Depresión

New France French possessions in present-day Canada from the 1500s to 1763 (p. 482)

Nueva Francia posesiones francesas en el actual Canadá desde el siglo XVI a 1763

New Stone Age the final era of prehistory, which began about 9000 B.C.; also called the Neolithic Period (p. 11)

Nueva Edad de Piedra era final de la prehistoria que empezó aproximadamente hacia el 9000 A.C.; también llamado período Neolítico

nirvana in Buddhist belief, union with the universe and release from the cycle of rebirth (p. 80)

nirvana en el budismo, unión con el universo y liberación del ciclo de la reencarnación

no-fly zones in Iraq, areas where the United States and its allies banned flights by Iraqi aircraft after the 1991 Gulf War (p. 1059)

zonas de exclusión del espacio aéreo zonas de Iraq en las que Estados Unidos y sus aliados prohibieron el vuelo a la aviación iraquí después de la Guerra del Golfo en 1991

nomad a person who moves from place to place in search of food (p. 11)

nómada persona que se traslada de un lugar a otro en busca de alimentos

nonalignment political and diplomatic independence from both Cold War powers (p. 1019)

no alineación independencia política y diplomática de ambas potencias de la guerra fría

North Atlantic Treaty Organization (NATO) a military alliance between several North Atlantic states to safeguard them from the presumed threat of the Soviet Union's communist bloc; countries from other regions later joined the alliance (p. 956)

Organización del Tratado del Atlántico Norte (OTAN) alianza militar entre varios estados del Atlántico norte para salvaguardarlos de la supuesta amenaza del bloque comunista liderado por la Unión Soviética; más tarde se incorporarían a la alianza países de otras regiones

Northern Ireland the northern portion of the island of Ireland, a part of the United Kingdom that has had a long religious conflict (p. 1045)

Irlanda del Norte parte norte de la isla de Irlanda y territorio del Reino Unido, que ha sufrido un conflicto religioso durante mucho tiempo

Nubia ancient kingdom in northeastern Africa, also called Kush (p. 343)

Nubia antiguo reino del noreste africano, también llamado Kush

nuclear family family unit consisting of parents and children (p. 357)

familia nuclear unidad familiar que consta de los padres y sus hijos

Nuremberg Germany city where Hitler staged Nazi rallies in the 1930s, and where Nazi war crimes trials were held after WWII (p. 953)

Nuremberg ciudad del sur de Alemania donde Hitler escenificó manifestaciones nazis durante la década de 1930, y donde se celebraron los juicios por crímenes de guerra nazis después de la Segunda Guerra Mundial

Nuremberg Laws laws approved by the Nazi Party in 1935, depriving Jews of German citizenship and taking some rights away from them (p. 915)

Leyes de Nuremberg leyes aprobadas por el partido nazi en 1935, que eliminaba algunos de los derechos de los judíos en Alemania

O

occupied territories areas controlled by a nation that are part of another entity; Palestinians use this term for certain lands Israel gained after the 1967 war. (p. 1055)

territorios ocupados zonas controladas por una nación que forman parte de otra entidad. Los palestinos usan esta palabra para referirse a los territorios ocupados por Israel después de la guerra de 1967

Old Stone Age the era of prehistory that lasted from 2 million B.C. to about 9000 B.C. (p. 11)

Antigua Edad de Piedra era de la prehistoria que duró desde aproximadamente 2 millones de años A.C. hasta el 9000 A.C.; también llamado período Paleolítico

Olduvai Gorge a gorge in Tanzania in which many hominid remains have been found (p. 8)

desfiladero Olduvai desfiladero en Tanzania donde se han encontrado muchos restos de homínidos

oligarchy government in which ruling power belongs to a few people (pp. 120, 523)

oligarquía gobierno en el que el poder está en manos de unas pocas personas

Olmecs the earliest American civilization, located along the Gulf Coast of Mexico from about 1500 B.C. to 400 B.C. (p. 188)

olmecas la primera civilización americana, ubicada a lo largo de la costa del Golfo de México, desde alrededor de 1500 A.C. a 400 A.C.

one-child policy a Chinese government policy limiting urban families to a single child (p. 1077)

política de un sólo hijo medida del gobierno chino que limita a las familias urbanas a tener únicamente un hijo

Open Door Policy American approach to China around 1900, favoring open trade relations between China and other nations (p. 776)

Política de puertas abiertas política estadounidense con respecto a China a principios del siglo XX, que abogaba por las libres relaciones comerciales entre China y otras naciones

Opium War war between Great Britain and China over restrictions to foreign trade (p. 774)

Guerra del opio guerra librada entre Gran Bretaña y China por las restricciones sobre el comercio exterior

oracle bone in Shang China, animal bone or turtle shell used by priests to predict the future (p. 100)

hueso de oráculo en la China Shang, hueso de animal o caparazón de tortuga usado por los sacerdotes para predecir el futuro

Organization of American States (OAS) a group formed in 1948 to promote democracy, economic cooperation, and human rights in the Americas (p. 1086)

Organización de los Estados Americanos grupo formado en 1948 con el fin de promover la democracia, la cooperación económica y los derechos humanos en las Américas

ostracism practice used in ancient Greece to banish or send away a public figure who threatened democracy (p. 126)

ostracismo en la antigua Grecia, el acto de desterrar o enviar lejos a una figura pública que amenazaba la democracia

Ottomans Turkish-speaking nomadic people who migrated from Central Asia into northwestern Asia Minor (p. 329)

otomanos grupo nómada de habla turca que emigró de Asia Central al noroeste de Asia Menor

outpost a distant military station or a remote settlement (p. 458)

fuerte fronterizo estación militar distante o asentamiento lejano

outsourcing the practice of sending work to companies in the developing world in order to save money or increase efficiency (p. 1100)

subcontratación práctica empresarial de enviar trabajo a compañías de países en vías de desarrollo con el fin de ahorrar dinero o aumentar el rendimiento

overproduction condition in which production of goods exceeds the demand for them (p. 895)

superproducción condición en la que la producción de mercancías excede la demanda

Oyo empire Yoruba empire that arose in the 1600s in present-day Nigeria and dominated its neighbors for a hundred years (p. 455)

imperio Oyo el imperio Yoruba que surgió en el siglo XVII en la actual Nigeria y dominó a sus vecinos durante cien años

ENGLISH/SPANISH GLOSSARY

P

Pacific Rim vast region of nations, including countries in Southeast Asia, East Asia, and the Americas, that border the Pacific Ocean (p. 1099)
Cuenca del Pacífico vasta región de naciones, que incluye los países del sureste y este asiático y de las Américas, que limitan con el océano Pacífico

pacifism opposition to all war (p. 925)
pacifismo oposición a las guerras

paddy rice field (p. 401)
arrozal campo de arroz

pagoda multistoried Buddhist temple with eaves that curve up at the corners (p. 372)
pagoda templo budista de varios pisos con aleros que se curvan en las esquinas

Paleolithic Period the era of prehistory that lasted from at least 2 million B.C. to about 9000 B.C.; also called the Old Stone Age (p. 11)
período Paleolítico era de la prehistoria que duró desde aproximadamente 2 millones de años A.C. hasta el 9000 A.C.; también llamado la Antigua Edad de Piedra

Pan-Africanism movement which began in the 1920s that emphasized the unity and strength of Africans and people of African descent around the world (p. 859)
Panafricanismo movimiento que empezó en la década de 1920 que se centraba en la unidad y fuerza de los africanos y personas con ascendencia africana en todo el mundo

Panama Canal man-made waterway connecting the Atlantic and Pacific oceans (p. 807)
Canal de Panamá canal artificial que conecta los océanos Atlántico y Pacífico

Pan-Arabism movement in which Arabs sought to unite all Arabs into one state (p. 862)
Panarabismo movimiento en el que los árabes pretendían unir a todos los árabes en un sólo estado

pandemic spread of a disease across a large area, country, continent, or the entire world (p. 834)
pandemia propagación de una enfermedad a una gran área, país, continente o al mundo entero

papal supremacy the claim of medieval popes that they had authority over all secular rulers (p. 228)
supremacía papal demanda de los papas medievales de que ellos tenían autoridad sobre todos los gobernantes laicos

Parthenon the chief temple of the Greek goddess Athena on the Acropolis in Athens, Greece (p. 132)

Partenón el principal templo de la diosa griega Atena, situado en la Acrópolis de Atenas en Grecia

papyrus plant used to make a paper-like writing material in ancient Egypt (p. 54)
papiro planta usada por los antiguos egipcios para hacer un material de escritura parecido al papel

Parliament the legislature of England, and later of Great Britain (p. 247)
Parlamento asamblea legislativa de Inglaterra, y más tarde de Gran Bretaña

parliamentary democracy a form of government in which the executive leaders (usually a prime minister and cabinet) are chosen by and responsible to the legislature (parliament), are also members of it (p. 724)
democracia parlamentaria forma de gobierno en la que la dirección ejecutiva (normalmente un primer ministro y un gabinete) es elegida por la asamblea legislativa (parlamento) y controlada por la misma, además de formar parte de ella

partition a division into pieces (pp. 535, 1015)
partición división en partes

partnership a group of merchants who joined together to finance a large-scale venture that would have been too costly for any individual trader (p. 234)
asociación grupo de mercaderes que se unen para financiar una empresa más grande que hubiera sido demasiado costosa para un solo comerciante

pasha provincial ruler in the Ottoman empire (p. 763)
bajá gobernante provincial del imperio otomano

paternalistic the system of governing a country as a father would a child (p. 756)
paternalista sistema de gobernar un país como un padre lo hace con su hijo

patriarch in the Roman and Byzantine empires, highest church official in a major city (pp. 171, 286)
patriarca en el Imperio Romano y imperio bizantino, el funcionario de rango más alto en la iglesia de una ciudad importante

patriarchal relating to a society in which men hold the greatest legal and moral authority (p. 59)
patriarcal relacionado con una sociedad en la que los hombres tienen la autoridad legal y moral

patrician in ancient Rome, member of the landholding upper class (p. 152)
patricio miembro de la clase alta terrateniente en la antigua Roma

patrilineal term for a family organization in which kinship ties are traced through the father (p. 358)

patrilineal organización familiar en la que los lazos de parentesco se siguen a través del padre

patron a person who provides financial support for the arts (p. 412)

mecenas persona que proporciona apoyo financiero a la cultura y las artes

Peace of Westphalia series of treaties that ended the Thirty Years' War (p. 527)

Paz de Westfalia serie de tratados por los que se puso fin a la Guerra de los Treinta Años

penal colony place where people convicted of crimes are sent (pp. 727, 798)

colonia penal lugar al que se manda a los condenados por crímenes

peninsulare member of the highest class in Spain's colonies in the Americas (pp. 480, 645)

peninsular miembro de la clase más alta en las colonias españolas de América

peon worker forced to labor for a landlord in order to pay off a debt (p. 478)

peón trabajador forzado a trabajar para un terrateniente para pagar una deuda

peonage system by which workers owe labor to pay their debts (p. 803)

peonaje sistema en el que los trabajadores deben trabajo como pago por sus deudas

perestroika a Soviet policy of democratic and free-market reforms introduced by Mikhail Gorbachev in the late 1980s (p. 1002)

perestroika "reestructuración" en ruso; política soviética de reformas democráticas y de libre mercado que introdujo Mikhail Gorbachev a finales de la década de 1980

personal computer (PC) a small computer meant to be used by individuals or small businesses (p. 1123)

computadora personal (PC, por sus siglas en inglés) pequeña computadora diseñada para uso individual o por parte de pequeñas empresas

perspective artistic technique used to give paintings and drawings a three-dimensional effect (p. 412)

perspectiva técnica artística usada para lograr el efecto de tercera dimensión en dibujos y pinturas

phalanx in ancient Greece, a massive tactical formation of heavily armed foot soldiers (p. 120)

falange en la antigua Grecia, sólida formación táctica de soldados a pie fuertemente armados

pharaoh title of the rulers of ancient Egypt (p. 45)

faraón título de los gobernantes del antiguo Egipto

Philippines a country in southeastern Asia made up of several thousand islands (p. 459)

Filipinas país al sudeste de Asia formado por varios miles de islas

philosophe French for "philosopher"; French thinker who desired reform in society during the Enlightenment (p. 546)

philosophe palabra francesa que significa "filósofo"; pensador francés que abogaba por reformas en la sociedad durante la Ilustración

philosopher someone who seeks to understand and explain life; a person who studies philosophy (p. 130)

filósofo persona que trata de comprender y explicar la vida; persona que estudia la filosofía

philosophy system of ideas (p. 97)

filosofía sistema de ideas

pictograph a simple drawing that looks like the object it represents (p. 22)

pictografía dibujo sencillo que se parece al objeto que representa (also called pictograms)

Pilgrims English Protestants who rejected the Church of England (p. 484)

peregrinos protestantes ingleses que rechazaron la Iglesia de Inglaterra

plantation large estate run by an owner or overseer and worked by laborers who live there (p. 453)

plantación gran propiedad administrada por un dueño o capataz y cultivada por trabajadores que viven en ella

plateau raised area of level land (p. 69)

meseta área elevada de tierra plana

plebeian in ancient Rome, member of the lower class, including farmers, merchants, artisans, and traders (p. 152)

plebeyo en la antigua Roma, miembro de clase baja, que incluía granjeros, mercaderes, artesanos y comerciantes

plebiscite ballot in which voters have a direct say on an issue (p. 593)

plebiscito votación en la que los votantes expresan su opinión sobre un tema en particular

pogrom violent attack on a Jewish community (p. 713)

pogrom ataque violento de una multitud hacia una comunidad judía

polis city-state in ancient Greece (p. 118)

polis ciudad-estado de la antigua Grecia

polytheistic believing in many gods (p. 20)

politeísta creencia en muchos dioses

ENGLISH/SPANISH GLOSSARY

pope head of the Roman Catholic Church; in ancient Rome, bishop of Rome who claimed authority over all other bishops (p. 171)

papa cabeza de la iglesia Católica Romana; obispo de Roma que afirmaba tener autoridad sobre los otros obispos

popular sovereignty basic principle of the American system of government which asserts that the people are the source of any and all governmental power, and government can exist only with the consent of the governed (p. 560)

soberanía popular principio básico del sistema de gobierno estadounidense en el que se determina que el pueblo es la fuente de todo poder gubernamental, y que el gobierno sólo puede existir con el consentimiento de los gobernados

potlatch among Native American groups of the Northwest Coast, ceremonial gift-giving by people of high rank and wealth (p. 205)

potlatch entre los grupos indígenas de la costa noroeste, ceremonia en que la gente de alto rango o riqueza hacía regalos

predestination Calvinist belief that God long ago determined who would gain salvation (p. 427)

predestinación creencia calvinista de que Dios decidió hace mucho tiempo quién conseguiría la salvación

prehistory the period of time before writing was invented (p. 4)

prehistoria período anterior a la invención de los sistemas de escritura

premier prime minister (p. 736)

premier primer ministro

price revolution period in European history when inflation rose rapidly (p. 492)

revolución del precio período en la historia de Europa en que la inflación aumentó rápidamente

privateer privately owned ship commissioned by a government to attack and capture enemy ships, especially merchant's ships (p. 481)

corsario barco privado comisionado por un gobierno para atacar y capturar barcos enemigos, especialmentelos barcos mercantes

Prohibition a ban on the manufacture and sale of alcohol in the U. S. from 1920 to 1933 (p. 885)

Prohibición restricción de la fabricación y venta de bebidas alcohólicas en Estados Unidos desde 1920 a 1933

proletariat working class (pp. 625, 840)

proletariado clase trabajadora

proliferate to multiply rapidly (p. 1115)

proliferar multiplicarse rápidamente

propaganda spreading of ideas to promote a cause or to damage an opposing cause (p. 830)

propaganda divulgación de ideas para promover cierta causa o para perjudicar una causa opuesta

prophet spiritual leader who interprets God's will (p. 60)

profeta líder espiritual a quien se le atribuye la interpretación de la voluntad de Dios

protectionism the use of tariffs and other restrictions to protect a country's home industries against competition (p. 1103)

proteccionismo el uso de aranceles y otras medidas restrictivas para proteger a las empresas de un país de la competencia

protectorate country with its own government but under the control of an outside power (p. 753)

protectorado país con su propio gobierno pero que está bajo el control de una potencia exterior

provisional temporary (p. 735)

provisional temporal

Prussia a strong military state in central Europe that emerged in the late 1600s (p. 528)

Prusia estado centroeuropeo militarmente poderoso que emergió a finales del siglo XVII

psychoanalysis a method of studying how the mind works and treating mental disorders (p. 888)

psicoanálisis método que estudia el funcionamiento de la mente y trata los trastornos mentales

pueblo Native American village of the United States Southwest (p. 203)

pueblo poblado indígena del sudoeste de Estados Unidos

Pueblo Bonito the largest Anasazi pueblo, built in New Mexico in the A.D. 900s (p. 203)

Pueblo Bonito el mayor poblado anazasi, construido en Nuevo México en el siglo X D.C.

Punjab state in northwestern India with a largely Sikh population (p. 1016)

Punjab estado del noroeste de India de población mayoritariamente sikh

purdah isolation of women in separate quarters (p. 770)

purdah aislamiento de las mujeres en recintos separadas

Puritans members of an English Protestant group who wanted to "purify" the Church of England by making it more simple and more morally strict (p. 517)

puritanos miembros de un grupo de protestantes ingleses que querían "purificar" la Iglesia de Inglaterra, haciéndola más sencilla y moralmente más estricta

Pusan Perimeter a defensive line around the city of Pusan, in the southeast corner of Korea, held by South Korean and United Nations forces in 1950 during the Korean War; marks the farthest advance of North Korean forces (p. 990)

Perímetro de Pusan línea defensiva alrededor de la ciudad de Pusan, en el sudeste de Corea, custodiada por Corea del Sur y las fuerzas de las Naciones Unidas en 1950 durante la Guerra de Corea; marca el mayor avance de las fuerzas de Corea del Norte

putting-out system a system developed in the 18th century in which tasks were distributed to individuals who completed the work in their own homes; also known as cottage industry (p. 614)

sistema de trabajo a domicilio sistema desarrolla do en el siglo XVIII en el que las tareas se distribúan a individuos quienes completaban el trabajo en sus hogares; tambien se conoce como industria familiar

Q

Qajars members of the dynasty that ruled present-day Iran from the late 1700s until 1925 (p. 333)

Qajars miembros de la dinastía que gobernó la zona del actual Irán desde fines del siglo XVIII hasta 1925

Qing dynasty dynasty established by the Manchus in the mid 1600s and lasted until the early 1900s; China's last dynasty (p. 463)

dinastía Chin dinastía establecida por los manchus a mediados del siglo XVII que duró hasta principios del siglo XX; fue la última dinastía china

Quran the holy book of Islam (p. 306)

Corán el libro sagrado del islam

quipu knotted strings used by Inca officials for record-keeping (p. 197)

quipu cuerdas con nudos que usaban los incas como llevar registros

R

racism belief that one racial group is superior to another (p. 680)

racismo creencia de que un grupo racial es superior a otro

radicals those who favor extreme changes (pp. 638, 835)

radicales persona que quiere hacer cambios extremos

rajah in ancient India, the elected warrior chief of an Aryan tribe (pp. 72, 326)

rajah jefe guerrero electo de una tribu aria en la antigua India

realism 19th-century artistic movement whose aim was to represent the world as it is (p. 682)

realismo movimiento artístico del siglo XIX cuyo objetivo era representar el mundo tal como es

Realpolitik realistic politics based on the needs of the state (p. 694)

Realpolitik política realista basada en las necesidades del estado

recession period of reduced economic activity (pp. 640, 977)

recesión periodo de reducción de la actividad económica

Reconquista during the 1400s, the campaign by European Christians to drive the Muslims from present-day Spain (p. 260)

Reconquista durante el siglo XV, campaña por parte de cristianos europeos para expulsar a los musulmanes de la actual España

refugee a person who flees from home or country to seek refuge elsewhere, often because of political upheaval or famine (pp. 713, 1108)

refugiado persona que abandona su hogar o país en busca de refugio en otro lugar, a menudo como consecuencia de inestabilidad política o hambruna

regionalism loyalty to a local area (p. 802)

regionalismo lealtad a un área local

Reich German empire (p. 695)

Reich imperio alemán

Reign of Terror time period during the French Revolution from September 1793 to July 1794 when people in France were arrested for not supporting the revolution and many were executed (p. 587)

Reinado del terror período durante la Revolución Francesa desde septiembre de 1793 a julio de 1794, en el que la gente en Francia era arresta da por no apoyar la revolución; mucha gente fue ejecutada

reincarnation in Hindu belief, the rebirth of the soul in another bodily form (p. 77)

reencarnación según la creencia hindú, renacimiento del alma en otra forma corporal

reparation payment for war damage, or damage caused by imprisonment (p. 834)

indemnización pago por daños causados por guerra o encarcelamiento

repeal cancel (p. 727)
revocar cancelar

republic system of government in which officials are chosen by the people (pp. 151, 583)
república sistema de gobierno en el que los gobernantes son elegidos por el pueblo

revenue money taken in through taxes (p. 483)
rentas públicas dinero que se recauda por impuestos

rhetoric art of skillful speaking (p. 130)
retórica arte de hablar con habilidad

rococo personal, elegant style of art and architecture made popular during the mid-1700s that featured designs with the shapes of leaves, shells, and flowers (p. 551)
rococó estilo de arte y arquitectura elegante y personal que se hizo popular a mediados del siglo XVIII y que incluía diseños con formas de hojas, conchas y flores

romanticism 19th-century artistic movement that appealed to emotion rather than reason (p. 681)
romanticismo movimiento artístico del siglo XIX que apelaba a la emoción más que a la razón

Rosetta Stone stone monument that includes the same passage carved in hieroglyphics, demotic script, and Greek and that was used to decipher the meanings of many hieroglyphs (p. 55)
piedra de Rosetta piedra arquitectónica que incluye el mismo pasaje esculpido con caracteres jeroglíficos, demóticos y en escritura griega que se usó para descifrar el significado de muchos jeroglíficos

Rosie the Riveter popular name for women who worked in war industries during WWII (p. 940)
Rosita la Remachadora nombre popularmente dado a las mujeres que trabajaban en las fábricas de armamento durante la Segunda Guerra Mundial

rotten borough rural town in England that sent members to Parliament despite having few or no voters (p. 722)
"distrito podrido" en Inglaterra, ciudad rural que enviaba miembros al parlamento a pesar de no tener o tener pocos votantes

Ruhr Valley coal-rich industrial region of Germany (p. 913)
Valle del Ruhr región industrial alemana rica en carbón

russification making a nationality's culture more ethnically Russian (p. 908)

rusificación hacer la cultura nacionalista más étnicamente rusa

Russo-Japanese War conflict between Russia and Japan in 1904–1905 over control of Korea and Manchuria (p. 790)
Guerra ruso-japonesa conflicto entre Rusia y Japón de 1904 a 1905 por el control de Corea y Manchuria

S

Sabbath a holy day for rest and worship (p. 60)
sabbat día sagrado para descansar y rendir culto

sacrament sacred ritual of the Roman Catholic Church (p. 225)
sacramento ritual sagrado de la Iglesia Católica Romana

Safavid Shiite Muslim empire that ruled much of present-day Iran from the 1500s into the 1700s (p. 333)
Safávida imperio musulmán chiíta que gobernó la mayor parte del actual Irán desde el siglo XVI hasta el siglo XVIII

Sahara largest desert in the world, covering almost all of North Africa (p. 340)
Sahara desierto más grande del mundo que cubre casi todo el norte de África

salon informal social gathering at which writers, artists, *philosophes,* and others exchanged ideas (p. 551)
salón reuniones sociales informales en las que escritores, artistas, filósofos y otros intercambiaban ideas

samurai member of the warrior class in Japanese feudal society (p. 391)
samurai miembro de la clase guerrera en la sociedad japonesa feudal

Sandinistas a socialist political movement and party that held power in Nicaragua during the 1980s (p. 1086)
sandinistas partido y movimiento político socialista que gobernó Nicaragua durante la década de 1980

sans-culotte working-class man or woman who made the French Revolution more radical; called such because he or she wore long trousers instead of the fancy knee breeches that the upper class wore (p. 583)
sans-culotte hombre o mujer de la clase obrera que hicieron la Revolución Francesa más radical; llamados así porque llevaban pantalones largos a la rodilla como los que llevaba en vez

de los pantalones ajustados la clase altas a la rodilla como los que llevaba la clase alta

Sapa Inca the title of the Inca emperor (p. 197)

Sapa Inca título del emperador inca

sati Hindu custom that called for a widow to join her husband in death by throwing herself on his funeral pyre (p. 768)

sati costumbre hindú que requería que la esposa se uniera a su marido en la muerte arrojándose a su pira funeraria

satirize make fun of (p. 162)

satirizar burlarse de algo

savanna grassy plain with irregular patterns of rainfall (pp. 340, 1024)

sabana planicie con pastizales cuyo régimen de lluvias es irregular

schism permanent division in a church (p. 270)

cisma división permanente de una iglesia

scholasticism in medieval Europe, the school of thought that used logic and reason to support Christian belief (p. 264)

escolástica en la Edad Media europea, escuela de pensamiento que usaba la lógica y el razonamiento para apoyar las creencias cristianas

scientific method careful, step-by-step process used to confirm findings and to prove or disprove a hypothesis (p. 436)

método científico proceso cuidadoso y de varios pasos que se usa para confirmar descubrimientos y para aprobar o desaprobar una hipótesis

scorched-earth policy military tactic in which soldiers destroy everything in their path to hurt the enemy (p. 597)

política de tierra quemada táctica militar en la que los soldados destruyen todo lo que tienen a su paso para perjudicar al enemigo

scribe in ancient civilizations, a person specially trained to read, write, and keep records (p. 22)

escriba en las civilizaciones antiguas, persona especialmente educada para leer, escribir y mantener registros

secede withdraw (p. 541)

separar retirarse

secret ballot votes cast without announcing them publicly (p. 723)

voto secreto votos que se dan sin hacerlos públicos

sect a subgroup of a major religious group (pp. 82, 428)

secta subgrupo de un grupo religioso importante

secular having to do with worldly, rather than religious, matters; nonreligious (pp. 228, 1035)

secular que tiene que ver más con asuntos mundanos que religiosos; no religioso

segregation forced separation by race, sex, religion, or ethnicity (pp. 741, 978)

segregación separación forzada por razón de raza, sexo, religión o etnia

selective borrowing adopting or adapting some cultural traits but discarding others (p. 390)

préstamo selectivo adoptar o adaptar algunos rasgos culturales y descartar otros

self-determination right of people to choose their own form of government (p. 833)

autodeterminación derecho de los pueblos a elegir su propia forma de gobierno

sepoy Indian soldier who served in an army set up by the French or English trading companies (pp. 460, 768)

sepoy soldado indio que sirvió en un ejército establecido por las compañías de comercio francesas o inglesas

serf in medieval Europe, a peasant bound to the lord's land (p. 222)

siervo en la Europa medieval, campesino vinculado a las tierras del señor

shah king (p. 333)

sha rey

shantytowns slums of flimsy shacks (p. 1070)

barrio de chabolas barrios muy pobres de casuchas endebles

Sharia body of Islamic law that includes interpretation of the Quran and applies Islamic principles to everyday life (p. 308)

Sharía ley canónica del islam que incluye la interpretación del Corán y que aplica los principios islámicos a la vida diaria

Sharpeville a black township in South Africa where the government killed anti-apartheid demonstrators in 1960 (p. 1049)

Sharpeville municipio sudafricano habitado por personas de raza negra donde el gobierno mató a decenas de manifestantes antiapartheid en 1960

Shiite a member of one of the two major Muslim sects; believe that the descendents of Muhammad's daughter and son-in-law, Ali, are the true Muslim leaders (p. 311)

chiíta miembro de una de las dos sectas musulmanas principales; creedor de que los descendientes de la hija y el yerno de Mahoma, Alí, son los verdaderos líderes musulmanes

Shinto principal religion in Japan that emphasizes the worship of nature (p. 389)

Shinto principal religión de Japón que enfatiza la adoración a la naturaleza

shogun in Japanese feudal society, supreme military commander, who held more power than the emperor (p. 391)

shogún en la sociedad feudal japonesa, jefe military supremo con más poder que el emperador

shrine altar, chapel, or other sacred place (p. 114)

santuario altar, capilla u otro lugar sagrado

Sikhism religion founded by Nanak that blended Islamic and Hindu beliefs (p. 327)

sikhismo religión fundada por Nanak que incorpora creencias islámicas e hindúes

Sikhs members of an Indian religious minority (p. 1015)

sikhs miembros de una minoría religiosa de India

Silla dynasty Korean dynasty that ruled from 668 to 935 (p. 385)

dinastía Silla dinastía coreana que gobernó desde 668 a 935

Sino-Japanese War war between China and Japan in which Japan gained Taiwan (p. 776)

Guerra Sinojaponesa guerra entre China y Japón por la que Japón obtuvo el control de Taiwán

smelt melt in order to get the pure metal away from its waste matter (p. 611)

refinar fundir mineral para separar el mineral puro de las impurezas

social contract an agreement by which people gave up their freedom to a powerful government in order to avoid chaos (p. 545)

contrato social acuerdo mediante el cual el pueblo cede sus libertades a un gobierno poderoso para evitar el caos

social democracy political ideology in which there is a gradual transition from capitalism to socialism instead of a sudden violent overthrow of the system (p. 626)

democracia social ideología política en la que hay una transición gradual del capitalismo al socialismo en vez de un derrocamiento violento del sistema

social gospel movement of the 1800s that urged Christians to do social service (p. 680)

evangelio social movimiento del siglo XIX que urgía a los cristianos a que hicieran servicios sociales

social mobility the ability to move in social class (p. 318)

movilidad social la capacidad de cambiar de clase social

social welfare programs to help certain groups of people (p. 699)

bienestar social programas para ayudar a ciertos grupos de personas

socialism system in which the people as a whole rather than private individuals own all property and operate all businesses (pp. 625, 1072)

socialismo sistema en el que el pueblo como un todo, en vez de los individuos, son dueños de todas la propiedades y manejan todos los negocios

socialist realism artistic style whose goal was to promote socialism by showing Soviet life in a positive light (p. 908)

realismo socialista estilo artistico cuyo objetvo era promover el socialismo mostrando la vila en la Union Sovietica desde un perspectiva postiva

Solidarity a Polish labor union and democracy movement (p. 1003)

Solidaridad sindicato laboral y moviriento democrático polaco

Song dynasty Chinese dynasty from 960 t 1279; known for its artistic achievements (p. 30)

dinastía Song dinastía china desde 960 a 1279; conocida por sus grandes logros artístics

Songhai medieval West African kingdo located in present-day Mali, Niger and Niger (p. 349)

Songhai reino medieval de África occidental ubicado en el presente Mali, Níger y Nigeria

sovereign having full, independent pwer (p. 458)

soberano tener poder pleno e independiente

soviet council of workers and soldirs set up by Russian revolutionaries in 1917 (840)

soviet consejo de trabajadores y soldados establecido por los revolucionarios usos en 1917

Spanish-American War conflict between the United States and Spain in 18 over Cuban independence (p. 793)

Guerra entre Estados Udos y España (Guerra hispano-estadou dense) conflicto entre Estados Unidos y Esña en 1898 por la independencia de Cuba

Sparta city-state in ancien reece (p. 120)

Esparta antigua ciudad-ado en Grecia

speakeasies illegal bars (385)

speakeasies bares ilegs

sphere of influence are in which an outside power claims exclusi investment or trading privileges (p. 753)

esfera de influen área sobre la que un poder exterior se res a privilegios comerciales o la exclusividad de alizar inversiones

St. Petersburg capital city and major port that Peter the Great established in 1703 (p. 532)
San Petersburgo ciudad y capital con un puerto importante, establecida en 1703 por Pedro el Grande

stalemate deadlock in which neither side is able to defeat the other (p. 822)
estancamiento punto muerto en una confrontación, en el que ninguna de las partes puede vencer a la otra

Stalingrad now Volgograd, a city in SW Russia that was the site of a fierce battle during WWII (p. 942)
Stalingrado actual Volgogrado; ciudad del sudoeste de Rusia donde se libró una encarnizada batalla durante la Segunda Guerra Mundial

Stamp Act law passed in 1765 by the British Parliament that imposed taxes on items such as newspapers and pamphlets in the American colonies; repealed in 1766 (p. 559)
Ley del Timbre ley promulgada en 1765 por el Parlamento Británico que imponía gravá menes a artículos como diarios y panfletos en las colonias americanas; revocada en 1766

standard of living measures the quality and availability of necessities and comforts in a society (p. 671)
estándar de vida medida de la calidad y disponibilidad de las necesidades básicas y de los lujos en una sociedad

stela in the ancient world, a tall, commemorative monument that was often decorated (p. 190)
estela en el mundo antiguo, gran monumento monolítico conmemorativo que comúnmente estaba decorado

steppe sparse, dry, treeless grassland (pp. 19, 289, 376)
estepa tierra de pastos escasos y secos sin árboles

stipend a fixed salary given to public office holders (p. 126)
estipendio salario fijo de los funcionarios públicos

stock shares in a company (p. 665)
acciones títulos o valores de una compañía

strait narrow water passage (p. 116)
estrecho paso angosto de agua

stupa large domelike Buddhist shrine (p. 400)
stupa gran altar budista en forma de cúpula

subcontinent large landmass that juts out from a continent (p. 68)
subcontinente gran masa de tierra que sobresale de un continente

suburbanization the movement to built-up areas outside of central cities (p. 977)

suburbanización proceso de construcción en áreas fuera del centro de la ciudad

Sudetenland a region of western Czechoslovakia (p. 927)
Sudetenland región occidental de la antigua Checoslovaquia

Suez Canal a canal linking the Red Sea and Indian Ocean to the Mediterranean Sea, which also links Europe to Asia and East Africa (pp. 734, 1036)
Canal de Suez canal que une el Mar Rojo y el Océano índico con el Mar Mediterráneo, que a la vez une Europa con Asia y África Oriental

suffrage right to vote (p. 586)
sufragio derecho al voto

Sufis Muslim mystics who seek communion with God through meditation, fasting, and other rituals (p. 312)
sufis místicos musulmanes que buscan la comunión con dios mediante la meditación, el ayuno y otros rituals

sultan Muslim ruler (pp. 316, 324, 764)
sultán gobernante musulmán

Sumer site of the world's first civilization, located in southeastern Mesopotamia (p. 30)
Sumeria lugar de la primera civilización del mundo, ubicada en el sureste de Mesopotamia

Sunni a member of one of the largest Muslim sects; Sunnis believe that inspiration came from the example of Muhammad as recorded by his early followers (p. 311)
sunita miembro de una de las dos sectas musulmanas principales; los sunitas creen que la inspiración proviene del ejemplo de Mahoma según fue registrada por sus primeros seguidores

superpower a nation stronger than other powerful nations (p. 966)
superpotencia nación suficientemente poderosa para influir en los actos y políticas de otras naciones poderosas

surplus an amount that is more than needed, excess (pp. 17, 346, 1098)
excedente cantidad de algo superior a lo que se necesita; exceso

surrealism artistic movement that attempts to portray the workings of the unconscious mind (p. 889)
surrealismo movimiento artístico que trata de mostrar el funcionamiento del inconsciente

sustainability the ability to meet the needs of the present without compromising the needs of future generations (p. 1104)

sostenibilidad capacidad de satisfacer las necesidades actuales sin poner en peligro las necesidades de generaciones futuras

sustainable development development that meets the needs of the present without compromising the ability of future generations to meet their own needs (p. 1074)

desarrollo sostenible desarrollo que cubre las necesidades del presente sin perjudicar la capacidad de las generaciones futuras de cubrir sus necesidades

Swahili an East African culture that emerged about 1000 A.D.; also a Bantu-based language, blending Arabic words and written in Arabic script (p. 355)

swahili cultura del este de África que emergió alrededor del año 1000 D.C.; también un idioma basado en el Bantú, que mezcla palabras árabes y usa la escritura árabe

T

Taiping Rebellion peasant revolt in China (p. 775)

Rebelión Taiping revuelta campesina en China

Taliban Islamic fundamentalist faction that ruled Afghanistan for nearly ten years until ousted by the United States in 2002 (p. 1119)

Talibán facción islámica fundamentalista que gobernó Afganistán durante casi diez años hasta que fue expulsada por Estados Unidos en 2002

Taj Mahal a tomb built by Shah Jahan for his wife (p. 328)

Taj Mahal tumba construida por Shah Jahan para su esposa; considerado como uno de los monumentos más importantes del imperio mughal

Tang dynasty Chinese dynasty from 618 to 907 (p. 368)

dinastía Tang dinastía china desde 618 a 907

tariff tax on imported goods (p. 495)

tasa impuesto a mercancías importadas

technology the skills and tools people use to meet their basic needs (p. 8)

tecnología herramientas y destrezas que usan las personas para satisfacer sus necesidades básicas

Tehran capital of the Qajar dynasty and present-day Iran (p. 333)

Teherán capital de la dinastía Qajar y del actual Irán

temperance movement campaign to limit or ban the use of alcoholic beverages (p. 676)

campaña de moderación campaña para limitar o prohibir el uso de bebidas alcohólicas

tenant farmer someone who would pay rent to a lord to farm part of the lord's land (p. 235)

agricultor arrendatario alguien que paga un alquiler a un señor para poder cultivar la tierra de éste

tenement multistory building divided into crowded apartments (p. 618)

apartamento de vecindad edificio de varios pisos dividido en apartamentos donde vive mucha gente

Tennis Court Oath famous oath made on a tennis court by members of the Third Estate in France (p. 576)

Juramento del juego de pelota famoso juramento hecho en una cancha de frontón por los miembros del Tercer Estado en Francia

Tenochtitlán capital city of the Aztec empire, on which modern-day Mexico City was built (pp. 192, 473)

Tenochtitlán capital del imperio azteca, sobre la cual se construyó la actual Ciudad de México

Teotihuacán city that dominated the Valley of Mexico from about A.D. 200 to A.D. 750 and that influenced the culture of later Mesoamerican peoples (p. 193)

Teotihuacán ciudad que dominó el Valle de México desde alrededor de 200 D.C. a 750 D.C., y que influyó en la cultura de los pueblos mesoamericanos posteriores

terrorism deliberate use of random violence, especially against civilians, to achieve political goals (p. 1116)

terrorismo uso deliberado de la violencia indiscriminada, especialmente en contra de civiles, para lograr fines políticos

Tet Offensive a massive and bloody offensive by communist guerrillas against South Vietnamese and American forces on Tet, the Vietnamese New Year, 1968; helped turn American public opinion against military involvement in Vietnam (p. 996)

Ofensiva Tet ofensiva masiva y sangrienta de las guerrillas comunistas contra los sudvietnamitas y las fuerzas estadounidenses durante el Tet, el Nuevo Año vietnamita, en 1968; ayudó a que la opinión pública estadouniden se se volviera en contra de la ocupación militar en Vietnam

theocracy government run by religious leaders (pp. 427, 1036)

teocracia gobierno administrado por líderes religiosos

Third Reich official name of the Nazi party for its regime in Germany; held power from 1933 to 1945 (p. 915)

Tercer Reich nombre oficial del partido nazi durante su mandato en Alemania; mantuvo el poder desde 1933 a 1945

38th parallel an imaginary line marking 38 degrees of latitude, particularly the line across the Korean Peninsula, dividing Soviet forces to the north and American forces to the south after WWII (p. 989)

paralelo 38 línea imaginaria que marca los 38 grados de latitud, en particular la línea a 38 grados de latitud norte que cruza la península coreana, que dividía las fuerzas soviéticas al norte y las fuerzas estadounindenses al sur después de la Segunda Guerra Mundial

Tiahuanaco a culture that thrived in the Andean region from about A.D. 200–A.D. 1000 (p. 196)

tiahuanaco cultura preincaica que tuvo su apogeo en la región andina desde alrededor de 200 D.C. a 1000 D.C.

Tiananmen Square a huge public plaza at the center of China's capital, Beijing (p. 1077)

Plaza de Tiananmen inmensa plaza pública en el centro de Beijing, la capital de China

Tokyo capital of Japan (p. 786)

Tokio capital de Japón

Torah the most sacred text of the Hebrew Bible, including its first five books (p. 57)

Tora el texto más sagrado de la Biblia judía que incluye sus cinco primeros libros

total war channeling of a nation's entire resources into a war effort (p. 829)

estado de guerra canalización de todos los recursos de una nación hacia la guerra

totalitarian state government in which a one-party dictatorship regulates every aspect of citizens' lives (p. 901)

estado totalitario gobierno en el que una dictadura de partido único regula todos los aspectos de la vida de los ciudadanos

tournament a mock battle in which knights would compete against one another to display their fighting skills (p. 221)

torneo batalla simulada en la que los caballeros competían entre ellos para lucir sus destrezas de lucha

trade deficit situation in which a country imports more than it exports (p. 773)

déficit comercial situación en la que un país importa más de lo que exporta

trade surplus situation in which a country exports more than it imports (p. 773)

excedente commercial situación en la que un país exporta más de lo que importa

traditional economy undeveloped economic systems that rely on custom and tradition (p. 17)

economía tradicional sistemas económicos sin desarrollar dependen de costumbres y tradiciones

tragedy in ancient Greece, a play about human suffering often ending in disaster (p. 134)

tragedia en la antigua Grecia, obra teatral que trataba del sufrimiento humano y que a menudo terminaba con un desastre

Treaty of Paris treaty of 1763 that ended the Seven Years' War and resulted in British dominance of the Americas (p. 486)

Tratado de París en 1763, tratado que terminó con la Guerra de los Siete Años y resultó en el dominio británico de las Américas

Treaty of Paris peace treaty made final in 1783 that ended the American Revolution (p. 562)

Tratado de París tratado de paz de 1783 que dio final a la Revolución Americana

Treaty of Tordesillas treaty signed between Spain and Portugal in 1494 which divided the non-European world between them (p. 450)

Tratado de Tordesillas tratado firmado por España y Portugal en 1494 por el que se dividían entre ellos el mundo fuera de Europa

triangular trade colonial trade routes among Europe and its colonies, the West Indies, and Africa in which goods were exchanged for slaves (p. 487)

comercio triangular ruta colonial de comercio entre Europa y sus colonias en las Indias Occidentales y África, en donde las mercancías se cambiaban por esclavos

tribunes in ancient Rome, official who was elected by the plebeians to protect their interests (p. 152)

tribuno en la antigua Roma, funcionario elegido por los plebeyos para proteger sus intereses

tributary state independent state that has to acknowledge the supremacy of another state and pay tribute to its ruler (p. 369)

estado tributario estado independiente que debe reconocer la supremacía de otro estado y pagar tributo a su gobernante

ENGLISH/SPANISH GLOSSARY

tribute payment that conquered peoples may be forced to pay their conquerors (p. 193)

tributo pago que los conquistadores podían obligar a pagar a los pueblos conquistados

Trojan War in Greek epic poems and myths, a ten-year war between Mycenae and the city of Troy in Asia Minor (p. 116)

Guerra de Troya en los mitos y poemas griegos, guerra de diez años de duración entre Micenas y la ciudad de Troya situada en Asia Menor

troubadour a wandering poet or singer of medieval Europe (p. 222)

trovador poeta o cantante itinerante de la Europa medieval

Truman Doctrine United States policy, established in 1947, of trying to contain the spread of communism (p. 955)

Doctrina Truman estrategia política establecida en 1947 con el propósito de contener la expansión del comunismo

tsar title of the ruler of the Russian empire (p. 293)

zar título del regente del imperio ruso

tsunami very large, damaging wave caused by an earthquake or very strong wind (pp. 388, 1107)

tsunami ola enorme y destructiva causada por un terremoto o vientos muy fuertes

turnpike private road built by entrepreneurs who charged a toll to travelers who used it (p. 614)

autopista de peaje carretera construida con capital privado; el dueño de la carretera cobra una tarifa a los viajeros por usarla

Tutsis the main minority group in Rwanda and Burundi (p. 1051)

Tutsis principal minoría de Ruanda y Burundi

Twenty-One Demands list of demands given to China by Japan in 1915 that would have made China a protectorate of Japan (p. 870)

Veintiuna Exigencias lista de exigencias dadas por Japón a China en 1915 por las que, si hubiera estado de acuerdo, China se habría convertido en un protectorado de Japón

tyrant in ancient Greece, ruler who gained power by force (p. 122)

tirano en la antigua Grecia, gobernante que llegó al poder por medio de la fuerza

U

U-boat German submarine (p. 825)
U-Boat submarino alemán

ultimatum final set of demands (p. 819)

ultimátum serie final de exigencias

ultranationalist extreme nationalist (p. 876)

ultranacionalista nacionalista radical

Umayyads members of the Sunni dynasty of caliphs that ruled a Muslim empire from 661 to 750 (p. 312)

omeyas miembros de la dinastía Sunita de califas que gobernó un imperio musulmán de 661 a 750

United Nations (UN) international organization established after World War II with the goal of maintaining peace and cooperation in the international community (p. 953)

Naciones Unidas (ONU) organización internacional establecida después de la Segunda Guerra Mundial con el propósito de preservar la paz y la cooperación en la comunidad internacional

universal manhood suffrage right of all adult men to vote (p. 635)

sufragio universal masculino derecho de todos los hombres adultos a votar

untouchable in India, a member of the lowest caste (p. 866)

intocable en India, miembro de la casta más baja

urban renewal the process of fixing up the poor areas of a city (p. 668)

renovación urbana reconstrucción de las áreas pobres de una ciudad

urbanization movement of people from rural areas to cities (pp. 616, 1073)

urbanización movimiento de personas de las áreas rurales a las ciudades

utilitarianism idea that the goal of society should be to bring about the greatest happiness for the greatest number of people (p. 623)

utilitarismo idea de que el objetivo de la sociedad debería ser lograr la mayor felicidad para el mayor número de personas

utopian idealistic or visionary, usually used to describe a perfect society (p. 420)

utópico idealista o visionario, normalmente se usa para describir una sociedad perfecta

V

V-E Day Victory in Europe Day, May 8, 1945, the day the Allies won WWII in Europe (p. 948)

Día de la Victoria en Europa (Día del Armisticio) (8 de mayo de 1945) día en que los aliados vencieron en Europa durante la Segunda Guerra Mundial

Valley of Mexico valley in Mexico in which the numerous Mesoamerican civilizations, including the Aztecs, arose (p. 192)

Valle de México valle en México en el cual se desarrollaron numerosas civilizaciones mesoamericanas, incluyendo los aztecas

vanguard group of elite leaders (p. 870)

vanguardia grupo de líderes de la élite

vassal in medieval Europe, a lord who was granted land in exchange for service and loyalty to a greater lord (p. 219)

vasallo durante la Edad Media, señor a quien se le cedía un terreno a cambio de servicio y lealtad al señor más importante

Vedas a collection of prayers, hymns, and other religious teachings developed in ancient India beginning around 1500 B.C. (p. 72)

Vedas con onjunto de oraciones, himnos y otras enseñanzas religiosas desarrolladas en la antigua India a partir de alrededor del siglo XVI a. de C.

veneration special regard (p. 71)

veneración estima especial

vernacular everyday language of ordinary people (pp. 265, 419)

vernáculo lenguaje diario de la gente corriente

Versailles royal French residence and seat of government established by King Louis XIV (p. 512)

Versalles residencia de la realeza francesa y sede de gobierno establecidos por el rey Luis XIV

veto block a government action (p. 152)

veto bloquear una acción del gobierno

viceroy representative who ruled one of Spain's provinces in the Americas in the king's name; one who governed in India in the name of the British monarch (pp. 477, 769)

virrey representante que regía una de las provincias de España en las Américas en nombre del rey; quien gobernaba en India en nombre del monarca británico

Vichy city in central France where a puppet state governed unoccupied France and the French colonies (p. 931)

Vichy ciudad en el centro de Francia desde donde un gobierno títere dirigió la Francia no ocupada y las colonias francesas

Viet Cong communist rebels in South Vietnam who sought to overthrow South Vietnam's government; received assistance from North Vietnam (p. 993)

Vietcong rebeldes comunistas en Vietnam del Sur que buscaban derrotar el gobierno de Vietnam del Sur; recibieron ayuda de Vietnam del Norte

Vikings Scandinavian peoples whose sailors raided Europe from the 700s through the 1100s (p. 218)

vikingo pueblo escandinavo cuyos marineros asaltaron Europa durante los siglos VIII al XII

vizier chief minister who supervised the business of government in ancient Egypt (p. 45)

visir ministro principal que supervisaba los asuntos de gobierno en el antiguo Egipto

W

War of the Austrian Succession series of wars in which various European nations competed for power in Central Europe after the death of Hapsburg emperor Charles VI (p. 528)

Guerra de Sucesión Austriaca serie de guerras en las que diversos países europeos lucharon por la hegemonía en centroeuropa después de la muerte de Carlos IV, emperador Habsburgo

warlord local military ruler (p. 105)

jefe militar cabeza de un ejército local

warm-water port port that is free of ice year-round (p. 532)

puerto de aguas templadas puerto en el que sus aguas nunca se congelan a lo largo del año

Warsaw Pact mutual-defense alliance between the Soviet Union and seven satellites in Eastern Europe set up in 1955 (p. 956)

Pacto de Varsovia alianza de defensa mutua establecida en 1955 entre la Unión Soviética y siete países de Europa del Este pertenecientes a su esfera de influencia

weapons of mass destruction (WMDs) biological, nuclear, or chemical weapons (p. 1059)

armas de destrucción masiva (ADM) armas biológicas, nucleares o químicas

welfare state a country with a market economy but with increased government responsibility for the social and economic needs of its people (p. 982)

estado de bienestar país con una economía de Mercado, pero con un gobierno con mayor responsabilidad sobre las nece sidades económicas de su pueblo

westernization adoption of western ideas, technology, and culture (p. 531)

occidentalización adopción de ideas, tecnología y cultura occidentales

Wittenberg a city in northern Germany, where Luther drew up his 95 theses (p. 425)

Wittenberg ciudad al norte de Alemania donde Lutero redactó sus 95 tesis

women's suffrage right of women to vote (p. 676)
sufragio femenino derecho de las mujeres a votar

World Trade Organization (WTO) international organization set up to facilitate global trade (p. 1103)
Organización Mundial del Comercio (OMC) organización internacional constituida para facilitar el comercio en el ámbito mundial

Y

Yalta Conference meeting between Churchill, Roosevelt, and Stalin in February 1945 where the three leaders made agreements regarding the end of World War II (p. 945)
Conferencia de Yalta reunión mantenida en febrero de 1945 entre Churchill, Roosevelt y Stalin en la que los tres mandatarios alcanzaron un acuerdo con respecto a la finalización de la Segunda Guerra Mundial

Yathrib final destination of Muhammad's hijra and the home of the first community of Muslims; later renamed Medina; located in the northwest of present-day Saudi Arabia (p. 305)
Yathrib destino final de la hégira de Mahoma y hogar de la primera comunidad de musulmanes; posteriormente rebautizada como Medina; ubicada en el noroeste de la actual Arabia Saudita

Yorktown, Virginia location where the British army surrendered in the American Revolution (p. 562)
Yorktown, Virginia lugar donde el ejército británico se rindió en la Revolución Americana

Yuan dynasty Chinese dynasty ruled by the Mongols from 1279 to 1368; best known ruler was Kublai Khan (p. 378)
dinastía Yuan dinastía china gobernada por los mongoles desde 1279 a 1368; su gobernante más conocido fue Kublai Khan

Z

zaibatsu since the late 1800s, powerful banking and industrial families in Japan (p. 788)
zaibatsu familias japonesas de banqueros e industriales poderosos desde finales del siglo XIX

zemstvos local elected assembly set up in Russia under Alexander II (p. 711)
zemstvos asambla local electa que se estableció en Rusia en la época de Alejandro II

Zen the practice of meditation; a school of Buddhism in Japan (p. 394)
zen práctica de meditación; escuela del budismo en Japón

zeppelin large gas-filled balloon (p. 825)
zepelín dirigible, globo grande lleno de gas

ziggurat in ancient Mesopotamia, a large, stepped platform thought to have been topped by a temple dedicated to a city's chief god or goddess (p. 32)
zigurat templo piramidal de la antigua Mesopotamia dedicado al dios o diosa principal de una ciudad

Zionism a movement devoted to rebuilding a Jewish state in Palestine (p. 737)
zionismo movimiento dedicado a la reconstrucción del estado judío en Palestina

INDEX

Italicized letters after page numbers refer to the following:
c = chart; *g* = graph; *m* = map; *p* = picture; *q* = primary source

Aachen   **Amazon River**

INDEX

D

INDEX

INDEX

INDEX

INDEX

INDEX

INDEX

ACKNOWLEDGMENTS

Staff Credits
The people who make up the **World History © 07** team—representing design services, editorial, editorial services, educational technology, marketing, market research, photo research and art development, production services, publishing processes, and rights & permissions—are listed below. Bold type denotes core team members.

Marla Abramson, Leann Davis Alspaugh, Scott Andrews, Helene Avraham, Renee Beach, Eytan Bernstein, Suzanne Biron, Stephanie Bradley, **Peter Brooks**, Kerry Lyn Buckley, Lynn Burke, Kerry Cashman, Geoffrey Cassar, Todd Christy, Lori-Anne Cohen, Alan Dalgleish, Laura Edgerton Riser, Anne Falzone, Tom Ferreira, Lara Fox, Elizabeth Good, Ellen Welch Granter, **Diane Grossman,** Julie Gurdin, **Mary Ann Gundersen,** Mary Hanisco, Salena Hastings, Lance Hatch, Brian Heyward, Margaret Higgins, Katharine Ingram, Tim Jones, Judie Jozokos, Lynne Kalkanajian, Courtney Lane, Ruth Lopriore, **Grace Massey, Constance J. McCarty,** Michael McLaughlin, Claudi Mimo, Xavier Niz, Carrie O'Connor, Mark O'Malley, Linda Punskovsky, **Deborah Nicholls,** Jen Paley, Jonathan Penyack, **Gabriela Perez-Fiato,** Judi Pinkham, Jennifer Ribnicky, Marcy Rose, Rashid Ross, Robyn Salbo, **Colleen Searson,** Greg Slook, Laurel Smith, **Lisa Smith-Ruvalcaba,** Kara Stokes, Ana Sofia Villaveces, Rachel Winter, **Sarah Yezzi**

Vendor
Pronk & Associates Inc.

Maps
XNR Productions, Inc.: **SH25, SH27, SH28, SH29,** 10, 18, 31, 37, 40–41, 45, 47, 63, 69, 74–75, 81, 85, 93, 103, 105, 119, 125, 127, 138, 151, 156, 164, 169, 174, 178–179, 181, 187, 189, 196, 202, 206, 210–211, 215, 217, 222, 226, 232, 248, 257, 261, 271, 275, 286, 292, 295, 298, 307, 315, 325, 332, 341, 342, 345, 349, 355, 380, 384, 388, 398, 406–407, 413, 432, 443, 447, 454, 462–463, 475, 485, 489, 496–497, 498, 505, 526, 532, 536, 540–541, 554, 558, 565, 595, 599, 613, 640, 647, 649, 656–657, 661, 678–679, 693, 703, 707, 716, 735, 742, 757, 765, 769, 774, 778, 793, 797, 799, 804, 806, 812–813, 821, 827, 830, 841, 852, 853, 860, 863, 872, 876, 879, 892, 907, 928, 934, 940, 943, 946, 949, 955, 957, 958, 961, 962–963, 969, 971, 975, 988, 989, 995, 998, 999, 1011, 1015, 1022, 1027, 1033, 1038, 1041, 1046, 1051, 1056, 1060, 1063, 1067, 1074, 1083, 1097, 1099, 1101, 1107, 1111, 1117, 1131, 1134–1135, 1136, 1137, 1138, 1139, 1140, 1141, 1142, 1143, 1144, 1145, 1152–1153, 1156–1157

Illustrations
Kenneth Batelman **929, 946–947;** Kerry Cashman **SH13, SH26, SH39,** 6–7, 10, 12, 21, 24–25, 34, 39, 42, 47, 49, 52, 54, 58, 62–63, 77, 79, 87, 95, 97, 99, 104–105, 127, 132–133, 140–141, 143, 144–145, 163, 172, 174–175, 180, 180–181, 192, 206–207, 227, 232, 234, 238–239, 247, 259, 264, 272, 274–275, 276–277, 284, 295, 298–299, 307, 321, 323, 334–335, 349, 351, 354–355, 358–359, 362–363, 370, 373, 378–379, 380, 390, 393, 396, 402–403, 414–415, 420–421, 430–431, 436, 437, 440–441, 448–449, 462–463, 466–467, 474–475, 480, 488–489, 496–497, 498–499, 506, 509, 513, 518–519, 534, 536–537, 552, 558, 562, 564–565, 566–567, 574, 581, 588–589, 602–603, 614, 624, 628–629, 640–641, 649, 652–653, 666, 674–675, 675, 677, 683, 686–687, 703, 712–713, 716–717, 724–725, 730, 734–735, 740, 744–745, 765, 768–769, 774–775, 778–779, 786–787, 794, 806, 808-809, 828–829, 828–829, 839, 846–847, 852–853, 853, 860–861, 878–879, 886–887, 894, 894–895, 900–901, 918–919, 932–933, 934–935, 941, 946–947, 946–947, 958–959, 969, 971, 988–989, 994–995, 1008–1009, 1038–1039, 1050, 1054–1055, 1060–1061, 1074, 1078, 108–109, 1084–1085, 1090–1091, 1102–1103, 1107, 1111, 1121, 1122–1123, 1124, 1126–1127, 1132–1133, 1146–1147, 1147, 1148–1149, 1158–1159, 1160–1161, 1163, 1168–1169; Ellen Welch Granter **SH2, SH3, SH4, SH9, SH10, SH12, SH13, SH15, SH16, SH17, SH21, SH30, SH41;** Kevin Jones Associates 12, 14, 21, 33, 39, 49, 52, 179, 204, 220–221, 582, 614, 635, 664, 712–713; Jen Paley **SH5, SH20, SH23, SH37,** 4, 5, 8, 11, 17, 20, 22, 24, 30, 33, 36, 44, 49, 50, 54, 57, 59, 62, 68, 76, 84, 92, 101, 108, 114, 118, 119, 124, 130, 137, 144, 150, 155, 159, 161, 166, 171, 173, 175, 180, 186, 188, 195, 201, 202, 206, 214, 216, 219, 225, 231, 238, 244, 246, 247, 251, 255, 262, 269, 271, 276, 282, 289, 294, 296, 298, 304, 306, 307, 310, 311, 317, 322, 324, 326, 329, 334, 340, 346, 352, 357, 362, 368, 376, 383, 387, 397, 402, 410, 418, 423, 426, 428, 434, 440, 446, 452, 457, 461, 466, 472, 477, 480, 482, 487, 491, 493, 496, 497, 498, 504, 506, 510, 516, 522, 525, 530, 534, 544, 550, 554, 555, 557, 563, 566, 569, 572, 578, 585, 592, 602, 608, 609, 612, 616, 617, 622, 628, 634, 637, 638, 642, 645, 652, 660, 662, 667, 670, 674, 675, 681, 686, 689, 692, 696, 700, 705, 710, 716, 722, 726, 730, 733, 739, 744, 750, 754, 762, 767, 772, 773, 778, 779, 784, 788, 791, 796, 801, 804, 806, 808, 809, 824, 826, 828, 833, 838, 839, 840, 843, 852, 853, 854, 855, 858, 865, 869, 870, 874, 878, 884, 886, 891, 895, 897, 898, 901, 904, 905, 906, 912, 917, 918, 924, 927, 929, 930, 934, 935, 938, 939, 947, 948, 952, 953, 958, 959, 961, 968, 972, 976, 985, 992, 1000, 1008, 1014, 1017, 1020, 1022, 1024, 1032, 1035, 1041, 1044, 1045, 1048, 1050, 1051, 1054, 1057, 1060, 1061, 1066, 1067, 1072, 1076, 1077, 1078, 1082, 1085, 1090, 1096, 1100, 1102, 1106, 1108, 1111, 1115, 1120, 1126, 1129, 1148, 1150, 1151, 1154, 1155, 1162, 1163, 1166, 1167; Ted Smykal **SH4, SH6, SH7, SH8, SH9, SH10, SH11, SH14, SH15, SH16, SH17, SH18, SH19, SH21, 33, 493, 554, 678–679, 998–999, 1022, 1034–1035, 1089**

Photographs
Every effort has been made to secure permission and provide appropriate credit for photographic material. The publisher deeply regrets any omission and pledges to correct errors called to its attention in subsequent editions.

Unless otherwise acknowledged, all photographs are the property of Pearson Education, Inc.

Photo locators denoted as follows: Top (T), Center (C), Bottom (B), Left (L), Right (R), Background (Bkgd)

Cover Art Resource, NY; **Front Matter v** National Geographic Image Collection; **vi** (T) Alan Hills and Barbara Winter ©The British Museum/©DK Images; **vii** (B) Ace Stock Limited/Alamy Images, The Image Works, Inc.; **viii** (B) Musee de la Tapisserie, Bayeux, France/ /Bridgeman Art Library; **ix** (T) Art Resource, NY; **x** (T, B) Victoria & Albert Museum, London/Art Resource, NY; **xi** (T) AKG London Ltd., (B) Science Museum/Science & Society Picture Library; **xii** Mary Evans Picture Library; **xiii** Corbis; **xiv** Kapoor Baldev/Sygma/Corbis; **xv** Alison Wright/Corbis; **xvi** (L) Wanda's Pie in the Sky; **xvii** Alamy Images; **xix** British Museum/The Art Archive; **xx** (Inset) AKG London Ltd., Charles & Josette Lenars/Corbis; **xxi** New York Daily News/Getty Images; **xxiv** bpk, Berlin/Antikensammlung, Staatliche Museen, Berlin, Germany/Art Resource, NY; **xxix** (R) Time & Life Pictures/Getty Images; **SH1** Jose Luis Pelaez, Inc./Corbis; **SH2** IT Stock Free/AGE Fotostock; **SH3** Ed Bock/Corbis; **SH6** Jupiter Images; **SH13** Public Record Office/HIP/The Image Works, Inc.; **SH22** Arthur Tilley/Getty Images; **SH24** Roger Wood/Corbis; **SH29** Getty Images; **SH30** (T) ©DK Images, (B) North Wind Picture Archives; **SH31** Arcadio/Cartoon Web, Cartoon & Writers Syndicate; **SH33** Science Museum/Science & Society Picture Library; **SH36** (L) ©The Granger Collection, NY, (R) Corbis; **SH38** ©Dana White/PhotoEdit; **2** Time & Life Pictures/Getty Images; **3** (T) ©Images of Africa Photobank/Alamy Images, (C) ©MELBA PHOTO AGENCY/Alamy, Reunion des Musees Nationaux/Art Resource, NY; **4** (R) ©Gallo Images/Corbis, (L) Kenneth Garrett/National Geographic Image Collection; **5** ©The Granger Collection, NY; **6** National Geographic Image Collection; **7** (R) ©Caro/Alamy Images, (BL) Michael P. Fogden/Photoshot, (TL) Peabody Museum, Harvard University, (R) Roger M. Richards; **8** Robert F. Sisson/National Geographic Image Collection; **9** Institute of Human Origins; **10** ©Wave Royalty Free/Alamy; **11** BibleLandPictures/Alamy Images; **12** (B) ©DK Images, (C) ©SSPL/The Image Works, Inc., (T) Steve Gorton/©DK Images; **13** Reunion des Musees Nationaux/Art Resource, NY; **16** (CR) ©JM Labat/Photo Researchers, Inc., (BR) DK Images, (BL) Harry Taylor/©DK Images, (CL) Réunion des Musées Nationaux/Art Resource, NY, (T) Sisse Brimberg/National Geographic Image Collection, (BC) Ted Kinsman/Photo Researchers, Inc.; **17** Art Resource, NY; **21** (T) ©Best View Stock/Alamy, (B) Juan Silva/Getty Images; **23** Alinari/Art Resource, NY; **24** ©Gallo Images/Corbis; **25** ©MELBA PHOTO AGENCY/Alamy; **26** (T) Cartoon Stock, (B) Time & Life Pictures/Getty Images; **27** Peter Brown; **28** The Gallery Collection/Corbis; **29** (T) ©The Granger Collection, NY, (C) ©The Trustees of The British Museum/Art Resource, NY, (R) Private Collection/The Art Archive, (B) Staatliche Sammlung Ägyptischer Kunst Munich/Gianni Dagli Orti/The Art Archive; **30** (R) ©Ancient Art & Architecture Collection Ltd/Alamy Images, (L) ©The Trustees of The British Museum/Art Resource, NY; **32** ©DK Images; **33** (C) Ashmolean Museum, University of Oxford, UK/Bridgeman Art Library, (TR, TL) Réunion des Musées Nationaux/Art Resource, NY, (B) The Art Archive; **34** (T, B) ©Planetary Exclusives/Alamy; **35** (T) Ronald Sheridan/Ancient Art & Architecture Collection Ltd.; **36** Réunion des Musées Nationaux/Art Resource, NY, (Bkgrd) The Art Archive/Musée du Louvre Paris/Gianni Dagli Orti/The Kobal Collection; **37** Erich Lessing/Art Resource, NY; **38** ©Topham/Image Works; **39** (T) ©CM Dixon/HIP/The Image Works, Inc., (BR, BL) Erich Lessing/Art Resource, NY; **42** (TR) ©The Granger Collection, NY, (C) ©The Trustees of the

British Museum/Art Resource, NY, (BL) Alan Hills and Barbara Winter ©The British Museum/©DK Images, (TL) Ian O'Leary/©DK Images, (BR) The Granger Collection, NY; **43** Ronald Sheridan/Ancient Art & Architecture Collection Ltd.; **44** Werner Forman/Art Resource, NY; **45** ©Nik Wheeler/Corbis; **47** Andrea Jemolo/AKG London Ltd.; **48** Dagli Orti/Egyptian Museum Cairo/The Art Archive; **49** ©The Granger Collection, NY; **50** (R) Alistair Duncan/©DK Images, (L) Réunion des Musées Nationaux/Art Resource, NY; **51** ©The Trustees of The British Museum/Art Resource, NY; **52** (B) ©The Trustees of The British Museum/Art Resource, NY, (Border) Egyptian Museum Cairo/Collection Dagli Orti/The Art Archive, (T) Réunion des Musées Nationaux/Art Resource, NY; **53** ©Roger Wood/Corbis; **54** (R) ©The British Museum/Topham/The Image Works, Inc., (C) akg-images/Werner Forman/NewsCom, (L) Werner Forman/AKG London Ltd.; **55** (T) Gianni Dagli Orti/The Art Archive, (B) KENNETH GARRETT/National Geographic Image Collection; **56** (T) ©Oscar Elias/Alamy Images, (B) ©Robert Harding Picture Library Ltd/Alamy Images, (TR) Staatliche Sammlung Ägyptischer Kunst Munich/Gianni Dagli Orti/The Art Archive; **57** West London Synagogue, London, UK/Bridgeman Art Library; **58** (CL) ©Nathan Benn/Corbis, (TL, Bkgrd) ©The Granger Collection, NY, (CR) The Israel Museum, Jerusalem; **61** (B) ©Peter Hvizdak/The Image Works, Inc.; **62** ©Michael S. Yamashita/Corbis; **63** (B) ©Asian Art & Archaeology, Inc/Corbis, (T) Réunion des Musées Nationaux/Art Resource, NY; **64** The Gallery Collection/Corbis; **65** (B) Erich Lessing/Art Resource, NY, (T) Zen Radovan/Z. Radovan, Jerusalem; **66** Eddie Gerald/Eddie Gerald, Hung Chung Chih/Shutterstock, Korobanova/Shutterstock; **67** (T) ©British Library Board. All Rights Reserved., (C) Image copyright ©The Metropolitan Museum of Art/Art Resource, NY, (B) Kamat's Potpourri/CyberCrow Inc.; **68** (R) Ronald Sheridan/Ancient Art & Architecture Collection Ltd., (L) Scala/Art Resource, NY; **70** Getty Images; **71** (B) ©Angelo Hornak/Alamy Images, (B) Copyright J.M. Kenoyer, Courtesy Dept. of Archaeology and Museums, Govt. of Pakistan/Harappa, (C) The Art Archive, (T) The Image Works, Inc.; **73** (R) ©Zhao Xuan/Alamy, (L) Angelo Hornak/Corbis, (R) Photo by Ling Long/Imaginechina; **75** (B) ©Rubin Museum of Art/Art Resource, NY, (T) bpk, Berlin/Museum fuer Asiatische Kunst, Staatliche Museen, Germany/Art Resource, NY; **76** (R) ©mark downey/Alamy Images, (B) ©Robert Maass/Corbis; **77** (TC) ©Angelo Hornak/Corbis, (T) ©Lindsay Hebberd/Corbis, (B) ©Sheldan Collins/Corbis, (B) Image copyright ©The Metropolitan Museum of Art/Art Resource, NY; **79** (BL) ©Asia Alan King/Alamy Images,

(BR) ©Greg Martin/SuperStock, (T) Jobon Rendaiji Temple Kyoto/Laurie Platt Winfrey/The Art Archive; **81** Tibor Hirsch/Photo Researchers, Inc.; **82** ©Profimedia International s.r.o./Alamy Images; **83** Corbis; **84** Kamat's Potpourri/CyberCrow Inc.; **87** (TR) ©Corbis Premium RF/Alamy, (Border) ©Karen Kasmauski/Corbis, (B) ©Lindsay Hebberd/Corbis, (TC) ©The Trustees of The British Museum/Art Resource, NY, (TL) Jean-Louis Nou/AKG London Ltd.; **88** H. Hansum/Bucknell University; **90** ©Associated Press; **91** (L) Borromeo/Art Resource, NY, (T) Getty Images, (BR) Sudharak Olwe/Dinodia Photo Library/Dinodia Picture Agency; **92** ©The Granger Collection, NY; **94** (T, B) ©Asian Art & Archaeology, Inc./Corbis; **97** ©The Granger Collection, NY; **98** Réunion des Musées Nationaux/Art Resource, NY; **99** (T) ©inga spence/Alamy Images, (BR, Border) ©The Trustees of The British Museum/Art Resource, NY, (C) Bibliotheque Municipale, Poitiers, France/Giraudon/Bridgeman Art Library, (BL) Bob Gibbons/Photo Researchers, Inc., (BC) Maryann Frazier/Photo Researchers, Inc., (C) Museum of Fine Arts, Boston, Massachusetts, USA/Special Chinese and Japanese Fund/Bridgeman Art Library; **100** (T) ©British Library Board. All Rights Reserved., (B) Ashmolean Museum, University of Oxford, UK/Bridgeman Art Library; **101** (R, L) ©British Library Board. All Rights Reserved.; **102** The Art Archive/Bibliothèque Nationale Paris/The Kobal Collection; **103** Corbis; **104** (Bkgrd) Art Wolfe/Getty Images, Bildarchiv Preussischer Kulturbesitz/Art Resource, NY; **105** ©The Granger Collection, NY; **106** Tek Image/Photo Researchers, Inc.; **107** Victoria & Albert Museum, London/Art Resource, NY; **108** (L) The Image Works, Inc., (R) Werner Forman/Art Resource, NY; **109** ©Bettmann/Corbis; **110** ©Greg Martin/SuperStock; **111** Ashmolean Museum, University of Oxford, UK/Bridgeman Art Library; **112** Erich Lessing/Art Resource, NY; **113** (C) ©akg-images/The Image Works, Inc., (B) ©Alinari Archives/Corbis, (T) Alinari/Art Resource, NY; **114** Scala/Art Resource, NY; **115** (T) Nimatallah/Art Resource, NY; **116** Erich Lessing/Art Resource, NY; **117** ©Kevin Fleming/Corbis; **118** (R) ©akg-images/The Image Works, Inc., (L) Peter Connolly/AKG London Ltd.; **119** ©Elio Ciol/Corbis; **120** Réunion des Musées Nationaux/Art Resource, NY; **121** Ace Stock Limited/Alamy Images; **122** bpk, Berlin/Antikensammlung, Staatliche Museen, Berlin, Germany/Art Resource, NY; **123** ©Steve Vidler/SuperStock; **124** Louvre, Paris, France/Giraudon/Bridgeman Art Library; **125** Scala/Art Resource, NY; **127** (C) ©2004 AAAC/Topham/The Image Works, Inc., (TL) ©Gianni Dagli Orti/Corbis, (TR) AKG London Ltd., (B) Ancient Art and Architecture Collection Ltd./Bridgeman Art Library; **128** bpk, Berlin/Antikensam-

mlung, Staatliche Museen, Berlin, Germany/Art Resource, NY; **129** ©Martin Beddal/Alamy Images, ©The British Museum/Heritage-Images; **130** Alinari/Art Resource, NY; **131** The Metropolitan Museum of Art/Art Resource, NY; **132** (B) ©SuperStock/SuperStock, (T) Erich Lessing/Art Resource, NY, (C) Image copyright ©The Metropolitan Museum of Art/Art Resource, NY; **133** (R) ©Carl & Ann Purcell/Corbis, (BL) ©Neil Setchfield/Lonely Planet Images, (TL) Nick Nicholls ©The British Museum/©DK Images; **134** (BT) ©Ruggero Vanni/Corbis, ©The Granger Collection, NY, (T) Erich Lessing/Art Resource, NY; **135** Nimatallah/Art Resource, NY; **136** Alinari/Art Resource, NY; **137** ©INTERFOTO/Alamy Images; **138** (B) Ancient Art & Architecture Collection Ltd., (T) BibleLandPictures/Alamy Images; **139** bpk, Berlin/Museum fuer Asiatische Kunst, Staatliche Museen, Berlin, Germany/Art Resource, NY; **140** ©The Granger Collection, NY, (Bkgrd) Photoaisa; **141** (C) ©SSPL/The Image Works, Inc., (L) National Archaeological Museum Athens/Gianni Dagli Orti/The Art Archive, (R) Time & Life Pictures/Getty Images; **142** ©Exactostock/SuperStock; **143** (B) ©Hubert Stadler/Corbis, (TL) ©Lebrecht Music and Arts Photo Library/Alamy Images; **144** Réunion des Musées Nationaux/Art Resource, NY; **145** (B) BibleLandPictures/Alamy Images, (T) Michael Ventura Photography; **146** ©Elio Ciol/Corbis; **147** Scala/Art Resource, NY; **148** Villa of the Mysteries Pompeii/Collection Dagli Ort/The Art Archive; **149** (C) ©Iberfoto/The Image Works, Inc., (T) bpk, Berlin/Antikensammlung, Staatliche Museen, Berlin, Germany/Art Resource, NY, (B) The Art Archive/Archaeological Museum Split Croatia/Alfredo Dagli Orti/The Kobal Collection; **150** Musée du Louvre Paris/Dagli Orti/The Art Archive; **151** Galleria di Storia ed Arte Udine/Collection Dagli Orti/The Art Archive; **154** Art Resource, NY; **155** (R) ©Mimmo Jodice/Corbis, (L) Archaeological Museum Venice/Collection Dagli Orti/The Art Archive; **156** Gianni Dagli Orti/Corbis; **157** (B) ©The Trustees of The British Museum/Art Resource, NY, (T) Scala/Ministero per i Beni e le Attività culturali/Art Resource, NY; **158** Gianni Dagli Orti/The Art Archive; **160** ©Iberfoto/The Image Works, Inc.; **161** Mary Evans Picture Library; **162** ©Topham/The Image Works, Inc., (BR) ©Topham/The Image Works, Inc., (TL) Erich Lessing/Art Resource, NY, (CL) Erich Lessing/Art Resource, NY, (BL) Gianni Dagli Orti/The Art Archive, (TR) Metropolitan Museum of Art, New York, USA/Bridgeman Art Library; **164** Jupiterimages/Thinkstock; **166** (R) Art Resource, NY, (L) Scala/Art Resource, NY; **167** (B) ©Nathan Benn/Corbis, (T) Private Collection/The Stapleton Collection/Bridgeman Art Library; **168** Mary Evans Picture Library; **170**

©Christie's Images Ltd./SuperStock; **172** ©The British Library/HIP/The Image Works, Inc.; **173** (L) ©The Granger Collection, NY, (R) Kunstmuseum, Bern, Switzerland/Bridgeman Art Library; **174** (Bkgrd) ©Historical Picture Archive/Corbis, Scala/Art Resource, NY; **175** (L) Pinacoteca Comunale Fermo Ascoli Piceno/Gianni Dagli Orti/The Art Archive, (R) The Art Archive/Archaeological Museum Split Croatia/Alfredo Dagli Orti/The Kobal Collection; **176** Bryan Reinhart/Masterfile Corporation; **179** (T) Image copyright ©The Metropolitan Museum of Art/Art Resource, NY; **180** (T) Gianni Dagli Orti/Corbis, (B) Kamat's Potpourri/CyberCrow Inc.; **181** (T) Scala/Art Resource, NY; **182** Villa of the Mysteries Pompeii/Collection Dagli Ort/The Art Archive; **183** bpk, Berlin/Antikensammlung, Staatliche Museen, Berlin, Germany/Art Resource, NY; **184** ©Charles & Josette Lenars/Corbis; **185** (B) ©Canadian Museum of Civilization, (C) Archaeological Museum Lima/Mireille Vautier/The Art Archive, (T) Werner Forman Archive/National Museum of Anthropology, Mexico City. Location: 12. ©Werner Forman/Topham/The Image Works, Inc.; **186** (C) ©Matthias Kulka/Corbis, (L) John Bigelow Taylor/Art Resource, NY; **187** Archaeological Museum Lima/Mireille Vautier/The Art Archive, (T) Réunion des Musées Nationaux/Art Resource, NY; **188** ©Danny Lehman/Corbis, (TL,) The Art Archive, (BR) The Image Works, Inc., (TR) Werner Forman/Art Resource, NY; **189** (T) Corbis, (T) The Art Archive, (B) Werner Forman Archive/National Museum of Anthropology, Mexico City. Location: 12. ©Werner Forman/Topham/The Image Works, Inc.; **190** Art Resource, NY, Throckmorton Fine Art; **191** (B) ©Danny Lehman/Corbis, (BR) ©Macduff Everton/Corbis, (CL) ©Paul Almasy/Corbis, (CR) ©Peter Arnold, Inc./Alamy Images, (TR) ©Werner Forman/Topham/The Image Works, Inc., (TL) François Guénet/AKG London Ltd., (CR) Museum of Fine Arts, Boston, Massachusetts, USA/Gift of Landon T. Clay/Bridgeman Art Library, Werner Forman Archive/Collection: Edward H. Merrin Gallery, New York. Location: 12. ©Werner Foreman/Topham/The Image Works, Inc.; **192** (B) ©DK Images, (T) ©The Granger Collection, NY, BeBa/Iberfoto/Photoaisa; **193** (L) Archaeological Museum Teotihuacan Mexico/Gianni Dagli Orti/The Art Archive, (R) PRISMA/Ancient Art & Architecture Collection Ltd.; **194** Image copyright ©The Metropolitan Museum of Art/Art Resource, NY; **195** (R) ©Werner Forman/Topham/The Image Works, Inc., (L) Archaeological Museum Lima/Gianni Dagli Orti/The Art Archive; **196** (B) ©Art Directors & TRIP/Alamy Images, (L) Archaeological Museum Lima/Gianni Dagli Orti/The Art Archive; **197** ©The Granger Collection, NY, Corbis, (Inset) Rick Browne/Photo Researchers, Inc.;

198 (B) ©Danny Lehman/Corbis, (T) Ronald Sheridan/Ancient Art & Architecture Collection Ltd., The Image Works, Inc.; 199 (L) ©British Library Board. All Rights Reserved., ©The Trustees of The British Museum/Art Resource, NY, (C) Art Resource, NY, (BR) Corbis, (T) John Bigelow Taylor/Art Resource, NY; 200 (B) Corbis, (T) Photo Researchers, Inc., Photri Images; 201 The Raven and the First Men, by Bill Reid (Haida), 1980. Collection of the UBC Museum of Anthropology, Vancouver, Canada. Photo: Bill McLennan/©University of British Columbia Museum of Anthropology; 202 (B) ©Canadian Museum of Civilization, (TR) ©Richard A. Cooke/Corbis, (TL) ©The Granger Collection, NY, Réunion des Musées Nationaux/Art Resource, NY; 203 George H. H. Huey/Corbis; 204 (T) ©Canadian Museum of Civilization, Art Resource, NY; 205 Art Resource, NY; 206 (B) ©Royalty-Free/Corbis, Francois Guénet/AKG London Ltd., (T) The Art Archive; 207 ©Gianni Dagli Orti/Corbis; 208 (B) ©Charles & Josette Lenars/Corbis, (T) Bodleian Library; 209 The Ann Ronan Picture Library/Heritage-Images; 212 ©The Granger Collection, NY; 213 (T) ©British Library Board. All Rights Reserved., (B) Scala/Art Resource, NY, (C) Snark/Art Resource, NY, (L) Corbis, (R) Reunion des Musee Nationaux/Art Resource, NY; 214 (L) Corbis, (R) Reunion des Musee Nationaux/Art Resource, NY; 216 Reunion des Musee Nationaux/Art Resource, NY; 218 The British Library/Topham-HIP/The Image Works, Inc.; 219 BeBa/Iberfoto/Photoaisa; 222 Topham/The Image Works, Inc.; 223 (R) North Wind Picture Archives, (L) The British Library/HIP/The Image Works, Inc.; 224 (R) The British Library/HIP/The Image Works, Inc., (L) Torla Evans ©The Museum of London/©DK Images; 225 (L) ADO/Iberfoto/Photoaisa, (R) HIP/Art Resource, NY; 227 (C) Erich Lessing/Art Resource, NY, (T) Kunsthistorisches Museum, Vienna, Austria/Bridgeman Art Library, (C) Lambeth Palace Library, London, UK/Bridgeman Art Library; 228 Scala/Art Resource, NY; 229 Louvre, Paris, France/Bridgeman Art Library; 230 Musee du Judaisme/RMN/Art Resource, NY; 231 British Library/The Art Archive; 232 (L) Erich Lessing/Art Resource, NY, (R) Judith Miller/Lennox Gallery Ltd/©DK Images; 233 The Pierpont Morgan Library, New York, NY/Art Resource, NY; 234 ©Mary Evans Picture Library/The Image Works, Inc., (R) Bridgeman Art Library; 235 Scala/Art Resource, NY; 237 (C) SuperStock, (T, B) The British Library/The Image Works, Inc.; 239 (T) ©Associated Press, (B) Judith Miller/Lennox Gallery Ltd/©DK Images; 240 ©The Granger Collection, NY; 241 (R) D.Y./Art Resource, NY, (L) Scala/Art Resource, NY; 242 Gianni Dagli Orti/Corbis; 243 (B) ©DK Images, (C) AKG London Ltd., (T) Musée Municipal Vaucouleurs/Dagli Orti/The Art Archive, (B) York Archaeological Trust for Excavation and Research Ltd./

©DK Images; 244 (R) AKG London Ltd., (L) Archives Nationales Paris/JFB/The Art Archive; 245 Franz-Marc Frei/Corbis; 247 The Royal Collection ©2006 Her Majesty Queen Elizabeth II; 249 The Art Archive/Corbis; 250 (B) ©The Granger Collection, NY, (T) Bridgeman Art Library; 251 (R) Erich Lessing/Art Resource, NY, (L) SEF/Art Resource, NY; 252 Foto Marburg/Art Resource, NY; 253 The British Library/HIP/The Image Works, Inc.; 254 San Francesco Assisi/Dagli Orti/The Art Archive; 255 Scala/Art Resource, NY; 257 (B) Bibliotheque des Arts Decoratifs, Paris, France/Bridgeman Art Library; 258 Galleria degli Uffizi Florence/Dagli Orti/The Art Archive; 259 (BL) Amos Zezmer/Omni Photo Communications, (TL) David Turnley/Corbis, (BR) Ellen Howdon/Courtesy of Glasgow Museum/©DK Images, (TR) Reuters/Corbis, (BR) University Library Coimbra/Dagli Orti/The Art Archive; 261 (T) Biblioteca Nacional Madrid/Laurie Platt Winfrey/The Art Archive, (B) Getty Images; 262 (R) ©DK Images, (L) Corbis, (R) York Archaeological Trust for Excavation and Research Ltd./©DK Images; 263 The British Library/HIP/The Image Works, Inc.; 264 (CR) Araldo de Luca/Corbis, (CL) Dave G. Houser/Corbis, (T) Peter Anderson/Courtesy of Saxon Village Crafts, Battle, East Sussex/DK Images, (B) The Pierpont Morgan Library/Art Resource, NY; 266 (B) Giraudon/Art Resource, NY, (T) Musee de la Tapisserie, Bayeux, France//Bridgeman Art Library; 268 (C) ©DK Images, (CR) Michel Setboun/Corbis, (B) Neil Lukas/©DK Images, (T) Vanni/Art Resource, NY; 269 (T, B) The Image Works, Inc.; 270 Musee Conde, Chantilly, France/Bridgeman Art Library; 272 (TR, TL) Geoff Dann/©DK Images, (BL) Snark/Art Resource, NY, (BR) The Board of Trustees of the Armouries/HIP/The Image Works, Inc.; 274 (Inset) ©DK Images, (TR) Bettmann/Corbis, (B) Frank Greenaway/©DK Images, (L) Stock Montage/SuperStock; 275 (L) ©The Granger Collection, NY, (R) Bibliotheque Royale de Belgique, Brussels, Belgium//Bridgeman Art Library; 276 The Board of Trustees of the Armouries/HIP/The Image Works, Inc.; 277 (T) Reuters/Wilson Chu/Corbis, (B) The Image Works, Inc.; 278 Galleria degli Uffizi Florence/Dagli Orti/The Art Archive; 279 Gianni Dagli Orti/Corbis; 280 Art Resource, NY; 281 (C) Art Resource, NY, (B) Bridgeman Art Library, (T) N. Carter/North Wind Picture Archives; 282 (L) ©The Granger Collection, NY, (R) Art Resource, NY; 284 (T) Adrian Zenz/Shutterstock, (Inset) Michele Burgess/PhotoLibrary Group, Inc.; 285 San Vitale, Ravenna, Italy/Bridgeman Art Library; 287 Alamy Images; 288 Giraudon/Art Resource, NY; 289 (L) ©DK Images, (R) Bridgeman Art Library; 290 Museum of History of Sofia, Sofia, Bulgaria/Archives Charmet/Bridgeman Art Library; 291 Doug Page/Index Stock/PhotoLibrary

Group, Inc.; 292 Andy Crawford/Courtesy of the History Museum, Moscow/©DK Images; 293 Tretyakov Gallery, Moscow, Russia/Bridgeman Art Library; 294 (L) Erich Lessing/Art Resource, NY, (R) Historical Museum of Republic of Crimea Simferopol/Dagli Orti (A)/The Art Archive; 295 (L) ©The Granger Collection, NY; 296 ©Pegaz/Alamy Images; 297 Erich Lessing/Art Resource, NY; 298 (B) Art Resource, NY; 299 (B) AKG London Ltd., (T) Elvis Barukcic/©Associated Press; 300 (B) Alamy Images, (T) British Library, London, Great Britain/Art Resource, NY; 301 PRISMA/Ancient Art & Architecture Collection Ltd.; 303 (B) ©DK Images, (C) ©The Granger Collection, NY, (T) Bridgeman Art Library; 304 (R) Art Directors & TRIP Photo Library, (L) Peter Sanders Photography Limited; 305 (T) Fitzwilliam Museum, University of Cambridge, UK/Bridgeman Art Library, (B) Kurt Stier/Corbis; 307 (CR) ©Associated Press, (CC) Prisma/Ancient Art & Architecture Collection Ltd., (TR) Reuters/Corbis, (TL) Steven Rubin/The Image Works, Inc., (B) Trip/Alamy Images; 308 ©The Granger Collection, NY; 309 (BL) ©DK Images, (BR) 2005 Richard l'Anson/Lonely Planet Images, (T) Bridgeman Art Library; 310 Monasterio de El Escorial/Index/Bridgeman Art Library; 311 Gary Cross/©DK Images; 312 Expuesto - Nicolas Randall/Alamy Images; 313 ©The Granger Collection, NY; 314 Snark/Art Resource, NY; 315 (B) José Fuste Raga/zefa/Corbis, (TR) Photographer's Choice/Getty Images, (TL) Roger Wood/Corbis; 316 Peter M. Wilson/Corbis; 317 (Inset) Topkapi Palace Museum, Istanbul, Turkey/Bridgeman Art Library, (Bkgrd) Werner Forman/Art Resource, NY; 318 (T) Peter Harholdt/Corbis, (B) Werner Forman/TopFoto/The Image Works, Inc.; 319 Royal Asiatic Society, London, UK/Bridgeman Art Library; 320 Ancient Art & Architecture Collection Ltd.; 321 (Bkgrd) ©British Library Board. All Rights Reserved., (T) ©The Granger Collection, NY, Bridgeman Art Library, (CL) Kharbine-Tapabor/Boistesselin/The Art Archive, (CC) The British Museum/HIP/The Image Works, Inc., (B) The Image Bank/Getty Images, (CR) University Library, Istanbul, Turkey/Bridgeman Art Library; 323 (TR) BeBa/Iberfoto/Photoaisa, (Bkgrd) Charles & Josette Lenars/Corbis, (B) Corbis, (TL) Victoria & Albert Museum, London/Art Resource, NY; 324 Getty Images; 325 Victoria and Albert Museum London/Eileen Tweedy/The Art Archive; 326 (L) Annie Griffiths Belt/Corbis, (R) Burstein Collection/Corbis; 327 Bridgeman Art Library; 328 Taxi/Getty Images; 329 (L) Moldovita Monastery Romania/Dagli Orti/The Art Archive, (R) Topkapi Palace Museum, Istanbul, Turkey, Giraudon/Bridgeman Art Library; 330 Ancient Art & Architecture Collection Ltd.; 331 (B) Private Collection, Archives Charmet/Bridgeman Art Library, (T) Topkapi Palace

Museum, Istanbul, Turkey/Bridgeman Art Library; 332 Nat & Yanna Brandt/Photo Researchers, Inc.; 334 Snark/Art Resource, NY; 335 Getty Images; 336 Bridgeman Art Library; 337 (R) Private Collection/Bridgeman Art Library, (L) rochaphoto/Alamy Images; 338 (B) André Held/AKG London Ltd.; 339 (B) Hamill Gallery of African Art, (T) The Metropolitan Museum/Art Resource, NY, (C) The Nasli M. Heeramaneck Collection, gift of Joan Palevsky/Art Resource, NY; 340 (R) Bibliotheque Nationale, Paris, France/Bridgeman Art Library, (L) Good-Shoot/Corbis; 341 David Keith Jones/Images of Africa Photobank/Alamy Images; 342 (R) A van Zandbergen/Afri-Pics Images, (C) Christopher and Sally Gable/©DK Images, (L) Michele Westmorland/Corbis; 343 (T) ©DK Images, (B) Bildarchiv Preussischer Kulturbesitz/Art Resource, NY; 344 The Nasli M. Heeramaneck Collection, gift of Joan Palevsky/Art Resource, NY; 345 Shizuo Kambayashi/©Associated Press; 346 (L) Nik Wheeler/Corbis, (R) The Metropolitan Museum/Art Resource, NY; 347 (B) Masterfile Corporation, (T) Werner Forman/Art Resource, NY; 348 Werner Forman/Art Resource, NY; 349 (BL) Bridgeman Art Library, (C) The Granger Collection, NY, (Bkgrd) Topham/The Image Works, Inc.; 350 Betty Press/Woodfin Camp & Associates; 351 AKG London Ltd., (Bkgrd) Annebicque Bernard/Sygma/Corbis, (R) National Museum Lagos, Nigeria/Held Collection/Bridgeman Art Library, (L) Werner Forman/Corbis; 352 (R) Art Resource, NY, (L) The Metropolitan Museum of Art, Rogers Fund, 1998 (1998.66). Photograph 1998/Art Resource, NY; 353 Mike Andrews/Ancient Art & Architecture Collection Ltd.; 354 AKG London Ltd.; 355 Suzanne Porter/Rough Guides/©DK Images; 356 Alamy Images; 357 ©Images & Stories/Alamy Images; 358 (R) ©The Trustees of the British Museum/Art Resource, NY, (TL, CL, C, Bkgrd) Hamill Gallery of African Art, (Bkgrd) Seattle Art Museum/Seattle Art Museum, (Inset) The Newark Museum/Art Resource, NY; 359 (C) Ellen Howdon/St Mungo, Glasgow Museums/©DK Images, (R) Glen Allison/Mira, (L) Hamill Gallery of African Art; 361 Brian Seed & Associates; 362 (T) ©DK Images, (B) Bibliotheque Nationale, Paris, France/Bridgeman Art Library; 363 (T) Art Resource, NY, (B) Werner Forman/Art Resource, NY; 364 ©Images & Stories/Alamy Images; 365 The Granger Collection, NY; 366 AAAC/Topham/The Image Works, Inc.; 367 (T) China Legacy Images, (C) Rick Browne/Photo Researchers, Inc., (B) Sekai Bunka/Ancient Art & Architecture Collection Ltd.; 368 British Library/The Art Archive; 369 (R) ©The Granger Collection, NY, (L) China Legacy Images; 370 (B) ©SSPL/The Image Works, Inc., (TL, R) China Legacy Images; **372** Norma Joseph/Robert Harding World Imagery; **373** (B) ©The Granger Collection, NY, (T) Bildarchiv Preussischer Kulturbesitz/Art Resource, NY; **374** British Library/The Art Archive; **375** (T) Edifice/Corbis, (BL) Peter Yates/Science Photo Library/Photo Researchers, Inc.; **376** (L) Art Resource, NY, (R) The British Museum/©DK Images; **377** ©The Granger Collection, NY; **378** (R) AKG London Ltd., (L) Bridgeman Art Library, Palazzo Farnese Caprarola/Dagli Orti/The Art Archive, (L) SuperStock; **380** (R) China Legacy Images, (C) Nigel Tudor, (L) Werner Forman/Art Resource, NY; **382** ©ChinaStock; **383** (Bkgrd) Rick Browne/Photo Researchers, Inc.; **385** Steve Vidler/Iberfoto/Photoaisa; **386** Alon Reininger/Contact Press Images; **387** (R) Erich Lessing/Art Resource, NY; **389** The Art Archive; **390** Musee des Beaux-Arts, Angers, France/Bridgeman Art Library; **391** Mary Evans Picture Library; **392** (B) British Museum, London, UK/Bridgeman Art Library; **393** (R, L) Art Resource, NY; **394** ©Catherine Karnow/Corbis; **396** (R) Asian Art & Archaeology, Inc./Corbis; **397** (B) Eric Trachtenberg; **398** (L) British Library, London, UK/Bridgeman Art Library, (B) C. Jopp/Robert Harding World Imagery; **399** Massimo Listri/Corbis; **400** Digital Vision/Getty Images, (Inset) Frank Carter/Lonely Planet Images; **402** Scala/Art Resource, NY; **403** (L) Art Resource, NY, (R) The Art Archive; **404** (L) ©The Granger Collection, NY, (R) AKG London Ltd.; **405** (B) Art Resource, NY, Peter Wilson/©DK Images; **408** Corbis; **409** (C) Art Resource, NY, (T) Arte & Immagini srl/Corbis; **410** (R) Ashley Simmons/Alamy Images, (L) Scala/Art Resource, NY; **411** The Bridgeman Art Library/Getty Images; **412** Archivio di Stato di Siena/Gianni Dagli Orti/The Art Archive; **414** (C, Bkgrd) ©DK Images, (R) Private Collection/Bridgeman Art Library, (L) Scala/Art Resource, NY, The Image Bank/Getty Images; **415** (L) ©DK Images, (R) Mary Evans Picture Library; **416** Mary Evans Picture Library; **417** Iberfoto/Photoaisa; **418** (R) Art Resource, NY, (L) Mary Evans Picture Library; **419** M. C. Esteban/Iberfoto/Photoaisa; 420 Scala/Art Resource, NY; **421** (TR) ©DK Images, (L, C) Erich Lessing/Art Resource, NY, (BR) Susannah Price/©DK Images; **422** (C) ©DK Images, (B) Andrea Pistolesi/Getty Images, (T) Mary Evans Picture Library; **423** (L) AAAC/Topham/The Image Works, Inc., (R) London College of Printing/©DK Images; **424** Bildarchiv Preussischer Kulturbesitz/Art Resource, NY; **425** The Corcoran Gallery of Art/Corbis; **427** Erich Lessing/Art Resource, NY, (L) National Trust Photographic Library/Derrick E. Witty/The Image Works, Inc.; **429** Corbis; **430** ©The Granger Collection, NY, (Bkgrd) Michael Busselle/Corbis; **431** (R) ©The Granger Collection, NY, (L) Mary Evans

Picture Library; **433** Erich Lessing/Art Resource, NY; **434** (R) ©Gustavo Tomsich/Corbis, (L) ©The Granger Collection, NY; **435** (L) ©The Granger Collection, NY, (R) Reuters/Corbis; **436** (BL) Corbis, (TL) Kevin Fleming/Corbis, (R) Maximilian Stock Ltd./Photo Researchers, Inc.; **437** (R) AAAC/Topham/The Image Works, Inc., (L) Glasgow University Library, Scotland/Bridgeman Art Library; **439** (T) Galileo Galilei (1564–1642) before members of the Holy Office in the Vatican in 1633, 1847, Robert-Fleury, Joseph-Nicolas (1797–1890)/Louvre, Paris, France/Peter Willi/Bridgeman Art Library, (B) Gildas Raffenel/epa/Corbis; **440** Scala/Art Resource, NY; **441** (BR) ©The Granger Collection, NY, (BL) Art Resource, NY, Cartoon Stock; **442** (Bkgrd) Corbis, Scala/Art Resource, NY; **444** Instituto Portugues de Museus; **445** (T) Art Resource, NY, (TR) China Legacy Images, (B) Christie's Images/Corbis; **446** (L) Ann Ronan Picture Library/The Image Works, Inc., (R) Bridgeman Art Library; **448** (R) ©National Maritime Museum, London, (L, Bkgrd) ©The Granger Collection, NY; **449** (TR) Alfredo Dagli Orti/The Art Archive, (TL) Antiquarian Images, (BR) Art Resource, NY, (BR) Museu de Marinha; **450** Preussischer Kulturbesitz/Art Resource, NY; **452** (R) Smithsonian Institution, (L) Topham/The Image Works, Inc.; **453** Private Collection/Photo ©Heini Schneebeli/Bridgeman Art Library; **455** Werner Forman/Art Resource, NY; **456** (T) Gift of Ernest Anspach, 1999 (199.295.4) Photograph (c) 2002/Art Resource, NY, (B) Museo de Arte Antiga/The Art Archive; **457** (L) Art Resource, NY, (R) Rainer Daehnhardt/Portuguese Academy of Antique Arms; **458** (R) Maritime Museum of Rotterdam, (L) The Royal Collection ©2006 Her Majesty Queen Elizabeth II; **459** Rijks Museum Amsterdam; **460** ©British Library Board. All Rights Reserved., ©The Granger Collection, NY; **461** (B) Biblioteca Apostolica Vaticana, (L) Ricci Institute; **462** The British Museum/The Image Works, Inc.; **463** (L) ©The Granger Collection, NY, (C) Christie's Images/Corbis, (R) The British Museum/HIP/The Image Works, Inc.; **464** ©The Cleveland Museum of Art, ©The Granger Collection, NY; **465** ©The Granger Collection, NY, Michael Holford; **466** (T) Art Resource, NY, (B) The British Museum/The Image Works, Inc.; **467** ©The Granger Collection, NY; **468** (T) ©The Granger Collection, NY, (B) Instituto Portugues de Museus; **469** (B) ©The Granger Collection, NY, (T) Giraudon/Art Resource, NY; **470** Schalkwijk/Art Resource, NY; **471** (C) Bridgeman Art Library, (T) Erich Lessing/Art Resource, NY, (B) Library of Congress; **472** Biblioteca Medicea-Laurenziana/Florence/Bridgeman Art Library; **473** (B) ©akg-images/The Image Works, Inc., (T) ©The Granger Collection, NY; **474** (Inset) AKG London Ltd., (Bkgrd) Charles & Josette

Lenars/Corbis; **475** ©Frank Nowikowski Photography; **476** Ira Block Photography; **477** Hispanic Society of America; **478** Instituto Portugues de Museus; **479** Danny Lehman/Corbis; **480** Joseph Martin/AKG London Ltd.; **481** Bridgeman Art Library; **482** Lee Snider/Photo Images/Corbis; **483** Bettmann/Corbis; **484** Michael Schwarz/The Image Works, Inc.; **485** (BR) Collection of The New-York Historical Society, (TR) National Museum of the American Indian, Smithsonian Institution, (BC) The Newark Museum/Art Resource, NY, (BL) Victoria & Albert Museum, London/Art Resource, NY; **486** Gunter Marx Stock Photos; **487** (R) Chicago History Museum, (L) Royal Albert Museum/Bridgeman Art Library; **488** (B) Ariadne Van Zandbergen/Lonely Planet Images, Bettmann/Corbis, Corbis, Image Source/Corbis; **489** (B) ©British Library Board. All Rights Reserved., (TR) Library of Congress; **491** The Art Archive; **492** (L) ©Courtesy of the Bancroft Library, University of California, Berkeley, (R) Francis C. Mayer/Corbis; **493** (C) Corbis, (L) Darrell Guiin/Corbis, (R) Ocean/Corbis; **494** (B) Journal-Courier/Steve Warmowski/The Image Works, Inc., Robert Harding World Imagery; **495** Erich Lessing/Art Resource, NY; **496** (CR) ©Julie Habel/Corbis, (L) Carlos Goldin/Corbis, (R) PoodlesRock/Corbis; **497** (TL) Bettmann/Corbis, (BR) Ira Block Photography, (BL) Kim Blaxland/Getty Images, (TR) Liba Taylor/Corbis, (BC) Ron Giling/PhotoLibrary Group, Inc.; **498** Steve Vidler/eStock Photo; **499** (BR) baur/Shutterstock, (TR) RICHARD B. LEVINE/NewsCom, (L) Stock Montage Inc.; **500** (T) ©The Art Gallery Collection/Alamy Images; **501** Mary Evans Picture Library; **502** Erich Lessing/Art Resource, NY; **503** (T) Erich Lessing/Art Resource, NY, (C) Rob Reichenfeld/©DK Images; **504** (R) Bettman/Corbis, (Bkgrd) Bettmann/Corbis, (R) J.Bedmar/Iberfoto/Photoaisa; **506** (Bkgrd) ©National Maritime Museum, London, (L) Bridgeman Art Library, (BR) British Library/Bridgeman Art Library, (TR) J.Bedmari/Iberfoto/Photoaisa; **508** Bridgeman Art Library; **509** (T) Art Resource, NY, (B) Mary Evans Picture Library; **510** Art Resource, NY; **511** ©Lebrecht Music and Arts Photo Library/Alamy Images; **513** (TR) ©Peter Willi/SuperStock, (BL) Reunion des Musees Nationaux/Art Resource, NY, (TL) Scala/Art Resource, NY, (BR) Topham/The Image Works, Inc., (CL) Victoria & Albert Museum/Art Resource, NY; **515** (B) STEPHEN MORRISON/epa/Corbis, (T) The Gallery Collection/Corbis; **516** Art Resource, NY; **517** J. Bedmar/Iberfoto/Photoaisa; **518** (TR) ©The Granger Collection, NY, (L) Corbis, (BR) The British Museum/HIP/The Image Works, Inc.; **519** (BR) ©The Granger Collection, NY, (TR) Bridgeman Art Library, (L) Mary Evans Picture Library; **520** (Bkgrd) HIP/The Image Works, Inc., Rob Reichenfeld/©DK

Images; **521** (B) ©The Granger Collection, NY, (T) Atwater Kent Museum/Bridgeman Art Library; **524** (T) Bettmann/Corbis, (B) The Parliamentary Archives; **525** (R) ©The Board of Trustees of the Armouries/HIP/The Image Works, Inc., (L) Erich Lessing/Art Resource, NY; **528** Photoaisa; **529** Mary Evans Picture Library; **530** (R, L) Corbis; **531** The Granger Collection, NY; **532** (BL) ©The Granger Collection, NY, (TR) AKG London Ltd., (Bkgrd) Sovfoto/Eastfoto; **533** ©Photos 12/Alamy Images; **536** (L) ©The Board of Trustees of the Armouries/HIP/The Image Works, Inc., (R) Mary Evans Picture Library; **537** (T) ©The Granger Collection, NY; **538** Photoaisa; **539** Bridgeman Art Library; **542** Réunion des Musées Nationaux/Art Resource, NY; **543** (C) Bridgeman Art Library, (T) Réunion des Musées Nationaux/Art Resource, NY, (B) The Granger Collection, New York; **544** (L) BeBa/Iberfoto/Photoaisa, (B) Musee Marmottan/©DK Images; **545** ©The Granger Collection, NY; **546** (R) Chateau de Versailles, France, Lauros/Giraudon/Bridgeman Art Library, (L) Réunion des Musées Nationaux/Art Resource, NY; **547** (L) ©The Granger Collection, NY, (R) Corbis; **548** BeBa/Iberfoto/Photoaisa; **549** (T) ©The Granger Collection, NY, (B) Iberfoto/Photoaisa; **550** (Inset) Bettmann/Corbis; **551** ©The Granger Collection, NY; **552** (B) Bridgeman Art Library, (Border, Bkgrd) Russ Lappa, (L) Victoria & Albert Museum, London/Art Resource, NY; **553** (R) ©DK Images, (C) Francis G. Mayer/Corbis, (L) John Heseltine/Corbis; **554** (C) BeBa/Iberfoto/Photoaisa, (R) Bridgeman Art Library, (L) Kurpfalzisches Museum, Heidelberg, Germany/Bridgeman Art Library; **556** (BL) Reuters/Corbis, (Bkgrd) The Art Archive, (TL) Zuma/Corbis; **557** (L) ©The Granger Collection, NY, (R) The Granger Collection, New York; **558** (L) Stock Connection; **559** SuperStock; **560** (L) National Portrait Gallery, Smithsonian Institution/Art Resource, NY, (C) Reunion des Musees Nationaux/Art Resource, NY, (R) The Corcoran Gallery of Art/Corbis; **561** Bridgeman Art Library; **562** The Granger Collection, NY; **564** (Inset) ©Bettmann/Corbis, (Bkgrd) Bettmann/Corbis; **565** (TL) Bettmann/Corbis, (TL) Library of Congress, (TC) MPI/Getty Images; **566** ©The Granger Collection, NY; **567** (B) Bridgeman Art Library, Steven G Artley/Artley Cartoons; **568** (B) ©The Granger Collection, NY, (T) Christie's Images/Corbis; **569** Bettmann/Corbis; **570** Bridgeman-Giraudon/Art Resource, NY; **571** (C, B) Art Resource, NY, (T) Musee de L'Histoire Vivante, Montreuil, France, Archives Charmet/Bridgeman Art Library; **572** (B) ©The Granger Collection, NY, (T) Erich Lessing/Art Resource, NY; **573** Snark/Art Resource, NY; **574** (TR) Giraudon/Art Resource, NY, (B) Musee de la Ville de Paris, Musee Carnavalet, Paris, France, Archives Charmet/

Bridgeman Art Library, (TL) Musee du Ranquet, Clermont-Ferrand, France/Giraudon/Bridgeman Art Library; **575** Musee Carnavalet, Paris, France, Lauros/Giraudon/Bridgeman Art Library; **576** (B) Chateau de Versailles, France/Bridgeman Art Library, (T) Giraudon/Art Resource, NY; **577** RÈunion des MusÈes Nationaux/Art Resource, NY; **578** Réunion des Musées Nationaux/Art Resource, NY; **579** Judith Miller/Bill & Myrtle Aquillino/©DK Images; **580** (T) AKG London Ltd., (B) Chateau de Versailles, France, Giraudon/Bridgeman Art Library; **583** Giraudon/Art Resource, NY; **584** Musee de la Ville de Paris, Musee Carnavalet, Paris, France, Giraudon/Bridgeman Art Library; **585** Bibliothèque des Arts Décoratifs Paris/Dagli Orti/The Art Archive; **586** Leonard de Selva/Corbis; **587** Giraudon/Art Resource, NY; **588** (L) Bridgeman Art Library, (C) Hulton Archive/Getty Images, (R) Musée Carnavalet Paris/Dagli Orti/The Art Archive; **589** (TL) Hulton-Deutsch Collection/Corbis, (R) Max Alexander/©DK Images, (BL) Musee de la Revolution Francaise, Vizille, France/Bridgeman Art Library; **590** (B) Art Resource, NY, (T) Bridgeman Art Library; **591** (T) Erich Lessing/Art Resource, NY, (B) Réunion des Musées Nationaux/Art Resource, NY; **592** (B) Private Collection/Bridgeman Art Library, (T) Scala/Art Resource, NY; **593** Giraudon/Art Resource, NY; **595** Art Resource, NY; **596** Musee des Beaux-Arts, Rouen, France Lauros/Giraudon/Bridgeman Art Library; **597** Giraudon/Art Resource, NY; **598** Bibliotheque Nationale, Paris, France, Archives Charmet/Bridgeman Art Library; **600** Giraudon/Art Resource, NY; **601** Randy Faris/Corbis; **602** ©The Granger Collection, NY; **603** (B) Private Collection/Bridgeman Art Library, (T) Riyadh Biji/Reuters/Corbis; **604** (R) ©The Granger Collection, NY, (L) Bridgeman-Giraudon/Art Resource, NY, (R) The Image Works, Inc.; **605** Giraudon/Art Resource, NY; **606** ©NRM/Pictorial Collection/SSPL/The Image Works, Inc.; **607** (C, B) Corbis, (T) National Railway Museum/Science & Society Picture Library; **608** NRM/SSPL/The Image Works, Inc.; **610** ©The Granger Collection, NY; **611** Oxford Scientific Films,Ltd./Photolibrary Group Inc.; **612** (L) Fine Art Photographic Library, London/Art Resource, NY, (R) National Railway Museum/Science & Society Picture Library; **613** Science Museum/Science & Society Picture Library; **616** Mary Evans Picture Library; **617** Hulton Archives/Getty Images; **619** (B) Manchester Archives and Local Studies, (T) Mary Evans Picture Library; **620** ©The Granger Collection, NY; **621** Hulton-Deutsch Collection/Corbis; **622** Hulton-Deutsch Collection/Corbis; **623** (B) ©The Granger Collection, NY, (T) Fine Art Photographic Library/Art Resource, NY; **624** (R) The Stapleton Collection/Bridgeman Art Library, (L) Topham/The Image Works,

Inc.; **626** (T) ©The Granger Collection, NY, (B) Corbis; **627** (B) Daniel Leclair/Reuters/Corbis, (T) Mary Evans Picture Library Ltd /The Image Works, Inc.; **628** (L) AKG London Ltd.; **629** (B) Museo Historico Nacional Buenos Aires/Dagli Orti/The Art Archive, (T) Peter Titmuss/Alamy Images; **630** /NRM/Pictorial Collection/SSPL/The Image Works, Inc.; **631** Image Select/Art Resource, NY; **632** Simon Bolivar Amphitheatre Mexico/Dagli Orti/The Art Archive; **633** (B) ©The Granger Collection, NY, (C) Gary Ombler/Courtesy of 1er Chasseurs a Cheval de la Lighne, 2e Compagnie/©DK Images, (T) Museo National De Colombia; **634** Hadtorteneti Muzeum, Budapest, Hungary/Archives Charmet/Bridgeman Art Library; **636** (R) ©Mary Evans/GROSVENOR PRINTS/The Image Works, Inc., (L) Georgios Kollidas/Shutterstock; **638** (R) Gary Ombler/Courtesy of 1er Chasseurs a Cheval de la Lighne, 2e Compagnie/©DK Images, (L) North Wind Picture Archives; **639** Musee de la Ville de Paris, Musee Carnavalet, Paris, France, Lauros/Giraudon/Bridgeman Art Library; **640** (Bkgrd) ullstein bild/©The Granger Collection, NY; **641** (R) Louvre, Paris, France/Bridgeman Art Library, (L) Private Collection, Archives Charmet/Bridgeman Art Library, (C, Bkgrd) ullstein bild/©The Granger Collection, NY; **642** Scala/Art Resource, NY; **643** ©The Granger Collection, NY; **644** (T) ©The Granger Collection, NY, (B) Gleb Garanich/Reuters/Corbis; **645** (L) Museo Nacional Bogota/Dagli Orti/The Art Archive, (R) Museo National De Colombia; **646** Chateau de Versailles, France/Bridgeman Art Library; **647** Corbis; **649** (BL) ©The Granger Collection, NY, (TR) Bettmann/Corbis, (BR) Museo Bolivar Caracas/Gianni Dagli Orti/The Art Archive, (TL) The Granger Collection, NY; **650** Miramare Museum Trieste/Dagli Orti/The Art Archive; **651** North Wind Picture Archives; **652** North Wind Picture Archives; **653** (C) Bibliothéque des Art Décoratifs Paris/Marc Charmet/The Art Archive, (B) Masterfile Corporation, (T) Reuters/Corbis; **654** (TR) AGE Fotostock/SuperStock, (BL) Simon Bolivar Amphitheatre Mexico/Dagli Orti/The Art Archive; **658** Lewis W. Hine/George Eastman House/Getty Images; **659** (T) Private Collection/Bridgeman Art Library, (B) The Image Works, Inc., (C) The Women's Library/Mary Evans Picture Library; **660** Mary Evans Picture Library; **661** Lewis B. Hine/AKG London Ltd.; **662** The Image Works, Inc.; **663** (B) Mary Evans Picture Library; **664** (TR) ©SSPL/Science Museum/The Image Works, Inc., (CR) Dagli Orti/The Art Archive, (L) The Image Works, Inc.; **665** Hulton-Deutsch Collection/Corbis; **666** Library of Congress; **667** (T) Bettmann/Corbis, (B) Topham/The Image Works, Inc.; **668** ©Bettmann/Corbis; **669** Hulton-Deutsch Collection/Corbis; **671** Musée de l´Affiche Paris/Dagli Orti/The Art Archive; **672** (T) Leland

J. Prater/Corbis, (B) SSPL/The Image Works, Inc., (C) The Advertising Archive; **673** (TR) Michael Nicholson/Corbis, (TL) Scala/Art Resource, NY, (B) Sirl Schwartzman; **674** (R) The Women's Library/Mary Evans Picture Library, (L) Underwood & Underwood/Corbis; **675** (BR) Corbis, (TL) Museum of London/Topham-HIP/The Image Works, Inc., Museum of London, UK/Bridgeman Art Library, (Bkgrd) Philip de Bay/Corbis; **676** ©Hulton Archive/MPI/Getty Images; **677** Topham/The Image Works, Inc.; **678** (TR) Kevin Schafer/Corbis, (BR) Oriol Alamany/Corbis, (BL) Renee Lynn/Photo Researchers, Inc., (TL) Tui De Roy/Minden Pictures; **679** (BR) ©The Granger Collection, NY, (C) Kevin Schafer/Corbis, (TL) Mary Evans Picture Library, (TR) Michael Nicholson/Corbis, (CL) Tom Brakefield/SuperStock, (BL) Tony Arruza/Corbis; **680** Underwood & Underwood/Corbis; **681** Albert Bierstadt (American, 1830–1902), Hetch Hetchy Canyon Oil on canvas, 1875 Gift of Mrs. E. H. Sawyer and Mrs. A. L. Williston/Mount Holyoke College Art Museum; **682** The Art Archive; **683** Art Resource, NY, (BC) Bettmann/Corbis, (TC) Erich Lessing/Art Resource, NY, (T) Philadelphia Museum of Art, (B) Private Collection, Archives Charmet/Bridgeman Art Library; **684** Erich Lessing/Art Resource, NY; **685** (BL) Art Resource, NY, (T) Réunion des Musées Nationaux/Art Resource, NY, (BR) SuperStock; **686** ©DK Images; **687** Private Collection/Bridgeman Art Library; **688** (T) Christie's Images/SuperStock, (B) Jacqui Hurst/Corbis; **689** North Wind Picture Archives; **690** AKG London Ltd.; **691** (B) ©DK Images, (C) DK Images, (T) Judith Miller Archive/©DK Images; **692** (TR) Judith Miller Archive/©DK Images, (L) PhotoLibrary Group, Inc.; **694** (T) AKG London Ltd.; **696** (R) Alison Harris/©DK Images, (L) Popperfoto/Getty Images; **697** ©The Granger Collection, NY; **698** WEIMAR ARCHIVE/Mary Evans Picture Library; **699** AKG London Ltd.; **700** (L) Alinari/Art Resource, NY; **701** ©Roger-Viollet/The Image Works, Inc.; **703** (B) ©The Granger Collection, NY, (TR) Alinari/Art Resource, NY, (C) Private Collection, Alinari/Bridgeman Art Library, (TL) Private Collection, Ken Welsh/Bridgeman Art Library; **704** Alinari/Art Resource, NY; **705** (R) DK Images, (L) Private Collection, Archives Charmet/Bridgeman Art Library; **708** Mary Evans Picture Library; **709** (B) Brooks Kraft/Sygma/Corbis, (T) The Art Archive/Corbis; **710** North Wind Picture Archives; **711** (T) ©DK Images, (B) Private Collection/Bridgeman Art Library; **712** HIP/Art Resource, NY; **713** ©The Granger Collection, NY; **714** (T) Mary Evans Picture Library, (B) Snark/Art Resource, NY; **716** Corbis; **717** (B) ©The Granger Collection, NY, (T) Musée Carnavalet Paris/Dagli Orti/The Art Archive; **718** (B) AKG London Ltd., (T) Giraudon/Art Resource, NY; **719** Greater London

Council, UK/Bridgeman Art Library; **720** Blackburn Museum and Art Gallery, Lancashire, UK/Bridgeman Art Library; **721** (T) AKG London Ltd., (B) Bettmann/Corbis, (C) Trades Union Congress Library Collections; **722** (L) Hulton Archive/Getty Images, (R) Victoria & Albert Museum, London/Art Resource, NY; **723** ©Birmingham Museums and Art Gallery/Bridgeman Art Library; **724** (R, CL) AKG London Ltd., (L) Corbis, (CR) Palace of Westminster, London, UK/Bridgeman Art Library; **725** (C) Mary Evans Picture Library, (L) Private Collection/Bridgeman Art Library; **726** Bettmann/Corbis; **727** Anti-Slavery International; **728** Mary Evans Picture Library; **729** Trades Union Congress Library Collections; **730** (Bkgrd) ©Dave Ashwin/Alamy, (TR) Holt Studios Int./Photo Researchers, Inc., (CL) Sean Sexton Collection/Corbis, (CR) The Illustrated London News Picture Library, London, UK/Bridgeman Art Library, (B) Trustees of the Watts Gallery, Compton, Surrey, UK/Bridgeman Art Library; **732** (T) Bradford Art Galleries and Museums, West Yorkshire, UK/Bridgeman Art Library, (B) Getty Images; **733** (R) Erich Lessing/Art Resource, NY, (L) Hulton Archive/Getty Images; **734** (Inset, Bkgrd) Hulton Archive/Getty Images; **735** (T) ©The Granger Collection, NY, (B) Musee de la Poste, Paris, France, Archives Charmet/Bridgeman Art Library; **736** ©Dave G. Houser/Corbis; **737** AKG London Ltd.; **738** Musee National de l'Education, Rouen, France, Archives Charmet/Bridgeman Art Library; **739** Stockbyte/Getty Images; **740** (BL, Bkgrd) American Philosophical Society, (BR) Division of Political History/National Museum of American History/Smithsonian Institution, (TR) Kevin R. Morris/Bohemian Nomad Picturemakers/Corbis; **741** New-York Historical Society/Bridgeman Art Library; **744** Mary Evans Picture Library; **745** The Women's Library/Mary Evans Picture Library; **746** (T) ©The Granger Collection, NY, (B) AKG London Ltd.; **747** Musee de la Ville de Paris, Musee Carnavalet, Paris, France, Archives Charmet/Bridgeman Art Library; **748** Hulton-Deutsch Collection/Corbis; **749** (T) ©British Library Board. All Rights Reserved., (B) Bridgeman Art Library, (C) Private Collection/Bridgeman Art Library; **750** (R) AKG London Ltd., (L) Mary Evans Picture Library; **751** National Archives UK; **752** (R, BL) ©The Granger Collection, NY, Roger Viollet/Topham/The Image Works, Inc.; **753** Hulton Archive/Getty Images; **754** AKG London Ltd.; **755** The Royal Collection ©2006 Her Majesty Queen Elizabeth II; **756** (B) AKG London Ltd., (T) Mary Evans Picture Library; **758** ©The Granger Collection, NY; **759** Mary Evans Picture Library; **760** Popperfoto/Getty Images; **761** Mansell/Time Life Pictures/Getty Images; **762** (R) Bridgeman Art Library, (L) Swim Ink 2, LLC/Corbis; **763** AKG London Ltd.; **765** (L) ©The Granger

Collection, NY, (Bkgrd) Public Record Office/HIP/The Image Works, Inc.; **766** Hulton Archive/Getty Images; **767** (R) ©British Library Board. All Rights Reserved., (L) Hulton Archive/Getty Images; **768** (T) Company of Girdlers/ Eileen Tweedy/The Art Archive, (C) Photo ©Civil War Archive/Bridgeman Art Library, (TR, BC) Royal Armouries Museum, (BR) The Image Works, Inc.; **769** (R) Mary Evans Picture Library; **770** (T) AFP/Getty Images, (C) Colin Garatt/ Corbis, (B) Paul A. Souders/Corbis; **772** (B) Alexander Popov/ITAR-TASS/ABACA-PRESS/NewsCom, Roy Miles Fine Paintings/Bridgeman Art Library; **773** (R) Bridgeman Art Library, (L) Masterfile Corporation; **774** The Image Works, Inc.; **775** (L) Panorama Stock, (R) Private Collection/The Art Archive; **776** Corbis; **777** Time- Life Pictures/Getty Images; **778** (L) Bridgeman Art Library, (R) The Image Works, Inc.; **779** Topham/The Image Works, Inc.; **780** (T) ©The Granger Collection, NY, (B) Time- Life Pictures/Getty Images; **782** Peter Harholdt/Corbis; **783** (T) ©The Granger Collection, NY, (C) Index Stock Imagery/Photolibrary Group, Inc., (B) The Image Works, Inc.; **784** (L) Topham/The Image Works, Inc.; **785** British Museum/The Art Archive; **786** Réunion des Musées Nationaux/Art Resource, NY; **787** (R) ©directphoto.bz/ Alamy Images, (L) Index Stock Imagery/ PhotoLibrary Group, Inc.; **788** Old Japan; **789** Rykoff Collection/Corbis; 790 Mary Evans Picture Library; **791** (R) Mary Evans Picture Library; **792** (L) Bettmann/ Corbis, (R) National Archives; **794** (TR) Getty Images, (TL) Horace Bristol/Corbis, (BR) Ray Moller/Royal Pavilion Museum and Art Galleries, Brighton/©DK Images, (TC) Roy Miles Fine Paintings/Bridgeman Art Library; **796** (R) ©Royalty-Free/Corbis, (L) Art Gallery of Ontario, Toronto, Canada/Bridgeman Art Library; **798** (B) Mary Evans Picture Library, (T) Photolibrary Group, Inc.; **800** (Inset) ©mediacolor's/Alamy Images, (B) Historical Picture Archive/Corbis; **801** (L) National History Museum Mexico City/Gianni Dagli Orti/The Art Archive, (R) Ocean/Corbis; **802** National History Museum Mexico City/Dagli Orti/The Art Archive; **803** (L) National History Museum Mexico City/Dagli Orti/The Art Archive, (R) Private Collection/Bridgeman Art Library; **805** Bettmann/Corbis; **806** (Bkgrd) Corbis, (TR, BC) Office of Imaging, Printing & Photographic Services/Smithsonian Institution, (BR) The Image Works, Inc.; **808** (L) ©DK Images, (R) Werner Forman/Corbis; **809** ©Royalty-Free/Corbis; **810** (R) Asian Art & Archaeology, Inc./Corbis, (L) National History Museum Mexico City/ Dagli Orti/The Art Archive; **814** Imperial War Museum/The Art Archive; **815** (C) ©DK Images, (T) Getty Images, (B) SSPL/ The Image Works, Inc.; **816** (L) bettman/ Corbis, (R) ullstein bild/©The Granger Collection, NY; **818** Corbis; **819** ©The Granger Collection, NY; **820** Chicago Tri-

bune; **821** Jacques Moreau/Archives Larousse, Paris, France/Bridgeman Art Library; **822** (L) Hulton-Deutsch Collection/Corbis, (R) Imperial War Museum, London/©DK Images; **823** Art Resource, NY; **824** (BR) Foto Marburg/Art Resource, NY, (T) SSPL/The Image Works, Inc., (T) ullstein bild/©The Granger Collection, NY; **825** (T) Popperfoto/Getty Images, (B) The Tank Museum; **827** Bettmann/Corbis; **828** Mary Evans Picture Library; **829** (R) ©The Granger Collection, NY, (L) Bettmann/Corbis; **830** (T) David Pollack/Corbis, (B) Snark/Art Resource, NY; **831** Hulton-Deutsch Collection/Corbis; **832** (B) ©The Granger Collection, NY, (T) A. R. Coster/Hulton Archive/Getty Images; **833** Bettmann/ Corbis; **834** (L) Corbis; **835** (Bkgrd) Bettmann/Corbis, Corbis; **838** SSPL/The Image Works, Inc.; **839** (L) ©DK Images, (R) AKG London Ltd.; **840** (L) The Image Works, Inc., (R) Wonders Exhibit/©Associated Press; **841** Hulton Archive/Getty Images; **842** (R) AKG London Ltd., (L) Christie's Images, London, UK/Bridgeman Art Library; **843** (L) Novosti/Bridgeman Art Library, (R) Topham/The Image Works, Inc.; **844** Eric Miller/Panos Pictures; **845** Topical Press Agency/Hulton Archive/ Getty Images; **846** (C) Art Resource, NY, (L) bettman/Corbis, (R) Imperial War Museum, London/©DK Images; **847** (L) ©The Granger Collection, NY, (R) Corbis; **848** (T) Eileen Tweedy/The Art Archive, (B) The Image Works, Inc.; **850** Corbis; **851** (C) Bridgeman Art Library, (B) Martin Plomer/©DK Images, (T) Paul Franklin ©Dorling Kindersley, Courtesy of the Castillo de Chapultepec/©DK Images; **852** (R) Bill Manns/The Art Archive, (L) Fernando Bueno/Getty Images; **853** (TR, TL, CC,) Bettmann/Corbis, (TR, CL, B) Corbis; **854** Corbis; **856** Paul Franklin ©Dorling Kindersley, Courtesy of the Castillo de Chapultepec/©DK Images; **857** (B) Schalkwijk/Art Resource, NY, (T) Time Life Pictures/Getty Images; **858** (L) The Advertising Archive; **859** National Library of South Africa; **860** (B) ©The Granger Collection, NY, (C) WorldSat International Inc./Photo Researchers, Inc.; **861** (R) Bettmann/Corbis, (L) Harry Thuku/Bettmann/Corbis; **862** ©The Granger Collection, NY; **864** Library of Congress; **865** Underwood & Underwood/Corbis; **866** DAP/The Image Works, Inc.; **868** Hulton-Deutsch Collection/Corbis; **869** (R) Corbis, (L) Panorama Stock; **870** ©The Granger Collection, NY; **871** Bettmann/Corbis; **872** Sovfoto/ Eastfoto; **875** (T) ©Random House Inc., (B) Mansell/Time Life Pictures/Getty Images; **877** Hulton/Getty Images; **878** ©The Granger Collection, NY, (L) Corbis; **879** (B) ©The Granger Collection, NY; **880** ©The Granger Collection, NY, (B) Corbis; **881** DPA/The Image Works, Inc.; **882** Time Life Pictures/Getty Images; **883** (C) Library of Congress, (B) ullstein bild/©The Granger Collection, NY; **884** ©Bettmann/Corbis; **885** (R) Culver Pic-

tures/The Art Archive, (L) Drug Enforcement Administration; **886** (TR, L) Bettmann/Corbis, (R) Library of Congress, (BR) Topham/The Image Works, Inc., (L) Underwood & Underwood/Corbis; **888** New York Daily News/Getty Images; **889** Tate Gallery/Art Resource, NY; **890** (BR) Art Resource, NY, (BC) Fogg Art Museum, Harvard University Art Museums, USA/ Bequest from the Collection of Maurice Wertheim, Class 1906/Bridgeman Art Library, (T) Roger Viollet/Topham/The Image Works, Inc., (BL) Scala/Art Resource, NY; **891** (R) ©DK Images, (L) Corbis; **892** Bettmann/Corbis; **893** ©The Granger Collection, NY; **894** (R) AKG London Ltd., (L) Archive Holdings Inc/ Getty Images, (B) Museum of American Finance; **895** (B) Bettmann/Corbis, (T) Mary Evans Picture Library; **896** (R) Roger-Viollet/Topham/The Image Works, Inc., (L) The Granger Collection, NY; **898** (L) ©DK Images, (R) Mary Evans Picture Library; **899** Time Life Pictures/Getty Images; **900** (R) Imperial War Museum, London/©DK Images, (TL) Museum of the Revolution, Moscow/©DK Images, (BL) Stefano Bianchetti/Corbis, (Inset) ullstein bild/©The Granger Collection, NY; **901** (Bkgrd,) Bettmann/Corbis; **903** Korea News Service/Reuters/Corbis; **904** ullstein bild/©The Granger Collection, NY; **905** ©The Granger Collection, NY; **906** London Express/Getty Images; **907** Rue des Archives/©The Granger Collection, NY; **908** ©DK Images; **909** ©The Granger Collection, NY; **910** akg-images/RIA Nowosti/AKG London Ltd.; **912** Corbis; **913** (B) Bettmann/Corbis, (T) Corbis; **914** Mary Evans Picture Library; **915** United States Holocaust Museum; **916** Feltz/Topham/The Image Works, Inc.; **918** (R, L) ©DK Images; **919** (T) ©Associated Press, (B) Drug Enforcement Administration; **920** Corbis; **922** Time & Life Pictures/Getty Images; **923** (B) The Advertising Archive; **924** (R) Getty Images, (L) London Express/Getty Images; **925** (L) Getty Images; **926** (TC, BC, B) Corbis; **927** (L) Getty Images, (R) Time Life Pictures/Getty Images; **930** Museum of Flight/Corbis, (L) Wanda's Pie in the Sky; **932** (BR) Bettmann/Corbis, (BL) Eric L. Johnson; **933** (B) Bettmann/ Corbis; **934** ©Hulton-Deutsch Collection/Corbis, (Bkgrd) United States Holocaust Museum; **935** Topham/The Image Works, Inc.; **936** Panorama Stock; **937** ©Associated Press; **938** ©AP Images; **939** (L) ©The Granger Collection, NY; **940** (L) Bettmann/Corbis, (R) Corbis; **941** (Bkgrd) Bettmann/Corbis, (B) Geoff Dann/Imperial War Museum, London/ ©DK Images, (R, L) Hulton Archive/Getty Images; **942** Corbis; **944** Bettmann/Corbis; **946** Topham/The Image Works, Inc.; **947** (B) Bettmann/Corbis; **948** (L) ©Associated Press, (R) Painting by Don Troiani, Military & Historical Image Bank; **949** ©Associated Press; **950** ©AP Images; **951** (B) Richard Klune/Corbis, (T) Time Life Pictures/Getty Images; **952**

(R) Alfred Eisenstaedt/Time Life Pictures/ Getty Images, (L) Imperial War Museum/ DK Images; **953** Hulton Deutsch/Corbis; **954** (T) Corbis, (B) Library of Congress; **955** Bettmann/Corbis; **956** The Michael Barson Collection; **957** (T) Bildarchiv Preussischer Kulturbesitz/Art Resource, NY, (B) THOMAS COEX/AFP/Getty Images/NewsCom; **958** (L) Corbis; **960** (T) Eric L. Johnson, (B) Time & Life Pictures/Getty Images; **964** Photos12/ Polaris Images; **965** (B) Corbis, (T) Jacques M. Chenet/Corbis; **966** (R) Getty Images, (L) Photos12/Polaris Images; **967** Alamy Images; **968** Bettmann/Corbis; **969** Patrick Robert/Sygma/Corbis; **971** (BR) ©Associated Press, (TR, BL) Bettmann/Corbis, (TL) Keystone/Gamma Rapho; **972** (R) Bob Rowan/Progressive Image/Corbis, (L) Peter Turnley/Corbis; **973** ©Associated Press; **974** Everett Collection, Inc.; **975** (TL) "LET'S GET A LOCK FOR THIS THING"—A 1962 Herblock Cartoon/The Herb Block Foundation, (B) ©Associated Press, (TR) Getty Images; **976** (B) David Seymour/©Magnum Photos, (T) Library of Congress; **977** (B) Bettmann/Corbis, (T) Lambert/Archive Photos/Getty Images; **978** (R) ©Associated Press, (L) ©Owen Franken/Corbis; **979** Bob Adelman/©Magnum Photos; **980** Polaris Images; **981** Brian Rose; **982** Topham/The Image Works, Inc.; **983** (B) Horace Bristol/Corbis; **984** Charles Gupton/Getty Images; **985** (L) Baldwin H. Ward and Kathryn C. Ward/Corbis, (R) Corbis; **986** Bettmann/Corbis; **987** (R) Corbis, (L) Gamma Rapho; **988** Bettmann/Corbis; **990** Bettmann/Corbis; **992** (R) Corbis, (L) Hulton Archive/Getty Images; **993** Time Life Pictures/Getty Images; **994** (TR, BR) ©Associated Press, (Bkgrd) Bettmann/Corbis, (BL) Nathan Benn/Corbis; **996** Russ Lappa; **997** Dirck Halstead/Getty Images; **998** (R) ©Associated Press, (L) Gamma Rapho; **999** (T) ©Associated Press, (B) Hires Chip/Gamma Rapho; **1000** (L) ©Associated Press; **1001** Bettmann/Corbis; **1003** (T) ©Mark Richards/PhotoEdit, Inc., Pascal Le Segretain/Sygma/Corbis; **1004** (L) Gamma Rapho, (R) Time Life Pictures/Getty Images; **1005** Ricky Wong/Bloomberg News/Landov LLC; **1007** (B) Jacques Langevin/Sygma/Corbis, (T) Liba Taylor/Corbis; **1008** Corbis; **1009** (L) Bettmann/Corbis, (R) Gamma Rapho; **1010** Photos12/Polaris Images; **1011** Martyn Goddard/Corbis; **1012** Alexis Orand/Gamma Rapho; **1013** (B) ©Associated Press, (T) Andrew England/ ©Associated Press, (C) PhotoDisc/Getty Images; **1014** (R) ©Associated Press, (L) Henri Cartier-Bresson/©Magnum Photos; **1016** Bettman/Corbis; **1017** Phoenix Art Museum, Arizona, Gift of George P. Bickford/Bridgeman Art Library; **1018** Mike Goldwater/Alamy Images; **1020** (R) Bernard Napthine/Lonely Planet Images, (L) Howard Sochurek//Time Life Pictures/ Getty Images; **1021** Getty Images; **1022** ©Hes Mundt/Alamy, (R) Sakchai Lalit/

©Associated Press; **1024** (R) Corbis; **1025** Fredrik Naumann/Panos Pictures; **1026** ©Danita Delimont/Alamy Images; **1028** Keystone/Getty Images; **1029** Ben Curtis/©Associated Press, (B) Plambeck/NewsCom; **1031** (T) Bettmann/Corbis, (B) Mark Kauffman/Time Life Pictures/Getty Images; **1032** (B) Corbis, (R) Patrick Ben Luke Syder/Lonely Planet Images; **1034** (T) Hassan Massoudy/ARS/Banque d'Images, ADAGP//Art Resource, NY, (B) Marco Di Lauro/Getty Images; **1035** (L) Richard Vogel/©Associated Press; **1036** ©AP Images; **1038** (R) Bettmann/Corbis, (TL) Corbis, (BL) Rick Barrentine/Corbis; **1039** (BR) ©AP Images, (BL) Getty Images, (T) Mindaugas Kulbis/©Associated Press; **1040** ©Hes Mundt/Alamy, (T) Henri Cartier-Bresson/©Magnum Photos; **1041** AFP/NewsCom; **1042** Gamma Rapho; **1043** (C) ©Tyler Cody/Alamy Images, (B) Olivier Coret/In Visu/Corbis; **1044** Corbis; **1045** Turesson/Pressens Bild/Gamma Rapho; **1047** OTHoNIEL/Gamma Rapho; **1048** Dieter Telemans/Panos Pictures; **1049** ©Magnum Photos; **1050** (TR) ©Associated Press, (TL) David Turnley/Corbis, (B) Frankenfeld/South Light/Gamma Rapho; **1052** Getty Images; **1053** (B) David Turnley/Corbis, (T) Owen Franken/Corbis; **1054** Nasser Shiyoukhi/©Associated Press; **1055** Ziv Koren/Polaris Images; **1056** ©Associated Press; **1057** (R, L) ©Associated Press; **1058** Laurent Rebours/©Associated Press; **1059** Wissam Al-Okaili/AFP/Getty Images; **1060** ©Magnum Photos, (TL) ©SSPL/Science Museum/The Image Works, Inc., Bettmann/Corbis; **1061** Michael Evstafiev/AFP/Getty Images; **1062** (T) CARLSON©2004 Milwaukee Sentinel. Reprinted with permission of UNIVERSAL PRESS SYNDICATE. All rights reserved./Universal Press Syndicate, Gamma Rapho; **1064** Tischler Fotografen/PhotoLibrary Group, Inc.; **1065** (C) Evaristo SA/AFP/Getty Images, (B) Paul C. Pet/Corbis; **1066** (L) Zed Nelson/Panos Pictures; **1068** Ron Giling/PhotoLibrary Group, Inc.; **1069** (Inset) Clive Shirley/Panos Pictures; **1070** Mark Henley/Panos Pictures; **1071** (T) Betty Press-Woodfin Camp/AURORA, Richard Hainebach; **1072** Mark Edwards/PhotoLibrary Group, Inc.; **1073** Liba Taylor/Panos Pictures; **1074** (CR) ABPL/Nigel Dennis/Animals Animals/Earth Scenes, (T) Betty Press/Panos Pictures, (B) Cyril Ruoso/Minden Pictures, (CL) Fiona Teede-UNEP/PhotoLibrary Group, Inc.; **1075** William Campbell/Corbis; **1076** (T) Jeff Widener/©Associated Press, (B) Peter Turnley/Corbis; **1077** Greg Baker/©Associated Press; **1078** (L) Eugene Hoshiko/©Associated Press, (R) Findlay Kember/Polaris Images; **1079** Christopher Brown/Polaris Images; **1081** (B) Corbis, (T) Steve Northup/Timepix/Time Life Pictures/Getty Images; **1082** Janet Jarman/Corbis; **1083** (B) David Rochkind/Polaris Images, (T) Russell Gordon/

Das Fotoarchiv./PhotoLibrary Group, Inc.; **1084** (R) Paulo Santos/©Associated Press, (L) Paulo Santos-Interfoto/©Associated Press; **1085** Anders Gunnartz/PhotoLibrary Group, Inc.; **1086** Dado Galdieri/©Associated Press; **1087** (B) Dario Lopez-Mills/©Associated Press; **1088** (L) ALI BURAFI/AFP/Getty Images, (R) Rafael Wollmann/Gamma Rapho; **1089** Barriopedro, EFE/©Associated Press; **1090** (L) Bettmann/Corbis, (R) Image Port/PhotoLibrary Group, Inc.; **1091** Dennis Galante/Corbis; **1092** Jorgen Schytte/PhotoLibrary Group, Inc.; **1093** China Photos/Reuters/Corbis; **1094** Alison Wright/Corbis; **1095** (T) CARE USA, (B) NASA; **1096** (R) ©Matthias Kulka/Corbis, (L) AFP/Getty Images; **1098** Anthony Devlin/©Associated Press; **1100** David Grossman/The Image Works, Inc.; **1102** (Bkgrd) Corel, (Bkgrd) Russell Gordon/Das Fotoarchiv/PhotoLibrary Group, Inc.; **1103** (L) ©simon kolton/Alamy Images, (R) Bananastock/Jupiter Images, (L) Michael Yamashita Photography; **1104** Paul A. Souders/Corbis; **1105** (B) AFP/Getty Images, (T) NewsCom/NewsCom, (C) Rafiqur Rahman/Reuters Media; **1106** (R) CARE USA, (L) Getty Images; **1107** (C) ©Noah Poritz/Photo Researchers, Inc., (L) Andy Crump, TDR, World Health Organization/Photo Researchers, Inc., (R) Caroline Penn/Corbis; **1109** (T) Phil Huber/Black Star; **1110** Demotix Demotix/PhotoLibrary Group, Inc., Russell Sadur/©DK Images; **1111** (B) ©Mike Goldwater/Alamy Images; **1112** ©Associated Press; **1114** (T) Alison Wright/The Image Works, Inc., (B) Shawkat Khan/AFP/Getty Images; **1115** Larry Downing/Reuters/Corbis; **1116** Lynn Johnson/AURORA; **1118** (T) ©Reuters/Corbis; **1119** Raheb Homavandi/Reuters/Landov LLC; **1120** (R) NASA, (L) Photo Researchers, Inc.; **1121** (Bkgrd) Bettmann/Corbis, (Inset) ESA/PLI/Corbis; **1122** (Border) ©James King-Holmes/Photo Researchers, Inc., (R) Bettmann/Corbis, (L) Getty Images, (Bkgrd) Los Alamos National Laboratory/Photo Researchers, Inc.; **1123** (R) ©A. Barrington Brown/Photo Researchers, Inc., (L) ©James King-Holmes/Photo Researchers, Inc., (B) Dr. Linda M. Stannard, University of Cape Town/Photo Researchers, Inc.; **1124** (BL) Jim Richardson/Corbis, (T) R. Gino Santa Maria/Shutterstock; **1126** ©Reuters/Corbis; **1127** (T) Custom Medical Stock Photo, (B) Rafiq Maqbool/©Associated Press; **1128** (B) AFP/Getty Images, (T) Cartoon Stock; **1130** (TR) J.Bedmar/Iberfoto/Photoaisa, (BR) Musee de la Tapisserie, Bayeux, France//Bridgeman Art Library, (BL) Pascal Le Segretain/Sygma/Corbis; **1131** Corbis; **1146** The Art Archive; **1149** Anders Blomqvist/Lonely Planet Images; **1150** (B) ©The Art Gallery Collection/Alamy Images, (T) DK Images; **1151** Giraudon/Art Resource, NY; **1153** ©Associated Press; **1154** Corbis; **1155** Rafiqur Rahman/Reuters Media; **1156** baur/Shutterstock; **1158** (TL) ©The Granger Collection, NY, (TR) Ancient Art &

Architecture Collection Ltd., (B) Art Resource, NY, (CL) Musée du Louvre Paris/Gianni Dagli Orti/The Art Archive; **1159** (TL) ©National Maritime Museum, London, (CL) Art Resource, NY, (TR) Getty Images, (CR) Mary Evans Picture Library/Photo Researchers, Inc., (B) Museu de Marinha; **1160** (C) Dagli Orti/The Art Archive, (TL) Getty Images, (B) The Image Works, Inc.; **1161** (T) ©James King-Holmes/Photo Researchers, Inc., (B) ESA/PLI/Corbis, (C) Getty Images; **1162** Alexander Zemlianichenko/©Associated Press; **1163** (T) Corbis; **1164** (TL, BL) Art Resource, NY, (TR) Bridgeman Art Library; **1165** (BL) Corbis, (BR) Laurent Rebours/©Associated Press; **1166** (B) ©The Granger Collection, NY, (T) Gunter Marx Stock Photos; **1168** (TL) Art Resource, NY, (BR) Erich Lessing/Art Resource, NY, (TR) Fitzwilliam Museum, University of Cambridge, UK/Bridgeman Art Library, (BL) The Art Archive; **1169** (TC) Copyright ARS, NY./Art Resource, NY, (TR) Historical Picture Archive/Corbis, (B) Jeff Greenberg/eStock Photo, (TL) The Museum of Modern Art/Art Resource, NY.

Text

Grateful acknowledgment is made to the following for copyrighted material:

ACT, Inc. Excerpt from "Writing Test Scores" from *www.act.org*. Copyright © 2005 by Act, Inc. All rights reserved. Used by permission.

Anglo-Norman Text Society c/o Birkbeck College Excerpt from "Test of Skill and Courage" from *History of William Marshall, Volume I - Text & Translation (11. 1-10031)* edited by A.J. Holden, with English translation by S. Gregory and historical notes by D. Crouch. © Anglo-Norman Text Society 2002. All rights reserved. Used by permission.

Ardis Publishing
From "Requiem" from *Selected Poems* by Anna Ahkmatova, translation copyright © 1974 by Robin Kemball. Reprinted with the permission of The Overlook Press (Ardis Publishers).

BBCi c/o BBC News Online
Excerpt "Black Death (Poem: "We see death coming…")" by Dr. Mike Ibeji from *www.bbc.co.uk*. British Broadcasting Corporation © 2002–2005.

Cambridge University Press
From *Hind Swaraj* by Mohandas K. Gandhi (Anthony J. Parel, editor.), copyright © 1997 by Anthony J. Parel, editor. Reprinted with the permission of Cambridge University Press.

The College Board Excerpt from "Scoring Guide" from *www.collegeboard.com*. Copyright © 2005 collegeboard.com. All rights reserved. Used by permission.

Columbia University Press
"3," "The Teachings of Confucius, Government by Personal Virtue, 43 and 97" by Wm. Theodore de Bary, et

al. from *Sources of Chinese Tradition Volume 1*. Copyright © 1960 by Columbia University Press. "55. Nothing Can Be Worse" by Sei Shonagon, translated by Ivan Morris from *The Pillow Book of Sei Shonagon*. Copyright © 1967 by Columbia University Press. Used by permission.

Doubleday A division of Random House, Inc. Excerpt from "Ja Nus Hons Pris" by Richard the 1st of England from *Warriors Of God, Richard The Lionheart And Saladin In The Third Crusade* by James Reston, Jr. Copyright © 2001 by James Reston, Jr. All rights reserved. Used by permission.

Farrar, Straus & Giroux, LLC. Excerpt from "Book Twenty: The Ranging of Powers" from *The Iliad* by Homer, translated by Robert Fitzgerald. Translation copyright © 1974 by Robert Fitzgerald. Reprinted by permission of Farrar, Straus and Giroux, LLC.

The Free Press, A Division of Simon & Schuster, Inc. Excerpts from "The Republic" by Plato from *Greek Philosophy: Thales To Aristotle, Second Edition, Revised and Expanded* edited by Reginald E. Allen. Copyright © 1966, 1985 by Reginald E. Allen. All rights reserved.

Georges Borchardt, Inc. "55 Nothing Can Be Worse" from *The Pillow Book of Sei Shonagon* translated and edited by Ivan Morris. Copyright © 1967, 1991 by Ivan Morris. Used by permission of Georges Borchardt, Inc., on behalf of the Estate of Ivan Morris.

Greenwich Workshop Press "Heavenly Reflections" by Alan Bean with Andrew Chaikin from *Apollo: An Eyewitness Account by Astronaut/Explorer/Artist/Moonwalker*. Copyright © 2009 Alan Bean. Courtesy of The Greenwich Workshop, Inc. Used by permission.

Harcourt Education Ltd. From *On Trial for my Country* by Stanlake Samkange. Reprinted by permission of Harcourt Education Limited.

Henry Holt and Company, Inc. From "Aeneid" by Virgil (Publius Vergilius Maro) from *The Classical Roman Reader, New Encounters With Ancient Rome* edited by Kenneth J. Atchity, copyright ©1997 by Kenneth J. Atchity. Reprinted by permission of Henry Holt and Company.

Houghton Mifflin Company From *Stolen Continents* by Ronald Wright. Copyright © 1992 by Ronald Wright. Reprinted by permission of Houghton Mifflin Company. All rights reserved.

Indiana University Press Song: "Our homes and humble dwellings …" from *The Mexican Corrido as a Source for Interpretive Study of Modern Mexico (1870–1950)* by Merle E.